Alan Rogers' Guides

EUROPE
2003

Quality Camping and Caravanning Sites

INSPECTED CAMPSITES & SELECTED

Compiled by: Alan Rogers' Guides Ltd

Cover design: Paul Effenberg, Vine Cottage Design
Maps created by Customised Mapping (01985 844092)
contain background data provided by GisDATA Ltd.
Maps are © Alan Rogers' Guides and GisDATA Ltd 2002

Clive Edwards, Lois Edwards & Sue Smart have asserted
their rights to be identified as the authors of this work.

First published in this format 2002

© Alan Rogers' Guides Ltd 2002

Published by: Alan Rogers' Guides Ltd, Burton Bradstock, Bridport, Dorset DT6 4QA

British Library Cataloguing-in-Publication Data:
A catalogue record for this book is available from the British Library.

ISBN: 0 901586 91 9

Printed in Great Britain by J H Haynes & Co Ltd

Contents

Introduction

Alan Rogers published the first of our guides in 1968, introducing it with the words 'I would like to stress that the camps which are included in this book have been chosen entirely on merit, and no payment of any sort is made by them for their inclusion'. As campers and caravanners ourselves, it was this objective approach that convinced the present authors to become regular users of Alan Rogers' Guides, and which eventually lead to our taking over the editing and publishing of the guides when Alan retired in 1986. Although the content and scope of the guides have expanded considerably in the fifteen years since we took over, Alan's philosophy and his rigorous selection criteria remain exactly the same as he defined some thirty years ago.

'With the Alan Rogers' Guide, what you read is what you get'. So said Cassandra Jardine writing in the Daily Telegraph earlier this year and there is no better endorsement of the Alan Rogers' philosophy of featuring only those sites which have been inspected by one of our team of experienced Site Assessors.

The 2003 edition of our Europe Guide features reports on 21 countries in Europe, including Scandinavia and many countries in Eastern Europe. However, it does not include sites in Britain for which we publish a separate guide and it contains only a limited selection of sites in France as we also publish a separate guide (featuring over 600 sites) for France alone as it is the most popular camping and caravanning destination in the world.

The Alan Rogers' Travel Service allows readers to book many of the sites in our Guides, and their ferry crossing, simply by telephoning our UK Travel Service number. Full details of the Alan Rogers' Travel Service can be found on page 7. A free Travel Service booking guide is included with this guide. As for savings, we are also pleased to draw readers' attention to the 'Camping Cheques' scheme. This scheme has operated successfully in France for some time, and has now been greatly expanded to cover sites in other European countries, the majority of which are featured in this guide. Now running in conjunction with the Alan Rogers' Travel Service, for those of our readers who are able to take their holidays outside of the peak months of July and August, this scheme offers very substantial savings. Our new guide - 'Alan Rogers' Mobile Homes and Chalets' - features details of accommodation for rent in mobile homes, chalets or bungalows on over 100 campsites in Europe.

The Alan Rogers' Approach to Selecting Sites

There are many thousands of officially recognised campsites in Europe, so to an extent the camper or caravanner is spoiled for choice. In fact the huge number of sites from which to choose is actually a serious problem as the facilities available, and more importantly the quality varies from the excellent to the downright poor, so any campsite guide that lists all these sites is less than really helpful.

By including only a select number of sites, all of which have been inspected by our own team of professional Inspectors, the Alan Rogers' Guide is specifically designed to help you to choose sites which meet your and your family's needs. Our selection of sites includes not just the most expensive ones, but a range of sites designed to cater for a wide variety of preferences, from the simple to the 'all-singing, all-dancing' holiday site.

The criteria which we use when selecting sites are rigorous, but the most important by far is the question of 'quality' - whatever the size of the site, whether it's part of a campsite chain, or even a municipal site makes no difference in terms of it being required to meet our exacting standards in terms of its quality - in other words, irrespective of the size of the site or the number of facilities offered, the essentials (the welcome, the pitches, the sanitary facilities and the maintenance) must all be of a good standard.

Since none of the campsites have to pay to be featured in our guides, we are free to select exactly those which we think our readers will enjoy, rejecting any that don't meet our standards and to write our own honest descriptions. This is an on-going process and depends on sites not only meeting our standards when they're initially selected, but also on their continuing to do so year after year. Looking back over our guides for the past thirty-five years provides an illuminating insight into just how much standards have changed. Many sites that were able to meet our standards in years past are no longer able to do so now and have therefore been 'dropped' in favour of better ones - one very good reason, amongst several, for making sure you have the latest edition of the Guide rather than an out-of-date one!

As you will see, and hopefully appreciate, unlike most other guides we don't rely on 'icons' or symbols to describe the sites featured in our Guides - partly because we prefer to write our descriptions in plain English, and partly because it is virtually impossible to express an opinion about the quality, or the ambience, for example by means of symbols. Those candid descriptions and opinions are what make the Alan Rogers' Guides unique. We also aim to provide a geographical spread that is as wide as possible within the confines of our selection process. We do find that at sites in very popular tourist destinations or city locations and those with direct access to a beach, standards can sometimes be a little variable due to the heavy demands on them. We have to balance the need for a site in that area with the maintenance of standards.

Hints on using the Alan Rogers' Guides

The Guide is divided firstly by country, subsequently (in the case of larger countries) by region. These are both indicated by the page title lines which should help readers locate their area of interest fairly quickly, although for a particular area the town index provides more direct access. Regions appearing in the title lines are either defined political entities, or simply geographical descriptions (i.e. north, south, etc.).

Indexes

Our three indexes allow you to find sites by country, site number and name, by country, region and site name or by the town or village where the site is situated.

Campsite Maps

The maps of each country are designed to show the country in relation to others and will help you to identify the approximate position of each campsite.

The Site Reports

Example of an entry:

Country – Region
Site name
number Address

Site report
A description of the site in which we try to give an idea its general features - its size, its situation, its strengths and weaknesses. This column should provide a picture of the site itself with reference to the facilities provided if they impact on its appearance or character. We refer to pitch numbers, electricity (with amp-erage), hardstandings etc. in this section as pitch design, planning and terracing affects the site's overall appearance. Similarly we continue to include reference to mobile homes, chalets, etc. but no longer indicate if they are available to let (this type of information appears in our 'Mobile Homes and Chalets' guide). Importantly at the end of this column we indicate if there are any restrictions, e.g. no tents, naturist sites, etc.

Facilities:
The second column in smaller print contains all the more specific information on the site facilities.

Please see the notes below.

Charges

Given in the local currency

Tel/Fax/E-mail:
Reservations:
Open:
Directions:
Separated from the main text in order that they may be read and assimilated more easily by a navigator en-route. Bear in mind that road improvement schemes can result in some road numbers being altered.

Facilities:

Toilet blocks: are covered in less detail than in previous editions. We assume that toilet blocks will be equipped with at least some British style WCs, washbasins with hot and cold water and hot showers with dividers or curtains, and will have all necessary shelves, hooks, plugs and mirrors. We assume that there will be an identified chemical toilet disposal point, and that the campsite will provide water and waste water points and bin areas. If not the case, we comment. We continue to mention certain features that some readers find important: washbasins in cubicles, facilities for babies, facilities for those with disabilities and motorcaravan service points. Disabled readers are advised to telephone the site of their choice to ensure that facilities are appropriate to their needs.

Shop: basic or full supplies, and opening dates.

Bars, restaurants, takeaway facilities and entertainment: we try hard to supply opening and closing dates and to identify if there are discos or other noisy entertainment.

Children's play areas: fenced and with safety surface (e.g. sand or bark).

Swimming pools: if particularly special, we cover in detail in the first column but reference is always included in the second column. Opening dates and levels of supervision are provided where we have been notified.

Leisure facilities: e.g. playing fields, bicycle hire, organised activities and entertainment.

Dogs: If dogs are not accepted or restrictions apply, we state it here. Check the quick reference list on page 519.

Off site: This briefly covers leisure facilities, tourist attractions, restaurants etc nearby. Geographical tourist information is more likely to be in the first column.

Charges: are the latest provided by the sites. In those few cases where 2002 or 2003 prices are not given, we try to give a general guide. Since January 2002, the unit of currency in 12 European countries has been the EURO (€) and for those countries we show prices in Euros per night. For the other countries we show charges in the local currency. We indicate if sites do not accept payment by credit card.

Telephone numbers: are given for most sites, but the numbers quoted assume you are actually IN the country concerned, and are normally nine or ten digit numbers beginning with an '0' (or in Spain a '9'). If you are 'phoning from the UK remember that this '0' is usually disregarded and replaced by the appropriate Country Code - this system is currently undergoing changes, and for the latest details you should refer to an up-to-date telephone directory, or in case of difficulty, to the telephone operator.

Opening dates: are those advised to us during the early autumn of the previous year - site owners can, and sometimes do, alter these dates before the start of the following season - often for good reasons - so if you intend to visit shortly after a published opening date, or shortly before the closing date, it is wise to check that it will actually be open at the time required. Similarly some sites operate a restricted service during the low season, only opening some of their facilities (e.g. swimming pools) during the main season - where we know about this, and have the relevant dates, we indicate it. Remember that many European campsites close for 'siesta' for two hours at mid-day.

Reservations: Necessary for high season (roughly mid-July to mid-August) in popular holiday areas. You can reserve via our own Travel Service, through tour operators or be wholly independent and contact the campsite(s) of your choice direct, using the phone, fax or e-mail numbers shown in the site reports, but please bear in mind that many sites are closed all winter. For the latest information, and/or to book, you may like to refer to our website – www.alanrogers.com – which is up-dated through the year.

Directions: Given last, with a coloured background, in order that they may be read and assimilated more easily by a navigator en route.

Points to bear in mind

Some site owners are very laid back when it comes to opening and closing dates. They may not be fully ready by their opening date - grass and hedges may not all be cut and perhaps only limited sanitary facilities open. At the end of the season they also tend to close down some facilities and generally wind down prior to the closing date. Bear this mind if you are travelling early or late in the season - it is worth ringing ahead.

The 'Camping Cheque' system addresses this as it requires participating campsites to guarantee to have all facilities open and running by the opening date and to remain fully operational until the closing date. Participating sites are  marked in this guide with the Camping Cheque logo.

Whether you're an 'old hand' in terms of camping or caravanning in Europe, or contemplating your first caravan holiday abroad, a regular reader of our Guides or a new reader, we hope you will find that this latest, full colour edition with 104 new sites has plenty to interest you and to help you make your choices for your 2003 holiday,

Alan Rogers	Lois Edwards MAEd, FTS
	Clive Edwards BEd, FTS
	Sue Smart Directors

The Alan Rogers' Travel Service

For the 2003 season we have added many more top quality sites to our Alan Rogers Travel Service. This unique service enables our readers to reserve their holidays as well as channel crossings and comprehensive insurance cover at extremely competitive rates. Whilst the majority are in France, we are also able to offer a selection of the very best sites in nine other European countries.

One simple telephone call to our Travel Service on **01892 55 98 98** is all that is needed to make all the arrangements. Why not take advantage of our years' of experience of camping and caravanning. We would be delighted to discuss your holiday plans with you, and offer advice and recommendations.

In brief, the following is a summary by country of what we are able to offer for 2003:

Austria
At the heart of Europe, this is a country of striking contrast - from Vienna's magnificent, fading imperial glories, to some of Europe's most dramatic Alpine scenery, particularly in the Tirol. Two sites.

Belgium
Three sites in this land of rolling countryside, dense forests and splendid, historic cities, as well as some excellent sandy beaches.

Germany
A vast land of scenic and cultural interest. Our six sites here offer a chance to appreciate some of the great contrasts, from the great mountains and forests in the south to the northern flatlands.

Ireland
A warm welcome is guaranteed at our three selected sites on the 'Emerald Isle'. The scenery is stunning and the pace of life refreshingly slow - your chosen destination may well be close to golden sands or at the foot of dramatic mountains.

Italy
Twelve sites in Italy's northern regions. Some excellent sites in Tuscany's rolling countryside and amongst some of Europe's finest historical cities, such as Rome, Florence, Pisa or Siena. As well as the dramatic northern lakelands.

Luxembourg
A tiny independent sovereign state with two distinct regions, to the north the uplands and forests of the Ardennes, and to the south, rolling farmland leading to the vineyards of the Mosel. Three sites.

Netherlands
A good selection of seven sites inviting the opportunity to explore some of The Netherlands' picturesque villages, dramatic coastline and lovely old provincial towns.

Spain
Europe's fourth largest country and a land of very great diversity. A country too which houses some of Europe's best campsites - many to be found on the 'Costas' or amidst the mountains to the north. Nine sites

Switzerland
Three sites in this landlocked country offering some of Europe's most outstanding scenery. Our chosen sites here are in the Berner Oberland and Valais cantons, regions which boast countless picturesque peaks and pretty mountain villages.

Don't forget - we are also able to take bookings for over 200 of the very best sites in France.

Get the site you want - Get the dates you want
Get the ferry you want - Get the price you want

01892 55 98 98   www.alanrogers.com

Save Money, and Take It Easy!
- No more trying to contact foreign sites direct
- No more doubt as to whether your pitch really is booked
- No more ringing round the ferry companies for the best price
- No more foreign currency booking fees

Andorra

UK Andorran Delegation, 63 Westover Road, London SW18 2RF Tel: 0181 874 4806
(Personal visits by appointment only, telephone morning only)

Andorra is situated high in the Pyrenees between France and Spain and is an independent principality covering 181 sq. miles. It is a sovereign country and the main occupations are agriculture and tourism. It is probably best known for skiing and tax free goods. The population is 55,000 (1991), density 117 per sq. km. and the capital is Andorra la Vella. The climate is temperate, with cold winters with a lot of snow and warm summers.The language is Catalan, with French and Spanish widely spoken. French francs and Spanish pesetas are both used.

Andorra
7144 Camping International

Carretera de Vila, Encamp

The site is approximately 6 km. from Andorra la Vella and tucked in the middle of town. Take care on the signed approach as the entrance road is a little tight with a sharp left turn into the entrance. As you would expect in this situation, the site is overlooked on two sides by town buildings and there is some traffic noise, but there are views of the mountains. Large terraced bar, over looking pool area with snack bar, really a restaurant but not operated as one. It is beautifully decorated and has some fine hunting weapons and trophies along with specimens of past hunting in the region mounted on the walls. There is a choice of restaurants a short walk from the gate. The pitches are level and in terraced rows with some shade from mature trees. This location is ideal for exploring the local area and indulging in the favourite pastime of Andorra - duty free shopping!

Facilities: One sanitary block in main building, second larger sanitary block situated at the lower end of site. They include some washbasins in cabins and mixed Turkish and British style WCs. Washing machine. The blocks have been refurbished but are unheated. Small shop for basics accessed from bar. Bar/snack bar (open all year). Satellite TV. Swimming pool and paddling pool (June - Sept). Petanque. Small children's play area. Electronic games. English spoken. **Off site:** Town shops 1 km. Municipal sports centre near.

Charges guide

Per person	€ 3.46
child (under 14)	€ 2.85
caravan or tent	€ 3.46
car	€ 3.46
motorcaravan	€ 6.61
electricity	€ 3.31

Tel: 831 609. Fax: 831 609. **Reservations:** Advisable in August. **Open** all year.

Directions: Leaving Andorra la Vella going north to Ax-les-Therm on the CG2, Encamp is approx. 6 km. The site is signed at one of the first left turns - keep a sharp eye out for the small sign put at bus roof level on the corner. Follow signs around a roundabout to the left and the site is on the left.

Andorra
Camping Valira
7145 Avinguda Salou, s/n, Andorra La Vella

This is a small and unusual site in the town of Andorra La Vella, with a steep curving entrance which can become congested at peak times. You pass the pleasant restaurant and bar and the heated indoor pool as you enter the site. Maximum use has been made of space here and it is worth looking at the picture of the site in reception as it was in 1969. The 160 pitches are mostly level on terraces and one of the family will guide you to your place which can be an interesting experience if the site is busy. All pitches have electricity and there are water points around the site. As this is a town site there is some ambient noise but the site is ideal for duty free shopping.

Facilities: The new facilities are modern and spotless, with provision for disabled campers, plus separate room with toddler's toilet and good baby room. Two washing machines and dryer. The two blocks can be heated in winter. Bar/restaurant. Small shop (town shops less than 1 km). Small heated indoor pool. Paddling pool. Children's play area.

Charges guide

Per person	€ 3,46
child (under 14)	€ 2,85
car	€ 3,46
caravan or tent	€ 3,46
motorcaravan	€ 6,61
electricity	€ 3,31

Tel/Fax: 822384. E-mail: campvalina@andorra.ad.
Reservations: Not necessary. **Open** all year.

Directions: Site is on the south side of Andorra La Vella, well signed off the N145. Watch signs carefully – an error with a diversion round town will cost you dear at rush hour.

Andorra
Camping Xixerella
7143 Carretera de Pals, Erts (La Massana)

Andorra is a country of narrow valleys and pine and birch forested mountains. Xixerella is attractively situated in just such a valley below towering mountains and beside a river. The site is made up of several sections, accessed by tarmac or gravel roads. There are some terraced pitches, although generally they are not marked out which results in very informal patterns of pitching. They are on grass, mainly with a small degree of slope. Electricity (3/6A) is available for most of the 220 places. Barbecues and picnic area with bridge access to walks in the woods. Pleasant bar and restaurant with pool-side terrace The site can be very busy from mid-July to mid-August, but otherwise it is usually quite peaceful. Do not forget to explore Andorra for that duty free shopping.

Facilities: The satisfactory main sanitary building is fully equipped, including British style WCs (no paper) and some children's toilets, some washbasins in cabins, showers with curtains. Laundry and dishwashing facilities under cover. Further modern facilities are in a novel round building by the pool, including a laundry, baby bath and dishwashing sinks. Small shop. Bar/restaurant. Swimming pool and paddling pool (open mid-June - mid-Sept). Sauna planned. Children's play area. Minigolf. Volleyball. Basketball. Table football. Electronic games. Disco in season. Torch useful. **Off site:** Volleyball and basketball pitch close by. Riding 3 km. Skiing possible at Pal (6 km) or Arinsal (5 km).

Charges guide

Per person	€ 3,01
child	€ 2,85
car	€ 3,01
caravan or tent	€ 3,01
motorcaravan	€ 5,71
electricity (3A)	€ 3,01

Tel: 836 613. Fax: 839 113. E-mail: xixerella@jaire.ad.
Reservations: Contact site. **Open** all year, as are shop, restaurant and bar.

Directions: Site is 8 km. from Andorra la Vella on the road to Pal (this road can only be accessed on the north side of town), via La Massana.

Austria

Austrian National Tourist Office, 13-14 Cork Street, London W1S 3NS
Tel: 020 7629 0461. Fax: 020 7499 6038. E-mail: info@anto.co.uk

Centrally situated in Europe, Austria is primarily known for two contrasting attractions - its capital Vienna with its fading Imperial glories, and the variety of its Alpine hinterland. Ideally suitable for all year round visiting, either viewing the spectacular scenery and enjoying the various opportunities for winter sports or visiting the historical sites and sampling the cultural attractions.

Population

7,915,000 (1993), density 94.2 per sq. km.

Capital

Vienna (Wien).

Climate

Austria has a moderate Central European climate. The winter season is from December to March (in higher regions the end of May) and warm clothing, including waterproof shoes or boots, is a necessity. Even in summer the evenings in mountain resorts can be quite cool.

Language

German is the usual language but English is widely spoken and understood.

Currency

From January 2002, in common with 11 other European countries, the Austrian unit of currency is the EURO (€).
€ 1 = schilling 13.76.

Banks

Banking hours are mainly 08.00 - 12.30 hrs and 13.30 - 15.00 hrs on Mon, Tues, Wed and Fri. Thurs hours are 08.00 - 12.30 and 13.30 - 17.30.
Credit Cards: Most cards are accepted in the larger cities and tourist areas. Travellers cheques are widely accepted.

Post Offices

Offices are open Monday to Friday 08.00 - 12.00 hrs and 14.00 - 18.00 hrs.

Time

GMT plus 1 (summer BST plus 1).

Telephone

To Austria from the UK the code is 0043, ignoring the '0' at the start of the area code. For calls from Austria to the UK the code is 0044.

Public Holidays

New Year; Epiphany; Easter Mon; Labour Day; Ascension; Whit Mon; Corpus Christi; Assumption, 15 Aug; National Day, 26 Oct; All Saints, 1 Nov; Immaculate Conception, 8 Dec; Christmas, 25, 26 Dec.

Shops

Shops open 08.00-18.30 hrs but many close for 2 hours at lunch and 13.00 on Sats except first Sat in every month, when they open to 17.00.

Motoring

Tolls: It is now compulsory to purchase a motorway disc. For visiting cars, motorhomes and towed caravans with a combined weight under 3.5 tons a 'weekly' disc (valid up to 10 days Thursday midnight to midnight two Sundays later) or 'monthly' (valid for two consecutive months) at is available. Motorbikes can only purchase a 'monthly'. They are available at major border crossings, petrol stations and post offices at present and for cash only. Fines for non-compliance are heavy. Previously levied road and tunnel tolls still apply, but a discount of 15% applies to discholders on the S16 Arlberg Tunnel, A13 Brenner - A9 Pyhon and A10 Tauern motorways.

Speed limits: For caravans and motorhomes (3.5t): 31 mph (50 kph) in built up areas, 62 mph (100 kph) other roads (including motorways for caravans) and 81 mph (130 kph) for motorhomes on motorways. There is a lower limit of 68 mph (110 kph) between 2200 - 0500 on the A8, A9, A10, A12, A13 and A14. A min. speed of 37 mph (60 kph) applies on roads with a blue sign showing a white car.

Towing Restrictions: The maximum overall length for car and caravan is restricted to 12 metres. It is also important that your caravan or motorhome is not overloaded.

Parking: Limited parking (blue zones) with max. parking time of 1.5-3 hrs. Parking clocks can be obtained free of charge from tobacconists (Tabak-Trafik), shops or local police stations. However in Vienna, Graz, Linz, Klagenfurt, Salzburg, Innsbruck and a few other cities there is a charge for parking vouchers. They must be clearly displayed on the inside of the windscreen.

Overnighting

It is possible to park outside campsites if permission has been obtained from the landowner. Except in Vienna and protected rural areas visitors may sleep in the vehicle but local restrictions can apply and you may not set up equipment beside vehicles.

Alpencamping Nenzing

001 Garfrenga 1, A-6710 Nenzing (Vorarlberg)

Although best known for its ski-ing resorts, the forests and mountains of the Vorarlberg province make it equally suitable for a peaceful summer visit. Alpencamping Nenzing, at 690 m. above sea level and away from all the noise and bustle of modern life, is truly an oasis of calm set in a natural bowl surrounded by trees with splendid views across the pleasant countryside. You wind your way up from the main road or motorway, turn the final corner to be confronted by the delightful campsite. On the left is a large building with the reception and restaurant and in front an old farm cart loaded with brightly coloured flowers. These are repeated around the site in hanging baskets and borders. Some of the 166 level tourist pitches are in a flat area with others on neat terraces beyond. All have electricity (12-16A) and 100 also have water, drainage, sewage, TV, gas and phone connections. As a member of the Top Camping Austria association, the site has a 'Topi' club providing a range of activities, sport and competitions for children and a widely ranging daily programme for adults that includes a variety of guided walks for different ages, the Bernina Glacier Express, sports and music. Being open all year, the site can be a base from which to ski in winter. The site is owned and run by the English speaking, friendly, Morik family who would like to welcome more British guests.

Facilities: Two excellent, heated, sanitary blocks - one under the reception building and another in the centre of the site. Baby room. Facilities for disabled visitors. Motorcaravan service point. Shop. Bar. Restaurant with terrace. Heated swimming pool (20 x 8 m) and small children's play area with another larger one on the top terrace. Topi Club for children. Practice climbing wall and large football field. Indoor pool planned which will link to the outdoor one and including fitness and sauna rooms and another sanitary block and family bathrooms. **Off site:** Bicycle hire, riding, tennis and fishing near.

Charges 2003

Per unit incl. 2 persons	€ 15.00 - € 26.20
incl. 1 child	€ 21.00 - € 27.40
incl. 2 children	€ 24.60 - € 31.80
electricity	€ 0.65
full services	€ 1.50
dog	€ 2.50 - € 4.40
local tax (over 15 yrs)	€ 0.65

No credit cards. **Tel:** 05525 62491. Fax: 05525 635 676. E-mail: josef.morik@vol.at. **Reservations:** Only accepted for 8/7-16/8 and necessary for that time. **Open** all year except Easter - 10 May.

Directions: From A14 Feldkirch - Bludenz motorway take exit for Nenzing on B190 road and then follow the small 'Camping' signs which have the site logo - a butterfly.

Waldcamping Feldkirch

023 Postfach 564, A-6803 Feldkirch (Vorarlberg)

The town of Feldkirch lies near the borders with Germany, Switzerland and Liechtenstein and this municipal site is part of the Gisingen sports stadium on the edge of the town. The Vorarlberg mountains and Bodensee (Lake Constance) are nearby and there are good sporting facilities, including a large outdoor pool with waterslides, at the stadium next to the site. Set in a quiet residential suburb, about 4 km from the centre, tall trees surround the site. The 170 tourist pitches are on flat grass, either in the centre, or to the side of the hard road which runs round the camping area, with electricity (6A) available. In high season an overflow area may be brought into use (without electricity). This is a neat, tidy site which caters for winter skiing and summer touring guests.

Facilities: Two well constructed sanitary blocks near the entrance, one open and heated in winter and an older block at the back of the site. Washing machines and dryers. Motorcaravan services. Shop (May - Sept). Large, heated swimming pool (free for campers). Children's pool and playground. Tennis. Football. Club room with TV and drinks machine. **Off site:** Bar/restaurant 1 km.

Charges 2002

Per person	€ 4.15 - € 4.95
child (6-14 yrs)	€ 2.00 - € 2.85
caravan or tent	€ 3.15 - € 4.20
car	€ 2.50 - € 3.45
small tent	€ 2.20 - € 2.80
motorcaravan	€ 4.95 - € 6.30
electricity	€ 1.90
local tax	€ 0.44 - € 0.87

Tel: 05522 74308. Fax: 05522 74308. E-mail: kkf@feldkirch.at. **Reservations:** Write to site. **Open** all year.

Directions: Follow signs from centre of town for Gisingen Stadium (4 km.) and Wildbad.

Camping Riffler

015 Bruggenfeldstraße 2, A-6500 Landeck (Tirol)

This small, pretty site is almost in the centre of the small town of Landeck and, being on the main through route from the Vorarlberg to the Tirol, would serve as a good overnight stop. Square in shape, it has just 50 pitches on either side of hard access roads on level grass, with the main road on one side and the fast flowing River Sanna on the other edge. Trees and flowers adorn the site giving good shade and all pitches have electricity (10A). Activities in the area include walking, mountain biking, paragliding, kite flying, rafting, canoeing and climbing.

Facilities: The single toilet block has been rebuilt to an excellent standard. Washing machine and dryer. Motorcaravan services. Restaurant (closed Oct). Shop. Small general room. Children's play area. Table tennis. Fishing. **Off site:** Bicycle hire 500 m. Swimming pool 500 m. Supermarket just outside the gate, other shops and restaurants about 100 m.

Charges 2003

Per person	€ 4.20
child (5-14 yrs)	€ 3.60
pitch	€ 4.30 - € 8.00
car on pitch	€ 2.20
local tax	€ 0.70
electricity	€ 2.20

Winter prices slightly more. No credit cards. **Tel:** 05442 64898. Fax: 05442 648984. E-mail: d.springeth@tirol.com. **Reservations:** Write to site. **Open** all year except May.

Directions: Site is at the western end of Landeck on the main no. 316 road.

Ötztal Arena Camp Krismer

022 Dorf 387, A-6441 Umhausen (Tirol)

This is a delightful site in the beautiful Ötz valley, on the edge of the village of Umhausen. Situated on a gentle slope in an open valley, it has an air of peace and tranquillity and makes an excellent base for mountain walking, particularly in spring and autumn, skiing in winter or a relaxing holiday. The 98 pitches are all marked and numbered and have electrical connections (12/16A); charges relate to the area available. The new reception building houses an attractive bar/restaurant, a TV room (with Sky) and the sanitary facilities. The young, enthusiastic man and wife management team speak good English.

Facilities: With under-floor heating, some washbasins in cabins and showers on payment, the toilet facilities are of exceptional quality. A small toilet/wash block at the far end of the site has been refurbished for summer use. Baby room. Washing machine and dryer, iron from reception, drying room. Motorcara-van services. Bar/restaurant (May-Sept, Dec-April). No shop but bread can be ordered at reception. TV room with satellite. Ski room. Fishing. Bicycle hire. **Off site:** Shops in village 200 m.

Charges 2002

Per person	€ 6.10
pitch	€ 3.63 - € 5.09
electricity (plus 0.73 per kw)	€ 2.54
dog	€ 2.54
local tax	€ 0.87

Tel: 05255 5390. Fax: 05255 5390. E-mail: info@oetztal-camp.com. **Reservations:** Write with deposit (€ 37). **Open** all year.

Directions: Take Ötztal Valley exit from Imst - Innsbruck motorway, and Umhausen is 13 km. towards Solden; well signed in village.

Ferienanlage Tiroler Zugspitze

004 Obermoos 1, A-6632 Ehrwald (Tirol)

Although Ehrwald is in Austria, it is from the entrance of Zugspitzcamping that the cable car runs to the summit of Germany's highest mountain. Standing at 1,200 feet above sea level at the foot of the mountain, the 200 pitches (120 for tourists), mainly of grass over stones, are on flat terraces with fine panoramic views in parts. All have electricity connections. The modern reception building at the entrance also houses a fine restaurant with a terrace which is open to those using the cable car, as well as those staying on the site. A further large modern building, heated in cool weather, has an indoor pool and fitness centre. This excellent mountain site with its superb facilities provides a good base from which to explore this interesting part of Austria and Bavaria.

Facilities: Two excellent sanitary blocks provide some washbasins in cabins and 20 private bathrooms for rent. Baby room. Washing machines and dryers. Shop. Bar. Restaurant. Indoor pool with sauna, whirlpool and fitness centre. Outdoor pool and children's pool with slide. Table tennis. Bicycle hire. Play area. Organised activities in season. **Off site:** Hotel 100 m. Sports in Ehrwald.

Charges guide

Per person	€ 10.17 - € 11.63
child (4-14 yrs)	€ 7.41 - € 8.36
pitch	€ 5.81 - € 7.63
electricity per kw.	€ 0.73
local taxes	€ 1.27 - € 1.64

Special seasonal weekly offers. No credit cards. **Tel:** 05673 2309. Fax: 05673 230 951. E-mail: ferienanlage@zugspitze.com. **Reservations:** Write to site with deposit (€ 73). **Open** all year.

Directions: Follow signs in Ehrwald to Tiroler Zugspitzbahn and then signs to site.

Sport Camp Tirol

020 Mühlkanal 1, A-6500 Landeck (Tirol)

There are several medium sized sites in this area bordering the Vorarlberg and Tirol, of which this and Camping Riffler are good, well run examples. The district is popular for winter skiing and summer watersports and mountain walking. White water sports are organised on the Rivers Inn and the Sanna (which runs alongside the site, with access). On the other side of the narrow site are fir clad mountains which, with many trees on the site, make it a very pleasant place to stop, either for one night whilst passing through, or for longer stays to explore the region. The 100 pitches (70-100 sq.m) are on either side of gravel roads which run from the asphalt central road and there are electricity connections throughout. The pitches are marked and visitors are shown where to go. There is further space for about 20 tents at the far end of the site. Good English is spoken by the enthusiastic man and wife team who run the site.

Facilities: As with most Austrian sites that open all year, the sanitary facilities are heated and of a good standard. The block for ladies is in a central position, with the men`s block behind reception. Facilities for disabled visitors. Children`s washroom. Washing machine and dryer. Motorcaravan services. Pizzeria/café. Shop. Table tennis. Playground. Volleyball. Programme of watersports, canyoning, rafting, kayak, etc. Roller skating rink. Bicycle hire and mountain biking. Fishing. **Off site:** Shop and restaurant just outside entrance. Swimming pool 1 km. Riding 1 km.

Charges 2003

Per adult	€ 5.20
child (5-10 yrs)	€ 3.60
caravan or family tent	€ 7.80
small tent	€ 3.30 - € 5.50
car	€ 3.40
motorcaravan	€ 9.30
electricity	€ 2.20
local tax	€ 0.60

Special winter rates. **Tel:** 05442 64636. Fax: 05442 64037. E-mail: info@sportcamptirol.at. **Reservations:** Write to site, no deposit or fee required. **Open** all year.

Directions: Site is on the main Vorarlberg - Tirol road by the river bridge, 1 km. west of Landeck. Signed Camping Huber and/or Sport Camp Tirol.

Holiday Camping

003 Reindlau 230B, A-6105 Leutasch (Tirol)

In a mountain setting north of Seefeld and away from the main routes (particularly for caravans), Holiday Camping is not for single night stops but is well suited for those wanting to spend a few days or longer in a quiet setting (no groups are accepted) with opportunities for walking, climbing or touring. Although there are mountains on either side, the site itself is level and offers fine views. Trees decorate the site (but not much shade) and it has a pleasant appearance with plants and shrubs. There are 145 level, numbered pitches of grass on stones, all with electricity (6/12A), water, drainage and TV sockets. The site works closely with the local tourist board to offer a variety of excursions, walking, mountain biking and games for children. Good English is spoken by the friendly owners.

Facilities: Two modern, heated sanitary blocks (one recently refurbished to a high standard) provide all washbasins in cabins. Baby room. Facilities for disabled visitors. Washing machines, dryers, irons. Motorcaravan services. Mini-market. Good restaurant with music twice weekly in high season. Excellent indoor heated swimming pool also has a sauna, steam bath, whirlpool and sun beds. Children's playground. Games room with pool, table tennis, etc. Bicycle hire. Fishing. Activities and excursions. Baby sitting service.

Charges 2003

Per adult	€ 8.50 - € 9.50
child 10-15 yrs	€ 7.50
child 2-10 yrs	€ 4.50
pitch incl. electricity, TV, water and drainage	€ 7.00 - € 10.50
dog	€ 2.00
private toilet unit	€ 12.50
local tax	€ 1.10 - € 1.20

Tel: 05214 65700. Fax: 05214 657 030. E-mail: info@holiday-camping.at. **Reservations:** Made for any length with deposit. **Open** all year except Nov.

Directions: Site is 4 km north of Leutasch; caravans should approach either from Seefeld from the north or via Telfs - Mosern - Seefeld from the south as Littenwald - Leutasch and Zirlerberg on the Innsbruck to Seefeld road are banned to trailers.

Tirol and the West

This is the best known area of Austria as far as British visitors are concerned and the most easily accessible part of the country. It has considerable charm and a wealth of scenic, sporting and historical interest as a centre for both winter and summer tourism. Folk-lore entertainment (Tirolerabend) is on offer outdoors in summer and in Gasthof bars and hotels in winter. Mountain paths are well marked and local authorities provide information centres in towns and lay-bys. Innsbruck is the famous capital of the region, good camp sites abound and there are many pleasant valleys to explore.

Ferienparadies Natterer See

Natterer See 1, A-6161 Natters (Tirol)

Above Innsbruck, 7 km. southwest of the town, this excellent site is in a quiet and isolated location around two small lakes. One of these is for bathing with a long 67 m. slide (free to campers, on payment to day visitors), while boats such as inflatables can be put on either lake. There are many fine mountain views and a wide variety of scenic excursions. For the more active, signed walks start from the site. There are 210 individual pitches (165 for tourists) of varying size. Some are quite small, either on flat ground by the lake or on higher, level terraces where views can be obscured by trees in the summer and some access roads are narrow. All pitches have electricity (6A), with 28 also having water and drain. Many are reinforced by gravel (possibly tricky for tents). For winter camping the site offers ski and drying rooms and a free ski-bus service. A toboggan run and langlauf have been developed on the site, with ice skating, ice hockey and curling on the lake. Occasional services are held in the small chapel. The excellent restaurant with bar and large terrace overlooking the lake has a good menu. Three 'theme pavillions' overlooking the water provide special dinners (4-8 persons). Very good English is spoken. This family-run campsite must rate as one of the best in Austria and can therefore become very busy. It was awarded Camping Cheques' Campsite of the Year 2001. Used by a tour operator (35 pitches).

Facilities: Two excellent sanitary blocks have underfloor heating, some washbasins in cabins, plus facilities for babies, children and disabled people. Laundry facilities. Motorcaravan services. Bar/restaurant (15/3-30/9).Takeaway. Good small shop (15/3-30/9). Children's playgrounds.Children's activity programme with Indian 'topi' tents. Child minding (day nursery) in high season. Sports field. Basketball, beach volleyball and water polo. Table tennis.Youth room with games, pool and billiards. TV room with Sky. Mountain bike hire. 'Aquapark' with water trampoline, slide and other attractions (1/5-30/9). Surfbikes and wind-glider. Canoes and mini sailboats for rent. During high season extensive daily entertainment programme for children and adults offers different sports, competitions, amusement and excursions. No dogs are accepted in high season (11/6-31/8). **Off site:** Tennis, minigolf nearby.

Charges 2002

Per person	€ 5.30 - € 7.10
child (under 14 yrs)	€ 4.00 - € 4.90
pitch	€ 7.20 - € 9.70
electricity (6A)	€ 3.20 - € 3.50
water and drainage plus	€ 1.50
dog (excl 11/06-31/08)	€ 3.00 - € 3.70
local tax	€ 0.60

Special weekly, winter, summer or Christmas packages. **Tel:** 0512 546732. Fax: 0512 5467 3216. E-mail: info@natterersee.com. **Reservations:** made for min. 7 days with deposit (€ 37). **Open** all year.

Directions: From Inntal autobahn (A12) take Brenner autobahn (A13) as far as Innsbruck-sud/Natters exit (no. 3) without payment. From Italy, take exit for Innsbruck-Sud/Natters. Site is signed from the exit (4 km). Care is needed when negotiating the site entrance.

Camping Innsbruck-Kranebitten

Kranebitter Allee 214, A-6020 Innsbruck (Tirol)

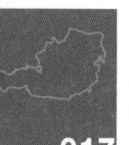

With good facilities, this site is in a pleasant situation just outside Innsbruck. The 120 pitches are numbered, but not marked out, on a partly sloping meadow with good shade cover, There are three separate terraces for caravans and motorcaravans and all pitches have electricity (6A, 2 and 3 pin; long leads are on loan for some). By the side of the site, with access to it, is a large open field with a good playground and plenty of space for ball games. Being so near to the attractive town of Innsbruck, the site makes an excellent base from which to visit the ancient city and also to explore the many attractions nearby. The 'Innsbruck-Card', available from the site, gives various discounts for attractions in the city, plus free travel on public transport (park-and-ride from the site, even if you don't stay overnight).

Facilities: The large, toilet block, although showing signs of age, is heated, clean and acceptable, with some washbasins in cabins. Washing machines and dryers. Motorcaravan services. Bar/ restaurant with terrace. Internet point. Shop for basic supplies. Children's playground, large play field adjoining. Games for children and barbecues in summer. Mountain hiking in summer, free ski bus in winter. **Off site:** Swimming pool 2 km.

Charges 2002

Per person	€ 4.94
child (4-14 yrs)	€ 3.27
caravan	€ 3.27
car	€ 2.91
motorcaravan	€ 5.09
electricity	€ 2.91

Less 10% for stays over 10 days. Special offers for sporting groups. **Tel:** 0512 284 180. Fax: 0512 284 180. E-mail: campinnsbruck@hotmail.com. **Reservations:** Contact site. **Open** all year.

Directions: From A12 Innsbruck - Arlberg motorway, take Innsbruck-Kranebitten exit from where site is well signed, directly on B171 (Telfs-Innsbruck non-toll road).

Your ★★★★★ Holiday Paradise in the Tirol Alps near Innsbruck...

full of life

Natterer See

8 convincing reasons for you to spend your holiday with us:

- the **unique scenic location** in the middle of unspoilt nature
- the **well-placed situation** - also perfect when en route to the South
- the **thrilling water experience** of our own swimming lake (average 22°C)
- the **guarantee of sport, amusement, fun, animation** - ideal for all the family
- the **weekly discounted prices for senior citizens** and bargain hunters and our special mountain-bike-packages
- the comfortable **apartments and guest rooms** for friends and relatives
- the central position in the „Olympia" ski region Innsbruck / Seefeld / Stubaital
- the **high praise from ADAC** for the facilities at our site

Facilities • **individual terraced pitches** with electricity and telephone hook-up partly water and drainage Sat-TV • motorhome service station • top quality sanitation facilities • mini-market • restaurant with lake terrace • **comfortable guest rooms** • **holiday apartments** • mini-club • pool room • youth room • sport & games areas • streetball • beach volleyball • **swimming lake** with 66m giant waterslide • water-trampoline• windglider • surfbikes • canoes• bumper boats • children's swimming bay • archery • mountainbike and cycle hire • indian camp • table-tennis • open-air chess • **top animation programme** • attractive walks

• ski an drying room • ice skating • ice hockey • curling and tobogganing on-site • cross country skiing
• „Olympia" ski region • ski bus

ADAC 2002 Superplatz

We will be pleased to send you our detailed brochure.

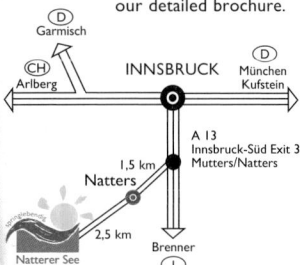

D Garmisch
CH Arlberg — INNSBRUCK — München Kufstein D
A 13 Innsbruck-Süd Exit 3 Mutters/Natters
1,5 km
Natters
2,5 km
Natterer See
Brenner I

Ferienparadies Natterer See

A-6161 Natters/Tirol/Austria
Tel. ++43(0)512/546732
Fax ++43(0)512/546732-16

email: info@natterersee.com
http://www.natterersee.com

Servus in Österreich

TOP CAMPING AUSTRIA

Schloß-Camping

A-6111 Volders (Tirol)

The Inn valley is not only central to the Tirol, but is a very beautiful and popular part of Austria. Volders, some 15 km. from Innsbruck, is one of the little villages on the banks of the Inn river and is perhaps best known for the 17C Baroque Servite Church and monastery. Conveniently situated here is the very pleasant Schloss-Camping, dominated by the castle from which it gets its name that towers at the back of the site with mountains beyond. The 160 grass pitches are on level or slightly sloping ground. Electricity connections throughout (16A). The well laid out camping area is closely mown making this a most attractive site and the English speaking Baron who owns and runs it gives a most friendly welcome. There are rooms to let in the castle. This is an excellent base from which to explore the region and visit Innsbruck, Salzburg, the Royal Castles at Schwangau, the Bavarian Alps and northern Italy over the Brenner Pass for day trips.

Facilities: The refurbished toilet block near the entrance has some washbasins in cabins. Bar/restaurant. Snack bar with terrace. Shop for basics (all May - end Sept). Heated swimming pool (8/5-8/9). Minigolf. Playground. Games and entertainment for children in high season. **Off site:** Supermarket 400 m.

Charges 2002

Per person	€ 4.95
child (3-14 yrs)	€ 3.25
caravan or tent	€ 3.25
car	€ 3.25
m/cycle	€ 1.10
motorcaravan	€ 6.50
electricity	€ 1.80
dog	€ 1.45
local tax	€ 0.51

No credit cards. **Tel:** 05224 52333. E-mail: campingvolders@utanet.at. **Reservations:** made for any length of stay with deposit and small fee. **Open** 15 April - 15 October.

Directions: From A12 motorway, travelling east, leave at exit for Hall, going westwards, take exit for Wattens and follow signs for Volders where site is signed.

Camping Seeblick Toni Brantlhof

Reintalersee 23, A-6233 Kramsach (Tirol)

Austria has some of the finest sites in Europe and Seeblick Toni-Brantlhof is one of the best. In a quiet, rural situation on the edge of the small Reintalersee lake, it is well worth considering for holidays in the Tirol with so many varied excursion possibilities nearby. Kramsach, a pleasant, busy tourist resort is some 3 km. from the site. The mountains which surround the site give scenic views and the campsite has a neat and tidy appearance. The 243 level pitches (215 for tourists) are in regular rows off hard access roads and are of good size with grass and hardstanding. Electricity is available on all pitches (10A) and there are cable TV and phone connections. The large, well appointed restaurant has a rooftop terrace where one can enjoy a meal, drink or snack and admire the lovely scenery. A path leads to the lake for swimming, boating and a sunbathing meadow. With a good solarium, sauna and fitness centre, this site provides for an excellent summer holiday and, with ski areas near, an excellent winter holiday also. Family run wirh good English spoken, there is a friendly welcome.

Facilities: Two heated sanitary blocks of quite outstanding quality include some washbasins in cabins. The main block has been extended to include en-suite toilet/basin/shower rooms (free), the second one, on the opposite side of the camping area, also has individual bathrooms to let. Both blocks are heated in cool weather. Facilities for disabled visitors. Baby room. Washing machines and dryers. Drying rooms. Motorcaravan services. Restaurant. Bar. Snack kiosk. Well stocked minimarket. Fitness centre. Children's playground. Tepi club, kindergarten and organised activities for children in high season. Youth room. Fishing. Bicycle hire. Riding.

Charges 2002

Per pitch	€ 7.05 - € 10.17
person	€ 5.23 - € 6.47
child (under 14 yrs)	€ 4.07 - € 4.65
electricity	€ 3.12
dog	€ 4.14 - € 5.09
local tax	€ 0.73

Tel: 05337 63544. Fax: 05337 63544 305. E-mail: camping@seeblick.co.at. **Reservations:** advised for main season and made for min. 1 week with deposit **Open** all year.

Directions: Directions: Take exit for Kramsach from A12 autobahn and follow signs 'Zu den Seen' in village. After 3 km. turn right at camp sign. Note: there are two sites side by side at the lake - ignore the first and continue through to Seeblick Toni.

AlpencampingMark

025 Bundesstraße 12, Maholmhof, A-6114 Weer bei Schwaz (Tirol)

This pleasant Tirol site is run by a family who provide not only a neat, friendly site and a warm welcome, but also a variety of outdoor activities. Formerly a farm, they now breed horses, giving a free ride each day to youngsters and organising treks. Herr Mark junior (a certified alpine ski guide and ski instructor) runs courses for individuals or groups in climbing (there are practise climbing walls on site), rafting, mountain bike riding, tracking, hiking, etc. Guided alpine tours can be arranged and there are pleasant walks up the lower slopes of the mountains directly from the site. Set in the Inn valley, between mountain ranges, the site has 96 flat, grass pitches (most for touring units) on either side of gravel roads, with electricity connections (6/10A). Trees provide shade in some areas. This site could be used for a night stop when passing through from Innsbruck to Salzburg, but is even better for a longer stay for adventurous youngsters or for a holiday in the Tirol area. The Mark family would very much welcome visits by rallies in the Spring season and are happy to arrange programmes of entertainment and excursions. Good English is spoken.

Facilities: First class, heated sanitary facilities are provided in the old farm buildings. Freezer. Washing machines and dryer. Motorcaravan services. Small, cheerful bar/restaurant and shop (1/6-1/9). Small heated pool (15/5-15/9). An attractive wooden chalet houses reception and the activities are administered from here. Activity programme with instruction. Bicycle hire. Riding. Glacier tours. Table tennis. Large children's play area with good equipment. A further chalet is for use by children in wet weather.

Charges 2002

Per person	€ 4.30 - € 5.00
child (under 14 yrs)	€ 3.00 - € 3.50
pitch	€ 4.50 - € 6.00
electricity	€ 2.00
dog	€ 1.50
local tax	€ 0.50

Tel: 05224 68146. **Fax:** 05224 681 466. **E-mail:** alpcamp.mark@aon.at. **Reservations:** Necessary for 1/7-15/8 and made without deposit. **Open** 1 April - 31 October.

Directions: irections: Site is 200 m. east of the village of Weer on Wattens - Schwaz road no. B171 which runs parallel to the A12, just 10 km. east of Innsbruck.

Erlebnis-Comfort-Camping Aufenfeld

012 Distelberg 1, A-6274 Aschau im Zillertal (Tirol)

This site is attractively situated in a mountain region with fine views and good facilities. The main area of the site itself is flat with pitches of 100 sq.m. on grass between made-up access roads, with further pitches on terraces at the rear. There are now 350 pitches (300 for touring units with 6A electricity) including some with individual sanitary cubicles. The site can become full mid-July until mid-August and at Christmas, but usually has space at other times. Ski lifts are nearby, one for beginners particularly close. A splendid, indoor swimming pool has been added and there is a heated outdoor pool, paddling pool, and a tennis court for summer use. A lake and leisure area has been created alongside the site.

Facilities: The well kept, heated toilet block in the main building is of excellent quality and size with several washbasins in cabins for each sex, one with a baby bath and one with a full bath for ladies. Additional units, some new, provide private cabins and family rooms. Washing machines, dryers. Motorcaravan services. Small shop. Restaurant. General room. TV. Indoor pool, sauna and sun-beds. Outdoor pool (May - Sept). Football field. Playground. Beach volleyball. Tennis. Riding. Fishing. Bicycle hire. Cash point machine.

Charges 2002

Per person	€ 4.50 - € 7.50
child (under 12 yrs)	€ 3.30 - € 5.50
pitch incl. electricity and TV hook-up	€ 6.60 - € 9.00
with water	€ 7.30 - € 10.50
with private sanitary cabin	€ 14.60 - € 20.00
electricity	€ 2.20 - € 3.00
dog	€ 3.00 - € 3.70
local tax	€ 1.00

Winter prices are higher. **Tel:** 05282 29160. **Fax:** 05282 291 611. **E-mail:** camping.fiegl@tirol.com. **Reservations:** made with deposit and fee for min. 1 week. **Open** all year except 7 Nov - 12 Dec.

Directions: From Inntal motorway, take Zillertal exit, 32 km. northeast of Innsbruck. Follow road no. 169 to village of Aschau from which site is well signed.

Camping Mayrhofen

Laubichl 125, Laubühel, A-6290 Mayrhofen (Tirol)

005

The town of Mayrhofen, in the pretty Zillertal Valley that runs south from the A12 Innsbruck - Worgl autobahn and then east over the Gerlos Pass through to the A10 Salzburg - Spittal motorway, is a very popular summer and winter resort. The picturesque narrow gauge Zillertalbahn winds its way along the valley following the River Ziller. Camping Mayrhofen (formerly Camping Kröll) stands back from the B169 road 1 km. north of Mayrhofen between the mountains on either side of the valley. The site has 170 level pitches for tourists, of grass on gravel, all with electricity (6A). There are a few trees, but little shade, although there are pleasant views. A new building houses reception and a small heated pool which extends from here to the outside where there is a grass area.

Facilities: Good quality sanitary provision has been refurbished to include private wash cabins. Washing machine and dryer. Shop (limited supplies). Bar/restaurant (also with rooms to let) provides limited food supplies. Grill. Children's playground. Small but good heated pool. Sauna and solarium. Games, TV and children's rooms.

Charges 2002

Per person	€ 5.20
child (under 14 yrs)	€ 3.30
tent or caravan	€ 3.00
car	€ 2.50
motorcaravan	€ 5.50
dog	€ 2.00
local tax	€ 0.60

Electricity on meter. No credit cards. **Tel:** 05285 62580-51. Fax: 05285 62580-60. E-mail: kroell.hermann@netwing.at. **Reservations:** Are made to guarantee admission (no deposit). **Open** all year.

Directions: Site is on northern side of Mayrhofen and signed from the B169 (approaching from the north, on your left hand side).

Camping Hofer

A-6280 Zell-am-Ziller (Tirol)

007

Zell am Ziller is in the heart of the Zillertal valley at the junction of the B169 and B165 Gerlos Pass road and nestles round the unusual 18th century church. Camping Hofer, owned by the same family for over 50 years, is on the edge of the village just five minutes walk from the centre on a quiet side road. The 100 pitches, all with electricity (6/10A), are grass on gravel. A few trees decorate the site and offer some shade. A pleasant development provides a bar/restaurant, games and TV room and a small heated pool which can be covered. A little road train gives a free service round the village. The pleasant owner, who speaks good English, does his best to provide a friendly, family atmosphere.

Facilities: Good quality, heated sanitary provision is on the ground floor of the apartment building and has some washbasins in cabins. Baby room. Washing machines, dryers and irons. Gas supplies. Motorcaravan services. Restaurant with bar (closed 1/11-10/12 and 30/4-31/5). Shop opposite. Swimming pool (1/4-31/10). Bicycle hire. Organised entertainment and activities in high season. Guided walks, cycle tours, barbecues, biking, skiing.

Charges 2002

Per person	€ 4.50 - € 7.00
pitch and electricity	€ 7.00 - € 10.50
local tax	€ 1.00

Special winter packages. No credit cards (debit cards accepted). **Tel:** 05282 2248. Fax: 05282 22488. E-mail: office@campinghofer.at. **Reservations:** Needed for July/Aug and Christmas; made for any length of stay with deposit. **Open** all year.

Directions: Site is well signed from the main B169 road at Zell am Ziller.

Camping Zillertal-Hell

A-6263 Fügen (Tirol)

009

The village of Fügen lies about 7 km. from the A12 autobahn at the start of the Zillertal, so is well placed for exploring the valley and the area around Schwaz. Easy to reach, Camping Zillertal-Hell is an attractive small site with excellent facilities and 127 marked pitches on flat grass. All have electricity (6/10A), nine also have water and drainage and there are hard-standings for motorcaravans. A programme of games and entertainment for children is organised in summer, at Christmas and at Easter with bicycle trips and hiking for adults. The site could make a good overnight stop or for a longer stay but, being on a main road, there is some road noise.

Facilities: New modern heated sanitary block of top quality has some washbasins in cabins, a children's wash room, and private bathrooms for hire. Washing machine, dryer, iron and drying room. Motorcaravan services. Attractive bar with terrace and small restaurant. Shop for basic supplies. Swimming pool (20 x 10 m, 1/5-15/10). Games room with TV. Playground. Organised games, activities and entertainment. Bicycle hire. Dogs are not accepted. **Off site:** Fishing 500 m. Shops and restaurants in the village 800 m.

Charges 2002

Per person	€ 4.20 - € 6.80
pitch and electricity	€ 8.50 - € 12.00
local tax	€ 0.51

Less for longer stays. **Tel:** 05288 62203. Fax: 05288 64615. E-mail: camping-hell@tirol.com. **Reservations:** Min. 7 days. **Open** all year.

Directions: Site is beside the no. 169 road, 7 km. south of the exit for Gagering (also signed Zillertal) from the A12 Innsbruck - Worgl motorway.

Terrassen-Camping Schloßberg Itter

Itter 140, A-6361 Hopfgarten (Tirol)

With some 200 pitches, this well kept site with good facilities is suitable both as a base for longer stays and also for overnight stops, as it lies right by a main road west of Kitzbühel. It is on a slight slope but most of the 200 numbered pitches are on level terraces. All have electricity and cable TV connections, 150 have water and drainage and 25 have telephone sockets. Space is usually available. The site has two remarkable features - the large children's playground has a huge collection of most ingeniously devised fixed apparatus, and secondly, the excellent sanitary facilities which have been added on the floor above the older provision. Good walks and a wealth of excursions by car are available nearby. There is a free ski-lift from the site in winter, especially suitable for beginners and children, and a toboggan run. There is some road and rail noise.

Facilities: Both sanitary units heated and of very high standard. The new section has a large room with private cubicles placed around the walls and as free standing units. Some of these have washbasins set in flat surfaces with others having baths, one a massage type, or showers, with two slightly larger units for families, with baby baths. Pots of artificial flowers complete the hotel-like atmosphere of 'Washland'. Facilities for disabled visitors. Washing machine and dryer. Motorcaravan services.Cooking facilities. Small shop, bar/restaurant (both closed Nov). Pleasant open-air, solar heated swimming pool (16 x 8 m.) and paddling pool (1/5-30/9). Sauna and solarium. Excellent children's playground. Refrigerator boxes for hire. Youth room. **Off site:** Tennis, fishing, riding, bicycle hire within 2 km. Golf 10 km.

Charges 2003

Per person	€ 5.50
child (1-13 yrs)	€ 3.40
tent or caravan	€ 7.60
motorcaravan	€ 6.40 - € 7.80
electricity	€ 2.60 - € .00
dog	€ 3.50
local tax (over 14 yrs)	€ 1.58

Prices higher for winter. Less 50% on pitch fee in mid-seasons. No credit cards. **Tel:** 05335 2181. Fax: 05335 2182. E-mail: info@camping-itter.at.
Reservations: made with deposit and fee; usually min. 1 week (2 weeks at Christmas). **Open** all year except 6 Nov - 1 Dec.

Directions: Site is 2 km. northwest of Hopfgarten on B170 road to Worgl (not up by Schloss Itter). The entrance is on a bend opposite a Peugeot/ Talbot garage and as much of the site is hidden from the road by trees, care is needed to spot it.

Tirol Camp

Lindau 20, A-6391 Fieberbrunn (Tirol)

This is one of many Tirol campsites that cater equally for summer and winter (here seemingly more for winter, when reservation is essential and prices 50% higher). Tirol Camp is in a quiet and attractive mountain situation and has 307 pitches all on wide flat terraces, set on a gentle slope (220 for touring units). Marked out mainly by the electricity boxes, they are said to be 80-100 sq.m. and all have electricity (6A), gas, water/drainage, TV and telephone connections. A small, heated swimming pool with a paddling pool is open in summer. For winter stays, the site is very close to a ski lift centre and a 'langlauf' piste.

Facilities: Original toilet block in the main building excellent, including some washbasins in cabins and some private bathrooms on payment, supplemented by a splendid heated block at the top end of the site, with spacious showers and all the washbasins in cabins. Washing machines, dryers and drying room. Motorcaravan services. Self-service shop and snacks. Restaurant (closed Oct, Nov and May). Separate general room. Sauna. Tennis. Swimming pool ((12 x 8 m; 1/6-30/9). Lake fishing. Riding. Bicycle hire. Outdoor chess. Children's playground and zoo. Entertainment and activity programmes for adults and children (July/Aug).

Charges 2002

Per pitch	€ 6.00 - € 12.00
adult	€ 4.00 - € 8.00
child (4-15 yrs)	free - € 4.00
dog	€ 4.00 - € 5.00
electricity (per kw/h on meter)	€ 0.70
local taxes	€ 1.00

Winter charges higher. Special weekly package deals with half-board offered in summer. **Tel:** 05354 56666. Fax: 05354 52516. E-mail: office@tirol-camp.at.
Reservations: made for any length (with deposit in winter only). **Open** all year.

Directions: Site is on the east side of Fieberbrunn, which is on the St Johann-Saalfelden road.

Euro Camping Wilder Kaiser

014 A-6345 Kössen (Tirol)

The village of Kössen lies to the south of the A8 Munich - Salzburg autobahn and east of the A12 motorway near Kufstein. It is therefore well situated for overnight stops but even more for longer stays. Wilder Kaiser is located at the foot of the Unterberg with views of the Kaisergebirge (the Emperor's mountains) and surrounded by forests. Being about 2 km. north of the village, it is a quiet location, away from main roads. The well constructed main building at the entrance houses reception, a fine restaurant with terrace, well stocked shop and the sanitary facilities overlooking heated swimming pool and children's pool. About 150 of the 250 pitches (grass over gravel) are available for tourists. Of a good size, with electricity (6/10A), water, drainage, TV and gas points, they are arranged on either side of decorative brick paved roads. Some have shade from the attractive trees and all have good views. One of the top ten best campsites in Austria, this can be recommended without reservation.

Facilities: The heated, central sanitary block is of excellent quality with generously sized showers and sinks. Nicely tiled, it is kept exceptionally clean. Baby room. Washing machines and dryers. Motorcaravan services. Shop. Large restaurant/bar (closed Nov). Snack bar (high season). Club room with TV. Heated swimming pool (May - Oct). Youth room. Sauna and solarium. Tennis. Large imaginative adventure playground. In high season, special staff run a Tepi club and other activities for adults and children, with the weekly programme displayed on notice boards.

Charges 2002

Per person	€ 4.65 - € 5.89
child (under 14)	€ 2.91 - € 3.63
pitch with electricity and TV	€ 5.16 - € 7.05
pitch with all services	€ 5.89 - € 8.14
electricity	€ 1.69 - € 2.33
dog	€ 2.69 - € 3.42
local tax	€ 0.65

Reductions for long off-season stays. **Tel:** 05375 6444. Fax: 053751 2113. E-mail: info@eurocamp-koessen.com. **Reservations:** made with deposit and fee for exact dates in high season; no minimum stay except at Christmas (3 weeks). **Open** all year.

Directions: From A8 autobahn (München - Salzburg), take Grabenstatt exit and go south on B307/B176 to Kössen where site is signed. From the south go north on B176. From A93 (Rosenheim- - Kufstein) autobahn take Oberaudorf exit and go east on B172 to Walchsee and Kössen.

Salzburg and the Centre

There is more to Salzburg than 'The Sound of Music' and Mozart, although memorabilia of its most famous composer dominate from confectionery to souvenirs. Pastureland, curative spas and interesting castles and monasteries abound. The Lake District, set amidst rolling hills, is near, along with salt mines to visit and music, art and drama festivals to enjoy. Salzburg has splendid gardens and ancient castles.

Seecamp Zell am See

016 Thumersbacherstraße 34, A-5700 Zell-am-See (Salzburg)

Zellersee, delightfully situated in the south of Salzburg province and near the start of the Grossglocknerstrasse, is ideally placed for enjoying the splendid southern Austria countryside. Seecamp is right by the water about 2 km. from the town of Zell and with fine views to the south end of the lake. One is immediately struck by the order and appearance of the site, with 176 good level, mainly grass-on-gravel pitches of above average size, all with electricity (10/16A). About half have water, drainage and TV connections. A large, modern building in the centre, houses the amenities. The lake is accessible for watersports, including both surfing and sailing schools. All in all, this is a splendid site for a relaxing or active holiday.

Facilities: Excellent, heated sanitary facilities include facilities for disabled visitors and a baby room. Washing machines, dryers and irons. Motorcaravan services. Restaurant (closed Oct-Nov). Shop (June-Aug. and Dec-mid Jan). Beach volleyball. Play area. Fishing. Bicycle hire. Summer entertainment for children. Activity programme for adults with rafting, canoeing, mountain biking, water ski-ing and hiking. Winter ski packages. Glacier ski-ing possible in summer. **Off site:** Free entry to nearby lake beach, swimming pool and ice skating.

Charges 2002

Per pitch	€ 7.97 - € 9.91
adult	€ 7.07
child (2-15 yrs)	€ 3.87
car	€ 2.25
electricity	€ 0.65
local tax (over 15 yrs)	€ 0,90

Less 20% in low season. Special winter package prices. **Tel:** 06542 72115. Fax: 06542 721 1515. E-mail: zell@seecamp.at. **Reservations:** Made for min. 7 days - contact site for form. **Open** all year.

Directions: Follow signs for Thumersbach where site is signed on north side of lake.

Kur Camping Erlengrund

Erlengrundstraße 6, A-5640 Badgastein (Salzburg)

Although in a fairly remote area, Badgastein became popular in the last century with those 'taking cures' in the waters from the hot natural springs that still fill the unique indoor swimming pool. The town is on a steep slope with the River Ache cascading down into the centre and under the main street. It also lies on the route to the south using the Tauern rail tunnel (which will take caravans) to travel between the Tirol and Carinthia. Camping Erlungrund is on flat ground just north of the town, surrounded by wooded mountains. It provides 180 pitches (118 for touring units in summer, 90 in winter), most with hardstanding under the grass. All pitches have electricity (16A) and 60 are fully serviced.

Facilities: The main apartment building also houses the good quality, heated sanitary facilities. Family bathrooms for hire. Washing machine and drying room. Small shop (mornings). Small heated swimming pool (high season). TV room. Table tennis. Football. Children's playground. **Off site:** Restaurant is just outside entrance. Site belongs to Hotel Europaischer Hof, campers may use the hotel's recreational facilities.

Charges 2002

Per person	€ 4.58 - € 5.09
child	€ 3.56 - € 3.92
pitch acc. to season and size	€ 4.94 - € 6.54
dog	€ 3.78
local tax (over 15 yrs)	€ 1.24

Electricity and gas on meter Tel: 06434 2790. Fax: 06434 30175. **Reservations:** made for min 1 week with deposit. **Open** all year.

Directions: Turn off B167 road at sign 1 km before Badgastein.

Camping Hirschenwirt

Bundesstraße 1, A-5600 St Johann im Pongau (Salzburg)

This small, but very pleasant site is ideally placed for those wanting a night stop when travelling on the Salzburg - Badgastein road, but could also make an excellent base for seeing this interesting area of mountains, lakes, salt mines, ice caves and famous towns. The flat, open site lies behind the Gasthof Hirschenwirt, with 40 tourist pitches on grass on either side of gravel roads. This attractive mountain area has outstanding cycle and mountain bike tracks and sporting opportunities locally include rafting, riding or paragliding. Being on a major road route there is traffic noise.

Facilities: Excellent sanitary facilities in the basement of the Gasthof have under-floor heating and include some private bathrooms for hire. Sauna and solarium also here. Washing machine, dryer and drying room. Bar/restaurant. Small swimming pool (May - Sept). Bicycle hire. Children's playground. Music (in restaurant) at weekends.

Charges 2002

Per person	€ 4.00
child (3-14 yrs)	€ 2.00
pitch	€ 6.00
electricity (per kw)	€ 0.44

No credit cards. **Tel:** 06412 6012. Fax: 06412 60128. E-mail: hirschenwirt@aon.at. **Reservations:** Write to site. **Open** all year except Nov.

Directions: Site is behind Gasthof Hirschenwirt at St Johann im Pongau on main B311 (Salzburg - Badgastein) road.

Camping Nord-Sam

Samstrasse 22a, A-5023 Salzburg (Salzburg)

A neat little site in the town suburbs, Nord-Sam is very close to the Salzburg-Nord autobahn exit, and so makes a convenient stopover. It is also acceptable for a longer stay, being on the edge of the town and with its own small swimming pool. It is divided into 100 individual pitches (with 16A electricity), which are not very large but are separated by hedges, etc. which offer some privacy and are also attractive to wild life (including red squirrels). Pitches are quite well shaded and the site is well tended, with flowers and shrubs. You should find space if you arrive reasonably early. Salzburg is a major railway junction so expect some train noise at night.

Facilities: The small, heated sanitary block, situated below the house, is of excellent quality with some washbasins in cabins. Washing machine and dryer. Motorcaravan services. Small shop. Room for general use where drinks served. Swimming pool (14 x 7 m). Meals in high season. Unusual small children's play area. Bicycle hire. **Off site:** Cycle path directly to the city centre. Bus service to city (tickets from reception, change at railway station).

Charges 2003

Per person	€ 4.00 - € 5.50
child (2-14 yrs)	€ 2.50 - € 4.00
pitch	€ 6.50 - € 8.00
electricity	€ 2.25

Tel: 0662 660 494. Fax: 0662 660 494. E-mail: christinelex@camping-nord-sam.com. **Reservations:** are made - contact site. **Open** 1 May - 30 September.

Directions: Site is signed from Salzburg-Nord autobahn exit and city centre; follow signs carefully.

Sport-Camp Woferlgut

Kroessenbach 40, A-5671 Bruck (Salzburg)

018

The village of Bruck lies at the junction of the B311 and the Grossglocknerstrasse in the Hohe Tauern National Park, with Salzburg to the north and Innsbruck to the northwest. Sport Camp Woferlgut, a family run site, is one of the best in Austria. Although surrounded by mountains, the site is quite flat with pleasant views. The 370 level, grass pitches are generously sized and marked out by shrubs (300 for touring units) and each has electricity (16A), water, drainage, cable TV socket and gas point. The fitness centre has a fully equipped gym, whilst the other building contains a sauna and cold dip, Turkish bath, solarium (all free) massage on payment and a bar. In summer there is a free activity programme, evenings with live music, club for children, weekly barbecues and guided cycle and mountain tours. The site's own lake is used for swimming and fishing, surrounded by a landscaped sunbathing area. In winter a cross-country skiing trail and toboggan run lead from the site and a free bus service is provided to nearby skiing facilities. A high grass bank separates the site and the road. The management is pleased to advise on local attractions and tours, making this a splendid base for a family holiday. Used by tour operators (20 pitches).

Facilities: Three modern sanitary blocks - the newest in a class of its own - have excellent facilities, providing private cabins, under-floor heating and music. Washing machines and dryers. Facilities for disabled visitors. Motorcaravan services. Cooking facilities. Fridge hire. Well stocked shop, restaurant (both 20/12-20/4 and 13/5-1/11). Small, heated outdoor pool and children's pool (15/5-30/9). Fitness centre. Two children's playgrounds and indoor play room. General room. Tennis. Volleyball. Football area. Bicycle hire. Hobby room with billiards, table tennis and TV. Fishing. Watersports and lake swimming. Hiking and skiing (all year) nearby. Collection of small animals with pony rides for young children. Motorcycles not accepted. **Off site:** Golf 3 km. Skiing 2.5 km. Boat launching and sailing 3.5 km.

Charges 2002

Per person	€ 4.40 - € 5.70
child (under 10 yrs)	€ 3.70 - € 4.90
tent or caravan	€ 4.70 - € 6.00
car	€ 4.00 - € 5.20
motorcaravan	€ 7.10 - € 11.20
electricity (plus meter)	€ 2.00
cable TV (once)	€ 7.80
dog	€ 2.90 - € 4.00

Special prices for senior citizens and families. No credit cards. **Tel:** 06545 73030. Fax: 06545 73033. E-mail: info@sportcamp.at. **Reservations:** Contact site. **Open** all year.

Directions: Site is southwest of Bruck. From road B311, Bruck by-pass, take southern exit (Grossglockner) and site is well signed.

Seecamp Neumarkt

027

Uferstrasse 3, A-5202 Neumarkt (Salzburg)

Surrounded by gentle hills and adorned with trees and flowers, Seecamp is separated from the lake by a narrow public road, although there is access to the water through the municipal bathing area. When seen in mid-week it was very quiet, but one would imagine that it is more lively during weekends in high season. The 170 grass pitches (90 for tourists, the remainder for long stay units) are on either side of gravel roads on a very gentle slope. They are not marked out or numbered but the position of electricity boxes allows sufficient space. All pitches have electricity (6A) and connections are available for TV/radio, water and drainage.

Facilities: Very good sanitary facilities, heated in winter with a first aid room are housed in a modern, underground block near the lake. There are ramps by the steps to the toilets for disabled visitors but these are rather steep. Some facilities are used by non-camping members of the public. Restaurant with terrace. Shop. Minigolf. Volleyball. Children's playground. General room with TV. Bathing at lake station. Fishing.

Charges 2002

Per pitch	€ 6.90
adult	€ 4.72
child (2-15 yrs)	€ 4.72
electricity (plus 0.58 per kw)	€ 1.82
dog	€ 1.09
local tax	€ 0.51

No credit cards **Tel:** 06216 4400. Fax: 06216 44004. **Reservations:** Write to site. **Open** Easter - 31 October.

Directions: Approx. 26 km. from Salzburg, on B1/A1 Salzburg - Linz road, take turning for Neumarkt. Follow signs for Strandcamping just before the small town itself. If using motorway use Wallersee Ost exit.

Camping Appesbach

024

Au 99, A-5360 St Wolfgang (Upper Austria)

St Wolfgang, a pretty little village on the lake of the same name which was made famous by the operetta 'White Horse Inn', is ringed round by hills in a delightful situation. The location of Appesbach, on the banks of the lake with a good frontage, is one of its main assets. The lake is used for all types of sailing and wind-surfing and bathing is possible if it's not too cool. The site has 170 pitches, with 80 for tourists with some in regular rows and the rest on open meadows that could become full in high season. Pitches near the lakeside have higher charges. All have electricity (10A) with a mix of German and European sockets. The welcoming owners, Maria and Christian, both speak good English.

Facilities: The two toilet blocks have been combined into one, extended and refurbished to a good standard. Motorcaravan services. Good shop. Bar/restaurant with TV (1/5-31/8). Snack bar with terrace (Easter-30/9). Small children's playground. Table tennis, billards, darts. **Off site:** Village 1 km. Many excursions possible including Salzburg 50 km.

Charges 2002

Per person	€ 4.43 - € 4.94
child (3-15 yrs)	€ 2.58 - € 3.20
pitch acc. to position and unit	€ 3.63 - € 10.17
electricity	€ 2.18
dog	€ 1.45
local tax	€ 0.65 - € 0.87

Tel: 06138 2206. Fax: 06138 220 633. E-mail: camping@appesbach.at. **Reservations:** min. 1 week with deposit. **Open** Easter - 31 October.

Directions: From B158 Salzburg-Bad Ischl road, turn towards St Wolfgang just east of Strobl and site is on the left 1 km. before St Wolfgang.

Camp Mond See Land

035

Wiedlroither KEG, PunzAu 21, A-5310 Mondsee (Upper Austria)

Mond See Land underwent a make-over in 2000 and now offers excellent facilities in a pleasant part of Austria, to the east of Salzburg, between the lakes of Mondsee and Irrsee. It is peacefully situated in a natural setting, with mountain views, yet less than 10 minutes drive from the autobahn. There are 60 good sized, level touring pitches (80 long stay), set amongst the trees at the lower level and on terraces, each with water, waste water and 16A electricity. The heated swimming pool is covered and has a sunbathing terrace, and there is a small fishing lake (unfenced).

Facilities: Two sanitary buildings, one new and the other completely renovated, offer first class facilities including some washbasins in cabins. Good unit for disabled visitors. Laundry with washing machines and dryer. Motorcaravan service point. Shop and restaurant, both all season. Swimming pool. Playground. Riding. **Off site:** Mondsee is a popular large lake with many sport opportunities. Golf 5 km.

Charges 2002

Per person	€ 4.22
pitch	€ 5.40 - € 5.80
electricity	€ 2.18

Tel: (0)6232/2600. Fax: (0)6232/27218. E-mail: austria@campmondsee.at. **Reservations:** Contact site. **Open** 1 April - 10 October.

Directions: From A1/E55 take exit 265 signed Straßwalchen onto B154. In approx 1.5 m. turn left owards Haidermühle and then 2 km to site (signed).

Camping am See

034 A-4831 Obertraun (Upper Austria)

It is unusual to locate a campsite so deep in the heart of spectacular mountain scenery, yet with such easy access. Directly on the shores of Halstattersee, near to Obertraun and the Dachstein range of mountains, this 2.5 hectare, flat site is an excellent, peaceful holiday base which is being upgraded. Owners cum professional artists, Carola and Lorenzo, both speak English and their talents are reflected around the central amenity building. The grass site is basically divided into two, with tents in a more shady area, whilst caravans and motorcaravans are more in the open. There are no specific pitches although the owners, within reason, control where you place your unit. Hallstratt is an attractive UNESCO listed alpine village with the oldest salt mines in the world.

Facilities: Completely refurbished, fully equipped and modern, the toilet block includes a small baby room. Washing machine. New, open barn style area for dishwashing and a similar area with purpose built barbecues, seating and tables. Bar and limited restaurant. Basic daily provisions kept such as bread and milk. **Off site:** Activities nearby include walking for all ages and abilities, bird watching, fishing, mountain biking, rock climbing, scuba diving and much more. For naturists, 100 m. from the site there is a delightful popular area designated as an FKK strand (naturist beach).

Charges 2002

Per unit incl. 2 persons and tax	€ 18.82 - € 19.19
child	€ 3.42 - € 2.91
electricity	€ 2.91
tent incl. 2 persons	€ 17.37 - € 19.55

Tel: 06131 265. **Fax:** 06134 8369. **E-mail:** camping. am.see@chello.at. **Reservations:** Necessary for high season. **Open** 1 May - 30 September.

Directions: Due south from Bad Ischi on road 145, take road 166 to Hallstatt. After single carriageway tunnel, site is 4 km. on left on entering village of Winkl.

Camping Stumpfer

028 A-3392 Schönbühel (Lower Austria)

This small, well appointed site with just 60 pitches is directly on the River Danube, near the small town of Schönbühel, and could make a convenient night stop being near the Salzburg - Vienna autobahn. The 50 unmarked pitches for touring units, all with electricity (16A), are on flat grass and the site is lit at night. There is shade in most parts and a landing stage for boat trips on the Danube. The main building also houses a Gasthof, with a bar/restaurant of the same name, that can be used by campers. This is very much a family run site.

Facilities: Part of the main building, the toilet block is of good quality with hot water on payment. Facilities for disabled visitors include ramps by the side of steps up to the block. Washing machine and dryer. Motorcaravan services. Small shop for basics. Playground. Fishing. **Off site:** Swimming pool, bicycle hire or riding within 5 km.

Charges 2003

Per person	€ 4.60
pitch	€ 2.50 - € 5.20
electricity	€ 2.20
local tax (over 16 yrs)	€ 0.76

Less 2% for cash payment, 5% after 7 days. **Tel:** 02752 8510. **Fax:** 02752 851017. **E-mail:** office@stumpfer.com. **Reservations:** Write to site. **Open** 1 April - 31 October.

Directions: Leave Salzburg - Vienna autobahn at Melk exit. Continue towards Melk Nord. Just before bridge turn right (Schönbühel and St Polten), at T-junction turn right again and continue down hill. Turn right just before filling station (Schönbühel) and site is 3 km. on left with narrow entrance.

Camping Rodaun

030 Breitenfurter Straße 487, An der Au 2, A-1236 Wien-Südwest-Rodaun (Vienna)

This good quality site is within the Vienna city boundary and is an excellent base for visiting this old, interesting and world famous city. Just 9 km. from the centre, there is an excellent public transport system for viewing the sights as car parking is almost impossible in the city. Set in a southern suburb, it is a very pleasant site in its own right with space for about 100 units on flat grass pitches. With little shade, pitches are not marked, either in the centre or outside the tarmac road running round the camping area, with electricity. There is also a hardstanding area for motorcaravans (but no space for awnings).

Facilities: The toilet block has some washbasins in cabins and hot showers on payment. Washing machines, dryers and irons. Motorcaravan service point. **Off site:** Supermarket and restaurant within 250 m. Swimming pool, 2 km.

Charges 2002

Per person	€ 5.45
child (3-13 yrs)	€ 3.27
pitch	€ 4.36 - € 5.01
car or motorcycle	€ 1.09
electricity	€ 0.65

Tel: 01 8884 154. **Fax:** 01 8884 154. **Reservations:** advised; write to site. **Open** 1 April - 5 November.

Directions: Take Pressbaum exit from West-autobahn or Vosendorf exit from Sudautobahn and follow signs. It is worth writing for a brochure which gives a good map showing how to find the site.

Donaupark Camping Tulln

Hafenstraße, A-3430 Tulln (Lower Austria)

029

The ancient town of Tulln (the 'city of roses') lies on the southern bank of the River Danube, about 20 miles northwest of Vienna. The city can be reached by train in about 30 minutes and one can sail on the river through the Wachau vineyards, orchards and charming villages viewing the ruined castles and church belfries. Tulln was founded by the Romans and was the capital until replaced, first by Klosterneuburg and then Vienna. Donaupark Camping, owned and run by the Austrian Motor Club (OAMTC), is imaginatively laid out 'village-style' with unmarked grass pitches grouped around six circular gravel areas. Further pitches are to the side of the hard road which links the circles and these include some with grill facilities for tents; 100 of the 130 tourist pitches have electricity(6A) and cable TV sockets. Tall trees surrounding the site offer shade in parts. Tucked neatly away at the back of the site, are 120 long stay caravans.This is a quiet location some 100 m. from the Danube. The manager speaks good English and is pleased to advise on tourist matters.

Facilities: Three identical, modern, octagonal sanitary blocks can be heated. One is at reception and the other two which are linked by a cover, at the far end. Facilities for disabled visitors. Washing machines and dryers .Cooking rings. Gas supplies. Bar and restaurantwith terrace which keeps open quite late.(1/5-15/9). Shop (15/5-15/9). Children's play areas, space for ball games and Topi club (July/Aug). Tennis. Volleyball. Bicycle and canoe hire. Excursion programme. Activities are organised in high season with guided tours around Tulln on foot, by bike and on the river by canoe. **Off site:** Lake swimming in adjacent park.Entry free for campers. Fishing 500 m. Bus service into Vienna 9/7-24/8. Half-hourly train service to Vienna. Steamer excursions.

Charges 2002

Per person	€ 5.09
child (5-14 yrs)	€ 2.90
pitch	€ 7.99 - € 10.17
small tent with car or motorcycle	€ 4.36
bicycle	€ 2.18
electricity	€ 1.45

Tel: 02272 65200. Fax: 02272 65201. E-mail: camp-tulln@oeamtc.at. **Reservations:** Write to site. **Open** Easter - 15 October.

Directions: From Vienna follow south bank of the Danube on B14; from the west, leave the A1 autobahn at either St Christophen or Altenbach exits and go north on B19 to Tulln. Site is on the east side of Tulln and well signed.

Donaupark Camping Klosterneuburg

In der Au, A-3400 Klosterneuburg (Lower Austria)

032

Klosterneuburg lies just to the north of Vienna on the Danube, outside the city boundary away from the noise and bustle of the famous city but only minutes away by train. Donaupark Camping is only a few hundred metres from the river, a walk away from Klosterneuburg and its well known Baroque abbey and the Wienerwald. Owned and run by the Austrian Motor Club (OAMTC), the site is in a park-like situation, surrounded by trees but with little shade. The 130 pitches of varying size (some small) are on grass or hardstanding, accessed from hard roads and with electricity (6A). Alongside the site is 'Happyland', an amusement park which also has a large swimming pool (discounts for campers). This is a good spot for families with the glories of historic Vienna easily reached and Happyland for the children. The friendly manager speaks good English.

Facilities: There are two modern sanitary units, one at reception and the other by the pitches. Facilities for disabled visitors. Motorcaravan services. Washing machines and dryer. Electric cooking rings. Freezer for ice packs. Restaurant/snack bar incl. small shop for basics (1/5-31/10). Play area. Bicycle hire. **Off site:** Organised excursions with bikes or guided sightseeing tours of Vienna.

Charges 2002

Per person	€ 5.50
child (5-14 yrs)	€ 3.00
pitch	€ 7.50 - € 11.00
electricity	€ 1.80
small tent with car or m/cycle	€ 4.50
local tax	€ 0.80

Tel: 02243 258 77. Fax: 02243 258 78. E-mail: camp-klosterneuburg@oeamtc.at. **Reservations:** Write to site. **Open** 15 March - 10 November.

Directions: Leave Vienna on the west bank of the Danube following signs for Klosterneuburg, site is signed in the town from the main road B14 and is 400 m. behind the railway station.

Vienna and the East

Although Vienna (Wien) is a vibrant centre for culture today, with museums, opera, famous choirs, well known cafés and the Danube, its glories lie in its illustrious past and the giants of music, architecture and psychology who lived and worked in the Austrian capital during its hey-day. This, coupled with its Imperial history, make it a gracious and interesting city to visit. The provinces of Lower Austria, Burgenland and Styria, land of vineyards, mountains and farmland, are off the tourist routes, although walkers are attracted to the forested hills where paths meander for hundreds of miles.

Thermenland Camping Fürstenfeld

050 Campingweg 1, A-8280 Fürstenfeld (Steiermark)

Fürstenfeld is the last village on the main route from Graz to Hungary and this site, although small with basic facilities, makes a good staging post. The site is quietly situated on the edge of the village next to a large, well mown, play area with a playground, space for all types of ball games and a really huge open air pool complex. The size of a football pitch, it has a shallow end for paddling, a larger part for swimming or pool games, an Olympic size racing pool and a diving pool. The 60 touring pitches on the site are on terraces on either side of hard access roads, under a covering of trees and with electricity in all areas.

Facilities: The single toilet block is rather cramped and not as good as on most Austrian sites, but is clean and acceptable. Washing machines and dryers. Baby room. Small bar with TV, but no other facilities on site. Fishing. **Off site:** Village shops and restaurants 500 m. Large sports park adjacent with kiosks for drinks and ice creams and a café. Golf 5 km.

Charges 2003

Per person	€ 4.80
child (2-14 yrs)	€ 1.50
pitch	€ 4.80
electricity (10A)	€ 1.80
local tax	€ 1.00

Tel: 03382 54940. Fax: 03382 54940. E-mail: camping.fuerstenfeld@twin.at. **Reservations:** Write to site. **Open** 15 April - 15 October.

Directions: From Graz - Vienna motorway, take exit for Fürstenfeld. Site is at western end of village and is signed.

Camping Central

033 Martinhofstraße 3, A-8054 Graz (Steiermark)

Although not as well known as Vienna, Salzburg and Innsbruck, Graz in the southern province of Styria is Austria's second largest city. Camping Central's name is misleading as it is in the southwest of the town, some 6 km. from the centre. The 136 level tourist pitches are either in regular rows either side of tarmac roads under a cover of tall trees or on an open meadow. All have electricity (6A). Adjoining the site is the town sports stadium which includes a huge open air pool, rebuilt to a high standard although the base of cobbles remains. Measuring 110 x 100 metres, it is reputed to be the largest pool in Europe. Except when there are activities at the stadium, this is a quiet place which makes a good night stop.

Facilities: The new, well built sanitary provision is of good quality and the other two blocks have been refurbished. Each can be heated in cool weather. Washing machines & dryer Facilities for disabled visitors. Huge swimming pool with special entry to the water for disabled people (open May - end Sept, when the small restaurant is also available to campers). Tennis, table tennis, playground, jogging track and minigolf. **Off site:** Two other restaurants within 300 m. Good shop about 400 m.

Charges 2002

Per unit incl. 2 persons	€ 21.44
extra person	€ 4.00 - € 6.18
local tax	€ 0.36

No credit cards. **Tel:** 06763 785 102. Fax: 0316 697 824. E-mail: freizeit@netway.at. **Reservations:** Reservation: not necessary. **Open** 1 April - 31 October.

Directions: From the west take the exit 'Graz-west', from Salzburg exit 'Graz-sud' follow signs Central and Strassgang and turn right for site at signs.

Camping Terrassen Maltatal

049 Malta 6, A-9854 Maltatal (Carinthia)

Just 6 km. from the autobahn and 15 from Millstättersee, this site is good for an overnight stop but its pleasant situation and the good-sized swimming pool on site encourage many to stay longer. The pool is over 300 sq.m. with a grassy lying out area and is open to all (free for campers). There are 200 grassy pitches on shallow terraces (70-100 sq.m.) and mostly in rows on either side of access roads. Numbered and marked, but not separated, all have electricity (6/10A) and 20 have water and drainage connections. The 'Kärnten-card' is available from the site which gives free travel on public transport and free entry to various attractions.

Facilities: Two toilet blocks, one with under-floor heating, have about half the washbasins in cabins and six family washcabins. A good supply with facilities for babies and children. Washing machines, dryers and irons. Motorcaravan services. Only basic provisions kept. Restaurant (all season). Swimming pool (20/5-15/9). Sauna. Playground. Bicycle hire. Riding. Entertainment programme, walks and excursions. **Off site:** Village 500 m. Fishing or golf 6 km.

Charges 2002

Per person	€ 5.20 - € 6.60
child (3-14 yrs)	€ 3.40 - € 4.10
pitch with electricity	€ 6.60 - € 8.90
local tax (over 18 yrs)	€ 1.25

Electricity included. Less for longer stays. **Tel:** 04733 234. Fax: 04733 23416. E-mail: info@maltacamp.at. **Reservations:** Made with deposit. **Open** 12 April - 31 October.

Directions: Site is 6 km. up a mountain valley from an exit at the southern end of the A10 Salzburg - Carinthia autobahn. Take autobahn exit for Gmund and Maltatal and proceed up Maltatal 6 km. to site.

Rutar Lido FKK Naturist See-Camping

036N A-9141 Eberndorf (Carinthia)

This 15 ha. site, affiliated to the International Naturist Federation (INF) is in a peaceful location adjacent to both open countryside and forested hills. Its main feature is no less than six swimming pools, two being indoors. These are both heated, as are two of the others. There are three lakes within the site, one for swimming and dinghies, whilst the other two provide pleasure for those who enjoy fishing. The area around the lakes has been left to nature with many wild flowers and other plants creating colour and interest. The 365 pitches (300 for tourers) are either on an open area of grass marked out by low hedges or in a more established area of pine trees. There are electrical connections throughout (10A) and some pitches have their own water supply and waste point. One area is set aside for those with dogs. Remember, this is a naturist site. Membership of the INF is not a requirement but visitors are expected to comply with their rules and ideals.

Facilities: The four sanitary blocks are not modern, but are adequate and clean with some private wash-cabins. Facilities for disabled visitors. Laundry facilities. Well stocked supermarket (1/4-30/9). Two bar/restaurants (all year). Outdoor pools (1/4-30/9). Indoor pools (all year). Two saunas. Children's play area, club and activities. Table tennis. Fitness room. Disco room. Bowling alley. Live music evenings and dances are held in high season. Small chapel. Fishing. **Off site:** The village of Eberndorf is twenty minutes walk.

Charges 2002

Per adult	€ 6.50
child (3-11 yrs)	€ 4.50
young person (12-18 yrs)	€ 5.50
pitch	€ 6.00 - € 10.00
dog	€ 4.00
local tax	€ 1.00

Tel: 04236 22620. Fax: 04236 2220. E-mail: fkkurlaub@rutarlido.at. **Reservations:** Write to site with €50 deposit. **Open** all year.

Directions: From A2 (Graz - Klagenfurt) road, take B82 south at Volkermarkt to roundabout at Eberndorf and follow signs to site.

FKK-Naturist Camping Müllerhof

042N Dobein 10, A-9074 Keutschach am See (Carinthia)

Müllerhof is an excellent naturist site, very well run with families in mind by its owners, the Safron family. Backed by a pine forest, on the southern side of the Keutschacher lake in Carinthia, the gently sloping site of almost 6 ha. provides for 270 touring units. Manicured grass with neat rows of varied, mature trees, light coloured compacted gravel access roads and a security barrier at the entrance give the impression that all is well maintained. Three grass sunbathing areas (one large, two small), each have direct access to the crystal clear waters of the lake which are edged with flowering lilies and rushes. Shallow areas are safe for children with parental observation. Jetties with steps and a handrail allow entry to deeper water which can reach 26 degrees in the height of the summer. One area of the site is deliberately untouched to follow nature, playing home to many species of wild flowers, frogs, butterflies and the like. Minimundus, on the western approach to Klagnefurt is a first class model village, the nearby Pyramidenkogel Observation tower (alt. 905 m) provides breathtaking views, whilst castles such as Hochosterwitz (40 km) are impressive.

Facilities: Two large, fully equipped toilet blocks are of the highest order and kept very clean. Washing machines, dryer and ironing facilities. The block at the centre of the site has a really high quality baby room. Sauna and massage. Small shop. Restaurant with waiter service or takeaway food. Large children's playroom filled with toys and well appointed play area. Welcome pack includes brochures on attractions and discount vouchers.

Charges 2003

Per person	€ 6.00 - € 7.00
child (3-11 yrs)	€ 3.00 - € 4.00
pitch	€ 7.50 - € 8.00

Plus local tax. No credit cards. **Tel:** 04273 2517. Fax: 04273 25175. E-mail: fkk_camp_muellerhof@aon.at. **Reservations:** Are necessary - contact site. **Open** 1 May - 30 September.

Directions: From A2 motorway take exit 335 signed Velden. Follow signs for Keutschach (or Keutschacher See). Approx. 4 km. after village of Schiefling, turn right at signs for FKK Centre. Site is on left in just over 1 km.

Strandcamping Turnersee

A-9123 St Primus (Carinthia)

041

The southern Austrian province of Karnten is a gentle rural area of mountains, valleys and lakes. Strandcamping lies between Villach and Graz just south of the A2 Villach - Vienna motorway giving the opportunity to visit Croatia and northern Italy. The neat, tidy site is situated in a valley with views of the surrounding mountains. The 315 marked and numbered pitches for touring units vary in size, on level grass terraces. Although there are many trees, not all parts have shade. All pitches have electricity (6A) and 50 also have water, drainage, TV and phone connections. There are 100 static caravans. At the lakeside is a large well-mown grass area for with a wooden decking area right next to the water with steps down for swimming in the lake. Although at almost 500 m. above sea level, the water in early June was warm enough for swimming, possibly because the area is known for its warm springs. It is very much a site for families where children are catered for rather than just tolerated and has a pleasant atmosphere.

Facilities: Four modern sanitary blocks spread around the site, providing the usual facilities including special provision for young children and babies in the largest block. Facilities for disabled people. Large, central building housing well stocked shop, pleasant restaurant with terrace (10/5-14/9), take-away (7/6-23/8) and play room for small children. Good play areas and small zoo with goats and rabbits. Topi club and organised activities for adults and children. Table tennis, games room, bicycle hire, watersports and volleyball. **Off site:** Fishing and golf 1.5 km. Riding 3 km. Boat launching 5 km.

Charges 2002

Per person	€ 4.30 - € 7.30
child (4-14 yrs)	€ 3.00 - € 5.00
pitch	€ 5.90 - € 9.00
dog	€ 1.50 - € 3.00
local tax	€ 1.09

Special deals for families. **Tel:** 04239 2350. **Fax:** 04239 2350 32. **E-mail:** info@breznik.at.
Reservations: Necessary for high season. **Open** 12 April - 4 October.

Directions: Leave A2 Klagenfurt - Volkermark motorway taking 'Volkermark-West' exit. Go via Tainach and St Kanzian towards St Primus and follow site signs.

Camping Arneitz

Seeuferlandesstraße 53, A-9583 Faak am See (Carinthia)

040

Directly on Faakersee, Camping Arneitz is one of the best sites in this area, central for the attractions of the region, watersports and walking. Family run, Arneitz led the way with good quality and comprehensive facilities. A newly built reception building at the entrance reflects the quality of the site and, apart from reception facilities, has a good collection of tourist literature and three desks with telephones for guests to use. The 400 level, marked pitches are mainly of gravel, off hard roads, with electricity available. Some have good shade from mature trees. Grass pitches are available for tents. There is a delightfully appointed restaurant at the entrance where there is entertainment in high season. Day trips can be made to Venice and many other parts of northern Italy, and the surrounding countryside.

Facilities: A splendid family washroom is large, heated and airy. There are family cubicles around the walls and in the centre, washbasins at child height in a circle with a working carousel in the middle. An extra small toilet block is nearer the lake. Hair washing salon with special basins and hairdryers. Washing machines, spin dryer, irons. Motorcaravan services. Supermarket. Self-service restaurant, bar and terrace. General room with TV. Small cinema for children's films. Beauty salon. Large sauna/solarium. Minigolf. Well equipped playground. Football field. Fishing. Riding. Bicycle hire. **Off site:** Golf 10 km.

Charges 2002

Per person	€ 6.40 - € 6.98
child (under 10 yrs)	€ 6.03 - € 6.61
pitch incl. electricity	€ 8.72 - € 10.90

Tel: 04254 2137. **Fax:** 04254 3044. **E-mail:** camping@arneitz.at. **Reservations:** only made outside main season. **Open** 28 April - 30 September.

Directions: Site is southeast of Villach, southwest of Veldon. Follow signs for Faakersee and Egg rather than for Faak village.

Carinthia and the South

This gentle, tranquil land of some 200 lakes and mountain scenery deserves to be better known than just as a through route from Salzburg to Italy. The beautiful scenery and rural way of life make it an attractive holiday destination to those who know it. Unfortunately, few British have yet discovered its charms and those who have probably wish to keep the secret to themselves. There are few large towns, but many pleasant villages, good, often uncrowded roads and excellent sites.

Naturpark Schluga Seecamping

A-9620 Hermagor (Carinthia)

045

This site is pleasantly situated on natural wooded hillside. It is about 300 m. from a small lake with clean water, where the site has a beach of coarse sand and a large grassy meadow where inflatable boats can be kept, also a sunbathing area for naturists. Many walks and attractive car drives are available in the area. This part of Carinthia is a little off the beaten track but the site still becomes full in season. The 336 pitches for touring units are individual and level, many with light shade and electricity (6A). Close by is Schluga Camping, under the same ownership, which is open all year (no. 044). English is spoken.

Facilities: Heated modern toilet blocks are well constructed, with some washbasins in cabins and family washrooms for rent. Washing machines and dryer. Motorcaravan services. Shop (20/5-10/9). Restaurant/bar by entrance and takeaway (all 20/5-10/9). Playground. Film room. Kiosk at beach. Surf school. Aqua jump. Pony rides. Bicycle hire. Badminton and volleyball court. Fishing. Weekly activity programme with mountain walks and climbs. **Off site:** Tennis (indoor and outdoor) near.

Charges 2002

Per person	€ 4.90 - € 7.10
child (5-14 yrs)	€ 3.00 - € 4.90
pitch	€ 4.30 - € 7.10
pitch with electricity	€ 6.40 - € 10.00
dog	€ 1.20 - € 4.10
local tax (over 18 yrs)	€ 1.00

Tel: 04282 2051. Fax: 04282 288 120. E-mail: camping@schluga.com. **Reservations:** Contact site for details. **Open** 20 May - 20 September.

Directions: Site is on the B111 road (Villach-Hermagor) 6 km. east of Hermagor town.

Schluga Camping

Obervellach 15, A-9620 Hermagor-Presseggersee (Carinthia)

044

Schluga Camping is under the same ownership as Schluga Seecamping, some 4 km. to the west of that site in a flat valley with views of the surrounding mountains. The 300 tourist pitches are of varying size, 87 with water and satellite TV connections. Electricity connections throughout (10A). Mainly on grass covered gravel on either side of the hard surfaced access road, they are divided by shrubs and hedges. Entertainment in the high season includes a disco and cinema. A weekly programme sheet details events at both Schluga sites and nearby. The site is open all year, to include the winter sports season, and has a well kept tidy appearance, although it may be busy in high seasons. English is spoken.

Facilities: Four sanitary blocks (one splendid new one, three good older ones) are well constructed and heated in cold weather. Some washbasins in cabins, showers (with small dressing space) and family washrooms for rent. Washing machines and dryers. Motorcaravan services. Well stocked shop (1/5-30/9). Bar/restaurant with terrace (closed Nov). Kiosk for snacks/ice creams. Heated pool (12 x 7 m; 1/5-30/9). Playground. Games room. Bicycle hire. Sauna. Fitness centre.TV room. Badminton. Kindergarten.

Charges 2002

Per person	€ 4.90 - € 7.10
child (5-14 yrs)	€ 3.00 - € 4.90
pitch	€ 4.30 - € 7.10
pitch with electricity	€ 6.40 - € 10.00
dog	€ 1.20 - € 4.10
local tax (over 18 yrs)	€ 1.00

Tel: 04282 2051. Fax: 04282 288 120. E-mail: camping@schluga.com. **Reservations:** Contact site. **Open** all year.

Directions: Site is on the B111 Villach-Hermagor road (which is better quality than it appears on most maps) just east of Hermagor town.

Camping Mössler

A-9873 Döbriach am Millstättersee (Carinthia)

047

Mössler is a friendly family site, fairly small, flat, grassy and set in very pleasant surroundings with mountain views. It is close to the Millstättersee, a reputedly warm lake. However, as the camp has a free, well heated swimming pool of 200 sq.m., the 600 m. stroll to the lake, where campers usually have free entry to swimming and boating facilities, is not so important. It is an excellent touring area with mountain lifts and many possible excursions to lakes and mountains near at hand. The site has about 200 pitches of two different sizes but both adequate, on flat ground with connections for electricity, water, TV, telephone, gas and drainage.

Facilities: Two modern toilet blocks are of an exceptional standard and quite luxurious, including under-floor heating. Washbasins in cabins, good free showers and private bathrooms (with bath, shower, basin and WC) usually let by the week. Facilities for disabled visitors. Washing machine. Motorcaravan services. Shop and restaurant (both 1/6-30/9). Swimming pools and children's pool (20/5-30/9). Children's playground. Sauna. TV room.

Charges 2002

Per pitch	€ 6.47 - € 12.14
adult	€ 5.38 - € 6.90
child (5-14 yrs)	€ 3.71 - € 5.01
local tax (over 18's)	€ 1.27

Tel: 04246 7735. Fax: 04246 773513. E-mail: camping@moessler.at. **Reservations:** can be made Sat. - Sat. with deposit. **Open** 1 April - 31 October.

Directions: Go to Döbriach, at east end of Millstättersee, and camp is signed.

Terrassen Camping Ossiachersee

046 Ostriach 67, A-9570 Ossiach (Carinthia)

As its name implies, this modern site has been constructed with terraces on ground thatslopes gently down to the lake shore. Because of the thick growth of reeds at the water's edge, access is limited to the lake via two small clearings. One of these has a beach for bathing and a jetty, and boats may be launched from the other. The site is protected by rising hills and enjoys lovely views across the lake to the mountains beyond. Trees, flowers, hedges and bushes abound, adding atmosphere to this neat, tidy site. The 550 pitches (485 for touring units) are in rows on the level grass terraces, separated by hard roads and marked by hedges. There is shade in parts and electricity connections throughout (4/6A). The site does become full in high season and although there is sufficient room on the pitches, it may give the initial impression of being overcrowded. A friendly, lively site, all ages and sports inclinations are catered for in a scenic location in a very beautiful part of Austria.

Facilities: Although the facilities in the five sanitary blocks vary, they are all of good quality, heated in cool weather, and with some washbasins in cabins. The newest block has family washrooms. Washing machines, dryers and irons. Motorcaravan services. Restaurant (15/5-30/9). Well stocked supermarket. High season entertainment programme for children and adults, giving a wide range of sports and activities. Children's playgrounds, games rooms and disco dancing courtyard. Watersports including water-skiing and windsurfing schools and boats for hire. Tennis, volleyball and badminton. Football field. Bicycle and moped hire. Fishing. Riding.

Charges 2003

Per person	€ 4.70 - € 7.00
child (3-9 yrs)	free - € 4.50
pitch acc. to season and location	€ 6.50 - € 10.50
small tent pitch	€ 4.00 - € 6.00
local tax (over 18 yrs)	€ 0.90 - € 1.25

No credit cards. **Tel:** 04243 436. Fax: 04243 8171. E-mail: martinz@camping.at. **Reservations:** Advisable 15 July-15 Aug weekends. Write with deposit (€ 240) and fee (€ 7,27). **Open** 1 May - 30 September.

Directions: Site is directly on the lake shore just south of Ossiach village. Leave the A10 autobahn at exit for Ossiachersee, turn left onto road 94 towards Feldkirchen and shortly right to Ossiach Sud. The site is shortly before Ossiach.

Komfort-Campingpark Burgstaller

048 Seefeldstraße 16, A-9873 Döbriach (Carinthia)

This part of Austria deserves to be better known as it is a most attractive region and has some excellent camp sites. An excellent site, Burgstaller is the largest of these and makes a peaceful base from which to explore Carinthia, northeast Italy and Slovenia. The site entrance is directly opposite the lawns leading to the bathing lido, to which campers have free access. There is also a heated swimming pool. The 450 pitches are on flat, well drained grass, backing onto hedges and marked out, on either side of gravel access roads. These vary in size (65-120 sq.m.), all with electricity, water and drainage and there are special pitches for motorcaravans. Much activity is organised here, including games and competitions for children in summer with a winter programme of skiing, curling and skating. At Christmas, trees are gathered from the forest and there are special Easter and autumn events. This is an excellent family site for winter and summer camping with a very friendly atmosphere, particularly in the restaurant in the evenings.

Facilities: Two very good quality sanitary blocks, the larger part of the central complex. It has some washbasins in cabins, facilities for children and disabled visitors, dishwashers and under-floor heating for cool weather. Some private sanitary rooms are for rent. Motorcaravan services. Good restaurant with terrace (May-Oct). Shop (May-Sept). Bowling alley. Disco (July/Aug). TV room. Sauna and solarium. Secluded roof terrace used for nude sunbathing. Two children's play areas (one for under 6s, the other for 6-12 yrs). Beach volleyball. Basketball. Bathing and boating in lake. Special entrance rate for lake attractions. Fishing. Bicycle hire. Mountain bike area. Riding. Comprehensive entertainment programmes. Covered stage and outdoor arena provide for church services (Protestant and Catholic, in German) and folk and modern music concerts.

Charges 2002

Per person	€ 4.72 - € 7.12
child (4-14 yrs	€ 2.91 - € 5.67
pitch	€ 4.36 - € 9.45
dog	€ 1.45 - € 2.18
local tax (over 18)	€ 1.34

Discounts for retired people. No credit cards. **Tel:** 04246 7774. Fax: 04246 77744. E-mail: dieter. burgstaller@campingpark.telekom.at. **Reservations:** Write to site. **Open** all year.

Directions: The site is well signed from around Döbriach.

Belgium

Belgian Tourist Office - Brussels - Ardennes, 225 Marsh Wall, London E14 9FW
Tel: 0906 3020 245 (premium rate). E-mail: info@belgium-tourism.org

or Tourism Flanders - Brussels, 31 Pepper Street, London E14 9RW
Tel: 09001 887799 Fax: 020 7458 0045   E-mail: office@flanders-tourism.org

Belgium is a small and densely populated country divided on a federal basis into the Flemish north, Walloon south and Brussels the capital, a culturally varied city. Despite being heavily industrialised Belgium possesses some beautiful scenery, notably the great forest of the Ardennes with its rivers and gorges contrasting with the rolling plains and historic cities of Bruges and Ghent with their Flemish art and architecture and the 40 miles of coastline with safe sandy beaches.

Population

10,040,000 (1993), density 329 per sq km.

Capital

Brussels (Bruxelles)

Climate

Belgium's temperate climate is similar to Britain but the variation between summer and winter is lessened by the effects of the Gulf Stream.

Language

There are two official languages in Belgium. French is spoken in the south and Flemish in the north; however, in the eastern provinces, German is the predominant language. Brussels is officially bilingual. Road signs and place names maybe written in either language or in some cases both.

Currency

From January 2002, in common with 11 other European countries, the Belgian unit of currency is the EURO (€).
€ 1 = B. Francs 40.34.

Banks

Banking hours are Mon-Fri 09.00-15.30. Some banks open on Saturday mornings.
Credit Cards: Major credit cards are all widely accepted, as are travellers cheques.

Post Offices

Open Mon-Fri 09.00-12.00 and 14.00-17.00, some opening Saturday mornings.

Time

GMT plus 1 (in summer BST plus 1).

Public Holidays

New Year; Easter Mon; Labour Day; Ascension; Whit Mon; Flemish National Day, 21 July; Assumption, 15 Aug; All Saints, 1 Nov; Armistice Day, 11 Nov; Christmas, 25 Dec.

Telephone

From the UK the code is 00 32. For calls within Belgium use the local code followed by the number. For calls to the UK the code is 0044 followed by the local STD code omitting initial 0. Telephone cards available from newsagents, post offices and train stations for Fr. 100 or Fr. 500.

Shops

Shops open from 09.00-17.30/18.00 hrs - later on Thursday and Friday but earlier on Saturdays. Some close at midday (2 hrs).

Motoring

For cars with a caravan or trailer: motorways are toll free except for the Liefenshoek Tunnel in Antwerp. Maximum permitted overall length of vehicle/trailer or caravan combination is 18 m.
Speed Limits: Caravans and motorhomes (7.5 tons): 31 mph (50 kph) in built up areas, 56 mph (90 kph) on other roads and 75 mph (120 kph) 4 lane roads and motorways. Minimum speed on motorways on straight level stretches is 43 mph (70 kph). Parking: Blue Zone parking areas exist in Brussels, Ostend, Bruges, Liège, Antwerp and Gent. Parking discs can be obtained from police stations, garages, some shops and the Royal Automobile Club Belgique.

Overnighting

Only generally permitted at motorway rest areas.

Camping Jeugdstadion

057 Leopold III Laan 16, B-8900 Ieper (West Flanders)

Camping Jeugdstadion is a small developing municipal close to historic old town. At present there are only 21 pitches, some on hardstandings, all with electricity (16A), plus a separate area for tents. The barrier key also operates the lock for the toilet block. At the end of Leopold III Laan is the Menin Gate built in 1927, which bears the names of British and Commonwealth soldiers who lost their lives between 1914-1918. The last post is sounded beneath the gate at 8 pm. every evening in their honour. The interactive museum entitled 'The Flanders Experience' in the Cloth Hall is a moving experience. The Commonwealth War Graves Commission is a little further away in Elverdingestraat. In mid August each year there is a festival for young people in the town, when the campsite is usually fully booked.

Facilities: The modern, heated but fairly basic toilet block has cold water to washbasins and three sinks for dishwashing outside. Bicycle hire. Minigolf. Boules. **Off site:** The adjacent sports complex has volleyball and squash, whilst indoor and outdoor pools are 500 m. and there is a very large comprehensive playground. In school holidays these facilities are extensively used by local children and can therefore be fairly busy and lively.

Charges 2002

Per caravan pitch incl. electricity	€ 4.50
adult	€ 3.00
child (under 6-12 yrs)	€ 1.50
tent	€ 1.50

Tel: 057 21 72 82. Fax: 057 21 61 21. E-mail: info@jeugdstadion.be. **Reservations:** Write to site for details. **Open** 16 March - 31 October.

Directions: Site is southeast of the city centre. From N336 (Lille) at roundabout by the Lille Gate, turn east on Picanolaan and take first left into Leopold III laan. Site entrance is on the right. Use parking spaces at roadside and book in at 'Kantine' (open 08.00-19.00) on left inside gates. The vehicle access is at the rear of the site, signed from Steverlyncklaan (2nd left off Picanollaan), but you will be given a map and a barrier key (deposit £20 or € 24,79). Alternatively go straight to the vehicle gate and walk through site to book in (easier for large units). Signposting is difficult to follow.

Camping De Lombarde

056 Elisabethlaan 4, B-8434 Lombardsijde (West Flanders)

De Lombarde is a spacious, good value holiday site, between Lombardsijde and the coast. It has a pleasant atmosphere and modern buildings. The 360 pitches are set out in level, grassy bays surrounded by shrubs, all with electricity (16A, long leads may be needed). Vehicles are parked in separate car parks. There are many seasonal units and 20 holiday homes, leaving 180 tourist pitches. There is a range of activities (listed below) and an entertainment programme in season. This is a popular holiday area and the site becomes full at peak times. A pleasant stroll takes you into Lombardsijde or you can catch the tram to the town or beach.

Facilities: Three modern heated, clean sanitary units are of an acceptable standard, with some washbasins in cubicles. Facilities for disabled people. Dishwashing sinks and large laundry. Motorcaravan services. Shop (1/4-30/9). Restaurant/bar and take-away (July/Aug. plus weekends and holidays 21/3-11/11). Tennis. Table tennis. Basketball. Boules. Fishing lake. TV lounge. New playground. Torch useful. **Off site:** Sea 400 m. Bicycle hire 1 km. Riding and golf 500 m.

Charges 2002

Per unit incl. electricity	€ 13.00 - € 24.00
small pitch incl. 2 persons	€ 2.60 - € 3.10
dog (1 per pitch)	free

Tel: 058 23 68 39. Fax: 058 23 99 08. E-mail: info@delombarde.be. **Reservations:** Write or fax for details. **Open** all year.

Directions: From traffic lights in Lombarsijde, turn left (towards sea) at next junction, follow tram-lines into Zeelaan. Continue following tram-lines until crossroads and tram stop, turn right into Elisabethlaan. Site is on right after 200 m.

Belgium - North
Camping de Blekker
Jachtwakersstraat 12, B-8670 Koksijde aan Zee (West Flanders)

This family-owned site, adjacent to a 186-hectare nature reserve on the Belgium coast, is divided into two sections: Blekker and Blekkerdal. De Blekker has 178 pitches of which 75 are allocated for tourists. The pitches are grassy with some dividing hedges and trees, and all have 10A electricity connections. Visitors should drive to the Blekker reception but will be given a choice of where to park. Local attractions include the Koksijde annual Flower Market and Floral Pageant, National Fishery Museum and horseback shrimp fishing in Oostduinkerke, and Plopsaland (a small theme park) or Clown City in De Panne.

Facilities: Each section has a single modern sanitary unit including washbasins in cubicles, dishwashing and laundry sinks, washing machine and dryer, facilities for babies and a suite for disabled persons (other than for washbasins, hot water is on payment throughout). Laundry. Small infirmary with bed. **Off site:** Shop in nearest village 300 m. Restaurant and bars 300 m. - 2 km.

Charges 2002

Per unit incl. 4 persons	€ 15.00 - € 25.00
extra adult	€ 5.00
extra child (under 12 yrs)	€ 4.00

Special rates for Ascension, Pentecost and Easter weekends. Tel: 058 511 633. Fax: 058 511 307. E-mail: camping.deblekker@belgacom.net. **Reservations:** Advised for high season and peak weekends. Open 15 February - 15 November.

Directions: From A16 (E40) take junction 1A, then the N8 towards Koksijde. At roundabout take N396 towards Koksijde Dorp and then turn towards Koksijde-aan-zee. Follow small green camp signs. Site entrance road is on the left.

Belgium - North
IC-Camping Nieuwpoort
Brugsesteenweg 49, B-8620 Nieuwpoort (West Flanders)

Near to Ostend, this large site with 952 pitches caters particularly for families. There are many on site amenities including a heated pool complex with two pools, a children's pool and a water slide, many sporting activities, and a children's farm. The numbered pitches, all with electricity, are in regular rows on flat grass. With 386 seasonal units and 79 caravan holiday homes, the site becomes full during Belgian holidays and in July/August. A network of footpaths links all areas of the site and gates to the rear lead to a reservoir reserved for sailing, windsurfing and canoeing (canoes for hire) during certain hours only. The site is well fenced, with a card operated barrier and a night guard.

Facilities: Seven functional, clean and well maintained toilet blocks include washbasins in cubicles. The blocks are accessible to disabled people. Dishwashing and laundry facilities. Motorcaravan services. Supermarket, restaurant and café/bar (weekends and Belgian holidays outside July/Aug). Takeaway. Swimming pools with waterslide and pool games (19/5-15/9). Tennis. Football. Adventure playground. Minigolf. Sports hall. Entertainment programme July/Aug. **Off site:** Fishing and bicycle hire within 500 m. Riding 3 km. Golf driving range 5 km. Nearest village 2 km. Beach 4 km.

Charges 2002

Per family (max 6 persons)	€ 18.00 - € 27.00
electricity	€ 1.50

Largest unit accepted 2.5 x 8 m. Tel: 058 23 60 37. Fax: 058 23 26 82. E-mail: nieuwpoort@ic-camping.be. **Reservations:** Made with deposit (€75). Open 31 March - 12 November.

Directions: From E40 take exit 4 (Middelkerke-Diksmuide). Turn towards Diksmuide following signs to Nieuwpoort. Pass through Sint-Joris and IC-Camping is on the right.

Belgium - North
Camping Memling
Veltemweg 109, B-8310 Brugge (West Flanders)

This traditional site, ideal for visiting Brugge, is located behind a bistro in a quiet suburb. The 100 unmarked pitches (60 for tourists) are on slightly undulating grass, with gravel roads and trees and hedges providing some shade. Electricity (6A) is available to 40 pitches. There is a separate area for tents. Bars, restaurants, local shops and supermarkets are within walking distance. Brugge itself has a network of cycleways and for those on foot a bus runs into the centre from nearby. It may be best for visitors with large units to telephone in advance to ensure an adequate pitch.

Facilities: Heated toilet facilities are clean and tidy, including some washbasins in cubicles. Facilities for babies and disabled visitors. Dishwashing sinks (H&C). Laundry with washing machine and dryer. Freezer for campers' use. Tiny children's playground. Bicycle hire. **Off site:** Municipal swimming pool and park nearby. Supermarket 250 m, hypermarket 1 km.

Charges 2002

Per adult	€ 2.80
child (under 12 yrs)	€ 1.70
pitch	€ 5.80 - € 6.70
electricity	€2.00

Tel: 050 35 58 45. Fax: 050 35 58 45. E-mail: info@camping-memling.be. **Reservations:** Write or fax for details. Open all year.

Directions: From R30 Brugge ring road take exit 6 onto N9 towards Maldegem. At Sint-Kruis turn right at traffic lights, where site signed (close to garage and supermarket, opposite MacDonalds).

Camping Blaarmeersen

061

Zuiderlaan 12, B-9000 Gent (East Flanders)

the travel service
TO BOOK

Ferry	✓
Pitch	✓
Accommodation	✗

01892 55 98 98

Blaarneersen is a comfortable, well managed municipal site in the west of the city. It adjoins a sports complex and a fair-sized lake which provide facilities for a variety of watersports, tennis, squash, minigolf, football, athletics track, dry ski slope, roller skating and a playground. The 208 individual, flat, grassy touring pitches are separated by tall hedges and mostly arranged in circular groups; with electricity to 178. There are 26 hardstandings for motorcaravans, plus a separate area for tents with barbecue facility. Some noise is possible as the the city ring road is close. In Gent, tour the markets, free of charge, with the Town Crier (May-Sept, Sunday 10.30). Central Gent is 3 km. - the bus stop is 150 m. and buses run every 20 minutes to the city centre.

Facilities: Four sanitary units of a decent standard vary in size. Most of the 36 free hot showers are in one block. Showers and toilets for disabled people. Laundry. Motorcaravan services. Shop, café/bar (both daily March - Oct). Takeaway. Sports facilities. Playground. Fishing on site in winter, otherwise 500 m. Lake swimming. **Off site:** Bicycle hire 5 km. Riding and golf 10 km.

Charges 2002

Per unit incl. 2 persons	€ 10.75 - € 14.25
extra person	€ 3.00 - € 4.00
child (5-12 yrs)	€ 1.50 - € 2.00
electricity (10A)	€ 1.25

Tel: 092 21 5399. Fax: 092 22 41 84. E-mail: camping.blaarmeersen@gent.be. **Reservations:** Most advisable in main season; made for any period (no deposit) and kept until 5 pm. **Open** 1 March - 15 October.

Directions: From E40 take exit 13 (Gent-West) and follow dual carriageway for 5 km. Cross second bridge and look for Blaarmeersen sign, turning sharp right and following signs to leisure complex. In city avoid overpasses - most signs are on the lower levels.

Camping Groeneveld

060

Groenevelddreef, Bachte-Maria-Leerne, B-9800 Deinze (East Flanders)

Quiet and clean is how Rene Kuys describes his campsite. Groeneveld is a traditional site in a small village within easy reach of Gent. It has a friendly atmosphere and is also open over a long season. Although this site has 108 pitches, there are a fair number of seasonal units, leaving around 50 large tourist pitches with electricity (8A). Hedges and borders divide the grassy area, access roads are gravel and there is an area for tents. A range of family entertainment and activities is organised in high season. The city of Gent is just 15 km. north of the site and 5 km. to the south is the pleasant town of Deinze.

Facilities: Two clean sanitary units of differing age and design provide British style WCs, washbasins and free hot showers. Motorcaravan services. Bar/café (July/Aug. and weekends) with a good range of snacks, and a comprehensive range of speciality and local beers. Small coarse fishing lake. Floodlit petanque court. Adventure style play area. TV room. **Off site:** Shops and restaurants nearby. Swimming pool 5 km. Kayaking 5 km. Golf 3 km.

Charges 2002

| Per unit incl. electricity | € 13.60 - € 17.40 |
| hikers (2 persons and tent) | € 2.50 - € 3.00 |

No credit cards. **Tel:** 093 80 10 14. Fax: 09 38 01 760. E-mail: info@campinggroeneveld.be. **Reservations:** Write to site. **Open** 26 March - 12 November.

Directions: From A10 (E40) exit 13, turn south on N466. After 3 km. continue straight on at round about and site is on left on entering village (opposite a large factory). Note: yellow signs are very small.

Camping De Gavers

059

Onkerzelestraat 280, B-9500 Geraardsbergen (East Flanders)

Domein de Gavers is a modern, well organised holiday site in a peaceful location. It is adjacent to a large sports complex, located about 5 km. outside Geraardsbergen. It can be a busy site in season. There is good security and a card operated barrier. Most of the 448 grassy, level pitches are taken by seasonal units but about 80 are left for tourists. Pitches are arranged on either side of surfaced access roads with some hedges and few trees to provide shade in parts, with electricity (5/10A) available to most. The site offers an extensive range of sporting activities and entertainment over a long season.

Facilities: Six modern, heated and well equipped toilet blocks provide hot showers (€0,50). Rooms for disabled people and babies. Launderette. Motorcaravan services. Shop (July/Aug). Cafeteria, restaurant, bars and takeaway (daily April - Sept, otherwise weekends). Excellent playground. Tennis. Volleyball. Basketball. Mini-football. Boules. 'Midget' golf. Fishing. Canoe, windsurfer, row boat hire. Bicycle hire. Swimming pool should be ready for 2003. Swimming and beach area. Climbing.

Charges 2002

| Per unit incl. electricity | € 9.00 - € 18.00 |

Discounts of 5-30% for longer stays. **Tel:** 054 41 63 24. Fax: 054 41 03 88. E-mail: gavers@oost-vlaan-deren.be. **Reservations:** Contact site. **Open** all year.

Directions: From E429/A8 exit 26 towards Edingen, take N255 and N495 to Geraardsbergen. Down a steep hill, then left towards Onkerzele, through village and turn north to site.

Camping Druivenland

064 Nijvelsebaan 80, B-3090 Overijse (North Brabant)

This small, peaceful site is within easy reach of Brussels and also close to 25,000 hectares of woodland where you can enjoy some of the best Belgian countryside by foot or by cycle. Neat and mature, the site is well looked after and family run. It has a large open touring field or further pitches available in the sheltered area of the static park. In total there are 99 pitches, with 40 for touring units and 40 electricity connections (8A). A very pleasant relaxing site at which to stay and tour this part of Belgium. Perhaps of interesting note, there are over 60 eating places in the town of Overijse.

Facilities: The fully equipped toilet block has a new unisex extension. Some washbasins are in cabins. Well laid out provision for disabled visitors (shower room and toilet/washroom). Dishwashing sinks (€ 0,50). Laundry sinks, washing machine and dryer. Kept extremely clean at all times, it is of a very high standard. Limited shop with some fresh food.

Charges 2002

Per unit incl. electricity	€ 14.50

E-mail: camping.druivenland@pandora.be.
Reservations: Contact site. **Open** 1 April - 30 September.

Directions: From E411 Brussels - Namur road take exit 3 to Overijse (not exit 2). After 1 km turn right signed Tombeek, Waver and Terlanen. Site is 1 km. on right (is it is quite a long walk from the barrier to reception).

Camping Grimbergen

063 Veldkantsraat 64, B-1850 Grimbergen (North Brabant)

A popular little municipal site with a friendly atmosphere, Camping Grimbergen has 90 pitches on fairly level grass, of which around 50 have electricity (10A). The municipal sports facilities are adjacent and the site is well placed for visiting Brussels. The bus station is by the traffic lights at the junction of N202 and N211 and buses run into the city centre every 15 minutes. In Grimbergen itself visit Norbertine Abbey, St Servaas church, and the Sunday morning market. Also worth a visit are the nearby towns of Lier and Mechelen, and the botanical gardens at Meise. The site is not really suitable for large units.

Facilities: Older style sanitary facilities are acceptable, but not luxurious, and cleaning can be variable at times. They can be heated in colder months. Three dishwashing sinks under cover. Separate facilities for disabled people. Motorcaravan services. Adventure playground. **Off site:** Fishing 800 m.

Charges 2002

Per adult	€ 3.00
child (under 12 yrs)	€ 1.00
pitch	€ 4.50
electricity	€ 1.50

No credit cards. **Tel:** 0479 76 03 78. Fax: 02 270 12 15. **Reservations:** Contact site. **Open** 1 April - 31 October.

Directions: From Brussels ring road take exit 7 (N202) to Grimbergen for about 2.5 km, turn right at traffic lights on N211 towards Vilvoorde (site is signed), then left at second set of lights (slightly oblique turn). Site entrance is on right in approx. 500 m.

Camping de Molen

075 Thonetlaan, B-2050 Antwerp (Antwerp)

This is a convenient municipal site located on the bank of the River Scheldt opposite the city centre. It is possible to walk into the heart of this ancient and interesting city (the tunnel is approx. 2 km. from the campsite, and is about 500 metres long), although cycling may be a better option. Alternatively the nearest Metro station is about 2 km. - ask for a map at reception. The site is fairly level with tarmac roads, and has around 99 pitches, with a fair number of seasonal units, leaving around 70 for tourists, most with access to 10A electricity hook-ups. You will need the adapter cable (deposit payable) as the electric hook-ups are not like any you have seen before, and some long leads may be necessary. Antwerp's ancient city centre and the diamond district are well worth a visit.

Facilities: Basic toilet facilities, clean when visited, could be hard pressed at times, especially when everyone returns from a hard day's sightseeing. Basic facilities for disabled persons. Dishwashing and laundry sinks under cover. Overall the facilities are quite acceptable given the very modest campsite fees. Double axle caravans are not admitted. **Off site:** Shops 500 m.

Charges 2002

Per person	€ 1.61
caravan, tent or motorcaravan	€ 0.87
car	€ 0.87
electricity	€ 1.24

Tel: 03 219 8179. Fax: 03 238 22 30. **Reservations:** Not possible. **Open** April - September.

Directions: Approaching from Gent on A14 (E17) at junction 16, turn right on N419. After 1 km. turn left towards Oeverkant and Burcht. Follow main road through Burcht along river bank for 7 km. Pass St Annastrandens Tunnel, and the marina, and the site is a short distance on the right.

Belgium - North
Camping Roosendael

Schriekenstraat 27, B-9290 Berlare-Overmere (East Flanders)

At the time of our visit this site had not yet been finished, but it does show promise of being a top quality site in a very special situation. Less than 250 m. away is Donkmeer the site of Belgium's finest group of lakes offering all types of water-sports including fishing, with attractive bars and cafés at which to sit and watch the world go by. The site is on the outskirts of the busy village of Berlare-Overmere which has a shop. It is a neat, well laid out site with 80 piches in total (30 for touring units) connected by tarmac roads. All the pitches will be fully serviced with electricity (10A), water and waste water (hence the small toilet block). They are level and quite large with some shade near hedges or trees. The warden is extremely helpful with lots of local knowledge.

Facilities: The small, yet superb, toilet block has spacious shower rooms (Û 0,25 per minute) and good en-suite facilities for disabled visitors. All was very clean and tidy. Dishwashing and laundry sinks. Washing machines and dryers. Family room for wet days. Small play area for under fives. Playing field for games. Boules. Barbecues not permitted.

Charges 2002

Per unit all included	€ 16.00 - € 0.62

Tel: 0936 78742. **Fax:** 0936 57355. **Reservations:** Made with deposit (€ 14,30). **Open** all year.

Directions: From E17 Gent - Antwerp take exit 11 for Overmere. Take E445 signed Zele and after 6 km. turn right for Donkmeer (turn is on right just past supermarket and garage). Go through village past the lakes. At a right hand bend you is Café De-Kalvaar - turn left and site is at end of road

Belgium - North
Camping Zilverstrand

Kiezelweg 17, B-2400 Mol (Antwerp)

Zilverstrand offers something for everyone: a holiday environment for all age groups, with nothing lacking for the discerning holi-daymaker. The main attraction is a 'subtropical' pool complex with a central swirl-pool, two shallow pools for toddlers, long water flume, jacuzzi and sunbeds (cheaper to campers). There is provision for wheelchair users. An ultra-modern tavern, restaurant and snack bar overlook the lake with its beach. Another two lakes cater for fishermen. There are two sand-based play areas for small children and one among the trees with adventure equip-ment for older children. Furthermore there is an extensive entertainment programme in July and August. Camping facilities are equally as good. Of the 102 touring pitches, all with fresh water tap, waste water disposal and electricity connection, 13 are set aside for motorcaravans. These pitches are huge and each have a tarmac area suitable for the drive wheels during inclement weather.

Facilities: A single modern sanitary block includes an excellent children's room (bath in the shape of a car, 3 raised showers, child-size toilets, baby chang-ing station), and 2 family suites suitable for visitors with disabilities. Further toilet facilities in the pool complex. Restaurant, bar, tavern and takeaway. Supermarket. Play areas. Boules, volleyball, football. Lakes for fishing. Lake with beach area and slide. **Off site:** Supermarket 7 km. Bicycle hire and golf 1 km. Riding 2 km. Walking and cycling routes (maps from reception). Abbey and zoo 7 km.

Charges 2002

Per unit	€ 11.00 - € 16.50
person	€ 2.50
child (under 11 yrs)	€ 1.00
dog	€ 1.25

Tel: 014 81 00 98. **Fax:** 014 81 66 85. **E-mail:** zilverstrand.bvba@pandora.be. **Reservations:** Min. 7 nights (Sat. - Sat.) in July/Aug. **Open** 1 March - 1 November.

Directions: From Antwerp, take E313 and exit at junction 23. Take N71 to Mol (towards Lommel), turn left onto N712 signed Kielzelweg and Zilverstrand is on the left.

Camping Floreal-Club Het Veen

065 Eekhoornlaan 1, B-2960 St Job in't Goor (Antwerp)

Floréal Club Het Veen is a modern, good value site, 20 km. from Antwerp. In a woodland area and with many sports facilities, it has good security and an efficient reception. There are 319 marked pitches (60 for tourists) on level grass, most with some shade and electricity (10A, long leads in some places) and also 7 hard-standings. Amenities include an indoor sports hall (charged per hour) and courts for tennis, football, basketball and softball are outside. Good cycling and walking opportunities exist in the area. English is spoken.

Facilities: Four modern, spacious toilet blocks include a few washbasins in cubicles (only two are close to tourist pitches). Well equipped facilities for disabled people. Dishwashing and laundry facilities. Motorcaravan services. Well stocked shop. Restaurant, bar, café and takeaway (daily July/Aug. weekends only at other times). Tennis. Badminton. Volleyball. Softball. Basketball. Football. Table tennis. Boules. Exciting playgrounds and children's enter-tainment in season. Fishing. Canoeing. Bicycle hire. **Off site:** Riding or golf 8 km.

Charges 2002

Per person	€ 3.00
child (3-11 yrs)	€ 2.25
pitch incl. electricity	€ 7.50
hiker/cyclist and tent	€ 7.50

Tel: 036 36 13 27. Fax: 036 36 20 30. **Reservations:** Write or fax site. **Open** Easter - 30 September.

Directions: Sint Job In't Goor is northeast of Antwerp. From A1 (E19) exit 4, turn southeast towards Sint Jo, straight on at traffic lights and, immediately after canal bridge, left at campsite sign. Continue straight on for about 1.5 km. to site.

Camping Baalse Hei

066 Roodhuisstraat 10, B-2300 Turnhout (Antwerp)

The 'Campine' is an area covering three-quarters of the Province of Antwerp, noted for its nature reserves, pine forests, mead-ows and streams and is ideal for walking and cycling, while Turnhout itself is an interesting old town. Baalse Hei is a long-established friendly site with 454 pitches. A separate touring area of 61 large pitches (all with 16A electricity and TV connections and shared water point) on a large grass field has been thoughtfully developed with young trees and bushes planted. Cars are parked away from the pitches. Large motorhomes can be taken although it is best to phone in advance. It is 100 m. from the edge of the field to the modern, heated, sanitary building. There is a small lake for swimming with a beach, a boating lake and a large fishing lake. Entertainment and activities are organised July/Aug. Walk in the woods and you will come across red squirrels or take the pleasant 1.5 km. river-side walk to the next village.

Facilities: The toilet block provides hot showers on payment (€ 0,50), some washbasins in cabins and facilities for disabled visitors. Dishwashing facilities (hot water € 0,12), Launderette. Motorcaravan serv-ices. Café/restaurant (daily 1/6-30/9, w/ends only other times, closed 16/11-25/1). Breakfast served in high season. Shop (all year). Club/TV room. Lake swimming. Fishing. Two tennis courts. Table tennis. Boules. Volleyball. Basketball. Football. Adventure play area. Bicycle hire. Arrival after 4 pm. departure by 10 am. **Off site:** Riding or golf 1.5 km.

Charges 2002

Per unit all incl.	€ 14.00 - € 18.00
2 cyclists and tent	€ 9.00 - € 12.00
electricity	€ 1.00
dog	free

No credit cards. **Tel:** 014 42 19 31. Fax: 014 42 08 53. E-mail: info@baalsehei.be. **Reservations:** Contact site. **Open** all year.

Directions: Site is northeast of Turnhout off the N119. Approaching from Antwerp on E34/A12 go onto Turnhout ring road to the end (not a complete ring) and turn right. There is a small site sign to right in 1.5 km. then country lane.

Goolderheide Vakantiepark

Bosstraat 1, B-3950 Bocholt (Limburg)

076

A large family holiday site with 900 individual pitches with a friendly family atmosphere, Goolderheide has been owned and operated by the same family for many years and has an excellent pool complex and playgrounds. There are many seasonal and rental units, plus around 300 tourist pitches with 4/6A electric hook-ups, all in a forest setting. The pitches are of variable size and the access roads are quite narrow. The outdoor pool complex consists of two large pools, one of Olympic size, a water slide and a paddling pool. There is also a fishing lake, and a lake with a small sandy beach. An enormous area is devoted to a comprehensive children's playground with a vast range of equipment. During the main season there is also a weekly supervised 'assault' course complete with aerial ropeways, etc., a soundproofed over 16's disco, plus a 'younger kids' disco, and an extensive programme of varied activities to keep children and adults occupied. There are no extra charges for most of these activities.

Facilities: Four fairly modern sanitary buildings (three are near the main touring pitches) provide an ample supply of WCs and washbasins, but rather fewer showers, dishwashing and vegetable preparation sinks. Baby changing areas in both the ladies' and men's. Separate laundry with washing machines and dryers. Two suites for disabled people. Bar. Shop (open daily in July/Aug. but only at weekends and on public holidays in low season). Takeaway. Swimming pools. Tennis and badminton courts. Fishing lake. Boules courts. Mini golf (payment). Comprehensive play area and supervised 'assault' course. Children's discos. Varied programme of activities. Night security staff in main season. **Off site:** Bicycle hire 1 km.

Charges 2002

Per adult	€ 5.20
child (under 12 yrs)	€ 2.75
pitch incl. 4A electricity	€ 15.60 - € 25.00
extra 2A electricity	€ 3.10
dog	€ 2.50

Tel: 089 462 470. Fax: 089 464 619. E-mail: info@goolderheide.be. **Reservations:** Advisable for peak season and public holidays, contact site. **Open** 1 April - 30 September.

Directions: From A13 (E313) Antwerp-Liege motorway junction 25, take N141 to Leopoldsburg, then N73 through Peer, to outskirts of Bree (35 km. approx), and take N76 north for 3 km, turn left into Bocholt, and continue towards Kaulille. Site entrance road is on left towards edge of town, well signed.

Family-Camping Wilhelm Tell

078 Hoeverweg 87, B-3660 Opglabbeek (Limburg)

The Limburg region is a relaxing area with much to do, including shopping or touring the historic towns with a very enjoyable choice of food and drink! Wilhelm Tell is a family run site that caters particularly well for children with its indoor and outdoor pools and lots of entertainment on offer throughout the season. The entertainment team are very active. There is a total of 128 pitches with 70 available for touring units, some separated, others on open fields. There are 60 electricity connections (10A) and, for winter use, 20 hardstandings. The super bar/restaurant has access for wheelchair users. M. Lode Nulmans has a very special attitude towards his customers and tries to ensure they leave satisfied and want to return. For example, in his restaurant he says 'it serves until you are full'.

Facilities: Toilet facilities are good with adequate toilets and showers and two washcabins for ladies in the large block. Extra facilities around the pool supplement at busy times. Baby room in reception area. Two excellent modern en-suite units for disabled visitors. Two dishwashing and two laundry sinks. Washing machine and dryer. Motorcaravan service point. Bar/restaurant and snack bar (times vary acc. to season.). Swimming pools (well supervised) Outdoor pool has slide and wave machine. Children's play area. Table tennis.

Charges 2002

Per pitch	€ 12.00
adult	€ 6.00
child	€ 3.00
electricity per k/w	€ 0.25
dog	€ 4.00
TV connection	€ 2.00

Less 30% in low season. **Tel:** 0032 89854444. Fax: 0032 89810010. E-mail: receptie@wilhelmtell.com. **Reservations:** Necessary for high season. **Open** all year.

Directions: From E314 take exit 32 and follow 730 road towards Opglabbeek. After filling station on right continue for 2 km. Turn right at bollards, go straight on at crossroads. At T junction turn left and entrance is on left (tight turn, watch for tree).

The Alan Rogers' Travel Service

We have recently extended The Alan Rogers Travel Service. This unique service enables our readers to reserve their holidays as well as ferry crossings and comprehensive insurance cover at extremely competitive rates. The majority of participating sites are in France and we are able to offer a selection of some of the very best sites in this country.

the travel service TO BOOK

Ferry	✓
Pitch	✓
Accommodation	✓

01892 55 98 98

One simple telephone call to our Travel Service on 01892 55 98 98 is all that is needed to make all the arrangements. Why not take advantage of our years' of experience of camping and caravanning. We would be delighted to discuss your holiday plans with you, and offer advice and recommendations.

Share our experience and let us help to ensure that your holiday will be a complete success.

Alan Rogers Travel Service 01892 55 98 98 or www.alanrogers.com

Camping du Waux-Hall

053 avenue Saint-Pierre 17, B-7000 Mons (Hainault)

Waux-Hall is a useful and convenient site for a longer look at historic Mons and the surrounding area. It is a well laid out municipal site, close to the town centre and E42 motorway. The 75 pitches, most with electricity (10A), are arranged on either side of an oval road, on grass and divided by beds of small shrubs; the landscape maintenance is excellent. A large public park with refreshment bar, tennis, a children's playground and lake is adjacent, with direct access from the site when the gate is unlocked. Places to visit include the house of Van Gogh, the Fine Arts Museum, Decorative Arts Museum and the Collegiate church.

Facilities: A single, heated toilet block is of older style, basic but clean, with most washbasins in cubicles for ladies. Washing machine and dryer. Dishwashing and laundry sinks under cover. Soft drinks machine, ice cream. Bicycle hire. Tennis. Children's playground. **Off site:** Public park adjacent. Town centre shops and restaurants within easy walking distance. Fishing 300 m. Riding 2 km. Golf 4 km.

Charges 2003

Per adult	€ 3.35
child	€ 2.15
pitch incl. 2 nights electricity	€ 2.30 - € 2.80
car	€ 0.90
electricity more than 2 nights (10A) per k/w	€ 0.15

No credit cards. **Tel:** 065 33 79 23. Fax: 065 36 38 48. **Reservations:** Write or phone for details. **Open** all year.

Directions: From Mons inner ring road, follow signs for Charleroi, La Louviere, Binche, Beaumont. When turning off ring road, keep to right hand lane, turning for site is immediately first right. (signed Waux-Hall and camping).

Camping de L'Orient

054 Vieux Chemin de Mons, 8, B-7500 Tournai (Doornik) (Hainault)

L'Orient is an attractive, good quality municipal site in a quiet, green location close to the historic town of Tournai and convenient for the E42. It is immaculately kept by its manager. The 51 level, grassy, individual pitches (all for tourists) are separated by laurel hedges and have shade in some parts and electricity (16A). Adjoining the site is an attractive restaurant and bar with a superb terrace overlooking the lake where campers can fish and hire pedaloes. There is also a new, high quality pool complex with café, indoor pool and outdoor pool with water slides. Tournai has the oldest belfry in Europe and you can also see the cathedral and museums dedicated to decorative arts, folklore, tapestry and military history.

Facilities: Two modern sanitary units are of high quality, spotlessly clean and heated in cool weather. They include some washbasins in cubicles and roomy showers on payment. Facilities for laundry, dishwashing and disabled people. Basic provisions available from reception. **Off site:** Restaurant/bar adjoining site (10.00-22.00 hrs in season). Swimming pool (50% discount for campers) and waterslide complex. Lake with picnic and barbecue areas, lakeside walks, fishing, pedalor hire and playground.

Charges 2002

Per adult	€ 2.50
child (6-12 yrs)	€ 2.00
pitch	€ 4.50 - € 6.00

Tel: 069 22 26 35. **Fax:** 069 89 02 29. **E-mail:** tourisme@tournai.be. **Reservations:** Write or phone for details. **Open** all year.

Directions: From E42 exit 32 take N7 towards Tournai centre. Turn left at first traffic lights (site signed), left at small roundabout and site entrance is immediately on the left.

Camping L'Eau Rouge

074 Cheneux 25, B-4970 Stavelot (Liège)

A popular, lively and attractively situated site, L'Eau Rouge is in a sheltered valley close to Spa and the Grand Prix circuit. There are 140 grassy pitches of 110 sq.m. on sloping ground either side of a central road (speed bumps) - 70 are taken by permanent units. The main building houses the busy reception, shop, café, bar and the main sanitary facilities. There are plenty of sporting activities in the area including skiing and luge in winter. The site is close to the motor race circuit at Spa Francorchamps and is within walking distance for the fit. The site's Dutch owners are not only embarking on a five year programme upgrading the infrastructure, but also have other ideas in the pipeline.

Facilities: There is a main block but a smaller unit serves the touring area. It includes good numbers of British WCs, mostly open washbasins, but rather fewer hot showers (free) - which could be stretched at times. Additional facilities should be available in the near future. Dishwashing and laundry sinks. Shop. Baker calls daily at 9.30 am. in season. Café. Bar. Football. Boules. Table tennis. Archery (free lessons on site 10 am. daily in high season). Barbecues. Playground. Entertainment in season. **Off site:** Riding 10 km. Bicycle hire 6 km.

Charges 2002

Per unit	€ 10.00
adult	€ 2.25
child (4-12 yrs)	€ 2.00
electricity (10A)	€ 2.00

Tel: 080 86 30 75. **Fax:** 080 86 30 75. **E-mail:** info@camping-leaurouge.be. **Reservations:** Write to site. **Open** all year except 10 Dec - 31 Jan.

Directions: From E42 take exit 11 (Malmedy) in the direction of Stavelot. Site is signed.

Camping Spa d'Or

070 Stockay 17, B-4845 Sart-lez-Spa (Liège)

Although a campsite for more than thirty years, Spa d'Or has been owned by the Linnemann family for just three. They have a long-term plan to upgrade the site which had been rather neglected. The 230 touring pitches have an open aspect, most are slightly sloping and all have 10A electricity. A tree-filled hill with shallow river below provides shelter at the lower end of the camping area. The two sanitary blocks are old but clean. Most of the showers are very small with little or no room for changing. Three showers in the ladies section are equipped with a washbasin, otherwise they are communal. With a cosy bar/restaurant, this is an acceptable site within easy reach of many tourist attractions.

Facilties: Two old but clean sanitary blocks with acceptable rather than brilliant facilities. Family room with shower, WC and baby bath. Room for visitors with disabilities. Dishwashing sinks. Shop (1/4-1/10). Bar, restaurant and takeaway (1/4-1/11). Outdoor heated pool (15/5-15/9). Play area with good equipment. TV in bar. Boules Entertainment during July and August. **Off site:** Fishing 2 km. Golf and riding 5 km. Maps for cycling and walking on sale at reception. Caves, museums, historical buildings within a short distance. Spa 4 km.

Charges 2002

Per unit incl. 2 persons	€ 16.50
extra person over 3 yrs	€ 3.75
tent pitch incl. 2 persons	€ 12.00

Tel: 087 474400. **Fax:** 087 475277. **E-mail:** info@campingspador.be. **Reservations:** Contact site. **Open** all year.

Directions: From E42 take exit 9 and follow the signs to Spa d'Or.

Camping Moulin de Malempre

073 1 Malempre, B-6960 Manhay (Luxembourg)

This pleasant countryside site, very close to the E25, is well worth a visit and the Dutch owners will make you very welcome. The reception building houses the office and a small shop, above which is an attractive bar and restaurant with open fireplace. The 150 marked tourist pitches are separated by small shrubs and gravel roads on sloping terrain. All have electricity (6/10A), 40 have water and drainage as well and the site is well lit. The star of this site is the main sanitary unit, an ultra modern, two storey Scandinavian style building; this is complimented by a unisex unit. There is a little traffic noise from the nearby E25 (not too intrusive). English is spoken.

Facilities: Modern toilet facilities include some washbasins in cubicles and family bathrooms on payment. The unisex unit can be heated and has a family shower room. Unit for disabled people with automatic taps, hoists and rails. Baby room. Dishwashing and laundry. Motorcaravan services. Shop for basics (15/5-31/8). Baker calls daily. Restaurant (15/5-15/9). Bar (15/5-15/9 and weekends). Heated swimming pool and children's pools (15/5-15/9). TV. Table tennis. Pool table. Boules. Playground. **Off site:** Bicycle hire 3 km. Riding 6 km.

Charges 2002

Per unit incl. 2 adults	€ 16.98 - € 19.58
tent pitch incl. 2 persons	€ 14.38
extra adult	€ 3.72
child (3-11 yrs)	€ 2.60
electricity	€ 2.35

Less 20% in low season. **Tel:** 086 45 55 04. Fax: 086 45 56 74. E-mail: camping.malempre@cybernet.be. **Reservations:** Made with deposit of half the total fees - contact site. **Open** 1 April - 31 October.

Directions: From E25/A26 (Liege-Bastogne) exit 49, turn towards Lierneux on N822, follow signs to Malempré and site.

Camping Tonny

072 Tonny 35, B-6680 Amberloup (Luxembourg)

the travel service
TO BOOK
Ferry ✔
Pitch ✔
Accommodation ✗
01892 55 98 98

With a friendly atmosphere, this family campsite is in pleasant valley by the River Ourthe. It is an attractive small site with 75 grassy touring pitches, with wooden chalet buildings giving a Tyrolean feel. The pitches (80-100 sq.m.) are separated by small shrubs and fir trees and electricity (4/6A) is available. Cars are parked away from the units and there is a separate meadow for tents. Surrounded by natural woodland, Camping Tonny is an ideal base for outdoor activites. The main chalet has a café/bar and open fireplace, with a nice shady terrace for relaxing outside and is open all year (according to demand).

Facilities: Two fully equipped sanitary units (both heated in cool weather) include dishwashing and laundry sinks (all hot water is on payment). Baby area and laundry. Freezer for campers use. Small shop. Café/bar. TV lounge and library. Sports field. Boules. Games room. Playgrounds. Skittle alley. Bicycle hire. Fishing. Canoeing. Cross country skiing.

Charges 2002

Per person	€ 2.50
pitch	€ 6.75
electricity (4A)	€ 1.50
dog	€ 1.50

Off season discounts for over 55's and longer stays. **Tel:** 061 68 82 85. Fax: 061 68 82 85. E-mail: camping.tonny@belgacom.be. **Reservations:** Essential for high season; contact site. **Open** 15 February - 15 November.

Directions: From N4 take exit for Libramont (N826), then to Amberloup (4 km.) where site is signed.

Camping le Vieux Moulin

077 Petite Strument 62, B-6980 La Roche en Ardenne (Luxembourg)

Located in one of the most beautiful valleys in the heart of the Ardennes, Le Vieux Moulin has 187 pitches and, although there are 127 long stay units at the far end of the site, the 60 tourist pitches do have their own space. Some are separated by hedges, others for tents and smaller units are more open, all are on grass, and there are 50 electric hook-ups (6A). The 19th century water mill has been owned and operated by the owner's family for many years, but has now been converted into a small hotel and a fascinating mill museum. La Roche is a pretty little town in an unspoiled area, a very scenic region of rolling tree-clad hills and small deep valleys.

Facilities: A newly constructed, centrally located toilet block is between the tourist and long stay areas. It can be heated in cool weather and provides washbasins in cubicles and controllable hot showers on payment. Dishwashing and laundry sinks with washing machine. No facilities for disabled persons. A further older unit is at the end of the mill building. Restaurant and bar with hotel (8 rooms). Mill museum. **Off site:** Town facilities 800 m.

Charges 2002

Per person over 5 yrs	€ 2.50
tent, caravan or motorcaravan	€ 7.50
electricity	€ 2.50
dog	€ 2.00

Tel: 084 411 380. Fax: 084 411 080. E-mail: strument@skynet.be. **Reservations:** Advised for high season. **Open** 1 April - 11 November.

Directions: From town centre take N89 south towards St Hubert. Turn right towards Hives where site is signed. Site is 800 m. from town centre.

Belgium - South
Camping Parc La Clusure

067 chemin de la Clusure 30, B-6927 Bure-Tellin (Luxembourg)

Set in a river valley in the lovely wooded uplands of the Ardennes, known as the L'Homme Valley touring area, La Clusure has 425 large marked, grassy pitches (350 for touring units). All have access to electricity (16A), cable TV and water taps and are mostly in avenues off a central, tarmac road. It's a busy site that could feel crowded during the high season. There is a very pleasant, well lit riverside walk (the river is shallow in summer and popular for children to play in), a heated swimming pool and children's pool with pool-side bar/terrace. The site is used by a tour operator (number of pitches varies). The nearby main Brussels - Luxembourg railway line is due to be re-routed by 2003. The famous Grottes of Han are nearby.

Facilities: Four sanitary units (one heated in winter) include some washbasins in cubicles and facilities for babies. Dishwashing and laundry facilities may be stretched at times. Motorcaravan services.Well stocked shop, bar (closed 4/11 - 23/3). Restaurant.. Snack bar. Takeaway. Bicycle hire. Tennis. Badminton. Volleyball. Swimming pools (1/5-15/9). Playgrounds. Organised activity programme includes courses in canoeing, mountain biking and climbing (July/Aug). Fishing (licence essential). Barrier card deposit €12,39. **Off site:** Rding nearby.

Charges 2002

Per pitch incl. 2 persons	€ 18.00
extra person	€ 4.00
electricity (16A)	€ 3.00
dog	€ 4.00
local tax	€ 0.75

Tel: 084 36 60 80. Fax: 084 36 67 77. E-mail: info@parclaclusure.be. **Reservations:** Advisable for Easter, Whitsun and for July - mid-Aug. Made with deposit and fee (€ 15). **Open** all year.

Directions: Site is signed north off the N803 Rochefort - St Hubert road at Bure, 8 km. south-east of Rochefort with a narrow, steepish, winding descent to site.

Belgium - South
Camping Le Pirot

086 Route de Charleville, B-5580 Han-sur-Lesse (Namur)

Le Pirot is an attractive, rather basic site more suitable for small caravans or motor-caravans and tent campers, in the centre of Han on the banks of the Lesse. Camping de La Lesse, its sister site a short distance away caters for larger units. All local attractions and the shops are within walking distance of both sites. There are just 30 grass pitches in three rows (two rows along the edge of the water), some with an electricity hook-up. A fairly old building houses adequate sanitary facilities that are kept acceptably clean. There are ongoing improvements as money becomes available.

Facilities: A single sanitary block at the end of the camping area includes open washbasins, shower cubicles and British-style toilets in a separate room. External under cover dishwashing and vegetable preparation. Bicycle hire. **Off site:** Shops, `tram safari`, caves, museums and other attractions within walking distance.

Charges 2002

Per adult	€ 2.73
child	€ 1.86
pitch	€ 4.96

Tel: 084 37 72 90. E-mail: han.tourisme@euronet.be. **Reservations:** Contact site. **Open:** 1 April - 30 September.

Directions: Leave A4 at junction 23, turn left in 300 m. towards Han-sur-Lesse and follow signs to the town. Site is on left immediately before the river bridge. Camping de La Lesse is signed about 100 m. further on the right.

Belgium - South
Camping Vallée de Rabais

071 rue de Bonlieu, B-6760 Virton (Luxembourg)

Vallée de Rabais is a large, spacious site with an interesting lay-out. This consists of a circular road with smaller roads leading to circular pads with pitches. The site offers excellent facilities in a very pleasant setting surrounded by forest. A large sports complex is just a walk away, offering tennis, fishing and much more. The forest is open to walkers and cyclists alike The new owners took over two years ago and are gradually revamping the entire site. Now only modern units and tents owned by the site can be found along with over 200 level touring pitches. Some pitches are fully serviced and all have 16A electricity, with adequate water points.

Facilities: Three facility blocks include one which is modern and of a very high standard with superb showers (also with washbasin) and an excellent en-suite room for disabled people. Laundry sinks, washing machines and dryers. Motorcaravan service point. Bar/restaurant and shop (opening times vary). Outdoor swimming pool with wood decking for sunbathing. **Off site:** Tennis and fishing.

Charges 2002

Per unit incl. 2 persons	€ 16.50
extra person (over 3 yrs)	€ 3.75
electricity	€ 3.00

Tel: 0032 63 57 11 95. Fax: 0032 63 58 33 42. E-mail: info@campingvalleederabais.be. **Reservations:** Necessary for high season. **Open** all year.

Directions: From E25/E411 take exit 29 towards Etalle and Virton. Follow signs for Vallée de Rabais. Turn right at sports complex. At crossroads (with phone box) turn right and uphill to site at end of road.

Croatia

Croatian National Tourist Office
2 The Lanchesters, 162-164 Fulham Palace Road, London W6 9ER

Tel: 0208 563 7979   E-mail: info@cnto.freeserve.co.uk   Internet: www.htz.hr

Croatia, or Hrvatska to use its old name, was until the early 1990s one of the six provinces of the old Yugoslavia under Marshal Tito. Since attaining independence as a state in its own right, Croatia has thrown off old communist attitudes and blossomed into a go-ahead, lively and friendly place to visit. For campers and caravanners there is an extra welcome as there are between 275 and 300 official campsites in the country. These vary from a field converted by an enterprising farmer to enormous sites of several square kilometres. These larger sites are mostly run by large companies who also operate up to 14 hotels. Each company may have up to 7 or 8 sites which, although leading to some degree of standardisation, also means an equal quality of services. Site facilities are open to day visitors and sites are licensed as to how many people they are allowed to have within their boundaries at any one time rather than how many caravans or tents they are allowed. This can be as many as 10,000 people for a large site. All sites are graded using a star system with one star being the lowest rating and three stars the top. Rating depends on the facilities provided. Croatia was, in the 1950s, one of the first countries to openly welcome naturists. As a result almost one in three of the bigger sites is a clothes-free zone and many other sites have an area of beach set aside for nude sunbathing and swimming.

Population

4,784,265; density 84.6%.

Capital

Zagreb.

Climate

This is predominately warm with an average on the coast of 2,600 hours of sunshine per year. Summer sea temperature is 25O to 27OC. It can get very hot with temperatures over 40OC. Don't forget the sun cream! Spectacular thunder storms are not uncommon in summer. The most pleasant times are late May and June and the first three weeks of September.

Language

The most commonly spoken language after the native Croatian is German. Almost all sites have English speaking staff but the some German or Italian helps a lot with one's neighbours.

Currency

The local currency is the Croatian kuna which is quite stable at around 12 to the UK£. There are exchange facilities everywhere. The best erates and the lowest commission charges are available in the banks. A maximum of 2,000 kuna may be taken into Croatia and any kuna brought home will not be exchangeable. Almost all sites now quote charges in Euros (€). There is a daily tourist tax per person which varies with the time of year being highest in July and August.

Banks

Normally open 08.00 - 19.00 hrs, Mon - Friday.
Credit cards are welcome at most sites and in larger shops. All major cards are accepted.

Post Offices

Operate the same hours as shops.

Time

European standard time: GMT and BST +1 hour.

Public Holidays

New Year's day; Epiphany 6 Jan; Good Friday; Easter Monday; Labour Day 1 May; Statehood Day 30 May; Day of Anti-Fascist Victory 22 June; Thanksgiving Day 5 Aug; Assumption 15 Aug; All Saints 1 Nov; Christmas 25/26 Dec.

Telephone

The dialling code for Croatia is 00 385.

Shops

Mainly 08.00 - 20.00 hrs, closed on Sundays.

Motoring

Croatia is proceeding with a vast road improvement programme. There are still some roads which leave a lot to be desired but things have improved dramatically over the last 7 years.
Speed Limits are as signed with a maximum of 60 km/hr in towns and 80 km/hr on urban roads for cars towing caravans. Motorhomes have a maximum of 60 km/hr in towns 80 to l00 km/hr on ordinary roads, depending on the vehicle's weight, and 120 km/hr on highways.
To drive in Croatia drivers need:
A valid UK driving licence.
A current international insurance certificate

(Green Card) which includes the caravan if towing.

Written permission from the owner to use the vehicle (or caravan) or the vehicle registration document (V5) if owned. School buses must not be overtaken whilst stationary and passengers are getting on or off. Overtaking a queue of vehicles in one go is illegal. If it becomes necessary to report an incident to the police they will make a charge for the paperwork involved. Fuel prices are approximately 60% of those in the UK.

Useful phone numbers

First aid 94
Police 92
HAK (auto club) 987
Croatia Camping Union 052/451324.

Overnighting

Parking up at the side of the road or on car parks, etc. is forbidden. However, most sites have areas outside the site proper where late arrivals may stop overnight.

Note

The majority of tourists visiting Croatia originate from Germany, Austria, Italy, Slovenia, Scandinavia and the late Eastern Block countries. Very few Brits have ventured there in the last few years.

The area most likely to appeal to British caravanners is the long Adriatic coast and/or the islands just offshore (more than 1,180 of them). The most popular area of all is Istria with more than 90% of the country's campsites. Almost all of these are directly on the sea. It is on Istria that we are concentrating in this edition.

Visitors from Britain must not expect camp site regulations to be the same as at home. Most sites tend to get very busy during the peak season and spacing between units can get very tight. There is no rule stating minimum distances, etc. Most people are sensible though and problems rarely arise.

How to find Croatia

The trip to the Istrian Peninsula area of Croatia is around 1,000 miles from Calais by the shortest route. There are, of course, numerous variations on the route but it is possible to have motorway driving for all but the last few miles.

The easiest way is to head for Munich and once there pick up the signs for Salzburg. The German/Austrian border is just before Salzburg and it is necessary to stop and purchase a vignette to allow travel on Austrian motorways. These are available with various periods of validity – a ten day one costing about £3.50 (in €). Once into Austria follow the signs for Villach. This will take you over the Tauern autobahn and through two very long tunnels of 6.4 and 4.6 km. where a further toll is payable. This is about £7.50 for a car and caravan and credit cards are accepted. The scenery along this stretch of road is simply fabulous. Villach is a good place to stop overnight with several sites close to the motorway. Once back on the motorway head for Italy following signs for Udine and then later Trieste. This is again a toll road. Take a ticket from the dispenser at the start and pay when you leave. Again credit cards are accepted.

Approaching Trieste look for signs for Slovenia and Koper (also called Capodistra). Be very careful to follow the signs and they will take you to the border between Italy and Slovenia. Crossing the border continue to follow the signs for Koper. Arriving in Koper look for signs to Porec. The road from here on gets a little rough, twisty and with steep hills but take heart, you're almost there! The road signed to Porec will take you to the Slovenia - Croatia border. Crossing into Croatia the next town is Buje where care is needed – look for signs to Porec and Novigrad (Citanova). On reaching Novigrad turn left at the traffic lights and you are on the road which will take you to all the sites listed.

Umag

Umag is a small town on the north-western coast of Istria that rose from the Roman remains and has maintained, up to now, narrow and winding streets and a fascinating mediaeval town structure. The modern tourist resort with an enchanting indented coast and its pebble, rocky beaches, small inlets and harbours give many opportunities for practising various sports and recreational activities. Umag is famous for tennis where, every year, tournaments are held gathering the best world tennis players.

The Umag area enjoys an abundance of camping and caravanning sites, which with one exception, are all one star sites. However, most of these sites provide facilities that are well above the requirements for a one star award. The following is a selection.

Croatia
Naturist Camping Kanegra
Kanegra bb, 52470 Umag (Istria)

Sitting as it does, almost on the Slovenian border, this could be said to be the first and last campsite in Croatia. Attached to the Kanegra bungalow complex, it is able to share facilities. The site occupies a five hectare strip of land between the wall of an ancient quarry and the sea and is directly across the bay from the town of Portoroz (Port of Roses) which is Slovenia's major seaside resort. The site has a very open aspect with very little shade and it is best described as mature and neat, with a rocky beach running its total length. There are 190 level pitches on sandy soil with sparse grass of which 68 are long-stay, leaving 122 for visitors. Pitches vary in size (80-100 sq.m) and are marked out and numbered, with electricity hook-ups available (16A; Europlugs). There is no pool but the site boasts crystal clear sea water and a safe beach. This is a fairly small, pleasant naturist site which is worthy of consideration for short or longer stays. Unusually for naturist sites, there is no objection to single men. Its proximity to Slovenia (Portoroz 13 km. around the bay) makes it a possible base for visiting some of that country's delights as well as those of Croatia.

Facilitiea: Two well equipped toilet blocks with washing up and laundry sinks. Drive-over motorcaravan service point. Shop. Two bars, three snack bars and two restaurants, all open until late. Nightly disco in the adjacent bungalow complex but reportedly this doesn't disturb the campsite. Activities centre around watersports or tennis (in Umag). **Off site:** Riding 10 km.

Charges 2002

Per unit	€ 2.60 - € 6.10
person	€ 2.60 - € 4.40
child (5-11 yrs)	€ 1.40 - € 2.30
electricity	€ 2.10
dog	€ 2.60

For stays less than 3 nights in high season add 10%. **Tel:** 052 732186. Fax: 052 732212. E-mail: kanegra@istraturist.hr. **Reservations:** Contact site or Istraturist reservations service - tel: 052/719 100, fax: 052/719 999. **Open** 1 May - 1 October.

Directions: Site is signed off the Trieste - Koper road in Slovenia or may be reached by following directions in 'How to find Croatia' page and following signs from Umag (10 km).

Croatia
Auto Camp Pineta
Istarska bb, 52475 Savudrija (Istria)

One of the older sites at the western end of Istria, Pineta is a medium sized site of 17 hectares, getting its name from being set amongst a forest of fully mature pine trees around two sides of a coastal bay. This is a site for those who prefer the cool that shade affords. The site, being one star rated, does not have many facilities but for those who like the peaceful life this could be more than acceptable. There are 500 piches of which 300 are occupied on a long stay basis, leaving 200 for touring units. Pitches are 70-80 sq.m. with almost all having access to electricity (10A; German and Europlugs). The site has a sea water swimming pool and sea bathing is also possible, with tennis and fishing also popular. During our visit we saw a wide variety of wild birds and the over 100 year old trees provide an interest all of their own. Pineta is a busy site which appears to be very popular, particularly with long stay guests.

Facilities: Toilet blocks are mixed - one old, two modern and one refurbished - but are fully equipped. Hot and cold showers. All except two WCs per block are Turkish style. One unit is for disabled guests. Dishwashing and laundry sinks. Fresh water at toilet blocks only. Drive over motorcaravan service point. Supermarket. Six bars, three restaurants and a snack bar, all open long hours with reasonable prices. Swimming pool (16 x 24 m). Tennis. Fishing (subject to permit). Barbecues are banned in the camping area but may be held on the beach. No organised activities. **Off site:** Riding 3 km. Gas is available in local garage 500 m. from the site entrance.

Charges 2002

Per unit	€ 3.10 - € 5.60
person	€ 2.60 - € 4.40
child (5-11 yrs)	€ 1.40 - € 2.30
electricity	€ 2.10
dog	€ 2.60

Tel: 052 759 518. Fax: 052 759 526. E-mail: camp.pineta@istraturist.hr. **Reservations:** Contact site or Istraturist reservations service - tel: 052/719 100, fax: 052/719 999. **Open** 1 May - 30 September.

Directions: From Triest - Koper(Capodistra) - Umag road look for Savundrija signs. Site is 6 km. from Umag.

The nostalgic old town centre of Rovinj inspires with charming alleys, sites such as the cathedral of the holy Euphemia and a fascinating flair. Crystal clear sea and dreamy bays also guarantee perfect bathing fun. Three-star camping facilities near the coastal town also spoil the visitor with numerous amenities. Camp **"Vestar"** is considered a paradise with a wide range of leisure activities and its own harbour, the naturist camp **"Monsena"** is situated 3 km from Rovinj. In **"Polari"** campers are able to utilise the entertainment programme of the adjoining resort "Villas Rubin".

Rovinj

Vestar · Polari · Naturist Monsena

Jadran Turist, Rovinj, Croatia
Tel. 00 385 / 52 / 800 376
Fax 813 497, 815 722
E-Mail: jadrantur-rovinj@jadran.tdr.hr
www.istra.com/jadranturist

»Ladin Gaj«

Idyllic alleys and picturesque little squares give Umag on the northwest coast of Istria its nostalgic flair. With one of the most attractive tennis centres in Europe (in the resort facility "Stella Maris") the little town has an excellent reputation. Around Umag, **"Stella Maris"**, **"Finida"**, **"Pineta"**, **"Ladin Gaj"** and the naturist camp **"Kanegra"** invite to holidays under the southern sun, the facilities having been modernised – also in the area of sanitary facilities. "Ladin Gaj" now has a playground, while "Pineta" and "Finida" concentrated on the expansion of the leisure and gastronomic facilities.

Istraturist, Umag, Croatia
Tel. 00 385 / 52 / 719 100, Fax 719 999
E-Mail: crs@istraturist.hr
www.istra.com/istraturist

operated by ● *Sol Meliá* CROATIA

Umag

Stella Maris · Finida · Pineta
Ladin Gaj · Naturist Kanegra

Croatia
Camping Stella Maris
6712 Savudrijska cesta bb, 52470 Umag (Istria)

This small one star site of 4.5 hectares is part of the excellent Sol Stella Maris leisure complex where the Croatian open tennis tournament is held (amongst other competitions). Located some 2 km. from the centre of Umag, the site is around 70% heavily wooded with abundant shade. The remaining 30% is of open, level grass suitable for any outfit but especially for motorcaravans. Pitches are zoned and numbered but not all marked or separated. The normal pitch size is 60 sq.m. but some are larger, and 400 are available to touring units. Of these, 320 have electricity (10A; Europlugs). This site`s real advantage is its attachment to the leisure complex, across a busy road, with all its many facilities available to campers. Two swimming pools are a short walk away and a very pretty beach area where sun loungers may be hired for less than £1 per day. When we visited in July the site was busy but by no means full, especially in the unshaded areas.

Facilities: Three modern and one older sanitary blocks are very well kept and fully equipped. Half the washbasins have hot water and all the showers. Facilities for disabled visitors (key from a member of the cleaning staff or reception). Dishwashing and laundry sinks, some with hot water. Apart from the toilet blocks there is no supply of fresh water or waste water disposal facility on site. Supermarket (07.00-22.00 hrs). Range of bars and snack bars. Restaurnt at the leisure complex. Barbeces permitted but a fire extinguisher must be handy. Tennis centre. Water sports. Fishing (permit required from Umag). Animation programme for children. **Off site:** 'Land train' every 15 minutes into Umag and a local bus service to towns further along the coast.

Charges 2002

Per unit	€ 3.80 - € 6.10
person	€ 2.80 - € 4.40
child (5-11 yrs)	€ 1.50 - € 2.30
electricity	€ 2.10
dog	€ 1.70 - € 2.50

For stays less than 3 nights in high season add 10%. **Tel:** 052 710900. Fax: 052 710909. E-mail: camp. stella.maris@istraturist.hr. **Reservations:** Contact site or Istraturist reservations service - tel: 052/719 100, fax: 052/719 999. **Open** 12 April - 15 October.

Directions: Site is 2.5 km. from Umag. On entering Umag look for signs to campsites and follow Stella Maris signs.

Croatia
Camping Finida
6714 Finida 66, 52470 Umag (Istria)

This site is run by the same concern as Stella Maris, Ladin Gaj, Kanegra and Pineta and is situated on the Novigrad to Umag road only one kilometre from Ladin Gaj. Unlike Ladin Gaj however, this site is quite small by Croatian standards at only 3.3 hectares and, in line with most smaller sites in this area, is heavily wooded affording maximum shade. Large motorcaravans would experience difficulty reaching some areas of the site due to narrow roads and leaning trees. There are 239 touring pitches (60-90 sq.m) all with 10A electricity using Europlugs, (146 long-stay pitches). Some of the electric boxes are brand new and plans are afoot to replace others. There is no swimming pool but the site fronts onto the sea with a pleasant stony beach for sunbathing. There are pedaloes for hire, surfing (in the right weather) and there is a resident diving club where lessons can be purchased. This is a mature site which attracts a regular return clientelle, and will suit those who are attracted by the shade and the cosiness of a smaller site.

Facilities: Three clean and elderly (but in good condition) toilet blocks contain British style WCs (block 2 has some Turkish style WCs). Dishwashing and laundry sinks (hot and cold water). Only one chemical toilet disposal point. Motorcaravan service point a bit tight to drive onto. Small but well stocked supermarket (tardis-like). Bar, snack bar and restaurant (08.00-24.00 hrs). Table tennis and minigolf. Fishing (subject to permit). Boats may be moored off the beach. **Off site:** Five buses per day into Umag and Novigrad.

Charges 2002

Per pitch	€ 3.10 - € 5.40
person	€ 2.10 - € 3.30
child (5-11 yrs)	€ 1.50 - € 3.30
electricity	€ 2.10
dog	€ 1.70 - € 2.10
local tax	€ 0.70

Tel: 052/756 296. Fax 052/756 295. E-mail camp.finida@istraturist.hr. **Reservations:** Advised for high season; contact site or Istraturist reservations service - tel: 052/719 100, fax: 052/719 999. **Open** 15 April - 30 September.

Directions: Site is on the right off the Umag - Norigrad, 4 km. from Umag.

Autocamp Ladin Gaj

6715 Jadranska bb, 52470 Umag (Istria)

Situated five kilometres from Novigrad on the road to Umag and posted by enormous signs, this site is difficult to miss. At 127 hectares Ladin Gaj is a strong contender to be the largest site in Croatia. The level, grassy ground and sparse shade make it look even larger. It is divided into in two parts, the smaller part being reserved for naturists and separated from the 'textile' part by space and a fence. There are 1,389 pitches available for touring units, 330 of which are in the naturist section. Pitch sizes are generous (80-120 sq.m.) and almost all are level with 10/16A electric hook ups available (Europlugs). There is no pool but the site is directly on the sea with swimming, boating and watersports facilities, and tennis and fishing also popular. The ancient towns of Umag and Novigrad are worth exploring with their history and culture. If you like wide-open spaces and quiet (no disco!) this is the site for you but take a bike or some other on-site transport or you'll need to do some walking.

Facilities: The site's crowning glory is 10 recently built and superbly maintained toilet blocks which include 2 bathrooms with deep tubs. Two blocks have children's WCs and facilities for disabled people including shower, WC and washbasin. Dishwashing and laundry sinks. Fresh water and waste water points at toilet blocks. Drive over motor-caravan service point. Range of shops and super-market. Bar, snack bar and restaurant (musical entertainment some evenings) all open early morning to midnight. Tennis. Fishing (subject to permit purchased in Umag). Football, minigolf. **Off site:** Riding near. Infrequent bus service to Umag and Novigrad.

Charges 2002

Per pitch acc. to season and type	€ 2.30 - € 7.20
person	€ 1.70 - € 3.60
child (5-11 yrs)	€ 1.10 - € 1.90
electricity	€ 2.10
dog	€ 1.80 - € 2.60

For stays less than 3 nights in high season add 10%. **Tel:** 052 75 63 03. Fax: 052 75 62 30. E-mail: camp.ladin.gaj@istraturist.hr. **Reservations:** Contact site or Istraturist reservations service - tel: 052/719 100, fax: 052/719 999. **Open** 1 April - 1 October.

Directions: Site is located alongside Umag - Novigrad road. Look for large signs.

Porec

An ancient town, Porec is located in the central part of the western Istrian coast, almost across from Venice. The Istrian Peninsula has a mild, Mediterranean climate and a history going back to prehistoric times, and there is much evidence of Roman occupation. The town of Porec was built by the Romans and is surrounded by tiny islands and green hills. Venturing inland, you find picturesque Mediaeval villages and towns, and castles full of mysterious stories and legends. You can still hear the rattle coming from an old mill and meet old wooden carts drawn by 'Boskarin', an Istrian breed of ox.

Solaris Naturist Centre

N6718 Lanterna, 52440 Porec (Istria)

Although only half the size, this is the naturist sister camp to Lanterna (no. 6716), being run by the same organisation. The pitches here are similar to Lanterna's in size and lay-out, although only 983 are available to tourists, there being 350 long stay units. There are 147 fully serviced pitches available on a first-come, first-served basis, an ample supply of electric hook-ups (10A) and plentiful water points. As this is a naturist site, single men and groups consisting of men only are prohibited and there are restrictions on photography. Ball games are forbidden in camping areas. There is a very pleasant swimming pool which is attended for as long as it is open. Clothing is not allowed in the pool. For those who embrace the naturist regime or want to give it a try, this is a pleasant, quiet site with above average facilities in an area of outstanding natural beauty.

Facilities: Twelve excellent, fully equipped toilet blocks (ten new) provide toilets, washbasins and showers (hot and cold). All blocks have facilities for disabled visitors. Ample dishwashing and laundry sinks, some with hot water. Two washing machines and ironing facilities. Restaurants and supermarkets (1/5-30/9). Swimming pool (1/5-30/9). Tennis. Bicycle hire. Riding. Children's play areas. Dogs are restricted to a particular area of the site. **Off site:** Riding and fishing 0.5 km.

Charges 2002

Per person	€ 2.70 - € 5.10
2 children free, third child	€ 1.80 - € 3.60
pitch incl. electricity	€ 4.50 - € 10.20
dog	€ 1.80 - € 3.70
local tax	€ 0.50 - € 1.00

Prices for pitches by the sea are higher. **Tel:** 052 404 000. Fax: 052 404 091. E-mail: solaris@riviera.hr. **Reservations:** Contact the Riviera Group: Tel: 052/434 900 or 408 000. Fax: 052/451 440 or 451 331. **Open** 1 April - 7 October.

Directions: Site is signed off the Novigrad (9 km) - Porec (13 km) road.

See advertisement on page 50

Lanternacamp

6716 Lanterna, 52440 Porec (Istria)

This is the largest site in Croatia with plenty of activities and high standards. Set in 90 hectares with over 3 kilometres of beach, there are 2,930 pitches of which 2,200 are for touring units. Facilities at Lanterna are in keeping with its size - there are, for instance, 18 toilet blocks. The policy here is to build more small toilet blocks rather that fewer large ones to reduce walking distances. The land is undulating with a sparse covering of grass and the marked and numbered pitches are arranged to take advantage of the topography and reduce the apparent size of the site. All pitches are of adequate size (60-120 sq.m) with some overlooking the sea, although these tend to be snatched up first. Some recent terracing work has improved the view for those areas. There are electricity connections throughout (10A) and 486 pitches with electricity and water. Dozens of activities and entertainment for children and adults are available both on and off site - this site has all that other sites have and more. However, the prices are higher than other sites in the area but still considerably less than one would pay in the UK or Germany for equivalent facilities. The season here is from April to the end of October with the second half of June to the end of August being the peak period.

Facilities: Most blocks are new and of top quality, with private bathrooms and baby care areas, some Turkish style WCs and hot and cold showers. All blocks provide facilities for disabled people. Cleaning is carried out overnight with additional 'tidy ups' during the day. Three supermarkets sell most everyday requirements. Four restaurants, bars and snack bars (1/5-30/9). Three swimming pools. Sand-pit and play areas, with animation for over 4 yrs in high season. Tennis. Table tennis. Watersports. Boats for rent. Minigolf. Riding. Dogs are allowed on site but are restricted to a certain area. **Off site:** Nearest large supermarket in Novigrad, 9 km. An hourly bus service runs from the reception area.

Charges 2002

Per person	€ 2.70 - € 5.10
2 children free, 3rd child	€ 1.80 - € 3.60
pitch incl. electricity	€ 4.50 - € 10.20
dog	€ 1.80 - € 3.70
local tax	€ 0.80 - € 1.00

Prices for pitches by the sea are higher. **Tel:** 052 404 500. Fax: 052 404 591. E-mail: riviera@riviera.hr. **Reservations:** Not normally necessary, but will be made with €30,68 fee (non returnable). Contact the Riviera Group: address: Tel: 052/434 900 or 408 000. Fax: 052/451 440 or 451 331. **Open** 1 April - 15 October.

Directions: Site is signed off the Novigrad - Porec road.

Croatia
Naturist Camping Istra

52452 Funtana (Istria)

Located in the tiny and picturesque village of Funtana, this peaceful site is run by the same organisation as Lanterna and Solaris. Istra has all the facilities expected of a middle to large site run by a major leisure organisation, except that there is no swimming pool. Sea swimming is possible, however. The usual ban regarding single men and men only groups applies. Additionally motorcycles, although not banned, are not welcome. There are 827 pitches for tourists, most with ample shade and varying in size from about 60-120 sq.m. The ground is undulating and some areas have been cut into low terraces. There are 987 electricity hook-ups (10A), with ample water points scattered throughout the site. Around 3 km. in the opposite direction is Vrsar, a fine and very attractive example of an Istrian fishing port (with two small supermarkets). This is a pleasant site but without the multiple facilities of the other sites in the same group. It appears quiet and peaceful and eminently suitable for those who just want to relax in the sun.

Facilities: Five old and five new sanitary buildings provide toilets, washbasins, showers (hot and cold) and hair dryers. Adequate washing up and laundry sinks, some with hot water. Laundry facilities. Small supermarket. Restaurant and bar (1/5-30/9). Shop (1/5-30/9). Children's play areas. Entertainment for children in high season. Minigolf. Tennis. Table tennis. Fishing near. **Off site:** Shops and restaurants in Funtana short walk from the gate. Serious shopping is Porec, some 7 km. away with a regular bus service from the village. Riding 1 km.

Charges 2002

Per person	€ 2.70 - € 5.10
two children free, third	€ 1.80 - € 3.50
pitch	€ 3.20 - € 7.10
pitch incl. electricity	€ 4.50 - € 10.80
dog	€ 1.80 - € 3.70
local tax	€ 0.80 - € 1.00

Prices for pitches by the sea are higher. **Tel:** 052 445 123. Fax: 052 445 306. E-mail: riviera@riviera.hr. **Reservations:** Contact the Riviera Group: 052/434 900 or 408 000. Fax: 052/451 440 or 451 331. **Open** 1 April - 15 October.

Directions: Site is signed off the Porec - Vrsar road in village of Funtana. Access for large units could be difficult when turning off the main road from the direction of Porec. If this looks as if it might be difficult, go past the signed turning and turn around in the night club car park a few metres further on. The problem is less when approaching from Vrsar.

See advertisement opposite

Croatia
Autocamp Turist Vrsar

PP 166, 52450 Vrsar (Istria)

Run by the same group as Lanterna, Solaris and Istra, this site adjoins the fishing port of Vrsar to which there is direct access from the site. At 30 hectares in area, this is a medium to large site and provides 695 touring pitches. Marked and numbered pitches vary in size with 90 sq.m. being the average, and the ground is undulating with sandy soil and grass. Some pitches are terraced. There is ample shade from mature trees, 850 electricity connections (10A; German plug) and 42 water points. The site has no swimming pool but sea bathing is possible. The restaurant is excellent, with a lovely view and there is also a snack bar. Many people like the fact that there is direct access to Vrsar and its range of cafés, bars and restaurants. This site is popular but does not get as crowded as some sites with more facilities and would suit those who want to get away from it all, but not too far.

Facilities: Three old and four new toilet blocks provide a mixture of British and Turkish style WCs, and washbasins and showers, not all with hot water. Some private cabins and baby rooms. Dishwashing and laundry sinks, some with hot water. Laundry. All facilities cleaned several times per day. Supermarket. (1/5-30/9). Bar/restaurant (1/5-30/9). Sports centre. Bicycle hire. Only gas barbecues are permitted. **Off site:** Shops in Vrsar, although the nearest serious shopping centre is at Porec. Riding 3 km.

Charges 2002

Per person	€ 2.70 - € 5.60
two children, third child	€ 1.80 - € 4.00
pitch incl. electricity	€ 4.50 - € 13.70
dog	€ 1.80 - € 3.70
local tax	€ 0.77 - € 0.97

Highest prices are for pitches by the sea. **Tel:** 052 441 419. Fax: 052 441 010. E-mail: riviera@riviera.com. **Reservations:** Contact the Riviera Group, address as site. Tel: 052/434 900 or 408 000. Fax: 052/451 440 or 451 331. **Open** 22 March - 15 October.

Directions: Site is on the main Porec (7 km) - Vrsar (1 km) road, well signed.

See advertisement opposite

Autokamp Zelena Laguna

6722 52440 Porec (Istria)

A busy, medium sized site (by Croatian standards), Zelena Laguna (green lagoon) is very popular with families and boat owners. Run by the Plava Laguna group that also runs three other campsites and seven hotels in the vicinity, this site is long established, yet is modernised each year as finances permit. The 1,017 pitches (784 for touring units) are a mixture of level, moderately sloping and terraced and range in size from 40-120 sq.m. The site itself slopes with a quite steep hill leading to the highest point which has impressive views overlooking the sea. Access to the pitches is by hard roads and shingle tracks which allow adequate space to manoeuvre. There are plenty of electrical hook-ups (10A; German plugs in most with a few Europlugs). There is one water point to every four pitches. This site can get very crowded in late June, July and August with the space between units much less than would be normal in the UK. As it can get very hot in high summer (40ºC), the pitches nearest the sea and the sea breezes, are the most sought after. The site is fronted by several hundred metres of rocky beach into which paved sunbathing areas have been laid. At one end of the beach is a marina. About 25% of the Blue Flag beach area is reserved for naturists. Good English is spoken by several of the receptionists.

Facilities: : Some new sanitary blocks are a great improvement on the old ones (one of which remains). About half the washbasins have hot water and there are free hot controllable showers in all blocks. Toilets are mostly British style, although there are also Turkish ones in at least one block. Supermarket and 'corner shop' selling groceries, fruit and vegetables. Several restaurants and snack bars (from 1/5). Swimming pool. Sub-aqua diving (with instruction). Tennis (instruction available). Five-a-side football. Bicycle hire. Boat hire (motor and sailing). Beach volleyball. Riding. Aerobics. Animation programme for children (from June, 9.30 onwards). **Off site:** Fishing 5 km. Small market and parade of shops selling beach wares, souvenirs etc. immediately outside site. Nearest large supermarkets are in Porec (4 km). Regular bus service and also a small 'land train' known as the 'Bumble Zug' from the adjacent hotel complex into the centre of Porec (alternatively it is 15 minutes drive but parking tends to be somewhat chaotic) but for the adventurous a water taxi to Porec harbour.

Charges 2002

Per person	€ 2.40 - € 4.70
child (5-12 yrs)	free - € 3.27
pitch	€ 3.58 - € 6.80
pitch incl. electricity	€ 4.45 - € 9.20
dog	€ 2.10 - € 3.32
local tax	€ 0.77

Tel: 052 410 101. Fax: 052 451 044. E-mail: mail@plavalaguna.hr. **Reservations:** Only made for certain pitches, with € 25,56 fee. Contact Plava Laguna Group, Rade Koncara 12, 52440 Porec. Tel: 052/410 101. Fax: 052/451 044. **Open** 1 April - 30 September.

Directions: Site is between the coast road and the sea with turning approx. 2 km. from Porec towards Vrsar. It is very well signed and is part of a large multiple hotel complex.

Camping Bijela Uvala

6724 Bijela Uvala, Elena Laguna, 52440 Porec (Istria)

Adjoining Zelena Laguna and run by the same company in the 1980s, this site is larger but with fewer pitches (780) making for a less crowded situation when times get busy. Bijela Uvala is therefore very popular with those who prefer a quieter life. The site won a European Camp Site of the Year award in 1999. It is part wooded, the predominant trees being oaks, and the pitches (60-120 sq.m) are marked out and numbered. There is some flat ground, some undulating and some terraced so a choice is possible. Choice pitches overlooking the sea are the first to go and are often booked a year ahead. There is, however, no need to book for other pitches unless one wishes to be sure of a particular spot. There are ample electricity hookups (10A; German type plugs). Bijela Uvala has around 1 km. of rocky beach, with a section reserved for naturists. In places the rocks have been levelled and paved to provide sunbathing areas. There are showers and toilets near the beach and a small marina for boat owners. Facilities of Zelena Laguna available to visitors here.

Facilities: Modern toilet blocks are cleaned several times a day. Mainly British style toilets and showers in individual cubicles, half with free controllable hot water. Washbasins are similarly supplied, as are dishwashing and laundry sinks. Supermarkets and few stalls selling fruit, vegetables and beach requisites. Restaurants and snack bars. Two quite new swimming pools, the larger being quite impressive. Both have shallow areas for little ones and are supervised at all times. **Off site:** Nearest large supermarkets in Porec (regular bus service, by car or high season 'land train' from Zelena Laguna).

Charges 2001

Per person	€ 2,40 - 4,70
child (5-12 yrs)	free - € 3,27
pitch	€ 3,58 - 6,80
pitch incl. electricity	€ 4,45 - 9,20
dog	€ 2,10 - 3,32
local tax	€ 0,77 - 0,97

Tel: 052 410 551. Fax: 052 410 600. E-mail: mail@plavalaguna.hr. **Reservations:** Made with € 25,56 fee. Contact the Plava Laguna Group. **Open** Easter - end October.

Directions: The site adjoins Zelena Laguna, off the main Porec - Vrsar road.

Naturist Centre Ulika

N6720 Cervar, 52440 Porec (Istria)

One of the many naturist campsites in Croatia, Ulika is run by the same concern as Zelena Laguna (6722) and Bijela Uvala (6724) and offers similar facilities. The site is well located, occupying a small peninsula of some 15 hectares. This means that there is only a short walk to the sea from anywhere on the site. The ground is mostly gently sloping with a covering of rough grass and there are 388 pitches with electricity connections (10A). One side of the site is shaded with mature trees but the other side is almost devoid of shade and could become very hot. There are many activities on site (see below) and an excellent swimming pool. The reception office opens 24 hours for help and information. Single men are not accepted. All in all, this is a pleasant, uncomplicated site which is well situated, well managed and peaceful.

Facilities: Six toilet blocks provide mostly British style WCs, washbasins (half with hot water) and showers (around a third with controllable hot water). Each block has facilities for disabled visitors. Dishwashing and laundry sinks (half with hot water). Laundry. Supermarket (seven days per week). Restaurant, pizzeria and snacks. Bicycle hire. Swimming pool. Fishing. Tennis. Table tennis. Minigolf. Water sports - water skiing, windsurfing, etc. Volleyball. Boating - marina on site. **Off site:** Riding nearby. Porec the nearest town is 6 km. - a must to visit - a regular local bus service runs from site reception.

Charges guide

Per person	€ 2,40 - 4,70
child (5-12 yrs)	free - € 3,27
pitch	€ 3,58 - 6,80
pitch incl. electricity	€ 4,45 - 9,20
dog	€ 2,10 - 3,32
local tax	€ 0,77 - 0,97

Tel: 052 436 325. Fax: 052 436 352. E-mail: mail@plavalaguna.hr. **Reservations:** Only made for certain pitches, with € 25,56 fee. **Open** April - October.

Directions: Site is approx. 3 km. off the main Novigrad - Porec road, signed in village of Cevar.

Rovinj

Rovinj is an historic, traditional, fisherman's town with unspoilt nature. It is renowned as one of the most beautiful towns on the Adriatic coast. With some twenty small surrounding islands this area is one of the most popular Croatian tourist destinations. It is great for sailing and diving enthusiasts, due to a very interesting seabed and the little islands around it. Many international sailing regattas take place in Rovinj. It is also a popular place to learn to sail or dive. Rovinj has arranged cycle tracks in pinewoods where you can take a walk or cycle ride, avoiding the hot summer sun.

Naturist Camping Monsena

N6730 Monsena bb, 52210 Rovinj (Istria)

Situated 4 km. from the centre of the lovely old port town of Rovinj this naturist site has much to offer. Of 12.6 hectares and adjacent to the Monsena bungalow complex, campers can take advantage of the facilities afforded by both areas. There are 470 pitches for touring units on various types of ground and of 80-120 sq.m. Most are separated by foliage, 10A electricity is available (German type plug), but only 80 have a water supply. An open, level area marked out by numbered stones is popular with motorcaravans. Unlike most naturist sites Monsena has no objection to single men entering the site. In fact, there are very few restrictions at all, management preferring to leave things to peoples' common sense and judgement. It seems to work, as this is one of the happiest and most friendly sites visited to date and it is well kept and well managed. A rocky beach backed by a grassy sunbathing area is very popular, but site has its own superb round pool with slide. Boat owners have a mooring area and launching ramp.

Facilities: Thirteen toilet blocks house have a mixture of British style and Turkish toilets. Half the washbasins have hot water. Some showers have hot water, the rest have cold and are outside. Each block has one private cabin on the female side and a unit for disabled visitors (shower, toilet and washbasin). Plenty of dishwashing and laundry sinks all with hot water. Fridge boxes for hire. Washing machines. Drive over motorcaravan service point (key for hose from reception). Waste bins are emptied daily using an electric powered silent vehicle (there's consideration for you!) Supermarket - clothing must be worn in the shop. Small market selling beach wares, and fresh fruit and vegetables. Two restaurants, taverna, pizzeria and terrace grill. Swimming pool. Watersports. Bicycle hire. Fishing (subject to permit). Daily animation for children and entertainment for adults on a less regular basis **Off site:** Hourly minibus service to Rovinj. Riding near

Charges 2003

Per unit incl. electricity	€ 5.40 - € 8.30
person	€ 3.40 - € 5.40
child (5-11 yrs)	€ 1.70 - € 2.70
dog	€ 3.00

For stays less than 3 nights in high season add 10%.
Tel: 052 802 000. Fax: 052 813 354. E-mail: monsena@jadran.tdr.hr. **Reservations:** Contact site or Istraturist reservations service - tel: 052/5280 0376, fax: 052/5281 3497. **Open** 1 May - 30 September.

Directions: From Rovinj follow red/green signs to Monsena. Site at end of signposted lane.

Camping Polari

6732 Polari bb, 52210 Rovinj (Istria)

Open from mid-April to mid-October, this site is unusual in that it is has facilities for both textile and naturist campers, the latter having a reserved area called Punta Eva, of approximately 12 hectares. The total site area is some 60 hectares which makes it medium to large by Croatian standards. Polari is a mature site with 1,250 pitches available to touring units. Most pitches are numbered and separated by small trees or hedges. Quite a few pleasant gardens surround the 400 long stay pitches and the site is generally well kept and tidy. The average pitch occupies 70 sq.m. and all have 16A electricity (German and Europlugs). There are two motorcaravan service areas. This is a popular, mature site which will satisfy most people and delight some, in a good area for historic tourist attractions. Rovinj has good shops and restaurants, fish being a speciality.

Facilities: Two brand new toilet blocks, two recently renovated and nine older blocks which need and are under progressive renovation. The blocks contain British and Turkish style toilets. Washing up and laundry sinks. Disabled guests have three en-suite cabins (key from reception). Washing machines and dryers. Laundry service including ironing. Two shops, one large and one small. Cocktail bar, two restaurants and snack bar all open long hours. Tennis. Volleyball, basketball, minigolf and table tennis. Children's animation with all major European languages spoken. Further entertainment and sports facilities in the neighbouring associated complex, Villas Rubin. **Off site:** Swimming pool 150 m from gate. Five buses daily to and from Rovinj (3 km). Riding 1 km.

Charges 2003

Per unit incl. electricity	€ 4.00 - € 8.10
person	€ 3.00 - € 5.20
child (5-11 yrs)	€ 1.50 - € 2.60
dog	free - € 3.00

For stays less than 3 nights in high season add 10%.
Tel: 052 801 501. Fax: 052 811 395. E-mail: polari@jadran.tdr.hr. **Reservations:** Contact site or Istraturist reservations service - tel: 052/5280 0376, fax: 052/5281 3497. **Open** 1 April - 1 October.

Directions: From any access road to Rovinj look for red signs to AC Polari (amongst other destinations).

Pula

Situated at the southern tip of the Istrian Peninsula, Pula has been in existence for over 3,000 years. It is a combination of an old and modern city where many famous writers and composers have found inspiration.

Autocamp Medulin

6734 52203 Medulin (Istria)

Medulin is a medium to large sized, one-star site near Pula on the tip of the Istrian peninsula and definitely for those who want to get back to nature. Consisting of a peninsula about l.5 km. long and a small island accessed by a road bridge, the site is thickly wooded with mature pine trees and reportedly never gets over-crowded. Visited in July, the site was busy but not full. There is very little regimentation evident and pitches are not marked out or numbered, most people taking advantage of the heavy shade afforded by the trees. The land is undulating but there is no shortage of level areas. There are 2,275 touring pitches, most with 10A electricity. Underfoot is a carpet of pine needles. There is presently no swimming pool but the site is almost surrounded by the sea with a gently sloping rocky beach making it good for children and other paddlers. This is a fully mature site and as a result some of the facilities are showing signs of age but if one remembers that this is a one star site and prices are considerably less than at sites with higher ratings, a very pleasant stay can be had.

Facilities: Toilet blocks are clean and tidy but in need of structural renovation. Toilets are British style, washbasins and showers are a mixture of outdoors and under cover. Some have hot water, some not, and some rely on solar power for the temperature of the water. Shop, market and produce stalls. Eight restaurants or snack bars provide a range of fare. Tennis. Table tennis. Watersports. Fridge rental. **Off site:** Golf, fishing (with permit) and riding near. Further restaurants and hostelries in Medulin village or in Pula which is famous for its Roman remains, especially its well preserved amphitheatre. Regular bus service into Pula or a 20 minute drive to town centre.

Charges guide

Per person	€ 2,95 - 3,68
child (2-12 yrs)	€ 1,12 - 1,84
caravan or large tent	€ 1,53 - 2,45
small tent	€ 1,02 - 1,38
car	€ 1,23 - 1,84
motorcaravan	€ 3,02 - 4,91
dog	€ 1,02 - 2,04

Tel: 052 572 801. Fax: 052 576 042. E-mail: marketing@arenaturist.hr. **Reservations:** Made with deposit; contact site or Arenaturist, PO Box 110, 52100 Pula. Tel: 052/223 811. Fax: 052/211 853. **Open** Easter - end October.

Directions: Approaching from the north (Koper, Rovinj), on outskirts turn right at third lights. Follow signs for Medulin and site at far end of village.

Czech Republic

The Czech Tourist Authority, 95 Great Portland Street, London W1N 5RA
Tel: 09063 640 641 (premium rate). Internet: www.visitczech.cz
E-mail: ctainfo@czechcentre.org.uk

Although the country we have known as Czechoslovakia has a long and distinguished past, it has a chequered history. The combined country of Czechoslovakia only appeared under that name on maps after the Treaty of Versailles in 1918. The latest event in its turbulent history was the split in December 1992 into its two component parts - the Czech Republic in the west and the Slovak Republic in the east. The Czech Republic shares frontiers with Germany, Poland, Austria and Slovakia. It is picturesque and hilly, with attractive lakes and valleys, and with many spa towns. The two main regions are Bohemia, including the Giant Mountains (skiing in winter) and Moravia.

Campsites, previously state-owned and run, are being progressively privatised and modernised and are gradually offering facilities more in line with those expected in Western Europe. All the sites we have included have acceptable, if not luxurious, sanitary arrangements. We found them all to be clean with British style WCs and hot water in all washbasins, sinks and showers. However, many showers have no private dressing spaces and, even in the best blocks, often no divider or curtain with just a communal dressing area.

Population

10,323,690 (93) , density 131 per sq km.

Capital

Prague (Praha)

Climate

A continental climate with four distinct seasons, average temperatures in summer (July) are 19oC - 30oC max. and in winter (January) 1-15oC.

Language

The official language is Czech. In hotels and restaurants English or German may be spoken.

Currency

Koruna abbreviated to Kc. One Koruna is divided into 100 hellers.

Banks

Open 0830-1630 Mon-Fri. Only notes are exchanged at most border change offices.
Credit cards: The major cards can be used to obtain currency and in some hotels, restaurants, shops and some filling stations. Travellers and Eurocheques are widely accepted.

Post Offices

Offices are open Mon-Sat 08.00-16.00.

Telephone

The code for the Czech Republic is 0042.

Time

GMT plus one hour. Summer BST + 1.

Public Holidays

New Year; Easter Mon; May Day; National Day, 8 May; Saints Day, 5 July; Festival Day, 6 July; Independence Day, 28 Oct; Christmas, 24, 25, 26 Dec.

Shops

Shops are open Mon-Fri 09.00-12.00 and 14.00-18.00. Some shops remain open midday. Sat: 09.00 until midday.

Motoring

There is a good and well signposted road network throughout the Republic and, although stretches of cobbles still exist, surfaces are generally good. There is a motorway from Bratislava (Slovakia) to Prague and others, radiating from the capital. New filling stations with well stocked shops (some with snack bars) are replacing the old, rather scarce, ones all over the Republic.

An annual road tax is levied on all vehicles using Czech motorways and express roads. There are three categories: motor vehicle up to 3.5 tons including trailer; with total weight between 3.5 and 12 tons and above 12 tons. The label, which must be fixed to the windscreen, can be purchased at border crossings, post offices and filling stations. The leaflet giving details of this tax shows the designated roads. Anyone driving a vehicle on a toll road without an affixed label is likely to be fined.

Seat belts are compulsory. Full UK licences are acceptable. Drinking and driving is prohibited. Infringing traffic regulations is subject to on-the-spot fines and speed traps abound.

Speed Restrictions: The max. speed limit for cars is 37 mph (60 kph) in built up areas, 56 mph (90 kph) outside them and 69 mph (110 kph) on expressways.
Parking: Cars may be parked only on the right of the road. In Prague, parking is limited and in Wenceslas Square a charge is made.

Overnighting

Camping is forbidden in places which are not reserved for that purpose.

Camping Oase bei Prag

484 Zlatniky 47, 25241 Dolni Brezany (Prague)

Camping Oase bei Prag is a quiet site, yet it is only five kilometres from Prague, with easy access. The journey to the city by car takes you through an attractive forest, but alternatively you could take the bus (from outside the site) or drive to the underground stop (10 minutes). The site has 85 pitches, all with 10A electricity, on level, well kept fields. At 90 sq.m. the pitches are relatively small but the site is very well kept and has just everything one may expect, including a new Western style toilet block, a well maintained swimming pool, a restaurant and a bar. The main attraction here is, of course, the Czech capital, but this site will provide a relaxing environment to return to and another advantage is that Mr Hess, the owner, speaks English.

Facilities: An outstanding, new toilet block includes washbasins (open style and in cabins) with hot and cold water, spacious, controllable showers and child size toilets. Facilities for disabled visitors. Laundry. Campers' kitchen with hob, fridge and freezer. Motorcaravan services. Restaurant and bar (both 15/4-30/9). No shop (groceries available in the village). Swimming pool (9 x 15 m), paddling pool with slide. Adventure style playgrounds. Trampolines. Table tennis. Volleyball. Basketball. Internet point. TV and video. Bicycle hire. Riding. Closed circuit security cameras. **Off site:** Fishing 2 km. Golf 10 km.

Charges 2002

Per pitch	Kcs 380
adult	Kcs 90
child (2-12 yrs)	Kcs 60
local tax	Kcs 10

Less 20% 15/4-31/5 and 1/9-30/9. 3% discount for cash payment. **Tel:** 02 4193 2044. Fax: 02 4193 2044. E-mail: post@campoase.cz. **Reservations:** Made before 1/5 for min. 1 week (Sat. - Sat). **Open** 14 April - 30 September.

Directions: From Prague take D1 southeast towards Brno and take exit 11 to Jesenice via road 101. From Jesenice follow the camp signs to the site in Zlatníky.

Camp Sokol Troja

485 Trojská 171A, 171 00 Praha (Prague)

Camp Sokol Troja is without doubt one of the quietest sites we found in the Prague area. Nevertheless, it is only a 15 or 20 journey to the centre of the city by bus (stop in front of the site) or tram no. 17 (300 m. walk). Unlike many of the municipal sites near Prague, this site has few facilities and little entertainment. There are 75 touring pitches (40 with 16A electricity) and ten cabins to rent. The pitches are small (80-90 sq.m) and can become muddy with rain. The access road is narrow and manoeuvring space is limited so the site may be less suitable for large caravans and motorhomes. The restaurant serves Czech meals at reasonable prices.

Facilities: The single, refurbished toilet block is a good provision with toilets, washbasins (hot and cold water) and pre-set showers in cabins without curtain or door. Cleaning can be variable. Facilities for disabled people. Dishwashing and laundry sinks (free hot water). Campers' kitchen with hob. Good restaurant. **Off site:** Fishing 1 km.

Charges 2002

Per adult	Kcs. 105
child (under 18 yrs)	Kcs. 80
pitch	Kcs. 90 - 180
car	Kcs. 90
electricity (16A)	Kcs. 70

Tel: 02 3354 2908. Fax: 02 3354 2908. E-mail: info@camp-sokol-troja.cz. **Reservations:** contact site. **Open** all year.

Directions: From Dresden or Teplice, follow signs to the centre and turn right before the first bridge over the Moldau into the Kozlovka Pátkova, in the Troja district. Site is well signed from here.

Caravancamp usk Prague

480 Plzenská 279, 150 00 Praha 5 (Prague)

Caravancamp is on sloping ground with some terracing in a quiet location about 8 km. from the centre of Prague. With 400 pitches (100 used for mobile homes and chalet, electricity is available for most caravan places but the grass pitches are neither numbered nor marked out and the site may become crowded in high season. There are hard access roads. It is a pleasant situation with trees and a hill on one side and some shade in parts. Caravancamp is a simple site suitable for a couple of days to visit Prague.

Facilities: The toilet blocks are satisfactory . Bar (1/4-31/10). Swimming pool. Tennis. Minigolf. **Off site:** Shops 200 m. Golf 3 km. Riding 10 km. Bicycle hire 1 km.

Charges 2002

Per person	Kcs 120.00 - 150.00
child (6-12 yrs)	Kcs 60.00
caravan	Kcs 160.00 - 180.00
tent	Kcs 100.00 - 120.00
car	Kcs 110.00 - 130.00
motorcaravan	Kcs 200.00 - 230.00
electricity	Kcs 90.00
local tax	Kcs 15.00

No credit cards. **Tel:** 025 721 3080. Fax: 025 721 5084. E-mail: caravancamp@volny.cz. **Reservations:** Write to site. **Open** 1 April - 31 October.

Directions: Site is well signed on main highway from Pilsen, road no. 5/E50, near Hotel Golf.

Caravan Camp Valek

482 Chrustenice 155, 267 12 Lodenice (Stredocesky)

Only 2.5 kilometres from the E50 motorway, this well-maintained, family owned site creates a peaceful, friendly base enjoyed by families. Surrounded by delightful countryside, it is possible to visit Prague even though it is about 28 km. from the city centre. It is best to use public transport and at Zlicin, a ten minute drive the site there is a 'park and ride' with guarded car parks costing 20p per day (no height restriction, arrive before 09.00). This is also the start of the 'B' metro line transporting one rapidly to Mustek, the heart of the city and the main sights (return fare 50p! - tickets can be bought in advance from reception). On leaving the car park to return, there is a large shopping centre including a Tesco superstore! The medium sized, gently sloping grass site is divided in two by a row of well-established trees (some shade) and the toilet block. Most pitches are relatively flat, in the open and not specifically marked. However this does not appear to cause overcrowding and generally there is plenty of space. Electricity (10A) is available. Some places have pleasant views of the sunbathing area in front of the pool with a pine-forested hillock as a backdrop. The 20 x 60 metre pool is fed by a river and better classified as a lake with rough concrete sides, access steps and a water chute.

Facilities: The single clean toilet block has limited numbers of toilets and showers, but during our visit in high season coped well. Small shop with fresh rolls daily, plus milk, sweets and ice cream. Tastefully decorated waiter service restaurant with terrace has an extensive menu with customers praising, quality, quantity and price of the meals. Natural swimming pool (20 x 60 m) with constantly changing water checked regularly by the authorities to ensure its purity. **Off site:** Prague 28 km. Plzen 69 km.

Charges 2002

Per adult	Kcs 95.00
child (6-14 yrs)	Kcs 45.00
caravan	Kcs 115.00
tent	Kcs 65.00 - 115.00
car	Kcs 95.00
motorcycle	Kcs 75.00
motorcaravan	Kcs 145.00
electricity	Kcs 85.00
animal	Kcs 35.00
local tax	Kcs 10.00

Tel: 0311 672 147. Fax: 0311 6 2147. E-mail: info@campvalek.cz. **Reservations:** Contact site. Open 1 May - 30 September.

Directions: From E50 (D5) motorway take exit 10 for Lodenice. Follow camping signs and or Chrustenice. Site is 300 m. on right on leaving Chrustenice.

Autocamping Konopiste

478 256 01 Benesov u Prahy (Stredocesky)

Benesov's chief claim to fame is the Konopiste Palace, the last home of Archduke Franz Ferdinand whose assassination in Sarajevo sparked off the First World War in 1914. Autocamp Konopiste is part of a motel complex, with excellent facilities situated in a very quiet, tranquil location soth of Prague. On a hillside, rows of terraces separated by hedges provide 65 grassy pitches of average size, 50 with electricity (10A). One of the best Czech campsites, it has many different varieties of trees and much to offer those who stay there. A fitness centre and heated swimming pool are shared with motel guests. The whole complex has a well tended, cared for air. Near the motel, is the Stodola restaurant, open each evening from 6 pm. until 1 am. this attractive replica of an old Czech barn is well worth a visit. With local specialities served by girls in local costume in a candle lit atmosphere and accompanied by a small, live music quartet, it is an evening to remember (booking essential).

Facilities: The good quality sanitary block is central to the caravan pitches. Washing machine and irons. Kitchen. Site's own bar/buffet (high season) with simple meals and basic food items. Motel bar and two restaurant (all year). Swimming pool (1/6-31/8). Tennis. Minigolf. Volleyball. Table tennis. Bicycle hire. Badminton. Fitness centre. Children's playground. Club room with TV. Chateau and park. **Off site:** Shop 200 m. Fishing 1.5 km. Riding 5 km. Prague 48 km. (public transport available).

Charges 2002

Per person	Kcs 100.00 - 120.00
child (6-15 yrs)	Kcs 50.00 - 60.00
caravan	Kcs 200.00 - 350.00
large tent	Kcs 180.00 - 250.00
car	Kcs 120.00 - 150.00
motorcycle	Kcs 50.00 - 100.00
motorcaravan	Kcs 300.00 - 400.00

Electricity included. Tel: 0317 722 732. Fax: 0317 722 053. E-mail: hotel@hotelkonopiste.cz. **Reservations:** Contact site. Open 1 May - 30 September.

Directions: Site is signed near the village of Benesov at Hotel Konopiste (no connection) and Motel Konopiste on main Prague - Ceske Budejovic road no. 3/E55.

Autocamp Liberec - Pavolice

ul. Letná, 460 01 Liberec 12 (Severocesky)

470

Although Liberec does not have too much to write home about, it does have a zoo, botanical garden and a Renaissance château. It is set in grand countryside near the Jizera mountains and not far from the Polish town of Gorlitz. Autocamp Pavlovice is a good site, nicely situated on the edge of the town near the sports ground. Just outside the entrance are the inevitable drab multi-storey workers flats, but trees screen these from view on the site. The Jested mountain at 1,012 m. dominates the distant sky line and is accessible by cable way for winter ski-ing and summer sightseeing. There are 140 pitches, 80 with electricity (10/16A), between the excellent bungalows and different varieties of trees which give a peaceful air. Some caravan pitches are divided by low hedges on the edge of the site with views across open countryside. Tarmac roads lead to the camping places. A speedway track right next to the campsite could cause noise disturbance when meetings are held on Sundays. This is a neat, tidy and very pleasant site, good for a night stop or a longer stay. There is a good welcome and a nice bar and restaurant.

Facilities: The single, good quality sanitary block has a kitchen with electric rings. Restaurant, with café, snack bar and raised terrace. Good size swimming pool (June-Sept). Tennis. Table tennis. Playground. **Off site:** Shops outside entrance. 'Centrum Babylon' leisure park nearby.Fishing, golf, riding and bicycle hire within 5 km.

Charges 2002

Per person	Kcs 100.00
child (6-15 yrs)	Kcs 50.00
caravan	Kcs 120.00 - 140.00
tent	Kcs 100.00 - 120.00
car	Kcs 60.00
motorcycle	Kcs 40.00
motorcaravan	Kcs 100.00 - 140.00
electricity	Kcs 70.00
dog	Kcs 60.00
local tax	Kcs 15.00

Less in low season. **Tel:** 0485 123 468. Fax: 0485 123 468. E-mail: info@autocamp-liberec.cz. **Reservations:** Not possible or necessary for the touring pitches. **Open** 1 May - 30 September.

Directions: Follow the E992 to Liberec and take the Liberec/Frydlant exit. Continue to roundabout and take east exit for Pavolice. Site is signed from there, a few hundred metres on the left before traffic lights.

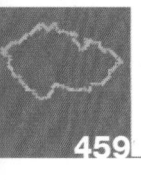

Eurocamp Lisci Farm

Dolni Branna 350, 54362 Vrchlabi (Vychodocesky)

459

This is truly a site that could be in Western Europe considering its amenities, pitches and welcome. However, Eurocamp Lisci Farma is a fully Czech site and has a pleasant Czech atmosphere. The 242 pitches are fairly flat, although the terrain is slightly sloping, and some pitches have shade. The pitches on the new area at the entrance are terraced. The site is well equipped for the whole family to enjoy with its adventurous playground with trampolines for children, archery, beach volleyball, Russian bowling and outdoor bowling court for older youngsters. A beautiful sandy, lakeside beach is 800 m. from the entrance. The real sportsmen amongst you can go paragliding or rock climbing, with experienced people to guide you. This site is very suitable for relaxing or exploring the culture of the area. Excursions to Prague are organised and, if all the sporting possibilities are not enough, the children can take part in the activities of the entertainment team, while you are walking or cycling or enjoying live music at the Fox Saloon.

Facilities: One old, but refurbished sanitary block and one modern block include spacious, controllable showers (on payment), child size toilets, baby room, facilities for disabled visitors, and a launderette with sinks, hot water and a washing machine. Motorcaravan service. Bar/snack bar with pool table. Games room. Swimming pool (6 x 12 m). Adventure style playground on grass. Trampolines. Tennis courts. Minigolf. Archery. Russian bowling. Bowling court. Beach volleyball. Paragliding. Rock climbing. Bicycle hire. Excursions to Prague. **Off site:** Fishing and beach 800 m. Golf 5 km. Riding 2 km.

Charges 2002

Per pitch (90-100 sq.m.)	Kcs. 260
adult	Kcs. 30 - 100
child (4-14 yrs)	Kcs. 10 - 70
electricity	free - Kcs. 70
animal	Kcs. 70
tourist tax	Kcs. 15

Tel: 0499 421 473. Fax: 0499 421 656. E-mail: hotel-camp@liscifarma.cz. **Reservations:** Contact site. **Open** all year excl. 1 Nov - 19 Dec.

Directions: Follow road no. 14 from Liberec to Vrchlabi and Dolni Branna. Site is signed in Vrchlabi in the direction of Prague.

Camping Slunce

471 07 Zandov (Severocesky)

469

Away from larger towns, near the border with the old East Germany this is pleasant rural country with a wealth of Gothic and Renaissance castles. Zandov has nothing of particular interest but Camping Slunce is a popular camp with local Czechs. There is room for about 50 touring units with 35 electrical connections (12A) on the level, circular camping area which has a hard road running round. Outside this circle are wooden bungalows and tall trees. The general building at the entrance houses all the facilities including reception.

Facilities: The satisfactory toilet block is good by Czech standards. Kitchen with electric rings, full gas cooker and fridges. Restaurant (open all year) with live music during high season. Kiosk for basics (May - Sept). Tennis. Table tennis. Swimming pool. Volleyball. Mountain bike hire. Playground. Large club room. Barbecues are not permitted. Dogs are not accepted. **Off site:** Fishing 1 km. Riding 2 km.

Charges 2002

Per person	Kcs 97.00
caravan or tent	Kcs 97.00
car	Kcs 97.00
motorcaravan	Kcs 189.00
electricity - plus meter	Kcs 22.00
local tax	Kcs 5.00

Tel: 0487 861116. **Fax:** 0487 861422. **Reservations:** Not made. **Open** 2 May - 30 September.

Directions: Zandov is 20 km. from Decin and 12 km. from Ceske Lipa (Ceské Lipy) on the minor road between these two towns. Signed in the centre of Zandov village.

Autocamping Orlice

PO Box 16, 517 41 Kostelec n Orlicí (Vychodocesky)

486

Kostelec does have an ancient castle, although not a lot else to commend it, but is a good centre from which to explore the interesting town of Hradec Kralove, East Bohemia, the Orlicke Hory and other high districts near the Polish border. On the edge of town near the swimming pool, this iste has a river running by and is in a quiet location and a pleasant appearance. Surrounded by tall trees, the grass pitches are of generous size although not marked or numbered, on each side of a concrete grid road which runs the length of this rectangular site. There is room for 80 units, half having electric points (16A) and with shade in parts. The friendly manageress speaks good English.

Facilities: The central sanitary block includes hot water in washbasins, sinks and good showers - it is of a standard for th Czech Republic. Unlike most Czech sites, showers have dividers, space for dressing, a door that locks, and even a chair! Limited food supplies are available in a bar/lounge during July/Aug. Café/bar (15/5-30/9). **Off site:** Town swimming pool near (15/6-31/8; new pool planned for 2003). Tennis 100 m. Fishing 0.5 km. Riding 5 km.

Charges 2002

Per person	Kcs 42.00 - 46.00
caravan or tent	Kcs 58.00 - 78.00
car	Kcs 58.00 - 68.00
motorcaravan	Kcs 84.00 - 95.00
electricity	Kcs 60.00
local tax	Kcs 5.00 - 6.00

Tel: 0494 323 970. **Fax:** 0494 322 768. **E-mail:** www.volny.cz/camp.orlice. **Reservations:** Write to site. **Open** 15 May - 30 September.

Directions: Site is signed from the centre of town.

Autocamping Morava

Bezrucova, 789 85 Mohelnice (Severomoravsky)

487

This is an interesting area of contrasts - heavy industry, fertile plains and soaring mountains. Mohelnice is a small industrial town but the campsite is in a peaceful setting surrounded by trees on the northern edge. The site is roughly in two halves with the camping area on a flat, open meadow with a hard access road. The 100 touring pitches are not numbered or marked so siting could be a little haphazard. There are 80 electricity connections (10A). There is little shade but the perimeter trees should screen out road noise. The other part of the site is given over to a two storey motel and bungalows with a good quality restaurant between the two. Good English is spoken at reception and it is a very pleasant, well organised site.

Facilities: The toilet block is satisfactory. Electric cooking rings. Restaurant (May - Oct). Kiosk/snack bar. Small shop (May - Oct). Live music (high season). Swimming pool (May - Oct). Tennis. Minigolf. Table tennis. Volleyball. Bicycle hire. Road track - driving and cycling learning area with tarmac roads, road signs, traffic lights and road markings well set up to give youngsters a practice area. Playground. TV room.

Charges 2002

Per person	Kcs 40.00
caravan or tent	Kcs 30.00 - 60.00
car	Kcs 30.00
electricity	Kcs 40.00

No credit cards. less 10% for 5 days or more, paid on arrival. **Tel:** 0583 430 129. **Fax:** 0583 433 011. **Reservations:** Write to site. **Open** 15 May - 15 October (motel all year).

Directions: Site is signed on the western edge of town on the Olomouc - Hradec Kralove road no. 35/E442.

Czech Republic
Camping Roznov

Horní Paseky 940, 756 61 Roznov pod Radhostem (Severomoravsky)

Roznov pod Radhostem is halfway up the Roznovska Becva valley amidst the Beskydy hills which extend from North Moravia into Poland in the extreme east of the Republic. It is a busy tourist centre which attracts visitors to the Wallachian open-air museum and those who enjoy hill walking. There are 300 pitches (200 for touring units), some of which are rather small, although there are some new landscaped pitches of 90-100 sq.m. Arranged on flat grass and set amidst a variety of fruit and other trees, there are 120 electrical connections (16A) and shade in some parts. Although right by a main road with some traffic noise, the site is surrounded by trees and hills and was reasonably quiet during our visit. The friendly manager will be pleased to advise on local attractions. Camping Roznov makes a good base for exploring this interesting part of Moravia.

Facilities: The good quality central toilet block has hot water in basins and sinks. This block also has a large, comfortable TV lounge/meeting room. A new, well equipped toilet block has been added with washbasins and WCs en-suite for ladies and a washing machine. Only very basic food items available in shop and restaurant, not always open. Swimming pool (25 m. and heated July/Aug). Tennis. Table tennis. Trampolines. **Off site:** Restaurant or snackbar night club at the modern Europlan Hotel some 300 m. towards the town. Fishing and golf 1 km. Riding 4 km.

Charges 2002

Per person	Kcs 99.00
child (3-15 yrs)	Kcs 83.00
caravan	Kcs 110.00
tent	Kcs 80.00
car	Kcs 83.00
motorcaravan	Kcs 170.00
electricity	Kcs 70.00
local tax	Kcs 17.00

Tel: 0571 648 001. Fax: 0571 648 002. E-mail: info@camproznov.cz. **Reservations:** Write to site. **Open** all year.

Directions: Site is at eastern end of Roznov on the main 18/E442 Zilina-Olomouc road opposite sports stadium.

Czech Republic
I.N.F. Naturist Camping Mlécna Dráha

Racov 15, 384 72 Zdikov (Jihocesky)

Opportunities for campers who enjoy a naturist lifestyle are extremely limited within the Czech Republic. We have explored all the possibilities and feel that this 12 ha. Dutch owned site with 65 pitches in southern Bohemia provides acceptable facilities near to interesting attractions and pleasant scenery. It is very popular with families. Previously a farm, this very open, sloping site has a number of well spaced mini-terraces creating both views and distance between you and your neighbours. Although all around is very green the majority of vegetation under foot is of weed content, not grass. The gradual descent through the site is via a track but the owners will help with a tractor should there be problems in siting a caravan. The focal point of the site is the main building and adjacent small river-fed lake. The latter is extremely popular with parents and children alike but used entirely at your own risk. A 'death slide' and the bases of windsurfing boards keep most entertained for long periods. The main building, some distance from most pitches houses all the facilities and accommodation. Electricity hook-ups (16A; French style connection) may need a long lead. Owners Wils and Bert have integrated well with the locals and this is reflected both in the quality of food at the restaurant and the prices of such services as a massage (approx. £3) or a haircut for £1! Within a reasonable distance are many places of interest.

Facilities: British style toilets and free hot showers are clean and acceptable. Sauna. The chemical disposal system is ecological and does not accept 'blue' chemicals. The product must be either green or none used. Bar, restaurant, terrace. Bread to order daily. **Off site:** Nearest shops 3.5 km. Prague is too far for a day visit but the site owners can arrange overnight accommodation and it is possible to travel by public transport. Nearby are the UNESCO World Monument town of Cesky Krumlov, Ceske Budejovice and the powerful impressive castle at Hluboka.

Charges guide

Per pitch	Kcs 200.00
adult	Kcs 160.00
child (under 15 yrs)	Kcs 90.00
electricity	Kcs 80.00

Tel: 03394 26222. Fax: 03394 26222. **Reservations:** Required to guarantee electric hook up; contact site. **Open** all year except 1 Oct - 19 Dec.

Directions: From no. 4 Prague - Passau road at Vimperk, take road 145 to Zdikov. On approach to village, site is well signed to the right. Follow to next village of Racov and site is on the outskirts on leaving the village.

Czech Republic
Camping Dlouhá Louka
477 Stromovka 8, 370 01 Ceské Budejovice (Jihocesky)

The medieval city of Céske Budejovice is the home of Budweiser beer and is also an industrial centre. It lies on the River Vltava with mountains and pleasant scenery nearby. Dlouhá Louka is a motel and camping complex 2 km. south of the town on the Céske Budejovice - Cesky Krumlov road. The camping part is a flat, rectangular meadow surrounded by trees which give some shade around the edges. There are some marked, hedged pitches and hardstanding, but many of the grass pitches are not marked or numbered so pitching can be rather haphazard. In total, 100 units are taken, 50 with electricity. This is a useful stop between Prague and Linz/

Facilities: The single sanitary block, with British style WCs, is at one end making a fair walk for some. Washing machine and irons. Kitchen with electric rings. Very pleasant bar/restaurant (all year). Small kiosk for basic supplies (1/7-3/8). Tennis. Volleyball. Table tennis. Playground. **Off site:** Shops 200 m. Bicycle hire 2 km. Fishing and golf 10 km.

Charges 2002

Per person	Kcs 70.00
child	Kcs 30.00
pitch	Kcs 50.00 - 110.00
electricity	Kcs 80.00
local tax	Kcs 15.00

No credit cards. **Tel:** 038 720 3601. Fax: 038 720 3595. **Reservations:** write to site. **Open** all year.

Directions: From town follow signs for Ceske Krumlov. After leaving ring road, turn right at Motel sign. Take this small road and turn right 60 m. before Camp Stromovky. Camp site name cannot be seen from the entrance - only the word Motel.

Czech Republic
Camping Frymburk
472 382 79, Frymburk (Jihocesky)

Camping Frymburk is beautifully located on the Lipno lake in southern Bohemia and is ideal for the active camper. From this site, activities could include walking, cycling, swimming, sailing, canoeing or rowing and afterwards you could relax in the small, cosy bar. The site has 170 level pitches on terraces (all with 6A electricity) and from the lower terraces on the edge of the lake there are lovely views over the water. A ferry crosses the lake from Frymburk where one can walk or cycle in the woods. The Dutch owner, Mr Wilzing, will welcome the whole family, personally siting your caravan. Children will be entertained by 'Kidstown' and the site has a small beach (the lake is not fenced or gated, so take care).

Facilities: Four toilet blocks, two old, one modern and one refurbished, with toilets, washbasins (open and in cabins) with cold water only, pre-set showers on payment (with curtain) and a bathroom with toilet, basin and shower. Launderette. Bar. Playground. Canoe, bicycle, pedaloes, rowing boat and surfboard hire. Kidstown. Bus trips to Prague. Torches useful. **Off site:** Shops and restaurants in the village 900 m.

Charges 2002

Per pitch incl. electricity	Kcs 380 - 480
person	Kcs 90
child (under 12 yrs)	Kcs 60
local tax	Kcs 10

Tel: 0380 735 284. **Reservations:** contact site. **Open:** 15 April - 1 October.

Directions: Take exit 114 at Passau in Germany (near the Austrian border) towards Freyung in the Czech Republic. Continue to Philipsreut and from there take no. 4 road towards Vimperk. Turn right a few kilometres after the border towards Volary on no. 141 road. From Volary follow the no. 163 road to Horni Plana, Cerna and Frymburk. Site is on the 163 road, right after the village.

Czech Republic
Camping Chvalsiny
471 Chvalsiny 321, 38208 Chvalsiny (Jihocesky)

Like Camping Horjany (483) Camping Chvalsiny is Dutch owned and has been developed from an old farm. Pitches at Chvalsiny are more or less flat, the grass is well cut, there's a new sanitary block and everything looks well maintained. The 200 pitches are of average size but look larger because of the open nature of the terrain which also means there is little shade. The location in the middle of the Blanky Les nature reserve, part of the vast Sumava forest, provides excellent opportunities for walking, cycling and fishing but it also has a rich culture and heritage. You can visit charming villages of which Cesky Krumlov with its impressive castle and scenic centre is the most important.

Facilities: Modern, clean and well kept toilet facilities include washbasins in cabins and controllable showers (coin operated). Laundry. Kiosk (1/6-15/9) with bread and essentials. Snack bar (1/6-15/9). Play attic. Lake swimming. Crafts, games, table tennis and soccer. Bicycle hire. Torches useful. **Off site:** Village restaurants close. Riding 10 km.

Charges 2002

Per person	Kcs 90
pitch	Kcs 180
electricity	Kcs 90
local tax	Kcs 10

No credit cards. **Tel:** 0380 739123. **Reservations:** possible via 0528 221137. **Open:** 15 May - 15 September.

Directions: Take exit 114 at Passau in Germany (near the Austrian border) towards Freyung in the Czech Republic. Continue to Philipsreut and take no. 4 road towards Vimperk. Turn right on no. 39 road to Horni Plana and Cesky Krumlov. Turn left 4 km. before Cesky Krumlov on no. 166 to Chvalsiny.

Czech Republic
Autocamping Luxor

465 353 01 Velká Hled'sebe (Zapadocesky)

An orderly site, near the German border, Luxor is adequate as a stopover for a couple of days. Like some other sites in the Czech Republic, it has now come under the management of a local hotel. It is in a quiet location by a small lake on the edge of the village of Velká Hled`sebe, 4 km. from Marianbad. The 100 pitches (60 for touring units) are in the open on one side of the entrance road (cars stand on a tarmac park opposite the caravans) or in a clearing under tall trees away from the road. All pitches have access to electricity (10A) but connection in the clearings section may require long leads. Forty bungalows occupy one side of the site. There is little to do here but it is a good location for visiting the spa town of Marianbad.

Facilities: Toilet buildings are old and should be refurbished, but the provision is more than adequate. Cleaning could be better. No chemical disposal point. Restaurant with self-service terrace (1/5-30/9). Rest room with TV, kitchen and dining area. Small playground. Fishing. Bicycle hire. **Off site:** Riding 5 km. Golf 8 km. Very good motel restaurant and shops 500 m. in village.

Charges 2002

Per unit incl. 2 adults and electricity	Kcs 380.00
extra adult	Kcs 53.00
child under 10 yrs	free

No credit cards. **Tel:** 0165 623 504. Fax: 0165 623 504. **Reservations:** For information write to Interhotel Cristal Palace, 353 44 Mariánské Lánzé or phone 0165/2056-7. Fax: 0165/2058. **Open** 1 April - 31 October.

Directions: Site is directly by the Stribo-Cheb road no. 21, 500 m. south of Velká Hled`sebe.

Czech Republic
Transkemp Hracholusky

474 330 33 Hracholusky (Zapadocesky)

Set beside the River Mzi where the Hracholusky dam has created a wide basin, Lodni Doprava enjoys a quiet location adjacent to an hotel amidst gentle hills and pleasant trees. The 200 pitches here are spread along three terraces looking over the water with 120 having electrical connections (6/10A). Two kiosks dispense drinks and basic supplies. There is swimming, boating and waterskiing on the lake and, during high season, a steamer makes 40 km. round trips along the river. This is a pleasant site but the presence of a large car park at the entrance may mean that it becomes crowded with day visitors in the summer.

Facilities: The large, single sanitary block also contains a rest room with TV, kitchen with electric rings and fridges. All was neat and clean when visited. Washing machines, dryers and irons. Bar and kiosks (July/Aug). Takeaway (April - Dec). Watersports. Swimming. Table tennis. Boat trips. Fishing. **Off site:** Riding 5 km.

Charges 2002

Per person	Kcs 30.00 - 40.00
caravan or tent	Kcs 80.00 - 120.00
car	Kcs 18.00 - 25.00
motorcaravan	Kcs 110.00 - 140.00
electricity	Kcs 60.00
local tax	Kcs 5.00 - 10.00

Less 10% for stays over 30 days. No credit cards. **Tel:** 0377 914 113. E-mail: info@hracholusky.com. **Reservations:** Write to site. **Open** 1 March - 31 December.

Directions: Take the E50/605 road west from Plzen (Pilsen). After Kozolupy turn right to Nord Jezna. 2 km. east of Ulice. Follow site signs from here.

Czech Republic
Camping Bila Hora

475 ul.28.rijna 49, 301 62 Plzen (Zapadocesky)

Even non-drinkers probably know that Pilsen is famous for its beer (Pils) and as the home of the Skoda car factory. Traffic in the town centre is heavy so, if you wish to visit the city where beer has been brewed since 1295, find a campsite and use the bus. Visits to the brewery may be arranged. Camping Bílá Hora is a suitable site and is situated amidst trees in the suburb of Bílá Hora, about 3 km. from the city centre on the edge of town. The 50 pitches are on a gentle slope in a clearing, but level concrete tracks have been made for caravans and motorcaravans, with electricity available at 30 pitches. It is a pleasant, quiet site with its own restaurant.

Facilities: A new sanitary block (British style WCs, bath and laundry) is in the camping area, plus another with the bungalows - they are good by Czech standards. Washing machine and iron. Motorcaravan services. Kitchen. Restaurant. Kiosk with small terrace (all year). Bicycle hire. Playground. Table tennis. Volleyball. **Off site:** Fishing 500 m. Swimming and tennis near. Shops 200 m. Bus stop at site entrance.

Charges 2002

Per person	Kcs 50.00
child (10-15 yrs)	Kcs 20.00
pitch	Kcs 140.00
electricity	Kcs 50.00

Tel: 0377 562 225. **Reservations:** Not necessary. **Open** 15 April - 30 September.

Directions: Site is to the north of the town on the Plzen(Pilsen) - Zruc no. 231 road where it is signed.

Czech Republic
Camping Horjany
483 Horejany 3, Tochovice, 26272 Breznice (Stredocesky)

Arthur and Jelly de Baan started Horjany about six years ago on old farm premises. The location of the site alone is worth a stay for a couple of days to enjoy, especially from the pitches at the back of the site under the trees, the wide views over the woods and the farming fields. Camping Horjany is truly a 'back to nature' campsite - not all of the 50 pitches are marked out and the grass between the pitches is not well cut. However, this doesn't cause any inconvenience because the site roads are cut well and if you need extra space on your pitch (adding up to 200 sq.m!) Arthur just mows an extra piece for you. The site breathes friendliness and cosiness and many campers come here every year. If you want to enjoy the true Czech country life on an authentic Czech farm, this is the place to go. A real piece of art is the perfectly designed bar in the old pigsty. With a warm and comfortable atmosphere, there are a few pleasant sofas to rest in after a long day's walking or cycling and a nice new bar where you can enjoy a beer or a glass of wine. You can even bring your own musical instruments and join in with the site's band. It is a pity this site is only open for eight weeks a year - it is a perfect place to relax, to enjoy and to make new friends.

Facilities: The single toilet block in a converted stable provides toilets, washbasins (open style and in cabins) with hot and cold water, controllable showers, child size washbasins, baby bath, sinks for washing up, a dryer, freezer and sinks (inside) with free hot water. No shop but bread to order. Swimming pool (12 x 6 m). Swings for children. Tennis. Live music. Disco. Soccer competitions against locals. Russian bowling. Library. Board games. Torches are necessary. **Off site:** Riding 2.5 km.

Charges 2002

Per unit incl. 2 persons	€ 10.00
extra person (max 6 per pitch)	€ 2.00
electricity	€ 2.00
dog	€ 1.50
local tax	€ 0.50

Tel: 0737 353785. E-mail: sophiartgouda.BV@12move.nl. **Reservations:** Necessary - contact the Dutch owners on 0031 182 530635. **Open** July and August only.

Directions: Follow road no. 20 Plzen - Pisek road and turn onto no. 19 road towards Rozmital and Breznice. Go left over the bridge in Breznice towards Tochovice and turn right in Tochovice to Horejany. Go through the village towards Tusovicky and you pass the site (not signed). Follow the A4 from Prague to Pribram and from there towards Strakonice. Turn right towards Kletice, Tusovice and Tusovicky which leads to Horejany and site.

Czech Republic
Recreacni Areal Jadran
464 35101 Frantiskovy (Zapadocesky)

Autokempink Koupaliste is on the outskirts of the spa town Frantiskovy Lázné and is the perfect base to visit the many restored spa baths with healing waters. Besides visiting the spa baths you can tour the beautiful West Bohemian countryside. Marie Novotny with her husband Jiri, owner of the site, welcomed us very warmly and is really looking forward to see you coming. She told us that the site has been open for eight years and that she loves to welcome British and Dutch campers. There are 150 pitches for tourers, all with 16A electricity, and the site has its own lake for cooling down in the hot summer months. The pitches are partly shaded and some are of at least 120 sq.m. Adjacent to the site is Hotel Jadran which serves fine meals for very reasonable prices and has a pleasant bar.

Facilities: The heated toilet blocks (two older, one refurbshed) are simple, but are clean and tidy. They include toilets, washbasins with hot and cold water, controllable showers, a launderette with 2 washing machines and sinks with free hot water (not covered). No shop but fresh bread available every morning in the restaurant. Giant chess, draughts and other games. Russian bowling. Volleyball. Fishing. Riding. Bicycle hire. Inflatables allowed in the lake. **Off site:** Fishing 6 km. Riding 400 m.

Charges 2002

Per adult	Kcs 75.00
child (3-12 yrs)	Kcs 45.00
tent or caravan	Kcs 90.00
motorcaravan	Kcs 120.00
pet	Kcs 30.00
electricity	Kcs 80.00

Less 10% for stays over 7 days or repeat visits. **Tel:** 0554 542 412. Fax: 0554 542 412. E-mail: atc.jadran@centrum.cz. **Reservations:** Possible but probably not necessary. **Open** all year.

Directions: Take the no. 6 road from Karlovy Vary to Frantiskovy Lázné and from there the signs to Hotel Jadran. Site is behind the hotel.

Denmark

The Danish Tourist Board, 55 Sloane Street, London SW1X 9SY
Tel: 020 7259 5959. Fax: 020 7259 5955. E-mail: dtb.london@dt.dk
Internet: www.visitdenmark.com

Denmark is the easiest of the Scandinavian countries to visit, both in terms of cost and distance. The countryside is green and varied with flat plains, rolling hills, fertile farmland, many lakes and fjords, wild moors and long beaches, interrupted by pretty villages and towns. There are many small islands but the main land masses which make up this country are the islands of Zealand (Sjælland), Funen (Fyn) and the peninsula of Jutland (Jylland), which extends northwards from the German border at Flensburg. Copenhagen, the capital and Denmark's largest city, is on Zealand and is an exciting city with a beautiful old centre, a good array of museums and a boisterous night life. Camping in Denmark is a delight, with many sites now having facilities that rival, and sometimes even surpass, the best in other parts of Europe. Most sites now offer well designed facilities for disabled people and babies, and many now have private family bathrooms. You will find kitchens on most sites, many with hobs, ovens, microwaves and the occasional dishwasher. All these facilities are often free. You will need either a valid International Camping Carnet, or a Danish Camping Pass (purchased at the first camp you visit in Denmark).

Population

5,162,000 (1992), density 120 per sq.km.

Capital

Copenhagen (København).

Climate

The climate can be changeable all year. In general April-May is mild. June-Aug. is usually warm and sunny. Autumn is often sunny but can be unreliable and the winter months Dec-March tend to be cold.

Language

The official language is Danish, but English is widely spoken.

Currency

The monetary unit is the Danish Krone (Dkr.) 1 Krone = 100 ore. Bank notes in circulation are: 1,000, 500, 100, and 50; coins are: 20, 10, 5, 2 and 1 krone, 50 and 25 ore.

Banks

In Copenhagen banks are open Mon-Wed & Fri 09.30-16.00. Thurs. to 18.00. Closed Sat. In the provinces opening hours vary from town to town. Danish banks may refuse to exchange large foreign bank notes. Traveller's cheques are cashed by banks and many restaurants and shops, which also accept most credit cards.

Post Offices

Open Mon-Fri 09.00/10.00-17.00/17.30, Sat 09.00/10.00-12.00 (some offices in Copenhagen are closed all day Saturday).

Telephone

The dialling code for Denmark is 0045. from Denmark to the UK dial 0044. Phone cards from Telecom shops (Telebutik).

Time

GMT plus 1 (summer BST plus 1).

Shops

Hours may vary in the main cities. Regular openings are Mon-Thu 09.00-17.30. Fri 09.00- 19.00/20.00. Sat 09.00-13.00/14.00. First Sat in every month most shops open 09.00-16.00/ 17.00.

Food and Restaurants

The cost of food is quite high and a stock of basic supplies is useful. However, supermarket prices are now fairly similar to London prices. The price of spirits is prohibitive but for wine and beer almost acceptable! Eating out can be expensive. Try sticking to 'Dagens Ret' - the day's speciality which is usually good value.

Motoring

Driving is much easier than at home as roads are much quieter. Driving is on the right. Do not drink and drive - any quantity is liable to immediate drastic action. Dipped headlights are compulsory at all times.
Speed limits: caravans and motorhomes (3.5 tons) 31 mph (50 kph) in built up areas, 44 mph (70 kph) for caravans on all other roads, for motorhomes 50 mph (80 kph) on other roads and 69 mph (110 kph) on motorways.
Parking: In Copenhagen parking discs are required where there are no meters. Meters coins or discs are available from post offices, petrol stations, and tourist offices.

Overnighting

Overnight stays outside camp sites is not permitted without the prior permission of the landowner. Camping in car parks and laybys is not permitted. Strong measures are taken against unauthorised parking on beaches - with on the spot fines.

Møgeltønder Camping

Sonderstregsvej 2, Mogeltonder, DK-6270 Tonder (Sønderjylland)

TThis site is only five minutes walk from one of Denmark`s oldest villages and ten minutes drive from Tønder with its well preserved old buildings and magnificent pedestrian shopping street. The old town of Ribe is just 43 km. It is also convenient for the ferry ports. A quiet family site, it has 285 large, level, numbered pitches on grass, most with electricity (10A), divided up by shrubs and small hedges. Only 35 pitches are occupied by long stay units, the remainder for tourists, and there are 15 cabins. The site also has an excellent outdoor heated pool, a good playground and a range of trolleys, carts and tricycles.

Facilities: Two superb, modern, sanitary units include roomy showers (on payment), washbasins with divider/curtain or in private cubicles, plus excellent bathrooms for families and disabled visitors. Two kitchens with hobs and dishwashing (all free). Washing machines and dryer. Motorcaravan services. Shop for essentials (bread ordered daily). Swimming pool. Playground. TV and games rooms. Minigolf. **Off site:** Golf and bicycle hire in nearby Tønder.

Charges 2003

Per adult	Dkr. 50.00
child (0-12 yrs)	Dkr. 25.00
electricity	Dkr. 20.00

Tel: 74.73.84.60. Fax: 74.73.80.43. **Reservations:** Not normally necessary. **Open** all year.

Directions: Turn left off no. 419 Tønder - Højer road, 4 km. from Tønder. Drive through Møgeltønder village and past the church where site is signed. The main street is cobbled so drive slowly.

Hvidbjerg Strand Camping

Hvidbjerg Strandvej 27, DK-6857 Blavand (Ribe)

A family owned, 'TopCamp' holiday site, Hvidbjerg Strand is on the west coast, 43 km. from Esbjerg. It is a high quality, seaside site with a wide range of amenities and facilities. All 650 pitches have electricity (6/10A) and 'comfort' pitches also have water, drain and satellite TV. Many are individual and divided by hedges, in rows on flat sandy grass, with areas also divided by small trees and hedges. On-site leisure facilities include an impressive, tropical style indoor pool complex with stalactite caves and 70 m. water chute, 'the black hole' with sounds and lights plus water slides, spa baths and a sauna. The latest indoor supervised play rooms is designed for all ages with Lego, computers, video games, TV, etc. The most recent sanitary facilities are also impressive, thatched in the traditional style. A Blue Flag beach is adjacent to the site.

Facilities: Four superb toilet units include washbasins (many in cubicles), roomy showers, spa baths, suites for disabled visitors, family bathrooms, kitchens and laundry facilities. The most recent units include bathrooms decorated with dinosaur or Disney characters, racing car baby baths, low height WCs, basins and showers, plus many high quality family bathrooms, suites for disabled visitors and an excellent kitchen. Some family bathrooms may be rented for private use. Motorcaravan services. Supermarket. Café/restaurant. TV rooms. Pool complex, solarium and sauna. Playgrounds. Supervised play rooms (09.00-16.00 daily). Barbecue areas. Minigolf, football, squash and badminton. Riding. Fishing. ATM machine.

Charges 2002

Per adult	Dkr. 62.00
child (0-11 yrs)	Dkr. 45.00
pitch	Dkr. 10.00 - 75.00
electricity (6/10A)	Dkr. 24.00 - 28.00

Tel: 75 27 90 40. Fax: 75 27 80 28. E-mail: info@hvidbjerg.dk. **Reservations:** Made without deposit. **Open** 16 March - 4 November.

Directions: From Varde take roads 181/431 to Blåvand. Site is signed left on entering the town.

Nordsø Camping

Tingodden 3, Årgab, 6960 Hvide Sande (Ringkøbing)

Located beside the North Sea, behind the sand dunes and next to a fjord, Nordsø not only has beach access but also provides a splendid indoor pool complex. There are 300 regularly laided out, level pitches, quite close together, most of which have 16 amp electricity with 80 fully serviced and 43 cabins. The site has a wide range of activites for children with a restaurant for evening use and a pizzeria for day time. The site is situated on the West Coast Path, a 40 km. long cycle path for children and adults. The site is very popular with German visitors.

Facilities: Two fully equipped toilet blocks one heated. Family bathrooms (charged). Facilities for the disabled visitors. Laundry. Restaurant, bar, pizzeria and takaway. Supermarket. Kitchen. Outdoor pool and indoor pool complex (Dkr. 10-20). Sauna, solarium and spa bath. Tennis, table tennis, minigolf. TV and games room. Play areas. **Off site:** Fishing near.

Charges 2002

Per adult	Dkr. 50 - 62
child under 12 yrs	Dkr. 35 - 42
pitch	Dkr. 20 - 50
electricity	Dkr. 30 - 24

Tel: 96.59.17.22 Fax: 96.59.17.17 E-mail: reception@city.dk. **Open:** 22 March - 1 September.

Directions: From E20 take exit 73, Korskroen. Take main road 11 to Varde then 181 towards Nymindegab and Hvide Sande. Site is 6 km. south of Hvide Sande.

Denmark - Jutland
Jesperhus Feriecenter & Camping

2140 Legindvej 30, DK-7900 Nykobing Mors (Viborg)

Jesperhus is an extensive, well organised and busy site with many leisure activities, adjacent to Blomsterpark. It is a 'TopCamp' site with 662 numbered pitches, mostly in rows with some terracing, divided by shrubs and trees and with shade in parts. Many pitches are taken by seasonal, tour operator or rental units, so advance booking is advised for peak periods. Electricity (6A) is available on all pitches and water points are in all areas. The indoor and outdoor pool complex (daily charge) has three pools, diving boards, water slides with the 'Black Hole', spa pools, saunas and a solarium. Although it may appear to be just part of Jutland, Mors is an island in its own right surrounded by the lovely Limfjord. It is joined to the mainland by a fine 2,000 m. bridge at the end of which are signs to Blomsterpark (Northern Europe's largest flower park which also houses a Bird Zoo, Butterfly World, Terrarium and Aquarium) and the camp site - both under the same ownership. The flower park, situated well to the north of Denmark, is an incredible sight from early spring to late autumn, attracting some 4,000 visitors a day to enjoy over half a million flowering plants and magnificent landscaped gardens. With all the activities at this site an entire holiday could be spent here regardless of weather, but Jesperhus is also an excellent centre for touring a lovely area of Denmark.

Facilities: Four first rate sanitary units are cleaned three times daily. Facilities include washbasins in cubicles or with divider/curtain, family and whirlpool bathrooms (on payment), suites for babies and disabled people. Superb kitchens with full cookers and hoods, microwaves, dishwashing sinks and a fully equipped laundry. Supermarket (1/4-1/11) with gas. Restaurant. Bar. Café, takeaway. Pool complex. Activities include a 10 lane bowling centre, 'space laser' game, minigolf, volleyball, tennis, go-carts and other outdoor sports. An indoor hall includes badminton, table tennis, and children's 'play-world'. Playgrounds. Pets corner. Golf. Fishing. **Off site:** Riding 2 km. Bicycle hire 6 km.

Charges 2002

Per adult	Dkr. 62.00
child (1-11 yrs)	Dkr. 48.00
pitch (July, B.Hs and weekends only)	Dkr. 50.00
electricity	Dkr. 28.00
environment tax per person	Dkr. 5.00

Tel: 967 01400. Fax: 967 01417. E-mail: jesperhus@jesperhus.dk. **Reservations:** Advised for holiday periods - write for details. **Open** all year.

Directions: From south or north, take road no. 26 to Salling Sund bridge, site is signed Jesperhus, just north of the bridge.

Denmark - Jutland
Solyst Camping

2150 Logstorvej 2, DK-9240 Nibe (Nordjylland)

You will always be near to the water in Denmark, either open sea or, as here, alongside the more sheltered waters of a fjord - Limfjord. Sølyst is a family run site providing 200 numbered pitches, most with electricity (6A), on gently sloping grass arranged in fairly narrow rows separated by hedges (140 for touring units). There are facilities for watersports and swimming in the fjord, the site also has a small heated swimming pool (8 x 16 m), waterslide and splash poolwith a children's pool all with paved sunbathing area, and paddle boats can be rented. A little train provides rides for children. Good paths have been provided for superb, easy walks in either direction, and indeed right into the nearby town of Nibe. This is a delightful example of an old Danish town with picturesque cottages and handsome 15th century church. Its harbour, once prosperous from local herring boats, is now more concerned with pleasure craft.

Facilities: A central sanitary unit includes washbasins in cubicles, four family bathrooms, a baby room and facilities for disabled visitors. Kitchen with gas hobs, microwave, oven and dishwashing sinks. Fully equipped laundry. A second unit provides extra facilities including two more family bathrooms. Hot water (except in washbasins) is charged for. Motorcaravan services. Mini-market. Snack bar and takeaway (open main season). Swimming pool. Solarium. Children's playground. Minigolf. Boules. TV room. Fishing. **Off site:** Bicycle hire or riding 1 km. Golf 4 km. Town of Nibe 1 km.

Charges 2003

Per adult	Dkr. 54.00 - 62.00
child (under 12 yrs)	Dkr. 28.00 - 32.00
pitch	free
electricity	Dkr. 23.00

Tel: 98 35 10 62. Fax: 98 35 34 88. E-mail: soelyst-camping@ferie.dk. **Reservations:** Advised for peak periods - write for details. **Open** all year.

Directions: Site is clearly signed from the no. 187 road west of Nibe town, with a wide entrance.

Klim Strand Camping

2170 Havvejen 167, Klim Strand, DK-9690 Fjerritslev (Nordjylland)

A large coastal, family holiday site, Klim Strand is a paradise for children. It is a privately owned 'TopCamp' site with a full complement of quality facilities, including its own fire engine and trained staff. The site has 700 numbered pitches, all with electricity (10A), laid out in rows, many divided by trees and hedges and shade in parts. Some 300 of these are fully serviced with electricity, water, drain and 18 channel TV hook-up. On site activities include an outdoor water-slide complex, indoor heated swimming pool complex, tennis courts, pony riding (all free), numerous play areas, an adventure playground with aerial cable ride, roller skating area and ramp. Live music and dancing are organised twice a week in high season, and an 18 hole golf course is nearby. Suggested excursions include trips to offshore islands, visits to local potteries, a brewery museum and bird watching on the Bygholm Vejle.

Facilities: Two large, central sanitary buildings are heated and include spacious showers and some washbasins in cubicles. A popular feature is the separate children's room with child size/height WCs, basins and half height shower cubicles. Baby rooms, bathrooms for families (some charged) and disabled visitors. Sauna, solariums, whirlpool bath, hairdressing rooms, fitness room. Dog bathroom. Two smaller units are by reception and beach. Laundry. Well equipped kitchens and barbecue areas with dishwashing sinks, microwaves, gas hobs, and two TV lounges. Motorcaravan services. Supermarket. Pizzeria. Restaurant and bar (17.00 Mon-Fri, 12.00 Sat/Sun). Internet cafe. TV rental. Pool complex. Children's playgrounds. Crèche. Bicycle hire. **Off site:** Golf 10 km.

Charges 2003

Per adult	Dkr. 65.00
child (0-11 yrs)	Dkr. 45.00
pitch	Dkr. 60.00
electricity	Dkr. 28.00
dog	Dkr. 18.00

Tel: 98 22 53 40. Fax: 98 22 57 77. E-mail: ksc@klim-strand.dk. **Reservations:** Essential for mid June - end August. **Open** 1 April - 20 October.

Directions: Turn off Thisted-Fjerritslev no. 11 road to Klim from where site is signed.

Nordstrand Camping

2180 Apholmenvej 40, DK-9900 Frederikshaven (Nordjylland)

An excellent site, Nordstrand is 2 km. from Frederikshaven and the ferries to Sweden and Norway. It is another 'TopCamp' site and provides all the comforts one could possibly need with all the attractions of the nearby beach, town and port. The 430 large pitches are attractively arranged in small enclosures of 9-13 units surrounded by hedges and trees. Many hedges are of flowering shrubs and this makes for a very pleasant atmosphere. 250 pitches have electricity and drainage, a further 20 have water and there are 16 on hardstandings. There are 64 seasonal units, plus 23 site owned cabins. The roads are all paved and the site is well lit and fenced with the barrier locked at night. The reception complex also houses a café (high season), with a telephone pizza service available at other times. The beach is a level, paved 200 m. walk. There is much to see in this area of Denmark and this site would make a very comfortable holiday base.

Facilities: Centrally located, modern, large toilet blocks provide spacious showers (on payment) and washbasins in cubicles, together with some family bathrooms, rooms for disabled people and babies. Laundry with free ironing. All are spotlessly clean. Good kitchens at each block provide mini-ovens, microwaves, hobs (free) and dishwashing sinks with free hot water. Motorcaravan services. Supermarket (all season). Cafè (15/6-15/8). Pizza service. Indoor swimming pool (charged). Sauna. Solarium. 'Short' golf course, minigolf, tennis, table tennis, billiards and chess. Bicycle hire. Children's playgrounds. **Off site:** Fishing 200 m.

Charges 2003

Per adult	Dkr. 62.00 - 56.00
child (0-11 yrs)	Dkr. 42.00 - 36.00
pitch	Dkr. 26.00 - 35.00
electricity 6/10A	Dkr. 25.00 - 26.00
dog	Dkr. 10.00

Tel: 98 42 93 50. Fax: 98 43 47 85. E-mail: nord-strand-camping@post10.tele.dk. **Reservations:** Essential for high season and made with deposit (Dkr. 400). **Open** 1 April - 20 October.

Directions: Turn off the main no. 40 road 2 km. north of Frederikshavn at roundabout just north of railway bridge. Site is signed.

Hobro Camping Gattenborg

2130 Skivevej 35, DK-9500 Hobro (Nordjylland)

This neat and very well tended municipal site is imaginatively landscaped and has 130 pitches on terraces arranged around a bowl shaped central activity area. Most pitches (100 for touring units) have electricity (10A) and there are many trees and shrubs. Footpaths connect the various terraces and activity areas. There are 30 seasonal units and 10 cabins. The reception building with a small shop and tourist information, has a covered picnic terrace behind, and houses a large TV lounge. The small, heated, outdoor swimming pool with water-slide is free to campers and open in high season weather permitting. Extra unusual facilities include billiards, giant chess, and a woodland moon-buggy track. The site is 500 m. walk from the town, close to the Viking Castle of Fyrkat.

Facilities: The main heated sanitary building towards the rear of the site includes washbasins in cubicles and hot showers (on payment). Two family bathrooms. Kitchen with hobs and dishwashing sinks, and small laundry with sink, washing machine and dryer. Facilities for disabled people and baby room. A tiny unit in the centre of the site has two unisex WCs and basins (cold water only) and a small kitchen. Motorcaravan services. Shop (order bread before 9 pm). Swimming pool (high season). Children's play areas. Table tennis. Basketball. Football. Minigolf. TV lounge. **Off site:** Bicycle hire near. Fishing 7 km. Town 500 m.

Charges 2003

Per adult	Dkr. 53.00 - 62.00
child (2-11 yrs)	Dkr. 28.00 - 32.00
electricity	Dkr. 22.00

Tel: 98 52 32 88. **Fax:** 98 52 56 61. E-mail: hobro@dk-camp.dk. **Reservations:** Contact site. **Open** 26 March - 1 October.

Directions: From E45 exit 35, take road 579 towards Hobro Centrum. Site is well signed to the right, just after railway bridge.

Terrassen Camping

2050 Himmelbjergvej 9 A, Laven, DK-8600 Silkeborg (Århus)

Terrassen Camping is a family run site arranged on terraces, overlooking Lake Julso and the countryside. There are 260 pitches most with electricity (6/10A). A small area for tents (without electricity) is at the top of the site where torches may be required. There are also 29 seasonal units, and some site owned cabins. The solar heated swimming pool (8 x 16 m, open June-end August) has a paved terrace and is well fenced. This is a comfortable base from which to explore this area of Denmark where a warm welcome and good English will greet you. Don`t forget to take a trip on Lake Julso on Hjejen, the world`s oldest paddle steamer.

Facilities: The main modern sanitary unit includes washbasins in cubicles, showers (on payment), family bathrooms and facilities for disabled visitors. Kitchen with hobs, ovens and dishwashing. An older unit contains another kitchen, plus 4 more shower cubicles with external access - despite their outward appearance they are immaculate. Motorcaravan services. Shop. Swimming pool (15/5-31/8). Adventure playground, toddlers play room and pets corner. Basketball, volleyball and boules. Canoe hire.

Charges 2003

Per adult	Dkr. 59.00
child (1-11 yrs)	Dkr. 35.00
pitch	free - Dkr. 60.00
electricity	Dkr. 25.00

Tel: 86 84 13 01. **Fax:** 86 84 16 55. E-mail: info@terrassen.dk. **Reservations:** essential for high season. **Open** 4 April - 14 September.

Directions: From the harbour in centre of Silkeborg follow signs and minor road towards Sejs (5 km.) and Ry (20 km.). Site is at village of Laven (13 km.). Note: Height restriction of 3 m. on this road.

Hampen Sø Camping

2044 Hovedgaden 31, 7362 Hampen (Vejle)

If you are heading up towards Denmark to cross to Norway or Sweden, then this site in a natural setting close to lakes and moors could be a useful stop-over. There are 230 pitches in total, with 80 seasonal units plus 34 cabins, but there will always be space for touring units. The pitches are arranged in large grassy bays taking around 15 units, and there are 10A electric hook-ups (some long leads may be needed). One sanitary block located at the upper end of the site and the second by the entrance road. The nearby Hampen See lake is a pleasant walk through the forest. English is spoken.

Facilities: Somewhat basic toilet facilities could be pressed at peak times. En-suite facilities for disabled people. Laundry. Good mini-market and cafeteria open all year and to the general public. Takeaway. Kitchen. Games and TV rooms. Small outdoor pool. Minigolf. Playground. Trampolines. Table tennis. Bicycle hire. **Off site:** Fishing nearby.

Charges 2002

Per adult	Dkr. 55
child (0-11 yrs)	Dkr. 28
electricity	Dkr. 25

Tel: 75.77.52.55 **Fax:** 75.77.52.66 E-mail: info@hampen-soe-camping.dk. **Reservations:** Contact site. **Open** all year.

Directions: Site lies on road no.176, approx. 500 m. southwest of its junction with road no.13 between Vejle and Viborg (around 50 km. south of Viborg). Look for Spar minimarket and camping signs.

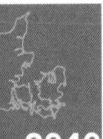

Denmark - Jutland
Blushoj Camping

2100 Elsegårdevej 55, DK-8400 Ebeltoft (Århus)

This is a traditional site where the owners are making a conscious effort to keep mainly to touring units - there are only 6 seasonal units and 4 rental cabins. The site has 200 pitches on levelled grassy terraces surrounded by mature hedging and shrubs. Some have glorious views of the Kattegat and others overlook peaceful rural countryside. Most pitches have electricity (10A), but long leads may be required. There is a heated pool (14 x 7 m) with a water-slide and terrace and the beach below the site provides opportunities for swimming, windsurfing and sea fishing. The owners also arrange traditional entertainment some weekends in high season. This is a fine location for a relaxed family holiday, with numerous excursion possibilities.

Facilities: One toilet unit includes washbasins with dividers and showers with divider and seat (on payment).The other unit has a kitchen with electric hobs, dishwashing sinks, dining/TV room, laundry and baby facilities. A heated extension provides six very smart family bathrooms, and additional WCs and washbasins. Motorcaravan service point. Well stocked shop. Swimming pool (20/5-20/8). Minigolf. Children's playground. Beach. Fishing.

Charges 2003

Per adult	Dkr. 58.00 - 66.00
child	Dkr. 30.00 - 34.00
electricity	Dkr. 22.00

No credit cards. **Tel:** 86 34 12 38. Fax: 86 34 12 38. **Reservations:** Contact site. **Open** 1 April - 15 September.

Directions: From road 21 northwest of Ebeltoft turn off at junction where several sites are signed. Follow signs through the outskirts of Ebeltoft turning southeast to Elsegårde village. Turn left for Blushøj and follow camp signs.

Denmark - Jutland
Riis Camping & Fritidscenter

2040 Osterhovedveg 43, DK-7323 Give (Vejle)

Riis is a good quality touring site ideal for visiting Legoland (18 km) and Lion Park (3 km). It is a friendly, family run 'TopCamp' site with 270 large touring pitches on sheltered, gently sloping, well tended lawns surrounded by trees and shrubs. Electricity (6A) is available to 220 pitches, and there are 51 site owned cabins. The outdoor heated pool and water-slide complex and the adjacent small bar that serves beer, ice cream, soft drinks and snacks are only open in main season. There is also a small, well stocked shop next to reception for necessities. More comprehensive shopping and restaurants are in nearby Give. This is a top class site suitable for stays in this very attractive part of Denmark.

Facilities: Two excellent sanitary units include washbasins with divider/curtain and controllable showers (on payment). Suites for babies and disabled visitors, family bathrooms (on payment), and solarium. Two excellent kitchens (on payment). Large dining room/sitting room with TV. Laundry. Motorcaravan services. Shop. Pool complex (charged in July). Cafe/bar. Table tennis. Minigolf. Outdoor bowling alley. Playground. TV lounge. Bicycle hire.

Charges 2002

Per adult	Dkr. 58.00
child (under 12 yrs)	Dkr. 35.00
pitch	Dkr. 35.00
electricity	Dkr. 25.00

Tel: 75 73 14 33. Fax: 75 73 58 66. E-mail: info@riis-camping.dk. **Reservations:** Advised for July/Aug. **Open** 30 April - 5 September.

Directions: Turn onto Osterhovedvej southeast of Give town centre at sign to Riis and site. After 4 km. turn left into tarmac drive which runs through the forest to the site. Alternatively, turn off the 442 Brande-Jelling road at Riis village north of Givskud.

Denmark - Jutland
Sandersvig Camping

2030 Espagervej 15-17, DK-6100 Haderslev (Sønderjylland)

An attractively laid out, family run site, Sandersvig offers the very best of modern facilities in a peaceful and beautiful countryside location, 300 m. from the beach. The 470 very large grassy pitches (270 for tourers) are divided up by hedges, shrubs and small trees into small enclosures, many housing only four units, most with electricity (10A). This site makes a very comfortable base for excursions. Visit the restored windmill at Sillerup (4 km.) or nearby historic Kolding with its castle, museums and shops. There are miles of country lanes around the site for cycling and walking.

Facilities: Four heated sanitary blocks offer some washbasins in cubicles and roomy showers (on payment). Suites for disabled visitors, family bathrooms and baby rooms. Excellent kitchens. Laundry. Motorcaravan services. Supermarket and fast food service, with dining room adjacent. (Easter-15/9). Takeaway (15/6-15/8). Outdoor heated pool (15/5-1/9). Solarium. Playground. Games room. TV lounge.

Charges 2003

Per adult	Dkr. 52.00
child (0-11 yrs)	Dkr. 30.00
pitch	Dkr. 10.00 - 25.00
electricity (10A)	Dkr. 22.00

Tel: 74 56 62 25. Fax: 74 56 62 25. E-mail: sandersvig@dk-camp.dk. **Reservations:** Essential for high season (25/6-7/8). **Open** 27 March - 15 September.

Directions: Leave E45 at exit 66 and turn towards Christianfeld. Turn right on 170 and follow signs for Fjelstrup and Knud, turning right in 1 km. to site.

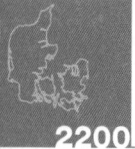

Denmark - Islands
Logismosestrand Camping
2205 Logismoseskov 7, DK-5683 Hårby (Fyn)

A countryside site with its own beach and pool, Løgismosestrand is surrounded by picturesque villages. The owner of this site is the son of another Alan Rogers' site owner, and was the youngest campsite owner in Denmark when he purchased this site. Since that time he has completely refitted the original sanitary unit, also built a new unit and, more recently, a new swimming pool (8 x 14 m) with a paddling pool (6 x 6 m), for which there is a small charge. The 230 pitches, some with a little shade, are arranged in rows and groups divided by hedges and small trees, 190 with electricity (10A). A barbecue area has been developed with gas grills.

Facilities: Heated toilet units, kept very clean, include washbasins in cubicles, roomy showers (on payment), a baby room, bathrooms for families and disabled people. Good laundry with washing machine and dryer. Excellent kitchen with inset gas hobs, microwave (cooking facilities charged for) and dishwashing sinks. Motorcaravan services. Well stocked shop. Snackbar/takeaway (in season). Swimming pool (1/6-1/9). Minigolf. Table tennis. Bicycle and boat hire. Pony riding. Adventure playground, large undercover games room, and play field. **Off site:** Riding 2 km. Golf 12 km.

Charges 2002

Per adult	Dkr. 54.00
child (under 12 yrs)	Dkr. 30.00
pitch	Dkr. 30.00
electricity	Dkr. 22.00

Credit cards accepted with 5% surcharge. **Tel:** 64 77 12 50. Fax: 64 77 12 51. E-mail: info@logismose.dk. **Reservations:** Essential for high season - write for details. **Open** 27 March - 18 September.

Directions: Southwest of Hårby via Sarup and Nellemose to Løgismose Skov, site is well signed. Lanes are narrow, large outfits should take care.

Denmark - Islands
DCU Camping Odense
2215 Odensevej 102, DK-5260 Odense S (Fyn)

Although within the confines of the city, this site is hidden away amongst mature trees and is therefore fairly quiet and is an ideal base from which to explore the fairytale city of Odense. The 225 pitches, of which 145 have electricity (10A), are on level grass with small hedges and shrubs dividing the area into bays. There are a number of seasonal units on site together with 14 cabins. A good network of cycle paths lead into the city. The Odense Adventure Pass (available at the site) allows unrestricted free travel on public transport within the city limits, free admission to the pool and a free newspaper, with varying discounts on other attractions.

Facilities: he large sanitary unit provides up to the minute facilities including washbasins in cubicles, family bathrooms, baby room and excellent suite for disabled visitors. Well appointed kitchen with gas hobs and dishwashing sinks. Laundry with washing machines and dryer. Motorcaravan services. Shop. Small swimmimg pool and children's pool. Games marquee. Table tennis. TV room. Large playground. Ball games field. Minigolf. Bicycle hire.

Charges 2002

Per adult	Dkr. 58.00
child (0-11 yrs)	Dkr. 29.00
pitch	Dkr. 20.00
electricity	Dkr. 20.00 - 27.00

Tel: 66 11 47 02. Fax: 65 91 73 43. E-mail: odense@dcu.dk. **Reservations:** Contact site. **Open** 22 March - 20 October.

Directions: From E20 exit 50, turn towards Odense Centrum, site entrance is 3 km. on left immediately beside the Texaco Garage.

Denmark - Islands
Bojden Strandcamping
2200 Bojden Landevej 12, Bojden, DK-5600 Fåborg (Fyn)

Bøjden is located in one of the most beautiful corners of southwest Fyn, known as the 'Garden of Denmark'. It is a well equipped site separated from the beach only by a hedge, and many pitches have sea views as the site slopes gently down from the road. Arranged in rows on mainly level grassy terraces and divided into groups by hedges and some trees, the 295 pitches (195 for touring units) all have electricity (10A). Four motorcaravan pitches also have water and waste points. Everyone will enjoy the beach (Blue Flag) for bathing, boating and water sports. Bøjden is a delightful site for an entire holiday, while remaining a very good centre for excursions.

Facilities: The high quality, heated toilet blocks include washbasins in cubicles, controllable showers, three family bathrooms, a baby room and excellent facilities for disabled people. Well appointed kitchen, plus a laundry. Motorcaravan services. Shop. Takeaway. Swimming pool (20/5-20/8). Solarium. Playgrounds. TV and games rooms. Bicycle and boat hire. Fishing. Riding. Minigolf.

Charges 2002

Per adult	Dkr. 55.00
child (under 12 yrs)	Dkr. 30.00
pitch	Dkr. 30.00
electricity	Dkr. 23.00

Credit cards accepted with 5% surcharge. **Tel:** 62 60 12 84. Fax: 62 60 12 94. E-mail: bojden@dk-camp.dk. **Reservations:** Advised for high season. **Open** 1 April - 15 September.

Directions: From Faaborg follow road no. 8 to Bøjden and site is on right 500 m. before ferry terminal (from Fynshav).

Denmark - Islands
Bøsøre Strand Camping

Bøsørevej 16, DK-5874 Hesselager (Fyn)

2210

A themed holiday site on the eastern coast of Fyn, the tales of Hans Christian Andersen are evident in the design of the heated indoor pool complex and the main outdoor children's playground at this site. The former has two pools on different levels, two hot tubs and a sauna and features characters from the stories, the latter has a fairytale castle with moat as its centrepiece. There are 300 pitches in total, and with only 80 seasonal units there should always be room for tourists out of main season. All have 6A electric hook-ups, there are 90 multi-serviced pitches and 20 hardstandings. Bøsøre operates a debit card system which is becoming increasingly popular on Danish campsites. Upon payment of a minimum Dkr. 100, the card will allow use of the facilities (showers, sauna, solarium, washing machine etc.) until the credit amount has been fully used. The card also operates the barriers and opens doors to other facilities.

Facilities: Sanitary facilities are housed in one main central block and a smaller unit close to reception. They provide all usual facilities plus some family bathrooms, baby rooms, facilities for dishwashing, laundry and disabled people. They could be stretched during high season. Motorcaravan service point. Shop. Restaurant. Pizzeria. Take-away in peak season. Kitchen (water charged). Solarium. Indoor pool complex. Games and TV rooms. Children's playground with moat. Bicycle hire. Entertainment three times per week in main season.

Charges 2002

Per adult	Dkr. 60.00
child (0-11 yrs)	Dkr. 40.00
serviced pitch	Dkr. 25.00
electricity	Dkr. 25.00
high season supplement (24/6-15/8)	Dkr. 40.00

Tel: 62.25.11.45. Fax: 62.25.11.46. E-mail: info@bosore.dk. **Reservations:** Contact site - advised for high season. **Open** Easter - 29 October.

Directions: The site lies on the coast about midway between Nyborg and Svendborg. From road no. 163 just north of Hesselager, take turning towards coast signed Bøsøre Strand.

Denmark - Islands
Hillerød Camping
Blytækkervej 18, DK-3400 Hillerod (Sjælland)

2250

The northern-most corner of Sjælland is packed with interest, based not only on fascinating parts of Denmark's history but also its attractive scenery. Centrally situated, Hillerød is a hub of main roads from all directions, with this neat campsite clearly signed. It has a park-like setting in a residential area with 5 acres of well kept grass and some attractive trees. There are 96 pitches, of which 50 have electricity (10A) and these are marked. The site amenities are all centrally located in modern, well maintained buildings which are kept very clean. The centre of Hillerød, like so many Danish towns, has been pedestrianised making shopping or outdoor refreshment a pleasure. Visit Frederiksborg Slot, a fine Renaissance Castle and home of the Museum of Danish national history. Hillerød, however is a fine base for visiting Copenhagen and only 25 km. from the ferries at Helsingør and the crossing to Sweden.

Facilities: The bright, airy toilet block is older in style and includes washbasins with partitions and curtain. Facilities for babies can be used by disabled people. Campers' kitchen adjoins the club room and includes free new electric hot plates and coffee making machine. Dishwashing sinks. Laundry room (free iron). Motorcaravan services. Small shop with basic supplies. Good comfortable club room with TV and children's corner. Playground. Bicycles provided free (some with buggy for small children). **Off site:** Tennis courts and indoor swimming pool 1 km. Riding 2 km. Golf 3 km. Excellent new electric train service every 10 minutes (20 mins. walk) to Copenhagen. The site sells the Copenhagen card.

Charges 2002

Per person	Dkr. 60.00
child (2-11 yrs)	Dkr. 30.00
electricity	Dkr. 25.00

Tel: 48 26 48 54. E-mail: hillcamp@post8.tele.dk. **Reservations:** Not made. **Open** Easter - 30 September.

Directions: Follow road no. 6 bypassing town to south until sign for Hillerod S. Turn towards town at sign for 'Centrum' on Roskildvej road no. 233 and site is signed to the right.

DCU Nærum Camping

2260 Ravnbakken, DK-2850 Nærum (Sjælland)

Obviously everyone arriving in Sjælland will want to visit 'wonderful, wonderful Copenhagen', but like all capital cities, it draws crowds during the holiday season and traffic to match. The site is near enough to be convenient but distant enough to afford peace and quiet (apart from the noise of nearby traffic) and a chance of relaxing after sightseeing. Nærum, one of the Danish Camping Union sites, is only 15 km.and very near a suburban railway that takes you to the city centre.It is a sheltered, friendly site with enthusiastic management. The long narrow site covers a large area alongside the ancient royal hunting forests, adjacent to the small railway line and the main road. Power lines do cross the site but there is lots of grassy open space. The 275 touring pitches are in two areas - in wooded glades taking about 6 units each (mostly used by tents) or on more open meadows where electrical connections (6A) are available. Nærum is a useful site to know for Copenhagen, but is also very near to the interesting shopping complex of Rødøvre and the amusement park at Bakken. Note: Should you wish to drive into the city, there is a very useful cheap car park on the quay-side. It is within easy walking distance of the centre and is located where the Kalvebød Brygge meets the Langebrø bridge (suitable for motorcaravans and caravans).

Facilities: Two modern toilet blocks, one in the meadow area has been refurbished and includes partitioned washbasins. The very good block at reception can be heated and also provides a laundry, dishwashing and a campers' kitchen. Good facilities for babies and disabled people. Four new family bathrooms (free). Motorcaravan service point. Shop. Reception and shop (closed 12.00-14.00 and 22.00-07.00). Café/restaurant near. Club room and TV. Barbecue. Children's play field and adventure playground. **Off site:** Full range of sporting facilities within easy reach of the site and café/restaurant within a few hundred metres. Train service to Copenhagen (400 m. on foot).

Charges 2002

Per adult high season	Dkr. 54.00
child (0-11 yrs)	Dkr. 27.00
electricity	Dkr. 18.00
environmental charge	Dkr. 10.00

Tel: 45 80 19 57. Fax: 45 80 11 78. E-mail: info@dcu.dk. **Reservations:** Write for details. **Open** early April - mid September.

Directions: From E55/E47, take Nærum exit (no. 14), 15 km. north of Copenhagen. Turn right at first set of traffic lights (site signed), right on road 19 at second lights, cross bridge and turn left, following signs to site.

Camping Charlottenlund Fort

2265 Strandvejen 144B, DK-2920 Charlottenlund (Sjælland)

On the northern outskirts of Copenhagen, this unique site is within the walls of an old fort which still retains its main armament of twelve 29 mm. howitzers (disabled, of course). The fort was constructed during 1886-1887 and was an integral link in the Copenhagen fortifications until 1932. The site is only 8 km. from the centre of Copenhagen, with a regular bus service (every 20 minutes) from just outside the site. Alternatively you could use the excellent cycle network to visit the city. The site sells the Copenhagen card, valid for 24, 48 or 72 hours, that includes unlimited travel on rail and bus transportation. There are 63 pitches, mostly on grass, all with 10A electric hook-ups. The obvious limitation on the space available means that pitches are relatively close together, but many are quite deep. The site is very popular and is usually full every night, so we suggest that you either make a reservation or arrive well before mid-day.

Facilities: Sanitary facilities located in the old armoury are rather basic, but acceptable and can be heated in cool weather. Showers on payment, but kitchen facilities include gas hobs and a dining area free of charge. Laundry. Motorcaravan service point. **Off site:** Small restaurant (separate management) is adjacent to the site, with good sea views to Sweden and the spectacular Øresund Bridge.

Charges 2003

Per adult	Dkr. 67.00
child (3-12 yrs)	Dkr. 25.00
caravan or motorcaravan	Dkr. 25.00
electricity	Dkr. 23.00
tent	free

Tel: 39.62.36.88. Fax: 39.61.08.16. E-mail: camping-fort@mail.dk. **Reservations:** Contact site - essential for high season. **Open** 15 May - 14 September.

Directions: Leave E47/E55 at junction 17, and turn southeast on Jægersborgvej. After a short distance turn left (east) on Jægersborg Allé, following signs for Charlottenlund (3 km). Finally turn right (south) on to Strandvejen, and site entrance is on left after 500 m.

Topcamp Feddet

2255 Feddet 12, DK-4640 Fakse (Sjælland)

This interesting spacious site with ecological principles is located on the Baltic coast. It has a fine, white, sandy beach (Blue Flag) which runs the full length of one side, with the Præstø fjord on the opposite side of the peninsula. There are 400 pitches, generally on sandy grass, with mature pine trees giving adequate shade. All have 10A electricity and 52 are fully serviced. Two, recently constructed sanitary buildings have been specially designed to have natural ventilation, with ventilators controlled by sensors for heat, humidity and smell. The shaped blades on the roof increase ventilation on windy days. All this saves power and provides a comfortable climate inside. Heating is by a wood chip furnace (backed up by an oil seed rape furnace), is CO2 neutral, and replaces 40,000 litres of heating oil annually. The buildings are clad with larch panels from sustainable local trees, and are insulated with flax mats. Rainwater is used for toilet flushing, but showers and basins are supplied from the normal mains, and urinals are water free. Water saving taps have an automatic turn off, and lighting is by low wattage bulbs with PIR switching. Recycling is very important here, with separate bins for glass, metal, paper, cardboard and batteries. The site has a Danish Green Key award for its environmental standards.

Facilities: Both sanitary buildings are impressive, equipped to very high standard and include family bathrooms (with twin showers), complete small children and baby suites. Facilities for disabled people. Laundry. Kitchens with ovens, hobs and rental fridges, dining room and a TV lounge. Each block has a chemical disposal facility complete with hand-basin, soap, and paper towel. Excellent drive-over motorcaravan service point. Well stocked licensed shop. Licensed bistro and takeaway (1/5-20/10 but weekends only outside peak season). Minigolf, games room and table tennis. Indoor toddlers playroom and several playgrounds for all ages, trampolines and bouncing cushion. Watersports. Fishing. **Off site:** Many other activities with guides or instructors, including Land Rover safaris, abseiling, Icelandic pony riding, educational courses, ocean kayaking, and seal watching in Fakse Bay.

Charges 2003

Per adult	Dkr. 65.00
child (0-11 yrs)	Dkr. 45.00
pitch	Dkr. 45.00
electricity	Dkr. 30.00
serviced pitch	Dkr. 75.00

Tel: 56.72.52.06. Fax: 56.72.57.90. E-mail: info@feddetcamping.dk. **Reservations:** Contact site - recommended for high season. **Open** 1 April - 19 October.

Directions: From south on E47/55 jcn. 38 take road to Tappernoje, continue straight on at crossroads, after 3 km. turn left on to road 209 (Præsto-Fakse), turn right 12 km. north of Præsto following signs to Feddet and campsite (4 km. along country roads). Alternatively, from the north, take exit 37, follow road 154 to Fakse, turn right on road 209 for 9 km, and follow signs to Feddet as before.

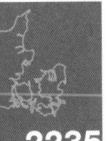

Sakskobing Gron Camping

2235 Saxes Allé 15, DK-4990 Sakskobing (Lolland)

This small, traditional style site provides a useful stop-over on the route from Germany to Sweden within easy reach of the Puttgarden - Rødby ferry. There are 125 level grassy pitches, most with electricity (10A) and, although there are a fair number of seasonal units, one can usually find space. The pool at the nearby sports centre is said to be the most modern in Europe. The site has a well stocked shop, which is open long hours, but the attractive town centre is semi-pedestrianised, and has good range of shops and a supermarket. The town is noted for its unusual 'smiling' water tower, which you pass on the way to the site.

Facilities: Two sanitary units provide basic, older style facilities, including push-button hot showers on payment, some curtained washbasin cubicles and a baby room, plus cooking, dishwashing and laundry facilities. Motorcaravan services. Shop. Children's playground.

Charges 2002

Per adult	Dkr. 55.00
child	Dkr. 28.00
electricity	Dkr. 20.00

Tel: 54 70 47 57. Fax: 54 70 70 90. **Reservations:** Advised for last week June to end of July. **Open** 1 April - 27 October.

Directions: From E47, exit 46, turn towards town on road 9. Turn right at crossroads towards town centre (site is signed), cross railway and then turn right again, and site entrance is 250 m. on left.

France

The French Government Tourist Office (FGTO), 178 Piccadilly, London W1V 0AL

Tel: 0906 8244 123 (premium rate) Mon-Fri, 08.30-20.00 hrs. Fax: 0207 493 6594

Population

57,800,000 (94), density 106 per sq.km.

Capital

Paris.

Climate

France has a temperate climate but it varies considerably, for example, Brittany has a climate similar to that of Devon and Cornwall, whilst the Mediterranean coast enjoys a subtropical climate.

Language

Obviously French is spoken throughout the country but there are many local dialects and variations so do not despair if you have greater problems understanding in some areas than in others. We notice an increase in the amount of English understood and spoken.

Currency

From January 2002, in common with 11 other European countries, the French unit of currency is the EURO (€).
€ 1 = Fr. Francs 6.56.

Banks

Open weekdays 09.00-1200 and 14.00-16.00. Some provincial banks are open Tues-Sat 09.00-12.00 and 14.00-16.00. Credit Cards: Most major credit cards accepted in most outlets and for motorway tolls.

Post Offices

The French term for post office is either PTT or Bureau de Poste. They are generally open Mon-Fri 08.00-19.00 and Saturday 08.00-12.00 and can close for lunch 12.00-14.00. You can buy stamps with less queuing from Tabacs (tobacconists).

Time

GMT plus 1 (summer BST + 1) but there is a period of about three to four weeks in October when the times coincide.

Telephone

From the UK dial 00 33, followed by the 10 figure local number MINUS the initial "0" - in other words from the UK you will dial 0033 followed by the last NINE digits of the telephone number. To the UK from France dial 0044. Many public phone boxes now only take phone cards. (Telecarte) These can be purchased from post offices, tabacs, and some campsites.

Public Holidays

New Year; Easter Mon; Labour Day; VE Day, 8 May; Ascension; Whit Mon; Bastille Day, 14 July; Assumption, 15 Aug; All Saints, 1 Nov; Armistice Day, 11 Nov; Christmas, 25 Dec.

Shops

Often close on Mon, all or half day and for 2 hours daily for lunch. Food shops open on Sun morning.

Motoring

France has a comprehensive road system from motorways (Autoroutes), Routes Nationales (N roads), Routes Départmentales (D roads) down to purely local C class roads.

Tolls: Payable on the autoroute network which is extensive but expensive. Tolls are also payable on certain bridges such as the one from the Ile de Ré to the mainland and the Pont de St Nazaire.

Speed Restrictions: Built-up areas 31 mph (50 kph), on normal roads 56 mph (90 kph); on dual carriageways separated by a central reservation 69 mph (110 kph), on toll motorways 80 mph (130 kph). In wet weather, limits outside built-up areas are reduced to 50mph (80 kph), 62 mph (100 kph) and 69 mph (110 kph) on motorways. A minimum speed limit of 50 mph (80 kph) exists in the outside lane of motorways during daylight, on level ground and with good visibility.
These limits also apply to private cars towing a caravan, if the latter's weight does not exceed that of the car. Where it does by 30%, limit is 40 mph (65 kph) and if more than 30%, 28 mph (45 kph).

Fuel: Diesel sold at pumps marked 'gaz-oil'.

Parking: Usual restrictions as in UK. In Paris and larger cities, there is a Blue Zone where parking discs must be used, obtainable from police stations, tourist offices and some shops.

Overnighting

Allowed provided permission has been obtained, except near the water's edge or at a large seaside resort. Casual camping is prohibited in state forests, national parks in the Départements of the Landes and Gironde, in the Camargue and also restricted in the south because of the danger of fire. However overnight stops on parking areas of a motorway are tolerated but not in a lay-by.

The Regions and Départements of France

For administrative purposes France is actually divided into 23 official Regions covering the 95 'départements' (similar to our counties).

However, these do not always coincide with the needs of tourists (for example the area we think of as 'The Dordogne' is split between two of the official regions. We have, therefore, opted to feature our campsites within unofficial 'tourist regions'.

We use the département numbers as the first two digits of our campsite numbers, so any campsite in the Manche département will start with the number 50.

Alan Rogers' FRANCE

The French sites featured in this guide are only a selection of over 600 featured in our Good Camps Guide - France.

**Available from
all good bookshops or
online at www.alanrogers.com**

France - Brittany
Camping des Abers

2913 Dunes de Ste Marguerite, 29870 Landéda

the **travel service** TO BOOK

Ferry ✓
Pitch ✓
Accommodation ✗
01892 55 98 98

This delightful 12 acre site is beautifully situated almost at the tip of the Sainte Marguerite peninsula on the north-western shores of Brittany in a wide bay formed between the mouths (abers) of two rivers, L`Aber Wrac`h and L`Aber Benoit. With soft, white sandy beaches and rocky outcrops and islands at high tide, the setting is ideal for those with younger children and this quiet, rural area provides a wonderful, tranquil escape from the busier areas of France, even in high season. Camping des Abers is set just back from the beach, the lower pitches sheltered from the wind by high hedges or with panoramic views of the bay from the higher places. There are 180 pitches arranged in distinct areas, partly shaded and sheltered by mature hedges, trees and flowering shrubs, all planted and carefully tended over 30 years by the Le Cuff family. Landscaping and terracing where appropriate on the different levels avoids any regimentation or crowding. Easily accessed by good internal roads, electricity is available to all (5A, long leads may be needed). Speaking several languages, the family who own and run this site with `TLC` will make you very welcome.

Facilities: Three toilet blocks (one part of the reception building and all recently refurbished) are very clean, providing washbasins in cubicles and roomy showers (token from reception). Good new facilities for disabled visitors and babies have been added at the reception block. Dishwashing sinks. Fully equipped laundry. Motorcaravan service point. Mini-market stocks essentials (1/5-15/9). Simple takeaway dishes (1/7-31/8). Pizzeria and restaurant next door. Table tennis. Good play area (on sand). Indoor TV and games room. Live music, Breton dancing and Breton cooking classes, and guided walks arranged. Splendid beach reached direct from the site with good bathing (best at high tide), fishing, windsurfing and other watersports. Miles of superb coastal walks. Torch useful. Gates locked 22.30-07.00 hrs. **Off site:** Tennis and riding close. The nearby town of L`Aber Wrac`h, a well known yachting centre, has many memorable restaurants

Charges 2003

Per person	€ 3.10
child (-17 yrs)	€ 1.70
pitch	€ 4.70
car	€ 1.40
electricity	€ 2.20
dog	€ 1.50

Less 20% until 15 June and Sept. **Tel:** 02 98 04 93 35. Fax: 02 98 04 84 35. E-mail: camping-des-abers@wanadoo.fr. **Reservations:** Write to site. **Open** 18 April - 28 September.

Directions: From Roscoff (D10, then D13), cross river bridge (L'Aber Wrac'h) to Lannilis. Go through town taking road to Landéda and from there signs for Dunes de Ste Marguerite, 'camping' and des Abers.

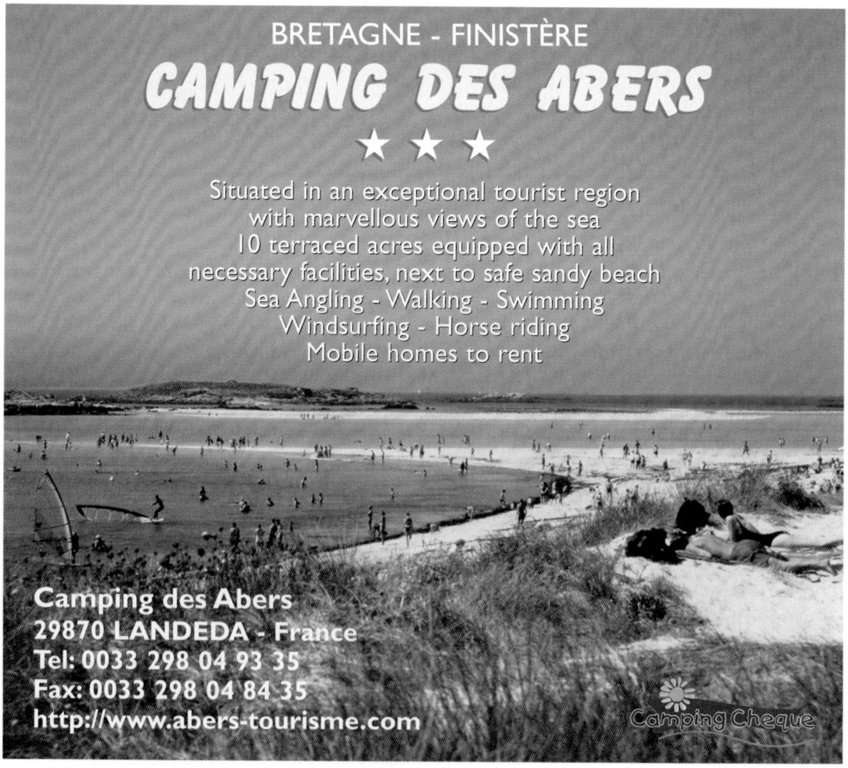

Camping Ty-Nadan

2901 route d'Arzano, 29310 Locunolé

Ty Nadan is a well organised site set amongst wooded countryside along the bank of the River Elle. The 183 pitches for touring units are grassy, many with shade and 152 with 10A electricity. An exciting and varied programme of activities is offered throughout the season - canoeing, rock climbing, mountain biking, aqua-gym, riding or walking - all supervised by qualified staff. A full programme of entertainment for all ages is provided in high season including concerts, Breton evenings with pig roasts, dancing, etc. (be warned, you will be actively encouraged to join in!) Recent developments include a new toilet block and extensions to the shop and bar. The swimming pool complex with its slides and paddling pool is very popular and now has an attractive viewing platform. Several tour operators use the site (90 pitches).

Facilities: Two older, split-level toilet blocks are of fair quality and unusual design. They include washbasins in cabins, and baby rooms. A new, impressively equipped block was opened in 2002 which provides easier access for disabled people. Dishwashing facilities in two attractive gazebo style units. Laundry room with washing machines and dryers. Good sized restaurant, takeaway, bar and well stocked shop (all open all season). Heated swimming pool (17 x 8 m), pool with water slides and paddling pool. Small beach on the river (unfenced). Tennis courts, table tennis, pool tables, archery and trampolines. Exciting adventure play park. Riding. Small roller skating rink. Bicycle hire. Skateboards, roller skates and boat hire. Fishing. Canoe expeditions. High season entertainment.

Charges 2002

Per person	€ 5.70
child (under 7 yrs)	€ 3.60
pitch	€ 12.20
electricity	€ 4.60
water/drainage	€ 6.50
animal	€ 3.00

Less 15-30% outside July/Aug. **Tel:** 02 98 71 75 47. Fax: 02 98 71 77 31. E-mail: TY-NADAN@wanadoo.fr. **Reservations:** Made for exact dates with deposit (€ 50) and fee (€ 25). **Open** 15 May - 5 September.

Directions: Make for Arzano which is northeast of Quimperlé on the Pontivy road and turn off D22 just west of village at camp sign. Site is approx. 3 km.

the only campsite where you can do this...

i comme... 33(2) 98 10 19 20

www.camping-ty-nadan.fr

Camping-Caravaning Le Pil-Koad
route de Douarnenez, Poullan-sur-Mer, 29100 Douarnenez

Pil Koad is an attractive, family run site just back from the sea near Douarnenez in Finistère. It has 190 pitches on fairly flat ground, marked out by separating hedges and of quite good, though varying, size and shape. The site also has a number of mobile homes and chalets. Nearly all pitches have electrical connections (10A) and original trees provide shade in some areas. A large room, the 'Woodpecker Bar', is used for entertainment with discos and cabaret in July and August. The gates are closed 10.30 - 07.00 hrs. A variety of beaches is within easy reach, with the coast offering some wonderful scenery and good for walking.

Facilities: Two main toilet blocks in modern style include mainly British style WCs and washbasins mostly in cabins. Laundry facilities. Motorcaravan service point. Gas supplies. Small shop for basics (16/6-8/9). Takeaway (23/6-1/9). Heated swimming pool and paddling pool (no bermuda-style shorts). Tennis court. Table tennis, minigolf and volleyball. Fishing. Bicycle hire. Playground. Weekly outings and clubs for children (30/6-30/8) with charge included in tariff. **Off site:** Riding 4 km. Restaurants in village 500 m. Nearest sandy beach 4 km. Douarnenez 6 km.

Charges 2002

Per person	€ 3.00 - € 5.00
child (under 7 yrs)	€ 1.50 - € 3.00
pitch	€ 6.00 - € 12.00
electricity (10A)	€ 3.50
dog	€ 1.50 - € 2.50
local tax (over 16 yrs from 1/7-31/8)	€ 0.15

Tel: 02 98 74 26 39. Fax: 02 98 74 55 97. E-mail: camping.pil.koad@wanadoo.fr. **Reservations:** Made for min. 1 week with 25% deposit and fee (€ 19). **Open** 1 May - 15 September.

Directions: Site is 500 m. east from the centre of Poullan on D7 road towards Douarnenez. From Douarnenez take circular bypass route towards Audierne; if you see road for Poullan sign at round about, take it, otherwise there is camping sign at turning to Poullan from the D765 road.

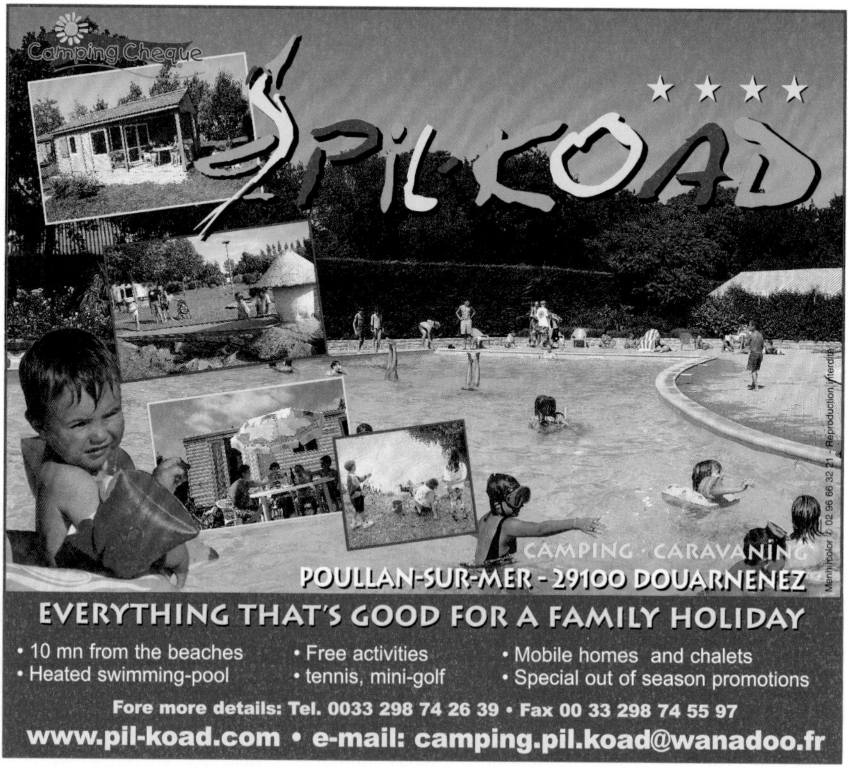

France - Brittany
Camping Le Panoramic
route de la Plage Penker, 29560 Telgruc-sur-Mer

This medium sized, ten acre site is situated on quite a steep hillside, with fine views along the coast. It is well tended and personally run by M. Jacq and his family who all speak good English. The site is in two parts, divided by a fairly quiet road leading to a good beach. The main upper site is where most of the facilities are situated, with the swimming pool, terrace and a playground located with the lower pitches across the road. Some up-and-down walking is therefore necessary, but this is a small price to pay for such pleasant and comfortable surroundings. The 220 pitches are arranged on flat, shady terraces, mostly in small groups with hedges and flowering shrubs and 20 pitches have services for motorcaravans. A good area for lovely coastal footpaths. Used by tour operators (20 pitches). A `Sites et Paysages` member.

Facilities: The main site has two well kept toilet blocks with another good block across the road. All include washbasins in cubicles, facilities for disabled people, baby baths, dishwashing, plus washing machines and dryers. Motorcaravan services. Small shop (1/7-31/8). Bar/restaurant withtakeaway (1/7-31/8). Barbecue area. Heated swimming pool, children`s pool and jacuzzi (all 15/5-7/9). Playground. Games and TV rooms. Children`s club in season. Tennis courts, volleyball. Bicycle hire. **Off site:** Riding 6 km, golf 14 km. Sailing school nearby. Good sandy beach 700 m. downhill by road, bit less on foot.

Charges 2003

Per person	€ 5.00
child (under 7 yrs)	€ 3.00
pitch	€ 10.00
electricity (6-10A)	€ 3.10 - € 4.50
local tax (over 10 yrs)	€ 0.40

Less 20% outside July/Aug. No credit cards. **Tel:** 02 98 27 78 41. Fax: 02 98 27 36 10. **Reservations:** Contact site. **Open** 15 June- 10 September.

Directions: Site is south of Telgruc-sur-Mer. On D887 pass through Ste Marie du Ménez Horn. In 11 km. turn left on D208 signed Telgruc-sur-Mer. Continue through the town and site is 1 km.

France - Brittany
Camping Village La Plage
rue de Men-Meur BP 9, 29730 Le Guilvinec

La Plage is a friendly site located beside a long sandy beach between the fishing town of Le Guilvinec and the watersports beaches of Penmarc'h on the southwest tip of Brittany. It is spacious and surrounded by tall trees, which provide shelter, and is made up of several flat, sandy meadows. The 410 pitches (189 for touring units) are arranged on either side of sandy access roads, mostly not separated but all numbered. There is less shade in the newer areas. Electricity is available on most pitches (2, 6 or 10A). Like all beachside sites, the facilities receive heavy usage. There is plenty to occupy one at this friendly site but the bustling fishing harbour at Le Guilvinec and the watersports of Penmarc'h and Pointe de la Torche are within easy travelling distance. Used by tour operators (89 pitches). A Yelloh Village member.

Facilities: Five sanitary blocks are of differing designs but all provide modern, bright facilities including washbasins in cabins, good facilities for children and toilets for disabled people. Laundry facilities. Motorcaravan service point. Shop with gas supplies. Bar, crêperie and takeaway. Heated swimming pool with paddling pool and water slide. Sauna. Play area. TV room. Tennis courts. Volleyball, basketball, minigolf, badminton, petanque, table tennis, giant chess/draughts. Bicycle hire. **Off site:** Fishing and watersports near. Riding 5 km. Golf 20 km.

Charges 2002

Per unit incl. 2 persons, electricity	€ 17.00 - € 31.00
extra person	€ 2.00 - € 5.00
electricity (10A)	€ 0.70
local tax (over 16 yrs)	€ 0.15

Tel: 02 98 58 61 90. Fax: 02 98 58 89 06. E-mail: info@campingsbretagnesud.com. **Reservations:** Advised and accepted until 15/6 with deposit (25%) and fee (€ 19). **Open** 4 May - 8 September.

Directions: Site is west of Guilvinec. From Pont l'Abbé, take the D785 road towards Penmarc'h. In Plomeur, turn left on D57 signed Guilvinec. On entering Guilvinec fork right signed Port and camping. Follow road along coast to site on left.

Camping Village Le Manoir de Kerlut

29740 Plobannalec-Lesconil

2912

the travel service
TO BOOK
Ferry ✔
Pitch ✔
Accommodation ✗
01892 55 98 98

Le Manoir de Kerlut is a comfortable site in the grounds of a manor house on a river estuary near Pont l'Abbe. The old 'manoir' is not open to the public, but is used occasionally for weddings and private functions. Opened in '89, the campsite has neat, modern buildings and is laid out on flat grass providing 240 pitches (90 for touring units). All have electricity connections (5, 6 or 10A), some also have water and drainage and around ten pitches have hardstanding. One area is rather open with separating hedges planted, the other part being amongst more mature bushes and some trees which provide shade. Site amenities are of good quality. Used by tour operators (38 pitches). A Yelloh Village member.

Facilities: Toilet facilities in two good blocks, each with several rooms (not all open outside July/Aug) include washbasins all in cabins, and facilities for babies and disabled people. Laundry. Small shop. Takeaway. Large modern bar with TV (satellite) and entertainment all season. Bar in the Manoir. Two heated swimming pools, children's pool and water slide. Sauna, solarium and small gym. Play area. Tennis, volleyball, badminton and petanque. Games room. Bicycle hire. Gates closed 22.30 - 7.30 hrs.
Off site: Fishing 2 km, riding 5 km, golf 15 km.

Charges 2002

Per unit incl. 2 persons and 5A electricity	€ 17.00 - € 31.00
extra person	€ 3.00 - € 5.00
child (under 7 yrs)	€ 2.00 - € 3.00
electricity (10A)	€ 0.70
dog	€ 2.00 - € 3.00
local tax (over 16 yrs)	€ 0.15

Tel: 02 98 82 23 89. Fax: 02 98 82 26 49. E-mail: info@campingsbretagnesud.com. **Reservations:** Write to site with deposit (€ 45) and fee (€ 19). **Open** 1 May - 9 September, with all services.

Directions: From Pont l'Abbé, on D785, take D102 road towards Lesconil. Site is signed on the left, shortly after the village of Plobannalec.

Camping Les Prés Verts

Kernous-Plage, 29900 Concarneau

2919

What sets this family site apart from the many others in this region are its more unusual features - its stylish pool complex with Romanesque style columns and statue, and its plants and flower tubs. The 150 pitches are mostly arranged on long, open, grassy areas either side of main access roads. Specimen trees, shrubs or hedges divide the site into smaller areas. There are a few individual pitches and an area towards the rear of the site where the pitches have sea views. Concarneau is just 2.5 km. and there are numerous marked coastal walks to enjoy in the area, plus watersports or boat and fishing trips available nearby. A 'Sites et Paysages' member.

Facilities: Two toilet blocks provide unisex WCs, but separate washing facilities for ladies and men. Preset hot showers and washbasins in cabins for ladies, both closed 21.00 - 08.00 hrs. Some child size toilets. Dishwashing and laundry sinks, washing machine and dryer. Pizza service twice weekly. Swimming pool (1/6-31/8; around 18 x 11 m.) and children's pool. Playground (0-5 yrs only). Minigolf. Path to sandy/rocky beach (300 m.) and coastal path. **Off site:** Supermarket 2 km. Riding 1 km, bicycle hire 3 km, golf 5 km.

Charges 2003

Per unit incl. 2 adults	€ 16.48 - € 20.60
extra adult	€ 4.76 - € 5.95
child (2-7 yrs)	€ 3.12 - € 3.90
dog	€ 1.16 - € 1.45
electricity (2-6A)	€ 2.90 - € 4.43
local tax	€ 0.25

Tel: 02 98 97 09 74. Fax: 02 98 97 32 06. E-mail: info@pres-verts.com. **Reservations:** Contact site for details. **Open** 1 May - 22 September.

Directions: Turn off C7 road, 2.5 km. north of Concarneau, where site is signed. Take third left after Hotel de l'Océan.

Camping Club du Saint-Laurent

Kerleven, 29940 La Forêt-Fouesnant

2902

Saint-Laurent is a well established site, situated on a sheltered wooded slope bordering one of the many attractive little inlets that typify the Brittany coastline. There is direct access from the site to two small sandy bays, which empty at low tide to reveal numerous rockpools (ideal for children to explore), and the site is on the coastal footpath that leads from Kerleven to Concarneau. The 260 pitches are on levelled terraces, under tall trees. All pitches are divided by hedging, have electrical connections (6A), are partly shaded and are of average size (100 sq.m.). Pitches with the best sea views tend to be adjacent to the cliff edge, and may not be suitable for families with young children. Access to some pitches can also be a little difficult, but the friendly site owners ensure that this is not a problem by offering to site any caravan using their own 4 x 4 vehicle. The swimming pool (complete with paddling pool and two water slides) is overlooked by the bar terrace. With organised activities and entertainment in high season, this site is an ideal choice for a lively family holiday, particularly for older children. Around 50% of the pitches are occupied by tour operators or site owned mobile homes.

Facilities: Two sanitary blocks provide combined shower and washbasin cubicles, separate washbasin cubicles, baby changing and facilities for disabled people. Laundry and dishwashing sinks. Washing machines, dryers and ironing facilities in newly refurbished room. Small shop at reception provides essentials. Bar,snack bar and takeaway (all 12/5-10/9). Swimming pools. Gym and sauna. Canoe hire. Basketball, two tennis courts (no charge), and table tennis. Children's play area. During July and August daily children's clubs and adult entertainments are organised (in English as well as in French), with discos in the bar each evening.

Charges 2002

Per unit incl. 1 or 2 persons, electricity and water	€ 15.24 - € 23.63
extra person over 7 yrs	€ 2.29 - € 4.27
child 2-7 yrs	€ 1.52 - € 3.05
dog	free - € 1.83
extra car	€ 1.52 - € 3.05

Tel: 02 98 56 97 65. Fax: 02 98 56 92 51.
Reservations: Advised for July/Aug. and made with deposit (€ 77) and fee (€ 22,87). **Open** 11 May - 14 September.

Directions: From N165 take D70 Concarneau exit. At first roundabout take first exit D44 (Fouesnant). After 2.5 km. turn right at T junction, follow for 2.5 km, then turn left (Port La Forêt - take care - 200 m. before the junction is a sign that implies Port La Forêt is straight on, and it isn't). Continue to round about, straight ahead (Port La Forêt) and after 1 km. turn left (site signed here). In 400 m left turn to site at end of this road.

Castel Camping L'Orangerie de Lanniron

Château de Lanniron, 29336 Quimper

2905

the travel service
TO BOOK
Ferry ✔
Pitch ✔
Accommodation ✔
01892 55 98 98

L'Orangerie is a beautiful and peaceful, family site in 10 acres of a XVIIth century, 42 acre country estate on the banks of the Odet river. It is just to the south of Quimper and about 15 km. from the sea and beaches at Bénodet. The family have a five year programme to restore and rehabilitate the park, the original canal, fountains, ornamental Lake of Neptune, the boat-house and the gardens and avenues. The original outbuildings have been attractively converted around a walled courtyard. The site has 200 grassy pitches, 149 for touring units, of three types (varying in size and services) on fairly flat ground laid out in rows alongside access roads. Most have electricity and 32 have all three services, with shrubs and bushes providing pleasant pitches. The restaurant in the beautiful XVIIth century Orangerie, and the Gardens are both open to the public and in Spring the rhododendrons and azaleas are magnificent, with lovely walks within the grounds and a riverside walk to town. Used by tour operators (45 pitches). All facilities are available when the site is open.

Facilities: The main heated block in the courtyard has been totally refurbished and is excellent. A second modern block serves the newer pitches at the top of the site and includes facilities for disabled people and babies. Washing machines and dryers. Motorcaravan service point. Shop (all season), Gas supplies. Bar, snacks and takeaway, plus restaurant (open daily from 20/5, reasonably priced with children's menu). Heated swimming pool (144 sq.m.) with children's pool. New pool planned. Small play area. Tennis. Minigolf, attractively set among mature trees. Table tennis. Fishing. Archery. Bicycle hire. General reading, games and billiards rooms. TV/video room (cable and satellite). Karaoke. Animation provided including outdoor activities with large room for indoor activities. **Off site:** Sea 15 km. Historic town of Quimper under 3 km. Two hypermarkets 1 km.

Charges 2002

Per adult	€ 5.40
child (2-7 yrs)	€ 3.50
pitch (100 sq.m.)	€ 12.50
with electricity (10A)	€ 16.20
special pitch (120/150sq.m.)	
with water and electricity	€ 19.00
animal	€ 3.50

Less 15% outside July/Aug. **Tel:** 02 98 90 62 02. Fax: 02 98 52 15 56. E-mail: camping@lanniron.com. **Reservations:** Made with deposit (€ 61) and fee (€ 19). **Open** 15 May - 15 September.

Directions: From Quimper follow 'Quimper Sud' signs, then 'Toutes Directions' and general camping signs, finally signs for Lanniron.

Camping du Letty

2903 29950 Bénodet

Built around their former farm, the Guyader family have ensured that this excellent and attractive site, with direct beach access, has plenty to offer for all the family. The site on the outskirts of the popular resort of Bénodet spreads over 22 acres with 493 pitches, all for touring units. Groups of eight to ten pitches are set in cul-de-sacs with mature hedging and trees to divide each cul-de-sac. Markers indicate the limits of each pitch which are slightly smaller than average (none more than about 80 sq.m), although they do not feel too small since they are not hedged or fenced. Most pitches have electricity (up to 10A), fresh and waste water connections. At the attractive floral entrance, former farm buildings provide a host of facilities including an extensively equipped fitness room. There is also a modern, purpose built nightclub and bar providing high quality live entertainment most evenings (situated well away from most pitches to avoid disturbance). Although there is no swimming pool here, the site has direct access to a small sandy beach, and has provided a floating pontoon with diving platform and water slides into the sea (safe bathing depends on the tides).

Facilities: Six well placed toilet blocks around the site, are of good quality with modern fittings. They include mixed style WCs, washbasins in large cabins and controllable hot showers (charged). Laundry and dishwashing sinks. Three well equipped baby changing rooms. Separate facility for disabled visitors. Launderette. Hairdressing room. Motorcaravan service points. Well stocked and reasonably priced minimarket, including butchery counter. Extensive snack bar and takeaway (22/6-30/8). Bar with games room and night club. Library/reading room. Games lounge with billiard and card tables and entertainment room with satellite TV. Fitness centre (no charge). Saunas, jacuzzis and solarium (all on payment). Table tennis. Two tennis and two squash courts (charged). Boules, volleyball, basketball and archery. Well equipped children's play area. In July/Aug. entertainment and activities organised for the whole family.

Charges 2003

Per adult	€ 4.50
child (under 7 yrs)	€ 2.25
pitch	€ 7.00
car or motorcaravan	€ 1.70
m/cycle	€ 1.20
electricity (1, 2, 5 or 10A)	€ 1.50 - € 4.00
dog	€ 2.30
local tax	€ 0.23 - € 0.46

Tel: 02 98 57 04 69. **Fax:** 02 98 66 22 56. **E-mail:** reception@campingduletty.com. **Reservations:** Not made. **Open** 15 June - 6 September.

Directions: From N165 take D70 Concarneau exit. At first roundabout take D44 to Fouesnant. Turn right at T junction. After about 2 km. turn left to Fouesnant (still D44). Continue through La Forêt Fouesnant and Fouesnant, picking up signs for Bénodet. Shortly before Benodet at roundabout turn left (signed Le Letty). Turn right at next mini round about and site is 500 m. on left.

Camping Village Le Grand Large

2929 48 route du Grand Large, Mousterlin, 29170 Fouesnant

the travel service
TO BOOK
Ferry ✓
Pitch ✓
Accommodation ✗
01892 55 98 98

Le Grand Large is a beach-side site situated on the Pointe de Mousterlin in natural surroundings. The site is separated from the beach by the road that follows the coast around the point. It is also protected from the wind by an earth bank with trees and a fence. The beach itself looks over the bay towards the Isles de Glénan. There are 300 level grass pitches of average size and rather sandy in places with some shrubs and mature trees. Tour operators take 44 places and the site itself has 96 tents and mobile homes to rent. Electricity is available everywhere (long leads useful) and some pitches have drainage. A small river runs through the site but it is fenced. Benodet (7 km) and Fouesnant (5 km) are near in different directions and the sandy beach is just up the steps and across the road. A family site, would also suit walkers and nature lovers in the low seasons as it is adjacent to a large tract of protected land, Marais de Mousterlin, ideal for walking, cycling and birdwatching.

Facilities: Two neat, new sanitary blocks include plenty of washbasins in cabins (warm water only). Two baby baths in the larger block with children's shower and toilet and facilities for disabled people in both blocks. Two washing machines, two dryers and plenty of laundry and washing up sinks (hot water only). Bar overlooks the sea with attractive terrace and a crêperie/grill restaurant that also provides takeaway food. Swimming pool with paddling pool, water slides in a separate pool. Tennis court and multi-sport court where it is possible to play 5-a-side football, badminton, volleyball, handball or basketball. Small play area. TV room and games room with table tennis and billiards.

Charges 2002

Per unit incl. 2 persons and 5A electricity	€ 17.00 - € 31.00
extra person	€ 3.00 - € 5.00
child (under 7 yrs)	€ 2.00 - € 3.00
electricity (10A)	€ 0.70
local tax (over 16 yrs)	€ 0.15
dog	€ 2.00 - € 3.00

Tel: 02 98 56 04 06. **Fax:** 02 98 56 58 26. **E-mail:** info@campingsbretagnesud.com. **Reservations:** Made with deposit (€ 45) and non-refundable fee (€ 19). **Open** 4 May (may be later for 2003) - 8 September.

Directions: Site is 7 km. south of Fouesnant. Turn off N165 expressway at Coat Conq, signed Concarneau and Fouesnant. At Fouesnant take A45 signed Beg Meil, then follow signs to Mousterlin. In Mousterlin turn left and follow camping signs.

Camping Le Vieux Chêne

3500 Baguer-Pican, 35120 Dol-de-Bretagne

the travel service
TO BOOK
Ferry ✓
Pitch ✓
Accommodation ✗
01892 55 98 98

This attractive, family owned site is situated between St Malo and Mont St Michel. Developed in the grounds of a country farmhouse dating from 1638, its young and enthusiastic owner has created a really pleasant, traditional atmosphere with a very personal feel. It offers 200 good sized pitches, most with electricity, water tap and light, in spacious rural surroundings on gently sloping grass. They are separated by bushes and flowers, with mature trees for shade. A very attractive tenting area (without electricity) is in the orchard. There are three lakes in the grounds and centrally located leisure facilities include an attractive pool complex. Some entertainment is provided in high season, free for children. Used by a Dutch tour operator (10 pitches).

Facilities: Three very good, unisex toilet blocks include washbasins in cabins, a baby room and facilities for disabled people. All recently been refurbished and can be heated. Small laundry with washing machine, dryer and iron. Motorcaravan services. Shop. Takeaway. Café with terrace overlooking the pools (all season). Medium sized, heated swimming pool, children's pool, toboggans, slides, etc. (17/5-14/9; lifeguard July/Aug). TV (satellite) and games rooms. Tennis court, minigolf, giant chess. Play area. Riding in July/Aug. Fishing is possible in two of the three lakes. **Off site:** Supermarket 3 km. Golf 12 km.

Charges 2002

Per unit	€ 7.00 - € 13.50
adult	€ 4.50
child (under 10 yrs)	€ 3.00
electricity (5A)	€ 3.50

Tel: 02 99 48 09 55. Fax: 02 99 48 13 37. E-mail: vieux.chene@wanadoo.fr. **Reservations:** Made with deposit (€ 30) and fee (€ 15). **Open** 1 April - 1 October.

Directions: Site is by the D576 Dol-de-Bretagne - Pontorson road, just east of Baguer-Pican. It can be reached from the new N176 taking exit for Dol-Est and Baguer-Pican.

BRITTANY

★★★★
Camping - Caravaning
le Vieux Chêne

BAGUER PICAN
35120 DOL DE BRETAGNE
TÉL. 0033 2 99 48 09 55
FAX 0033 2 99 48 13 37
Website: www.camping-vieuxchene.fr

- *200 pitches,*
- *Tennis,*
- *Aquatic Park,*
- *Fishing ponds,*
- *Mini-golf,*
- *Mini-club,*
- *Snack-bar, Shop,*
- *Ponies...*

Castel Camping Le Pré du Château de Careil

4403 33 rue du Château, Careil, 44350 Guérande

This site is totally different from the more usual Castel sites. It is the smallest site in the group and has few of the facilities or activities usually associated with these sites. It has a quiet atmosphere and is very popular with couples, retired people and those with young children (it is not really recommended for families with older children or teenagers). In the grounds of the Château de Careil, a building dating from the 14th century which may be visited, this small site, shaded by mature trees, contains just 50 good sized pitches. All are equipped with electricity (6/10A) and water, some with drainage also.

Facilities: The main refurbished toilet facilities in the main building include four unisex shower and washbasin rooms. En-suite facilities for disabled people, baby room and washing machine. In season (15/6-5/9) some emergency provisions are kept and bread can be ordered. Small pool (11 x 5 m. open 15/6-5/9). Playground. TV room. Volleyball and table tennis. Archery occasionally. **Off site:** Supermarket near. Fishing or golf 10 km, bicycle hire 2 km, riding 5 km. In July/Aug. tours of the Château are possible.

Charges 2002

Per unit incl. 2 persons, electricity	€ 17.00 - € 20.00
extra person	€ 3.00 - € 4.50
electricity (10A)	€ 1.60
local tax	€ 0.23 - € 0.46

No credit cards. **Tel:** 02 40 60 22 99. Fax: 02 40 60 22 99. E-mail: chateau.careil@free.fr. **Reservations:** Possible with deposit (€ 21,34) and booking fee (€ 15,24). **Open** 1 May - 30 September.

Directions: Take D92 from Guérande to La Baule and turn east to Careil before the town. From D99 Guérande - St Nazaire road, turn onto D92, following signs to 'Intermarche' and for Château de Careil. Take care as gate is fairly narrow and between two bends making access a little awkward.

Castel Camping Château du Deffay

BP 18 Le Deffay, Ste Reine de Bretagne, 44160 Pontchâteau

4409

A family owned site, Château de Deffay is a refreshing departure from the usual Castel formula in that it is not over organised or supervised and has no tour operator units. The landscape is natural to encourage wildlife, right down to the molehills, and the site blends well with the rural environment of the estate, lake and farmland which surround it. For these reasons it is enjoyed by many. However, with the temptation of free pedaloes and the fairly deep, unfenced lake, parents should ensure that children are supervised. The 120 good sized, somewhat uneven pitches have pleasant views and are either on open grass, on shallow terraces divided by hedges, or informally arranged in a central, slightly sloping wooded area. Most have 6A electricity. The facilities are situated within the old courtyard area of the smaller château (that dates from before 1400). The larger château (built 1880) and another lake stand away from this area providing pleasant walking. The reception has been built separately to contain the camping area. Alpine type chalets overlook the lake and fit well with the environment.

Facilities: The main sanitary unit, housed in a converted barn, is well equipped including washbasins in cabins, provision for disabled people and a baby bathroom. Washing machines, and dryer. Maintenance can be variable and, with the boiler located at one end of the block, hot water can take time to reach the other in low season. Extra facilities are in the courtyard area where the well stocked shop, bar, small restaurant with takeaway and solar heated swimming pool and paddling pool are located (all 15/5-15/9). Play area for children. TV in the bar, separate room for table tennis. English language animation in season including children's mini club. Torches useful. **Off site:** Golf 5 km. Close to the Brière Regional Park, the Guérande Peninsula, and La Baule with its magnificent beach.

Charges guide

Per pitch	€ 5.95 - € 8.99
with electricity (6A)	€ 9.15 - € 12.20
with 3 services	€ 10.52 - € 13.72
per adult	€ 2.44 - € 3.90
child (2-12 yrs)	€ 1.68 - € 2.59

Tel: 02 40 88 00 57. Fax: 02 40 01 66 55. E-mail: info@camping-le-deffay.com. **Reservations:** Accepted with deposit (€ 10 per day) and fee (€ 16). **Open** 1 May - 21 September.

Directions: Site is signed from D33 Pontchâteau - Herbignac road near Ste. Reine. Also signed from the D773 and N165.

France - Brittany
Camping de La Plage

5602 Plage de Kervilaine, 56470 La Trinité-sur-Mer

The area of Carnac/La Trinité is popular with holiday makers and the two La Trinité sites of La Plage and La Baie have the great advantage of direct access to a good sandy beach. Both sites are owned by the same family, and each is very well maintained, both having a small (12m.) heated pool with a slide. The grassy pitches, which have electricity (6/10A) and water (70% with drainage also), are separated by hedges and shrubs and at La Plage there are attractive flower beds. Situated on a low cliff, the terrace with its views across the bay is a very popular place for a meal or a drink. Reception areas are welcoming and friendly with tourist information on display. The village of La Trinité is about an hours walk away along the cliff path and ten minutes (approx) by car. Carnac is about 10-15 minutes drive in the opposite direction.

Facilities: The sanitary blocks have washbasins in cubicles, facilities for the disabled and small children. Washing machines and dryers. Well provided shop with bakery outlet. Bar, restaurant, crêperie, take-away. Lively entertainment programme in high season that caters for all ages and some evening entertainment in nearby disco. Good children's play areas including ball pool. Tennis, basketball, minigolf, table tennis. Large TV screen. Hire of sailboards and bikes. Guided tours on foot or bicycle. Internet access available. Small communal barbecue areas, otherwise only gas ones are allowed on pitches. Both sites have a number of tour operators.

Charges 2002

Per pitch incl. 2 persons	€ 15.60 - € 27.60
extra adult	€ 4.00
child (2-18 yrs)	€ 2.00
electricity (6/10A)	€ 1.80 - € 3.25
dog	free - 1.05

Tel: 02 97 55 73 28. Fax: 02 97 55 88 31. E-mail: laplage@club-internet.fr. **Reservations:** Contact site. **Open** 8 May - 15 September.

Directions: Site is signed in different places from D186 coast road from La Trinité to Carnac-Plage.

France - Brittany
Camping La Vallée du Ninian

5616 Le Rocher, 56800 Taupont

M. and Mme. Joubaud developed this peaceful family run site in central Brittany from a farm area in the eighties and take care to ensure that everyone has an enjoyable holiday. The level site falls into the three areas - the orchard with 32 large, hedged pitches with electricity, the wood with about 13 pitches more suited to tents, and the meadow by the river providing a further 35 pitches delineated by small trees and shrubs, some with electricity. The shop has, as a centre-piece, a working cider press with which M. Joubaud makes his own 'potion magique'. The adjoining covered bar area is the venue for song and dance evenings with a Breton flavour and occasional camp fire sing-songs are organised.

Facilities: The central building houses unisex toilet facilities including washbasins in cubicles, large cubicle with facilities for disabled visitors and laundry area with washing machines, dryer and ironing board. Covered dishwashing area with hot water. Shop selling basic provisions. Small (7 x 12 m) heated swimming pool. Swings and slides, large trampoline, popular with children.

Charges 2002

Per pitch incl. vehicle	€ 5.00
adult	€ 3.10
child (under 7 yrs)	€ 2.30
electricity 3/6A	€ 1.60 - € 3.10
local tax	€ 0.08 - € 0.15

Tel: 02 97 93 53 01. Fax: 02 97 93 57 27. **Reservations:** Contact site. **Open** 1 May - 30 September.

Directions: From Ploërmel centre follow signs to Taupont north on the N8. Continue through village of Taupont and turn left (east) signed Vallée du Ninian. Follow road until 1 km. before Hellean. From Josselin follow signs for Hellean. Go through village and turn sharp right after the bridge over the river Ninian. Site is 400 m. on the right.

France - Normandy
Camping de la Vallée

88 rue de la Vallée, 14510 Houlgate

Camping de la Vallée is an attractive site with good, well maintained facilities. Situated on a grassy hillside overlooking Houlgate, the 278 pitches (180 for touring units) are large and open. Hedges have been planted and all have electricity. Part of the site is sloping, the rest level, with gravel or tarmac roads. An old farmhouse has been converted to house a new bar and comfortable TV lounge and billiards room. English is spoken in season. Used by tour operators (55 pitches). Very busy in high season, maintenance and cleaning could be variable at that time. The town is 900 m, the beach 1 km.

Facilities: Three good toilet blocks include washbasins in cabins, mainly British style toilets, facilities for disabled people and baby room. Dishwashing, laundry with machines, dryers and ironing boards (no washing lines allowed). Motorcaravan services. Shop (from 1/5). Bar. Snack bar with takeaway in season (from 15/5). Heated pool (from 15/5; no shorts). Playground. Bicycle hire. Volleyball, football field, tennis, petanque. Entertainment in July/Aug. **Off site:** Fishing 1 km. Riding 500 m. Golf 2 km.

Charges 2002

Per unit incl. 2 persons, electricity	€ 16.00 - € 25.00
extra adult	€ 5.00 - € 6.00
child (under 7 yrs)	€ 2.50 - € 3.00
dog	€ 3.00

Credit card minimum € 76. **Tel:** 02 31 24 40 69. Fax: 02 31 24 42 42. E-mail: camping.lavallee@wanadoo.fr. **Reservations:** Made with deposit and fee. **Open** 1 April - 30 September.

Directions: From A13 take exit for Cabourg and follow signs for Dives/Houlgate going straight on at roundabout. Follow road straight on at next round about, and then four sets of traffic lights. Turn left along seafront. After 1 km. at lights turn right, carry on for about 1 km. and over mini-roundabout - look for site sign and flag poles on right.

CAMPING CARAVANING

LA VALLÉE
★★★★

88, Rue de la Vallée
14510 Houlgate
Tel: 0033 231.24.40.69
Fax: 0033 231.28.08.29

□ SHOP □ BAR □ GAMES ROOM
□ TENNIS □ HEATED SWIMMING POOL
□ CHILDREN'S POOL □ ENTERTAINMENT

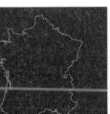

France - Normandy
Camping Municipal Cany-Barville

76450 Cany-Barville

This good quality site, first opened in 1997 adjacent to the municipal sports stadium, has a floral entrance and tarmac roads. Of the 100 individual hedged pitches around 74 are available for tourists. There are around 40 concrete hardstandings and the remainder are on grass, all are fully serviced with water, drain and electric hook-ups (10A). As yet, there is not very much shade from the young specimen trees. Cany-Barville is a bustling small town with a traditional Normandy market on Monday mornings. There is a Château and an Eco-museum (1/4-30/10), and the Durdent valley has numerous other châteaux, mills, churches and 'colombiers'.

Facilities: The modern, centrally located, sanitary unit can be heated and has some washbasins in cubicles. Dishwashing and laundry sinks. Separate suites for disabled people. Motorcaravan service point with chemical disposal facility. Table tennis, volleyball, boules. **Off site:** Sailing and windsurfing centre 2 km. Beach 10 km. Supermarket 1 km.

Charges 2002

Per adult	€ 2.20
child (under 14 yrs)	€ 0.95
pitch	€ 2.40
animal	€ 0.80
electricity	€ 2.40

Tel: 02 35 97 70 37. **Reservations:** Advisable in July and August. **Open** all year.

Directions: From traffic lights on eastern side of town turn off D925 on to D268 towards Yvetot. Go under railway arch and continue straight on. Site is 600 m. from town centre adjacent to sports field.

Camping du Domaine Catinière

2702 Route de Honfleur, 27210 Fiquefleur-Equainville

A peaceful, friendly site, convenient for Le Havre ferries, this is a developing site with new owners (1998) who are intent on improving this countryside site which lies in the middle of a very long village. The site is steadily achieving a modern look, whilst retaining its original French flavour. There some privately owned mobile homes, but there should be around 85 pitches for tourists including a large open field for tents and units not needing electricity. Caravan pitches are separated, some with shade, others are more open and all have electricity hook-ups (4, 6, or 10A). The site is divided by well fenced streams, popular with young anglers. The site is a good base for a short break to visit this part of Normandy, with the pretty harbour town of Honfleur less than 5 km., and the nearby Vallée de la Risle. It is only a short distance from the ferry terminal, and makes every effort to meet the demands of ferry users.

Facilities: Already modernised, the toilet facilities include some washbasins in cubicles, and facilities for disabled people and babies. Reception with shop. Small bar/restaurant with regional dishes and snacks. Heated swimming pool (mid-June - end Aug). Two children's playgrounds, trampoline, table tennis, and boules court. New barrier (card deposit). **Off site:** Large supermarket is also close to the southern end of the bridge.

Charges 2003

Per adult	€ 4.20
child (under 7 yrs)	€ 2.50
pitch	€ 5.00
electricity (4/10A)	€ 3.50 - € 4.70
dog	€ 2.00

Tel: (0)2 32 57 63 51. **Fax:** (0)2 32 42 12 57. **E-mail:** info@camping-catiniere.com. **Reservations:** Advisable for high season, made with deposit of € 39 per week. **Open** 1 April - 30 September.

Directions: From Le Havre ferry terminal follow signs to the Pont de Normandie. From the southern end of the bridge, take D580 / D180 towards Toutainville for 2.5 km., then take D22 (right) towards Beuzeville for 1 km., and site is on right.

Domaine de la Catinière

Is situated 5 km from Honfleur and 25 km from le Havre in a quiet and green valley.

You are welcome from the 1st April till the 30th september.

MOBILE HOMES FOR HIRE

Route d'Honfleur D22
27210 Fiquefleur Equainville
Tel: 0033 232 576 351 - Fax: 0033 232 421 257
E-mail: info@camping-catiniere.com
Website: www.camping-catiniere.com

Camping Municipal Guignicourt

0206M 02190 Guignicourt

This very pleasant little municipal site has 100 pitches, 50 for long stay units and 50 for tourists. The manager takes great pride in his site, which is clean and tidy with many floral displays. Pitches are generally large and level, although you might need an extra long electric lead for some, but there are few dividing hedges. Pitches along the river bank have most shade, with a few specimen trees providing a little shade to some of the more open pitches. The town is quite attractive and is worthy of an evening stroll. At the junction of the N44 and D925, 7 km. west of the town, is the Chemin des Dames, Monument des Chars d'Assaut - a memorial to the WW1 tank campaign at Berry-au-Bac.

Facilities: The modern sanitary unit has British and Turkish style Toilets, washbasins (cold only except for the one in a cubicle), push-button hot showers, dishwashing and laundry sinks. Playground, tennis and boules courts, and fishing. **Off site:** The town has all services including a supermarket and bank. You may notice a low level hum from the nearby Generale Sucrière factory, a major industry of the town. Golf nearby.

Charges 2002

Per adult	€ 1.80
child (2-10 yrs)	€ 1.00
pitch	€ 2.00 - € 3.10
animal	€ 1.15
electricity (6/10A)	€ 2.75 - € 4.60

Tel: 03 23 79 74 58. **Reservations:** Contact site for details. **Open** 1 April - 30 September.

Directions: Guignicourt is about 20 km. north of Reims, just east of the A26, junction 14. The site is well signed from D925 in the village.

Camping-Caravaning du Vivier aux Carpes

10 rue Charles Voyeux, 02790 Seraucourt-le-Grand

0200

the travel service
TO BOOK
Ferry ✓
Pitch ✓
Accommodation ✗
01892 55 98 98

Vivier aux Carpes is a small quiet site, close to the A26, two hours from Calais, so it is ideal for an overnight stop but is also worthy of a longer stay. A neat, purpose designed site is imaginatively set out taking full benefit of large ponds which are well stocked for fishing. There is also abundant wild life. The 60 well spaced pitches, are at least 100 sq.m. on flat grass with dividing hedges. The 45 for touring units all have electricity (6A), some also with water points, and there are special pitches for motorcaravans. This peaceful site has a comfortable feel and is close to the village centre. The enthusiastic owners and the manager speak excellent English and are keen to welcome British visitors. The cathedral cities of St Quentin, Reims, Amiens and Laon are close, Disneyland just over an hour away, Compiegne and the WW1 battlefields are near and Paris easily reached by train (1 hr 15 mins from St Quentin). This site is good for couples or fishing enthusiasts.

Facilities: The spacious, clean toilet block has separate, heated facilities for disabled visitors, which are made available to other campers in the winter months. Laundry facilities. Motorcaravan service point (fresh water for large vans is charged). Above the toilet block is a large TV/games room with table tennis and snooker. Small children's play area. Bicycle hire. Petanque. Fishing (about € 5,50 p/day). Gates close 22.00 hrs, office open 09.00-21.30. Rallies welcome. **Off site:** Village has post office, doctor, chemist and small supermarket. Riding 500 m. Golf 12 km.

Charges 2003

Per unit incl. 2 persons and electricity	€ 15.00
extra person	€ 2.80
child (under 10 yrs)	€ 2.00
pet	€ 0.60

Monthly, weekly or weekend rates available. Discounts for students with tents. No credit cards. **Tel:** 03 23 60 50 10. Fax: 03 23 60 51 69. E-mail: camping.du.vivier@wanadoo.fr. **Reservations:** Advised for peak season. **Open** 1 March - 30 October.

Directions: Leave A26 (Calais - Reims) road at exit 11 and take D1 left towards Soissons for 4 km. Take D8 and on entering Essigny-la-Grand (4 km.) turn sharp right on D72 signed Seraucourt-le-Grand (5 km). Site is clearly signed - it is in the centre of the village.

Camping Campix

BP 37, 60340 St-Leu-d'Esserent

6001

Opened in 1991, this informal site has been unusually developed in a former sandstone quarry on the outskirts of the small town. The quarry walls provide very different boundaries to most of the site, giving it a sheltered, peaceful environment. Trees have grown to soften the slopes. Not a neat, manicured site, the 160 pitches are arranged in small groups on the different levels with stone and gravel access roads (some fairly steep and possibly muddy in poor weather). Electricity (6A) is available to approximately 140 pitches. Torches are advised. There are very many secluded corners mostly for smaller units and tents and plenty of space for children to explore (parents must supervise - some areas, although fenced, could be dangerous). A footpath leads from the site to the town where there are shops, restaurants and an outdoor pool (in season). This site is best suited to those not needing sophisticated on-site facilities, or for visiting local places of interest and the friendly, English speaking owner will advise. These include Chantilly, the Asterix Park and the Mer de Sable, a Western theme amusements park, both 20 km. Disneyland is 70 km. It is also possible to visit Paris by train (information at reception).

Facilities: At the entrance to the site a large building houses reception and two clean, heated sanitary units - one for tourers, the other usually reserved for groups. Two suites for disabled people double as baby rooms. Laundry facilities with washing machine and dryer. At quieter times only one unit is opened but facilities may be congested at peak times. Motorcaravan service facilities. Bread and milk delivered daily. Basic snack bar operates from mobile unit (July/Aug). **Off site:** Fishing 1 or 5 km, riding or golf 5 km.

Charges 2003

Per unit	€ 3.00 - € 5.00
person	€ 3.00 - € 5.00
child (under 9 yrs)	€ 2.00 - € 3.00
small tent	€ 2.50 - € 4.00
dog	€ 1.00 - € 2.00
electricity	€ 2.50 - € 3.50

Tel: 03 44 56 08 48. Fax: 03 44 56 28 75. E-mail: campixfr@aol.com. **Reservations:** Advisable for July/Aug. **Open** 7 March - 30 November.

Directions: St Leu-d'Esserent is 11 km. west of Senlis, 5 km. northwest of Chantilly. From the north on the A1 autoroute take the Senlis exit, from Paris the Chantilly exit. Site is north of the town off the D12 towards Cramoisy, and is signed or in the village.

From St Leu via Creil
or drive 2 Creil 4 direct service

Camping Le Royon

8004 1271 route de Quend, 80790 Fort-Mahon-Plage

This busy family run site, some two kilometres from the sea, has 280 pitches of which 110 are used for touring units. Of either 95 or 120 sq.m, the marked and numbered pitches are divided by hedges and arranged either side of access roads. Electricity (6A) and water points are available to all. The site is well lit, fenced and guarded at night (€ 30 deposit for barrier card). A friendly clubroom and bar serves drinks and ices, sells bread and newspapers and has the usual games machines. Entertainment is organised for adults and children in July/Aug. The site is close to a the Baie de L'Authie which is an area noted for migrating birds.

Facilities: Four toilet blocks provide mostly unisex facilities with British or Turkish style WCs and some washbasins in cubicles. Units for disabled people. Baby baths. Dishwashing and laundry sinks under cover. Small shop (July/Aug). Mobile takeaway calls each evening in July/Aug. Clubroom. Attractive, heated, covered swimming pool (16 x 8 m; 29/4-15/9) with open air children's pool and terrace. Playground. Table tennis, multi-court, tennis court and boules. Bicycle hire. **Off site:** Fishing, riding or golf within 1 km. Windsurfing, sailing, sand yachting, canoeing nearby. Cinema, disco and casino near.

Charges 2002

Per pitch incl. water tap, electricity (6A) and 3 persons	€ 13.00 - € 25.00
extra person over 1 yr	€ 6.00
local tax (over 10 yrs)	€ 0.30
dog	€ 2.00

Tel: 03 22 23 40 30. **Fax:** 03 22 23 65 15. **E-mail:** barbara.dutot@wanadoo.fr. **Reservations:** Essential for July/Aug; made with deposit (€ 40 p/week) and fee (€ 10). **Open** 1 March - 31 October.

Directions: Site is on outskirts of Fort Mahon Plage, on D32 towards Quend.

Camping Le Val de Trie

8006 Bouillancourt-sous-Miannay, 80870 Moyenneville

the travel service
TO BOOK
Ferry ✔
Pitch ✔
Accommodation ✔
01892 55 98 98

Le Val de Trie is a natural countryside site in a woodland location, near a small village. It is maturing into a well managed site with modern facilities. The 100 numbered, grassy pitches are of a good size, divided by hedges and shrubs with mature trees providing good shade in most areas, and all have electricity (6A) and water. Access roads are gravel (the site is possibly not suitable for the largest motorcaravans). There are good walks around the area and a notice board keeps campers up to date with local market, shopping and activity news. The site has a friendly, relaxed atmosphere and English is spoken. Very much off the beaten track, it can be very quiet in April, June, September and October. If you visit at these times and there is no-one on site, just choose a pitch or call at the farm to book in. There are a few Dutch tour operator tents (5).

Facilities: The original sanitary building has been extended and a second unit opened. They include washbasins in cubicles, units for disabled people, babies and children, plus laundry and dishwashing facilities. Washing machine and dryer. Basic motorcaravan services. Small shop (from 1/5) provides basic necessities, farm produce and wine, bread can be ordered each evening and butcher visits twice weekly in season. Bar, takeaway and terrace (15/5-15/9). Pleasant small swimming pool (6 x 12 m. open 1/6-31/8). Table tennis, boules and volleyball. Fishing lake (free). Bicycle hire. Play areas and small animal enclosure. **Off site:** Riding 2 km, golf 5 km.

Charges 2002

Per unit incl. 2 persons	€ 10.00 - € 13.00
with electricity	€ 13.00 - € 16.50
extra person	€ 2.90 - € 3.70
child (under 7 yrs)	€ 1.90 - € 2.20
dog	€ 0.80

No credit cards. **Tel:** 03 22 31 48 88. **Fax:** 03 22 31 35 33. **E-mail:** raphael@camping-levaldetrie.fr. **Reservations:** Made with dates, plus deposit (€ 31; no fee for AR readers). **Open** 1 April - 1 November.

Directions: From A28 exit 3 turn northwest on D173 to Moyenneville. In town take road towards Miannay. After 2 km. turn left to Bouillancourt sous Miannay and site is signed in village.

Camping International de Jablines

Base de Loisirs, 77450 Jablines

7703M

Redesigned in 1997, Jablines replaces an older site in an upmarket, modern style which, with the accompanying leisure facilities of the adjacent 'Espace Loisirs', provides an interesting, if a little impersonal alternative to other sites in the region. The whole complex close to the Marne has been developed around old gravel workings. Man-made lakes provide marvellous water activities - dinghy sailing, windsurfing, canoeing, fishing and supervised bathing, plus a large equestrian centre. In season the activities at the leisure complex are supplemented by a bar/restaurant and a range of very French style group activities. The 'Great Lake' as it is called, is said to have the largest beach on the Ile-de-France! The site itself provides 150 pitches, all of a good size with gravel hardstanding and grass, accessed by tarmac roads and clearly marked by fencing panels and newly planted shrubs. All have 10A electricity, nearly half water and waste connections.

Facilities: Two identical toilet blocks, heated in cool weather, are solidly built and well equipped. They include some washbasins in cubicles, indoor dishwashing and laundry facilities with washing machine and dryer. Motorcaravan service (charged). Shop (high season). Play area. Bar/restaurant adjacent at leisure centre/lake complex along with a range of watersports including 'water cable ski', and riding activities. Whilst staying on the site, admission to the leisure complex is free. Internet point. Ticket sales for Disneyland, Asterix and Sea Life.

Charges 2003

Per standard pitch incl. 2 persons and 10A electricity	€ 17.50 - € 20.00
pitch incl. water and waste	€ 18.50 - € 21.00
extra person	€ 4.50 - € 5.00
child (under 12 yrs)	€ 3.00 - € 3.50
dog	€ 1.00

Tel: 01 60 26 09 37. Fax: 01 60 26 43 33. E-mail: Jablines@free.fr. **Reservations:** Essential for July/Aug. and made with booking form from site and 30% deposit. **Open** 28 March - 2 November.

Directions: From A4 Paris - Reims autoroute take A104 north before Disneyland. From the A1 going south, follow signs for Disneyland immediately after Charles de Gaulle airport using the A104. Take exit 8 off the A104 and follow D404 and signs to Base de Loisirs Jablines (8 km). At park entry péage go to campsite lane.

France - East
Camping Lac de la Liez

5203 Peigney, 52200 Langres

Managed by the enthusiastic Baude family, this newly renovated lakeside site is near the city of Langres. With its old ramparts and ancient city centre, Langres was elected one of the 50 most historic cities in France. Situated only 10 minutes from the A5, Camping Des Lacs provides an ideal spot for an overnight stay en-route to the south of France. There is also a lot on offer for a longer stay, including the lake and an indoor pool complex. The site provides 135 fully serviced, terraced pitches with panoramic views of the 500 acre lake. There is direct access to the lake for swimming with a sandy beach and a harbour where boats and pedaloes may be hired.

Facilities: Three brand new toilet blocks have all facilities in cabins. Shop, bar and restaurant. Indoor pool complex with spa and sauna, Extensive children's games area and tennis court. Lake with beach and boat hire.

Charges 2002

Per pitch	€ 5.00 - € 8.00
person	€ 4.00 - € 6.00
child (under 7 yrs)	€ 2.00 - € 3.00
electricity	€ 3.00 - € 4.00
dog	€ 1.50

Tel: 03 25 90 27 79. **Fax:** 03 25 90 66 79. **E-mail:** campingliez@free.fr. **Reservations:** Contact site. **Open** 15 June - 31 October.

Directions: From A5 use Langres north exit and follow signs.

Eastern France
Camping Club du Lac de Bouzey

8804 19 rue du Lac, 88390 Sanchey

Camping-Club Lac de Bouzey is 8 km. west of Épinal, overlooking the lake, at the beginning of the Vosges Massif. It is well placed for exploring the hills, valleys, lakes and waterfalls of the south of Alsace Lorraine The word 'Club' has been added to the name to indicate the number of activities organised in high season. The 160 fairly small, level, back-to-back grass pitches are arranged on either side of tarmac roads with electricity (4-12A). They are on a gentle slope, divided by beech hedging, under a cover of tall, silver birch trees and overlooking the 130 ha. lake. The lake has a number of sandy beaches. Many water sports may be enjoyed, from pedaloes to canoes, windsurfing and sailing. The large, imposing building at the entrance to the site houses a restaurant and bar with terraces overlooking the lake. Two bars by the lake would indicate that the lake-side is popular with the public in summer but the camping area is quiet, separated by a road and well back and above the main entrance. An 'all year' site, there is lots going on for teenagers. English is spoken. A 'Sites et Paysages' member.

Facilities: The central sanitary block, partly below ground level, includes a baby room and one for disabled people (although there is up and down hill walking on the site). In winter a small, heated section in the main building with toilet, washbasin and shower is used. Well stocked shop. Bar, restaurant. Heated swimming pool of an original shape and backed by two sunbathing terraces (1/4-30/9). Fishing, riding and bicycle hire on site. Below ground, under the restaurant, is a sound-proof room for cinema shows and discos for those staying on site only. Staff escort young people back to their pitch at the end of the evening. High season programme of activities for all ages, including excursions, entertainment, sports and a mini-club. **Off site:** Golf 8 km

Charges 2002

Per unit incl. 2 adults	€ 15.00 - € 22.00
extra person	€ 3.50 - € 6.50
child (4-7 yrs)	free - € 4.50
electricity (6A)	€ 4.00
dog	free - € 2.00

Tel: 03 29 82 49 41. **Fax:** 03 29 64 28 03. **E-mail:** camping.lac.de.bouzey@wanadoo.fr. **Reservations:** Made with deposit (€ 10 per day booked) and fee (€ 25). **Open** all year.

Directions: Site is 8 km. west of Épinal on D460 and is signed from some parts of Épinal. Follow signs for Lac de Bouzey and Sanchey.

Alan Rogers' FRANCE

The French sites featured in this guide are only a selection of over 600 featured in our Good Camps Guide - France.

Available from all good bookshops or online at www.alanrogers.com

Camping du Lac de la Liez

Open 14th June - 1st November

Close to the Champagne and Ardennes regions of France, Lac de Liez is a top quality 4 star site, ideal for the whole family

 Comfort: spacious toilet blocks and modern facilities

 Sport: covered pool complex, tennis courts, lake

 Fun: organised activities for both adults and children

 Relaxation: sauna, spa

 Conviviality: bar, restaurant, warm welcome

✔ **Beautiful lakeside setting**
✔ **Beach for swimming**
✔ **Pedalos, water-bikes, boats...**

Peigney, F-52200 Langres, tel 0033 (0)325 90 27 79, fax 0033 (0)325 90 66 79
campingliez@free.fr, http://www.camping-liez.com

France - East
Camping Municipal Châlons-sur-Marne

5102M rue de Plaisance, 51000 Châlons-en Champagne

The location of Châlons, south of Reims and near both the A4 and A26 autoroutes, about 200 miles from Calais and Boulogne, make this an ideal stopover. It is also ideally situated for exploring this famous region in the plain of the River Marne and its historical connections. This site on the southwest edge of town is an example of a good municipal site. The wide entrance with its well tended appearance of neatly mown grass and flower beds sets the tone for the rest of the site. About half of the 130 pitches, accessed from hard roads, are on a gravel base with the rest on grass. Most have electricity (10/15A). The generously sized gravel pitches are separated by hedges and each group of four shares a water tap and drain. Trees abound although there is no shade in some parts.

Facilities: The two toilet blocks, one behind reception, the other at the far end of the site, have been refurbished. Sections of these facilities are of varying standards due to an ongoing programme of refurbishment. Some washbasins in cabins, facilities for disabled visitors, plus a washing machine and dryer. Bread to order. Snack bar. Gas supplies. Games and TV rooms. Playground. Tennis, table tennis, volleyball, boules and place for mini-football. **Off site:** Fishing (free for campers) near. Bus stop at entrance.

Charges 2002

Per person	€ 4.00
child (under 7)	€ 1.65
pitch and vehicle	€ 7.05
electricity	€ 2.95

Tel: 03 26 68 38 00. Fax: 03 26 68 38 00. E-mail: camping.mairie.chalons@wnadoo.fr. **Reservations:** Write to site. **Open** 30 March - 31 October.

Directions: From north on the A4, take La Veuve exit (27) onto N44 which by-passes the town. Leave at last exit signed St Memmie and follow camp signs. From south on A26, take exit 28 on N77 and, head towards town. Site is well signed 'Camping'.

France - East
Camping-Caravaning du Ried

6703 route de Rhinau, 67860 Boofzheim

The area between the main road from Strasbourg to Colmar and the river Rhine is usually bypassed by those who are exploring Alsace or passing through to Switzerland and Italy. However, if looking for a night stop or a different base in the region, Camping du Ried could well fit the bill. Situated on the edge of a small, picturesque village, it has 150 tourist pitches amongst the 120 static caravans. Most of these are under tall trees, on grass and separated by hedges. One might think that this is just another reasonable campsite until one sees the excellent pool complex just inside the site entrance which has an attractive outdoor pool for use in July and August and a heated indoor one open from May to September. We found this a pleasant site with very friendly management who would like to welcome more British visitors even though no English is spoken.

Facilities: The single toilet block is quite a large building and, although old, is well tiled and has all the usual facilities including for disabled people. Washing machines and dryer. Bar/restaurant. Splendid indoor and outdoor pools. Children's playground. Boules. Minigolf. Canoeing. High season animation for children and daily programme including a variety of excursions, guided canoe trips and competitions. Library. **Off site:** Supermarket outside gates.

Charges 2002

Per unit incl. 2 persons	€ 13.00
extra person	€ 4.00
child (under 7 yrs)	€ 2.00
animal	€ 2.00
electricity (3/6A)	€ 3.50 - € 5.00
caravan over 5.5 m. plus	€ 4.00

Tel: (0)3 88 74 68 27. Fax: (0)3 88 74 62 89. E-mail: info@camping-ried.com. **Reservations:** Made with deposit and fee; contact site. **Open** 1 April - 30 October.

Directions: Leave N83 Strasbourg - Colmar road at Benfeld and go east on D5 to Boofzheim. Site is 500 m. beyond village towards Rhinau.

BETWEEN STRASBOURG AND COLMAR
AT 2 KM FROM THE RHINE
2 HEATED SWIMMING POOL (which one is covered)
MOBILE HOMES WITH TERRACE FOR HIRE

CAMPING CARAVANING du RIED
1 RUE du CAMPING 67860 BOOFZHEIM
Tel : 0033 388 74 68 27 Fax : 0033 388 74 62 89
WWW.CAMPING-RIED.COM
FREE BROCHURES ON REQUEST

Castel Camping Sequoia Parc

La Josephtrie, 17320 Saint Just-Luzac

1714

Approached by an impressive avenue of flowers, shrubs and trees, Séquoia Parc is a Castel site set in the grounds of La Josephtrie, a striking château with beautifully restored outbuildings and a spacious courtyard. The site itself is designed to a high specification with reception in a large, light and airy room retaining its original beams and leading to the courtyard area where you find the shop, bar and restaurant. The pitches are 140 sq.m. in size with 6A electricity connections and separated by young shrubs. The pool complex with water slides, large children's pool and sunbathing area is impressive. The site has a good number of mobile homes and chalets. Used by tour operators (125 pitches). This is a popular site with entertainment and reservation is necessary in high season. A Yelloh Village member.

Facilities: Three luxurious toilet blocks, maintained to a high standard, include units with washbasin and shower, a laundry, dishwashing sinks, facilities for disabled visitors and baby baths. Motorcaravan service point. Gas supplies. Shop. Restaurant/bar and takeaway. Impressive swimming pool complex with paddling pool. Tennis, volleyball, football field. Games and TV rooms. Bicycle hire. Pony trekking. Organised entertainment in July/Aug.

Charges 2002

Per unit incl. 2 persons and electricity	€ 15.00 - € 31.00
extra person	€ 5.00 - € 7.00
child (3-7 yrs)	€ 3.00 - € 5.00
dog	€ 3.00
local tax	€ 0.30

Tel: 05 46 85 55 55. Fax: 05 46 85 55 56. E-mail: sequoia.parc@wanadoo.fr. **Reservations:** Made with 30% deposit and € 30 booking fee. **Open** 18 May - 9 September.

Directions: Site is 2.5 km. southeast of Marennes. From Rochefort take D733 south for 12 km. Turn west on D123 to Ile d'Oléron. Continue for 12 km. and turn southeast on D728 towards Saintes. Site clearly signed, in 1 km. on the left.

the travel service
TO BOOK
Ferry ✓
Pitch ✓
Accommodation ✓
01892 55 98 98

The Island of Ré, which is no more than 30 km. long and 5 km. wide, lies off the coast at La Rochelle and is reached by a toll bridge. It is a paradise for cyclists, walkers and those who wish to commune with nature. Here you will find the well managed Camping Interlude which offers first class facilities and enjoys a pleasant location with access to an excellent beach. A popular site even in low season, it is has 387 pitches, 136 of which are for touring outfits. Pitches are sand based, vary in size from 80 - 120 sq.m. and are mostly divided by hedged on part undulating terrain. Many are placed to the left of the site in a pine forest setting, others mingle with the tour operators and mobile homes. Choosing a shady pitch is not a problem for there are many tree varieties. Interlude makes an ideal base for exploring the island of Ré and for those planning an early holiday, the facilities on site are all operational from the end of March. It is a suitable site for all ages, with plenty of recreational pursuits to keep the entire family happy, both on and off site.

Facilities: Two modern, clean and well equipped sanitary blocks provide washbasins in cabins and some showers units, suitable for families, with twin washbasins. Baby room, child size toilets, en suite facilities for visitors with disabilities, laundry sinks, washing machines and dryers, plus dishwashing areas. Motorcaravan service point. Restaurant/bar and shop (all season). Two swimming pools, one outdoor and one inside. Children's play area. Volleyball, boules. Organised events and entertainment for young and old. Games/TV room. Tennis courts. Bicycle hire.

Charges 2002

Per unit incl. 2 persons	
100 sq.m. pitch	€ 12.00 - € 23.00
120 sq.m. incl. water & electricity	€ 16.00 - € 29.00
140 sq.m. pitch incl. drainage also	€ 16.00 - € 32.50
extra person	€ 4.60 - € 8.90
pet	€ 2.25 - € 6.65

Tel: (0)5 46 09 18 22. Fax: (0)5 46 09 23 38. E-mail: interlude@iledere.com. **Reservations:** Advisable all season; contact site. **Open** 29 March - 21 September.

Directions: After crossing toll bridge to Ile de Ré follow sign for Le Bois Plage. Turn left at first round about and continue straight on at second and third roundabout, then left at fourth roundabout where site is signed (charges toll bridge: low season 1/1-19/6 car and caravan € 15 return; high season € 27; motorcaravan € 9-16).

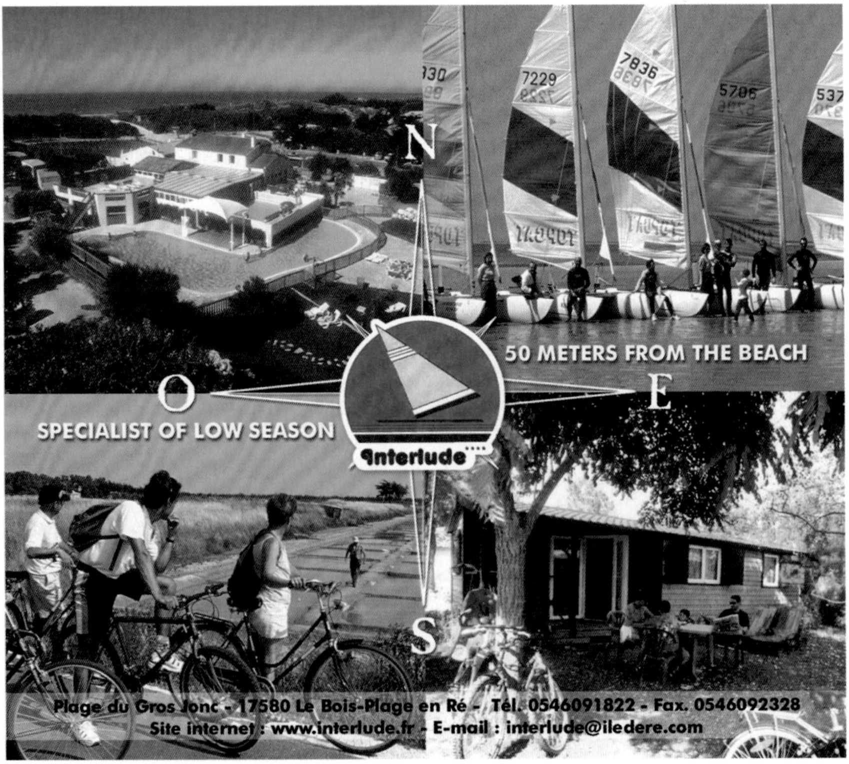

Vendée

Let yourself go...

NANTES

CHOLET

-JEAN-DE-MONTS

LA ROCHE-SUR-YON

S SABLES-D'OLONNE

FONTENAY-LE-COMTE

JARD-SUR-MER

LA ROCHELLE

Call today for your free brochure

01892 55 98 05

- ☀ Long sandy shores, clear blue skies, brilliant sunshine and historical towns. With an enviable sunshine record, watersports galore and the warm Atlantic waves, it's easy to see why the Vendée is one of the most popular areas of France for couples and families alike.

- ☀ Beach lovers will discover 140 kilometres of sandy shores backed by fragrant pine forests running alongside and, as a change, Le Puy du Fou spectacle is a must.

- ☀ You'll find a superb selection of accommodation to suit all tastes, ranging from hotels, châteaux, holiday apartments, villages and campsites. All with on site amenities to keep everyone happily occupied.

- ☀ And with so much to see, you'll be pleased that the Vendée is a comfortable drive from the port of St Malo.

Why not let yourself go?

VENDÉE
TRAVEL SERVICE

www.vendee.org.uk

Camping Bois Soleil

1701 2 avenue de Suzac, 17110 St Georges-de-Didonne

Close to the sea and the resort of St Georges, Bois Soleil is a fairly large site in three separate parts, with 208 serviced pitches for touring caravans and several for tents. The main part, 'Les Pins', is mature and attractive with ornamental trees and shrubs providing shade. Opposite is 'La Mer' which has direct access to the beach and is used only in the main season. It has some areas with rather less shade and a raised central area for tents. The sandy beach here is a wide public one, sheltered from the Atlantic breakers although the sea goes out some way at low tide. The third and largest part of the site, 'La Forêt', is mainly for static holiday homes (many privately owned), although there are some touring pitches here for both tents and caravans. The areas are well tended with the named pitches (not numbered) cleared and raked between clients and with an all-in-charge including electricity and water. This lively site offers something for everyone, whether they like a beach-side spot or a traditional pitch, plenty of activities or the quiet life - it is best to book for the area you prefer. It can be full mid-June - late August.

Facilities: Each area is served by one large sanitary block, supplemented by smaller blocks providing toilets only. Another heated block is near reception. Well designed and appointed buildings, cleaned twice daily, they include washbasins in cubicles, facilities for disabled people (WC, basin and shower) and for babies. Launderette. Nursery for babies. Supermarket, bakery (July/Aug) and beach shop. Upstairs restaurant and bar with terrace, excellent takeaway (from April). Little pool for small children. 'Parc des Jeux' with tennis, table tennis, bicycle hire, boules and children's playground. TV room and library. Comprehensive tourist information and entertainment office. Internet terminal. Charcoal barbecues are not permitted but gas ones can be hired by the evening. Dogs or other animals are not accepted. **Off site:** Fishing and riding within 500 m, golf 2 km.

Charges 2002

Per unit incl. 2 persons, electricity	€ 16.00 - € 27.50
3 persons	€ 19.00 - € 27.50
tent incl. 2 persons	€ 13.00 - € 24.50
extra person	€ 3.50 - € 5.00
child (3-7 yrs)	€ 1.50 - € 3.50
electricity 10A	€ 3.40 - € 5.00
local tax (1/7-31/8)	€ 0.25

Tel: 05 46 05 05 94. **Fax:** 05 46 06 27 43. **E-mail:** camping.bois.soleil@wanadoo.fr. **Reservations:** Made with 25% deposit and € 26 fee. **Open** 1 April - 15 September.

Directions: From Royan centre take coast road (D25) along the sea-front of St Georges-de-Didonne towards Meschers. Site is signed at roundabout at end of the main beach.

Camping Naturiste Cap Natur'

N8533 151 ave de la Faye, 85270 St Hilaire-de-Riez

Situated on the northern outskirts of the busy resort of St Hilaire-de-Riez, and only about 1 kilometre from the nearest beach (6 km. from the nearest official naturist beach beside Plage des 60 Bornes) this family campsite for naturists is in an area of undulating sand dunes and pine trees. The 120 touring pitches nestle among the dunes and trees and offer a wide choice to suit most tastes, including the possibility of electrical connections (4/10A), although in some cases long leads are needed. Despite the undulating terrain, some pitches are quite level and thus suitable for motorcaravans. The modern facilities are excellent and include both open air and indoor pools, and a jacuzzi. Around the pool is an ample paved sunbathing area, including a stepped 'solarium'. The whole of the indoor complex is a designated non-smoking area. In season a regular Saturday evening 'soirée' is held with a set Vendéen meal, wine and entertainment. There is an air of peace and quiet about this site which contrasts with the somewhat frenzied activity which pervades many of the resorts in this popular tourist area, with a friendly, warm welcome from the family that own it.

Facilities: Sanitary facilities are basic, but clean, consisting of one indoor and one outdoor (but roofed) block. Both blocks have open plan hot showers, British style WCs, washbasins, baby baths and children's toilets. Small shop and restaurant (menu includes some local specialities), good sized bar, with TV, pool tables and various indoor table games. Indoor and outdoor swimming pools. Children's play area on soft sand. Volleyball and archery. Torches useful. A number of apartments, tents and mobile homes are on site.

Charges 2002

Per unit incl. 2 adults	€ 14.00 - € 25.00
extra person	€ 2.50 - € 5.20
child (under 10 yrs)	€ 1.60 - € 3.40
animal	€ 2.20
electricity (10A)	€ 4.20

Tel: 02 51 60 11 66. **Fax:** 02 51 60 17 48. **E-mail:** info@cap-natur.com. **Reservations:** Advised in high season and for French holidays. Made with 25% deposit and booking fee (€ 27,44). **Open** 24 March - 3 or 11 November.

Directions: Site is on the north side of St Hilaire-de-Riez. From Le Pissot roundabout go south on the D38, follow signs for St Hilaire at first roundabout you come to (first exit off roundabout), then at second roundabout (garage) turn right signed 'Terre Fort'. At third Y-shaped junction turn right again signed 'Parée Prèneau' (also site sign here). The site is 2 km along this road on the left.

Bois Soleil

Camping ★★★★
Charente-Maritime

Surrounded by pine trees and a sandy beach on the Atlantic Coast, with one direct access to the beach, Bois Soleil proposes to you many attractions like tennis, tabletennis, children playgrounds andentertainment.

Shops, take-away and snack-bar with big TV screen.

Camping Qualité

Spring and Summer 2003

PROJECT 2003
SWIMMING POOL

240 m2
Heated Swimming Pool
BALNEO & PADDLING POOL

2, avenue de Suzac - 17110 ST GEORGES DE DIDONNE
Tel: 0033 546 05 05 94 - Fax: 0033 546 06 27 43
www.bois-soleil.com / e-mail: camping.bois.soleil@wanadoo.fr

8504

La Garangeoire is one of a relatively small number of seriously good sites in the Vendée, situated some 15 km. inland near the village of St Julien des Landes. One of its more memorable qualities is the view of the château through the gates as you drive in. Imaginative use has been made of the old Noirmoutiers 'main road' which passes through the centre of the site and now forms a delightful, quaint thoroughfare, nicknamed the Champs Elysée. Providing a village like atmosphere, it is busy at most times with the facilities opening directly off it. The site is set in the 200 ha. of parkland which surrounds the small château of La Garangeoire. The peaceful fields and woods, where campers may walk, include three lakes, one of which is used for fishing and boating (life jackets supplied from reception). The site has a spacious, relaxed atmosphere and many use it as a quiet base. The main camping areas are arranged on either side of the old road, edged with mature trees. The 300 pitches, each with a name not a number and individually hedged, are especially large (most 150-200 sq.m.) and are well spaced. Most have electricity (12A), some water and drainage also. The site is popular with British tour operators (144 pitches).

Facilities: Ample sanitary facilities are of good standard, well situated for all areas. One excellent block has facilities for babies and disabled people. All have washbasins in cabins. Good laundry facilities. Motorcaravan service point. Good shop. Full restaurant, takeaway and a separate crêperie with bars and attractive courtyard terrace overlooking the swimming pool complex (from 1/5) with water slides, fountains and a children's pool. Large playing field with play equipment for children's activities, whether organised or not. Games room. Two tennis courts. Bicycle hire. Table tennis, crazy golf, archery and volleyball. Riding in July/Aug. Fishing and boating. **Off site:** Beaches 15 km.

Charges 2003

Per unit incl. 2 persons	€ 14.00 - € 24.00
with electricity	€ 17.00 - € 28.00
with services	€ 18.50 - € 30.00
extra person	€ 3.50 - € 5.50
child (under 10 yrs)	€ 2.00 - € 2.50
dog	€ 2.00 - € 3.00
local tax	free - € 0.50

Tel: 02 51 46 65 39. Fax: 02 51 46 69 85. E-mail: garangeoire@wanadoo.fr. **Reservations:** Made for min. 7 days with deposit (€ 61) and fee (€ 22,87). **Open** 5 April - 24 September.

Directions: Site is signed from St Julien; the entrance is to the north off the D21 road.

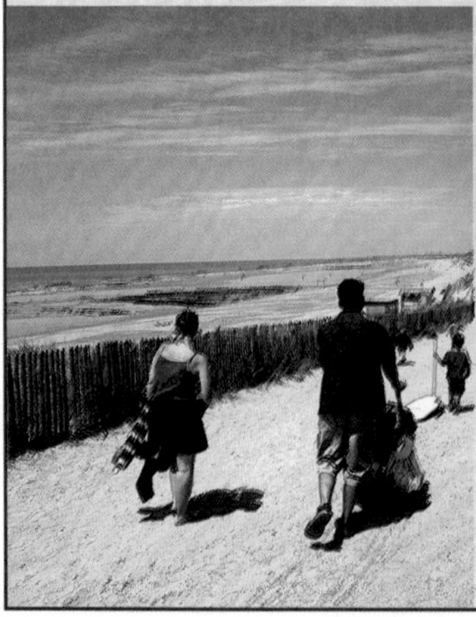

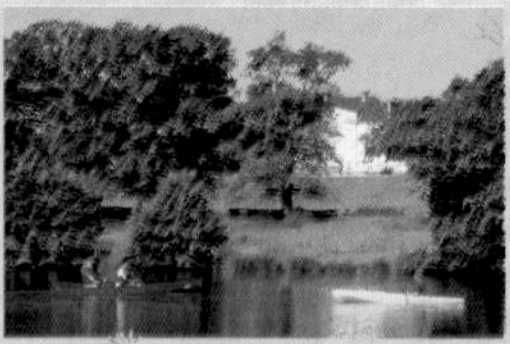

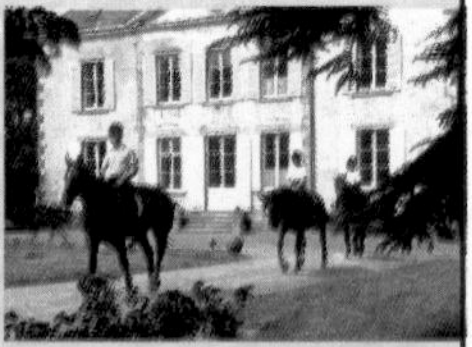

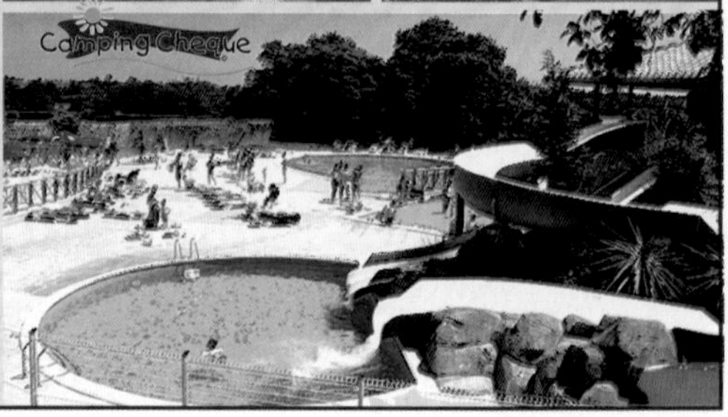

Camping La Yole

chemin des Bosses, Orouet, 85160 St-Jean-de-Monts

La Yole is an attractive, popular and well run site, 1 km. from a sandy beach. It offers 278 pitches, the majority under trees with ample shade and separated by bushes and the trees. All have electricity, water and drainage and are of 100 sq.m. or more. The pool complex is surrounded by a paved sunbathing area and over-looked by a new bar and restaurant which have a large terrace. A pleasant walk through pine woods then by road leads to two sandy beaches. The security barrier is closed at night. Used by tour operators (50%). A Sites et Paysages member. This a friendly, popular site with welcoming owners.

Facilities: Two toilet blocks of older design, one refurbished, include washbasins in cabins, units for disabled people and new baby baths, all kept very clean. The third block in the newer part of site is very modern with baby room. Laundry with washing machine, dryer and iron. Well stocked shop. Takeaway. Bar (all season) and restaurant (18/5-31/8). Swimming pool with water slide, paddling pool and an indoor heated pool with jacuzzi. Children have exceptional space with a play area on sand, large field for ball games, picnics and a club room. Tennis. Table tennis, pool and video games. Organised entertainment in high season. No dogs are accepted. Only gas barbecues are permitted. **Off site:** Fishing, golf and watersports 6 km. at St Jean

Charges 2002

Per tent incl. 2 persons, electricity and water	€ 14.48 - € 22.25
or for caravan incl. drainage also	€ 16.65 - € 26.45
extra person	€ 3.51 - € 5.60
extra child (2-9 yrs)	€ 1.98 -€ 4.00
baby (0-2 yrs)	free - € 3.05
local tax (July/Aug. over 10 yrs)	€ 0.34

Tel: 02 51 58 67 17. Fax: 02 51 59 05 35. E-mail: contact@la-yole.com. **Reservations:** Advised, particularly for July/Aug. **Open** 8 May - 15 September.

Directions: Signed off the D38, 6 km. south of St Jean de Monts in the village of Orouet.

Camping Les Ecureuils

8521 route des Goffineaux, 85520 Jard-sur-Mer

Les Ecureuils is a wooded site in a quieter part of the southern Vendée. It is undoubtedly one of the prettiest sites on this stretch of coast, with an elegant reception area, attractive vegetation and large pitches separated by low hedges with plenty of shade. Of the 261 pitches, some 120 are for touring units, each with water and drainage, as well as easy access to 10A electricity. Jard is rated among the most pleasant and least hectic of Vendée towns. The harbour is home to some fishing boats and rather more pleasure craft, and has a public slipway for those bringing their own boats. This site is very popular with tour operators (126 pitches). And in case you are curious, yes there are squirrels on site, including red ones! A new indoor pool and spa should now be complete.

Facilities: Two toilet blocks, well equipped and kept very clean, include baby baths, and laundry rooms. Small shop. Takeaway service (pre-order). Snacks and ice-creams available from the friendly bar. Good sized L-shaped swimming pool and separate paddling pool. Modern children's play area. Minigolf, table tennis and a pool table. Club for children (5-10 yrs) daily in July/Aug. Bicycle hire. Only gas barbecues are allowed. Dogs are not accepted. **Off site:** Nearest beach 400 m. Fishing 400 m. Range of places to eat at nearby marina or in town which has good supermarket and weekly market.

Charges 2002

Per pitch	€ 11.00
Per pitch with electricity (10A)	€ 14.50
person over 10 yrs	€ 5.50
child 0-4 yrs	€ 2.00
child 5-9 yrs	€ 4.00
local tax (July/Aug, over 10 yrs)	€ 0.50

Tel: 02 51 33 42 74. Fax: 02 51 33 91 14. E-mail: camping-ecureuils@wanadoo.fr. **Reservations:** Advised for July/Aug. **Open** 15 May - 15 September.

Directions: Jard-sur-Mer is on the D21 road between Talmont St Hilaire and Longeville sur Mer. Site is well signed from the main road - caravanners will need to follow these signs to avoid tight bends and narrow roads.

Camping Bois Soleil

8540 chemin des Barres, 85340 Olonne-sur-Mer

This site has a very French feel, the majority of the population when we visited seeming to be French. It is a traditionally laid out site with 170 marked pitches, separated by hedges, on flat or gently sloping ground. There is just one (French) tour operator and a scattering of mobile homes and chalets, leaving some 100 pitches available for tourers and tents. All have electricity (6A, French style sockets) and water points adjacent and many also have waste water pipes. The main buildings house a small reception and tourist information room as well as the bar and attached shop. There is an excellent new swimming pool complex with sunbathing areas, paddling pool and a separate pool for the two water slides and impressive flume. In July and August a range of daily activities is organised for adults and children.

Facilities: The two well equipped and maintained toilet blocks have copious hot water, mainly British style toilets, with washbasins in cubicles in the new block. This block is locked overnight, but basic toilet facilities are provided. Covered dishwashing and laundry sinks. Two washing machines. Shop in July and August only with `eat in` or takeaway food service; bread (and cooked chicken) must to be ordered the previous day. Swimming and paddling pools. Sandy children's play area (caged), trampoline and table tennis. **Off site:** Beaches are just 2 km. The thriving resort of Les Sables d'Olonne is 5 km along the coast.

Charges guide

Per unit incl. 2 persons	€ 7.30 - € 14.20
with electricity	€ 13.75 - € 17.25
extra adult	€ 2.45 - € 3.00
child (under 7 yrs)	€ 1.85 - € 2.15
animal	€ 1.85

Tel: (0)2 51 33 11 97. Fax: (0)2 51 33 14 85.
Reservations: Advised for July/Aug. and made with 25% deposit and booking fee in July/Aug of € 12,20.
Open 1 May - 16 September.

Directions: Site is off the D80 coast road between Olonne-sur-Mer and is clearly signed on the inland side.

Bois Soleil ★★★
94, chemin des Barres
85340 Olonne sur Mer
Tel: 0033 251 33 11 97
Fax: 0033 251 33 14 85
Email: camping.boissoleil@wanadoo.fr
Site: www.campingboissoleil.com

The Alan Rogers' Travel Service

the travel service
TO BOOK
Ferry ✓
Pitch ✓
Accommodation ✓
01892 55 98 98

We have recently extended The Alan Rogers Travel Service. This unique service enables our readers to reserve their holidays as well as ferry crossings and comprehensive insurance cover at extremely competitive rates. The majority of participating sites are in France and we are able to offer a selection of some of the very best sites in this country.

One simple telephone call to our Travel Service on 01892 55 98 98 is all that is needed to make all the arrangements. Why not take advantage of our years' of experience of camping and caravanning. We would be delighted to discuss your holiday plans with you, and offer advice and recommendations.

Share our experience and let us help to ensure
that your holiday will be a complete success.

Alan Rogers Travel Service 01892 55 98 98 or www.alanrogers.com

Camping La Grand' Métairie

8530 8 rue de la Vineuse en Plaine, 85440 St Hilaire la Forêt

Just 5 kilometres from the super sandy beach at Jard sur Mer, La Grand' Métairie offers many of the amenities of its seaside counterparts, but with the important advantage of being on the edge of a delightful, sleepy village, otherwise untouched by tourism. It is a busy well run site with a lively entertainment programme in high season and a new covered pool planned. The site has 172 pitches (72 touring pitches), all with electricity (6A), water and drainage. The pitches as yet have little shade but are all separated by small trees and bushes and are generous in size.

Facilities: Two modern toilet blocks are kept very clean and include washbasins mainly in cabins. Units for disabled people. Washing machines and dryers. Fridge hire. Basic provisions kept on site (village store 100 m). Smart bar/restaurant (15/5-15/9). Attractive, kidney-shaped heated pool with jacuzzi and paddling pool. Tennis, minigolf (both free in low season). Visiting hairdresser. **Off site:** High season free minibus service runs to the beach and to a number of local markets. Riding, fishing within 5 km.

Charges 2002

Per unit incl. 2 persons, electricity	€ 12.96 - € 18.29
extra person	€ 3.35 - € 4.57
child (under 5 yrs)	€ 2.13 - € 3.05
dog	€ 2.29

Tel: 02 51 33 32 38. **Fax:** 02 51 33 25 69. **E-mail:** grand-metairie@wanadoo.fr. **Reservations:** Advised for high season with 25% deposit and fee (€ 18,29). **Open** 1 April - 30 September.

Directions: Site is in centre of St Hilaire la Forêt. From Les Sables d'Olonne take D949 (La Rochelle) towards Talmont St Hilaire and Luçon. 7 km. after Talmont turn right on D70 to St Hilaire la Forêt. Site is on the left before village centre.

Camping Municipal Les Vieux Chênes

3605M 36310 Chaillac

A delightful site on the outskirts of an attractive village, this is another little gem - a small site within walking distance of the centre, where there are shops, bars, cafés, restaurants, etc. The 34 grass pitches, all with electricity (15A), are very generous in size, slightly sloping, with hedging and some mature trees. The well manicured appearance and relaxed atmosphere add to the attraction of this peaceful environment. The adjacent lake is for fishing only, although there is access to a larger lake just 1 km. away where varied watersports - swimming, windsurfing, canoeing and pedaloes - can be enjoyed. In high season it is possible some noise may carry from this area to the site.

Facilities: Heated sanitary facilities are insulated for winter use and include washbasins in private cabins. Bicycle hire. Winter caravan storage. **Off site:** Shops 200 m. Fishing 25m. Watersports 1 km.

Charges 2002

Per person (over 14 yrs)	€ 1.52
child	free
pitch	€ 1.52 - € 2.29
electricity	€ 1.52

Tel: 02 54 25 61 39. **Fax:** 02 54 25 65 41. **Reservations:** Not made. **Open** all year.

Directions: From the north leave A20, south of Argenton sur Creuse, take D1 to St Benoit (16 km.) and then west to Chaillac on D36 (8.5 km). From the south leave A20 at exit 21, take D10 to St Benoit, then D36 as before. Go through the village and turn left by the Mairie.

Camping L'Arada Parc

rue de la Baratière, 37360 Sonzay

3706

Although Camping L'Arada Parc is a relatively new site (only in its second full year) it has already become popular as an overnight stop, or as a quiet location from which to visit the numerous châteaux in this beautiful part of France. The 87 grass pitches all have a 10A hook-up, and 28 of them have fresh water and waste disposal points. Pitches are clearly marked and separated by maturing trees, shrubs and flowers that will, in time, provide some shade. Snacks and meals in the restaurant are cooked to order with barbecue chicken available at weekends. Campers can enjoy a snack or drink on the terrace overlooking the attractive (unheated) swimming pool.

Facilities: Two modern toilet blocks provide unisex toilets, showers and washbasins in cubicles. Excellent baby/toddler room and en suite facilities for disabled visitors). Dishwashing and laundry sinks under cover at each block. Laundry with washing machine, dryer and ironing board. Shop (1/4-3/11). Bar, restaurant and takeaway (1/4-3/11). Swimming pools. Play area, covered games area. Boules, volleyball, badminton and table tennis. TV room. Bicycle hire. Entertainment, themed evenings and activities for children organised in July/Aug. **Off site:** Tennis 200 m. Fishing 9 km. Riding 7 km.

Charges 2002

Per unit incl. 2 persons	€ 14.00
extra person	€ 4.00
child 2-7 yrs	€ 3.00
electricity (10A)	43.00

Tel: (0)2 47 24 72 69. Fax: (0)2 47 24 72 69. E-mail: laradaparc@free.fr. **Reservations:** Made with deposit (€ 45); contact site. **Open** 1 April - 3 November.

Directions: Sonzay is northwest of Tours. Take D959 Tours - Château-la-Vallière road, then D6 to Sonzay and follow camping signs. Site is signed from the D959.

Le Parc du Val de Loire

route de Fleuray, 41150 Mesland

4101

Between Blois and Tours, quietly situated among vineyards away from the main roads and towns, this family owned site is nevertheless centrally placed for visits to the châteaux; Chaumont, Amboise and Blois (21 km.) are the nearest in that order. There are 174 touring pitches of reasonable size, either in light woodland marked by trees or on open meadow with separators. All of the pitches have electricity (6A), and 77 of them also have water and drainage. Sports and competitions are organised in July/Aug. with weekly disco and dance for adults. Wine tasting opportunities each Friday and a coach to Paris one day each week. There are local walks on marked footpaths (maps € 0,30). Used by tour operators (100 pitches).

Facilities: Two original toilet blocks of varying standards include washbasins in cabins. A third block is more modern. Units for disabled visitors, baby bathrooms and laundry facilities. Motorcaravan service point. Large shop with bakery. Bar adjacent to the pools, with restaurant, snack service, pizzeria and takeaway, TV room and large recreation room. Three swimming pools, smaller pool with popular water slide, and small children's pool. Tennis court, good playgrounds with skate board facilities, bicycle hire, table tennis, minigolf, BMX track, football pitch, volleyball, badminton and basketball. Pony rides. **Off site:** Fishing or golf 2 km, riding 10 km.

Charges 2002

Per unit incl. 2 persons (100 sq.m.)	€ 14.10 - € 21.70
large pitch (150 sq.m.)	€ 18.80 - € 27.00
extra person	€ 3.60 - € 5.50
child (2-7 yrs)	€ 2.00 - € 3.10
electricity 6-10A	€ 2.00 - € 3.50
animal	€ 1.90

Tel: 02 54 70 27 18. Fax: 02 54 70 21 71. **Reservations:** Made for min. 4 days with deposit (€ 77) and fee (€ 20). **Open** 30 March - 11 November.

Directions: Mesland village is 5 km. northwest of Onzain, accessible from Château-Renault/Amboise exit of A10 autoroute via D31 to Autrèche, Continue for 5 km, left at La Hargardière and 8 km. to site.

Camping-Caravaning La Grande Tortue

4107 3, route de Pontlevoy, 41120 Candé-sur-Beuvron

This is a pleasant, rustic site that has been tastefully developed in an old forest. It provides 106 touring pitches are set amongst trees which provide shade as well as some sunshine. The grass is kept a little longer than normal, especially during the early season, to maintain the forest environment. The majority of the pitches are more than 100 sq.m. and all have 6/10A electricity. During July and August, the family owners organise a programme of trips including wine/cheese tastings, canoeing, and an all-day visit to the Loire Valley. There are markets at Amboise (Sunday), Montrichard (Monday) and Blois (Monday). Used by tour operators.

Facilities: Three sanitary blocks offer British and Turkish style WCs, washbasins in cabins, showers (chain operated in two blocks and press button in the third), plus a very basic chemical emptying point. Laundry with deep sinks, washing machine, dryer and ironing board. Shop selling provisions, cards and small gifts. Terraced bar and restaurant with reasonably priced food and drink (15/5-15/9). Trampolines, a ball crawl with slide and climbing wall, bouncy castle, table tennis, an adult swimming pool, and two shallower pools for children (all 15/5-15/9). **Off site:** Walking and cycling. Fishing 500 m. Golf 7 km. Riding 8 km.

Charges 2002

Per pitch and 2 people	€ 12.00 - € 18.50
with electricity	€ 15.00 - € 21.50
extra adult	€ 4.00 - € 5.50
child (under 7 yrs)	€ 3.00 - € 4.00
local tax	€ 0.08 - € 0.15

Tel: 02 54 44 15 20. Fax: 02 54 44 19 45. E-mail: grandtortue@libertysurf.fr. **Reservations:** Necessary in July/Aug. **Open** 5 April - 30 September.

Directions: Site is just outside Candé-sur-Beuvron on the D751, midway between Amboise and Blois. From Amboise, turn right just before entering Candé, then immediately left into the campsite - well signed from the road.

Camping de Chantepie

4902 St Hilaire-St Florent, 49400 Saumur

The drive along the winding road bordered by apple orchards and vineyards is well rewarded on arriving at the floral entrance to Camping de Chantepie. Reception at this friendly site is housed in a tastefully restored ancient farmhouse. Linked by gravel roadways (can be dusty), the 150 grass pitches are all level and spacious. They are separated by low hedges of flowers and trees which offer some shade and most have electrical connections (5A). The panoramic views over the Loire from the pitches on the terraced perimeter of the meadow are stunning. There is, from here, a footpath leading to the river valley. Leisure activities for all ages are catered for in July/Aug. by the Chantepie Club, including wine tastings, excursions and canoeing. This is a good site for families.

Facilities: The toilet block is very clean and facilities are adequate with washbasins in cubicles and facilities for disabled visitors. Well stocked shop. Bar and terraced restaurant and separate takeaway (from 5/5). Paddling pool and two heated swimming pools are protected from the wind by a stone wall. Play area. Minigolf. Volleyball, TV, video games and table tennis. Pony rides. Bicycle and mountain bike hire. **Off site:** Fishing 200 m, riding 6 km, golf 2 km.

Charges 2002

Per unit incl. 2 persons	€ 15.85 - € 19.82
extra adult	€ 3.78 - € 4.25
child (2-10 yrs)	€ 2.20 - € 2.74
electricity	€ 2.32 - € 2.90
local tax	€ 0.15 - € 0.30

Tel: 02 41 67 95 34. Fax: 02 41 67 95 85. E-mail: camping.chantepie@wanadoo.fr. **Reservations:** Made with € 11 fee; contact site for details. **Open** 29 April - 14 September.

Directions: From Saumur take D751 signed Gennes. Turn right at roundabout in St Hilaire-St Florent and continue until Le Poitrinea and campsite sign, then turn left. Continue for about 3 km. and then turn right into road leading to site.

Camping Caravaning International ★★★★

La Grande Tortue

3, route de Pontlevoy
41120 CANDÉ-sur-BEUVRON
Tel: 0033 254 44 15 20 - Fax: 0033 254 44 19 45
Website: www.la-grande-tortue.com

France - Loire Valley
Camping de L'Etang
St Saturnin sur Loire, 49320 Brissac

4904

Originally the farm of the ancient Château de Brissac, the tasteful conversion has retained the tranquillity and ambience of bye-gone days and added the necessary comforts expected by today's campers. A rural campsite with pleasant views across the countryside, there are over 150 good sized, level touring pitches. Separated and numbered, some have shade and all have 10A electricity with water and drainage nearby. A small bridge crosses the river Aubance which runs through the site and there are two lakes where fisherman can enjoy free fishing. The site has its own vineyard and the wine produced is highly recommended and can be purchased on the campsite. The production of the wine and the maintenance of the campsite, vineyards and the adjacent pleasure park offer, under guidance, employment to handicapped personnel.

Facilities: Three well maintained sanitary blocks are of a high standard. Laundry room with washing machines, dryer, together with baby and toddler facilities. Disabled visitors are well catered for. Motorcaravan service point. The adapted farmhouse houses reception, small shop, bar and takeaway (from 15/6). Restaurant planned. Two swimming pools, one heated, and paddling pool. Wide variety of evening entertainment in high season. **Off site:** The adjacent Parc de Loisirs is a paradise for children with activities including boating, pony rides, miniature train, water slide, bouncy castle and swings (free entry for campers). Golf 10 km.

Charges 2003

Per unit incl. 2 persons	€ 16.25 - € 20.30
extra adult	€ 3.85 - € 4.85
child (2-10 yrs)	€ 2.25 - € 2.80
electricity	€ 2.40 - € 3.00
local tax	€ 0.15 - € 0.30

Tel: 02 41 91 70 61. Fax: 02 41 91 72 65. E-mail: info@campingetang.com. **Reservations:** Contact site. **Open** 25 May - 13 September.

Directions: Take D748 south from Angers. Follow signs to Brissac-Quincé but do not enter the town, proceed to site along D55 (well signed) in direction of St Mathurin.

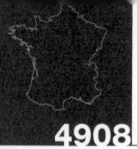

France - Loire Valley
Camping Ile d'Offard

4908 rue de Verden, Ile d'Offard, 49400 Saumur

Situated on an island between the banks of the Loire and within walking distance of the centre of Saumur, this site is useful as an overnight stop en-route south or as a short-term base from which to visit the region's châteaux. The 190 touring pitches are on grass at the far end or hardstanding nearer the entrance. Some 67 pitches are occupied by tour operators and holiday homes – these can be intrusive in some areas. As the site only closes mid- Dec. until mid-Jan, it is ideal for winter travellers. Some pitches have electricity. The adjacent town swimming pools and minigolf (July/Aug) are free for campers.

Facilities: Three sanitary blocks, one heated, include provision for disabled visitors. Toilets in all blocks are unisex. Block 1 has a well equipped laundry. The other blocks are only open in high season. Basic restaurant and bar (end April - early Sept) with take-away. Table tennis, volleyball. Play area. Some activities in high season. Torches useful. **Off site:** Thursday market 500 m, Saturday market 2 km.

Charges 2002

Per unit incl. 2 adults	€ 13.50 - € 18.50
extra person	€ 2.00 - € 4.00
electricity	€ 3.00

Tel: 02 41 40 30 00. **Fax:** 02 41 67 37 81. **E-mail:** iledoffard@wanadoo.fr. **Reservations:** Advised for July/Aug. **Open** all year excl. 15 Dec - 15 Jan.

Directions: From N147 take 'Saumur Centre' exit. At roundabout follow signs for Châtellerault and Chinon and continue alongside river towards town centre. At next roundabout left over bridge onto island. Just before next bridge turn right to site.

France - Loire Valley
Camping L'Etang de la Brèche

4901 route Nationale 152, 5 Impasse de la Breche, 49730 Varennes-sur-Loire

The Saint Cast family have developed L'Etang de la Brèche with loving care and attention on a 25 ha. estate 4 km. southeast of Saumur on the edge of the Loire behind the dykes. It is a peaceful base from which to explore the famous châteaux and wine cellars in this region. The site provides 201 large, level pitches with shade from mixed tall trees and bushes, facing central, less shaded grass areas. There are electrical connections to most pitches (long cables may be needed), with water and drainaway on some. The restaurant, also open to the public, blends well with the existing architecture and, together with the bar area and terrace, provides a social base and is probably one of the reasons why the site is popular with British visitors. The swimming complex includes three pools: one with a removable cover, one outdoor, and a lovely pool for toddlers. The small lake and wooded area ensure a relaxed, rural atmosphere and make this a comfortable holiday base for couples and families. A Les Castels site, used by tour operators (85 pitches).

Facilities: Three toilet blocks, modernised to good standards, include facilities for babies with two units for people with disabilities. Washing up sinks and laundry. Shop and epicerie. Good, reasonably priced restaurant, pizzeria and takeaway. Three heated pools. Tennis, basketball, minigolf and a field for football. Bicycle hire. General room, games and TV rooms. Well organised, varied sporting and entertainment programme (10/7-25/8). Child minding is arranged in afternoons. Low season excursions 'Getting to know the Area' and wine tastings are organised. Torch useful. **Off site:** Riding 2 km, golf 8 km.

Charges 2002

Per unit incl. 2 persons	€ 15.00 - € 22.00
incl. 3 persons	€ 18.50 - € 25.00
extra adult	€ 3.50 - € 5.00
hild (under 10 yrs)	€ 2.00 - € 3.00
electricity (10A)	free - € 3.00
water and drainage	€ 2.00

Tel: 02 41 51 22 92. **Fax:** 02 41 51 27 24. **E-mail:** mail@etang.breche.com. **Reservations:** Made for min. 7 nights in high season (3 days in low season) with deposit and fee. **Open** 17 May - 9 September.

Directions: Site is 100 m. north off the main N152, about 4 km. southeast of Saumur on the north bank of the Loire.

Castel Camping
LES CASTELS
L'Etang de la Brèche

49730 Varennes sur Loire
Tel : 0033 241 51 22 92
Fax : 0033 241 51 27 24
mail@etang-breche.com
www.etang-breche.com

Camping Qualité©

AT 5 KM OF SAUMUR

France - Loire Valley
Camping L'Européen de Montsabert
Montsabert, 49320 Coutures

4906

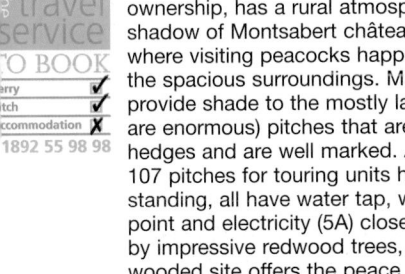

This extensive campsite, now under new ownership, has a rural atmosphere in the shadow of Montsabert château, from where visiting peacocks happily roam in the spacious surroundings. Mature trees provide shade to the mostly large (some are enormous) pitches that are divided by hedges and are well marked. A few of the 107 pitches for touring units have a hard-standing, all have water tap, waste water point and electricity (5A) close by. Fringed by impressive redwood trees, this partially wooded site offers the peace of the countryside and yet easy access to Saumur and Angers. It is an ideal base for exploring, whether by foot, bicycle or car. Used by tour operators (19 pitches).

Facilities: The main central toilet block can be heated and has washbasins and bidets in cabins. Outside dishwashing and laundry facilities. Washing machine and dryer. A second block serves the pool and another unit provides more WCs. Restaurant and takeaway (both 15/6-15/9). Bar (1/6-15/9). Shop (1/6-30/8). Large 25 m. heated swimming pool (1/6-15/9; no bermuda style shorts). Sports hall, minigolf, volley and basketball, table tennis and tennis. Bicycle hire. Picnic tables are provided in the shade near the entrance with a communal barbecue area. Torch useful. **Off site:** Windsurfing, canoeing and sailing near. Fishing 5 km, golf 5km, riding 8 km.

Charges 2002

Per pitch incl. 2 persons	€ 13.00 - € 18.30
extra person	€ 3.30 - € 4.25
electricity (5A)	€ 2.75
cyclists (1 or 2 persons)	€ 10.70

Tel: 02 41 57 91 63. Fax: 02 41 57 90 02. E-mail: anjoucamp@wanadoo.fr. **Reservations:** Made with 30% deposit and fee (€ 7,62). **Open** 15 May - 15 September.

Directions: From Le Mans, direction Angers, take exit 12 direction Seiches s Loire. Turn left to the D74 signed Bauné, Château Montgeoffroy, Mazé. In Mazé take the D55 towards St Maturin s Loire, pass the bridge and follow the signs L'Européen and Coutures.

On raised ground with panoramic views over the strikingly modern buildings and night-time bright lights that comprise the popular attraction of Futuroscope, Le Futuriste is a neat, modern site, open all year. It is ideal for a short stay to visit the park which is only 1.5 km. away (tickets can be bought at the site) but it is equally good for longer stays to see the region. With a busy atmosphere, there are early departures and late arrivals. Reception is open 08.00-22.00 hrs. There are 112 individual, flat, grass pitches divided by young trees and shrubs which are beginning to provide some shelter for this elevated and otherwise rather open site (possibly windy). There are 28 pitches without electricity for tents, 22 with electricity (16A) and a further 62 with electricity, water, waste water and sewage connections. All are accessed via neat, level and firmly rolled gravel roads. Of course, the area has other attractions and details are available from the enthusiastic young couple who run the site. Note: it is best to see the first evening show at Futuroscope otherwise you will find youself locked out of the site - the gates are closed at 23.30 hrs.

Facilities: Excellent, very clean sanitary facilities are housed in two modern blocks which are insulated and can be heated in cool weather. The facilities in the newest block are unisex. and include some washbasins in cabins and facilities for disabled people. Dishwashing and laundry sinks. Washing machine and dryer. Small shop (1/5-30/9) provides essentials (order bread the night before). New bar/restaurant. Snack bar and takeaway. Two outdoor pools, one with a slide (1/5-30/9). Free fishing in lake on site. Youth groups are not accepted. **Off site:** Bicycle hire 500 m, golf 5 km. Supermarkets near.

Charges 2002

Per pitch incl. 1-3 persons	€ 12.00 - € 16.50
extra person	€ 1.50 - € 2.20
local tax	€ 0.15
dog	€ 1.60
electricity	€ 2.20 - € 3.00

Tel: 05 49 52 47 52. Fax: 05 49 52 47 52. E-mail: d.Radet@libertysurf.fr. **Reservations:** Phone bookings accepted for min. 2 nights. **Open** all year.

Directions: From either A10 autoroute or the N10, take Futuroscope exit. Site is located east of both roads, off the D20 to St Georges-Les-Baillargeaux. From all directions follow signs to St Georges. The site si on the hill; turn by the water tower and site is on the left.

Open all year.
Panoramic view over the Futuroscope situated at 2 kms.
Heated swimming pool, pond, snack, bar, restaurant.
Chalets for hire.

86130 St-Georges les Baillargeaux
Tel/Fax: 0033 549 52 47 52
Website: www.camping-le-futuriste.fr

Camping du Parc de Saint Cyr

86130 Saint Cyr

8609

This well organised, five hectare campsite is part of a 300 hectare leisure park, based around a large lake with sailing and associated sports, and an area for swimming (supervised July/Aug). Land based activities include tennis, two half-courts, table tennis, fishing, badminton, pétanque, TV room, and a well equipped fitness suite, all of which are free of charge. In high season there are extra free activities including a kids club, beach club, archery and an entertainment programme. Also in high season but charged for are fly-fishing, sailing school, aquatic toboggan, windsurfing, canoe, kayak, water bikes and stunt bikes. Campers also get 20% discount on green fees at both the 9 and 18 hole golf courses. If all this sounds a bit too exhausting, you could escape to the small, peaceful formal garden in the centre of the site. The campsite has around 185 tourist pitches and 13 mobile homes for rent. The marked and generally separated pitches are all fully serviced with electricity (10A), water and drain.

Facilities: The main toilet block is modern and is supplemented for peak season by a second, recently refitted unit, which should prove adequate for demand, although they do attract some use by day-trippers to the leisure facilities. They include wash-basins in cubicles, dishwashing and laundry sinks, washing machines and dryers, and facilities for babies and disabled persons. Shop, restaurant and takeaway (April - Sept). Children's playground on the beach. Many activities as detailed above. Bicycle hire. Barrier locked 22.00-07.00 hrs (€ 7,62 deposit for card).

Charges 2002

Per pitch incl. electricity, water and drainage	€ 4.60 - € 10.00
adult	€ 2.40 - € 4.00
child (under 7 yrs)	€ 1.50 - € 2.00
animal	free - € 1.50
local tax	€ 0.30

Tel: (0)5 49 62 57 22. Fax: (0)5 49 52 28 58. E-mail: contact@parcdesaintcyr.com. **Reservations:** Advisable for high season, made with fee (€ 7,62). **Open** 1 April - 30 September.

Directions: Saint Cyr is approx. midway between Châtellerault and Poitiers. Site is signed to the east of the N10 and St Cyr village, off the D82 towards Bonneuil-Matours, and is part of the Parc de Loisirs de Saint Cyr.

Camping ★★★★
parc de Saint-Cyr

The campsite is situated in the beautiful setting of a 750 acre leisure Park.

Free entertainment – Beach – Kid and beach club – Tennis courts...

www.parcdesaintcyr.com
Tél : 00.33(0)549.62.57.22 - Fax : 00.33(0)549.52.28.58

Golf
du Haut-Poitou

Offers 9 and 18 holes golf course

The well-tended courses provide a wide variety of challenges and are situated in an exceptionally beautiful seting of lakes and woods.

Driving range, buggies, clubs rental ...

www.golfduhautpoitou.com
Tel : 00.33. (0)549.62.53.62 Fax : 00.33.(0)549.88.77.14

The Campsite and the Golf are situated a few minutes from Poitiers, which is famous for its Romanesque architecture, and for Futuroscope, the theme park of film and visual communication.

-20%

discount is given for green-fees at Haut-Poitou Golf Course if you are staying at the Campsite★★★★.

SAGA - Parc de Saint-Cyr - 86130 Saint-Cyr - FRANCE

An attractively situated lakeside site in Bungundy countryside, Camping Lac de Panthier is in fact two distinct campsites - one where the site activities take place and the other where the reception and other facilities can be found, the latter offering a quieter and more attractive setting. The 207 pitches (167 for touring units) all have electricity connections (6A) and are mostly on level grass, although in parts there are shallow terraces. The site has a swimming pool complex but the most obvious attraction is its proximity to the lake with its many watersports facilities. This site is in beautiful countryside within 2 km. of the lovely Canal de Bourgogne, which links the Seine and the Saône rivers. Used by tour operators (50 pitches). A 'Sites et Paysages' member.

Facilities: Four good quality toilet blocks (two for each site) also provide for babies and disabled people. Shop, bar and restaurant (all 15/5-22/9). Swimming pool complex with adults' pool, children's pool and water-slide (15/5-15/9). Watersports. **Off site:** Boat excursions from Pouilly en Auxois (8 km). Dijon, Autun and Beaune are also within easy reach.

Charges 2003

Per pitch	€ 4.10 - € 6.80
adult	€ 3.70 - € 6.10
child (under 7 yrs)	€ 1.80 - € 3.00
electricity	€ 4.00
dog	€ 1.50
local tax (over 17 yrs)	€ 0.30

Tel: 03 80 49 21 94. Fax: 03 80 49 25 80. E-mail: info@lac-de-panthier.com. **Reservations:** Contact site. **Open** 20 April - 29 September.

Directions: From the A6 use exit 24 (where the A6 joins the A38). Take the N81 towards Arnay Le Duc (back over the A6), then almost immediately turn left on D977 for 5 km. Fork left again for Vandenesse en Auxois. Continue through village on D977 for 2.5 km, turn left again and site is on left.

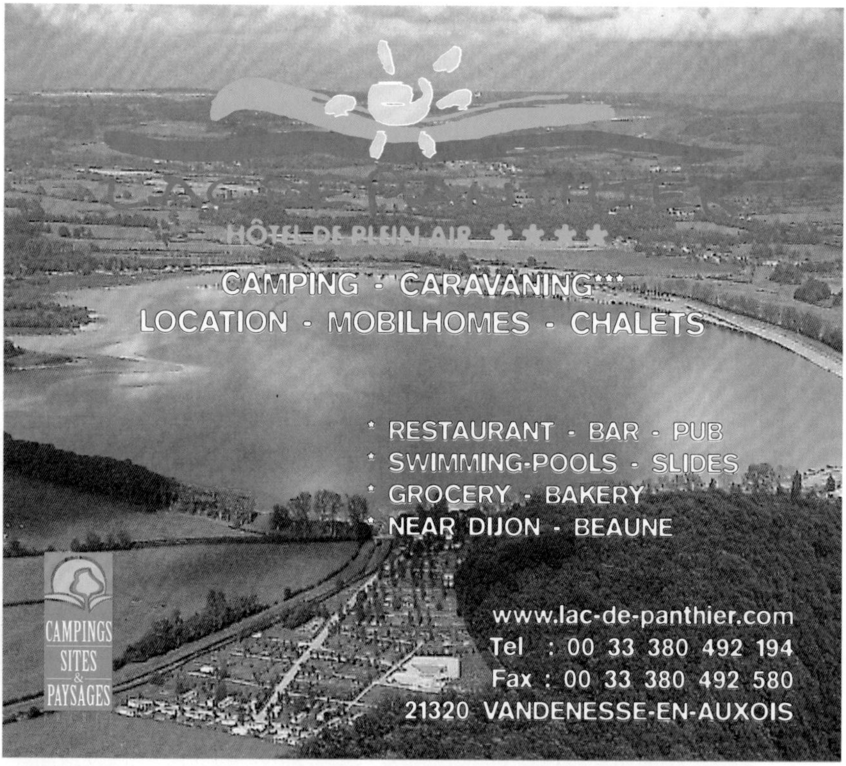

France - Burgundy
Camping La Grappe d'Or
2105 2 route de Volnay, 21190 Meursault

Meursault, the capital of the great white wines of Burgundy, is southwest of Beaune and Camping La Grappe d'Or offers terraced pitches overlooking acres of vineyards. Most of the 118 touring pitches are flat, of varying sizes, and some have shade from mature trees. They all have electricity (15A). There is an outdoor pool and flume and, in high season, aqua gym and other water activities are organised. A second part of the site is 100 m. towards the village in the grounds of the owners' house. Here there are caravan holiday homes for rent. This is a reasonable site from which to enjoy cycle/walking tours that take you around the local vineyards.

Facilities: Sanitary facilities are in three blocks with some washbasins in cabins. Child/baby room, facilities for visitors with disabilities, laundry and undercover dishwashing sinks. Shop, bar, restaurant, takeaway and swimming pool, all open from 15/5 - 15/9 although hours may vary. Play area, volleyball, tennis courts. Bicycle hire. **Off site:** Fishing 8 km, golf or riding 7 km. Indoor swimming pool 7 km.

Charges 2002

Per unit incl. 2 persons	€ 11.00 - € 14.50
extra person	€ 3.00 - € 3.70
child up to 7 yrs	€ 1.50 - € 1.90
electricity	€ 3.50
large motorhome in high season plus	€ 8.00

Tel: (0)3 80 21 22 48. Fax: (0)3 80 21 65 74.
Reservations: Made with € 25 deposit plus € 5 fee.
Open 1 April - 15 October.

Directions: Site is north of Meursault. Take N74 from Beaune and follow the sign for Meursault; campsite is well signed from the town.

France - Burgundy
Camping des Bains
5801 15 avenue Jean Mermoz, 58360 Saint-Honoré-les-Bains

the travel service TO BOOK
erry ✓
itch ✓
ccommodation ✗
1892 55 98 98

This is an attractive site, owned and run by the Luneau family who are keen to welcome British visitors. As the site is low-lying, pitches can be rather soft in wet weather and it can also be quite cold at night in early or late season. That said, it is well situated for exploring the Morvan area. Most of the 120 large, separated pitches (100 sq.m) have a 6A electricity connection, although some may require a long cable. The actual thermal park is next door and there are opportunities locally for `taking the waters` which, combined with the clean, pollution free environment, is said to be very good for asthma sufferers (`cures` run for three week periods). A `Sites et Paysages` member.

Facilities: The two main units have washbasins in separate cabins and ample hot showers (one block may be closed in low season). Dishwashing, baby bath, laundry. Facilities for disabled people. Traditional bar (1/6-30/9) with food and takeaway (1/6-15/9). Small swimming pool (12 x 12 m) with a separate slide (15/6-15/9). Excellent play area and two small streams for children to fish. Table tennis, minigolf and entertainment weekly for children in July/Aug. **Off site:** Canal-side cycle route from Vandenesse (6 km). Bicycle hire or riding 500 m.

Charges 2003

Per unit incl. 2 persons	€ 14.50
extra person	€ 4.20
electricity (6A)	€ 3.00
local tax	€ 0.30

Tel: 03 86 30 73 44. Fax: 03 86 30 61 88. E-mail: camping-les-bains@wanadoo.fr. **Reservations:** Write to site with deposit (€ 65) and fee (€ 12,20). **Open** 1 May - 10 October

Directions: From Nevers, travel east on D978; turn right onto D985 towards St Honoré-les-Bains, from where site is signed `Village des Bains`.

France - Burgundy
Castel Camping Manoir de Bezolle
5803 58110 St-Pereuse-en-Morvan

the travel service TO BOOK
erry ✓
itch ✓
ccommodation ✗
1892 55 98 98

Manoir de Bezolle is well situated to explore the Morvan Natural Park and the Nivernais area. It has been attractively landscaped to provide a number of different areas, some giving pleasant views over the surrounding countryside. Pitches of varying sizes are on level grass with some terracing and most have access to electricity (6A or more). Features worthy of special mention include two small lakes, one used for fishing and a Red Indian village with ponies for children. This site is good for families with a range of activities provided for them.

Facilities: Two main toilet blocks (open as needed) provide washbasins in cabins, a bath, provision for disabled visitors and a baby bath. A smaller, older block is by the pools. Laundry. Motorcaravan services. Shop (15/5-15/9; bread to order at other times). Bar and restaurant (15/5-15/9). Pizza and takeaway (high season). Internet point. Two swimming pools (1/6-15/9). Riding (June-Sept). Table tennis, minigolf. Fishing. Animation in season.

Charges 2002

Per pitch incl. 2 persons	€ 12.00 - € 20.00
extra person	€ 2.00 - € 5.00
electricity 10A	€ 4.00
local taxes	€ 0.50

Tel: 03 86 84 42 55. Fax: 03 86 84 43 77. E-mail: info@bezolle.com. **Reservations:** With deposit (€ 46) and fee (€ 15,20). **Open** 15 April - 30 September.

Directions: Site is between Nevers and Autun (mid-way between Châtillon-en-Bazois and Château-Chinon), just north of the D978 by the small village of St Péreuse-en-Morvan.

Castel Camping Château de L'Epervière

71240 Gigny-sur-Saône

7107

Peacefully situated on the edge of the little village of Gigny-sur-Saône, yet within easy distance of the A6 autoroute, this site sits in a natural woodland area near the Saône river (subject to flooding in winter months). With 135 pitches, nearly all with 6A electricity, the site is in two fairly distinct areas. The original part has semi-hedged pitches on part-level ground with plenty of shade from mature trees, close to the château and fishing lake - you may need earplugs in the mornings because of the ducks! The centre of the second area has a more open aspect, with large hedged pitches and mature trees offering shade around the periphery and central open grass area. An unfenced road across the lake connects the two areas of the site (care is needed with children). The managers, Gert-Jan and Francois, and their team enthusiastically organise a range of activities for visitors that includes wine tastings in the cellars of the château and a Kids' Club in July/Aug. The site is actually owned by Christophe Gay the founder and driving force behind 'Camping Cheques', the low season 'Go as you please' package that gives flexibility to visit Camping Cheque sites in Europe. Used by tour operators (60 pitches). A member of 'Les Castels' group.

Facilities: Two well equipped toilet blocks, one beside the château and a newer one on the lower section include washbasins in cabins, dishwashing and laundry areas under cover. Washing machine and dryer. Shop providing bread and basic provisions (1/5-30/9). Tastefully refurbished restaurant in the château with a distinctly French menu (1/4-30/9). Second restaurant with more basic menu and takeaway service. A converted barn houses an attractive bar, large screen TV and games room. Unheated swimming pool (1/5-30/9), partly enclosed by old stone walls protecting it from the wind, plus a smaller indoor heated pool with jacuzzi, sauna and paddling pool. Children's play area. Bicycle hire. **Off site:** Riding 15 km, golf 20 km.

Charges 2003

Per adult	€ 5.10 - € 6.10
child (under 7 yrs)	€ 3.10 - € 4.10
pitch	€ 6.60 - € 9.20
dog	€ 2.10 - € 2.60
electricity	€ 3.10 - € 4.10

Tel: 03 85 94 16 90. Fax: 03 85 94 16 97. E-mail: domaine-de-lepervière@wanadoo.fr. **Reservations:** Contact site. **Open** 1 April - 15 October.

Directions: From N6 between Châlon-sur-Saône and Tournus, turn east on D18 (just north of Sennecey-le-Grand) and follow site signs for 6.5 km. From A6, exit Châlon-Sud from the north, or Tournus from the south.

Welcome to the heart of Burgundy

Camping Cheque

Camping Caravaning

★★★★

Château de l'Epervière

71240 Gigny sur Saône
Tel: 0033 385 94 16 90
Fax: 0033 385 94 16 97
domaine-de-lepervière@wanadoo.fr

LES CASTELS
★★★★

Camping Les Lanchettes

7303 73210 Peisey-Nancroix

This site is in the beautiful Vanoise National Park and at 1,470 m. is one of the highest campsites in this guide. The steep climb to the site, not recommended for underpowered units, through spectacular scenery is well worth the effort. This natural site is terraced and has 90 good size, reasonably level and well drained, grassy/stony pitches. With 80 used for touring units, all have electricity (3-10A). Because it is very cold in winter and quite cold on some spring and autumn evenings there are no outside taps. In winter about 30 pitches at the bottom of the site become part of a cross country ski run. For those who love wonderful scenery, flora and fauna and for those wanting a walking/biking summer holiday, this is the site for you.

Facilities: Comprehensive facilities are all in the basement of the house, very cosy in winter. Restaurant with takeaway (July/Aug. and mid Dec-mid April). Playground. Club/TV room. Large tent/marquee used in bad weather for a meeting place and as a dormitory by tenters. Motorcaravan service point. In winter a bus runs to all the hotels, bars, ski tows etc and calls at the site. Accompanied walks (one free) in the National Park. **Off site:** Riding next to site. Bicycle hire 6 km. Golf 8 km.

Charges 2002

Per unit incl. 2 persons	€ 10.80 - € 11.90
electricity 3, 5 or 10A	€ 2.90 - € 7.30

Tel: (0)4 79 07 93 07. Fax: (0)4 79 07 88 33. E-mail: lanchettes@free.fr. **Reservations:** Contact site. **Open** all year, 15 Oct - 15 Dec.

Directions: From Albertville take N90 towards Bourg-St-Maurice, through Moûtiers and Aime and about 5 km. further turn right, signed Landry and Peisey-Nancroix. Follow road down, then up a fairly wide, steep, winding hill (a few hairpin bends) for 10 km. Site on right in 1 km. beyond Nancroix.

Camping-Caravaning Les Grands Pins

3313 33680 Lacanau-Océan

This Atlantic coast holiday site with direct access to fine sandy beach, is on undulating terrain amongst tall pine trees. A large site, it provides 570 pitches, with about 44 private and rental mobile homes, leaving around 525 pitches of varying sizes for touring units. The site is well served by tarmac access roads, and although not noticeably divided, one half of the site is a traffic free zone (except for arrival or departure day, caravans are placed on the pitch, with separate areas outside the zone for car parking). There is a good number of tent pitches, those in the centre of the site having some of the best views, and especially useful for tenters are safety deposit and fridge boxes which are available for rent. The large sandy beach is a 350 m. stroll from the gate at the back of the site.

Facilities: Five toilet blocks, including an excellent new one, include washbasins in cubicles, dishwashing and laundry sinks, a dog and wetsuit washing area, baby room and facilities for disabled people (not all units open in low season). Launderette. Motorcaravan services. Good supermarket, surf boutique. Bar, restaurant and snack bar with takeaway. Heated pool (20 x 10 m, from 1/5 with lifeguard in July/Aug). Jacuzzi. Games room. Fitness suite. Tennis (charge in July/Aug). Two playgrounds. Bicycle hire. Organised activities for children (July/Aug). Entrance barrier with keypad access. Only gas barbecues are permitted. **Off site:** Fishing, golf, riding and bicycle hire 5 km.

Charges 2002

Per pitch incl. 2 persons, electricity	€ 23.00 - € 30.00
extra person	€ 6.50 - € 8.50
child (2-12 yrs)	free - € 4.00

Tel: (0)5 56 03 20 77. Fax: (0)5 57 70 03 89. E-mail: reception@lesgrandspins.com. **Reservations:** Essential for high season, made with deposit and reservation fee. Discounts for early booking. **Open** 19 April - 15 September, full facilities from 1/5.

Directions: From Bordeaux take N125/D6 west to Lacanau, continue on D6 to Lacanau Océan. Follow signs to camp sites, passing several other sites, and Les Grand Pins is signed to the right at the far end of the road. From northern France you could use the ferry from Royan to Le Verdon.

Camping **Les Grands Pins** ✳ ✳ ✳ ✳
F-33680 Lacanau Ocean   Tél : (33) 5 56 03 20 77   Fax (33) 5 57 70 03 89
E-mail : reception@lesgrandspins.com   www.lesgrandspins.com

Camping
and
Mobile-homes
350m
from
the beach

Airotel Camping de la Côte d'Argent

33990 Hourtin-Plage

the travel service
TO BOOK

Ferry ✔
Pitch ✔
Accommodation ✘

01892 55 98 98

Spread over 20 hectares of undulating sand-based terrain and in the midst of a pine forest, this large site is well placed and well equipped for leisurely family holidays. It also makes an ideal base for walkers and cyclists, with over 100 km. of cycle lanes leading through the Medoc countryside. Hourtin-Plage is a pleasant invigorating resort on the Atlantic coast and a popular location for watersports enthusiasts, or those who prefer spending their days on the beach. More appealing though may be to stay on site, for Côte d'Argent's top attraction is its swimming pool complex with wooden bridges connecting the pools and islands, on which there are sunbathing patios and children's play areas. There are 750 touring pitches which are not clearly defined and in the trees, some on soft sand-based ground (night lighting provided). When we visited 48 hardstandings for motorcaravans were almost complete. Due to the work on the site the access roads were in a poor condition, but we were told would be repaired in the near future. A reader tells us that the site is well organised and ideal for children, akthough it can be noisy at night in high season.

Facilities: Five very clean sanitary blocks of various ages include provision for disabled visitors. Plenty of laundry machines. Motorcaravan service points. Large supermarket. Restaurant, takeaway and pizzeria bar. Four swimming pools, waterslides and flumes. Two tennis courts, pool tables and four play areas. Mini-club and organised entertainment in season. Charcoal barbecues are not permitted. **Off site:** Walkway to the beach.

Charges guide

Per unit incl. 2 persons	€ 18.60 - € 25.15
extra person	€ 2.74 - € 4.57
child (2-10 yrs)	€ 1.83 - € 3.35
tent incl. 2 persons	€ 15.24 - € 22.26
electricity (6A)	€ 3.81
dog	€ 1.68 - € 3.05
local tax over 10 yrs	€ 0.50

Tel: 05 56 09 10 25. Fax: 05 56 09 24 96. E-mail: info@camping-cote-dargent.com. **Reservations:** Necessary for July/August. **Open** 11 May - 15 September.

Directions: Turn off D101 Hourtin-Soulac road 3 km. north of Hourtin. Then join D101E signed Hourtin-Plage. Site is 300 m. from the beach.

Camping Le Vieux Port

Plage sud, 40660 Messanges

the travel service
TO BOOK

Ferry ✔
Pitch ✔
Accommodation ✔

01892 55 98 98

The area to the north of Bayonne is heavily forested and a number of very large campsites are attractively located close to the superb Atlantic beaches. Le Vieux Port is probably the largest and certainly one of the most impressive of these. Appealing particularly to families with teenagers, this lively site has no fewer than 1,406 open pitches of mixed size, most with electricity and some with water and drainage. Sprawling beneath the pines, the camping area is well shaded and pitches are generally of a good size, attractively grouped around the toilet blocks. At least a third of the site is taken up with mobile homes and there are a large number of tour operators here (30%). The heated pool complex is exceptional boasting no less than five outdoor pools and three large water slides. There is also a heated indoor pool. At the back of the site a path leads across the dunes to a superb beach. A little train also trundles to the beach on a fairly regular basis in high season. All in all, a lively site with a great deal to offer an active family.

Facilities: Nine well appointed toilet blocks are all of modern design and well maintained. Facilities for disabled people. Motorcaravan service point. Good shopping facilities, including a well stocked supermarket and various smaller shops. Several restaurants (including takeaway service) and bars (all open throughout the season). Large swimming pool complex (no bermuda shorts). Three tennis courts, two football pitches, a multi-sport pitch, minigolf etc. Bicycle hire. Well run and popular riding centre. Large animation team organise a wide range of activities in high season including frequent discos and karaoke evenings. Only communal barbecues are allowed.

Charges 2002

Per unit incl. 2 persons	€ 11.00 - € 26.00
extra person over 10 yrs	€ 2.50 - € 5.00
child under 10 yrs	€ 1.50 - € 3.00
electricity (6/10A)	€ 2.50 - € 6.00
local tax (June-Sept)	€ 0.42
animal	€ 1.25 - € 2.50

Tel: 05 58 48 22 00. Fax: 05 58 48 01 69. E-mail: levieuxport@wanadoo.fr. **Reservations:** Essential in high season. **Open** 1 April - 30 September.

Directions: Leave RN 10 at Magescq exit heading for Soustons. Pass through Soustons following signs for Vieux-Boucau. Bypass this town and site is clearly signed to the left at second roundabout.

Airotel Camping Caravaning de la Côte d'Argent

33990 Hourtin Plage

Tél :(+ 33)5.56.09.10.25 Fax :(+ 33)5.56.09.24.96

Internet : www.camping-cote-dargent.com

Swimming pool complex of 3500 m² with water slides

Caravans and mobile homes to rent

Camping de la Côte d'Argent occupies an area of 20 hectares situated in the heart of a pine forest, but only 300 m from a huge beach, and just 4 km away from one of the biggest natural lakes in the whole of the France. A characterful site, protected from the wind by the forest and nearby sand dunes, this site is natural surroundings also enjoys the benefit of an ideal climate.

ESE COMMUNICATION : 04 94 67 06 00

Free brochures on request - Alan Rogers 2003

Name.. First name................................

Adress..

Town..Post code...............................

Camping du Domaine de la Rive

route de Bordeaux, 40600 Biscarosse

4010

Set in pine woods, La Rive has a superb beach-side loaction on Lac de Sanguient. It provides mostly level, numbered and clearly defined pitches of 100 sq.m. All have electricity connections (6A) and there is good shade. The swimming pool complex is wonderful, with various pools linked by water channels and bridges, the four-slide pool having a wide staircase to the top to speed up enjoyment. There is also a jacuzzi, paddling pool and two large, unusually shaped swimming pools, all surrounded by paved sunbathing areas and decorated with palm trees. An indoor pool is planned. The beach is excellent, shelving gently to provide safe bathing for all ages. There are windsurfers and small craft can be launched from the site's slip-way. This is a friendly site with a good mix of nationalities and lots of activities for the family, although it can be noisy at night in high season.

Facilities: Five modern, very good quality toilet blocks have washbasins in cabins and mainly British style toilets. Visitors with disabilities well catered for in three blocks. Baby baths. We found the facilities very clean. Motorcaravan service point. Well stocked shop with gas (15/5-15/9). Bar serving snacks and takeaway. Games room. Restaurant with reasonably priced family meals (1/6-15/9). Pool complex supervised July/Aug (15/5-15/9). Play area. Two tennis courts. Bicycle hire. Basketball court, table tennis, boules, archery and football. Fishing. Water skiing. Watersports equipment hire. Sports tournaments June-Aug. Discos and karaoke evenings organised outside bar with stage. Mini-club for children. Charcoal barbecues not permitted on pitches (central area available). **Off site:** Riding 5 km, golf 10 km.

Charges 2002

Per pitch incl. 2 persons, electricity	€ 20.00 - € 30.00
with water and drainage	€ 23.00 - € 33.00
extra person	€ 3.40 - € 5.00
child (3-10 yrs)	€ 2.30 - € 3.50
local tax	€ 0.50

Tel: 05 58 78 12 33. Fax: 05 58 78 12 92. E-mail: info@camping-de-la-rive.fr. **Reservations:** Advised for July/Aug. (deposit €100). **Open** 1 April - 30 September.

Directions: Take D652 from Sanguinet to Biscarrosse and site signed on the right in 6 km.

Camping Les Vignes

Route de la Plage du Cap de L'Homy, 40170 Lit-et-Mixe

4016

Les Vignes is a large holiday site close to the Atlantic coast with 420 pitches, of which 240 are occupied by a mix of mobile homes, bungalows and tents, most of which are for rent. The 180 tourist pitches are relatively level on a sandy base, all serviced with electricity (10A) and water, some with waste water drains. The site's amenities, including a supermarket, restaurant and bar, are located at the entrance to the site. The rather stylish swimming pool complex includes a six lane water slide. A wide range of activities is provided and during July and August a great variety of entertainment options for both adults and children, some of which takes place in the new entertainment 'Big Top'. There are many cycle tracks in the area.

Facilities: Four sanitary units (not all open in low season) provide combined washbasin and shower cubicles, dishwashing and laundry sinks, washing machines and dryers, facilities for babies and disabled people. Large supermarket. Restaurant, bar and takeaway (all from mid-June). Pool complex (1/6-15/9, large pool from 21/6). Tennis. Table tennis. Golf driving range. Minigolf. Volleyball, basketball. Pétanque. Kids' club and playground. Bicycle hire. **Off site:** Golf, canoeing, kayaking, surfing, riding.

Charges 2002

Per pitch incl. 2 persons	€ 12.00 - € 27.50
water and electricity (mandatory)	€ 2.50 - € 5.00
extra person (over 5 yrs)	€ 4.00 - € 5.00
child (under 5 yrs)	€ 1.50 - € 3.00

Tel: (0)5 58 42 85 60. Fax: (0)5 58 42 74 36. E-mail: contact@les-vignes.com. **Reservations:** Advisable for high season, made with deposit and fee. **Open** 1 June - 15 September.

Directions: Lit-et-Mixe is 20 km. south of Mimizan. From Lit-et-Mixe take D652 south for 1 km., then turn west on D88 towards Cap de l'Homy for 1.5 km. where site entrance is on left.

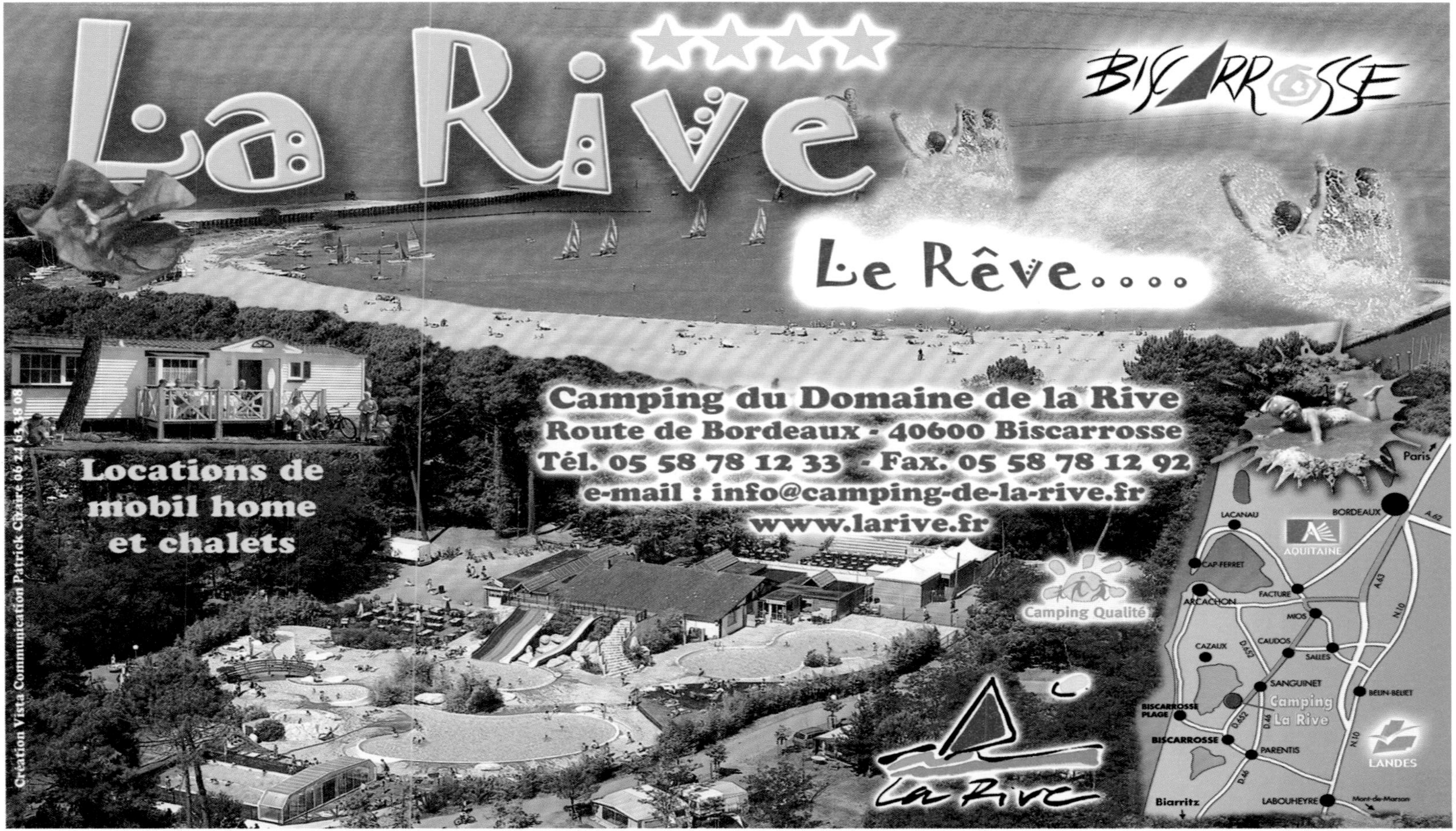
La Rive
Biscarrosse
Le Rêve....
Camping du Domaine de la Rive
Route de Bordeaux - 40600 Biscarrosse
Tél. 05 58 78 12 33 - Fax. 05 58 78 12 92
e-mail : info@camping-de-la-rive.fr
www.larive.fr
Locations de mobil home et chalets
Camping Qualité
La Rive
Paris
Bordeaux
Lacanau
Aquitaine
Cap-Ferret
Arcachon
Facture
Mios
Cazaux
Caudos
Salles
Sanguinet
Camping La Rive
Belin-Beliet
Biscarrosse Plage
Biscarrosse
Parentis
Landes
Biarritz
Labouheyre
Mont-de-Marsan
Création Vista Communication Patrick Cizaire 06 24 63 38 08

Sunêlia Le Col-Vert

4005 Lac de Leon, 40560 Vielle-St-Girons

the travel service
TO BOOK
Ferry ✔
Pitch ✔
Accommodation ✔

01892 55 98 98

This extensive but natural site edges a nature reserve and stretches right along the Lac de Léon, a conservation area, for 1 km. on a narrow frontage. This makes it particularly suitable for those who want to practise water sports such as sailing and windsurfing. Bathing is also possible (although there are pools on site as well) as the lake bed shelves gently making it easy for children. The site has a supervised beach, sail-boarding courses are arranged and there are some boats and boards for hire. There are some 800 pitches in total, the 380 pitches for touring units being flat and covered by light pinewood, most with good shade. They are of around 100 sq.m, only partly separated and some 72 have water and electricity points. Much 'animation' is organised in season: children's games, tournaments, etc. by day and dancing or shows in the evenings. Used by tour operators (80 pitches).

Facilities: The four toilet blocks include a very large one towards the far end of the site. Not all are open in low season. Cleaning can be variable and the hot water supply is not reliable. Mostly British WCs, washbasins in cabins. Dishwashing sinks (mainly cold water but with hot tap to draw from). Washing machines, dryer and dishwasher. Good facilities for disabled people. Motorcaravan services. Shops (15/5-15/9). Good bar/restaurant by the lake (open to all). Simple takeaway. Two heated pools (all season and supervised), one open air with whirl pool and a covered one, with sunbathing areas. Children's playground. TV room, table tennis, amusement machines. Sports area with tennis and volleyball. Fitness centre and sauna/solarium. Two jogging tracks. Safety deposit boxes. Note: An overall charge is made for the leisure activities but this excludes certain facilities, eg. riding, bicycle hire, sauna, tennis, minigolf. Fishing (lessons for children). Riding. Sailing school (15/6-15/9). Several areas for barbecues. **Off site:** Walking and cycle ways in the forest. Golf 10 km. Atlantic beaches 5 km.

Charges 2002

Per unit incl. 2 persons	
acc to season, type and location	€ 8.50 - € 28.50
extra person	€ 2.00 - € 4.50
child (3-7 yrs)	€ 1.50 - € 3.50
dog	€ 1.00 - € 3.00
electricity (3/10A)	€ 3.35 - € 5.00
local tax€	0.41

Tel: 05 58 42 94 06. Fax: 05 58 42 91 88. E-mail: contact@colvert.com. **Reservations:** Any length with UK£42 deposit per week booked and £25 fee. **Open** Easter - 15 September.

Directions: Roads to lake and site lead off D652 St Girons - Léon road at Vielle-St-Girons (signed).

Domaine Naturiste Arnaoutchot

N4012 40560 Vielle-St-Girons

the travel service
TO BOOK
Ferry ✔
Pitch ✔
Accommodation ✔

01892 55 98 98

'Arna' is a large naturist site with extensive facilities and direct access to the beach. Even with 500 pitches, its layout in the form of a number of sections, each with its own character, make it quite relaxing and very natural. These sections amongst the trees and bushes of the Landes provide a variety of reasonably sized pitches, most with electricity, although the hilly terrain means that only a limited number are flat enough for motorcaravans. The centrally located amenities are extensive and of excellent quality. The site has the advantage of direct access to a large, sandy naturist beach, although access from some parts of the site may involve a walk of perhaps 600-700 m. The 'Arna Club' provides more than 30 activities and workshops (in the main season). English is spoken. Chalets, mobile homes and tents for rent. The site is used by a tour operator (20 pitches). Member 'France 4 Naturisme'.

Facilities: Sanitary facilities include the usual naturist site type of blocks with communal hot showers, but also a number of tiny blocks with one hot shower, WC and washbasin each in an individual cabin. All blocks provide fully tiled, modern facilities, one block is heated in low season. Laundry. Motorcaravan service point. Large supermarket and a range of other shops. Bar/restaurant, pizzeria and tapita (fish) bar. Pizza delivery to pitches or to telephone point on beach. Heated indoor pool with solarium, whirlpool and slide. Outdoor pool and terraced sunbathing area. Sauna, steam, whirlpool and massage. Arna Club (main season) with riding, archery, golf practise, tennis, petanque, swimming, rambling, cycling, sailing, handicrafts, excursions and activities for children. TV, video and games rooms. Cinema. Library. Hairdresser and chiropodist. Internet point. Bicycle hire. Fishing. Barbecues are not permitted. Torches useful. **Off site:** Riding or golf 5 km.

Charges 2002

Per unit incl. 2 persons	€ 12.50 - € 27.50
extra person over 3 yrs	€ 3.00 - € 6.00
leisure club	€ 0.40 - € 1.20
electricity (3A)	€ 3.50

Tel: 05 58 49 11 11. Fax: 05 58 48 57 12. E-mail: contact@arna.com. **Reservations:** Made with 25% deposit and fee (€ 27,44). **Open** 1 April - 15 September.

Directions: Site is signed off D652 road at Vielle-Saint-Girons - follow D328 for 3-4 km.

France - Atlantic Coast
Camping Les Tamaris Plage
6408 Quartier Acotz, 64500 Saint-Jean-de-Luz

This is a small, pleasant and well kept site. It is situated well outside the town but just across the road from a sandy beach with 79 numbered pitches, 45 with electricity, including some mobile homes and bungalows. They are of very good size and separated by hedges, on slightly sloping ground with some shade. It becomes full for nearly all July and August with families on long stays, so reservation then is advisable. No shop, bread daily across the road

Facilities: Single toilet block of superb quality and unusual design should be an ample provision. Washbasins and showers in private cabins, mainly British style WCs, dishwashing sinks, facilities for disabled people. Washing machine. Covered terrace with views of the sea. Adult TV room and children's room with TV and games. Playground. **Off site:** Fishing 30 m, bicycle hire, golf 4 km, riding 7 km.

Charges 2002

Per unit (100 sq.m. pitch) incl. 2 persons and electricity (5A)	€ 21.00 - € 27.50
tent pitch (80 sq.m.) incl. 2 persons	€ 16.50 - € 23.00
extra person (over 2 yrs)	€ 3.50 - € 5.00

Tel: 05 59 26 55 90. **Fax:** 05 59 47 70 15. **E-mail:** tamaris1@clubinternet.fr. **Reservations:** Made with 20% deposit and fee (€ 18.30). **Open** 1 April - 30 September.

Directions: Proceed south on N10 and 1.5 km. after Guethary take first road on right (before access to the motorway and Carrefour centre commercial) and follow camp signs.

France - Atlantic Coast
Camping Airotel La Chêneraie
6409 chemin Cazenave, 64100 Bayonne

La Chêneraie is only 8 km. from the coast at Anglet with its long sandy beach and large car park, but you would think you were much further away from all the hustle and bustle of the coast. The distant views of the Pyrénées from various points all add to the feeling of peace. The 210 pitches are arranged on neat grass, with most partially divided by trees and shrubs, so quite well shaded. Many have electricity connections, some with water and drainage. One area is very sloping but it has been terraced to give level pitches. Wooded walks lead to a small lake which can be used for inflatables or fishing (no swimming). A tour operator uses 20 pitches. English is spoken.

Facilities: The large, central sanitary block includes washbasins in cabins, with three smaller blocks around the site providing additional facilities. In high season these facilities may be under pressure and maintenance and cleaning could be variable. Dishwashing and laundry sinks. Washing machine and dryers, baby baths, and facilities for disabled people. Shop, restaurant with all day snacks and a takeaway (all main season). Medium sized swimming pool open June - end August (longer if the weather is good). Children's playground. Tennis courts (free outside July/Aug). TV room. Table tennis. **Off site:** Bicycle hire 5 km, riding 6 km, golf 7 km.

Charges 2002

Per pitch	€ 9.45 - € 11.43
with water and electricity	€ 10.67 - € 16.01
person	€ 3.66 - € 4.27
child (under 10 yrs)	€ 2.13 - € 2.74
dog	€ 2.29
local tax (over 18s)	€ 0.17

Tel: 05 59 55 01 31. **Fax:** 05 59 55 11 17. **Reservations:** Made for min. 1 week with deposit (€ 62) and fee (€ 15,24). **Open** Easter - 30 September (full services 1/6-15/9).

Directions: Site is 4 km. northeast of Bayonne just off main N117 road to Pau, signed at traffic lights. From new autoroute A63 take exit 6 marked 'Bayonne St Esprit'.

The Alan Rogers' Travel Service

We have recently extended The Alan Rogers Travel Service. This unique service enables our readers to reserve their holidays as well as ferry crossings and comprehensive insurance cover at extremely competitive rates. The majority of participating sites are in France and we are able to offer a selection of some of the very best sites in this country.

One simple telephone call to our Travel Service on 01892 55 98 98 is all that is needed to make all the arrangements. Why not take advantage of our years' of experience of camping and caravanning. We would be delighted to discuss your holiday plans with you, and offer advice and recommendations.

Share our experience and let us help to ensure your holiday will be a complete success.

Alan Rogers Travel Service 01892 55 98 98 or www.alanrogers.com

1201

the travel service
TO BOOK

Ferry	✓
Pitch	✓
Accommodation	✗

01892 55 98 98

This pleasant terraced site has been imaginatively and tastefully developed by the Dupond family over a 25 year period. In particular, the magnificent carved features in the bar create a delightful ambience. True, the ground is hard in summer but reception staff supply robust nails if your awning pegs prove a problem. Most of the 200 pitches (all with electricity and water) are peaceful, generous in size and with views of the valley. The pools are bedecked by flowers and crowned by a large urn which dispenses water into the paddling pool. But it is the activity programme that is unique at Val de Cantobre, supervised by qualified instructors, some arranged by the owners and some at a fair distance from the site. Passive recreationists appreciate the scenery, especially Cantobre, a medieval village that clings to a cliff in view of the site. Nature lovers will be delighted to see the vultures wheeling in the Tarn gorge. Butterflies in profusion, orchids, huge edible snails, glow worms, beavers and the natterjack toad all live here. It is easy to see why - the place is magnificent. Although tour operators occupy around 40% of the pitches, the terrace design provides some peace and privacy, especially on the upper levels and a warm welcome awaits from the Dupond family.

Facilities: The fully equipped impressive toilet block is beautifully appointed with a huge indoor dishwashing area. Shop, although small, offers a wide variety of provisions; including many regional specialities (comparing well with local shops and markets). Attractive new bar, restaurant, pizzeria and takeaway facility. Three adjoining swimming pools. Around 15 types of activity including river rafting, white water canoeing, rock climbing or jumps from Millau's hill tops on twin seater steerable parachutes. All weather sports pitch. Fishing. Torch useful.

Charges 2002

Per unit incl. 2 persons and 4A electricity	€ 18.00 - € 26.00
extra person (4 yrs and over)	€ 3.00 - € 6.00
dog	free - € 3.00

Tel: 05 65 58 43 00. Fax: 05 65 62 10 36.
Reservations: Made for any length with 25% deposit, fee (€ 18,29) and optional cancellation insurance. **Open** 18 May - 15 September, with all facilities.

Directions: Site is 4 km. north of Nant, on D991 road to Millau. From Millau direction take D991 signed Gorge du Dourbie.

Camping-Caravaning Les Rivages

1202 avenue de l'Aigoual, route de Nant, 12100 Millau

Les Rivages is a large site on the outskirts of the town. It is well organised and well situated, being close to the high limestone Causses and the dramatic gorges of the Tarn and Dourbie, the latter of which runs past the back of the site. Smaller pitches, used for tents and small units, abut a pleasant riverside space suitable for sunbathing, fishing or picnics. Most of the 314 pitches are large, 100 sq.m. or more, and well shaded. A newer part of the site (on the right as you enter) has less shade but pitches are larger. All pitches have electricity (6A), and 100 have water and drainage. The site offers a very wide range of sporting activities close to 30 in all (see facilities). Millau is a bustling and pleasant town. Don't miss the night markets, but don't eat before you get there - there are thousands of things to taste, many of them grilled or spit roasted. The gates are shut 10 pm.- 8 am, with night-watchman.

Facilities: Four well kept modern toilet blocks have all necessary facilities. A special block for children includes baby baths, small showers, children's toilets as well as ironing facilities. Shop for most essentials (20/5-15/9). Terrace restaurant and bar overlooking a good-sized main swimming pool and children's pool (from 10/5). Children's play area. Much evening entertainment, largely for children, along with child-minding and a mini-club. Tennis (indoor and outdoor). Squash (can be viewed from the bar). Table tennis. Floodlit petanque. Many river activities, walking, bird watching and fishing. **Off site:** Rafting and canoeing arranged. Bicycle hire 1 km, riding 10 km, golf 40 km. Hypermarket in Millau.

Charges 2002

Per pitch incl. 2 persons	€ 12.50 - € 19.50
with electricity	€ 14.50 - € 22.50
with water and drainage	€ 16.50 - € 24.50
extra person (over 3 yrs)	€ 3.00 - € 4.00
pet	€ 2.50 - € 3.00
local tax (15/6-15/9)	€ 0.30

Tel: 05 65 61 01 07. Fax: 05 65 59 03 56. E-mail: campinglesrivages@wanadoo.fr. **Reservations:** Advisable for Jul/Aug. with deposit (€ 61) and fee (€ 15,24). **Open** 1 May - 30 September.

Directions: From Millau, take D991 road south towards Nant. Site is about 400 m. on the right.

France - Dordogne/Aveyron

Camping Club Les Genêts

Lac de Pareloup, 12410 Salles Curan

the travel service
TO BOOK
Ferry ✓
Pitch ✓
Accommodation ✓
01892 55 98 98

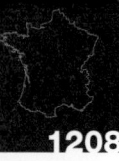

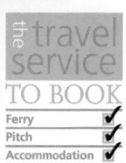

This family run site is on the shores of Lac de Pareloup and offers both family holiday and watersports facilities. The 162 pitches include 102 grassy, mostly individual pitches for touring units. These are in two areas, one on each side of the entrance lane, and are divided by hedges, shrubs and trees. Most have electricity (6A) and many also have water and waste water drain. The site slopes gently down to the beach and lake with facilities for all watersports including waterskiing. A full animation and activities programme is organised in high season, and there is much to see and do in this very attractive corner of Aveyron. Used by tour operators (40 pitches). A `Sites et Paysages' member.

Facilities: Two main sanitary units include washbasins in cubicles and a suite for disabled people. Refurbishment of the older unit is planned, whilst the other unit is new. Baby room. Dishwashing and laundry sinks. Laundry room. Very well stocked shop. Bar and restaurant. Snack bar serving pizzas and other snacks in main season. Swimming pool and spa pool (both 1/6-15/9; unsupervised). Children's playground. Minigolf, volleyball and boules. Bicycle hire. Red Indian style tee-pees. Hire of pedaloes, windsurfers and kayaks. Fishing licences available.

Charges 2002

Per unit incl. 1 or 2 persons and 6A electricity	€ 11.00 - € 24.00
lakeside pitch	€ 11.00 - € 32.00
extra person over 7 yrs	€ 3.00 - € 5.50
child 2-7 yrs	free - € 5.50
pet	€ 3.00 - € 4.00

Tel: 05 65 46 35 34. Fax: 05 65 78 00 72. E-mail: contact@camping-les-genets.fr. **Reservations:** Advised for July/Aug. and made with deposit (€ 155) and fee (€ 29). **Open** 25 May - 15 September.

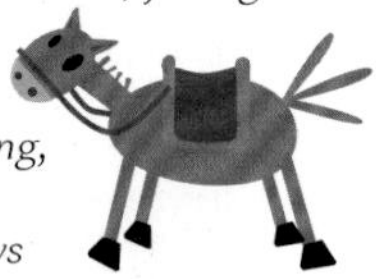

Directions: From Salles-Curan take D577 for about 4 km. and turn right into a narrow lane immediately after a sharp right hand bend. Site is signed at junction.

Camping Marmotel

12130 Saint Geniez d'Olt

The road into Marmotel passes various industrial buildings and is a little off-putting - persevere, they are soon left behind. The campsite itself is a mixture of old and new. The old part provides many pitches with lots of shade and separated by hedges. The new area is sunny until the trees grow. These pitches each have a personal sanitary unit, with shower, WC, washbasin and dishwashing. New and very well designed, they are reasonably priced for such luxury. All pitches have electricity (10A). A lovely new restaurant with terrace overlooks the new heated swimming and paddling pools which have fountains, a toboggan and sun beds on either grass or the tiled surrounds. The bar/reception area is also new with comfortable seating and internet access.

Facilities: Good sanitary facilities include baby baths and facilities for disabled visitors. Washing machines. Bar/restaurant and takeaway (all season). Swimming pools. Fishing. Bicycle hire. Tennis. Small play area. Entertainment for all ages in July/Aug. including a disco under the bar, cinema screen, karaoke, dances and a mini club for 4-10 yr olds. **Off site:** Large supermarket 500 m. Riding 500 m. Bicycle tours and canoe trips on the Lot and rafting on the Tarn.

Charges 2002

Per unit incl. 1 or 2 persons, 10A electricity	€ 21.50
with sanitary unit	€ 24.50
extra person	€ 3.80 - € 4.50
child under 3 yrs	€ 2.30
animal	€ 1.00

Tel: 05 65 70 46 51. Fax: 05 65 47 41 38. E-mail: info@marmotel.com. **Reservations:** Made with deposit (€ 100) and fee (€ 15). **Open** 7 May - 21 September.

Directions: Heading south on autoroute A75 (free) take exit 40 and follow signs for St Geniez d'Olt. Site is at western end of village. Site is signed onto D19 to Prades d'Aubrac, then 500 m. on left.

"VERY COMFORTABLE, VERY NATURAL."
5 ha in the Lot Valley, by the riverside. 180 pitches, 42 of which have individual toilet. Chalets and Mobile homes for hire. 350 sqm swimming pools, waterslides, tennis, animations, kids club, bar, restaurant.
Open 30/04 – 21/09
www.marmotel.com

Camping Marco de Bignac

Lieudit 'Les Sablons', 16170 Bignac

The small village of Bignac is set in peaceful countryside not too far from the N10 road, north of Angoulême. Since buying the campsite in 1994, the Marshall family have worked hard to improve this tranquil site which is arranged along one side of an attractive lake on a level, grassy meadow. The 89 pitches are marked at each corner by a tree so there is shade, and electricity (3/6A) is available. At the far end of the site is a hedged swimming pool and plenty of grassy space for ball games. The lake shores are home to ducks and the lake itself is used for fishing and small boats. The reception office is part of the owner's home and near here is a bar and snack bar with tables outside and views across the lake. This site is popular with British visitors and is a peaceful, relaxing location for couples or young families. There is no noisy entertainment and all the activities are free of charge.

Facilities: Two traditional French style toilet blocks have functional facilities all in cabins opening from the outside. Dishwashing or laundry sinks at either end of each block. Washing machine. Bar and snack bar (1/6-31/8; closed Mon. until high season). Essentials kept in the bar and baker calls daily (high season). Swimming pool (15/6-31/8, unsupervised). Football field, badminton, tennis, table tennis, pedaloes, minigolf and boule pitch (boules provided), all free. Play area. Pets corner. Fishing. Special evenings, outings and competitions organised in high season. A torch may be useful. **Off site:** Local markets. Riding 5 km.

Charges guide

Per pitch incl. 2 persons	€ 10.67 - € 14.48
extra person	€ 2.29 - € 3.81
child (2-7 yrs)	free - € 2.29
electricity 3-6A	€ 2.29 - € 3.81

Tel: 05 45 21 78 41. Fax: 05 45 21 52 74. **Reservations:** Made with deposit. **Open** 15 May - 15 September.

Directions: From N10 south of Poitiers, 14 km. north of Angoulême, take D11 west for Vars and Basse. Go through Vars to Basse where turn right onto D117 to Bignac. Site is signed at several junctions and in village (Camping Bignac).

Owned and run by a French family who continually seek to improve it, this pleasant and attractive site is one for those who enjoy peace, away from the hustle and bustle of the main Dordogne attractions, yet sufficiently close for them to be accessible. Set in a 14 ha. wooded valley, it has 160 pitches split into two sections; 108 are for touring vans - 35 below the central reception complex in a shaded situation, and 73 above on partly terraced ground with varying degrees of shade. All pitches have electricity. Spacing is good and there is no crowding. The site has been attractively planted with a pleasing variety of shrubs and trees, and combined with the small stream that runs through the centre of the site they create a beautiful and tranquil setting. There is a delightful wooded walk via a long distance footpath (GR 36) to Château Biron (2-3 km), and the Bastide town of Monpazier is also within walking distance. A `Sites et Paysages' member.

Facilities: All three sanitary blocks are of a good standard, including washbasins in cabins, facilities for disabled visitors and babies in each. Adequate dishwashing and laundry sinks. Laundry room. Good shop. Bar/restaurant with shaded patio and take-away. Swimming pool and children's paddling pool, plus freshwater pool with waterslide. Play area. Boules, half-court tennis, table tennis, volleyball, basketball, trampolining and football area. Library. Bicycle hire. Events, games and canoe trips organised (1/7-31/8).

Charges 2002

Per normal pitch	€ 4.90 - € 9.00
large pitch incl. water and drainage	€ 7.85 - € 11.70
person (over 2 yrs)	€ 3.55 - € 6.20
electricity (3/10A)	€ 3.25 - € 5.50
animal	€ 1.30 - € 2.45
local tax (over 13 yrs)	€ 0.23

Tel: 05 53 22 65 25. Fax: 05 53 23 99 76. E-mail: courrier@moulin-de-david.com. **Reservations:** Advisable for Jul/Aug, with deposit (€ 61 per week reserved) and booking fee (€ 19) for stays between 29/06 and 24/08). **Open** 18 May - 7 September.

Directions: From Monpazier take the D2 Villeréal road. Take third turning left (after about 2 km), signed to Moulin de David and 'Gaugeac mairie'. Site is about 500 m. along this road on the left.

MOULIN DE DAVID ****

A good Campsite !

Web: moulin-de-david.com Mail: courrier@moulin-de-david.com
England: Kay SALE, 40 Lindale Mount, Wakefield, West Yorkshire WF2 OBH, Tel: 01924 781503

Camping Domaine de la Paille Basse

46200 Souillac-sur-Dordogne

4601

Lying some 8 km. from Souillac, this family owned, high quality site is easily accessible from the N20 and well placed to take advantage of excursions into the Dordogne. It is part of a large domaine of 80 hectares, which is available to campers for walks and recreation. The site is quite high up and there are excellent views over the surrounding countryside. The 250 pitches are in two main areas - one is level in cleared woodland with good shade, and the other on grass in open ground without shade. Numbered and marked, the pitches are a minimum 100 sq.m. and often considerably more. About 80 have individual electricity, water and drainage, and electricity is available to all the others. Activities and entertainment are organised in season (animation was of a very high standard when we stayed). For good reason, the site can get very busy in high season and is popular with tour operators (20%), but there is more space available from mid August.

Facilities: The main toilet facilities are in three different sections, all centrally located close to reception (there is also a small night unit at one end of site). All have modern equipment and are kept very clean. Laundry facilities. Shop for essentials. Good restaurant, bar with terrace and takeaway. Crêperie. Good swimming pool complex, with main pool (25 x 10 m), second one (10 x 6 m) and paddling pool (unheated). Solarium. Sound-proofed disco room (twice weekly in season). TV rooms (with satellite). Cinema room below swimming pool area. Archery, tennis (charged), football, volleyball and table tennis. Children's playground. **Off site:** Golf 4 km.

Charges 2002

Per person	€ 5.50
child (under 7)	€ 3.50
pitch	€ 8.50
electricity (3A)	€ 3.50
local tax	€ 0.15

Tel: 05 65 37 85 48. Fax: 05 65 37 09 58. E-mail: paille.basse@wanadoo.fr. **Reservations:** Advised mid-July - mid-Aug. and made for min. 1 week with deposit and € 18,29 booking fee. **Open** 15 May - 15 September.

Directions: From Souillac take D15 road leading northwest towards Salignac-Eyvignes and after 6 km. turn right at camp sign and follow steep and narrow approach road for 2 km.

Le Domaine de la Paille Basse, half way between Rocamadour and the caves of Lascaux, is an excellent base for excursions enabling you to visit the highlights of two régions. Situated at the top of a hill, La Paille Basse is a restored medieval village in the heart of 200 acres of wooded land. La Paille Basse has carefully combined architectural beauty and modernity, fitting its facilities within the original buildings.

Castel Camping La Paille Basse

★★★★

46200 Souillac

Tel: 0033 565 37 85 48
Fax: 0033 565 37 09 58

LES CASTELS

Camping-Caravaning Moulin du Périé

4701 47500 Sauveterre-la-Lemance

Set in a quiet area and surrounded by woodlands this peaceful little site is well away from much of the tourist bustle. Its 125 grass pitches, divided by mixed trees and bushes, are reasonably sized and extremely well kept, as indeed is the entire site. All pitches have electricity (6A) and most enjoy good shade, with younger trees and shrubs rapidly filling out in the new area. The picturesque old mill buildings, adorned with flowers and creepers, now home to the restaurant etc. and the food is to be recommended as is the owner's extensive knowledge of wine that he is pleased to share with visitors. The attractive front courtyard is complemented by an equally pleasant terrace at the rear. A quiet, friendly site with regular visitors - reservation is advised for July/Aug. A 'Sites et Paysages' member.

Facilities: Three clean, modern and well maintained toilet blocks incorporate facilities for disabled visitors, babies and laundry. Motorcaravan service facilities. Shop for essentials (with gas). Bar/reception and restaurant (including takeaway). Two small, clean swimming pools (no bermuda-style shorts) overlook a shallow, spring water lake, ideal for inflatable boats and paddling. Bordering the lake, a large grass field is popular for football and volleyball. Boules, table tennis, outdoor chess. New children's playground and trampoline. Small, indoor play area. Bicycle hire. In season various activities, on and off site are arranged; including canoeing, riding, wine tasting visits, sight seeing trips plus weekly barbecues and gastronomic meals. Winter caravan storage. **Off site:** Fishing 1 km. Small supermarket in village and larger stores in Fumel.

Charges 2002

Per unit incl. 2 persons	€ 11.00 - € 18.80
with electricity	€ 14.30 - € 22.10
extra person	€ 3.55 - € 5.60
child (under 7 yrs)	€ 1.50 - € 3.00
animal	€ 1.80 - € 3.40

Tel: 05 53 40 67 26. Fax: 05 53 40 62 46. E-mail: moulinduperie@wanadoo.fr. **Reservations:** Advised for July/Aug. and made with deposit (€ 130) and fee (€ 18). **Open** 4 May - 24 September.

Directions: Sauveterre-la -Lémance lies by the Fumel - Périgueux (D710) road, midway between the Dordogne and Lot rivers. From D710, cross railway line, straight through village and turn left (north east) at far end on C201 minor road signed Château Sauveterre, Loubejec and site. Site is 3 km. up this road on right.

Camping-Caravaning Le Val Saint Jean

15200 Mauriac

1503

La Val Saint-Jean is part of a typical, newly developed 'Centre de Loisirs' which the French do so well, set beside a lake in the heart of the département of Cantal. The campsite is situated at a height of 700 m. and provides 100 generously sized touring pitches (with 10A electricity), terraced with good views and organised for the maximum of privacy, on a hill above the lake. The site is well planned so that you are never far from a sanitary block and it has an impressive number of good quality facilities. Most of the activities are situated by the lake where you can use all the facilities of the leisure club including canoeing, kayaking and pedalos. The lake has a sandy beach and an area for swimming. There is a large swimming pool, plus one for children on the campsite with sunbathing areas (free to campers). Both the pool and the lake have lifeguards most of the time and can get very busy in the main season. This less well known region is well worth exploring and the local gastronomy can be experienced in the village of Mauriac with its attractive architecture typical of the area.

Facilities: The two sanitary blocks (4 and 6 years old) are well equipped with hot water throughout, providing some washbasins in cabins, dishwashing sinks and a laundry room with washing machine and dryer. Facilities for people with disabilities. Limited shop. Bar, snack bar and restaurant (all May - Sept). Swimming and paddling pools (1/6-15/9). Children's play area, playing field and table tennis. Watersports. Fishing. Activities organised for children (8-16 yrs) in July/Aug. **Off site:** A nine-hole golf course is next to site. Mauriac village 600 m. Riding 2 km.

Charges 2002

Per unit incl. 2 persons	€ 7.80 - € 15.00
extra adult	€ 3.00 - € 4.50
child 10-18 yrs	€ 3.00 - € 3.80
child under 10 yrs	free - € 1.60
dog	€ 1.50
electricity (10A)	€ 3.00

Tel: 04 71 67 31 13. Fax: 04 71 68 17 34. E-mail: sogeval@wanadoo.fr. **Reservations:** Contact site. **Open** 11 May - 15 September.

Directions: From Clermont-Ferrand take RN 89 towards Bordeaux, then D922 towards Bort-les-Orgues-Mauriac. Site is well signed in Mauriac.

Camping Val St-Jean ★★★
Mauriac   Auvergne

Tel: 0033 471 67 31 13 - Fax: 0033 471 68 17 34
E-mail: SOGEVAL@wanadoo.fr
Website: www.camping-massifcentral.com

2301

Le Château de Poinsouze is a recently developed site with 136 pitches arranged on the open, gently sloping, grassy park to one side of the château's main drive - a beautiful plane tree avenue. It is a well designed, high quality site. The 94 touring pitches, some with lake frontage, all have electricity (6, 10 or 16A), with water, waste water and sewage connections to many. The château (not open to the public) lies across the lake from the site. The exceptionally well restored outbuildings on the opposite side of the drive house a new restaurant, other facilities and the pool area. The site has a friendly family atmosphere, there are organised activities in main season including dances, children's games and crafts, family triathlons, and there are marked walks around the park and woods. All facilities are open all season, though times may vary. This is a top class site with a formula which should ensure a stress-free, enjoyable family holiday. Boussac (2.5 km) has a market every Thursday morning. The massive 12/15th century fortress, Château de Boussac, is open daily all year.

Facilities: The high quality, double glazed sanitary unit is entered via a large utility area equipped with dishwashing and laundry sinks, foot-pedal operated taps, sinks accessible for wheelchair users, drinks machine and two smaller rooms with washing machines, dryer and ironing. Four spacious rooms are very well equipped including some washbasins in cubicles, baby baths, changing mats and child's WC, and two suites for disabled people. Good motorcaravan service point. Well stocked shop. Takeaway, Comfortable bar with games, TV and library room above. New restaurant. Well fenced swimming pool with slide, children's pool (children wear colour coded bracelets, deposit required). Fenced playground designed with safety in mind. Table tennis, petanque, pool table and table football games. Bicycle hire. Free fishing in the lake (if you put the fish back); boats and lifejackets can be hired. Football, volleyball, basketball, badminton and other games. Dogs are not accepted in high season (6/7-23/8).

Charges 2003

Per pitch incl. 2 persons	€ 12.00 - € 19.00
with electricity (6A), water, drain	€ 19.00 - € 25.00
with electricity (10A), water, waste water, sewage connection	€ 21.00 - € 26.00
extra adult	€ 3.50 - € 5.50
child (2-7 yrs)	€ 2.00 - € 4.00
electricity 10-25A	€ 2.00 - € 4.50
dog (low and mid-season only)	€ 3.00

Tel: 05 55 65 02 21. Fax: 05 55 65 86 49. E-mail: info.camping-de.poinsouze@wanadoo.fr. **Reservations:** Advisable during July/Aug; made with 30% deposit and € 18,29 fee. **Open** 16 May - 14 September.

Directions: Site entrance is 2.5 km north of Boussac on D917 (towards La Châtre).

Centre of France
Château de Poinsouze
★★★★

New Family Campsite. Calm & Nature. Exceptional fully enclosed sanitary facilities. Heated swimming pool. Chalets & mobil-homes for hire. Gites all year long.
Route de la Châtre 23600 Boussac-Bourg - Tel: 0033 555 65 02 21 - Fax: 0033 555 65 86 49
info.camping-de.poinsouze@wanadoo.fr / www.camping-de-poinsouze.com

Camping Soleil Vivarais
Sampzon, 07120 Ruoms

A large, quality site bordering the River Ardèche, complete with beach, Soleil Vivarais offers much to visitors, particularly families with children. A popular feature is the 'barrage' with its canoe ramp, used by children with rubber boats more than canoeists, and providing an invigorating shower for bathers. Water is shallow in high season, but swimming is then best attempted in one of the pools. Of the 270 pitches, 50 generously sized, level pitches are for tourers, all with 10A electricity. Many are shaded and 30 have full services. During the day the proximity of the swimming pools to the terraces of the bar and restaurant make it a pleasantly social area. In the evening the purpose built stage, with professional lighting and sound system, provides an ideal platform for a regular family entertainment programme, mostly mimed musical shows. A new section beyond the beach houses good quality chalets, and an very attractive new pool complex, which all may use. Used by tour operators (80 pitches). A 'Sites et Paysages' and 'Yelloh Village' member.

Facilities: Three fairly modern and one very modern toilet block are clean and cope adequately with demands placed upon them. Baby and child room and four units for people with disabilities. Washing machines and dryers. Small supermarket, well stocked and sensibly priced. Bright, modern bar/restaurant complex with takeaway and occasional pizzas. Sound-proof disco adjacent to the bar (capacity 100-120), popular with teenagers. Heated main pool and paddling pool (no bermuda style shorts). Water polo, aqua-aerobics, pool games. Tennis (charged). Basketball, volleyball and football. Fishing. Petanque, table tennis and archery. Bicycle hire. Extensive animation programme for all ages in June, July and August. **Off site:** Activities nearby, many with qualified instruction and supervision, include mountain biking, walking, canoeing, rafting, climbing and caving. Riding 2 km, golf 10 km.

Charges 2002

Per unit incl. 2 persons, electricity	€ 19.00 - € 34.00
extra person	€ 4.00 - € 7.00
child (1-10 yrs)	free - € 6.50
pet	free - € 3.00
local tax (over 10s)	€ 0.30

Tel: 04 75 39 67 56. Fax: 04 75 39 64 69. E-mail: camping-soleil-vivarais@wanadoo.fr. **Reservations:** Made by fax and credit card or write to site with deposit (€ 92) and fee (€ 30). **Open** week before Easter - 20 September.

Directions: From Le Teil, just west of Montelimar, turn off the N86 and take the N102 westwards through Villeneuve-de-Berg. Disregard the first sign for Vallon-Pont-d'Arc and continue for about 5 km. on N102 before turning left on D103, toward Vogue, then left on D579 and through Ruoms. Still on the D579, follow Vallon Pont D'Arc signs towards Sampzon. Site is on right via a bridge across the river controlled by lights.

0707 route de Valgorge, Chassiers, 07110 Largentière

the travel service TO BOOK

Ferry	✔
Pitch	✔
Accommodation	✔

01892 55 98 98

Combining farming, wine-making, running an Auberge and a friendly family campsite is no simple task, but the Chevalier family seem to manage it quite effortlessly. Well run and with the emphasis on personal attention, this site is highly recommended. In a somewhat lesser known area of the Ardèche at Chassiers, in a peaceful location on the Route de Valgorge (there may be some road noise), the site has developed from an original 'camping à la ferme' into a very well equipped modern campsite. There are 150 good-sized, level, grassy pitches, 88 for tourists with electricity and including 42 serviced pitches (electricity, water, waste water). Pitches are in two distinct areas - the original site which is well shaded, and the lower part which is more open. There is an unfenced frontage onto a small lake connected to the river, providing opportunities for bathing, fishing or canoeing (free life jackets) with one part of the bathing area quite safe for youngsters (supervision essential). The site's own Auberge is set in a room of the original 1824 building that once used to house silk worms. You may dine either inside the cave-like restaurant or outside on the attractive, shaded terrace. The traditional food is recommended, being both reasonably priced and of extremely good quality. A reader reports some noise until midnight.

Facilities: Two modern, comprehensively equipped toilet buildings include washbasins in cubicles, dish-washing and laundry sinks and facilities for babies and disabled persons. It is an excellent provision, kept immaculate. Laundry in separate building. Motorcaravan service point. Small shop, takeaway and bar with terrace (all 20/4-22/9). Excellent pool complex with two large pools (20 x 10 m. and 15 x 7.5 m, both heated and open all season) and paddling pool. Adventure style playground. Organised amusements for children in high season. Bicycle hire. Tennis court. Minigolf. Table tennis. Boules. Canoeing. **Off site:** Medieval village of Largentière (1.5 km.) with Tuesday market and medieval festival in July. Canoe and kayaking on the Ardèche arranged from the site each Wednesday (mid -June - end Aug).

Charges 2002

Per unit incl. 2 persons	€ 18.00 - € 22.50
serviced pitch	€ 23.00 - € 28.50
extra person	€ 4.00 - € 5.50
child (1-10 yrs)	€ 3.00 - € 4.40
dog	free - € 2.00
electricity	€ 4.00
local tax	€ 0.15

Tel: 04 75 88 31 97. Fax: 04 75 88 32 73. E-mail: reception@lesranchisses.fr. **Reservations:** Made with 30% deposit plus booking/insurance fee (€ 30). **Open** 14 April - end September.

Directions: Largentière is southwest of Aubenas and is best approached using the D104. 16 km. south of Aubenas turn northwest on the D5 and, immediately, on leaving Largentière, fork left signed Valgorge. Site is first on left, in about 1.8 km.

Domaine des Plantas

,07360 Les Ollières-sur-Eyrieux

A good quality site in a spectacular setting on the steep banks of the Eyrieux river, Domaine des Plantas offers an attractive alternative to those in the more popular southern parts of the Ardèche. The Eyrieux valley is less well known, but arguably just as attractive as those further south and a good deal less crowded, particularly in the main season. Perhaps the only drawback to this site is the narrow twisting three kilometre approach road which, although by no means frightening, may present something of a challenge to those with large outfits - however, the helpful owners have an ingenious convoy system designed to assist campers on departure. There is a sandy beach beside the quite fast-flowing, but fairly shallow, river (used for bathing) and a swimming pool and paddling pool with tiled surrounds for sunbathing. Facilities are housed in an original building which is quite impressive with its Protestant history and visible from the main road across the river long before you reach it. The restaurant terrace provides a stunning viewpoint. The 162 pitches (35 new in 2002, with electricity, water and drain) are terraced and shaded, so some up and down walking is required. They have electricity connections (10A, long leads may be needed) and water points are very accessible.

Facilities: One large, modern toilet block, centrally situated in courtyard style, is well equipped with washbasins in cubicles and good facilities for children with small toilets and baby baths. An additional smaller block serves the higher terraces. Dishwashing and laundry sinks. Washing machine. Motorcaravan service point. Small shop (bread to order). Bar, restaurant and disco. Heated kidney shaped swimming pool and paddling pool. Adventure play area beside river. Mountain biking, canoeing, canyoning, riding and 'randonnées pedestres' (sounds better in French!). In high season animation for children organised six days a week, and discos for 14-18 year olds held in cellar twice weekly (strictly no alcohol). Many activities are possible and are arranged according to the campers' motivations, including excursions. Only gas barbecues are allowed. **Off site:** Riding 15 km.

Charges 2002

Per unit incl. 2 persons, electricity	€ 18.00 - € 26.00
extra person over 4 yrs	€ 4.00 - € 6.00
animal	€ 2.00
local tax	€ 0.31

Tel: 04 75 66 21 53. Fax: 04 75 66 23 65. E-mail: plantas.ardeche@wanadoo.fr. **Reservations:** Made with deposit (€ 110) and fee (€ 20). **Open** 15 June - 15 September.

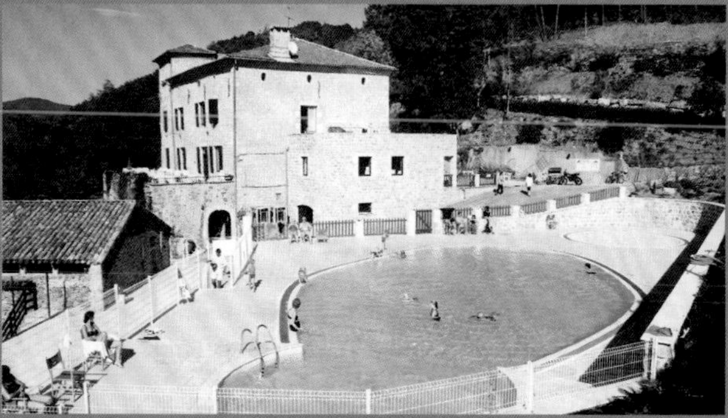

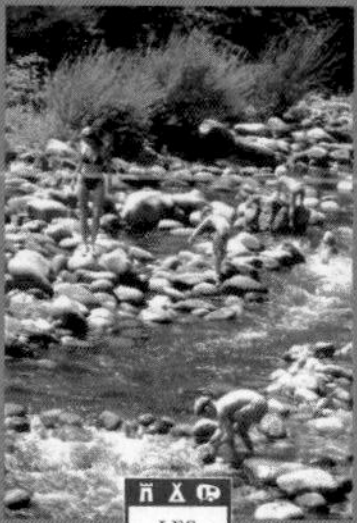

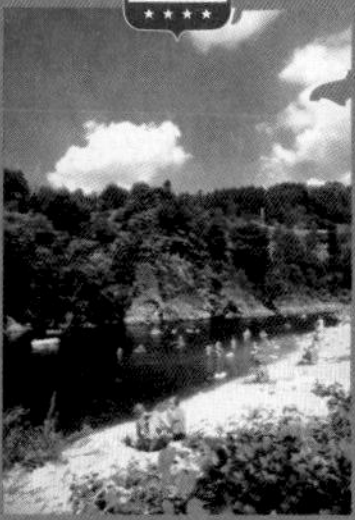

Directions: From A7 take exit 15 (Valence Sud). Immediately after the péage turn right to Valence centre, then follow signs to Montélimar via the N7 for 7 km. Turn right towards Charmes sur Rhône, thence to Beauchastel. On leaving Beauchastel follow signs to Ollieres sur Eyrieux.

Sunêlia Le Grand Lierne

2603 BP 8, 26120 Chabeuil

In addition to its obvious attraction as an overnight stop, fairly convenient for the A7 autoroute, this site provides a pleasant base to explore this little known area (worth discovering) between the Ardèche and the Vercors mountains and the Côte du Rhône wine area. It has 140 marked pitches, 76 for touring units, mainly separated by developing hedges or oak trees. They have good shade, some are on flat ground and all have electricity (6/10A). A more open area exists for those who prefer less shade and a view of the mountains. A varied entertainment programme has a particular emphasis on activities for children, with a range of activities and excursions. The owners wish to keep a balance between nationalities and are also keen to encourage rallies and will arrange visit programmes. English spoken. Used by tour operators (30%). A 'Sites et Paysages' member.

Facilities: Two sanitary blocks include washbasins in cabins, facilities for disabled people and a small WC for children. Dishwashing under cover. Washing machines (powder provided), dryers and outdoor lines by the blocks. Motorcaravan services. Shop. Bar/snack bar with terrace for eating in and take-away (all season). Fridge rental. Two swimming pools, one covered and heated in low season (no bermuda shorts), paddling pool and 50 m. water slide. Children's playgrounds and trampoline. Mini-tennis, minigolf, table tennis, volleyball, archery and football field. Bicycle hire. Library. Barbecues are permitted in special areas. Dogs and other pets are not accepted in high season (6/7-24/8). Caravan storage. **Off site:** Fishing 3 km, riding 7 km, golf 3 km, canoe/kayak near.

Charges 2002

Per unit incl. 2 adults	€ 15.00 - € 24.00
extra person	€ 6.00 - € 7.00
child (2-7 yrs)	€ 3.00 - € 5.00
electricity (6/10A)	€ 4.00 - € 5.50
animal	€ 2.50
local tax	€ 0.20

Tel: 04 75 59 83 14. Fax: 04 75 59 87 95. E-mail: contact@grandlierne.com. **Reservations:** Accepted with deposit (€ 92) and fee (€ 27,50). **Open** 27 April - 7 September, with all services.

Directions: Site signed in Chabeuil about 11 km. east of Valence (18 km. from autoroute). It is best to approach Chabeuil from the south side of Valence via the Valence ring road, thence onto the D68 to Chabeuil itself. Site is off the D125 to Charpey, 5 km. from Chabeuil, but well signed.

Castel Camping du Château de Senaud

2602 26140 Albon

Château du Sénaud, near the N7 south of Vienne, makes a useful stopover on the way south, but one could enjoy a longer stay to explore the surrounding villages and mountains. It is one of the original sites in the Castel chain and is still run with character and hands-on attention by Mme. Comtesse d'Armagnac. There are a fair number of permanent caravans used at weekends, but it also has some 85 pitches in tourist areas. Some have shade, some have views across the Rhône valley, and electricity and water connections are available on all pitches. There may be some noise from the autoroute.

Facilities: Four toilet blocks include British and one Turkish style toilets, washbasins in cabins, some en-suite with shower in one block. Facilities for babies. Washing machines. Motorcaravan service point. Shop (15/5-15/9). Bar, takeaway and good value small restaurant with simple menu (all 15/6-15/9). Swimming pool with water toboggan (1/5-15/9, depending on the weather) and new jacuzzi. Tennis court. Fishing. Bicycle hire. Table tennis, bowling alley and minigolf. **Off site:** Riding 10 km. Golf course and walks adjacent.

Charges guide

Per person	€ 3.96 - € 4.88
child (under 7)	€ 2.44
pitch	€ 6.10
dog	€ 1.52
electricity (10A)	€ 3.20 - € 3.66

Tel: 04 75 03 11 31. Fax: 04 75 03 08 06. E-mail: camping.de.senaud@libertysurf.fr. **Reservations:** Made with deposit for min. 3 nights. **Open** 15 March - 31 October.

Directions: Leave autoroute at Chanas exit, proceed south on N7 for 8 km. then east on D301 from Le Creux de la Thine to site. From south, exit autoroute for Tain-Tournon and proceed north, approaching site on D122 through St Vallier then D132 towards Anneyron to site.

Camping Le Gallo Romain

2608 route du Col de Tourniol, 26300 Barbières

Surrounded by wooded hills and mountains, this small simple site makes a good base from which to explore the spectacular Vercors plateau. It is quiet and peaceful, in an attractive location with pitches set on terraces that descend to a small stream. There are 80 pitches, some with a little grass, all with electricity (6A) and most with some shade at some part of the day. The area is ideal for walking or mountain biking with many special cycle tracks in the hills, or for wild flower or butterfly enthusiasts. English is spoken.

Facilities: Two sanitary blocks including washbasins in cubicles, are kept reasonably clean but could be stretched in peak season. Small shop high season only but fresh bread available all season. Small bar/restaurant (booking essential), plus takeaway. Swimming pool (17 x 8 m) and paddling pool. Games room, pool table, table tennis and volleyball. Small play area. **Off site:** Bicycle hire in the village 1 km, riding or golf 6 km. Shops at Barbières 1 km.

Charges 2002

Per adult	€ 2.80 - € 3.50
child (under 7 yrs)	€ 1.60 - € 2.00
pitch	€ 9.60 - € 12.00
electricity (6A)	€ 2.00 - € 2.50

Tel: 04 75 47 44 07. Fax: 04 75 47 44 07. E-mail: info@legalloromain.net. **Reservations:** Advised for high season; made for exact dates with deposit and fee. **Open** 1 May - 15 September.

Directions: Leave A49/E713 autoroute at exit 7 (Romans-sur-Isère) and turn south on D149, follow ing signs to Col de Tourniol. Barbières is approx. 12 km. along this road. Drive carefully through narrow village streets; the site is a little way past on right.

the travel service
TO BOOK

Ferry	✔
Pitch	✔
Accommodation	✔

01892 55 98 98

The Alan Rogers' Travel Service

This unique service enables our readers to reserve their holidays as well as ferry crossings and comprehensive insurance cover at extremely competitive rates. The majority of participating sites are in France and we are able to offer a selection of some of the very best sites in this country.

Share our experience and let us help
to ensure that your holiday will be a complete success.

Alan Rogers Travel Service 01892 55 98 98 or www.alanrogers.com

France - Provence
Camping International

Route Napoleon, 04120 Castellane

0410

Camping International has very friendly, English speaking owners and is a reasonably priced, less commercialised site situated in some of the most dramatic scenery in France with good views. The 250 pitches, 130 good sized ones for touring, are clearly marked, separated by trees and small hedges, and all have electricity and water. The bar/restaurant overlooks the swimming pool with its sunbathing area set in a sunny location, and all have fantastic views. In high season English speaking young people entertain children (3-8 years) and teenagers. On some evenings the teenagers are taken to the woods for campfire 'sing-alongs' which can go on till the early hours without disturbing the rest of the site. There are twice weekly guided walks into the surrounding hills in the nearby Gorges du Verdon - a very popular excursion. The weather in the hills here is very pleasant without the excessive heat of the coast. Access is good for larger units.

Facilities: Several small toilet blocks are of an older design with small cubicles and, although they are quite basic, the showers are fully controllable. One newer block has modern facilities, including those for disabled visitors, but this is not open early and late in the season. Washing machines, dryer and irons and a baby room. Chemical disposal at motorcaravan service point. Fridge hire. Shop. Restaurant/takeaway. Swimming pool (all 1/5-30/9). Club/TV room. Children's animation and occasional evening entertainment in July/Aug. Play area. Volleyball, football and boules pitches. Internet access. **Off site:** Castellane (1.5 km) is an very attractive little town with a superb river, canyon and rapids, ideal for canoeing, rafting and canyoning etc. Ideal country for walking and biking. Riding 800 m. Boat launching 5 km.

Charges 2002

Per unit incl. 2 persons	€ 12.00 - € 17.00
extra person over 10 yrs	€ 3.00 - € 4.50
child 4-10 yrs	€ 1.80 - € 3.50
child under 4 yrs	€ 1.65 - € 3.35
dog	€ 2.50
local tax	€ 0.15 - € 0.30

Tel: (0)4 92 83 66 67. Fax: (0)4 92 83 77 67. E-mail: info@campinginternational.fr. **Reservations:** Necessary for July/Aug. and made with deposit (€ 45), no booking fee. **Open** 1 April - 30 September.

Directions: Site is 1 km. north of Castellane on the N85 'Route Napoleon'.

France - Provence
Camp du Verdon

Domaine de la Salaou, 04120 Castellane

0402

Close to 'Route des Alpes' and the Gorges du Verdon, this is a very popular holiday area, the gorge, canoeing and rafting being the main attractions, ideal for active families. Two heated swimming pools and numerous on-site activities help to keep non-canoeists here. Du Verdon is a large level site, part meadow, part wooded, with 500 grassy, partly shaded pitches (350 for tourists). Numbered and separated by newly planted bushes, they vary in size (but mostly over the average), have 6A electricity, and 120 also have water and waste water. They are mostly separate from the mobile homes (45) and pitches used by tour operators (110). Some overlook the unfenced river Verdon, so watch the children. One can walk to Castellane without using the main road. With the facilities open all season, the site is very popular. Patrols after 11pm. make sure that the site is quiet.

Facilities: The toilet blocks are being refurbished, the finished ones having British style WCs and all the latest equipment. As other blocks are upgraded, Turkish style toilets will be replaced. One block has facilities for disabled visitors. Washing machines and irons. Motorcaravan service and car wash points. Popular restaurant with terrace and bar including room with log fire for cooler evenings. Large well stocked shop. Pizzeria/crêperie. Takeaway (open twice daily). Two heated swimming pools and new paddling pool with 'mushroom' style fountain (all open all season). Entertainers provide games and competitions for all (July and August). Dances and discos (July and Aug) suit all age groups - the latest finishing time is around 11 pm. Playgrounds. Minigolf, table tennis, archery, basketball and volleyball. Organised walks. Bicycle hire. Riding. Small fishing lake. **Off site:** Castellane (1 km) and the Ardèche Gorge. Riding 2 km, boat launching 4.5 km, golf 20 km. River Ardèche and many water sports.

Charges 2002

Per unit with up to 3 persons	€ 14.00 - € 24.00
with 6A electricity	€ 18.00 - € 28.00
large 150 sq.m. serviced pitch	€ 25.00 - € 35.00
extra person over 4 yrs	€ 6.00 - € 8.00

Tel: 04 92 83 61 29. Fax: 04 92 83 69 37. E-mail: contact@camp-du-verdon.com. **Reservations:** Made for any length with deposit (€ 80-110 depending on pitch) and fee (€ 20). **Open** 15 May - 15 September.

Directions: From Castellane take D952 westwards towards Gorges du Verdon and Moustiers. Site is 1 km. on left.

Hotel de Plein Air L'Hippocampe

route de Napoléon, 04290 Volonne

04010

Hippocampe is a friendly, lakeside site situated in a beautiful area of France. The perfumes of thyme, lavender and wild herbs are everywhere and the higher hills of Haute Provence are not too far away. There are 447 level, numbered pitches (271 for touring units), medium to very large (140 sq.m.) in size. All have electricity (10A) and 206 have water and a drain, most separated by bushes and cherry trees (June is the time for the cherries and you may help yourself). Some of the best pitches border the lake. This is a family run site with families in mind, with games, aerobics, competitions, entertainment and shows, plus a daily club for younger family members in July/August. A soundproof underground disco is set well away from the pitches and is very popular with teenage customers. Staff tour the site at night ensuring a good night's sleep. The site is, however, much quieter in low season and, with its good discounts, is the time for those who do not want or need entertaining. The Gorges du Verdon is a sight not to be missed and rafting, paragliding or canoe trips can be booked from the site. Being on the lower slopes of the hills of Haute-Provence, the surrounding area is good for both walking and mountain biking. Used by tour operators (20 pitches). English is spoken.

Facilities: Toilet blocks vary from old to modern, all with good facilities that include washbasins in cabins. They were very clean when we visited in June. Washing machines. Motorcaravan service point. Fridge rental. Bread available from reception (from 28/4), small shop (29/6-1/9). Bar (27/4-30/9). Restaurant, pizzeria and barbecue chicken shop (all 12/5-15/9). Large, attractive pool complex (from 27/4-30/9) with various pools of differing sizes and depths, heated in early and late seasons. Tennis (free outside 3/7- 21/8). Fishing, canoeing, boules. Bicycle and pedalo hire (high season). Large selection of sports facilities to choose from, some with free instruction, including archery (high season). Charcoal barbecues are not permitted. **Off site:** Village of Volonne 600 m. Riding 500 m. Monuments, ancient churches, museums, markets, festivals and vineyards. Rafting, canoeing, canyoning, torrent walking, mountain biking, paragliding and hang gliding.

Charges 2002

Per unit with 2 persons	€ 12.00 - € 20.00
with electricity	€ 15.00 - € 24.50
with water/drainage 100 sq.m.	€ 15.00 - € 26.70
with water/drainage 140 sq.m.	€ 15.00 - € 30.50
extra person (over 4 yrs)	€ 2.50 - € 5.50
dog	free - € 3.00
local tax (June-Sept)	€ 0.15 - € 0.38

Tel: 04 92 33 50 00. Fax: 04 92 33 50 49. E-mail: camping@l-hippocampe.com. **Reservations:** Made with deposit (varies with size of pitch from € 50 - € 95) and booking fee (€ 25). **Open** 1 April - 30 September.

Directions: Approaching from the north turn off N85 across river bridge to Volonne, then right to site. From the south right on D4, 1 km. before Château Arnoux.

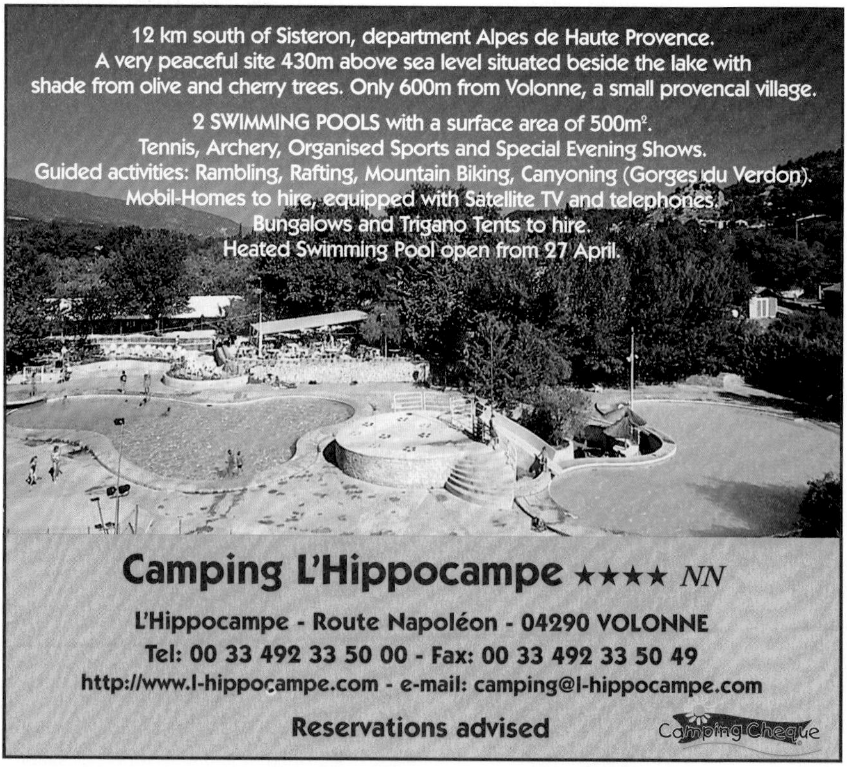

Domaine Naturiste de Bélézy

84410 Bédoin

N8402

Bélézy is an excellent naturist site with many amenities and activities at the foot of Mt Ventoux. We continue to be impressed by its policy of annual refurbishment, its management, the French approach to naturism and the extent to which the natural environment has been managed in harmony with the Provencal countryside. The ambience is essentially relaxed and comfortable. English is spoken widely amongst staff and customers although some activities may be conducted solely in French. The site has two areas joined by a short pedestrian tunnel and the 171 marked and numbered pitches are set amongst many varieties of trees and shrubs - oaks, olives, pines, acacias, broom, lavender, etc. Electricity points (12A) are plentiful but you may need a long cable in places. The emphasis is on informality and concern for the environment and during high season cars are banned from the camping area to the supervised parking areas nearby. This not only provides an air of tranquillity, but safety for children. So far as naturism is concerned, the emphasis is on personal choice (and weather conditions!), the only stipulation being the requirement for complete nudity in the pools and pool area. The leisure park side of the site is an area of natural parkland including an orchard, fishpond and woodland (complete with red squirrels), and a good range of sports facilities including tennis courts and swimming pools. The largest pool is for swimming and relaxation (you may enjoy a musical serenade), the smaller pool (heated 25/3-30/9) is also used for watersports and aquarobics. The smallest is for children supervised by their parents. Near the pool area is the smart restaurant, with terrace, and the mellow old Mas (Provencal farmhouse) that houses many activities, as well as the library, near soundproof disco, information centre and children's club. Member 'France 4 Naturisme'.

Facilities: Sanitary blocks are a little different. The newer ones are of a standard type and excellent quality, with free hot showers in cubicles with separators, and washbasins in cabins. One block has an attractive children's section with baby baths, sinks and showers at different heights, children's toilets and is decorated with tiles painted with animals. In the same area the adult block has hot showers in the open air, separated by natural stone dividers and washing up areas again mostly in the open air. Shop (1/4-30/9). Restaurant provides excellent food, waiter service, and takeaway meals at affordable prices. Three swimming pools. Sauna. Hydrotherapy centre (1/4-30/9) to tone up and revitalise with qualified diagnosis; treatments include steam baths, massage and seaweed packs, osteopathy and Chinese medicine (including acupuncture). Two tennis courts. Boules and table tennis. Adventure play area. Activities include painting and pottery courses, language lessons, archery, music (bring your own instrument) and guided walks. Children's clubs in holiday periods. Barbecues are prohibited but there is a central barbecue area. Weekly handout 'Bélézy Scoop' outlines forthcoming events. Dogs and pets are not accepted. **Off site:** It is possible to walk into Bédoin (excellent street market - Monday mornings).

Charges 2002

Per unit incl. 1 adult	€ 13.00 - € 22.50
2 adults	€ 18.30 - € 28.50
3 adults	€ 25.50 - € 35.70
extra adult	€ 5.50 - € 8.50
child (3-8 yrs)	€ 4.00 - € 6.50
electricity (12A)	€ 3.50
large pitch	€ 4.00
pitch with water, drainage and sink	€ 5.00

Tel: 04 90 65 60 18. Fax: 04 90 65 94 45. E-mail: info@belezy.com. **Reservations:** Write with deposit (25%) and fee (€ 30) - contact site. **Open** 15 March - 4 October.

Directions: From A7 autoroute or RN7 at Orange, take D950 southeast to Carpentras, then northeast via D974 to Bédoin. Site is signed in Bédoin, being about 1.5 km. northeast of the village

Domaine Naturiste L'Eglantière

Aries-Espenan, 65230 Castelnau-Magnoac

N6501

This pretty site is situated in the valley between the Pyrénées and the plain, within easy reach of Lourdes and the mountains. Alongside a small, fast flowing river, in wooded surroundings it comprises 12 ha. for camping and caravanning, with a further 32 for walking and relaxing in the woods and fields. The river is said to be suitable for swimming and canoeing, with fishing nearby. The 120 pitches are of mixed size on fairly level grass, the older ones secluded and separated by a variety of tall trees and bushes, the newer ones more open, with a natural tenting area across the river. About 100 pitches have 8A electrical connections. The site has is an attractive, central, medium sized swimming pool with sunbathing areas both on paving and grass, and a children's pool, overlooked by the attractive style clubhouse and terrace. A small health centre (massage, sauna) is being developed in the old farmhouse. A range of studios, mobile homes, chalets and tents is on site. Used by a tour operator (5 pitches). Member of France 4 Naturisme.

Facilities: Two main sanitary blocks at each end of the site are in typically naturist style, providing under cover, open plan, controllable hot showers, and sinks for washing up. A small centrally located sanitary block has individual cubicles. Shop (June-Sept). Clubhouse with bar, small restaurant, pizzeria and takeaway (June-mid Sept), internet access and indoor soundproofed activities/disco area, play room for younger children and table tennis for older ones. Swimming pool (April - end Sept). Play area and children's animation in season. Volleyball, badminton, table tennis, petanque and archery. Activities on the river. Canoe and mountain bike hire. Trekking and cross country cycling. Barbecues are officially forbidden. Torches useful. **Off site:** Restaurants in the nearby village.

Charges guide

Per pitch incl. 2 persons	€ 11.89 - € 21.19
'wild' pitch (July/Aug. only)	€ 15.09
extra person	€ 3.09 - € 4.42
child (3-8 yrs)	€ 1.52 - € 2.74
animal	€ 1.22 - € 1.98
electricity (10A)	€ 3.81
leisure card (obligatory)	€ 0.38 - € 0.76

Tel: 05 62 99 83 64. Fax: 05 62 39 82 99.
Reservations: Made with deposit (25%) and fee (€ 27.44). **Open** Easter - October.

Directions: From Auch take D929 south towards Lannemezan. Just after Castelnau-Magnoac watch for signs to hamlet of Ariès-Espénan on left and follow site signs.

Sunêlia Les Trois Vallées

Ave des Pyrenees, 65400 Argelès-Gazost

6502

We felt this was the most promising site along the valley road from Lourdes into the Pyrénées, and one of few with room and plans for development. It has a rather unprepossessing entrance and pitches near the road suffer from noise, but at the back, open fields allow views of surrounding mountains on all sides. Recent additions include an indoor pool and two jacuzzis. Recently extended, the site now has 400 flat, grassy, marked out pitches of reasonable size, all with electricity. Water points were scarce, but the owner hoped to remedy this, given the go-ahead by local officialdom. The proximity to the road is at least advantageous for touring the area, being by a roundabout with Lourdes one way, Luz-St-Sauveur and mountains another way, and the dramatic Pyrénées Corniche Col d'Aubisque going off to the west. Argelès-Gazost is an attractive town with excellent restaurants and cultural interests. The site is popular with young people and could be quite lively at times.

Facilities: The two unisex toilet blocks are fairly modern and include facilities for disabled people and a laundry room. Cleaning can be variable and facilities could be under pressure at peak times. Bread available on site. Bar/disco. Café and takeaway. Swimming pool complex (from 1/6) with paddling pool and two water slides. TV room. Good children's playground. Volleyball, football, boules and archery. **Off site:** Supermarket across the road. Fishing 500 m, bicycle hire 50 m, riding 3 km.

Charges 2002

Per pitch incl. 2 persons	€ 10.00 - € 20.00
with electricity (3A)	€ 13.00 - € 23.00
extra person	€ 3.40 - € 6.00
child (under 7 yrs)	€ 1.80 - € 5.00
electricity 6A	€ 2.50

Tel: 05 62 90 35 47. Fax: 05 62 90 35 48. E-mail: 3_valees@wanadoo.fr. **Reservations:** Advised for July/Aug. and made with deposit (€ 77) and fee (€ 15,24). **Open** 1 April - 30 September.

Directions: Take N21 from Lourdes to Argelès-Gazost. As you approach Argelès, pass a Champion supermarket on your right, and then a roundabout - take the furthest left exit and the site entrance is 100 m. or so on the left.

Castel Camping Pyrénées Natura

6506 route du Lac, 65400 Estaing

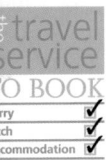

The travel
service
'O BOOK
rry ✓
tch ✓
commodation ✓
1892 55 98 98

Pyrénées Natura, at an altitude of 1,000 metres, on the edge of the National Park, is the perfect site for lovers of nature. Eagles and vultures soar above the site and a small open air observatory is provided. The Ruysschaert family's aim is that you go home from a holiday here feeling at peace with the world, having learned something about the flora and fauna of the High Pyrénées. Tristan, their son, is qualified to take groups walking in the mountains to see chamois, marmots and the varied flora and fauna (there are even a few bears but they are seen rarely). The 60 pitches, all with electricity, are in a large, level, open and sunny field. Around 75 varieties of trees and shrubs have been planted - not too many to spoil the view though, which can only be described as fantastic. Reception is in a traditional style stone building with timber floors. The small shop is quite unique. Housed in the old water mill, it stocks a variety of produce, including wine. This is left unmanned and open all day and, after you have chosen your goods, you pay at reception - very trusting. The last weekend in May is a special time when the local shepherds take their flocks up to the high pastures. Campers help by walking up with them and then helping to separate the different flocks. Returning to the site by bus, with a good old sing-song with the shepherds, the site provides food for everyone. That sounds like a trip worth making.

Facilities: First class toilet facilities with high quality fittings include a cubicle for children with shower, WC and washbasin, full facilities for disabled visitors and, in the same large room, baby bath, shower and changing mat. WCs have individual paper seat covers. Dishwashing and laundry sinks. Washing machine and airers are provided to avoid unsightly washing lines. Motorcaravan service point. Dog shower. Small shop. Small bar (15/5-15/9) and lounge area, extra upstairs lounge, library and TV (mainly used for videos of the National Park). Small play area for the very young. Table tennis, boule and giant chess. Weekly evening meal in May, June and Sept. **Off site:** Village has two restaurants.

Charges 2003

Per unit incl. 2 persons and electricity (3A)	€ 19.50
extra person	€ 3.50
child (under 8 yrs)	€ 2.00
electricity (6/10A)	€ 1.50 - € 3.00
animal	€ 1.50
local tax	€ 0.45

Tel: 05 62 97 45 44. Fax: 05 62 97 45 81. E-mail: info@campping-pyrenes-natura.com. **Reservations:** Made with deposit (€ 55). **Open** 1 May - 20 September.

Directions: From Lourdes take N21 to Argelès-Gazost. At the roundabout at Argelès, take D918 signed Aucun, turning left after 5.5 km. onto D13 to Bun. After Bun cross the river and right onto D103 to site (5.5 km). Some parts are narrow but with passing places.

Domaine Naturiste Club Origan

N0607 06260 Puget-Theniers

Origan is a naturist site set in the mountains behind Nice. Despite its rather spectacular location, it is easily accessible from the coast and you only discover that you are at a height of 500 m. when you arrive! The access road is single track and winding with a few passing places for about a mile, so arrival is not recommended until late afternoon. The terrain within the extensive confines of the site is fairly wild and the roads distinctly stony. The site is not suitable for caravans longer than six metres due to the steep slopes, although the site will assist with a 4x4 vehicle if requested. The scenery is impressive and footpaths in and around the site offer good, if fairly strenuous, walks up to a height of 1,000 m. The 50 touring pitches, in three different areas with many wild flowers, are of irregular size and shape and all have good views. Electricity connection (6A) is possible on most pitches (by long cable). Member 'France 4 Naturisme'

Facilities: Sanitary facilities, exceptionally clean when we visited, are of a standard and type associated with most good naturist sites - mainly British type WCs, mostly open plan hot showers and ample washbasins with hot and cold water. Laundry facilities. Shop (15/6-21/8). Bar/restaurant (all season). Takeaway. Heated swimming pools, one for children (1/5-31/8). Jacuzzi and sauna. Disco in cellars. Tennis. Fishing. Bicycle hire. Organised activities for adults and children (high season). Individual barbecues are not permitted. Torches advised. **Off site:** The nearby small town of Puget-Theniers is very pleasant and offers choice of bars, cafés, shops, etc.

Charges 2002

Per unit incl. 1 person	€ 12.00 - € 17.00
incl. 2 persons	€ 14.00 - € 24.00
incl. 3 persons	€ 17.00 - € 29.00
extra person	€ 5.00 - € 8.00
child (4-10 yrs)	free - € 5.00
electricity	€ 4.00
leisure package	€ 0.46 - € 0.92

Tel: 04 93 05 06 00. Fax: 04 93 05 09 34. E-mail: info@club-origan.com. **Reservations:** Needed in high season; 25% deposit and fee (€ 30). **Open** 12 April - 30 September.

Directions: Heading west on the N202, just past the town of Puget-Theniers, turn right at camp sign at level crossing; site is 1.5 km.

Camping-Caravaning Les Cigales

0608 505 ave. de la Mer, 06210 Mandelieu la Napoule

It is hard to imagine that such a quiet, peaceful site could be in the middle of such a busy town and so near to Cannes - we were delighted with it. The entrance (easily missed) with reception and parking has large electronic gates that ensure that the site is very secure. There are only 115 pitches (20 used for mobile homes) so this is really quite a small, personal site. There are three pitch sizes, from small ones for tents to pitches for larger units. All are level with much needed shade in summer, although the sun will get through in winter when it is needed, and all have electricity (6A). The site is alongside the Canal de Siagne and for a fee small boats can be launched at La Napoule, then moored outside the campsite's side gate. Les Cigales is open all year so it is useful for the Monte Carlo Rally, the Cannes Film Festival and the Mimosa Festival, all held out of the main season. English is spoken.

Facilities: Two well appointed unisex toilet blocks are kept very clean, one heated for the winter months. Washbasins in cabins and facilities for babies and disabled visitors. Dishwashing and laundry sinks. Washing machine. Motorcaravan service point. Restaurant at entrance with takeaways (April - 30 Sept). Swimming pool (March - Oct). Small play area. Table tennis. Fishing possible in the canal (but not many fish!) **Off site:** The town is an easy walk. Centre commercial 2 km. Bus stop 10 minutes. Railway station 1 km. for trains to Cannes, Nice, Antibes and Monte Carlo. Riverside and canal walks. Two golf courses within 1 km. Beach 800 m.

Charges guide

Per adult	€ 3.50
child (under 5 yrs)	€ 2.30
pitch	€ 10.67 - € 22.11
electricity (3-6A)	€ 2.30 - € 3.81

Tel: 04 93 49 23 53. **Fax:** 04 93 49 30 45. **E-mail:** campingcigales@wanadoo.fr. **Reservations:** Made with deposit (€ 77). **Open** all year.

Directions: From A8 take exit 40 and bear right. Remain in right hand lane and continue right signed Plages-Ports and Creche-Campings. New Casino supermarket is on the right. Continue under motor way to T-junction. Turn left and site is 60 m. on left opposite Chinese restaurant.

The Alan Rogers' Travel Service

This unique service enables our readers to reserve their holidays as well as ferry crossings and comprehensive insurance cover at extremely competitive rates. The majority of participating sites are in France and we are able to offer a selection of some of the very best sites in this country.

Share our experience and let us help
to ensure that your holiday will be a complete success.

Alan Rogers Travel Service 01892 55 98 98 or www.alanrogers.com

Alan Rogers' FRANCE

The French sites featured in this guide are only a selection of over 600 featured in our Good Camps Guide - France.

**Available from
all good bookshops or
online at www.alanrogers.com**

Domaine d'Arnauteille
11250 Montclar

Enjoying some beautiful and varied views, this rather unusual site is ideally situated for exploring, by foot or car, the little known Aude Département, the area of the Cathars and for visiting the walled city of Carcassonne (10 minutes drive). However, access could be difficult for large, twin axle vans. The site itself is set in 115 hectares of farmland and is on hilly ground with the original pitches on gently sloping, lightly wooded land and newer ones with water, drainage and electricity (5/10A), semi-terraced and partly hedged. The facilities are quite spread out with the swimming pool set in a hollow basin surrounded by green fields and some newly developed pitches. The reception building is vast; originally a farm building, with a newer top floor being converted to apartments. Although architecturally rather strange, from some angles it is quite attractive and mature trees soften the outlines. This is a developing site with enthusiastic owners for whom riding is the principle theme with stables on site (remember that the French are more relaxed about hard hats, etc). Some up and down walking between the pitches and facilities is unavoidable. A 'Sites et Paysages' member.

Facilities: The main, heated sanitary block is now a distinctive feature, rebuilt to a very high specification with a Roman theme. Three other smaller blocks are located at various points. They include washbasins in cabins, dishwashing under cover (hot water), washing machines, facilities for disabled people and a baby bath. Facilities can be stretched at peak times. Motorcaravan service point and gas. Small shop (15/5-30/9 - the site is a little out of the way). Restaurant in converted stable block offers plat du jour, grills, takeaway (15/5-15/9). Swimming pool (25 x 10 m.) with children's pool. Play area. Table tennis and volleyball. Riding (stables open 15/6-15/9). **Off site:** Bicycle hire 8 km, fishing 3 km, golf 10 km, rafting and canoeing near, plus many walks with marked paths.

Charges 2003

Per pitch incl. 2 persons	€ 13.50 - € 20.00
with 5A electricity	€ 17.00 - € 23.50
with electricity, water and drainage	€ 20.00 - € 27.50
extra person	€ 4.00 - € 5.50
child (under 7 yrs)	€ 2.50 - € 3.60
dog	€ 1.50 - € 2.20
electricity 10A, plus	€ 1.60

Tel: 04 68 26 84 53. Fax: 04 68 26 91 10. E-mail: arnauteille@mnet.fr. **Reservations:** Made with deposit (25%) and fee (€ 23). **Open** 1 April - 30 September.

Directions: Using D118 from Carcassonne, after bypassing the small village of Rouffiac d'Aude, there is a small section of dual carriageway. Before the end of this, turn right to Montclar up a rather narrow road for 2.5 km. Site is signed sharp left and up hill before the village.

Domaine d'Arnauteille

11250 Montclar

(15 mins from the city of Carcassonne and 9 miles from the airport with direct flights to Paris and London)

In the heart of a 115 ha estate with 7 ha for camping in an exceptional setting with magnificient views of the surrounding hills.
25m swimming pool, walking, rambling & riding.
Comfortable sanitary facilities.
Restaurant & shop.
Mobil-homes, chalets and André Trigano canvas bungalows, all fully equipped for hire.
Open: 01/04 - 30/09

Tel: 0033 468 26 84 53
Fax: 0033 468 26 91 10
E-mail: Arnauteille@mnet.fr
www.arnauteille.com

Camping La Nautique

1108 La Nautique, 11100 Narbonne

This extremely spacious site is situated on the Etang de Bages, where flat water combined with strong winds make it one of the best windsurfing areas in France and is owned and run by a very welcoming Dutch family. The site is fenced off from the water for the protection of children and wind-surfers can have a key for the gate (with deposit) that leads to launching points on the lake. La Nautique has 390 huge, level pitches (a small one is 130 sq.m), with many used for site owned mobile homes and chalets and 30 tour operator pitches. There are also 6 or 7 overnight pitches with electricity in a separate area. The wide range of evergreens, flowering shrubs and trees on site give a pleasant feel and each pitch is separated by hedges making some quite private. All have electricity (10A) and water. The difference between this and other sites is that each pitch has an indi-vidual toilet cabin. Tent campers may find the ground rather rocky. A variety of enter-tainment is organised in July/Aug, plus a sports club for supervised surfing, sailing, rafting, walking and canoeing (some activi-ties are charged for). English is spoken by the welcoming Schutjes family. This site caters for families with children including teenagers (in fact they say 8 months to 86 years!)

Facilities: Each individual cabin has a toilet, shower and washbasin (key deposit) and, as each pitch empties, the facilities are cleaned in readiness for the next. Special pitches for disabled people with facili-ties fitted out to cater for their needs. Two fully equipped laundry areas. Additional dishwashing sinks strategically placed. Shop at entrance (1/6-15/9) with reasonable stock. Bar/restaurant (evenings only May and Sept) plus large TV. Snack bar 1/7 - 31/8. Takeaway. Swimming pools (solar heated), water slide and paddling pool with fountain and slide, and poolside bar (1/7-31/8). New children's play areas and active children's club. Tennis, table tennis, basketball, volleyball, football, minigolf and boules. Teenagers' disco organised in high season. Recreation area with TV for youngsters. Internet connection. Only electric barbecues are permitted. Torch useful. **Off site:** Large sandy beaches at Gruissan (10 km) and Narbonne Plage (15 km). Narbonne is only 4 km. Walking and cycling. Riding. Canoeing, sailing and windsurfing on the Etang.

Charges 2002

Per unit incl. 1 or 2 persons, electricity, water and sanitary unit	€ 14.15 - € 24.50
extra person	€ 3.65 - € 4.75
child (1-7 yrs)	€ 1.55 - € 2.74
dog or cat	€ 1.25 - € 1.90
local tax	€ 3.00

Tel: 04 68 90 48 19. **Fax:** 04 68 90 73 39. E-mail: info@campinglanautique.com. **Reservations:** Made with deposit (€ 104) and fee (€ 16). **Open** 1 March - 17 November.

Directions: From A9 take exit 38 (Narbonne Sud). Go round roundabout to last exit and follow signs for La Nautique and site, then further site signs to site on right in 3 km.

Camping-Caravaning Le Boucanet

30240 Le Grau du Roi

On the beach between Grande Motte and Le Grau-du-Roi, this is a sunny site with only a little shade. Many trees have been planted but as yet most are not tall enough to give much shade. As to be expected, the 462 pitches are sandy and level. The 357 for touring units are separated by small bushes, most with electricity (6A). The pleasant restaurant overlooks the large pool and is open lunchtimes and evenings. An excellent shopping arcade provides groceries, fruit, newspapers, a butcher and cooked meats, rotisserie and pizzas. In July and August organised activities include games, competitions, gymnastics, water polo, jogging and volleyball for adults. Horse riding on the white horses of the Camargue is to be found within a few kilometres.

Facilities: The toilet blocks are convenient for the pitches providing washbasins in cubicles and some British style toilets in two blocks, the remainder Turkish style (about 70%). Facilities for disabled people at two blocks. Baby rooms. Dishwashing and laundry sinks have warm water. Washing machines, dryers, irons and fridge hire. Motorcaravan service point. Range of shops. Restaurant. Bar with snacks (all these facilities open all season). Large swimming pool and paddling pool. Play area on sand and mini-club in July/Aug. Table tennis, tennis. Bicycle hire. Dogs are not accepted. **Off site:** Golf 1.5 km. Riding 500 m.

Charges 2002

Per unit incl. 2 persons	€ 18.50 - € 25.00
with electricity	€ 21.50 - € 28.00
supplement for pitch on first row of beach	€ 4.65 - € 8.40
extra adult	€ 6.80 - € 8.20
child (under 7 yrs)	€ 5.40 - € 6.60
local tax	€ 0.10 - € 0.20

Tel: (0)4 66 51 41 48. Fax: (0)4 66 51 41 87. E-mail: campingboucanet@wanadoo.fr. **Reservations:** Necessary for July/Aug. and made with 25% deposit and booking fee (€ 23); by money order or cheque only. **Open** 4 May - 28 September.

Directions: Site is between La Grand Motte and Le Grau-du-Roi on the D255 coastal road, on the seaward side of the road.

Camping Naturiste de la Sablière

N3010   Domaine de la Sablière, St Privat de Champclos, 30430 Barjac

Spectacularly situated in the Cèze Gorges, this naturist site occupies a much larger area than its 250 pitches might suggest. It offers a wide variety of facilities, all within a really peaceful, wooded and dramatic setting. Pitches are grouped in areas - 'Mesange' (mainly for tents with cars banned in high season and parking provided 200 m. away) and 'Fauvette' at the bottom of the gorge alongside the river at some points close to the main access road, which is well surfaced but steep and winding. A newer area, 'Pinson', is near the top of the hill, the side of which forms part of the site. The pitches themselves are mainly flat on terraces, attractively situated among a variety of trees and shrubs. Some with low overhang. Many are of a good size and have electricity. A pool complex provides a children's pool and two large pools, one of which can be covered by a sliding glass dome, bar, sauna, TV room and disco. This is essentially a family run and orientated site and Gaby Cespedes, and her team provide a personal touch that is unusual in a large site. This no doubt contributes to the relaxed and very informal atmosphere - first time naturists would find this a gentle introduction into naturism without any pressure. You must expect some fairly steep walking between pitches, pool complex, restaurant and supermarket, although there is a minibus service in high season. Member of France 4 Naturisme.

Facilities: Six good unisex sanitary blocks (two new in 2001) have excellent free hot showers in typical open plan, naturist site style, washbasins (cold water), baby baths and facilities for people with disabilities. Washing up and laundry sinks. Laundry. Supermarket and charcuterie. Open air, covered restaurant (all season) with good value waiter service meals and a takeaway in an attractive setting. Swimming pool complex. Small café/crêperie. Varied and numerous activities include walking, climbing, swimming, canoeing, fitness trail, fishing (permit required), archery, tennis, minigolf and volleyball, book binding, pottery, yoga etc. Entertainment programme for adults and children (mid June - end Aug). Torch useful. **Off site:** Barjac with its Antiques Fair at Easter and mid-August. Alès, Chemin de Fer des Cevennes.

Charges 2003

Per pitch incl. 2 persons	€ 11.00 - € 28.00
extra person	€ 3.00 - € 6.10
child under 8 yrs	free - € 5.60
electricity	€ 3.60
dog	€ 1.00 - € 2.50

Tel: 04 66 24 51 16. Fax: 04 66 24 58 69. E-mail: sabliere@club-internet.fr. **Reservations:** Made with deposit (25%) and fee (€ 30)- contact site. **Open** Easter - end September.

Directions: From Barjac take D901 east for 3 km. Site is signed just before St Privat-de-Champclos and is approx. 3 km. on narrow roads following camp signs.

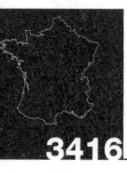

Camping-Club Charlemagne

3416   34340 Marseillan Plage

Charlemagne is under the same family ownership as Nouvelle Floride and situated across the road from it, 200 metres from the beach. It boasts a large range of amenities, consisting of a large supermarket, bakery, takeaway/fast food, bar, restaurant and disco. Facing the main street, these facilities are open to the public and are consequently well stocked, well equipped and open for the whole season. The site is traditionally laid out under the shade of tall trees providing 480 level pitches. Of these 270 are available for touring units, neatly hedged and all with electricity (6A) and water. Access to the beach is by a footpath past Nouvelle Floride but the site also has a good, well used pool complex. This is a site which caters for all ages with a wide range of activities.

Facilities: There are four toilet blocks, two of the same modern design and quality as at Nouvelle Floride, with washbasins in cabins, dishwashing under cover, laundry sinks and washing machine. The two more traditional blocks have some Turkish toilets. Motorcaravan service point. Fridge hire. Full range of shops, bar/cafe, restaurant, takeaway and disco, all open all season. Swimming pool (all season). Good fenced play area. Mini-club (May-Sept). Range of evening entertainment covering concerts, cabarets, dances and discos. **Off site:** Nearby tennis, golf, karting, riding, bicycle hire and water sports.

Charges 2003

Per unit incl. up to 2 persons,	
water and electricity	€ 15.00 - € 38.00
extra person (over 1 yr)	€ 5.00 - € 8.00
pet	€ 3.00 - € 3.50
local tax	€ 0.33

Tel: (0)4 67 21 92 49. Fax: (0)4 67 21 86 11. E-mail: info@charlemagne-camping.com. **Reservations:** Needed for July/Aug. **Open** 5 April - 27 September.

Directions: From A9 exit 34, follow N314 to Agde then N112 towards Sete and watch for signs to Marseillan Plage from where site is well signed.

Camping-Club Nouvelle Floride
34340 Marseillan Plage

Marseillan Plage is a small, busy resort just east of Cap d'Adge and La Nouvelle Floride enjoys a super position immediately beside a long gently shelving sandy beach. It is a good quality site, very traditional in style and set under tall trees with neat hedges to separate the 520 pitches (370 for tourers). These are on sandy soil and all have water and electricity (6A). Some of the pitches in the newer area (across a small lane) and the hardstanding pitches near the beach have little shade as yet. There are a number of mobile homes but the site is mainly for tourers. Amenities and facilities are generally of excellent quality and include a strikingly attractive bar area overlooking the beach with a raised stage for entertainment. Alongside the play area is a multi-purpose ball court and fitness centre, also on sand with robust machines with the idea of keeping Mum and Dad fit whilst still keeping an eye on the children. Essentially a `holiday site`, there is an extensive programme of entertainment and activities catering for all ages, and a new, 'state of the art' pool complex. However, the main attraction for most will almost certainly be the direct access to a fine beach. The gates on the beach entrance are locked at 9 pm. for security. This is a well run, family run site aimed at families.

Facilities: The four toilet blocks are impressive, including two with a number of en-suite showers and washbasins, otherwise washbasins all in cabins. Baby rooms, excellent facilities for disabled visitors and even a dog shower. The showers and washing up areas are closed between 23.00-07.00 hrs. Motorcaravan service point. Bar and restaurant. Shop all season, plus a range of shops at Charlemagne across the road. Pool complex with slides, jacuzzi, paddling pools, etc (all season). Play area, fitness centre and multi-purpose ball court. Table tennis. Weekly films (DVD) and variety of organised games, competitions, dances and discos. Mini-club in school holidays. Bicycle hire. **Off site:** Riding and bicycle hire 500 m. Golf 5 km.

Charges 2003

Per unit incl. 1 or 2 persons, water and electricity	€ 19.00 - € 38.00
extra person	€ 5.00 - € 8.00
child under 1 yr	free
pet	€ 3.00 - € 3.50
local tax	€ 0.30

Tel: (0)4 67 21 94 49. Fax: (0)4 67 21 81 05. E-mail: info@nouvelle-floride.com. **Reservations:** Contact site. **Open** 12 April - 28 September.

Directions: From A9 autoroute exit 34, follow N312 to Agde then take N112 towards Sete. Watch for signs to Marseillan Plage from where site is well signed.

Camping Le Sérignan Plage

Le Sérignan Plage, 34410 Sérignan

the travel service
TO BOOK
Ferry ✓
Pitch ✓
Accommodation ✗
01892 55 98 98

This is the sister site to Sérignan Plage Naturist (no. 3408N), owned by Jean Paul Amat and his family who you will see around the site. Have a chat - his English is excellent and he likes to practise. It is a large, but very comfortable site, built in a genuinely unique style with direct access to a beautiful sandy beach. You will normally find room even in the high season, with 450 touring pitches in several different areas and three different styles to choose from, with the benefit of some of the most comprehensive amenities we have encountered. The touring pitches by the beach have little shade, are sandy and a little smaller. The others are mostly of a very good size on level grass with plenty of shade. All pitches have electricity (5A) and are mostly separate from a similar number of seasonal pitches and rented accommodation in the centre section of the site. Perhaps the most remarkable aspect of this site is the cluster of attractive buildings which form the central 'village' area with shops, pretty bars and a smart restaurant, amongst which is a small indoor heated swimming pool of unusual design mainly for out of season use. To complement this an amazing outdoor pool complex has now been added near the touring area. With interlinked pool areas, deep parts for swimmers, exciting children's areas with slides, bridges and islands, it is attractively landscaped and surrounded by a very large grass sunbathing area complete with sun loungers. The village area with inner and outer courtyards, has a lively, international atmosphere (well used and perhaps showing some wear and tear). Entertainment is provided every evening in high season, including shows at the outdoor stage in the outer courtyard, discos most nights and daily sporting activities. Wine and food tastings with tourist information presentations each Monday at 5 pm. Giant screen for news and current affairs. There is something for everyone here and you will not need to leave the site if you do not wish to. Remember, this is a seaside site in a natural coastal environment, so do not expect it to be neat and manicured; in parts nature still predominates. The site has direct access to a superb, large sandy beach and to the adjoining naturist beach, both of which slope very gently and offer safe bathing at most times. Used by tour operators (99 pitches).

Facilities: Nine unisex toilet blocks. The older circular ones with a mixture of British and Turkish style WCs are nearest the sea and central 'village' area, seasonal units and mobile homes, etc. and thus take the brunt of the wear and tear. The touring area, furthest from the sea but near the pool complex has three modern toilet blocks of individual design. Well planned with good facilities, these include a number of large controllable hot showers with washbasin (non-slip floor) and WC en-suite, well equipped baby rooms, facilities for disabled people. Dishwashing and laundry facilities in all blocks and central launderette. At peak times maintenance can be a little variable. Well stocked supermarket, bakery, newsagent/tabac, ATM and range of market stalls. Poissonnerie and boucherie (7/6-8/9). Hairdresser. Bars, restaurant serving local specialities plus takeaway choices (all 7/4-10/9). Much animation for children, amusement machines and a range of evening entertainment in the amphitheatre and even a separate, secluded roof-top bar (9 pm - 1 am) - ask for a 'Cucaracha'! Soundproof disco. Heated indoor pool and landscaped outdoor pool complex (also heated) with lifeguards in the main season and an ID card system to prevent abuse (April - Sept). Range of sporting activities organised by site staff. Bicycle hire. **Off site:** Riding 2 km, golf 10 km. Bicycle hire. Sailing and windsurfing school on beach (lifeguard in high season).

Charges 2002

Per unit incl. 1 or 2 persons and 5A electricity	€ 17.00 - € 29.00
extra person	€ 3.00 - € 5.00
pet	€ 3.00

Tel: 04 67 32 35 33. Fax: 04 67 32 26 36. E-mail: info@leserignanplage.com. **Reservations:** Made from 1 Feb. with deposit (25%) and fee (€ 30). **Open** 10 April - 22 September.

Directions: From A9 exit 35 (Béziers Est) follow signs for Sérignan on D64 (9 km). Don't go into Sérignan, but take sign for Sérignan Plage for 4 km. At small multi sign (blue) turn right on single carriageway. At T-junction turn left over small road bridge and after left hand bend, site is 100 m. after naturist site and also Sérignan Plage Nature.

YOUR HOLIDAYS BY THE SEA

Sérignan-Plage can be likened to an open-air auberge with the Mediterranean on your doorstep

FROM APRIL TO SEPTEMBER: 850 m² heated lagoon pool • heated indoor pool • activities and shows • mini-club • restaurant • bar • shops...

Sunshine Guarantee

For bookings made in April, May and September you only pay for the nights you stay, if exceptionally the sun should not shine. For further information, refer to the general conditions of sale.

Le Sérignan Plage
34410 Sérignan
Languedoc-Roussillon
tél. 00 33 467 32 35 33
fax. 00 33 467 32 26 36
info@leserignanplage.com
www.leserignanplage.com

BORD DE MER

Le sérignan plage

CAMPING AUBERGE
MÉDITERRANÉE

DDB Nouveau monde LE TOURISME

CAMPING VILLAGES
yelloh!
VILLAGE

Camping Le Sérignan Plage Nature

34410 Sérignan

Sérignan Plage Nature is a very comfortable and distinctly characterful naturist site beside a large sandy beach. It was for many years run as a private club but in recent years the charming, English speaking owner, Jean Guy Amat, has improved facilities here to make the site a comfortable, relaxed and friendly naturist campsite. Jean Guy also owns Sérignan Plage next door. The site has 260 touring pitches (out of 500) on level grass and all with 5A electricity. The pitches vary in size (80-120 sq.m), the smaller ones nearest to the beach with less shade and sandy, whilst many of the larger grassy ones further back are of a comfortable size with varying shade from the varieties of trees that have been encouraged to grow to a good size (utilising waste water for irrigation). A new area away from the beach and this has younger saplings only. The Romanesque architectural style of several of the buildings (one is called the Forum) has been preserved. There is a warm and friendly ambience at the bar and restaurant and evening entertainment is provided. This atmosphere is helped in no small measure by the enthusiasm of the managers. This is a well equipped family oriented campsite, with many facilities and good entertainment in season. It has direct access to a superb, safe and virtually private naturist beach of fine sand (with lifeguard in high season). Member 'France 4 Naturisme'.

Facilities: The toilet blocks of differing design have all been refurbished, and all offer modern facilities with some washbasins in cabins and both British and Turkish style WCs. All is clean and well maintained. Dishwashing under cover. Washing machines. Large supermarket, market for fresh fruit and vegetables, newsagent/souvenir shop and ice cream kiosk. Bar, restaurant with reasonably priced menu. Evening entertainment. Children's disco. **Off site:** Riding 2 km.

Charges 2002

Per unit incl. 1 or 2 persons	€ 13.00 - € 26.00
extra person	€ 3.50 - € 4.00
electricity (5A)	€ 3.00
dog	€ 3.00

Tel: 04 67 32 09 61. Fax: 04 67 32 26 36. E-mail: info@serignsnnaturisme.com. **Reservations:** Made from 1 Feb. with deposit (€ 61), fee (€ 15,24) and cancellation insurance (€ 70). **Open** 1 May - 30 September.

Directions: From A9 exit 35 (Béziers Est) follow signs for Sérignan on D64 (9 km). Prior to Sérignan, take road to Sérignan Plage. At small multi sign (blue) turn right onto one-way single carriageway (poorly surfaced) for 500 m. At T-junction turn left over small bridge and site is 75 m. on right immediately after left hand bend (not the first, but the second naturist site).

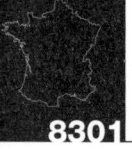

Camping-Caravaning Les Pins Parasol

route de Bagnols, 83600 Fréjus

Not everyone likes very big sites, and Les Pins Parasols with its 189 pitches is of a size which is quite easy to walk around. It is family owned and run. Although on very slightly undulating ground, virtually all the pitches are levelled or terraced and separated by hedges or bushes with pine trees for shade. They are around 100 sq.m. and all have electricity. What is particularly interesting, as it is the most unusual feature, is that 48 of the pitches are equipped with their own fully enclosed, tiled sanitary unit, consisting of British WC, washbasin, hot shower and washing up sink, all quite close together. These pitches naturally cost more but may well be of interest to those seeking extra comfort. The nearest beach is the once very long Fréjus-Plage (5.5 km) now reduced a little by the new marina, and adjoins St. Raphaël. (See note on La Baume entry concerning traffic delays at the D4/N7 road junction.) Used by tour operators (10%).

Facilities: Besides the individual units there are three toilet blocks of good average quality providing washbasins in cabins and facilities for disabled people. One block can be heated when necessary. Small shop with reasonable stocks and restaurant with takeaway (both 1/5-20/9). General room with TV. Swimming pool (200 sq.m) with attractive rock backdrop and separate long slide with landing pool and small children's pool. Half-court tennis. **Off site:** Bicycle hire or riding 2 km, fishing 6 km, golf 10 km. Bus from the gate into Fréjus 5km.

Charges 2002

Per normal pitch with electricity	
incl. 2 persons	€ 17.30 - € 22.00
with sanitary unit incl. 2 persons	€ 21.50 - € 27.00
extra person	€ 4.40 - € 5.50
child (under 7 yrs)	€ 2.90 - € 3.50
dog	€ 1.70 - € 2.00
local tax	€ 0.15 - € 0.30

Tel: 04 94 40 88 43. Fax: 04 94 40 81 99. E-mail: lespinsparasol@wanadoo.fr. **Reservations:** Necessary for July/Aug. only and made for min. 10 days for exact dates with deposit (€ 92) but no fee. **Open** Easter - 30 September.

Directions: From autoroute A8 take exit 38 for Fréjus Est. Turn right immediately on leaving pay booths on a small road which leads across to D4, where right again and under 1 km. to site.

Camping Domaine de la Bergerie

Vallée du Fournel, 83520 Roquebrune sur Argens

8317

This is yet another site near the Côte d'Azur which will take you away from all the bustle of the Mediterranean to total relaxation amongst the cork, oak, pine and mimosa. The 60 hectare site is quite spread out. The terrain varies from natural, rocky semi-landscaped areas for mobile homes to flat, grassy terrain with avenues of 200 separated pitches for touring caravans and tents. All pitches average over 80 sq.m. and have electrical connections, with those in one area also having water and drainage. The restaurant/bar, a converted farm building, is surrounded by shady patios, whilst inside it oozes character with high beams and archways leading to intimate corners. Tournaments and programmes are organised daily and, in the evening, shows, cabarets, discos, cinema, karaoke and dancing at the amphitheatre prove popular until very late - it can be noisy.

Facilities: Four sanitary blocks are kept clean and include washbasins in cubicles, facilities for disabled people and babies, plus dishwashing and laundry areas with washing machines. Well stocked supermarket. Bar/restaurant. Takeaway. New pool complex (1/4-30/9) with indoor pool to be added for 2003. Fitness centre (body building, sauna, gym, etc). Five tennis courts and two half courts. Archery, roller skating and minigolf. Volleyball and mini football. Mini-farm for children. Fishing. Only gas barbecues are permitted. **Off site:** Riding or golf 4 km, bicycle hire 7 km. Water skiing and rock climbing nearby. St Aygulf or Ste Maxime are 7 km.

Charges 2002

Per unit incl. 2 adults, electricity	€ 16.00 - € 25.00
3 persons and electricity	€ 20.00 - € 33.00
extra adult	€ 4.00 - € 6.50
child (under 7 yrs)	€ 3.00 - € 5.00
electricity (10A)	€ 1.80 - € 2.50
dog	free - € 2.50
local tax (over 10 yrs)	€ 0.30

Tel: 04 98 11 45 45. Fax: 04 98 11 45 46. E-mail: info@domainelabergerie.com. **Reservations:** Made with deposit (€ 200) and fee (€ 20). (Mobile homes available 15 February - 15 November). **Open** 1 June - 15 September.

Directions: Leave A8 at Le Muy exit on N7 towards Fréjus. Proceed for 9 km., then right onto D7 signed St Aygulf. Continue for 8 km. and then right at roundabout onto D8; site is on the right.

Between Frejus and Saint Tropez and just 10 minutes drive from the sea, in a wooded setting amongst cork oaks, pines and mimosas, the spell of the Var's area is waiting for you at.....

DOMAINE de la bergerie

★★★★

April, May, June and September : Special offer for 2 persons for 2, 3 weeks or 1 Month.

VERY COMFORTABLE MOBILES HOMES TO RENT
sited on large landscaped terraces of 200 m².

6 Tennis   Fitnesscenter   Children'sclub

Camping - Caravaning - Club Vallée du Fournel
83520 Roquebrune sur Argens - FRANCE
✆.: (33)4 98 11 45 45 Fax.: (33)4 98 11 45 46
www.domainelabergerie.com

Coupon for a free brochure

Name : _____
First name : _____
Address : _____
Postcode : _____
City : _____

Caravaning L'Etoile d'Argens

8307

83370 St. Aygulf

the travel service
TO BOOK

Ferry	✔
Pitch	✔
Accommodation	✗

01892 55 98 98

First impressions of L'Etoile d'Argens are of space, cleanliness and calm. Reception staff are very friendly and English is spoken (open 24 hrs). This is a site run with families in mind and many of the activities are free, making for a good value holiday. There are 493 level grass pitches laid out in typical French style, separated by hedges. There are five sizes of pitch, ranging from 50 sq.m. (for small tents) to 100, 130, 180 or 250 sq.m. These are exceptionally large and two families could easily fit two caravans and cars or one family could have a very spacious plot with a garden like atmosphere. All pitches are fully serviced with fresh and waste water and 10A electricity, with some shade although the site is not overpowered by trees which leads to a spacious feeling. The pool and bar area is attractively land-scaped with old olive and palm trees on beautifully manicured and watered grass. The river runs along one side of the site and a free boat service (15/6-15/9) runs every 40 minutes to the beach. It is also possible to moor a boat or fish. This is a good family site for the summer but also good in low season for a quiet stay in a superb location with excellent pitches. Tour operators take 85 pitches and there are 130 mobile homes but for a large site it is usually calm and peaceful even in July.

Facilities: Two new toilet blocks were added in 2000, whilst some of the original small unisex blocks have been retiled making a big improvement. All are well kept and include some washbasins in cubicles. Dishwashing sinks and laundry with outside clothes line. Supermarket and gas supplies. Bar, restaurant, pizzeria, takeaway. Two adult pools, children's paddling pool and solarium. Tennis (two of the four courts are floodlit) with coaching and minigolf (both free in low season), aerobics, archery (July/Aug), football and swimming lessons. Volleyball, basket-ball, table tennis and boule. Play area with rubber safety base. Children's entertainer in July/Aug. Activity programme includes games, dances for adults and escorted walking trips to the surrounding hills. within 3 km. **Off site:** Golf, riding or bicycle hire

Charges 2002

Per tent pitch (100 sq.m.)	
with electricity and 2 persons	€ 20.00 - € 35.00
'comfort' pitch (100 sq.m), 3 persons	
with water and drainage	€ 26.00 - € 40.00
'luxury' pitch, 4 persons 180 sq.m	€ 37.00 - € 55.00
extra person	€ 5.50 - € 7.00
child (under 7)	€ 3.50 - € 5.00
dog	€ 3.00 - € 3.50

Tel: 04 94 81 01 41. Fax: 04 94 81 21 45. E-mail: letoiledargens@wanadoo.fr. **Reservations:** Made for any period with substantial deposit and fee. **Open** Easter - 30 September, with all services.

Directions: Leave A8 at exit 36 and take N7 to Le Muy and Fréjus. After about 8 km. at roundabout take D7 signed Roquebrune and St Aygulf. In 9.5 km. (after roundabout) turn left signed Fréjus. Watch for site sign and ignore width and height limit signs as site is 500 m. to right.

Camping-Caravaning Moulin des Iscles

8324

83520 Roquebrune-sur-Argens

A haven of peace and tranquillity, Moulin des Iscles is hidden down 0.5 km. of private, unmade road - an unusual find in this often quite hectic part of Provence. Based around a former mill, it is a small, pretty site beside the river Argens with access to the river in places for fishing, canoeing and swimming, with a concrete bank and fenced where deemed necessary (some sought after pitches overlook the river). The 90 grassy, level pitches with electricity (6A) and water to all, radiate out from M. Dumarcet's attractive, centrally situated home which is where the restau-rant and shop are situated. A nice mixture of deciduous trees provide natural shade and colour and the old mill house rests comfortably near the entrance which has a security barrier closed at night. This is a quiet site with little on site entertainment, but with a nice little restaurant. An effort has been made to welcome handicapped visitors. It is a real campsite not a 'camp-ing village'.

Facilities: The toilet block is fully equipped, includ-ing ramped access for disabled visitors. Some Turkish style toilets. Washbasins have cold water, some in cubicles. Baby bath and changing facilities en-suite. Covered laundry and dishwashing sinks. Small separate unisex provision for pitches near the entrance. Washing machine. Restaurant with home cooked dish-of-the-day on a weekly rotation. Surprisingly well stocked shop. Library - some English books. TV room incl. satellite, Pool table, table tennis. Play area, minigolf and boules all outside the barrier for more peace and quiet on site. Internet terminal.

Charges 2002

Per unit incl. 2 or 3 persons	€ 17.60
extra adult	€ 3.20
child (over 10 yrs)	€ 2.20
local tax	€ 0.30
electricity	€ 2.70

Tel: 04 94 45 70 74. Fax: 04 94 45 46 09. E-mail: moulin.iscles@wanadoo.fr. **Reservations:** Contact site. **Open** 1 April - 30 September.

Directions: Follow as for site no. 8320, Les Pecheurs, but continue past it through the village of Roquebrune towards St Aygulf for 1 km. Site signed on left. Follow private unmade road for approx. 500 m. to site entrance in front of you.

L'Etoile d'Argens

★★★★

TENNIS AND

GOLF FREE

LOW-SEASON

TEL : +33 4 94 81 01 41   FAX :+33 4 94 81 21 45
83370 ST AYGULF

www.provence-campings.com/frejus/etoile-argens
E-mail : letoiledargens@wanadoo.fr

ESE communication: 04 94 67 06 00

France - Mediterranean
Camping-Caravaning Esterel

avenue des Golf, 83700 Saint-Raphael

8302

For caravans only, Esterel is a quality site east of St Raphaël, set among the hills at the back of Agay. It is an attractive quiet situation with good views around. The site is 3.5 km. from the sandy beach at Agay where parking is perhaps a little easier than at most places on this coast. In addition to a section for permanent caravans, it has some 250 pitches for tourists, on which caravans of any type are taken but not tents. Pitches are on shallow terraces, attractively landscaped with good shade and a variety of flowering plants, giving a feeling of spaciousness. Each pitch has an electricity connection and tap, and 18 special ones have their own individual en-suite washroom adjoining. A pleasant courtyard area contains the shop and bar, with a terrace overlooking the attractively landscaped (floodlit at night) pool complex. Wild boar come to the perimeter fence each evening to be fed by visitors. This is a good site, well run and organised in a deservedly popular area. A member of 'Les Castels' group.

Facilities: Two refurbished and well maintained toilet blocks, plus one smaller one by the tourist section, are very satisfactory. They can be heated and include washbasins mostly in cabins. Individual toilet units on 18 pitches. Facilities for disabled people. Laundry room. Motorcaravan service point. Shop. Takeaway. Bar/restaurant. Five heated, circular swimming pools, one large for adults, one smaller for children and three arranged as a waterfall (1/4-30/9). New disco. Archery, volleyball, minigolf, two tennis courts, pony rides, petanque and squash court. Playground. Bicycle hire. Events and entertainment are organised in season. Barbecues are forbidden. **Off site:** Good golf courses very close. Trekking by foot, bicycle or by pony in the surrounding L'Esterel forest park.

Charges 2002

Per pitch incl. 2 persons	€ 25.92 - € 29.73
de-luxe pitch	€ 32.78 - € 36.59
extra person	€ 6.86
child (1-7 yrs)	€ 4.57
local tax	€ 0.30

Tel: 04 94 82 03 28. Fax: 04 94 82 87 37. E-mail: contact@esterel-caravaning.fr. **Reservations:** Needed for high season and made for min. 1 week with deposit (€ 80) and fee (€ 15,24). CD brochure available from site. **Open** 1 April - 30 September.

Directions: You can approach from St Raphaël via Valescure but easiest is to turn off coast road at Agay where there are good signs. From Fréjus exit from A8, follow signs for Valescure throughout, then for Agay, and site is on left.

France - Mediterranean
Au Paradis des Campeurs

La Gaillarde-Plage, 83380 Les Issambres

8308

Having direct access to a sandy beach (via an underpass) and being so well maintained are just two of the reasons that Au Paradis des Campeurs is popular. Family owned and run, it now has 180 pitches, all with 6A electricity and 132 with water tap and drainaway. The original pitches vary in size and shape but all are satisfactory and most have some shade. The new pitches are all large but at present have little shade although trees and bushes have been planted and shade is developing. There is no entertainment which gives peaceful nights. The gates are surveyed by TV (especially the beach gate) and a security man patrols all day. The site has become popular and it is essential to book for June to August.

Facilities: Two toilet blocks, refurbished to an excellent standard with high quality fittings and well maintained, include most washbasins in cabins. Facilities for babies. Dishwashing, laundry sinks, two washing machines and dryer. Motorcaravan service point. Shop and restaurant (with takeaway) front onto main road and open all season. TV room. Two excellent play areas, catering for the under and over 5s. **Off site:** Bicycle hire 2.5 km, riding 3 km, golf 6 km.

Charges guide

Per unit incl. up to 3 persons	€ 12.35 - € 19.21
extra person	€ 4.88
child (under 4 yrs)	€ 2.74
electricity (6A)	€ 3.35

Tel: 04 94 96 93 55. Fax: 04 94 49 62 99. **Reservations:** Advised for main season. **Open** 20 March - 15 October.

Directions: Site is signed from N98 coast road at La Gaillarde, 2 km. south of St Aygulf.

A SAMPLE OF YOUR HOLIDAY...

ON THE COTE D'AZUR – BETWEEN CANNES AND SAINT-TROPEZ
5 MN AWAY FROM THE SEA

Luxury mobile homes for rental and vast pitches for caravans !

The Club formula !

The children's paradise

NON STOP Animation !

LES CASTELS

Esterel Caravaning ★★★★

Avenue des Golfs - 83530 Agay - FRANCE
Tel : +33 4.94.82.03.28 - Fax : +33 4.94.82.87.37
www.esterel-caravaning.fr - contact@esterel-caravaning.fr

Open from 01.04 to 04.10.2003

the travel service
TO BOOK
Ferry ✔
Pitch ✔
Accommodation ✔
01892 55 98 98

Developed over three generations by the Simoncini family, this peaceful, friendly site is set in more than four ha. of mature, well shaded countryside at the foot of the Roquebrune Rock. It will appeal to families who appreciate natural surroundings together with many activities, cultural and sporting. Interspersed with a number of mobile homes, the 103 touring pitches are all of a good size with electricity (6/10A) and separated by trees or flowering bushes. The Provencal style buildings are delightful, especially the bar, restaurant and games room, with its terrace down to the river and the site's own canoe station (locked gate). Adjacent to the site and beside the lake (path under road bridge) is another restaurant, also open to the public. This is near a sandy beach, minigolf and half-court tennis. Other than the beach area (no lifeguard), the lake is used exclusively for water skiing. Activities include climbing the 'Rock' with a guide. We became intrigued with stories about the Rock, as unfolded by Sabine Simoncini. The Holy Hole, the Three Crosses and the Hermit all call for further exploration which Sabine is happy to arrange, likewise trips to Monte Carlo, Ventiniglia (Italy) and the Gorges du Verdon. Used by tour operators (75 pitches).

Facilities: Modern, well designed toilet facilities are in three blocks, one new and attractively designed in the local style, the other two refurbished. Overall, it is a good provision, open as required, with washbasins in cabins (warm water only), baby baths and facilities for disabled visitors. Dishwashing and laundry sinks (H&C) and washing machines. Sheltered swimming pool (25 x 10 m) with separate paddling pool (child-proof gates and lifeguard in high season) with ice cream bar. Shop. Bar, restaurant and games room. Children's play area. Fishing. Canoeing (free) and water skiing. Animation arranged in main season for children and adults, visits to local wine caves and sessions at rafting and diving schools. Charcoal barbecues are not permitted. Only one dog per pitch is accepted. **Off site:** Riding 6 km. Golf 6 km (reduced fees). Bicycle hire 1 km. The medieval village of Roquebrune is within walking distance.

Charges 2002

Per unit incl. 2 persons	€ 15.00 - € 27.00
incl. 3 persons	€ 17.50 - € 28.50
extra person	€ 3.40 - € 5.50
child (under 7 yrs)	€ 2.50 - € 4.20
dog (max 1)	€ 2.00
electricity (6/10A)	€ 4.00 - € 5.00
local tax	€ 0.30

Tel: 04 94 45 71 25. Fax: 04 94 81 65 13. E-mail: pecheurs@worldonline.fr. **Reservations:** Made for touring pitches with deposit and fee. **Open** 23 March - 29 September.

Directions: From A8 autoroute take Le Muy exit and follow N7 towards Frèjus for approx. 13 km. bypassing Le Muy. After crossing over the A8, turn right at roundabout towards Roquebrune sur Argens. Site is on left after 2 km. just before bridge over river (watch carefully for fairly narrow entrance).

*Camping Les Pêcheurs*****

Family campsite with warm atmosphere, situated at the foot of the Rock of Roquebrune, Côte d'Azur beaches at short distance. Large and shady pitches, river, swimming pools.

83520 Roquebrune sur Argens
Tel: 0033 494 45 71 25 - Fax: 0033 494 81 65 13
E-mail: pecheurs@worldonline.fr
www.camping-les-pecheurs.com

Camping-Caravaning Cros de Mouton

BP.116, 83240 Cavalaire-sur-Mer

8322

Cros de Mouton is a reasonably priced campsite in a popular area. High in the hills on a steep hillside, 1.5 km. from Cavalaire and its popular beaches, the site is a calm oasis away from the hectic coast. Unfortunately, due to the nature of the terrain, some of the site roads are very steep - the higher pitches with the best views are especially so. However, Olivier and Andre are happy to take your caravan up with their 4x4 Jeep if you are worried. There are 199 terraced pitches under cork trees which include 39 for mobile homes, 80 suitable only for tents with parking close by, and 80 for touring caravans. These have electricity (10A), some also have water. The restaurant terrace and the pools have wonderful view of Cavalaire and the bay. English is spoken.

Facilities: Two clean and well maintained toilet blocks have all the usual facilities including wash-basins in cubicles. Washing machine at each and a fully fitted facility for disabled customers (although site is perhaps a little steep in places for wheel-chairs). Bar/restaurant serving reasonably priced meals, plus takeaways. Swimming and paddling pools with lots of sun-beds on the terrace and small bar serving snacks and cold drinks. Small play area and games room.

Charges 2003

Per adult	€ 5.70 - € 7.00
child (under 7 yrs)	€ 4.00
pitch	€ 5.70 - € 7.00
electricity (10A)	€ 4.00
local tax	€ 0.15 - € 0.30
dog	free - € 2.00

Tel: 04 94 64 10 87. Fax: 04 94 05 46 38. E-mail: campingcrosdemouton@wanadoo.fr. **Reservations:** Made with deposit (€ 84) and fee (€ 16). **Open** 15 March - 31 October.

Directions: Site is very well signed from the centre of Cavalaire.

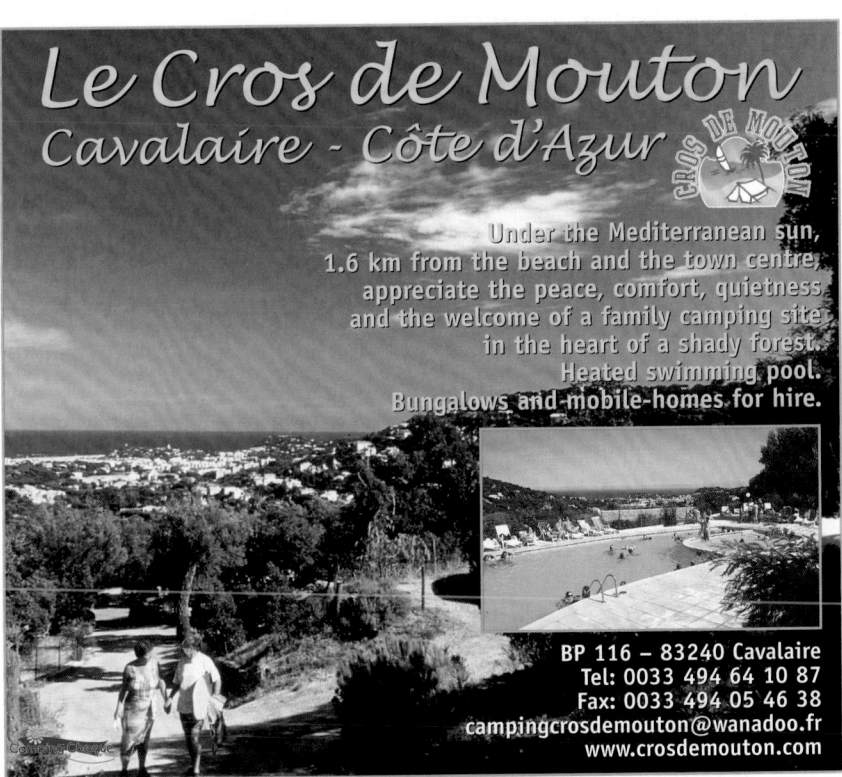

Le Cros de Mouton
Cavalaire - Côte d'Azur

Under the Mediterranean sun, 1.6 km from the beach and the town centre, appreciate the peace, comfort, quietness and the welcome of a family camping site in the heart of a shady forest. Heated swimming pool. Bungalows and mobile-homes for hire.

BP 116 – 83240 Cavalaire
Tel: 0033 494 64 10 87
Fax: 0033 494 05 46 38
campingcrosdemouton@wanadoo.fr
www.crosdemouton.com

the travel service
TO BOOK

Ferry	✔
Pitch	✔
Accommodation	✔

01892 55 98 98

The Alan Rogers' Travel Service

This unique service enables our readers to reserve their holidays as well as ferry crossings and comprehensive insurance cover at extremely competitive rates. The majority of participating sites are in France and we are able to offer a selection of some of the very best sites in this country.

Share our experience and let us help to ensure that your holiday will be a complete success.

Alan Rogers Travel Service 01892 55 98 98 or www.alanrogers.com

Camping Les Lacs du Verdon

8314 Domaine de Roquelande, 83630 Régusse

In beautiful countryside and within easy reach of the Grand Canyon du Verdon and its nearby lakes, this site is only 90 minutes from Cannes. This bustling and possible noisy campsite is suitable for active families and teenagers. The 30 acre wooded park is divided in two by a minor road. The 480 very stony, but level pitches (rock pegs advised) are marked and separated by trees and lines of stones. There are 130 pitches for tourists which are scattered amongst the trees and often have an irregular shape, although all are of average to good size. There are plenty of electricity boxes but long leads may be necessary. Water taps are few. The part across the road is used mainly for mobile homes but has some pitches for tourers, mostly at the far end. There are toilet blocks close by but the pitches are a long way from all the other site facilities. The main site is much more pleasant and closer to all the activities. Tour operators and mobile homes, for hire and privately owned, take up nearly three quarters of the site.

Facilities: The toilet blocks are old and much of the equipment is looking very jaded, but they are just about acceptable. They mainly have British style WCs and some washbasins in cubicles with warm water only. The block we tried had fairly hot water but campers complained they were not so lucky. All blocks have sinks for laundry and dishes. Washing machines and dryers. At the end of May very little was open and the level of cleanliness was just about adequate. Motorcaravan service point (with charge). Shop. Bar. Restaurant (recently rebuilt) and pizzeria (all 18/5-13/9). TV and teenage games. Discos, dances and theme nights. Excellent swimming pool/paddling pool complex (all season) and new artificial grass tennis courts - the highlight of this campsite. Volleyball, table tennis, archery and boules. Bicycle hire. Playground. Daily animations, for all the family, in May and June with a more extensive programme in high season. Only electric barbecues are permitted. **Off site:** Fishing, beach, sailing and windsurfing at the site's club at Saint Croix (15 km). The village of Régusse is about 2.5 km. and the small town of Aups is 7 km. Riding 10 km.

Charges 2002

Per pitch incl. 1 or 2 persons	€ 17.00 - € 20.00
extra person over 7 yrs	€ 5.00 - € 6.00
child (3-7 yrs)	€ 4.00 - € 5.00
dog	€ 2.00
electricity 10A	€ 4.00
local tax	€ 0.30

Tel: 04 94 70 17 95. Fax: 04 94 70 51 79. E-mail: info@lacs-verdon.com. **Reservations:** Made with 25% deposit and fee (€ 20). **Open** 27 April - 28 September.

Directions: Leave the A8 motorway at St Maximin and take the D560 northeast to Barjols. At Barjols turn left on D71 to Montmeyan, turn right on D30 to Regusse and follow site signs.

Village Camping

Les Lacs du Verdon

Domaine de Roquelande
83630 Régusse - FRANCE
tél:+33 (0)4 94 70 17 95
fax:+33 (0)4 94 70 51 79
www.lacs-verdon.com

- A beautifully preserved site
- Mobil homes and cottages with modern conveniences
- Large and shady places for camping and caravans
- Places for camping cars

In the middle of the National Park of the Verdon
At 15km from the lake and the Gorges

- Activities for all (children, teenagers and adults)

- Quality facilities : restaurants, pizzeria, snack, self service, bar, night club, tennis, mini-golf and a children's playground

New ! heated pool

- A friendly atmosphere, lot's of sun, beautiful beaches and to top it all, our nice and helpful team at your service.

Holiday Green Village Club Camping-Caravaning
Route de Bagnols-en-Forêt, 83600 Fréjus

8360

Holiday Green is seven kilometres inland from the busy resort of Fréjus. It is a large, modern campsite with a fantastic view of the red Estérel massif. The site has been developed on a hillside and by reception at the top of hill is a large Californian style heated swimming pool and a wide range of other facilities. This is where everything happens and it is said there are activities and entertainment from morning until closing. The rest of the site is terraced into the hillside and almost completely hidden in the 15 hectares of pine woods which absorbs about 500 large touring pitches and some 200 mobile homes. Sloping in parts, there is plenty of shade and electricity connections (3A) available.

Facilities: Modern toilet facilities include good hot showers. Laundry. Shopping centre. Bar, restaurant and fast food. Sound proof disco. Swimming pool. Three tennis courts. Archery. Petanque. All facilities are open all season. Excursions organised on foot, on horse-back and on mountain bikes. Entertainment programme. Playground. Children's club (July/Aug). **Off site:** Beach 7 km. Golf and riding 8 km. Free daily bus to the beach and free access to Aquatica, the biggest aqua park in the region.

Charges 2002

Per pitch	€ 34.00
extra person	€ 8.00
child (0-5 yrs)	€ 5.00

Tel: 04 94 19 88 30. Fax: 04 94 19 88 31. E-mail: info @holiday-green.com. **Reservations:** Advanced booking necessary for high season. **Open** 30 March - 30 September.

Directions: From A8 autoroute exit 38 follow signs for Bagnols-en-Forêt and pick up site signs.

Route de Bagnols
83600 Fréjus
Tel: 0033 494 198 830
Fax: 0033 494 198 831   www.holiday-green.com

Domaine Naturiste Riva Bella
BP 21, 20270 Alèria

N2004

A relaxed, informal naturist site beside a glorious beach, Riva Bella is arguably camping and caravanning at its very best. The site is divided into several distinct areas - pitches and bungalows, alongside the sandy beach, in a wooded glade with ample shade, behind the beach, or beside the lake/lagoon which is a feature of this site. The ground is undulating, so getting an absolutely level pitch could be a problem in the main season. Although electric hook-ups are available in most parts, a long cable is probably a necessity. A recent addition is a therapy centre with treatments based on marine products. Noël Pasqual is proud of his site and the fairly unobtrusive rules are designed to ensure that everyone is able to relax, whilst preserving the natural beauty of the environment. There is, for example, a restriction on the movement of cars in certain areas (but ample free parking). Generally the ambience is relaxed and informal with nudity only obligatory on the beach itself. Member 'France 4 Naturisme'.

Facilities: Toilet facilities in several blocks have been completely refurbished. Whilst fairly typical in design for naturist sites, they are fitted and decorated to the highest standards facilities for disabled people and babies. Large well stocked shop (15/5-30/9). Fridge hire. Excellent restaurant (all season) with reasonable prices overlooks the lagoon. Snack bar beside the beach during the main season (1/6-30/9). Watersports including sailing school, fishing, sub-aqua etc. Therapy centre. Sauna. Volleyball, aerobics, table tennis, giant draughts and archery. Fishing. Mountain bike hire. Half-court tennis. Herd of llamas to watch. The police/fire service ban barbecues during the summer as a safety precaution. **Off site:** Riding 5 km.

Charges 2003

Per unit incl. 2 persons	€ 17.00 - € 29.00
1 person	€ 13.00 - € 21.00
extra person	€ 4.00 - € 8.00
child (0-8 yrs)	€ 2.00 - € 4.50
electricity	€ 3.50
dog	€ 2.50 - € 3.00
local tax	€ 0.15

Tel: 04 95 38 81 10. Fax: 04 95 38 91 29. E-mail: riva-bella@wanadoo.fr. **Reservations:** Made with deposit and fee/cancellation insurance. **Open** 12 April - 11 October.

Directions: Site is approx. 8 km. north of Aleria on N198 (Bastia) road. Watch for signs and unmade road to it and follow for 4 km.

LES CASTELS

★ ★ ★ ★

CAMPING & CARAVANING

A DIFFERENT FRANCE

There are 45 4-star Castels caravan
and camp sites dotted round the
most beautiful regions of France.
Many are set in the grounds of
chateaux or manor houses and offer :

• amenities of the highest standards,

• activities and entertainment for
the young and not so young,

• a broad choice of pitches and
different types of very comfortable
accommodation.

15 € *a night for a pitch for 2 people,
with electricity, whatever the site and lenght of stay
when you present your Privilege Card.*

To find out more, contact us and

• receive our brochure-road map free of charge
• book your Privilege Card for the year 2003 (10 €)
• order the presentation guidebook for our 45 Castels
camp sites (contribution to expenses : 10 €).

*offer valid at most camp sites from opening up until 30/06 and from 1/09 until the closing of the comp sites
for anyone who has ordered the Privilege Card from our secretary.

Address : Secretariat LES CASTELS - C.P. 3751 - 56037 VANNES Cedex - France
Internet sites : www.les-castels.com- www.castels-campings.com
Tel : + 33 (0)2 97 42 57 12 - Fax : + 33 (0)2 97 42 57 67

Holidays with complete Freedom

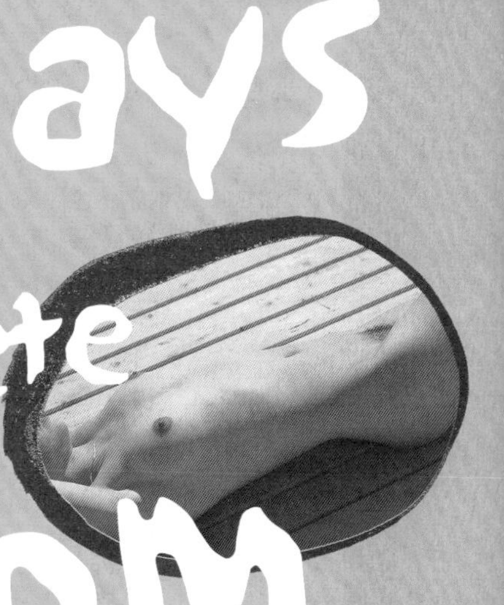

Ten French camping villages together in the same catalogue!
From the Atlantic Ocean to the Mediterranean Sea, through the countryside and mountains, all these centres, approved by FEN (France Espaces Naturistes), guarantee high quality reception, services, activities and entertainment. You can request your France 4 Naturism catalogue now and book the camping site of your choice directly or with your France 4 Naturism agent in England.

GREAT BRITAIN
Suzanne Piper
73, Williamson Road
Lydd on Sea - Romney Marsh
TN29 9NZ - GB
Tel.: 01797 364315 - Fax: 01797 361480

www.france4naturisme.com

THE NATURIST HOLIDAY SPECIALIST

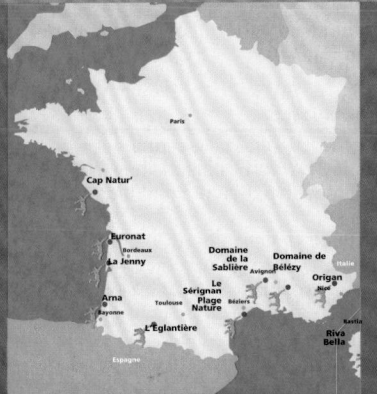

France 4 naturisme

VENDÉE Cap Natur' - 151, av. de la Faye 85270 ST HILAIRE DE RIEZ - tel. 00 33 (0)2 51 60 11 66 - fax 00 33 (0)2 51 60 17 48 **GIRONDE OCÉAN** La Jenny - Route de La Jenny - 33680 LE PORGE - tel. 00 33 (0)5 56 26 56 90 - fax 00 33 (0)5 56 26 56 51 **MÉDOC OCÉAN** Euronat - 33590 GRAYAN-L'HÔPITAL - tel. 00 33 (0)5 56 09 33 33 - fax 00 33 (0)5 56 09 30 27 **LANDES OCÉAN** Arna - Arnaoutchot - 40560 VIELLE, ST GIRONS - tel. 00 33 (0)5 58 49 11 11 - fax 00 33 (0)5 58 48 57 12 **PYRÉNÉES GASCOGNE** L'Eglantière - Aries Espenan - 65230 CASTELNAU-MAGNOAC - tel. 00 33 (0)5 62 39 88 00 - fax 00 33 (0)5 62 39 81 44 **MÉDITERRANÉE** Le Sérignan Plage Nature - 34410 SERIGNAN - tel. 00 33 (0)4 67 32 09 61 - fax 00 33 (0)4 67 32 68 41 **ARDÈCHE** Domaine de la Sablière - St Privat de Champclos - 30430 BARJAC - tel. 00 33 (0)4 66 24 51 16 - fax 00 33 (0)4 66 24 58 69 **PROVENCE** Domaine de Bélézy - 84410 BEDOIN - tel. 00 33 (0)4 90 65 60 18 - fax 00 33 (0)4 90 65 94 45 **ALPES D'AZUR** Origan - 06260 PUGET-THENIERS - tel. 00 33 (0)4 93 05 06 00 - fax 00 33 (0)4 93 87 47 49 **CORSE** Riva Bella - BP 21 - 20270 ALÉRIA - tel. 00 33 (0)4 95 38 81 10 - fax 00 33 (0)4 95 38 91 29

vendée • atlantique • pyrénées • méditerranée • ardèche • provence • alpes d'azur • corse

Germany

German National Tourist Office, PO Box 2695, London W1A 3TN
Tel: 020 7317 0908   Fax: 020 7495 6129
E-mail: gntolon@d-z-t.com   www.germany-tourism.de

As a holiday destination Germany provides a rich variety of scenic and cultural interest. Although the German people are great travellers and can be found on holiday all over Europe, they nevertheless enjoy camping in their own country and good campsites can be discovered throughout the 16 'Länder'. Not only does the scenery provide great contrast - from the flat lands of the north to the mountains of the south and the forests of the west and east - but as it was only fully unified as one state in 1871, regional characteristics are a strong feature of German life and give a rich variety of folklore and customs. Medieval towns, ancient buildings and picturesque villages abound all over the country and add to the fascination of visiting Germany. Reunification may have provided many problems for politicians and people but has opened up a whole new area which was previously difficult to explore. Great strides are being made, particularly where investment has been attracted, to improve and modernise campsites.

Population
80,767,591 (1993); density 226 per sq.km.

Capital
Berlin. After unification in 1990, the German parliament chose Berlin as the national capital and voted to move the seat of government from Bonn to Berlin over a 12 year period.

Climate
In general winters are a little colder and summers a little warmer than in the UK.

Language
German. Most Germans speak some English, but it is appreciated if you try to use any knowledge of German that you have retained.

Currency
From January 2002, in common with 11 other European countries, the German unit of currency is the EURO (€).
€ 1 = DM 1.96.

Banks
Banking hours are Mon-Fri 08.30-12.30 and 14.00-16.00 with late opening on Thursdays until 18.00 hrs. Closed Sat.
Credit Cards: are becoming widely accepted but only the major cards are accepted in main department stores and restaurants in the large cities. Girocheques are widely accepted.

Post Offices
Open Mon-Fri 08.00-18.00 and Sat 08.00-12.00.

Time
GMT + 1, or BST + 1 in summer.

Telephone
The code to dial Germany from the UK is 0049.

Public Holidays
New Year's Day; Good Fri; Easter Mon; Labour Day; Ascension; Whit Mon; Unification Day (3 Oct); Christmas, 25, 26 Dec; plus, in some areas, Epiphany (6 Jan), Corpus Christi (22 Jun), Assumption (15 Aug), Reformation (31 Oct) and All Saints (1 Nov).

Shops
Open Mon-Fri 08.30/09.00 to 18.00/18.30, closed Saturday 14.00 (sometimes earlier).

Motoring
An excellent network of (toll-free) motorways (Autobahns) exists in the 'West' and the traffic moves fast. Remember in the 'East' a lot of road building is going on amongst other works so allow plenty of time when travelling and be prepared for poor road surfaces.
Speed limits: Caravans and motorhomes (2.8 tons) 31 mph (50 kph) or 19 mph (30 kph) in built up areas, 50 mph (80 kph) all other roads for caravans, 63 mph (100 kph) other roads and 81 mph (130 kph) motorways for motorhomes. Lower limits for heavier vehicles.
Parking: Don't park on roads with Priority Road signs. Meters and parking disc zones are in use.

Overnighting
If not forbidden by local regulations, then permitted at 'Rast platz' and on streets, but not open spaces.

Useful Addresses
National Motoring Organisations:
Automobil-Club von Deutschland (AVD) Lyoner Strasse 16, 60528 Frankfurt am Main
Tel: 069 6606-0. Office hours 08.00-17.00
Allgemeiner Deutscher Automobil-Club (ADAC) Am Westpark 8, 81373 München.

Camping Wulfener Hals

23769 Wulfen auf Fehmarn (Schleswig-Holstein)

3003

If you are travelling to Denmark or on to Sweden, taking the E47/A1 then B207 from Hamburg, and the ferry from Puttgarden to Rødbyhavn, this is a top class all year round site, either to rest overnight or as a base for a longer stay. Attractively situated by the sea, it is a large, mature site (34 hectares) and is well-maintained. It has over 800 individual pitches of up to 160 sq.m. (half for touring) in glades and some separated by bushes, with shade in the older parts, less in the newer areas nearer the sea. There are many hardstandings and 462 pitches have electricity, water and drainage. There is much to do for old and young alike with a small outdoor heated pool (unsupervised), but the sea is naturally popular as well. The site also has many sporting facilities including its own golf courses and schools for watersports.

Facilities: The four heated sanitary buildings have first class facilities including showers on payment (€ 0,51) and both open washbasins and private cabins (more of these for ladies). Facilities for disabled people, dishwashing and laundry, each available in most but not all the buildings. Motorcaravan services. Shop, bar and restaurants, (one waiter, one self-service and takeaway (all year). Swimming pool (May - Oct). Sauna. Solarium. Sailing and windsurfing school. Diving school. Golf courses (18 hole, par 72 and 9 hole, par 27). Roller skating. Riding. Fishing. Archery. Football area. Table tennis. Good play equipment for younger children. Bicycle hire. Only small dogs are accepted. **Off site:** Village mini-market 2 km. Naturist beach 500 m.

Charges 2002

Per adult	€ 3.30 - € 6.50
child (2-14 yrs)	€ 1.60 - € 4.50
pitch	€ 6.50 - € 17.40
(plus surcharges over 110 or 130 sq.m.)	
electricity (10A)	€ 2.30
dog	€ 1.00 - € 6.50

Many discounts available and special family prices. **Tel:** 04371 86280. Fax: 04371 3723. E-mail: camping@wulfenerhals.de. **Reservations:** Probably not necessary for short stay. **Open** all year.

Directions: From Hamburg take A1/E47 north to Puttgarden, cross the bridge onto the island of Fenmark and turn right twice to Avendorf and follow the signs for Wulfen and the site.

Germany - North West
Ferienpark Schlei-Karschau

Karschau 56, 24407 Rabenkirchen-Faulück (Schleswig-Holstein)

3002

Schlei-Karschau is a pleasant, quiet site on the only Baltic Sea fjord in Germany. All you will hear is the wind from the sea and the calls of the birds. This site is ideal if you enjoy fishing or sailing, or you could visit one of the beaches on this coast, just 10 kilometres further down. The site has 160 open pitches, 100 for touring units, all with at least 4A electricity. Part of the Rohloff group, Schlei-Karschau is not yet fully developed. Already completed are a new, fully equipped sanitary block and a new playground, and in the near future it will be possible to rent mobile homes or chalets. There is no shop as yet (but the baker calls twice a week). Students provide an entertainment programme for children in high season with painting and crafts for toddlers and sporting events for older youngsters. There is no evening entertainment for adults but, after a hard day fighting with large fish or sails at sea you may prefer to relax in the restaurant or bar. Relaxing in front of your caravan or tent is another possibility - you are likely to see many rabbits passing by.

Facilities: The single, new sanitary block includes controllable hot showers in cabins with washbasin, child size toilets and washbasins and facilities for disabled visitors. Launderette with washing machines and dryers. Campers' kitchen with fridge. Motorcaravan services. Restaurant and bar (daily in high season). New playground. Sports field. Table tennis. Table football. Children's actvity programme 6 days a week in high season. Fishing. Bicycle hire. Motor boat hire. **Off site:** Golf 4 km. Riding 6 km. Beach 10 km.

Charges 2002

Per pitch	€ 8.00
adult	€ 4.00
child (1-14 yrs)	€ 2.00
electricity and water	€ 2,00
pet	€ 2,00
boat mooring	€ 2,00
boat anchorage	€ 10,00

Discount (5-15%) for senior campers. **Tel:** 04642 920820. **Reservations:** contact site. **Open** all year.

Directions: Follow the A7 from Hamburg north to Flensburg and take exit Schleswig - Schuby. Take the B201 road towards Kappeln. Drive through Süderbrarup and turn right after 5 km. to Faulück. Follow signs to site.

Germany - North West
Camping Schnelsen Nord

Wunderbrunnen, 22457 Hamburg (Hamburg)

3005

Situated some 15 km. from the centre of Hamburg on the northern edge of the town, Schnelsen Nord is a suitable base either for visiting this famous German city, or as a night stop before catching the Harwich ferry or travelling to Denmark. A large number of trees and shrubs offer shade and privacy. There is some traffic noise because the autobahn runs along-side (despite efforts to screen it out) and also some aircraft noise. However, the proximity of the A7 (E45) does make it easy to find. The 145 pitches, which are all for short-term touring only, are of good size (100 sq.m.), on grass with access from gravel roads. All have 6A electricity, are numbered and marked out with small trees and hedges. Only very basic food supplies are stocked in reception as the site is only about 10 minutes walk from the restaurants and shops in town. Apart from some road traffic 'hum', as previously mentioned, this is a quiet, well laid out site.

Facilities: A deposit is required for the key to the single sanitary block, which is a well constructed modern building with good quality facilities and heated in cool weather. Hot water is free for the washbasins (some in cabins) and dishwashing. Good facilities for disabled visitors, with special pitches close to the block. Washing machines and dryers. Motorcaravan service point. Shop (basics only). Table tennis. Children's playground. **Off site:** Swimming pool, tennis courts, golf and fishing nearby.

Charges 2002

Per adult	€ 4.35
child (under 13 yrs)	€ 2.85
caravan	€ 7.45
tent	€ 6.65 - € 7.20
car	€ 2.30
motorcaravan	€ 9.75 - € 11.25
electricity	€ 2.30
dog	€ 1.60

Tel: 040 5594225. Fax: 040 5507334. E-mail: service@campingplatz-hamburg.de. **Reservations:** Said to be unnecessary. **Open** 1 April - 31 October.

Directions: From A7 autobahn take Schnelsen Nord exit. Stay in outside lane as you will soon need to turn back left; follow signs for Ikea store and site signs.

Campingplatz Freie Hansestadt Bremen

Am Stadtwaldsee 1, 28359 Bremen (Bremen)

Five kilometres from the city centre and in pleasant 'green belt' surroundings near the university, this is a useful small site. There is no need to take your vehicle into the city, as the site has excellent public transport connections. There is bus stop in front of the site. Despite the easy accessibility of the city, the site has a distinctly rural feel with quite an abundance of wildlife. It has 115 large pitches (75 for touring units) of at least 100 sq.m on flat grass and marked out by stones, all with 6A electricity and 12 with hardstanding for motorcaravans. What helps make this site appealing is the pleasant reception accorded to guests and the helpful English speaking staff. Being a popular spot, it can become very busy and full here over a long season and on certain pitches road noise may be experienced.

Facilities: An excellent, heated building includes some washbasins in cabins, provision for disabled visitors and a baby room. Washing machines and dryer. Motorcaravan services. Gas supplies. Cooking facilities. Good reasonably priced restaurant/bar (March - Oct). Takeaway (all year). Small shop, open all year, but limited in low season - fresh bread to order. General room. Playground. Sports Field. Bicycle hire. Barbecue area. **Off site:** 20 hectare lake suitable for swimming and boating 500 m. Bus stop at the entrance, tram service only minutes away. Good cycling and walks in the municipal woodland adjacent.

Charges 2002

Per person	€ 4.10
child (under 16 yrs)	€ 2.50
pitch	€ 5.40 - € 8.50
dog	1.50

Tel: 0421 212002. Fax: 0421 219857. E-mail: campingplatz-bremen@t-online.de. **Reservations:** made for any length with deposit. **Open** all year.

Directions: From A27 autobahn northeast of Bremen take exit 19 for 'Universitat' and follow signs for university and site.

Knaus Camping Park Wingst

Schwimmbadallee 13, 21789 Wingst (Lower Saxony)

With an impressive landscaped entrance, a shop and restaurant to one side and reception to the other and a barrier which is closed in the evening, this is a good quality site. It is a rural area with attractive villages, plenty of water and woodland, near to the interesting old port of Bremerhaven with its 29 km. of quays and maritime and fishing museums. The heart of this site is a deep set, small fishing lake and beach. Lightly wooded, pitches are accessed by circular roadways on differing levels and terraced where necessary. Because of the design you don't realise that there are 380 pitches, nearly all with electricity (6A) and clearly defined by shrubs and trees (250 for touring units).

Facilities: Two heated toilet blocks, one adjoining reception and one nearer the lake (access to this is by steps from the varying levels). The provision is good and well kept, with one block recently renovated. Motorcaravan services. Shop, restaurant, bar and takaway (all year). Playground. Minigolf. Table tennis. Fishing. Beach volleyball. Bicycle hire. Large screen TV. Barbecue facility with roof. **Off site:** Swimming pool behind the hotel opposite the site is open to campers, paid at reception. Riding 2 km.

Charges 2002

Per person	€ 5.00
child (3-14 yrs)	€ 2.50
pitch	€ 3.00 - € 7.50
electricity	€ 1.80

No credit cards. **Tel:** 04778 7604. Fax: 04778 7608. **Reservations:** Contact site. **Open** all year except Nov.

Directions: Follow B 73 North from Hamburg and take exit for Wingst (Spiel and Sportpark) signed 'camping platz'. Then take first left.

Azur Camping Lüneburger Heide

Kesselstrasse 36, D-21272, Egestorf (Lower Saxony)

This Azur site is quietly located in woods forming part of the Lüneburger moors. There are 540 pitches (240 for touring units), all with 6-16A electricity. The generally very spacious touring pitches are on sloping ground shaded by trees. The pitches themselves are flat and some have hardstanding for caravans and motorcaravans. The site's location makes it an exellent base for walking and cycling on the moors. With few activities on site, we feel it is not likely to appeal to families with children. There are facilities for disabled visitors, but the ground would be difficult for people in wheelchairs or less mobile.

Facilities: Two older style, but well maintained, toilet blocks include washbasins (some in cabins), controlable showers, baby room and facilities for disabled people. Launderette. Dishwashing under cover with free hot water. Fridge hire. Motorcaravan services. Shop and restaurant (April - Oct). Swimming pool. Sports field. Playground. **Off site:** Golf 25 km. Fishing 20 km. Riding 1.5 km. Bicycle hire 1.5 km.

Charges 2002

Per adult	€ 3.00 - € 6.00
pitch	€ 4.00 - € 7.50
electricity	€2.10

No credit cards. **Tel:** 04175- 661. E-mail: egestorf@azur-camping.de. **Reservations:** Made with deposit (€45). **Open** April - October

Directions: From the A3 (Hannover - Hamburg) take exit 41 for Egestorf. Drive through Egestorf and site is about 1 km. after the village on the left.

Kur und Feriencamping Röders Park

3010 Ebsmoor 8, 29614 Soltau (Lower Saxony)

Although near Soltau centre (1.5 km), Ebsmoor is a peaceful location, ideal for visits to the famous Luneburg Heath or as a stop on the route to Denmark. The site is run by the 3rd generation of the Röders family who make their visitors most welcome and speak excellent English. The central feature of the wooded site is a small lake crossed by a wooden bridge. An abundance of trees and shrubs gives a secluded setting to an already well cared for appearance. Röders' Park only offers a tranquil stay - there is no entertainment. Many sports activities are available locally. The site has 100 pitches (75 touring), all with 6A electricity and 50 with water and drainage. Most have hardstanding and reasonable privacy between pitches.

Facilities: Two modern, very clean sanitary blocks (one with under-floor heating) contain all necessary facilities with a laundry room and an excellent, separate unit (including shower) for wheelchair users. En-suite facilities planned for 2003. Motorcaravan services. Gas supplies. Simple shop. Restaurant (both Easter - Oct). Children's play area. Bicycle hire. **Off site:** Fishing and riding 1.5 km. Golf 3 km. Thermal swimming pool 1 km. 999 km. of cycle paths in the surrounding area.

Charges 2002

Per person	€ 4.50
child (4-14 yrs)	€ 3.50
pitch	€ 10.00
dog	€ 1.50
electricity (6A)	€ 1.00

Tel: 05191 2141. Fax: 05191 17952. E-mail: info@roeders-park.de. **Reservations:** Contact site. **Open** all year.

Directions: From Soltau take B3 road north and turning to site is on left after 1.5 km. (opposite DCC camping sign) at yellow town boundary sign.

DCC Kur-Campingpark

3035 Braunschweigerstraße 12, 37581 Bad Gandersheim (Lower Saxony)

Attractively situated between a tree-covered hill and the B64 road, this is a well run site with a stream running through the middle and plenty of trees but little shade. It has 460 level pitches of which 300 are for touring units, most with 10A electricity. They are all well marked and easily accessible, divided into long and short stay areas and a section for those with animals. The site provides good amenities for both summer walkers and winter skiers. On the edge of the Harz area,you can exploring the twisty and busy roads of the main resort towns or participate in one of the organised walks. The pretty, old town is a 15 minute stroll. Some road noise is possible, mainly affecting the overnight area.

Facilities: Toilet facilities are modern and heated, with showers on payment, plus facilities for babies and child toilets. Laundry facilities. Solarium. Motorcaravan services. Gas supplies. Restaurant (excl. Monday). Shop (not Nov). Table tennis. Play areas. Bicycle hire. **Off site:** Riding, fishing, swimming, sailing, windsurfing all near.

Charges 2002

Per pitch	€ 8.50
adult	€ 4.00
child (4-13 yrs)	€ 2.50
electricity (plus meter)	€ 0.30
local tax	€ 0.51

Special overnight price (after 3 pm - leave before 12 noon) € 15 (16 with electricity). No credit cards. **Tel:** 05382 1595. Fax: 05382 1599. **Reservations:** Contact site. **Open** all year.

Directions: From autobahn A7 (E45), leave at Seesen, then road 64 to Bad Gandersheim. Site is on right, about 2 km before town and is signed as a no through road to the right.

Knaus Camping Park Walkenried

3045 Ellricher Straße 7, 37445 Walkenried (Lower Saxony)

The southern Harz area offers much for walkers and anglers and this site organises many outings ranging from free walks to coach trips to the highest mountain in the area at Brocken (1,142 m). It also has the benefit of an indoor pool, sauna and solarium. Outdoor activities available in the area include tennis, riding and watersports. There are 160 touring pitches here of 80-100 sq.m. and arranged in well shaded groups on mainly slightly sloping grass and gravel. Most are separated by bushes or trees and have 4A, 2 pin electrical connections. There are some smaller hardstandings for motorhomes and a separate area for visitors with dogs.

Facilities: The satisfactory tiled and heated sanitary facilities are in the main building by the entrance, with washbasins in cabins for ladies (some curtained for men) and a toilet for disabled visitors. Laundry and cooking facilities. Gas supplies. Motorcaravan services. Shop and restaurant (closed Tuesdays). Order bread at reception. Indoor swimming pool, free for campers (all year excl. 1/11-15/12). Sauna and solarium. Large play area. Barbecue area. Large screen TV. Bicycle hire. **Off site:** Fishing 2 km.

Charges 2002

Per person	€ 5.00
pitch	€ 3.00 - € 7.50
electricity	€ 1.80

No credit cards. **Tel:** 05525 778. Fax: 05525 2332. **Reservations:** Contact the site. **Open** all year except November

Directions: Walkenried is signed from B4 Erfurt-Magdeburg road just north of Nordhausen and from B243 (Seesen-Nordhausen). Site signed in town.

Alfsee Ferien-und Erholungspark

Am Campingpark 10, 49597 Rieste (Lower Saxony)

3025

There have continued to be major improvements to this already well-equipped site. There are now over 800 pitches (many long stay but with 400 for tourers) on flat grass, 120 with 16A electricity, with some shade for those in the original area. A new camping area provides 100 large, serviced pitches. Alfsee offers a really good base for enjoying the many watersports activities available here on the two lakes. The smaller one has a 780 m. water-ski 'tug' ski-lift style (on payment) and there is also a separate swimming area here with a sandy beach (and beach volleyball). A little further along is a 600 m. go-kart track and a smaller track for youngsters. The Alfsee itself is a very large stretch of water with a sailing school, windsurfing, motor boats, row boats, canoes and pedaloes as well as fishing and a cafe/restaurant open daily. This site has plenty to offer for the active family and children of all ages.

Facilities: Three older, but still very good sanitary blocks serve the original area with two new first class, heated buildings with family bathrooms, baby rooms and laundry facilities. Washing machines and dryers. Cooking facilities. All is nicely decorated and well maintained. Motorcaravan services. Gas supplies. Shop, restaurants and takeaway (all year). New pub and internet point. Watersports. Football practice field. Children's playground and entertainment. Grass tennis courts. Trampoline. Minigolf. Go-kart track. General room with amusement machines. Fishing. Bicycle hire. Riding. **Off site:** Golf 8 km.

Charges 2002

Per unit incl. 2 adults	€ 11.63 - € 16.62
extra adult	€ 2.71 - € 3.89
child or student	€ 1.94 - € 2.76
dog	€ 1.53 - € 2.56
electricity (once only plus meter	€ 1.53
overnight pitch (17.00 - 10.00 hrs)	€ 9.20 - € 12.78

Tel: 05464 5166. Fax: 05464 5837. E-mail: info@alfsee.com. **Reservations:** Made for any length without deposit. **Open** all year.

Directions: From A1 autobahn north of Osnabrück take exit 67 for Neuenkirchen and follow signs for Rieste, Alfsee and site.

Erholungszentrum Grav-Insel

Gravinsel 1, 46487 Wesel (North Rhine-Westphalia)

3202

Grav-Insel claims to be the biggest family camping site in Germany, providing entertainment and activities to match, with over 2,000 permanent units as well as those for touring. It is a well maintained site, attractively situated on an island in the Rhine and is a good base for swimming (with a sandy beach by a quiet inlet), fishing, boating (with boat park). A long section for the touring units runs beside the water to the left of the entrance. The pitches are flat, grassy, mostly without shade and of about 100 sq.m. Some are marked by water points and there are electricity boxes with multiple outlets (10/16A). A brand new building behind the modern reception is enormous and houses excellent sanitary facilities including some for disabled visitors, a restaurant with wheelchair access, terraces for a snack bar and ices, play rooms (including a large area for wet weather play) and a supermarket. This is a busy, well managed site where the peacocks add to the holiday atmosphere.

Facilities: Excellent, new sanitary facilities, augmented by older portakabin units in the touring area, have toilets with washbasins, some very large showers with triple sprays, baby room, launderette, dishwashing. Solarium. Supermarket (hours acc. to season). Restaurant (all year). Riding. Fishing. Swimming. Large play area on sand plus wet weather indoor area. Animation in high season. Boat park. Sailing. **Off site:** Warner Bros. Movie-World-Park 20 minutes drive.

Charges 2002

Per person	€ 2.00
child (under 14 yrs)	€ 1.00
pitch	€ 4.50

Tel: 0281 972830. Fax: 0281 9728340. E-mail: grav-insel@t-online.de. **Reservations:** Not made. **Open** all year.

Directions From the A3 Arnhem - Düsseldorf exit 6 take B58 towards Wesel, at the 4th roundabout right towards Rees then left at sign for Flüren, through town and left to site after 1.5 km.

Germany - North West
DCC Truma Campingpark

3030 49545 Tecklenburg (North Rhine-Westphalia)

This is a large site near Osnabrück, taking some 900 units and covering a wide area. Over half the pitches are for permanent caravans, but space is usually available for touring units and there is a 'quick stop' overnight facility. The individual pitches are on mostly flat grassy areas, but not separated and there are many electrical connections (16A). A swimming pool complex and leisure area with heated indoor and outdoor pools is a recent addition. Little English is spoken. There are good walks from the site, with woodland not used for camping. Osnabrück is 15 km.

Facilities: Four good modern toilet blocks (heated in cool weather) have some washbasins in cabins. Sinks for laundry and dishes on payment. Facilities for disabled visitors. Washing machine and dryer in each block. Cooking facilities. Motorcaravan services. Shop (March - Oct). Restaurant/bar (March - Oct and Dec - Jan). Snacks (July/Aug). Swimming pools. Sports field. Minigolf. Children's playground. Dry ski in summer. Youth room with table tennis; occasional disco. **Off site:** Riding near.

Charges 2002

Per person	€ 3.83 - € 4.35
pitch	€ 6.39 - € 8.44
electricity (0,51 per kw)	€ 1.79
overnight stop on parking area	€ 10.00

Tel: 05405 1007. **Reservations:** Formal ones are complicated and probably unnecessary; send a card to site before arrival. **Open** all year.

Directions: From south, leave A1 at exit 73 (Tecklenburg/Lengerich). Turn right, immediately left and then right again towards Lengerich. Turn left at fourth traffic lights to 'Leeden-Lotte' site is signed from Leedon village. From north take exit 72 onto E30, then exit 14 for Lotte and Leeden.

Germany - North West
Campingplatz Biggesee Sondern

3210 Am Sonderner Kopf 3, 57462 Olpe-Sondern (North Rhine-Westphalia)

Biggesee-Sondern is a high quality leisure complex site, in an attractive setting on the shores of a large lake in the Südsauerland National Park, offering many leisure opportunities, as well as excellent camping facilities. It is therefore deservedly popular, and reservation is almost always advisable. Well managed, the same company also operates two other sites on the shores of the lake, where space may be available, which is useful as it is also popular for a short stay, being quite near the A45 and A4 roads. There are 300 flat or sloping numbered pitches of 100 sq.m, of which about 250 are for tourists, either in rows or in circles, on terraces, with 6A electricity and water points grouped throughout.

Facilities: Excellent sanitary facilities are in two areas, heated when necessary (no paper). Many washbasins in cabins. Facilities for babies, laundry and disabled people. Motorcaravan services. Cooking facilities. Roller-skating. Playroom and playground. Skiing. Watersports. Walks around the lake. Football. Table tennis. Fishing. Bicycle hire. Solarium and sauna. Entertainment and excursions. **Off site:** Tennis near. Riding 8 km. Golf 12 km. Restaurant and snacks 300 m (Easter - 31/10).

Charges 2002

Per unit incl. electricity	€ 10.50 - € 13.10
person	€ 3.10 - € 3.90
child (3-15 yrs)	€ 1.80 - € 2.40

No credit cards. **Tel:** 02761 944111. Fax: 02761 944 122. E-mail: biggesee@t-online.de. **Reservations:** Advised for much of the year. **Open** all year.

Directions: From A45 (Siegen-Hagen) autobahn, take exit 18 to Olpe (N), and turn towards Attendorn. After 6 km. turn to Bigge-Stausee. Site is well signed.

Germany - North West
Campingplatz der Stadt Köln

3205 Weidenweg 35, 51105 Köln-Poll (North Rhine-Westphalia)

The ancient city of Cologne offers much with many museums, art galleries, opera and open-air concerts, as well as the famous Cathedral. This site is pleasantly situated along the river bank, with wide grass areas on either side of narrow tarmac access roads with low metal barriers separating it from the public park and riverside walks. Of 140 unmarked, level or slightly undulating touring pitches, 50 have 10A electricity and there is shade for some from mature trees. Because of its position close to the Autobahn bridge over the Rhine, there is road and river noise, but when we stayed the location and friendly atmosphere more than made up for it.

Facilities: The small toilet block has fairly basic facilities, but is heated with free hot water (06.00-12.00, 17.00-23.00 hrs) in washing troughs and in the showers. Washing machine and dryer. Small shop opens in the mornings for bread and basic supplies and microwave evening snacks (mid May-Sept). Fishing. Bicycle hire. **Off site:** Bar/café by entrance. Trams and buses to city centre 1 km.

Charges 2002

Per adult	€ 4.09
pitch	€ 4.10 - € 6.65
electricity	€ 1.53

Tel: 0221 831966. Fax: 0221 831966. **Reservations:** Write to site. **Open** 25 April - 5 October.

Directions: Leave autobahn A4 at exit no. 13 for Köln-Poll (just to west off intersection of A3 and A4). Turn left at first traffic lights and follow site signs through a sometimes fairly narrow one-way system to the riverside, back towards the motorway bridge.

Germany - South West
Camping und Ferienpark Teichmann

3280 An der B252, 34516 Vöhl-Herzhausen (Hesse)

Situated by a 6 hectare lake (the Edersee) with tree-covered hills all around, this well cared for site blends in attractively with its surroundings. Windsurfing, rowing boats, pedaloes (no motor-boats), swimming and fishing are possible, all in different areas, and the site is also suitable for a winter sports holiday (with ski runs near). There are many local walks and the opportunity exists for taking a pleasure boat trip and riding home by bicycle. The 460 pitches (half for touring units) are mainly on flat grass, all with 6A electricity and with some hardstandings. There is a separate area for tents. The many amenities include a mini-market and café. A good site for families, there are many activities (listed below) and a pitch can usually be found even for a one night stay. A very large open air model railway is a special attraction.

Facilities: Three good quality sanitary blocks can be heated and have some private cabins, with baby rooms in two with facilities for wheelchair users. Café and shop (both summer only). Restaurant by entrance open all day (Feb-Dec). Watersports. Boat and bicycle hire. Lake swimming. Football. Fishing. Minigolf. Beach volleyball (high season). Tennis. Table tennis. Playground. Large working model railway. Sauna and solarium. High season disco. **Off site:** Cable car (you can take bikes), Aquapark, museums, boat trips and much else.

Charges 2002

Per unit with 2 persons, electricity, water and waste water	€ 9.50 - € 14.00
extra person over 16 yrs	€ 3.60 - € 5.70
extra person 3-16 yrs	€ 2.60 - € 3.60
6A electricity	€ 2.10

Tel: 05635 245. **Fax:** 05635 8145. **E-mail:** camping-teichmann@t-online.de. **Reservations:** Made with deposit (€50) and fee (€ 5). **Open** all year.

Directions: From A44 Oberhausen - Kassel autobahn, take exit for Korbach. Site is between Korbach and Frankenberg on the B252 road, 1 km. to the south of Herzhausen, about 45 km. from the A44.

Germany - South West
Lahn Camping

3265 Schleusenweg 16, 65549 Limburg an der Lahn (Hesse)

Pleasantly situated on the bank of the river Lahn (with direct access to it) between the autobahn and the town - both the autobahn viaduct and the cathedral are visible - this is a useful overnight stop for travellers along the Köln-Frankfurt stretch of the A3. You may, however, be tempted to stay longer as there are other attractions here, notably a very fine swimming pool complex nearby and the attractive old town of medieval buildings a gentle stroll away. The site is on level grass with 200 touring pitches (out of 250 altogether and 140 have 6A electricity - may need long cable) on either side of gravel tracks at right angles from the main tarmac road, which runs the length of the site. There are some trees but it is mainly open. It is very popular with many nationalities and can become crowded at peak times, so arrive early. Some road and rail noise.

Facilities: The main sanitary block near reception is rather old but improvements have been made (showers need a token). A new, high quality heated block at the other end of the site is a welcome addition. Washing machines, dryers, cookers. Gas supplies. Motorcaravan services. Bar/restaurant (open evenings and Sundays) offers drinks, simple meals and takeaway. Small shop for basic supplies (not Sunday p.m.). Fishing (permit on payment). Play area. Bicycle and motorcycle hire. **Off site:** Swimming pool opposite. Riding 5 km. Golf 15 km. Supermarkets and good range of shops and restaurants in town. Pleasure cruises.

Charges 2002

Per person	€ 3.50
child (3-14 yrs)	€ 2.00
pitch	€ 5.10
electricity	€ 2.00
waste tax	€ 1.00

No credit cards. **Tel:** 06431 22610. **Reservations:** May be possible - phone site. **Open** 18 April - 26 October.

Directions: Leave A3 autobahn at Limburg-Nord exit and follow road into town and then signs for 'Camping-Swimming'.

Camping Seepark

3275 36275 Kirchheim (Hesse)

Kirchheim is just 5 km. from the A7 (50 km. south of Kassel) and also close to the Frankfurt to Dresden autobahns A5-A4 in eastern Hesse, which has the largest forested area in Germany. Pleasantly situated on the side of a valley, this is a large terraced park and is probably unique in offering a service for diabetics, with special food available and dialysis arranged in Bad Hersfeld hospital. There are 170 touring pitches (5 for people with disabilities) generally in their own areas (out of 370 altogether), varying in size from about 80 to 110 sq.m many marked with young trees in the corners. All have 16A electricity, just under half with water and drainage. They are mostly numbered in cul-de-sacs with access from tarmac roads leading up to an open area for larger vehicles and a tent field at the top. Thousands of bushes and trees have been planted over the years (but providing little shade for the pitches) and flowers are prominent around the service buildings. Opposite the entrance is a mainly sloping overnight area (including electricity and shower). This area of eastern Hesse has many areas of interest - Bad Hersfeld is an ancient town with an annual Festival of Drama and Opera from mid June to mid August, Fulda is an ecclesiastical centre and near it is Schloss Fasanerie, a good example of baroque architecture with a fine collection of porcelain and beautifully furnished.

Facilities: The original sanitary facilities are in the complex at the entrance with further very good facilities at the modern restaurant building higher up the site (high season and holidays). They have under-floor heating and private cabins. The tent area is currently served by a portable unit. Launderette. Drive over motorcaravan service point. Shop. Restaurant (breakfast available) open all year. Small free heated open air raised swimming pool (June-Aug; 1 m. deep; parents must supervise children which also applies to the lake swimming area at the left side of the site). Tennis. Table-tennis. Football. Volleyball. Minigolf. Diabetic service. Play areas. Tennis. Fishing. Volleyball. Football field. Water-skiing. Barbecue area. **Off site:** Close by on the lake there is water-skiing, boat hire, trampolining, adventure pool, roller skating rink, indoor tennis and fishing. Golf 3 km.

Charges 2002

Per unit incl. up to 6 persons	€ 17.50
electricity	€ 2.00
water	€ 0.80
rubbish tax	€ 0.30

Tel: 06628 1525. **Fax:** 06628 8664. **E-mail:** info@campseepark.de. **Reservations:** Advisable Easter, Whitsun and June - September, although overnight should be possible if arriving early. **Open** all year.

Directions: From A7 Kassel - Fulda/Wurzburg take exit 87 for Kirchheim and follow signs to Seepark for 4.5 km. The park is on a minor road between the small villages of Rimboldshausen and Kemmerode, just west of the lake.

Camping Gülser Moselbogen

3222 Am Gülser Moselbogen 20, Güls, 56072 Koblenz (Rhineland Palatinate)

The provision of first class sanitary facilities here, combined with the location being very convenient for sightseeing along the rivers Mosel and Rhein and the easy access to Koblenz, the A48 and A61, make this an attractive proposition for a short or longer-term stay. The site is set quite high up from the river (safe from flooding) but with no direct access to it, and has a pleasant outlook to the forested valley slopes. A large proportion of the 16 acre site is taken up by privately owned bungalows, but the touring section of 60 large individual pitches, near the entrance, is self contained and accessed by gravel paths leading off the main tiled roads. The flat pitches have little shade yet, but all have connections for TV and 16A electricity and there are water points in each section. A new area of gravel hardstanding has been developed and RVs are accepted.

Facilities: Entry to the really excellent, heated sanitary building is by a coded card that also operates the hot water to the showers (free to the washbasins, many of which are in cabins). Unit for disabled visitors, baby room, dishwashing and cooking rings (charged). Laundry. Gas supplies. Motorcaravan services. Bread and milk may be ordered at reception. Play area. Bicycle hire. **Off site:** Restaurant 500 m. Güls village 1.5 km. Fishing 200 m, riding 3 km.

Charges 2002

Per person	€ 4.50
child (3-14 yrs)	€ 2.50
pitch	€ 5.50
dog	€ 1.50
electricity (plus 1.00 connection)	€ 1.50
chip card deposit	€ 5.11

Tel: 0261 44474. **Fax:** 0261 44494. **E-mail:** moselbogen@paffhausen.com. **Reservations:** Not normally necessary. **Open** all year.

Directions: Site is 1.5 km. west of village of Güls, and is accessed from the B416 that runs along the north bank of the Mosel from Koblenz (where it joins the B9) towards Cochem. From the A61 take exit 38 towards Koblenz-Metternich. After 2 km. turn right towards Winningen/Flughaven/Güls (white sign) and keep on main road for Güls till the B416, turn right towards Cochem and watch for site signs in 1.5 km.

Naturpark Camping Suleika

3225 Lorch bei Rüdesheim am Rhein, 65382 Rüdesheim am Rhein (Hesse)

On a steep hillside in the Rhine-Taunus Nature Park and approached by a narrow and steep system of lanes through the vineyards, this situation is not for the faint hearted. Having said that, it is a popular site for caravan rallies. Once you reach the site, it is steeply arranged in small terraces up the side of the wooded hill with a stream flowing through - the water supply is direct from springs. The surroundings are most attractive, with views over the vineyards to the river below. The Riesling Walk footpath passes above the site. Of the 100 pitches, 50 are for tourists. These are mostly on the lower terraces, in numbered groups of up to four units. There is a special area for younger campers. All have electricity and there are water points around. Cars have to be parked away from the pitches near the entrance. A central block contains a very pleasant restaurant and small shop for basics (bread to order), with sanitary facilities alongside. With steep walks from most pitches to the facilities, this is probably not a site for visitors with disabilities; however, it is an attractive situation and reception staff are very friendly. This particular area is famous as it was briefly a 'Free State' (1919-23) and you will be able to taste and buy the site owner's wine and other items as souvenirs. There are many local attractions (as well as the Lorelei) shown on a large map, and the helpful owner speaks good English.

Facilities: The excellent toilet block is heated in cool weather and provides some washbasins in cabins for each sex and a nicely furnished baby washroom, with WC, shower and bath. Laundry service. Motorcaravan services. Gas supplies. Restaurant (closed Mon. and Thu.). Small shop (bread to order). Children's playground. Some entertainment in season. **Off site:** Fishing 300 m. Bicycle hire. Riding 4 km.

Charges 2003

Per adult	€ 4.50
child	€ 2.50
caravan or tent	€ 3.00 - € 4.50
car	€ 1.50
motorcaravan	€ 7.00
dog	€ 1.50
electricity (plus meter)	€ 1.00
rubbish tax	€ 0.50

No credit cards. **Tel:** 06726 9464. Fax: 06726 9440. **Reservations:** made with €26 deposit, so only worthwhile for a longer stay. **Open** 15 March - 31 October.

Directions: There is a direct entrance road from the B42 (for cars only), between Rudesheim and Lorch, with a height limitation of 2.25 m. under a railway bridge. Higher vehicles will find the site signed on the south side of Lorch. Site is reached via a one-way system of lanes - follow the signs.

Germany

Landal GreenParks Wirfttal

3212 Wirftstraße, 54589 Stadtkyll (Rhineland Palatinate)

the travel service
TO BOOK
erry ✓
itch ✓
Accommodation ✗
01892 55 98 98

Peacefully set in a small valley in the heath and forest of the hills of the northern Eifel, near the Belgian border Wirfttal has 250 numbered pitches of which 150 are for tourers. They mostly back onto fences, hedges etc. on fairly flat ground of different levels (steel pegs are required for tents and awnings). The pitches are 80 sq.m or more, and all have electricity (6A) and TV aerial points with water points around, 17 individual pitches have their own water and waste water points. Also part of the site, but separate from the camping, is a large holiday bungalow complex. A short walk up the hill is an outdoor swimming pool complex with three pools, one heated, and minigolf. Additionally, at the site entrance, is a small indoor pool, and a sports centre with two outdoor tennis courts (floodlit), a super adventure playground, bowling and an indoor tennis and squash centre. Fishing (but not swimming) is allowed in the small lake.

Facilities: There is one main toilet block (the only one open out of main season), and two small units, all heated. All ladies' washbasins and one for men in the main block are in cabins. Shop. Restaurant and snacks (high season). Swimming pool complex (with discount for campers). Indoor pool (free) and sauna and solarium (on payment) Tennis (indoor and outdoor). Riding. Fishing (free). Bicycle hire. Sports centre adjacent with squash hall. Children's play equipment around site and main adventure playground. Winter sports. Bicycle and sledge hire. Animation in season in activity hut.

Charges 2002

Per unit incl. 2 persons and electricity	€ 26.00
extra person	€ 2.50
dog	€ 3.00
electricity (6A)	€ 2.30
local tax	€ 0.90

Less in low season. Special 5, 8 or 10 day rates. **Tel:** 06597 92920. Fax: 06597 929250. E-mail: info@landal.de. **Reservations:** Made (Fri.- Fri. only in high season) with 50% deposit. Office open 7 days/week. **Open** all year.

Directions: Site is 1.5 km. south of Stadtkyll on road towards Schüller.

Germany - South West
Campingplatz am Rhein

3224 65385 Rüdesheim am Rhein (Hesse)

Relaxed and informal, this site is quietly located on edge of town right by the Rhine. This is a major tourist area so it will become very busy here at certain times, but the owner says there is almost always room on the site. The 7 acre touring site (no permanent units are accepted) is flat and grassy, with quite a lot of attractive, old tall trees that offer some shade. Caravan and tent pitches are on grass (no plastic groundsheets) and the owner firmly believes in unmarked camping so that the grass can grow. A separate area of hardstanding is provided for motorcaravans. Electricity (10A) is available to most pitches and there are many water points.

Facilities: Satisfactory toilet facilities are in a modernised building with token operated showers (5 mins) and almost half the washbasins in cabins. Washing machines and dryer. Motorcaravan services. Shop. Bar and snacks. Children's play area. Gates closed to vehicles and riverside 22.00-08.00 hrs. **Off site:** Heated outdoor pool 100 m. Amenities of Rüdesheim 600 m. Boat trips on the Rhine and many other sightseeing opportunities are close by.

Charges 2002

Per person	€ 4.10
child (under 15 yrs)	€ 2.50
pitch	€ 7.00 - € 8.00
electricity	€ 2.30
local tax	€ 1.50

No credit cards. **Tel:** 06722 2528. Fax: 06722 941046. **Reservations:** Not made (no brochure either). **Open** 1 May - 3 October.

Directions: Site is signed in several places from the B42 in the east of Rüdesheim and is alongside the river.

Germany
Camping Goldene Meile

3215 Simrockweg 9 - 13, 53424 Remagen (Rhineland Palatinate)

This site is on the banks of the Rhine between Bonn and Koblenz, and adjacent to a large complex of open-air public swimming pools (campers pay the normal entrance). Although there is an emphasis on permanent caravans, there are about 300 pitches for tourists (from 550), 50 with water and waste water connections (more extra large ones are being added) and 14 with waste water, and an area for tents. They are either in the central, more mature area or in a newer area where the numbered pitches of 80-100 sq. m. are arranged around an attractively landscaped small fishing lake. Just 5 are by the busy river, but it is more peaceful the further back you are. There are electricity connections in most areas (8A). They claim always to find space for odd nights, except perhaps at B.Hs. This site is in a popular area and, although busy in high season, appears to be well run.

Facilities: The main toilet block to one side of the site is a good quality building, heated and kept clean, with some washbasins in cabins, showers with token from machine and facilities for wheelchair users. Shower and wash rooms are locked at 10 pm. A smaller block serves the pitches near the lake (no showers). Washing machine and dryer. Cooking facilities. Motorcaravan services. Gas supplies. Small shop with bread to order, bar and restaurant (all 1/4-30/10 and some weekends). Playgrounds. Entertainment for children in July/Aug. Bicycle hire. Main gate locked at 10 pm. (also 1-3 pm). **Off site:** Swimming pools adjacent (May-Sept).

Charges 2003

Per person	€ 5.00
child (6-16 yrs)	€ 4.00
pitch	€ 7.00
with services	€ 8.50
electricity	€ 2.25
rubbish tax	€ 0.50

Tel: 02642 22222. Fax: 02642 1555. E-mail: info@camping-goldene-meile.de. **Reservations:** can be made for at least a few days. **Open** all year.

Directions: Remagen is 23 km. south of Bonn on no. 9 road towards Koblenz. Site is on road running close to the Rhine from Remagen to Kripp and is signed from the N9 south of Remagen, which avoids the congested town (signs also for Allwetterbad). From A61 autobahn take Sinzig exit.

On one of the most beautiful and modern camp sites in the romantic Rhine valley between Bonn (20 km) and Koblenz (40 km) you will find ideal conditions.

For a holiday: water sports on the Rhine and in the heated all-weather pool (86 m chute), sports and keep-fit (indoor and outdoor tennis courts, playing field, volleyball court, football ground), hiking in the Eifel and the Westerwald, boat trips on the Rhine and the Mosel, numerous wine festivals.

For a short stop: convenient location only 7 km from the A 61 motorway (Sinzig-Remagen exit), 2 km to the B 9. Shop, restaurant with terrace, first-class rating from ADAC for many years.

Campingplatz »Goldene Meile«
D-53424 Remagen
Tel. (0 26 42) 2 22 22
http://www.camping-goldene-meile.de
e-mail: info@camping-goldene-meile.de

Camping Harfenmühle

55758 Asbacherhütte (Rhineland Palatinate)

3254

Harfenmühle is situated in a wooded valley in the Hunsrück, an attractive area of Germany just below the Mosel. It is also unusual to find a site which has its own gourmet restaurant and wine cellar. It is essentially a friendly, relaxed partly terraced site, with 70 touring pitches, mostly individual and ranging in size up to 150 sq.m, with 16A electrical connections and a separate meadow for tents. There are also 70 permanent units and 35 chalets. There is plenty to keep youngsters happy and many sightseeing opportunities. Precious stones (Edel-steinen) and minerals can be searched for here and nearby and there are 1500 km. of marked walks through the Naturpark Saar-Hunsrück.

Facilities: Satisfactory, heated all year round, sanitary facilities are in the main building, with some private cabins, curtained showers on payment. Sauna and solarium. Launderette. Tennis. Play area. Boules. Trout fishing. Swimming lake. Table tennis. Ski hire. Aviary. Kiosk with fresh bread daily and takeaway in season. Gourmet. Restaurant (closed 18/2-7/3). Wine cellar/bar. **Off site:** Riding 3 km.

Charges 2002

Per person	€ 3,80
child (2-15 yrs)	€ 2,50
pitch	€ 7,50
electricity per kwh.	€ 0,40

Discounts in low season for stays over 5 nights. **Tel:** 06786 7076. Fax: 06786 7570. E-mail: camping-harfenmuehle@t-online.de. **Reservations:** contact site. **Open** all year.

Directions: From the B41 Saarbrücken - Bad Kreuznach, exit north at Fischbach signed towards Herrstein and then on tthrough Morschied to Asbacherhütte, with site entrance on right.

Azur Camping Hunsrück

54421 Reinsfeld (Rhineland Palatinate)

3256

Hunsrück is very large (20 ha.) site taking nearly 1,000 units. There are 600 touring pitches and 380 permanent units arranged in 29 circular glades, each of which is surrounded by trees, with an open central area for short stay visitors. They are reasonably flat, on grass but not marked out, with 10A electrical connections (euro plugs in the central area). A stream runs through the park into the lake. The restaurant provides good value meals and a bar.

Facilities: Several old sanitary buildings provide similar but not identical facilities, with a total of 8 cabins for general use and 144 for hire. Showers are a little small. One block has facilities for disabled people. Washing machines and dryers. Outdoor heated pool June to Sept. unsupervised (hat compulsory). Play areas, large minigolf, smallish football pitch, volleyball, tennis. Animation 13/7-10/8. Basic supplies in reception. Bread to order. Restaurant/bar. Games room. **Off site:** Riding 10 km.

Charges 2002

Per person	€ 4,50 - € 6,00
child (2-12 yrs)	€ 3,50 € 4,50
pitch	€ 5,50 - € 7,50
electricity	€ 2,10

Tel: 06503 95123. Fax: 06503 95124. E-mail: info@azur-camping.de. **Reservations:** contact site. **Open** all year.

Directions: From A1/E422 Saarbrücken - Trier, take exit 132 Reinsfeld. Follow to town and site (signed).

Family Camping Club

Moselufer, 56820 Mesenich bei Cochem (Rhineland Palatinate)

3232

Situated beside the Mosel river, with views of forest and vineyard, this site has the added advantage of being on a stretch of the river well away from the railway. Formerly run for long-term units, it has been acquired by a progressive young family who are rapidly updating the facilities to turn it into a comfortable touring location. The 68 touring pitches are among the vines, mainly level, individual ones with electricity connections (6/8A), separated by bushes and the older ones with shade. On arrival you must stop on the fairly narrow site road while booking in at the new reception. It is very popular in July and August with many activities organised for youngsters, but they do insist on no noise after midnight. Good English is spoken.

Facilities: Well equipped, heated toilet facilities provide washbasins mainly in cubicles or curtained. Washing machines and dryer. Shop, bar and restaurant (1/7-1/9). Swimming pools (19/6-12/9). Play equipment. Fishing. Disco evenings and wine tours in July/Aug. Dogs are not accepted in July/Aug. **Off site:** Bicycle hire 300 metres. Golf or riding 10 km.

Charges 2002

Per unit incl. 2 persons	€ 12.00 - € 20.50
extra person (over 2 yrs)	€ 4.00
electricity	€ 2.00

No credit cards. **Tel:** 02673 4556. Fax: 02673 1751. E-mail: info@familycamping.de. **Reservations:** Essential for July/Aug. Office tel: 02673 4556 or 1589. Fax: 02673 1751. **Open** 15 April - 3 October.

Directions: Mesenich is on the opposite side of the Mosel from Cochem and can be reached from the B49, crossing the river bridge at either Cochem to the northeast or Senheim to the southwest. It can also be reached from the scenic B421 Kirchberg to Zell road, turning to Senheim 15 km. after Kirchberg (rather winding and steep road at the end).

Camping Am Mühlenteich

3235 56291 Lingerhahn (Rhineland Palatinate)

Set among trees and fields in the hills at the eastern end of the Hunsrück, this friendly site is only 15 km. from the Rhine at Oberwesel. Bingen, Boppard and Koblenz are also reached easily via the A61 autobahn. In addition to 350 pitches for permanent caravans, there are 100 touring pitches with electricity connections (6A). Some are in the main part (for longer stays), others are in a more open situation opposite (caravans and tents are mixed together) and space is usually available. On site is an unusual pool for swimming (free of charge) fashioned from a natural basin and fed by springs. A splendid new building houses reception, a shop and café and there is very good provision for children, including some very popular children's play equipment and a video room, plus entertainment in July/August.

Facilities: The central sanitary block, in two sections, is large, heated and of good quality. With a further building for high season, the supply is satisfactory, with some private cabins for ladies in two blocks and for men in one. Gas supplies. Motorcaravan services. Small shop. Café (Easter-Oct and holidays). Baker calls daily at 8.30 am. Cable/satellite TV. Youth disco room. Tennis. Basketball. Table tennis. Large adventure playground. Football field. Wagon rides in season. Bicycle hire. Barbecue. Animation in high season. **Off site:** Riding or fishing 4 km. Golf 15 km.

Charges 2003

Per person	€ 4.00
child (2-16 yrs)	€ 3.00
pitch	€ 8.00
electricity	€ 2.00
local taxes	€ 1.00

No credit cards. **Tel:** 06746 533. Fax: 06746 1566. E-mail: info@muehlenteich.de. **Reservations:** Write to site. **Open** all year.

Directions: From A61 autobahn take exit for Laudert. Follow signs into Lingerhahn village, between Laudert and Kastellaun. Site is signed in middle of the village

A very well kept site with every comfort, open all year. Electrical connections for 400 pitches. Restaurant. Shop. Games Room. Youth Room and adventure playground. Tennis. Cable TV on all pitches.

6 km from Koblenz-Mainz autobahn - take exit for Laudert.

Proprietor: Willi Christ. Tel. 06746 533. National Gold Medal in for outstanding camp blending with the landscape. Winner of A.D.A.C. Touristic Prize 81.

Camping 'Am Mühlenteich' – 56291 Lingerhahn/Hunsrück

Camping Burgen

 3230 Moselstraße, 56332 Burgen (Rhineland Palatinate)

Camping Burgen is pleasantly situated between the road and the river on the flat grassy bank of the Mosel between Koblenz and Cochem. It has attractive views and, like many sites alongside the Mosel, it may very occasionally be flooded. Most of the pitches on the river's edge are occupied by permanent caravans and attendant boats, but there are 120 individual numbered hardstanding pitches for tourists plus a meadow at one end, both with electricity available (10A), The site fills up for much of July and August but a few pitches are kept for short stay visitors. With a railway across the water, the road and commercial boats, some noise may be expected. You can swim and fish in the Mosel (there is also a small pool on site) or just use the site as a base for visiting local attractions. A floodlit castle on the opposite bank of the Mosel provides an attractive view.

Facilities: The single central toilet block is quite good, with washbasins (5 in cabins), and 9 showers (on payment, token from reception or shop) which might be hard pressed in high season. Washing machine and dryer. Gas supplies. Motorcaravan services. Shop (essentials only all season). General room with TV and games, drinks served. Small swimming pool (9.5 x 6.5 m. open May-Aug). Fishing and swimming in the river. Slipway for boats. Table tennis. Children's playground. **Off site:** Restaurant 200 m. Bicycle hire 4 km. Boat trips.

Charges 2003

Per person	€ 4.50
child (1-13 yrs)	€ 2.00
pitch	€ 6.50
motorcycle and tent	€ 5.00
electricity	€ 1.50
local tax	€ 1.00 - € 2.00

Tel: 02605 2396. Fax: 02605 4919. **Reservations:** made for any length with deposit and fee. **Open** 1 April - 15 October.

Directions: Site is on eastern edge of town, 30 km. from Koblenz (a tight turn into the site if approaching from Koblenz).

Country Camping Schinderhannes

3242 56291 Hausbay-Pfalzfeld (Rhineland Palatinate)

Country Camping could be a useful transit stop en-route to the Black Forest, Bavaria, Austria and Switzerland, as well as a family holiday. High in the Hunsruck (a large area with forests, ideal for walking and cycling), Schinderhannes himself was a legendary 'Robin Hood' character, whose activities were curtailed in Mainz, at the end of a rope. Lying about 30 km south of Koblenz, west of the Rhine and south of the Mosel, it is set in a 'bowl' of land which catches the sun all day long and with trees and parkland all around. This is a very peaceful and picturesque setting, very close to, but rather different from, no. 3235. There are 250 permanent caravans in a separate area from 90 overnight pitches on hardstanding, which are on two areas near reception. For those staying longer, the site becomes visually more attractive as you drive down into the area around the lake to a further 160 numbered pitches. These are of over 80 sq.m. on grass, some with hardstanding and all with European electrical connections (10A) and with water points around. You can position yourself for shade or sun. The lake is used for swimming and inflatable boats and for fishing. English is spoken by the helpful reception staff.

Facilities: The sanitary buildings, which can be heated, are of a high standard with one section, in the reception/shop building, for the overnight pitches and the remainder close to the longer stay places. Facilities for disabled people. Laundry. Bar. Pleasant large restaurant featuring an open fire, a rest area with TV and a bowling alley downstairs. Shop (all amenities 15/3-31/10 and maybe Xmas). Tennis (on payment). Basketball. Fishing. Children's play area and fort. Rallies welcome. Barrier closed 22.00-07.00 hrs. **Off site:** Bicycle hire 1 km. (cycle down to the Rhine and catch the train back).

Charges 2002

Per adult	€ 5.00
child	€ 3.00
pitch incl. electricity	€ 8.00
dog	€ 1.50

Tel: 06746 80280. Fax: 06746 802814. E-mail: info@countrycamping.de. **Reservations:** For groups only, contact site. **Open** all year.

Directions: From A61 Koblenz - Ludwigshafen road, take exit 43 Pfalzfeld (30 km. south of Koblenz) and on to Hausbay where site is signed.

Country Camping
Schinderhannes
HOLIDAY - RALLY & FAMILYCAMP
Between Rhine and Mosel
Free Brochure

GPS: N 50.1060 E 07.5679

see no. 3242

Germany - South West
Camping Burg Lahneck

3220 Ortsteil Oberlahnstein, 56112 Lahnstein (Rhineland Palatinate)

The location of this site is splendid, high up overlooking the Rhine valley and the town of Lahnstein - many of the pitches have their own super views. Adjacent is a good outdoor swimming pool with extensive grassy areas, and the mediaeval castle Burg Lahneck (the home of the camp proprietor, which may be visited) with its smart restaurant. It is in the best part of the Rhine valley, and close to Koblenz and the Mosel. A 'Kurcentrum', under 2 km. from the site, has a thermal pool from warm springs (reduced admission to campers) with sauna and solarium. The site, which consists partly of terraces and partly of open grassy areas, has a cared for look and all is very neat and clean. One can usually find a space here, though from early July to mid-August it can become full. There are 115 individual touring pitches (out of 125 altogether) marked but not separated and mostly level, all with electricity (16A). Campers are sited by the management. Reception staff at the site are friendly and charges reasonable. There are some tour operator pitches.

Facilities: The single central, heated toilet block is of a good standard, and well maintained and cleaned. There are some cabins for both sexes. Showers are on payment (€ 0,50). Washing machine and dryer. Motorcaravan services. Gas supplies. Small shop. Small playground. **Off site:** Cafe/restaurant adjoining site serves drinks, snacks, ices, etc. with some hot evening food; meals also in Burg Lahneck restaurant. Town swimming pool (reduced charges for campers, 15/5-31/8). Tennis nearby. Riding 500 m. Fishing 3 km. Bicycle hire 2 km.

Charges 2003

Per person	€ 5.50
child (3-14 yrs)	€ 3.00
trailer tent or caravan	€ 5.50
tent	€ 4.50 - € 5.50
car	€ 3.50
motorcycle	€ 1.50
motorcaravan	€ 7.50 - € 8.50
dog	€ 1.00
electricity (plus meter)	€ 0.50

No credit cards. **Tel:** 02621 2765. Fax: 02621 18290. **Reservations:** made without deposit for exact dates. **Open** Easter/1 April - 31 October.

Directions: From B42 road bypassing the town, take Oberlahnstein exit and follow signs 'Kurcentrum' and Burg Lahneck.

Germany - South West
Landal GreenParks Sonnenberg

3245 54340 Leiwen (Rhineland Palatinate)

the travel service
TO BOOK

Ferry	✓
Pitch	✓
Accommodation	✗

01892 55 98 98

With attractive views over the Mosel as you climb the approach road, 4 km. from the wine village of Leiwen and the river, this pleasant site is on top of a hill. It has a splendid free leisure centre incorporating an indoor activity pool with child's paddling pool, whirlpool, cascade and slides. Also in this building are ten-pin bowling, a sauna, solarium and fitness room, tennis and badminton, plus a snack bar. Combining a bungalow complex (separate) with camping, the site has 150 large, individual and numbered grassy pitches on terraces with electricity (6A) and TV connections. Excursions and entertainment are organised in season, with ranger guided walks, wine-tasting, daily cruises from Leiwen to Bernkastel and coach trips to the Rhine (both May-Oct). There are two good restaurants and shop, and the site is efficiently managed with a friendly and helpful English speaking reception staff.

Facilities: The single toilet block has under-floor heating, washbasins in cabins (all for women, a couple for men). It is stretched in busy times. Large laundry. Motorcaravan services. Shop. Restaurant, bistro, bar and snacks (one restaurant only in low season). Indoor multi-purpose leisure centre with activity pool, climbing wall, 10 pin bowling, tennis and badminton. Volleyball. Football pitch. Minigolf. Children's playground. Bicycle hire in high season. Disco, entertainment and excursions at busy times (not all every day). Deer park. **Off site:** Fishing 5 km. Riding or golf 12 km.

Charges 2003

Per unit incl. 2 persons, electricity	€ 18.00 - € 31.00
extra person	€ 2.50
dog	€ 3.00

Special 5, 8 or 10 day rates. **Tel:** 06507 93690. Fax: 06507 936936. E-mail: info@landal.de. **Reservations:** Essential mid July - end August. Write with deposit (Fri. - Fri. only in high season). **Open** 21 February - 3 November.

Directions: From Trier-Koblenz A48/A1 take new exit 128 for Bekond, Föhren, Hetzerath and Leiwen. Follow signs for Leiwen and in town follow signs for Ferienpark, Sonnenberg or Freibad on very winding road up hill 4 km. to site.

Camping Sägmühle

3258 67705 Trippstadt (Rhineland Palatinate)

Sägmühle has been in the same family for over 50 years, during which time it has undergone several major developments which have turned it into a first class site. It is peacefully situated beside a lake, in a wooded valley in the heart of the Palatinate Nature Park, and there are many kilometers of walks to enjoy, as well as castles to explore. A first class restaurant offers some fine local wines, and there is plenty for children to enjoy with fishing, swimming and boating in the lake, a fort, minigolf and tennis. The 200 touring pitches (half the total) are at least 80 sq.m. or more on flat grass, each with electricity and TV connections, with plenty of water points around. There are three separate areas of pitches, one of which is close to the lake – it is a pleasant change to find a site that keeps the lakeside pitches for tourers.

Facilities: Each area has its own sanitary facilities, those beside the lake and the back being first class, with those at the side being renovated. Private cabins, baby bathroom, facilities for disabled people, launderette. Motorcaravan services. Restaurant and takeaway. Bread available from the accessory shop in high season. Solarium. Two tennis courts. Play areas. Table tennis, football area, basketball. Mountain bike hire. Entertainment in high season. **Off site:** Shops 10 minutes walk in Trippstadt.

Charges 2002

Per person	€ 5.00 - € 6.00
child (under 14 yrs)	€ 1.90 - € 2.00
pitch incl. electricity (4A)	€ 5.70 - € 7.20
local tax (adults only)	€ 0.15

Tel: 06306 92190. Fax: 06306 2000. E-mail: info@saegmuehle.de. **Reservations:** Contact site. **Open** all year.

Directions: From Saarbrücken on A6, take exit 15 (Kaiserslautern West) on B270 towards Pirmasens. Turn left after 8 km. towards Karlstal/Trippstadt and follow site signs. From A65 between Karlsruhe and Neustadt take exit 15 or 17 towards Annweiler on B10. After Annweiler right on B48 to Rinnthal and on towards Kaiserslautern/Johanniskreuz. After 20 km left to Kaiserslautern/Trippstadt and the next left to Trippstadt. Follow site signs into the valley.

★ ★ ★ ★ ★

One of the most popular Holiday Campsites in the Palatinate forest, both in summer and winter

400 km of waymarked walks, swimming in freshwater lake (heated open air pool 1 km) large adventure play area, 2 tennis courts, 1 basketball court, minigolf, boules, comfortable restaurant with local specialities (250 seat room available for groups). In Summer an extensive entertainment programme. Fishing. Table-tennis. Barbecue hut. Hairdressing salon. Solarium. Massage. Permanent Motorcaravan and Caravan exhibition. Accessories and workshop. Motorcaravan waste disposal facility. Newly opened Sanitary building with family cabins and baby-changing room.

67705 Trippstadt • Tel. 06306 / 9 21 90 • Fax 06306 / 20 00
www.saegmuehle.de • e-mail: info@saegmuehle.de

Landal GreenParks Warsberg

3250 54439 Saarburg (Rhineland Palatinate)

On top of a steep hill in an attractive location, this site and the winding approach road offer pleasant views over the town and surrounding area. A chair lift links the site to the town - it is well worth a ride, as is the 530 m. 'Rodelbahn' toboggan (both with small fee). A large, well organised site, there are 500 numbered touring pitches of quite reasonable size on flat or slightly sloping ground, separated in small groups by trees and shrubs, with electricity in most places. There are some tour operator pitches and a separate area of bungalows. There are plenty of games facilities, a restaurant, large shop and a magnificent indoor pool. With friendly, English speaking staff, this site should appeal to all age groups. July and August are very busy.

Facilities: Three toilet blocks of very good quality provide washbasins (many in private cabins) and a unit for disabled visitors. Large launderette. Gas supplies. Motorcaravan services. Shop. Restaurant and takeaway, games rooms adjacent. Swimming pools (15/5-15/9). Tennis. Minigolf. Bicycle hire. Football field. Large playground. Bowling. Outdoor chess and draughts. Entertainment in season for all ages. Reception opens 9 - 12 and 2 - 5.30 (Sunday 10-12 only). **Off site:** Riding and fishing 5 km.

Charges 2003

Per unit incl. 2 persons	€ 17.00 - € 22.00
with electricity (6A)	€ 19.00 - € 25.00
extra person	€ 2.50

Tel: 06581 91460. Fax: 06581 914646. E-mail: info@landal.nl. **Reservations:** Advisable and made for July/Aug. Sat-Sat with 50% deposit. **Open** 29 March - 4 November.

Directions: From Trier on road 51 site well signed in the northwest outskirts of Saarburg off the Trierstrasse (signs also for 'Ferienzentrum') and from all round town. Follow signs up hill for 3 km.

Germany - South West
Knaus Camping Park Bad Dürkheim

3260 In den Almen 3, 67098 Bad Dürkheim (Rhineland Palatinate)

This large site is comfortable and has some 550 pitches (about half occupied by permanent caravans) but, being the best site at this well known wine town, it is very busy in main season. However, with some emergency areas they can usually find space. The site is long with individual pitches of fair size arranged on each side of the central road, which is decorated with arches of growing vines. There is some shade with trees growing and electricity throughout (16A). A lake runs along one side and swimming is possible (much of the lake has a sandy floor and there is a little beach) and non-powered boats can be launched. An activity programme offers guided tours, biking, canoeing and climbing. There is some noise from light aircraft, especially at weekends.

Facilities: Three large sanitary blocks are spaced out along the central avenue. They are of a high standard (private cabins, automatic taps, etc)and are heated in cool weather. Washing machine and dryer in each block. Gas supplies. Motorcaravan services. Cooking facilities. Shop (all year). Restaurant. Sports programme. Tennis. Beach volleyball. Sports field. Children's playground. Garden chess. Sauna and solarium. Dogs are not accepted.

Charges 2002

Per person	€ 5.00
child (3-14 yrs)	€ 2.50
pitch	€ 9.00
tent and motorcycle	€ 4.00
electricity	€ 1.80

No credit cards. **Tel:** 06322 61356. Fax: 06322 8161. E-mail: knaus-camping-duerkheim@t-online.de. **Reservations:** made for any length without deposit. **Open** all year except. November

Directions: Bad Dürkheim is on the no. 37 road west of Ludwigshafen. Site is on the eastern outskirts, signed from the Ludwigshafen road.

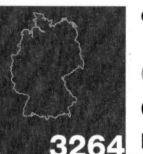

Germany - South West
Camping Büttelwoog

3264 Im Büttelwoog 3, 66994 Dahn (Rhineland Palatinate)

Many visitors come here for an overnight stay and then stop for longer or return on their journey home, as it is both peaceful and in an attractive area close to the border with France. In a long, narrow valley with tall trees on either side, a hard access road leads from reception and shop and the bar/restaurant to flat, numbered, grassy pitches, all of which have electricity connections (4A, mainly 2 pin). Some 80 long stay pitches are further along and another section behind reception gives 120 touring pitches in all. This is a pleasant site in an interesting setting and the welcome is friendly.

Facilities: Heated sanitary facilities are quite good, with most in private cabins. Washing machine. Small shop for essentials; café/bar for meals incl. breakfast (both 1/3-1/11). Playground on sand. Minigolf. Bicycle hire. Riding. Torches are useful at night. **Off site:** Swimming pools (indoor and outdoor) 300 m. Town 800 m.

Charges 2003

Per adult	€ 5.00
child (under 16 yrs)	€ 3.50 - € 4.00
pitch	€ 6.00
electricity	€ 1.80
local tax	€ 3.00

Less 10% from 3rd night with camping carnet. No credit cards. **Tel:** 06391 5622. Fax: 06391 5326. E-mail: buettelwoog@t-online.de. **Reservations:** Contact site. **Open** all year.

Directions: From Saarbrücken go towards Kaiserslauten on A6/E50 or road 423. Take Zweibrücken exit, then Pirmasens, finally turning to Dahn at Hinterweidenthal. Site is well signed in Dahn.

Germany - South West
Camping Haide bei Heidelberg

3403 Ziegelhäuser-Landstraße 91, 69151 Neckargemünd (Baden-Württemberg)

Haide is attractively situated beside the river Neckar, just west of the ancient university city and its famous castle. There is direct access to the river from the site, so children would need to be supervised. Safe from flooding, there is, however, some noise from the railway and road on the opposite bank, but it was not intrusive when we stayed. The site has 250 pitches, mainly without shade, with just under 200 for touring units. They are not marked out but there is plenty of space and there are 80 electricity connections (16A). The whole site is well maintained and is a good base from which to explore Heidelberg or the motor racing track at Hockenheim.

Facilities: Two satisfactory sanitary buildings include showers on payment. washing machines and dryers, dishwashing sinks and facilities for disabled visitors. Motorcaravan service point. Bicycle hire. Small play area for young children. **Off site:** Shop 2 km.

Charges 2003

Per person	€ 4.60
child (up to 15 yrs)	€ 2.30
pitch	€ 3.00
electricity	€ 1.50

Tel: 06223 2111. Fax: 06223 71959. E-mail: camping.haide@t-online.de. **Reservations:** Not usually necessary, but arrive early mid July - mid August. **Open** 1 April - 31 October.

Directions: From the 'Kreuz Heidelberg' exit on the A5, take B37 towards the city. Cross the bridge and turn right along the river bank towards Neckasteinach.

Camping Romantische Straße

3602 97993 Creglingen-Münster (Baden-Württemberg)

The small village of Münster is on a scenic road just 3 km. from Creglingen (also the 100 km. long Tauber valley cycle route) and about 16 km. from the tourist town of Rothenburg which, although fascinating, is also extremely busy and commercialised. This site would, therefore, be much appreciated for its peaceful situation in a wooded valley just outside Münster, with 90 grass touring pitches (out of 130), many level, others with a small degree of slope. They are not hedged or fenced, to keep the natural appearance of the woodland. All the pitches have electricity (16A), some shade, and are situated either side of a stream (fenced off from a weir at the top of the site). Good English is spoken by the friendly owners, who also own the restaurant. They have plans to further develop this attractive site, having already renovated the pool and made an open air chess and boules area in a peaceful spot. Bird watchers will be interested that the White-throated Dipper is regularly seen.

Facilities: The main sanitary facilities are of good quality, with free hot water for washbasins (two for each male/female in private cabins) and showers. A small unit further into the site is not of the same quality. Launderette. Motorcaravan services. Small shop for basic supplies. Gas supplies. Large, pleasant bar/restaurant at the entrance (closed Mondays). Barbecue and covered sitting area. Heated indoor swimming pool (bathing caps required), sauna and solarium. Minigolf. Play area. Table tennis. Bicycle hire. Rooms to let. **Off site:** Large lakes for swimming 100 m. and fishing 1 km. Riding 3 km.

Charges 2002

Per adult	€ 4.30 - € 5.30
child (2-12 yrs)	€ 3.30 - € 3.80
pitch	€ 5.90 - € 6.90
small tent pitch	€ 2.80 - € 3.50
electricity	€ 2.00
local tax	€ 0.35

No credit cards. **Tel:** 07933 20289. Fax: 07993 990019. E-mail: camping.hausotter@web.de. **Reservations:** Advised for Whitsun, July/Aug. and made without deposit for British visitors. **Open** 15 March - 15 November.

Directions: From the Romantische Strasse between Rothenburg and Bad Mergentheim, exit at Creglingen to Münster (3 km) and site is just beyond this village.

Azur Camping Ellwangen

3627 Rotenbacher Strasse, 73479 Ellwangen (Baden-Württemberg)

In a quiet position on the edge of town, with the river Jagst along one side, this modern six hectare site, from which you can see the large hilltop castle, has a park-like appearance with mature trees giving some shade. The 95 large, flat, grassy pitches (8 hardstandings) are unmarked off tarmac access roads. Electricity is available for about half the pitches from central boxes (16A). All the facilities are in one area to the left of the site entrance in modern units, with reception, the small shop for basic supplies and a bar/restaurant with terrace open all year.

Facilities: Heated sanitary facilities provide some private cabins. Dishwashing facilities, both inside and out, a small laundry, and room for babies and disabled visitors. Laundry facilities. Gas supplies. Motorcaravan service point. Shop. Restaurant/bar. Play equipment on sand. Fishing is very popular. **Off site:** Cycle paths. Indoor wave-pool 200 m.

Charges 2002

Per adult	€ 4.50 - € 6.00
pitch	€ 5.50 - € 7.50
electricity	€ 2.10

No credit cards. **Tel:** 07961 7921. Fax: 0796 562330. E-mail: info@azur-camping.de. **Reservations:** Contact site. **Open** all year (18/11- 28/2 by reservation only).

Directions: From A7 Ulm - Würzburg autobahn take exit 113. Go into Ellwangen from where site signed towrds Rotenbach village (tight turn into site).

Campingplatz Cannstatter Wasen

3402 Mercedesstraße 40, 70372 Stuttgart (Baden-Württemberg)

This is an attractively modernised, well managed city municipal site. On the outskirts of the city, but only a ten minute drive from the centre and with bus and train links just 500 m. away, it is a very convenient location. Completely fenced, the site is beside the river Neckar, with a walkway into the city, and is surprisingly green, with pretty flower beds, bushes and trees. Even though all the 234 pitches are on hardstanding, they appear green with grass growing through honeycomb tiles. They are unmarked, have electricity hook-ups and 25 also have water.

Facilities: Showers and washbasins (only a couple of private cabins) are of quite good quality in older buildings with heating. Modern unit for disabled visitors. New dishwashing and laundry facilities. Laundry. Motorcaravan services. Bistro with terrace (closed 20 Dec - 15 Jan). Play area. In low season the barrier is only open 08.00-10.00 and 17.00-19.00 hrs.

Charges 2002

Per unit incl.2 persons	€ 16.80

Tel: 0711 556696. Fax: 0711 557454. **Reservations:** Contact site for details. **Open** all year.

Directions: Site is in Bad Cannstatt close to the Daimler Benz Stadium in the east of the city. Signed from the B10 which is reached from the A8 exit 55 via the B313, or the A81 exit 17 via the B327.

Germany - South West
Camping Bad Liebenzell

3405 Pforzheimer Straße 34, 75378 Bad Liebenzell (Baden-Württemberg)

Now privately owned, this former municipal site is attractively situated on the outskirts of the pleasant little spa town of Bad Liebenzell in the northeast Black Forest. It has direct access to an excellent, large, heated swimming pool complex which is free to campers. Recently rebuilt, this includes swimming pools, wave pool and a long slide. There is also a children's pool and grassy sunbathing area and several tennis courts. The site is often full in high season when reservation is advisable (if not reserved arrive early). There may be some noise from the nearby roads and railway. The 235 pitches (150 for tourists) all have 16A electricity and are neatly arranged in rows on flat grass between hedges, trees and the good access roads. This is a well run and orderly site.

Facilities: Three heated toilet blocks are well maintained with washbasins mostly in cabins in two blocks, showers mainly in the end building. Provision for disabled visitors. Washing machines and dryers. Cooking facilities. Gas supplies. Motorcaravan services. Bar/restaurant. Small shop (excl. Nov) - bread to order. Swimming pool complex (15/5-15/9). Cafe/bar by pool (closed Nov). Large room with TV. Tennis. Fishing. Playground. Dogs are not accepted. **Off site:** Cycle tracks, nature trails, cross country skiing 8 km. Riding 5 km. Golf 2 km.

Charges 2002

Per person	€ 5.50
child (4-16 yrs)	€ 3.00
pitch	€ 4.00 - € 6.00
electricity	€ 2.10
local tax	€ 2.10 - € 2.60

Tel: 07052 935680. Fax: 07052 935681. E-mail: campingpark.bl@gmx.de. **Reservations:** Contact site (no deposit). **Open** all year.

Directions: From A8 exits 43, 44 or 45 to Pforzheim then B463 road south (25 km). From A81 exit 28 to Herrenberg then B296 to Calw and B463 to Bad Liebenzell. Site is just north of town.

Germany - South West
Freizeitcenter Oberrhein

3420 79244 Rheinmunster (Baden-Württemberg)

This large, well equipped holiday site provides much to do and is also a good base for visiting the Black Forest. To the left of reception are a touring area and a section of hardstanding for motorcaravans. The 250 touring pitches - out of 700 overall - all have electricity connections (mostly 16A, 3 pin, a few with 2 pin), and include 86 with water and drainage, but little shade. Two of the site's lakes are for swimming (with roped-off areas for toddlers) and non-powered boating (the water was very clean when we visited), the third small one is for fishing. This site is well worth considering for a holiday, especially for families with young and early teenage children. Occasional live music til late.

Facilities: Seven top quality, heated toilet buildings have free hot water and very smart fittings. Some have special rooms for families. Family washcabins to rent. Motorcaravan services. Gas supplies. Shop (1/4-31/10). Lakeside restaurant; snack bar (both 1/4-31/10). Modern play areas on sand. Small zoo. Tennis. Table tennis. Bicycle hire. Minigolf. Windsurf school. Swimming and boating lakes. Fishing (charged). **Off site:** Riding 4 km. Golf 5 km.

Charges 2002

Per pitch incl. electricity	€ 7.00 - € 9.00
adult	€ 5.00 - € 8.00
child (under 15 yrs)	€ 2.50 - € 6.00

Tel: 07227 2500. Fax: 07227 2400. E-mail: info@ freizeitcenter-oberrhein.de. **Reservations:** Made for min. 1 week with deposit and fee. **Open** all year.

Directions: Site signed from Rheinmünster, 16 km. southwest of Rastatt on B36. From north on A5/ E35-52 take exit 51 (Baden-Baden) via Hügelsheim then south onto B36; from south exit 52 (Bühl) and via Schwarzach and Rheinmünster or exit 52 to Rheinau then north on B36 to Stollhofen.

Germany - South West
Camping Aichelberg / Schwabenalb

3410 Bunzenberg 1, 73101 Aichelberg (Baden-Württemberg)

This small, pleasant and friendly municipal site is a very convenient night-stop, just off the Stuttgart-München autobahn, roughly midway between Stuttgart and Ulm, and a reasonable drive from the German border at Aachen. On the edge of a wood, the 60 shaded touring pitches on flat grass and hardstanding are not marked out but adequate space is allowed and all have electrical connections (10A). There are 90 static units and separate area for tents opposite the entrance.

Facilities: The main toilet block is well constructed and should be sufficient with free hot water for washbasins and sinks plus one private cabin. Two showers for each sex (by token) and a family washroom. Washing machine and dryer, dishwashing room. Small shop and restaurant, both all year (order bread). Bar. Playground. **Off site:** Village shops 4 km.

Charges 2002

Per person	€ 4.35
pitch	€ 5.11
electricity (plus meter)	€ 1.53

No credit cards. **Tel:** 07164 2700. Fax: 07164 2700. **Reservations:** Write to site (not necessary for overnight). **Open** all year.

Directions: Take exit 58 from autobahn A8 just to the west of Kirchheim towards Goppingen. If coming from München turn right then immediately left to site, if from Stuttgart follow signs.

Camping Adam

3415 Campingstraße 1, 77815 Bühl (Baden-Württemberg)

This very convenient lakeside site is by the A5 Karlsruhe-Basle autobahn near Baden-Baden, very easily accessed from exit 52 Bühl (also from the French autoroute A35 just northeast of Strasbourg). It is also a useful base for the Black Forest. There is a lake that is divided into separate areas for bathing or boating and windsurfing, with a long slide - the public are admitted on payment and it attracts many people on fine weekends. All the touring pitches (250 from 600 total) have electricity (10A). Those for caravans are individual ones, with some special ones near the lake with water and drainage. Tents go along the lake surrounds and there are some places with hard paved centres to eliminate wet weather problems. At very busy times, units staying overnight only may be placed close together on a lakeside area of hard-standing. The shop and restaurant/bar remain open virtually all year (not Monday or Tuesday in low season), so this is a useful site to use out of season. In general the site has a well tended look and good English is spoken by the pleasant staff.

Facilities: Two heated sanitary buildings for tourers, one rebuilt to a high standard, have mostly private cabins in the new block, hot showers on payment, facilities for babies and disabled people. Laundry and dishwashing sinks. Washing machine and dryer. Gas supplies. Motorcaravan services. Shop (1/4-31/10). Restaurant (1/3-30/10). Takeaway (1/5-31/8). Football. Volleyball. Tennis. Bowling alley and games room with terrace. Playground. Bicycle hire. Fishing. **Off site:** Riding or golf 5 km.

Charges 2003

Per person	€ 4.50 - € 6.50
child (10-16 yrs)	€ 3.00 - € 3.50
child (3-10 yrs)	€ 2.00 - € 2.50
pitch with services	€ 6.50 - € 8.00
electricity	€ 2.00

Tel: 07223 23194. **Fax:** 07223 8982. **E-mail:** webmaster@campingplatz-adam.de. **Reservations:** Write to site. **Open** all year.

Directions: Take A5/E35-52, exit 52 (Bühl), turn towards Lichtenau, go through Oberbruch and left to site. From French autoroute A35 take exits 52 or 56 onto D2 and D4 respectively then turn onto A5 as above.

Camping ADAM
D-77815 Bühl-Oberbruch
bei Baden-Baden
Tel. (0 72 23) 2 31 94 · Fax (0 72 23) 89 82

www.campingplatz-adam.de
webmaster@campingplatz-adam.de

On the edge of the Black Forest, by a clean swimming and surfing lake, only 20 minutes drive from Strasbourg and 15 minutes from Baden-Baden. The lovely surroundings guarantee to refresh you at any time of the year. +Cycling +Swimming +Surfing +Skiing +Rambling +Fishing +Health care in Baden-Baden. Exemplary sanitary facilities, for handicapped also, each pitch with electricity and waste water. New restaurant with cosy atmosphere and spacious sun terrace. Self-service shop with extensive choice. New children's playground. Beach volleyball. Football. Boccia. Tennis court. Bicycle hire. New, first-class, spacious mobile homes with 2 bedrooms, fully fitted kitchen, bathroom, separate W.C, heating, hot water, sat.-TV. *Open all year.*
Directions: Autobahn A5 Karlsruhe - Basel, exit Bühl towards Oberbruch-Moos.

Bonath Schwarzwald Camping Wolfach

3432 Schiltacher Straße 80, 77709 Wolfach-Halbmeil (Baden-Württemberg)

This brand new site, which is still being developed, is set on the side of an attractive valley in the Black Forest, set back from the road in a quiet position with a pleasant outlook. Terraced but with little shade yet, it has fairly level pitches, many with electricity (20A), water and waste water, and an area which can also be used for tents. In front of the main building is an area of hardstanding for overnight visitors, also with electricity connections. Linda and Bob, the Dutch managers are very helpful and will advise on local attractions.

Facilities: First class sanitary facilities include private cabins, large free showers including one multi-head, laundry, dishwashing, family bathrooms for hire and a kitchen, in the main building close to the entrance. It also houses reception with a small shop, the restaurant open daily all year.

Charges 2003

Per pitch	€ 4.80 - € 5.30
adult (inc. tax)	€ 5.90 - € 6.30
child (2-13 yrs)	€ 2.50 - € 3.20

Tel: 07834 859309. **Fax:** 07834 859310. **E-mail:** info@camping-online.de. **Reservations:** May be advisable for July/August. **Open** all year.

Directions: From A5 Karlsruhe - Freiburg, take exit 55 Offenburg on B33/E531 to Haslach, then on 33/294 through Hausach, soon after which left on 294 to Wolfach and on about 3 km. to Halbmeil. Site is on the left at the end of the village

Camping Hochschwarzwald

3437 Kiefer-Ortlieb, 79674 Todtnau-Muggenbrunn (Baden-Württemberg)

Hochschwarzwald is a small, peaceful, quality site in an attractive wooded valley high up in the Black Forest. This is an extremely popular area, with many summer visitors enjoying walking and cycling, but it is also ideal for winter stays, with skiing from the site. At the back of the park, as well as being able to walk in the woods, you can paddle in a flat area of the stream which tumbles town the hill and there is an attractive barbecue area with seating as well as table tennis. Of 85 marked pitches (some with shade), 50 are for tourers (all with 10A electrical connections) on level terraces of grass and gravel. There is an area at the entrance for overnight stays in high season.

Facilities: Two modern, heated sanitary buildings have good installations, with a few private cabins, a family room, a unit for the disabled, washing machine, dryer and spin dryer, plus dishwashing, inside or out. Small shop and restaurant/bar (closed Thursdays) are both closed for 2 weeks in March and November. **Off site:** Indoor pool, tennis court and ski school in Muggenbrunn. Todtnau waterfalls 3 km.

Charges 2002

Per person	€ 4,10 - € 4,60
child (2-12 jaar)	€ 2,30 - € 2,50
pitch	€ 5,10 - € 5,60
electricity per kwh.	€ 0,50
local tax	€ 0,90

Tel: 07671 1288. Fax: 07671 95190. E-mail: camping.hochschwarzwald@web.de. **Reservations:** Contact site. **Open** all year.

Directions: Site is about 1 km. beyond Muggenbrunn on the road from Todtnau towards Freiburg.

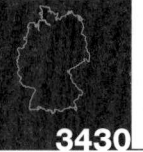

Schwarzwaldcamping Alisehof

3430 Schapbach, 77776 Bad Rippoldsau (Baden-Württemberg)

Alisehof is a pleasant site quite high up in the heart of the Black Forest, about 20 km from Freudenstadt. In an attractive, generally peaceful setting in a wooded valley (daytime noise from the adjacent saw-mill is possible) it is away from the main routes and big towns, with walks available from the site. The 180 individually numbered pitches vary in size from moderate to quite large and all have electricity (16A). Arranged in rows on terraces (the slope is only steep towards the top), 120 pitches on the lower slopes are available for tourists. In high season there is an entertainment programme for children and organised walks for adults. The friendly management speak English.

Facilities: An excellent toilet block has family cabins for hire, facilities for disabled visitors, a separate section for children and baby rooms. The original facilities in the main building are of very good quality, with a laundry, dishwashing and cooking hobs. Beauty and fitness centre. Shop (all year). Pleasant bar lounge in old farmhouse (all year except when very quiet and Mondays). Playground. Fishing. Gas supplies. Motorcaravan services. Cooking facilities. **Off site:** Schapbach (1 km). Riding 2 km. Golf 1 km.

Charges 2003

Per person	€ 5.80 - € 6.20
pitch	€ 4.80 - € 5.30
electricity (plus meter)	€ 1.60
local tax	€ 0.70

No credit cards. **Tel:** 07839 203. Fax: 07839 1263. E-mail: info@camping-online.de. **Reservations:** Write to site before 31 May, with deposit (€5,11) and fee (5,11). **Open** all year.

Directions: Site is 1 km. northeast of Schapbach, which is southwest from Freudenstadt. From A5 take Appelweier/Oberkirch exit towards Freudenstadt turning right to Schapbach.

Azur Camping Schwäbische Alb

3407 Rosencamping-Erpfingen, 72820 Sonnenbühl (Baden-Württemberg)

This is a popular, all year park for families in the summer and holiday times, but it is also pleasant for visits in the quieter periods during the rest of the year, with interesting scenery and the famous Castle Hohenzollern, the seat of the Kaisers, 30 km. away high up on a rocky promontory. Of the 450 pitches, 325 are taken by long stay units, leaving the tourers, for the most part, on an undulating field at the top of the park. This does give the best views, but can be exposed to the wind. The pitches are unmarked but there are lots of electrical connections. A quite large adventure play area is up here too. To the left of the site entrance are some more short stay pitches on gently sloping grass.

Facilities: Good quality sanitary facilities, just down from the touring area, include washbasins (some private cabins) and showers (changing space maybe a little small) and baby room. Dishwashing, cooking and laundry. Motorcaravan services. Small shop. Café/bar (not when site very quiet). Heated outdoor pool (unsupervised, unfenced). Table tennis, volleyball and outdoor chess. Animation in high season. Playground. Evangelical church in high season.

Charges 2002

Per adult	€ 4.50 - € 6.00
child (2-12 yrs)	€ 3.50 - € 4.50
pitch	€ 5.50 - € 7.50
electricity	€ 2.10

No credit cards. **Tel:** 07128 466. Fax: 07128 30137. E-mail: info@azur-camping.de. **Reservations:** For high season contact site. **Open** all year.

Directions: From B312 south from Reutlingen, go on to B313 towards Gammertingen for about 4 km. then follow signs to Erpfingen.

Ferien-Campingplatz Münstertal

3450 Dietzelbachstr. 6, 79244 Münstertal (Baden-Württemberg)

Münstertal is an impressive site pleasantly situated in a valley on the western edge of the Black Forest. It has been one of the top graded sites in Germany for 20 years, and first time visitors will soon realise why when they see the standard of the facilities here. There are 300 individual pitches in two areas, either side of the entrance road on flat gravel, their size varying from 70-100 sq.m. All have electricity (16A) and 200 have waste water drains, many also with water, TV and radio connections. The large indoor swimming pool with sauna and solarium, and the outdoor pool, are both heated and free and there is a large, grass sunbathing area. A recent addition is a health and fitness centre with a range of treatments, massages, etc. Children are very well catered for here with a play area and play equipment, tennis courts, minigolf, a games room with table tennis, table football and pool table and fishing. Riding is popular and the site has its own stables. There are 250 km. of walks, with some guided ones organised, and winter sports with cross-country skiing directly from the site (courses in winter - for children or adults and ski hire). The site becomes full in season and reservations, especially in July, are necessary.

Facilities: The three toilet blocks are of truly first class quality, with washbasins, all in cabins, showers with full glass dividers, baby bath, a unit for disabled visitors and individual bathrooms, some for hire, others for general use. Dishwashers in two blocks. Laundry with washing machines, spin and tumble dryers. Drying room. Motorcaravan services. Well stocked shop (all year). Restaurant, particularly good and well patronised (closed Nov.). Heated swimming pools, indoor all year 0730-2100, outdoor (with children's area) May-Oct. New health and fitness centre. Sauna and solarium. Bicycle hire. Tennis courses in summer. **Off site:** Village amenities near. Golf 15 km. Freiburg and Basel easy driving distances for day trips.

Charges 2002

Per person	€ 6.20 - € 7.40
child (2-10 yrs)	€ 4.10 - € 4.65
pitch	€ 9.85 - € 11.80
local tax (16 plus)	€ 0.77

No credit cards. **Tel:** 07636 7080. Fax: 07636 7448. E-mail: info@camping-muenstertal.de. **Reservations:** made without deposit. **Open** all year.

Directions: Münstertal is south of Freiburg. From A5 autobahn take exit 64, turn southeast via Bad Krozingen and Staufen and continue 5 km. to the start of Münstertal, where camp is signed from the main road on the left.

Terrassen Campingplatz Herbolzheim

3442 Im Laue, 79336 Herbolzheim (Baden-Württemberg)

the travel service
TO BOOK
Ferry   ✔
Pitch   ✔
Accommodation ✘
01892 55 98 98

This well equipped campsite is in a quiet location on a wooded slope to the north of Freiburg. It is useful as a night stop when travelling between Frankfurt and Basel, and is just 10 km. from Europa Park, only a short way from the A5 autobahn. There are 73 caravan or motorcaravan pitches for tourists plus a few for motorcyclists, all with electricity (10A) and grass surfaces, on terraces linked by hard access roads with a little shade for some. A separate meadow for tents is at the top of the site (with three cabin toilets) and some pitches are used by a tour operator. This is good walking country and with only occasional entertainment, the site makes a very pleasant place in which to relax between daily activities, the many trees, shrubs and plants giving a pleasant, peaceful atmosphere.

Facilities: The main toilet facilities are modern, with new facilities for babies and disabled visitors. Laundry and dishwashing facilities. Motorcaravan services. Bar/restaurant (Easter - 1/10 daily). Shop for basics (order bread). Table tennis. Volleyball. Football. New playground planned. Dogs are not accepted 15/7-15/8. **Off site:** Large open-air heated municipal swimming pool complex adjacent (1/4-15/9). Bicycle hire 1 km. Riding 5 km. Restaurants and shops in the village (3 km). Local market on Friday mornings.

Charges 2002

Per person	€ 5.00
child (0-15 yrs)	€ 3.00
pitch	€ 6.00 - € 8.00
tent pitch	€ 5.00
electricity	€ 1.50

Tel: 07643 1460. Fax: 07643 913382. E-mail: s.hugoschmidt@t-online.de. **Reservations:** rom A5 Frankfurt - Basel autobahn take exit 57, 58 or 59 and follow signs to Herbolzheim. Site is signed in south side of town near the swimming pool. **Open** 14 April - 3 October.

Directions: From A5 Frankfurt - Basel autobahn take exit 57, 58 or 59 and follow signs to Herbolzheim. Site is signed in south side of town near the swimming pool.

Terrassen-Camping Alte Sägemühle

3452 79295 Sulzburg (Baden-Württemberg)

By a peaceful road leading only to a natural swimming pool and an hotel, beyond the picturesque old town of Sulzburg with its narrow streets, this attractive location is perfect for those seeking peace and quiet. Set in a tree-covered valley with a stream running through the centre, the site has been kept as natural as possible. It is divided into terraced areas - tents have their own - and the 50 pitches (90% are 125 sq.m.) all have electrical connections (16A) mainly German type, although long leads may be needed. The main building by the entrance houses reception, a small shop and the sanitary facilities. Run by the Geuss family (Frau Geuss speaks reasonable English) the site has won an award from the state for having been kept natural, for example, no tarmac roads, no minigolf, no playgrounds, etc. There are opportunities for walking straight from the site into the forest, and many walks and cycle rides are shown on maps available at reception. The tiny 500 year old Jewish Cemetery reached through the site has an interesting history.

Facilities: In the main building, facilities are of good quality with two private cabins, separate toilets, dishwashing, washing machine and dryer. Small shop for basics, beer and local wines (all year). Natural, unheated swimming pool adjacent (June-Aug) free to campers. Torch may be useful. **Off site:** Restaurants and other shops in Sulzburg (1.5 km). Bicycle hire in Sulzburg. Riding 5 km. Europa Park is less than an hour away.

Charges 2003

Per person	€ 5.00
child (1-15 yrs)	€ 3.00
pitch	€ 4.00 - € 6.50
electricity (plus meter)	€ 0.50
local tax (from 16 yrs)	€ 0.50

Tel: 07634 551181. Fax: 07634 551182. **Reservations:** Advised in high season. **Open** all year.

Directions: Site is easily reached (25 minutes) from autobahn A5/E35. Take exit 64 for Bad Krozingen just south of Freiburg onto the B3 south to Heitersheim, then on through Sulzburg, or if coming from the south, exit 65 through Müllheim, Heitersheim and Sulzburg.

Camping Kirchzarten

3440 Dietenbacher Str. 17, 79199 Kirchzarten (Baden-Württemberg)

There are pleasant views of the Black Forest from this municipal site which is within easy reach by car of Titisee, Feldberg and Todtnau, and 8 km. from the large town of Freiburg in Breisgau. It is divided into 473 numbered pitches with electricity, 370 of which are for tourists (some used by tour operators). Most pitches, which are side by side on level ground, are of quite reasonable size and marked out at the corners, though there is nothing to separate them and there are some hardstanding motorcaravan pitches. From about late June to mid-August it does become full. The fine pool complex adjoining the site is free to campers and is a main attraction, with pools for diving, fun, swimming and children, surrounded by spacious sunbathing areas and a children's play area on sand. It is only a short stroll from the site to the village centre, which has supermarkets, restaurants, etc.

Facilities: The new sanitary building is a splendid addition and includes a large, central chidren's section, private cabins (some for hire), 2 dishwashing sections and a laundry room. Cooking stoves, washing machines, dryers, irons, sewing machines (all on payment by meter) are available among the other buildings. Restaurant/bar. Shop. Swimming pool complex (15/5-15/9). Large playground. Table tennis. Organised recreation programme in high season. Dogs are not accepted. **Off site:** Tennis (covered court, can be booked from site). Adventure playground, fitness track, tennis and minigolf near. Golf 3 km.

Charges 2002

Per person incl. tax	€ 5.00 - € 7.90
child (4-16 yrs)	€ 2.90 - € 4.20
third child or more	€ 1.85 - € 2.35
pitch	€ 5.30 - € 6.60
electricity	€ 1.10
unreserved pitch	€ 1.10 - € 15.40

Every 15th day free. **Tel:** 07661 9040910. Fax: 07661 61624. E-mail: info@camping-kirchzarten.de. **Reservations:** made for min. 1 week without deposit. **Open** all year.

Directions: From Freiburg take B31 road signed Donaueschingen to Kirchzarten where site is signed (it is south of the village).

CAMPING KIRCHZARTEN

A site in the southern Black Forest with every comfort for wonderful holidays. New heated outdoor swimming pool complex. Kurhaus with restaurant and reading room nearby. Riding, tennis, minigolf, children's playground in the wood. Fine walking country. Caravans for hire.

Terrassen-Camping Sandbank

3435 Seerundweg, 79822 Titisee (Baden-Württemberg)

This is a pleasant site overlooking Lake Titisee in this lovely area of the Black Forest. There are 190 marked pitches for tourists, with electricity (16A) and on gravel terraces with good views over the lake. Trees provide good shade in some parts. The small town of Titisee is a 20 minute walk along the lakeside and with the attractions of this part of the Forest near - Freiburg, the Rhine Falls at Schaffhausen, the source of the Danube at Donaueschingen, Basle in Switzerland - it is ideal for a long or short stay. Access to the lake is possible for swimming, boating and carp fishing. Walks are organised and there is some music in high season. Reception staff are friendly and English is spoken.

Facilities: The large, heated toilet block provides many washbasins in cabins, hot showers on payment, baby room (key from management) and facilities for disabled people. Washing machines and dryer. Motorcaravan services. Gas supplies. Shop. Pleasant lakeside bar/restaurant with terrace, also providing takeaway food. Playground. Bicycle hire. Fishing. Organised walks. Lake swimming. Boat excursions from Titisee. Music in season. Motorcycles are not accepted.

Charges 2003

Per person	€ 3.40 - € 4.40
child	€ 2.30 - € 2.60
pitch	€ 5.10 - € 6.70
electricity	€ 1.30
local tax	€ 1.00

Tel: 07651 8243. Fax: 07651 8286. E-mail: info@camping-sandbank.com. **Reservations:** Not made. **Open** 28 March - 20 October.

Directions: From Freiburg take road 31 to Titisee. From the centre follow camping signs then signs for Bankenhof, continuing on less well made up road past this site to Sandbank.

Camping Belchenblick

3445 Münstertäler Straße 43, 79219 Staufen (Baden-Württemberg)

the travel service
TO BOOK
Ferry ✓
Pitch ✓
Accommodation ✗
01892 55 98 98

The quality site stands at the gateway, so to speak, to the Black Forest. Not very high up itself, it is just at the start of the long road climb which leads to the top of Belchen, one of the highest summits of the forest. It is well situated for excursions by car to the best areas of the forest, for example the Feldberg-Titisee-Höllental circuit, and many excellent walks are possible nearby. Staufen is a pleasant little place with character. The site has 210 pitches (180 for touring units) with many electrical connections (10-15A), and 50 pitches have TV, water and waste water connections. On site is a small heated indoor pool and adjacent is a municipal sports complex, including an open-air pool and tennis courts. Reservation is necessary from early June to late August at this popular site, which is not cheap. However, charges do include hot water and the pool. A tractor will site your caravan if required.

Facilities: Three high quality sanitary blocks are heated and have free hot water, individual wash-basins (6 in private cabins), plus 21 family cabins with WC, basin and shower (some on payment per night for exclusive use). Washing machine. Gas supplies. Motorcaravan services. Shop (1/5-31/10). Bar (all year). Snacks (1/5-31/10). Indoor and outdoor pools. Sauna and solarium. Tennis. Play area with barbecue section. Volleyball. Basketball. Skating. Hockey and football fields. Bicycle hire. **Off site:** Restaurant near. Fishing 500 m. Riding 2 km.

Charges 2002

Per person	€ 6.00 - € 7.50
child (2-12 yrs)	€ 4.00
pitch	€ 8.00
electricity (p/kw per hour)	€ 0.60
water connection	€ 0.50
local tax	€ 0.62 - € 0.77

Tel: 07633 7045. Fax: 07633 7908. E-mail: camping.belchenblick@t-online.de. **Reservations:** made without charge. **Open** all year.

Directions: Take autobahn exit for Bad Krozingen, south of Freiburg, and continue to Staufen. Site is southeast of the town and signed, across an unmanned local railway crossing near the entrance.

Campingplatz Belchenblick
D-79219 Staufen i. Br.
Telephone 07633-7045
Telefax 07633-7908
Internet: www.camping-belchenblick.de
E-Mail: camping.belchenblick@t-online.de

- modern sanitary facilities (also for disabled)
- indoor- and outdoor pool
- sauna • solarium • tennis
- children's playground
- TV- and water connection at the pitches • shop
- guided tours and footwalks
- excursions
- physio-therapy

Kur- und Feriencamping Badenweiler

3454 Weilertalstrasse 73, 79410 Badenweiler (Baden-Württemberg)

Badenweiler is a very pretty village on the edge of the southern Black Forest, easily accessed from the A5 or B3, but far enough from them to be peaceful. This campsite is on a hillside close to the village, with pleasant views, and is owned and run by the Wiesler family, with a little English spoken. Reception is part of a building which also houses a bar/café, opening hours as for reception, with take-away snacks in the evenings in high season, basic supplies and a downstairs children's room. There are four terraces with 100 large, individual grass pitches, 90 for touring and all with electricity (16A), water and waste water connections. The municipal heated outdoor pool, 200 m. away, is free for campers.

Facilities: Top quality sanitary facilities are contained in two fully tiled buildings, one with toilets (soap and paper towels) and the other with free, controllable hot showers with full glass dividers and washbasins (cabins and vanity style). Family washrooms, facilities for babies and disabled visitors. Washing machines and dryers. Motorcaravan services. Gas supplies. Shop for basics. Play area and play room. **Off site:** Shop 300 m. Restaurants 200 m. Golf 12 km.

Charges 2003

Per person	€ 5.90
child (under 15 yrs)	€ 3.50 - € 5.10
pitch	€ 8.00 - € 8.50
electricity (per kwh)	€ 0.40
local tax	€ 1.28 - € 1.79

No credit cards. **Tel:** (0)7632 1550. Fax: (0)7632 5268. E-mail: camping.badenweiler@t-online.de. **Reservations:** Highly recommended throughout the summer. **Open** all year except 15 Dec - 15 Jan.

Directions: From the A5 about midway between Freiburg and Basel take exit 65 onto the B378 to Müllheim, then onto the L131 signed to Badenweiler-Ost from where the site is well signed.

Gugel's Dreiländer Camping

Oberer Wald 3, 79395 Neuenburg (Baden-Württemberg)

3455

Neuenburg is ideally placed not only for enjoying and exploring the south of the Black Forest, but also for night stops when travelling from Frankfurt to Basel on the A5 autobahn. Set in natural heath and woodland, Gugel's is an attractive site where the permanent caravans, away from the tourist area, with their well-tended gardens, enhance rather than detract from the natural beauty. There are 220 places for tourists either in small clearings in the tall trees which cover the site, in open areas or on hardstanding section used for single night stays. All have electricity connections (6A), and there are now individual pitches, including one group of 30 with electricity, water, waste water and satellite TV connections. Opposite the entrance is a meadow where late arrivals and those who wish to depart before 7 am. may spend the night. A social room has been added with satellite TV where guests are welcomed with a glass of wine and a slide presentation of the attractions of the area. The Rhine is within walking distance. There may be some road noise near the entrance. The site may become very busy in high season but you should always find room. In general there is a good atmosphere and it can be recommended for both short and long stays.

Facilities: Three good quality heated sanitary blocks include some washbasins in cabins, one baby room and one for disabled visitors. Washing machines and dryers. Motorcaravan services. Enlarged shop (all year). Excellent restaurant, popular with both campers and non-residents (open all year). Indoor pools (all year). Boules. Tennis courts with racquet and ball hire. Fishing. Minigolf. Table tennis. Chess. Barbecue. Bicycle hire. Community room with TV. Activity programme with organised walks, excursions, etc. and sports and competitions for children (high season). Large, new play area and another with electric cars and motorcycles (on payment). **Off site:** Golf 5 km. Riding 1.5 km. Neuenburg, Breisach, Freiburg and Basel are just some of the interesting places to visit as well as the Black Forest.

Charges 2002

Per person	€ 5.75
child (2-15 yrs)	€ 2.90
caravan or tent	€ 5.20
small tent	€ 3.50
car	€ 4.00
motorcaravan	€ 5.20 - € 8.40
electricity	€ 2.00

Discount every 10th night, persons free. No credit cards. **Tel:** 07631 7719. Fax: 07635 3393. E-mail: info@camping-gugel.de. **Reservations:** Made for min 2 weeks in July/Aug. with deposit. Write specifying tent or caravan. **Open** all year.

Directions: From autobahn A5 take Neuenburg exit, turn left at traffic lights, left at next junction and follow signs for 2 km. to site (called 'Neuenburg' on most signs).

FKK-Naturist Camping Drei-Länder-Eck

N3457 Steinenstadt, 79395 Neuenburg (Baden-Württemberg)

Established in 1919, Drei-Länder-Eck is the largest privately owned naturist site in Germany. Close to both the Black Forest and the Rhine, it offers a base allowing the opportunity to explore in three countries, Germany, Switzerland and France. It also offers facilities and amenities to the highest of standards. Throughout the well-maintained grounds, many different deciduous and pine trees create a degree of shade and home for a variety of wildlife. Three specifically designated, separate areas within the park provide visitors with 120 level pitches of average size each with 16A hook-up, some with hardstanding for both unit and awning with each pitch fronted by a grassed area for sunbathing. The other camping areas are mainly grass although some pitches almost equate to a hardstanding. All are made welcome at reception where you receive both a warm welcome (English spoken) and an information pack. Single men require membership of the International Naturist Federation. Opening for 2002, is a large 'natural' swimming pool complex for all ages and a fitness centre. The children's play area is built on the lines of a huge galleon to theme park standards. Between 13.00-15.00 hrs the site closes and it is deemed a quiet period and during these times, sports, play areas and the banging in of pegs come to a halt. Do remember this is a naturist site.

Facilities: Two heated, modern, fully tiled sanitary blocks are fully equipped. Dishwashing. Washing machine and dryer. Mother and baby room. Full facilities for disabled people. Sauna, solarium, relaxation room, manicure, pedicure, massage and hairdresser. Small shop. Bar. Restaurant with canopied terrace. Outdoor chess. Basement for young people. Children's play area. Animation programme in high season. Badminton, boule, archery, football, tennis, volleyball and table tennis. Naturist jogging and cycle track. **Off site:** Small supermarket at Steinenstadt (15 minute walk)

Charges guide

Per person	€ 5.11
child (5-15 yrs)	€ 3.07
caravan or tent	€ 5.11
car	€ 1.79
motorcaravan	€ 7.16
electricity	€ 1.53

Tel: 07635 9576. Fax: 07635 2600. E-mail: fkkdle@ aol.com. **Reservations:** Contact site. **Open** 1 March - 1 October.

Directions: From road 3, 7 km. south of Mullheim take exit for Bad Bellingen and Steinenstadt (Penny Markt supermarket). Follow signs for Steinenstadt. Turn left before bridge and at crossroads straight ahead to site (signed).

Camping Wirthshof

3465 Steibensteg 12, 88677 Markdorf (Baden-Württemberg)

Lying 7 km. back from the Bodensee, 12 km. from Friedrichshafen, this friendly site with good facilities could well be of interest to Britons with young children. The 324 individual touring pitches have electrical connections (10A) and are of about 80 sq.m. on well tended flat grass, adjoining access roads. There are some larger pitches with water, waste water and electricity. No dogs are accepted in July/Aug. and there is a special section for campers with dogs at other times. On site is a pleasant heated outdoor pool with a grassy lying-out area; it is free to campers but is also open to outsiders on payment so can be busy in season. Many activities are organised for children and adults over a long season.

Facilities: The three heated toilet blocks provide washbasins in cubicles, a unit for disabled people and a children's bathroom. Solar heated unit for dishwashing and laundry. Gas supplies. Motorcaravan services. Shop. Restaurant/bar. Swimming pool (25 x 12.5 m; open 10/5-10/9). Sports field with goal posts. Adventure playground. Bicycle hire. Normal minigolf; also 'pit-pat', played at table height with billiard cues. Activity programme. Dogs not accepted July/Aug. **Off site:** Tennis near. Riding 8 km. Golf and fishing 10 km.

Charges 2003

Per person	€ 5.50
child (1-14 yrs)	€ 4.50
pitch incl. electricity	€ 10.50
serviced pitch incl. electricity	€ 13.00

No credit cards. **Tel:** 07544 2325. Fax: 07544 3982. **Reservations:** made with deposit and fee. **Open** 15 March - 30 October.

Directions: Site is on eastern edge of Markdorf, turn south off B33 Ravensburg road. The site is signed (but not named) from Markdorf.

Germany - South West
Isnycamping

3467 Lohbauerstr. 59-69, 88316 Isny (Baden-Württemberg)

Isny is a delightful spot for families and for others looking for a peaceful stay in a very well-managed environment. The site has been developed to a high standard by the former owner of Donau-Lech (3630) and lies just south of the village, in a wood by a lake. Leading down from reception, with the lake to your left, you come to an open area of individual 100 sq.m. hardstanding pitches (just beyond the toilet block), with a circular access road. To the left is a woodland section for tents and other units wanting shade. A café with light snacks during the week and meals at the week-ends is open long hours in high season. It has a terrace that overlooks the lake, which is used for swimming (unsupervised) daily until early evening, and was pleasantly warm when we swam in it.

Facilities: The sanitary unit (deposit required for the key) is new and first class, and is cleaned a minimum of 5 times a day. It has private cabins as well as vanity style washbasins, large controllable showers, with full curtain, token operated. Good unit for disabled visitors. Dishwashing room. Laundry is in the ladies' section of the building by the entrance. Motorcaravan service point. Café/bar. Reception keeps a few basic supplies. Bicycles to borrow. **Off site:** Restaurant and supermarket 1.5 km.

Charges 2002

Per adult	€ 5.00
child per year of age	€ 0.30
pitch	€ 7.00
electricity per kw	€ 0.50
rubbish tax	€ 0.36

Tel: (0)7562 2389. Fax: (0)7562 2004. **Reservations:** Contact site. **Open** all year except November and December.

Directions: From the B12 between Lindau and Kempten, turn south at sign in Isny and follow signs up into the woods.

Germany - South East
Bavaria Sport Camping Park

3725 Grafenauerstraße 31, 94535 Eging am See (Bavaria (S))

Eging is a Kurbad village of the type found in many parts of Germany where warm and cold water baths are used in a variety of treatments. It is located in the southwest tip of the Bavarian Forest, in good walking country and occupies an open hilltop position amidst rolling forest countryside on slightly sloping ground about 600 m. from the small lake, treatment and sports centre. Mainly level numbered pitches on terraces of grass or fine gravel are divided by bushes and saplings on either side of tarmac roads (but with little or no shade). Water and electricity points are widely spaced (long cables may be needed).

Facilities: The single sanitary block is of good quality with some private cabins. Facilities for disabled people are provided. Bar/Restaurant (May to October). Small shop by reception. Flipper, table football and computer games. Play area. **Off site:** Apart from the Kur facilities, there are opportunities for a wide variety of sports nearby - swimming, tennis, curling, fishing, walking and winter sports.

Charges 2002

Per unit incl electricity	€ 3.90 - € 4.50
person	€ 5.10 - € 7.50
local tax (over 16 yrs)	€ 0.50

Tel: 08544/8089. Fax: 08544/7964. **Reservations:** Write to site. **Open** all year.

Directions: Take exit 113 (Garham) from A3 Regensburg - Passau autobahn. Pass turn to Eging, continuing to main road and turn right, then almost immediately left. Cross level crossing and site is on left by hotel. Site is also signed in Eging.

Germany - South East
Azur Ferienzentrum Zwiesel

3710 94227 Zwiesel (Bavaria (S))

Bayerischerwald is a large site on the edge of town with views to the hills and a stream running through it. Pleasantly situated nearly 2,000 feet up (it can be cool at night) on a slight slope, there are around 500 pitches, just under 400 of which are individual numbered ones for tourers, but there is not much shade. There are various areas, with motorhomes taken on a flat open, grassy section, whilst for caravans there are some flat and many sloping or undulating pitches, all with electricity and water points along the central road. One side of the park is for dog owners and there is an overnight area of hardstanding just outside. The site is also open for winter camping, with ski-lifts quite near.

Facilities: The two tiled sanitary blocks (one part modernised) have some private cabins. Facilities for the disabled. Baby room. Launderette. Bread orders at reception. Pleasant restaurant/bar (closed Nov). Badminton/basketball area. Open air chess, table-tennis, small football area, hopscotch. **Off site:** Large swimming pool complex next door, open June-Sept. and an indoor pool (all are free for campers).

Charges 2002

Per adult	€ 4.50 - € 6.00
child (2-12 yrs)	€ 3.50 - € 4.50
pitch	€ 5.50 - € 7.50
electricity	€ 2.10

Tel: 09922 802 595. Fax: 09922 802 594. E-mail: info@azur-camping.de. **Reservations:** write to site. **Open** all year.

Directions: Site is on north side of Zwiesel. From autobahn A3 Regensburg-Passau, take Deggendorf exit and then B11 to Zwiesel. Take Zwiesel Nord exit and follow Azur signs.

Camping Gitzenweiler Hof

3650 Gitzenweiler 88, 88131 Lindau-Oberreitnau (Bavaria (S))

Gitzenweiler Hof has been developed into a really well-equipped, first-class site for a family holiday. In a country setting it has about 350 permanent caravans as well as about 350 places for touring units (it is advisable to book for July/Aug). In the tourist section many pitches are without markings with siting left to campers, the others in rows between access roads. There are 350 electricity connections (6A) and 39 pitches for motorcaravans with water, drainage, telephone and TV connections. A large open-air swimming pool has attractive surrounds with seats (free for campers). Lindau is an interesting town, especially by the harbour, and possible excursions include the whole of the Bodensee (Lake Constance), the German Alpine Road, the Austrian Vorarlberg and Switzerland. This is a pleasant, friendly, well-run site with a separate area just outside for overnight stops.

Facilities: The toilet blocks have been beautifully renovated and include some washbasins in cabins, a children's bathroom and baby bath, plus a dog shower. Washing machines, dryers and dishwasher. Motorcaravan services. Shop (limited hours in low season). Two restaurants (closed Feb). Large swimming pool in summer (33 x 25 m). Volleyball. Playground and play room with entertainment in summer. Organised activities for adults and children all year. Hens, rabbits, ducks and ponies for the children. Ground for football, etc. Free fishing in lake. Table tennis. Minigolf. Club room. Doctor comes if needed; hospital near. American motorhomes accepted up to 10 tons.

Charges 2002

Per person	€ 6.00
child (3-9 yrs)	€ 2.00
pitch	€ 8.00 - € 14.00
tent pitch	€ 5.00 - € 8.00
electricity	€ 2.00
local tax	€ 0.30 - € 0.60

Discounts for stays over 14 days and in low season. Overnight hardstanding with electricity outside site barrier € 12,00 plus tax. **Tel:** 08382 94940. Fax: 08382 949415. E-mail: info@gitzenweiler-hof.de. **Reservations:** made with deposit (€103). **Open** all year.

Directions: Site is signed from the B12 about 4 km. north of Lindau. Also from A96 exit 3 (Weißensberg), and from in and around Lindau.

Familien Sport Gemeinschaft Allgäu

N3655 Haldenmühle 1, 87463 Dietmannsried (Bavaria (S))

The majority of naturist camping facilities for visitors to Germany are at grounds owned and run by clubs. Haldenmühle is one such long established club with extremely good facilities. (single men are not allowed). On the approach, with the Alps behind you, the rolling countryside is quite open, yet a small pine forest surrounds the 13 ha. site providing the necessary privacy for a naturist environment. A tarmac road descendsquite steeply into an attractive setting where you will immediately see a typical alpine style building housing some of the facilities and a miniature in respect of the sites origin, a water wheel. The majority of the grassed pitches are level and in the open. Several near the fast flowing river Iller are suitable for canoe enthusiasts (not recommended for swimming). Although there are places for some 50 units, only 30 can have electricity (16A). The mill pond, dating back to 1632 has been transformed into a well-constructed swimming pool complete with diving board and plate sized fish. Being at the bottom of a steep valley, mobile phone reception can be extremely poor but a public phone is available. The site is within distance of such sites as Kempten (oldest recorded city in Germany), Lake Constance, the Alps and the fairy tale castle of Neuschwanstein. Help is available in siting or exiting with your unit.

Facilities: The fully tiled modern sanitary unit has free hot communal showers. Dishwashing. Washing machine and dryer. Solarium, relaxation area and large sauna. All water on site originiates from a spring and exceeds the necessary standards for drinking, including the pool. Bar and restaurant. Small shop. Large function hall. Swimming pool. Comprehensive play area and animation in high season. Badminton, volleyball, football, and boule.

Charges 2003

Per unit	€ 4.50
adult with FKK card	€ 4.00
adult without FKK card	€ 5.50
electricity	€ 1.50

Tel: 08374 5991. Fax: 08374 586610. **Reservations:** Contact site. **Open** all year.

Directions: Exit A7 (Memming-Kempten) for Dietmannsried. After a short distance travelling west toward Leutkirch turn right to Reicholzried. After church, take second turn left (Schmiedstrasse) signed Kiesels and Haudenmühle. Follow Haldenmühle signs.

Camping Hopfensee

3670 Hopfen am See, 87629 Füssen im Königswinkel (Bavaria (S))

Hopfensee is a high class site with excellent facilities, catering for discerning visitors, by a lake. It is well placed to explore the very attractive Bavarian Alpine region which, along with the architecture and historical interest of the Royal Castles at Hohenswangau and the Baroque church at Wies, makes it a very popular holiday area.The 377 tourist pitches for caravans and motorhomes, most with shade, each have 16A electricity, water, drain and cable TV connections. They are marked, numbered and of a good size. At the centre of the site is a large building with an open village-like square in the middle, adorned with cascading flowers. It houses the exceptional sanitary facilities and, on the upper floors, a swimming pool, treatment and physiotherapy suites, fitness centre, cinema and children's play room. There is direct access to the lake for sailing, canoeing etc. and a place for parking boats. Charges are high, but include the pool, super sports building, cinema, etc. Tents are not accepted.

Facilities: The exceptionally good, heated sanitary facilities provide British style WCs, free hot water in washbasins (some in cabins), large showers and sinks, laundry and washing-up rooms, as well as baby and children's wash rooms. Some private units are for hire. Motorcaravan services. Restaurant with terrace faces across the lake towards the setting sun. Bar. Shop. Indoor pool and fitness centre. Supervised courses of remedial water treatments, massage, etc. Sauna, solarium and steam bath. Children's playground and kindergarten. Large games room with table tennis, pool, etc. Bicycle hire. Tennis. Table tennis. Fishing. Ski school in winter. No tents taken. **Off site:** Riding 1 km.

Charges 2002

Per person	€ 7.00 - € 8.00
child (2-12 yrs)	€ 4.25 - € 5.00
12-18 yrs	€ 5.50 - € 7.50
pitch with cable TV, electricity	€ 10.50 - € 11.50
local tax (over 18)	€ 1.23

No credit cards. **Tel:** 08362 917710. Fax: 08362 917720. E-mail: info@camping-hopfensee.com. **Reservations:** made without deposit; min. 14 days 16 June - 1 Sept (unless shorter time fits into charts). **Open** all year except 4 Nov - 16 Dec.

Directions: Site is 4 km. north of Füssen. Turn off B16 to Hopfen and site is on the left through a car park. If approaching from the west on B310, turn towards Füssen at T-junction with the B16 and immediately turn right again for the road to Hopfen.

Alpen-Caravanpark Tennsee

3680 82493 Krün / Obb (Bavaria (S))

Tennsee is an excellent site in beautiful surroundings high up (1,000 m.) in the Karwendel Alps with super mountain views, and close to many famous places of which Innsbruck (44 km) and Oberammergau (26 km) are two. Mountain walks are plentiful, with several lifts close by. It is an attractive site with good facilities including 139 serviced pitches with individual connections for electricity (up to 16A), gas, TV, radio, telephone, water and waste water. The other 111 pitches all have electricity and some of these are available for overnight guests at a reduced rate. Reception and restaurants, bar, cellar youth room and a well stocked shop are all housed in attractive buildings. Many activities and excursions are organised to local attractions by the Zick family, who run the site in a friendly and efficient manner.

Facilities: The first class sanitary block has underfloor heating, washbasins in cabins and private units with WC, shower, basin and bidet for rent. Unit for disabled people with the latest in flushing and warm air drying. Baby bath, dog bathroom and a heated room for ski equipment (with lockers). Washing machines, free dryers and irons. Gas supplies. Motorcaravan services. Cooking facilities. Shop. Restaurants with takeaway (waiter, self service and takeaway). Bar. Youth room with table tennis, amusements. Solarium. Bicycle hire. Playground. Organised activities and excursions. Bus service to ski slopes in winter. **Off site:** Fishing 400 m. Riding or golf 3 km.

Charges 2003

Per person	€ 7.00 - € 7.50
1-3 children (3-15 yrs)	€ 3.50 - € 5.00
other children	€ 3.50
pitch	€ 8.00 - € 12.50
local tax	€ 1.10
waste tax	€ 0.50
family motorcaravan overnight rate on certain pitches	€ 12.50 - € 17.50
Easter family package	€ 21.00

Senior citizens special rates (not winter). **Tel:** 08825 170. Fax: 08825 17236. E-mail: info@camping-tennsee.de. **Reservations:** Advised for July - Sept and Xmas and made for exact dates (no fee). **Open** all year except 8 Nov - 15 Dec.

Directions: Site is just off main Garmisch-Partenkirchen/Innsbruck road number 2 between Klais and Krün, 15 km. from Garmisch, (watch for small sign `Tennsee + Barmersee').

Germany - South East
Terrassencamping am Richterbichl

3675 82401 Rottenbuch / Ammer (Bavaria (S))

This friendly little site, beside the main B23 Garmisch-Augsburg road, has all the features required of a good transit site. About 110 pitches (40 for permanent units and 70 for tourists) are on flat terraces in rows on either side of access roads. They are not marked out but a minimum of 80 sq.m. is allowed per unit and there are electrical connections (10A) in all parts. There could possibly be some road noise. A little lake (quite deep with a small shallow area) beside the site can be used for swimming or boating with inflatables.

Facilities: The toilet block is underneath the main building and is heated. It is satisfactory and provides washbasins, four in cabins and showers on payment. Washing machine and dryer. Motorcaravan services. Gas supplies. Shop (basics kept, bread to order). Bar with breakfast (all year). TV. Games room. Playground. Bicycle hire. **Off site:** Shops and restaurants 5 minutes walk. Fishing 4 km. Riding 5 km.

Charges 2003

Per person	€ 4.10 - € 4.60
child (3-16 yrs)	€ 2.30 - € 2.60
pitch	€ 4.70 - € 5.20
electricity (plus meter)	€ 1.00
local tax	€ 0.50

Tel: 08867 1500. Fax: 08867 8300. E-mail: christof.echtler@t-online.de. **Reservations:** made for any period without deposit. **Open** all year.

Directions: Site is beside the B23 road on south side of Rottenbuch (12 km. south of Schongau).

Germany - South East
Camping Brunnen

3665 Seestraße 81, 87645 Schwangau-Brunnen (Bavaria (S))

Quietly situated - but very busy in high season - this lakeside site with mountain views is a useful base for excursions, with Füssen and the famous castles of Neuschwanstein and Hohenschwangau close by. Right by the Forggensee, with a beach and jetty (the water level of the reservoir can vary), it is on slightly undulating ground. The 300 pitches (230 for touring units) are all individual ones with some terracing, most have hardstanding and are from 60-120 sq.m, with 16A electrical connections (long leads may be necessary), and there is a separate meadow for tents in summer.

Facilities: Excellent toilet facilities are on different floors in a modern, heated building, with several washrooms and toilet rooms (only some opened in low season). Half the washbasins are in private cabins. Free hairdryers. Some bathrooms for hire. Facilities for disabled visitors. Baby bathroom and good children's room. Washing machines and dryers. Drying room. Cooking facilities. Dishwasher. Gas supplies. Motorcaravan services. Small shop. Restaurant with good value meals. Playground. Games and TV room. Sports field. Fishing. Bicycle hire. Riding. **Off site:** Golf 2 km.

Charges 2003

Per person incl. tax	€ 6.00 - € 7.00
child (2-15 yrs)	€ 3.00 - € 5.00
pitch	€ 5.00 - € 6.00
electricity (1 night charge)	€ 1.50

Tel: 08362 8273. Fax: 08362 8630. E-mail: info@ camping-brunnen.de. **Reservations:** made for winter only, not summer, so arrive early especially when the weather is good. **Open** all year excl. Nov - 20 Dec.

Directions: At Schwangau, 3 km. northeast of Füssen on no. 17 Munich road, turn off at crossroads at the eastern end of the village, by the Spar shop, where there are signs to Brunnen and site.

Germany - South East
Camping Allweglehen

3685 83471 Berchtesgaden (Bavaria (S))

Berchtesgaden is a National Park with magnificent scenery, in an area of mountains, lakes, castles and churches. Hitler built his 'Eagles Nest' on top of the Kehlstein, which is visible from the site and open to the public (bus service, no cars). This all year site occupies a hillside position, with spectacular mountain views. The site access road is steep (14%), particularly at the entrance, but the proprietor will use his tractor to tow caravans. There are 180 pitches (160 for touring), arranged on a series of gravel terraces, all with good views and electricity(16A). The pleasant restaurant, with terrace, offers Bavarian specialities at reasonable prices. This is a splendid base for sightseeing or relaxing.

Facilities: Two adjacent toilet blocks near the restaurant can be heated. Washing machines, dryers and iron. Motorcaravan services. Gas supplies. Restaurant. Kiosk for essentials. Play area. Small heated pool (small charge, 15/5-15/10). Solarium. Minigolf. Table tennis. Fishing. Excursions. Dogs are not accepted. **Off site:** Riding 2 km. Golf 5 km.

Charges 2002

Per pitch	€ 6.14
person	€ 4.35
electricity (per kw)	0.46
local taxes	1.79

Tel: 08652 2396. Fax: 08562 63503. **Reservations:** Write to site (in German!). **Open** all year.

Directions: Easiest is via the Austrian autobahn A10 (vignette necessary) Salzburg Sud exit and the B305 towards Berchtesgaden. Or the B305 from Ruhpolding (the pretty but winding with 3.1 m. height limit), or the B20 from Bad Reichenhall. Site is 4 km. northeast of Berchtesgaden.

Panorama Camping Harras

3688 Harrasser Strasse 135, 83209 Prien am Chiemsee (Bavaria (S))

Panorama Harras is a popular, friendly site on a small wooded peninsula by the Chiemsee, with good views to the mountains across the lake. Sailing and windsurfing are very popular here and you can swim from the shingle beach. It is also a useful base for exploring this attractive area, with boat trips to the `Herrenchiemsee` island with its castle, cycle trips and mountains to walk in. Pitches vary between 60 and 100 sq.m. (some available by the lake) with a separate, all numbered section of gravel hardstanding for motorhomes, and an area for tents also on gravelly grass. Most have electricty (6A), and 80 numbered pitches are marked by trees, which give some shade, but with no hedges, it can give a crowded look if full.

Facilities: Good quality sanitary facilities include family shower rooms with washbasin and toilet (no paper). Showers need a token. Baby room, launderette, inside dishwashing and a good unit for disabled people. Well stocked shop. Restaurant with bar and takeaway (all open for the whole season). **Off site:** Boat trips on the lake. Automobile museum 20 km.

Charges 2002

Per person	€ 4.90
child (under 14 yrs)	€ 3.20
per unit	€ 4.90
tent	€ 3.00
electricity	€ 1.80
local tax	€ 0.20 - 0.60

Surcharge 15% for stays of less than 4 nights. **Tel:** 08051 90460. Fax: 08051 904616. E-mail: info@camping-harras.de. **Reservations:** Contact site. **Open** 28 April - 31 October.

Directions The Chiemsee is north of the A8 (E52,E60) between Munich and Salzburg. Take exit 106 north towards Prien and turn towards Harras in approx. 2.5 km. Follow signs for another 2 km.

★ ★ ★ ★
An idyllic holiday by the lake

New: luxury sanitary facilities

Panorama-Camping Harras • 83209 Prien / Chiemsee • 0049-8051/9046-0 • Fax -16
Internet: http://www.camping-harras.de • E-Mail: info@camping-harras.de

Camping Wagnerhof

3690 Campingstraße 11, 83346 Bergen (Bavaria (S))

Bergen is a pretty little village 3 km. south of the A8 München - Salzburg and about 10 km. from the Chiemsee, Germany`s largest lake. Wagnerhof is a well organised and very pleasant site with a good variety of trees, plants and shrubs in a quiet location on the edge of Bergen and with views of the hills and mountains which surround this area. The site is owned and run by two brothers, one of whom speaks good English. Most of the 140 tourist pitches have some shade and are part hardstanding, part grass, all have 16A electricity and are separated by hedges. With no organised entertainment, this is an ideal site for those who find this intrusive, but it can make a good night stop between Munich and Salzburg and you may well be tempted to stay longer and explore the Chiemsee, Bavarian mountains, Salzburg - or just relax!

Facilities: Two first-class sanitary blocks, the larger in the centre of the site and the other by reception, provide some washbasins in cabins and are heated in cool weather. Washing machine, dryer, drying room, cooking facilities. Small shop (May - Oct). General room where drinks are served. Swimming pool adjacent (May - Sept). Tennis. Playground. **Off site:** Bicycle hire 1 km. Fishing 8 km. Village a short stroll.

Charges 2002

Per person	€ 4.00 - € 5.00
child (under 14 yrs)	€ 2.50 - € 3.00
pitch	€ 5.00 - € 6.50
electricity - 1 night stay	€ 2.00
local taxes	€ 1.20 - 1.55

No credit cards. **Tel:** 08662 8557. Fax: 08662 5924. E-mail: info@camping-bergen.de. **Reservations:** made with deposit. **Open** all year.

Directions: From A8 autobahn take exit 110 for Bergen, follow signs to village and the camp is signed and on your right on the edge of Bergen.

Camping Municipal München-Thalkirchen

3640 Zentralländstraße 49, 81379 München (Bavaria (S))

Now under new management, this well cared for municipal site is pleasantly and quietly situated on the southern side of Munich in parkland formed by the River Isar conservation area, 4 km. from the city centre (there are subway and bus links) and tall trees offer shade in parts. The large city of Munich has much to offer and the Thalkirchen site becomes quite crowded during the season, There are 550 pitches (150 for caravans, most with 10A electricity, water and waste water shared; 100 for motorcaravans, mostly with electricity and a small area of hardstanding) of various sizes (some quite small), marked by metal or wooden posts and rails. Like many city sites, groups are put in one area. and American motorhomes are accepted. The site is very busy (and probably noisy) during the Beer Festival (14 Sept - 5 Oct), but is well maintained and kept clean.

Facilities: There are five refurbished toilet blocks, two of which can be heated, with seatless toilets, washbasins with shelf, mirror and cold water. Hot water for showers and sinks is on payment. Facilities for disabled people. Shop (7 am - 8.30 pm). Snack bar with covered terrace (7 am - 10 pm), Drinks machine incl. Beer. General room with TV pool and games. Good small children's playground. Tourist information, souvenirs and other services. Treatment room. Washing machines and dryers. Maximum stay 14 days. Bikes for hire. Dormitory accommodation for groups (schools, scouts and guides etc.) Office hours 7 am - 11 pm. **Off site:** Pleasant walks may be taken in the adjacent park and the world famous Munich zoo is just 15 minutes walk along the river from the site. Restaurant 200 m.

Charges 2002

Per person	€ 4.40
child (2-14 yrs)	€ 1.30
tent (acc. to size)	€ 2.80 - € 3.60
car	€ 4.30
motorcycle	€ 2.00
caravan incl. car	€ 9.70
motorcaravan (acc. to size)	€ 5.60 - € 6.70
electricity	€ 1.80
Bier fest surcharge	€ 3.60

Credit cards only accepted for souvenirs. **Tel:** 089 7231707. Fax: 089 7243177. **Reservations:** Not made except for groups - said to be room up to 4 pm. daily. **Open** 15 March - end October.

Directions: From autobahns follow 'Mittel' ringroad to SSE of the city centre where site is signed; also follow signs for Thalkirchen or the Zoo and site is close. Well signed now from all over the City.

Camping Donau-Lech

3630 Campingweg 1, 86698 Eggelstetten (Bavaria (S))

the travel service
TO BOOK

Ferry	✓
Pitch	✓
Accommodation	✗

01892 55 98 98

The Haas family have developed this friendly site just off the 'Romantische Strasse' well and run it very much as a family site, providing a useful information sheet in English. The lake provides swimming and wildlife for children and adults to enjoy. Alongside it are 50 marked touring pitches with 16A electricity, on flat grass arranged in rows either side of a tarred access road. With an average of 120 sq.m. per unit, it is a comfortable site with an open feeling and developing shade. There are three separate pleasant, flat, grass areas near the entrance for people with tents (including youngsters, cyclists or motorcyclists) with unmarked pitches. Pitches for long stay visitors are located beyond the tourers. Very basic food supplies are kept with bread to order. Suitable not only as a night stop on the way south, the site is also not far from Augsburg or Munich (Family Railticket availablle, valid for the return journey to Munich and the city's transport system) and the local area is very attractive.

Facilities: All amenities are housed in the main building at the entrance with reception. Sanitary facilities are downstairs with free showers now, warm water washbasins, (no cabins), dishwashing and laundry room, all of a satisfactory standard. Sauna. Washing machine and dryer. Motorcaravan services. Large bar area with terrace. Small shop for basics (1/4-31/10). General room. Youth room. Table tennis. Children's play area. Lake for swimming on site (own risk). **Off site:** Restaurants and other amenities a short drive. Golf course and driving range 1 km. Larger lake used for sailboarding 400 m.

Charges 2002

Per person	€ 4.50
child (2-15 yrs)	€ 2.50
caravan	€ 5.00 - € 6.00
tent	€ 3.50 - € 5.00
car	€ 1.28
motorcaravan	€ 5.00 - € 6.00
electricity (plus meter)	€ 2.00

Tel: 09090 4046. Fax: 09090 4046. E-mail: info@ donau-lech-camping.de. **Reservations:** not needed - said to be always space at present. **Open** all year except. November.

Directions: Turn off main B2 road about 5 km. south of Donauwörth at signs for Asbach-Bäumenheim Nord towards Eggelstetten, then follow camp signs for over 1 km. to site.

Germany - South East
Camping München-Obermenzing
3635 Lochhausenerstraße 59, 81247 München (Bavaria (S))

On the northwest edge of Munich, this site makes a good stopover for those wishing to see the city or pass the night. The flat terrain is mostly covered by mature trees, giving shade to most pitches. Caravan owners are well off here as they have a special section of 130 individual drive-through pitches, mainly separated from each other by high hedges and opening off the hard site roads with easy access. These have 10A electricity connections and about 30 have water and waste water connections also. About 200 tents and motorcaravans are taken on quite large, level grass areas, with an overflow section so space is usually available. There is a shop and rest room with TV and a drinks machine (including beer). There is some road noise, but we spent another reasonably undisturbed night here, helped by the new earth bank, and it is a very convenient site.

Facilities: The single central sanitary block is large, having been extended, and it should now be adequate in size. Cleaning appears satisfactory and there is heating in the low season. It provides individual washbasins, many in curtained cubicles and most with free hot water. Hot showers require tokens (meter outside so make sure taps are turned off). Cooking facilities on payment. Washing machine and dryers. Gas supplies. Motorcaravan services. Shop (from May). TV room. **Off site:** Baker and café nearby. Riding or golf 6 km. Public transport services are available to the city from very close by. By car the journey might take 20-30 minutes depending on the density of traffic.

Charges 2002

Per person	€ 4.35
child (2-14 yrs)	€ 2.00
car	€ 3.00
tent	€ 3.85
caravan or motorcaravan	€ 6.00
motorcycle	€ 2.00
electricity (plus slot meter)	€ 1.00
dog (1 only)	€ 1.00
Bier fest surcharge per person (14/09-05/10)	€ 2.00

No credit cards. **Tel:** 089 8112235. Fax: 089 8140748. E-mail: campingplatz-obermenzing@ t-online.de. **Reservations:** Are not made. **Open** 15 March - 31 October.

Directions: Site is in northwest of the city. From Stuttgart, Nuremberg, Deggendorf or Salzburg, leave A99 at München - Lochhausen 'Kreiss-West'.

Germany - South East
Azur Camping Altmühltal
Am Festplatz 3, 85110 Kipfenberg (Bavaria (N))

In the beautiful Altmühltal river valley, this Azur site is in pretty woodland, with lots of shade for much of it. On flat grassland with direct access to the river, one looks from the entrance across to the old Schloss on the hill. Outside the main entrance is a large, flat, grass/gravel field for 60 overnight tourers (with electricity). The main site has 277 pitches, of which 178 are for touring, plus two small areas for tents and one large one. Ranging in size up to 90 sq.m. they are generally in small groups marked by trees or bushes. This well-run site is a popular base for walking, cycling, fishing, canoeing and other water-sports. This area of northern Bavaria is really attractive, with pretty villages and towns, both to the west to Treuchtlingen and beyond, and to the east to Kelheim where the river Altmühl joins the Danube.

Facilities: The main sanitary facilities are good, with free hot water (no private cabins), baby room, unit for wheelchair users, plus dishwashing. Launderette. Kitchen with ovens and cooking rings. These facilities are mostly duplicated 'portacabin' style at the other end of the site (toilets only in low season). Motorcaravan services. Shop combined with reception and vending machine for drinks (including beer). Beer garden/snacks July-August. Play area. Table tennis. Fishing. **Off site:** Two restaurants within 300 m. Supermarket 100 m. Bicycle and canoe hire in town.

Charges 2002

Per adult	€ 4.50 - € 6.00
child (2-12 yrs)	€ 3.50 - € 4.50
pitch	€ 5.50 - € 7.50
electricity	€ 2.10

Tel: 08465 905167. Fax: 08465 3745. E-mail: info@azur-camping.de. **Reservations:** Probably not needed for overnight. For longer stays in high season and school holidays contact site. **Open** all year.

Directions: From the A9/E45 Munich - Nuremberg, take exit 59 Denkendorf or 58 Eichstätt and follow the signs to Kipfenberg.

Germany - South East
DCC Campingpark Romantische Straße
91550 Dinkelsbühl (Bavaria (N))

Run by the German Camping Club (DCC), this is a modern site, very close to one of Germany`s best known mediaeval towns, from which of course visits can be made to other places on the Romantic Road. There are 475 pitches (half of which are for touring and most with a gentle slope) on broad grassy terraces overlooking a small lake, with a separate area for tents by the water. All are numbered and of about 80 sq.m., with 10A electricity. A special area is kept for overnight stays. The lake can be used for bathing or your own non-powered boat.

Facilities: Two large modern toilet blocks are of good quality and should satisfy all demands with some washbasins in cabins. Washing machines, dryers and dishwashing. Cooking facilities. Shop. Restaurant (at least Easter, then May - end Sept). General/TV room. Playgrounds on sand and grass. Minigolf. Organised activities in season. Bicycle hire.

Charges 2002

Per person	€ 4.00
pitch	€ 8.50
electricity	€ 1.50
local tax (over 4 yrs)	€ 0.70

Tel: 09851 7817. **Reservations:** Only through DCC and rather complex; try phoning site shortly before arrival, or arive early in high season. **Open** all year.

Directions: Site is in the northeast of town signed towards Dürrwangen from the Dinkelsbühl - Feuchtwangen road no. 25.

Germany - South East
Knaus Camping Park Lackenhäuser
Lackenhäuser 127, 94089 Neureichenau (Bavaria (S))

This extensive site is some 40 km. from Passau, right at the southeast tip of Germany - the border with Austria runs through one side of the site and the Czech Republic is very close too. It is very popular and reservations may be advisable from mid-June to Sept. and it is very busy in winter with skiing etc. Mainly on sloping ground with good views from some parts, it has 500 pitches with terracing in some areas, nearly all for tourists, and 40 chalets or caravans. 4A electricity connections are available and water points are fed from pure springs. It is a beautiful setting with 7 km. of walks available within the campsite perimeters and an attractive fishing lake. There is a friendly atmosphere here.

Facilities: Three good sanitary buildings, all refurbished have some washbasins in cabins and under floor heating for cool weather. Baby room. Washing machines and dryers. Gas supplies. Motorcaravan services. Cooking facilities. Supermarket. Restaurant/bar. Hairdressing salon. Heated indoor pool (free), sauna and fitness room, and outdoor spring water pool. Small lake. Fishing. Bowling alley. Church. Organised activities (July/Aug. and Xmas). Ski hire. Dog free area. **Off site:** Golf 12 km.

Charges 2002

Per person	€ 5.00
pitch	€ 3.00 - € 7.50
electricity	€ 1.80

No credit cards. **Tel:** 08583 311. Fax: 08583 91079. **Reservations:** made for any period without deposit. **Open** all year except November

Directions: From Regensburg on A3 take exit 115 into Passau, then road 12 (Freyung). Turn off just before Röhrnbach for Waldkirchen, through Jandelsbrunn to Lackenhaüser.

Dreiflüsse Camping

3695

94113 Irring b. Passau (Bavaria (S))

Although the site overlooks the Danube, it is in fact some 9 km. from the confluence of the Danube, Inn and Ilz. Dreiflüsse Camping occupies a hillside position to the west of Passau with pitches, flat or with a little slope on several rows of terraces. The 180 places for touring units are not all numbered or marked, although 16A electricity boxes determine where units pitch, and half have water and waste water connections. Trees and low banks separate the terraces which are of gravel with a thin covering of grass. The energetic and very jolly owner is most popular with his regular visitors and he gives the site a very friendly air. This is a useful en-route stop or for a longer stay to explore the delights of Passau and the southern Bavarian forest, and is popular with cyclists. There may some road and rail noise (24 hrs).

Facilities: The sanitary facilities are acceptable, if a little old, with two private cabins for women, one for men). Laundry. Motorcaravan services. Gas supplies. Pleasant, modern Gasthof restaurant with terrace at site entrance, where the reception, shop and sanitary buildings are also located. Shop all season. Small heated indoor swimming pool (May - 15 Sept on payment). Play area. Table tennis. Bicycle hire. **Off site:** Riding 3 km. Bus service for Passau from outside site (a little erratic and finishes at 6 pm).

Charges 2002

Per person	€ 4.50
child (4-12 yrs)	€ 3.00
pitch	€ 5.00 - € 8.00
electricity (plus kw charge)	€ 2.00

No credit cards. **Tel:** 08546 633. Fax: 08546 2686. **Reservations:** Write to site. **Open** 1 April - 31 October.

Directions: From autobahn A3, take exit 115 (Passau-Nord) from where site is signed. Follow signs from Passau on road to west of city and north bank of Danube towards Windorf and Irring.

DREIFLÜSSE CAMPING - JOSEF PITSCHENEDER

From A3 exit North for all visitors to this refreshing international Holiday and Touring camp site. Very modern, hygienic facilities. Shady, terraced pitches and separate, peaceful recreation area with attractive views. Ideal young persons tent area. Kiosk. Restaurant. Bar. Terrace. Beer garden. Youth room. Play area. Modern swimming pool. Fishing. Tennis. Rooms, bungalows and mobile homes for hire. 4 bikes for hire. Barbecue area. Lourdes grotto. Public guest-room. Danube cycleway passes by 300 m. away. Ideal staring point for Passau shops and culture visits (Museum, Cathedral, Old Town), and attractive surrounding area. Thermal baths in Bad Füssing, Bad Griessbach, or Bad Bimbach, and in Bavarian National Forest Park. 'Special attraction' take a boat trip on the Danube. Game and Bird park at Ortenburg plus aquarium.

IRRING 23, D 94113 PASSAU
Tel: 08546 633 Fax: 08546 2686 www.ecamp.com

Knaus Campingpark Nürnberg

3610

Hans Kalb Strasse 56, 90471 Nürnberg (Bavaria (N))

This is an ideal site for visiting the fascinating and historically important city of Nuremberg. Since acquiring this pleasantly situated site, the Knaus group have undertaken various improvements, and it now ranks as one of the best city sites anywhere. There are 140 shaded pitches on mainly flat grass among the tall trees, some marked out with 'ranch' style boards, others still attractively 'wild', some others with hardstanding. 112 have 10A electrical connections with water taps in groups. There is sufficient space for them to be quite big and many have the advantage of being drive through. Some mobile homes and a few long term units. All the Knaus parks are well run and they are pleased to welcome British tourers. Red squirrels are a common sight. There may be some noise if there is an event on at the Stadion, so it may be worthwhile checking.

Facilities: A brand new heated sanitary building offers first class facilities Washing machines and dryers, cooking facilities, unit for disabled visitors. Gas supplies. Motorcaravan services. Shop. Bar/bistro area with terrace and light meals served. Play area in woodland. Tennis court Table tennis. Bicycle hire. Large screen TV. **Off site:** City centre 4 km. (a 20 minute walk following signs takes you to the underground station). Swimming pool and football stadium 200 m.

Charges 2002

Per person	€ 5.00
child (3-14 yrs)	€ 2.50
pitch	€ 8.50
electricity	€ 1.80

No credit cards. **Tel:** 0911 9812717. Fax: 0911 9812718. **Reservations:** Not made and said to be unnecessary. **Open** all year.

Directions: From autobahns, take Nürnberg-Fischbach exit from A9 München-Bayreuth east of Nürnberg. Proceed 3 km. on dual carriageway towards city then left at camp sign. From city follow 'Stadion-Messe' signs and site is well signed (near a large Grundig office block), and along from the Stadion.

Knaus Camping-Park Viechtach

3715 Waldfrieden 22, 94234 Viechtach (Bavaria (S))

Camping-Park Viechtach, although reached via a small industrial area, is a relaxing place at which to stay, well laid out in a woodland setting on the edge of the village. The various trees and shrubs give a garden effect and there is good shade in most parts. A tarmac road winds its way between the grass pitches (most terraced) which are separated by rocks and trees and marked by plaques. There are 250 pitches (130 for touring units), all with 6A electricity, and size varies from small for some motorcaravans to quite large for bigger units (100 sq.m.). Whether for a night stop or for a longer stay to visit the Bavarian Forest, this site is well worth considering. English is spoken by the friendly reception staff.

Facilities: Two heated sanitary blocks have been renovated recently. One is central to the touring pitches, the other at the top end of the site on the ground floor of a larger building, with a drying room. Facilities are similar with washbasins (some private cabins), sinks and showers. Bread to order. There is an attractive bar/restaurant with reasonable prices, a small shop for basic supplies and a camping equipment shop. A heated indoor swimming pool has a sauna and solarium. Children's playgrounds for all ages. Table tennis. Beach volleyball. Bicycle hire. 2 Small games rooms. Large screen TV. Several rooms for wet weather. Washing machines, dryers and irons. Gas supplies. **Off site:** Outdoor pool and tennis nearby.

Charges 2002

Per unit incl. 2 persons and electricity	€ 10.00
extra person	€ 5.00
child (3-14 yrs)	€ 2.50
tent and motorcycle	€ 4.00
electricity	€ 1.80

No credit cards. **Tel:** 09942 1095. Fax: 09942 902222. **Reservations:** Write to site. **Open** all year except Nov.

Directions: Take Viechtach exit from B85 Weiden - Passau road, and follow site signs for some way.

Internationaler Campingplatz Naabtal

3720 93188 Pielenhofen (Bavaria (S))

Regensburg is an ancient city on the Danube, near the Bavarian Forest which, although not as well known as the Black Forest, is a lovely area of natural beauty. Naabtal is a very pleasant, attractive riverside site in a beautiful tree-covered valley and makes an excellent night stop when travelling to or from Austria or Hungary or a base for exploring this interesting part of Germany. Sixty per cent of the site is taken up by static caravans used for weekends and holidays. The 130 large, flat or gently sloping pitches for tourists (all with 10A electricity, some individual) are mostly under willow and other types of trees by the riverside or in an open field. There is good shade in some parts and hills covered with trees rise all around - this is good walking and mountain biking country, with marked trails. Small boats can be launched on the placid river (where you may also swim at your own risk) and there are two good size tennis courts.

Facilities: A new sanitary building serves the tent area so thay have their own showers now, while two original, heated toilet blocks are part of larger buildings. Some washbasins are in cabins, showers are on payment. Washing machines, dryers and irons. New, first class unit for disabled people. Gas supplies. Motorcaravan services. Sauna and solarium. Bar/restaurant (1/4-31/10 plus Xmas/New Year). Small shop (Easter - end Sept.). Skittle alley and tarmac curling rink. Children's playground with imaginative fixed apparatus. Large meeting room with catering facilities, a stage and a youth room with table tennis and video games. Tennis. Football field. Volleyball. Bicycle hire. Fishing (permit required). Small boats on river. Reception will advise on local excursions, walks, cycle routes and sports. **Off site:** Golf 15 km. Village shop 1.5 km

Charges 2002

Per person	€ 4.75
child	€ 2.95
pitch	€ 5.50
electricity (plus meter)	€ 0.50

No credit cards. **Tel:** 09409 373. Fax: 09409 723. E-mail: camping.pielenhofen@t-online.de. **Reservations:** Needed in high season; contact site. **Open** all year.

Directions: Take exit 97 Nittendorf from A3 Nürnberg - Regensburg, and follow road to Pielenhofen (Camping Naabtal is signed from exit). Cross river and turn right to site. Site is about 11 km. from autobahn exit. From A93 exit 39 onto B8 towards Nittendorf, then at Etterzhausen turn towards Pielenhofen.

Camping Rangau

3605 Campingstraße 44, 91056 Erlangen-Dechsendorf (Bavaria (N))

Run by the same family for many years now, this site makes a convenient stopover, quickly and easily reached from the A3 Würzburg-Nürnberg and A73 Bamberg - Nürnberg autobahns and is pleasant enough to stay a bit longer. It has 110 pitches which are mainly for tourists on flat ground, under trees, numbered and partly marked but only about 60-80 sq.m. so it can look cramped when busy. There are also 60 permanent units. There is usually space and, in peak season, overnight visitors can often be put on the adjacent football pitch. A fair sized lake with access from the site through a gate can be used for sailing or windsurfing or for fishing on permit; boats are for hire.

Facilities: A satisfactory sanitary block, heated when cold, has well spaced washbasins (some cabins for ladies) and showers. Good facilities for disabled visitors. A new facility provides washbasins in cabins and WCs. Laundry facilities. Gas supplies. Restaurant with terrace for meals or drinks. Order bread from reception. Playground. Club/TV room. **Off site:** Erlangen centre 5 km. Swimming 200 m.

Charges 2002

Per person	€ 4.10
child (6-12 yrs)	€ 2.10
pitch	€ 4.10
electricity (6A)	€ 1.60
rubbish tax	€ 0.60

Tel: 09135 8866. Fax: 09135 724743. E-mail: infos@camping-rangau.de. **Reservations:** Made without deposit and kept until 6 pm. **Open** 1 April - 30 September.

Directions: Take exit for Erlangen-West from A3 autobahn, turn towards Erlangen but after less than 1 km. at Dechsendorf turn left by camp signs and follow to site.

Spessart-Camping Schönrain

3735 Schönrainstraße 4-18, 97737 Gemünden-Hofstetten (Bavaria (N))

Situated a short distance from the town of Gemünden, with views of forested hills beside the river Main, this is a very friendly, family run site, with excellent facilities. There are just 200 pitches, half of which are for touring. They are at least 100 sq.m. with some up to 200, most have 10A electricity and some also have water. A new area has been developed for tents. The site has an outdoor pool open from Whitsun to end Sept (weather permitting). A pleasant small restaurant and bar and a shop are on site with the local full-bodied Franconian wine and schnaps for sale. Frau Endres welcomes British guests and speaks a little English. There are opportunities for walking and riding in the adjacent woods, excursions are organised in the main season and it is possible to hire a bicycle, ride to Würzburg and catch the pleasure boat back, or take a combined bus and cycle ride. Fishing and boating are both very popular in the locality.

Facilities: A super new sanitary building has card operated entry - the card is pre-paid and operates the showers, washing machines and dryers, coffee machine, dishwashing, gas cooker, baby bathroom, jacuzzi etc. Two private bathrooms (complete with wine and balcony!) for rent. Motorcaravan services. General room with sections for very young children, a pool table and arcade games and a TV. Upstairs is a library and internet café, fitness room and solarium. Bar/restaurant (closed Tuesdays). Shop. Swimming pool. Playground. Outdoor chess. Table tennis. Bicycle hire. Excursions. **Off site:** Fishing 400 m. Riding 200 m. Canoeing, cycling and walking near.

Charges 2002

Per pitch 100 sq.m.	€ 6.00
pitch 150 sq.m.	€ 8.50
hikers or cyclists and small tent	€ 4.00
person	€ 5.00
child (under 14 yrs)	€ 3.00
electricity	€ 2.00

Less 10% for stays over 14 days in mid and low seasons. **Tel:** 09351 8645. Fax: 09351 8721. E-mail: info@spessart-camping.de. **Reservations:** Write to site. **Open** 1 April - 30 September.

Directions: From Frankfurt - Würzburg autobahn, take Weibersbrunn-Lohr exit and B26 to Gemünden. Turn over Main bridge to Hofstetten. From Kassel - Wurzburg autobahn, leave at Hammelburg and take B27 to Gemünden, and as above.

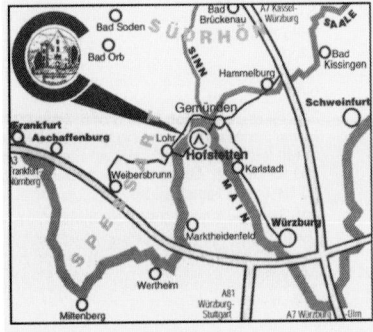

Knaus Campingpark Frickenhausen

3625 Ochsenfurter Straße 49, 97252 Frickenhausen (Bavaria (N))

This is a pleasant riverside site with good facilities just south of Würzburg, situated towards the northern end of the 'Romantische Strasse' and not far from the A3 Frankfurt to Nürnberg. There are 115 fair sized, numbered touring pitches on generally flat grass, arranged in sections leading from tarred access roads with flowers around. Most have 6A electricity connections. About 80 long stay places are mostly separate nearer the river. All the amenities are in a long block opposite reception. Upstairs is a little shop and a restaurant with a terrace for candle-lit meals, whilst downstairs is a cosy café/bar. There is a small, heated, open-air swimming pool (for adults only at specific times), whilst on an 'island' surrounded by attractive trees alongside the River Main is a large play area. The ducks are very friendly and will invite you to feed them.

Facilities: The modernised, heated, sanitary facilities have washbasins (some private cabins), and dishwashing sinks. Soap and paper towels are provided for the toilets. Washing machine and dryer. Gas supplies. Restaurant, cafe/wine bar and shop (weekends only in low season). Bread to order. Club room. Large screen TV. Small, free swimming pool. Children's play area and beach volleyball on river island. Table tennis. Bicycle hire. Fishing. Boat marina. Cooking facilities. **Off site:** Public swimming pool 300 m.

Charges 2002

Per person	€ 5.00
child (3-14 yrs)	€ 2.50
pitch	€ 3.00 - € 7.50
small tent and motorcycle	€ 4.00
electricity	€ 1.80
rubbish tax	€ 1.00

No credit cards. **Tel:** 09331 3171. Fax: 09331 5784. **Reservations:** Not made. **Open** all year except November.

Directions: Take exit 71 (Ochsenfurt) from the A3 autobahn at Würzburg and continue on the B13. Do not cross the Main into town but follow Frickenhausen and site signs; the site is shortly on the right.

Azur Camping Odenwald

3470 63931 Kirchzell (Bavaria (N))

Between the rivers Neckar and Main, in the nature reserve of the Odenwald with lots of rambling opportunities and only 7 km. from Amorbach with its 700 year old Benedictine Abbey, the site gives the impression of being deep in the forest and will appeal most to those who like the peaceful attractions of hills, trees and meadows. It is situated by a stream in a low lying valley, away from main through routes, although Heidelberg, Frankfurt and Würzburg are only an hour away. Miltenberg is a handy base for pleasure cruises on the Main and a few miles down the Neckar, Bad Wimpfen is a fine example of a mediaeval town. Just over half the pitches are taken by permanent caravans but there are 120 grassy and shaded tourist pitches spread out around the site, with a separate area for tents and a section with electrical connections for overnight stays. There is usually space but it can be full at Easter and Whitsun and in late July.

Facilities: Toilet facilities, in three main blocks, vary from satisfactory to above average quality and are kept clean, with heating in cooler weather. There are some washbasins in cabins for both sexes, plus a toilet and shower for disabled visitors in one, baby and drying rooms. Washing machines and dryer. Motorcaravan services. Gas supplies. Small shop (April - Oct, at other times order bread at reception). Restaurant. Children's playground. Table tennis. Indoor swimming pool, sauna and solarium (closed Tuesdays). Bicycle hire. Barbecue. General room with TV (satellite). Entertainment in high season.

Charges 2002

Per adult	€ 4.50 - € 6.00
child (2-12 yrs)	€ 3.50 - € 4.50
pitch	€ 5.50 - € 7.50
small tent pitch	€ 3.50 - € 4.50
electricity	€ 2.10

No credit cards. **Tel:** 09373 566. Fax: 09373 7375. E-mail: info@azur-camping.de. **Reservations:** are made with deposit (€ 7,67) and fee (€ 7,67); write to site for details. **Open** all year (reduced facilities 16 Nov. - 14 March).

Directions: Site is 2 km. south of Kirchzell on the Eberbach - Amorbach road. Caravans approaching from Eberbach may choose to go on for 1 km. and turn back.

Germany - South East
Camping Schloss Issigau

3750 95188 Issigau (Bavaria (N))

This is a handy, pleasant little family run site with very good facilities, of a type not common in Germany - less than 50 pitches and all for tourers. It is just over 5 km. from the A9 Berlin - Nuremberg in north-east Bavaria, on the edge of the pretty village with views across it and fields to woods. Entering a large grassed courtyard there are several sections, part terraced and with some old trees giving a little shade in places. As you go through the site it opens up to a largish, sloping tent area beside the small ponds, beyond which is the new young children's play area There are 45 pitches - around half are individual ranging up to 120 sq.m.- all with 16A electricity, plus three also with water and waste water. There is a delightful café/bar and restaurant in the interesting old 'Schloss' (circa 1398 - a large fortified house is how we might describe it) with a museum of old armour, etc.

Facilities: Satisfactory heated sanitary facilities are in an old building with some modern fittings and some washbasins in cabins. Dishwashing and laundry facilities (washing machine, dryer, spin dryer, iron and board) and a baby room. Café/bar and restaurant (open daily from 12.00 to 22.00). Table tennis and games room. Hotel accommodation available. **Off site:** Small supermarket 300 m. The Naturpark Frankenwald is on the doorstep to the southwest.

Charges 2002

Per adult	€ 4.20
child (4-14 yrs)	€ 1.80
caravan or motorcaravan	€ 5.00
tent	€ 4.00 - € 5.00
electricity plus meter	€ 1.00

No credit cards. **Tel:** 09293 7173. **Fax:** 09293 7050. **Reservations:** Probably unnecessary. **Open** 15 March - 31 October and 18 December - 9 January.

Directions: From A9 Berlin - Nuremberg, 45 km. north of Dreieck Bayreuth/Kulmbach take exit 31 Berg/Bad Steben to Issigau and follow the signs in the village - narrow in places.

Germany - North East
Camping Oberhof

3855 Am Stausee (Bergstrasse 14), Oberhof, 99330 Frankenhain (Thuringia)

Oberhof has been purchased by the owners of 3242 Schinderhannes and they have already begun upgrading the site. 150 pitches for tourers and electricity connections are available, of which 20 are on hardstanding with water and waste water. Situated just 2 km. from the German winter sports centre, with cross country skiing possible from the site, there are also over 100 km. of waymarked walks, the Beerberg and Schneekopf mountains (978 m) nearby and many famous towns within a half hour drive (Erfurt, Weimar etc).

Facilities: Takeaway. Lakeside beach, fishing, boat hire and diving school. Children's play area. Table tennis, volleyball. Bicycle hire.

Charges 2002

Per person	€ 4.00
child	€ 2.00
pitch	€ 5.00
electricity	€ 1.50

Tel: 036205 76518. **Fax:** 036205 71768. **E-mail:** info@countrycamping.de. **Reservations:** Contact site. **Open** all year.

Directions: From A4 autobahn between Eisenach and Dresden, take exit 42 (Gotha) onto the B247 south towards Oberhof. At the 'Wegscheide' guest house (approx. 3 km. before Oberhof) turn left into the parking area and take the track on the right for 1 km. downhill to site (fairly steep in places). From Erfurt on the A71 take the Ilmenau/Geschwanda exit onto B88 towards Ohrdruf/Gotha to Frankenhain from where turn left onto the track towards Lütsche Talsperre and the site.

Camping Strandbad Aga

3850 Reichenbacherstrasse 14, 07554 Gera-Aga (Thuringia)

Strandbad Aga is a useful night stop near the A4/A9 and within reach of Dresden, Leipzig and Meissen. It is in open country-side on the edge of a small lake, with 350 individual, fenced pitches, mostly fairly level, without shade. The 200 touring pitches all have 16A electricity - for stays of more than a couple of days, over-nighters going on an open area. The lake is used for swimming, boating and fishing (popular with day visitors at weekends and with a separate naturist area) and there is a small playground on one side (close to a deep part). Entertainment is organised in July and the friendly, enthusiastic owner improves the facilities each year.

Facilities: The sanitary building is at one side, with some washbasins in cabins and hot showers on payment. Large (4 x 4 m.) room for wheelchair users. Washing machines and dryers. Motorcaravan serv-ices. Modern restaurant/bar open long hours. High season kiosk for drinks, ice creams, etc. Playground. Small lake used for inflatables and fishing. Swimming and watersports in the lake. Entertainment in high season. No English spoken. **Off site:** Tennis 1 km. Football 200 m. Shop in village (200 m).

Charges 2002

Per adult	€ 4.00
child (3-13 yrs)	€ 2.00
pitch	€ 5.50 - € 6.00
electricity plus meter	€ 1.50

No credit cards. **Tel:** 036695 20209. Fax: 036695 20209. **Reservations:** Write to site. **Open** 1 April - 1 November.

Directions: From A4/E40 Chemnitz - Erfurt auto-bahn take Gera exit 58 then B2 towards Zeitz, first following Bad Köstritz signs, then site signs.

Camping am Schlosspark

3842 03222 Lubennau (Brandenburg)

Situated about halfway between Berlin and Dresden, this is an attractive proposition for a short visit as well as a night stop, in a delightful, woodland setting, about 10 minutes walk from the centre of the much visited old town. Taking 125 units (rather close together at very busy times), all have electricity. They are mainly on flat grass but with a central hardstanding area for motor-caravans and a long area for tents at the end. You can go for a trip in a gondola, explore the Spreewald or just look round the interesting old town from this pleasant site. A public path passes between the site and the river. At public holidays and during the high season, the site can be very busy and facilities may be stretched.

Facilities: The refurbished, heated sanitary facilities are quite good with free hot water for the wash-basins (some private cabins), but the showers require tokens from reception. A kitchen is provided as well as dishwashing and laundry. Small children's play area. Boat and bicycle hire. Fishing. Motorcaravan service point. **Off site:** Shops in the adjacent town. Café 200 m. Riding 5 km.

Charges 2002

Per person	€ 4.00
caravan or motorcaravan	€ 7.00
tent	€ 2.56 - € 4.09
electricity (plus meter)	€ 1.50

Tel: 03542 3533. Fax: 03542 3533. **Reservations:** Essential probably only for May Day and Whitsun weekends. **Open** all year.

Directions: From A13 (Berlin - Dresden) take exit 9, turning right on B115 into Lübbenau then following site signs. At weekends the town is busy, requiring extra patience. It may be easier to enter Lübbenau from the southeast via the A15 exit 2 (Boblitz).

Camping Havelberge am Woblitzsee

3820 17237 Groß Quassow (Mecklenburg-West Pomerania)

The Müritz National Park is a very large area of lakes and marshes, popular for birdwatching as well as watersports, and Havelberge is a large, well-equipped site to use as a base for enjoying the area. It is quite steep in places here with many terraces, most with shade, less in newer areas, with views over the lake. There are 250 pitches in total with 80 good sized, numbered touring pitches most with 10A electrical connections. Over 170 seasonal pitches with a number of attractive chalets and an equal number of mobile homes in a separate areas. In the high season this is a busy park with lots going on to entertain families of all ages, whilst in the low seasons this is a peaceful base for explor-ing an unspoilt area of nature.

Facilities: Three sanitary buildings provide very good facilities, with a few private cabins, and showers on payment. Dishwashing, cooking rings and laundry. Motorcaravan service point. Small shop and modern restaurant (May - Sept). The lake provides fishing, swimming from a small beach and non-powered boats can be launched - canoes, rowing boats, windsurfers and bikes can be hired. Play areas and animation in high season. Volleyball. **Off site:** Riding 3.5 km.

Charges 2002

Per adult	€ 2.05 - € 5.01
child (2-14)	€ 1.02 - € 3.32
pitch	€ 3.07 - € 9.20
electricity	1.99

Tel: 03981 24790. Fax: 03981 247999. E-mail: havel-tourist@t-online.de. **Reservations:** Contact site for high season and school holidays. **Open** all year.

Directions: From A19 Rostock - Berlin road take exit 18 and follow B198 to Wesenberg and go left to Klein Quassow and follow site signs.

Camping Sanssouci-Gaisberg

3827 An der Pirschheide, Templiner See 41, 14471 Potsdam (Brandenburg)

Sanssouci is an excellent base for visiting Potsdam and Berlin, about 2 km. from Sanssouci Park on the banks of the Templiner See in a quiet woodland setting. Looking very attractive, reflecting the effort which has been put into its development, with modern reception, shop, takeaway, restaurant and bar. There are 240 pitches in total with some 90 odd being seasonal pitches but all the 150 touring pitches s now have 6/10amp electricity, many also with their own water and waste water connections. Tall trees mark out the tourist pitches, and access is good for larger units. There is a separate area for tents by the lake. Reception staff are helpful with English spoken and a comprehensive English language information pack has been prepared by the owners for local attractions. Free transport in the mornings and evenings is operated by the site to the nearby station. Tickets for public transport, boat trips and fishing can be bought at reception.

Facilities: Top class sanitary facilities are in an excellent, modern, heated block containing hot showers, washbasins in cabins and facilities for babies. Dishwashing on payment and laundry, plus a very good facility for wheelchair users. A separate smaller toilet building also. New building with bathroom to rent, kitchen, hairdressers and solarium. Gas supplies. Motorcaravan services. Restaurant/bar. Shop. Rowing boats, motorboats and pedaloes for hire. Fishing. Swimming in the lake. Play area in central woods. Bicycle hire. Internet café. Site closed to vehicles 13.00-15.00 hrs. **Off site:** Riding 3 km. Golf 10 km. The pool, sauna, solarium and skittle alley at the nearby Hotel Semiramis may (100 m.) be used by campers at a discount.

Charges 2002

Per adult	€ 5.88 - € 7.16
child (2-15 yrs)	€ 0.46
pitch	€ 6.54 - € 7.21
electricity	€ 1.79
local tax	€ 0.77

Special low season offers. No credit cards. **Tel:** 03327 55680. Fax: 03327 55680. E-mail: info@ recra.de. **Reservations:** Not normally necessary. **Open** 1 April - 4 November.

Directions: From A10 take Potsdam exit 7, follow B1 to within 4 km. of city centre then sign to right for camp just before the railway bridge. Or A10 exit 12 on the B2 into town and follow signs for Brandenburg/Werder. Site is southwest of Sanssouci Park on the banks of the Templiner See off Zeppelinstrasse 1.2 km. along a woodland drive.

Germany - North East
Camping und Freizeitpark LuxOase

3833 Arnsdorfer Straße 1, Kleinröhrsdorf, 01900 Dresden (Saxony)

This is a pleasantly situated new park about half an hour from the centre of Dresden, in a very peaceful location with good facilities. It is owned and run by a progressive young family. On open grass-land with views across the lake (access to which is through a gate in the site fence) to the woods and low hills beyond, this is a sun-trap with little shade at present. There are 138 large touring pitches (plus 50 seasonal in a separate area), marked by bushes or posts on generally flat or slightly sloping grass. All have 10A electricity and 92 have water and waste water facilities. At the entrance is an area of hardstanding (with electricity) for late arrivals. The main entrance building houses the amenities and in front of the building is some very modern play equipment on bark. You may swim, fish or use inflatables in the lake. There are many interesting places to visit apart from Dresden and Meissen, with the fascinating National Park Sächsische Schweiz (Saxon Switzerland) on the border with the Czech Republic offering some spectacular scenery. Boat trips on the Danube can be taken from the tourist centres of Königstein and Bad Schandau and Saxony is also famous for its many old castles. Bus trips are organised to Prague

Facilities: A brand new sanitary building provides modern, heated facilities with private cabins, a family room, baby changing room, units for disabled visitors and two units for hire. Rooms for cooking, laundry and dishwashing. Gas supplies. Motorcaravan services. Shop (am. all year, pm. in high season). Bar and restaurant with good value meals (Apr - Oct evenings and w/end lunchtimes). Bicycle hire. Lake swimming. Sports field with basketball and volleyball. Fishing. Children's play area. Sauna. Train, bus and theatre tickets from reception. Minigolf. **Off site:** Riding 1 km. Golf 7.5 km. Public transport to Dresden 1 km. Nearby Dinosaur park, zoo and indoor karting etc.

Charges 2002

Per person	€ 4.00 - € 4.50
child (2-14 yrs)	€ 2.20 - € 2.50
motorcaravan or caravan	€ 7.00 - € 7.80
tent	€ 5.00 - € 5.60
car or motorcycle	€ 1.70
electricity	€ 1.70 - € 2.00

Various special offers in low season. **Tel:** 035952 56666. Fax: 035952 56024. E-mail: camping. luxoase@t-online.de. **Reservations:** Advisable for July/August. **Open** all year except 11 Jan - 28 Feb.

Directions: From A4 (Dresden - Görlitz) take exit 85 towards Radeberg, soon following signs to site via Leppersdorf and Kleinröhrsdorf.

Germany - North East
Campingplatz Auensee

3847 Gustav-Esche Strasse 5, 04159 Leipzig (Saxony)

It is unusual to find a first-class site in a city, but this large, neat and tidy site is one. It is far enough away from roads and the airport to be reasonably peaceful during the day and very quiet overnight and has 168 pitches of which about 150 are for short-term tourers. It is set in a mainly open area with tall trees and very attractive flower arrangements around, with some chalets and 'trekker' huts for rent in the adjoining woodland, home to the shoe-stealing foxes. The individual, numbered, flat grassy pitches are large (at least 100 sq.m.), all 16A electrical connec-tions and five on hardstanding, arranged in several sections with a separate area for young people with tents. Three central points supply water and barbecue areas are provided. Children of all ages are well catered for with forts, an ultra-modern climbing frame all on sand, a super-swing and an enclosed court with tennis, football and basketball. A modern restaurant and a small shop are open all year round. A popular site, it is best to arrive early.

Facilities: Five sanitary buildings (all in one area and mind your head if you are over 6 feet tall) have differ-ing mixtures of very modern equipment and offer many washbasins in cabins and showers on payment (token). Well equipped rooms for babies and disabled visitors (key from reception). Dishwashing facilities (open air and inside). Kitchen and laundry rooms. All the buildings can be heated. Shop in restaurant and snack bar (all year). Entertainment rooms. Several play areas. Bicycle hire. Fishing close by. Barbecue with seating. Kitchen. Motorcaravan service point. Dog walk. English usually spoken. **Off site:** Public transport to the city centre goes every 10 minutes from just outside the site.

Charges 2002

Per person	€ 4.09
child (3-18 yrs)	€ 2.95 - € 3.07
pitch	€ 7.67 - € 8.80
electricity (per kwh)	€ 0.38

Tel: 0341 4651 600. **Reservations:** Contact site. **Open** all year.

Directions: Signs to site are hard to find but it is signed 5 km. from Leipzig centre on the B6 to Halle. From the A9 Berlin - Nurnberg take exit 17 at Schkeuditz onto the B6 towards Leipzig. Turn right to Auensee at the Church just 3 km before the centre of the town. If you pass the railway station you are too far. Turn back and turn left at Church.

Hungary

Hungarian National Tourist Ofice, 46 Eaton Place, London SW1X 8AL
Tel: 020 7823 1032 Fax: 020 7823 1459
E-mail: htlondon@btinternet.com Internet: www.hungarytourism.com

There are many interesting areas of Hungary for the tourist apart from Budapest (for which you should allow at least a couple of days) and Lake Balaton (around 70% of the visitors here are German) and the British are warmly received. The Danube Bend in the north-west is justifiably popular, as is the north-east hills area (Eger and Miskolc), with the spectacular stalactites in the large cave system at the border with Slovakia in Aggtelek (north of Eger). The interesting towns of the Great Plain to the east of the Danube have a great Magyar tradition and there are many Thermal baths (often at campsites) to enjoy. There are also several notable wine areas and you can purchase quality wines at low prices. West of the Danube appears rather more advanced, while in the east and north it is still common to see agricultural workers with scythes and few tractors. There has been a rapid advance in the general standard of campsites, although the majority still have communal (single sex) changing for show-ers. All sites have British style WCs. Most sites require payment in cash.

Population
10,471,000 (1995); density 113 per sq. km.

Capital
Budapest.

Climate
There are four fairly distinct seasons - hot summer (June-Aug), mild spring and autumn, very cold winter with snow.

Language
The official language is Magyar, but German is widely spoken, and English and French are also spoken particularly by those engaged in the tourist industry in the west of the country.

Currency
Hungarian forints (ft) come in notes of 10, 20, 50, 100 and 500 ft. When you change cash keep receipts - to convert money at the end of your visit - it is illegal to export Hungarian currency. You can change money at tourist offices, at most large hotels or campsites. Banks can be slow and exchange rates are the same every-where.

Banks
Open Mon-Fri 09.00-14.00, Sat 09.00-12.00.

Post Offices
Usually open Mon-Fri 08.00-17.00/18.00, Sat. 12.00-14.00/18.00, but it is quicker to buy stamps at tobacconists.

Telephone
To call from the UK the code is 0036 followed by area code less initial 0, and number. From Hungary dial 06 followed by the area code. International calls from Hungary can be dialled direct from red or grey phone boxes but it may be easier through the international operator (09).

Public Holidays
New Year; 15 March; Easter Mon; Labour Day; Whitsun; Constitution Day, 20 Aug; Republic Day, 23 Oct; Christmas, 25, 26 Dec.

Time
GMT plus 1 (summer BST plus 1).

Shopping
Open Mon-Fri 10.00-18.00, Sat 10.00-14.00. Food shops open Mon-Fri 07.00-19.00, Sat 07.00-14.00. Home produced products, including food and restaurant meals are cheap by western standards. Traditionally main meals are taken at midday so there is a better range of dishes in the restaurants then. All eating places display signs indicating their class from I to IV which gives some guide to comparative prices. Set menus are good value.

Motoring
Main roads are very good, as is sign-post-ing. Dipped headlights are compulsory at all times. Most of the few motorways are single carriage, single lane -care is needed.
Fuel: On motorways and in large towns petrol stations open 24 hours otherwise 06.00-20.00. Eurocard accepted at some petrol stations.
Tolls: are payable on the M1 from the Austrian border to Györ and on the full length of the M5 (Budapest - Kiskunfelegy-haza); also on the M3 (Budapest - Fuzesabony) eastward.
Speed Restrictions: Caravans and motorhomes (3.5 tons) 31 mph (50 kph) in built up areas, caravans 44 mph (70 kph) and 50 mph (80 kph) on other roads and motorways respectively, motorhomes 50 mph (80 kph) and 75 mph (120 kph).
Parking: Do not park in places where you would not park in the UK.

Siotour Camping Autós I

504 Szent István út, 8622 Szantod (Somogy County)

If you have young children or non-swimmers in your party, then the southern shores of the lake where this Siotour is situated are ideal as you can walk out for nearly a kilometre before the water rises to more than a metre in depth. It is a large site with its own direct access to the lake offering 480 pitches, most with 16A electricity, but there must be the possibility of noise in high season, although it was peaceful during our visit in early June. There are many tall trees and the more attractive pitches are near the lakeside, including some unshaded ones alongside the water. The rest, in a large central area which comprises the majority of the site, are flat, individual ones on grass and these are hedged and vary from small to quite large. A separate tent area is at the back of the site.

Facilities: Three very modern, tiled sanitary buildings and one older one. Three en-suite private bathrooms can be rented including bath and shower. Warm water to washbasins with single tap. Showers with private changing area. No toilet paper. Facilities for disabled visitors. Satisfactory dishwashing and laundry facilities (key from reception). Supermarket. Restaurant with excellent menu. Three snack bars and a bar all with terraces (from June). Lake swimming, fishing and non-powered boating. Children's wooden play equipment on sandy grass by the lake. Table tennis. Moped, roller skate and bicycle hire. **Off site:** Shop 50 m. Adjacent large water slide area and boats for hire.

Charges 2003

Per person	€ 4.20 - € 5.80
child (2-14 yrs)	€ 2.10 - € 2.90
caravan	€ 9.30 - € 17.60
tent	€ 4.00 - € 5.80
local tax (over 18 yrs)	€ 1.30 - € 1.50

Electricity and car incl. **Tel:** 84 348 863. Fax: 84 348 931. E-mail: siotour.autos1@axelero.hu.
Reservations: Write to site. When closed write to Siotour AG Hauptbüro, 8600 Siófok, Batthyány u. 2/6. Tel: 84/310 806. Fax: 84/310 803. **Open** 16 May - 7 September.

Directions: Exit road no. 7/E71 between Balaton-földvár and Siófok towards Tihany, and the site is well signed.

SIOTOUR - your partner in South-Balaton.
We look forward to welcoming you at our 13 well equipped campsites on the south shores of Lake Balaton.

Our campsites:

Ifjúság Camping
Aranypart Camping
Autós I. Camping
Autós II. Camping
Rév Camping
Lídó Camping
Vadvirág Camping

Napsugár Camping
Aranyhid Camping
Magyar Tenger Camp.
Kék Tó Camping
Höforrás Camping
Deseda Camping

The services we offer:
• Facilities for sport and relaxation
• Recreation programmes for the children
• Modern sanitary facilities
• Excursions available and facilities for money exchange

Contact our central reservations office: SIOTOUR, H-8600 Siófok, Batthyány u. 2/b.
Tel.: 36-84-310 806 Fax: 36-84-310 803
E.mail: siotour@mail.datanet.hu, Internet address: http\\www.siotour.hu

Siotour Camping Aranypart

506 Szent László u.183-185, 8600 Siófok (Somogy County)

Situated right by the famous lake, and near to the main tourist town, this very well run site has 680 flat, grassy pitches - 255 for caravans and 425 for tents, just over half being fairly small individual ones. There are 400 electrical connections (16A). At the far end of the site is a fenced area where there are 70 excellent bungalows for rent. Also at this end is a camping area where groups of young people are pitched. A superb restaurant offers a good menu and there are many sports and entertainment facilities making it very popular with the younger generation. The site is fenced from the lake with good security.

Facilities: Five very well equipped amenity blocks are situated throughout this long site. Dishwashing and laundry facilities at either end with free hot water. Five washing machines. Four two burner cookers in the middle of the site. Shops. Snack bars and bars. Restaurant. Two play areas and one animator. Bicycle hire. Lake swimming. **Off site:** Riding 0.5 km.

Charges 2003

Per person	€ 3.90 - € 5.80
child (2-14 yrs)	€ 1.95 - € 2.90
caravan incl. electricity	€ 5.10 - € 14.60
tent	€ 3.30 - € 4.40
local tax	€ 1.30 - € 1.50

No credit cards. **Tel:** 84 352 519. Fax: 84 352 801. E-mail: siotour.aranypart@axelero.hu. **Reservations:** Contact site or Siotour (see advert). Necessary for July and August. **Open** 18 April - 22 September.

Directions: Site is 3 km. north of Siófok. From road no. 70, exit at km. 108, cross railway and site is 200 m. well signed.

Siotour Camping Vadvirág

500 Arany j.u., 8636 Balatonszemes (Somogy County)

This large Siotour site (14 ha) on the southern shore of Lake Balaton has a beach almost one kilometre long, which is also used by day visitors. On flat grass, just over half the 600 touring pitches are individual with electricity connections available (16A) and 270 are for tents with some shade. A range of watersports is possible with all sorts of boats for hire including windsurfers and pedaloes, and there is excellent swimming in the lake. Note that the train line runs along the back of the site. No English is spoken.

Facilities: Three modern sanitary blocks include some washbasins in cabins, a few private bathrooms for hire and facilities for disabled visitors. Launderette. Motorcaravan services. Shop and gift shop. Snack bars, two restaurant, and pizzeria. Lake swimming with water slide, boat hire. Three tennis courts. Table tennis. Minigolf. Bicycle hire. Playground and trampoline at lakeside.

Charges 2003

Per person	€ 4.10 - € 5.60
caravan incl. electricity	€ 6.30 - € 16.70
tent	€ 4.00 - € 5.10
local tax (over 18 yrs)	€ 1.30 - € 1.50

Electricity and car incl. No credit cards. **Tel:** 84 360 114. Fax: 84 360 114. E-mail: siotour.vadviragk@ axelero.hu. **Reservations:** Contact site or Siotour (see advert). **Open** 6 June - 7 September.

Directions: Balatonszemes is about halfway round the southern side of Lake Balaton. Access site from road 7/E71 turning towards lake at km. 134, over the railway and then just 300 m.

Balatontourist Camping Kristof

507 8220 Balatonalmadi (Veszprem County)

This is a delightfully small site with just 33 marked pitches and many tall trees. Square in shape, the generously sized pitches are on either side of hard roads, on level grass. There is some shade and 12 electricity points (6A). The site lies between the main road and railway line and the lake. There is no direct access to the lake, but a public lakeside area adjoins the site, and site fees include the entry price. This is a neat little site with a kiosk with terrace for breakfast and dinner (steaks, etc) drinks, bread, milk and ice cream. Balatonalmádi is at the northern end of the lake and well placed for excursions around the lake or to Budapest. Kristof is very suitable for anyone seeking a small, friendly site without the bustle of the larger sites. Good English is spoken.

Facilities: The excellent, fully equipped toilet facility is part of the reception building. Laundry room with washing machine (small charge), kitchen and sitting room with TV. Café (19/4-23/9). Children's playground and organized entertainment every day except Sunday Tennis court. **Off site:** Fishing, bicycle hire 500 m. Riding 5 km. Village shops and supermarket 500 m.

Charges 2002

Per pitch	€ 6.72 - € 13.52
adult	€ 2.23 - € 3.89
child (2-14 yrs)	€ 1.78 - € 3.20
local tax (over 18 yrs)	€ 0.77

Tel: 88 584 201. Fax: 88 584 202. E-mail: ckristof@ balatontourist.hu. **Reservations:** Essential July - 20 Aug. Write for booking form. **Open** 19 April - 23 September.

Directions: Site is on road no. 71 at Balatonalmádi, between the railway line and the lake and is signed.

Panorama Camping

513 Fenyvesalza 4/a, 9090 Pannonhalma (Zala County)

In 1982 this became the first private enterprise campsite in Hungary. It offers a very pleasant outlook and peaceful stay at the start or end of your visit to this country, situated just 20 km. southeast of Gyȯr, on a hillside with views across the valley to the Sokoro hills. On the edge of the village, it is just below the 1,000 year old monastery, which has guided tours. The 75 numbered, hedged pitches (30 with 10A electricity) are on terraces, generally fairly level but reached by steepish concrete access roads, with many trees and plants around. There are benches provided and a small, grass terrace from where you can purchase beer, local wine and soft drinks.

Facilities: Sanitary facilities quite satisfactory with a small building near reception and a larger unit halfway up the site. Curtained, hot showers with curtained communal changing. Hot water for dishwashing and laundry. Cooking facilities. Bar and meals (1/6-30/9). Shop. Recreation room with TV and games. Small play area and small pool (cleaned once per week). Table tennis. No English spoken. **Off site:** Hourly bus service to Gyȯr. Good value restaurant 400 m. Shop for essentials 150 m. Fishing 4 km.

Charges 2002

Per unit incl. 2 persons	HUF 1200.00
electricity	HUF 500.00

No credit cards. **Tel:** 96 471 240. Fax: 96 470 561. **Reservations:** Advisable for high season - write in German. **Open** Easter, then 1 May - 15 September.

Directions: From no. 82 Gyȯr - Veszprém road turn to Pannonhalma at Ecs. Site is well signed - the final approach road is fairly steep

Naturista Camping Balatonbereny

N502 Balaton u.12, 8649 Balatonberény (Somogy County)

A holiday anywhere on the shore of Lake Balaton almost equates to being beside the sea. With a length of 77 km. and a surface area of 600 sq.km. it is the largest fresh water lake in western and central Europe. The quieter, less commercial southern end of Balaton provides location for this very acceptable 6 ha. naturist site with direct access to the lake. The 267 numbered flat grass pitches each with electricity (16A), are of a good size, many divided by neatly boxed privet hedges. Well-spaced mature trees provide a degree of shade. An INF naturist card is not a requirement but gives a 10% reduction. A unique circular pier, that doubles as a sunbathing area, permits access to the shallow waters. One has to walk almost 200 m. into the lake for a suitable swimming depth. Canoes, dinghies and windsurfing are all very popular. This is a quiet site with no entertainment programme but possibly two or three social evenings during the season. Within an acceptable driving distance one can visit Festetics mansion at Keszthely and the internationally famous hot water lake at Heviz. Kanyavar island at Kis-Balaton providing an excellent location for bird watching. Only limited English is spoken.

Facilities: Two central sanitary blocks are not modern but are adequate and clean, with British style toilets and open washbasins. Water temperature to the showers can be variable. Cold showers by the lake. Dishwashing and laundry sinks with hot water. Washing machine. Two cookers. Small shop for basics. Restaurants. Takeaway. Massage. Pre-arranged tours may be booked. Play area. Volleyball. Kayak and pedalo hire. **Off site:** Two small supermarkets at Balatonbereny (400 m). Restaurant near entrance.

Charges 2002

Per person	HUF 750.00 - 870.00
child (2-14 yrs)	HUF 530.00 - 610.00
pitch incl. electricity	HUF 1600.00 - 1980.00
electricity	HUF 500.00
local tax	HUF 300.00

Less 10% with INF naturist card. **Tel:** 085 377 715. Fax: 085 377 715. E-mail: naturista@matavnet.hu. **Reservations:** Should not be necessary. **Open** 15 May- 15 September.

Directions: Travelling southeast from Zalaegerszeg on road 76 take left turn signed Balatonbereny. Site is signed in 3.5 km. marked FKK. Turn left to site on right in 150 m

Balatontourist Diana Camping

508 8241 Aszófô (Veszprem County)

Once a very large site of about 12 ha. Diana was developed many years ago as a retreat for the 'party faithful'. Now just 4 ha.s are used by Mr and Mrs Keller-Toth, who have leased it from the Balatontourist organisation and run it as a quiet, friendly site. There is a great feeling of space and naturally, much woodland around in which you may wander. There are 27 hedged pitches of 120 sq.m. (where two 60 sq.m. ones have been joined) on grass. Many have shade from trees including about 65 smaller individual ones. The remainder are amongst the trees which mark them out. There is no exact number of pitches, but about 200 units are taken in all, with 156 electrical connections (2 pin, 6 or 10A) on sloping ground. The fair-sized restaurant, open all season, has tables, benches and flowers in troughs outside. Animation is organised in high season with Hungarian musicians and animators.

Facilities: Toilet facilities are old but kept very clean with chemical disposal in the men`s. Shower block open 06.00-12.00 and 15.00-23.00. Very smart, new ladies` section has large showers with private dressing, whilst the facilities for men are older with communal changing. Washbasins, for both men and women, are older with just two with hot water for each, the rest withcold water. Splendid, new children's washroom (key from reception), with 3 shower/baths, 2 of designed for handicapped children. Laundry with washing machines (key from reception). Large kitchen with 3 cookers but cold water dishwashing only. Well stocked shop (open 08.00-17.00 low season or 22.00 high season). Restaurant (all season). Play area, with animation in high season. Volleyball. Tennis. Under cover table tennis. **Off site:** Many walking opportunities. Lake fishing 3 km. Riding or bicycle 5 km.

Charges 2003

Per pitch incl. electricity	€ 6.15 - € 10.25
extra person	€ 1.84 - € 2.87
child (2-14 yrs)	€ 1.02 - € 1.64
local tax	€ 0.53

Special rates for disabled persons. **Tel:** 87 445 013. Fax: 87 445 013. E-mail: dianacamping@freemail.hu. **Reservations:** Write to site. **Open** 3 May - 21 September.

Directions: From road 71 on the north side of the lake, turn towards Aszófö just west of Balatonfüred, through the village and follow the signs for about 1 km. along access road (bumpy in places).

Balatontourist Camping Füred

8230 Balatonfüred (Veszprem County)

This is a large international holiday village rather than just a campsite, pleasantly decorated with flowers and shrubs, with a very wide range of facilities and sporting activities. All that one could want for a family holiday can be found on this site. Directly on the lake with 800 m. of access for boats and bathing, it has a large, grassy lying out area, a small beach area for children with various watersports organised. There is also a swimming pool on site with lifeguards. Mature trees cover about two-thirds of the site giving shade, with the remaining area being in the open. The 954 individual pitches (60-120 sq.m), all with electricity (4-10A), are on either side of hard access roads on which pitch numbers are painted. Many bungalows are also on the site. Along the main road that runs through the site, are shops and kiosks, with the main bar/restaurant and terrace overlooking the lake. Other bars and restaurants are around the site. A water ski drag lift is most spectacular with its four towers erected in the lake to pull skiers around the circuit. Coach trips and pleasure cruises are organised. The site is part of the Balatontourist organisation and, while public access is allowed for the amenities, security is good. Some tour operators - Danish and German.

Facilities: Six toilet blocks are at various points around the site, fully equipped and including and hot water for dishwashing and laundry. Washing machines. Gas supplies Numerous bars, restaurants, cafés, food bars and supermarket (all 12/4-10/10). Stalls and kiosks with wide range of goods, souvenirs, photo processing. Hairdresser. Excellent swimming pool with separate children's pool (1/5-30/9). Sauna. Fishing. Water ski school. Sailing. Pedaloes. Children's play area on sand. Bicycle hire. Dodgem cars. Tennis. Minigolf. Video games. Dogs are not accepted. **Off site:** Riding 5 km. Close by a street of fast food bars, about 10 in all, offering a variety of Hungarian and international dishes with attractive outdoor terraces under trees.

Charges 2002

Per person	€ 2.46 - € 5.33
child (2-14 yrs)	€ 2.05 - € 4.30
pitch incl. electricity (120 sq m)	€ 11.89 - € 20.08
100 sq.m.	€ 11.07 - € 18.36
70 sq m	€ 9.22 - € 14.14
60 sq m	€ 7.17 - € 11.68

Plus local tax over 18 yrs. **Tel:** 87 343 823. Fax: 87 342 341. E-mail: cfured@balatontourist.hu. **Reservations:** Write to site. **Open** 12 April - 10 October.

Directions: Site is just south of Balatonfüred, on Balatonfüred - Tihany road and is well signed. Gates closed 1-3 pm. except Sat/Sun.

Camping Napfény

8253 Révfülöp (Veszprem County)

Camping Napfény is the larger, sister site of Camping Venus (no. 538). Designed for families with children of all ages looking for an active holiday, the site has a 200 m. frontage on Lake Balaton. There are steps to get into the lake and canoes, boats and pedaloes for hire. An extensive entertainment programme is designed for all ages and there are several bars and restaurants of various styles. There are souvenir shops and a supermarket. In fact, you need not leave the site at all during your holiday, although there are several excursions on offer, including to Budapest or to one of the many Hungarian spas, a trip over Lake Balaton or a traditional wine tour. The site's 450 pitches vary in size (60-110 sq.m). Located further from the water than the pitches at the Venus site, almost all have shade – very welcome during the hot Hungarian summers – and 4-10A electricity. This site is larger and therefore more crowded than the Venus site. As with most of the sites on Lake Balaton, a train line runs just outside the site boundary.

Facilities: The three sanitary blocks, two new and one partly refurbished, include washbasins (open style and in cabins) with hot and cold water, spacious, pre-set and controllable showers, child size toilets and basins, 2 bathrooms with bath, basin and toilet (hourly charge). Heated, unisex baby room. Facilities for disabled visitors. Launderette with washing machines, a dryer, spin dryer, and ironing board (irons for hire). Dishwashing under cover with free hot water. Dog shower. Motorcaravan services. Supermarket. Several bars and restaurants and souvenir shops (open when site is open). Fenced sports field with tennis court on tarmac, basketball and handball. Minigolf. Fishing. Bicycle hire. Canoes, rowing boats and pedaloes for hire. Extensive entertainment for all ages. **Off site:** Riding 3 km.

Charges 2002

Per pitch incl. electricity	HUF 2720 - 4240
tent and car	HUF 1030
motorcaravan	HUF 2110
person	HUF 1050
child (2-14 yrs)	HUF 830

Tel: 088 54 44 44. E-mail: cnapfeny@balatontourist. hu. **Reservations:** Made before mid-May; contact site. **Open** 8 May - 8 September.

Directions: Take the M71 from Veszprém southeast to Keszthely. Site is in Révfülöp on the left hand side of the road.

Hungary

Camping Venus

8252 Balatonszepezd (Veszprem County)

For those who want to be directly beside Lake Balaton, but would like a reasonably quiet location, Camping Venus site is probably the best spot. Apart from the rather noisy train that passes the site a few times an hour, this is a quiet site with views of the lake from almost all the pitches. From the front row of pitches you could almost dangle your feet from your caravan in the warm water of the lake. Varying in size from 70 to 100 sq.m, there are 150 flat pitches, all with at least 4A electricity and almost all with shade. Given the small size of the site, Mária Ékes, the manager, gets to know every guest in person and she will make you very welcome. This is a well managed site with modern, well kept sanitary blocks and 24 hour security at the gate. Lake Balaton with its water temperature of about 25 degrees Celsius in summer, is obviously the main attraction here, but you can also make several excursions, for example a trip to Budapest or a gipsy night in Riza.

Facilities: Two sanitary blocks, one new, provide toilets, washbasins (open style and in cabins) with hot and cold water, pre-set showers, facilities for disabled people and child size toilets and basins. Launderette with washing machine, sinks and ironing board (iron for hire at reception). Motorcaravan services. Shop for basics. Bar. Restaurant. Snack bar. Playground. Table tennis. Daily activity program with pottery, fairy tale reading, horse shows, tournaments in Sümeg, trips over the lake and to Budapest. Canoe, pedalo, rowing boats and bicycle hire. Dogs are not accepted. **Off site:** Riding 2 km.

Charges 2002

Per pitch incl. electricity	HUF 3250 - 3750
adult	HUF 1050
child (2-14 yrs)	HUF 830

Plus local tax. **Tel:** 00 36 87 568 067. Fax: 00 36 87 568 062. E-mail: cvenus@balatontourist.hu. **Reservations:** Made before mid-May; contact site. **Open** 14 May - 10 September.

Directions: Follow the M71 from Veszprém to the southeast towards Keszthely. Site is in Balatonszepezd on the left hand side of the road.

Hungary

Panoráma Camping

Panoráma Köz 1, 8372 Cserszegtomaj (Zala County)

Campsites around Lake Balaton generally have the disadvantage of being close to the main road and/or the railway, as well as being extremely busy in high season. Panorama is popular too, but is essentially a quiet site near the western end of the lake. It also has the benefit of extensive views from the flat, grass terraces. Only the young or very fit are advised to take the higher levels with the best views of all. The original 50 pitches vary in size from fairly small to quite large (100 sq.m.), all with 10A electricity, with the lower terraces having fairly easy access. A further 30 pitches have been added. The site is a sun-trap and there is not much shade from the trees. It also has a delightful restaurant, with terrace, offering really good value meals at lunchtime and in the evenings. The friendly proprietors speak no English but are keen to welcome British visitors and have a dictionary. As at many Hungarian sites, you will probably find German and or Dutch visitors who would assist if you speak no German at all.

Facilities: A new sanitary block, with the original block, are heated and very satisfactory, with large, curtained, controllable showers (communal changing). Dishwashing. Washing machine. Ladies' hairdresser. Massage. Small shop (Mon - Sat, 07.30-10.00). Restaurant with bar. **Off site:** Many walking and cycling opportunities. Riding, bicycle hire and tennis 3 km. fishing and boat launching 6 km. Lake Balaton 7 km. Héviz is the famous, large, thermal, warm water lake and there are castles to visit.

Charges 2002

Per person	HUF 520.00
child (under 14 yrs)	HUF 420.00
caravan	HUF 830.00 - 1300.00
tent	HUF 750.00 - 850.00
car or m/cycle	HUF 260.00
motorcaravan	HUF 1300.00
electricity	HUF 600.00

Electricity included. No credit cards. **Tel:** 83 314 412. Fax: 83 330 215. **Reservations:** Advisable for May and Sept (the busiest months), and made in German. **Open** 1 April - 31 October.

Directions: Site is about 2 km. north of Héviz on the road signed to Sümeg. There is a long, hard access road with a large sign.

Hungary

Ozon Camping

510

Erdei Malom köz 3, 9400 Sopron (Gyor-Moson-Sopron County)

Sopron, close to the border, was not over-run by the Turks or bombed in WW2, so 350 historic buildings and monuments remain intact, making it the second major tourist centre after Budapest. It also has a music festival from mid-June to mid-July and is close to the Löverek hills. This surprisingly pleasant campsite is just over 4 km. from the centre, with the modern, chalet style reception at the entrance from where the oval site opens out into a little green valley surrounded by trees. It is peaceful and comfortable with many trees within the site offering shade. Concrete access roads lead to 60 numbered grass pitches, all with electricity (6A). Some with water and waste water are in the lower level on the left, where siting is more diffi-cult for caravans. Mostly flat, some with a slight slope, they are separated by hedges and of up to 80 sq.m.

Facilities: Sanitary facilities in two heated buildings are identical except that one has a laundry (free) whilst the other, near the swimming pool, has a sauna. Curtained showers with communal changing, close to washbasins therefore could be a little cramped. Both blocks have free cookers, fridges and dishwashing. Gas supplies.Restaurant with good value meals (all season). Room with TV. Basic essen-tials and money exchange at reception. Small swim-ming pool and paddling pool (15/5-11/10). **Off site:** Shops 150 m. Bicycle hire 1 km. Tennis 2 km. Fishing 2 km. Riding 3 km. Bus service to town centre.

Charges 2003

Per person	HUF 1020.00
child (under 10 yrs)	HUF 750.00
pitch	HUF 1400.00
dog	HUF 750.00
local tax	HUF 150.00

No credit cards. **Tel:** 99 331 144. **Fax:** 99 331 145. **Reservations:** May be advisable in high season and are made if you write in German. **Open** 15 April - 15 October.

Directions: From A3 south of Wien, follow roads 16 (Kingenbach) and 84 to Sopron. Site is on road to Brennerberganya, well signed in Sopron.

Hungary

Gasthof Camping Pihenö

512

I-es fout, 9011 Györszentivan-Kertváros (Gyor-Moson-Sopron County)

This privately owned site makes an excel-lent night stop when travelling to and from Hungary as it lies beside the main no. 1 road, near to the end of the motorway to the east of Györ. It is set amidst pine trees with pitches which are not numbered, but marked out by small shrubs, in a small clearing or between the trees. With space for about 40 touring units, all with electric-ity (6A), and a dozen simple, one roomed bungalows. On one side of the camp, fronting the road, is the reception, bar and pleasant restuarant with terrace. A very friendly German speaking owner runs the site and restaurant with his wife who speaks a little English.

Facilities: A single, small toilet block has just two showers for each sex (charge) and curtained, communal dressing space. Room for washing clothes and dishes with small cooking facility. Bar. Restaurant with good menu and reasonable prices. Solar heated swimming pool (10 x 5 m, open June - Sept). Bread orders at reception previous evening.

Charges 2003

Per person	€ 1.74
pitch	€ 2.26
electricity	€ 0.87

Less 10% for stays over 4 days, 20% after 8. **Tel:** 96 523 008. **Fax:** 96 523 008. **E-mail:** piheno@ arrabonet.gyor.hu. **Reservations:** Write to site. **Open** 1 April - 30 October.

Directions: Coming from Austria, continue through Györ following signs for Budapest. Continue on road no. 1 past start of motorway for 3 km. and site is on left. From Budapest, turn right onto road no. 10 at end of motorway, then as above.

Hungary

Dömös Camping

511

Duna-Part, 2027 Dömös (Komarom-Esztergom County)

The area of the Danube Bend is a major tourist attraction and here at Dömös is a modern, well maintained and peaceful site with large pitches and easy access. The Danube is just over 50 m. away and quite fast flowing. With Budapest just 45 km, Esztergom (the ancient capital of Hungary) 15 km. and the small town of Visegrad, with its impressive cliff fortress close by, this could make an ideal base. There are about 100 quite large pitches, of which 80 have 6A electricity, in sections on flat grass, divided by small plants and some with little shade. At the top of the site is an inviting open-air swimming pool.

Facilities: Modern sanitary building includes very satisfactory, large showers with individual changing. Laundry. Motorcaravan services. Small café with terrace (restaurant planned). Bar. Shop (1/6-26/8). Swimming pool (20 x 10 m, all season). Small play area. Sightseeing tours. English is spoken. **Off site:** Village facilities 300 m. Fishing 50 m. Riding 2 km.

Charges 2003

Per pitch incl. electricity	1750
person	750
local tax	400

No credit cards (cash only). **Tel:** 33 482 319. **Fax:** 33 414 800. **E-mail:** domoscamping@mail.uti.hu. **Reservations:** Not normally made, but may for British visitors. **Open** 1 May - 15 September.

Directions: Site is between village and the Danube, off road 11 Esztergom - Visegrad - Szentendre.

Camping Rosengarten

Pilisi út 7, 1106 Budapest (Pest County)

517

Camping Rosengarten is a charming, small family site with only 25 pitches on the outskirts of Budapest. It is a better option than some other sites for visiting the Hungarian capital as it has more amenities. In addition to a swimming pool, Rosengarten also has a play area for young children and a bar with TV. The 25 pitches are on flat, well kept grass and you can relax the shade of large trees. The bar is packed with memorabilia from former guests and the Heiszer family will be glad to advise you on sightseeing in the city. The bus to the closest underground station stops in front of the site - it takes about half an hour from the site to the city centre. On your return the swimming pool will be welcome after a day in the city and afterwards you can enjoy the Hungarian hospitality of the Heiszer family in the cosy bar. The site is open all year and one sanitary block is heated.

Facilities: The two sanitary blocks are fairly simple but very clean and one can be heated. They have controllable showers, two en-suite rooms with basin, toilet and shower. Dishwashing sinks under cover with free hot water. Washing machine. Bar with TV. No shop but bread to order Outdoor swimming pool (11 x 5 m). Playground. Table tennis. Cabins to rent. **Off site:** Budapest (30 minutes with public transport, tickets from reception). Riding 3 km.

Charges 2002

Per person	HUF 1200.00
child	HUF 800.00
caravan or motorcaravan	HUF 1200.00
with electricity	HUF 1400.00
tentHUF	1100.00

No credit cards. **Tel:** 00 36 1 261 95 37. Fax: 00 36 1 261 96 37. E-mail: camping@mail.externet.hu. **Reservations:** Call, write or e-mail site. **Open** all year.

Directions: Take the no. 3 road (not the M3) east towards Miskolc and turn immediately right after passing the railway bridge at the Opel garage. Site is on right in 200 m.

Fortuna Camping

Dózsa György út 164, 2045 Törökbálint (Pest County)

515

This superb and pretty site lies at the foot of a hill with views of the vineyards, but Budapest is only 25 minutes away by bus. Surrounded by mature trees, the owner, Csaba Szücs, will proudly name all 150 varieties of bushes and shrubs which edge some of the pitches. The site has a small restaurant with very reasonable prices but it is only open from 18.00-20.00 (although when we visited the last order was taken at 21.00). A new, open air swimming pool with flume will help you to cool off in summer with an indoor pool for cooler weather. Concrete and gravel access roads lead to terraces where there are 170 individual pitches most bordered with hedges, all with electricity (16A, long leads may be needed), and 14 with water, on slightly sloping ground. A special field area provides for group bookings, and has separate facilities. Herr Szücs and his family will endeavour to make your stay a comfortable one. His daughter organises tours to Budapest or the surrounding countryside, and will also explain the mysteries of public transport in Budapest.

Facilities: Four fully equipped sanitary blocks (one with heating) with extra toilets for disabled people. Washing up facilities, plus six cookers in sheltered area. Washing machine. Gas supplies. Motorcaravan services. Restaurant and bar (all year). Snack bar. Shop (1/6-20/8 or essentials from reception, order bread previous day). Outdoor swimming pool with slide (15/5-15/9). New indoor pool. Small children's play area. Excursions organised. English is spoken. **Off site:** Close to bus terminal for city centre 1 km.

Charges 2002

Per person	€ 5.00
child (4-14 yrs)	€ 4.00
pitch	€ 5.00
electricity	€ 2.00
dog	€ 2.00

No credit cards. **Tel:** 23 335 364. Fax: 23 339 697. **Reservations:** Advisedfor high season - write to site. **Open** all year.

Directions: From M1 Györ - Budapest, exit for Törökbálint following signs for town and then site. Also accessible from M7 Budapest - Balaton road.

Jumbo Camping

518 Budakalászi út 23-25, 2096 Üröm (Pest County)

Jumbo Camping is a modern, thoughfully developed site in the northern outskirts of Budapest. Situated on a hillside 15 km from Budapest centre, with attractive views of the Buda hills and with public transport to the city near, this is a pleasant and comfortable, small site (despite the name) where you will receive a very warm welcome. It is possible to park outside the short, steepish entrance which has a chain across. Reception, where you are given a comprehensive English language information sheet, doubles as a café/bar area. The concrete and gravel access roads lead shortly to 55 terraced pitches of varying size, a little on the small size for large units, and some with a fair degree of slope. Hardstanding for cars and caravan wheels, as well as large hardstandings for motorhomes. There is a steep incline to some pitches and use of the site's 4x4 may be required. All pitches have 6A electricity (may require long leads) and there are some caravan pitches with water and waste water. They are mostly divided by small hedges and the whole area is fenced.

Facilities: Sanitary facilities are most satisfactory, with large showers (communal changing). Dishwashing undercover, Terrace with chairs and tables. Washing machine, iron and cooking facilities on payment. Motorcaravan services. Café where bread (orders taken), milk and butter available. Small swimming pool (10/6-10/9). Children's play area. Barbecue area. English spoken and information sheet provided in English. **Off site:** Shop and restaurant 500 m. The 'Old Swabian Wine-Cellar' said to serve extremely good food. Bus to city 500 m. every 30 minutes. Riding (4 km) and tennis can be arranged. Fishing 8 km.

Charges 2002

Per pitch acc to size and season	HUF 600 - 1400
adult	HUF 890
child (3-14 yrs)	HUF 580
electricity	HUF 560
dog	HUF 280
local tax	HUF 120

No credit cards (cash only). **Tel:** 26 351 251. Fax: 26 351 251. **Reservations:** Write to site. **Open** 1 April - 31 October.

Directions: Site is signed on roads to Budapest - nos. 11 from Szentendre and 10 from Komaron. If approaching from Budapest use 11 but note that the site sign appears very quickly after a sharp right and bend (site signs and entry are clearer if using road 10). You can also approach via Györ on M1/E60 and Lake Balaton on M7/E71. The turn into the site is quite acute and uphill.

Farm Lator

519 Rózsavari út 95, 3425 Sály-Lator (Heves County)

Farm Lator is a small, privately run site on the edge of one of the Hungarian National Parks, near the Bükk mountains, more or less in the middle of nowhere! This keeps the site really quiet and the surroundings very suitable for many different types of bird and butterfly that you won't find anywhere else in Europe. The Dutch/ Hungarian owners of Farm Lator, Rob de Jong and Barbara Borostyankoi, try to keep the site and its surroundings as natural as possible. This means the site has few amenities, other than a clean and well kept sanitary block, and electricity (16A) is only provided for three pitches. The charm of this site is the peace and quiet of the natural environment that one enjoys here but they also organise excursions. Barbara would love to take you on a trip to the 'real' Eger to show you much more than just the castle and the world famous red wine cellars. You can also visit the char-coal-burners who show you how to burn chalk and charcoal the old fashioned way - something that would be hard to find anywhere else in Europe.

Facilities: One small unisex sanitary block provides a toilet, two washbasins and three controllable showers, all very clean and well maintained. Sinks under cover. Three pitches with 16A electricity. Sitting room with library and table tennis. Weekly meal organised. No shop but bread to order. Torches useful. **Off site:** Eger 1 hour drive.

Charges 2002

Per person	€ 4.00
child (4-16 yrs)	€ 2.00
tent	€ 4.00 - 5.00
caravan or motorcaravan	€ 8.00
electricity	€ 2.00

No credit cards. **Tel:** 0036 49 33 61 33. E-mail: farmlator@hotmail.com. **Reservations:** Contact site. **Open** all year.

Directions: From Budapest take M3 motorway to Miskolc. Take exit for Füzesabony and follow the no. 3 road towards Miskolc. In Bükkabrany, at Total petrol station, take exit to Sály and follow road all the way to the end.

Hungary
Pelsoczy-Tiszavirág Camping

P.f.27, 3910 Tokaj (Szabolcs-Szatmar-Bereg Co)

From mid-June to mid-September, this site gets quite busy, but either side of these dates it is quiet and very relaxing. Set on the banks of the wide River Tisza, the level grass pitches, 120 in number, are close together and narrow but quite long, off a hard circular access road so siting should be quite easy. All the pitches have electricity mostly 6 Amp and there is much shade. There is a high season reception, but at other times, you site yourself and a gentleman calls during the evening to collect the fee. There may well be some day-time noise from watersports on the river but it is very quiet by night. This is a useful base for visiting northeast Hungary, not far from the Ukraine and Romania. Tokai the plans are afoot to rebuild the toilet block.

Facilities: The toilet block has external entry WCs (British style) and curtained showers with communal undressing. They are cleam, but basic and a little tired looking. Kiosk and bar. River sports. No English spoken (German is). **Off site:** Shops for basics outside the main season are in the town over the bridge, a 600 m. walk. Bicycle and boat hire 200 m. Riding 3 km.

Charges 2002

Per unit incl. 2 persons	HUF 2200
tent	HUF 1800

Tel: 47 352 626. Fax: 47 352 017. **Reservations:** Advised for high season, but in German - otherwise arrive early. **Open** 1 April - 30 October.

Directions: Tokaj is east of Miskolc and north of Debrecen. Site is just south of the river bridge on road no. 38. (Note: beware the noisy campsite signed on the other side of the road).

Hungary
Diófaház

Ady Endreút 12, 3348 Szilvásvárad (Heves County)

Diófaház is an ideal base in northeast Hungary for exploring this wooded part of the country, to visit the stud farm of the famous Lippizaner horses (one of only five in the world) or to visit the town of Eger, world famous for its culture and red wine. The site is in private grounds on the edge of the village and provides a maximum of 15 pitches, 6 with electricity, which makes it quiet and peaceful. Gyöngyi and Simon de Heij, the Dutch/Hungarian owners provide a warm welcome and if you're lucky you may arrive for weekly barbecue or the home made Hungarian goulash soup. There are plenty of opportunities for cycling or walking. In winter this is a skiing resort and there is a local spa.

Facilities: The single toilet block includes washbasins in cabins with hot and cold water, controllable showers and sinks with free hot water. Fresh rolls to order every day with home made jam but no shop. Discounts at two restaurants in the village if you show your campers card. Barbecues are not permitted. English is spoken. **Off site:** Riding 200 m. Bicycle hire 500 m. Fishing 6 km.

Charges 2002

Per unit incl. 2 persons	€ 8.50
extra person	€ 2.50

Tel: 00 36 36 35 55 95. Fax: 00 36 36 35 55 95. E-mail: info@diofahaz.hu. **Reservations:** Contact site. **Open** all year.

Directions: Take the no. 25 road from Eger north to Szilvásvárad. Site is signed when entering the village.

Hungary
Dorcas Christian Camping Centre

Vekeri Tó, 4002 Debrecen (Hajdu-Bihar County)

Debrecen is an interesting old town, close to the Hortobagy National Park and convenient if you are looking for a break travelling to Romania or the Ukraine. Dorcas is a Dutch Christian organisation and the campsite provides holidays for special causes. The site is about 10 km. from Debrecen in a forest location, fenced and covered with trees. The 40 flat and grassy touring pitches are off tarmac access roads, arranged in four groups. Some pitches are divided by hedges, others marked out by trees and all have electricity available (6A). A very pleasant restaurant and terrace offers good value meals. Through the site is an area for walks and a lake for fishing.

Facilities: The central large tiled sanitary building is of a rather open design and of acceptable quality with large, curtained showers (external changing). Facilities for dishwashing and laundry (key at reception). Shop for basics. Good value restaurant (menu in English) with terrace. Small swimming pool (June-Aug). Playgrounds. Church services (in English) . Conference hall and meeting rooms. Bicycle hire. TV rental. Good walks. English spoken. **Off site:** Riding 2 km. Lake nearby with fishing.

Charges 2002

Per unit incl. 2 adults and electricity	10.00
extra person	3.00

Plus local tax. **Tel:** 52 441 119. Fax: 52 441 119. E-mail: dorcasaidhungary@debrecen.com. **Reservations:** Probably unnecessary, but contact site. **Open** 1 May - 30 September.

Directions: From Debrecen take road no. 47 south for 4 km. then left towards Hosszupalyi for 6 km. Site is signed on the right.

Hungary
Kek-Duna Camping
530 Hösök Tere 12, 7020 Dunafoldvar (Tolna County)

Dunaföldvár is a most attractive town of 10,000 people and you are in the heart of it in just two or three minutes by foot from this site, easily reached via the wide towpath on the west bank of the Danube. For a town site, Kék-Duna is remarkably peaceful. Apart from the obvious attractions of the river, with a large island opposite and pleasant walks possible, the ancient town has a most interesting museum, the 'Burg', with a genuine dungeon and cells, Roman relics and with a panoramic view of the town and river from its top floor. There are in fact too many places of interest within easy reach to list here. This is a pleasant small site on the banks of the Danube, fenced all round and locked at night, with flat concrete access roads to 50 pitches. All have electricity (16A), the first half being open, the remainder well shaded.

Facilities: Modern, tiled sanitary building with nicely decorated ladies' section offers curtained showers with communal changing. The rest of the facilities are of above average standard. Dishwashing outside with cold water. Washing machine. Shop and café (from mid June), town shops close. Bicycle hire. Excursion information. **Off site:** Tennis 50 m. Riding 5 km. Thermal swimming pool 200 m (under the same ownership).

Charges 2002

Per adult	HUF 500.00
pensioner, student or child	HUF 250.00
caravan, car and electricity	HUF 1200.00
motorcaravan and electricity	HUF 1100.00
tent and car	HUF 550.00
electricity for tent	HUF 220.00

Tel: 75 541 107. **Fax:** 75 541 107. **Reservations:** Advisable for July/Aug. or arrive early. **Open** all year.

Directions: From no. 6 Budapest - Pecs road take exit at Dunaföldvár for Kecskemed road no. 52, and follow until slip road on right which leads on to the riverside towpath. Site is well signed.

Hungary
Jonathermál Motel-Camping
526 Kökút 26, 6120 Kiskunmajsa (Bacs-Kiskun County)

Situated three kilometres to the north of the town of Kiskunmajsa, a few kilometres west of road no. 5 (E75) from Budapest (140 km.) to Szeged (35 km.) this is one of the best Hungarian campsites. The camping area is large, reached by tarmac access roads with 250 unmarked pitches are in several areas around the motel and sanitary buildings. All the 120 large pitches have electricity (6A) and are set on flat grass. Entrance to the pool complex is charged (weekly tickets available) which gives you a huge 100 x 70 m. open air pool with a beach along one side, the indoor pool, children's pool, thermal, sauna and cold dip and an open air thermal pool, plus various places to eat and drink.

Facilities: A heated sanitary block provides first class facilities including washbasins in cabins and a unit for disabled visitors. Launderette. Gas supplies. Kiosk on site for bread and basics. Smart bar and rest room. Restaurant by pool complex. Large swimming and thermal complex with other facilities (1/5-1/10). Massage (on payment). Playground. Volleyball, tennis and minigolf. Fishing. Bicycle hire. Riding. German spoken. **Off site:** Shop 120 m.

Charges 2002

Per unit incl. 2 persons	HUF 1560 - 2080
child (6-14 yrs)	HUF 200.00 - 300.00
electricity	HUF 650.00

Plus local tax. Less 5-10% for longer stays. No credit cards. **Tel:** 77 481 855. **Fax:** 77 481 013. E-mail: jonathermal@mail.datanet.hu. **Reservations:** Possibly necessary mid-July - mid-Aug. **Open** all year.

Directions: From no. 5 (E75) Budapest - Szeged road take Kiskunmajsa exit and site is well signed 3 km. north of the town.

Hungary
Sugovica Camping
531 Petöfi-sziget, 6500 Baja (Bacs-Kiskun County)

If you are exploring Southern Transdanubia or en-route south, then Baja is an acceptable stop, on the east banks of the Danube. The site is on a small island, quiet and relaxed, next to the hotel which owns it, where there is a small swimming pool on payment and a terraced restaurant. The 180 fair sized pitches (80 sq.m), all with 10A electricity and 7 with hardstandings for motorhomes, are on flat, grassy, firm ground, easily accessed from tarred roads and with some shade from the many trees.

Facilities: Sanitary facilities are just about adequate. Showers have communal changing, but all was clean when seen. Laundry and kitchen with fridge and freezer. Small shop. TV room. Tennis. Table tennis. Riverside walks. Fishing. Boat Launching. No English spoken. **Off site:** Town facilities close.

Charges 2002

Per unit incl. 2 persons	HUF 2100
electricity	300.00
local tax	70.00

Tel: 79 321 755. **Fax:** 79 323 155. **Reservations:** not made. **Open** 1 May - 30 September.

Directions: Site is on Petoti island (sziget), well signed from just southwest of the junction of roads 51 from Budapest and 55 from Szeged, the bridge being close to a cobbled town square.

Ireland

Northern Ireland Tourist Board

24 Haymarket, London SW1Y 4DG. Tel: 020 7766 9920 Fax: 020 7766 9929
E-mail: infogb@nitb.com Internet: www.ni-tourism.com

The Republic of Ireland Tourist Board

Bord Failte, Ireland House, 150-151 New Bond Street, London W15 2AQ
Tel: 0800 039 7000 Fax: 020 7493 9065
E-mail: info@irishtouristboard.co.uk   Internet: www.ireland.travel.ie

'You're welcome' is not said lightly to the visitor who sets foot in Ireland, it is said with sincerity. On this 'Emerald Isle' you will find friendly and hospitable people, spectacular scenery and a selection of good campsites, in both north and south of the country, to suit your particular needs. Whether you choose to be sited by a lough shore, at the foothills of a mountain range or close by golden sands and mysterious rock formations, the scenery is stunning and the pace of life slow. With the help of information and maps available from both Tourist Offices you discover for yourself, not only the beauty spots, but also many historic and interesting routes to follow. For more campsites in both Northern Ireland and the Irish Republic, see the **Alan Rogers' Good Camps Guide - Britain & Ireland.**

The notes below refer to the Irish Republic. For information on travel in the North contact the address above.

Population

3,500,000, density 50 per sq. km.

Climate

Similar to the UK but even wetter!

Language

English. The traditional tongue Gaelic (Gaeltacht) is spoken mainly in the south-west.

Currency

From January 2002, in common with 11 other European countries, the Irish unit of currency will be the EURO (€).
€ 1 = Irish£ 0.79.

Banks

Open Mon-Fri 10.00-12.30 and 13.30-15.00 (Thur 13.30-17.00), but note many small country towns are served by sub-offices open only certain days.

Post Offices

Main offices open Mon-Fri 09.00-17.30 and Sat 09.00-13.00.

Telephone

To call the UK dial 00 44 followed by the local STD code omitting initial 0. From the UK dial 00 353 omitting the first 0 of the code plus number.

Public Holidays

New Year; St Patrick's Day, 17 Mar; Easter; 1st Mon in June; 1st Mon in Aug; last Mon in Oct; Christmas, 25 Dec.

Shops

Open Mon-Sat 09.00-17.30 or 18.00.

Motoring

Allow plenty of time when travelling in Ireland even though the roads are relatively uncongested. Poor road surfaces, unmarked junctions and poor weather conditions can delay. Signposting or the lack of them can be a problem. A good map is a necessity. Drive on the left as in the UK. A Green Card is advised as most policies provide only minimum coverage in the Republic of Ireland

Speed Limits: On certain roads, clearly marked, the speed limits are 40 mph (65 kph) or 50 mph (80 kph) - applying to a car and trailer as well.

Ferry Services

The following ferry services are expected to operate between the UK mainland and Ireland in 2002:

Irish Ferries
08705 171717

P&O Irish Sea
0870 24 24 777

Sea Cat Scotland
08705 523 523

Swansea Cork Ferries
01792 45 61 16

Stena Line
08705 70 70 70

Norse Merchant Ferries
0870 600 4321

Northern Ireland
Drumaheglis Caravan Park

834 36 Glenstall Road, Ballymoney BT53 7QN (Co. Antrim)

A caravan park which maintains high standards, Drumaheglis is popular throughout the season. On the banks of the lower River Bann, 4 miles from Ballymoney, it appeals to watersports enthusiasts or makes an ideal base for exploring this scenic corner of Northern Ireland. The marina offers facilities for boat launching, water-skiing, canoeing or fishing, whilst getting out and about can take you to the Giant's Causeway, Portstewart or Portrush, the sands of Whitepark Bay, the Glens of Antrim or the picturesque villages of the Antrim coast road. For tourers only, this site iis well laid out with trees, shrubs, flower beds and tarmac roads. There are now 53 serviced pitches with hardstanding, electricity (5/10A) and water points.

Facilities: Modern toilet blocks, spotlessly clean when we visited, include individual wash cubicles, and facilities for disabled visitors, plus four family shower rooms. Dishwashing sinks. Washing machine and dryer. Children's play area. Volleyball and table tennis. Barbecue and picnic areas. **Off site:** Bicycle hire and golf 4 miles, riding 0.5 miles.

Charges 2002

Per unit incl. electricity	£ 13.00
for 7 days	£ 78.00
pitch without services	£ 10.00
for 7 days	£ 60.00

Tel: 028 2766 6466. Fax: 028 2766 7659. E-mail: info@ballymoney.gov.uk. **Reservations:** Essential for peak periods and weekends. **Open** Easter - 1 October.

Directions: From A26/B62 Portrush - Ballymoney roundabout continue for approx. 1 mile on the A26 towards Coleraine. Site is clearly signed - follow International camping signs.

Northern Ireland
Tullans Farm Caravan Park

859 46 Newmills Road, Coleraine BT52 2JB (Co. Londonderry)

A quality, well run family park convenient for the Causeway coast, Tullans Farm is one of the most popular in the area. It has a quiet, heart of the country feel, yet the town of Coleraine is within a mile, the seaside resort Portrush and Portstewart five miles. Tullans Farm has earned a reputation for its clean toilet block, attractive flower displays and its well cared for appearance. In a central position, fronted by a parking space, stands a long white building housing the sanitary facilities and reception. Around the park roads are gravel and 32 pitches are on hardstanding, all with electric hook-ups (10A). In season the owners organise barbecues, barn dances and line dancing.

Facilities: The toilet and shower rooms, including a family shower unit, are spacious, modern and include facilities for people with disabilities. Laundry and washing up room with sinks, washing machine, dryers and a large fridge. Play area. TV lounge and barn used for indoor recreation.

Charges 2002

Per unit incl. all persons, electricity	£ 10.00 - £ 11.00
awning	£ 1.00
family tent	£ 10.00
2 man tent	£ 7.00

No credit cards. **Tel:** 028 7034 2309. Fax: 028 7034 2309. **Reservations:** Advised for peak times. **Open** March - 31 October.

Directions: From the Lodge Road roundabout (south end of Coleraine) turn east onto A29 Portrush ring road and proceed for 0.5 miles. Turn right at sign for park and Windy Hall. Park is clearly signed on left.

Irish Republic
Roundwood Caravan & Camping Park

913 Roundwood (Co. Wicklow)

In the heart of the Wicklow mountains, this park is under new management, but still maintains high standards. It is neatly laid out with rows of trees dividing the different areas and giving an attractive appearance. There are 31 hardstanding pitches for caravans and 8 motorcaravans, all with electricity (6A), plus 40 pitches for tents, arranged off tarmac access roads. There are excellent walks around the Varty Lakes and a daily bus service to Dublin city. Close by are the Wicklow and Sally Gap, Glendalough, Powerscourt Gardens, plus many other places of natural beauty. Apart from its scenic location, this site is well placed for the ferry ports.

Facilities: The sanitary block is kept clean, with adequate washing and toilet facilities, plus spacious showers on payment. Two dishwashing sinks and good laundry facilities, but ask at reception as machines are not self-service. Campers' kitchen and dining room. TV room. Adventure playground. Bicycle hire. **Off site:** Fishing or golf 1 km.

Charges 2002

Per unit	€ 8.90 - € 10.20
adult	€ 2.55
child (under 14 yrs)	€ 1.90
electricity	€ 1.90

No credit cards. **Tel:** 01 2818163. Fax: 01 2818196. E-mail: roundwoodcaravancamp@yahoo.co.uk. **Reservations:** Accepted without deposit and advisable for July/Aug. **Open** 31 March - 1 October.

Directions: Turn off N11 Dublin - Wexford road at Kilmacanogue towards Glendalough and then 15 km. to Roundwood.

Irish Republic
Moat Farm Caravan and Camping Park
916 Donard (Co. Wicklow)

Providing a true feel of the countryside, this park is part of a working sheep farm. It offers incredible vistas across a scenic landscape, yet is within driving distance of Dublin and Rosslare. Driving into the village of Donard you little suspect that alongside the main street lies a pleasant, well cared for and tranquil five-acre site. There are 40 pitches for caravans and tents. Spacious pitches with hardstanding line both sides of a broad avenue, incorporating ample space for awning and all with 10A electricity and drainage points. A large field takes tents and further caravans. The site makes a good base for touring or going on foot, for this area is a walker's paradise with a 30 minute circular walk around the perimeter of the site.

Facilities: The toilet block is kept very clean and includes spacious showers, facilities for visitors with disabilities, and a well equipped laundry room. There is a good quality campers' kitchen and a large recreation/entertainment room with an open fire. Three large barbecues. **Off site:** Fishing 3 km, bicycle hire 15 km, golf 13 km.

Charges 2002

Per caravan, motorcaravan or family tent	€ 11.00
person	€ 1.50
tent (1 or 2 persons)	€ 8.00
electricity	€ 2.00

No credit cards. **Tel:** 045 404727. Fax: 045 404727. E-mail: moatfarm@ireland.com. **Reservations:** Contact site. **Open** 1 March - 31 October.

Directions: Park is 16.5 km. south of Blessington. Leave M50 Dublin ring motorway at exit 10 to join N81 southwest for 19 km. to Blessington. Continue on N81 for a further 16.5 km. and turn left at Old Toll House pub onto local road and follow signs to park in Donard village (3.5 km.)

Irish Republic
Casey's Caravan Park
933 Clonea, Dungarvan (Co. Waterford)

Set on 20 acres of flat grass, edged by mature trees, this family run park offers 284 pitches which include 154 touring pitches, 118 with electrical hook-ups (5A) and 30 with hardstanding. The remainder are occupied by caravan holiday homes. There is direct access from the park to a sandy beach (lifeguard in July/Aug). A highly recommended leisure centre is adjacent should the weather be inclement. The park is 5.5 km. from Dungarvan, a popular town for deep sea angling and three 18 hole golf courses are within easy distance. Recommended drives include the scenic Vee, the Comeragh Drive and the coast road to Tramore.

Facilities: The central toilet block (key system), has good facilities kept spotlessly clean, with showers on payment (€1), washing up sinks and small laundry with machine and dryer. A further luxurious and modern block provides an excellent campers' kitchen, laundry room and toilet for disabled visitors. Large play area with bark surface in its own field (not supervised by staff). Games room with pool table, table tennis and amusements. TV lounge. Crazy golf. Gas supplies. Full time security staff in high season. **Off site:** Two village stores near the beach. Golf.

Charges 2002

Per unit incl. all persons	€ 16.50
hiker, cyclist or m/cyclist incl. tent	€ 6.35
electricity	€ 1.50

No credit cards. **Tel:** 058 41919. **Reservations:** Are made in low season, but not between 9 July - 15 Aug; contact park. **Open** 3 May - 14 September.

Directions: From Dungarvan centre follow R675 east for 3.5 km. Look for signs on the right to Clonea Bay and site. Site is approx. 1.5 km.

Irish Republic
Blarney Caravan & Camping Park

948 Stone View, Blarney (Co. Cork)

There is a heart of the country feel about this 'on the farm' site, yet the city of Cork is only 8 km. A friendly, family run park it has secluded location and neatly laid out, open appearance. The terrain is elevated and gently sloping, commanding views towards Blarney Castle and the surrounding mountainous countryside. The 40 pitches, 30 of which have hardstanding and 10A electricity, are with caravans sited to the centre and left and tents to the right. There are gravel roads, well tended young shrubs, and a screen of mature trees and hedging marks the park's perimeter. In the Blarney area, apart from the castle, house and gardens, there are shops, restaurants, pubs and outdoor pursuits such as walking, riding and fishing.

Facilities: Well kept toilet areas, one new, are housed in converted farm buildings with reception and small shop. Facilities for disabled visitors. Laundry room. Dishwashing area in the large campers' kitchen. Motorcaravan service point. Shop (1/6-31/8). TV lounge. 18 hole golf and pitch and putt course. Night lighting. **Off site:** Public bar and restaurant 100 m. serving food all day.

Charges 2003

Per caravan, family tent, motorhome	€ 6.50 - € 8.00
adult	€ 4.00
child	€ 2.00
hiker/cyclist and tent	€ 5.50 - € 6.00
electricity	€ 3.00

7 nights for price of 6, if pre-paid. **Tel:** 021 451 6519. Fax: 021 438 5167. E-mail: con.quill@camping-ireland.ie. **Reservations:** Contact park. **Open** 1 February - 15 November.

Directions: Site is 8 km. northwest of Cork, just off the N20. Take N20 from Cork for approx. 6 km. and then left on R617 to Blarney. Site clearly signed at Esso station in village, in approx. 2 km.

Irish Republic
Eagle Point Caravan & Camping Park

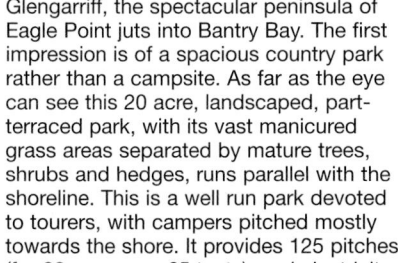

951 Ballylickey, Bantry (Co. Cork)

Midway between the towns of Bantry and Glengarriff, the spectacular peninsula of Eagle Point juts into Bantry Bay. The first impression is of a spacious country park rather than a campsite. As far as the eye can see this 20 acre, landscaped, part-terraced park, with its vast manicured grass areas separated by mature trees, shrubs and hedges, runs parallel with the shoreline. This is a well run park devoted to tourers, with campers pitched mostly towards the shore. It provides 125 pitches (for 60 caravans, 65 tents), and electricity hook-ups (6A). Eagle Point makes an excellent base for watersports enthusiasts - swimming is safe and there is a slipway for small craft.

Facilities: Three well maintained, well designed toilet blocks are above expected standards. Laundry and dishwashing. Motorcaravan services. Children's play area. Tennis courts. Football field to the far right, well away from the pitches. Fishing. Supermarket at park entrance. Dogs are not accepted. **Off site:** Bicycle hire 6 km, riding 10 km, golf 2 km.

Charges 2002

Per family unit	€ 17.50 - € 18.50
unit incl. 2 persons	€ 15.00 - € 16.00
motorcyclist, hiker or cyclist (per person)	€ 6.50
extra car	€ 2.50
electricity	€ 1.50

Tel: 027 50630. E-mail: eaglepointcamping@eircom.net. **Reservations:** Bookings not essential. **Open** 26 April - 30 September.

Directions: Take N71 to Bandon, then R586 Bandon to Bantry, N71 Bantry to Glengarriff. 6.4 km. from Bantry; park entrance is opposite Burmah petrol station.

Irish Republic
Creveen Lodge Caravan & Camping Park

957 Healy Pass, Lauragh (Co. Kerry)

The address of this park is rather confusing, but Healy Pass is the well known scenic summit of the road (R574) crossing the Beara Peninsula, which lies between Kenmare Bay to the north and Bantry Bay to the south. Several kilometres inland from the north coast road (R571), the R574 starts to climb steeply southward towards the Healy Pass. Here, on the mountain foothills, is Creveen Lodge, a working hill farm with a quiet, homely atmosphere. To allow easy access, the steep farm track is divided into a simple one-way system. There are 20 pitches, 16 for tents, 4 for caravans, with an area of hardstanding for motorcaravans, and electricity (5A). This is walking and climbing countryside.

Facilities: Well appointed and immaculately maintained, the small toilet block provides showers on payment (€0.65), plus a communal room with a fridge, freezer, TV, ironing board, fireplace, tables and chairs. Reception is in the farmhouse which also offers guests a comfortable sitting room. Full Irish breakfast is served on request. Play area. **Off site:** Fishing 2 km, bicycle hire 9 km.

Charges 2002

Per unit	€ 9.00
adult	€ 1.50
child	€ 0.75
hiker or cyclist incl. tent	€ 4.75
electricity	€ 1.50

No credit cards. **Tel:** 064 83131. Fax: 064 83998. E-mail: info@creveenlodge.com. **Reservations:** Write to site with an S.A.E. **Open** Easter - 31 October.

Directions: Park is on the Healy Pass road (R574) 1.5 km. southeast of Lauragh.

Irish Republic
Fossa Caravan & Camping Park

Killarney (Co. Kerry)

the **travel service**
TO BOOK
Ferry ✓
Pitch ✓
Accommodation ✗
01892 55 98 98

This mature, well equipped park is in a scenic location, ten minutes drive from the town centre. Fossa Caravan Park is recognisable by its forecourt on which stands a distinctive building housing a roof top restaurant, reception area, shop and petrol pumps. The well laid out park is divided in two - the touring area to the right, tucked behind the main building, and to the left an open grass area mainly for campers. Touring pitches, with electricity and drainage, have hardstanding and are angled between shrubs and trees in a tranquil, well cared for garden setting. At a lhigher level are 50 caravan holiday homes, unobtrusive and sheltered by the thick foliage of the wooded slopes which climb high behind the park. Fossa is convenient for Killarney (5.5 km) and is also en-route for the famed 'Ring of Kerry', making it an ideal base for walkers and golfers.

Facilities: Modern toilet facilities kept spotlessly clean include showers on payment. Laundry room, washing up area. Campers' kitchen. Shop (April - Sept). Restaurant (1 June - end Aug) and takeaway (July/Aug). TV lounge. Play area. Picnic area. Games room. Bicycle hire. Night lighting and security patrol. **Off site:** Fishing or golf 2 km, riding 3 km.

Charges 2002

Per unit	€ 5.00 - € 6.50
adult	€ 4.50
child (under 14 yrs)	€ 1.50
motorcycle and tent per person	€ 6.75 - € 7.50
hiker/cyclist and tent per person	€ 5.00 - € 6.00
awning	€ 3.00
electricity (5/10A)	€ 3.00

Tel: 064 31497. **Fax:** 064 34459. **E-mail:** fossaholidays@eircom.net. **Reservations:** Advisable in high season and made for min. 3 nights with deposit. **Open** 1 April - 30 September.

Directions: Approaching Killarney from all directions, follow signs for N72 Ring of Kerry/Killorglin. At last roundabout join R562/N72. Continue for 5.5 km. and Fossa is the second park to the right.

FOSSA CARAVAN & CAMPING PARK

★ Ample hardstanding & electric hook-up ★ Separate tent area
★ Modern toilets ★ Shaving points ★ Hairdryers ★ Hot showers
★ Facilities for the disabled ★ Full laundry facilities ★ Campers kitchen
★ Free wash-up facilities ★ On site shop open 7 days Easter to Sept.
★ Restaurant (June-Aug) ★ Take away (July/Aug)
★ Children's playground ★ Tennis court ★ Games room ★ TV room ★ Bicycles for hire
★ Mobile homes for hire ★ Hostel accommodation

FOR FREE COLOUR BROCHURE WRITE TO:
Brosnan Family, Fossa Caravan & Camping Park, Fossa, Killarney, Co. Kerry, Ireland
Telephone: (064) 31497   Fax: (064) 34459

Irish Republic
Cong Caravan and Camping Park

Lisloughrey, Quay Road, Cong (Co. Mayo)

the **travel service**
TO BOOK
Ferry ✓
Pitch ✓
Accommodation ✗
01892 55 98 98

It would be difficult to find a more idyllic and famous spot for a caravan park than Cong. Situated close to the shores of Lough Corrib, Cong's scenic beauty was immortalised in the film 'The Quiet Man'. This well kept park is 1.6 km. from the village of Cong, near the grounds of the magnificent and renowned Ashford Castle. The owner's house that incorporates reception, shop and the hostel, stands to the fore of the site. Toilet facilities and the holiday hostel accommodation are entered from the courtyard area. The 40 grass pitches, 36 with electricity, are at a higher level to the rear, with the tent areas below and to the side. The park can be crowded and busy in high season. There is much to keep the active camper happy. Cycling, walking, climbing, caving and scenic drives can all be pursued. A mini cinema shows 'The Quiet Man' film nightly all season.

Facilities: Toilet facilities for the campsite are tastefully decorated, kept clean and are heated when necessary. They include hot showers with curtains (charge), hairdryers, soap and hand towels. Dishwashing area (charge for hot water). Campers' kitchen. Launderette service. Central bin depot. Barbecue, games room and extensive children's play area. Shop. Full Irish or continental breakfast, dinner or packed lunch may be ordered. Bicycle hire. **Off site:** Riding or golf within 2 km, fishing and boat slipway 500 m.

Charges 2002

Per pitch	€ 10.00
adult	€ 2.00
child	€ 1.60
electricity	€ 3.00
hiker/cyclist incl. tent and 1 person	€ 8.50

Tel: 092 46089. **Fax:** 092 46448. **E-mail:** quiet.man.cong@iol.ie. **Reservations:** Contact park. **Open** all year.

Directions: Leave N84 road at Ballinrobe to join R334/345 signed Cong. Turn left at end of the R345 (opposite entrance to Ashford Castle), take next road on right (approx. 300 m) and the park is on right (200 m).

Italy

Italian State Tourist Board, 1, Princes Street, London W1R 8AY

Tel: 020 7408 1254 Fax: 020 7493 6695 Brochures: 09065 508925 (60p per minute)

E-mail: enitlond@globalnet.co.uk   Internet: www.enit.it

Italy only became a unified state in 1861, hence the regional nature of the country today. There are 20 distinct regions and each one retains its own relics of an artistic tradition generally acknowledged to be the world's richest. However, the sharpest division is between north and south. The north is an advanced industrial area, relatively wealthy, whereas the south is one of the economically less developed areas of Europe. Central Italy probably represents the most commonly perceived image of the country and Tuscany, with its classic rolling countryside and the historical towns of Florence, Siena and Pisa, is one of the most visited areas. Venice is unique and as beautiful as its reputation suggests. Rome, Italy's capital, on its seven hills with its Roman legacy, is independent of both north and south. Naples, the natural heart of the south, is close to some of Italy's ancient sites such as Pompei.

Population

58,000,000, density 191.7 per sq. km.

Climate

Varying considerably between north and south; the south enjoys extremely hot summers and relatively mild and fairly dry winters, whilst the mountainous regions of the north are much cooler with heavy snowfalls in winter.

Language

The language is Italian derived directly from Latin. There are several dialect forms and some German is spoken near the Austrian border.

Currency

From January 2002, in common with 11 other European countries, the Italian unit of currency is the EURO (€).
€ 1 = Lire 1,936.

Banks

Open Mon-Fri 08.30-13.30 and 15.00-16.00.

Post Offices

Open Mon-Sat 08.00-17.00/18.30. Smaller towns may not have a service on Saturday. Stamps can also be bought in 'tabacchi'.

Time

GMT plus 1 (summer BST +1).

Public Holidays

New Year; Easter Mon; Liberation Day, 25 Apr; Labour Day; Assumption, 15 Aug; All Saints, 1 Nov; Immaculate Conception, 8 Dec; Christmas, 25, 26 Dec; plus some special local feast days.

Shops

Open Mon-Sat 08.30/09.00-13.00 and 16.00- 19.30/20.00, with some variations in the north.

Telephone

To call Italy the code is 0039. You then do need to include the `0' in the area code. To phone the UK dial 00 44 followed by the UK code minus the initial 0. As well as coins, tokens (gettone) or phone cards from bars and news stands are used.

Motoring

Driving Licence: A valid EC (pink) UK driving licence is acceptable. The older green UK licence must be accompanied by an official Italian translation (from the Italian Tourist Office or the AA). However, DVLA will exchange licences for the pink EC version with the appropriate fee.

Penalties: If you have a projection from the rear of your vehicle - such as a bicycle rack - it is obligtory to have a large 'continental' red/white hatched warning square. There are fixed penalties for not having this or for not wearing a seat belt.

Tolls: Payable on the extensive and expensive Autostrada network. If travelling distances, save time by purchasing a 'Viacard' from pay booths or service areas.

Speed limits: Caravans and motorhomes (3.5 tons) 31 mph (50 kph) in built up areas, 44 mph (70 kph) and 50 mph (80 kph) for caravans on other roads and motorways respectively, 56 mph (90 kph) and 80 mph (130 kph) for motorhomes.

Fuel: Petrol stations on the Autostrada open 24 hours. Elsewhere times are 07.00-13.00 and 16.00-19.30; only 25% open on Sundays. Most motorway service stations accept credit cards, apart from American Express and Diners.

Parking: There are 'Blue Zones' in all major towns. Discs can be obtained from tourist and motoring organisations or petrol stations. In Venice use the special car parks on the mainland, linked by ferry and bus to Venice.

Camping Villaggio dei Fiori

6401 Via Tiro a Volo 3, 18038 San Remo (Ligúria)

Open all year round, this open and spacious site has high standards and is ideal for exploring the Italian Riviera or for just relaxing by the enjoyable, filtered sea water pools. If you prefer, there is a path to a secluded and pleasant beach overlooked by a large patio area. The beach surrounds are excellent for snorkelling and fishing. Unusually, most of the pitch areas at the site are totally paved and there are some extremely large pitches for large units (ask reception to open another gate for entry). There is ample shade from mature trees and shrubs, which are constantly watered and cared for in summer, and pleasant views over the sea from the western pitches. All pitches have electricity (only 3A) and there is an outside sink and cold water for every four Some super pitches overlook the beach edge. The friendly management speak excellent English and will supply detailed tourist plans. Excursions are offered (extra cost) along the Italian Riviera dei Fiori and the French Côte d'Azur. Buses run from outside the site to Monte Carlo, Nice, Cannes, Eze and many other places of interest. This is a very good site for visiting all the attractions in the local area.

Facilities: Three clean and modern sanitary blocks have British and Turkish style WCs and hot water throughout and two private cabins in each. Facilities for disabled campers. Washing machines, dryer and irons. Motorcaravan services. Large restaurant with fine menu and extensive terrace with giant children's toys close by. Bar sells essential supplies. Pizzeria and takeaway (all year). Sea water swimming pools (one for children, and both with a small extra charge in high season) and sophisticated whirlpool spa (June-Sept). Tennis. Table tennis. Volleyball. Children's play area. Fishing. Animation for children and adults in high season. Excursions. Bicycle hire. Dogs or other animals are not accepted. **Off site:** Shop 150 m. Riding 2 km. Golf 2 km.

Charges 2002

Per pitch incl. up to 4 persons	€ 24.00 - € 44.00
half pitch incl. 2 persons, no car	€ 14.00 - € 23.00
electricity	€ 2.00

Some charges due on arrival. Discounts for stays in excess of 7 days. Discount for readers 10% in low season. **Tel:** 0184 660635. Fax: 0184 662377. E-mail: info@villaggiodeifiori.it. **Reservations:** Contact site for details. **Open** all year.

Directions: From main SS1 Ventimiglia - Imperia road, site is on right side of road just before town of San Remo. There is a sharp right turn if the site is approached from the west. from autostrada A10 take San Remo Ouest exit. Site is well signed.

6404 Camping Dei Fiori

Viale Riviera 11, 17027 Pietra Ligure (Ligúria)

Recommended by our agent - this site will be inspected in 2003.

This site is situated some 500 metres from the beach, in a quiet and peaceful setting. Facilities include a swimming pool, solarium, bar, pizzeria, children's play area and a games room, There is an entertainment programme in season. Mobile homes and bungalows are available for rent, as well as a range of different size touring pitches.

Charges guide

Per pitch incl. 3 persons	€ 18.00 - € 33.00

Tel: 019 625636. Fax: 019 6294105. **Reservations:** contact site. **Open** all year.

Camping Baciccia

6403 Via Torino 19, 17023 Ceriale (Ligúria)

This friendly, family run site is a popular holiday destination. There is always a family member by the gate to greet you, and Vincenzina and Giovanni work tirelessly so ensure that you enjoy your stay. Tall eucalyptus trees shade the 120 tightly packed pitches which encircle the central facilities block. The pitches are on flat ground and all have electricity. Baciccia was the nick-name of the present owner's grandfather who grew fruit trees and tomatoes on the site. The informal restaurant overlooks a large pool and, as no frozen food is served, the menu is necessarily simple but is traditional Italian food cooked to perfection. If you have forgotten anything by way of camping equipment just ask and the family will loan it to you. The beach is a short walk and the town has the usual seaside attractions but it is worth visiting the tiny traditional villages close by. This will suit campers who are looking for a family atmosphere.

Facilities: Two clean and modern sanitary blocks near reception have British and Turkish style WCs and hot water throughout. Washing machines, dryer and irons. Motorcaravan services. Restaurant/bar. Pizzeria and takeaway (all year). Sea water swimming pools (June-Sept). Tennis. Table tennis. Volleyball. Play area. Fishing. Animation for children and adults in high season. Excursions. Bicycle hire. **Off site:** Shop 150 m. Riding 2 km. Golf 2 km.

Charges 2002

Per unit incl. up to 3 persons	€ 21.00 - € 39.00
extra person (over 2 yrs)	€ 4.00 - € 8.00
half pitch incl. 2 persons, no car	€ 14.00 - € 26.00
dog	€ 2.00 - € 4.00

Discounts for stays in excess of 7 days. Discount for readers 10% in low season. **Tel:** 0182 990 743. Fax: 0182 993 839. E-mail: info@campingbaciccia.it. **Reservations:** Contact site. **Open** all year.

Directions: From the A10 (E80) between Imperia and Savona, take Albenga exit. Turn left towards Ceriale and Savona, turning left after 3 km. at traffic lights and follow signs to site.

Camping Genova Est

6410 Via Marconi-loc Cassa, 16031 Bogliasco (Ligúria)

This wooded site is set on steep slopes close to the Genoa motorways coming from the north or west and, although it has very limited facilities, it is quite near the town. There is a regular free bus service to the beach in high season, or if you are extremely fit a set of steep stairs will take you there in 15 minutes. The Buteros who run and own the site both speak good English. The approach from the main road twists and climbs steeply with a tight final turn at the site entrance. There are 54 touring pitches with electricity (3/5A). The small play area is set on a narrow terrace and children should be supervised. A pretty bar and a little restaurant with a terrace give fine views over the sea. This is a site to be used for exploring Genoa and Riviera di Levante, rather than for extended stays.

Facilities: One of the two sanitary blocks provides free hot showers and en-suite cabins (WC, washbasin and shower). Washing machine. Motorcaravan services. Shop and bar/restaurant (both Easter - 30/9). Essential daily goods form restaurant. Towing vehicle available. Gas supplies. Site is not suitable for disabled people. Torches necessary in many areas. **Off site:** Fishing 1.5 km.

Charges 2002

Per person	€ 5.00
child (3-10 yrs)	€ 3.20
caravan or tent	€ 4.30 - € 5.90
car	€ 2.60
motorcaravan	€ 7.50
electricity	€ 1.70

Less 5% discount for holders of the current Alan Rogers Guide. **Reservations:** Contact site. **Open** 1 March - 30 October.

Directions: From autostrada A10 take Nervi exit and turn left (south) on the SS1 towards La Spezia. In Bogliasco look for a sharp left turn with a large sign for the site. Follow narrow winding road for 2 km. to site.

Villaggio Camping Valdeiva

6412 Loc. Ronco, 19013 Deiva Marina (Ligúria)

A mature and peaceful site 3 km. from the sea between the famous Cinque Terre and Portofino, Valdiva is open all year. It is situated in a valley amongst dense pines so views are restricted. On flat ground and separated, most of the 125 pitches are used for permanent Italian units, the remaining 30 or so shared between tourers and tents (some tent pitches are on high terraces) with shade in most parts. Of varying size, they have electricity (3A) connections. Cars may be required to park in a separate area depending on the pitch. The site does have a small pool, which is very welcome if you do not wish to take the free bus to the beach. The play area has dated metal equipment with sharp edges and we strongly recommend the closest parental supervision if you choose to use the area. The beach is pleasant and the surrounding village has several bars and restaurants. There are pleasant walks in the unspoilt woods of Liguria nearby or the most interesting tourist option is a visit to Cinque Terre, five villages, some of which can only be reached by rail, boat or by cliff footpath. Their history is one of fishing but now they also specialise in wines. We see this as a transit site rather than for extended stays.

Facilities: Three sanitary blocks are provided for the tourers and tents, and they are all very different. One block is more modern, the others are dated. WCs are mainly Turkish, but there are some of British style. Washbasins have hot water and there are free hot showers. Shop for basics only (15/6-15/9). Bar/restaurant with reasonable menu and pizzas cooked in a traditional wood fired oven (15/6-15/9). Small swimming pool. Poor children's play area. Table tennis. Electronic games. Excursions. Free bus to the beach. Torches required.

Charges 2002

Per pitch incl. 2 persons	€ 14.98 - € 22.21
3 persons	€ 18.08 - € 29.95
4 persons	€ 21.17 - € 34.09

Tel: 0187 824174. Fax: 0187 825352. E-mail: valdeiva@libero.it. **Reservations:** Contact site. **Open** all year.

Directions: Leave autostrada A12 at Deiva Marina exit and follow signs to Deiva Marina. Signs are clear at the first junction and site is on left approx. 3 km. down this road.

Camping Mombarone

6220 Settimo Vittone Reg, 10010 Torre Daniele (Piedmont)

This is a small rustic all year site alongside the SS26 road. It has 120 pitches, 80 of which are given over to permanent units, but there will always be a space for tourers. The Peretto family take pride in looking after their guests and English is spoken. The site is thoughtfully laid out with attractive plants and shrubs and trees for shade. It is surrounded by very attractive mountains and wooded hills, with vines bedecking the eastern slopes. This is an ideal base for climbers as the mountains in this area are extremely popular. The many famous valleys including Valle di Champorcher and Valle di Gressony are within easy driving distance, as is the Parco Nazionale del Gran Paradiso. There is a small wooden bar on site but shops and good restaurants are close by in the village of Quincinetto. There is a small framed and supported pool for children or they can paddle in the shallow river and catch tiddlers on the northern boundary. If you are here in October help the family pick their own grapes, make the wine (in the Nebbiolo style) and share the fun. The wine is sold at the bar - it is good!

Facilities: The sanitary facilities are spotless with both British and Turkish WCs and a washing machine. When you leave tell them how many showers taken and settle up accordingly! Bar. Toddlers pool. Volleyball, table tennis, table football. Fishing. **Off site:** Riding 5 km. Shops and restaurants in the town.

Charges 2003

Per person	€ 3.00
child (under 10 yrs)	€ 2.50
caravan	€ 3.00
car	€ 1.50
motorcaravan	€ 4.50
electricity	€ 1.50

No credit cards. **Tel:** 0125 757907. Fax: 0125 757396. E-mail: campingmombarone@libero.it. **Reservations:** Write to site. **Open** all year.

Directions: Take the SS26 north from Ivrea. Site between 45 and 46 km. markers just before entering the town of Torre Daniele. From motorway take Quiuinetto A5 exit (Milan-Aosta).

Camping Valle Romantica

Via Valle Cannobina, 28822 Cannobio (Piedmont)

6240

The pretty little town of Cannobio is situated between Verbania and Locarno on the western shore of Lake Maggiore. It could make a base for exploring the Lake and its islands, although progress along the winding lakeside road, hemmed in by mountains, is slow. Serious mountain walkers are well catered for, and the Swiss resort of Locarno is not far. Steamers cross the Lake, but the only car ferry across is between Verbania and Laveno. In a scenic situation, this lovely site was established about 40 years ago by the present owner's father, who planted some 20,000 plants, trees and shrubs, and there is much to interest botanists in this tree-clad mountain valley. The site's swimming pool is in a sunny position and there is a pool in the river, where, except after heavy rain, children can play. The 130 numbered pitches for touring units are on flat grass among the trees, which provide good shade and serve to separate the pitches (but mean some narrow site roads). Electricity (4A) is available on most pitches, although long cables are necessary in some parts. Used by tour operators (30 pitches). The owner takes a keen and active personal interest in the site, and English is spoken.

Facilities: The three sanitary blocks provide good facilities with free showers of a reasonable size, with hooks, screen and a small dressing space, controlled by taps. Washing machines. Gas supplies. Motorcaravan services. Small, well stocked supermarket. Pleasant bar/restaurant with waiter service and takeaway. Entertainment (folk music) is provided one night per week in the high season. Pizzeria. Swimming pool (1/5-15/9). Fishing (licence required). Boat slipway. Sailing and windsurfing schools. Fridge boxes for hire. **Off site:** Bicycle hire 500 m.

Charges 2003

Per person	€ 5.50 - € 6.50
child (1-12 yrs)	€ 3.50 - € 4.00
pitch	€ 9.00 - € 11.50
dog	€ 3.50
electricity (4A)	€ 3.00

No credit cards. **Tel:** 0323 71249. Fax: 0323 71249. E-mail: info@riviera-valleromantica.com. **Reservations:** Contact site. **Open** 29 March - 30 September.

Directions: After crossing the border from Switzerland, continue for 4 km. to outskirts of Cannobio. Turn right to Valle Cannobine and continue for 1 km. (do not turn right for Treffume).

Camping Riviera

Via Casali Darbedo 2, 28822 Cannobio (Piedmont)

6245

With scenic views across the water and surrounding mountains, this 22,000 sq.m. site is directly beside Lake Maggiore. Under the same active ownership as Valle Romantica, the whole site has a well cared for appearance and it is certainly one of the best lakeside sites in the area. Over 250 numbered pitches are on flat grass, either side of hard surfaced access roads and divided by trees and shrubs. There are 220 with 4A electricity (long cables may be needed). There is a small jetty and easy access to the lake for boats, swimming and other watersports. Sailing and windsurfing regattas are organised. The site could make a suitable base for exploring the area, although progress on the busy winding road may be slow!

Facilities: The five sanitary blocks, one new and two with facilities for disabled visitors, are of good quality. Washing machines. Fridge boxes for hire. Gas supplies. Motorcaravan services. Well stocked site shop. Pleasant bar/restaurant with covered terrace, providing waiter service and takeaway. Pizzeria. Swimming pool (1/5-15/9). Fishing (licence required). Boat slipway. Sailing and windsurfing schools. **Off site:** The town is only a short distance. Bicycle hire 500 m.

Charges 2003

Per person	€ 5.50 - € 6.50
child (1-12 yrs)	€ 3.50 - € 4.00
pitch	€ 9.00 - € 11.50
dog	€ 3.50
electricity (4A)	€ 3.00

No credit cards. **Tel:** 0323 71360. Fax: 0323 71360. E-mail: info@riviera-valleromantica.com. **Reservations:** Made for min. 11 nights with deposit (€ 62) and fee (€ 41,32). **Open** 29 March - 31 October.

Directions: After the border crossing from Switzerland, continue for 4 km. to the outskirts of the town of Cannobio. There are several sites nearby - Riviera is the last site before the bridge, at the lakeside.

Camping Tranquilla

6247 Via Cave 2, 28831 Baveno (Piedmont)

Tranquilla is a family run site on the western slopes above Baveno, close to Lake Maggiore. Reception is housed in an attractive old railway carriage from where the Luca family will make you welcome to the site with excellent English spoken. The site is in two terraced sections, both with electricity connections (4/5A). The pitches, both permanent (55) and touring (56) are of average size and are randomly mixed, with trees offering some shade. Although on the small side, the site's two swimming pools are very welcome in the height of summer as the 1.5 km. walk to the lake, where swimming can be difficult, is down a steep slope, and would prove difficult for older or disabled visitors. The site has an unusually large restaurant with two terraces, a large menu at reasonable prices and live entertainment in season. The terrace has a fountain, some views and is very popular. Tourist information is available and reception will book any of the local activities and facilities including watersports. The site is an ideal base to explore the local area which is most attractive but vehicular transport is necessary as there is no bus service.

Facilities: The southern site has a recently built ladies' sanitary block, which is spotless and includes facilities for disabled campers, whilst the male side is more mature, but very clean. The northern side (with all the support facilities) has several older sanitary blocks that have recently been modernised and have an improved hot water supply and are again kept clean. British and Turkish style WCs. Freezer and refrigerator service. Laundry. Motorcaravan services. Bar. Restaurant, pizzeria and takeaway. Swimming pools (10/5-30/9). Play area. Table tennis. Table football. Electronic games. Excursions arranged. **Off site:** Fishing 800 m, golf or riding 3 km. Bus service 800 m. Camping items in adjoining store, shops nearby.

Charges 2003

Per person	€ 3.65 - € 4.65
child (1-3 yrs)	€ 2.30 - € 3.00
child (4-12 yrs)	€ 2.85 - € 3.50
pitch	€ 5.70 - € 8.25
dog	€ 1.81
electricity	€ 2.00

Low season offers. No credit cards, but travellers cheques and British currency accepted. **Tel:** 0323 923452. Fax: 0323 923452. E-mail: info@tranquilla.com. **Reservations:** Write to site. **Open** 1 March - 31 October.

Directions: From Avora follow SS33 road north to Baveno, site is signed to the left in the northern part of the town. Site is approx. 1.5 km. uphill and well signed.

Camping Parisi

6248 Via Piave 50, 28831 Baveno (Piedmont)

Camping Parisi is a quiet, family run site on the western shore of Lake Maggiore within the town of Baveno. The small and compact site has just 61 pitches, all for tourers. The pitches are shaded by mature trees and there are stunning views over the lake which is this site's real strength. An early reservation would be necessary if you wish to occupy one of the lakeside pitches (extra charge). Whilst there is no swimming pool, it is possible to paddle and swim from the lake shore which is also good for sunbathing (but care must be taken with children). The site has a restaurant and bar, reached through a gate on the northern boundary. The public also have the use of these facilities through a separate access which is secured by night. This shared community complex also has limited fixed entertainment such as five-a-side soccer on sand, satellite TV in the bar, volleyball, table tennis, a small children's play area and a large beach area with sun-beds. Live entertainment is offered adjacent to the restaurant at weekends during high season.

Facilities: Central sanitary facilities are clean with free hot showers and British style WCs but, as yet, no facilities for disabled campers. These facilities are supplemented by day in the 'community area' where a modern complex offers coin slot showers, British toilets and sinks. The site has no shop or washing machine as the town is 100 m. distant. Freezer service. Community complex with bar, TV. Restaurant (from 1/5). Volleyball. Five-a-side soccer. Children's play area. Table tennis. Reception will make bookings for local activities. **Off site:** Shops nearby.

Charges 2002

Per person	€ 5.15 - € 5.70
baby (1-3 yrs)	€ 2.05 - € 2.30
child (4-12 yrs)	€ 4.15 - € 4.90
caravan	€ 4.65 - € 4.90
tent	€ 4.15 - € 4.65
motorcaravan	€ 7.75 - € 8.80
car	€ 3.60 - € 4.14
motorcycle	€ 2.85 - € 3.10
dog	€ 1.55 - € 2.05
electricity	€ 2.10

Tel: 0323 923156. Fax: 0323 924160. **Reservations:** Write to site. **Open** 20 March - 10 October.

Directions: From A26 Genoa - Gravellona take Baveno exit and turn right on main road to site. From Simplon or Gothard the first site sign is in Feriolo. From Arona follow SS33 road north to Baveno. Site is signed to the right in the centre of the town on the right but a sharp eye is needed to pick out the small sign high on the wall at a narrow part of the street.

Camping Continental Lido

 Via 42 Martiri, 156, 28924 Fondotoce di Verbania (Piedmont)

Continental Lido is situated on the shore of the small Lake Mergozzo, about one kilometer from the better known Lake Maggiore. The 500 small to normal sized tourist pitches are back-to-back in regular rows on grass. All have electricity (6A) and there is shade from a variety of trees in some parts. There is no swimming pool but a small sandy beach slopes gently into the lake where swimming and watersports can also be enjoyed (no powered craft may be used). Fir-clad mountains provide a scenic background. An unusual feature is the 9-hole golf course. Under the same ownership as Isolino Camping Village, this site is managed by son Giano Paolo who speaks good English.

Facilities: Five refurbished toilet blocks have free hot water, facilities for disabled visitors and washing machines and dryers. Well stocked shop. Bar/restaurant with terrace and takeaway. TV. Tennis courts. Volleyball, basketball and 9-hole golf course. Children's playground. Watersports canoes, kayaks. Games room. Bicycle hire. Entertainment and activities (mid-June to mid-September). **Off site:** Site is within easy range of botanical gardens and the Swiss Ticano canton.

Charges 2002

Per person	€ 3.75 - € 5.55
child (3-11 yrs)	€ 2.95 - € 4.00
pitch	€ 13.50 - € 21.95

Tel: 0323 496300. Fax: 0323 496218. E-mail: info@ campingcontinental.com. **Reservations:** Contact site. **Open** 23 March - 22 September.

Directions: Site is on the SS34 road between Fondotoce and Gravellona.

Camping Village Isolino

Via per Feriolo 25, 28924 Verbania Fondotoce (Piedmont)

Lake Maggiore is one of the most attractive Italian lakes and Isolino Camping Village is one of the largest sites in the region. The long entrance road to the site - rolled gravel and fairly uneven - is rather off-putting but then the stunning location and attractive swimming pool with its lovely views across the lake to the fir-clad mountains beyond is breathtaking and worth finding. Most of the 710 tourist pitches have shade from a variety of trees and are of a good size in regular back-to-back rows. All have electrical connections (6A). There is a small sandy beach and a wide range of watersports (no jet-skis) can be enjoyed on the lake. The social life of the campsite is centred around the large bar which has a stage for musical entertainment, pool-side terrace and takeaway with a restaurant on the floor above sharing the magnificent views across the lake. The site is owned by the friendly Manoni family who also own Camping Continental Lido at nearby Lake Mergozzo and good English is spoken.

Facilities: Six well-built toilet blocks, most refurbished, have free hot water. Washing machines and dryers. Fridge boxes for hire. Motorcaravan service point. Large well stocked supermarket. Most attractive swimming pool with children's pool at one end and sunbathing area. Football pitch. Tennis courts. Fishing. Watersports. Bicycle hire and guided mountain bike tours. Beach volleyball and organised activities for children and adults and weekly disco in July/Aug. **Off site:** It is well situated for visiting the many attractions of the region which include famous gardens on the islands in the lake and at the Villa Taranto, Verbania. The Swiss mountains and resort of Locarno are quite near.

Charges 2002

Per person	€ 3.80 - € 6.00
child (3-11 yrs)	€ 2.90 - € 4.90
pitch	€ 15.60 - € 27.00
dog	€ 2.90 - € 5.40

Tel: 0323 496 080. Fax: 0323 496 414. E-mail: info@isolino.com. **Reservations:** Contact site. **Open** 23 March - 22 September.

Directions Leave A26 motorway at exit for Stresa/ Baveno, turn left towards Fondotoce and follow signs to site on right.

The Alan Rogers' Travel Service

We have recently extended The Alan Rogers Travel Service. This unique service enables our readers to reserve their holidays as well as ferry crossings and comprehensive insurance cover at extremely competitive rates. One simple telephone call to our Travel Service on 01892 55 98 98 is all that is needed to make all the arrangements. Why not take advantage of our years' of experience of camping and caravanning. We would be delighted to discuss your holiday plans with you, and offer advice and recommendations.

Alan Rogers Travel Service 01892 55 98 98 or www.alanrogers.com

Camping Au Lac de Como

6250 Via Cesare Battisti 18, 22010 Sorico (Lombardy)

Au Lac du Como is situated in a most pleasant location at the head of Lake Como in the centre of the village of Sorico facing south down the water and surrounded by wooded mountains. There is direct access to the lake for swimming, boating and other watersports, with windsurfing appearing to be the most popular pastime. Static units predominate but the camping area is directly by the lake where there is said to be room for 74 touring units, with 3A electricity connections. However, as pitches are not marked out, pitching can be a little haphazard and the area may become crowded at times, particularly in high season when advanced booking is advised. Cars are parked just away from tents and caravans and there is further parking outside the entrance. The owner speaks good English and insists on respect for other residents so ball games, barbecues and loud music are not allowed. The site is well situated for exploring the area, with Switzerland nearby via the Splugen Pass. There are also marked paths and trails for walking and biking in the mountains with an interesting nature park close with a variety of flora and fauna. Although it makes a good night stop when passing this way, many visitors find it interesting and stay longer.

Facilities: There is one good sanitary block in the centre of the static part and two smaller basic ones, all with mainly British style WCs. Hot water in the larger block is on payment but free in the other two except for washing up and laundry. Washing machine and dryer. Motorcaravan services. Supermarket. Hotel bar and restaurant open all day, offering excellent buffet breakfast service and evening meals. Heated swimming pool (21 x 7 m). Sauna and solarium. Fishing. Range of watersports possible. Canoe, kayak and bicycle hire.

Charges 2002

Per person	€ 6.50
child	€ 4.50
pitch	€ 11.00
dog	€ 6.00
extra car	€ 6.00

Less 10-50% for over 1 night outside July/August. **Tel:** 0344 84035. Fax: 0344 84802. E-mail: infoaulac@aulacdecomo.com. **Reservations:** Advised for high season; write to site. **Open** all year.

Directions: Easiest route is north on SS36 from Lecco to Nuovo Olonio and west on SS402 (signed Gravelona) to Sorico; site is then on the left in centre of village. Can be approached on SS340 from Como on lake-side road which is quite narrow in places but an interesting drive (not advised for larger units).

Azur Camping Idro Rio Vantone

6258 Via Vantome, 45, 25074 Idro (Lombardy)

The German company AZUR have some 30 sites in the home country and just two in Italy, of which this is one. Lake Idro, one of the smaller of the northern Italian lakes, is tucked away in the mountains to the west of the better known Lake Garda. Rio Vantone is situated on the southeast shore of the lake with marvellous views across the water to the small villages on the opposite bank and surrounding mountains. The ground slopes gently down to the water's edge with most of the 240 tourist pitches in level rows divided by hedges and a wire fence, with others between tall trees. All have electricity (6/10A) and there are 10 with water and drainage as well. The ones nearest the lake attract a higher charge. Being away from the main highways the site is more suitable for longer stays than one night stops but it is a peaceful spot in which to relax and from which to explore the countryside and nearby small towns. The lake is ideal for windsurfing and the surrounding countryside for walking and climbing. Thirty tour operator tents are not intrusive.

Facilities: The main, heated sanitary block occupies the ground floor of a large building and is of excellent quality with all the usual facilities, including en-suite cabins (WC, washbasin and shower) and special ones for children. A smaller block is also open in high season. Facilities for disabled people. Washing machines and dryer. Motorcaravan services. Gas supplies. Cooking rings. Well stocked shop (all season). Excellent restaurant just outside the entrance (1/6-10/9). Daily programme for children in high season. Windsurf school. Boat and mountain bike hire. Volleyball and badminton. Paddling pool and playground (supervision is needed as the entry is near a boat slip-way down to the lake). Torches useful in some areas. **Off site:** Fishing 1.5 km.

Charges 2002

Per person	€ 4.50 - € 6.50
child (2-12 yrs)	€ 3.50 - € 5.00
pitch (acc. to position, facilities and season)	€ 5.00 - € 26.00
electricity	€ 2.20
dog	€ 2.20

Tel: 036 583125. Fax: 036 5823663. E-mail: idro@azur-camping.de. **Reservations:** Write to site. **Open** 15 April - 15 November.

Directions: From A4 Milan - Venice motorway, take 'Brescia Est' exit. Go north on SS 45bis towards Salo then SS237 via Vobarno and Barge to Lemprato. Rio Vantone is at the southeast corner of the lake after camps Belvedere and Pineta. From Brescia, follow signs 'Lago d'Idro'.

Camping Punta d'Oro

6259 Via Antonioli 51 - 53, 25049 Iseo (Lombardy)

Lago d'Iseo is the fifth largest of the northern lakes and one of the least known outside Italy. However, it is a popular tourist spot for Italians and many others and therefore has not escaped exploitation. Camping Punta d'Oro, at the town of Iseo in the southeast corner of the lake, is a small, delightful campsite, which has been run by the professional Brescianini-Zatti family for the last 30 years. It slopes gently down to the lake from the railway line (they say, an infrequent local service) and there could be some road noise. The very pretty site, adorned with trees and plants, has 64 grass pitches (with just 15 static caravans) on either side of decorative brick roads. Electrical connections (5A) are available. There is a lakeside area on the northeast boundary but pitches at the water's edge are more expensive. There are excellent views across the lake to wooded mountains on the opposite shore where small villages shelter down by the water and further mountains rise behind the site. It is a good centre for exploring around the lake, Monte Isola (Italy's largest lake island) by ferry from Iseo or to ascend Monte Gugliemo (1,949 m). With no entertainment programme, this could well suit those who are looking for a very pleasant base without the activity of a larger site.

Facilities: The two small sanitary blocks have been refurbished to a high standard with a mix of British and Turkish style WCs and hot water in washbasins, showers, dishwashing and laundry sinks. All these services were immaculate when seen. Washing machine. Motorcaravan services. Shop. Small bar/restaurant with a terrace. Games room. TV in bar. Access to lake for swimming, fishing with two narrow slipways for boat launching. **Off site:** Bicycle hire 500 m. Riding 1.5 km. Golf 5 km.

Charges 2002

Per person	€ 4.10 - € 5.80
child (1-9 yrs)	€ 3.30 - € 4.50
pitch acc. to size and season	€ 8.30 - € 14.50
dog	€ 1.70 - € 2.60

Electricity included. **Tel:** 030 980084. Fax: 030 980084. E-mail: punta@franciacorta.it. **Reservations:** Write to site. **Open** 1 April - 31 October.

Directions: Leave A4 (Milan-Venice) autostrada at Ospitaletto exit, go north to Rodengo and then take SS510 to Iseo. Punta d'Oro is at northern end of town - cross the railway line and turn right at corner where site is signed. Care should be taken on entry as this is tight for large units.

Camping San Francesco

6252 Strada Vicinale, 25015 Rivoltella (Lombardy)

This large, well organised site is situated to the west of the Simione peninsula on the southwest shores of Lake Garda. This position allows wonderful views of the lake, the most attractive Grotte di Cattulo, the far shores, Bardolini, the wooded slopes and mountains beyond. The Facchini family used to grow grapes for Lagana wine on this land, their aim is now to ensure you enjoy your stay. This impressive site has 292 marked pitches which are generally on flat gravel and sand, enjoying natural shade from mature trees. The pitches are generally of average size, a new system in part of the site offering three types of pitch from 'lakeside large', through superior to standard. All have electricity (3A) and easy access. A private wooded beach area of about 400 m. on the lake can be used for sunbathing, windsurfing, canoeing, sailing and power-boating The management maintain rescue boats for water activities on the lake. The site's well equipped sports centre, accessed via a tunnel under the road, includes three large, supervised pools. Near the pool complex is an equally impressive entertainment area. There may be some noise disturbance from an adjoining holiday complex in high season (but not after 23.00).

Facilities: Sanitary facilities are in two large, identical, centrally located buildings. Very clean when seen, they offer every facility a camper could want with hot water at all points. Excellent facilities for disabled campers. Shop. Restaurant. Bar. Pizzeria and snacks. Swimming pools (15/4-20/9) and jacuzzis. Sports centre, football stadium, tennis. Children's playground. Entertainment programme, organised activities and excursions. Big screen satellite TV. RC chapel in high season. Torches required in some areas. The large, busy reception will advise and organise any of the myriad of activities, tours and ferry trips. **Off site:** Golf 10 km. Riding 5 km.

Charges 2003

Per person	€ 5.20 - € 8.50
child (under 6 yrs)	€ 4.70 - € 7.70
pitch incl. electricity	€ 10.90 - € 18.50
superior pitch	€ 12.90 - € 26.00

Tel: 0309 110245. Fax: 0309 119464. E-mail: info@campingsanfrancesco.it. **Reservations:** Contact site. **Open** 1 April - 30 September.

Directions: From autostrada A4, between Brescia and Verona, exit towards Sirmione and take S11 to Rivoltella. Site is well signed.

Camping Europa Silvella

6260 Via Silvella 10, 25010 San Felice del Benaco (Lombardy)

This large, modern, lakeside site was formed from the merger of two different sites with the result that the 323 pitches (about 295 for tourists) are spread among a number of different sections of varying type. The chief difference between them is that the marked pitches alongside the lake are in smaller groups and closer together so that one has less space. However, in the larger, very slightly sloping or terraced grassy meadows further back one can have 80 sq. m. or more instead of 50. There is reasonable shade in many parts and all pitches have 4A electricity, 45 with water and drainage. Some areas also contain bungalows, mobile homes and log cabins. The site has frontage to the lake in two places (with some other property in between), with a beach, jetty and moorings. The private beach is very pleasant, with all manner of watersports available. There is a windsurfing school in season, along with an organised animation programme with live entertainment. A new, large modern swimming pool complex has a jacuzzi and a children's pool.

Facilities: Toilet blocks include washbasins in cabins, facilities for disabled visitors and a superb children's room with small showers. Laundry. Supermarket. Bazaar. Restaurant/bar. Swimming pools (hats required). Tennis courts. Volleyball courts and five-a-side soccer pitch. Table tennis. New children's playground. Bowling alley. Surf boards, canoes and bicycles for hire. Animation and entertainment (every night in season). Disco. Tournaments, swimming, windsurfing and tennis lessons. First aid room.

Charges 2002

Per person	€ 3.87 - € 6.35
child (2-9 yrs)	€ 3.36 - € 5.32
pitch with electricity only	€ 9.55 - € 13.94
with electricity, water and drainage	€ 11.10 - € 16.53
dog	€ 5.16

Tel: 0365 651095. Fax: 0365 654395. **Reservations:** not usually necessary for caravans and tents, but will be made for min. 7 days with 30% deposit and € 20,66 fee. **Open** 23 April - 27 September.

Directions: From Desenzano at southerly end of Lake Garda follow S572 north towards Salo. Following signs for San Felice turn off towards lake. Then follow yellow tourist signs bearing campsite name.

camping
SanFrancesco ★★★★

The camping site is located at the beginning of Sirmione peninsula, the Garda Lake pearl. Restaurant and pizzeria are completely renewed. The camping site is situated on a shaded surface of 104.000 sm. right by the sea, with a 300m long beach. In the sport area (35.000 sm.) you can enjoy the swimming pool (1.400 sm.) with a kid's pool and water games. In addition there is the possibility to practise more than 10 sports. To reach us follow exit Sirmione on the highway Milan-Venice. The camping site is an ideal starting point to reach Gardaland and Caneva.

ADAC
ERLEBNIS
Camping

Strada Vic. S. Francesco - I-25015 Desenzano del Garda (BS)
Tel. 0039/0309110245 - Fax 0039/0309119464
E-mail: info@campingsanfrancesco.it/com
Http: //www.campingsanfrancesco.it/com

Fornella Camping

6275 Via Fornella 1, 25010 San Felice del Benaco (Lombardy)

the **travel service**
TO BOOK
Ferry	✓
Pitch	✓
Accommodation	✓

01892 55 98 98

Fornella Camping is another of the good sites in this region where one is spoilt for choice. It is the sister site of Fontanelle (no. 6277) and of similar high standards. An open site, it is surrounded by olive and other trees with a backdrop of mountains and good views. Although there is access to the lake, this cannot be seen from all parts of the site as a tree covered hill intervenes. There are 230 marked and numbered pitches for tourers, separated by access roads on flat grass and terraced where necessary, all with electricity. Many pitches are shaded by young trees. Mobile homes and bungalows edge the touring pitches but do not intrude. The well appointed bar/restaurant and the shop are by the lakeside with a terrace giving splendid views over the lake. A new swimming pool is a super addition for the 2003 season. The lakeside area and private pebble beach is pleasant and there are two separate lake accesses for boats and windsurfers. Being well away from the main road, this is a quiet, peaceful site. The friendly management speak excellent English. Used by tour operators (30%)..

Facilities: Three very clean, modern sanitary blocks, well dispersed around the site, have mainly British type WCs and hot water in washbasins (some in cabins), showers and sinks. Facilities for disabled people. Washing machines, dryer and irons. Motorcaravan services. Bar/restaurant. Pizzeria and takeaway at certain times. Shop. Supervised swimming pool and children's pool (15/5-15/9). Tennis. Table tennis. Volleyball. Two playgrounds and animation for children in season. Beach. Fishing. **Off site:** Bicycle hire 4 km. Riding 10 km. Golf 8 km.

Charges 2003

Per person	€ 4.60 - € 8.80
child (3-7 yrs)	€ 3.60 - € 6.80
pitch incl. electricity (6A)	€ 9.30 - € 16.50
dog	free - € 5.90
boat	€ 6.00 - € 11.50

Charges acc. to season and pitch location. Various low season discounts. **Tel:** 0365 62294. Fax: 0365 559418. E-mail: fornella@fornella.it. **Reservations:** Made with deposit and fee; contact site. **Open** 1 May - 21 September.

Directions: From main SS572 Desenzano-Salo road on the west side of the lake, head for San Felice and follow signs.

Camping Fontanelle

6277 Via Del Magone 13, 25080 Moniga del Garda (Lombardy)

Camping Fontanelle is a sister site to Fornella (no. 6275), situated near the historic village of Moniga and enjoying excellent views across the lake. The site sits on the south-western slopes of Lake Garda and has 200 pitches on flat and terraced ground. Approximately 25% of these are given over to tour operators but there is little impingement. All are marked and have electrical connections (6A) and there are some very pleasant lakeside pitches (extra cost). Some for tents and tourers are very secluded but are distant from the campsite facilities, although small blocks with toilets are close by. The swimming pools are superb, one for adults with the children's pool alongside (closed 13.00-15.00 hrs). The lakeside pitches have access to the beach through gates in the safety fence. The lake is a public area and there is no lifeguard, although the local equivalent to the RNLI is active on the lake. We are told there is no problem with security here although the public gain access to the beach along fenced paths through the site. Good English is spoken.

Facilities: The two main toilet blocks are modern and clean, with hot water throughout. Facilities for disabled campers in these blocks. Washing machines and dryers. Motorcaravan services. Large mini-market with prices to compete with local supermarkets. Restaurant/bar. Takeaway (from 15/5). Shop. Swimming pools (from 15/5, supervised). Table tennis. Tennis. TV room. Electronic games. Animation and live entertainment in season. **Off site:** Bicycle hire 1 km. Golf 5 km. Riding 10 km.

Charges 2002

Per adult	€ 4.50 - € 8.53
child (3-7 yrs)	€ 3.50 - € 6.70
pitch incl. electricity	€ 9.00 - € 15.40
boat	€ 8.00 - € 13.50
dog	€ 4.10 - € 5.10

Tel: 0365 502079. Fax: 0365 503324. E-mail: info@campingfontanelle.it. **Reservations:** Made for min 7 days from November onwards with fee and deposit; write to site. **Open** 1 May - 21 September.

Directions: From A4 or E70 Milano - Verona road travel north on the west side of the lake to Moniga - site is well signed.

Camping Ideal Molino

Via Gardiola 1, 25010 San Felice del Benaco (Lombardy)

Molino is a small, garden-like site with charm and character, which may appeal to those who do not like the larger and more ordered sites. A friendly family atmosphere is being maintained at the site by the daughter of the original owners. Ingeborg is delightful and speaks perfect English. The family house, of which the charming restaurant is part, has a huge water wheel constantly turning which was used to crush the olives from the local area. This explains the name of the campsite and the old mill equipment can still be seen under the house. The site is mainly on fairly level ground beside Lake Garda with a hill rising quite sharply behind. It is in two main parts divided by the site buildings, and pitches vary in character, some by the lake, some for tents on terraces, and many in rows with pergolas, flowering shrubs, etc. All pitches are well shaded, have electricity (4A), water and drainage. The excellent restaurant has superb lake views and huge lakeside barbecue operates twice weekly producing meat and fish to order. Accompany these with the delicious local Lugana wines. There is a pleasant stony beach at one end; elsewhere one steps straight down into shallow water. Boats can be launched and there is a floating pontoon for sunbathing, diving or boat landing. The management bans loud radios or TVs, or any noise after 11 p.m.

Facilities: All three small sanitary blocks have been rebuilt to a very high standard, with automatic lighting and facilities for disabled visitors. They have British style WCs, individual washbasins with hot water and adjustable hot showers. Laundry (attended). Motorcaravan services. Shop. Restaurant/bar. Bicycle hire. Table tennis. Fishing. Water ski-ing. Free organised entertainment in season. Boat excursions to markets in lakeside towns. Dogs are not accepted.

Charges 2002

Per unit incl. electricity	€ 9.00 - € 14.00
adult	€ 4.35 - € 7.00
child (2-9 yrs)	€ 3.80 - € 5.50

No credit cards. **Tel:** 0365 62023. Fax: 0365 559395. E-mail: info@campingmolino.it. **Reservations:** Made for min 7 days from January onwards with fee and deposit. **Open** 16 March - 30 September.

Directions: From Desenzano at southerly end of lake Garda follow S572 north towards Salô. Turn off towards lake, following signs for San Felice. Then follow yellow signs bearing camp name. Watch for sudden stop sign on final descent to site! Site is about 4 km. outside Salô.

6284 Camping Belvedere

Via Cavalle 5, I-25080 Manerba del Garda (BS)

Recommended by our agent – this site will be inspected in 2003.

Situated on Lake Garda's Gulf of Manerba, this campsite offers pitches on terraces with good shade. Many have views of the lake and there is a beach with moorings available for those with their own small boats. Facilities include a restaurant with terrace, a bar, mini-market, children's playground and tennis court.

Charges 2002

Per pitch	€ 10.85 - € 13.45
adult	€ 5.69
child	€ 4.65

Substantial reductions outside high season. **Tel:** 0365 551175. E-mail info@camping-belvedere.it. **Open** 1 April - mid October.

Directions: From A4 autostrada take Desenzano exit towards Manerba, until you pick up camping signs.

Villaggio Turistico La Gardiola

6270 Via Gardiola, 36, 25010 San Felice del Benaco (Lombardy)

This small, modern site is set directly beside the lake in a very popular area. The 40 pitches (25 for tourers) are on flat, shaded terraces and all pitches have electricity and water. The site is separated from the shingle beach by a small private service road. The views from the site are stunning across the lake and the family atmosphere, and friendly owners give the site a very homely feel. English is spoken. If you enjoy small sites with an uncomplicated atmosphere, then this could be for you. Reservations are accepted.

Facilities: An innovative sanitary block just below ground level has a lift system for disabled visitors. The facilities are quite adequate and there is free hot water throughout. Laundry. Small kiosk with terrace for coffee and snacks. Small playground. Table tennis. Fishing. **Off site:** Restaurants, shops, pizzerias nearby.

Charges 2002

Per unit incl. electricity	€ 9.30 - € 16.53
adult	€ 3.10 - € 5.94
child and over 60s	€ 2.58 - € 4.91
dog	€ 1.55 - € 3.10

Tel: 0365 559240. Fax: 0365 559240. E-mail: info@lagardiola.com. **Reservations:** Contact site. **Open** 10 April - 30 September.

Directions: Near San Felice on SS572 Salo - San Felice road, site is well signed at San Felice. Take care from the town as the road is very narrow and the locals move swiftly!

6283 Camping La Rocca

37017 Lazise sul Garda (Venetia)

Recommended by our agent – this site will be inspected in 2003.

This is a family-orientated campsite with 175 touring pitches. It is in a pleasant location in the quiet Gulf of Manerba on Lake Garda, near the La Rocca natural park. It has a range of facilities including swimming pools, a tennis court, bar, shop and bicycles to rent.

Charges 2002

Per pitch	€ 7.00 - € 12.00
adult	€ 3.80 - € 6.50
child	€ 3.00 - € 5.00

Tel: 0365 551738. E-mail: info@laroccacamp.it. **Open** 29 March - 5 October.

Directions: From A4 autostrada take Desenzano exit and the SS572 to pick up camping signs.

Camping LA ROCCA ✱✱✱✱
Via Cavalle, 22 • I-25080 MANERBA
LAGO DI GARDA (BS)

Tel. 0039/0365/551738
Fax 0039/0365/552045
Http: www.laroccacamp.it
E-mail: info@laroccacamp.it

Opening: from 29.03. to 05.10.03

The camping site is situated between the peninsula S. Biagio and Rocca Manerba.
It provides two swimming pools and two tennis courts.
The beach is right by the lake. At disposal bar, mini market, post service and telephone box, playground and table tennis.
The camping site is open from 29/03/03 till 05/10/03. Reservations possible.

Camping Week-End

6280 Via Vallone della Selva 2, 25010 San Felice del Benaco (Lombardy)

Created among the olive groves and terraced vineyards of the Chateau Villa Louisa, which overlooks it, this modern well equipped site enjoys some superb views over the small bay which forms this part of Lake Garda. Although the site is 400 m from the lake for many campers the views resulting from its situation on higher ground will be ample compensation. Set in quiet countryside, it provides an unusually tranquil environment, although even here it can be very busy in the high season. There are some 220 pitches, all with electricity (from 3A), of which about 30% are taken by tour operators and statics. The touring pitches are in several different areas, and many enjoy views. Some pitches for larger units are on the upper terraces on steep slopes and manoeuvring can be challenging, and low olive branches may cause problems. The attractive restaurant has a thoughtfully laid out terrace and lawn.

Facilities: The three sanitary blocks, one below the restaurant/shop, are modern, well maintained and include hot water to showers, basins and washing-up areas. Mainly British style WCs, a few washbasins in cabins and facilities for disabled people. We have had reports of congestion in the facilities at peak periods. Washing machines and dryer. Motorcaravan services. Bar/restaurant (waiter service). Takeaway. Shop. Supervised swimming pool and children's pool. Volleyball. Barbecues. Entertainment programme in season. Two playgrounds. First aid room. English spoken. **Off site:** Fishing 2 km. Golf 6 km. Riding 8 km. Windsurfing, water skiing and tennis near.

Charges 2002

Per unit incl. electricity	€ 9.55 - € 13.43
adult	€ 4.65 - € 6.71
child (3-10 yrs)	€ 3.62 - € 5.61
dog	€ 3.62 - € 5.42

No credit cards. **Tel:** 0365 43712. **Fax:** 0365 42196. E-mail: cweekend@tin.it. **Reservations:** Contact site. **Open** 28 April - 23 September.

Directions: Approach from Saló (easier when towing) and follow site signs. From Milano - Venezia autostrada take Desenzano exit towards Saló and Localita Cisano - S. Felice.

...so unique!!
★★★★
camping villaggio

WEEKEND

Via Vallone della Selva, 2
25010 San Felice del Benaco
(BRESCIA) - Italy
Tel. 0039/036543712
Fax 0039/036542196
Http: //www.weekend.it
E-mail: info@weekend.it

Quiet family site, well maintained. Modern sanitary facilities. Free hot water in the showers and basins. Washing machine, bar, restaurant, pizzeria, small shop. Very scenic. 2 swimming pools, children's playing area, volleyball, table tennis, music and dancing in the evenings. Ask for our brochure. Reservations accepted. Caravan, tent and bungalow for hire. New 6 person mobile-homes. Individual washing cubicles.

Camping Zocco

6285 Via del Zocco 43, 25080 Manerba del Garda (Lombardy)

Camping Zocco is an excellent site in a quiet, scenic location sloping gently down to the lake where there is a jetty and a long pleasant shingle beach. There are 200 pitches for tourists, all with electricity (4A), and sized from 60-80 sq.m., the pitches are either on slightly sloping ground, on terraces or around the perimeters of two open meadows. A variety of trees, including olives, give shade in some parts. The site has a well cared for appearance. Watersports can be enjoyed on the lake and boats may be launched from the site. The Fratelli family who run this site give British visitors a warm welcome and English is spoken. A superb new pool complex and an administrative block make Zocco a most attractive option if you prefer a smaller site with excellent facilities. Used by tour operators (20 pitches).

Facilities: Three tiled sanitary blocks, amongst the cleanest we have seen, are well spaced around the site. Mainly British style WCs, hot water in the washbasins, sinks and showers. Facilities for disabled people. Washing machines. Motorcaravan services. Good restaurant/pizzeria with terrace and bar. New coffee shop. Well stocked shop (1/5-15/9). Bar on beach (reduced hours in low season). New swimming pool complex with jacuzzi (free to campers). Watersports. Fishing. Tennis. Football. Play area. Entertainment for children during July/Aug. **Off site:** Bicycle hire 1.5 km. Riding and golf 4 km.

Charges 2002

Per person	€ 4.20 - € 6.20
child (3-11 yrs)	€ 3.40 - € 5.20
pitch incl. electricity	€ 8.50 - € 12.00
dog	€ 2.10 - € 3.70

Tel: 0365 551605. **Fax:** 0365 552053. E-mail: info@campingzocco.it. **Reservations:** Made for min. 7 days with deposit (€ 78) deducted from final bill. **Open** 12 April - 21 September.

Directions: From Desenzano head north on road 572 towards Salo and take minor road to Manerba from where Zocco is signed.

Camping Bella Italia

6263 Via Bella Italia 2, 37019 Peschiera del Garda (Venetia)

Peschiera is a picturesque village on the southern shore of Lake Garda and Camping Bella Italia is a large, well organised site, just 1 km. west from the centre of the village. In the grounds of a former farm, the site slopes gently down to the lake with access to the water for swimming and boating. Although about one third of the total area is taken by the site's own accommodation (apartments and bungalows) and tour operators, there are some 850 tourist pitches, most towards the lakeside and reasonably level on grass under trees. All have electricity (3A), are separated by shrubs and numbered on the campsite plan but not on the ground. They are grouped in regular rows on either side of hard access roads which are named after composers (east side) and artists (west side) of the wide central road which leads to the shops, pleasant restaurants and terrace. There are fine views across the lake from many parts. A feature of the site is the group of pools of varying shape and size with an entertainment area at the road end of the site. Strict regulations (a long list is given on arrival) are in place to ensure a peaceful site.

Facilities: Seven good sanitary blocks, including two new ones, have British style toilets, free hot water in washbasins (some in cabins), showers and sinks, facilities for disabled visitors, and good provision for washing up and laundry. Washing machines. Motorcaravan services. Shops. Bars. Waiter service restaurant and terrace with splendid views across to the opposite shore and new restaurant in the old farm building. Swimming pools. Tennis. Football. Volleyball. Basketball. Playgrounds (small). Games and TV room. Watersports. Bicycle hire. Organised activities. Dogs are not accepted. **Off site:** Fishing 1 km. Numerous excursions possible and Gardaland, Italy's most popular theme park is about 2 km. east of Peschiera.

Charges 2003

Per person	€ 4.00 - € 8.50
child (under 5 yrs)	gratis - € 5.00
pitch	€ 9.00 - € 17.00

Four charging seasons. **Tel:** 045 640 0688. Fax: 045 640 1410. E-mail: bellaitalia@camping-bellaitalia.it. **Reservations:** Advised for high season; contact site. **Open** 1 April - 7 October.

Directions: From Peschiera exit on A4 (Milan - Venice) autostrada, turn left and drive through town to site 1 km. from centre, on the right.

Camping Piani di Clodia

6253 Localita Bagatta, 37017 Lazise (Venetia)

As might be expected in a popular area like Lake Garda, there are many campsites. Piani di Clodia is one of the best large sites giving a positive impression of space and cleanliness. It is located on a slope between Lazise and Peschiera in the southeast corner of the lake, with lovely views across the water to Sirmione's peninsula and the opposite shore. The site is very close to Gardaland, one of the biggest theme parks in Europe and the huge Caneva aqua park. The rectangular site slopes down to the water's edge and has over 1,000 pitches, all with electricity (5A), terraced where necessary and back to back from hard access roads. There is some shade from mature and young trees. The pool complex is truly wonderful with three pools, the whole area being fenced and supervised, with a pleasant sunbathing area and bar. At the centre of the site is a quality rooftop restaurant, huge lower self service restaurant plus a pizzeria. From most of this area you will be able to enjoy the free entertainment on the large stage. There is a fence between the site and the lake with access points to a private beach and opportunities for a variety of watersports.

Facilities: Seven modern, immaculate sanitary blocks are well spaced around the site with a mix of British and Turkish style WCs and hot water in washbasins, sinks and showers. All have facilities for disabled visitors and one has a baby room. Washing machines, dryers and laundry service. Motorcaravan services. Shopping complex with supermarket, general shops for clothes, etc. Two bars. Self-service restaurant with takeaway and pizzeria and gelaterie. Swimming pools - one for straightforward swimming which can be heated, another with a variety of slides and hydro-massage and the third for children. Tennis. Table tennis. Gymnastics. Bicycle hire. Large grass space for volleyball and other ball games. Large playground. Outdoor theatre with animation programme. **Off site:** Riding near. Golf 12 km. Caneva aqua park, Gardaland theme park close by.

Charges 2002

Per person	€ 3.39 - € 7.75
child (1-9 yrs)	€ 2.58 - € 5.16
pitch with electricity	€ 8.78 - € 18.08
pitch with electricity and water	€ 9.81 - € 19.63

Tel: 045 7590456. Fax: 045 7590939. E-mail: info@pianidiclodia.it. **Reservations:** Write to site. **Open** 20 March - 5 October.

Directions: Site is south of Lazise on road SS249 before Peschiera.

Camping La Quercia

6255 37017 Lazise sul Garda (Venetia)

A spacious, popular site on a slight slope leading down to Lake Garda, La Quercia can accommodate around 1,000 units and is decorated by palm trees and elegantly trimmed hedges. There is a strict security regime in high season with passes required at all times including the beach security points. Pitches are in regular double rows between access roads, all with electricity (4/6A). Most are shaded by mature trees, although those furthest from the lake are more open to the sun. Although siting is not always easy, but staff do help in high season. La Quercia has a fine sandy beach on the lake, with diving jetties. Much of the site activity centres around the Olympic-size pool and terrace bar, restaurant and pizzeria which overlook the animation stage. A second self service restaurant is nearer the beach, part of which is dominated by a large screen TV (can have high volume settings) plus an ice-cream bar. The evening entertainment is a little daunting at first, with the young team working hard to involve everyone - smaller children love it! The site is a short distance from the exquisite lakeside towns of Lazise and Peschiera and is a short drive from Verona, one of Italy's finest cultural centres. La Quercia has always been a popular site and, although its prices have been quite high, it does offer a great deal for your money, including a wide choice of organised activities and amenities, most free. Many of the courses require enrolment on a Sunday. A reader reports that on Saturday nights in high season there may be some late night noise from a disco outside the site. English is spoken. Used by tour operators.

Facilities: The six toilet blocks are perfectly sufficient and are of a very high standard. Laundry. Supermarket. General shop. Bar, restaurant, self-service restaurant and pizzeria. Swimming pool, children's pool and a large, landscaped spa pool (small charge). Tennis court. Table tennis. Riding stables. Football. Aerobics and yoga. Facilities for boats on the lake. Scuba club. Children's playground with water play. Organised events (sports competitions, games, etc.) and free courses in swimming, surfboard. canoeing, Roller blading. tennis, archery, climbing, judo, with multi-gym, volleyball and tennis courts also available. Minigolf. Evening entertainment or dancing. Baby sitting service. Internet. ATM. Free weekly excursion. Medical service. **Off site:** Supermarkets en-route to Verona. 'Guardaland' supposedly the largest theme park in Italy and the enormous Caneva Aqua Park nearby.

Charges 2002

Per person	€ 4.80 - € 8.01
child (under 5)	€ 2.79 - € 5.37
pitch	€ 9.55 - € 18.33
reserved pitch	€ 10.59 - € 21.95

No credit cards. Low season discount for pensioners. **Tel:** 045/6470577. **Fax:** 045/6470243. **Reservations:** made Sat - Sat for certain pitches. **Open** 10 days before Easter - 30 September.

Directions: Site is on south side of Lazise. From north on Trento - Verona A22 autostrada take Affi exit then follow signs for Lazise and site. From south take Peschiera exit and site is 7 km. towards Garda and Lazise.

Camping Gasparina

6266 Via Gasparina 13, 37010 Cavalcaselle (Venetia)

Camping Gasparina is of average size for this area and of reasonable quality, but a little away from the towns around the lake in a peaceful location giving the appearance of being in the countryside. As the site slopes towards the lake, levellers are needed in some parts. There are 430 grass tourist pitches in back-to-back rows separated by gravel roads. Many trees and flowers adorn the site, with shade in most parts. Near reception are the supermarket, bar/restaurant and swimming pool (30 x 10 m) which is enclosed by a neat well clipped hedge and has a comprehensive set of rules for safety and enjoyment of guests. There is a small beach and boats can be launched here.

Facilities: Two refurbished and one new toilet block have the usual facilities with warm water in two blocks. Facilities for disabled visitors. Washing machines and dryer Shop. Bar/restaurant with terrace.. Swimming pool. Playground. Tennis courts. Watersports. Animation in high season. **Off site:** Riding 3 km. Bicycle hire 2 km.

Charges 2002

Per person	€ 3.00 - € 7.00
child (up to 10 yrs)	€ 2.00 - € 3.50
pitch	€ 5.50 - € 10.00
boat trailer	€ 13.00 - € 18.00

Tel: 045 7550775. **Fax:** 045 7552815. **E-mail:** info@gasparina.com. **Reservations:** Contact site. **Open** 25 March - 28 September.

Directions: Leave A4 [Milan-Venice] motorway at exit for Peschiera, go north on east side of lake on SS249 towards Lazise for entrance road on your left.

Camping del Garda

6256 Via Marzan 6, 37019 Peschiera del Garda (Venetia)

Although Camping del Garda is not directly on the lake (a cul-de-sac leading to a watersports centre runs between camp and water) it has access via a large gate to the beach and for launching boats. This is one of the largest campsites around Lake Garda and more a self contained holiday village. There are many trees, some providing shade on the 800 level grass tourist pitches which are back-to-back in 59 numbered rows. With access from hard roads and trees marking corners, all have electrical connections (4A). Several days of heavy rain immediately before our visit had prevented the mowing of some pitches but otherwise it was a neat, tidy site with flower beds adding to its attraction. It is within easy walking distance of the picturesque little town of Peschiera and the busy waterfront from where boat trips can be made. There are two large swimming pools (from 1 June) with lifeguards. A wide variety of sports is available, entertainment programmes for children and adults are provided and there is provision for boat enthusiasts to launch boats.

Facilities: Eleven good quality toilet blocks have the usual facilities with free hot water in sinks, wash-basins and showers. Facilities for disabled visitors in two blocks. Washing machines and dryers. Bars, restaurant and takeaway. Supermarket. Swimming pools. Tennis courts and tennis school. Minigolf. Watersports including windsurf school. Fishing. Playground. Full programme of organised activities in high season. Table tennis. Bowls. Dogs or motorcycles are not accepted. **Off site:** Gardaland, Zoo Safari, Verona etc.

Charges 2002

Per person	€ 4.00 - € 7.00
child (under 5 yrs)	free - € 4.50
pitch incl. electricity (4A)	€ 9.00 - € 15.00

Tel: 045 755 0540. Fax: 045 640 0711. E-mail: campinggelgarda@icmnet.net. **Reservations:** Contact site. **Open** 1 April - 30 September.

Directions: Leave the A4 (Milan-Venice) motorway at exit for Peschiera, head towards town and follow signs from roundabout.

Camping Lido

6254 Via Peschiera 2, 37017 Pacengo (Venetia)

Camping Lido is one of the largest and best of the 120 campsites around Lake Garda and is situated in the southeast corner of the lake. There is quite a slope from the entrance down to the lake so many of the 700 grass touring are on terraces which give lovely views across the lake. The pitches are of varying size, separated by hedges and all have electrical connections (5A). This is a most attractive site with tall, neatly trimmed trees standing like sentinels on either side of the broad avenue which runs from the entrance right down to the lake. A wide variety of trees provide shade on some pitches and flowers add to the overall appearance. Near the top of the site is a large, well designed pool and a fitness centre. The site has its own beach with a landing stage that marks off a large area for swimming on one side and on the other an area where boats can be moored. Every night in high season there is a free bus service for teenagers to a local disco returning at 2 a.m. One could happily spend all the holiday here without leaving the site but with so many attractions nearby this would be a pity.

Facilities: Seven modern toilet blocks have the usual facilities including provision for disabled visitors and three family rooms with baths. Washing machines and dryer. Restaurant, bars, pizzeria, takeaway and well stocked supermarket. Swimming pool and children's pool. Fitness centre with fully equipped gym, sauna and Turkish bath. Playground. Football field. Tennis. Bicycle hire. Watersports. Fishing (permit required). Volleyball. High season organised activities for children and adults. Shingle beach with private landing stage for boats. **Off site:** Gardaland Theme Park, Verona, other parts of Lake Garda.

Charges 2002

Per person	€ 3.50 - € 6.75
child (under 10 yrs)	free - € 4.10
senior (over 60 yrs)	€ 3.00 - € 5.75
pitch incl. services	€ 8.00 - € 15.00

Tel: 045 759 0030. Fax: 045 759 0030. E-mail: info@campinglido.it. **Reservations:** Contact site. **Open** 23 March - 29 September.

Directions: Leave A4 Milan - Venice motorway at exit for Peschiera. Head north on east side of lake on SS249. Site entrance on left after Gardaland Theme Park.

Camping Al Porto

6237

38069 Torbole (Trentino - Alto Adige)

This is a small unassuming site built on what was the family farm fifty years ago. It is peaceful, set back from the main road, and close to the water. Lake access is about 80 m. along a road to the rear of the site and here there is a slow shelving beach ideal for windsurfers. Although the services on site are limited it is in the heart of Torbole where there is a choice of places to eat. The grass pitches are level with mature trees providing shade. Hedges separate two areas, one with numbered pitches with electricity for tourers. The other less formal area is for tents (no electricity) with a secure hut for wind-surfing equipment to one side. A no frills site which is good for stop-overs and excellent for windsurfers.

Facilities: The clean, modern sanitary block has British and Turkish style WCs and hot water throughout. Facilities for disabled campers. Washing machines. Motorcaravan services. Bar with snacks incl. light breakfasts. Play area. **Off site:** Swimming and windsurfing in the lake. Mountain biking, hiking, climbing, canoeing, canyoning and fishing nearby. Shops and cafés a short walk.

Charges 2003

Per pitch	€ 8.50
adult	€ 6.00
child (1-12 yrs)	€ 4.56
electricity	€ 0.50

Discounts in low season. No credit cards. **Tel:** 0464 505891. Fax: 0464 505891. E-mail: alporto@torbole.com. **Reservations:** not taken. **Open** 5 April - 2 November.

Directions: Site is on the northeast tip of Lake Garda. Take Roverto south exit for Lake Garda north, then A240 for Nago. From Nago to Torbole and leave Torbole in direction of Riva del Garda. Site is on left before the town exit bridge.

Camping Al Sole

6232

Loc. Besta, 38060 Molina di Ledro (Trentino-Alto Adige)

Lake Ledro is only 9 km. from Lake Garda, its sparkling waters and breathtaking scenery offering a low key alternative for those who enjoy a natural setting. This site has been owned by the same friendly family for over 30 years and their experience shows in the layout of the site with its mature trees and the array of facilities. Situated on the lake with its own pretty grass and sand beach, the facilities are constantly upgraded and include a new pool and a play area. It came as no surprise to hear that many people choose to return year after year. The local community welcomes tourists and offers free hiking programmes. A very nice peaceful site for extended stays or sightseeing.

Facilities: The new sanitary block has plenty of hot water and good facilities for disabled campers. Washing machines. Freezer. Small supermarket. Pleasant restaurant with terrace. Bar serving snacks and takeaway. Large screen TV. New swimming pool. Play area. Table tennis. Lake for swimming, boating, windsurfing, fishing and canoeing. Live music and dancing in July/Aug. Torches needed in some areas. **Off site:** Pedalo hire nearby. The area is also ideal for hiking, mountain biking, climbing and canyoning.

Charges guide

Per pitch incl. electricity	€ 5.68 - € 7.23
person	€ 4,13 - € 5,68
child (3-12 yrs)	€ 3,35 - € 4,64

Tel/Fax: 0464/508496. Email info@campingalsole.it. **Reservations:** contact site. **Open** 20 April - 30 Sept.

Directions: From Torbole on Lake Garda follow Limone signs north of Riva to access the tunnel to Mollina di Ledro and Lago di Ledra on the N240. (care must be taken north of Riva as signs are very sparse). Site is signed approaching Lago di Ledra.

Camping Steiner

6210

Kennedy Straße 32, 39055 Laives (Bolzano) (Trentino - Alto Adige)

Being on the main S12 which now has a motorway alternative, Camping Steiner is very central for touring with the whole of the Dolomite region within easy reach, as well as Bolzano, Merano and other attractive places. It has its share of overnight trade but, with much on site activity, one could spend an enjoyable holiday. It is a smallish site with part taken up by bungalows. The tourist pitches, mostly with good shade and hardstanding, are in rows on either side of access roads. The site becomes full in season. It is run personally by the proprietor's family who provide friendly reception, with English spoken.

Facilities: The two sanitary blocks, one new, can be heated in cool weather. Excellent small restaurant and takeaway. Cellar bar. Shop. Two free swimming pools - an open air one, 20 x 10 m. (May-Sept), and a 12 x 6 m. enclosed, heated pool (open all season, except July/Aug). Playground and paddling pool. Table tennis. **Off site:** Golf course 30 minutes away.

Charges 2002

Per person	€ 5.00 - € 6.00
pitch incl. car and 6A electricity	€ 10.00 - € 12.00

Less in low season. Less 5-10% after 2 weeks stay. **Tel:** 0471 950105. Fax: 0471 951572. E-mail: steiner@dnet.it. **Reservations:** Min. one week with reasonable deposit. **Open** 28 March - 7 November.

Directions: Site is on S12 in northern part of Leifers, 8 km. south of Bolzano. From motorway if approaching from north, take Bolzano-Süd exit and follow Trento signs for 7 km; from south take Ora exit and proceed for 14 km. towards Bolzano.

Camping Monte Brione

6235 Via Brione 32, 38066 Riva del Garda (Trentino - Alto Adige)

The small resort of Riva at the head of Lake Garda shelters under a rocky escarpment and from ancient times has been an important communication and trading centre on the route between Verona and the Alps. Although it lacks the sophistication of the southern end of the lake, today it is a picturesque tourist resort and recognised as one of the European windsurfing Meccas due to a combination of strong winds with flat water. Thus, this end of the lake tends to have a younger clientele and there is a late night vibrancy which follows a day spent speeding across the lake amongst fellow windsurfers. A municipal site, Camping Monte Brione is situated on the edge of town at the foot of an olive covered hill, about 500 m. from the town centre and lake side. There are 131 pitches on flat, well mown grass, marked by trees and posts in groups of four around a water and electricity (6A) service point. Unmarked terraces on the hillside take 21 tents. Good tarmac roads dissect the site which has a neat, well tended air. Although near residential developments, there are good views of the mountains.

Facilities: Two sanitary blocks, which will be due for refurbishment soon, are at either end of the site and have mixed Turkish and British style WCs, washbasins in cabins, and facilities for disabled people. Motorcaravan services. Shop for basic supplies. Snack bar, bar and covered terrace. Good sized swimming pool with a sunbathing area (1/6-30/9). Minigolf. Table tennis. Bowls. TV/video. Bicycle hire. Two play areas. **Off site:** The town has many shops and restaurants and is popular with the young windsurfers. Fishing 1 km. Riding 3 km. Sailing, boating and tennis near.

Charges 2002

Per person	€ 6.70
child (4-12 yrs)	€ 4.40
pitch	€ 8.80 - € 10.35
dog	€ 3.30

Less 15% in low season. **Tel:** 0464 520885. **Fax:** 0464 520890. **E-mail:** campingbrione@rivadelgarda.com. **Reservations:** Write to site with 20% deposit (refundable) of anticipated bill. **Open** Easter/1 April - early October.

Directions: Leave A22 at Garda-Nord exit for Torbole and Riva. Just before Riva, through short tunnel, then turn right at camp signs.

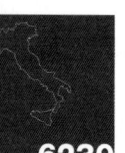

Camping San Cristoforo

6230 Via dei Pescatori, 38057 Pergine Valsugana (Trentino - Alto Adige)

This part of Italy is becoming better known by those wishing to spend time by a lake in splendid countryside, but away from the more crowded, better-known resorts. Lake Caldonazzo is one of the smaller lakes, but is excellent for watersports, with lifeguards on duty in the season. Camping San Cristoforo is a relatively new site on the edge of the small town of the same name and is separated from the lake by a minor road, but with easy access. Owned by the friendly Oss family whose policy is to get to know their guests and build a family atmosphere, the site has 160 pitches. On flat grass on either side of hard access roads and separated by trees, the pitches are of a good size, numbered in front and with 3A electricity. The lake is very close offering watersports and fishing - we sighted several large trout during our visit! This quiet mountain site has a well cared for air and English is spoken. Used by a tour operator.

Facilities: The modern sanitary block provides some washbasins in cabins. Dishwashing and laundry sinks. Facilities for disabled people. Washing machine and dryer. Small well stocked shop. Attractive bar/restaurant (all year) by the pool with terrace, serving reasonably priced meals and takeaway. Swimming pool (20 x 20 m.) with sunbathing area and small children's pool. Bicycle hire. Minigolf. **Off site:** Village shops close. Fishing and boating 200 m. Riding 5 km. Golf 2 km.

Charges 2002

Per person	€ 5.10 - € 6.40
child (2-5 yrs)	€ 3.10 - € 4.10
child (6-11 yrs)	€ 3.60 - € 5.10
pitch	€ 9.20 - € 11.30
dog	€ 3.10

Discounts for longer stays in low season. **Tel:** 0461 512707. **Fax:** 0461 707381. **E-mail:** campingscristoforo@campingclub.nu. **Reservations:** Not accepted. **Open** 19 May - 7 September.

Directions: Site is southeast of Trento, just off the SS47 road; well signed from the village of San Cristoforo.

Camping Al Pescatore

6227 Via dei Pescatori 1, 38050 Calceranica al Lago (Trentino - Alto Adige)

The small lake Calceranica lies just to the east of Trento in the foothills of the Dolomites amidst splendid scenery. Camping Al Pescatore is a very pretty, small campsite about 50 m. from the lake where swimming and watersports can be enjoyed. There are 173 tourist pitches on grass under tall trees some of which are in an over-flow section immediately opposite the entrance and all have electric connections (4A). The lakeside is very popular at weekends and during our visit on a Sunday in mid-June, a many people were enjoying the scenery and the two large restaurants opposite the beach were both very busy, although it was peaceful on the site. In July and August a small bar and shop are open. The site could make a suitable night stop if travelling between Austria and Italy via the Brenner but you might be tempted to stay a little longer as there are many places of interest nearby. A friendly site, English is spoken at reception.

Facilities: The two toilet blocks on the main site provide the usual facilities and there is a single unisex block in the overflow section. Facilities for disabled visitors. Washing machines. Shop and bar July/Aug. Playground. In July and August there are organised activities for children and music and dancing for adults.

Charges 2002

Per adult	€ 6.00
child (under 12 yrs)	€ 5.50
pitch	free - € 8.30
dog	€ 2.60

Tel: 0461 723062. **Fax:** 0461 724212. **E-mail:** trentino@campingpescatore.it. **Reservations:** Contact site. **Open** 16 May - 16 September.

Directions: Leave A22 (Brenner - Modena) motorway at Trento Nord, follow SS47 in the direction of Padova to S. Christoforo and follow signs to Calceranica and site.

Camping Spiaggia Lago di Molveno

6214 Via Lungolago 25, 38018 Molveno (Trentino - Alto Adige)

This site was recommended to us by a reader and when we visited it we could see why. Camping Spiaggia is on the edge of the pretty little village of Molveno on the lake of the same name and is run by a company set up and controlled by the local authority to promote tourism in the area. It occupies a most scenic location at the foot of the Brenta mountains with views across the lake. It is a most attractive site, adorned with plants and trees and has 132 tourist pitches, with about the same number of static caravans, on level grass, marked and separated with each having an electrical connection (4A). Right next to the site is a sports complex with free access for campers to the tennis courts and heated swimming pool [15/6 - 8/9]. In June and September and weekends during May and October a free return ticket is given for the funicular to Pradel in the Brenta Parco Naturali. Being open all year it is an ideal location from which to ski in winter and go walking and climbing in summer.

Facilities: Three modern, heated toilet blocks have free hot water. Facilities for disabled visitors. Well stocked shop (open all year). Attractive bar/restaurant with takeaway (closed October, November and weekends in winter). Playground. In June, August and September entertainment is organised in the village for children and adults. **Off site:** Just outside the site is a football field, bowls, volleyball, basketball, minigolf and pedalos and boats for hire.

Charges 2002

Per person	€ 4.50 - € 8.00
child (3-12 yrs)	€ 3.00 - € 5.50
pitch	€ 5.50 - € 12.00
dog	€ 1.00 - € 2.50

Tel: 0461 586 978. **Fax:** 0461 586 330. **E-mail:** camping@molveno.it. **Reservations:** Contact site. **Open** all year.

Directions: From A22 (Brenner - Modena) motorway leave at exit for S. Michele north of Trento and head northwest on SS43 - signed Val di Non - and then SP64 following signs to Moveno and site.

Camping Due Laghi

6225 Localita Costa 3, 38056 Levico Terme (Trentino - Alto Adige)

This good, modern site is close to the main road but is quiet, with mountain views and only five minutes walk from the Levico lake where it has a small private beach where one can put boats. A most attractive site with a variety of trees and flowers, there are 426 numbered pitches on flat grass, in rows marked by slabs and all with electricity (3/6A). Most are said to be around 80 sq.m. but there are 60 larger pitches (90 sq.m) with electricity, water, TV and phone connections. The site has a good swimming pool, so it may be suitable for a stay as well as overnight. It is said to become full from 15/7 - 15/8 but there is always a chance of finding space. The site supplies a comprehensive descriptive guide to the attractions of the region. English is spoken.

Facilities: The central toilet block is both of good quality and very large, with British and Turkish type WCs, some washbasins in cubicles and a unit for disabled people. The hot water supply can be variable. Some private WCs may be hired. Laundry. Gas supplies. Motorcaravan services. Shop. Restaurant, pizzeria and café/bar with takeaway. Music weekly in high season. Swimming pool (over 300 sq.m) and children's pool. Sauna. Playground. Tennis. Bicycle hire. **Off site:** Walks from site. Fishing 500 m. Riding 2 km. Golf 5 km.

Charges 2003

Per person	€ 6.00 - 7.50
child (2-5 yrs)	€ 4.00 - € 5.00
child (6-11 yrs)	€ 5.00 - € 6.00
pitch	€ 10.00 - € 14.50
dog	€ 2.00 - € 3.00

Club card for entertainment, etc. obligatory in July/Aug. Discounts for longer stays in low season. No credit cards. **Tel:** 0461 706290. Fax: 0461 707381. E-mail: cduelaghi@tin.it. **Reservations:** made for at least 1 week in peak season, with deposit and fee. **Open** 18 May - 15 September.

Directions: Site is 20 km. southeast of Trento just off S47 road towards Padova (camp sign at turning).

Camping Latsch an der Etsch

6212 Reichstraße 4, 39021 Laces-Latsch (Trentino - Alto Adige)

An enthusiastic reader's report on this site prompted a visit and we found, as suggested, a delightful little campsite. The Alto Adige or Sud-Tirol is the most northerly province of Italy bordering on Switzerland and Austria and was ceded to Italy in 1918. German is the first language and villages and towns bear both the German and Italian names. Latsch (or Laces) is in the Venosta Valley which runs from Merano to Spondigna. Gasthof Camping Latsch is 640 m. above sea level between the SS38 road and the river, with splendid views across to the surrounding mountains. About 20 of the 120 tourist pitches are on a terrace by reception with the remainder on a lower terrace alongside the river. They are in regular rows which are separated by hedges with thin grass on gravel. All have electricity (6A) and 47 also have water, drainage, sewage and TV points. Trees provide shade to some parts. A unique feature of the site is the large underground car park which protects vehicles from winter snow and summer sun and, if used, gives a reduction in pitch charges. Although right by a main road, the Gasthof and terracing screen out most of the road noise. The friendly, English speaking owner has created a very pleasant ambience and appeared very popular with those staying there. Mountain walkers will be in their element and chair-lifts give access to higher slopes. Interesting drives can be made over nearby passes with Merano, Bolzano, the Dolomites and the duty-free town of Livigno within range.

Facilities: The modern sanitary block is on two floors (to serve each section) has all the usual facilities and is heated in cool weather. Twenty excellent private bathrooms (basin, shower, toilet) are for hire. Motorcaravan service point. Washing machine and dryer. Bar and pleasant restaurant (all season). Shop. Small heated indoor pool, plus sauna, solarium and fitness room. Larger, irregularly shaped outdoor pool with marble surrounds, small waterfall and sunbathing area. Children's playground. **Off site:** Bowling, fishing (licence), tennis, golf and riding near.

Charges 2003

Per person	€ 5.20 - € 6.20
child (2-12 yrs)	€ 4.20 - € 5.70
electricity	€ 2.10
dog	€ 4.40 - € 5.20

Tel: 0473 623 217. Fax: 0473 622 333. E-mail: camping.latsch@dnet.it. **Reservations:** contact site. **Open** all year except 8 November-15 December.

Directions: Latsch/Laces is 28 km. east of Merano on SS38 Bolzano-Silandro road. Site entrance on the right of the Gasthof (keep on main road, don't turn off to village).

Camping Olympia

6200 39034 Toblach-Dobbiaco (Trentino-Alto Adige)

In the Dolomite mountains, Camping Olympia, always good, has been given a face-lift by the redesigning of the camping area and the refurbishment of the already excellent sanitary accommodation. Tall trees at each end of the site have been left, but most of those in the centre have been removed and the pitches re-laid in a regular pattern. They include 12 fully serviced ones with electricity, water, waste, gas and TV and telephone points. The static caravans are grouped together at one end leaving the centre for tourists and with a grass area at the other end for tents. An attractive centre piece has fountain surrounded by flowers. On the far side of the site, where campers can walk amidst the woods, is a little play area.

Facilities: Excellent sanitary provision, on two floor levels, is in the main building. Seven cabins with WC, washbasin and shower to rent. Two small blocks at each end of the site with further WCs and showers. Shop. Attractive restaurant is open all day, all year. Snack bar (not April/May or Oct/Nov). Tennis. Swimming pool (open when weather permits). Sauna, solarium, steam bath and whirl pools. Table tennis. Minigolf. Fishing (on payment). Bicycle hire. Play area. Animation programme in high season.

Charges 2002

Per person	€ 6.20 - € 7.23
child (3-12 yrs)	€ 3.62 - € 5.17
pitch	€ 8.26 - € 11.36

Tel: 0474/972147. Fax: 0474/972713. E-mail: intercamp@dnet.it. **Reservations:** Write to site. **Open** all year.

Directions: Site is between Villabassa and Toblach/Dobbiaco. From A22 Innsbruck-Bolzano autostrada, take Bressanone/Brixen exit and travel east on SS49 for about 60 km. From Cortina take SS48 and SS51 northwards then west on SS49.

Camping Antholz

6201 39030 Antholz (Trentino - Alto Adige)

Appearances can be deceptive and this is the case with Camping Antholz, an all year campsite in the heart of the Dolomites. At first sight the 130 pitches, numbered but only roughly marked out, make this a very ordinary looking site. Inside the entrance is a pleasant looking building with reception and a smart restaurant. It is when one investigates the sanitary accommodation that one realises that this is no ordinary site, as the provision is superb. High up in the Anterselva valley, the site has splendid views of near and distant peaks. There are few trees on the site but many provide a nice background. This is good skiing country in winter and, with a new National Park near. provides good walking in summer.

Facilities: The toilet block with under-floor heating, in addition to the normal facilities, also provides a hair salon, cosmetics room and a baby room. Washing machine and dryer. Motorcaravan services. Restaurant (all year). Shop for basics. Playground. TV room. Table tennis. Bicycle hire. Limited entertainment programme for children in high season. **Off site:** Tennis near. Winter sports, summer walking.

Charges 2002

Per unit incl. 2 persons, electricity	€ 18.07 - € 22.21
extra person	€ 4.39 - € 5.68
child (2-12 yrs)	€ 3.09 - € 3.87
dog	€ 2.32 - € 2.58

Tel: 0474 492204. Fax: 0494 492444. E-mail: info@camping-antholz.com. **Reservations:** Write to site. **Open** all year.

Directions: From Bressanone exit on A22, go east on SS49 through Brunico and turn north (signed Antholz) for about 12 km. Pass Antholz village and site is on right.

Camping International Dolomiti

6205 via Campo di Sotto, 32043 Cortina d'Ampezzo (Venetia)

The Cortina region boasts several good sites and this family run site is one of the nearest to the town. Beside a fast flowing river in a broad flat, grassy area surrounded by mountain scenery, it is a quiet situation 3 km. from the town centre. The 390 good sized pitches are marked out by white stones on either sides of access roads and most have electricity (4A). Half the site is well shaded. There is a heated swimming pool on site. It makes a good centre for touring the Dolomites or for more active pursuits such as mountain walking. With no reservations made, arrive early in the day in the first three weeks of August.

Facilities: The main toilet block is large and should be adequate, including mainly Turkish style WCs, with some British, and washbasins with hot water sprinkler taps. A heated block has been added with facilities for disabled visitors. Washing machines and ironing. Gas supplies. Small shop (open long hours) and coffee bar. Swimming pool (1/7-31/8). Basic playground (hard base). **Off site:** Restaurant 600 m. Fishing 1 km. Bicycle hire or riding 3 km. Golf 2 km.

Charges 2002

Per person	€ 4.50 - € 7.50
child (under 6 yrs)	€ 2.50 - € 4.00
pitch	€ 7.00 - € 9.00

Tel: 0436 2485. Fax: 0436 5403. E-mail: campeggiodolomiti@tin.it. **Reservations:** Not made; contact site for information only. **Open** 1 June - 15 September.

Directions: Site is south of Cortina, to west of main S51. There are signs from the road.

Camping Toblacher See

6202 Toblacher See 3, 39034 Toblach-Dobbiaco (Trentino - Alto Adige)

Although the Dolomite region of northern Italy is best known as a winter sports area, it is also popular during the summer with climbers, walkers and mountain bike enthusiasts. Camping Toblachersee is situated between the busy SS51 and a small, quiet lake surrounded by mountains. The 190 pitches, except for a small grass area for tents, are all on hardstandings of sharp, white gravel and, as these slope, levellers are required. The bar, restaurant and takeaway with terrace is pleasantly situated by the lakeside with scenic views across the water to the mountains beyond.
Undoubtedly the crowning glory of this site is its splendid toilet block where all facilities are in private cabins with family bathrooms for hire. Unless you wish to linger by the lake or are a bird watcher, this is more a site from which to explore the area, go climbing, walking or mountain biking or skiing in winter than stay on all day although there is some entertainment during August. At certain times of year a package deal is available for 3, 4 or 6 days including half-board, an excursion and guided mountain bike tour.

Facilities: A single toilet block (mentioned above) also includes a washing machine and dryer and facilities for disabled visitors. Shop with basic supplies. Bicycle hire. Fishing. Bar/restaurant and takeaway (closed Mondays). Cross country ski slopes. Guided walks.

Charges 2002

Per person	€ 5.20 - € 8.30
child (10-16 yrs)	€ 4.40 - € 7.30
child (2-9 yrs)	€ 2.60 - € 4.70
pitch for caravan or motorcaravan	€ 7.00 - € 9.60
pitch for tent	€ 4.20 - € 6.70
electricity per kw.	€ 0.52
local tax	€ 0.52

Tel: 0474 972294. Fax: 0474 976647. E-mail: camping@toblachersee.com. **Reservations:** Contact site. **Open** all year.

Directions: Leave the A22 [Brenner-Bolzano] motorway at Bressanone. Go east on SS49 to Toblach/Dobbiacho and south on SS51 towards Cortina for 2.5 km. - site on right.

Villaggio Turistico Isamar

6055 Isolaverde, via Isamar, 9, 30010 S. Anna di Chioggia (Venetia)

Many improvements have been made here over the years and these continue, making it quite difficult to itemise all the amenities. Although directly by the sea, with its own sandy beach, it is a fair way from the entrance to the sea. The largest camping area, which may be cramped at times, is under pines and grouped around the swimming pool, the large modern sanitary block, shops, etc. near reception. A smaller area is under artificial shade near the beach with an Olympic size, salt-water swimming pool, children's pool and four new pools, a covered entertainment section, pizzeria, bar/restaurant and a small toilet block. Between these sections are well constructed holiday bungalows. A third camping area has been developed mainly for the site's own accommodation. The pitches, on either side of hard access roads, vary in size and all have electrical connections. The site has a much higher proportion of Italian holidaymakers than many other sites. It is also popular with the Germans and Dutch and may become crowded in high season.

Facilities: The main toilet blocks are fully equipped and of good quality with British style WCs (small block has only Turkish style). Dishwashing and laundry sinks. Laundry. Motorcaravan services. Gas supplies. Fridges for hire. Hairdresser. Supermarket and general shopping centre. Large bar/pizzeria and self-service restaurant. Swimming pools. Tennis. Playground. Disco. Games room with pin tables. Riding. Bicycle hire. Extensive entertainment and fitness programme offered for adults and supervised play for children over 4 years of age. Dogs are not accepted. **Off site:** Fishing 500 m.

Charges 2002

Per person	€ 3.50 - € 8.80
child (2-5 yrs)	€ 2.50 - € 7.40
pitch with full facilities	€ 5.00 - € 20.00
tent pitch	€ 4.00 - € 10.50

Less 10% for stays in low season for over 2 weeks.
Tel: 041 5535 811. Fax: 041 490440. E-mail: info@villaggioisamar.com. **Reservations:** Made for min. 7 days with deposit from Sat. **Open** 13 May - 16 September.

Directions: Turn off main 309 road towards sea just south of Adige river about 10 km. south of Chioggia, and proceed 5 km. to site.

Camping Della Serenissima

6050 Via Padana 334/a, 30030 Oriago (Venetia)

This is a delightful little site of some 140 pitches (all with 16A electricity) where one could stay for a number of days whilst visiting Venice (12 km), Padova (24), Lake Garda (135) or the Dolomites. There is a good service by bus to Venice and the site is situated on the Riviera del Brenta, a section of a river with some very large old villas. It is used mainly by Dutch and British visitors, with some Germans, and is calm and quiet. A long, narrow and flat site, numbered pitches are on each side of a central road. There is good shade in most parts with many trees, plants and grass. The management is very friendly and good English is spoken.

Facilities: The single sanitary block is just adequate, has been and still is being improved, with hot water in washbasins, showers and sinks. Mainly Turkish style WCs. Motorcaravan services. Gas supplies. Shop (all season). Bar. Restaurant and takeaway (1/6-31/10). Play area. Fishing. Bicycle hire. Reduced price bus ticket to Venice if staying for 3 days. No organised entertainment but local markets etc. all well publicised. **Off site:** Golf or riding 3 km.

Charges 2002

Per adult	€ 5.60 - € 6.60
child (3-10 yrs)	€ 4.00 - € 5.00
caravan and car	€ 9.80 - € 10.80
tent and car	€ 8.80 - € 9.80
motorcaravan	€ 9.80 - € 10.80

Tel: 041 921850. Fax: 041 920286. E-mail: camping.serenissima@shineline.it. **Reservations:** Are made; contact site. **Open** Easter - 10 November.

Directions: From the east take road S11 at roundabout SSW of Mestre towards Padova and site is 2 km. on right. From west, leave autostrada A4 at Dolo exit, follow signs to Dolo, continue on main road through this small village and turn left at T-junction (traffic lights). Continue towards Venice on S11 for site about 6 km on left.

6053 Camping Fusina

Via Moranzani, 79, 30030 Fusina (Venetia)

Recommended by our agent – this site will be inspected in 2003.

A pleasant site with helpful staff, Camping Fusina is located on a peninsula at the end of the lagoon south of Venice. With good access from all major routes there are around 200 touring pitches, partly shaded and with 5A electricity, together with some 100 mobile homes. There could be some factory or boat noise.

Facilities: Fully equipped toilet facilities include a washing machine and motorcaravan service point. Restaurant, bar and shop (March - Nov). Children's playground. Volleyball. Entertainment in season. Boat hire possible. **Off site:** Good public transport or boat connections to Venice.

Charges 2002

Per unit	€ 14.00
person	€ 7.00
child (5-12 yrs)	€ 4.00

Tel: 0415 470055. Fax: 0415 470050. E-mail: info@camping-fusina.com. **Reservations:** No need to book for motorcaravans or tents, otherwise contact site. **Open** all year.

Directions: From SSII Padua to Venice road follow site sign on road east of Mira, turning right as signed. Site in Fusina at end of peninsula.

Camping Marina di Venezia

6045 Via Montello 6, 30010 Punta Sabbioni (Venetia)

This is a very large site (2,300 pitches) with much the same atmosphere as many other large sites along this appealing stretch of coastline. Marina di Venezia, however, has the advantage of being within walking distance of the ferry to Venice. It will appeal particularly to those who enjoy an extensive range of entertainment and activities, and a lively atmosphere. The site's excellent sandy beach is one of the widest along this stretch of coast and has a pleasant beach bar. The main pool is Olympic sized and there is also a very large children's pool adjacent. Pitches are marked out individually on sandy terrain and most are separated by trees or hedges. They are of an average size for the region (around 80 sq.m). Most are equipped with electricity, and some have water and drainage.

Facilities: Ten modern toilet blocks are maintained to a high standard with good hot showers and a reasonable proportion of British-style toilets. Good provision for disabled visitors. Washing machines and dryers. Shopping facilities include a fish shop, sports shop and a shoe shop, to name but three! Several bars, restaurants and takeaway facilities. Swimming pools (no slides). Several play areas including bouncy castle. Tennis, football, beach volleyball, windsurf and catamaran hire. Wide range of organised entertainment including a good childrens' club in high season. Church on site.

Charges 2002

Per person	€ 3.75 - € 7.40
child or senior (under 5 and over 60)	€ 3.20 - € 6.05
pitch incl. services	€ 9.45 - € 18.10
pitch incl. satellite TV connection	€ 11.40 - € 21.70
dog	€ 0.90 - € 2.35

Tel: 041 530 2511. Fax: 041 966 036. E-mail: camping@marinadivenezia.it. **Reservations:** essential for high season - contact site. **Open** 20 April - 30 September.

Directions: From A4 motorway, take Jesolo exit. After Jesolo continue towards Punta Sabbioni. Site is clearly signed to the left towards the end of this road, close to the embarkation point for Venice ferries.

Camping Cavallino

6032 Via delle Batterie 164, 30013 Cavallino (Venetia)

This large, well ordered site is run by a friendly, experienced family who have other sites in this guide. It lies beside the sea with direct access to a superb beach of fine sand, which is very safe and enjoys the cover of several lifeguards. The site is thoughtfully laid out with large numbers of unusually large pitches shaded by olives and pines. All pitches have electricity (4A) and there is a 10% tour operator presence. If you wish to visit Venice a bus service runs to the ferry at Punta Sabbioni, some 20 minutes away. You then catch an interconnecting ferry which, after a charming journey of 40 minutes, drops you directly at St Marco Square after negotiating its way around the gondolas. A late return will mean a 2 km. walk at the end of a different bus service, but the night views of Venice from the sea are wonderful. Be sure to pay independently at the ferry rather than using the supposed cheap 'all-in' tickets which in fact are more expensive.

Facilities: Clean and modern toilet blocks are well spaced and provide a mixture of Turkish and British style WCs with facilities for disabled campers. Launderette. Motorcaravan services. Large shop providing most requirements. Swimming pools (May-Sept). Restaurant with large terrace, offering rapid service and takeaway. The menu is varied and reasonably priced with some excellent shell-fish and pasta dishes. Pizzeria. Table tennis. Minigolf. Play area. Ambitious animation programme is provided, aimed mostly at younger guests. Dogs are not accepted.

Charges 2002

Per person	€ 3.30 - € 7.30
child (1-6 yrs) or over 60s	€ 2.80 - € 5.90
pitch incl. electricity	€ 9.30 - € 18.50

Min. stay in high season I week. No credit cards. **Tel:** 041 966133. Fax: 041 5300827. E-mail: info@ campingcavallino.com. **Reservations:** Made for letting units only, but site provides priority cards for previous visitors. **Open** 11 April - 11 October.

Directions: From Venice - Trieste autostrada leave at exit for airport or Quarto and Altino. Follow signs, first for Jesolo and then Punta Sabbiono, and site signs will be seen just after Cavallino on the left.

Visiting Venice

If you are visiting Italy a trip to Venice is a must. It is said that you will either love it or find it totally distasteful, but you will walk away enchanted. The Basilica di San Marco and the Palazzo Ducale certainly draw the largest crowds, but to itemise the other sights would be too lengthy, let alone explaining the history behind this fascinating part of Italy. We prefer to visit in the late afternoon, after the crowds have thinned. When looking for somewhere to eat or drink, beware of some overpriced restaurants - Venice can be a very expensive city. Venture away to quieter areas where it is possible to find reasonably priced menus. Be sure to allow lots of time for getting around as we guarantee that you will get lost at some point. A good map is essential and we found a compass a help in navigating the fascinating labyrinths of alleys, canals and bridges.

Camping dei Fiori

6030 Via Pisani 52, Ca'Vio, 30010 Ca' Vio Treporti (Venetia)

The Lido del Cavallino peninsula, stretching from the outskirts of Lido del Jesolo to Punta Sabbioni, has over 30 good sites directly on the Adriatic sea and convenient for visiting Venice and other interesting places in northeast Italy. Dei Fiori stands out amongst the other small camps in the area. As its name implies, it is aflame with colourful flowers and shrubs in summer and presents a neat and tidy appearance whilst providing a quiet atmosphere. The 420 pitches, with electricity (5/6A), are either in woodland where space varies according to the trees which have been left in their natural state, or under artificial shade where regular shaped pitches are of reasonable size. Well built bungalows for rent enhance the site and are in no way intrusive, giving a village-like effect. About a quarter of the pitches are taken by static units, many for hire. Shops and a restaurant are in the centre next to the swimming pools. Nearby is the hydro-massage bath which is splendidly appointed and reputed to be the largest in Italy. The long beach is of fine sand and shelves gently into the sea. Regulations ensure the site is quiet between 11 pm. - 7.30 am. and during the afternoon siesta period. Venice is about 40 minutes away by bus and boat and excursions are arranged from the site. The site is well maintained by friendly, English speaking management.

Facilities: Three sanitary blocks are conveniently situated around the site and are of exceptional quality with British style WCs, well equipped baby rooms, good facilities for disabled people and washing machines and dryers. Motorcaravan services. Restaurant. Snack bar. Shops. Swimming pools and whirl pools. Fitness centre, hydro-massage bath and programmes (1/5-30/9) under the supervision of qualified staff (a charge is made during middle and high seasons but not in low season). Tennis. Table tennis. Minigolf. Basketball. Children's club and play area. Windsurfing. Organised activities, entertainment and excursions. Dogs are not accepted. **Off site:** Bicycle hire 2 km. Riding 4 km.

Charges 2002

Per person	€ 4.20 - € 8.50
child (1-4 yrs) or senior (over 65)	€ 3.20 - € 7.50
pitch with 3 services	€ 9.30 - € 19.80
pinewood pitch with electricity	€ 8.00 - € 18.40
tent in pinewood with electricity	€ 6.60 - € 16.50

Min. stay 7 days in high season (4/7-29/8). **Tel:** 041 966448. Fax: 041 966724. E-mail: fiori@vacanze-natura.it. **Reservations:** Advised for high season (incl. Whitsun) and made for min. 7 days. Write for application form as early as possible. **Open** 12 April - 4 October.

Directions: Leave A4 Venice-Trieste autostrada either by taking exit for airport or Quarto d'Altino and follow signs for Jesolo and then Punta Sabbioni and camp signs just after Ca'Ballarin.

Camping Mediterraneo

Via delle Batterie 38 Ca'Vio, 30010 Cavallino-Treporti (Venetia)

This large site has been considerably improved in recent years and is near Punta Sabbioni from where boats go to Venice. Mediterraneo is directly on the Adriatic Sea with a 480 m. long beach of fine sand which shelves gently and also two large pools (one for adults, the other for children) and a whirlpool. Sporting, fitness and entertainment programmes are arranged and sea swimming is supervised at designated hours by lifeguards. The 750 touring pitches, of which 500 have electricity (from 4A), water and drainaway, are partly in boxes with artificial shade, some larger without shade, with others in unmarked zones under natural woodland equipped with electric hook ups where tents must go. Used by tour operators (145 pitches). This is an organised and efficient site.

Facilities: Eight modern sanitary blocks are of good quality with British type WCs and free hot water in washbasins, showers and sinks. Washing machines. Motorcaravan services. Refrigerator hire. Commercial centre with supermarket and other shops with a restaurant, bars and a pizzeria near the pools. Swimming pool. Playground. Tennis court. Minigolf. Table tennis. Bicycle hire. Surf and swimming school. Regular monthly programme of sports, organised games, excursions etc; dancing or shows 3 times weekly in main season. Fitness programme. Dogs are not accepted. **Off site:** Riding and golf 3 km.

Charges 2002

Per person	€ 3.60 - € 7.80
child (3-5 yrs) or senior (over 60)	€ 2.60 - € 6.30
pitch with electricity	€ 7.00 - € 17.80
pitch with 3 services	€ 7.80 - € 19.50
tent pitch with electricity	€ 5.60 - € 16.00

Four rates. **Tel:** 041 966721. Fax: 041 966944. E-mail: mediterraneo@vacanze-natura.it. **Reservations:** made with large deposit. **Open** 4 May - 22 September.

Directions: Site is well signed from Jesolo-Punta Sabbioni road near its end after Ca' Ballarin and before Ca' Savio. Follow camp signs, not those for Treporti as this village is some way from the site.

GRUPPO
vacanze & natura
www.vacanze-natura.it
A sea of...
Amusement
Relax
Fun
Entertainment
Prà delle Torri
centro vacanze
ferienzentrum
Apart Hotel
Camping
Village
Hotel
Golf
Prà delle Torri
★★★★
Centro Vacanze
I-30021 Caorle
VENEZIA
Tel. 0039/0421299063
Fax 0039/0421299035
torri@vacanze-natura.it
www.pradelletorri.it
Dei Fiori
★★★★
Camping Village
I-30010 Treporti - Ca'Vio
VENEZIA
Tel. 0039/041966448
Fax 0039/041966724
fiori@vacanze-natura.it
www.deifiori.it
Garden Paradiso
★★★★
Camping Village
I-30013 Lido del Cavallino
VENEZIA
Tel. 0039/041968075
Fax 0039/0415370382
garden@vacanze-natura.it
www.gardenparadiso.it
Mediterraneo
★★★★
Camping Village
I-30010 Treporti - Ca'Vio
VENEZIA
Tel. 0039/041966721
Fax 0039/041966944
mediterraneo@vacanze-natura.it
www.campingmediterraneo.it

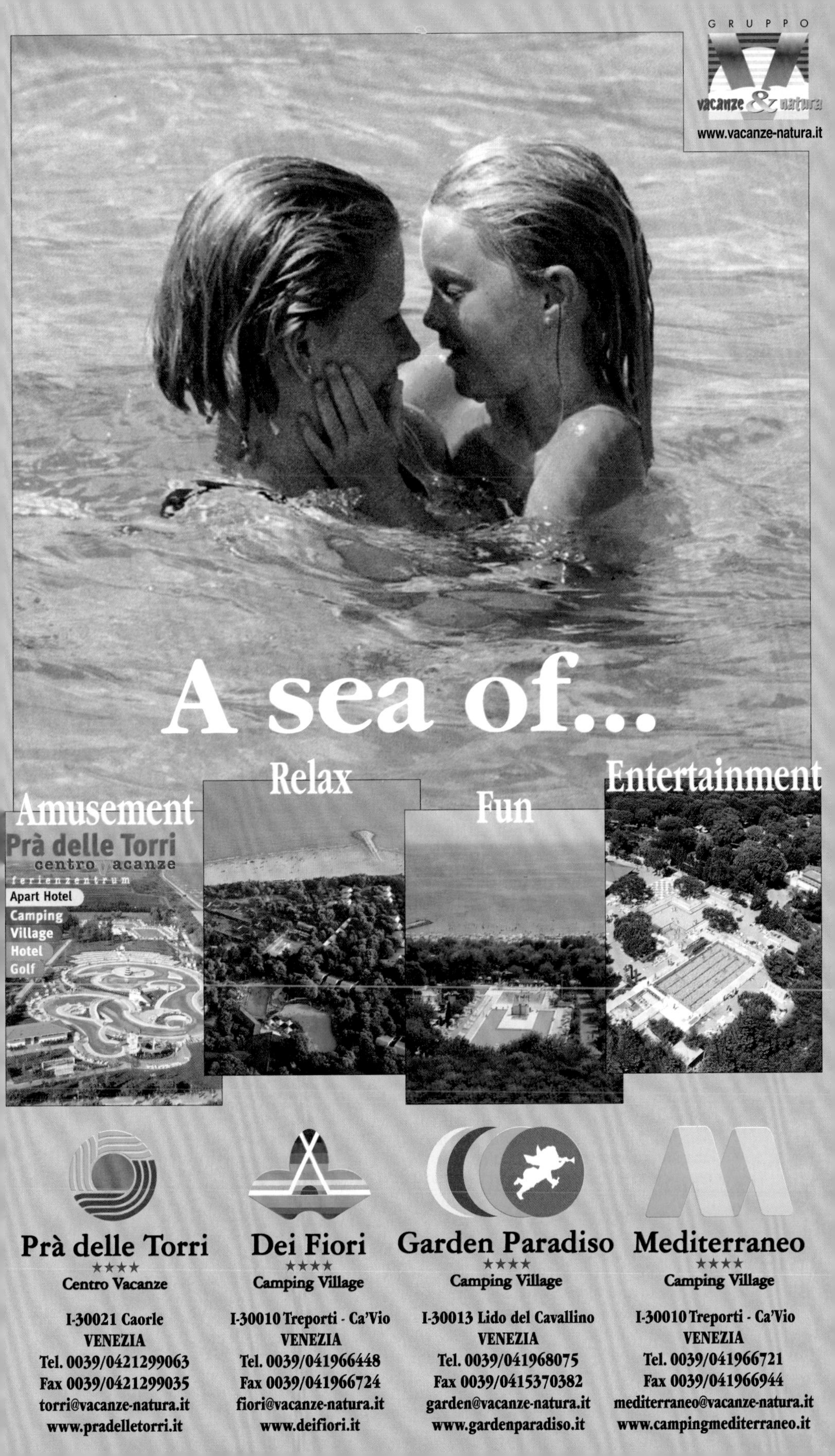

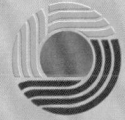

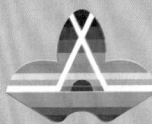

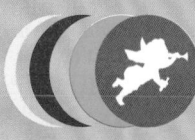

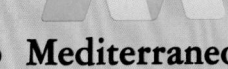

Camping Village Garden Paradiso

6040 Via Baracca 55, 30013 Cavallino (Venetia)

There are many sites in this area and there is much competition in providing a range of facilities. Garden Paradiso is a very good seaside site also providing three excellent centrally situated swimming pools. Compared with other sites here, this one is of medium size with 835 pitches. Most have electricity (from 6A), water and drainage points and all are marked and numbered with hard access roads, under a good cover of trees. Flowers and shrubs abound giving a pleasant and peaceful appearance. The site is directly on the sea with a beach of fine sand. The restaurant is near the beach with a bar/snack bar in the centre of the site. Used by tour operators (35 pitches). *See advertisement on page 249*

Facilities: Four brick, tiled toilet blocks are fully equipped with a mix of British and Turkish style toilets. Facilities for babies. Dishwashing and laundry sinks. Washing machines and dryers. Motorcaravan services. Shopping complex. Restaurant (22/4-28/9). Snack bar and takeaway. Swimming pools. Tennis. Table tennis. Minigolf. Play area. Organised entertainment and excursions. Bicycle hire. Dogs are not accepted. **Off site:** Fishing 2.5 km. Riding 2 km.

Charges 2002

Per person	€ 4.13 - € 8.00
junior (3-6 yrs) or senior (over 60)	€ 2.58 - € 6.20
pitch	€ 9.30 - € 20.00

Less 10% for over 30 days (early), or 20 days (late) season. **Tel:** 041 968075. Fax: 041 5370382. E-mail: garden@vacanze-natura.it. **Reservations:** Made with deposit (€155). **Open** 28 March - 30 September.

Directions: Leave Venice-Trieste autostrada either by taking the airport or Quarto d'Altino exits; follow signs to Jesolo and Punta Sabbioni. Take the first road on the left after Cavallino and site is a little way along on the right.

Camping Union Lido Vacanze

6020 Via Fausta 258, 30013 Cavallino (Venetia)

This well known site is extremely large but has first class organisation and it has been said that it sets the standard that others follow. It lies right by the sea with direct access to a long and broad sandy beach which fronts the camp. Shelving very gradually, the beach, which is well cleaned by the site, provides very safe bathing. The site is regularly laid out with parallel access roads under a covering of poplars, pine and other trees typical of this area providing good shade. These mark out the numbered pitches of adequate size (2,600 for touring units), all with electricity (5A) and 1,476 also with water and drainage. There are separate parts for caravans, tents and motorcaravans, plus one mixed part. The entrance provides a large off-road overnight parking area with electrical connections, toilets and showers for those arriving after 9 pm. An aqua-park includes a swimming pool, lagoon pool for children, heated whirlpool and a slow flowing 160 m. long 'river'. Covering 5,000 sq.m. this is supervised by lifeguards and is open mornings and afternoons. There is also a heated pool for hotel and apartment guests, available to others on payment. A selection of sports is offered in the annexe across the road and fitness programmes are available in season. The golf 'academy' with professional, has a driving range, pitching green, putting green and practise bunker, and a diving centre has a school and the possibilty of open water dives. Union Lido is above all an orderly and clean site and this is achieved partly by strict adherence to regulations suiting those who like comfortable camping undisturbed by others and good management.

Facilities: Sixteen well kept, fully equipped toilet blocks which open and close progressively during the season include hot water to all facilities, footbaths and deep sinks for washing dishes and clothes. Eleven blocks have facilities for disabled people. Launderette. Motorcaravan service points. Gas supplies. Comprehensive shopping area set around a pleasant piazza has wide range of shops including a large supermarket (all open till late). There are seven restaurants and several pleasant and lively bars. Aqua-park (from 15/5). Tennis. Riding. Table tennis. Minigolf. Skating rink. Bicycle hire. Archery. Two fitness tracks in 4 ha. natural park with play area and supervised play for children. Boat excursions. Recreational events for adults and children, day and evening. Italian language lessons. Golf academy. Diving centre and school. Windsurfing school in season. Church service in English in Jul/Aug. Exchange facilities and cash machine. Ladies' and gent's hairdressers. First aid centre, doctor's surgery with treatment room and camp ambulance. Dogs are not accepted.

Charges 2003

Per person	€ 5.90 - € 8.50
child (under 3 yrs)	€ 3.50 - € 5.90
child (3-12 yrs)	€ 4.90 - € 7.40
pitch with electricity	€ 10.60 - € 19.10
pitch with water and drainage	€ 13.30 - € 21.80

Three different seasons: (i) high season 29/6-31/8; (ii) mid-season 18/5-29/6 and 31/8-14/9, and (iii) off-season, outside these dates. **Tel:** 041 968080. Fax: 041 5370355. E-mail: info@unionlido.com. **Reservations:** Made for the letting units only, but site provides 'priority cards' for previous visitors. **Open** 1 May - 30 September.

Directions: From Venice-Trieste autostrada leave at exit for airport or Quarto d'Altino and follow signs first for Jesolo and then Punta Sabbioni, and camp will be seen just after Cavallino on the left.

Il Parco delle Vacanze

The pleasant holiday park with quality, style and atmosphere in a friendly environment right on to the Venetian Cavallino coast.
Open from 1st May to 30th September.

Camping - Caravan - Bungalow

Spacious, fitted pitches on grass under pines and poplars, for tents, caravans and motorcaravans. Many caravan pitches have water and drainage points. Caravans and mobile homes for hire, with shower and WC. Bungalow "Lido" with kitchen-living room, 2 double bedrooms (twin beds), shower and separate WC and terrace including some for disabled guests.

Fitness - Sport - Play Park

Spacious area with games and keep-fit equipment, with trained staff, multi-use sportsground for roller blading and other activities, volley ball, swimming instruction, wind surfing school, diving centre with school and diving excursions at sea, table tennis, minigolf, tennis and riding school. Archery and football competition.
Golf Academy. The Happy Place! Children's play area with much equipment. Climbing games and supervised play programme.

Animation - Entertainment - Activities

Open air theatre for entertainment program. Concerts and music performances. Painting course. Artistic activities. Plays and hobbies with supervisor. Mini club and activities for kids. Scout camp (July and August). Football school from 6 till 12 years. Assistance for children and baby area.

I-30013 CAVALLINO - VENEZIA
Tel. Camping 0039/0412575111-041968080
Tel. Hotel 0039/041968043-041968884
Telefax 0039/0415370355
E-mail: info@unionlido.com
Http://www.unionlido.it

Park Hotel Union Lido

The only 4-star-hotel in Cavallino. 78 rooms with air conditioning, completely refurnished. Self-catering complex with 24 two-storey flatlets. Heated swimming pool, with splash and whirlpool also available in the early and late season for our Hotel and self-catering guests. Sauna, massages and physiotherapy.

Aqua Park

An experience! 5000 sq metres of water landscape with a gentle river, a lagoon for the children, swimmingpool, a waterfall, wellness facilities with shiatzupool and some whirlpools (15.5. - 20.9 and later weather permitting).

Camping-Village Capalonga

6010 Via della Laguna 16, 30020 Bibione-Pineda (Venetia)

A quality site right beside the sea, Capalonga is a large site with 1,350 pitches of variable size (70-90 sq.m). Nearly all marked out, all have electrical connections (4/10A), some have water and drainage, and there is good shade almost everywhere. The site is pleasantly laid out - roads run in arcs which avoids the square box effect. Some pitches where trees define the pitch area may be tricky for large units. The very wide, sandy beach is cleaned by the site and never becomes too crowded; a concrete path leads out towards the sea to avoid too much sand-walking. The sea bed shelves extremely gently so is very safe for children and the water is much cleaner here than at most places along this coast. A large lagoon runs along the other side of the site where boating (motor or sail) can be practised and a landing stage and moorings are provided. There is also a swimming pool on site. Capalonga is an excellent site, with comprehensive facilities.

Facilities: The seven toilet blocks are well and frequently cleaned. Two newer blocks built side by side have facilities for disabled people and very fine children's rooms with basins and showers at the right height. British and some Turkish style toilets, some washbasins in private cabins and a whole wall of mirrors. Launderette. Motorcaravan services. Large supermarket. General shop for campers and beach goods, cards, papers, etc. Self-service restaurant and separate bar. Swimming pool (25 x 12-5 m; 19/5-15/9). Boating. Fishing. Children's playground. Large playing field provides exercise stations, football pitch and a general area for ball games and there are play areas with equipment on the beach. Free animation programme with wide range of sport, fitness and entertainment. First-aid room. Dogs are not accepted.

Charges 2003

Per person	€ 5.70 - € 9.80
child (1-4 yrs)	gratis - € 4.50
child (5-10 yrs)	gratis - € 6.50
pitch with electricity	€ 10.50 - € 19.00
pitch with water and drainage	€ 11.00 - € 20.00
boat	€ 6.50 - € 12.00

Tel: 0431 438351. **Fax:** 0431 438370. **E-mail:** capalonga@bibionemare.com. **Reservations:** Advised for July/Aug. and made for Sat. to Sat. only, with large deposit and fee. **Open** 1 May - 28 September.

Directions: Bibione is about 80 km. east of Venice, well signed from afar on approach roads. 1 km. before Bibione turn right towards Bibione Pineda and follow camp signs.

Camping Village Il Tridente

6015 Via Baseleghe 12, 30020 Bibione-Pineda (Venetia)

This is an unusual site as only half the area is used for camping. Formerly a holiday centre for deprived children, it occupies a strip of woodland 200 m. wide and 400 m. long stretching from the main road to the sea. It is divided into two parts by the Residence, an apartment block of first class rooms with air conditioning and full cooking and bathroom facilities which are for hire. The 250 tourist pitches are located amongst tall pines in the area between the entrance and the Residence. Pitch size varies according to the positions of the trees, but they are of sufficient size and have 4A electrical connections. The ground slopes gently from the main building to the beach of fine sand and this is used as the recreation area with two swimming pools - one 25 x 12.5 m. and a smaller children's pool - tennis courts, table tennis and sitting and play places. With thick woodland on both sides, Il Tridente is a quiet, restful site with excellent facilities.

Facilities: The three sanitary blocks, two in the main camping area and one near the sea, are of excellent quality. All have similar facilities with mixed British and Turkish style WCs in cabins with washbasins and facilities for disabled people. Washing machines and dryers. Motorcaravan services. The Residence includes an excellent restaurant, bar and well stocked supermarket. Swimming pools. Children's playground. Tennis. Table tennis. Mini-football. Volleyball. Animation programme includes activities for children in high season. Boats may be kept at the quay on the sister site, Capalonga (no. 6010), about 1 km. away. Dogs are not accepted.

Charges 2003

Per person	€ 5.70 - € 9.00
child (1-4 yrs)	gratis - € 4.20
child (5-10 yrs)	gratis - € 6.30
pitch incl. electricity	€ 10.50 - € 18.00

Tel: 0431 439600. **Fax:** 0431 439193. **E-mail:** tridente@bibionemare.com. **Reservations:** Contact site. **Open** 12 April - 28 September.

Directions: From A4 Venice - Trieste autostrada, take Latisana exit and follow signs to Bibione and then Bibione Pineda and camp signs.

Camping Residence

6025 Via F. Baracca 47, 30013 Cavallino (Venetia)

The Litorale del Cavallino has a large number of excellent sites, giving a good choice for those wishing to visit and stay in this area near Venice. Camping Residence is a very good site with a sandy beach directly on the Adriatic and is well kept, with many floral displays. Pitches are marked out with small fences or pines, which give good shade, and are laid out in regular rows on level sand. They vary in size, with those for caravans larger than those for tents, and all have electricity connections (6A). A medium size site (for this region) of 300 tourist pitches, it is smaller than 6020 but has the same strict rules regarding noise (no radios or dogs, quiet periods and no unaccompanied under 18s) but is less formal and more personal. The beach fronting has been enlarged and improved and the sea bed shelves gradually making it safe for children. Excellent pools have been added and there is a good animation programme in high season for both children and adults. Venice can be easily reached by bus to Punta Sabbioni and ferry across the lagoon and there are organised excursions to places of interest.

Facilities: The three large sanitary blocks are very clean with full facilities including British style WCs. Although of good quality, they are being refurbished. Supermarket, separate shops for fruit and other goods. Well appointed restaurant with separate bar. Takeaway. Swimming pools with sunbathing areas. Children's playground. Table tennis. Tennis court. Minigolf. Fitness programme. Video games room. Dancing or disco by beach until 11 pm three times weekly June-August and entertainment programme. Post office. Bureau de change. Doctor will call. Ladies hairdresser. Car wash. Chemical disposal. Dogs are not accepted. **Off site:** Boat moorings for hire at nearby marina. Fishing or bicycle hire 1 km.

Charges 2002

Per person	€ 3.80 - € 7.70
child (under 5 yrs)	gratis - € 5.80
pitch	€ 8.00 - € 17.90

Less 10% on pitch fee for over 60s. **Tel:** 041 968027. Fax: 041 5370164. E-mail: info@compres.it.
Reservations: Made for min. 1 week; contact site.
Open: 24 April - 22 September.

Directions: From A4 Venice-Trieste autostrada leave at exit for Airport or Quarto D'Altino, follow signs for Jesolo and then Punta Sabbioni. Take first left after Cavallino bridge and site is about 800 m. on right hand side (well signed).

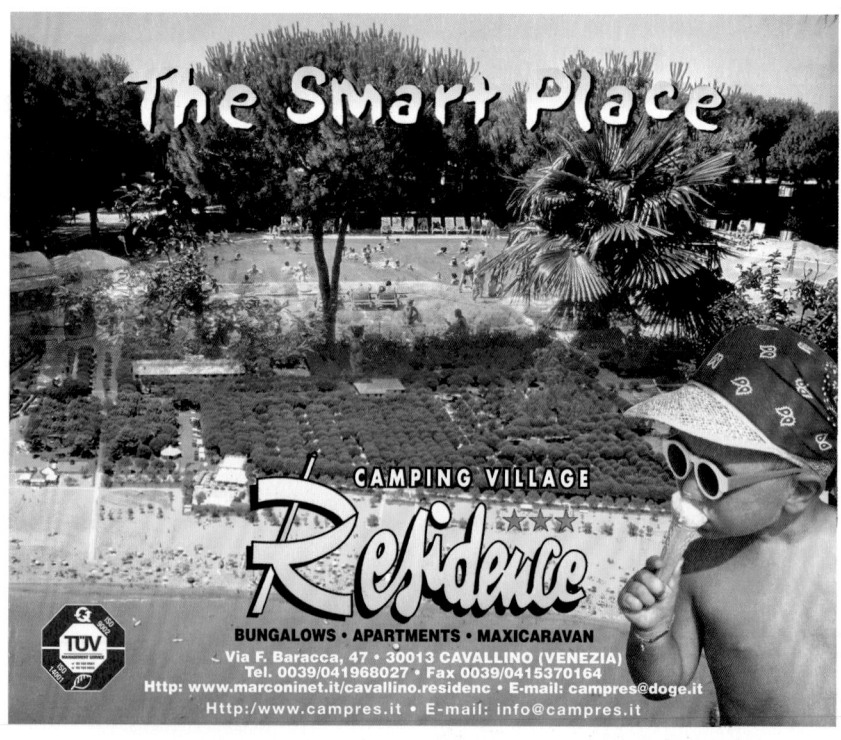

The Smart Place

CAMPING VILLAGE

Residence

BUNGALOWS • APARTMENTS • MAXICARAVAN

Via F. Baracca, 47 • 30013 CAVALLINO (VENEZIA)
Tel. 0039/041968027 • Fax 0039/0415370164
Http: www.marconinet.it/cavallino.residenc • E-mail: campres@doge.it
Http:/www.campres.it • E-mail: info@campres.it

Camping Italy

Via Fausta 272, 30013 Cavallino (Venetia)

6021

There are over 30 campsites on the Littorale del Cavallino between Lido di Jesolo and Punta Sabbioni and Camping Italy, under the same ownership as the better known Union Lido which it adjoins, is suggested for those who prefer a smaller site where less activities are available (although those at Union Lido may be used). The 144 tourist pitches are on either side of sand tracts from hard access roads under a cover of trees. Being on the small size (60-70 sq.m), they may be difficult for large units, particularly in high season when cars may have to be parked away from some pitches. All have electricity connections (5A) and some have water as well. There is direct access to a gently sloping sandy beach and a good, heated, swimming pool which has a whirlpool at one end. Strict regulations regarding undue noise make this a peaceful site and with lower charges than some in the area, this a good site for families with young children where it is possible to book in advance.

Facilities: Two good quality, fully equipped sanitary blocks include facilities for disabled visitors. Washing machines. Shop. Restaurant. Bar beside beach. Heated swimming pool (17 x 7 m). Small children's playground, mini-club and children's disco. Weekly dance for adults. Barbecues are only permitted in a designated area. Dogs are not accepted. **Off site:** Sports centre 500 m. Golf or riding 500 m.

Charges 2003

Per person	€ 4.40 - € 6.70
child (under 6 yrs)	€ 2.90 - € 5.40
pitch with electricity	€ 7.30 - € 16.20
pitch with electricity and water	€ 7.80 - € 17.40

Three charging seasons. **Tel:** 041 968 090. Fax: 041 537 0076. E-mail: info@campitaly.it. **Reservations:** Contact site. **Open** Easter - 16 September.

Directions: From Venice - Trieste A4 autostrada leave at exit for airport or Quarto d' Altino and follow signs for Jesolo and Punta Sabbioni. Site is on left after Cavallino.

Camping Vela Blu

Via Radaelli, 10, 30013 Cavallino (Venetia)

6028

Compared to most other campsite in this area, Vela Blu is small with just 230 tourist pitches. On sand under tall pines which give shade in most parts, these vary in size as some are in natural woodland. All have electricity connections (4A). Flowers, shrubs and roads paved with decorative bricks add to the pleasant appearance of the site. It has its own beach of fine sand although a fence between here and the camping area hides this (access is through a single gate). There is no swimming pool as yet although permission was applied for in 1995! Evening social life revolves around the pleasant restaurant with the terrace overlooking the stage where activities and entertainment take place next to the children's playground. A walking area and shower are provided for dogs which are not allowed on the beach. There is a shop and bar with others nearby. This is a very pleasant site in a quiet location within easy reach of Venice and other attractions of northern Italy and particularly suitable for those who prefer a small campsite.

Facilities: Two modern toilet include an attractive baby room and rooms for disabled guests. Washing machines and dryers. Motorcaravan service point. Medical room. Shop. Bar, restaurant and takeaway. Games room. TV room with satellite. Table tennis. Volleyball. Windsurfing. Fishing. Bicycle hire. Entertainment for adults and children by trained animators.

Charges 2002

Per person	€ 0.43 - € 6.50
child or senior (over 60 yrs)	€ 2.90 - € 5.70
pitch	€ 7.70 - € 14.00
dog	€ 4.20

Tel: 041 968068. Fax: 041 5371003. E-mail: info@velablu.it. **Reservations:** Contact site. **Open** 20 April - 16 September.

Directions: Leave A4 (Venice - Trieste) motorway at exit for Aeroporto and follow signs for Jesolo and Punta Sabbioni. Site is signed after village of Cavallino.

Camping Alba d'Oro

6042 Via Tristina, Ca,Noghera, 30030 Mestre (Venetia)

This well managed site is ideal for visiting Venice and a private bus from the site takes you directly to the bus station on the west side of the city. There is always room here and on arrival you can select your own pitch. There is a separate area for backpackers and yet another for families. The 350 pitches, 130 with electricity connections (4A), are of good size and easy to manoeuvre on to. The good sized pool is especially welcome after a hot day spent visiting Venice. The east side of the site is bordered by a canal and if you wish to take your own boat to Venice it can be launched here (max. 2 m. draught) with access to Venice gained by a charming canal journey. The site is close to the airport and aircraft will be heard on some pitches especially to the east. However, as there is no night flying allowed it is worth staying here to be close to the city rather than driving to the sites in Cavallino and having the resultant long journey into Venice. The clientele staying here changes rapidly and is very cosmopolitan, with a young backpacker element, but the site is not noisy.

Facilities: The four modern sanitary blocks are kept very clean. One block has facilities for disabled campers. Sinks for washing dishes and clothes. Launderette. Motorcaravan services. Restaurant with a most pleasant terrace overlooking the pool and serving good food at reasonable prices is very busy every night. Part of the same complex, is a lively bar with entertainment in season including pool parties and 'happy hours'. Pizzerias. Table tennis. Bicycle hire.

Charges 2002

Per person	€ 6.00 - € 7.10
pitch incl. electricity	€ 9.90 - € 10.60
child (2-10 yrs)	€ 3.80 - € 4.90
tent	€ 8.50 - € 9.50

Tel: 041 5415102. Fax: 041 5415971. E-mail: albadoro@tin.it. **Reservations:** Contact site. **Open** 20 March - 31 October.

Directions: From Venice-Trieste autostrada leave at exit for airport and follow signs for Jesolo on the SS14. Site is on right at 10 km. marker.

Portofelice Camping Village

1222 Viale Dei Fiori 15, 30020 Eraclea Mare (Venetia)

the travel service
TO BOOK
Ferry ✔
Pitch ✔
Accommodation ✘
01892 55 98 98

Portofelice is a typical Italian coastal site with a sandy beach and plenty of well organised activity. It is unusual in being separated from the sea by a protected pine wood with a gravel path between the two. It is of medium size for this part of Italy with 540 tourist pitches and 230 occupied by static caravans, bungalows and tour operators' accommodation. The pitches are arranged in rectangular blocks or zones in regular rows, separated by hedges from hard access roads and with either natural or artificial shade. Cars are parked in numbered places under shade at the side of the zones. All have electricity (6A) and 170 also have water, drainage and TV sockets. The social life of the site is centred around the pool complex where the shops, pizzeria, bar, café and restaurant are also located. A wide range of entertainment and activities are organised for adults and children. If you can drag yourself away from the holiday village, you can explore the region by car with Venice, the Dolomites and the Italian Lakes within range.

Facilities: Two modern sanitary blocks have the usual facilities with slightly more Turkish style toilets than British. New toilet block for children (0-12 yrs). Facilities for disabled people. Shops. Pizzeria. Restaurant with a good menu at reasonable prices and most tables on a covered terrace with waiter service. Swimming pools with an area specifically equipped for disabled guests, whirlpool massage and sunbathing. Playgrounds. Tennis, football, basket and volleyball, open spaces and a sandy beach. Bicycle hire. Organised activities for children. Activity and entertainment programmes, with evening shows and music. **Off site:** Golf 6 km. Riding 200 m.

Charges 2002

Per person	€ 2.80 - € 7.90
senior (over 60 yrs)	€ 2.30 - € 6.30
child (1-5 yrs)	gratis - € 5.90
pitch depending on type	€ 8.40 - € 17.90

Tel: 0421 66411. Fax: 0421 66021. E-mail: info@portofelice.it. **Reservations:** Write to site. **Open** 10 May - 21 September.

Directions: From A4 Venice-Trieste motorway take exit 'St Dona/Noventa' and go south through St Dona di Piave and Eraclea to Eraclea Mare where site is signed.

Italy - North East
Centro Vacanze Pra' Delle Torri
P.O. Box 176, 30021 Caorle (Venetia)

6003

Pra' delle Torre is another Italian Adriatic site which has just about everything! Pitches for camping, hotel, accommodation to rent, one of the largest and best equipped swimming pools in the country and a golf course where lessons for beginners are also available. Many of the 910 grass pitches have shade and are arranged in zones and when you book in at reception you are taken by electric golf buggy to select your pitch. All have electricity (5A) and many water and drainage as well. There are two good restaurants, bars and a range of shops arranged around an attractive square. There is a large grass area for ball games but the swimming pool complex is the crowning glory. There is a good children's playground, a babies' car track, and a whole range of sports, fitness and entertainment programmes, along with a medical centre, skincare and other therapies. They have their own sandy beach and Porto St Margherita and Caorle are nearby. One could quite happily spend a whole holiday here without leaving the site but the attractions of Venice, Verona etc might well tempt one to explore the area.

Facilities: Sixteen excellent, high quality toilet blocks with the usual facilities including very attractive 'Junior Stations', units for disabled visitors, washing machines and dryers. Motorcaravan service point. Large supermarket and wide range of shops, restaurants, bars and takeaways. Tennis courts. Football field. Minigolf. Table tennis. Fishing. Watersports. Archery. Basketball and volleyball. Diving. Aqua gym, fitness programmes and keep fit track. Bowls. Mountain bike track. Wide range of organised sports and entertainment.

Charges 2002

Per person	€ 3,35 - € 7,75
child (1-5 yrs)	€ 2,35 - € 5,70
pitch incl. electricity	€ 6,50 - € 19,65
tent pitch	€ 4,65 - 14,50

Min. stay 2 nights. **Tel:** 0421 299035. Fax: 0421 299036. E-mail: torri@vacanze-natura.it.
Reservations: Contact site. **Open** 26 April - 28 September.

Directions: From A4 (Venice - Trieste) motorway leave at exit for Ste Stino di Livenze and follow signs to Caorle then St Margherita and signs to site.

See advertisement on page 249

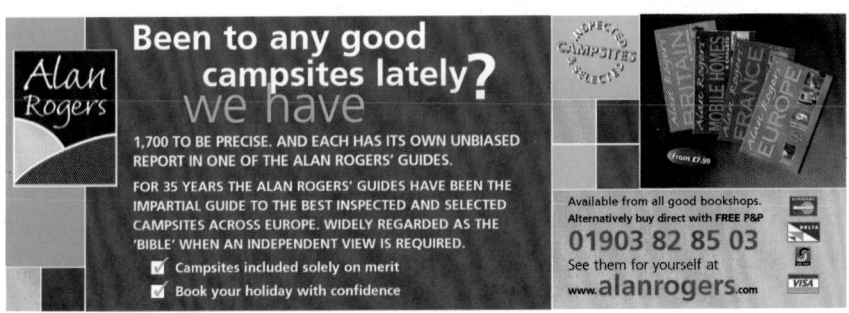

Camping Village Belvedere Pineta

6007 33051 Grado (Friuli - Venézia Giúlia)

Belvedere Pineta is situated on the edge of an almost entirely land-locked lagoon, five kilometres from Grado on the northern Adriatic Sea. A minor road runs between the site and the lagoon and a bridge over this connects the site with the beach of fine sand. It is a large site with 900 tourist pitches arranged in regular rows with most under shade provided by the many tall pine trees which cover the site. Most are of reasonable size and all have electricity (4A). An area of letting accommodation is to one side of the camping area. With two pools, an area for ball games, tennis courts, minigolf, table tennis and the beach there are plenty activities to enjoy and during high season (July/Aug) there is a large programme of sport and entertainment for both children and adults organised. Aquileia, once the fourth city of the Roman Empire is near with interesting remains of this period and excursions can be made by sea and rail to Venice and other places in the region.

Facilities: Most of the six toilet blocks have been refurbished to a good standard with all the usual facilities including some for children and free hot water in all basins, showers and sinks. Facilities for disabled visitors. Motorcaravan service point. Range of shops. Restaurant, pizzeria and takeaway. Swimming pools. Sports facilities. Children's play areas. Organised entertainment in high season.

Charges 2002

Per person	€ 4,00 - 7,90
child (2-10 yrs)	gratis - € 5,65
pitch	€ 11,20 - € 18,40
dog	€ 3,45 - € 5,70

Tel: 0431 91007. Fax: 0431 918641. E-mail: info@belvederepineta.it. **Reservations:** Contact site. **Open** 1 May - 30 September.

Directions: Leave A4 (Venice - Trieste) motorway at exit for Palmanova and go south on SS352 towards Grado. Camp is signed after Aquileia and is on the left.

6008 Camping Sabbiadoro

Via Sabbiadora 8, 33054 Lignano Sabbiadoro

Recommended by our agent – this site will be inspected in 2003.

A large site, Camping Sabbiadora provides over 1,250 pitches, mostly individual and partly shaded. Electricity (4/6A) is available, but the pitches are on the small side being 60-80 sq m. Amenities provided include a shop, a bar, restaurant and a takaway. There is a heated outdoor pool and facilities for tennis, minigolf, table tennis and bicycle hire. A range of entertainment is organised in the main season. Sanitary facilities are fully equipped and include a washing machine and dryer, and facilities for disabled visitors. No dogs are accepted in high season. A fine beach nearby is particularly good for children.

Charges 2002

per adult	€ 7.23
child (3-12 yrs)	€ 4.23
pitch	€ 11.36

Tel: 0431 71455. Fax: 0431 721355. E-mail: campsab@dns.ngtanday.it. **Open** 23 March - 29 September.

Directions: From Latisano follow straight road to Lignano for 20 km. Bear left and follow signs to Sabbiadoro. After 3 km through pine trees on the edge of town turn right. After 400 m. at roundabout with BP garage, the site is opposite.

Villaggio Turistico Camping Europa

6005 PO Box 129, 34073 Grado (Friuli - Venézia Giúlia)

This large flat site beside the sea can take almost 600 units. All the pitches are marked, nearly all with good shade, and there are electrical connections (4/8A) in all areas. The terrain is undulating and sandy in the areas nearer the sea, where cars have to be left in parking places and not by your pitch. There is direct access to the beach but the water is shallow up to 200 m. from beach, with growing seaweed. However, a narrow wooden jetty is provided which one can walk along to deeper water. For those who prefer, there is a swimming pool near the sea and, on the site, a medium sized heated pool and smaller children`s pool. This is a good honest site which, after recent improvements, is probably the best in the area.

Facilities: Six toilet blocks are identical and should make up a good supply, with free hot water in all facilities, half British style WCs and facilities for disabled people. A new block opened in 2001. Washing machines. Motorcaravan services. Large supermarket; small general shop (May - Sept). Large bar and self-service restaurant, with takeaway (all season). Swimming pools (May - Sept, 10 am.-7 pm). Two tennis courts. Football pitch. Table tennis. Fishing. Bicycle hire. Playground. Dancing, at times, in season; some organised activities July/Aug. Dogs are taken only in a special section and in limited numbers. **Off site:** Golf 0.5 km. Riding 4 km.

Charges 2003

Per person	€ 5.50 - € 8.00
child (3-12 yrs)	gratis - € 5.50
pitch incl. electricity	
acc. to season and location	€ 8.00 - € 16.00
dog	€ 2.50 - € 6.00

Less 10% for longer stays out of season.
Tel: 0431 80877. Fax: 0431 82284. E-mail: info@ campingeuropa.it. **Reservations:** Advised for high season and made for min. 1 week from Sat. to Sat., with deposit in high season (50% of total). **Open** 12 April - 21 September.

Directions: Site is 4 km. east of Grado on road to Monfalcone. If road 35L is taken to Grado from west, continue through the town to Grado Pineta.

Camping Mare Pineta

6000 Sistiana 60 D, Duino - Aurisina, 34019 Trieste (Friuli - Venézia Giúlia)

This site is 18 km. west of Trieste, and is on raised ground near the sea with views over the Sistiana Bay, Miramare Castle and the Gulf of Trieste. A pebbly beach, with a car park, lies just beyond the site, a drive of about 1 km. (a free bus service runs every 40 mins from 9 am.-7 pm). Alternatively there is a large swimming pool (unheated) on site with a new terrace. The development of this site continues with modern reception buildings and improved sanitary facilities. Over 350 of the 500 individual pitches are available for tourists. They are on gravel hardstanding (awnings possible) in light woodland, all with electricity (from 3A) and with water nearby. Space is nearly always available (1-15 Aug. is the busiest). For arrivals outside office hours, a waiting area has water and toilet facilities. The Rilke footpath runs along the seaside border of the site. It is reported that a weekend disco on the beach below the campsite involves noisy vehicle departures at 3 am. The site is used by a tour operator.

Facilities: Six toilet blocks of varying quality, some recently modernised and extended, provide some washbasins in cabins and some for children (the hot water supply does not always cope with the demand) and WCs of both British and Turkish style. Facilities for disabled people. Sinks for laundry and dishwashing, most with hot water. Laundry with dryer and ironing. Motorcaravan service point. Shop (all season). Bars. Pizzeria with terrace. Disco. Swimming pool (1/6-15/9) with lessons. Children's playground. Facilities for football, volleyball and mini-basket. Tennis. Table tennis. Games room. Organised entertainment in season. No dogs or animals are accepted. **Off site:** Fishing 1 km. Bicycle hire 500 m. Riding 2 km. Golf 10 km.

Charges 2002

Per person	€ 3.61 - € 6.20
child (3-12 yrs)	€ 2.58 - € 4.65
pitch incl. electricity and water	€ 7.23 - € 13.94
pitch with view of the bay	€ 10.33 - € 18.07

No credit cards. **Tel:** 040 299264. Fax: 040 299265. E-mail: info@marepineta.com. **Reservations:** Made with 40% deposit and € 15,49 fee. **Open** 1 May - 30 September.

Directions: From west take Sistiana exit from A4 autostrada, turn right and site is 1 km. on right; from east approach on S14.

Camping Bungalow Park Tahiti

6065 viale Libia 133, 44020 Lido delle Nazioni (Emília-Romagna)

Tahiti is an excellent, extremely well run site, thoughtfully laid out less than a mile from the sea (a continuous small fun road-train link is provided). Flowers, shrubs, ponds and attractive wooded structures enhance its appearance and, unlike many campsites of this size, it is family owned and run. They have thought of everything here and the manager Stefano is a dynamo who seems to be everywhere, ensuring the impressive standards are maintained. The staff are smart and attentive. As well as the 25 x 12 m. swimming pool, there is a Caribbean style water-play fun area with palms, plus a jacuzzi, bar and terrace (small extra charge for 'wet' activities). The 400 pitches are of varying size, back to back from hard roads and defined by trees with shade in most areas. There are 30 pitches with a private unit containing a WC and washbasin. Electricity (6A) is available throughout. English is spoken by the friendly management, although the British have not yet really discovered this site. The site is very busy in season with much to-ing and fro-ing, but all is always under control it is superb, especially for families with children.

Facilities: All sanitary blocks are of a very high standard, nicely decorated with plants and potted shrubs. They have a mix of British and Turkish style WCs and free hot water for washbasins, sinks and showers. The new block has a baby room and make-up/hairdressing room. Two waiter service restaurants with extensive menus. Bar. Pizzeria, takeaway. Large supermarket and kiosk. Swimming pools. New fitness centre with thermal baths. Several children`s playgrounds and mini-club, bouncy castles and mini go-carts. Well equipped gym. Archery. Tennis. Floodlit sports area. Table tennis. Minigolf. Basketball. Volleyball. Football pitch. Bicycle hire. Electronic games. Free transport to the beach. Organised entertainment in ourdoor theatre and excursions in high season. Daily medical service. ATM. Internet terminals. Dogs are not accepted. Torches needed in some areas. **Off site:** Fishing 300 m. Riding 500 m.

Charges 2002

Per person	€ 4.50 - € 8.10
child (2-8 yrs)	gratis - € 6.10
pitch acc. to season and type and facilities	€ 8.20 - € 26.90
pitch with sanitary facility	€ 22.90 - € 35.90

Tel: 0533 379500. Fax: 0533 379700. E-mail: info@ campingtahiti.com. **Reservations:** Made for min. 1 week (2 weeks in high season) with deposit. **Open** 11 May - 21 September.

Directions: Turn off SS309 35 km. north of Ravenna to Lido delle Nazioni (north of Lido di Pomposa) and follow camp signs.

Camping Classe

N6063 Lido di Dante, 48020 Ravenna (Emília-Romagna)

The flat, open farmland approach to family owned Camping Classe is not dissimilar to our own East Anglia, with a patchwork of crops and orchards, but here you are by the Italian Adriatic, not the North Sea! Lido di Dante is not a major tourist resort and is therefore more peaceful than many locations along Italy's eastern coastline. Between the site and the shoreline (200 m) a large, delightful natural area provides a habitat for many species of birds and other wildlife. On the site a variety of well spaced trees offer shade over 430 good sized flat grass pitches each with electricity (4A). Part of the campsite (2.5 ha) is screened devoting 225 places for those that enjoy naturism (electricity only 2A). This area has a sanitary block and a small bar. Naturists must dress to visit any other part of the site, to make use of the 'free' facilities or when walking to the sandy beach. Italy does not have any official naturist beaches although this particular section of the coast is recognised as being such. Having walked through the nature reserve, those that prefer to remain clothed should walk to the left while for nude sunbathing walk in the opposite direction (naturists require an INF card and no singles allowed).

Facilities: Sanitary facilities in six blocks are not modern but are adequate and generally clean. Toilets are a mix of British and Turkish style. Baby bath and mini toilet. One small block is reserved for disabled visitors. Dishwashing and laundry sinks. Washing machine. Shop. Restaurant (all season, all day). Swimming pool (bathing hats required). Minigolf, tennis and gym. Fitness programmes and sporting competitions. Fitness trail. Children's play areas. English spoken. High season animation programme for adults and children. **Off site:** Small village adjacent to site has a couple of shops and very popular restaurants.

Charges 2002

Per person	€ 5.68 - € 7.30
child (0-8 yrs)	€ 4.60 - € 5.00
tent pitch	€ 6.00 - € 14.00
caravan	€ 10.33 - € 15.00
motorcaravan	€ 9.00 - € 14.00
dog	€ 3.10
electricity	€ 2.32

Tel: 0544 492005. Fax: 0544 492058. E-mail: info@ campingclasse.it. **Reservations:** Necessary in high season. Low season address: Via del Fringuello 10, 47900 Rimini.

Directions: Travelling south from Ravenna towards Rimini on S16, after passing 'Ravenna Sud' service area, take next exit signed Classe (km. 157). Continue on this road passing over 516. Do not turn right into Classe. Prior to hump-back bridge turn right signed Lido di Dante and site is signed from this junction.

Camping Adriatico

6622 Via Pinarella 90, 48015 Cervia (Emília-Romagna)

Adriatico, on the Italian Riviera, is owned and run by the pleasant Fabbri family. It is a busy seaside type of site popular with the Italians. English is spoken and all facilities are clean and well kept. As you would expect there is some noise from the local resort (nearest disco is 200 m), and on the western side you will be serenaded by the voluble frogs in the adjacent allotment. The pitches vary in size, are on flat ground, well shaded with lots of room to manoeuvre. The self service restaurant and bar complex is close to the entrance, as are the supervised pools. In a pleasant situation and a short walk from the busy beach, this site would be be good for families who enjoy bustling seaside sites. There are limited sports here and some live music in the bar during high season, but the town of Cervia offers all you could want in this sort of holiday area. Reasonably priced food and wine can be found in the town, along with spa treatments which are popular here. The canal harbours are interesting.

Facilities: Four sanitary blocks, two large two small, have some British style WCs, individual washbasins with cold water and free hot showers. One hot tap in washing areas. Baby rooms. Washing machines and a dryer. Facilities for disabled campers. TV room. Restaurant/bar, snack bar and takeaway. Swimming pool (15/6-31/8; free in low seasons). Market. Electronic games. Table tennis. Play area. Excursions to local areas of interest. **Off site:** Fishing, boat launching and bicycle hire within 1 km. Golf 4 km. Riding 3 km.

Charges 2003

Per person	€ 4.40 - € 7.20
child (2-8 yrs)	€ 3.30 - € 5.50
pitch	€ 9.20 - € 13.00
tent pitch	€ 7.20 - € 11.00
dog	€ 2.70 - € 5.00

Tel: 0544 71537. Fax: 0544 72346. E-mail: info@ campingadriatico.net. **Reservations:** made with deposit. **Open** 19 April - 14 September.

Directions: Site lies midway between Ravenna and Rimini. From A14 autoroute take exit for Cesena or Ravenna and head for Cervia on SS16. Site is south of Cervia, well signed. Drive along the sea-front and the signs are between the 167/169 markers. From the sea front to the site (800 m) there are some interesting turns away from the sea around corners with cars parked in very casual Italian style everywhere.

Camping Villaggio Rubicone

6624 Via Matrice Destra 1, 47039 Savignano (FO) (Emília-Romagna)

This is a sophisticated, professionally run site where the very friendly owners, Sandro and Paolo Grotti are keen to fulfil your every need. The reception area is most attractive, spacious and efficient, operating an effective security system and offering a booking service for local attractions including trips to Venice, Rimini and other places of interest. Rubicone covers over 30 acres of thoughtfully landscaped, level ground by the sea and has a large private beach where guests can enjoy the luxurious facilities, including free parasols. There is shade from poplar trees for some of the 600 touring pitches which vary in size (up to 90 sq.m). Arranged in back to back double rows, in some areas the central pitches are a little tight for manoeuvring larger units. All the pitches are kept very neat with hedges and all have electrical connections (5A), 40 with water and waste water facilities, and 20 with private sanitary facilities. There are many bars around the site from beach bars to night club bars and the restaurant offers excellent food and efficient service at very reasonable prices. The animation programme is staged in a circular terraced area near the main bar. The site has an array of activities on offer (e.g. judo lessons) and many sporting opportunities. Across the railway line (via an underpass) is a huge complex including excellent pools for adults and children.

Facilities: In addition to the 20 private sanitary units, there are modern toilet blocks with hot water for the showers and washbasins (half in private cabins), mainly British style toilets, baby rooms and two excellent units for disabled visitors. Washing machines. Motorcaravan services. Bars. Restaurant, snack bar and excellent shop (from 10/5). Pizzeria (all season). Swimming pools (from 1/5; bathing caps mandatory). Children's play equipment. Tennis. Solarium. Jacuzzi. Mini racing track. Water motorbikes. 'Powered' trampolines. Beach with lifeguard and showers. Fishing. Boat launching. Sailing and windsurfing schools. Gas supplies. Dogs are not accepted. **Off site:** Bicycle hire 500 m. Riding 2 km. Golf 15 km.

Charges 2002

Per person	€ 4.60 - € 8.25
child (2-8 yrs)	€ 3.50 - € 6.90
pitch (small, medium, large)	€ 9.60 - € 14.40
electricity	€ 2.10

No credit cards. **Tel:** 0541 346377. Fax: 0541 346999. E-mail: info@campingrubicone.com. **Reservations:** Contact site. **Open** 1 May - 30 September.

Directions: Site is 15 km. northwest of Rimini. From Bologna exit the A14 at Rimini north and head for the S16 to Bellaria and San Mauro a Mare; site is well signed.

Centro Turistico San Marino

6623 Strada San Michele 50, Cailungo, 47893 San Marino (Emília-Romagna)

According to one guide book, the Republic of San Marino is 'an unashamed tourist trap which trades on its falsely preserved autonomy'. It has its own mint, produces its own postage stamps, issues its own car registration plates, has a small army and a unique E-mail address, but in all other respects, is part of Italy. However, tourists do seem to find it interesting, particularly those with patience to climb to the battlemented castles on the three highest ridges. Centro Turistico San Marino is 4 km. below this, standing at 400 m. above sea level and spreading gently down a hillside, with lovely views across to the Adriatic. This excellent, modern site has a variety of well cared for trees offering shade. The main grass pitches are roomy, on level terraces accessed from tarmac or gravel roads. Separated by hedges, all have water, waste and electricity connections (5A), 10 with satellite TV connections. There are smaller pitches on lower terraces for tents. All pitches have visitors in the form of well fed Italian rabbits which enjoy your company. The irregularly shaped swimming pool has an pretty flower bedecked island. There is a pleasant open feel to this site. Used by a tour operator (30 pitches).

Facilities: Four high quality heated sanitary blocks, kept very clean, are well located around the site with British and Turkish style WCs and hot water in washbasins, sinks and showers. Washing machines and dryers. Motorcaravan services. Gas supplies. Shop with limited supplies (all year, closed Tuesday in winter). Kitchen with fridge and gas cooker used by campers and TV room (satellite). Attractive restaurant/pizzeria with good menu and pleasant terrace overlooking the pools (all year). Swimming pool (20/5-31/8) with jacuzzi and solarium. Several children's play areas. Video games. Table tennis. Volleyball. Football. Archery. Boules. Tennis. Bicycle hire. Small amphitheatre for entertainment. Animation programme for children (high season). Bus service on market days and Sundays. Minibus and car hire at extremely competitive rates (local taxis are very expensive).

Charges 2002

Per person	€ 5.00 - € 8.00
child (4-10 yrs)	€ 3.00 - € 6.00
caravan	€ 4.00 - € 11.00
tent	€ 3.00 - € 8.00
car	€ 2.00 - € 4.00
motorcaravan	€ 6.00 - € 13.00
dog	€ 1.00 - € 4.00

Tel: 0549 903964. Fax: 0549 907120. E-mail: info@ centroturisticosanmarino.com. **Reservations:** Write to site. **Open** all year.

Directions: Leave autostrada A14 at exit Rimini-Sud (or SS16 where signed), follow SS72 west to San Marino. Site is signed from about 15 km. This is the only campsite in this strange little republic.

Camping Stella Maris

6618 via A Cappellini 5, 61032 Torrette di Fano (Marche)

This clean, modern Adriatic coast site is, in our opinion, the best in the area. The owner Francesco Mantoni is friendly, enthusiastic and proud of his site. For swimming and relaxing there is the choice of an excellent long fine soft sand beach or an excellent pool complex with loungers, umbrellas, jacuzzi and children's paddling pool. Alongside the pool is a most attractive restaurant (white linen tablecloths) with table service, a varied menu and good selection of wine. The nearby paved terrace area has its own separate bar and snack service. Cleverly incorporated in this area is the entertainment stage, its attractive striped canvas hood matching the nearby pool umbrellas. The pitches are of a good size with some touring pitches. Beach access is gained through a security gate. In this informal setting touring pitches, permanent sites and cabins are blended together but the mixture works. The beach is excellent and unlike many hereabouts is not packed with umbrellas and sun-loungers. English is spoken and the site has a crisp efficient feel about it. A site for holidays and for touring, a high standard of service is provided in all areas.

Facilities: Clean, modern sanitary blocks are nicely decorated with a separate ladies room including hair dryers. Children's facilities are locked for security and parents are given keys. Facilities for disabled campers. Washing machines, dryers and ironing boards. Motorcaravan services. Excellent large supermarket. Restaurant/bar. Snacks. Large swimming pool. Games room, billiards,TV room. Hard court with arena style seating used for organized games (volleyball and five-a side-soccer). Animation in season. Dogs or other animals are not accepted.

Charges 2002

Per pitch	€ 11.88 - € 12.91
person	€ 6.20 - € 7.23
child (2-6 yrs)	€ 4.13 - € 5.42

Electricity (6A) included. **Tel:** 0721 884231. Fax: 0721 884269. E-mail: stellamaris@camping.it. **Reservations:** Advised in high season. **Open** April - September.

Directions: Site is between Fano and Falconara. From autostrada take Pesaro exit and follow signs on the SS16 for Ancona, site is approx 3 km. past Fano on waters edge.

Camping Communale Estense

6060 Via Gramicia 76, 44100 Ferrara (Emília-Romagna)

Ferrara is an interesting and historic city, well worth a short visit. The old city, surrounded by ancient walls, is attractive and mainly pedestrianised, with several museums, a cathedral and a wealth of architectural interest, but as a result of an apparent lack of publicity, has relatively few foreign visitors. This pretty municipal campsite on the northern outskirts offers comfortable facilities for all types of units and includes 50 fairly large, grass pitches, with numerous electrical connections. Trees are used to provide shade and to screen the site. Unusual concrete portals around the site are covered in roses. And shrubs and other flowers give a cheerful atmosphere. The site is good for exploring local attractions, reception staff are professional with English spoken and prices are reasonable. On-site facilities are limited, with machines for snacks and cold drinks, but there is an excellent trattoria within walking distance (1 km.) and a wide choice of other eating places in the city itself.

Facilities: Two acceptable, adjacent toilet blocks are fully equipped, one heated with British and Turkish style toilets. Separate facilities for disabled visitors. Drinks and snacks machines. Torches required in places. **Off site:** Restaurant close by. Fishing 500 m. Golf 100 m. Riding 3 km.

Charges 2003

Per person (over 8 yrs)	€ 4.50
pitch	€ 6.50
dog	€ 1.50
electricity	€ 1.50

No credit cards. **Tel:** 0532 752396. **Fax:** 0532 752396. E-mail: campeggio.estense@libero.it. **Reservations:** Not required. **Open** all year.

Directions: Site is well signed from the city and is on the northern side of the ring road.

Camping Ecochiocciola

6603 via Testa 70, 41050 Maserno di Montese (Emília-Romagna)

Tucked away in the Appennines in a small village, this interesting little campsite is open all year and has many surprises. 'Ecochiocciola' (named for the camper after the snail wearing his house on his back) is being developed by the owner Ottavio Mazzanti as a place to enjoy the natural geographic, geological, botanical and zoological features of the area. Comforts such as the swimming pool are designed to enhance the experience. Ottavio speaks excellent English and there are mementos of his extensive travels in the reasonably priced restaurant, which serves Indian as well as Italian dishes. The 50 small touring pitches are on level or gently sloping ground with some terraces, many enjoying superb views. Ottavio has begun to develop many of his unique ideas into features which will entertain and interest his guests, including a guided tour through the adjacent 'didactic' park complete with illustrative boards, which analyse the environment. There is also an orchard with ancient fruits and a garden with kitchen and medicinal herbs. The region is only 60 km. from historic Bologna, the surrounding area is very pretty and there are many areas of interest nearby including the Ferrari gallery at Maranello. This is a peaceful site with a distinctly rustic feel for people who enjoy natural settings.

Facilities: Two mature but clean sanitary blocks have some British style WCs and coin-operated hot showers. Facilities for disabled campers. Washing machine. Motorcaravan services. Restaurant. Bar. Pizzeria. Games room, large multipurpose room for entertainment. Swimming pool with shallow area for children (14/6-31/8) with nearby barbecue and grill. Football, volleyball tennis and skating area. Torches necessary. **Off site:** Riding trails, guided tours and mountain biking. No shop on the site but the village is 300 m. Local bus stop in village. Riding 3 km.

Charges 2003

Per person	€ 4.00 - € 6.00
child (2-8 yrs)	€ 3.00 - € 5.00
pitch	€ 8.00 - € 12.00
electricity (6A)	gratis
dog	€ 1.50 - € 3.00

Tel: 059 980065. **Fax:** 059 980025. E-mail: ecochiocciola@misterweb.it. **Reservations:** Contact site. **Open** all year excl. 3/2- 7/3 and 10/11 - 19/12).

Directions: From tha A1 take Moderna South exit through Vignola, Montese, Sesta la Fanano, to Maserno di Montese. Site is 200 m. from the village, well signed.

Camping Hotel Città di Bologna

6602 Via Romita 12 - 4A, 40127 Bologna (Emília-Romagna)

This spacious site was established in `93 on the edge of the Trade Fair Centre of this ancient and historic city and is very clean and modern. The reception is impressively efficient and friendly with excellent English spoken. Although near enough to the motorway to be aware of vague traffic hum, the site is surrounded by fields and trees giving a peaceful atmosphere. The intention was not only to make a campsite, but to provide high quality motel-type rooms for use by those visiting trade fairs. The 120 pitches are numbered and marked out by trees giving some shade. On level grass with hardstandings (open fretwork of concrete through which grass can grow) in two areas, there are electrical connections (6A) in all areas. You will always find space here as there is huge over capacity. The site is excellent for an overnight stop or for longer stays to explore the most attractive and unusual city of Bologna and Emilia-Romagna. Bologna is obviously not Venice or Verona but it has a beauty of its own, we think a visit is a must. There are 40 km. of porticos so you can even sight-see in the rain! In every corner there is something of historic interest. Talk to the manager Doctor Osti - he is an enthusiast.

Facilities: The modern sanitary block for campers' use is in the centre of the camping area (some WCs are Turkish style). Excellent provision for disabled visitors (some British style WCs with free showers and alarms that ring in reception). Washing machines. Motorcaravan services. Smart bar with adjoining terrace where snacks are offered. Superb new heated and supervised swimming pool (small charge). Small children's play area. Table tennis. Football. Minigolf. Volleyball. Medical room - doctor will call. **Off site:** Bus service to city centre from site. Shops and restaurant 500 m.

Charges 2003

Per person	€ 4.00 - € 7.00
child (5-9 yrs)	€ 3.00 - € 4.50
pitch	€ 8.00 - € 11.00
single person and tent	€ 8.00 - € 12.50
dog	€ 2.00

Electricity included. **Tel:** 051 325016. Fax: 051 325318. E-mail: info@hotelcamping.com. **Reservations:** Write to site. **Open** all year (except 10 days at Christmas).

Directions: Site is well signed from `Fiera` (fair) exit on the autostrada on the northeast of the city.

6607 Camping International La Versilia

Via Vittorio Apuana 33, 55042 Forte dei Marmi (Tuscany)

Recommended by our agent – this site will be inspected in 2003.

La Versilia is a campsite with 296 pitches in a mainly wooded setting, only 1300 metres from a Blue Flag beach. It has a range of facilities on-site including modern toilet facilities, a bar, restaurant, pizzeria and shop. Off-site are a nearby disco, tennis, sailing school and an 18 hole golf course.

Charges 2002

Per pitch	€ 6,70 - € 11,00
adult	€ 4,40 - € 7,50
child	€ 3,50 - € 6,00

Tel: 0584 880764. E-mail campingversilia@camping. it. **Open** 1 April - 15 September.

Directions: From autostrada A12, exit Versilia, in the direction of Vittoria Apuana, and follow signs - Ferroviaria-Stazione-Forte dei Marmi.

TUSCANY IN CAMPING

Only 1500 meter from the sea, that is reachable by bus, the wonderful beach of Forte dei Marmi is waiting for you and is inviting you to take a bath in a sea to that the Bandiere Blu awarded lots of prizes. The camping site is situated on the countryside and offers excellent services, a quite place and fist class accommodation. An holiday spent here is an unique holiday: the sea of Versilia, the wonderful mountains of Alpi Apuane with the fantastic Natural Park, the most interesting nightlife in Italy and some incredible artistic, wine and food routes. *OPEN FROM APRIL TO SEPTEMBER.*

CAMPING INTERNATIONAL VERSILIA
Via Vittoria Apuana, 33 • I-55042 Forte dei Marmi (LU) • Italy
Tel. 0039/0584880764 • Tel. en Fax 0039/0584752118
Http: www.campingversilia.it • E-mail: info@campingversilia.it

Camping Barco Reale

6600 Via Nardini 11 - 13, 51030 San Baronto (Tuscany)

Just 40 minutes from Florence and an hour from Pisa, this site is beautifully situated high in the Tuscan hills close to the birthplace of Leornado da Vinci, and the fascinating town of Pistoia. Part of an old walled estate, there are impressive views of the surrounding countryside and pleasant walks in the grounds. It is a quiet site of 15 ha. with 175 sprawling pitches with good shade from mature pines and oaks, Some are pitches are huge with great views and others are very private. Most are for tourists, but some have difficult access (tractor assistance available). All have electricity (3, 5 or 10A) and 50 have water and waste water drainage. The site has an attractive bar, a smart leased restaurant and a leased shop (prices are a little high). The pools have really stunning views to the west (on a clear day you may see the island of Capraia) A most attractive and popular site, it will appeal to those who prefer a quiet site but with plenty to do for all age groups. Used by tour operators.

Facilities: Two modern sanitary blocks are well positioned and kept very clean. Good facilities for disabled people (dedicated pitches close by) and a pretty baby room. Laundry facilities. Motorcaravan services. Restaurant. Bar. Disco. Shop. Supervised swimming pool and children's pool (caps required; 15/5-15/9). Playgrounds. Table tennis. Volleyball. Football. Chess. Bowls. Bicycle hire. Entertainment and adventure park. The large Roman style amphitheatre provides a full programme of animation for children in high season. Cooking lessons for Tuscan style food. Excursions on foot and by bus (all season). No charcoal fires are permitted. **Off site:** Village and shops 1 km. Golf 15 km. Fishing 8 km.

Charges 2003

Per person	€ 6.40 - € 8.30
child (0-12 yrs)	€ 2.80 - € 5.00
pitch and car	€ 8.90 - € 12.20

Credit cards accepted for amounts over € 155. Discounts for longer stays. **Tel:** 0573 88332. Fax: 0573 856003. E-mail: info@barcoreale.com. **Reservations:** Write to site. **Open** 1 April - 30 September.

Directions: From Pistoia take Vinci - Empoli - Lamporecchio signs to San Baronto. From Empoli follow signs to Vinci and San Baronto. Final approach is around a sharp bend and up a steep slope. The drive from the autoroute is pretty but very winding and extremely time consuming!

CAMPING BARCO REALE

Via Nardini, 11/13 • I-51030 S. Baronto (PT)
Tel. 0039/057388332 • Fax 0039/0573856003
E-mail: barcore@tin.it • E-mail: info@barcoreale.com
Http: www.barcoreale.com

IN THE HEART OF TUSCANY

- 2 swimming pools (1 for adults, 1 for children)
- Volleyball
- Outdoor draughts
- Skittle alley - Trekking
- Football field - "Boccia"
- Children's playground
- Supermarket
- Restaurant
- Tennis (3 km)

The campsite lies on a hill in a pine and oak wood with a lovely panorama. The house where Leonardo da Vinci was born and the famous towns of Tuscany are not far away, excursions by bus are organised. Barco Reale is an ideal site for a pleasant holiday from April to September owing to guided walks among the olive groves and wine country, the wonderful scenery, the local culture and the climate.

Camping Torre Pendente

6608 viale delle Cascine 86, 56122 Pisa (Tuscany)

Torre Pendente is a friendly site, well run by the Signorini family who speak good English and make everyone feel welcome. It is within walking distance of the famous leaning tower of Pisa (but via a dimly lit underpass). Obviously its position means it is busy throughout the main season. A medium sized site, it is on level, grassy ground with tarmac or gravel access roads and some shade. There are 220 touring pitches, 160 with 5A electricity. All site facilities are near the entrance. A swimming pool has been added recently. The small shop, bar and restaurant cater for all pockets. We consider this unsophisticated site suitable for short stays to explore Pisa rather than for an extended visit.

Facilities: Sanitary facilities are basic with hot showers and mainly British style toilets (cleaning may be variable). New toilet blocks should be completed for 2002. Washing machine. Motorcaravan services. Shop. Bar. Restaurant. New swimming pool. Basic children's playground. Boules. Bicycle hire. **Off site:** Riding 3 km.

Charges 2002

Per adult	€ 6.75
child (3-10 yrs)	€ 3.20
pitch and car	€ 8.60 - € 10.90
dog	€ 1.60

Tel: 050 561704. Fax: 050 561734. E-mail: torrepen@campingtoscana.it. **Reservations:** Contact site. **Open** 25 March - 15 October.

Directions: From autostrada A12, exit at Pisa Nord and follow signs for 5 km. to Pisa. Do not take first sign to town centre. Site is well signed at a later left turn into the town centre (Viale delle Cascine) and is then a short distance on the left hand side.

Camping Mugello Verde

6605 Via Massorondinaio 39, 50037 San Piero a Sieve (Tuscany)

Mugello Verde is a country, hillside site with long curving terraces and one tarmac access road. Some pitches offer good views. English is spoken at reception where much tourist information is available - ask for the dates of the Ferrari team practices and the racing on the nearby International Mugello racing track! There are 200 good sized pitches for motorcaravans and caravans with smaller areas for tents. All pitches have electricity (6A) and mature olive and other trees provide shade. Some permanent pitches are scattered among the tourist pitches.

Facilities: Two sanitary blocks on the terraces have been refurbished to a good standard and facilities are clean and relatively modern with mixed British and Turkish style WCs. Most washbasins have hot water. Dishwashing and laundry facilities (hot water throughout). Comprehensive facilities for disabled campers. Shop. Restaurant/bar with varied menu and pizzeria (all season). Swimming pool (15/6-15/9; no paddling pool). New play area. Electronic games. Tennis. **Off site:** Riding, golf, bicycle hire and fishing, all within 5 km.

Charges 2002

Per person	€ 5.40 - € 8.30
child	€ 2.60 - € 5.16
pitch	€ 6.20 - € 13.90

Tel: 055 848 511. Fax: 055 848 6910. E-mail: mugelloverde@florencecamping.com. **Reservations:** Write to site. **Open** all year.

Directions: From A1 autostrada take Barberino del Mugello exit and follow SS65 to San Piero a Sieve. Site is well signed from the town.

Camping Norcenni Girasole Club

6612 Via Norcenni 7, 50063 Figline Valdarno (Tuscany)

The Norcenni Girasole Club is an excellent, busy and well run site in a picturesque, secluded situation with great views of Tuscan landscapes 19 km. south of Florence. Owned by the dynamic Cardini-Vannucchi family, care has been taken in its development and the buildings and infrastructure are most attractive and in sympathy with the surrounds. Absolutely everything is to hand and guests will only need to leave the site if they wish to explore the local attractions. There is an amazing choice of swimming pools on site and at the 'Lagoon' in the sister site which is 100 m. walk. Children can ride the large, exciting water flume free, play in the waterfall and feature pool or revert to other themed pools with slides. A modern health complex provides saunas, jacuzzi, steam bath, a fitness centre, hydro-massage, Shiatzu massage or a straight massage (extra cost). Three attractive restaurants with terraces serve wonderful food, the Vecchio specialises in typical Tuscan fare. There are 470 clean and roomy pitches for touring units, all with electricity (4A) and water, most shaded by well tended trees. The ground is hard and stony (tent pegs can be difficult). Although on a fairly steep hillside, pitches are on level terraces accessed from good, hard roads. Tour operators occupy another 150 pitches and there are a few (20) permanent pitches. An extensive animation programme is published each week with music and lots of activities for children. Courses in the Italian language, Tuscan cooking and wine tasting are provided. There are many English visitors and all information and most of the animation is in English.

Facilities: Sanitary facilities are very good with mixed British and Turkish style WCs. Hot water is available throughout. Five family bathrooms are for rent but, being very popular, these need to be booked in advance. Facilities for disabled visitors. Washing machines and dryers. Supermarket and gift shops. Wine shop. Bar and superb restaurants with terrace. Pizzeria. Gelateria. Two flood-lit tennis courts. Riding. Wonderful swimming pools, one covered and heated (supervised; hats required). Fitness centre with jacuzzi and Turkish bath (charged). Soundproof disco. Riding. Internet café. ATM. **Off site:** Several excursions are on offer with one evening tour of Florence that includes a five course dinner in an historic palace. Daily bus direct to Florence and shuttle buses to the local railway station.

Charges 2003

Per person	€ 6.70 - € 9.30
child (2-12 yrs)	€ 4.00 - € 5.50
caravan or trailer tent	€ 6.00 - € 8.10
tent	€ 5.60 - € 7.50
car	€ 3.80 - € 5.20
motorcaravan	€ 9.80 - € 13.30

Tel: 055 915141. Fax: 055 9151402. E-mail: girasole@ecvacanze.it. **Reservations:** Made with deposit. **Open** 30 March - 2 November.

Directions: From Florence take Rome A1/E35 autostrada and take Incisa exit. Turn south on route 69 towards Arezzo. In Figline turn right for Greve and watch for Norcenni signs - site is 4 km up a twisting, climbing road. If approached from the west it is a very long narrow winding road.

Camping Panoramico Fiesole

6610 Via Peramonda 1, 50014 Fiesole (Tuscany)

This is a mature but pleasant site in a fine hilltop situation offering wonderful views over Florence - on some evenings you can hear music from the nearby Roman amphitheatre famous for its classical entertainment in summer. The site is appreciably fresher and quieter than nearer the very busy city. It can become crowded in the main season and a very steep final access can be difficult for larger units although the site will assist with a jeep. Pitches are separated, motorcaravans and caravans in the upper area. The last approach to the site take you through the charming village of Fiesole but there are some challenging turns and tight squeezes (look for the wall mounted mirrors) A bus service operates one way from the site to the centre of town (0845 - 1145) to connect with the service to Florence (tickets from site office). However, it is an extremely long uphill walk back to the campsite from the town and thus the local bus (to within 300 m) or taxi may be essential. The 120 pitches, all with electricity (5A), are on terraces and steep walks to and from the various facilities could cause problems for people with mobility or breathing problems. There is shade in many parts. At the entrance, a large aviary houses a mixture of sad looking birds, tortoises and guinea pigs. Dine on the terraces of the pleasant restaurant and enjoy the romantic views.

Facilities: Two tastefully refurbished toilet blocks have mainly British style WCs, free hot water in washbasins and good showers. Washing machines and dryers. Shop (1/4-31/10). Bar and restaurant (1/4-31/10). Swimming pool (1/6-30/9). New children's play area reported. Electronic games. Fridges, irons and little cookers available for campers' use. English spoken. Torches required in some parts.

Charges 2002

Per person	€ 8.50
child (3-12 yrs)	€ 6.50
pitch incl. electricity	€ 14.00

Tel: 055 599069. Fax: 055 59186. E-mail: panoramico@florencecamping.com. **Reservations:** Not taken and said to be unnecessary if you arrive by early afternoon. **Open** all year.

Directions: From A1 take Firenze-Sud exit and follow signs to Fiesole (which lies NNE of central Firenze). From Fiesole centre follow camping signs out of town for approx. 1 km; the roads are very narrow both through the town and the final steep access. Site is signed on the right. If approaching from the north in a large unit you will need to pass the entrance road, proceed to the town and turn at the bus terminus as the access road is too sharp and steep for a left turn.

Camping Il Poggetto

6611 Via Il Poggetto 143, 50010 Troghi (Tuscany)

This superb new site has a lot to offer. It benefits from a wonderful panorama of the Colli Fiorentioni hills with acres of the Zecchi family vineyards to the east adding to its charm. It is just 15 km. from Florence. The charming and hard-working owners Marchiello and Daniella have a wine producing background and you can purchase their fine wines at the site's shop. Their aim is to provide an enjoyable and peaceful atmosphere for families. All 90 pitches are of a good size and have electricity (7A) and there are a few in excess of 100 sq.m for larger units. On arrival you are escorted to view available pitches then assisted in taking up that place. The restaurant offers some fine Tuscan fare along with pizzas, pastas and delicate 'cucina casalinga'. An attractive large terrace overlooks the two pools. Enjoy the typically Tuscan views and revel in the choice of Chianti from the region. A regular bus service runs directly from the site to the city (discounted tickets).

Facilities: Two spotless sanitary blocks with subtle piped music are a pleasure to use with a mix of British and Turkish style WCs, washbasins and showers. Three private sanitary units for hire. Five very well equipped units for disabled campers. Hot water throughout including for dishwashing. Washing machines, dryers, irons and clean ironing boards. Motorcaravan services. Gas supplies. Shop. Bar. Restaurant. Takeaway. Volleyball. Swimming pools and jacuzzi (15/5-30/9). Games room. Table tennis. Bicycle and scooter hire. Children's playground. Animation and excursions twice weekly. English spoken. Site barrier closed 13.00-15.00 hrs. **Off site:** Tennis 100 m. Fishing or riding 2 km. Golf 12 km.

Charges 2002

Per person	€ 7.00
pitch	€ 12.50
child (0-12 yrs)	€ 5.00
small tent pitch	€ 9.00

Tel: 055 8307323. Fax: 055 8307323. E-mail: poggetto@tin.it. **Reservations:** Contact site. **Open** 16 March - 15 October.

Directions: Leave A1 at 'Incisa Valdarno' exit and turn left towards Incisa after 400 m turn right on Sp1 towards Firenze. Site is 5 km. at Troghi, well signed.

Camping Toscana Colliverdi

6664 via Marcialla 349, Loc. Marcialla, 50020 Certaldo (Tuscany)

Very much a 'no frills' country hillside site, 20 km. north of Siena, Toscana Colliverdi has space for 60 large units on deep terraces and two small areas for tents. All the terrace pitches have electricity (3/5A). One part of the access road is tarmac the other rough gravel - large units should use the tarmac for ease of access on the steep slopes. There are excellent views of the surrounding countryside (unfortunately marred by overhead wires). The site is well positioned to visit the many places of interest in the area, including the birthplace of Leonardo de Vinci which is very close. This site's strength is the owner, Constantino who is there to please whatever the situation. He is an expert on the local history and culture and has an extensive array of tourist information and many fascinating snippets that are not in the guide books. Nothing is too much trouble and a comprehensive pack is given to all. There are no supporting facilities but he is in close liaison with suppliers in the local village and all requisites are available.

Facilities: A small, but clean and good quality sanitary block is on the second terrace, providing British and Turkish syle toilets. Showers, exterior washbasins, dishwashing and laundry sinks all have hot and cold water. These facilities are very limited for the campsite size and can become very busy at peak periods. No washing machines or facilities for disabled campers. Play area. Bicycle hire. No other on site facilities but see text. The site is dark at night and the centre steps are a challenge as some are of differing depths, thus a good torch is required. **Off site:** Restaurant shop, butchers, greengrocer, post office 2 km.

Charges 2002

Per person	€ 5.16 - € 5.68
child (1-8 yrs)	€ 3.10 - € 3.62
motorcaravan	€ 9.30 - € 9.81
tent or caravan	€ 5.16 - € 5.68
car	€ 2.07
motorcycle	€ 1.55
electricity	€ 2.07

No credit cards. **Tel:** 0571 669334. Fax: 0571 669334. **Reservations:** Write to site. **Open** 1 week before Easter - 30 September.

Directions: From A1 autostrada Florence - Siena, take Tavarnelle exit and head for Tavarnelle. At the village follow signs for Marcialla. Site entrance is on the left approx. 700 m. after the village of Marcialla.

The ideal stopover to Get to Know Tuscany.
New campsite between Florence and Siena, between the green hills of the Chianti wine route. Florence 24 km - Siena 30 km - Pisa 67 km - Vinci 29 km - Certaldo 6 km - S.Gimignano 19 km - Volterra 39 km. Set amongst woods, hills and vineyards, Camping Toscana Colliverdi is very quiet and comfortable. Modern sanitary facilities with free hot showers. The pitches of 70 mq are situated on varoius levels. Directions: motor-wat Florence-Siena and Tavernelle. In Tavernelle follow direction Marcialla-Certaldo where site is signposted.

Panorama-Camping
Toscana Colliverdi
Via Marcialla, 349 • I-50020 Marcialla Certaldo (FI)
Tel. and fax 0039/0571669334 • Http:www.campingtoscana.it/toscanacolliverdi • E-mail: toscolverdi@virgilio.it

BOLOGNA NORD
PISA
VINCI
VOLTERRA
CERTALDO
SAN GIMIGNANO — MARCIALLA
TAVERNELLE
SIENA — FIRENZE (CERTOSA)
SUD ROMA
AUTOSTRADA DEL SOLE A1 - HIGHWAY A1

Camping La Montagnola

6625 53018 Sovicille (Tuscany)

An agreeable alternative to sites closer to the centre of Siena, La Montagnola is set in secluded woodland to the north of the village of Sovicille. The owners have worked hard to provide a good basic standard of amenities. The 66 pitches are of good size (80 sq.m) and offer considerable privacy. Clearly marked with shade, all are suitable for caravans and motorcaravans, and have electricity (5A). However, there are just three water points on the site. Some higher pitches are around a central barbecue area along with mobile homes. This unsophisticated site could make an excellent touring base for central Tuscany and is not too far from the motorway for a short stay.

Facilities: A single toilet block provides free hot showers and sufficient washbasins (cold water) and mainly British style toilets - not luxurious, but adequate and clean. Small well stocked shop and bar. Play area. Volleyball. Table tennis. Torches definitely required in tented areas. **Off site:** Large supermarket 6 km. (San Rocco a Philli or Rosia), a small one 6 km (Sovicille). Two restaurants in the village.

Charges 2002

Per person	€ 6.00
child (4-12 yrs)	€ 3.90
pitch	€ 7.00

Tel: 0577 314473. Fax: 0577 314473. **Reservations:** Not necessary. **Open** Easter - 30 September.

Directions: From north on Firenze - Siena motorway take Siena Ovest exit, turn left on SS73, at the village Voltebass turn right following signs for Sovicille from where site is signed. From south (Grosseto) take SS223 turning at crossroads to Rosia from where site is also signed.

Camping Montescudaio

6630 Via del Poggetto km 2, 56040 Montescudaio (Tuscany)

This well developed site, south of Livorno, is fashioned out of a very extensive area of natural undulating woodland (with low trees) and has its own character. The fact that the site is cleverly divided into separate areas for families and couples, including those in tourers, shows the owner's desire to reduce any possibility of noise for families on site. There are 372 pitches for touring units with shade, most of a good size, plus 170 seasonal units, bungalows or large caravans, in separate clearings. Electricity (5A) is available in all parts, long leads required in some pitches. The restaurant is good with a Tuscan menu. A piano bar operates through the season along with various other entertainment in July/Aug. This is an attractive site which is being developed with great style. The owner is keen to please his clients and has tried to think of most needs. It is 4 km. from the sea at the nearest point but there is a pleasant large free pool on the site with a separate children's pool. A miniature botanical garden is at the centre of the site. Used by tour operators (25 pitches). There is much to see in this area ranging from the amazing Etruscan tombs and ruins to sampling the wines of the area.

Facilities: Top quality sanitary blocks are comprehensively appointed and have hot water in all the blocks. Baby baths in the two main blocks. This is one of the few sites we have seen using steam cleaning as a matter of routine. Motorcaravan services. Freezer for campers. Excellent laundry service. Shops. Bar. Restaurant and takeaway in main season. Open-air pizzeria with bar and small dance floor (from mid-June). Swimming pool. Tennis. Several comprehensive play areas scattered around the site. Table tennis. Fitness field. Excursions. Organised events programme in main season. Medical service. Dogs are not accepted (kennels available outside). Torches required in some areas.

Charges 2003

Per person (any age)	€ 5.00 - € 6.90
pitch incl. electricity	€ 10.80 - € 19.20

Tel: 0586 683477. Fax: 0586 630932. E-mail: info@camping-montescudaio.it. **Reservations:** Min. stay in July/Aug. 7 days. Write with € 50 deposit. **Open** 9 May - 21 September.

Directions: From the Genova - Livorno autostrada take exit for Rosignano Marittimo. Take the highway (Livorno-Grosseto) towards Roma and exit for Cecina. Follow signs for Guardistallo (not Montescudaio) and site is located on the Cecina-Guardistallo road, 2 km. from Cecina.

Camping Semifonte

6663 Via Foscola 4, 50021 Barberino Val d'Elsa (Tuscany)

Barberino lies in the heart of Tuscany between Florence and Siena, an area rich in history and known for that special Italian wine Chianti. Camping Semifonte is a terraced site with fine views over the surrounding hills. The pitches are a little on the small side with some tight manoeuvring possibly required on the narrow terraces and a steep pull out from the site. Staff are helpful and there is a small but adequate shop. A nice restaurant is 500 m. outside the site with another in the village, a short walk away, but well worth trying.

Facilities: The fully equipped toilet block was new in 2000. Laundry facilities and a motorcaravan service point. Swimming pool with children's pool on site. Regular bus route to/from Florence and Siena.

Charges 2002

Per adult	€ 5.50 - € 6.50
child (3-10 yrs)	€ 3.50 - € 4.00
pitch	€ 5.50 - € 9.00
electricity (4A)	€ 2.00

Tel: 055 8075454. Fax: 055 8075454. E-mail: semifonte@semifonte.it. **Reservations:** made with € 5.50 fee. **Open** 1 April - 20 October.

Directions: Exit Florence-Siena autostrada at Tavarmelle junction to Barberina Val d'Elsa. Take first left on entering village and site is 500 m.

Camping Il Gineprino

6637 Via dei Platani, 56a.b.c, 57020 Marina di Bibbona (Tuscany)

This is a pleasant part of Tuscany with many interesting places within visiting distance. Il Gineprino, a small, new family run site is on the edge of Bibbona but not directly on the coast. The friendly owner, Roberto was an architect and designed the entire site, which has a nice family atmosphere. When we visited there was lots of fun and dancing by the floodlit pool. Trees planted in '95 now provide shade for most of the pitches. There are 70 pitches (10 with private sanitary facilities) on the main site plus 50 bungalows, watch for low branches if you are around 3.5 m. high. A further area for 50 motorhomes, with electricity and another sanitary block is directly across the quiet beach access road. The site has an unusually shaped pool and an excellent restaurant with terrace, serving local cuisine. Cars have to be parked in a separate area opposite the site entrance. The 130 touring pitches are numbered and marked by trees at the corners and all have a water tap and electricity (4A). Entertainment is provided on two or three evenings each week in high season and excursions can be arranged. The beach is about 400 m. and can be reached on foot through a pinewood. British guests are welcome and English is spoken.

Facilities: Three sanitary blocks have British and Turkish style WCs, hot water in washbasins and showers, with cold for dishwashing and laundry. Family room (on payment) with WC, washbasin and shower and facilities for disabled people. Motorcaravan services. Shop, restaurant with terrace (both 1/5-15/9). Swimming pool with children's pool and aquagym (1/5-15/9). Games room. TV room. Table tennis. Bicycle hire. Football ground. 'Bocce'. Volleyball. Some entertainment in high season. Excursions. **Off site:** Fishing 500 m. Riding 1 km.

Charges 2002

Per person	€ 5.50 - € 9.50
child (0-8 yrs)	€ 4.00 - € 6.00
pitch with electricity	€ 8.00 - € 12.50
dog	€ 3.00 - € 5.00

No credit cards. **Tel:** 0586 600550. Fax: 0586 600550. E-mail: ilginepnino@tiscalinet.it. **Reservations:** Write to site. **Open** April - end September.

Directions: Site is signed on the approach from the main SS1 coast road between La California and Marina di Bibbona. Follow signs to Marina di Bibbona where there are no campsite signs.

Camping Le Pianacce

6635 Via Bolgherese, 57022 Castagneto Carducci (Tuscany)

In a quiet situation in the Tuscan hills, 6 km. from sea at Donoratico, this high quality site has an attractive medium-sized pool, overlooked by the restaurant/bar terrace that also has commanding views over the area. The site is on steeply rising ground and has 113 pitches for tourists, all with 3A electricity, in tiered rows on fairly narrow terraces. Access to most is not easy because the limited space between the small dividing hedges and the high bank of the next terrace restricts manoeuvring so installation is now made by the site's tractor. All pitches are shady. The site is almost entirely for tourists, with very few seasonal units, but it is likely to be full from about mid-July to 20 Aug. It is a quiet site and peaceful at night. There is a nature reserve adjacent and if you care to travel to the sandy beach it is 20 km. long and beautiful. The local area is famous for its wine routes through the vine covered hills (try the Paleo or Ornellaia!) Also explore the local Etruscan ruins and six medieval villages close by. Used by tour operators (40 pitches).

Facilities: There are three toilet blocks, including a small one at the top of the site, all refurbished to a high standard. British style WCs, individual washbasins with hot water and free hot showers. Baby room with bath and child sized facilities. Motorcaravan services. Shop. Restaurant/bar. Swimming pool and children's pool with water games. Archery. Tennis. Minigolf. Bicycle hire. Playground. Information point. Internet point. Free bus service to beach. Gas supplies. Animation is provided in season for children and adults. Barbecues are only permitted on the communal area. Torches required in some areas. Dogs are not accepted. **Off site:** Fishing or riding 6 km.

Charges 2002

Per person	€ 4.30 - € 7.90
child (0-10 yrs)	€ 3.20 - € 6.30
pitch	€ 7.50 - € 12.90
2 man tent incl. motorcycle	€ 5.30 - € 9.60

Some special offers in low season. No credit cards. **Tel:** 0565 763667. Fax: 0565 766085. E-mail: info@ campinglepianacce.it. **Reservations:** Made with deposit; contact site. **Open** 13 April - 12 October.

Directions: Turn off main S1 just north of Donoratico in hamlet of Il Bambolo at sign to Castagneto Carducci. After 3 km. turn left at signs to Bolgheri and site, then follow camp signs. Single track final approach.

Italy - Central

Camping Pappasole

6640 Carbonifera 14, 57020 Vignale Riotorto (Tuscany)

This lively site offers plenty of sporting activities and is located 250 m. from its own sandy beach facing the island of Elba. It is a large site on flat, fairly open ground offering 409 pitches of 90 sq.m. many with electricity (3A) and water, others fully serviced. Some 344 pitches have their own cosy individual sanitary facility with WC, shower and washbasin, and next to these a compartment with gas stove, fridge and sink (extra cost). Pitches are separated by bushes with shade from mature trees and artificial shade in other areas. There may be some road or rail noise in certain parts. The excellent pools are a strong feature. However, the central focus of the site is an attractive covered area (floodlit at night) for music and entertainment.

Facilities: Three modern sanitary blocks have free hot water and mainly Turkish, but with some British style WCs. These facilities may be a fair walk from some pitches. Laundry facilities. Motorcaravan services. Gas supplies. Fridge hire. Hairdresser. Restaurant. Snacks. Bar. Shop. Swimming pools (from 26/4). Play area. Tennis. Table tennis. Bowls. Handball. Watersports. Minigolf. Bicycle hire. Fishing. Medical services. Safety deposit boxes. Impressive animation programme. **Off site:** Riding 5 km. Sub-aqua diving. Excursion programme (26/5-8/9).

Charges 2002

Per person	€ 4.50 - € 10.50
child (3-10 yrs)	€ 3.00 - € 7.00
pitch	€ 9.00 - € 22.00
pitch with services	€ 13.50 - € 35.00

Tel: 0565 20420. Fax: 0565 20346. E-mail: info@pappasole.it. **Reservations:** Made for whole weeks, Sat. - Sat. **Open** 5 April - 13 October.

Directions: Site is north of Follonica just off the SS1 (Follonica Nord exit). Follow signs for 'Torre Mozza' and site. You must cross the bridge over the railway line to access the site.

Italy - Central

Camping Le Capanne

6636 Via Aurelia Km 273, 57020 Bibbona (Tuscany)

Marina di Bibbona is a relatively little known resort situated a little to the south of Livorno and close to the better known resort of Cecina. The area retains much charm and a number of popular beaches are close at hand. A member of the 'Camping di Charme' group, the site's new owners have some ambitious development plans, many of which are already fulfilled. The site is very easily accessed from the main S1 Via Aurelia road (Livorno - Rome). There are 320 good sized pitches, most with electricity (5A). The pitches are nearly all well shaded by pine, olive and eucalyptus trees. A modern mobile home area has a sunnier, more open setting .

Facilities: Toilet blocks are of a traditional design but kept clean, with plenty of hot water. Toilets are mixed British and Turkish style. Dishwashing and laundry sinks. Washing machines. Mini-market and 'bazaar'. Bar and popular restaurant near site entrance. Large swimming pool and play area. Bicycle hire. Entertainment programme in high season. **Off site:** Beach 2 km. with bus from the site in high season.

Charges 2002

Per adult	€ 3.36 - € 6.71
child (under 10 yrs)	€ 2.32 - € 5.16
pitch (incl. electricity)	€ 5.68 - € 11.36

No credit cards. **Tel:** 0586 600 064. Fax: 0586 600 198. E-mail: info@campinglecapanne.it. **Reservations:** Necessary for the high season. **Open** 1 April - 30 September.

Directions: Take A12 autostrada (Livorno - Rossignano Marittimo) to its end and join the Via Aurelia (S1) heading south. Exit at Bibbona and follow signs to the campsite.

Italy - Central

Camping Valle Gaia

6632 via Cecinese 87, 56040 Casale Marittimo (Tuscany)

Valle Gaia is a delightful family site with a friendly, laid back atmosphere, which is in marked contrast to some of the busy sites on the coast. Yet it is located just 9 km. from the sandy beaches at Cecina. This pretty site has two enticing pool complexes, both with childrens` pools and generous sunbathing terraces, and is just a short drive away from the mediaeval Manhattan of San Gimignano, Volterra and Siena. The 150 pitches are of a reasonable size (90 sq.m.), well shaded by pine or cypress trees and surrounded by oleanders. Most have electricity. The bar and restaurant are both very popular, the latter located in a splendidly converted farmhouse, and specialising in local cuisine.

Facilities: Three toilet blocks of modern construction are maintained to a high standard with mainly British style toilets. Some washbasins in cubicles. Washing and drying machines. Shop stocks a good range of provisions including local produce. Tennis courts, 5-a-side pitch, table tennis and games room. Bicycle hire. Only gas barbecues are permitted. **Off site:** Shops at Casale Marittimo 3.5 km. Riding 4 km.

Charges 2002

Per pitch	€ 7.90 - € 12.95
adult	€ 4.20 - € 7.15
child (under 10 yrs)	€ 3.10 - € 5.25

Tel: 0586 681 236. Fax: 0586 683 551. E-mail: info@vallegaia.it. **Reservations:** essential for high season - made with deposit **Open** 23 March - 26 October.

Directions: From A12 autostrada, take Rossignano Marittimo exit, following signs to Roma, joining the E80. Take Casale Marittimo exit and follow signs to the town. The site is clearly signed from here.

Blucamp

6641 57021 Campiglia Marittima (Tuscany)

Blucamp is a relatively new, simple site in a tranquil setting near the pretty village of Campiglia Marittima. Owned and run by a partnership of two charming Italians who are keen to welcome British guests, good English is spoken. The famous islands of Elba and Capraia can be sighted whilst checking in at the reception block, and there are fabulous views over green hills and the sea from the upper pitches. The 100 pitches (all with 3A electricity, 12 fully serviced) are terraced and on steep slopes; one area is for tents only and has the most amazing views. There is a tractor (free) to help you install your unit if required. Cars are parked off the pitches in numbered bays. All pitches have young trees that provide some shade but others are more open. The site is entirely for tourists, with just four bungalows for rent. It is busy in high season, but is very quietly situated, 8 km. back from the sea, just 700 m. from the old medieval village of Campiglia Marittima. After the stifling beach sites, which are dusty under huge pines, this is a most refreshing experience as there is invariably a cooling breeze. The local area has a history of Etruscan metal mining, with the fascinating miner's castle of the Temperino Valley. There is a ferry connection to Elba and Corsica 19 km. distant.

Facilities: Two satisfactory sanitary blocks have British and Turkish style WCs, individual washbasins with cold water and free hot showers. Six private sanitary units for hire. Washing machine. Small friendly restaurant/bar with a pretty terrace is run by a separate family and offers wonderful Tuscan cuisine specialising in fish. Attractive medium-sized swimming pool. Electronic games. Table tennis. Internet. Torches required in some areas. **Off site:** Fishing 8 km. Riding 2 km.

Charges 2002

Per person	€ 7.10
child (0-8 yrs)	€ 4.90
pitch	€ 9.00 - € 13.00
water and drain	€ 4.30
private sanitary unit	€ 8.00
dog	€ 5.00

Less 30% outside July/Aug. **Tel:** 0565 838553. Fax: 0574 574272. E-mail: info@blucamp.it.
Reservations: Made with deposit; contact site.
Open 17 May - 7 September.

Directions: Take exit for S. Vincenzo Sud off the main S1 road Livono to Follonica. Follow signs for Campiglia Marittima where site is signed.

Camping Le Marze

6662 Strada Statale 322, della Collacchie km 30,200, 58046 Marina di Grosseto (Tuscany)

This natural site is situated 4 km. north of Marina di Grosseto and has 180 generously sized pitches for touring units. Separated by hedges, all have electricity (3A) and most enjoy natural shade from mature pine trees. On sand and with easy access, there is a background noise of 'cicadas' (crickets) from the lofty pines and squirrels entertain high above. A private beach is across the main road. Bicycles are an asset and you can also enjoy a cycle ride to the town along a beach track. The beach is worth the walk as it is the strongest feature here, being soft sand which shelves slowly. There are secluded dunes, and a lifeguard. The beach bar is excellent and operates as a disco at night thus protecting the site from noise. The site layout is circular with the restaurant, bar and shop complex in the centre. Le Marze is well placed to visit local Etruscan villages, such as Ventulania and Roselle, or Pienza, a late Romanesque town created by Pope Pio II. There is a large tour operator presence but these are on the outer ring of the site and not intrusive.

Facilities: The four sanitary facilities are of a good standard, two of them new and excellent with British style WCs (some Turkish in the older blocks). Facilities for disabled campers in the new blocks along with baby facilities and private bathrooms. Motorcaravan service point. Market with amazing choice of goods and a bazaar alongside. Bar, restaurant, pizzeria and takeaway. Two identical swimming pools, unusual in that they are in supported structures (1.3 m. deep). Two children's play areas. Ambitious entertainment programme in season, excursions and activities including gym with a personal trainer (extra charge). Barbeque areas. Evening entertainment. Swimming pools with aqua-aerobics and watersports. Torches required in some areas.

Charges 2002

Per person	€ 5.68 - € 8.26
child (2-12 yrs)	€ 3.36 - € 6.61
caravan	€ 5.16 - € 7.33
car	€ 4.75 - € 6.61
motorcycle	€ 2.84 - € 3.87
motorcaravan	€ 8.88 - € 11.05

Tel: 0564 35501. Fax: 0564 35534. E-mail: lemarze@ecvacanze.it. **Reservations:** Contact site.
Open 1 May - 15 October.

Directions: At Grosseto on S1 Livorno - Rome road take road signed to Marina di Grosseto. Take S327 road to Castiglione della Pescaia, 1.4 km before the Marina. Site is well signed on the right about 3 km. towards Castiglione della Pescaia.

Camping Maremma Sans Souci

6660 (Grosseto), 58043 Castiglione della Pescaia (Tuscany)

This seaside site is owned and run by the Perduca family and sits in natural woodland on the coast between Livorno and Rome. The minimum amount of undergrowth has been cleared to provide 400 individually marked and hedged, flat pitches for camping enthusiasts. This offers considerable privacy in individual settings. A positive feature of this site is that there are no seasonal pitches. Some pitches are small and cars may not remain with tents or caravans but must go to a shaded and secure car park. There is a wide road for motorhomes but other roads are mostly narrow and bordered by trees (this is a protected area, and they cannot fell the trees). Access to some parts is difficult therefore for caravans and each pitch is earmarked either for caravans or for tents. There are electrical connections (3A) for all caravan pitches. An excellent sandy beach is less than 100 m. from one end of the site (400 m. from the other) and is used only by campers. The restaurant with several terraces offers Italian food at extremely good prices along with a fine choice of wines. Maremma is a friendly site right by the sea which should appeal to many people who like a relaxed style of camping and a real personal touch.

Facilities: Five small, mature toilet blocks are well situated around the site. Free showers and hot water at the sinks, plus lots of little extras such as hair dryers and soap dispensers, etc. Three blocks have additional, private cabins each with WC, basin and shower and there are separate facilities for disabled campers. Baby showers and baths. Washing machines. Motorcaravan services. Laundry. New reception incl. doctor's surgery and facilities for disabled visitors. Cash point. Shop. Excellent restaurant (self service in season) serving a range of local fish and fresh pasta. Bar with pizzas and other snacks. Well stocked shop. Free freezer. Volleyball. Car wash. Sailing school. Good English spoken. Torches required in some areas. No dogs are taken between 16/6-31/8. **Off site:** Excursions organised to Elba and Rome.

Charges 2002

Per person	€ 5.00 - € 7.75
child (2- 6 yrs)	€ 4.00 - € 5.15
pitch and car	€ 6.50 - € 13.00

Tel: 0564 933765. Fax: 0564/935759. E-mail: info@maremmasanssouci.it. **Reservations:** necessary for July/Aug. and will be made for min. 1 week with deposit (€ 2,58). **Open** 1 April - 31 October.

Directions: Site is 2.5 km. northwest of Castiglione on road to Follonica.

6669 Camping Village Baia Azzurra

Via Provinciale di Rocchette, 58043 Castiglione della Pescáia (Tuscany)

Recommended by our agent – this site will be inspected in 2003.

This site is being improved and is in a beautiful location to the north of Castiglione. Some English is spoken and there is 24 hour security. There are 120 pitches of around 80 sq. m. with 3A electricity available and plenty of shade. Some bungalows are available to rent. A sandy beach is adjacent, with swimming pool and paddling pools on site (caps essential). Entertainment is organised in high season. Separate car park. Bus service near.

Charges guide

Per unit incl. 2 adults	€ 31.00

Tel: 0564/941092. Fax: 0564/941242. E-mail: info@baiadellerocchette.com. **Reservations:** advisable in high season. **Open** 1 April - 31 October.

Directions: Following the S322 north from Castiglione della Pescaia turn left at sign for Rocchette. Site is on right in 3 km.

6671 Camping International Argentario

Torre Saline, Via Aurelia, 58010 Albinia (Tuscany)

Recommended by our agent – this site will be inspected in 2003.

Argentario provides 404 pitches for touring units along with some 100 bungalows for hire. The pitches are on the small side - 60 or 70 sq.m. but there is shade and 4A electricity connections. The adjacent beach is of sand and shingle and there is a swimming pool and a paddling pool on the site. Boat hire is possible and amenities include minigolf, volleyball, basketball and archery. There is a shop, a restaurant, bar and takeaway and fully equipped sanitary facilities. Cars are parked in a separate car park in high season, when dogs are not accepted either.

Charges 2000

per unit incl. 2 adults	€ 16,01 - € 26,86

Tel: 0564 870302. Fax: 0564 871380. E-mail: info@argentariocampingvillage.com. **Reservations:** contact site. **Open** Easter/1April - 30 September.

Directions:off Via Aurelia at the 150 km. mark, signed Porto S. Stefano. Site is on the right, clearly marked.

See advertisement opposite

6667 Camping La Finoria

Via Monticello 66, 58023 Gavorrano (Tuscany)

Recommended by our agent – this site will be inspected in 2003.

Finoria stands on top of a hill, surrounded by trees, and close to the Mediterranean, the Gulf of Fallonica and Elba. It offers a range of facilities including a pool, tennis court, archery etc. The campsite itself has pitches with electrical connections, modern sanitary facilities, and a small shop. The site restaurant overlooks the Gulf and Elba and serves traditional, local dishes. Excursions are organised, including sailing, riding or mountain biking, and trips to Elba. In the appropriate season it is possible to participate in harvesting chest-nuts and olives, and even to make and take home your own olive oil!

Charges 2003

Per pitch	€ 4.00 - € 10.00
person	€ 2.50 - € 8.50
child (1-6 yrs)	€ 2.00 - € 4.50

Tel: 0566 846248. E-mail: finoria@ouverture.it. **Reservations:** Contact site. **Open** all year.

Directions: From the 'Via Aurelia' a few km. north-west of Grosseto, take Gavorrano exit. Pass through Bagno di Gavorrano into Gavorrano to site at top of hill on the right.

Parco Delle Piscine

6645 Via del Bagno Santo 29, 53047 Sarteano (Tuscany)

On the spur of Monte Cetona, Sarteano is a spa, and this large smart site utilises that spa in its very own environs. The novel feature here is the three unique swimming pools fed by the natural thermo-mineral springs. These springs have been known since antiquity as 'del Bango Santo'. Two of these pools (the largest is superb with water cacade and hydro-massage, and the other large shallow pool is just for children), are set in a huge park-like ground with many picnic tables. They are free to all those staying on the site. A third excellent pool is on the site itself and is opened in main season for the exclusive use of campers. A very big building alongside the spa-pool houses a select restaurant on the first floor and a pizzeria on the second floor. Delle Piscine is really good as a sightseeing base or as an overnight stop from the Florence - Rome motorway (site is 6 km. from the exit). The attractive town is directly outside the site gate, and is worth exploring, especially the massive fortress with its drawbridge (straight out of a toy-box!) This spacious site is well run, the infrastructure is excellent and there is lots of room to manoeuvre everywhere. There are 450 individual, flat pitches, all of good size and fully marked out with high neat hedging giving really private pitches. There is a friendly welcome.

Facilities: The two heated toilet blocks are of high quality with mainly British style WCs, and numerous sinks for laundry and dishwashing (with hot water). Motorcaravan services. Restaurant/pizzeria/bar. Takeaway. Coffee bar. Newspaper kiosk. Swimming pools (one all season). TV room, satellite TV room and mini-cinema with 100 seats and a very large screen. Tennis. Soccer field. Table tennis. Volleyball. Exchange facilities. Free guided cultural tours. Local market on Fridays. Internet. Gas supplies. Dogs are not accepted. **Off site:** Bicycle hire 100 m. Riding 3 km.

Charges 2003

Per adult	€ 9.00 - € 11.50
child (3-10 yrs)	€ 5.00 - € 7.00
tent or caravan	€ 9.00 - € 11.50
car	€ 4.00 - € 5.00
motorcaravan	€ 12.00 - € 16.50
electricity	€ 3.50

Tel: 0578 26971. Fax: 0578 265889. E-mail: info@ bagnosanto.it. **Reservations:** Write to site, or book by e-mail. **Open** 23 March - 30 September.

Directions: From autostrada A1 take exit for Chiusi and Chianciano, from where Sarteano (6 km.) and site are signed.

Camping Le Soline

6665 via delle Soline, 51, 53010 Casciano di Murlo (Tuscany)

Le Soline is a country hillside site with wonderful views of the Tuscan hills from its steep slopes. Just 20 km. south of Siena and 800 m. from the village of Casciano, it has 80 neat pitches for large units and 60 tents on seven terraces with 6A electricity. Many trees including olives provide shade for the pitches, most having views. Ducks wander the site whilst geese are the gate-keepers. There is a full entertainment programme in high season and some free guided tours of the area (includes a dip in the lake). The kind and attentive Broggini family spare no efforts in making your stay a pleasant memory and are extremely hard working to this end. The elegant restaurant has an excellent menu (we tried the seafood - superb!) and the terraces look over the pool to the colourful hills beyond. The heated pools are clean with sunbathing areas loungers and umbrellas. The site is well positioned to visit the many historic and cultural places in the area and will suit families who wish for a peaceful break.

Facilities: A good quality, heated sanitary block (recently refurbished) is on the third terrace, providing mixed British and Turkish style WCs, facilities for disabled campers and hot water in the basins but showers are on payment. A few small private sanitary blocks are for hire. Motorcaravan services. Gas supplies. Laundry. Freezer for campers use. Restaurant. Pizzeria (all season). Well stocked shop (15/3-10/11). Swimming pools (Easter-15/10). Playground. Volleyball. Mini-football field. Archery. Bicycle hire. Organised excursions (June-Aug). Barbecue area (not allowed on pitches). Car wash area. Mobile homes and bungalows to rent. Cats are not accepted. **Off site:** Riding 600 m. Fishing 3 km.

Charges 2002

Per person	€ 7.00
child (2-12 yrs)	€ 4.50
caravan	€ 6.00
tent	€ 4.50 - € 5.50
motorcaravan	€ 6.50
car	€ 1.50
motorcycle	€ 1.00

Tel: 0577 817410. Fax: 0577 817415. E-mail: camping@lesoline.it. **Reservations:** contact site. **Open** all year.

Directions: From Siena, turn off SS223 (Siena - Grosseto) to the left to Fontazzi (about 20 km.) and keep right for Casciano, following signs. Alternatively, from Via Cassia SS2 turn at Lucignano d'Arbia for Murlo.

Camping Badiaccia

6654 via Trasimeno 1, Voc. Badiaccia 91, 06061 Castiglione del Lago (Umbria)

A lakeside site, Camping Badiaccia has excellent views of the surrounding hills and the islands of the lake. It provides a base from which to visit interesting places in this part of central Italy or as a night stop when travelling to Rome, as it is near the A1 autostrada. Being directly on the lake gives an almost seaside atmosphere - unusually they use a birdcage as the postbox! There is a protected swimming area along the beach with lots of sunbathing space and sunloungers and some reed areas close by and a jetty that provides a base for fishing. The site also has a protected mooring for small boats and offers a good selection of sporting opportunities with four special staff in high season to organise activities for children and adults. Well tended and maintained, Baddiaccia has a pleasant appearance enhanced by a variety of plants and flowers and English is spoke by the friendly staff. Some of the 150 numbered pitches are smaller than average but there is good shade in most parts, all have 4A electricity and are separated by trees and bushes in rows from hard access roads. A pleasant, large swimming pool is by the restaurant and a children's pool in the beach area. Excursions to Rome and Florence are organised in high season.

Facilities: The two centrally positioned sanitary blocks can be heated and are fully equipped. Washing machines. Motorcaravan services. Gas supplies. Restaurant, snack bar and shop - all open all season. Gelateria. Swimming pool (20 x 10 m) and children's pool (1/6-30/9). Play areas. Tennis. Table tennis. Minigolf. Boules. Minigolf. Volleyball. Football. Beach volleyball. Windsurfing. Watersports. Fishing. Boat hire. Entertainment and excursions in high season. Large barbecue area by lake. English spoken. Torches required in places. Dogs accepted but not by the lakeside. **Off site:** Riding 3 km. Golf 20 km.

Charges 2002

Per person	€ 4.65 - € 5.68
child (under 10 yrs)	€ 3.10 - € 4.65
caravan	€ 5.16 - € 5.68
tent	€ 4.65 - € 5.16
car	€ 1.55
motorcaravan	€ 5.68 - € 6.20

Electricity included. **Tel:** 075 9659097. Fax: 075 9659019. E-mail: camping@badiaccia.com. **Reservations:** Write to site. **Open** 1 April - 30 September.

Directions: From A11 Milan-Rome autostrada take Val di Chiana exit and turn east towards Perugia on the SS75bis. Leave this at Castiglione exit and go south on SS71 in the direction of Castiglione where site is well signed about 5 km. north of the town.

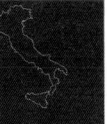

Camping Villaggio Italgest

6652 Via Martiri di Cefalonia, 06060 Sant' Arcangelo di Magione (Umbria)

Directly on the shore on the south side of Lake Trasimeno, which is almost midway between the Mediterranean and the Adriatic, San Arcangelo is ideally placed for exploring Umbria and Tuscany. The area around the lake is fairly flat but has views of the distant hills and can become very hot during summer. Villaggio Italgest is a pleasant site with 200 tourist pitches on level grass and, except for the area next to the lake, under a cover of tall trees. All pitches have 4/6A electrical connections and most places have their own water points. In high season cars are parked away from the pitches. The site offers a wide variety of activities, tours are organised daily and there is entertainment for children and adults in high season. The bar/restaurant is reputed to remain open until 2 am. There is a good sized swimming pool area with one pool with slides, a smaller children's pool and a whirlpool. Whether you wish to use this site as a base for exploration, as a place to relax, you will find this a most pleasant place to stay. The lady owner speaks good English and would welcome more British visitors.

Facilities: The one large and one smaller sanitary block have been renewed and were clean when seen, with mainly British style WCs and free hot water in the washbasins and (small) showers. Facilities for disabled people. Motorcaravan services. Washing machines and dryers. Community room with stoves, fridges and freezers. Bar, restaurant, pizzeria and takeaway(all season). Mini-market. Wide range of activities, entertainment and excursions. Small marina for boats. Swimming pool (25 x 12.5 m; open all season). Tennis. Football. Volleyball. Table tennis. Play area. TV (satellite) and games rooms. Sound-proof disco. Films. Watersports, motor boat hire and lake swimming. Fishing. Mountain bike hire. Entertainment for adults and children and mini club (July/Aug). Italian language and civilisation couses. Excursions. **Off site:** Golf, parachuting, riding, canoeing and sailing close.

Charges 2003

Per person	€ 5.70 - € 7.70
child (3-9 yrs)	€ 4.00 - € 5.70
pitch	€ 6.00 - € 9.50
car	€ 1.80 - € 2.50

Tel: 075 848 238. Fax: 075 848 085. E-mail: camping@italgest.com. **Reservations:** During winter telephone 075/5847422 or write to site with 30% deposit (deducted from final account). **Open** 1 April - 30 September.

Directions: Site is on the southern shore of Lake Trasimeno. Take exit 'Magione' from the Perugia spur from the Florence - Rome autostrada, proceed southwest round the lake to S. Arcangelo where the site is signed.

Camping Listro

6653 Via Lungolago, 06061 Castiglione del Lago (Umbria)

This is a simple, pleasant, flat site with the best beach (private to the campsite) on Lake Trasimeno. As the lake is very shallow with some reeds (7 m. at its deepest), it has very gradually sloping beaches making it very safe for children to play and swim. This also results in very warm water, which is kept clean as fishing and tourism are the major industries hereabouts. Camping Listro is a few hundred yards north of the historic town of Castiglione and the attractive town can be seen rising up the hillside from the site. It provides 110 pitches all with electricity (3A) with 70% of the pitches enjoying the shade of mature trees. Younger campers are in a separate area of the site, ensuring no noise disturbance and some of the motorcaravan pitches are right on the lakeside giving stunning views out of your windows. Facilities on the site are fairly limited with a small shop and bar and snack bar, and there is no organised entertainment. English is spoken and British guests are particularly welcome. If you enjoy the simple life and peace and quiet in camping terms then this site is for you.

Facilities: Two screened sanitary facilities are very clean with British and Turkish style WCs. Facilities for disabled visitors. Washing machine. Motorcaravan services. Bar. Shop. Snack bar. Children's play area. Table tennis. Volleyball. Private beach. **Off site:** The town is 800 m. and many bars and restaurants are near, as are sporting facilities including a good swimming pool and tennis courts (discounts using the camp-site card).

Charges 2003

Per person (over 3 yrs)	€ 3.50 - € 4.20
pitch	€ 3.50 - € 4.20
car	€ 1.10 - € 1.60
motorcycle	€ 0.80 - € 1.05

Less 10% for stays over 8 days in low season.
Tel: 075 951193. Fax: 075 951193. E-mail: listro@listro.it. **Reservations:** Contact site. **Open** 1 April - 30 September.

Directions: From A1/E35 Florence-Rome autostrada take Val di Chiana exit and join the Perugia (75 bis) superstrada. After 24 km. take Castiglione exit and follow town signs. Signs to site are clearly marked just before the town.

CAMPING LISTRO ★★

In a green setting on the shore of Lake Trasimeno
· Private beach · Free hot water and electricity
· Newly renovated shower and toilet facilities
· Shop for essentials · Bar · Play area for children
By the site exit are: Swimming pool, Tennis courts, Athletics track, Football field, Windsurfing, Canoeing, Disco, Restaurant. Only 500 m. from the historic centre of Castiglione del Lago, the site is an ideal base for visits to Rome, Umbria and Tuscany.

www.listro.it

I-06061 Castiglione del Lago (PG) • Tel. + Fax 0039/075951193

6801 Camping Holiday & 6802 Camping Baviera

Nuovo Centro Turistico Hoba, Lungomare Nord, 64022 Giulianova Lido (TE)

Recommended by our agent – these sites will be inspected in 2003.

Situated midway along the Adriatic coast at Giulianova, these are seaside sites with access to a sandy beach. They have a good range of facilities, including swimming pools, a restaurant and takeaway, pizzeria, three bars, and a supermarket. There are facilities for tennis and many activities are organised.

Charges 2002

Per pitch	€ 7.06 - € 14.93
adult	€ 3.21 - € 6.46
child	€ 2.28 - € 4.61

Tel: Camping Holiday 08 58 004420, Camping Baviera 08 58 008928. E-mail: info@hoba.it. **Reservations:** Contact sites. **Open** 1 June - 15 September.

Directions: From A14 autostrada take Giulianova exit. Follow this road for 10 km. and the sites are to be found at the end of the promenade.

See advertisement opposite

Camping Il Collaccio

6656 Azienda Agricola 11 Collaccio, 06047 Castelvecchio di Preci (Umbria)

Tuscany has grabbed the imagination and publicity, but parts of nearby Umbria are just as beautiful. Castlevecchio di Preci is tucked away in the tranquil depths of the Umbrian countryside. The natural beauty of the Monti Sibillini National Park is near (excursions are organised) and there are walking and cycling opportunities with many marked paths. Historic Assisi and Perugia and the walled market town of Norcia are worth exploring. Il Collaccio is owned and run by the Baldoni family who bought the farm over 30 years ago, rebuilt the derelict farmhouse in its original style and then decided to share it with holiday makers by developing a campsite and accommodation for rent. The farming aspect was kept, along with a unit producing salami (they run very popular salami making and Umbrian cookery courses over Easter and New Year - no preservatives!) and its products can be bought in the shop and sampled in the excellent restaurant. The camping area has been carved out of the hillside which forms a natural amphitheatre with splendid views. At first sight the narrow steep entrance seems daunting (the owner will assist) and the road which leads down to the somewhat steep camping terraces takes one to the exit. A pleasant restaurant and bar overlooks the upper pools and a bar is alongside the lower pools. The 93 large pitches are on level terraces with stunning views. Electrical connections (6A) are available - long leads useful. Thousands of trees, planted to replace those cut down by the previous owner, are maturing and provide some shade. An interesting feature is a tree plantation on a lower slope where they are experimenting in cultivating truffles - much patience is needed. With sparsely populated villages across the valley on the mountain slopes and embraced by stunning scenery, Il Collaccio and its surrounds are unusual and different. Small, but not intrusive, tour operator presence.

Facilities: Three modern sanitary blocks are spaced through the site with British and Turkish styled WCs, cold water in washbasins and hot, pre-mixed water in showers and sinks. Facilities for disabled visitors. Washing machine. Motorcaravan service point. Restaurant (all season). Shop (basics, 1/7-31/8). Two new swimming pools both with children's pool (15/5-30/9). Play area. Tennis. Volley and basketball. Football. Table tennis. Boules. Entertainment in high season. Excursion opportunities with small numbers on gourmet visits to olive oil and wine making organisations. **Off site:** Cycling and walking. Canoeing and rafting 2 km. Fishing 10 km.

Charges 2002

Per person	€ 5.50 - € 7.25
child (3-12 yrs)	€ 2.25 - € 3.50
caravan or motorcaravan	€ 6.50 - € 8.50
tent	€ 5.50 - € 7.25
car	€ 2.00 - € 3.00
motorcycle	€ 1.00 - € 2.00

Electricity included. **Tel:** 0743 939005. Fax: 0743 939094. E-mail: info@ilcollaccio.com. **Reservations:** Write to site. **Open** 1 April - 30 September.

Directions: From SS77 Foligno-Civitonova Marche road turn south at Muccia for Visso from where Preci is signed. There is a direct route (saving a long and extremely winding approach) through a new tunnel, if the site is approached north of Eggi which is approx. 10 km. north of Spoleto. The tunnel exit is at Sant Anatolia di Narco SS209, where a left turn will take you to Preci (when we visited there were few signs but it is worth asking for directions).

Italy - Central

Camping Internazionale Assisi

6655 S Giovanni in Campiglione 110, 06081 Assisi (Umbria)

Camping Internazionale is situated on the west side of Assisi and has high grade facilities which provide tourers with a good base to visit both St Francis` city and nearby Perugia and Lake Trasimeno. The excellent restaurant has a large terrace which can be completely enclosed serving reasonably priced meals, ranging from pizzas to local Umbrian dishes. The city is lit up in the evenings to provide a beautiful backdrop from some areas in the site. The 175 pitches are large and clearly marked on flat grass, all with electricity (3A). There is shade as it can be very hot in this part of Italy, and a welcome relief is the site`s pleasant, large pool. The site is pleasantly out of the city bustle and heat and offers a regular shuttle bus service. Assisi boasts a fine cathedral, among many other attractions, and a stay should not be cut short.

Facilities: The well appointed and clean toilet block has free hot showers, plenty of washbasins, mainly Turkish style WCs (only 4 British style in each block) and facilities for disabled people. Washing machine. Motorcaravan services. Restaurant/pizzeria (closed Wednesdays). Bar with snacks. Shop. Ice cream bar. Kitchen for campers. Free swimming pool, jacuzzi and circular children`s pool (caps mandatory). Table tennis. Bicycle hire. Tennis. Volleyball. Gas supplies. **Off site:** Riding 2 km. Excursions to Assisi centre, Rome and Siena. Bus to city from outside the site.

Charges 2003

Per adult	€ 6.00 - € 7.00
child (3-10 yrs)	€ 4.00 - € 5.00
pitch and electricity	€ 7.00 - € 10.00

Credit card min. €50. **Tel:** 075 813710. Fax: 075 812 335. E-mail: info@campingassisi.it. **Reservations:** Made for 1 week stays in high season, but not really necessary. **Open** 1 April - October.

Directions: Site is on the south side of the SS147, which branches left off SS75 Perugia-Foligno road. Follow Assisi signs and look for the un-named camping sign going off to the left (downhill) as you enter the city. Site is 4 km. from the city. At Violi a village just before Assisi there is a warning of a low bridge of 3.3 m. - in fact it is higher at the centre.

Italy - South

Camping Europe Garden

6800 Abruzzo, via Belvedere 11, 64028 Silvi (Abruzzo)

This site is 13 km. northwest of Pescara and, lying just back from the coast (2 km.) up a very steep hill with pleasant views over the sea. The 204 pitches, all with 10A electricity, are mainly on good terraces - access may be difficult on some pitches. However, a tractor will help. When we visited the site was dry but we suspect life might become difficult on some pitches after heavy rain. Cars stand by units on over half of the pitches or in nearby parking spaces for the remainder, most pitches are shaded. There is a good pool at the bottom of the site, with a small bar and entertainment in season on a small stage and associated area within the pool boundary. The restaurant has large olive trees penetrating the floor and ceilings and good views but the terrace views are fabulous. The site has very steep slopes and is not suitable for infirm campers.

Facilities: Two good toilet blocks are well cleaned and provide mixed British and Turkish style WCs. Washing machines. Restaurant. Bar. Tennis. Children`s playground. Swimming pool (300 sq.m; swimming caps compulsory), small children`s pool and jacuzzi. Free bus service (18/5-7/9) to beach. Entertainment programme. Free weekly excursions (15/6-8/9) to different parts of the Province. Electronic money is used throughout the site (credit bought on swipe cards). Dogs are not accepted.

Charges 2002

Per person	€ 4.10 - € 6.70
child (3-8 yrs)	€ 3.60 - € 5.15
pitch	€ 9.30 - € 12.90
electricity	€ 1.80

No credit cards. Discounts for longer stays outside high season. **Tel:** 085 930137. Fax: 085/932846. E-mail: egarden@camping.it. **Reservations:** Made with €103 deposit for first 2 weeks of August (min. 2 weeks), at other times without deposit. **Open** 27 April - 20 September.

Directions: Turn off inland S16 coast road at km. 433 stone for Silvi Alta and follow camp signs. From A14 take Pineto exit from north or Pescara Nord exit from the south. Signing is good.

Camping Heliopolis

6805 Contrada Villa Fumosa 1, 64025 Pineto (Abruzzo)

Heliopolis is an attractive, well run site with a charming English speaking lady owner named Gigliola who is delighted to receive British customers in her site which is very popular with Italians. This is an unusual site for the Adriatic as most of the pitches have their own neat, clean and covered private units with shower/WC and washing facilities. The pitches are of average size arranged in rows at right angles to the beach and most have artificial shade provided. All have electricity (4A). Cars may be parked off the pitch. The site opens directly onto a wide pleasant sand and shingle beach that shelves gently in most conditions. Like many Adriatic sites, there is some noise from passing trains especially on the western side. An attractive covered restaurant makes local dishes and the house wine is very good. A separate bar overlooks the clean pools. From the terraces you can enjoy the organised entertainment which the Italians love. The fun is contagious, you can get involved as much as you wish. If you would like to experience what we consider to be a 'real' Italian campsite then this may be for you.

Facilities: Two excellent toilet blocks, one for men and one for women, also have facilities for disabled campers. Laundry facilities. Individual units for 120 of the 160 pitches. Bar/coffee shop. Restaurant (weekends only until 1/6). Shops (from 1/6). Swimming pool and children's pool (from 15/6). Volleyball. Tennis and play pitches. Playground. Games room and electronic games. Entertainment organised in high season. Hairdresser and massage on site in season. Doctor attends 2 hrs daily. Torches required near beach areas. **Off site:** Trips to Rome, Napoli, Capri, the Republic of San Marino and other local attractions can be organized.

Charges 2002

Per person	€ 4.00 - € 7.00
child (3-12 yrs)	€ 3.50 - € 6.50
standard pitch	€ 9.50 - € 21.50
pitch with private facilities	€ 16.53 - € 28.00
small tent pitch	€ 4.00 - € 7.50
dog	€ 1.55

Electricity included. **Tel:** 085 9492720. Fax: 085 9492171. E-mail: info@heliopolis.it. **Reservations:** Write to site for details. **Open** 1 April - 30 September.

Directions: Site is to the north of the town sharing an approach with Camping Pineto Beach; both sites are clearly signed from A14 road (exit Pineto) and SS16 (in town).

Ipini Camping

6811 Via Delle Sassete-1/A, Fiano Romano, 00065 Roma (Lázio)

This excellent family site is ideal for visiting Rome. Roberto and Judy McKeever (Italian and Australian) and their partner Antonella created this wonderful homely site in a quiet area, 20 km. north of the city. They spare no effort to make you welcome. A thoughtfully designed and decorated central block houses the restaurant, bar and snack bar. The grass terrace enjoys fine views of the distant mountains and live entertainment is staged in season. Tour buses pass through weekly and things become busier and more lively. The weekly pig roast and buffet is great! Some of the 150 large pitches have excellent views, arranged on terraces with some enjoying shade from mature trees. Electricity (10A) is available. Some 80 mobile homes, plus tour operator pitches are also on site. The swimming pool, spa, and children's pool are most welcome in the heat of summer. The site is some distance from Rome but this does ensure a tranquil existence away from the city heat and bustle and all rates here are very competitive including the return trip to Rome by air conditioned bus. It is ideal for exploring Rome or the attractions close by including the medieval town of Fiano Romano or the archaeological site of 'Lucus Feronial'.

Facilities: The one excellent sanitary block is of hotel standard down to the decorative fittings in all cubicles. All facilities are spotless and hot water is free in showers, washbasins and dishwashing sinks. Two extremely large and well equipped units for disabled visitors. New washing machines. Motorcaravan services. Bar. Restaurant. Large, well stocked shop. Snack bar. Boule. Swimming pool. Tennis. Children's play area. Paddle tennis. Mountain biking. Trekking. Canoeing. Torches required in some areas. **Off site:** Free initial pick-up from the local station.

Charges 2002

Per person	€ 7.80 - € 8.70
child (3-12 yrs)	€ 5.20 - € 5.70
caravan	€ 5.50 - € 6.50
tent	€ 3.10 - € 3.90
car	€ 3.10 - € 3.90
motorcaravan	€ 7.50 - € 8.70

Electricity included. **Tel:** 0765 453349. Fax: 0765 453057. E-mail: ipini@camping.it. **Reservations:** Contact site. **Open** 15 March - 15 November.

Directions: ring road (GRA) take A1 exit to Fiano Romano. Just before the town take a right along via Belvedere - it is opposite a petrol station. and follow the camping signs - there is only the one site.

Roma Flash Sporting

6812 Via Settevene Palo km 19,800, 00062 Bracciano (Lázio)

The dynamic Monni family greet you with a smile at this clean and pleasant site on the western side of Lake Bracciano which supplies Rome's drinking water. Mature trees provide cover for the 200 pitches, some of which have fine lake side views. Elide and Edoardo, who both speak English, have built their site on flat ground with the bar/restaurant facilities to the southern side, again with lake views. The rustic restaurant shares a building with the very small shop. There is one covered and one terraced area where you can sample the pizzas or the daily dish on offer. The lake panorama is very pleasant. You can swim in the pool or from the two 'beaches' on the lake which both have grass areas for sunbathing. Boats and windsurfers can be launched (no powered vessels). You are 40 km. from Rome and the site provides a bus (extra charge) to travel to Piazzale Flaminio in the city centre. There are regular excursions to local areas of interest.

Facilities: Two toilet blocks of traditional construction have some British type WCs. Showers, washbasins and dishwashing sinks have free hot and cold water (two new luxury units planned for 2002). Facilities for disabled visitors. Washing machine. Gas supplies. Bar/pizzeria (all season). Small shop. Swimming pool and small paddling pool (caps compulsory). Table tennis. Beach handball. Play area. Water-sports. Canoes-kayaks. Games room. Boule. Animation for children in high season. Excursions possible. Torches required in some areas. Dogs are accepted but not allowed on beach areas.

Charges 2002

Per person	€ 4.13 - € 6.19
child (3-10 yrs)	€ 3.10 - € 4.64
caravan	€ 5.16 - € 6.71
tent	€ 4.13 - € 6.71
car	€ 2.06 - € 3.10
motorcaravan	€ 5.16 - € 6.71
dog	€ 2.60 - € 3.60

Tel: 0699 805458. **Fax:** 0699 809350. **E-mail:** info@ romaflash.it. **Reservations:** Contact site. **Open** 1 April - 30 September.

Directions: From E35/E45 north of Rome, take Settebagni exit. Follow GRU (Rome's equlvalent of the M25) west to Cassia exit. Follow sign for Lago Bracciana to town of Bracciano. Site is well signed from town.

Camping Seven Hills

6810 Via Cassia 1216, 00191 Roma (Lázio)

If you are looking for a very lively site with many young people, which tends towards the impersonal then Seven Hills may be for you. It is situated in a delightful valley, flanked by two of the seven hills of Rome and is just off the autostrada ring road to the north of the city (4 km. from the city centre - the site runs a bus service with a frequency dictated by demand; extra charge). Arranged in two sections, the top half, near the entrance, restaurant and shop, consists of small, flat, grass terraces with two to four pitches on each, with smaller terraces for tents. Access to some pitches may be tricky. The flat section at the lower part of the site is reserved mainly for ready erected tents used by international tour operators who bring guests by coach. These tend to be younger people and the site, along with its very busy pool, has a distinctly youthful feel. Consequently there may be a little extra noise. The site is a profusion of colour with flowering trees, plants and shrubs and a good covering of trees provide shade. The 80 pitches for tourers (3A electricity to some) are not marked, but the management supervise in busy periods. English is spoken and many notices are in English. All cash transactions on the site are made with a metal tag on a necklace from reception and there is a tight regime of passes and indelible ink wrist stamping at the pool (disco music, no paddling pool and an extra charge). This is an extremely busy and bustling site with up to 15 touring buses with their occupants on the site during high season, in addition to a very busy camping routine. There are bungalows, chalets and cabins to hire, all of varying standards adding to the large number of people and the feeling of constant changeover, also some may find the pools a little crowded in summer.

Facilities: Three soundly constructed sanitary blocks are well situated around the site, with open plan washbasins, and hot water in the average sized showers. Dishwashing under cover with cold water. Facilities for disabled campers. Washing machines and irons. Well stocked shop. Bar/restaurant and terrace. Money exchange. Table tennis. Volleyball. Swimming pool at the bottom of the site with bar/snack bar and a room where the younger element tends to congregate. Disco. **Off site:** Golf (good course) 4 km. Bus service to Rome. Excursions and cruises arranged. Internet. Torches required in some areas.

Charges 2002

Per person (over 4 yrs)	€ 7.23
caravan	€ 7.75
tent	€ 4.39
car	€ 3.62
motorcycle	€ 2.07
motorcaravan	€ 7.75

No credit cards. **Tel:** 0630 310826. Fax: 0630 310039. E-mail: seven_hills@camping.it. **Reservations:** Write to site. **Open** all year.

Directions: Take exit 3 from the autostrada ring-road on to Via Cassia (signed SS2 Viterbo - NOT Via Cassia Bis) and look for camp signs. Turn right after 1 km (13 km. stone) and follow small road for about 1 km. to site.

6809 Camping Tiber

Via Tiberina km. 1,400, 00188 Roma (Prima Porta)

Recommended by our agent – this site will be inspected in 2003.

An excellent, quiet site, Camping Tiber is ideally located for visiting Rome with an easy train service and a good bus service. There are 300 tourist pitches, part shaded, with 3/6A electricity and some 100 bungalows to rent. Fully equipped sanitary facilities include a washing machine. There is a drive-over motorhome service point. Shop, bar, restaurant and takeaway. An outdoor pool is open June to Sept. (caps said to be essential).

Charges 2002

Per adult	€ 8.78
child (3-12 yrs)	€ 6.71
car	€ 4.39
caravan	€ 6.20
tent	€ 5.68
motorhome	€ 10.07

Tel: 06/33610733 Fax. 06/33612314 E-mail info@ campingtiber.com. **Reservations:** Contact site. **Open** 15 March - 31 October.

Directions: From Florence, exit at Rome Nord Fiano on A1 and immediately turn south onto Via Tibernia and site is signed. From other directions on Rome ring road take exit 6 northbound on S3 Via Flaminia.

See advertisement opposite

Camping Porticciolo

6813 Via Porticciolo, 00062 Bracciano (Lázio)

This small family run site, useful for visiting Rome, has its own private beach on the southwest side of Lake Bracciano. The owners and his wife are charming and speak English. Alessandro is a Roman classical history expert. The site is over-looked by the impressive castle in the village of Bracciano. There are 170 pitches (150 for tourers) split into two sections, some with lake views and 120 having elec-tricity (6/15A). Pitches are large and shaded by very green trees which are continuously watered in summer. The friendly bar has two large terraces, shared by the trattoria which opens lunch-times and the pizzeria with its wood fired oven in the evenings. A small amount of entertain-ment is offered during the season and the lake is clean for swimming with power-boats banned. As an uncomplicated, lake-side site away from the heat and hassle of the city, it is ideal.

Facilities: Two somewhat rustic, but clean, sanitary units are usefully placed, one on each side of the site. Hot showers (by token), laundry facilities and washing machines. Motorcaravan services. Shop (basics). Bar. Trattoria/pizzeria (1/6-5/9). Tennis. Five-a-side soccer. Small play area. Table tennis. Volleyball. Fishing. Gas supplies. Tourist information (from computer terminal by reception). Internet point. Torches required in some areas. **Off site:** Riding 2 km. Bus service from outside the gate runs to central Rome. Air conditioned train service from Bracciano (1.5 km) into the city and the site runs a morning connecting bus

Charges 2002

Per person	€ 4.13 - € 5.50
child (3-10 yrs)	€ 3.36 - € 4.50
pitch and car	€ 5.73 - € 9.20

Tel: 06 99803060. Fax: 06 99803030. E-mail: romalake@libero.it. **Reservations:** Write to site. **Open** 1 April - 30 September.

Directions: From Rome ring road (GRA) northwest side take Cassia exit to Bracciano S493 (be careful not to confuse this exit with 'Cassia bis' which is further northeast). Follow signs to village of Bracciano on southwest shore of Lago di Bracciano and site is clearly signed.

Camping Flaminio

6814 Via Flaminia 821, 00191 Roma (Lázio)

We were impressed with Camping Flaminio - it is ideally situated for visiting 'the Eternal City'. An attractive, quite large campsite with some shade, it is on ground which is sloping in parts. It is located about 400 metres up a lane leading off the main road, which results in its being surprisingly quiet. There is a regular bus/underground service into the centre of Rome from outside the site entrance, which operates until late evening. It is a site for those with culture in mind and the nearest antiquities, etc.are only 500 m. away. There is limited space allocated to touring units, but the majority of these pitches are of average size, have electrical connections (3/6A) and are approached by brick access roads. There are also some 80 well-equipped bungalows.

Facilities: The sanitary facilities are currently housed in somewhat ancient blocks, but a new block is planned for the 2003 season. Bar-pizzeria and restaurant. Shop. Swimming pool and solarium (15/6-5/9 charged for in peak season). Fitness centre. Play area. **Off site:** The Vatican City, shops, supermarket, service station, bank and access to cycle route alongside river into the City. Buses and trains outside the gate.

Charges 2002

per person	€ 8,50 - € 9,50
child (under 12 yrs)	€ 6,00 - € 7,00
caravan or camper	€ 10,50 - € 12,00

Tel: 06 333 2604. Fax: 06 333 0653. E-mail: info@villageflaminio.com. **Reservations:** Contact site. **Open** all year.

Directions: From the ring road due north of the city take the Via Flaminia exit (6) south towards the city centre, and after 3 km. bear left to avoid tunnel - site is 150 m. on the right after tunnel entrance.

Holiday Village
6815 Via Flacca Km 6,800, 04020 Salto di Fondi (Lázio)

This is a picturesque seaside site with unusual cultural activity, midway between Rome and Naples. Set in a pinewood area, the carefully tended flowers and trees and the white painted buildings make it a very pleasant location. The facilities are on a natural raised area between the beach and the tourers area. During high season there are cultural and sporting activities, for example, ballet dancers, and plays, shows and films staged on one of the open-air stages. As well as the beach, there are two pools. The 100 large pitches for tourists are at the rear of the site under effective, but sombre, green shading, but close to the amenities. They are on flat grass, all with 3/5A electricity. The large beach is of fine sand (with lifeguard) and there is a pleasant grass promenade between the beach and the restaurant complex.

Facilities: One large and five smaller toilet blocks are of modern construction and have some British type WCs. Showers have hot water on payment, with cold water in washbasins and dishwashing sinks. Two family washrooms have hot water. Facilities for disabled visitors. Washing machines and dryers. Gas supplies. Bar/restaurant, pizzeria and snack bar (all June-Sept). Supermarket. Greengrocer. Boutique. Hairdresser. Swimming pools (instructor). Tennis. Table tennis. Handball. Disco. TV. Live theatre and ballet. Organised excursions to Rome, Capri, Naples, Pompei, Monte Cassino (with local agency). Doctor on site daily. Dogs and pets are not accepted. Torches required in some areas.

Charges 2002

Per pitch incl. 2 adults	€ 15.00 - € 46.00
extra person	€ 5.00 - € 14.00

No credit cards. **Tel:** 0771 555009. Fax: 0771 555029. E-mail: holidayvillage@tiscalinet.it. **Reservations:** Contact site. **Open** all year.

Directions: Site is well signed on coast road SS213 between Gaeta and Terracina, 7 km. south of Terracina. It is reached from the Rome - Naples autostrada, depending on approach, from several exits between Frosinone and Ceprana.

Camping Villaggio Baia Domizia
6820 81030 Baia Domizia (Campania)

This large well kept, seaside site is about 70 km. north west of Naples, and is within a pinewood, cleverly left in a natural state. There are 1,200 touring pitches in clearings, either of grass and sand, or on hardstanding, all with electricity (5A). Finding a pitch may take time, but staff help in season. The entire site is beautifully kept with shrubs, flowers and green areas. Most pitches are well shaded, but others near the beach are not. There is never very far to walk to the beach, though it may be some 300 m. to the central shops and restaurant. The central complex is superb with well designed buildings containing all your needs. Charges are high, but this site is well above average and most suitable for families with children.

Facilities: Seven good toilet blocks have hot water in washbasins (many cabins) and showers, and facilities for disabled people. Washing machines, spin dryers. Motorcaravan services. Gas supplies. Huge supermarket and general shop. Large bar and restaurants with pizzeria and takeaway. Sports ground. TV. Playground. Bicycle hire. Windsurfing hire and school. Disco. Church. Tennis. Excursions. Torches required in some areas. Barrier closed 14.00 -16.00 - no entry. Dogs are not accepted. **Off site:** Fishing or riding 3 km.

Charges 2002

Per person (12 yrs and over)	€ 4.10 - € 9.30
pitch and car	€ 9.80 - € 17.80

Electricity included. **Tel:** 0823 930164. Fax: 0823 930375. E-mail: baiadomizia@iol.it. **Reservations:** Not taken, but min. 1 week stay in high season (July/Aug). **Open** 1 May - 21 September.

Directions: Turn to Baia Domizia leads off Formia - Naples road 23 km. from Formia. From Rome - Naples autostrada, take Cassino exit to Formia. Site is to the north of Baia Domizia and well signed.

Camping Riposo
6835 Via Cassano 12 - 14, 80063 Piano di Sorrento (Campania)

Just 500 m. from the picturesque port of Piano di Sorrento is the tiny site of Camping Riposo. Simple, pretty and clean, this is only for those who just want a secluded place to park their unit whilst they explore this famous area. The Scalici family offer a courteous and helpful service. The site is shaded by citrus trees, there are electrical connections available and hot water is is free. Like most Italian sites, Riposo is very crowded in August.

Facilities: There are no entertainments and no pool - just a tiny bar and shop. Three excellent food shops nearby

Charges 2002

Per person	€ 4.65
child (1-6 yrs)	€3.10
pitch and car	€ 7.49 - € 9.29

Electricity and tax included. Less 10% for AR readers. **Tel:** 081 8787374. **Reservations:** Write to site. **Open** 1 June - 30 September.

Directions: From Meta follow plentiful directions off main road SS145 (to Sorrento from autostrada at Castellamare). Access could be tricky for large units but gates can be opened wide.

International Villagio I Pini

Corso Italia 242, 80063 Piano di Sorrento (Campania)

This pleasant shady site is just 3 km. before Sorrento centre and we have selected it because it is open all year and is conveniently situated for public services into Sorrento, Pompei or Naples. It also avoids taking caravans into the astonishing traffic chaos of Sorrento town. There are 130 touring pitches all contained by hedges. There is a free bus service to a pay beach in nearby Meta. Camping I Pini is owned and operated by the Maresca family. Signora Maresca is English and they all offer you a warm welcome.

Facilities: Two sanitary blocks (one closed in low season) provide hot and cold showers (hot water is free), dishwashing and laundry sinks, and facilities for disabled visitors. These facilities are to be upgraded. Bar/restaurant. Large supermarket 200 m. Good swimming pool (covered in winter). Play area. Free entertainment (Aug. only). Dogs are not accepted in July/August.

Charges 2002

Per person	€ 6.00 - € 9.00
caravan, motorcaravan or large tent	€ 6.00 - € 9.00
small tent	€ 4.00 - € 5.00
car	€ 3.00 - € 4.00

Electricity included. **Tel:** 081 8786891. E-mail: info@ campingipini.com. **Reservations:** Not usually necessary but write to site. **Open** all year.

Directions: From A3 Naples - Salerno motorway take Castellamare exit and SS145 Sorrento road. After 20 km, just past Meta town, look for large campsite sign on the right.

Camping Zeus

6830

via Villa dei Misteri, 80045 Pompei (Campania)

This site is just 50 m. from the entrance to the fantastic ruins at Pompei. It is a reasonably priced, city type site with no frills but it is perfect for visiting the famous archaeological sites here. After experiencing Pompei, if you wish to then see Herculaneum (we think it is amazing -the preservation is so much better) the train station is just outside the gate and it is just a 20 minute journey. The site's 80 pitches, all for tourers, are under mature trees which give shade. Pitching is informal with lines of trees dictating where large units park - ensure you liaise with other units so that you can get out in the morning! All are on flat grass, with 5A electricity and an energetic watering programme keeps the trees and grass green. It is worth noting that the ruins have limited disabled access.

Facilities: The single sanitary block is clean and modernised, with British and Turkish type WCs. Showers have hot water, with cold water in washbasins and dishwashing sinks. Facilities for disabled campers. Washing machines Gas supplies. Bar/restaurant with good value daily menu. Shop.

Charges 2002

Per unit incl. 2 persons	€ 16.00 - € 18.60

Tel: 081 8655320. Fax: 081 8508778. E-mail: campingzeus@libero.it. **Reservations:** Not taken. **Open** all year .

Directions: Leave Napoli -Salerno autostrada at Scavi di Pompei exit. Turn hard left at sign for Gran Camping Zeus. It is an uphill approach for approximately 200 m.

Camping Sant' Antonio

Via Marina d'Equa 21, Seiano, 80069 Vico Equense (Campania)

A base from which to explore Pompei, Herculaneum and Sorrento, this pretty little site, just across the road from Seiano beach, would suit caravanners who like a peaceful (for Italy) location. There are only 150 pitches which are in shade offered by orange, lemon and walnut trees. All pitches have electricity (5A) and access is easy on the flat ground. In summer (mid-June - end Sept) there is a regular 15 minute bus service to the Circumvesuviana railway which runs frequently to Sorrento, Pompei, Herculaneum and Naples - the only sensible way to travel for non-party sightseeing. English is spoken by the Maresca family who run the site.

Facilities: The single sanitary block provides hot and cold showers, washbasins and British style WCs. Hot water is on payment. Small shop, bar and restaurant. Dogs are not accepted in August. **Off site:** Fishing and boat slipway 100 m.

Charges 2002

Per person	€ 6.20 - € 7.23
child (up to 8 yrs)	€ 4.13 - € 5.68
pitch and car	€ 6.71 - € 10.33

Tel: 081 8028570. Fax: 081 8028570. **Reservations:** Contact site. **Open** 15 March - 30 October.

Directions: Take route SS163 from Castellamare to Sorrento. Just 50 m. after tunnel by-pass around Vico Equense, watch for very hard right turn for Seiano beach and follow signs down the narrow road.

Camping Villagio Athena

6853 Via Ponte di Ferro, 84063 Paestum (Campania)

This level site, which has direct access to the beach, has most facilities to hand. Much of the site is in woodland, but sun worshippers will have no problem here. The access is easy and the staff are friendly. There are 150 pitches, of which only 20 are used for static units and these are unobtrusive. There is no disco, although cabaret shows are staged in July/Aug. The management, the Prearo brothers, aim for a pleasant and happy environment.

Facilities: Toilet facilities in three blocks have mixed British and Turkish style WCs, washbasins and showers (cold water only) and hot showers on payment. Dishwashing and laundry sinks. Toilets for disabled people. Shop. Bar and restaurant (1/5-30/9). Riding. Watersports. Dogs and barbecues are not permitted. **Off site:** Tennis 1 km. Hourly bus service. Greek temples nearby.

Charges 2002

Per person	€ 4.65 - € 6.50
pitch incl. electricity	€ 8.50 - € 13.00

Tel: 0828 851105. Fax: 0828 851105. E-mail: vathena@tiscalinet.it. **Reservations:** Contact site. **Open** 1 March - 30 October.

Directions: Take SS18 through Paestum and, at southern end of town before the antiquities, turn right as signed and follow road straight down to sea. Site is well signed.

Sea World Village

6850 San Giorgio - Padiglione Nauti, ss Adriatica 78, 70126 Bari (Puglia)

There are few good sites in this southern part of Italy, but Sea World Village (formerly Camping Internazionale San Giorgio) is very acceptable as a transit stop or short stay. The new owners have considerably improved the site. Bari is a busy city, but Sea World Village is on the southern edge. There are 20 tourist pitches, all with electricity, well separated from the static pitches. Access to the sea is via rocks and concrete platforms, with a small swimming pool at the water's edge, plus a separate, man-made, sandy beach which is cleaned daily. The large car park and many changing cabins means the site is crowded at weekends with day visitors. There are a number of bungalows built in local style.

Facilities: The sanitary blocks are of modern construction with mainly British style toilets and free hot showers. Restaurant, pizzeria and market (all year). Bar (15/6-15/9). Swimming pool (15/6-15/9). Roller skating, hockey, football and tennis areas. Bowling. Disco. Watersports. Writing room. Doctor calls. **Off site:** Riding or golf 10 km. Fishing 5 km.

Charges 2002

Per person	€ 5.16 - € 7.75
pitch	€ 7.75 - € 10.33
small tent with car	€ 5.16 - € 8.26
electricity	€ 1.55

Tel: 0805 491175. Fax: 0805 491202. **Reservations:** Only made for site bungalows. **Open** all year.

Directions: Take Bari exit from autostrada A14 and follow signs for Brindisi on the dual carriageway ring road (Tangenziole). After exit 15 watch carefully for the San Giorge exit. Turn left and site is signed 200 m. ahead, across traffic lights.

Village Camping Marina di Rossano

6852 C. da Leuca, CP 363, 87068 Rossano (Calabria)

This is the most welcoming site we have visited in this southern area of Italy. Most of the staff in reception, the shops, bar and restaurant speak English with a smile. The location is not so far as it seems - it can be reached by either the west or east autostrada, without the final tortuous or very busy roads to some nearer coastal sites. It took us about two hours from Naples and it is about two hours from Bari. There are about 250 pitches, all under tall, shady poplar trees and cars are parked in a secure area away from the pitches. It is entirely secluded and leads directly to a large stretch of private beach. Very suitable for disabled people, their own facilities are provided. There are many apartments and bungalows on site. The site has an excellent swimming pool and sporting facilities.

Facilities: Several toilet blocks, mostly with free hot water, include facilities for disabled visitors. Shop. Bars. Restaurant. Swimming pools. All facilities open from 1 June. Private beach. Tennis. Small football pitch. Basketball. Volleyball. Bicycle hire.

Charges 2002

Per pitch	€ 15.49 - € 23.24
adult	€ 3.62 - € 6.46
child (3-4 yrs)	€ 2.32 - € 5.16
dog	gratis - € 4.65

Electricity included. **Tel:** 0983 516054. Fax: 0983 512690. E-mail: marina.club@tiscalinet.it. **Reservations:** Contact site. **Open** 1 April - 30 September.

Directions: From the north take the east coast highway (route 106 - Ionica). Leave at Rossano exit and a football stadium is immediately opposite with a site sign to its left. Follow signs for 1 km. to site. From the south, at Rossano exit turn left under road bridge. Turn left immediately before stadium.

6858 Camping Il Salice

C/da Ricota grande, I-87060 Corigliano Calabro (Calabria)

Recommended by our agent – this site will be inspected in 2003.

This a very well thought of campsite with its own private beach in the south of Italy. It is a region enjoying a warm climate all year round. The site has an extensive range of modern facilities including a restaurant, pizzeria, takeaway and bar, a shop, laundry and a heated toilet block. Windsurfing is possible and there is an outdoor pool, solarium, games room and tennis courts.

Charges 2002

Per adult	€ 2.00- € 10.00
child (3-6 yrs)	free - € 8.00
pitch	€ 3.00 - € 14.00
small tent	€ 1.50 - € 13.00
electricity (3-6A)	€ 2.00 - € 3.00

Tel: 0983 851 169 Fax: 0983 851147. E-mail: info@saliceevacanze.it. **Open** all year.

Directions: From A3 Salerno-Reggio Calibria auto strada take Sibari exit, followed by the SS 106 road towards Crotone - at Km 19 take the turn for Centro Vacanze Il Salice.

C.da Ricota Grande • I-87060 CORIGLIANO CALABRO (CS)
Tel. and Fax 0039/0983851147 • Tel. 0039/0983851169
Http: www.salicevacanze.it
E-mail: info@salicevacanze.it

CAMPING - BUNGALOW - RESIDENCE

The "Il Salice" holiday centre is situated in Calabria, directly on the Ionian Sea, where one can still admire a magnificent stretch of the coast. Here in the heart of the Magna Graecia, there are traces of the customs, traditions and artistic objects of the ancient peoples from this place. Nearby there are the magnificent peaks of Monte Pollino, with its National Park and the fabulous Sila Massif. This area is particularly suitable for stupendous tourist excursions. Among our services we offer the following: English and German speaking staff - medical assistance on request - organised activities - washing machine and dryer - swimming pool - free hire of bicycles in period A - all credit cards - supermarket - butcher - hairdresser.

For further information about prices visit our website.

CAMPING: Special rates for families a day fully furnished. Minimum stay 7 days.
Period A) 28.10.02/30.03.03 € 8,00
Period B) 01.04.03/16.05.03 - 27.09.03/25.10.03 € 10,00
Period C) 17.05.03/27.06.03 - 08.09.03/26.09.03 € 15,00

Italy - South
Centro Turistico San Nicola

71010 Peschici (Puglia)

This is a really splendid site occupying a hill-side position, sloping down to a cove with a 500 m. beach of fine sand - a special feature is an attractive grotto at the eastern end. Surrounded by tree clad mountains, it is a quiet, well regulated site which is part of, but separate from, a tourist holiday complex in the same area. Hard access roads lead to spacious well constructed, grassy terraces, under shade from mature trees. Scores of pitches are on the beach fringes (no extra charge) and there is a separate area for campers with animals. There are 750 pitches of varying size, all with 5A electricity. Cars may have to be parked away from the pitches in high season. There are some bungalows on site. With a neat, tidy appearance, many flowerbeds provide a garden atmosphere and the site prides itself in its tranquillity despite its size.The site is popular with German campers (tannoy announcements and most notices in German only) although English is spoken. It is fairly remote with some interesting hairpins in the last 14 km. of the 75 km. journey from the autostrada. However, we think it is well worth the drive if you enjoy high quality beach sites and wish to explore the Gargano National Park.

Facilities: Six excellent, modern toilet blocks, two in the beach part, the others situated around the site, are of superb quality with British and Turkish style toilets, hot water in the washbasins (some with toilets in private cabins), showers and dishwashing facilities. Washing machines and dryers. Supermarket, fruit and fish shops, bazaar (all high season). Two beach bars (from 1 May). Large bar/restaurant with terraces and separate pizzeria (all season). Tennis. Watersports. Children's playground. Organised activities and entertainment for young and old (July/Aug). Coach and boat excursions.

Charges 2002

Per adult	€ 3.62 - € 7.64
child (1-8 yrs)	€ 2.48 - € 5.42
caravan or trailer tent	€ 4.65 - € 9.30
tent	€ 3.62 - € 7.49
car	€ 2.74 - € 4.65
motorcaravan	€ 6.51 - € 11.36

Tel: 0884 964024. Fax: 0884 964025. **Reservations:** Only made for site's own accommodation (min. 1 week). **Open** 1 April - 15 October.

Directions: Leave autostrada A14 at exit for Poggio Imperiale, and proceed towards Peschici and Vieste. When signs for Peschici and Vieste diverge, follow Vieste signs keeping a sharp look-out for San Nicola. Then follow black signs for Centro Turistico San Nicola and pass Camping Baia San Nicola (on your left) just before site. It will take at least 1.5 hrs from the motorway. Note: There is also a San Nicola Varano en-route which must be ignored.

6845

6848 Punta Lunga Camping Village

Localita defensola C.P.339, 71019 Vieste (Puglia)

Recommended by our agent – this site will be inspected in 2003.

This is a well organised coastal site in the heart of the Gargano National Park, which is an attractive region with pretty villages and warm waters. The on-site facilities include restaurant, pizzeria, takeaway, creperie, bar, shop, laundry and games room. There is a disco and entertainment is organised, also windsurfing. The swimming pool is charged for (€ 3) from 15 June - 14 Sept. Pets are not accepted.

Charges 2002

Per adult	€ 3.50 - € 9.25
child (2-12 yrs)	€ 2.30 - € 6.00
pitch	€ 3.70 - € 11.00
electricity	€ 1.50 - € 2.00

Tel: 0884 706031. Fax: 0884 706910. E-mail: puntalunga@puntalunga.com. **Open** 19 April - 19 October. **Reservations:** not made.

Directions: From the north take A14 exit for Poggio Imperiale, then to Vico Gargancio and Vieste. From the south take A14 exit Foggia, then towards Manfrendonia, Mattinata and Vieste.

Loc. Defensola • C.P. 339
I-71019 Vieste del Gargano (FG)
Tel. +39/0884706031
      +39/0884706032
Fax +39/0884706910
E-mail: puntalunga@puntalunga.com
www.puntalunga.com
www.puntalunga.it

VILLAGGIO CAMPING
★★★

Open until
20th October 2003

Modern campsite in an enchanting position, quiet, directly on the sea and on a limpid sandy bay, thickly wooded with pine, eucalyptus and acacia trees. Comfortable one and two room bungalows, with bathroom and kitchen. Washing machines with coins. Restaurant and pizzeria; beach and cellar bar; supermarket, tobacconist, Italian and foreign newspapers; medical assistance and infirmary; organised evening activities and sport; hire of mountain bikes; beach service, windsurfing and sailing school, spare parts and repairs for windsurfing and sailing equipment; fitness, wakeboard, kitesurfing: trips and excursions over the Gargano area.

6856 Camping Pineta al Mare

72012 Specchiolla di Carovigno (Brindisi)

Recommended by our agent – this site will be inspected in 2003.

Situated in the middle of a pine forest, and only about 300 metres from the beach, this is an attractive site with 200 pitches. It is close to the town and port of Brindisi and, for those en-route to Greece, it makes an excellent stop-over, especially as there are special ferry deals available. Facilities include a restaurant, pizzeria, bar and takeaway, and there is a shop and laundry, an outdoor swimming pool (with slide), tennis court, canoe hire, etc. Lots of attractions are within a range of 25 km.

Charges 2002

Per adult	€ 4.90 - € 6.70
child (2-8 yrs)	€ 3.60 - € 4.60
pitch	€ 4.20 - € 7.70

Tel: 0831 987 821. E-mail: info@campingpineta-mare.com. **Open** 1 March - 30 November.

Directions: From the Bari-Brindisi autostrada, take Specchiolla exit, approx. 20 km. from Brindisi.

6865 Camping Riva di Ugento

Litorania Gallipoli - S. Maria di Leuca, 73059 Ugento (LE)

Recommended by our agent – this site will be inspected in 2003.

Set on the coast of the warm Ionian Sea at Ugento, this is a large (1,000 pitch) site for 'enjoying the outdoors'. It has a good range of amenities including an outdoor swimming pool, games room, tennis court and minigolf, and there are canoes for hire and windsurfing. Facilities include a restaurant, pizzeria, bar and takeaway, a shop, laundry and heated toilet block.

Charges
Contact site.

Tel: 0833 933600. E-mail: rivadiugento@rivadiugento.it. **Open** 15 March - 30 September.

Directions: From Bari take the Brindisi road to Lecce, then route 101 to Gallipoli, followed by the SR274 towards S.Maria de Leuca, and exit at Ugento.

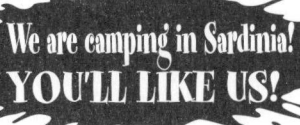

Sardegna

...APULCO ★★★
...U-PUNTA PALAU (SS) - Tel. 0789 709 497

CAPO D'ORSO ★★★
PALAU - GOLFO DELLE SALINE (SS) - Tel. 0789 702 007

ISOLA DEI GABBIANI ★★★
PALAU - PORTO POLLO (SS) - Tel. 0789 704 024 / 19

BAIA SARACENO ★★★
PALAU - PUNTA NERA (SS) - Tel. 0789 709 403

ISULEDDA ★★★★
CANNIGIONE - ARZACHENA (SS) - Tel. 078 986 003-86012

CUGNANA-PORTO ROTONDO ★★★
OLBIA - LOC. CUGNANA (SS) - Tel. 078 933 184

TAVOLARA ★★★
PORTO S. PAOLO (SS) -SS. 125 Km 300+300 Tel. 078 940 166

SAN TEODORO LA CINTA ★★★
SAN TEODORO (NU) - Tel. 0784 865 777

PEDRA E CUPA ★★★
BUDONI (NU) - Tel. 0784 844 004

SELEMA ★★★
S. Lucia di Siniscola (NU) - Tel. 0784 819068

LE CERNIE ★★★
Case Sparse - Lotzorai (NU) - Tel. 0782 669 472

SOS FLORES ★★★
TORTOLI - SAN GEMILIANO (NU) - Tel. 0782 667 485

ORRI' ★★★
TORTOLI - LOC. ORRI' (NU) - Tel. 0782 624 695

PORTO CORALLO ★★
VILLAPUTZU (CA) - Tel. 070 997 017

LE DUNE ★★★
Loc. Piscina Rei - Muravera (CA) -Tel. 0709 919 057

SPIAGGIA DEL RISO ★★★
VILLASIMIUS - CAMPOLONGU (CA) - Tel. 070 797 150

CAPO FERRATO ★★
Loc. Costa Rei - Muravera (CA) -Tel. 070 885653

MENDOSA ★★
...ARGHERITA PULA (CA) - SS 195 Km 33.800- Tel. 0709 208 364

GARDEN CALA SINZIAS ★★★
CASTIADAS - CALA SINZIAS (CA) - Tel. 070 995 037

Internet: www.faitasardegna.it - **e-mail:** faitasarda@foce.it

FAITA SARDEGNA
CAMPING & BUNGALOWS

Italy - Sardinia
Camping Capo d'Orso

6860 Loc Saline, Palau, 07020 Sardegna

Capo d'Orso is some 4.5 km. from the village of Palau on the northern edge of the Costa Smerelda in northern Sardinia. It is a well established and decidedly pretty site on a hillside sloping down to the sea, facing Caprera Island and several beaches. The terrain is fairly rocky but the 450 pitches are on level, sparsely grassed terraces, with quite good access roads. Most have 3A electricity and are of a fair size (40-80 sq.m). Cars are parked away from the pitches in July/Aug. This side of the island seems generally to be hotter and more sheltered from the wind, but there is not a lot of shade. This site could be a useful alternative to our other site on Sardinia, being somewhat cheaper, smaller and less formally organised, but with significantly less shade.

Facilities: Toilet facilities, in three blocks, are adequate, including hot showers (on payment in season, free at other times), washbasins, dishwashing and laundry sinks (cold water) and mainly Turkish, but with some British, type WCs. When seen in early June facilities were well maintained although not all the blocks are open at that time. Shop. Bar/restaurant. Pizzeria. Takeaway (all from 1/6). Scuba diving, windsurfing, sailing school, boat excursions, boat hire and moorings (all main season). Tennis. Underground disco. Entertainment programmes for children and adults. Excursions arranged in high season.

Charges 2002

Per adult	€ 6.20
child (6-12 yrs)	€ 5.16
large tent or caravan	€ 5.16 - € 18.08
car or motorcycle	gratis - € 3.10
motorcaravan	€ 5.16 - € 21.17
electricity	€ 2.07

Tel: 0789 702007. **Fax:** 0789 702006. **E-mail:** info@capodorso.it. **Reservations:** Contact site. **Open** 1 May - 30 September.

Directions: Site is 5 km. from Palau, in the northeast of Sardinia, on the coast opposite (southwest of) Caprera Island.

Italy - Sardinia
Camping Baia Blu La Tortuga

6855 Pineta di Vignola Mare, Aglientu, 07020 Sardegna

La Tortuga is a large site situated on a bay of startling blue sea and golden sand, in one of the nicest corners of this island, enjoying welcome breezes and convenient for the ferry at St Teresa di Gallura (for Corsica). The site is under the same ownership as Marepineta (no. 6000) and has excellent facilities including some of the most modern sanitary installations we have seen. The 800 pitches (550 for touring units) all have electricity connections (3A) and are arranged in rows between tall pines, eucalyptus and shrubs with good access avenues and plenty of shade. Catering facilities include an attractive restaurant, pizzeria and takeaway and a small, pleasant bar. A large site, there is direct access to the beach and an extensive range of amenities, both on site and nearby. Used by tour operators.

Facilities: Four blocks of a similarly unusual design provide an exceptionally good ratio of facilities to pitches including combined private shower/wash-basin cabins (for rent), free hot showers and mixed British and Turkish toilets. Numerous footbaths, basins for children, sinks for dishes and laundry (hot water: am. clothes, pm. dishes) and facilities for disabled people. Washing machines, dryers and irons. Motorcaravan services. Gas supplies. Bar. Restaurant, pizzeria, snack bar and takeaway (May-Sept). Supermarket. Children's playground. Tennis. Volleyball. Football. Table tennis. Games and TV rooms. Windsurfing school. Facilities and school for divers. Entertainment and sports activities organised in season. Excursions. Barbecue area (not permitted on pitches). **Off site:** Disco 50 m. Riding 5 km.

Charges 2002

Per person	€ 4.20 - € 9.60
junior (4-10 yrs) or	
senior (over 60 yrs)	€ 3.10 - € 7.30
pitch incl. electricity	€ 8.30 - € 21.20
tent pitch incl. electricity	€ 6.70 - € 13.40
dog	€ 1.00 - € 4.65

Tel: 079 602060. **Fax:** 079 602040. **E-mail:** info@baiablu.com. **Reservations:** Made with 30% deposit and € 15,50 fee. **Open** 12 April - 28 September.

Directions: Site is on the north coast between towns of Costa Paradiso and S. Teresa di Gallura (18 km.) at Pineta di Vignola Mare.

Luxembourg

Luxembourg Tourist Office, 122, Regent Street, London W1R 5FE Tel: 020 7434 2800
Fax: 020 7734 1205   E-mail: tourism@luxembourg.co.uk   www.luxembourg.co.uk

The Grand Duchy of Luxembourg is an independent sovereign state, 999 square miles in area lying between Belgium, France and Germany. Geographically, the Grand Duchy is divided into two sections: in the north the uplands of the Ardennes, a hilly and scenic region, in the south mainly rolling farmlands and woods, bordered on the east by the wine growing area of the Moselle Valley. Luxembourg City is one of the most spectacularly sited capitals in Europe and home to about one fifth of the population.

Population
389,800; density 151 per sq. km.

Capital
Luxembourg City.

Climate
A temperate climate prevails, the summer often extending from May to late October.

Language
Letzeburgesch is the national language, with French and German also being official languages.

Currency
From January 2002, in common with 11 other European countries, the Luxembourg unit of currency is the EURO (€).
€ 1 = Lux. Franc 40.34.

Banks
Open 08.30/09.00-12.00 and 13.30-16.30.
Credit Cards: are widely accepted.

Post Offices
Open 08.00-12.00 and 14.00-17.00 (but those in villages often operate more restricted hours).

Time
GMT plus 1 (summer BST +1).

Telephone
For calls from Luxembourg to the UK the code is 0044 followed by the STD code omitting initial 0. To call Luxembourg from the UK the code is 00 352 followed by the number (no area codes).

Public Holidays
New Year; Carnival Day, mid-Feb; Easter Mon; May Day; Ascension; Whit Mon; National Day, 23 June; Assumption, 15 Aug; All Saints; All Souls; Christmas, 25, 26 Dec.

Shops
Open Mon 14.00-18.30. Tues to Sat 08.30-12.00 and 14.00-18.30, (grocers and butchers close at 15.00 on Sat).

Motoring
Speed Limits: Caravans and motorhomes (3.5 tons) 31 mph (50 kph) in built up areas, caravans 46 mph (75 kph) and 56 mph (90 kph) on other roads and motor-ways respectively, motorhomes 56 mph (90 kph) and 75 mph (120 kph).
Fuel: Visa and Eurocard are accepted.
Parking: A Blue Zone area exists in Luxembourg City (discs from tourist offices) but parking meters are also used.

The Alan Rogers' Travel Service

We have recently extended The Alan Rogers Travel Service. This unique service enables our readers to reserve their holidays as well as ferry crossings and comprehensive insurance cover at extremely competitive rates. The majority of participating sites are in France and we are able to offer a selection of some of the very best sites in this country.

One simple telephone call to our Travel Service on 01892 55 98 98 is all that is needed to make all the arrangements. Why not take advantage of our years' of experience of camping and caravanning. We would be delighted to discuss your holiday plans with you, and offer advice and recommendations.

Share our experience and let us help to ensure that your holiday will be a complete success.

Alan Rogers Travel Service 01892 55 98 98 or www.alanrogers.com

Luxembourg
Camping des Ardennes
767 L-9809 Hosingen

A good value, small municipal site, Camping Ardennes is located on the edge of this attractive small town with an easy level walk to all amenities and parks and some floral arrangements to admire during the summer season. The 48 touring pitches are level, open and grassy. All have electricity (10A) and are arranged on either side of surfaced roads, with a few trees providing a little shade in places. Adjacent sports complex with tennis and football, etc. This site is useful as a stopover if travelling along the N7.

Facilities: The single well appointed, modern, clean sanitary block can be heated in winter includes separate men's and women's facilities. Facilities for dishwashing and laundry, with a washing machine, dryer and clothes lines. Café/bar (opening variable). Barbecue. Playground. Volleyball. Boule. Skis and winter sports equipment for hire. English spoken. Rooms for rent (B&B).

Charges 2002

Per pitch	€ 4.50
adult	€ 4.50
child (3-12 yrs)	€ 2.25
electricity	€ 2.25
dog	€ 2.25
local taxes	€ 0.25

Tel: 921 911. Fax: 929 896. E-mail: gaalcamp.pt.lu. **Reservations:** Write to site (no deposit). **Open** all year.

Directions: Site is off the main N7 road north of Diekirch and is signed from the centre of the town, with the sports complex.

Luxembourg
Camping de la Sûre
765 23 route de la Sûre, L-9390 Reisdorf

Camping de la Süre, on the banks of the river that separates Luxembourg and Germany, is a pleasant site close to Reisdorf. The 180 numbered pitches (120 with 10A electricity) are not separated but are marked with trees that provide some shade. There are caravan holiday homes in a fenced area towards the back of the site, leaving the prime pitches for tourists. Visitors should be aware that, due to long-term improvement plans, building work is on-going on the site.

Facilities: Modern, clean sanitary facilities recently refitted and extended, including some washbasins in cubicles. Laundry. Small shop. Café/bar. Takeaway. Playground. Minigolf. Sports field. Canoeing. Fishing. **Off site:** Town centre within easy walking distance, and cycle ways abound. Bicycle hire 200 m, golf 8 km.

Charges 2002

Per pitch	€ 5.50
adult	€ 5.00
child (under 14 yrs)	€ 2.50
electricity	€ 2.50
dog	€ 2.50

Discounts for long stays and off season. **Tel:** 836 246. Fax: 869 237. E-mail: ren2@pt.lu. **Reservations:** Write to site for details. **Open** 1 April - 30 October.

Directions: From the river bridge in Reisdorf, take the road to Echternach, de la Sûre is the second campsite on the left.

Luxembourg
Camping Kalkesdelt
791 chemin du Camping, L-9022 Ettelbruck

This agreeable, good value municipal site is situated on a hilltop overlooking the town. It is quietly located about 1 km. from the centre of Ettelbruck, with a nice atmosphere and well tended gardens and grass. The modern main building includes reception and a 'salle de séjour' (with library and TV). The 160 marked pitches are accessed from tarmac roadways and have electricity available (16A). Reception has good tourist information and English is spoken.

Facilities: A new sanitary unit using solar energy provides washbasins in cabins and a room for disabled people. Laundry. Motorcaravan services. Gas supplies. Restaurant. Snack bar and takeaway open evenings. Breakfasts can also be served. A baker calls daily at 7.30 am. (order day before). Bicycle hire. Playground. Table tennis. Entertainment in season.

Charges 2002

Per pitch	€ 4.00
adult	€ 3.00
child (3-14 yrs)	€ 1.80
electricity	€ 2.00

Plus local tax. No credit cards. **Tel:** 812 185. Fax: 813 186. E-mail: tstrijbos@internet.lu. **Reservations:** Write to site for details. **Open** 1 April - 31 October.

Directions: Site is signed on the western outskirts of Ettelbruck off the N15 and approached via a short one-way system.

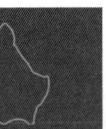

Luxembourg
Camping Trois Frontières
Maison 1, L-9972 Lieler

On a clear day, it's possible to see Belgium, Germany and Luxembourg from the campsite swimming pool, hence its name: Les Trois Frontières. Martin and Esther Van Aalst own and manage the site themselves and all visitors receive a personal welcome and immediately become part of a large happy family. Most of the facilities are close to the entrance, leaving the camping area quiet, except for the children's play area. The restaurant/ takeaway provides good quality food at reasonable prices, served either inside or on the pleasant terrace with flower borders and overlooking the pool. The pool, paddling pool and grass sunbathing area with recliners are screened by an ornamental balastrade. There is no shop, however, Martin and Esther sell basic provisions such as bread, milk, and newspapers.

Facilities: Unisex facilities include excellent showers, washbasins in cabins, British-style WCs, suite for visitors with disabilities, plus baby bath and changing station. More WCs in second building (down some steps). Dishwashing sinks. Laundry. Children's play area. Boules pitch, table tennis, games room, table football, table tennis, darts. Bicycle hire. **Off site:** Shops 2.3 km. Golf and riding 12 km. Clervaux 12 km, walking and cycling.

Charges 2002

Per pitch incl. 2 persons	€ 15.15 - € 17.50
extra adult	€ 5.10 - € 5.60
child (under 12 yrs)	€ 2.60 - € 3.10
electricity (4A)	€ 2.25
pet	€ 1.90

Reduction during low season for visitors over 55 yrs. **Tel:** 998 608. Fax: 979 184. E-mail: camp.3front@ cmdnet.lu. **Reservations:** Contact site. **Open** all year.

Directions: Take N7 northward from Dieker. Continue past Weiswampach, then turn right onto CR338 signed Lieler. Site is on right as you enter the village.

Luxembourg
Europacamping Nommerlayen
L-7465 Nommern

This is a top quality site, in central Luxembourg, with fees to match, but it has everything! A large, central building housing most of the services and amenities opens onto a terrace around an excellent swimming pool complex with two main pools and an imaginative watery playground. The 396 individual pitches (70-120 sq.m.) on grassy terraces, all have access to electricity (2/16A) and water taps. There is little shade on the newer open, grassy section - this is a deliberate policy so as not to obscure the views over the surrounding countryside. Interestingly enough the superb new sanitary block is called 'Badtemple' (it`s architecture suggesting this title as the entrance with colonnades supporting a canopy is reminiscent of a Greek temple). To gain entry to the sauna and to obtain hot water for washbasins, showers and sinks, one pays to have a cash equivalent charged into a plastic block which is inserted into a slot.

Facilities: A large, high quality, modern sanitary unit provides some washbasins cubicles, facilities for disabled people, and family and baby washrooms. The new block includes all the usual features, with special rooms for children and disabled visitors, plus a sauna. Laundry. Motorcaravan service point. Supermarket (Easter - 1/11). Restaurant. Snack bar. Bar. Swimming pools (1/5-1/11). Solarium. Fitness programmes. Bowling. Table tennis. Snooker. Billiards. Volleyball. Football. Children`s playground. Large screen TV. Entertainment in season. Bicycle hire. Bottle bank. **Off site:** Riding 1 km. Fishing and golf 5 km

Charges 2002

Per unit incl. 2 persons and 2A electricity, acc. to pitch and facilities	€ 17.00 - € 30.00
extra adult	€ 4.00
child (under 18 yrs)	€ 3.50
dog	€ 2.50
electricity (16A) plus	€ 3.00

Tel: 878 078. Fax: 879 678. E-mail: nommerlayen@ vo.lu. **Reservations:** Essential for high season only, with deposit. **Open** all year except 15 Dec. - 15 Jan.

Directions: Site is 5 km. from Larochette, on the west side of Nommern village.

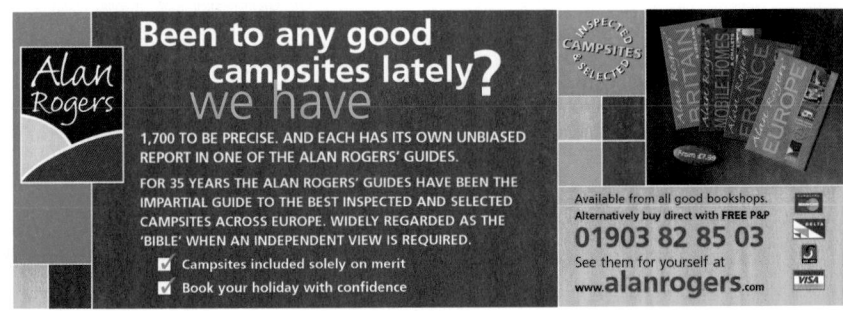

Luxembourg
Camping Auf Kengert

764 L-7633 Larochette / Medernach

A friendly welcome awaits you at this peacefully situated, family run site, 2 km. from Larochette, northeast of Luxembourg city, providing 180 individual pitches, all with electricity (4/16A). Some in a very shaded woodland setting, on a slight slope with fairly narrow access roads. There are also six hardened pitches for motorcaravans on a flat area of grass, complete with motorcaravan service facilities (space really only suitable for four motorhomes). Further pitches are in an adjacent and more open meadow area. There are also six site owned chalets and caravans. This site is popular in season, so early arrival is advisable, or you can reserve.

Facilities: The well maintained sanitary block in two parts includes a modern, heated unit with some washbasins in cubicles, and excellent, fully equipped cubicles for disabled visitors. The showers, facilities for babies, additional WCs and washbasins, plus laundry room are located below the central building which houses the shop, bar.and restaurant. Motorcaravan services. Gas supplies. Playground and indoor play room. Swimming pool (Easter - 30 Sept). Paddling pool. Open area for ball games. Fishing. Bicycle hire. **Off site:** Golf, fishing and riding 8 km.

Charges 2002

Per person	€ 10.00 - € 12.00
child (4-18 yrs)	€ 4.00 - € 6.00
electricity	€ 2.00
dog	€ 1.25

10% reduction for students, walkers and cyclists.
Tel: 837186. Fax: 878 323. E-mail: info@kengert.lu.
Reservations: Write to site. **Open** 1 March - 8 November.

Directions: From Larochette take the CR118/N8 (towards Mersch) and just outside town turn right on CR119 towards Schrondweiler, site is 2 km. on the right.

Moien ! *(which means hello in Luxembourg language)*

We would like to welcome you to our family run site, peacefully set in a splendid nature. We think it is ideal for overnight stops or longer stays, perfectly situated on your way South or East.
Our policy is to provide full service whole year round.
You may enjoy our solar-energy heated pool, our fine restaurant with real log-fire and our large supermarket. We can provide calor and other gas as well as unleaded petrol. For your laundry there are washing machines and dryers. New: indoor playground.

We look forward to meeting you in Luxembourg !

Camping Auf Kengert

L-7633 Larochette/Medernach   Grand Duché de Luxembourg
Tel. +352-837186   fax +352-878323
www.kengert.lu   e-mail: info@kengert.lu

Luxembourg
Camping Birkelt

761 1 rue de la Piscine, L-7601 Larochette

This is very much a family site, the price representing the range of facilities provided. It is well organised and well laid out, set in an elevated position in attractive undulating good walking countryside. A tarmac road runs around the site with 400 large grass pitches, some slightly sloping, many with a fair amount of shade, on either side of gravel access roads in straight rows or circles. All pitches have a 6A electric point. As well as the all weather swimming pool complex just outside the site entrance (free for campers), there is also a fitness centre with solarium and sauna. Entertainment is arranged in high season. The site is very popular with tour operators (140 pitches).

Facilities: Three modern sanitary buildings well situated around the site include mostly open washbasins (6 cabins in one block). Dishwashers (on payment), baby baths, facilities for wheelchair users. Washing machines and dryers. Motorcaravan service point. Shop. Restaurant with terrace. Children's playgrounds. All weather swimming pool. Outdoor pool for toddlers. Fitness centre). Table tennis. Roller blade skating, Minigolf. Tennis. Football ground. Riding. Balloon flights. **Off site:** Fishing 10 km. Golf 5 km. Bicycle hire 5 km. Kayak 10 km.

Charges 2003

Per unit incl. 2 persons	€ 26.00
extra person	€ 3.75
electricity	€ 2.50
dog	€ 2.50

Less 25% in low season. **Tel:** 879 040. Fax: 879 041.
E-mail: v.lux@pt.lu. **Reservations:** Write to site for reservation application form. **Open** 1 April - 31 October.

Directions: From N7 From N7 Diekirch - Luxembourg city, turn onto N8 at Berschblach (just past Mersch) towards Larochette. Site is signed on the right about 1.5 km. from Larochette. Approach road is fairly steep and narrow.

Camping Fuussekaul

785 4 Fussekaul, L-9156 Heiderscheid

Children who visit Fuusse Kaul (the name means fox hole) won't want to leave as there is so much for them to do. Apart from a fun pool, exciting play areas, and an entertainment programme, children and parents can bake their own pizzas in the open-air oven. Of the 530 pitches, 300 of varying sizes are for touring units, all with a 10A electricity connection. The touring area (separate from the chalets and seasonal pitches) is well endowed with modern facilities, although there is no provision for visitors with disabilities. An entertainment programme continues throughout the main holiday season and includes mini shows and theatre productions, and sports. On the opposite side of the road (pedestrian access via an under-road passage) is a service and parking area for six motorhomes. Each pitch has a hook-up, fresh water tap and waste water drain.

Facilities: Four excellent sanitary blocks provide showers (token € 0.50), washbasins (in cabins and communal) and children and baby rooms with small toilets, washbasins and showers. Laundry. Suite with sauna and sunbeds etc. Parking and service area for motorhomes. Well-stocked shop, bar, restaurant. Swimming pools, playgrounds, cross country skiing when snow permits. Bicycle hire. Motorhome hire. Children's club included in site fees. Oven for baking pizzas. **Off site:** Supermarket and shops in Ettelbruckk 7 km. Castles, museums and walks all within a reasonable distance. Bus stops outside site entrance. Fishing 3 km. Riding 500 m.

Charges 2002

Per unit incl. 2 persons	€ 13.50 - € 23.50
extra person	€ 2.00
electricity	€ 2.00
dog	€ 2.00

Tel: 268 8881. Fax: 268 88828. E-mail: info@ fuussekaul.lu. **Reservations:** Necessary in July and August with fee (€ 20). **Open** all year.

Directions: Take the N15 road from Deikirch to Heiderscheid. Site is on left at top of hill just before reaching the village. Motorhome service area is signed on the right.

A lovely holiday-park for young and old alike, situated in the Upper Sauer natural park. A favourite area with many footpaths across the wooded hills. A luxurious toilet building and sauna is at our guests' disposal all year round.

4, Fuussekaul, L-9156 Heiderscheid
Tel.: +352 –26 88 88-1
www.fuussekaul.lu nfo@fuussekaul.lu

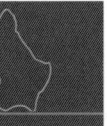

Naturistcamping de Reenert

N786 4 Fussekaul, L-9156 Heiderscheid

Lëtzeburger Naturistecamping de Reenert is located at Heiderscheid in the natural park of the Haute-Sûre. Visitors report to the reception at Camping Fuusse Kaul opposite, where they are given the code to enter the site. Pitches are large and flat, sanitary facilities are excellent. There's an outdoor heated swimming, children's play area, and a meeting room. An extensive entertainment programme including sports, games, body painting and many other activities is run during the high season. Visitors are welcome to use the bar, restaurant, sauna, tennis court and shop at Fuusse Kaul. Fresh bread is also baked daily at Fuusse Kaul.

Facilities: One modern and one 'portacabin' style unit provide excellent facilities, including one family and three low level showers. Heated outdoor swimming pool, play area. Entertainment /meeting room. Shop, bar, restaurant, sauna, tennis, bicycle hire at Fuusse Kaul. **Off site:** Supermarket and shops in Ettelbruckk 7 km. Bus stops outside entrance. Fishing 3 km. Riding 500 m.

Charges 2002

Per unit incl. 2 persons	€ 10.00 - € 17.50
extra person	€ 2.00
electricity	€ 2.00
dog	€ 2.00

Tel: 26 88 881. Fax: 26 88 8828. E-mail: info@ fuussekaul.lu. **Reservations:** Contact site. **Open** all year.

Directions: Take the N15 road from Deikirch to Heiderscheid. Site is on right at top of hill just before reaching the village - check in at Fuusse Kaul on the left.

Luxembourg
Camping de la Sûre
route de Gilsdorf, L-9234 Diekirch

The municipal Camping de la Sûre is within walking distance of the centre of Diekirch, a town that is brimming with things to see and do. Located on the banks of the Sûre, this site offers 175 flat grass pitches, most with a 16A electricity connection. One large building close to the entrance houses the reception and sanitary facilities, all of which were in pristine condition at the time of our visit. A walk/cycle path runs alongside the campsite; maps are available in the Syndicat d'Initiative in the town centre. Diekirch, with a donkey as its mascot, is a happy town and well worth a visit. A concert is held in the square every evening during the high season, there are free guided walks twice monthly during July and August, as well as a weekly entertainment programme for youngsters. Visitors to the campsite receive an information bag in their own language. There is an ongoing programme for improvements.

Facilities: One large building houses several heated rooms with modern facilities including showers and communal washbasins. Baby room and suite for visitors with disabilities. Laundry. Dishwashing. Children's play area. Children's entertainment organised during July and August. **Off site:** Diekirch has all leisure facilities within walking distance of campsite. Large park with skateboarding /bicycle ramps adjacent. Walk/cycle path along site boundary.

Charges 2002

Per adult	€ 4.70
child	€ 2.23
pitch	€ 3.72
dog	€ 0.74
electricity	€ 1.98

Tel: 80 9425. **Fax:** 80 2786. **E-mail:** tourisme@diekirch.lu. **Reservations:** Advisable in July and August, contact site. **Open** 1 April - 1 October.

Directions: Follow campsite signs from centre of Diekirch.

Luxembourg
Camping Kohnenhof
Maison 1, L-9838 Obereisenbach

Nestling in a valley with the River Our running through it, Camping Kohnenhof offers an agreeable location for a relaxing family holiday. From the minute you stop at the reception you are assured of a warm and friendly welcome. Numerous paths cross through the wooded hillside so this could be a haven for walkers. The river is shallow and safe for children to play in (parental supervision essential). The restaurant is part of an old farmhouse and, with its open fire to keep it warm, offers a wonderful ambiance to enjoy a meal. A large sports field and play area with a selection of equipment caters for younger campers. During the high season, an entertainment programme is organised for parent and children participation. Some campers may be quite a distance from the sanitary facilities, bar and restaurant which are grouped together near the site entrance. This site is not suitable for visitors with walking disabilities.

Facilities: Heated sanitary block with showers and washbasins in cabins. Motorhome service point. Laundry. Bar, restaurant, takeaway. Games and TV room. Baker calls daily. Sports field with play equipment. Boule court. Bicycle hire. **Off site:** Golf 15 km, riding 5 km. Bus to Clervaux and Vianden stops (4 times daily) outside site entrance. Castle at Vianden 14 km. Monastery at Clervaux 14 km.

Charges 2002

Per pitch	€ 9.00
person	€ 4.20
child (under 12 yrs)	€ 2.20
dog	€ 2.40
electricity	€ 2.50
local tax	€ 1.70

Tel: 929 464. **Fax:** 929 690. **E-mail:** kohnenho@pt.lu. **Reservations:** Advised in high season with € 10 deposit. **Open** 28 March - 2 November.

Directions: Take the N7 north from Diekirch. At Hosingen, turn right onto CR324 road signed to Eisenbach. Follow campsite signs from Eisenbach or Obereisenbach (the CR324 is a little narrow and winding in places).

Luxembourg
Camping Kockelscheuer

22 Rte de Bettembourg, L-1899 Kockelscheuer

This is a much larger site than Bettembourg (no. 775), closer to Luxembourg city (4 km. from the centre) and quietly situated (although there can be some aircraft noise at times). On a slight slope, there are 161 individual pitches of good size, either on flat ground at the bottom or on wide flat terraces with easy access, all with 16A electricity. There is also a special area for tents. For children there is a large area with modern play equipment on safety tiles and next door to the site is a sports centre. Charges are very reasonable. There is a friendly welcome although little English is spoken.

Facilities: Two fully equipped, identical sanitary buildings, both very clean at time of visit. Washing machines. Motorcaravan services. Shop. (order bread the previous day). Snack bar. Restaurant in adjacent sports centre also with minigolf, tennis, squash, etc. Rest room. No entry or exit for vehicles (reception closed) from 12.00-14.00 hrs. **Off site:** Swimming pool 5 km.

Charges 2002

Per person	€ 3.50
child (3-14 yrs)	€ 1.75
pitch	€ 4.00
electricity (1 or 2 days)	€ 1.75

Tel: 401 815. Fax: 401 243. **Reservations:** are made but site says you should find space if you arrive by 5 p.m. **Open** Easter - 31 October.

Directions: Site is SSW of Luxembourg city on the N13 to Bettembourg. Note: road is also known locally as the 186. From the south, exit A4 at junction signed Kockelscheuer onto N4. In 2 km. turn right (signed Kockelscheuer and campsite) and continue to follow the signs.

Camping Kockelscheuer – Luxembourg
22, route de Bettembourg, L-1899 Kockelscheuer
Telefon 47 18 15 • Fax 40 12 43 • www.camp-kockelscheuer.lu

A modern campsite situated at Kockelscheuer's Leisure Centre, with an ice skating rink, tennis, walking trails, boules, bowling, sauna, solarium whirlpool, restaurants. Spacious sanitary facilities. Large pitches with electric hook-up. Comfortable campers' lounge with terrace. Camping shop.

Luxembourg
Camping Bettembourg

Parc Jacquinot, B.P. 23, L-3201 Bettembourg

Bettembourg is a small municipal site with immaculate modern facilities, exclusively for tourists. It is situated on the southern outskirts of Bettembourg and is beautifully maintained. The 25 pitches, accessed from a central paved roadway, have some neatly trimmed dividing hedges and all have 16A electricity. Simple animation for children is organised in peak season. Brochures showing the local cycle path network and other tourist information may be obtained from reception. The site is near the railway station and marshalling yard so there is some noise at times. A good value site ideal as a stopover but only French is spoken.

Facilities: Toilet facilities are very good and include washbasins in cubicles, a suite for disabled visitors, fully equipped baby room, dishwashing and laundry facilities. The warden is justifiably proud of them. Clubroom with bar, coffee bar and TV. Bread daily (order by 9 pm the day before). Cooking hob for tent campers. Gas supplies. Reception closed 12.00-15.00; barrier closed 23.00-07.00 hrs. **Off site:** Fishing 20 km.

Charges 2002

Per pitch incl. electricity	€ 3.70
adult	€ 3.70
child (3-14 yrs)	€ 1.70
dog	free

No credit cards. **Tel:** 513 646. Fax: 520 357. E-mail: syndicat.bettembourg@vo.lu. **Reservations:** Write to site for details. **Open** 1 April - 30 September.

Directions: From town centre follow camping signs, site is to the south of the town, near the railway station, marshalling yard and Parc Municipal.

Luxembourg
Camping Gaalgebierg
L-4001 Esch-sur-Alzette

Occupying an elevated position on the edge of town, near the French border, this pleasant good quality site is run by the local camping and caravan club. Although surrounded by hills and with a good variety of trees, not all pitches have shade. There are 150 pitches (100 for tourists) 100 sq.m., most on grass, marked out by trees, some on a slight slope. There is a gravel area set aside for one night stays, plus four all-weather pitches for motorhomes although these are used mostly in the winter. All pitches have 16A electricity and TV points. The site operates its own minibus for visits to Luxembourg city and other excursions (free to campers) and also provides the Luxembourg card. Camping Gaalgebierg is justifiably of its new water saving policies and rubbish recycling system, and is one of only eight sites to receive the 'EcoLabel' from Luxembourg's Ministry of Tourisme.

Facilities: The modern, well equipped toilet blocks can be heated and include some washbasins in cubicles, hot showers on payment and excellent facilities for disabled people and babies. Dishwashing and laundry sinks. Laundry. These facilities have a key-card entry system. Motorhome service point. Gas available. Shop for basics. Small bar and take-away on demand. TV room. Excellent playground. Volleyball. Table tennis. Boules. Badminton. Room with keep fit equipment and indoor table tennis (free). Entertainment and activities programme in high season. **Off site:** Restaurant within walking distance. Swimming pool and tennis nearby.

Charges 2002

Per pitch	€ 5.00
adult	€ 3.50
child (3-12 yrs)	€ 1.75
electricity (16A)	€ 1.50
local tax per person	€ 0.25

Less 10% for stays of 7 days, 20% for 30 days excl. July/Aug. Deposit (refundable) for barier/key cards €12,39. No credit cards. **Tel:** 541 069. Fax: 549 630. E-mail: gaalcamp@pt.lu. **Reservations:** Write to site. **Open** all year.

Directions: Site is well signed from centre of Esch, but a sharp look out is needed as there are two acute right-handers on the approach to the site.

Luxembourg
Camping Bon Repos
39 rue de Consdorf, L-6551 Berdorf

In the Petite Suisse region of Luxembourg, an area of limestone gorges, which is popular with climbers and hikers, this attractive little peaceful family run site would make a good base from which to explore the eastern side of this tiny country. Located at the edge of the village of Berdorf, the site is gently sloping, with a central tarmac roadway. The 56 pitches for caravans and motorcaravans are mostly arranged in bays of four, each on a small terrace, and all have a 16A electric hook-up. Most are fairly open, a few have a little shade. There is a separate area for tents on a more level area at the bottom of the site. Activities for children are organised every Wednesday morning in high season. In the forest nearby, carved naturally in the limestone formations is an amphitheatre where concerts and other events are staged occasionally. The tourist town of Echternach is just 6 kilometres.

Facilities: Modern main sanitary building, well tiled and very clean, providing all the usual facilities. Smaller unit (without showers) by the tent field. Both units can be heated if necessary. Further ensuite unit above reception. Reception (open 09.00-10.00, 12.00-14.00, 19.00-20.00) sells wine, beer and soft drinks. TV and games room. Children's playground. Baker calls every morning between 08.30 & 09.00. Shops, hotel and sports centre with indoor pool close. Gas supplies. Dogs are not accepted. **Off site:** Local shops, hotels for drinks and meals, and municipal sports complex with indoor swimming pool, fitness centre, tennis courts, minigolf etc. are just a few minutes walk away.

Charges 2002

Per pitch	€ 4.00 - € 4.20
adult	€ 4.00 - € 4.20
child (3-13 yrs)	€ 1.75
electricity	€ 1.50

Reduction for pitch and adults from the 3rd week out of season. **Tel:** 790 631. Fax: 799 571. E-mail: irma@bonrepos.lu. **Reservations:** Advisable for high season, contact site for details. **Open** 1 April - 11 November.

Directions: Berdorf is 6 km. west of Echternach, the site is signed from village centre towards Consdorf. The entrance is just after a left-hand bend, take care.

Luxembourg
Camping La Pinède

763 33 rue Burgkapp, L-6211 Consdorf

La Pinède is a pleasant municipal site in the Mullerthal region. It is situated adjacent to the municipal sports field, with the main sanitary facilities under the stand. The site provides 110 individual, hedged, grassy spaces for tourists all with electricity (10A), plus 39 pitches housing static units. There is no shop on site but all necessary shops and services are in the town within walking distance. A baker calls Monday to Saturday (not on Wednesday in low season). The immediate area is popular for cycling and hiking and the river Moselle and vineyards are an easy day trip by car. Guided walks are organised in high season.

Facilities: Sanitary facilities provide washbasins and showers in a building which can be heated in cool weather. Further small, modern unit at the far end of the site open in July/Aug. Extra refurbished facilities are to the rear of the bar. Gas supplies. Café/bar. Small adventure-style playground. Minigolf. Tennis. Football field and volleyball. **Off site:** Fishing or bicycle hire 9 km. Riding 12 km. Golf 6 or 12 km. Echternach 10 km. Circular walk in the rocks with torches and candles - maps available at reception.

Charges 2002

Per pitch	€ 4.00
adult	€ 4.00
child (under 14 yrs)	€ 2.00
electricity	€ 1.50

Tel: 790 271. **Fax:** 799 001. **E-mail:** sit.consdorf@internet.lu. **Reservations:** Write to site for details. **Open** 15 March - 15 November.

Directions: Consdorf is southwest of Echternach. From N14 Diekirch - Grevenmacher road, turn left onto the CR121 signed Consdorf. Site is well signed from the town.

Luxembourg
Camping Belle-Vue 2000

759 29 rue de Consdorf, L-6551 Berdorf

Next door to Camping Bon Repos (no. 782) Belle Vue would be ideal for those wanting a winter stopover. Residential and seasonal pitches are at the top end of the site and those reserved for touring units at the bottom end with views of the surrounding hills (site is split 70% residential:30% touring). Two modern sanitary blocks serve the touring pitches, both equipped with all services. A large play area (hedged) offers a variety of equipment for pre-teens children. The reception is in the same buildiong as the shop, which closes from 12.00-13.00 daily and at noon on Sundays.

Facilities: Two modern sanitary blocks with good clean **Facilities:** showers, communal washbasins, British-style WCs, suite for visitors with disabilities, dishwashing sinks, and laundry. Hedged playground for pre-teen children. TV/meeting room. Table tennis. Well-stocked shop. **Off site:** Local shops, hotels for drinks and meals, and municipal sports complex with indoor swimming pool, fitness centre, tennis courts, minigolf etc. are just a few minutes walk away.

Charges 2002

Per adult	€ 4.00
child (3-14 yrs)	€ 2.00
pitch	€ 4.00
electricity	€ 2.00
dog	€ 2.00

Tel: 79 0635. **Fax:** 79 9349. **Reservations:** Contact site. **Open** all year.

Directions: Berdorf is 6 km. west of Echternach, the site is signed from centre of village in the direction of Consdorf.

Luxembourg
Camping Officiel de Drie Groene Harten

760 5 Route de Diekirch, L-6430 Echternach

This site is divided into three distinct camping areas, nestling on a hillside within a 10-minute walking distance from the centre of Echternach. The reception is at the lower level with facilities and pitches reserved for campers with disabilities. La Residence (on the next level) is for seasonal campers. La Jeunesse (midway) is for tent campers and provides a modern sanitary block, a barbecue area and some electric hook-ups. La Paradis (at the top) for touring caravans and motorhomes offers good-sized pitches with electricity and a sanitary block. The road up to La Jeunesse and La Paradis is very steep, but once you have pitched there are splendid views across the valley and shelter from the hill with plenty of trees.

Facilities: Two modern sanitary blocks in the tent and touring campings with acceptably clean facilities (showers, communal washbasins, British-style WCs). Dishwashing sinks. Further WCs and showers at the lower level. Washing machine and tumble dryer. Facilities for visitors with disabilities. A baker calls daily between 08.15 and 09.15. TV/meeting room. Playground for youngsters plus adventure equipment for older children. A 2.2 km. trim trail. Volleyball, basketball, football target, table tennis.

Charges 2002

Per adult	€ 4.00
child	€ 2.00
pitch	€ 4.00
electricity	€ 2.00

Tel: 72 02 72. **Fax:** 72 08 47. **E-mail:** info@camping-echternach.lu. **Reservations:** Contact site. **Open** 15 March - 1 November.

Directions: Follow camping official signs in Echternach.

Netherlands

Netherlands Board of Tourism, 18 Buckingham Gate, London SW1E 6NT
Tel: 0906 8717 777 (60p per minute) Fax: 020 7539 7953
E-mail: information@nbt.org.uk Internet: www.holland.com/uk

The Netherlands offers a warm welcome to British visitors, and the general standard of campsites has improved considerably during the last few years. There is more to the Netherlands than Amsterdam and the bulb fields. Granted, both are top attractions and no visitor should miss the city of Amsterdam with its delight of bridges, canals, museums and listed buildings or miss sighting the spring-time riot of colour that adorns the fields and gardens of South Holland. Curiosity has prompted us to venture further afield to touch on all of its twelve provinces. We discovered a country with a variety of holiday venues ranging from lively seaside resorts to picturesque villages, idyllic old fishing ports and areas where nature rules. Favourite places along the way include the Province of Overijssel, especially the Vecht valley, an area of natural beauty which centres around the town of Ommen. From here scenic routes, cycle tracks and footpaths lead to attractive hamlets and towns tucked into a woodland setting. Giethoorn, to the northwest of the province is justly dubbed the 'Venice of the North'. Another appealing spot is around Dordrecht, southeast of Rotterdam. Here the Alblasserwaard polder, a typically Dutch landscape offers time to discover the famed windmills of Kinderdijk, cheese farms and a a stork village. The lure of the islands of the Zeeland Provice is difficult to resist. These islands are joined by amazing feats of engineering, particularly the Oosterschelde storm surge barrier. Island hopping introduces lovely old towns such as Middelburg, the provincial capital Zierikzee with its old harbour or the quaint old town of Veere.

Population

15,200,000, density 447 per sq.km.

Climate

The sea has a great affect on the climate of the Netherlands. The average winter is mild - although a sudden cold snap in January or February will have the skaters out on the waterways. Summers are warm with temperatures averaging 16-17oC centigrade in July/August. In the east and southeast winters are colder and summers warmer. Spring is the driest season.

Time

GMT + 1 (summer BST + 1).

Language

Dutch is the native tongue. English is very widely spoken, so is German and to some extent French. In Friesland a Germanic language, Frisian is spoken. The Dutch are very language-conscious partly because they are great travellers, to be found in all parts of the world - often running sites!

Currency

From January 2002, in common with 11 other European countries, the Dutch unit of currency is the EURO (€).
€ 1 = NLG 2.21.

Banks

Open Mon-Fri 09.00-16.00/1700. Exchange offices (GWK) are often open longer hours.

Post Offices

Open Mon-Fri 08.30-17.00. Some offices open Sat 08.30-12.00.

Telephone

To call the Netherlands from the UK the code is 00 31, the UK from the Netherlands, 00 44.

Public Holidays

New Year; Good Fri; Easter Mon; Queen's Birthday, 30 Apr; Liberation Day, 5 May; Ascension; Whit Mon; Christmas, 25, 26 Dec.

Shops

Shops open Mon-Fri 09.00/09.30 - 17.30/18.00. Sat. closing 16.00/ 17.00. In big cities, stores have late opening Thurs. or Fri. and close Mon. morning. The Dutch are early diners - restaurants open 17.30-22.00/23.00.

Motoring

There is a comprehensive motorway system but, due to the high density of population, all main roads can become very busy, particularly in the morning and evening rush hours. There are many bridges which can cause congestion.
Tolls: There are no toll roads but there are a few toll bridges and tunnels notably the Zeeland Bridge, Europe's longest across the Oosterschelde.
Speed Limits: Built up areas 31 mph (50 kph), other roads 50 mph (80 kph) and motorways 62 mph (100 kph) or 75 mph (120 kph). Cars towing a caravan or trailer are limited to 50 mph (80 kph) outside built-up areas.

CAMPSITES

within a stone's throw of the city

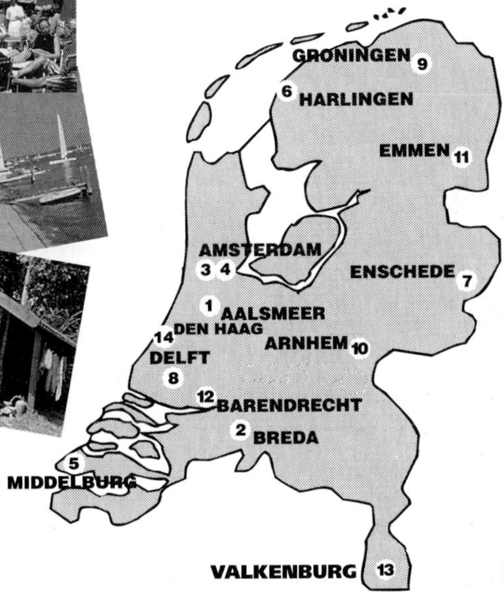

1 Het Amsterdamse Bos
Kleine Noorddijk 1
1432 CC Aalsmeer
Tel: 31 (0) 20-6416868
Fax: 31 (0) 20-6402378

2 De Bosweelde
Geersbroekseweg 3
4851 RD BREDA
(Ulvenhout)
Tel: 31 (0) 76-5612525
Fax: 31 (0) 76-5657565

3 Gaasper Camping
Loosdrechtdreef 7
1108 AZ AMSTERDAM
Tel: 31 (0) 20-6967326
Fax: 31 (0) 20-6969369

4 Vliegenbos
Meeuwenlaan 138
1022 AM AMSTERDAM
Tel: 31 (0) 20-6368855
Fax: 31 (0) 20-6322723

5 Camping Middelburg
Koninginnelaan 55
4335 HA MIDDELBURG
Tel: 31 (0) 118-625395

6 De Zeehoeve
Westerzeedijk 45
8862 PK HARLINGEN
Tel: 31 (0) 517-413465
Fax: 31 (0) 517-416971

7 De Twentse Es
Keppelerdijk 200
7534 PA ENSCHEDE
Tel: 31 (0) 53-4611372

8 Delftse Hout
Korftlaan 5
2616 LJ DELFT
Tel: 31 (0) 15-2130040
Fax: 31 (0) 15-2131293

9 Camping Stadspark
Campinglaan 6
9727 KH GRONINGEN
Tel: 31 (0) 50-5251624
Fax: 31 (0) 50-5250099

10 Camping Arnhem
Kemperbergerweg 771
6816 RW ARNHEM
Tel: 31 (0) 26-4431600
Fax: 31 (0) 26-4457705

11 Camping Emmen
Angeloërdijk 31
7822 HK EMMEN
Tel: 31 (0) 591-612080
Fax: 31 (0) 591-623726

12 De Oude Maas
Achterzeedijk 1a
2991 SB BARENDRECHT
Tel: 31 (0) 78-6772445
Fax: 31 (0) 78-6773013

13 Camping Den Driesch
Heunsbergerweg 1
6301 BN VALKENBURG
Tel: 31 (0) 43-6012025
Fax: 31 (0) 43-6016139

14 Vakantiecentrum
Kijkduinpark
Machiel Vrijenhoeklaan 450
2555 NW DEN HAAG
Tel: 31 (0) 70-4482100
Fax: 31 (0) 70-3232457

Are you looking for an unforgettable holiday within reach of culture, museums, nightlife but still giving you that real free feeling of camping?

What you are looking for could be a "city" campsite. The well thought-out campsites with all modern facilities are situated in an ideal place giving you the choice to explore the city and the surrounding areas.

Whether camping, caravanning or with your mobile home, you will always be welcomed by the City Campsites in the Netherlands,

For more information please contact the City Campsites directly.

e-mail: info@stadscampings.nl
www.citycamps.com

Stadscamping

Netherlands - West
Recreatiecentrum Pannenschuur

550 Zeedijk 19, 4504 PP Nieuwvliet (Zeeland)

This is one of several coastal sites on the narrow strip of the Netherlands between the Belgian frontier near Knokke and the Breskens ferry. Quickly reached from the ports of Ostend, Zeebrugge and Vlissingen, it is useful for overnight stops or for a few days to enjoy the seaside. A short walk across the quiet coast road and steps over the dike bring you to the open, sandy beach. Quite a large site, most of the 595 pitches are taken by seasonal caravans but there are also 165 pitches for tourists mostly in their own areas. In bays of six or eight units surrounded by hedges, all have electricity, water and drainage. Cars are parked in separate parking areas. A star attraction is the complex that provides a super indoor heated pool with children`s sections, jacuzzi, sauna, and solarium. Overall, this is a very good site.

Facilities: Five sanitary blocks including two new, heated buildings, provide first class facilities including children's washrooms, baby rooms and some cabins. Launderette. Motorcaravan services. Gas supplies. Supermarket (restricted hours in low seasons). Restaurant, snack bar and takeaway. Swimming pool, sauna and solarium. These amenities are closed 14/1-31/1. Games room with snooker, pool, amusement machines, soft drinks bar. Playground. Bicycle hire. Organised activities during season. **Off site:** Fishing 500 m. Riding 2 km.

Charges 2002

Per person (over 2 yrs)	€ 4.50
pitch incl. electricity	€ 14.85 - € 17.95
local tax	€ 0.65

Rates available for weekly stays. **Tel:** 0117 37 23 00. Fax: 0117 37 14 15. E-mail: info@pannenschuur.nl.
Reservations: Advised (high season Sat.- Sat. only) and made with deposit and fee. **Open** all year (all amenities closed 14/1-31/1).

Directions: At Nieuwvliet, on Breskens - Sluis minor road, 8 km. southwest of Breskens, turn towards the sea at sign for Nieuwvliet-Bad and follow signs to site.

Netherlands - West
Camping Groede

551 Zeeweg 1, 4503 PA Groede (Zeeland)

Camping Groede is a friendly, fair-sized site by the same stretch of sandy beach as no. 550. Family run, it aims to cater for the individual needs of visitors and to provide a good all-round holiday. Campers are sited as far as possible according to taste - in family areas, in larger groups or on more private pitches for those who prefer peace and quiet. In total, there are 570 pitches for tourists (plus 380 seasonal units), 570 with electrical connections (4/6/10A) and 300 with water and drainage connections. A new field has 63 fully serviced large pitches. Groede is ideally sited for ferry stopovers (Breskens) and short stay visitors are very welcome, as well as long stay holiday makers. Access to the beach is good for wheelchairs and baby buggies. Run by the family van Damme, who provide a good information booklet.

Facilities: Toilet facilities are excellent with a high standard of cleanliness, including some wash cabins, baby baths, family room and a dedicated unit for persons with disabilities. Motorcaravan services. Gas supplies. Shop, restaurant and snack bar (all weekends only in low seasons). Visitors are invited to join locals in archery and card games. Recreation room. Sports area. Play areas. Football, volleyball and activities for children in peak season. Bicycle hire. Fishing. **Off site:** Riding 1 km. Golf 11 km

Charges 2002

Per pitch incl. 2 persons	€ 12.00 - € 19.00
with 4A electricity	€ 13.50 - € 20.50
with water and drainage also	€ 15.25 - € 22.50
extra person	€ 2.00
local taxes	€ 0.80

No credit cards. **Tel:** 0117 37 13 84. Fax: 0117 37 22 77. E-mail: info@campinggroede.nl. **Reservations:** Will be made with € 12 fee, but half the pitches are kept unreserved. **Open** 28 March - 31 October.

Directions: From Breskens take the coast road for 5 km. to site. Alternatively, the site is signed from Groede village on the inland Breskens - Sluis road.

Camping de Molenhoek
Molenweg 69a, 4493 NC Kamperland (Zeeland)

567

This family run site makes a pleasant contrast to the livelier coastal sites in this popular holiday area. It is rurally situated 3 km. from the Veerse Meer which is very popular for all sorts of watersports. Catering both for 300 permanent or seasonal holiday caravans and for 100 touring units, it is neat, tidy and relatively spacious. The marked touring pitches are divided into small groups with surrounding hedges and trees giving privacy and some shade, and electrical connections are available. A large outdoor pool is Molenhoek's latest attraction. Entertainment is organised in season (dance evenings, bingo, etc.) as well as a disco for youngsters. Although the site is quietly situated, there are many excursion possibilities in the area including the towns of Middelburg, Veere and Goes and the Delta Expo exhibition.

Facilities: Sanitary facilities in one fully refurbished and one newer block, include some washbasins in cabins, dishwashing and laundry sinks. Toilet and shower facilities for disabled visitors and provision for babies. Motorcaravan services. Small shop. Simple bar/restaurant with terrace and TV room. Restaurant/bar. Swimming pool (15/5-15/9). Playground. Bicycle hire. **Off site:** Fishing 2.5 km. Riding 1 km. Tennis and watersports close.

Charges 2002

Per unit incl. 2 persons	€ 16.00 - € 22.00
extra person	€ 2.60 - € 3.20
dog	€ 2.20 - € 2.80
electricity	€ 2.50

No credit cards. **Tel:** 0113 37 12 02. E-mail: molenhoek@zeelandnet.nl. **Reservations:** Are made - details from site. **Open** 1 April - 28 October.

Directions: Site is west of the village of Kamperland on the 'island' of Noord Beveland. From the N256 Goes - Zierikzee road, exit west onto N255 Kamperland road. Site is signed south of this road.

Kampeer- en recreatiecentrum

DE MOLENHOEK

Only five minutes from the beach and Veerse Meer.
Quiet campsite with small fields separated by hedges.
Good restaurant and snackbar. Activity programme.
Young people's room and disco. Heated swimming pool.
Playground and swimming pool for children. A good campsite for the whole family for a short or long stay.
Close to the "Oosterschelde" works and the "Pijlerdam".
Caravans for hire.

A CAMPSITE WHERE EVERYONE IS HAPPY!

Molenweg 69A-4493 NC Kamperland Tel: (+31) 113 371202
Internet: www.zeelandnet.nl/molenhoek E-mail: molenhoek@zeelandnet.nl

Camping de Veerhoeve
Veerweg 48, 4471 NC Wolphaartsdijk (Zeeland)

558

This is a family run site near the shores of the Veerse Meer which is, ideal for family holidays. It is situated in a popular area for watersports and is well suited for sailing, windsurfing or fishing enthusiasts, with boat launching 1 km. away. As with most sites in this area there are many mature static and seasonal pitches. However, part of the friendly, relaxed site is reserved for touring units with 150 marked pitches on grassy ground, all with electrical connections. A member of the Holland Tulip Parcs group.

Facilities: Sanitary facilities in three blocks have been well modernised with full tiling. Hot showers are on payment. Laundry facilities. Motorcaravan services. Supermarket (all season). Restaurant and snack bar (July/Aug. otherwise at weekends). TV room. Tennis. Playground and play field. Bicycle hire. Fishing. Accommodation for groups. Max. 1 dog per pitch. **Off site:** Riding 1 km. Golf 7 km. Slipway for launching boats and riding 1 km.

Charges 2003

Per pitch incl. up to 4 persons	€ 19.00 - € 21.75
with electricity (6A), water and drainage	€ 20.00 - € 23.00
with TV connection	€ 21.00 - € 24.00
extra person	€ 7.50
local tax	incl.

Tel: 0113 58 11 55. Fax: 0113 58 19 44. E-mail: deveerhoeve@zeelandnet.nl. **Reservations:** Write to site. **Open** 3 April - 30 October.

Directions: From N256 Goes-Zierikzee road take Wolphaartsdijk exit. Follow through village and signs to site.

Camping Schoneveld
Schoneveld 1, 4511 HR Breskens (Zeeland)

This site is well situated within walking distance of Breskens and it has direct access to sand dunes. It has around 200 touring pitches and has many static vans, but these are kept apart. Touring outfits are placed behind reception and laid out in fields which are entered from long avenues that run through the site, there are also 12 car parking bays. One ultra modern and very clean toilet block serves this area of the site. The complex at the site entrance houses reception, a restaurant and a recreation room. It is to the fore of the site you also find the indoor swimming pool, tennis courts and a football field. The ferry link to Breskens from Vlissingen is scheduled in 2003 to take pedestrians and cyclists only, a tunnel is to open for motor vehicles. A member of the Tulip Parc group.

Facilities: One large sanitary block provides showers, wash cubicles, child size toilets and washbasins, baby room, en-suite unit for disabled visitors. Motorcaravan service point. Restaurant. Fun Food Plaza. Bowling. Swimming pool. Table tennis. Tennis. Football field. Play area. Organised entertainment in July/Aug. Bicycle hire.

Charges 2002

Per unit incl. 2 persons	€ 16.00 - € 27.00
incl. 3 persons	€ 20.00 - € 31.00
incl. 5 persons	€ 23.00 - € 34.00
tent pitch incl. 1 or 2 persons	€ 9.00 - € 14.50
extra person	€ 4.50

Weekly tariff available. **Tel:** 0117 38 32 20. Fax: 0117 383 650. E-mail: schoneveld@zeelandnet.nl. **Reservations:** Contact site. **Open** all year.

Directions: From Breskens port follow N58 south for approx. 1 km and turn right at camping sign. Site is 500 m.

Camping International Renesse
Scharendijkseweg 8, 4325 LD Renesse (Zeeland)

Situated 300 metres from the beach at Renesse in Zeeland, this is a friendly, family run site. Its owners have set high standards, which is demonstrated by the immaculate and tastefully decorated sanitary facilities. There are 200 pitches, with 100 for touring units. These are a generous size and laid out in bays and avenues surrounded by hedging. Around a courtyard area beyond reception is a supermarket and a bar which is attractively decorated with novel figures and the owner's personal memorabilia. Outside bench seating and umbrellas turns this corner of the camping into a popular meeting place. Being close to one of Zeeland's excellent beaches makes this site an ideal choice for families.

Facilities: Two luxury sanitary blocks provide showers, washbasins (some in cabins) and a baby room. Dishwashing sinks (hot water on payment). Laundry room with washing machine, dryer and ironing board. Motorcaravan service point. Supermarket. Bar. Games room, TV and table tennis. Play area. Bicycle hire. Entertainment in high season for children and adults.

Charges 2002

Per unit incl. 2 persons	€ 16.50
extra person	€ 4.00
child (2-9 yrs)	€ 3.50
dog	€ 2.50
electricity	€ 2.30
caravan over 7 m.	€ 4.10

Tel: 0111 461391. Fax: 0111 462571. E-mail: info@ camping-international.net. **Reservations:** Advisable in high season; contact site. **Open** 1 March - 31 October.

Directions: From Zierikzee follow N59 to Renesse for approx. 15 km. and turn right at roundabout (before town) onto local road signed R101. Continue for approx. 1 km. and turn left, then first right to site on right.

Camping 't Weergors

697 Zuiddijk 2, 3221 LJ Hellevoetsluis (Zuid-Holland)

A rustic style site built around old farm buildings, t'Weergors gives off a comfortable mature feel. At the front of the site is a well presented farmhouse which houses reception and includes the main site services. Around the courtyard area is one of the two sanitary blocks which is unsophisticated, but clean and functional with tiled walls and floor. There are 100 touring pitches, plus seasonal and static places. Some touring pitches are exceptionally large, divided by hedging with a 'drive in, drive out' system (cars charged if kept on pitch). Each pitch has a cable TV connection. An appealing feature of this site is the lake which lies to the rear, offering a quiet corner where you might head for an evening stroll. The old centre of Hellevoetsluis is worthy of a visit.

Facilities: Two sanitary blocks have showers (by token), washbasins, some in cabins, child size WCs and a baby bath. Dishwashing sinks (token) and laundry area with washing machine and dryer. Motorcaravan service point. Small shop. Restaurant, bar and snack bar. Tennis. Football field. Recreation room/TV. Play area. Paddling pool. Organised entertainment in high season. Fishing. Bicycle hire.

Charges 2002

Per person	€ 2.50
child (3-12 yrs)	€ 1.50
tent or caravan	€ 6.00
car on pitch	€ 2.50
electricity	€ 2.20
dog	€ 1.40
local tax	€ 0.45

Tel: 0181 312430. Fax: 0181 311010. E-mail: weergors@publishnet.nl. **Reservations:** Contact site. **Open** Easter - 31 October.

Directions: From Rotterdam join A15 west to Rozenburg junction 12 and join N57 south for 11 km. Turn left on N497 signed Hellevoetsluis and follow camp signs for 4.5 km. to roundabout. Turn right at roundabout and site is 1.5 km. on right.

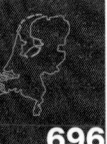

Camping De Klepperstee

696 Vrijheidsweg 1, 3253 ZG Ouddorp (Zuid-Holland)

De Klepperstee is a good quality, family site offering excellent recreation areas that are spread over the centre of the site, giving it an attractive open parkland appearance which is enhanced by many shrubs, trees and grass areas. The variety of children's play equipment ensures hours of non-stop fun and there is a special evening house for older children with a television, etc. The site itself is peacefully located in tranquil countryside amid renowned nature reserves and just outside the village of Ouddorp in Zuid Holland. The 338 spacious touring pitches are in named avenues, mostly separated by hedging and spread around the perimeter, together with the seasonal and static caravans.

Facilities: One main sanitary block and a number of WC/shower units around the touring area provide hot showers (on payment), washbasins, some in cabins (hot water only), baby bath and shower, child size toilets and a unit for people with disabilities. Dishwashing sinks (hot water on payment). Laundry machines. Motorcaravan service point. Supermarket. Restaurant, bar and takeaway. Small paddling pool. Play areas. Football field, netball, basketball and tennis. Table tennis. TV, pool and electronic games. Entertainment in high season. Bicycle hire. No animals are accepted and no single sex groups.

Charges 2002

Per unit incl. up to 4 persons, 6A electricity	€ 27.50
with 10A electricity	€ 30.00
tent pitch incl. 2 persons	€ 14.00
extra person	€ 2.50
local tax	€ 0.40

Tel: 0187 681511. Fax: 0187 683060. E-mail: info@klepperstee.com. **Reservations:** Contact site for booking form. **Open** Easter - 31 October.

Directions: From Rotterdam follow A15 west to Rozenburg exit 12 and join N57 south for 22 km. Turn right at end of dual carriageway signed to Ouddorp. Continue on local road following signs for Strand. Site on left after approx. 3 km.

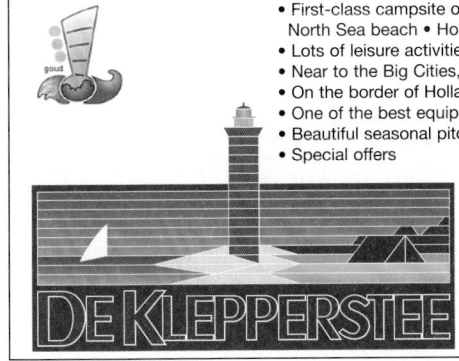

Netherlands - West
Camping De Oude Maas
561 Achterzeedijk 1A, 2991 SB Barendrecht (Zuid-Holland)

This site is easily accessed from the A15 southern Rotterdam ring road and is situated right by the river, so it is well worth considering if you are visiting the city or want a peaceful stop. The entrance is the least inspiring part here and you have to drive right up to the barrier in order to activate the intercom. Once through this, you pass a long strip of mixed seasonal and touring pitches. There are two more attractive touring areas, one for 12 units with electricity, water and waste water connections in a hedged group near to the reception and river. The third section is in a woodland setting, well back from the river.

Facilities: One small, mediocre sanitary building, a more modern one and a small 'portacabin' type facility provide all necessary facilities including a unit for disabled visitors, a baby room and dishwashing. Launderette. Fishing. **Off site:** Swimming pool near. Golf 10 km. Riding 8 km. Bicycle hire 5 km.

Charges 2002

Per adult	3.02
child (under 15 yrs)	1.62
pitch and car	6.04
electricity (10A)	1.62
dog	1.62

Tel: 0180 677 24 45. Fax: 0180 677 30 13. E-mail: de.oudemaas@worldonline.nl. **Reservations:** May be advisable high season. **Open** 1 March - 15 October.

Directions: Best approach is from the A29 Rotterdam/Bergen op Zoom motorway. Leave A29 at exit 20 (Barendrecht) and follow signs for Heerjansdam and site.

Netherlands - West
Recreatiecentrum Delftse Hout
560 Korftlaan 5, 2616 LJ Delft (Zuid-Holland)

Pleasantly situated in Delft's park and forest area on the eastern edge of the city, this well run, modern site is part of the Koningshof group. It has 200 tourist pitches quite formally arranged in groups of 4 to 6 and surrounded by attractive young trees and hedges. All have sufficient space and electrical connections (10A). Modern buildings near the entrance house the site amenities. A good sized first floor restaurant serves snacks or full meals and has an outdoor terrace overlooking the swimming pool and pitches. Walking and cycling tours are organised and there is a recreation programme in high season. A special package deal can be arranged including tickets to local 'royal' attractions and a visit to the Royal Delftware factory.

Facilities: Modern, heated toilet facilities include a spacious family room. Laundry. Motorcaravan services. Shop for basic food and camping items (1/4-1/11). Restaurant and bar (1/4-1/10). Small outdoor swimming pool (15/5-15/9). Adventure playground. Table tennis. Volleyball, basketball. Recreation room. Bicycle hire. Gas supplies. **Off site:** Fishing 1 km. Riding or golf 5 km. Bus service to Delft centre.

Charges 2003

Per unit incl. 2 persons	€ 22.00 - € 23.00
with services	€ 27.00 - € 29.00
extra person (3 yrs and older)	€ 1.50
electricity (10A)	€ 3.50
dog (1 per pitch)	€ 2.00
local tax	€ 0.50

Low season discounts and for senior citizens (over 55). Special packages. **Tel:** 0152 13 00 40. Fax: 0152 13 12 93. E-mail: info@delftsehout.nl. **Reservations:** Essential for high season (not made by telephone). **Open** all year.

Directions: Site is 1 km. east of Delft. From A13 motorway take Delft/Pijnacker (exit 9), turn towards Pijnacker and then right at first traffic lights, following camping signs through suburbs and park to site.

Netherlands - West
Camping Noordduinen
568 Campingweg 1, 2221 EW Katwijk (Zuid-Holland)

This is a large, well managed site surrounded by dunes and sheltered partly by trees and shrubbery, which also separate the various camping areas. The 200 touring pitches are marked and numbered but not divided. All have electricity (10A) and 45 are fully serviced with electricity, water, drainage and TV connection. There are also seasonal pitches and mobile homes for rent. The latter are placed mostly away from the touring areas and are unobtrusive. You are escorted to an allocated pitch and sited in a formal layout and cars are parked away from the pitches. Entertainment is organised in high season, bicycles can be hired nearby and worth a visit is Space Expo.

Facilities: The three sanitary blocks are modern and clean, with washbasins in cabins, a baby room and provision for people with disabilities. Hot water for showers and dishwashing is on payment. Laundry. Motorcaravan services. Supermarket. Restaurant/bar which doubles as a function room and a takeaway service. Games room. Play area. Only gas barbecues are permitted. No dogs are accepted. **Off site:** Beach and Katwijk within walking distance.

Charges 2002

Per standard pitch	€ 21.50 - € 27.00
electricity (10A)	€ 3.00
local tax	€ 0.40

Tel: 0714 02 52 95. Fax: 0714 03 39 77. E-mail: info@noordduinen.nl. **Reservations:** Contact site. **Open** 31 March - 28 October.

Directions: Leave A44 at exit 8 (Leiden/Katwijk) to join N206 to Katwijk. Take Katwijk Noord exit and follow signs to site.

Camping Duinrell

Duinrell 1, 2242 JP Wassenaar (Zuid-Holland)

A very large site, Duinrell's name means 'well in the dunes' and the water theme is continued in the adjoining amusement park and in the extensive indoor pool complex. Entry to the popular pleasure park is free for campers - indeed the camping areas surround and open out from the park. The 'Tiki' tropical pool complex has many attractions which include slides ranging from quite exciting to terrifying (according to your age!), whirlpools, saunas and many other features. There are also free outdoor pools and the centre has its own bar and café. Entry to the Tiki complex is at a reduced rate for campers. Duinrell is open all year and a ski school (langlauf and Alpine) with 12 artificial runs, is a winter attraction. The campsite itself is very large with 1,150 tourist places on several flat grassy areas and it can become very busy in high season. As part of a continuing improvement programme, 950 marked pitches have electricity, cable TV, water and drainage connections. Amenities shared with the park include restaurants, a pizzeria and pancake house, supermarket and a theatre. The original 900 permanent units have been reduced to around 150, gradually being replaced with smartly furnished self catering bungalows.

Facilities: Six toilet blocks, including two very good new ones, serve the tourist areas and can be heated in cool weather. Laundry facilities. Amusement park and Tiki tropical pool complex as detailed above. Restaurant, cafés, pizzeria and takeaways (weekends only in winter). Supermarket. Entertainment and theatre with shows in high season. Bicycle hire. Bowling. Winter ski school. Fishing.

Charges 2002

Per pitch incl. electricity	€ 9.50
with cable TV	€ 11.50
person over 3 yrs	€ 8.50
person over 65 yrs	€ 6.25
'nature' pitch	€ 8.00
dog	€ 5.00
local tax (over 3 yrs)	€ 0.68

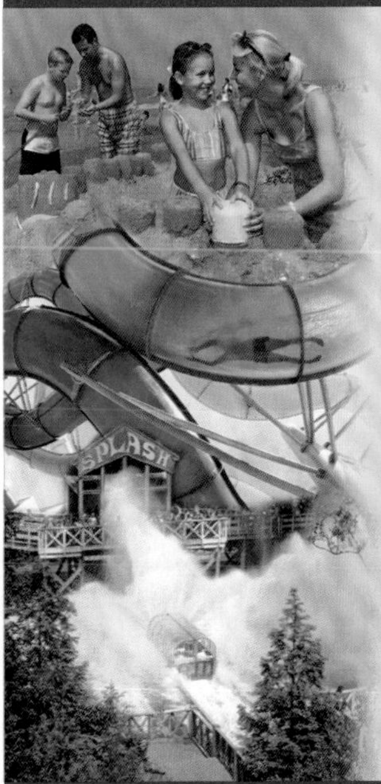

Overnight stays between 17.00-10.00 hrs (when amusement park closed) less 25%. **Tel:** 0705 15 52 57. Fax: 0705 15 53 71. **Reservations:** Advised for high season, Easter and Whitsun (min. 1 week), 50% payment required 6 weeks in advance plus fee (€ 6,81). **Open** all year.

Directions: Site is signed from N44/A44 Den Haag-Amsterdam road, but from the south the turning is about 5 km. after passing sign for start of Wassenaar town - then follow camp signs.

Netherlands - West
Camping Koningshof
Elsgeesterweg 8, 2231 NW Rijnsburg (Zuid-Holland)

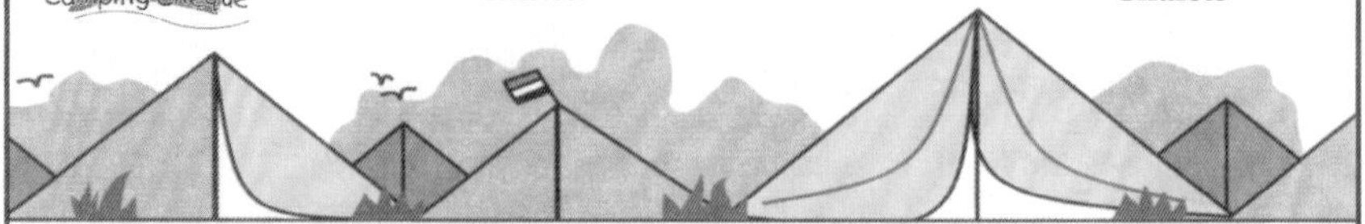

563

the travel service
TO BOOK
Ferry ✓
Pitch ✓
Accommodation ✓
01892 55 98 98

This popular site is run in a personal and friendly way. The 225 pitches for touring units are laid out in groups of four or twelve, divided by hedges and trees and all with electrical connections (10A). Cars are mostly parked in areas around the perimeter and 100 static caravans, confined to one section of the site, are entirely unobtrusive. Reception, a pleasant good quality restaurant, bar and a snack bar are grouped around a courtyard style entrance which is decorated with seasonal flowers. The site has a small outdoor, heated pool (13.5 x 7 m), with separate a paddling pool and imaginative children`s play equipment. Recent additions are a recreation hall, an indoor swimming pool and a unique children`s play pool with water streams, locks and play materials. The site has a number of regular British visitors from club connections who receive a friendly welcome, with English spoken. Used by tour operators (25 pitches). A very useful local information booklet (in English) is provided for visitors. A member of the Holland Tulip Parcs group.

Facilities: Three good toilet blocks, one with underfloor heating, include washbasins in cabins and provision for disabled visitors. Laundry room with washing machines and dryers. Motorcaravan services. Gas supplies. Shop (10/4-15/10). Bar (10/4-1/11). Restaurant (1/4-10/9). Snacks and takeaway (1/4-1/10). Small outdoor pool (unsupervised; 15/5-15/9). Indoor pool complex (15/3-15/11). Solarium. Adventure playground and sports area. Tennis courts. Fishing pond (free). Bicycle hire. Entertainment in high season. Room for shows. One dog per pitch accepted in a limited area of the site. **Off site:** Riding or golf 5 km. Sandy beach 5 km. Den Haag 15 km. and Amsterdam 30 km.

Charges 2002

Per pitch incl. 2 persons	€ 22.00
extra person (over 3 years)	€ 3.00
electricity (10A)	€ 2.00
dog (see text)	€ 2.00

Plus local tax. Low season and senior citizen discounts; special group rates. **Tel:** 0714 02 60 51. Fax: 0714 02 13 36. E-mail: info@koningshofholland.nl. **Reservations:** Necessary for July/Aug and made for any length with deposit and fee (payable by credit card). **Open** all year.

Directions: From N44/A44 Den Haag - Amsterdam motorway, take exit 7 for Oegstgeest and Rijnsburg. Turn towards Rijnsburg and follow camp signs.

Buone vacanze
Einen schönen urlaub
Felices vacaciones
Have a nice holiday
Trerlig Semester
God ferie
Prettige vakantie

KONINGSHOF
Camping
Caravanning
Chalets

NEW
indoor pool

DE NOORDDUINEN
Camping
Caravanning
Chalets

DE ZUIDDUINEN
Camping
Caravanning
Chalets

DELFTSE HOUT
Camping
Caravanning
Chalets

Elsgeesterweg 8	Campingweg 1	Zuidduinsweg 1	Korftlaan 5
2231 NW Rijnsburg	2221 EW Katwijk	2225 JS Katwijk	2616 LJ Delft
Netherlands	Netherlands	Netherlands	Netherlands
Tel. +31 (0)71 - 4026051	Tel. +31 (0)71 - 4025295	Tel. +31 (0)71 - 4014750	Tel. +31 (0)15 - 2130040
Fax. +31 (0)71 - 4021336	Fax. +31 (0)71 - 4033977	Fax. +31 (0)71 - 4077097	Fax. +31 (0)15 - 2131293
info@koningshofholland.nl	info@noordduinen.nl	info@zuidduinen.nl	info@delftsehout.nl
www.koningshofholland.nl	www.noordduinen.nl	www.zuidduinen.nl	www.delftsehout.nl

Vakantiecentrum Kijkduinpark

Machiel Vrijenhoeklaan 450, 2555 NW Den Haag (Zuid-Holland)

564

This former touring park has been transformed into an ultra-modern, all year round centre and family park, which is still developing. Many huts, villas and bungalows have been built, along with a brand new reception and large idoor swimming pool complex. The wooded touring area is immediately to the left of the entrance, with 450 pitches in shady glades of bark covered sand. There are simple pitches for tents, some pitches with electricity only and many with electricity 10A, water, waste water and cable TV connections. In a paved central area stands a supermarket, snack bar and restaurant. The main attraction here is the Meeresstrand, 500 m. from the site entrance. This is a long, wide sandy beach with flags to denote suitability for swimming. It is popular with windsurfers.

Facilities: There are now five modern sanitary blocks (key entry). Launderette. Snack bar. Shop. Restaurant. Supermarket (all year). Indoor pool. Bicycle hire. Special golfing breaks. Entertainment and activities organised in summer. **Off site:** Fishing 500 m. Riding 5 km,

Charges 2002

Per unit incl. 2 persons	€ 12.16 - € 26.13
with electricity, water and drainage	€ 15.77 - € 29.73
dog (max 1)	€ 2.70
local tax	€ 1.06

Less 10-30% in low season and 20% discount for over 55 yr olds. **Tel:** 0704 48 21 00. Fax: 0703 23 24 57. E-mail: info@kijkduinpark.nl. **Reservations:** Advisable for high season, write to site. **Open** all year.

Directions: Site is southwest of Den Haag on the coast and Kijkduin is well signed as an area from all round Den Haag.

Camping De Victorie

569 Broekseweg 75-77, 4231 VD Meerkerk (Zuid-Holland)

Within an hour's drive of the port of Rotterdam you can be pitched on this delightful, spacious site in the 'green heart' of Holland. De Victorie, a working farm and a member of a club of small, 'green' sites, offers an alternative to the bustling seaside sites. Everything about it is surprising and contrary to any preconceived ideas. To the left of the entrance, a modern building houses reception, open plan office and space with tables and chairs, where the friendly owners may well invite you to have a cup of coffee. The 70 grass pitches are level and generous in size with 4A electricity supply. You can choose to be pitched in the shade of one of the orchards, or in the more open meadow area. The freedom of the farmland is especially enjoyed by children with farm animals, wildlife and tractor rides.

Facilities: The main sanitary block is kept spotlessly clean, tastefully decorated and fully equipped. Showers are on payment. Dishwashing area and laundry room. Additional sanitary facilities are around the site. Farm shop selling milk, eggs, meat, cheese and ice cream. Children's play area. Trampoline, and play field for football. Bicycle hire. Fishing. Riding. **Off site:** Golf 2.5 km

Charges 2002

caravan, tent or motorcaravan	€ 1.25
Per person	€ 1.25
car	€ 0.50
large motorcaravan	€ 1.75
electricity (4-6A)	€ 1.25 - € 1.50
local tax	€ 0.60

No credit cards. **Tel:** 0183 35 27 41. Fax: 0183 35 12 34. E-mail: info@svr.nl. **Reservations:** Contact site. **Open** 15 March - 31 October.

Directions: From Rotterdam follow A15 to junction with A27. Proceed 6 km. north on A27 to exit 25 for Noordeloos and join N214. Site is signed approx. 200 m. after roundabout at Noordeloos (don't enter the village).

Camping Het Amsterdamse Bos

566 Kleine Noorddijk 1, 1432 CC Aalsmeer (Noord-Holland)

Het Amsterdamse Bos is a very large park to the southwest of Amsterdam, one corner of which has been specially laid out as the city's municipal site. Close to Schiphol Airport (we noticed little noise), it is about 12 km. from central Amsterdam. A high season bus service runs from the site every 35 minutes during the day to the city (a local service at other times is 300 m). The site is well laid out alongside a canal, with unmarked pitches on separate flat lawns mostly backing onto pleasant hedges and trees, with several areas of hardstanding. It takes 400 tourist units, with 100 electrical connections (10A). An additional area is available for tents and groups.

Facilities: Two older style sanitary blocks rather let the site down, appearing somewhat small and well used. A third block is good. Hot water is on payment to the washbasins but pre-set hot showers are free. Laundry facilities. Motorcaravan services. Gas supplies. Small shop. Cafe/bar and snack bar. Children's sand pit. Fishing, boating, pancake restaurant in the park. **Off site:** Riding and bicycle hire 5 km.

Charges guide

Per person over 4 yrs	€ 4.45
caravan	€ 3.30
tent	€ 2.80
car or motorcycle	€ 2.35
motorcaravan	€ 5.60
dog	€ 1.55
electricity (10A)	€ 3.40

Group reductions. **Tel:** 0206 41 68 68. Fax: 0206 40 23 78. E-mail: camping@dab.amsterdam.nl. **Reservations:** A limited number only will be made for 'serious enquirers'. **Open** 1 April - 15 October.

Directions: Amsterdamse Bos and site are west of Amstelveen. From the A9 motorway exit for either Amstelveen or Aalsmeer (easier), turn towards Aalsmeer and look out carefully for camp signs.

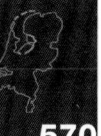

Netherlands - West
Gaasper Camping Amsterdam

567 Loosdrechtdreef 7, 1108 AZ Amsterdam (Noord-Holland)

Amsterdam is probably the most popular destination for visits in the Netherlands, and Gaasper Camping is on the southeast side, a short walk from a Metro station. On the edge of a large park with a lake, there are also opportunities for relaxation. The site is well kept and neatly laid out on flat grass with attractive trees and shrubs. There are 390 touring pitches in two areas - one more open and grassy, mainly kept for tents, the other more formal with numbered pitches divided by ditches or good hedges. Areas of hardstanding are available and all caravan pitches have electricity (4/10A). Some 60 seasonal and permanent units have their own area. In high season the site becomes very crowded and it is necessary to arrive during the day to find space (in July/Aug. check-ins start at 11.00 hrs). Although this is a typical, busy city site, there is a friendly welcome, with English spoken.

Facilities: Three modern, clean toilet blocks (one unisex) for the tourist sections are an adequate provision. Some washbasins in private cabins. Hot water for showers and some washing-up sinks on payment. Facilities for babies. Washing machine and dryer. Motorcaravan services. Gas supplies. New supermarket (1/4-15/10). Café/bar plus takeaway (1/4-15/10). Shopping centre and restaurant nearby. Children's play area on grass. **Off site:** Riding 200 m. Fishing 1 km. Golf 4 km.

Charges 2002

Per person	€ 4.00
child (0-11 yrs)	€ 1.75
caravan or tent	€ 4.25 - € 5.75
car	€ 3.50
motorcaravan	€ 7.00
electricity	€ 2.00

No credit cards. **Tel:** 0206 96 73 26. Fax: 0206 96 93 69. **Reservations:** Made only in writing for caravans or motorcaravans for min. stay of 7 nights (state whether single/double axle and with/without awning). **Open** all year except 1 January - 14 March.

Directions: Take exit for Gaasperplas/Weesp (S113) from the section of A9 motorway which is on the east side of the A2. Note: do not take the Gaasperdam exit (S112) which comes first if approaching from the west.

Netherlands - West
Molengroet Recreatieverblijven

570 Molengroet 1, 1723 PX Noord-Scharwoude (Noord-Holland)

Molengroet is a modern, pleasant site, close to a lake for watersports and 40 km. from Amsterdam. It is a useful stop on the way to the Afsluitdijk across the top of the Ijsselmeer or as an enjoyable stop for watersport enthusiasts. The 260 touring pitches are grouped according to services provided, ranging from simple pitches with no services, to those with electricity (4/10A), TV, water and waste water. The bar and restaurant are open all season and there is a snack bar in high season. The nearby lake with surf school is an attractive proposition, particularly for those with teenagers. A site bus can take you to the local pool or the beach. Friendly multi-lingual staff provide local information. A member of the Holland Tulip Parcs group.

Facilities: The best sanitary facilities, in a modern, heated building, are near the serviced pitches. Supplemented by two other blocks, all necessary facilities are provided. Motorcaravan services. Gas supplies. Shop (1/4-1/9), bread and milk from reception at other times. Restaurant/bar (1/4-1/9). Fishing. Bicycle hire. Surfboards and small boats for hire. Entertainment is organised in high season and at weekends. **Off site:** Watersports close. Tennis, squash and swimming nearby. Riding or golf 5 km.

Charges 2002

Per unit incl. 2 persons, electricity	€ 23.00
with private sanitary facility	€ 30.00
extra person (over 2 yrs)	€ 3.50

Reductions in low season and for longer stays. **Tel:** 0226 39 34 44. Fax: 0226 39 14 26. E-mail: info@molengroet.nl. **Reservations:** Made with 50% deposit on booking, balance 3 weeks before arrival. **Open** 1 April - 1 November.

Directions: From Haarlem on A9 to Alkmaar take N245 towards Schagen. Site is southwest of Noord Sharwoude, signed on Geestermerambacht road.

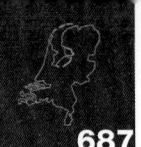

Kennemer Duincamping de Lakens

687 Zeeweg 60, 2051 EC Bloemendaal aan Zee (Noord-Holland)

De Lakens is part of the Kennemer Duincampings group and is beautifully located in the dunes at Bloemendaal aan Zee. De Lakens has 940 reasonably large, flat pitches with a hardstanding of shells. There are 410 are for tourers (235 with 10A electricity) and the sunny pitches are separated by low hedging. This site is a true oasis of peace in a part of the Netherlands usually bustling with activity. From this site it is possible to walk straight through the dunes to the North Sea. Although there is no pool, a lake on the site can be used for swimming or, of course, there is the sea. A separate area is provided for groups and youngsters to maintain the quiet atmosphere. We feel you could have an enjoyable holiday here - weather permitting.

Facilities: The six toilet blocks for tourers (two brand new) include controllable showers, washbasins (open style and in cabins), facilities for disabled people and a baby room. Launderette. Two motorcaravan service points. Bar/restaurant and snack bar. Supermarket. Adventure type playgrounds. Bicycle hire. Basketball, table football, table tennis and boules. Entertainment program in high season for all ages. Boat slipway. Fishing. Dogs are not accepted. **Off site:** Beach 1 km. Riding 1 km. Golf 10 km.

Charges 2003

Per pitch	€ 19,45 - € 23,85
with electricity	€ 22,35 - € 26,75

Tel: 023 573 2266. Fax: 023 573 2288. E-mail: delakens@kennemerduincampings.nl. **Reservations:** Made with deposit and fee. **Open** 1 April - 1 November.

Directions: From Amsterdam go west to Haarlem and follow the N200 from Haarlem towards Bloemendaal aan zee. Site is on the N200, on the right hand side.

Camping Sint Maartenszee

574 Westerduinweg 30, 1753 BA Sint Maartenszee (Noord-Holland)

Situated within easy travelling distance of the attractive and interesting towns of North Holland, especially Alkmaar, this excellent family site is separated from the sea by 900 m. of grassy dunes. With the dune environment, the ground is basically sandy but grass has grown well and hedges are now established. Specialising in family holidays, unusually for the Netherlands only touring units are taken (with a bungalow park adjacent). The 300 pitches are arranged in lines backed by high hedging; 200 have electricity and 150 are fully serviced with water, drainage and cable TV connections. A good restaurant/bar, with attractive terrace overlooking the minigolf, has a sitting area with open fire and board games provided. This is a pretty and interesting area of the Netherlands and Sint Maartenszee is quite near the fascinating man-made barrier built to form the Ijsselmeer which allowed the reclamation of so much land.

Facilities: Two first class modern toilet blocks are in low neat buildings. Hot water for showers is free (with a fascinating panel demonstrating how solar power helps to heat the water). They include washcabins, family shower rooms, baby bathrooms and raised level showers for children. Dishwashing and laundry room with hot water on payment and microwave. Each block has a couple resident on site to clean and maintain standards throughout the day. Motorcaravan services. Gas supplies. Restaurant/bar (all season). Supermarket (all season). Minigolf. Volleyball. Basketball. Children`s play areas. No dogs or transistors accepted. **Off site:** Bicycle hire 200 m. Fishing 1 km. Bus service from village to Alkmaar (cheese market on Fridays April - Sept).

Charges 2002

Per unit: 60 sq.m. pitch	€ 7.40 - € 11.75
90 sq.m. pitch with electricity	€ 12.25 - € 18.00
fully serviced	€ 13.80 - € 21.00
person	€ 3.15
local tax	€ 0.60

No credit cards. **Tel:** 0224 56 14 01. Fax: 0224 56 19 01. E-mail: info@campingsintmaartenszee.nl. **Reservations:** Made for some pitches (all with electricity) with deposit (details from site) but 40% are kept free from reservation for any length of stay. **Open** 28 March - 15 September.

Directions: From Alkmaar, take N9 northwards towards Den Helder. Site is signed after approx. 18 km. towards the sea at St-Maartensvlotbrug.

Camping Westerkogge

682 Kerkebuurt 202, 1647 MH Berkhout (Noord-Holland)

Camping Westerkogge is near the A7 motorway and Hoorn, and close to the Ijsselmeer. The 300 pitches (100 for touring units) are on grassy fields, surrounded by high trees and bushes that provide shade; 80 pitches have 4A electricity and 28 of these also have water and drainage. From this site you can cycle through the lovely West Friesland countryside, sail on the Ijsselmeer or visit the attractive old town of Hoorn. It is also a good base for visiting Amsterdam or the harbour of Den Helder. After that you could tour through the polder by boat or hire a canoe. Fishing is even easier because it's possible on site. Besides all the activities in the area, the site itself has a lot to offer. Take a dive in the covered swimming pool, join in at the shows or the bingo or for youngsters there's a special disco twice a week. This is a site for the whole family.

Facilities: Three toilet blocks include washbasins (open style and in cabins), child size washbasins and unisex showers (token). Facilities for disabled visitors. Laundry. Covered sinks with free hot water. Motorcaravan services. Shop (in reception). Café with bar and snacks. Covered pool (10 x 5 m) with separate paddling pool (also open to the public). Playground. Sports court. Tennis court. Bicycle hire. Go-kart and canoe hire. Boat trips through the polder. **Off site:** Golf 15 km. Riding 10 km. Beach 30 km.

Charges 2002

Per unit incl. 2 persons, and 4A electricity	€ 16.05 - € 17.97
extra person	€ 2.55 - € 2.80
pet	€ 1.80 - € 2.05

Tel: 0229 55 12 08. Fax: 0229 55 13 90. E-mail: info@camping-westerkogge.nl. **Reservations:** Contact site. **Open** 1 April - 30 October.

Directions: Follow the A7 from Amsterdam north towards Hoorn and take exit Berkhout/Hoorn. Follow signs for Berkhout and site.

Camping Jachthaven Uitdam

572 Zeedijk 2, 1154 PP Uitdam (Noord-Holland)

Situated beside the Markermeer which is used extensively for watersports, this large site has its own private yachting marina (300 yachts and boats). It has 200 seasonal and permanent pitches, many used by watersports enthusiasts, but also offers 260 marked tourist pitches (120 with 6A electricity) on open, grassy ground overlooking the water and 14 mobile homes to rent. There is a special area for campers with bicycles. Very much dominated by the marina, this site will appeal to watersports enthusiasts, with opportunities for sailing, windsurfing and swimming, but it is also on a pretty stretch of coast, 15 km. north east of Amsterdam.

Facilities: Two rather basic toilet blocks in fairly open buildings have hot showers on payment. A third block is of excellent quality. Motorcaravan services. Gas supplies. Shop (1/4-1/10). Bar/restaurant (weekends and high season). TV room. Tennis. Children's playground. Bicycle hire. Fishing. Yacht marina (with fuel) and slipway. Watersports facilities. Entertainment in high season.

Charges 2002

Per unit incl. 2 persons	€ 18.50
extra person (over 2 yrs)	€ 3.75
tent	€ 12.00 - € 15.00
dog	€ 3.00
boat on trailer	€ 6.00
boat in marina, per metre (min. € 7.75)	€ 1.30

Less 20% outside 1/5-7/9. **Tel:** 0204 03 14 33. Fax: 0204 03 36 92. E-mail: info@campinguitdam.nl. **Reservations:** Contact site. **Open** 1 March - 1 November.

Directions: From the A10, take the N247 towards Volendam then Monnickendam exit south in the direction of of Marken, then Uitdam.

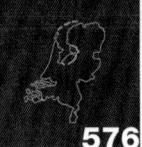

Nauticpark de Kuilart

576 Kuilart 1, 8723 CG Koudum (Friesland)

De Kuilart is a well run, modern site by Friesland`s largest lake and with its own marina and boating facilities, it attracts many watersports enthusiasts. The marina provides windsurfing and sailing lessons and boat hire, and there are special rates at the site for groups and sailing clubs. However, the site has an excellent indoor swimming pool as well as an area for lake swimming and on land there are sports facilities and woods for cycling and walking. It may also therefore appeal for a relaxing break in a pleasant area not much visited by British campers. The 560 pitches at De Kuilart are in groups of 10 to 16 on areas of grass surrounded by well established hedges. There are 225 for tourers, 200 with electricity, water, waste water and TV connections. The restaurant provides good views of the lake and woodland. A member of the Holland Tulip Parcs group.

Facilities: Four modern, heated sanitary blocks well spaced around the site are of above average quality, although showers are on payment and most wash-basins (half in private cabins) have only cold water. Launderette. Motorcaravan services. Gas supplies. Restaurant/bar (23/3-4/11). Supermarket (20/4-2/9). Indoor pool (3 sessions daily, 23/3-4/11). Sauna and solarium. Lake swimming area. Sports field. Children`s playground. Tennis. Bicycle hire. Fishing. Recreation team (high season). Marina (600 berth) with windsurfing, boat hire and boat shop. Garage at harbour. Dogs are accepted in certain areas (if booked). **Off site:** Riding or golf 4 km

Charges 2002

Per unit incl. 2 persons	€ 15.00 - € 19.00
pitch with services	€ 13.00 - € 20.50
extra person (over 1 yr)	€ 3.75

Tourist tax and babies under 1 year included. Special weekend rates at B.Hs. **Tel:** 0514 52 22 21. Fax: 0514 52 30 10. E-mail: info@kuilart.nl. **Reservations:** Advised as site is very popular; made from Sat. - Sat. only in peak season. **Open** all year.

Directions: Site is southeast of Koudum, on the Fluessen lake. Follow the camping sign off the N359 Bolsward - Lemmer road.

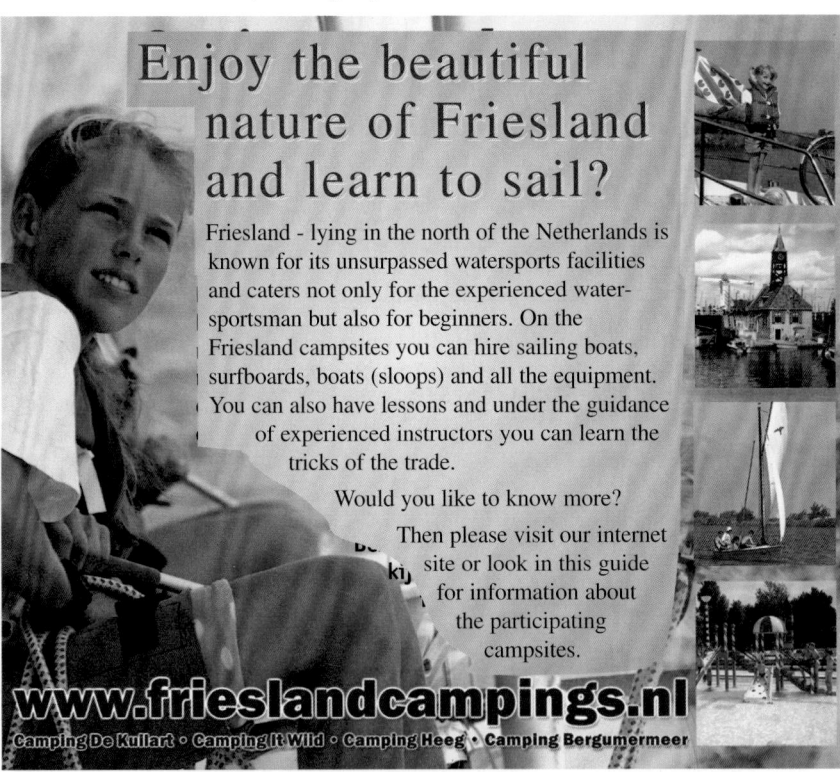

Enjoy the beautiful nature of Friesland and learn to sail?

Friesland - lying in the north of the Netherlands is known for its unsurpassed watersports facilities and caters not only for the experienced watersportsman but also for beginners. On the Friesland campsites you can hire sailing boats, surfboards, boats (sloops) and all the equipment. You can also have lessons and under the guidance of experienced instructors you can learn the tricks of the trade.

Would you like to know more?

Then please visit our internet site or look in this guide for information about the participating campsites.

www.frieslandcampings.nl

Camping De Kuilart • Camping It Wiid • Camping Heeg • Camping Bergumermeer

The Friesland Campings Group

There are four campsites in this group:

576 Nauticpark de Kuilart - see above.
Camping It Wiid, Kooidijk 10, 9264 TP Eernewoude/Earnewâld
Tel: 0511 53 92 23 Fax: 0511 53 93 35. E-mail: info@wiid.nl
Watersportcamping Heeg, de Burd 25a, NL-8621 JX Heeg
Tel: 0515 442328. Fax: 0515 442739. E-mail: wch@watersportcampingheeg.nl
Leisurepark Bergumermeer, Solcamastraat 30, 9262 ND Suameer
Tel: 0511-461385. Fax: 0511-463955. E-mail: info@bergumermeer.nl

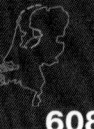

Netherlands - North
Camping De Zeehoeve

608 Westerzeedijk 45, 8862 PK Harlingen (Friesland)

Superbly located, directly behind the sea dyke of the Waddensea and just a kilometre from the harbour of Harlingen, De Zeehoeve is an attractive and spacious site. It has 300 pitches (125 for tourers), all with 6A electricity and 20 with water, drainage and electricity. This splendid location allows one the opportunity to watch the sun slowly setting from the sea dyke. You can also stroll through Harlingen or take the ferry to Vlieland or Terschelling. It is possible to moor your own boat at Harlingen, to hire a boat or book a sailing or sea fishing trip. De Zeehoeve is ideal for rest and relaxation, for watersports or visit the attractions of Harlingen and Friesland. After a day of activity, one can wine and dine in the site restaurant or one of the many pubs in Harlingen.

Facilities: Three sanitary blocks include open style washbasins with cold water only, washbasins in cabins with hot and cold water, controllable showers (on payment), family showers and a baby bath. Facilities for disabled people. Cooking hob. Launderette. Sinks with free hot water. Motorcaravan services. Bar/restaurant (1/7-31/8). Playground. Volleyball. Bicycle hire. Pedaloes and canoes for hire. Fishing. Extensive entertainment programme in July/Aug. **Off site:** Beach 200 m. Riding 10 km.

Charges 2002

Per adult	€ 3.50
child (4-11 yrs)	€ 3.00
caravan or tent	€ 3.50
car or m/cycle	€ 2.00
motorcaravan	€ 5.50
electricity	€ 2.00
pet	€ 2.00

Tel: 0517 41 34 65. **Fax:** 0517 41 69 71. **Reservations:** Contact site. **Open** 1 April - 15 October.

Directions: From Leeuwarden take A31 southwest to Harlingen, then follow site signs.

CAMPING *DE ZEEHOEVE*

Part of the famous Eleven-City skating route, "De Zeehoeve" is by the city of Harlingen, the only seaport in the beautiful, historical province of Friesland. You can make a day trip to Vlieland or Terschelling, two of the lovely Wadden Islands and our province has many places of interest, most close to the city itself - the Ald Faers Erf-route, Kazemattenmuseum, Technical Activity Centre Aeolus, the Planetarium in Franeker ans. You can rent bikes, canoe or use pedaloes, cycle, ramble or go sea fishing on the Waddensea - these are just some of the things to see and do in Friesland. The campsite is 1 km. south of Harlingen, with heated modern toilet facilities - launderette - animation in high season - an inland harbour with a trailer slip, and there is accommodation to hire.

Fam. Kleefstra, Westerzeedijk 45, 8862 PK Harlingen
Tel. +31 517-413465, fax +31 517-416971
E-mail: info@zeehoeve.nl www.zeehoeve.nl

Netherlands - North
Camping 't Strandheem

612 Parkweg 2, 9865 VP Opende (Groningen)

Camping Strandheem has some quite large, numbered pitches (110 sq.m.) some with hardstanding and suitable for motorcaravans. Of the 330 pitches, 180 are used for tourers, all with water, electricity and cable connections and partly separated by low hedges, although there is not much shade. This is a good base for some interesting excursions, including visits to the fishing harbour of Lauwersoog or the little village of Eenrum where you can learn how to make mustard in Abraham's Mosterdmakerij, design wax candles in a candle factory and visit a wooden shoe factory. The site itself also has a lot to offer. For youngsters there is an entertainment program in high season with water games in the lake next to the site, real life theatre, games and craft work; for adults there are card nights or films twice a week. De Bruinewoud family will give you a warm welcome.

Facilities: Two modern toilet buildings have washbasins (open style and in cabins), controllable showers, child size toilets and basins, a good baby room and fully equipped bathroom. Facilities for disabled people. Launderette. Motorcaravan service. Shop. Café with bar and snack bar. Covered swimming pool (5 x 5 m) with separate paddling pool and slide. Playgrounds. Minigolf. Fishing. Bicycle hire. Volleyball. Basketball. Boules. Lake with beach (€ 1 p/p per day). Extensive recreation program in July and August. Film and card nights. **Off site:** Lake with beach 100 m. Riding 6 km. Golf 15 km.

Charges 2002

Per unit incl. 2 persons	€ 17.00
extra person	€ 2.50
private sanitary facility	€ 6.50
electricity (4/10A)	€ 1.70 - € 2.30
dog	€ 2.50

Tel: 0594 65 95 55. **Fax:** 0594 65 85 92. **E-mail:** info@strandheem.nl. **Reservations:** Made with 50% deposit. **Open** 1 April - 1 October.

Directions: Follow the A7 west from Groningen towards Heereenveen and take exit 31. Follow camp signs from there.

Recreatiecentrum Barradeel

607 Buorren 43, 8851 EL Tzummarum (Friesland)

Camping Barradeel with its 160 pitches is not very large but, according to managing director Bouma, it is next to the largest nature reserve in Europe, the Waddensea. Of the 80 fairly spacious but not separated pitches for touring units, 60 have water, drainage, 6A electricity and cable TV connection. The other 20 pitches are for hikers. From the site it is an easy walk to the village of Tzummarum to buy the daily necessities (the site doesn't have a shop) but it is even shorter to the Waddensea. Also the fishing harbour Harlingen is close by and from here you can take the ferry to the islands of Vlieland and Terschelling. Another place worth visiting is Franeker, the oldest university city in the Netherlands, with the planetarium of Eise Eisinga. This small site, directly below the dykes of the Waddensea, offers peace and quiet and the chance to enjoy the sea air.

Facilities: Two older sanitary blocks have open style washbasins with cold water only, washbasins in cabins with hot and cold water, pre-set showers and a baby bath. Launderette. Restaurant and snack bar. Swimming pools with slide and fountain. Playground. Trampolines. Tennis courts. Sports court. Archery. Volleyball. Gym. Entertainment program in high season. Key deposit € 25. **Off site:** Large swimming pool, tennis courts and gym adjacent to site. Fishing and riding 1 km. Boat launching 6 km. Beach 13 km. Golf 20 km.

Charges 2002

per unit incl. 2 persons	€ 11,70 - € 15,00
extra person	€ 3,70
animal	€ 2,00

No credit cards. **Tel:** 0518 481600. E-mail: barradeel@nwfriesland.nl. **Reservations:** Made with 50% deposit. **Open** all year.

Directions: Take the A31 from Leeuwarden to the southwest to Harlingen and take exit 20 towards Dongjum/Tzummarum. Follow the N384 to the north to Tzummarum and follow the camp signs.

Camping Stadspark

577 Campinglaan 6, 9727 KH Groningen (Groningen)

The Stadspark is a large park to the south-west of the city, well signed and with easy access. The campsite is within the park with many trees and surrounded by water. It has 200 pitches with 150 for touring units, of which 75 have 6A electricity and 30 are fully serviced. The separate tent area is supervised directly by the manager. Buses for the city leave from right outside and timetables and maps are provided by Mrs Van der Veer, the helpful, English speaking manager. Groningen is a very lively city with lots to do.

Facilities: Two sanitary blocks, one totally refurbished, provide hot water for showers and dishwashing is now free. Motorcaravan service point. Shop (1/5-15/9). Café, bar and takeaway (1/5-15/9). Bicycle hire. Fishing. Canoeing. **Off site:** Riding and golf 10 km.

Charges 2002

Per unit incl. 2 adults	€ 11.80
extra adult	€ 2.30
child (2-12 yrs)	€ 1.50
electricity	€ 1.70
dog	€ 1.80
local tax	€ 0.40 - € 0.70

No credit cards. **Tel:** 0505 25 1624. Fax: 0505 25 00 99. E-mail: camping_stadspark@planet.nl. **Reservations:** Contact site. **Open** 15 March - 15 October.

Directions: From Assen on A28 turn left on the A7. Turn on N370 and follow site signs (Stadspark, quite close).

Netherlands - North
Camping Lauwersoog

609 Strandweg 5, 9976 VS Lauwersoog (Groningen)

The focus at Camping Lauwersoog is very much on the sea and watersports. One can have sailing lessons or hire canoes, sailing boats or fishing boats and it is a short stroll from the site to the beach. The site is also close to the harbour where you can take the ferry to Schiermonnikoog and let the wind blow away the cobwebs on the large beaches of this beautiful, almost car free island (only residents may take cars). The site's restaurant specialises in seafood and even the entertainment for all ages has a water theme. There are 450 numbered pitches with 225 for tourers. Electricity (4/6A) is available at 200 pitches and 80 have water, drainage, electricity and cable connections. The pitches are on level, grassy fields (some by the beach), partly separated by hedges.

Facilities: The two toilet blocks for tourers provide washbasins (open style and in cabins), pre-set showers and child size toilets. Facilities for disabled people. Laundry. Ice pack service. Covered sinks with free hot water. Motorcaravan service. Shop (daily in July/Aug) with delivery service. Seafood restaurant. Snack bar on the beach. Playground. Sailing school. Canoes, sailing boats and fishing boats for hire. Bicycle and go-kart hire. Volleyball. Boules. Extensive entertainment program for all ages in high season. Torch useful. **Off site:** Riding 5 km.

Charges 2002

Per unit incl. 2 persons, 6A electricity serviced pitch (125 sq.m)	€ 20.00 € 23.00
extra person	€ 3.00
local tax	€ 0.35

Tel: 0519 34 91 33. Fax: 0519 34 91 95.
Reservations: Made with 50% deposit. **Open** all year.

Directions: Follow N361 from Groningen north to Lauwersoog and then follow site signs.

Netherlands - North
Camping de Valkenhof

614 Beilerstraat 13a, 9431 GA Westerbork (Drenthe)

De Valkenhof is a spacious family site with 180 pitches, partly in the woods and partly on open fields without hedges to separate them. With 160 pitches for touring units, there are 143 with 4A electricity. With 500 km. of cycle paths, De Valkenhof and its surroundings are ideal for enjoying the woods and moors of Drente. The site is also close to the former concentration camp of Westerbork, which is well worth a visit and the museum village of Orvelte. De Valkenhof does not allow cars on the campsite itself and this, together with the large pitches, provides for a really quiet holiday. Other than a recreation room for youngsters, a pool and sanitary buildings, the site has few amenities but you'll find all you need in the village. The large outdoor pool (over 1,000 sq.m), with its giant slide will certainly appeal to children.

Facilities: Two modern toilet blocks have washbasins (open style and in cabins, only one block with hot water at the basins), pre-set showers, toilets, showers and basins for children and a baby room. Laundry. Sinks under cover. Some snacks from reception. Swimming pool with slide and paddling pool. Extensive entertainment program in high season for children. Boules. Library. Games room. Only gas barbecues are permitted. **Off site:** Bicycle hire 2 km.

Charges 2002

Per unit incl . 2 persons	€ 16.25
extra person	€ 3.00
local tax	€ 0.50

No credit cards. **Tel:** 0593 33 15 46. **Reservations:** Made with 50% deposit. **Open** 1 April - 1 October.

Directions: Travelling north from Zwolle on the A28, take exit Beilen/Westerbork. Follow N31 eastwards and take exit for Westerbork. From there follow the camp signs.

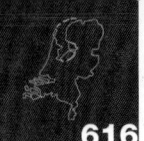

Recreatiecentrum Engeland

Oude Benderseweg 11, 7963 PX Ruinen (Drenthe)

616

Recreatiecentrum Engeland is a large, spacious site with 450 pitches in the woods in Drente. All 205 touring pitches have electricity (4/10A) and include 40 serviced pitches with water, drainage, cable TV and electricity. The numbered pitches are over 100 sq.m. in size and are on large, grassy fields, separated by hedges and in the shade of trees. This comfortable site in the heart of the province Drente allows you to relax and to bike or walk through the woods or over the moors. If you don`t want to find your way through the woods yourself the site provides guided biking trips and walks on a regular basis. Engel and Bengel arrange daily adventures, crafts or water games for children. Local attractions for children include Speelstad Oranje, a large play-town or Ponypark Slagharen. Adult activities include a `whisper tour` by boat through the `De Weerlibben` national park or a visit to the `water-town` of Giethoorn.

Facilities: Four well-spaced toilet blocks provide washbasins (open style and in cabins), child-size toilets, bathrooms, child-size baths and a baby room. Facilities for disabled visitors. Laundry. Motorcaravan services. Shop. Restaurant with Engel & Bengel menu. Pancake restaurant. Play areas between the pitches. Giant chess. Boules. Tennis courts. Minigolf. Bicycle hire. Full entertainment programme in high season. Dog are allowed on certain pitches only. **Off site:** Riding 500 m. Fishing 3 km. Golf 18 km.

Charges 2002

Per unit incl. 2 persons	€ 18.95
extra person	€ 3.00
serviced pitch, plus	€ 3.95
dog	€ 2.35
local tax	€ 0.50

No credit cards. **Tel:** 0522 47 17 70. Fax: 0522 47 26 14. E-mail: engeland@etrade.nl. **Reservations:** Made with € 5,75 booking fee; contact site. **Open** 1 April - 1 October.

Directions: From Zwolle follow A28 north and take Ruinen exit. Follow site signs from there.

Rekreatiepark 't Kuierpadtien

Oranjekanaal NZ 10, 7853 TA Wezuperbrug (Drenthe)

579

Professionally run, this all year round site is suitable as a night stop, or for longer if you wish to participate in all the activities offered in July and August (on payment). These encompass canoeing, windsurfing, water shutes and the dry-ski slope, which is also open during the winter so that the locals can practise before going en-masse to Austria. There are three opportunities for swimming with an indoor pool supplemented by a heated outdoor pool (June-Aug) and the lake itself. The site itself is in a woodland setting on the edge of the village. The 320 flat and grassy pitches for touring units (with 650 in total) are of reasonable size. All have 4A electricity and 10 are fully serviced A member of the Holland Tulip Parcs group.

Facilities: Eight quite acceptable sanitary blocks, including a new one, with hot showers (17.30 - 10.00 in July/Aug). Motorcaravan services Supermarket (1/4-15/9) but bread all year. Restaurant and bar (all year). Indoor pool. Outdoor pool (1/4-1/9). Sauna, solarium and whirlpool. Tennis. Dry ski slope. Play areas. Boules, volleyball and basketball.

Charges 2002

Per person (over 1 yr)	€ 4.10
pitch	€ 8.50 - € 16.75
car	€ 2.75
dog (max. 1)	€ 2.75
local tax	€ 0.50

No credit cards. **Tel:** 0591 38 14 15. Fax: 0591 38 22 35. E-mail: info@kuierpad.nl. **Reservations:** Advised for July/Aug. and made with deposit. **Open** all year.

Directions: From N34 Groningen-Emmen road exit near Emmen onto N31 towards Beilen. Turn right into Schoonord where left to Wezuperbrug. Site is at beginning of village on the right.

Netherlands - Central
Rekreatiepark Hazevreugd

619 Vormtweg 9, 8321 NC Urk (Flevoland)

Recreatiepark Hazevreugd, set in the Urkerbos on the former island Urk, is a true family site with lots of sporting facilities. You can hire go-karts and bikes, go surfing from the beaches of the Ijsselmeer or go riding in the woods. Besides the sporting activities, this site is an excellent base for a visit to the Batavia shipyard in Lelystad where you can see original 17th century ships that sailed to India. You can also make a boat trip to the Zuiderzee-museum in Enkhuizen or visit the `water-town' of Giethoorn. The site has 220 pitches, 192 for tourers, all with shade and 6A electricity. There are also 63 serviced pitches with water, electricity and drainage and separate pitches for motorcaravans.

Facilities: Two modern toilet blocks have wash-basins (open style and in cabins), pre-set showers, child size toilets, family showers and a baby room. Laundry. Sinks with free hot water. Motorcaravan services Shop (bread to order). Bar/restaurant (29/6-10/8) and snack bar. Outdoor pool (40 sq.m.) with paddling pool. Playground. Sports court. Boules. Bicycle and go-kart hire. **Off site:** Fishing, boat launching and beach 2 km.

Charges 2002

Per unit incl. up to 4 persons	€ 24.00 - € 27.00
extra person over 4 yrs	€ 3.00
dog	€ 2.50
serviced pitch, plus	€ 2.50
local tax	€ 0.57

No credit cards. **Tel:** 0527 68 17 85. E-mail: info@hazevreugd.nl. **Reservations:** Made with € 15 fee (Sat. - Sat. only). **Open** April - September.

Directions: Follow the A6 from Almere to the north and take exit 13 to Urk (N352). Site is next to the Urkerbos and well signed.

Netherlands - Central
Camping De Roos

598 Beerzerweg 10, 7736 PJ Beerze-Ommen (Overijssel)

De Roos is a family run site in a area of outstanding natural beauty, truly a nature lover's campsite. It is situated in Overijssel's Vecht Valley, a unique region set in a river dune landscape on the River Vecht. The river and its tributary wend their through this spacious campsite. It is a natural setting that the owners of De Roos have carefully preserved. Conserving the environment is paramount here and the 285 pitches and necessary amenities have been blended into the landscape with great care. Pitches, many with electricity, are naturally sited, some behind blackthorn thickets, in the shadow of an old oak, or in a clearing scattered with wild flowers. De Roos is a car-free campsite during peak periods - vehicles must be parked at the car park. Swimming, fishing and boating is possible in the Vecht. The enthusiastic owners have compiled walking and cycling routes in English.

Facilities: Four well maintained sanitary blocks are kept fresh and clean. The two larger blocks are heated and include baby bath/shower and wash cabins (no toilet paper). Dishwashing sinks. Launderette. Motorcaravan services. Health food shop and tea room (1/5-1/9). River swimming. Fishing. Bicycle hire. Volleyball. Basketball. Boules. Table tennis. Several small playgrounds and field for kite flying. Gas supplies. Dogs are not accepted (and cats must be kept on a lead!) Torch useful. **Off site:** Riding 6 km. Golf 10 km.

Charges 2002

Per pitch	€ 10.70 - € 12.50
person over 3 yrs	€ 2.40 - € 2.90
electricity	€ 2.00
tourist tax	€ 0.50

Discounts in low season and special packages. **Tel:** 0523 25 12 34. Fax: 0523 25 19 03. E-mail: info@camping-de-roos.nl. **Reservations:** Contact site; reservations made with € 6,81 fee. **Open** 30 March - 27 October.

Directions: Leave A28 at Ommen exit 21 and join N340 for 19 km. to Ommen. Turn right at traffic lights over bridge and immediately left on local road towards Beerze. Site on left after 7 km. just after Beerze village sign.

Netherlands - Central
Camping De Vechtstreek

599

Grote Beltenweg 17, 7794 RA Rheeze-Hardenberg (Overijssel)

It would be difficult for any child (or adult) to pass this site and not be curiously drawn to the oversized open story book which marks its entrance. From here young children turn the pages and enter the exciting world of Hannah and Bumpie, two of the nine characters around which this site's fairy-tale theme has been created. The young owners of De Vechtstreek have given their park a special identity by creating this fairy tale. The colourful characters appear on finger boards and signs throughout the site. Not only is the story acted out in the restaurant at the Saturday children's buffet, the story continues in the indoor water play park which is dominated by Hannah's Castle. It is also a campsite which offers top class facilities. There are 270 touring pitches mostly laid out in bays which accommodate around 12 units. In the centre of each is a small children's play area. There are many water points and pitches have electricity (4A). Although there are numerous static vans these are unobtrusive and placed away from the touring area. The site has a mature appearance with many trees and shrubs

Facilities: Three modern, well equipped and heated sanitary blocks include a baby room, family shower and outside washing-up area. Excellent laundry room Well stocked supermarket. Restaurant, snack bar and takeaway (all season). Play areas. Fairy-tale water play park. Daily activity club. Football field. Theatre. Access to a fishing, swimming and boating recreation area at rear of site (200 m).

Charges 2002

Per unit incl. 2 persons	€ 22.95 - € 28.95
3 persons	€ 25.10 - € 31.75
4 persons	€ 27.25 - € 34.65
extra person	€ 4.20
dog	€ 2.50
local tax	€ 0.35

Tel: 0523 26 13 69. Fax: 0523 26 59 42. E-mail: camp.vechtstreek@wxs.nl. **Reservations:** Contact site. **Open** 1 April - 15 September.

Directions: From Ommen take N34 Hardenberg road for 9 km. Turn right on N36 and proceed south for approx. 3.5 km. Turn left at first crossroads and immediately left again on local road. Site clearly signed on left in 2 km.

Netherlands - Central
Camping De Molenhof

648

Oude Bornsedijk 30, 7667 SC Reutum/Weerselo (Overijssel)

De Molenhof is a pleasant family site where you can enjoy the real Twent hospitality. It has 450 well laid out pitches of which 400 are for touring units, all with water, drainage, electricity (4/10A) and cable connections. The remaining 50 pitches are currently occupied by mobile homes, but these are to be replaced with touring pitches in the next two years. This is a real family site and children in the 12-14 year age group particularly will enjoy themselves in the covered, adventure playground, the two swimming pools (one outdoor, one covered) with a large slide on the outside and with the entertainment team that provides a full daily programme in high season. The highlight for youngsters will probably be the new sanitary block which has a special 'fairy tale' style children's area. Taking a shower here will be a real treat. Older guests are not forgotten - the site organises sports tournaments or you can take a tour with a tilt-cart through the woods. You can explore the rich Twent surroundings by bike or go shopping in Almelo, Hengelo, Enschede or even in Germany, since you are close to the border.

Facilities: Four toilet blocks, one in 'fairy tale style' for children, provide washbasins (open style and in cabins), adult and child size toilets and basins, controllable showers, bathrooms and a baby room. Laundrette. Motorcaravan service. Well stocked shop. Bar/restaurant. Pancake restaurant. Swimming pools. Playgrounds (1 covered). Sports court. Tennis court. Fishing. Bicycle and go-kart hire. Boules. Extensive entertainment program in high season. **Off site:** Golf 8 km. Beach 6 km. Riding 6 km.

Charges 2002

Per fully serviced pitch incl. 2 persons	€ 26.00
incl. 3 persons	€ 30.00
extra person	€ 4.00

Tel: 0541 66 12 01. E-mail: molenhof@wxs.nl. **Reservations:** Made with 50% deposit. **Open** all year.

Directions: Follow A1 from Amsterdam east to Hengelo and take exit 31, Hengelo Noord. Go through Deurningen to Weerselo and from there the N343 towards Tubbergen and site signs.

Rekreatiepark de Luttenberg

581 Heuvelweg 9, 8105 SZ Luttenberg (Overijssel)

This woodland site is near the Sallandse Heuvelrug nature reserve and is well placed for relaxing walking and cycling tours. It is a large park with 120 seasonal pitches around the perimeter and 220 touring pitches (all with 4A electricity) in a central area off tarmac access roads. The large, individual pitches are numbered and separated, in rows divided by hedges and trees, with easy access. A separate cluster is for dog owners. There is a large bar and eating area with terrace and a small, separate restaurant The new 25 metre swimming pool and a small one for children, with the on-site activities and an animal enclosure provide plenty to keep younger visitors happy. A member of the Holland Tulip Parcs group.

Facilities: New heated sanitary block with controllable showers gives a satisfactory overall provision together with two other blocks. All are heated and each provides hot showers on payment. Motorcaravan services. Gas supplies. Small shop for essentials including bread. Bar and restaurant (low season: Tues. and Fri-Sun). Barbecue with seating. Swimming pool (15/5-15/9). Tennis. Table tennis. Football. Volleyball. Boules. Bicycle hire. Minigolf. **Off site:** Fishing 1.5 km. Riding 6 km.

Charges 2003

Per unit incl. 2 persons and electricity	€ 19.75
hikers and cyclists (2 persons)	€ 13.40
extra person (over 3 yrs)	€ 3.65
dog	€ 3.65

Less 15% outside 15/7-1/9. No credit cards. **Tel:** 0572 30 14 05. Fax: 0572 30 17 57. E-mail: info@luttenberg.nl. **Reservations:** Made with fee; contact site. **Open** 31 March - 1 October.

Directions: From N35 Zwolle - Almelo turn on N348 Ommen road east of Raalte, then turn to Luttenberg and follow signs. From A1 (Amsterdam - Hengelo) take exit 23 at Deventer on N348, then as above.

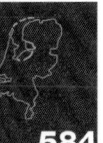

Camping de Pampel

584 Woeste Hoefweg 33-35, 7351 TN Hoenderloo (Gelderland)

A site with no static holiday caravans is rare in the Netherlands and this adds to the congenial atmosphere at De Pampel. This is enhanced by its situation deep in the forest, with 9 ha. of its own woods to explore. This peaceful park offers many opportunities for interesting outings with the two National Parks in the vicinity, the Kroller-Muller museum and the city of Arnhem. The area has excellent cycle paths which can be joined from a gate at the back of the site. There are 185 pitches (20 seasonal). You can choose to site yourself around the edge of a large open field with volleyball, etc. in the middle, or pick one of the individual places which are numbered, divided by trees and generally quite spacious. All have electricity (no heaters allowed) but the furthest pitches are some distance from the toilet facilities.

Facilities: Toilet facilities are good and modern, with free hot showers. Dishwashing. Laundry. Shop (1/4-31/10). Restaurant. Bar and snack bar open high season (July/Aug), otherwise at weekends only. Swimming pool and child's pool, heated by solar panels, are open Easter - Oct. Play area. Pets corner. Sports area. Barbecues by permission only, no open fires. Dogs are not accepted.

Charges 2003

Per unit incl. 2 persons	€ 22.50
without car	€ 16.50
extra person	€ 5.00
child (1-11 yrs)	€ 4.00
electricity (4/6A)	€ 3.00 - € 3.50
serviced pitch	€ 2.75

Less 20% (excl. electricity) in low seasons. **Tel:** 0553 78 17 60. Fax: 0553 78 19 92. E-mail: info@pampel.nl. **Reservations:** Made with deposit (50%). **Open** all year.

Directions: From the A50 Arnhem-Apeldoorn road exit for Hoenderloo and follow signs.

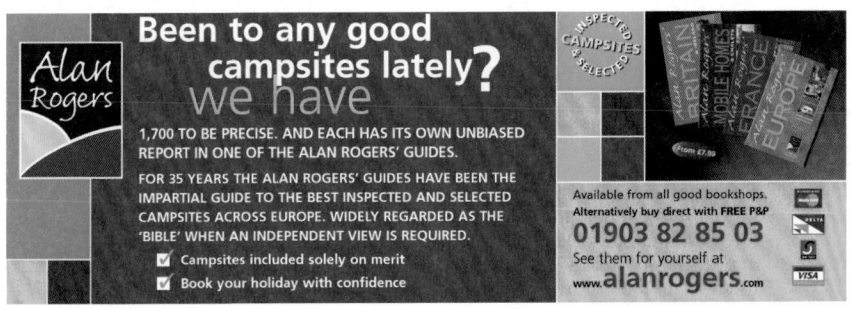

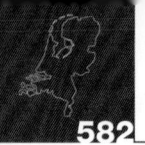

Netherlands - Central
Camping de Hertshoorn

582 Putterweg 68-70, 3886 PG Garderen (Gelderland)

Although this is quite a large site, this is not immediately apparent with its woodland location. Careful design has allowed both single pitches in little glades and groups on cleared grassy areas with plenty of gentle shade. Around 383 of the pitches are for tourists and all have electricity (6A), water, drainage and cable TV connection. Cars must be parked on the entrance car park. The very smart reception (more like a hotel than a camp site!) provides information packs in English, with a pleasant restaurant at the rear which the owners call 'a living room for guests'. Well kept small animal paddocks and stables entertain the children and a variety of play equipment is around the site, plus a play area with rocks, water and sand. Garderen is a pretty village, 1 km. away, and the area is very suitable for cycling. Adding a new word to the camping vocabulary, the site has three 'tree-tents' for hire. These drop-shaped, canvas tents with steel frames and wooden floors are suspended from pine trees and accommodate two people (with access by ladder!) - we have yet to try them!

Facilities: Four excellent toilet blocks provide comprehensive, heated facilities with a variety of cabins and showers (showers electronically timed), dishwashing facilities and freezers and one block houses a well equipped laundry. Gas supplies. Motorcaravan services Supermarket. Restaurant (closed Mondays). Snacks. Indoor heated swimming and paddling pools and outdoor paddling pools. Minigolf. Children's farm. Play areas. Entertainment for children in high season. Bicycle hire. Baby equipment hire. Tree tents for rent. Dogs are not accepted. **Off site:** Riding 2 km. Golf 8 km.

Charges 2003
Per unit incl. 2 persons, electricity	€ 20.00 - € 30.00
extra person	€ 2.50 - € 3.30
local tax	€ 0.60

Weekly family packages - details from site. No credit cards. **Tel:** 0577 461 529. Fax: 0577 461 556. E-mail: hertshoorn@vvc.nl. **Reservations:** Advised for high season. **Open** 29 March - 25 October.

Directions: From A1/E30 between Amersfoort and Apeldoorn, take Garderen exit no. 17. Cross the N344, through village and site is signed on the Putten road.

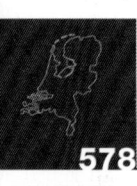

Netherlands - Central
Holiday Park de Zanding

578 Vijverlaan 1, 6731 CK Otterlo (Gelderland)

the travel service
TO BOOK
Ferry ✓
Pitch ✓
Accommodation ✓
01892 55 98 98

De Zanding is a family run, highly rated site that offers almost every recreational facility, either on site or nearby, that active families or couples might seek. Immediately after the entrance, a lake is to the left where you can swim, fish, sunbathe or try a two-person canoe. There are many sporting options and organised high season programmes for all ages. Minutes away is the Hoge Veluwe National Park, recommended for a great day out either cycling, walking or visiting the Kröller-Müller Museum (with the second largest collection of Van Gogh paintings after Amsterdam). There are 500 touring pitches spread around the site, some individual and separated, others in more open spaces shaded by trees. Most have electricity (4/10A). Some serviced pitches are in small groups between long stay units and there is another area for tents. Seasonal units and mobile homes take a further 470 pitches. In the village of Otterlo are a 14th century Dutch Reformed Church and the Netherlands Tile Museum. A member of the Holland Tulip Parcs group.

Facilities: First class sanitary facilities are housed in five modern blocks that are clean, well maintained and well rquipped. Good provision for babies and people with disabilities. Laundry. Kitchen. Motorcaravan services. Gas supplies. Supermarket. Restaurant/bar (15/5-15/9). Lake swimming. Fishing. Tennis. Minigolf. Boules. Volleyball. Five children's play areas. Bicycle hire. Organised activities. Dogs are not accepted.

Charges 2002
Per unit incl. 2 persons and 4A electricity	€ 15.00 - € 24.05
tent pitch incl. 2 persons	€ 10.50
extra person	€ 2.00 - € 3.00
10A electricity	€ 1.35

Tel: 0318 596111. Fax: 0318 596110. E-mail: zanding@vvc.nl. **Reservations:** not necessary. **Open** 29 March - 25 October.

Directions: Leave A12 Utrecht - Arnhem motorway at Oosterbeek at exit 25 and join N310 to Otterlo. Then follow camping signs to site, watching carefully for entrance.

Camping Eiland van Maurik

629 Rijnbandijk 20, 4021 GH Maurik (Gelderland)

Camping Eiland van Mourik is beside a lake at the Nederrijn, in the centre of an extensive nature and recreation area. These surroundings are ideal for all sorts of activities - swimming, wiindsurfing, water-skiing or para-sailing, relaxing on the beach or fishing. There is even an animal farm for the children. In the event of bad weather, the site has a gym including volleyball, badminton and table tennis and a covered 'play palace' - Avontura where, in high season, games and activities are organised for children. The site has 365 numbered, flat pitches. All the 155 for touring units have 10A electricity and cable TV connections and 64 also have water and drainage. There is direct access from the site onto the beach. You could enjoy the pancakes in the 'Oudhollandse' restaurant - also enjoy the views over the water if you do! This is a site for families.

Facilities: The three toilet blocks for tourers include washbasins (open style and in cabins), controllable showers and a baby room. Launderette with ironing board and iron. Dishwashing sinks. Shop. Bar/restaurant (1/4-1/10). Play areas (1 covered). Play field. Tennis. Minigolf. Table Bicycle hire. Riding (part of the entertainment programme). Tennis. Volleyball. Water skiing. Para-sailing. Animal farm. Entertainment program in high season. Gate key deposit € 50. **Off site:** Shop, restaurant and bar nearby. Golf 9 km.

Charges 2003

per unit incl. 2 persons, electricity and local tax	€ 22,00 - € 29,00
extra person (under 2 yrs free)	€ 3,00
dog	€ 3,50
boat per night (not on pitches)	€ 6,00
hikers and cyclists (2 persons)	€ 12,00

Tel: 0344 691502 or 691232. Fax: 0344 692248. E-mail: info@eilandvanmaurik.nl. **Reservations:** Made with 50% deposit, balance due on arrival. **Open** 1 April - 1 October.

Directions: From Rhenen follow the N320 road towards Mourik and signs for 'Eiland van Mourik'.

Camping De Wielerbaan

596 Zoomweg 7-9, 6705 DM Wageningen-Hoog (Gelderland)

This family run park has an interesting history and a natural setting at a point where the Veluwe, the valley of Gelderland and the picturesque area of Betuwe meet. Translated 'Wielerbaan' means 'cycle race-track' which still stands in the heart of this site. The present owners have utilised this area to accommodate recreation facilities which include an indoor pool. Touring pitches here are divided into two areas, one in the seclusion of a forest setting with the added luxury of individual toilet cabins, the other a meadow setting where the pitches are serviced with water, electricity and drainage. Planned cycles routes are available at reception, or maps to choose your own way. It is possible to go by boat to Arnhem and worth visiting is the Burgers Zoo or seeking out the nearby parks (discounted entrance cards from the site).

Facilities: Five sanitary blocks of a reasonable standard provide wash cabins, showers and a baby room. Some individual toilet units. Launderette. Gas supplies. Shop. Small restaurant. Snacks and take-away. Swimming pool. Minigolf. Boules. Ten small play areas and organised entertainment in high season. **Off site:** Golf 500 m. Fishing 5 km.

Charges 2002

Per unit incl. 2 persons, electricity	€ 15.80 - € 23.95
private toilet cabin	€ 3.60
dog (max. 2)	€ 2.80

Less 10% for over 55s at certain times. **Tel:** 0317 41 39 64. Fax: 0317 42 07 51. E-mail: wielerbaan@ vvc.nl. **Reservations:** Advisable in high season. **Open** all year.

Directions: Leave A12 at exit 24 towards Wageningen and continue for 4.5 km. to second roundabout, where site is clearly signed. Follow signs to site, 1.5 km. from the town.

Netherlands - Central
Camping de Vergarde
587 Erichemseweg 84, 4117 GL Erichem (Gelderland)

Situated north of `s Hertogenbosch and west of Nijmegen and Arnhem, De Vergarde has two sections on either side of a lake. Static holiday caravans are on the left, with 207 touring pitches in named sections on the right (about one third seasonal). With good access, pitches are numbered on flat grass and include 30 new ones with electricity (6A) and TV connections. There are trees all round the perimeter (but no shade on the pitches) and the site has a spacious, open feeling with the lake adding to its attractiveness. The shop opens daily and the restaurant/bar in high season plus weekends in low season. Lots of ducks and geese gather around the lake, which can be used for fishing (but not swimming). A member of the Holland Tulip Parcs group.

Facilities: Excellent sanitary facilities are in three blocks, including family showers and baby bathrooms. Most, but not all, hot water is on payment. Washing machines. Motorcaravan services. Heated swimming pools (1/5-1/9). Shop (1/5-1/10). Restaurant (1/5-1/10). Children`s play area and large indoor games room for wet days. Pony riding. Pets corner. Horse drawn wagons. Minigolf. Bicycle hire. Volleyball. Basketball. Games room. Two tennis courts. Fishing.

Charges 2002

Per unit incl. 2 adults	€ 16.30
with electricity, water and drainage	€ 18.20
with satellite TV	€ 20.40
extra person (over 2 yrs)	€ 3.00
dog (max 1)	€ 3.00

Special weekly rates. Low season less 20%. **Tel:** 0344 57 20 17. Fax: 0344 57 22 29. E-mail: info@ devergarde.nl. **Reservations:** Contact site. **Open** 1 March - 30 October.

Directions: From A15 Dordrecht - Nijmegen road exit at Tiel West (also MacDonald`s) and follow signs to Erichem village.

Netherlands - Central
Camping de Hooge Veluwe
585 Koningsweg 14, 6816 TC Arnhem (Gelderland)

Its situation at the entrance to the Hoge Veluwe National Park with its moors, forests, sand drifts, walking routes and cycle paths, makes this a highly desirable holiday base. The site itself is well managed and laid out in an orderly fashion, with 150 touring pitches. All have electricity (4/6A), are numbered and laid out in small fields which are divided by hedging. Some are traffic free which means cars must be left in a nearby car park. Mobile homes are discreetly placed mostly in the centre of the site, but the many trees and shrubbery make them unobtrusive, in fact, many have enviable garden areas. The adjacent National Park incorporates the Kroller Muller Museum and the Museonder Underground Museum. The Burgers Zoo and Safari Park and Burgers Park, are also near, all of which make interesting visits. There is some road noise.

Facilities: Five excellent, heated sanitary blocks with all facilities, are easily identified by colourful logos. Launderette. Motorcaravan services. Gas supplies. Supermarket. Restaurant. Takeaway. TV room. Heated outdoor and indoor pools, and a paddling pool. Several small children`s play areas. Recreation hall. Dedicated playground with football pitch, tennis, cycle track, basketball, minigolf, etc. Bicycle hire. Organised activities. **Off site:** Riding 50 m. Golf 6 km.

Charges 2002

Per unit incl. 2 persons, electricity	€ 15.00 - € 25.00
extra person	€ 3.00
tourist tax	€ 0.50
dog	€ 3.25

Tel: 0264 43 22 72. Fax: 0264 43 68 09. E-mail: info@dehoogeveluwe.nl. **Reservations:** necessary in high season. **Open** 28 March - 26 October.

Directions: Leave A12 motorway at exit 25 (Oosterbeck) and follow signs for Hooge Veluwe. Site is on right in approx. 6 km.

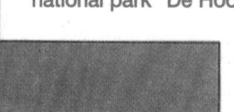

Nature Park Sikkeler

573 Sikkelerweg 8, 7261 LP Ruurlo (Gelderland)

Sikkeler is a well cared for and long-established family site, a paradise for nature lovers. It offers guests peaceful and natural surroundings with an emphasis on the fact that organised entertainment is 'taboo'. It is an award winning site surrounded by the fascinating landscape of the Achterhoek, an area tucked away in the far eastern corner of Gelderland. In a woodland setting it offers 145 touring pitches, 125 with electricity (4A) and 45 fully serviced with water, drainage, electricity and TV connection. These latter pitches are sited in a more open area, divided by shrubs and young trees. Sited away from the touring pitches are a number of site owned thatched cottages and quality bungalows. Nearby attractions include a castle, saw mill, cheese farm and wooden shoe factory. The friendly, welcoming owners speak good English.

Facilities: Four modern, heated, sanitary units, clean and well maintained include provision for babies and people with disabilities. Very clean campers' kitchen and launderette. Motorcaravan services. Small shop (1/4-15/9). Restaurant and takeaway (30/4-1/9). Paddling pool, animal enclosure and play area. Bicycle hire. Table tennis. Playing field. **Off site:** Golf, fishing or riding within 1 km.

Charges 2002

Per unit incl. 2 persons	€ 13.50 - € 17.75
extra person	€ 3.00
electricity (4A)	€ 2.00
serviced pitch	€ 13.50 - € 22.00
hikers/cyclists (2 persons) and tent	€ 14.25
dog (1 per pitch)	€ 3.00
local tax	€ 0.45

Tel: 0573 46 12 21. Fax: 0573 46 15 68. E-mail: info@sikkeler.nl. **Reservations:** Usually not essential. **Open** all year.

Directions: Leave A18 exit 4, on N315 towards Zelhem/Ruurlo. Site is on left 4 km. south of Ruurlo.

Camping Arnhem

631 Kemperbergerweg 771, 6816 RW Arnhem

Camping Arnhem is a wooded site in the Veluwe region of the Netherlands, close to the 'Hooge Veluwe' National Park. The 560 pitches are partly in the sun and partly in the shade of tall trees and there are 280 for touring units. This is a perfect base for visiting the National Park, the Kroller Moiler museum or the outdoor museum. You could also go riding or play golf close to the site or experience the silence high up in the air in a glider from the Terlet airport. There is also plenty to do on the site including tennis, table tennis, boules or minigolf. Children can be entertained by the professional entertainment team - if you don't look out, the clowns may take you for a healthy dive in the adventure pond.

Facilities: Modern sanitary blocks provide free hot showers, facilities for disabled visitors and a baby room. Launderette with washing machine, spin dryer, dryer and ironing facilities. Supermarket. Café. Bar. Tennis. Minigolf. Table tennis. Sports field. Boules. Open air theatre. Playground. Adventure pond. Swimming pool for children. Entertainment programme in high season. Bicycle hire. **Off site:** Arnhem for shopping. Burgers Zoo. Kroller Moiler museum. Airborn museum. Riding and golf. Gliding. Balloon trips and boat trips.

Charges 2002

Per unit incl. 2 adults, 2 children and 4A electricity	€ 13,50 - € 28,25
local tax	€ 0,37

Tel: 026 443 1600. Fax: 026 445 7705. E-mail: arnhem@holiday.nl. **Reservations:** contact the site. **Open** 1 April - 26 October.

Directions: From the A50 take exit 21 for Schaarsbergen. Go to Schaarsbergen and follow the camp signs.

Recreatiecentrum Heumens Bos

595 Vosseneindseweg 46, 6582 BR Heumen (Gelderland)

The area around Nijmegen, the oldest city in the Netherlands, has large forests for walking or cycling, nature reserves and old towns to explore, as well as being quite close to Arnhem. A warm welcome from the Grol family awaits you at this well run site. It covers 16 ha. and is open over a long season for touring families (no groups of youngsters allowed) and all year for bungalows. It offers 165 level, grass touring pitches for touring units, all with electricity (6A). Numbered but not separated, in glades of 10 and one large field, all have easy access with cars parked away from the caravans. One small section for motorcaravans has some hardstandings. The restaurant, which offers a quality menu (the owners are former restaurateurs) and a new terrace, is close to the comfortable bar and snack bar. An open air pool with a small children's pool is maintained at 28°C by a system of heat transfer from the air.

Facilities: The main, high quality sanitary building, plus another new block, are modern and heated, providing showers on payment, rooms for families and disabled people and hot water to private cabins and other washbasins. Another smaller building has acceptable facilities. External, covered dishwashing facilities. Smart launderette. Motorcaravan services. Gas supplies. Large shop. Bar, restaurant and snack bar (all season). Heated swimming pool (from 1/5). Bicycle hire. All weather tennis courts. Boules. Table tennis. For children a separate glade area with play equipment on sand and grass, Activity and excursion programme (high season). Large wet weather room. **Off site:** Fishing 2 km. Golf 10 km.

Charges 2002

Per pitch incl. 2 persons	€ 14.50 - € 25.00
extra person (over 3 yrs)	€ 3.50
electricity	€ 2.20
dog (max 1)	€ 3.00

Special low season weekends (incl. restaurant meal) and special deal for over 55 yr olds. **Tel:** 0243 58 14 81. Fax: 0243 58 38 62. E-mail: info@heumensbos.nl. **Reservations:** Made without charge and advisable for July/Aug. **Open** 1 April - 1 November.

Directions: From A73 (Nijmegen - Venlo) take exit no. 3 (4 km. south of Nijmegen) and follow site signs.

CAMPING-CARAVANNING HEUMENS BOS

HEUMENS BOS is situated just 8 km. south of Nijmegen and is an ideal base for visiting the area, including Arnhem and Germany. It is a perfect place to start your Holland discovery. Bicycles may be hired to try out the network of cycle paths in the area. Plenty of tourist information and advice are available from reception, such as information about the Liberation Museum, the Bicycle Museum, the Dutch Open Air Museum, The Efteling theme park, Burgers Zoo, Warner Brothers Movie World, and more. During high season we provide a special recreation programme for children.

Heumens Bos has many facilities, such as heated outdoor pools, tennis court, table tennis, boules pitch, playground, high quality sanitary buildings, a luxurious launderette, special motorcaravan service point, supermarket, à la carte restaurant and terraces. You can also rent a luxurious bungalow, tent or caravan. Special prices during low season.

Heumens Bos is easy to reach via motorway A73, Nijmegen/Venlo/Köln, exit 3, Heumen.

ADAC 2002

 ANWB Vosseneindseweg 46, NL-6582 BR Heumen
★ ★ ★ ★ ★ Tel.: +31 24 358 14 81 Fax +31 24 358 38 62
E-mail: info@heumensbos.nl Internet: www.heumensbos.nl **heumens bos**

Camping Betuwestrand

586 A Kraalweg 40, 4153 XC Beesd (Gelderland)

A pleasant site for night stop or longer stay, conveniently situated just off the A2/E25 motorway (Utrecht - 's Hertogenbosch, exit 14), It is a large site with 200 places for tourers (all with 6/10A electricity and drainage) in addition to its 450 well established permanent units. The touring pitches are in four distinct areas with many situated around the edges of an attractive lake with a large sandy beach. For families with young children there is another area away from the water with play areas. An area of the lake is cordoned off for swimming with a slide and diving boards and it is also suitable for windsurfing. Gelderland is the part of the Netherlands famous for fruit growing, situated between the rivers Maas and Waal and worthy perhaps of further consideration by British visitors.

Facilities: The toilet blocks are of a good standard and include family rooms and facilities for disabled visitors. Hot water is on payment in both showers and washbasins (in individual cabins). Launderette. Shop. Restaurant (open to the public). Bar/TV room. Playground. Good lake fishing. Tennis. Dogs are not accepted. **Off site:** Bicycle hire 500 m.

Charges 2002

Per unit incl. up to 2 persons, electricity and tourist tax	€ 18.00
tent pitch incl. 2 persons	€ 11.00
extra person	€ 3.00

Less 20% in low season. Special weekend or weekly prices. No credit cards. **Tel:** 0345 68 15 03. Fax: 0345 68 16 86. E-mail: info@betuwestrand.nl. **Reservations:** Necessary in high season - contact site. **Open** 1 April - 30 September.

Directions: Site is 25 km. SSE of Utrecht, clearly signed from both directions on the E25 road between Utrecht and 's Hertogenbosch. Take exit 14 (Beesd) and site is 200 m.

Recreatiecentrum Mijnden

683 Bloklaan 22A, 1231 AZ Loosdrecht (Utrecht)

Recreatiecentrum Mijnden is located amongst typical Dutch countryside and close to cities such as Amsterdam, Utrecht and Hilversum. The site has 195 level pitches for tourers, all with 4 or 6A electricity, and 30 with water and drainage. The pitches are on grassy fields and almost all provide lovely views over the lake. Mijnden is in a central position in the Vechtstreek, one of the most beautiful parts of the Netherlands, and you can explore this area by car, bike or on foot. Also, there are some famous country estates and several charming castles to visit. The site itself has a lot to offer with entertainment and activities including swimming, sailing, water skiing or boating. The site has its own boat slipway so you could bring your own boat and navigate on the Loosdrechtse Plassen. The waterfront is not fenced or gated.

Facilities: Three modern, heated sanitary blocks with showers on payment, washbasins, toilets and facilities for disabled visitors. Launderette with washing machines. Motorcaravan service point. Gas. Supermarket. Bar-café-restaurant. Snack bar. Room for teenagers. Zoo. Playground. Sports field. Boat slipway. Entertainment programme. Fishing. Bicycle hire. Caravan storage. **Off site:** Amsterdam and Utrecht 20 km. Loosdrechtse Plassen 100 m.

Charges 2002

Per week: tent/caravan incl. 2 persons	€ 16.95
3 persons	€ 21.95
4 persons	€ 25.95
hikers tent incl. 1 person	€ 7.95
extra person	€ 4.00
dog	€ 3.00

Tel: 0294 23 31 65. Fax: 0294 23 34 02. E-mail: info@mijnden.nl. **Reservations:** Contact site. **Open** 1 April - 15 October.

Directions: From Utrecht travel to Hilversum and then towards Loosdrecht. Follow signs from Loosdrecht towards Loenen and from there the camp signs.

REKREATIECENTRUM MIJNDEN ★★★★

Phone 0031-294233165 • Fax 0031-294233402 • www.mijnden.nl

Situated in typical Dutch countryside, right by the Loosdrecht lakes. The surrounding area is noted for its historical features (castles and country houses) and its beautiful scenery. Loosdrecht offers many opportunities for watersports enthusiasts and nature lovers will find much to enjoy in the local area.

The leisure centre has its own restaurant, with fish, grill and meat specialities. Mijnden lies between the 4 cities of Amsterdam, Den Haag, Rotterdam and Utrecht. They each offer lots to see and do for the whole family and are easily accessed by car or public transport

You will be made very welcome

Vakantiecentrum De Heigraaf

691 De Heygraeff 9, 3931 ML Woudenberg (Utrecht)

This family run site in rural environment is very close to a public lake with sandy beaches set in pine woods. With this popular attraction within walking distance the site has a fairly high proportion of mobile homes and seasonal caravans but provides 200 marked pitches for touring units out of the overall 500. Accessed by a central, tarmac road these are nicely situated around the edges of small hedged field areas on level grass with electricity available to most. The newer area at the top of the site has individual pitches (some with toilet units) overlooking the fields. The main facility area in the centre of the site provides entertainment for children during school holidays with a pleasant café and the usual small animal enclosure popular with the Dutch. The reception at the entrance is in the traditional farm house and is very well appointed in the style of the region. Some English is spoken.

Facilities: Four well spaced sanitary units of the same design are well equipped and of good quality. Facilities for disabled people, bathrooms and baby rooms shared between the units. Hot water is charged (€ 0.50) except in the washbasins (some in cubicles). Laundry room. Shop (all season but less hours in low season as is restaurant/bar and café. Many pieces of children's equipment on sand and grass. Swimming at lake within walking distance. **Off site:** Discounts arranged for local attractions such as the Zoo, swimming pool and amusement park, etc (if booked at reception).

Charges 2002

Per person	€ 2.50
child (3-12 yrs)	€ 2.20
caravan or tent	€ 4.00
car	€ 1.90
motorcaravan	€ 5.90
electricity	€ 2.00

Tel: 028 65 066. E-mail info@heigraaf.nl. **Reservations:** Contact site. **Open** 1 April/Easter - end October.

Directions: From A28 take exit for Amersfoort Zuid on N227 then follow N224 for Woudenberg. After 1.5 km take first right for site.

Netherlands - South
Camping De Katjeskelder

554 Katjeskelder 1, 4904 SG Oosterhout (Noord-Brabant)

This site is to be found in a wooded setting in a delightful area of Western Brabant. This is idyllic cycling and walking country-side and many known attractions such as the Efteling theme park and the Biesbosch nature park lie within a short drive. It is a well established, family run site offering extensive facilities with a new and impres-sive ultra-modern reception area. Around the 25 hectare site are mobile homes and bungalows but there are 200 touring pitches, all with electricity and water (between two pitches), plus 13 fully serv-iced pitches with hardstanding for motor-caravans. Cars are prohibited alongside the pitches, but may be parked nearby. The site has a 'cat' theme, hence the cat names including that of the restaurant, the 'Gelaarsde Kat' (Puss in Boots) which is situated in the 'Tropikat' complex. This tropical indoor water playground is free for campers and the site also has an outdoor swimming pool and children's pool, both supervised. A member of the Holland Tulip Parcs group.

Facilities: Three modern, heated sanitary blocks provide facilities including a family shower/wash room, baby room and provision for disabled people. Laundry. Motorcaravan services. Supermarket. Restaurant, bar, snack bar, pizzeria and takeaway (the 'Hapjeskat') Indoor tropical pool. Outdoor swim-ming pools (15/5-31/8). Play field. Tennis. Bicycle hire. Minigolf. Several play areas for small children, plus a large adventure playground and organised entertainment for children all season.

Charges 2003

Per unit incl. 1-2 persons and electricity,	
water and TV connections	€ 19.00 - € 33.00
3-4 persons	€ 23.50 - € 33.50
dog	€ 5.00

Tel: 0162 453 539. Fax: 0162 45 40 90. E-mail: kkinfo@katjeskelder.nl. **Reservations:** Necessary in high season. **Open** 1 January - 28 October.

Directions: From A27 Breda/Gorinchem motorway take Oosterhout Zuid exit 17 and follow signs for 7 km to site.

Beekse Bergen Safari Campsite

590 Beekse Bergen 1, 5081 NJ Hilvarenbeek (Noord-Brabant)

Beekse Bergen is a large impressive leisure park set around a very large, attractive lake near Tilberg. The park offers a range of amusements which should keep the most demanding of families happy! These include not only water based activities such as windsurfing, canoeing, jetski, rowing and fishing, but also a small amusement park, a cinema, tennis courts, minigolf and many more. The lake is bordered by sandy beaches, children's playgrounds, open-air swimming areas and water slides. Transport around and across the lake is provided by a little train or a sightseeing boat (in high season). These and most of the amenities are free to campers. Part of the resort is the Beekse Bergen Safari Park with reduced entry for campers, where you can see the many wild animals from either your own car, a safari bus or two safari boats, the Stanley and the Livingstone. On the far side of the lake, as well as the bungalows and tents, there are two distinct campsites - one on flat meadows surrounded by hedges and trees near the lake, the other in a more secluded wooded area reached by a tunnel under the nearby main road. The 600 numbered pitches are about 100 sq.m, and all have electrical connections. The Safari Campsite has a 'typical safari environment' and a viewpoint over the Safari Park (with free, unlimited entry for campers staying here. Open 24 April - 2 Sept). There is an independent central complex with catering, playground and launderette, plus an entertainment team.

Facilities: Sanitary facilities are quite adequate in terms of numbers, cleanliness and facilities including some washbasins in private cabins. Launderettes. Restaurants, cafés and takeaway (weekends only in low seasons). Supermarket. Children's playgrounds and indoor pool. Beaches and lake swimming. Watersports including rowing boats (free) and canoe hire. Amusements. Tennis. Minigolf. Fishing. Recreation programme. Bicycle hire. Riding. Twin axle caravans not accepted. **Off site:** Golf 5 km. This is an area with many other recreational activities, including the award winning Efteling amusement park.

Charges 2002

Per person (from 2 yrs)	€ 3.50
standard pitch incl. electricity	€ 10.35 - € 17.80
serviced pitch	€ 13.60 - € 21.05
local tax	€ 0.61

Discounts for weekly stays, camping packages available. **Tel:** 013 5491100. Fax: 0135 36 67 16. E-mail: beeksebergen@libema.nl. **Reservations:** Necessary for high season and B.Hs. **Open** 28 March - 26 October.

Directions: From A58/E312 Tilburg - Eindhoven motorway, take exit to Hilvarenbeek on the N269 road. Park and campsite are signed Beekse Bergen.

Vrijetijdspark Vinkeloord

588 Vinkeloord 1, 5382 JX Vinkeloord (Noord-Brabant)

Run by the same group as Beekse Bergen (590), Vinkeloord is a large site with motel accommodation and a bungalow park, in addition to its 500 camping pitches. These are divided into several grassy areas, many in an attractive wooded setting, 381 with electrical connections (4-10A) and also some with full services (water and TV connection). The site is a popular holiday choice with activities organised in the main seasons. The varied amenities are located in and around a modern, central complex. They include heated outdoor swimming pools, a new indoor leisure pool with slide, and ten-pin bowling alley. A small, landscaped lake has sandy beaches and is overlooked by a large, modern play area. Some of the touring pitches also overlook the water. Campers are entitled to free entry to the adjacent 'Autotron' attraction.

Facilities: Eight toilet blocks are well situated for all parts of the site with a mixture of clean and simple facilities (some unisex) with some warm water for washing and some individual washbasins. Supermarket. Bar. Modern, up-market restaurant. Snack bar/takeaway (high season only). Free outdoor heated swimming pools (1/6-1/9). Indoor leisure pool (on payment). Ten-pin bowling alley. Tennis courts. Minigolf. Table tennis. Sports field. Bicycle hire. Fishing. Barbecue area. Children's play areas on sand. Many organised activities in season. Conference facilities. Max. 1 dog per pitch.

Charges 2002

Per person (from 3 yrs)	€ 3.40 - € 4.55
standard pitch incl. electricity	€ 8.35 - € 13.60
serviced pitch (water and TV)	€ 13.10 - € 17.30
local tax	€ 0.50

Tel: 0735 34 35 36. Fax: 0735 32 16 98. E-mail: vinkeloord@libema.nl. **Reservations:** Advised for high season - write for details. **Open** 29 March - 3 November.

Directions: Site is signed from the N50/A50 road between 's Hertogenbosch and Nijmegen, approx. 10 km. east of s'Hertogenbosch at Vinkel.

Netherlands - South
Kampeerterrein De Achterste Hoef

671 Troprijt 10, 5531 NA Bladel (Noord-Brabant)

This quite large campsite is to be found off the N284 at Bladel in Noord-Bradant. It is an ideal location for cycling, walking and is close to the Belgian border. A family oriented site, it offers good quality facilities which are well maintained and kept very clean. On entering the site you find all the main service buildings alongside reception. There are about 300 touring pitches, many fully serviced and 28 with their own sanitation and sited near the lake. There are also seasonal and static caravan places, but these are kept apart and mostly in one area. The touring pitches are 100-150 sq.m. in size with many amongst the trees, but some are in open meadows and some divided by young shrubs. To the rear is the lake and beach area.

Facilities: Four sanitary blocks have showers, washbasins, both open and in cabins, a bathroom and a baby bath. Dishwashing sinks, laundry room, washing machine and dryer. Motorcaravan service point. Supermarket. Restaurant/bar and snack bar. Disco. Recreation room. Pitch and putt. Football. Tennis. Heated swimming pool. Minigolf. Bicycle hire. Watersports. Play areas. Animal corner. Organised activities in July/Aug.

Charges 2002

Per unit incl. 1 person	€ 11.50 - € 23.00
incl. 2 persons	€ 13.50 - € 27.00
extra person over 2 yrs	€ 4.00
dog (max 1)	€ 4.13
local tax	€ 0.63

Tel: 0497 381579. Fax: 0497 387776. E-mail: info@achterstehoef.nl. **Reservations:** Contact site. **Open** Easter - 31 October.

Directions: Travelling east or west on the N284 Eindhoven - Reusel road turn south at 2nd traffic lights in Bladel and follow camping signs to site.

Netherlands - South
Camping de Kienehoef

679 Zwembadweg 35 - 37, 5491 TE Sint-Oedenrode (Noord-Brabant)

De Kienehoef is at Sint Oedenrode in Noord Brabant, which boasts many historical sights, including two castles. The site is well cared for and attractively laid out with reception to the right of the entrance and the site facilities to the left. Behind this area is a heated pool. The generous pitches are mostly laid out in bays and placed between trees and shrubs to the right of a long avenue leading through the site. A few are to the left, alongside bungalows which are discreetly placed in the trees. In what is known as the red area, cars must be parked away from pitches.

Facilities: Two modern, clean and well maintained toilet blocks include pre-set showers and some shower/wash cubicles, also family and baby rooms. Separate dishwashing and laundry area. Shop, restaurant/bar and snacks (all1/5-15/9). Heated swimming pool (1/5-15/9). Lake fishing. Sports field, tennis court, volleyball. Dogs are not accepted.

Charges 2002

Per unit incl. 2 persons	€ 20.40 - € 24.40
extra person	€ 3.20 - € 27.60
hiker tent pitch	€ 6.70 - € 7.70

Tel: 0413 47 28 77. Fax: 0413 47 70 33. E-mail: info@kienehoef.nl. **Reservations:** Contact site. **Open** 28 March - 28 October.

Directions: Leave A2 s`Hertogenbosh - Eindhoven motorway at exit 27 and follow signs to Sint Oedenrode. Site is well signed from village.

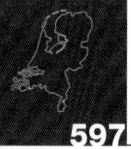

Netherlands - South
Camping De Paal

597 Paaldreef 14, 5571 TN Bergeyk (Noord-Brabant)

A first class campsite, De Paal is especially suitable for families with young children. Situated in 42 ha. of woodland, there are 530 touring pitches, ranging in size up to 150 sq.m. (plus 70 seasonal pitches). The pitches are numbered and separated by trees, with cars either parked on the pitch or in a parking area. All have 6A electricity, TV, water, drainage and a bin. There is a play area on each group of pitches, in addition to the large open sand-based adventure play area and large barn for wet weather. The high quality indoor heated pool consists of play pools for babies and children, with a deeper one for parents. Maps from reception show the many walking and cycling opportunities in this attractive area. Whilst catering foremost for families, outside high season there are many regular adult visitors to this friendly site.

Facilities: High quality sanitary facilities are ultra modern, including washcabins, family rooms and baby baths, all with lots of space. Facilities for disabled visitors. Launderette. Motorcaravan services. Underground supermarket. Restaurant (high season), bar and snack bar (all season). Indoor pool (all season, supervised in high season). Outdoor pool (May - Sept). Bicycle hire. Tennis. Play areas. Theatre. **Off site:** Tennis complex with 6 indoor courts (Sept-May) and pleasant lounge bar. Riding and covered wagons for hire 500 m.

Charges 2002

Per pitch incl. 2 persons and services	€ 21.00 - € 31.00
extra person (over 1 yr)	€ 4.00 - € 5.00
dog	€ 4.00

Discounts outside 5/7-16/8 daily 30%, over 7 days 35%. **Tel:** 0497 57 19 77. Fax: 0497 57 71 64. E-mail: info@depaal.nl. **Reservations:** Essential for July/Aug. and made for min. 1 week Sat to Sat. **Open** Easter/1 April - 31 October.

Directions: From E34 Antwerpen-Eindhoven road take exit 32 (Eersel) and follow signs for Bergeyk and site (2 km. from town).

Vakantiecentrum de Hertenwei

Wellenseind 7-9, 5094 EG Lage Mierde (Noord-Brabant)

Set in the southwest corner of the country quite close to the Belgian border, this relaxed site covers a large area. In addition to 100 quite substantial bungalows with their own gardens (some residential, 30 to let and 32 mobile homes), the site has some 350 touring pitches. These are in four different areas on oblong meadows surrounded by hedges and trees, with the numbered pitches around the perimeters. There is a choice of pitch size (100 or 150 sq.m.) and all have 6A electrical connections, many with water and drainage, and 70 with cable TV connection as well. The most pleasant area is probably the small one near the entrance and main buildings - these are a long walk from some of the furthest pitches. Indoor and outdoor pool and recreation programme in season with films, dances or disco, sports, bingo, etc.

Facilities: Four toilet blocks are of slightly differing types, all of quite good quality and well spaced around the site. Virtually all washbasins in private cabins and the blocks can be heated in cool weather. Units for disabled people, hair washing cabins and baby baths. Launderette. Gas supplies. Motorcaravan services. Supermarket (Easter - end Oct). Bar by indoor pool (12 x 6 m. open all year, admission charged). Three outdoor pools, the largest 25 x 10 m. (27/4-25/8). Restaurant, cafeteria (all year). Disco. Two tennis courts. Playgrounds and play meadows. Sauna, solarium and jacuzzi. Bicycle hire. **Off site:** Supermarket 2 km. Bus service to Tilburg or Eindhoven with stop at entrance. Fishing 4 km. Riding 4 km

Charges 2002

Per unit incl. 2 persons, electricity	€ 26.25 - € 28.50
extra person	€ 3.00
local tax	€ 0.55

Less 25-40% in low seasons. **Tel:** 0135 09 12 95. E-mail: mjmaille@bigfoot.com. **Reservations:** Made for min. 1 week, in summer Sat to Sat. only, with deposit. **Open** all year.

Directions: Site is by N269 Tilburg - Reusel road, 2 km. north of Lage Mierde and 16 km. south of Tilburg.

★ ★ ★ ★ ★

VAKANTIECENTRUM

de hertenwei

WELLENSEIND 7-9
5094 EG LAGE MIERDE
Tel. +31 13 509 12 95
WWW.HERTENWEI.NL

Situated 2 km north of Lage Mierde on the Tilburg - Reusel road (road Nr. 269) surrounded by beautiful woodland. Modern heated sanitary blocks with hot water in basins and showers. Heated swimming pool and children's pool. Indoor pool with hot whirlpool, sauna, solarium. Bar. Supermarket. Washing machines. Snack bar. Restaurant. Discotheque. Tennis courts. Also bungalows and mobile-homes to let: (4–6–8–16–20 persons)

Please send for our free brochure

Camping De Maasvallei

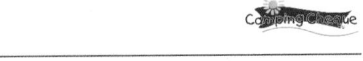

Dorperheideweg 34, 5944 NK Arcen (Limburg)

Set in the pretty countryside around Noord-Limburg and close to the German border this fairly large site has 463 pitches. There are also static caravans, a number of which are to rent. It is well situated for boating on the Maas, or if preferring to relax on site there is a lake and beach. Being a mature site it is surrounded by trees and some pitches benefit from shade. The main facilities such as the restaurant, bar, takeaway, shop, games room and swimming pool are a short walk from reception, with the lake towards the rear of the site. This is mainly a campsite geared for families, or it would appeal to those seeking a break where walking and cycling are the main attractions of the area. Arcen is a pretty village and draws many visitors.

Facilities: Two clean and heated sanitary blocks provide showers, washcabins, baby baths and a family room, Dishwashing and laundry sinks, washing machines and dryers. Motorcaravan service point. Restaurant and bar. Shop. Swimming pool. Table tennis, basketball, volleyball. Bicycle hire. Organised activities in July/August. Dogs are accepted, but only one per family and in a special area.

Charges 2002

Per unit incl. 2 persons	€ 24.00 - € 27.00
extra person (over 3 yrs)	€ 2.50
local tax	€ 0.91

Tel: 077 4731564. Fax: 077 4731573. **Reservations:** Contact site. **Open** all year.

Directions: Leave A77 Boxmeer - Goch motorway at exit 2 to join N271 south in the direction of Venlo. Follow N271 for 27 km. and turn left at traffic lights on dual-carriageway onto local road (signed Lingsfort). Continue on local road for 1.8 km. and turn left. Site is on right after 1.6 km.

Kampeercentrum Klein Canada

Dorpstraat 1, 5851 AG Afferden (Limburg)

Following the war, the family who own this site wanted to emigrate to Canada - they didn't go, but instead created this attractive site with the maple leaf theme decorating buildings, pool and play equipment. Pleasant, farm style buildings adorned with flowers house the main amenities near the entrance and the site has a sheltered atmosphere with many ornamental trees. There are three touring areas, one on an island surrounded by an attractive, landscaped moat used for fishing, the other on flat ground on the other side of the entrance. They provide 195 large, numbered pitches, all with electricity (6-10A), water, drainage and TV connections. The newest area will offer 80 pitches each with its own sanitary unit and car park space. Some 200 permanent and seasonal pitches form other areas to the back of the site. There is a small indoor pool, sauna and solarium and an outdoor pool (with large slide) and children's pool with a grassy sunbathing area. Cars are parked in separate areas. This is a good quality site with a lot to offer for a comfortable stay in charming surroundings. A member of the Holland Tulip Parcs group.

Facilities: Mixed toilet facilities include some with washbasins in cubicles, and family facilities in a fully tiled and heated room. Some pitches have individual units. Motorcaravan services. Gas supplies. Supermarket, Bar, restaurant, snack bar,and takeaway (all 1/4-31/10). Outdoor pool (May - Sept). Indoor pool (all year). Sauna and solarium. Pool table. Table top minigolf. Tennis. Fishing. Children's playground. Animals enclosure. Bicycle hire. **Off site:** Riding 5 km.

Charges 2002

Per unit incl. 4A electricity	€ 8.51 - € 13.61
'super comfort' pitch plus	€ 13.05 - € 18.15
person	€ 3.18
child (1-12 yrs)	€ 2.50
dog	€ 2.04
local tax	€ 0.79

Tel: 0485 531223. Fax: 0485 532218. E-mail: info@kleincanada.nl. **Reservations:** made with € 10 deposit. **Open** all year.

Directions: Afferden is on the N271 between Nijmegen and Venlo, just south of the A77/E31 motorway into Germany. Site is on the N271 and is signed.

Recreatiecentrum de Schatberg

Midden Peelweg 5, 5975 MZ Sevenum (Limburg)

In a woodland setting of 86 hectares, this family-run campsite is more reminiscent of a holiday village, with a superb range of activities, making it an ideal venue for families. It is well situated for visits to Germany and Belgium, also easily accessible from the port of Zeebrugge. The surrounding countryside offers the opportunity to commune with nature, either by cycling or walking. For the more 'stay on site' visitor the location is excellent with several lakes for fishing, windsurfing and swimming, plus an extensive range of activities and a heated outdoor swimming pool. The 600 touring pitches, with electricity (10A), water and drainage, average 100 sq.m. in size and are on rough grass terrain mostly with shade, but not separated. A range of rented and private accommodation is unobtrusively placed in separate areas and includes some very smart, brick-built bungalows for rent. A feature at De Schatberg is the attractive restaurant/bar area and the reception and indoor pool, manned by friendly staff. After a fire this area has been rebuilt to a modern design and is very user-friendly. Look out for the wallabies and the deer!

Facilities: Three modern, fully equipped toilet blocks, supplemented by two small wooden toilet units to save night time walks, receive heavy use in high season. There are showers, washbasins (some in cabins), family shower rooms, baby baths and en-suite units for disabled visitors. Dishwashing and laundry sinks. Washing machines and dryers. Motorcaravan service point. Supermarket. Restaurant, bar and takeaway. Indoor and outdoor swimming pools. Football. Tennis. Minigolf. Trampoline. Play areas. Fishing. Watersports. Bicycle hire. Bowling, casino, underground disco, entertainment for children and adults in high season. Dogs are not accepted.

Charges 2003

Per unit incl. up to 4 persons	€ 16.00 - € 28.00
extra person over 3 yrs	€ 4.00

Tel: 0774 67 77 77. Fax: 0774 67 77 99. E-mail: info@schatberg.nl. **Reservations:** Contact site. **Open** all year.

Directions: Leave A67 Eindhoven-Venlo motorway at Helden exit 38 and follow signs for 1 km. to site.

Terrassencamping Gulperberg Panorama

653 Berghem 1, 6271 NP Gulpen (Limburg)

Gulperberg Panorama is just three kilometres from the attractive village of Gulpen. Visitors are assured of a warm welcom and if arriving (or leaving) on a Saturday are welcomed (or bade farewell) by the 'Aartje Twinkle'. Pitches are large and flat on terraces overlooking the village on one side and open countryside on the other. Many have full services. English is spoken in the reception, although all written information is in Dutch - don't hesitate to ask if you require a translation. This is good walking country and maps are available for a small charge from the reception. Gulperberg Panorama is a haven for children. During the high season there is a weekly entertainment programme to keep them occupied. The site is not suitable for visitors with disabilities. Dogs are restricted to one section of the campsite.

Facilities: Four modern sanitary blocks have excellent facilities (showers require a token). Family shower room and baby room. Laundry. Shop (27/4-31/8). Bar (17/4-27/9). Takeaway 11/7-31/8). Swimming pool (15/5-15/9). Three play areas. TV and games room. Extensive entertainment programme for children plus family entertainment. **Off site:** Fishing 4 km. Golf and bicycle hire 3 km. Riding 5 km. Further afield are caves, museums and Maastricht with its large variety of shops.

Charges 2002

Per unit incl. 2 persons	11.60 - € 14.30
extra person (over 6 yrs)	€ 1.95 - € 2.60
child (2-6 yrs)	€ 1.80 - € 2.05
electricity (6A)	€ 1.70 - € 2.15
serviced pitch	€ 5.35 - € 5.80
pet (max 2)	€ 1.80 - € 2.30
local tax	€ 1.00

Reductions for the over-55s. **Tel:** 0434 50 23 30. Fax: 0434 50 46 09. E-mail: info@gulperberg.nl. **Reservations:** Advised in July and August. **Open** 17 April - 27 September.

Directions: Gulpen is east of Maastricht. Take N278 Maastricht - Aachen. Site is signed just as you enter Gulpen (look for them on the right). Turn right and follow camping signs for approx. 3 km.

Holiday Resort BreeBronne

652 Lange Heide 9, 5993 PB Maasbree (Limburg)

Said to be one of the top campsites in the Netherlands, BreeBronne is set in a forest region beside a large lake. There are 500 pitches, of which just under half are for touring units. They are at least 80 sq.m. in size and all have electricity (10A), water, waste water and cable TV connections. The lake provides a sandy beach and opportunities for swimming, sailing and windsurfing. Alternatively, you can swim in the heated open-air pool (May-Aug) or the 'sub-tropical' heated indoor pool with its special children's area (April-Oct).

Facilities: The sanitary facilities are top class with a special section for children and excellent provision for disabled visitors. Launderette. 'De Bronn' restaurant with regional specialities. Bar. Takeaway. Shop. Play area. Play room. Tennis. Animation. **Off site:** The local area has a rich history, with pretty villages, museums.

Charges 2003

Per unit incl. 4 persons	
fully serviced pitch	€ 21.50 - € 37.00
extra person	€ 4.20
dog	€ 4.70
local tax	€ 0.64

Tel: 0774 652360. Fax: 0774 652095. E-mail: info@breebronne.nl. **Reservations:** Contact site. **Open** 1 April - 31 October.

Directions: Breebronne lies between the towns of Sevenum and Maasbree. From autobahn A67 towards Venlo take exit 38 and fork right. After 3 km. take turn for Maasbree, then left (marked Maasbree) and continue to a roundabout. Take third exit and from here BreeBronne is signed. Go through town and fork right after 2 km. to site on the left.

Norway

Norwegian Tourist Board, Charles House, 5 Regent Street, London SW1Y 4LR

Tel: 020 7839 6255 Fax: 020 7839 6014 E-mail: infouk@ntr.no www.visitnorway.com

Norway has the lowest population density in Europe, which is not surprising when one realises that about one quarter of its land is above the Arctic Circle. It is a land of contrasts, from magnificent snow capped mountains, dramatic fjords, vast plateaux with wild untamed tracts, huge lakes and rich green countryside. Oslo is the oldest of the Scandinavian capitals and one of the most prettily sited, whilst Bergen is the fjord capital, Trondheim is an atmospheric city with its medieval heart intact, and Tromsø, with its stunning `Arctic Cathedral', likes to think of itself as the capital of the North. You can see the Northern Lights (Aurora Borealis) between November and February, north of the Arctic Circle, which lies between Mo i Rana and Bodø. During certain freak weather conditions it may be seen further south. The Midnight Sun is visible north of the Arctic Circle in summer - at Bodø between early June and early July, at Tromsø from late May to mid July, and at Nordkapp from mid May until late July. However you can never guarantee these experiences - it depends on meteorological conditions. Midsummer night's eve is celebrated all over the country, with thousands of bonfires along the fjords.

Population
4,300,000 (1997); density 13 per sq. km.

Capital
Oslo.

Climate
The Gulf Stream follows the coast and weather is less extreme on the west coast. Generally weather in summer and winter is unpredictable (it can be very wet). Average temperatures 18.2° in Oslo, 14.5° in Bergen, 12.7° in Tromso in July. In Jan. -3.7° in Oslo, 1.5° in Bergen, and -4.7° in Tromso. Daylight hours in Oslo are 6 hrs in Jan. and 18.5 hrs in July whilst Tromso in Jan. has no daylight and in July, 24 hours

Language
Norwegian, but English is widely spoken, particularly by the young.

Currency
The Norwegian krone, divided into 100 ore. Denominations are 10, 50, 100, 500, and 1000 kr.

Banks
Open Mon-Fri 09.00-15.00. Every largish village and town in Norway has a bank, although rural branches may have restricted opening hours.

Post Offices
Opening hours are generally 08.00/08.30-16.00/17.00 Mon-Fri, 08.00-13.00 on Sat.

Time
GMT plus 1 (BST plus 1 in summer).

Telephone
To phone from the UK, the code is 0047 plus the number. From Norway to the UK, the code is 095 44, plus the number (omitting the initial 0).

Shops
Normal hours: Mon-Fri 09.00-16.00/17.00, Thu 09.00-18.00/20.00 and Sat 09.00-13.00 /15.00.
There are 2,600 tax-free shops in Norway. If you buy goods for more than 308 kr make sure you get a tax refund. After deduction of a handling charge you'll get 11-18% of the buying price back in cash, at ports or major border crossings.
Food: more expensive than in the UK, except for very good vegetables, fruit and some fish. Smoked and fresh salmon are excellent and reindeer steak very tender. A small beer in a cafe can cost £3.
Camping Gaz: Not readily available. You can buy camping gaz from Statoil and AGA Progas, which have outlets throughout Norway.

Motoring
Roads are generally uncrowded around Oslo and Bergen but be prepared for tunnels and hairpin bends. Certain roads are forbidden to caravans or best avoided (advisory leaflet from the Norwegian Tourist Office). Vehicles must have sufficient road grip and in the winter it may be necessary to use winter tyres with or without studs or chains. Towed caravans up to 2.3 m. wide are permitted; if between 2.3 and 2.5 m. (max permitted width) the car towing it must be at least as wide as the caravan. Drink driving laws are extremely strict.
Tolls: Vehicles entering Bergen on weekdays must pay a toll. Vehicles up to 3.5 tonnes entering Oslo pay a toll, also to enter Kristiansand (ferry terminal). Tolls are also levied on certain roads.

Speed Limits: Caravans and motorhomes (3.5 tons) 31 mph (50 kph) in built up areas, caravans 50 mph (80 kph) on all other roads, motorhomes 50 mph (80 kph) on other roads and 56 mph (90 kph) on motorways.

Fuel: Mon-Fri petrol stations are closed between 19.00 and 05.00. At weekends stations are closed other than in closely populated areas. Major credit cards accepted in larger petrol stations.

Parking: Parking regulations in towns are very strict and subject to fines. Yellow parking meters give 1 hour, Grey -2 and Brown - 3 hours.

Camping in Norway

There are more than 1,000 campsites in Norway and you have the option to take your own tent, caravan or motorcaravan, or to use cabin (Hytte) accommodation. The Public Roads Administration (Statens Vegvesen), in conjunction with local authorities, has started creating roadside campsites with basic facilities (Bobil parks). These are primarily designed for motorcaravans to overnight, some are free, others operate an honesty box system.

So few British were going to Norway in the early 'nineties that it was an act of faith on our part to extend our guide north of Denmark. We must admit to have been heavily influenced by the arrival on the scene of Color Line (now Fjord Line) who adopted a positive approach to the British camping market. More recently, the Scandinavian Seaways service to Göteborg in Sweden, has become equally popular as an entry route to Norway, for those who live closer to Harwich. Our first entries were concentrated around Bergen, this being the area traditionally favoured by British visitors, but since then we have steadily expanded our coverage. To enable the more adventurous to reach the Arctic Circle and Nordkapp, we have expanded north with a small selection of sites including the most northerly campsite in the world.

We continue to give low priority to the coast to the south of Stavanger/Oslo or to the valleys to the east of Oslo/Trondheim, although these are deservedly popular among Norwegian campers, they are of least interest to British campers. Norway is primarily touring country, very few campers spend more than two nights in any one campsite, preferring to move on in search of wonderful scenery just around the corner. To fit in with this we have arranged our sites in a loose circuit starting at Stavanger and Haugesund, moving north via Bergen through fjordland to Trondheim. From here one can either travel north to the Arctic Circle or Nordkapp (returning through Norway or via our sites in Sweden), or turn south and continue the circuit via the eastern valleys and Oslo.

There are a few negatives which deserve mention. Norway can be very expensive. The west coast and central mountains and fells can also be very wet; only the well equipped should consider relying entirely on tented accommodation. Mosquitoes can be a problem in summer (from June) - go prepared.

Norway - Western Fjords

Mo Camping

Steinsdalsvegen 117, 5601 Norheimsund (Hordaland)

2340

The main road leading inland from Bergen (route 7) is pleasant but perhaps unexciting until it reaches Norheimsund where it joins Hardangerfjord, one of the 'Big Three' of Norway's spectacular fjords. Mo Camping is an attractive site on what appears to be a small lake but is actually an arm of the main fjord. At the head of this arm, within walking distance of the site are the spectacular Steinsdals Falls. This little site is part of a small working farm run by the Mo family. It has 35 unmarked touring places, with 25 electrical connections possible, on a curve of flat, well kept grass with two small areas of hardstanding for poor weather. The camping area is divided from the working farm by a line of charming, traditional, wooden farm buildings which include the family home, the office and the toilet facilities. Although offering only basic facilities, this site is well looked after.

Facilities: Heated sanitary facilities (in a converted barn) include for each sex a shower (on payment) and two WCs with washbasins opposite. Rather cramped, they are hard-pressed when the site is full. Laundry, plus dishwashing and drying facilities. Motorcaravan services. Gas supplies. Free fishing. **Off site:** Town 1 km. Shop and filling station 200 m. Bicycle hire 5 km. Riding 7 km.

Charges 2002

Per person	Nkr. 5
child (under 12 yrs)	Nkr. 3
pitch	Nkr. 80
tent without car	Nkr. 50
electricity (16A)	Nkr. 20

No credit cards. **Tel:** 56 55 17 27. **Reservations:** Not necessary. **Open** 1 June - 31 August only.

Directions: Site is by the no. 7 road just over 1 km. west of Norheimsund.

Sundal Camping

2325 P.O. Box 5476, 5476 Mauranger (Hordaland)

This is an excellent gateway site for fjord-land, from either Stavanger or Bergen. Maurangerfjord is a steep-sided arm leading off the eastern shore of the Hardangerfjord. Mauranger village commands magnificent views across the waters. Cutting through the village is a turbulent stream. Its waters are ice-cold, from the Folgefonn ice-cap and its renowned glacier, an hour's brisk walk from the village. Sundal is divided into two sections: a wooded, waterfront site between the local road and the fjord, with a small marina; and an open meadow uphill of the local road. Sundal is not only ideally situated for Folgefonn; it is also the nearest good site to the charming small town of Rosendal, famous for the stately home of the celebrated Rosenkrantz family.

Facilities: Well equipped toilet blocks provide most facilities. Stream and lake fishing. Canoe and rowing boat hire. Small shop. Pleasant small hotel adjacent with attractive restaurant and bar.

Charges 2003
not available

Tel: 53 48 41 86. **Reservations:** Contact site.

Directions: Route 48 crosses Hardangerfjord by ferry from Gjermundshavn to Lofallstrand from where a clearly marked local road runs northeast for 16 km. along the fjord waterfront to Mauranger.

Odda Camping

2320 Borsta, 5750 Odda (Hordaland)

Bordered by the Folgefonna glacier to the west and the Hardangervidda plateau to the east and south, Odda is now an industrial town. At the turn of the century it was one of the most popular destinations for the European upper classes - the magnificent and dramatic scenery is still there, together with the added interest of the industrial impact. This municipal site is on the town's southern outskirts, on the shores of the Sandvin lake and on the minor road leading up to the Buar glacier, Vidfoss Falls and Folgefonna ice-cap. It is possible to walk to the ice face. The site is spread over 2.5 acres of flat, mature woodland, divided into small clearings by massive boulders deposited long ago by the departing glacier. There are 50 tourist pitches including many with electricity.

Facilities: A single timber building at the entrance houses the reception office (often unattended) and the simple, but clean sanitary facilities which provide, for each sex, 2 WCs, one hot shower (on payment) and 3 open washbasins. Small kitchen with dishwashing facilities. Washing machine and dryer in the ladies washroom. **Off site:** Town facilities close.

Charges 2002

Per tent and car	Nkr. 75
caravan and car	Nkr. 90
motorcycle	Nkr. 65
electricity	Nkr. 20

Tel: 53 64 34 10. **Reservations:** write to site. **Open** 1 June - 31 August.

Directions: Site is on the southern outskirts of Odda, signed off road to Buar, with a well marked access.

Ringoy Camping

2315 5782 Ringoy (Hordaland)

There are several sites at the popular nearby resort town of Kinsarvik, but none compares for situation or atmosphere with the small, simple Ringoy site. This site is basically a steeply sloping field running down from the road to the tree-lined fjord, with flat areas for camping along the top and the bottom of the field. The owners, the Raunsgard family are particularly proud of the site's remarkable shore-side barbecue facilities. On arrival you find a place as there is no reception - someone will call between 8 and 9 pm.

Facilities: The toilet block is small and simple (with metered showers), but well designed, constructed and maintained. It is possibly inadequate during peak holiday weeks in July. Rowing boat (free). **Off site:** Village mini-market and garage within a minute's walk.

Charges 2002

Per unit	Nkr. 80
electricity (10A)	Nkr. 15

Tel: 53 66 39 17. **Reservations:** Write to site. **Open** all year.

Directions: Site is on route 13, midway between Kinsarvik and Brimnes.

Eikhamrane Camping

2330 5776 Nå (Hordaland)

Sorfjord has long been on a popular route for travellers across Norway via Utne (where Norway's oldest hotel is a tourist attraction in its own right) and a short ferry crossing across Hardangerfjord. Travellers are also attracted by the Folgefonn ice cap which lies at the head of Sorfjord. About halfway along the western shore of Sorfjord is Eikhamrane Camping. On a well landscaped and partly terraced field which slopes alongside the road to a pebbly beach, it was formerly part of an orchard. There is room for 50 units on unmarked, well kept grass with 20 electrical hook ups (10A). There are good gravel roads, with areas of gravel hardstanding for poor weather. Many pitches overlook the fjord.

Facilities: Two small timber toilet blocks, one for toilets with external access, the other for washbasins (open) and showers (on payment). Both are simple but very well kept. Small kitchen with dishwashing facilities (hot water on payment) and two laundry sinks outside, under cover. Some supplies kept at reception office in the old farmhouse, home of the owner (bread and milk to order). Watersports (sailing, canoeing and rowing), and fishing in lake. **Off site:** Digranes nature reserve (birdwatching) nearby.

Charges 2002

Per person	Nkr. 10
child (4-12 yrs)	Nkr. 5
pitch	Nkr. 70
electricity	Nkr. 15

No credit cards. **Tel:** 53 66 22 48. **Reservations:** write to site. **Open** 1 June - 31 August only.

Directions: Site is on road 550 just outside the village of Nå, on the western shore of Sorfjord, 32 km. south of Utne and 16 km. north of Odda.

Espelandsdalen Camping

2350 5736 Granvin (Hordaland)

The textbook upper glacial valley of Espelandsdalen runs from Granvin to Ulvik, both at the heads of their respective arms of Hardangerfjord. A minor road links the two small towns with sharp climbs at either end (tricky for caravans). The valley is occupied by a series of connected lakes and for generations farmers have struggled to make a living out of the narrow strip of land between water and rock. One of these farmers has converted a narrow, sloping field bisected by the road into a modest lake-side campsite taking about 40 units. The grassy meadow pitches below the road run right down to the lake-shore. There are a few electrical hook ups (8-10A). Campers come for fishing, walking or skiing, or just to marvel at the views of the valley and its towering mountain sides.

Facilities: A basic sanitary block consists of a washing trough with hot water, a shower on payment and WCs. Some basic foodstuffs are kept in the office. Swimming, fishing and boating in lake. Boat hire. **Off site:** Ski track 2 km.

Charges 2002

Per person	Nkr. 10
child (4-12 yrs)	Nkr.5
pitch	Nkr.60
electricity	Nkr.20

No credit cards. **Tel:** 56 52 51 67. **Fax:** 56 52 59 02. E-mail: kalsaas@online.no. **Reservations:** Contact site. **Open** 1 May - 31 August.

Directions: The northern loop of the 572 road follows Espelandsdalen and the campsite is on this road, about 6 km. from its junction with route 13 at Granvin (steep gradients - see above).

Botnen Camping

2370 5950 Brekke (Sogn og Fjordane)

For those setting forth north on route 1 from Bergen there are suprisingly few attractive sites until one reaches the southern shore of mighty Sognefjord. At Brekke is a well known tourist landmark, the Breekstranda Fjord Hotel, a traditional turf-roofed complex which tourist coaches are unable to resist. A mile or two beyond the hotel, also on the shore of the fjord, is the family run Botnen Camping. An isolated, simple (2-star) site which slopes steeply, it is well maintained. It has its own jetty and harbour, with rowing boats and canoes for hire, and commands a splendid view across the fjord to distant mountains.

Facilities: Children's play area. Swimming, fishing and boating in fjord. Boats and canoes for hire.

Charges 2002

Per person	Nkr. 10
child	Nkr. 5
caravan	Nkr. 40
tent	Nkr. 30
electricity	Nkr. 15

Tel: 57 78 54 71. **Reservations:** Contact site. **Open** May - 1 September.

Directions: Site is 2 km off the coast road running west from Brekke.

Ulvik Fjord Camping

2360 5730 Ulvik (Hordaland)

Ulvik was discovered by tourists 150 years ago when the first liners started operating to the head of Hardangerfjord, and to this day, regular cruise liners work their way into the heartland of Norway. A century and a half of visitors has meant that Ulvik is now an established tourist destination - but, with only just over 1,000 inhabitants, it still manages to retain an unspoilt village atmosphere. Access is by narrow, winding roads, either along the side of the fjord or up a steep road behind the town - probably not recommended for caravans. This pretty little site is 500 m. from the centre of the town. It occupies what was once a small orchard taking about 30 units on undulating ground which slopes towards the fjord, with some flat areas and a few electrical connections.

Facilities: There are no facilities other than a small wooden building which houses reception and the well kept sanitary facilities. For each sex there are 2 open washbasins, WCs and 2 modern showers on payment. Small kitchen with cooker and dishwashing sink. Boat slipway, fishing and swimming in fjord. **Off site:** Hotel opposite, shops and restaurants in town.

Charges 2002

Per motorcaravan or car plus tent	Nkr. 60
with caravan	Nkr. 65
person	Nkr. 15
child (4-12 yrs)	Nkr. 10
hiker or cyclist and tent	Nkr. 35
electricity	Nkr. 20

Tel: 05 52 65 77. **Reservations:** write to site. **Open** 20 May - 31 August.

Directions: Ulvik is reached by road no. 572; the site is on the southern side of the town, opposite the Ulvikfjord Pension. There is a ferry from road no. 7 at Brimnes. Cars and caravans can now connect with road 7 via a tunnel.

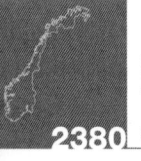

Tveit Camping

2380 6894 Vangsnes (Sogn og Fjordane)

In the district of Vik on the south shore of Sognefjord, 4 km. from the small port of Vangsnes, Tveit Camping is part of a small working farm and it is a charming neat site. Reception and a kiosk open most of the day in high season, with a phone to summon assistance at any time. Four terraces provide 40 pitches, 30 with electricity. On the campsite is a restored Iron Age burial mound dating from 350-550 AD, whilst the statue of 'Fritjov the Intrepid' towers over the landscape at Vangsnes. It is possible for families do do easy hikes on the glacier at Nigardsbreen but not at Fjaerland where it is more challenging.

Facilities: Modern, heated sanitary facilities provide showers on payment, a unit for disabled visitors, kitchens with facilities for dishwashing and cooking, and a laundry with washing machine, dryer and iron (hot water on payment). Motorcaravan services. Kiosk (15/6-15/8). TV rooms. Playground. Harbour for small boats, slipway and boat/canoe hire. Fishing. Bicycle hire. **Off site:** Shop, café and pub by ferry terminal in Vangsnes 4 km. Riding 15 km.

Charges 2002

Per person (over 5 yrs)	Nkr. 10
pitch	Nkr. 80
electricity	Nkr. 20

No credit cards. **Tel:** 57 69 66 00. E-mail: tveit@online.no. **Reservations:** Write to site. **Open** 10 May - 10 October.

Directions: Site is by Rv 13 between Vik and Vangsnes, 4 km. south of Vangsnes.

Kjornes Camping

2390 5800 Sogndal (Sogn og Fjordane)

A simple farm site in a prime fjordside location, ideal for those on a budget. Occupying a long open meadow which slopes down to the tree lined waterside this site is ideal for those who enjoy peace and quiet, lovely scenery or a spot of fishing. Access is via a narrow lane with passing places, which drops down towards the fjord 3 km. from Sogndal. The site takes 100 touring units, but there are only 36 electrical connections (16A). There are also some cabins for accommodation on site. A scenic route runs along the north shore of Sognefjord and the Sogndalfjord to Sogndal and then across the Jotunheimen mountain plateau towards Lom.

Facilities: The sanitary unit is basic but clean, providing mostly open washbasins, and 2 showers per sex (on payment). Small kitchen with dishwashing sink, double hot-plate and fridge. 'Al fresco' laundry with small roof covering the sink, washing machine and dryer.

Charges 2002

Per unit	Nkr. 45
adult	Nkr. 15
child	Nkr. 5
small tent	Nkr. 30
electricity	Nkr. 20

Tel: 57 67 45 80. Fax: 57 67 33 26. E-mail: camping@kjornes.no. **Reservations:** Write to site. **Open** 1 June - end August.

Directions: Site is off the Rv 5, 3 km. east of Sogndal, 8 km. west of Kaupanger.

PlusCamp Sandvik

2385 6868 Gaupne (Sogn og Fjordane)

Sandvik is a compact, small site on the edge of the town of Gaupne close to the Nigardsbreen Glacier. It provides 60 touring pitches, 32 with electrical connections (8/16A), arranged on fairly level grassy terrain either side of a gravel access road. A large supermarket, post office, banks, etc. are all within a level 500 m. stroll. A café in the reception building is open in summer for drinks and meals and the small shop sells groceries, ices, soft drinks, sweets, etc. This is a useful site for those using the spectacular Rv 55 high mountain road from Lom to Sogndal or for visiting the Nigardsbreen Glacier and Jostedalsbreen area of Norway.

Facilities: The single, fully equipped, central sanitary unit includes washbasins with dividers and two hot showers per sex (on payment). Multi-purpose unit for families or disabled people with facilities for baby changing and a further WC, basin and shower with ramp for access. Small campers' kitchen has dishwashing facilities, hot-plates, oven and fridge (all free of charge) together with tables, chairs and TV. Separate laundry with sinks, washing machine and dryer. Shop and small restaurant (1/6-31/8). Playground. Boat hire. Fishing.

Charges 2002

Per pitch incl. up to 4 persons	Nkr. 120
electricity	Nkr. 25

Tel: 57 68 11 53. Fax: 57 68 16 71. E-mail: sandvik@pluscamp.no. **Reservations:** Write to site. **Open** all year.

Directions: Signed just off Rv 55 Lom-Sogndal road on eastern outskirts of Gaupne.

Byrkjelo Camping

2436 6867 Byrkjelo (Sogn og Fjordane)

This neatly laid out and well equipped small site offers 50 large marked and numbered touring pitches, 40 with electrical connections (10A) and 15 with gravel hardstandings. It is a good value site in a village location with neatly mown grass, attractive trees and shrubs with a warm welcome from the young and enthusiastic owners. Fishing is possible in the river adjacent to the site. Reception and a small kiosk selling ices, sweets and soft drinks, are housed in an attractive cabin and there is a bell to summon the owners should they not be on site when you arrive. A garage, mini-market and cafe are 100 m. away and lively Sandane is 19 km.

Facilities: The good heated sanitary unit includes 5 shower rooms each with washbasin, on payment. A multi-purpose unit serves the needs of families with babies and disabled visitors, incorporating a WC, basin and shower with handrails, etc. Campers' kitchen with dishwashing sinks, hot-plates and dining area (all free). Separate laundry. Motorcaravan services. Kiosk. TV room. Minigolf. Small playground. Fishing. **Off site:** Riding 5 km. Ideal base for Nordfjord and Jostedalsbreen.

Charges 2002

Per unit	Nkr. 70
adult	Nkr. 10
electricity	Nkr. 20

No credit cards. **Tel:** 57 86 74 30. Fax: 57 86 71 54. E-mail: byrkjelocamping@sensewave.com. **Reservations:** Advisable in peak season. **Open** 20 May - 1 September.

Directions: Site is beside the Rv 1 in the village of Byrkjelo, 19 km. east of Sandane.

PlusCamp Jolstraholmen

2400 Jolstraholmen, 6847 Vassenden (Sogn og Fjordane)

This well presented, family run site is between Sognelfjord and Nordfjord. It is located between the road and the fast-flowing Jolstra River (renowned for its trout fishing), 1.5 km. from the lakeside village of Vassenden, behind the Statoil filling station, restaurant and supermarket complex which is also owned and run by the site owner and his family. The 80 pitches (some marked) are on grass or gravel hardstanding all with electricity (10A) and some have water and waste points. A river tributary runs through the site and forms an island on which some tent pitches are located. Guided walking tours are organised, and a riverside and woodland walk follows a 1.5 km. circular route from the site and has fishing platforms and picnic tables along the way.

Facilities: The main heated sanitary facilities, fully equipped in rooms below the complex, include showers on payment) plus one family bathroom per sex. Small unit located on the island. Two small kitchens provide dishwashing and cooking facilities (free of charge). Laundry has sinks, washing machine and dryer. Supermarket. Restaurant. Garage. Covered barbecue area. Playground. Voleyball. Water slide (open summer, weather permitting). Rafting. Fishing. Guided walks. Boat hire. **Off site:** Minigolf 50 m. Ski-slopes within 1 km.

Charges 2002

Per unit incl. 1-4 persons	Nkr. 105 - 140
small tent incl. 2 persons	Nkr. 60 - 80
electricity	Nkr. 30

Tel: 57 72 71 35. Fax: 57 72 75 05. E-mail: jostraholmen@pluscamp.no. **Reservations:** Write to site. **Open** all year.

Directions: Site is beside the E39 road, 1.5 km. west of Vassenden, 18 km. east of Førde.

Bjorkedal Camping

2480 6120 Folkestadbgd (Møre og Romsdal)

On the Rv 1 north of the Nordfjord is a lovely bowl shaped valley famous for traditional boat building. This site is on a grassy open plateau about 300 m. off the main road and overlooking the farmland and mountains around the lake. There is space for 25 tents or vans with 10 electric connections (16A), and 5 log cabins. For a thousand years boats have been hand built in this valley by the Bjorkedal family. Site owner, Jakob Bjorkedal, will be pleased to show you the old water powered saw mill that he has reconstructed, and there are usually some examples of his boat building craft in the magnificent workshop with a spectacular cathedral-style timber roof. There is a network of footpaths both in the valley and leading up into the surrounding circle of mountains.

Facilities: small, modern and spotlessly clean sanitary unit includes washbasins with dividers and curtains, one shower per sex (on payment), plus a WC and washbasin unit with ramped access for disabled people. Kitchen with dishwashing sink and full cooker (free). Laundry with sinks and washing machine. TV lounge. Small game hunting. Freshwater fishing. **Off site:** Site is convenient base from which to explore Geiranger, Runde, West Cape or Strynefjellet.

Charges 2002

Per unit	Nkr. 40
adult	Nkr. 10
child	Nkr. 5
electricity	Nkr. 15

Tel: 70 05 20 43. **Reservations:** Write to site. **Open** all year.

Directions: Signed off the Rv 1, midway along the western side of Bjorkedal lake and 21 km. north of Nordfjordeid.

Prinsen Strandcamping

2460 Ratvika, 6015 Alesund (Møre og Romsdal)

Prinsen is a lively, fjordside site, 5 km from the attractive small town of Alesund. It is a more attractive option to the crowded sites closer to town, even so, this is mainly a transit and short-stay site. Divided by trees and shrubs, and sloping gently to a small sandy beach with views down Borgundfjord, the site has 125 grassy pitches, 27 cabins, 110 electricity connections (16A) and 75 cable TV hook-ups. Reception houses a small shop, bread can be ordered daily, and English newspapers are also usually available. Alesund has lovely Art Nouveau architecture, Sunnmøre Folk Museum has 50 old houses, a boat collection and medieval and Viking artefacts.

Facilities: The main heated sanitary unit in the reception building is fully equipped with mostly open washbasins, showers on payment and a sauna for each sex. Small kitchen with cooking facilities and dishwashing sinks. Laundry with sink, washing machines and dryer. Extra older facilities mainly serving rooms and cabins, but include multi-purpose bathroom for disabled people, families and baby changing (key from reception). New motorcaravan service point. Shop (1/6-1/9). TV room. Barbecue areas. Playground. Slipway and boat hire. Fishing. Bicycle hire. **Off site:** Restaurant 800 m.

Charges 2002

Per unit incl. up to 6 persons	Nkr. 150
electricity	Nkr. 20

Tel: 70 15 52 04. Fax: 70 15 49 96. **Reservations:** Write to site. **Open** all year.

Directions: Turn off E136 at roundabout signed to Hatlane and site. Follow signs to site.

Åndalsnes Camping and Motel

2470 6300 Åndalsnes (Møre og Romsdal)

This attractive, popular site is situated in mature woodland beside the Rauma river, 1 km. from the town centre. It is close to Romsdalfjord and the breathtaking Trollstigen mountain road with its 11 giant hairpins that scale the sheer rock face. The reception, shop and cafeteria complex are on the opposite side of the road to the main touring area. Arranged informally between the many trees and shrubs, 180 of the 230 grassy pitches have electric hook-ups (16A, long leads may be required). The cafeteria, which doubles as a function room/TV lounge, serves breakfast and dinner and is open daily though times vary according to demand.

Facilities: Two heated sanitary units provide some washbasins in cubicles with showers (tokens on payment). Facilities for disabled visitors. Kitchens and laundries with facilities for cooking, dining, dishwashing and ironing. Washing machines and dryers. Well stocked shop (1/5-1/9). Cafeteria (1/5-1/9). Children's playground. Minigolf. Bicycle hire. Canoe and boat hire. Fishing.

Charges 2002

Per pitch	Nkr. 80 - 90
adult	Nkr. 15
child (4-12 yrs)	Nkr. 10
electricity	Nkr. 25

Tel: 71 22 16 29. Fax: 71 22 62 16. E-mail: acampi@online.no. **Reservations:** Write to site. **Open** 1 May - 15 September.

Directions: Turn off E136 by the bridge to southwest of town, towards Trollstigen and Romsdalfjord. Site is signed.

Bjølstad Camping

2450 6445 Malmefjorden (More og Romsdal)

This delightful small, rural site, which slopes down to Malmefjorden, has space for just 45 touring units on grassy, fairly level, terraces either side of the tarmac central access road. A delight for children is a large, old masted boat, plus the more conventional swings. At the foot of the site is a waterside barbecue area and a jetty. Boats can be hired, one can swim or fish in the fjord. This site is an ideal base for visiting the famous Varden viewpoint with its magnificent views over this 'Town of Roses', the fjord and 222 mountain peaks. Further afield, one can drive the fantastic and scenic Atlantic Highway as it threads its way across the many islands and bridges to the west of Kristiansund.

Facilities: The basic, clean, heated sanitary unit includes one shower per sex (token on payment), plus washbasins with dividers, and one in cubicle (for ladies). Small campers' kitchen with two dishwashing sinks and hot-plate. Laundry service at reception. Children's playground. Boat hire. Fjord fishing and swimming. Dogs are not accepted. **Off site:** Riding 9 km. Golf 12 km.

Charges 2002

Per caravan	Nkr. 95
tent or motorcaravan	Nkr. 80
adult	Nkr. 10
child	Nkr. 5
electricity	Nkr. 15

Tel: 71 26 56 56. Fax: 71 26 04 52. E-mail: bjoelstad.camping@c2i.net. **Reservations:** Write to site. **Open** 1 June - 30 September (may before on request).

Directions: Turn off Rv 64 on northern edge of Malmefjorden village towards village of Lindset (lane is oil bound gravel). Site is 1 km.

Skjerneset Camping

2490 Ekkilsoya, 6553 Bremsnes (More og Romsdal)

The tiny island of Ekkilsøya lies off the larger island of Averoy and is reached via a bridge (no toll) from the main Rv 64 just south of Bremsnes. Although the fishing industry here is not what it used to be it is still the dominant activity and Skjerneset Camping has been developed by the Otterlei family to give visitors an insight into this industry and its history. Most of the old 'Klippfisk' warehouse is now a fascinating museum, with the remainder housing the site facilities. There is space for 20 units on hardstandings around a rocky bluff and along the harbour's rocky frontage and all have electricity (16A). A small grassy area for 10 tents is under pine trees in a hollow on the top of the bluff. Note: this is a working harbour with deep unfenced water very close to the pitches.

Facilities: Unisex sanitary facilities are heated, but basic, and perhaps a little quirky in their layout but include washbasins in cubicles. Kitchen with two full cookers plus a hot-plate and dishwashing sinks. Small laundry with sink and washing machine. All were free when we visited. Motorcaravan service point planned. Kiosk for basic packet foods, crisps, ices, sweets, postcards etc. TV. Motor or rowing boat hire. Organised sea-fishing or sightseeing trips in the owner's new sea-going boat, and for non-anglers who want a fish supper, fresh fish are always available on site.

Charges 2002

Per unit (less 20% outside 20/6-20/8)	Nkr. 90
electricity	Nkr. 20

Tel: 71 51 18 94. Fax: 71 51 18 15. **Reservations:** Write to site. **Open** all year.

Directions: Site is on the little island of Ekkilsøya which is reached via a side road running west from the main Rv 64 road, 1.5 km. south of Bremsnes.

Magalaupe Camping

2505 Rute 5, 7340 Oppdal (Sør Trøndelag)

This is a rural, riverside site in a sheltered position with easy access from the E6. Fairly simple facilities are offered but there are a host of unusual activities in the surrounding area, including caving, rafting, mineral hunting, and reindeer and elk safaris. In winter the more adventurous can also go snow-mobiling or skiing in the high Dovrefjell National Park. The 75 unmarked and grassy touring pitches (36 with10/16A electricity) are in natural surroundings amongst birch trees and rocks on several different levels and served by gravel access roads. The simple facilities should be adequate at most times.

Facilities: Small, but very clean, heated sanitary unit fully equipped but the showers are on payment. Extra WC/washbasin units in reception building. Small kitchen with dishwashing, hot-plate and freezer, plus a washing/drying machine. Kiosk for ices, soft drinks, etc. Bar (mid June - Aug). TV lounge. Fishing. Bicycle hire. **Off site:** Supermarkets, etc. in Oppdal (11 km). Riding or golf 12 km.

Charges 2002

Per unit incl. 4 persons	Nkr. 80
small tent without electricity	Nkr. 50
electricity	Nkr. 20

No credit cards. **Tel:** 72 42 46 84. Fax: 72 42 46 84. E-mail: camp@magalaupe.no. **Reservations:** Write to site. **Open** all year.

Directions: Site is signed to western side of the E6, 11 km. south of Oppdal.

Håneset Camping

2510 7460 Roros (Sør Trondelag)

At first sight Håneset Camping it is not promising, lying between the main road and the railway, nor is the gritty sloping ground of the site very imaginatively landscaped - for grass, when it grows up here, is rather coarse and lumpy. However, as we soon discovered, it is the best equipped campsite in the town, and ideal to cope with the often cold, wet weather of this bleak 1,000m. high plateau. The 50 unmarked touring pitches all have access to electricity (10/16A), and most facilities are in the main complex building. People flock from all over Europe to visit this remarkably well preserved mining town. For over 300 years it was one of Europe's leading copper mines. As a result it occupies a special place on UNESCO's world heritage list for its unique concentration of historic wooden houses.

Facilities: Heated sanitary facilities provide three separate rooms for each sex, fully equipped with showers on payment. Washing machine and two clothes washing sinks. Kitchen. Shop and cafeteria (mid June-August) and huge sitting/TV room and two well equipped kitchens which the owners, the Moen family, share fully with their guests, plus rooms for rent. Playground. **Off site:** Town 20 minutes walk

Charges 2002

Per caravan or motorcaravan	Nkr. 110 - 135
tent	Nkr. 90
electricity	Nkr. 20

No credit cards. **Tel:** 72 41 06 00. Fax: 72 41 06 01. **Reservations:** Write to site. **Open** all year.

Directions: Site is on the Rv 30 leading south from Roros to Os, 3 km. from Roros.

Trasavika Camping

2500 7354 Viggja (Sør Trondelag)

On a headland jutting into the Trondheim-fjord and some 40 km. from Trondheim, Trasavika occupies such an attractive position with glorious views that the extra distance into town is bearable. The 65 pitches are on an open grassy field at the top of the site, or on a series of terraces below which run right down to the small sandy beach, and are easily accessed via a well designed gravel road. There are 48 electricity connections (10A). To one side, on a wooded bluff at the top of the site, are 14 cabins. A safer site entrance has been constructed leading down to the reception complex which also houses the small shop, and café. Nobody travelling as far as mid-Norway would dream of not visiting the interesting, historic city of Trondheim, for long the capital of Norway.

Facilities: The neat, fully equipped, sanitary unit includes two controllable hot showers per sex (on payment). Hot water on payment in kitchen and laundry which have a hot-plate, dish and clothes washing sinks, washing machine and dryer. Shop. Café (20/6-30/8). TV/sitting room. Children's playground. Jetty and boat hire. Free fjord fishing.

Charges 2002

Per caravan or motorcaravan	Nkr. 120
tent	Nkr. 80 - 110
electricity	Nkr. 30

Tel: 72 86 78 22. Fax: 72 86 79 79. E-mail: jowiggen@start.no. **Reservations:** Write to site. **Open** 1 May - 10 September.

Directions: Site is on the edge of Viggja on E39 between Orkanger and Buvik, 17 km. from the E6 and 40 km. west of Trondheim.

Vegset Camping

2495 7760 Snåsa (Nord-Trøndelag)

This pleasant site is seven kilometres north of Snåsa, beside the E6 road and on the banks of Lake Snåsavatn. It consists of 10 site owned chalets and an extensive area for touring units, mainly on quite a slope. Snåsa is a centre for the South Lapp people who have their own boarding school, museum and information centre there. The Bergasen Nature Reservation is close to the village and is famous for its rare flora, especially orchids. The Gressamoen National Park is also near.

Facilities: A new, well equipped sanitary block provides showers (Nkr. 5), plus a shower with toilet suitable for disabled people. Kiosk selling grociers. Kitchen. TV room. Swimming, fishing and boat hire.

Charges 2002

Per unit	Nkr. 80

Tel: 74 15 29 50. **Reservations:** Contact site. **Open** Easter - 10 October.

Directions: Site is just off the E6 road, 7 km. from Snåsa.

Krokstrand Camping

Krokstrand, 8630 Storforshei (Nordland)

Attractively arranged amongst the birch trees, with a fast flowing river and waterfall alongside, and views of snow covered mountains this site is a popular resting place for all nationalities on the long trek to Nordkapp. There are 40 unmarked pitches and electrical connections (16A) for 20 units. The small reception kiosk is open 16.00 - 22.00 hrs in high season, otherwise campers are invited to find a pitch and pay later. Directions in English are given to the owner's house (within walking distance) for emergencies. Being only 18 km. drive from the Arctic Circle with its Visitor Centre, this site is in an ideal location. and those interested in WW2 history will find the neatly tended grave of a Russian soldier by the site gate.

Facilities: The well maintained, spotlessly clean, small sanitary unit includes two showers per sex (on payment). Laundry with washing machine and dryer. Small kitchen with double hot-plate and dishwashing sink. Motorcaravan services. Brightly painted playground with trampoline, well maintained. Minigolf. Fishing. **Off site:** Small village just outside the camp entrance has a hotel with restaurant, a souvenir shop. The nearest town for shopping is Mo-i-Rana (60 km).

Charges 2002

Per unit	Nkr. 75
adult	Nkr. 10
child	Nkr. 5
electricity	Nkr. 20

No credit cards. **Tel:** 75 16 60 02. **Fax:** 75 16 60 02. **Reservations:** Write to site. **Open** 1 June - 20 September.

Directions: Entrance is off E6 at Krokstrand village opposite hotel, 18 km. south of the Arctic Circle.

Saltstraumen Camping

Boks 85, 8056 Saltstraumen (Nordland)

On a coastal route, this site is close to the largest Maelstrom in the world. It is within walking distance of this outstanding phenomenon - the strongest tidal current in the world, where in the course of 6 hours between 33,800 and 82,700 billion gallons of water are pressed through a narrow strait, at a rate of about 20 knots. The effect is greatest at new or full moons, check tide tables to determine the best time to visit. Otherwise a rather ordinary site, the 60 touring pitches are mostly level gravel hardstandings in rows, with electricity (10A) available to all. A few 'softer' pitches are available for tents. The site is 33 km. from Bodø and 50 km. from Fauske.

Facilities: Basic but heated sanitary facilities are clean, and fully equipped. Showers are just shower heads with dividers between and communal changing, but the ladies' room has some shower curtains. Kitchen with two full cookers. Laundry with washing machine and dryer. Motorcaravan service point. TV room. Children's playground. Minigolf. Fishing. **Off site:** Adjacent is a filling station with shop, hairdressers and nearby are a hotel and cafeteria.

Charges 2002

Per caravan	Nkr. 100
motorcaravan	Nkr. 85
tent	Nkr. 75
electricity	Nkr. 25

Tel: 75 58 75 60. **Fax:** 75 58 75 40. **Reservations:** Write to site. **Open** all year.

Directions: From Rv 80 (Fauske -Bodø) turn south on Rv 17, site is 12 km. at Saltstraumen adjacent to a Statoil station.

Lyngvær Lofoten Bobilcamping

Postboks 30, 8310 Kabelvåg (Nordland)

This is a superbly positioned campsite by the sea on the Lofoten Islands. It is well laid out, having only been built in '91/92, with room for 200 units, half with access to electrical connections. There are several play areas and boat hire is available (rowing and motor boats, canoes and pedaloes). The site has its own salmon and sea trout fishing. It is a good area for walking, both by the sea and in the mountains.

Facilities: Facilities are clean and good, although there are rather few of them. Showers, a little cramped, are on payment. Extra unisex showers and toilets are beside reception. Communal kitchen with cooking and washing up facilities. Large sitting area with satellite TV. Children's play areas. Boat hire. Fishing.

Charges 2002

Per unit	Nkr. 80
electricity	Nkr. 20

Fifth night free. **Tel:** 76 07 87 81. **Reservations:** Write to site. **Open** 15 March - 31 August.

Directions: Site is signed from the ferry terminal.

Ballangen Camping

2455 8540 Ballangen (Nordland)

A pleasant, lively site conveniently located on the edge of a fjord with a small rocky beach, with direct access off the main E6 road. The 150 marked pitches are mostly on sandy grass, with electricity (10/16A) available to 120. There are a few hard-standings, also 50 cabins for rent. A TV room has tourist information, a coffee and games machines and there is a small outdoor pool and waterslide with free fjord fishing, and boat hire. An interesting excursion is to the nearby Martinstollen mine where visitors are guided through the dimly lit Olav Shaft 500 m. into the mountain. Narvik with its wartime connections and museums is 40 km.

Facilities: Toilet facilities in a new building with modern fittings include some washbasins in cubicles. Facilities for disabled visitors, sauna and solarium. Kitchen with dishwashing sinks, full cooker, hot-plates and covered seating area. Laundry. Motorcaravan services. Well stocked shop. Café and takeaway (main season). TV/games room. Swimming pool and waterslide (charged). Tennis. Minigolf. Fishing. Boat and bicycle hire. **Off site:** Riding 2 km. Ballangen (4 km.) has supermarket and other services.

Charges 2002

Per unit incl. 4 persons	Nkr. 130
electricity	Nkr. 20

Tel: 76 92 76 90. Fax: 76 92 76 92. **Reservations:** Contact site. **Open** all year.

Directions: Access is off the E6, 4 km. north of Ballangen, 40 km. south of Narvik.

Slettnes Fjordcamp

2445 9047 Oteren (Troms)

Slettnes is a useful stopover southeast of Tromso beside the E6 road. Beside a narrow fjord and surrounded by snowy capped mountains, this is a large site mainly for permanent caravans but with room for 20 touring units. A very well kept site, there are neat flower beds outside reception.

Facilities: Sanitary facilities consist of two toilets each for male and female with washbasins with mirror, etc. There are three showers each, communal but with no charge and good hot water. A kitchen houses a sink unit, full size cooker and microwave.

Charges 2002

Per unit	Nkr. 100

Tel: 77 71 45 08. **Reservations:** Contact site.

Directions: Site is beside the E6 road near Oteren

Kirkeporten Camping

2425 9763 Skarsvåg, Nordkapp (Finnmark)

This is the most northerly campsite in the world (71° 06' 50") and considering the climate and the wild unspoilt location it has to be one of the best sites in Scandinavia, and also rivals the best in Europe. An added bonus is that the reindeer often come right into the campsite to graze. The 30 pitches, 22 with electricity (16A), are on grass or gravel hardstanding in natural 'tundra' terrain beside a small lake, together with 10 rental cabins and 5 rooms. Sea fishing and photographic trips by boat can be arranged and buses run 4 times a day to Honningsvåg or the Nordkapp Centre. We suggest you follow the marked footpath over the hillside behind the campsite, from where you can photograph Nordkapp at midnight if the weather is favourable. We also advise you pack warm clothing, bedding and maybe propane for this location. Note: Although overnighting at Nordkapp Centre is permitted, it is on the very exposed gravel car-park with no electric hook-ups or showers.

Facilities: Excellent modern fully sanitary installations in two under-floor heated buildings, linked by a covered timber walkway. They include a sauna, two family bathrooms, baby room, and excellent unit for disabled visitors. Laundry with washing machine and dryer. Kitchen, with hot-plates, sinks and a dining area. All have quality fittings, excellent tiling and beautiful woodwork - the owner is a carpenter by profession. Good motorcaravan service point. Reception/cafeteria at the entrance open daily (15/6-15/8).

Charges 2002

Per person	Nkr. 20
pitch	Nkr. 110
electricity	Nkr. 30

Tel: 78 47 52 33. Fax: 78 47 52 47. **Reservations:** Not usually necessary. **Open** 20 May - 1 September.

Directions: On the island of Magerøya, from Honningsvåg take the E69 for 20 km. then fork right signed Skarsvåg. Site is on the left after 3 km. just as you approach Skarsvåg.

Norway - North
Solvang Camping
Transfarelv, 9500 Alta (Finnmark)

2435

This is an old-style, restful little site with a welcoming atmosphere. It is set well back from the main road, so there is no noise. The site overlooks the tidal marshes of the Altafjord, which are home to a wide variety of bird-life, providing ornithologists with a grandstand view. The 30 pitches are on undulating grass amongst pine trees and shrubs, and are not marked, although there are 12 electric hook-ups (16A). The site is run by a church organisation and only limited funds are available for repairs and refurbishment. However, facilities are clean and in good order (out of season, the site provides holidays for needy children). Places of interest in the area are the Savco Canyon, with the controversial Alta Power Station and dam at its upper end.

Facilities: Basic, heated sanitary facilities in a fairly old building, include mostly open washbasins. Kitchen with two full cookers and dishwashing sinks. Small laundry with washing machine and spin dryer. In its own little kiosk outside is the modern stainless steel chemical disposal point and outside a waste water drain which, with a little ingenuity, is possible to use for draining a motorcaravan tank. TV lounge. Football field. Children's playground.

Charges 2002

Per unit	Nkr. 90
electricity	Nkr. 30
cyclist tent	Nkr. 70

No credit cards. **Tel:** 78 43 04 77. Fax: 78 44 30 20. **Reservations:** Write to site. **Open** 1 June - 10 August.

Directions: Site is signed off the E6, 10 km. north of Alta.

Norway - North
Kautokeino Fritidssenter & Camping
Suohpatjávri, 9520 Kautokeino (Finnmark)

2415

This is a newly developed, friendly, lake-side site, 8 km. south of Kautokeino. The 30 pitches are not marked but are gener-ally on a firm sandy base amongst low growing birch trees, with 20 electric hook-ups (10A) available. There are also cabins and motel rooms for rent. Although the grass is trying to grow, the ground is frozen from September until May so it takes many years to establish. During the season when there are enough guests, the owner arranges an evening campfire around two Sami tents, with 'lectures' about the Sami people. There are good walks to some special Sami sites. The site is 35 km. north of the Finnish Border.

Facilities: The modern sanitary building is heated and well maintained, with 2 British style WCs, 2 open washbasins and 2 showers (on payment) per sex. Small kitchen with full cooker, dishwashing sinks and refrigerator. Laundry with washing machine, dryer and ironing facilities. Separate bathroom for disabled people, also containing baby facilities. Football. Volleyball. Site rents canoes, boats and pedalos and free fishing available in lake.

Charges 2002

Per unit	Nkr. 65 - 75
adult	Nkr. 10
child	Nkr. 5
hikers tent	Nkr. 45
electricity	Nkr. 25

Tel: 78 48 57 33. Fax: 78 48 57 33. **Reservations:** Write to site. **Open** 1 June - 30 September.

Directions: Site is 8 km. south of Kautokeino on the Rv 93. (Do not confuse with another site of similar name in the town).

Norway - East
Gjelten Bru Camping
2560 Alvdal (Hedmark)

2515

Located just a few km. west of Alvdal, this peaceful little site with its traditional turf roof buildings, makes an excellent base from which to explore the area. The 50 touring pitches are on level neatly trimmed grass, served by gravel roads, and with electricity (10A) for 37. Some pitches are in the open and others under tall pine trees spread along the river bank. Across the bridge on the other side of the river and main road, the site owners also operate the local, extremely well stocked mini-market and post office. The UNESCO World Heritage town of Roros is 75 km. to the northeast, and the Dovrefjell National Park is also within driving distance.

Facilities: Heated toilet facilities are housed in two buildings. One unit has been refurbished, the other is of newer construction. There is a mix of conventional washbasins and stainless steel washing troughs, and hot showers on payment. Separate unit with WC, basin, shower and handrails for disabled campers. Two small kitchens, one at each block, provide dish-washing facilities, hot-plates and an oven all free of charge. Fishing. **Off site:** Supermarket and post office nearby. Bicycle hire 5 km.

Charges 2002

Per unit	Nkr. 115
electricity	Nkr. 15

No credit cards. **Tel:** 62 48 74 44. Fax: 62 78 70 20. **Reservations:** Write to site. **Open** all year.

Directions: On the Rv 29 at Gjelten 3.5 km. west of Alvdal. Turn over the river bridge opposite village store and post office, and site is immediately on the right.

Rustberg Hytteulerie & Camping

2545 | 2636 Øyer (Oppland)

Conveniently located beside the E6 and just 20 km. from Lillehammer, this attractive terraced site provides a comfortable base for exploring the area. Like all sites along this route it does suffer from road noise at times, but the site facilities and nearby attractions more than compensate for this. There are 90 pitches with 60 available for touring units, most reasonably level and with some gravel hardstandings available for motorcaravans. There are 50 electrical connections (10A). Small open air swimming pool with water-slide which is open June-Aug. (weather permitting). The Maihaugen Folkmuseum and Lillehammer town are 20 km, Hunderfossen (5 km.) has the Norwegian Road Museum and the more adventurous can ride the Olympic bobsleigh track.

Facilities: Heated, fully equipped sanitary facilities include washbasins in cubicles and showers on payment. Two luxurious family bathrooms. Unit for disabled people with WC, basin and shower. Campers' kitchen and dining room with dishwashing, a microwave oven and double hob (all free). Separate laundry provides sinks, washing machine, dryer and drying cupboard. Motorcaravan services. Kiosk stocking basic foods, beer, ices, sweets, postcards and stamps. Swimming pool and water-slide. Billiard golf. Children's playground.

Charges 2002

Per unit	Nkr. 125
small tent	Nkr. 110
electricity	Nkr. 20

Tel: 61 27 81 84. **Fax:** 61 27 87 05. **Reservations:** Write to site. **Open** all year.

Directions: Site is well signed from the E6, 20 km. north of Lillehammer.

Strandefjord Camping

2550 | 2920 Leira (Oppland)

Fagernes lies on the north shore of an impressive glacial lake - Strandefjorden, and just 4 km. to the southeast at Leira, on a corner of this lake, is Strandefjord Camping. This undulating, woodland site behind a light industrial estate, has 70 touring pitches, but can take up to 250 units in scattered clearings amongst the trees and beside the lake. Many pitches are only suitable for tents and only 75 have electricity (10A). Also 30 seasonal units, 31 cabins and rooms on site. Saunas (which are equipped with TV!) are to be found under the main site complex which also houses reception, a licensed restaurant, and conference room. Fishing and swimming in the lake are possible.

Facilities: The main heated, but rather basic, sanitary unit could be hard pressed in high season. It includes some washbasins in cubicles, but only 2 showers per sex (on payment). Separate rooms house a small kitchen with dishwashing and cooking facilities (free), and a laundry. Extra showers and WC's with saunas. Restaurant (June-Aug). Children's play areas. Lake swimming. Fitness track. Tennis. Beach volleyball. Minigolf. Boat hire. **Off site:** Village mini-market 2 minute walk.

Charges 2002

Per caravan or motorcaravan	Nkr. 120
tent and car	Nkr. 100
bicycle or motorcycle and tent	Nkr. 85
electricity	Nkr. 25

Tel: 61 36 23 65. **Fax:** 61 36 24 80. **Reservations:** Write to site. **Open** all year.

Directions: Turn off the E16 Oslo road onto the Rv 51, at Leira village 4 km. east of Fagernes. The site entrance is within 50 m.

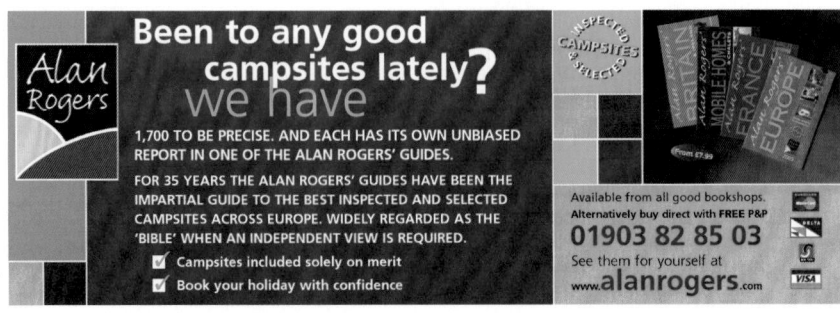

Fossheim Hytte & Camping
2570 3550 Gol (Buskerud)

Centred on the country town of Gol is one of Norway's favourite camping areas, Hallingdal. This small touring site lies just 4 km. west of the town, on the banks of the Hallingdal river bank, and is shaded by elegant tall birch trees. Despite being just below the main road and with a railway in the trees on the opposite side of the river, surprisingly little noise penetrates this idyllic setting. There are 50 grassy pitches, with electricity (10/16A) available to 40 and cable TV connections for some. Most overlook the river. In addition there are 14 cabins and 4 rooms for rent, but no static caravans are accepted. Trout fishing with a specially constructed wooden walkway and platform for anglers with disabilities.

Facilities: A modern heated toilet unit includes some washbasins in cubicles, separate unit for disabled people and a sauna. Small kitchen and laundry rooms provide cramped facilities for dishwashing and cooking (free of charge), plus sinks for clothes washing and a washing machine and dryer. Shop with bread to order (1/6-31/8). Large comfortable TV lounge. Children's play area. Bicycle and canoe hire. Trout fishing and canoeing. **Off site:** Riding 4 km. Golf 18 km.

Charges 2002
Per unit incl. 2 persons	Nkr. 105 - 145
extra person	Nkr. 10
electricity	Nkr. 30

Tel: 32 02 95 80. Fax: 32 02 95 85. E-mail: foshytte@online.no. **Reservations:** Write to site. **Open** all year.

Directions: Site is 4 km. west of Gol on route Rv 7 leading to Geilo. (Note: there is another site of similar name in the adjoining Hemsedal).

Olberg Camping
2615 Olberg, 1860 Trogstad (Østfold)

Olberg is a newly developed, delightful small farm site, close to lake Øyeren and within 70 km. of Oslo. There are 35 large, level pitches and electricity connections (16A) are available for 28 units located on neatly tended grassy meadow with newly planted trees and shrubs. The reception building also houses a small gallery with paintings, glasswork and other crafts. In high season fresh bread is available (except Sunday) and coffee, drinks, ices and snacks are provided. A short drive takes you to the beach on Lake Øyeren, and there are many woodland walks. The old church and museum at Trøgstad, and Båstad church are worth visiting. Please bear in mind that this is a working farm. Forest and elk 'safaris' are arranged.

Facilities: Excellent, heated sanitary facilities in a purpose built unit created in the end of a magnificent large, modern barn are fully equipped and include a ramp for wheelchair access and one bathroom for families or disabled visitors. Dishwashing under cover with hot and cold water. Washing machine and ironing board. Small kitchenette with full size cooker and food preparation area. Kiosk. Snacks available. Craft gallery. Children's playground. **Off site:** Tennis nearby. Riding 2 km. Fishing 3 km. Golf 20 km.

Charges 2002
Per unit incl. 2 adults	Nkr. 120 - 125
tent incl. 2 persons	Nkr. 80 - 120
electricity	Nkr. 25

Tel: 69 82 86 10. Fax: 69 82 85 55. E-mail: froesol@frisurf.no. **Reservations:** Write to site. **Open** 1 April - 1 October, other times by arrangement.

Directions: Site is signed on Rv 22, 20 km. north of Mysen on southern edge of Båstad village.

Sandviken Camping
2590 3650 Tinn Austbygd (Telemark)

Sandviken is a remote, lakeside site, in scenic location, suitable for exploring Hardangervidda. With its own shingle beach, at the head of Tinnsjo Lake, it provides 150 grassy, mostly level, pitches. In addition to 50 seasonal units and 12 cabins, there are 100 numbered tourist pitches with electricity (5A), plus an area for tents, under trees along the waterfront. The office/reception kiosk also sells sweets, soft drinks, ices etc. and a baker calls daily in July. A 1 km. stroll takes you to the tiny village of Tinn Austbygde which has a mini-market, bakery, café, bank, garage and post office.

Facilities: Tidy heated sanitary facilities includes some washbasins in cubicles, showers on payment, sauna, solarium and a dual-purpose disabled/family bathroom. Kitchen and laundry rooms (hot water on payment). Motorcaravan services. Kiosk (1/6-15/9). Playground. TV and games room. Minigolf. Fishing and watersports. Boat hire.

Charges 2002
Per person	Nkr. 15
child (4-18 yrs)	Nkr. 10
caravan or motorcaravan	Nkr. 80 - 95
tent	Nkr. 70 - 85
electricity	Nkr. 25

No credit cards. **Tel:** 35 09 81 73. E-mail: kontact@sandviken-camping.no. **Reservations:** Write to site. **Open** all year.

Directions: Easiest access is via the Rv 37 from Gransherad along the western side of the lake.

Rysstad Feriesenter

2600 Midt i Setesdal, 4748 Rysstad (Aust-Agder)

Setesdal, on the upper reaches of the Otra river, offers a wide range of scenery, often spectacular. It is an area famous for its colourful mining history (silver) and for its vibrant art and folklore. A spectacular mountain road links Setesdal with Sirdal to the west, bringing Setesdal within easy and pleasant driving range of Stavanger. At the junction of this road and Setesdal is the small village of Rysstad, named after the family who developed camping in this area. The site occupies a wide tract of woodland between the road and the river towards which it shelves gently, affording a splendid view of the valley and the towering mountains. The site is divided into two sections; one divided by trees and hedges into numbered pitches (20 electric hook-ups), the other is an open field.

Facilities: Good modern sanitary facilities under the reception block have showers on payment, wash-basins in cubicles, dishwashing sinks and a cooker. Laundry facilities with washing machine. Children's play area and amusement hut. Sports field. Fishing, swimming and boating (boats for hire). Fitness track. Bicycle hire. TV room. Centre includes café, shop, bank, garage and restaurant. Attractive area on the river's edge for barbecues and entertainment with an arena type setting. **Off site:** Village within walking distance.

Charges 2002

Per person	Nkr. 15
child	Nkr. 10
caravan or tent	Nkr. 120
hiker's tent	Nkr. 60
electricity	Nkr. 25

Tel: 37 93 61 30. Fax: 37 93 63 45. **Reservations:** Write to site. **Open** 1 May - 1 October.

Directions: Site is about 1 km. south of junction between route 9 (from Kristiansand) and the extended route 45 (from Stravanger).

Neset Camping

2610 4741 Byglandsfjord (Aust-Agder)

On a semi-promontory on the shores of the 40 km. long Byglandsfjord, Neset is a good centre for activities or as a stop en route north from the ferry port of Kristiansand (from England or Denmark). Byglandsfjord offers good fishing (mainly trout) and the area has marked trails for cycling, riding or walking in an area famous for its minerals. Neset is situated on well kept grassy meadows by the lake shore with the water on three sides and the road on the fourth and provides 200 unmarked pitches with electricity and cable TV available. The main building houses reception, a small shop and a restaurant with fine views over the water. This is a well run, friendly site where one could spend an active few days.

Facilities: Three modern sanitary blocks which can be heated, two with comfortable hot showers on payment, washing up facilities (metered hot water) and a kitchen. Restaurant and takeaway (1/7-15/8). Shop. Campers' kitchen. Children's playground. Lake swimming, boating and fishing. Barbecue area. Bicycle, canoe and pedalo hire. Climbing, rafting and canoeing courses arranged (including trips to see beavers and elk). Cross-country ski-ing possible in the area in winter.

Charges 2002

Per unit	Nkr. 135
adult	Nkr. 10
child (5-12 yrs)	Nkr. 5
electricity	Nkr. 30

Tel: 37 93 42 55. Fax: 37 93 43 93. **Reservations:** Write to site. **Open** all year.

Directions: Site is on route 9, 2.5 km. north of the town of Byglandsfjord on the eastern shores of the lake.

Holt Camping

2612 4900 Tvedestrand (Aust-Agder)

Tvedestrand is an attractive small resort with a pretty harbour, which is very popular with the Norwegians for their own holidays. Holt Camping is quite pleasantly situated beside the main E18 road, some 3 km. from the town - there is a little noise from the road during the day but we were not disturbed when staying overnight. The site is part level, part sloping grassland and about half of the pitches have 16A electrical connections with a number of cabins. This site could be very useful en-route to Oslo from the ferry at Kristiansand or for a break in this part of Norway.

Facilities: The single small sanitary block has excellent, well maintained facilities including hot showers on payment (1 per sex), washbasins (H&C) and provision for dishwashing and laundry (washing machine and dryer). Serving both the touring pitches and the cabins, the facilities may well be under pressure during busy times. Shop/café immediately outside site entrance. Children's play area.

Charges 2002

Per unit incl. 2 persons and electricity	Nkr. 100
without electricity	Nkr. 80

Tel: 37 16 02 65. **Reservations:** Contact site. **Open** 1 June - 31 August.

Directions: Site is beside the main E18 coast road (which actually bypasses the town), about 1 km. south of the turn off to the town itself.

Portugal

ICEP Portuguese Trade & Tourism Office, 22/25a Sackville Street, London W1X 2LY

Tel: 020 7494 1441   Fax: 020 7494 1868   E-mail: iceplondt@aol.com

Portugal occupies the southwest corner of the Iberian peninsula and is a relatively small country, bordered by Spain in the north and east and the Atlantic coast in the south and west. However, for a small country it has tremendous variety both in its way of life and traditions. The Portuguese consider the Minho area in northern Portugal to be the most beautiful part of their country with its wooded mountain slopes and wild coastline, a rural and conservative region with picturesque towns. Central Portugal (the Estremadura region) with its monuments, evidence of its role in the country's history, has fertile rolling hills and adjoins the bull-breeding lands of Ribatejo (banks of the Tagus). The huge, sparsely populated plains southeast of Lisbon, the cosmopolitan yet traditional capital, are dominated by vast cork planta-tions supplying nearly half the world's cork, but it is an impoverished area, and visitors usually head for Evora. The Algarve compensates for the dull plains south of Evora and has attracted more tourist development than the rest of the country. Portugal is therefore a land of contrasts - the sophisticated development of the Algarve as against the under-developed rural areas where time has stood still. For British visitors, with large distances to travel, longer stays out of season are particularly attractive.

Population

9,900,000, density 106.6 per sq.km.

Capital

Lisbon (Lisboa)

Climate

The country enjoys a maritime climate with hot summers (sub-tropical in the south) and mild winters with comparatively low rainfall in the south, heavy rain in the north.

Language

Portuguese, but English is widely spoken in cities, towns and larger resorts. French can be useful.

Currency

From January 2002, in common with 11 other European countries, the Portuguese unit of currency was the EURO (€). € 1 = Esc. 200.48.

Banks

Open Mon-Fri 08.30-11.45 and 13.00-14.45. Some large city banks operate a currency exchange 18.30-23.00

Post Offices

Offices (Correios) open Mon-Fri 09.00-18.00, some large ones on Sat. mornings.

Time

From the last Sunday in Sept to the last Sunday in March, the time in Portugal is GMT. In summer it is GMT + 1 hr (as UK).

Telephone

To telephone Portugal from the UK dial 00 351. To the UK from Portugal dial 00 44. You need to be patient to get a line. Phone cards available (500 /1200 esc) from post offices, and tobacconists.

Public Holidays

New Year; Carnival (Shrove Tues); Good Fri; Liberty Day, 25 Apr; Labour Day; Corpus Christi; National Day, 10 June; Saints Days: Lisbon 13 June, Porto 24 June; Assumption, 15 Aug; Republic Day 5 Oct; All Saints, 1 Nov; Immaculate Conception, 8 Dec; Christmas, 24-26 Dec.

Shops

Open Mon-Fri 0900-1300 and 1500-1900. Sat 0900-1300.

Motoring

The standard of roads is very variable - even some of the main roads can be very uneven. The authorities are making great efforts to improve matters, but other than on motorways or major highway routes (IP's) be prepared to make slow progress. Watch Portuguese drivers, as they tend to overtake when they feel like it.

Tolls: Tolls are levied on certain motorways (auto-estradas) out of Lisbon, and upon southbound traffic at the Lisbon end of the giant 25th Abril bridge over the Tagus.

Speed Limits: Car - Built-up areas 31 mph (50 kph), other roads 56 mph (90 kph), Motorways min. 25mph (40 kph) Max. 75mph (120 kph).

For towing vehicles in built-up areas 31 mph (50 kph), other roads 43/50 mph (70/80 kph) and Motorways min. 25 mph (40 kph) max. 62mph (100 kph)

Fuel: Petrol stations are open from 0700-2200/2400 and some 24 hours. Credit cards are accepted but Visa is preferred. Use of a credit card incurs a surcharge.

Parking: Parked vehicles must face the same direction as moving traffic. Some towns have 'Blue Zones', discs available from ACP or the police.

Overnighting

Generally not allowed and fines may be imposed.

Camping Olhao

Pinheiros de Marim, 8700 Olhao (Faro)

823

This site, taking around 1,000 units and open all year, has mature trees to provide reasonable shade. The pitches are marked, numbered and in rows divided by shrubs with electricity and water to all parts. Permanent and long stay units take 20% of the pitches and the tourist pitches fill up quickly June and August, so arrive early. Amenities include very pleasant swimming pools and tennis courts, a reasonable restaurant/bar, all very popular with the local Portuguese, and a café/bar with TV and games room. There is some noise nuisance from an adjacent railway. The large, sandy beaches in this area are on offshore islands reached by ferry and are, as a result, relatively quiet; some are reserved for naturists. This site can get very busy in peak periods and mainte-nance can be variable. There was a large, low season British contingent when we visited enjoying the low prices.

Facilities: Eleven sanitary blocks are adequate, clean when seen, and are specifically sited to be a maximum of 50 m. from any pitch. One block has facilities for disabled visitors. Laundry. Supermarket. Kiosk. Restaurant/bar (open all year). Café and general room with TV. Children's playgrounds. Swimming pools (April - Sep) and tennis courts (fees for both). Volleyball. Bicycle hire. Internet. **Off site:** Bus service 50 m to the nearest ferry at Olhao. Riding 1 km. Fishing 2 km. Golf 20 km.

Charges 2002

Per adult	€ 1.70 - € 3.30
child (5-12 yrs)	€ 0.90 - € 1.75
car	€ 1.40 - € 2.75
tent	€ 1.70 - € 5.50
caravan	€ 3.30 - € 6.60
motorcaravan	€ 2.25 - € 6.60
electricity	€ 1.05

Less for longer winter stays. **Tel:** 289 70 03 00. **Fax:** 289 70 03 90. **E-mail:** sbsicamping@mail.telepac.pt. **Reservations:** Contact site. **Open** all year, as are all facilities.

Directions: Just over 1 km. east of Olhão, on EN125, take turn to Pinheiros de Marim. Site is 300 m. on left. Look for white triangular entry arch as the site name is different on the outside wall - a foible of the owner.

Camping Olhão ★★★ SBSi — Open All Year
Tel: 351 289 700 300
Fax: 351 289 700 390

Orbitur Camping Quarteira

Estrada da Fonte Santa, 8125 Quarteira (Faro)

822

This is a large, busy attractive site on undulating ground with some terracing, taking 795 units. On the outskirts of the popular Algarve resort of Quarteira, it is 600 m. from a sandy beach which stretches for 1 km. to the town centre. Many of the unmarked pitches have shade from tall trees and there are a few small individual pitches of 50 sq.m. with electric-ity and water for reservation. There are 680 electrical connections (15A). Like others along this coast, the site encourages long winter stays. The swimming pools are excellent, featuring pools for adults (with a large flume) and children (fountains), (open in high season incurring an extra charge). There is a large restaurant and supermar-ket which have a separate entrance for local trade.

Facilities: Five sanitary blocks provide British and Turkish style toilets, individual washbasins with cold water, hot showers plus facilities for disabled visitors. Washing machines. Motorcaravan services. Gas supplies. Supermarket, self-service restaurant (Feb - Nov). Separate takeaway (from late May). Swimming pools (June - Sept). General room with bar and TV. Tennis. Kiosk. Open air disco. Medical room. **Off site:** Fishing 1 km. Bicycle hire (summer) 1 km. Golf 4 km.

Charges 2003

Per unit incl. 2 persons, electricity and water	€ 15.60 - € 29.70
extra adult	€ 2.50 - € 4.90
child (5-10 yrs)	€ 1.25 - € 2.45

Off season discounts. **Tel:** 289 30 28 26. **Fax:** 289 30 28 22. **E-mail:** info@orbitur.pt. **Reservations:** Contact Orbitur - Central de Reservas, Rua Diogo do Couto, 1149-042 Lisboa. **Tel:** 21/811 70 00 or 811 70 70. **Fax:** 21/814 80 45. **Open** all year.

Directions: Turn off N125 south towards Quarteira in Almancil (8 km. west of Faro). Site is 5 km. from the junction.

Parque de Campismo Albufeira

EN 125 Ferreiras-Albufeira, 8200-395 Albufeira (Faro)

821

The spacious entrance to this site will accommodate the largest of units (watch for severe speed bumps at the barrier!) One of the better sites on the Algarve, with installations and amenities well above the usual standard. The 1,500 pitches are on fairly flat ground with some terracing, trees and shrubs giving reasonable shade in most parts. There are some marked and numbered pitches of 50-80 sq.m. Winter stays are encouraged with many facilities remaining open including a heated pool. An attractively designed complex of traditional Portuguese style buildings on the hill forms the central area of the site, has pleasant views and is surrounded well watered lawns and a fountain.

Facilities: The toilet blocks include hot showers. Washing machines. Waiter and self-service restaurants, and pizzeria. Bars. Sound proof disco. Swimming pools. Children's playground. ATM. Car hire. **Off site:** Site bus service to Albufeira (2 km).

Charges 2002

Per adult	€ 4.76
child (410 yrs)	€ 2.32
caravan acc. to size	€ 4.67 - € 5.77
motorcaravan acc. to size	€ 4.67 - € 10.40
tent acc. to size	€ 4.37 - € 4.92
car	€ 4.17
motorcycle	€ 2.77 - € 10.40
electricity (10A)	€ 2.35

Tel: 289 58 76 29. Fax: 289 58 76 33. E-mail: campingalbufeira@mail.telepac.pt. **Reservations:** are made to give individual pitch, no deposit or fee. **Open** all year.

Directions: From N125 coast road or N264 (from Lisbon) at new junctions follow signs to Albufeira. Site is approx. 1 km. from junctions, on left.

Parque de Campismo de Armacao de Pera

8365 Armacao de Pera (Faro)

841

A modern site with a wide attractive entrance and a large external parking area, the 1,200 pitch areas are in zones on level grassy sand. They are marked by trees that provide some shade, and are easily accessed from tarmac and gravel roads. Electricity (10A) is available for most pitches. The facilities are good. The restaurant, self service café and bar, and well stocked supermarket should cater for most needs. The disco near to the entrance and café complex is soundproofed which should ensure a peaceful night for non-revellers. The site is within easy reach of Albufeira and is 40 km. from Faro and makes an excellent base for stays in this region and for winter sun-seekers.

Facilities: Three modern sanitary blocks provide British and Turkish style WCs, some with bidets, washbasins, showers with hot water on payment, and facilities for disabled campers. Laundry. Supermarket. Restaurant (1/5 - 30/9). Self service café. Three bars (1/5-30/9). Kiosk. Games and TV rooms. Tennis. Well maintained play area. Swimming pool and children's pool (May - Sept). ATM.

Charges 2002

Per adult	€ 4.10 - € 4.90
child (4-10 yrs)	€ 1.30 - € 2.70
pitch and car	€ 3.20 - € 5.00
electricity (6A)	€ 2.00 - € 3.50

Min. stay 3 nights 1 June - 31 Aug. **Tel:** 282 31 22 96. Fax: 282 31 53 79. **Reservations:** Write to site. **Open** all year.

Directions: Site is west of Albufeira. Turn off N125/ IC4 road in Alcantarilha, taking the EN269-1 towards the coast. Site is on left side before Armação de Pêra. There are other sites with similar names in the area, so be sure to find the right one.

Orbitur Camping Sagres

Cerro das Moitas, 8650 Sagres (Faro)

843

Camping de Sagres is a pleasant site at the western tip of the Algarve, not very far from the lighthouse in the relatively unspoilt southwest corner of Portugal. With 960 pitches for tents and 120 for tourers, the pitches are sandy and located amongst pine trees that give good shade. There are some hardstandings for motorhomes and electrical connections (5A) throughout. This is a reasonable site for those seeking winter sun, or as a base for exploring this 'Land's End' region of Portugal, as it is away from the hustle and bustle of the more crowded resorts. The beaches and the town of Sagres (the departure point of the Portuguese navigators) with its fort, are a short drive.

Facilities: Three spacious toilet blocks are showing some signs of wear but provide hot and cold showers, washbasins with cold water and footbaths. Dishwashing and laundry sinks (cold water) are under cover outside. Washing machines and ironing boards. Motorcaravan services. Supermarket (1/4-1/11). Restaurant/bar and café/grill (all 1/4-30/9). TV room. Bicycle hire. Barbecue area. Playground. Fishing. Medical post. Car wash.

Charges 2003

Per person	€ 2.40 - € 4.30
child (5-10 yrs)	€ 1.20 - € 2.15
pitch and car	€ 4.10 - € 6.30
electricity	€ 2.25

Off season discounts (up to 70%). **Tel:** 282 62 43 71. Fax: 282 62 44 45. **Reservations:** Write to site. **Open** all year.

Directions: Turn off road N268 East to EN268, after approx. 2 km. after turn to Sagres, site (as a camping site only - no name) is signed off to right.

Orbitur Camping Valverde

Estrada da Praia da Luz, Valverde, 8600 Lagos (Faro)

A little over 1 km. from the village of Praia da Luz and its beach and about 7 km. from Lagos, this large, well run site is certainly worth considering for your stay in the Algarve. It has 600 numbered pitches, of varying size which are enclosed by hedges. All are on flat ground or broad terraces with good shade in most parts from established trees and shrubs. On site is a swimming pool with long curling slide and children's pool (under 10's free, adults charged). This is an excellent site with well maintained facilities and good security. It attracts a good number of long-term winter visitors. The site, which is one of the better Orbitur sites, is extremely well managed by Sra. Pinto, who is helpful and friendly.

Facilities: Six large, clean, toilet blocks have some washbasins and sinks with cold water only, and hot showers. Units for disabled people. Laundry. Motorcaravan services. Supermarket, shops, restaurant and bar complex (all April - Oct). Takeaway. Swimming pool (Jun - Sep). Play-ground. Tennis court with markings for other sports. General room with TV. Excursions. Medical post. Disco. Pub. **Off site:** Fishing and bicycle hire 3 km. Golf 10 km. The road to the beach is quite narrow with fast traffic.

Charges 2003

Per unit incl. 2 persons, electricity, water	€ 15.60 - € 29.70
extra adult	€ 2.50 - € 4.90
child (5-10 yrs)	€ 1.25 - € 2.45

Off season discounts. **Tel:** 282 78 92 11. Fax: 282 78 92 13. E-mail: info@orbitur.pt. **Reservations:** Contact Orbitur - Central de Reservas, Rua Diogo do Couto, 1149-042 Lisboa. Tel: 21/811 70 00 or 811 70 70. Fax: 21/814 80 45. **Open** all year.

Directions: Fork left on N125 road 3 km. west of Lagos to Praia da Luz and site is under 1 km.

Parque de Campismo Quintos dos Carriços

Praia da Salema, Vila do Bispo, 8650-196 Budens (Faro)

This is an attractive and peaceful, valley site with a dedicated naturist area. A traditional tiled Portugese style entrance leads you down a steep incline into this excellent and well maintained site which has a village atmosphere. The site has been developed over the years by the Dutch owner. It is spread over two valleys), with the 300 partially terraced pitches marked and divided by trees and shrubs. A small stream (dry when seen) meanders through the site. Although the site is lit, torches may be required in more remote areas. The many fine beaches in the region provide ample opportunities for diving, swimming and fishing.

Facilities: Four modern, spacious sanitary blocks, well tiled with quality fittings, include washbasins with cold water and hot showers on payment. Excellent facility for disabled people. Gas supplies. Well stocked mini-market (all year). Bar (daily in season, once a week only 15/10-1/3). TV room. Bicycles, scooters, mopeds and m/cycles for hire. Internet. Library. Games room. **Off site:** Fishing and golf 1 km. Riding 8 km. Bus service operates from the site. Beach 1 km.

Charges 2002

Per adult	€ 3.80
child	€ 1.90
pitch and car	€ 5.40 - € 9.20
electricity	€ 1.50

Discounts for long winter stays. **Tel:** 282 69 52 01. Fax: 282 69 51 22. E-mail: quintacarrico@oninet.pt. **Reservations:** Contact site. **Open** all year.

Directions: Turn off RN125 (Lagos-Sagres) road at turn to Salema (17 km. from Lagos); site is signed.

Camping Sitava

Sitava Turismo, Brejo de Zimbreira, 7645 Vila Nova de Milfontes (Beja)

With a huge entrance off the road, then a 500 m. drive through a pine forest to the camping area, this is a very large site (50 hectares) complete with beach access. It has good sized, level pitches, although the numerous tall pines concentrate the mind when manoeuvring - on the other hand they provide shade. A large building houses reception, a bar with terrace and a restaurant with a second restaurant by the inner gate. An attractive feature is a fountain in a circle of lawn, that in turn is in the centre of a covered walkway supporting blooms of vivid colours, ideal for sitting and relaxing. The beaches are excellent, gently shelving, with rocks and cliffs surrounding a fine sandy bay.

Facilities: Two large, identical toilet blocks are cheerful in appearance but beginning to show signs of wear. Free hot showers. Restaurant/bar with snacks (all year). Large restaurant (summer only). Shop. Large children's play area. Table tennis. TV room with games area - darts, pool and electronic games. Five-a-side soccer pitches. Tennis courts. Barbecue area. Dogs are not accepted. Torches needed for some pitches. **Off site:** Buses to village.

Charges 2002

Per adult	€ 3.16
child	€ 1.60
pitch and car	€ 4.83 - € 5.40
electricity	€ 1.82

Plus 7% VAT. Reductions in low season. **Tel:** 283 89 93 43. Fax: 283 89 95 71. **Reservations:** Contact site. **Open** all year.

Directions: From E201-1 Cercal - Sines road (road changes from the E120 at Tanganheira), turn left (southwest) to Porto Covo and follow signs (south) to Vila Nova de Milfontes. Site is well signed.

Parque de Campismo de Milfontes

818 7645 Vila Nova de Milfontes (Beja)

This popular site with good facilities has the advantage of being open all year and being within walking distance of the town and beach. As such, it makes a perfect base for those visiting out of main season or for long winter stays when fees are heavily discounted. Well lit and fenced, it has around 500 shady pitches for touring units on sandy terrain, marked out and divided by hedges and nicely paved paths. Some pitches may be too small for caravan and car and cars may have to be parked in an internal car park. Electricity (6A) is available in all parts. There are opportunities for watersports fishing, canoeing and swimming from the resort beaches.

Facilities: The four toilet blocks are clean and well maintained. Two have complete suites for disabled visitors with ramped entrances. Mainly British style WCs, bidets, washbasins (some with hot water), hot and cold showers, footbaths and some children's facilities, in a mix of combinations and styles. Motorcaravan services. Supermarket (1/4-30/9). Bar and snacks (1/4-30/9). Restaurant (1/6-30/9). TV room. Playground. Gas supplies. **Off site:** Fishing and bicycle hire 1 km. Golf 20 km. Riding 15 km.

Charges 2002

Per person	€ 2.00 - € 3.30
child (5-10 yrs)	€ 1.00 - € 1.65
pitch and car	€ 3.25 - € 6.40
electricity	€ 1.75

Tel: 283 99 61 40. Fax: 283 99 61 04. **Reservations:** Contact site. **Open** all year.

Directions: From N120 coast road at Cercal, turn on E390 and continue into Vila Nova de Milfontes. Turn right in town and follow camp signs. Site is on right at end of no through road. Don't confuse it with another site on left just before Milfontes.

Parque de Campismo Porto Covo

816 7520-436 Porto Covo (Setubal)

This is a site in a popular, small seaside resort where a fairly large proportion of the pitches are occupied by Portuguese units. However, it has a reasonable sense of space as you pass the security barrier to reception which is part of an uncluttered and attractively designed 'village square' area. The pitches are small but are hedged, reasonably level, all have electricity (5/10A), and are shaded. A jolly bar and restaurant with terrace cleverly operates across the boundary of the site and it offers a varied Portuguese menu at very reasonable prices. A second smaller restaurant operates in low season. The beaches are a short walk and feature steep cliffs and pleasant sandy shores.

Facilities: The toilet blocks are clean with the usual amenities including hot showers, plus cold outside showers. Motorcaravan services. Restaurant/bar. Mini-market in season. Recreation room. Play area. Swimming pools. Tennis. Barbecue areas. Boat trips and fishing trips organised. **Off site:** The village is a short walk from a range of shops, bars and restaurants in pretty new roads. Fishing 500 m.

Charges 2002

Per adult	€ 2.60
child	€ 1.30
pitch and car	€ 3.00 - € 6.75
electricty	€ 1.75

All plus 7% VAT. Reductions in low season. **Tel:** 269 90 51 36. Fax: 269 90 52 39. **Reservations:** Write to site. **Open** all year.

Directions: From E120-1 Cercal - Sines road (note: the road changes from the E120 at Tanganheira). Take left turn (southwest) to Porto Covo. The signs are misleading hereon so look for a large white water tower with site logo.

Parque de Campismo Colina do Sol

845 2465 Sao Martinho do Porto (Leiria)

Colina do Sol is a well appointed site with its own pool and near to the beach. Only 1 km. from the small town of S. Martinho do Porto, it has around 350 pitches marked by fruit and ornamental trees on grassy terraces. Electricity (6/10A) is available to all, although some may need long leads. The attractive entrance with its beds of bright flowers, is wide enough for even the largest of outfits, and the surfaced roads are very pleasant for manoeuvring. There is a warm welcome and good English is spoken. A restaurant, cafeteria, and a bar with a delightful paved terrace are beside the large clean swimming pools. The beach is at the rear of the site, with access via a gate which is locked at night.

Facilities: Two large, clean and modern toilet blocks provide British style WCs (some with bidets), washbasins - some with hot water. Dishwashing and laundry sinks are outside but covered. Ironing facilities. Motorcaravan services. Supermarket, restaurant/café with bar. **Off site:** Shop, restaurant and bar within 200 m.

Charges 2002

Per adult	€ 2.87
child (4-10 yrs)	€ 1.37
pitch and car	€ 4.39 - € 6.04
electricity	€ 1.60

Less 25-50% in low seasons. **Tel:** 262 98 97 64. Fax: 262 98 97 63. **Reservations:** Contact site. **Open** all year except 15 Dec. -15 Jan.

Directions: Turn from EN 242 (Caldas-Nazaré) road northeast of San Martinho do Porto. Site is clearly signed.

Parque de Campismo São Miguel

São Miguel, Odeceixe, 7630-592 Odemira (Beja)

817

Nestled in green hills near two pretty white villages, four kilometres from the beautiful Praia Odeceixe (beach) is the attractive camping park Sao Miguel. The main building (with its traditional Portugese architecture) is built around two sides of a large grassy square, it houses reception, restaurant, bars and supermarket. There are 'Lisbon Arcade' style verandas to sit under and enjoy a drink, coffee or meal while enjoying the view across the square to the pool tennis courts and camping which is hidden under a canopy of trees. Unusually the site works on a maximum number of 700 campers, you find your own place (there are no defined pitches) under the tall trees, there are ample electrical points, the land slopes away gently. The wooden chalet style accomodation is in a separate area, but some mobile homes share the two traditional older style but clean sanitary blocks. An outdoor cinema operates in summer showing films for children and adults. The self serve restaurant and bars are excellent, there is a pizzeria by the pool with its own terrace (summer only) and for those who want to self cater the supermarket has a bakery, as well as wide range of goods including cooked chicken, fresh fruit and vegetables.

Facilities: Two older style sanitary buildings with British style WCs and free hot showers. Washing machines, dishwashing and laundry sinks are at the end of the block under cover. Toilets and basins for disabled campers but no shower. Shop (June -Sept). Restaurant/bar (March - Oct). Bar, snacks and pizzeria (June - Sept). Playground. Tennis courts (extra charge). Swimming pool (extra charge). No animals are accepted. Torches useful. **Off site:** Village has a range of shops bars and restaurants. Fishing/sailing 4 km. Riding 20 km. Historic village of Odemira 2 km. Campsite is situated inside the Nature Park of Alentejo.

Charges 2002

Per adult	€ 2.60 - € 4.00
child (5-10 yrs)	€ 1.40 - € 2.25
tent	€ 2.60 - € 6.00
caravan	€ 4.00 - € 5.50
car	€ 2.60 - € 3.50
motorcaravan	€ 5.00 - € 8.00
electricity	€ 2.10

Plus 7% VAT. **Tel:** 282 947145. Fax: 282 947285. E-mail: camping.sao.miguel@mail.telepac.pt. **Reservations:** Write to site. **Open** Easter - September.

Directions: Between Odemira and Lagos on the N120 just before the village of Odeceixe on the main road well signed.

Camping Markádia

Barragem de Odivelas, Apartado 17, 7920-999 Alvito (Beja)

835

A tranquil, lakeside site in an unspoilt setting, this will appeal most to those nature lovers who want to 'get away from it all' and to those who enjoy country pursuits such as walking, fishing or riding. The lake is in fact a 1,000 hectare reservoir, and more than 120 species of birds can be found in the area. The open countryside and lake provide excellent views and a very pleasant environment, albeit somewhat remote. The stellar views in the very low ambient lighting are wonderful at night. The site is lit but a torch is required. There are 130 casual unmarked pitches on undulating grass and sand with ample electricity connections (16A). The friendly Dutch owner has carefully planned the site so each pitch has its own oak tree to provide shade. The bar/restaurant with a terrace is open daily in season but weekends only during the winter. One can swim in the reservoir and rowing boats, pedaloes windsurfers are available for hire. You may bring your own boat, although power boats are not allowed on environmental grounds.

Facilities: Four modern, clean and well equipped toilet blocks are built in traditional Portuguese style with hot water throughout. Dishwashing and laundry sinks are open air. Washing machines and ironing boards. Laundry. Motorcaravan services. Bar and restaurant (1/4-30/9). Shop (all year). Lounge. Children's playground. Fishing. Boat hire. Tennis. Riding. Medical post. Car wash. Dogs are not accepted in July/August. Facilities and amenities may be reduced outside the main season.

Charges 2002

Per adult	€ 4.20
child (5-10 yrs)	€ 2.00
tent or caravan	€ 4.20
car or motorcycle	€ 4.20
motorcaravan	€ 8.40
electricity	€ 2.10

Discounts of 10-20% outside June - Aug, and for longer stays. No credit cards. **Tel:** 284 76 31 41. Fax: 284 76 31 02. **Reservations:** Contact site for details. **Open** all year.

Directions: From A2 between Setabul and the Algarve take N259 to Ferrira de Alentgo. Then take the N2 road to Torrao. 13 km. later at Odivepus, turn right towards Barragem and site is 3 km. along poor road after crossing head of reservoir (follow small signs).

Orbitur Camping Costa da Caparica

Ava. Alfonso de Albuquerque, Quinta de Ste Antonio, 2825 Costa da Caparica (Setubal)

815

This is very much a site for 600 permanent caravans but it has relatively easy access to Lisbon (just under 20 km.) via the motorway, by bus or even by bus and ferry if you wish. It is situated near a small resort, favoured by the Portuguese themselves, which has all the usual amenities plus a good sandy beach (200 m. from the site) and promenade walks. There is a small area for touring units which includes some larger pitches for motorcaravans. We see this very much as a site to visit Lisbon rather than for prolonged stays. Some activities and shows are organised in season in an outdoor disco and entertainment area.

Facilities: The three toilet blocks have mostly British style toilets, washbasins with cold water and some hot showers - they come under pressure when the site is full. Facilities for disabled visitors. Washing machine. Motorcaravan services. Supermarket. Large bar/restaurant (Feb-Nov). Playground. Doctor calls daily in season. Gas supplies. **Off site:** Fishing 1 km. Riding 4 km. Golf 5 km.

Charges 2003

Per unit incl. 2 persons	€ 15.20 - € 28.30
extra adult	€ 2.40 - € 4.40
child (5-10 yrs)	€ 1.20 - € 2.20

Off season discounts. **Tel:** 212 90 13 66. Fax: 212 90 06 61. E-mail: info@orbitur.pt. **Reservations:** Contact Orbitur - Central de Reservas, Rua Diogo do Couto, 1149-042 Lisboa. Tel: 21/811 70 00 or 811 70 70. Fax: 21/814 80 45. **Open** all year.

Directions: Cross the Tagus bridge (toll) on A2 motorway going south from Lisbon, immediately take the turning for Caparica and Trafaria. At 7 km. marker on IC20 turn right (no sign) - the site is at the second roundabout.

Orbitur Camping Guincho

E.N.247, Lugar da Areia - Guincho, 2750-053 Cascais (Lisbon)

813

Although this is a popular site for permanent Portugese occupants with 1,295 pitches, it is nevertheless quite attractively laid out among low pine trees and with the A5 autostrada connection to Lisbon (30 km), it provides a useful alternative to sites nearer the city. Located behind sand dunes and a wide, sandy but somewhat windswept beach, the site offers a wide range of facilities. These include a fairly plain bar/restaurant and a supermarket (all year). There is a choice of pitches (small - mainly about 50 sq.m.) mostly with electricity (15A), although siting amongst the trees may be tricky. This is viewed as an alternative for visiting Lisbon, not a holiday site.

Facilities: The three sanitary blocks, one refurbished, are in the older style but are clean and tidy. Washbasins with cold water but hot showers. Dishwashing sinks have cold water. Three washing machines, two dryers. Facilities for disabled visitors. Motorcaravan services. Supermarket. Restaurant, bar and terrace (all year). General room with TV. Tennis. Playground. Entertainment in summer.

Charges 2003

Per unit icl. 2 persons	€ 15.20 - € 28.30
extra adult	€ 2.40 - € 4.40
child (5-10 yrs)	€ 1.20 - € 2.20

Off season discounts. **Tel:** 214 87 04 50. Fax: 214 87 21 67. E-mail: info@orbitur.pt. **Reservations:** Contact Orbitur - Central de Reservas, Rua Diogo do Couto, 1149-042 Lisboa. Tel: 21/811 70 00 or 811 70 70. Fax: 21/814 80 45. **Open** all year.

Directions: Approach from either direction on the N247. Turn inland 6.5 km. west of Cascais at camp sign. Site is well signed from the A5 autopista.

Lisboa Camping-Parque Municipal de Monsanto

Estrada da Circunvalacao, 1400-061 Lisboa (Lisbon)

814

This is very large (38 ha.) site providing a quality service at a good price. The wide entrance with its ponds, fountains and the trees, lawns and flowering shrubs leading up to the pool, is a most attractive feature. On sloping ground, the site`s many terraces are well shaded by trees and shrubs. The 400 extremely good pitches include 170 on concrete hardstandings, each with its own services electricity (6/16A). There is a huge separate area for tents, and 70 chalet style bungalows are for hire. You are 8 km. from central Lisbon with two bus routes giving a regular service from the gate, and 10 km. from a decent beach. Although a city site it is big enough to generate a park atmosphere. This is a pleasant site for visiting Lisbon.

Facilities: Eight solar-powered toilet blocks contain quality facilities, including those for disabled people. Launderette. Motorcaravan service point and car wash. Shops, bar and restaurants (all year). Two superb swimming pools (with lifeguard; May - Sept). Tennis. Minigolf. Sports field. Playgrounds. Roman theatre. Entertainment in high season. General and TV rooms. Organised excursions. Travel agent on site. **Off site:** Lisbon city. Beaches 10 km. Golf 5 km. Riding 16 km. Bicycle hire 2 km.

Charges 2002

Per pitch incl. electricity	€ 15.00 - € 20.00
adult	€ 3.50 - € 4.70
child (6-12 yrs)	€ 1.75 - € 2.30

Electricity included. **Tel:** 217 623 100. Fax: 217 623 105. **Reservations:** Not made. **Open** all year.

Directions: From Lisbon take A5 towards Estoril and the site is signed from junction 4 onto the 1C17. The site has huge signs off this road at the first exit to Buraca. Site is immediately on the right Enter to the right of the fountain on the tiled road.

Orbitur Camping Foz do Arelho

848

Foz do Arelho, 2500 Caldas da Rainha (Leiria)

This is a large and roomy ex-municipal site, new to the Orbitur chain and improvements are still taking place. It is 2 km. from the beach and has a new central complex with a most impressive pool. The large two storey, brick-faced building contains all the site's leisure facilities but has no ramped access and there are no sanitary facilities for disabled campers. The building is somewhat sterile and the furniture is bland but there are pleasant views over the pool from the restaurant and terrace. Pitches are generally sandy with some hardstandings, vary in size and are unmarked on two main levels with wide tarmac roads. There is a little shade and some permanent units occupied in high season and weekends at other times. All touring pitches have electricity (5/15A).

Facilities: Four identical modern sanitary buildings (solar heating) with seatless British and Turkish style WCs and free showers. Washing machine in one, dishwashing and laundry sinks have cold water only. No facilities for disabled campers. No chemical disposal point. Supermarket. Children's club. Games room. Table tennis. Small new amphitheatre. Bar/snacks and restaurant. (April - Sept). Playground - supervision needed . Bus service. Doctor's room. Torches useful. **Off site:** Seaside town 2 km. Fishing 2 km. Watersports 3 km. Riding 15 km. Bus 500 m.

Charges 2003

Per adult	€ 2.10 - € 3.70
child	€ 1.05 - € 1.85
pitch and car	€ 3.90 - € 9.20
electricity	€ 2.25

Tel: 262 978683. Fax: 262 978685. **Reservations:** Contact Orbitur - Central de Reservas, Rua Diogo do Couto, 1149-042 Lisboa. Tel: 21/811 70 00 or 811 70 70. Fax: 21/814 80 45. **Open** all year.

Directions: Site is north of Lisbon west of Caldos. From A8 take N360 to Foz de Arelho. Site is well signed.

Camping-Caravaning Vale Paraiso

846

Estrada Nacional 242, 2450-138 Nazaré (Leiria)

A pleasant, well managed site, Vale Paraiso is by the main N242 road in 8 ha. of undulating pine woods. It provides over 600 shady pitches, many on sandy ground only suitable for tents. For other units there are around 250 individual pitches of varying size on harder ground with electricity (4-10A). A range of sporting and leisure activities includes a good outdoor pool with sunbathing areas a play area for children plus a small adventure playground. There is a bar, takeaway and a recently (2002) refurbished, slightly bland restaurant/bar. Several long beaches of white sand are within 2-15 km. allowing windsurfing, sailing, surfing or body-boarding. Nazaré is an old fishing village with narrow streets, a harbour and marina and many outdoor bars and cafés, with a lift to Sitio. There is much of historical interest in the area. The owners are keen to welcome British visitors and English is spoken.

Facilities: Toilet facilities are good, with hot water for washbasins, showers, laundry and dishwashing sinks. Nearly all WCs are British style. Facilities for disabled people. Baby baths to borrow. Washing machine and dryers. Motorcaravan services. Shop. Self-service and a la carte Electronic games. Restaurant (March - Sept). Café/bar with TV (all year). Takeaway. Tabac. Supermarket (March - Sept). Swimming pool (March - Sept; free for children under 11 yrs). Petanque. Volleyball. Basketball. Football. Badminton. Leisure games. Amusement hall. Bicycle hire. Safety deposit. Gas supplies. Tourist information. E-mail and fax facilities. Bus service from gate. **Off site:** Fishing 1.5 km. Riding 5 km. Golf 35 km. Boat launching 2.5 km.

Charges 2003

Per person	€ 2.90 - € 3.80
child (3-10 yrs)	€ 1.40 - € 1.80
caravan and car	€ 6.00 - € 7.20
tent	€ 2.50 - € 4.70
motorcaravan	€ 4.20 - € 4.90
electricity (4-10A)	€ 2.40

Tel: 262 56 18 00. Fax: 262 56 19 00. E-mail: camping.vp.nz@mail.telepac.pt. **Reservations:** Contact site. **Open** all year.

Directions: Site is 2 km. north of Nazaré, on the EN242 Marinha Grande road.

Animation and Nature
Reservations on-line: www.valeparaiso.com

Estrada Nacional 242
2450-138 Nazaré-PORTUGAL
Tel. 351 262 561 800
Fax. 351 262 561 900
info@valeparaiso.com

vale paraíso ***
camping

Orbitur Camping Valado
E.N.8 - 5 Alcobaca - Valado, 2450 Nazaré (Leiria)

811

This popular site is close to the old, traditional fishing port of Nazaré which has now become something of a holiday resort and popular with coach parties. The large sandy beach in the town (about 2 km. steeply downhill from the site) is sheltered by headlands and provides good swimming. The site is on undulating ground under tall pine trees, has 503 pitches and, although some smallish individual pitches with electricity and water can be reserved, the bulk of the site is not marked out and units could be close together especially during July/Aug. About 375 electrical connections are available. The functional restaurant, bar and supermarket are contained in one white-walled block.

Facilities: The three toilet blocks have British and Turkish style WCs, washbasins (some cold water), and 17 hot showers, all very clean when inspected. Dishwashing and laundry sinks under cover. Laundry. Motorcaravan services. Supermarket. Bar, snack bar and restaurant with terrace (Feb - Nov). TV/general room. Playground. Tennis. Medical post. Car wash. Gas supplies. **Off site:** Fishing and bicycle hire 2 km. Bus service 20 m.

Charges 2003

Per unit incl. 2 persons	€ 12.30 - € 22.20
extra adult	€ 1.90 - € 3.40
child (5-10 yrs)	€ 0.95 - € 1.70

Off season discounts (up to 70%). **Tel:** 262 56 11 11. Fax: 262 56 11 37. E-mail: info@orbitur.pt.
Reservations: Contact Orbitur - Central de Reservas, Rua Diogo do Couto, 1149 042 Lisboa. Tel: 21/811 70 00 or 811 70 70. Fax: 21/814 80 45. **Open** 1 February - 30 November.

Directions: Site is on the Nazaré - Alcobaca N8-5 road, 2 km. east of Nazaré.

Orbitur Camping Sao Pedro de Moel
Rua Volta do Sete, 2430 Sao Pedro de Moel (Leiria)

810

This quiet and very attractive site is situated under tall pines, on the edge of the rather select small resort of São Pedro de Moel. The attractive, sandy beach is about 500 m. walk downhill from the site (you can take the car, although parking may be difficult in the town) and is sheltered from the wind by low cliffs. The shady site can be crowded in July/Aug, and the 525 pitches are in blocks and unmarked (cars may be parked separately). There are 404 electrical connections (15A). Although there are areas of soft sand, there should be no problem in finding a firm place. The large restaurant and bar are modern as is the superb swimming pool.

Facilities: Four clean toilet blocks have mainly British style toilets (some with bidets), some washbasins with hot water. Hot showers are mostly in one block. Laundry. Motorcaravan services. Supermarket. Large restaurant and bar (Apr - Sept). Swimming pools (June - Sept). TV/games room. Playground. Tennis. Medical post. Car wash. Gas supplies. **Off site:** Bus service 100 m. Fishing 1 km. Beach 500 m.

Charges 2003

Per unit incl. 2 persons	€ 13.70 - € 24.90
extra adult	€ 2.10 - € 4.00
child (5-10 yrs)	€ 1.05 - € 2.00

Off season discounts. **Tel:** 244 59 91 68. Fax: 244 59 91 48. E-mail: info@orbitur.pt. **Reservations:** Contact Orbitur - Central de Reservas, Rua Diogo do Couto, 1149 -042 Lisboa. Tel: 21/811 70 00 or 811 70 70. Fax: 21/814 80 45. **Open** all year.

Directions: Site is 9 km. west of Marinha Grande, on the right as you enter São Pedro de Moel.

Campismo O Tamanco
Casas Brancas II, 3100-231 Louriçal (Leiria)

840

O Tamanco is a peaceful countryside site, with a homely atmosphere - chickens and ducks wander around and there is a Burro here. The young Dutch owners, Irene and Hans, are sure to give you a warm welcome at this delightful little site. The pool is very pleasant as is the small bar and a restaurant. Courses in printing and sculpture are arranged at certain times of the year. The site is very popular with the Dutch and winter campers. The 100 good sized pitches are separated by cordons of fruit trees, ornamental trees and flowering shrubs, on level grassy ground. There is electricity (6/16A) to 72 pitches and 5 pitches for large motorhomes. There may be some road noise on pitches at the front of the site.

Facilities: The single toilet block provides very clean and generously sized facilities including washbasins in cabins, with easy access for disabled visitors. As facilities are limited they may be busy in peak periods. Dishwashing and laundry sinks outside, under cover. Washing machine. Bar/restaurant. Roofed patio with fireplace. TV room/lounge. Swimming pool. **Off site:** Lake 2 km. Beach 11 km.

Charges 2002

Per adult	€ 2.75
child (up to 5 yrs)	€ 1.50
pitch and car	€ 4.20 - € 5.10
electricity (6A)	€ 1.90

Winter discounts up to 40%. No credit cards. **Tel:** 236 95 25 51. Fax: 236 95 25 51. E-mail: campismo.o.tamanco@mail.telepac.pt. **Reservations:** Contact site. **Open** 1 January - 31 October.

Directions: From N109/IC1 (Leira-Figuera de Foz) road, 25 km. south of Figuera in Matos de Carriço, turn on to N342 road (signed Louriçal 6 km). Site is directly off behind high hedges 1.5 km. on left.

Orbitur Camping Figueira da Foz

809

E.N. 109 - km 4 - Gala, 3080 Figueira da Foz (Coimbra)

This site of around 450 pitches is on sandy terrain under a canopy of pine trees and well cared for. Some pitches near the road may be rather noisy. One can drive or walk the 300 m. from the back of the site to a private beach; you should swim with caution when it is windy - the warden will advise. The site fills in July/August and units may be very close together, but there should be plenty of room at other times. Besides the beach, Coimbra and the nearby Roman remains are worth visiting.

Facilities: The three toilet blocks have British and Turkish style toilets, individual basins (some with hot water) and free hot showers. Motorcaravan services. Laundry. Supermarket and restaurant/bar with terrace (all May - Sept). Lounge. Children´s playground. Tennis. TV. Doctor visits in season. Car wash area. Gas supplies. **Off site:** Fishing 1 km. Bicycle hire and riding 3 km. Beach 300 m.

Charges 2003

Per person	€ 2.10 - € 3.70
child (5-10 yrs)	€ 1.05 - € 1.85
pitch and car	€ 3.90 - € 9.20
electricity (5/15A)	€ 2.25

Off season discounts. **Tel:** 233 43 14 92. Fax: 233 43 12 31. E-mail: info@orbitur.pt. **Reservations:** Contact Orbitur - Central de Reservas, Rua Diogo do Couto, 1149-042 Lisboa. **Open** all year.

Directions: Site is 4 km. south of Figueira da Foz beyond the two rivers; turn off N109 1 km. from bridge on southern edge of Gala, look for Orbitur sign on roundabout it is then 600 m. to site.

Camping Municipal Arganil

833

E.N. 17 - km5, Sarzedo, 3300 Arganil (Coimbra)

This quiet, inland site is attractively located in the hamlet of Sarzedo, some 2 km. from the town of Arganil. A spacious and well planned site, it is high quality for a municipal and prices are very reasonable! Delightfully situated among pine trees above the River Alva where one can swim, fish, canoe and windsurf. The 150 pitches, most with electricity (15A), are of a reasonable size, mainly on flat sandy grass terraces shaded by tall trees. The site is kept beautifully clean and neat and access roads are tarmac. An small but excellent restaurant serves local food and has an unusual attached bar with terrace.

Facilities: Sanitary facilities are clean and well maintained, with Turkish and British style WCs, controllable hot showers, washbasins in semi-private partitioned cabins and a hairdressing area with electric sockets. Washing machines. Bar, restaurant and snacks (all year). Shop (July - Sept). TV room. Tennis. Car wash. **Off site:** Fishing 100 m. Watersports 200 m. Bus service 50 m. River beach 100 m.

Charges 2002

Per person	€ 1.80 - € 3.20
child (5-10 yrs)	€ 0.90 - € 1.60
pitch and car	€ 3.00 - € 8.45
electricity (5/15A)	€ 2.25

Plus 7% VAT. **Tel:** 235 20 57 06. Fax: 235 20 54 23. E-mail: info@c.m.arganil.pt. **Reservations:** Contact site. **Open** all year.

Directions: From EN17/N2 Coimbra - Sarzedo at 324.4 km marker exit to Sarzedo site is signed. Ignore first campsite sign to Avelar as there is a better access 500 m. further on the right.

Orbitur Camping Mira

807

Estrada Florestal no. 1 - km 2, 3070 Mira (Coimbra)

A small seaside site set in pinewoods, Orbitur Camping Mira is situated to the south of Aveiro and Vagos, in a quieter and less crowded area. It fronts onto a lake at the head of the Ria de Mira, which eventually runs into the Aveiro Ria. A back gate leads directly to a wide, quiet beach 300 m. away, a road runs alongside the site where the restaurant complex is situated resulting in some road noise. The site has around 225 pitches on sand, which are not marked but with trees creating natural divisions. Electricity (15A) and water points are plentiful. The site provides an inexpensive restaurant, snack bar, lounge bar and TV lounge. A medium sized supermarket is well stocked. The Mira Ria is fascinating, with the brightly painted, decorative 'Moliceiros' (traditional fishing boats).

Facilities: The modern toilet blocks are clean, with 14 free hot showers and washing machines. Motorcaravan services. Shop, restaurant and bar (Feb - Nov). Snack bar. TV room. Smart playground. Gas supplies. **Off site:** Fishing 500 m. Bicycle hire 200 m. Golf 1 km. Bus service 150 m. Indoor pool, lake swimming and riding at Mira 7 km.

Charges 2003

Per person	€ 2.10 - € 3.70
child (5-10 yrs)	€ 1.05 - € 1.85
pitch and car	€ 3.70 - € 10.70
electricity (5/15A)	€ 2.25

Off season discounts. **Tel:** 231 47 12 34. Fax: 231 47 12 54. E-mail: info@orbitur.pt. **Reservations:** Contact Orbitur - Central de Reservas, Rua Diogo do Couto, 1149-042 Lisboa. Tel: 21/811 70 00 or 811 70 70. Fax: 21/814 80 45. **Open** 1 March - 30 November.

Directions: Turn off N109 at Mira, about 27 km. south of Aveiro towards Praia de Mira. After about 5 km. (watch for speed bumps) a small sign shows a left turn which leads direct to the site. If you miss it, the site is signed from the resort. Ask for the Orbitur site if stuck - others are not as pleasant!

ENJOY THE OPEN AIR

FOR CAMPING, CARAVANNING, AND RENTALS (CARAVANS AND BUNGALOWS), FOR YOUR WEEKENDS OR HOLIDAYS IN THE COUNTRYSIDE, THE MOUNTAINS OR THE BEACH, YOUR ENJOYMENT IS OUR PLEASURE.

1 ANGEIRAS
2 CAMINHA
3 COSTA DE CAPARICA
4 ÉVORA
6 GALA [FIGUEIRA DA FOZ]
7 GUINCHO
8 ILHA DE ARMONA
9 LUSO
10 MADALENA
11 MIRA
12 MONTARGIL
13 PORTALEGRE
14 QUARTEIRA
15 RIO ALTO [PÓVOA DE VARZIM]
16 S. JACINTO
17 S. PEDRO DE MOEL
18 SAGRES
19 VALADO [NAZARÉ]
20 VALVERDE [LAGOS]
21 VIANA DO CASTELO
22 VISEU

▲ CAMPING SITE   ■ ACCOMMODATION   ● CAMPING SITE + ACCOMMODATION

INFORMATION and RESERVATION:
R. Diogo do Couto, 1-8° F · 1149-042 Lisboa · Portugal Tel. +351.21 811 7000/70
Fax +351.21 8148045 e-mail: info@orbitur.pt www.orbitur.pt

ORBITUR · INTERCÂMBIO DE TURISMO, SA

ORBITUR

Orbitur Camping Sao Jacinto

805 E.N.327, km20, Sao Jacinto, 3800 Aveiro (Aveiro)

This small site is in the Sao Jacinto nature reserve, on a peninsula between the Atlantic and the Barrinha, with views to the mountains beyond. The area is a weekend resort for locals and can be crowded in high season - it may therefore be difficult to find space in July/Aug, particularly for larger units. Swimming and fishing are both possible in the adjacent Ria, or the sea, 20 minutes walk from a guarded back gate. There is a jetty for boats and the manager will organise hire of the decorative 'Moliceiros' boats used in days gone by to harvest seaweed for the land. This is not a large site, taking 169 units on unmarked pitches, but in most places trees provide natural limits and shade. A bore-hole supplies the site with drinking water.

Facilities: Two toilet blocks, very clean when inspected, contain the usual facilities. Dishwashing and laundry sinks. Washing machine and ironing board in a separate part of the sanitary block. Motorcaravan services. Shop. Restaurant/bar (all May - Sept). Playground. Table tennis. **Off site:** Bus service 20 m. Fishing 200 m.

Charges 2002

per unit incl. 2 persons	€ 12.30 - € 22.20
extra adult	€ 1.90 - € 3.40
child (5-10 yrs)	€ 0.95 - € 1.70

Off season discounts (up to 70%). **Tel:** 234 83 82 84. Fax: 234 83 81 22. E-mail: info@orbitur.pt. **Reservations:** Contact Orbitur - Central de Reservas, Rua Diogo do Couto, 1149-042 Lisboa. Tel: 21/811 70 00 or 811 70 70. Fax: 21/814 80 45. **Open** February - November.

Directions: Turn off N109 at Estarreja to n109-5 to cross bridge over Ria da Gosta Nova and on to Torreira and São Jacinto. From Porto go south N1/09 turn for Ovar on the N 327 to Sao Jacinto.

Parque de Campismo da Vagueira

804 Gafanha da Vagueira, Gafanha da Boa Hora, 3840-254 Vagos (Aveiro)

This is a large site set 1.5 km. from the beach and 500 m. from the river 'Ria da Gosta Nova'. Shaded under tall pine trees and with comprehensive facilites and reasonable prices. The 800 pitches are unmarked, on sand and pine needles with many permanent units in high season and weekends at other times. Groups are taken in high season. The modern buildings have clean lines and are in sympathy with the surroundings, the restaurant/bar/café complex has a disco area outside where music is played at weeknds. This is a good family site if you do not need a pool and have transport to get you to the beach.

Facilities: Seven modern sanitary buildings with British and Turkish style WCs. Washing machines, dishwashing and laundry sinks have cold water only. Facilities for disabled campers. Supermarket. Children's club. Games room. Bar/snacks and separate restaurant (Jun - Sept). Playground. Tennis. Torches useful. **Off site:** River fishing 500 m. Beach 1.5 km. Golf 1 km. Riding 1 km. Bus 500 m.

Charges 2002

Per person	€ 3.29
child	€ 1.65
pitch and car	€ 5.47 - € 6.05
electricity	€ 1.81

Tel: 234 797526. Fax: 234 797093. **Reservations:** Write to site. **Open** all year.

Directions: Site is south of Aveiro. Take N109 south from Aveiro towards Mira. At Vagos take N333 and turn right towards Vagueira. Site well signed just off the roundabout as you arrive at the beach road.

Orbitur Camping Rio Alto

803 E.N.13 - km13 - Rio Alto-Estela, 4490 Póvoa de Varzim (Porto)

This site makes an excellent base for visiting Porto (by car) which is some 35 km. south of Estela. It has around 700 pitches on sandy terrain and is adjacent to what is virtually a private beach (access via a novel double tunnel under the dunes). The beach shelves steeply at some tidal stages (life-guard 15/6-15/9). The 18 hole golf course is adjacent. There are some hardstandings for caravans and motorcaravans and electrical connections (5A -15A) to most pitches. The area for tents is furthest from the beach and windswept, stunted pines give some shade. There are arrangements for car parking away from camping areas in peak season. There is a quality restaurant, snack bar and a large swimming pool across the road from reception.

Facilities: Four well equipped toilet blocks have hot water. Washing machines and ironing. Facilities for disabled campers. Restaurant/bar and snack bar (1/1 -30/11), mini-market (15/5-15/9). Swimming pool (1/6-30/9). Tennis. Playground. Games room. Surfing. TV. Gas supplies. Evening entertainment weekly in season. **Off site:** Golf 1 km. Fishing 800 m.

Charges 2003

Per person	€ 2.10 - € 4.30
child (5-10 yrs)	€ 1.05 - € 2.15
pitch and car	€ 5.10 - € 11.30
electricity (5/15A)	€ 2.25

Off season discounts. **Tel:** 252 61 56 99. Fax: 252 61 55 99. E-mail: info@orbitur.pt. **Reservations:** Contact Orbitur - Central de Reservas, Rua Diogo do Couto, 1149-042 Lisboa. Tel: 21/811 70 00 or 811 70 70. Fax: 21/814 80 45. **Open** all year.

Directions: Site access is directly off EN13 coast road towards the sea (just north of Estela), 12 km. north of Póvoa de Varzim. Travel 2.6 km. along the narrow cobbled road and look right for Orbitur sign. Take this for 0.8 km. (speed bumps) to site.

Orbitur Camping Viana do Castelo

802 Rua Diogo Alvares, Cabadelo, 4900-161 Darque (Viana do Costelo)

This site in northern Portugal is worth considering as it has the advantage of direct access, through a gate in the fence (locked at night) to an large and excellent soft-sand beach (400 m), popular for wind-surfing. There are 225 pitches on undulating, sand, most with good shade. There are some flat good sized pitches for caravans and electricity (16A) in all parts. As usual with Orbitur sites, pitches are not marked and it could be crowded in July/Aug. A pleasant restaurant terrace overlooks the pool. A ferry crosses the river to the town centre. The site is also convenient for visiting the medieval town of Ponte de Lima (24 km), with its white-washed houses, towers and Roman bridge.

Facilities: Clean, well kept toilet facilities are in two blocks. Both blocks have washbasins with cold water and hot showers. Good facilities for disabled campers. Laundry. Motorcaravan services. Supermarket, small restaurant with terrace and bar (all May-Sept). Reading room with TV, video and fireplace. Playground. Tennis. Medical post. Gas supplies. **Off site:** Fishing 1 km. Riding 2 km.

Charges 2002

Per unit incl. 2 persons	€ 13.70 - € 24.90
extra adult	€ 2.10 - € 4.00
child (5-10 yrs)	€ 1.05 - € 2.00

Off season discounts. **Tel:** 258 32 21 67. Fax: 258 32 19 46. E-mail: info@orbitur.pt. **Reservations:** Contact Orbitur - Central de Reservas, Rua Diogo do Couto, 1149-042 Lisboa. Tel: 21/811 70 00 or 811 70 70. Fax: 21/814 80 45. **Open** 16 January - 30 November.

Directions: On N13 coast road driving north to south drive through Viana do Castelo and over estuary bridge, turn immediately right off N13 towards Cabedelo and the sea. Site is the third camp signed, the other two are not recommended.

Orbitur Camping Caminha

801 E.N.13 - km 90 - Mata do Camarido, 4910 Caminha (Viana do Costelo)

A pleasant site in northern Portugal close to the Spanish border; this site is just 200 m. from the beach with an attractive and peaceful setting in woods alongside the river estuary that marks the border with Spain. With a pleasant, open feel about it, fishing is possible in the estuary and bathing, either there or from the rather open, sandy beach. The site is shaded by tall pines with other small trees planted to mark the large sandy pitches. The roads throughout the site are extremely good as are the water, electrical supply and lighting and the buildings are picked out in white, resulting in the site having a pleasant sharp image.

Facilities: The clean, well maintained toilet block has British style toilets, washbasins (cold water) and hot showers, plus beach showers, extra dishwashing and laundry sinks (cold water). Laundry. Small restaurant, snacks and supermarket (all April - Sept). **Off site:** Fishing 1 km. Beach 100m. Bus service 800 m. Riding 5 km.

Charges 2003

Per person	€ 2.10 - € 3.50
child (5-10 yrs)	€ 1.05 - € 1.85
pitch and car	€ 4.00 - € 8.70
electricity	€ 2.25 - € 2.90

Off season discounts. **Tel:** 258 92 12 95. Fax: 258 92 14 73. E-mail: info@orbitur.pt. **Reservations:** Contact Orbitur - Central de Reservas, Rua Diogo do Couto, 1149 - 042- Lisboa. Tel: 21/811 70 00 or 811 70 70. Fax: 21/814 80 45. E-mail as site address. **Open** 16 January - 30 November.

Directions: Turn off main coast road (N13-E50) along estuary 3 km. south of Caminha at sign to site - indicated on right.

Parque Natural de Vilar de Mouros

838 4910 Vilar de Mouros (Viana do Costelo)

Located some 15 minutes walk above the village of Vilar de Mouros and very close to the Spanish border, this small site is ideal for those looking for an uncomplicated traditional campsite giving really good prices. The 45 marked pitches for caravans and motorcaravans, all with electricity (2 or 5A), are on slightly sloping, grass terraces, with a separate unmarked area for tents, all set amongst trees and vines on a hillside. This friendly site has a good range of other amenities which include a tennis court and unusual small stone swimming pools. By far the most popular attraction is the regular Saturday evening gastronomic and folklore trips (with free minibus transport) to the site owner's own hotel.

Facilities: The two toilet blocks, very much in the quainter, older Portuguese style, provide British style WCs (some with bidets), washbasins (cold water), and hot showers. Dishwashing and laundry sinks (cold water) are under cover. Washing machine and dryer. Mini-market. Café/bar. Self-service restaurant. Swimming pool. Tennis court. TV room. Children`s pool and playground. Medical post. Bicycle hire. Little English spoken. Dogs are not accepted. **Off site:** Fishing 4 km. Riding 5 km.

Charges 2002

Per adult	€ 3.39
child	€ 1.70
pitch and car	€ 5.73 - € 6.48
electricity (2/9A)	€ 2.24

Tel: 258 72 74 72. Fax: 258 72 74 72. **Reservations:** Contact site. **Open** all year.

Directions: Site is signed from the N13, just north of Seixas, turn towards Vilar de Mouros. Site is on right just before village.

Parque de Campismo de Cerdeira

837

4840 Campo do Gerês (Braga)

Placed in the National Park of Peneda Gerês, amidst spectacular mountain scenery, this excellent site offers modern facilities in a truly natural area. The National Park is home to all manner of flora, fauna and wildlife, including the roebuck, wolf and wild boar. The well fenced, professional and peaceful site has some 600 good sized unmarked, mostly level, grassy pitches in a shady woodland setting. Electricity (5/10A) is available for most pitches, though some long leads may be required. A very large timber complex, tastefully designed with the use of noble materials, granite and wood provides a superb restaurant with a comprehensive menu. (including breakfast). There are unlimited opportunities in the area for fishing, riding, canoeing, mountain biking and climbing take advantage of this quality mountain hospitality.

Facilities: Three very clean sanitary blocks provide mixed style WCs, controllable showers and hot water. Dishwashing and laundry sinks under cover. Laundry. Gas supplies. Mini-market. Restaurant/bar (15/4- 30/9, plus weekends and holidays). Children's playground. Bicycle hire. TV room. Medical post. Good tennis courts. Mini Golf. Car wash. Barbeque area. Torches useful. English spoken. Dogs are not accepted in July/August. **Off site:** Fishing 800 m. Riding 800 m.

Charges 2002

Per adult	€ 3.00 - € 4.00
child (5-11 yrs)	€ 1.80 - € 2.50
pitch and car	€ 5.80 - € 8.50
electricity (5/10A)	€ 2.00 - € 3.00

Tel: 253 35 1005. Fax: 253 35 33 15. E-mail: parque.cerdeira@portugalmail.pt. **Reservations:** Contact site. **Open** all year.

Directions: From north, N103 (Braga-Chaves road), turn left at N205 (7.5 km north of Braga). Follow N205 to Caldelas Terras de Bouro and Covide where the campsite is clearly marked to `Campo do Geres`. An alternate route from the N103 looks easier on the map but is in fact more difficult.

Parque Campismo de Municipal

836

Barragem de Idhana-a-Nova, 6060 Idanha-a-Nova (Castelo Branco)

With its high level of sophistication, this attractive and well laid out site is unlike most municipal sites. It is located in quiet, unspoilt countryside close to a reservoir, near the small town of Idanha-a-Nova. The site has around 500 spacious unmarked pitches on wide grassy terraces and there is a little shade from young trees. Electricity (16A) is included in the price. Amenities include tennis courts with stadium-style spectator seating and a medium sized swimming pool with child's pool, together with several children's playgrounds. A good supermarket, restaurant, bar and terrace complex is located centrally on site, open in high season.

Facilities: Four large toilet blocks, built in the traditional Portuguese style, provide quality installations with some washbasins in private cabins, hot showers with dividers, foot baths and facilities for disabled visitors. Dishwashing and laundry sinks (cold water). Laundry. Supermarket (1/7-30/9). Cafe, bar and restaurant (1/7-30/9). Swimming pool. Tennis courts. TV room. Vending machines. Medical post. Car wash. Canoe hire.

Charges 2002

Per adult	€ 1.25
child (4-10 yrs)	€ 0.62
pitch and car	€ 3.49
electricity	€ 0.60

Tel: 277 20 27 93. Fax: 277 20 29 45. **Reservations:** Write to site. **Open** all year.

Directions: Using the N240, turn off at Ladoeiro onto the N354 (32 km. east of Castelo Branco) and follow signs to Barragem and site. Do not approach via the town of Idanha-a-Nova.

The ORBITUR Chain of Campsites

Orbitur is the largest Portugese campsite chain which has sites all over Portugal and boasts a central booking agency and e-mail service which may be used to avoid disappointment at peak season. There are 22 sites which have prime camping pitches and supporting facilities along with bungalows and mobile homes for rent.

Reservations for any of the sites should be made through the central office (not to individual sites); write to Orbitur at:

Orbitur - Central de Reservas,
Rua Diogo do Couto, 1149-042 Lisboa.
Tel: 21/811 70 00 or 811 70 70. Fax: 21/814 80 45.
E-mail: info@orbitur.pt. Internet: http://www.orbitur.pt.

Membership of the Orbitur Camping Club, taken either with your booking or at any site (free for pensioners) grants a 10% discount on site charges. Camp charges are reasonable and there is a general reduction of 40% to 70% (depending on length of stay) from October to March inclusive.

see advertisement on page 361

Slovakia

Slovak Tourist Centre, 16 Frognal Parade, Finchley Road, London NW3 5HG
Tel: 020 7794 3263   Fax: 020 7794 3265   E-mail: cztc@cztc.demon.co.uk

Slovakia became an independent republic on 1 Jan 1993, following the split of the former Czechoslovakia into its two component parts - the Czech Republic in the west and Slovakia in the east. In central Europe, it shares boundaries with the Czech Republic, Austria, Poland, Hungary and the Ukraine. It is hilly and picturesque, with historic castles, forests, mountain streams, valleys and lakes, and the culture reflects a strong Hungarian influence.

Population
5,403,500 (94); density 110 per sq. km.

Capital
Bratislava

Climate
Cold winters and mild summers. Hot summers and some rain in the eastern lowlands.

Language
The official language is Slovak. Some English or German in hotels, etc.

Currency
Koruna or Crown (Skr) = 100 halierov. Notes are Sk. 50, 100, 200, 500 and 1000; coins are Sk. 1, 2, 5,10,20 and 50.

Banks
Hours are Mon-Fri 08.00-13.00 and 14.00-17.00; banks are closed on Sat. Only notes exchanged at most border change offices **Credit cards:** The major ones can be used to obtain currency and in some hotels, restaurants shops and some petrol stations in towns and tourist areas. Travellers cheques are widely accepted.

Post Offices
Offices are open Mon-Sat 08.00-16.00.

Telephones
The dialling code for Slovakia is 0042.

Time
GMT plus one hour, BST + 1 in summer.

Public Holidays
New Year; Easter Mon; May Day; Liberation Day, 8 May; Saints Day, 5 July; Festival Day, 6 July; 28 Oct; Christmas, 24, 25, 26 Dec.

Shops
Open Mon-Fri 09.00-12.00 and 14.00-18.00. Some remain open at midday. Sat: 09.00-midday.

Motoring
The major route runs from Bratislava via Trengin, Banska, Bystrica, Zilina and Poprad to Presov. A full UK driving licence is acceptable.

Tolls: A windscreen sticker which is valid for a year must be purchased at the border crossing for use on certain motorways.

Speed limits: Caravans 31 mph (50 kph) in built up areas and 50 mph (80 kph) on all other roads. Motorhomes (3.5 tons) 31 mph (50 kph) in built up areas 56 mph (90 kph) other roads and 69 mph (110 kph) on motorways.

Parking: Vehicles must be parked on the right.

Overnighting
Not allowed on open land. Elsewhere permissible where a toilet is in situ.

492 Autocamping Trencin
na Ostrove, PO Box 10, 91101 Trencin

Trencin is an interesting town with a long history and dominated by the partly restored castle which towers high above. The small site with room for 30 touring units (all with electricity) and rooms to let, stands on an island about 1 km. from town centre opposite a large sports complex. Pitches occupy a grass area surrounded by bungalows, with the castle high on one side and woods and hills on the other. There is some road and rail noise. A very neat, tidy friendly site with English spoken during our visit.

Facilities: Toilet block is old but tiled and clean with hot water in the washbasins (in cabins with curtains) and showers (doors and curtains) under cover but not enclosed. Electric cookers, fridge/freezer, tables and chairs. Bar in high season. Boating and fishing in river. **Off site:** Shops 300 m. Restaurants 200 m. Tennis, indoor and outdoor pools within 400 m.

Charges 2002

Per person	Sks. 120
pitch and car	Sks. 140 - 150
electricity	Sks. 80
local tax	Sks. 10

No credit cards. **Tel:** 0831/434013. E-mail: autocamping.tn@mail.put.sk. **Reservations:** Write to site. **Open** 15 May - 15 September.

Directions: Site is signed in places in town, otherwise head for town sports centre.

Slovakia
Autocamping Trusalová
03853 Turany (Zilina)

Autocamping Trusalová is situated right on the southern edge of the Malá Fatra National Park, northeast of the historic town of Martin which has much to offer to tourists. The town is perhaps best known for the engineering works which produced most of the tanks for the Warsaw Pact countries before the recent revolution and change to a more democratic regime. Paths from the site lead into the Park making it an ideal base for walkers and serious hikers who wish to enjoy this lovely region. The site is in two halves, one on the left of the entrance and the other behind reception on a slight slope. Surrounded by trees with a stream rushing along one side, pitches are grass from a hard road with room for about 150 units and there are some bungalows. We received a friendly welcome from the German speaking staff.

Facilities: Each half has its own old, but clean and acceptable, toilet provision including hot water in basins, sinks and showers. Motorcaravan service point. Each section has a covered barbecue area with raised fire box, chimney, tables and chairs. Volleyball. Table tennis. TV lounge. Playground. Outdoor chess board. Bicycle hire. **Off site:** Bar just outside site. Shops in the village 3 km. Restaurants 500 m. or 1 km.

Charges 2002

Per person	Sks. 95
child (6-15 yrs)	Sks. 45
pitch and car	Sks. 145 - 190
electricity	Sks. 90
local tax	Sks. 10

No credit cards. **Tel:** 0842/292636 or 292667.
Reservations: Write to site in German. **Open** 1 June - 15 September.

Directions: Turn north at Motorest Fatra on the road 18/E50 near village of Turany to site.

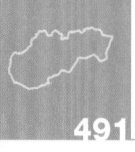

Slovakia
Autocamping Turiec
03608 Martin 8 (Zilina)

Turiec is situated in northeast Slovakia, 1.5 km. from the small village of Vrutky, 4 km. north of Martin, at the foot of the Lucanska Mala Fatra mountains and with castles nearby. Holiday activities include hiking in summer, skiing in winter. There is room for about 30 units on slightly sloping grass inside a circular tarmac road with shade from tall trees. Electrical connections are available for all places. A wooden chalet by the side of the camping area has a TV rest room and a small games room.

Facilities: One acceptable sanitary block to the side of the camping area, but in winter the facilities in the bungalow at the entrance are used. Cooking facilities. Snack bar in summer. Badminton. Volleyball. Swimming pool 1.5 km. Rest room with TV. Small games room. Covered barbecue. **Off site:** Shop outside entrance.

Charges 2002

Per unit	Sks. 100 - 150
electricity	Sks. 100

Tel: 0842/284215. **Reservations:** Contact site. **Open** all year.

Directions: Site is signed from E18 road (Zilina - Martin) in the village of Vrutky, 3 km. north of Martin. Follow signs to Martinské Hole.

Slovakia
Autocamping Zlaté Piesky
Senecka cesta c 2, 821 07 Bratislava (Bratislava)

Bratislava undoubtedly has charm, being on the Danube and having a number of interesting buildings and churches in its centre. However, industry around the city, particularly en-route to the camp from the south, presents an ugly picture and gives no hints of the hidden charms. Zlate piesky (golden sands) is part of a large, lakeside sports complex which is also used during the day in summer by locals. The site is on the edge of town with 200 touring pitches, 120 with electrical connections, on level grass under tall trees. Many bungalows to hire are spread around the site. The attractive lakeside recreation area also has pedaloes for hire and there is a fitness area in the park.

Facilities: Four toilet blocks, two for campers and two for day visitors, are of marginal quality and may be hard pressed. Two restaurants, one with waiter service, the other self service. Many small snack bars. Shops. Lake for swimming and watersports with large beach area. Table tennis. Minigolf. Children`s play areas. Room with billiards and electronic games. Disco.

Charges 2002

Per person60	Sks. 70
child (4-15 yrs)	Sks. 30 - 40
caravan	Sks. 80 - 90
motorcaravan	Sks. 90 - 140
tent	Sks. 30 - 60
electricity	Sks. 80

No credit cards. **Tel:** 0744 257 373. Fax: 0744 257 373. E-mail: kempi@netax.sk. **Reservations:** Write to site. **Open** 1 May - 15 October.

Directions: Follow signs on road no. 61 for Zillina and airport and pick up signs for camp. Zlaté piesky is on the left on entering the sports area.

Slovenia

Slovenian Tourist Office, 49 Conduit Street, London W1R 9FB

Tel: 020 7734 7133   Fax: 020 7287 5476   E-mail: slovenia@cpts.fsbusiness.co.uk

With the recovery of tourism in Slovenia we have included a small section of inspected sites. Despite the recovery very few British vehicles are yet to be seen in Slovenia. This is partly because the country has been concentrating its promotional efforts on its neighbours, in particular Germany, Austria and Italy. However, it is also because of the daunting driving distance from the UK. Whether via France or Germany, the Slovenian border is about 1,000 miles from Calais. Nevertheless, we are convinced that it fully deserves a place in our guide. The scenery almost everywhere is attractive, often spectacular; there is much of interest to enjoy; the road network is quite adequate; price levels are generally lower than Britain or mainland Europe; the people are relaxed and friendly; and last but not least, there is an ample choice of good campsites with sanitary facilities mainly on a par with those found in the more popular European destinations.

We have arbitrarily divided the country into four quarters, with the Ljubljana area in the centre. The northwest is the quarter of prime interest to British visitors as it is not only the usual entry from Austria but it includes the awesome Julian Alps with the lakes of Bohinj and Bled to the east and the Upper Soca Valley to the west. The southwest quarter includes Slovenia's short stretch of Adriatic coast in which the historic port of Piran and the adjacent resort of Portoroz will be of particular interest to visitors. Unfortunately the campsites on the coast are grossly overcrowded during the summer holiday season, mainly by Slovenes and Italians, and dominated by static caravans. Next the centrally situated capital Ljubljana - a convenient stopover. The northeast quarter has two very different areas of attraction. The Savinja valley, in particular its upper section in the Savinja Alps, is almost as spectacular as the Julian Alps. The far northeast, beyond the Savinja, is a gentle rural area, largely given over to vines (home of Lutomer Riesling). In the pleasant rolling countryside of the southeast, the main attractions are to be found on the banks of the slow flowing Krka river.

Population

Just over 2 million.

Capital

Ljubljana (pop. approx 1/4 million).

Language

Slovene, with German often spoken in the north and Italian in the west. English is generally understood except by the elderly.

Currency

The basic unit is the Slovene Tolar (abbreviated as SIT) of which there are several hundred to the pound sterling. Any unused Tolars should be exchanged on or soon after departure.

Banks

Now run on efficient conventional western lines. Cash machines in most towns. Banks open week-days 8.30-16.30 with a lunch break 12.30-14.00, plus Saturday mornings 8.30-11.30. Main credit cards accepted, including most filling stations.

Post Offices

Opening hours as for banks.

Time

Central European Time (one hour ahead of UK).

Telephone

To call Slovenia, prefix code is 386. To call the UK prefix code is 0044. Most call boxes require a phone card.

Shops

Shops usually open by 8 in the morning, sometimes 7. Closing times vary widely. Food: Readily available in shops and street markets. General quality a little below West European standards but rather cheaper. Drink: Usual range readily available. Prolific choice of Slovenian wines but confusingly labelled (in Slovene) and not generally cheaper than in Britain or western Europe.

Motoring

Small but expanding network of motorways radiating from Ljubljana (there may be tolls). Secondary roads often poorly maintained. Tertiary roads are often gravel (known locally as 'white roads' and shown thus on road maps).
Fuel: Filling stations readily available except in remote rural areas. Fuel is cheap.
Speed Limits: Driving standards mixed as privatisation of economy has resulted in presence of many high-performance cars with low-performance drivers. Overtaking on blind corners by adolescents is one result. The normal speed limit is 80 mph (130 kph), faster on motorways - slower in built up areas. Road markings and signs are generally good.

Camp Smlednik

436 Dragocajna 14a, 1216 Smlednik

Camp Smlednik is relatively close to the capital, Ljubljana, yet within striking distance of Lake Bled, the Karawanke mountains and Julian Alps. It provides a good touring base, set above the river Sava. This same site also provides a small, separate enclosure for those who enjoy naturism. Situated beside the peaceful tiny village of Dragocajni, in attractive countryside, the site provides 80 places for visiting tourers each with electricity (6/10A). Although terraced, it is probably better described as large plateau with tall pines and deciduous trees providing some shade. Amongst the many species of birds you have every chance of seeing the Golden Oriole. Near reception is a bar that provides limited food at weekends. Boasting a dartboard, it radiates an atmosphere typical of a British pub and is used by local villagers in the evenings accentuating that feeling. From a grass sunbathing area there is stepped access to the river for swimming. This is at your own risk and there are reservations as to the quality of river water in Slovenia. Good size fish can be caught by the angler (licence required). The Sava is excellent for canoeing or kayaking. The naturist area measuring only some 30 x l00 m. accommodates 15 units in a delightful setting adjacent to the river (INF card not required).

Facilities: Three fully equipped sanitary blocks are of varying standards, but it is an adequate and clean provision. In the main camping area a fairly new, solar powered two storey block has free hot showers, the lower half for use within the naturist area. Normally heated showers in the old block are on payment. Dishwashing and laundry sinks. Washing machine. Toilet for disabled visitors (level access). Bar (all year), limited food at weekends. Two good quality clay tennis courts (charged). Table tennis, basketball and area to kick a ball. Swings for children. River swimming and fishing. **Off site:** Village shop for basics. Two small supermarkets nearby at Medrode.

Charges 2003

Per person	SIT 1200
child (7-14 yrs)	SIT 600
electricity (6-10A)	SIT 650
local tax	SIT 83

Tel: 01362 7002. Fax: 01362 7002. **Reservations:** Only necessary for the naturist section. **Open** 1 May - 15 October.

Directions: Travelling on road no.1, both Smlednik and the site are well signed. From E61 motorway, Smlednik and site well signed at the Vodiice exit.

Camping Bled

420 Kidriceva 10c, Sl, 4260 Bled

Visitors to Bled are well provided with camping facilities, there being two very large sites nearby. About 3 km. to the east of the lake, in a flat pine forest just off the main road, is the heavily publicised Kamp Sobec. Although this is very professionally managed and equipped to a high standard, its location cannot compare with that of Camping Bled which is actually on the western tip of Lake Bled. The waterfront here is a small public beach immediately behind which gently runs a sloping narrow wooded valley. Visitors are free to pitch anywhere on the grass covered 6 ha site. Unlike many other Slovenian sites the number of statics appears to be carefully controlled with touring caravans, motorcaravans and tents predominating. Some visitors may be disturbed by the noise coming from above of trains as they hurtle out of a high tunnel overlooking the campsite but this is a small price to pay for the pleasure of being in a pleasant site from which the lake, its famous little island, its castle and town can be explored on foot or by boat.

Facilities: Toilet facilities in five blocks are of a very high standard (with free hot showers). Two blocks are heated. Solar energy used. Recycling bins. Laundry. Motorcaravan services. Gas supplies. Fridge hire. Supermarket. Restaurant. Play area and children`s zoo. Table tennis. Organised activities in July/Aug. including children`s club, excursions and sporting activities. Mountain bike tours. Live entertainment. Fishing. Bicycle hire. **Off site:** Golf or riding 3 km. Within walking distance of waterfront and town. Restaurants near.

Charges 2002

Per person	€ 5.53 - € 8.14
child (7-13 yrs)	€ 3.87 - € 5.70
electricity	€ 2.43 - € 2.63
dog	€ 1.50 - € 2.21
local tax	€ 0.50

Less 10% for stays over 6 days. **Tel:** 04 575 2000. Fax: 04 575 2002. E-mail: info@camping.bled.si. **Reservations:** Contact site. **Open** 1 April - 15 October.

Directions: From the town of Bled drive along south shore of lake to its western extremity (some 2 km). Zaka is behind the large public restaurant which faces the beach.

Autocamp Spik

Jezerci 21, 4282 Gozd Martuljek

410

Most British motorists enter Slovenia on the E55 from Villach over the demanding Wurzen pass, or through the easy Karawanken tunnel. Close by the turn to Kransjska Gora is the small village of Gozd Martuljek and here, directly on route 1, is Kamp Spik, named after the peak which dominates the spectacular view from the site. This is the highest site in Slovenia. It is large and flat, covering 8 ha of spruce woodland. The site is shared with the modern Spik Hotel and the facilities are extensive, including excellent recreational facilities. As a result of its spectacular location and its extensive facilities many pitches are occupied by seasonal units.

Facilities: All facilities expected of modern tourist complex. Swimming pool (1/7-31/8). Fishing. Bicycle hire. Climbing school. Mountaineering. **Off site:** Riding 6 km.

Charges 2002

Per person	€ 5.62 - € 7.16
child (5-12 yrs)	less 30%
electricity	€ 2.05
dog	€ 1.53
local tax	€ 0.51

Less 10% for stays over 7 days. **Tel:** 04 5880 120. Fax: 04 5880 115. **Reservations:** Contact site. **Open** all year.

Directions: Site is well signed on the A1 just outside Gozd Martuljek.

Kamp Kamne

Franc Voga, Dovje 9, 4281 Mojstrana

415

For visitors proceeding down the A1 towards the prime attractions of the twin lakes of Bled and Bohinj, a delightfully informal little site is to be found just outside the village of Mojstrana. Owner Frank Voga opened the site as recently as 1989, on a small terraced orchard. He has steadily developed the facilities, adding a small pool, then a tennis court. The little reception doubles as a local bar where locals wander up for a beer and a chat while enjoying the view across the valley of the Julian Alps. The site is popular with walkers as three valleys lead west into the mountains from Mojstrana, including the trail to the ascent of Triglav, at nearly 3,000 m. the highest point of the Julian Alps.

Facilities: Basic facilities only (classified as third class) but of high quality and well maintained. Reception/bar. Small swimming pool. Tennis court. Frank's English is rather basic, but his daughter Anna is fluent. **Off site:** Walking trails.

Charges guide

Per person	SIT 600 - 800
child (7-14 yrs)	SIT 300 - 400
electricity	SIT 400

Plus local tax. **Tel:** 064 891 105. **Reservations:** Contact site. **Open** all year.

Directions: Site is well marked on north side of the A1, just to west of exit for Mojstrana.

Kamp Koren

5222 Kobarid

427

British history teaches little of the terrible mountain warfare between Austria and Italy which went on in the Julian Alps throughout WW1. This macabre struggle, involving half a million casualties, is commemorated in the military museum at Kobarid and in the cemeteries in the neighbourhood. Kobarid itself is a pleasant country town, with easy access to nearby rivers, valleys and mountains which alone justify a visit to Koren. But most British visitors will remember it for the opportunity it provides to fill that gap in their knowledge of European history. The campsite occupies a flat, tree-lined meadow on a wide ledge which drops down sharply to the Soca river. A small, site with just 45 pitches, it is very popular with those interested in outdoor sports, including canoeing.

Facilities: An attractive log-built toilet block is of a standard worthy of a high class private sports club. Laundry facilities. Shop (June - Sept). Café for light meals, snacks and drinks apparently without much regard to closing hours. Bowling. Fishing. Bicycle hire. Canoe hire. **Off site:** Riding 5 km. Town within walking distance

Charges 2002

Per person	SIT 990 - 1550
child (7-14 yrs)	less 50%
electricity	SIT 400

Plus local tax. **Tel:** 05 389 1311. Fax: 05 389 1310. E-mail: lidija.koren@siol.net. **Reservations:** Contact site. **Open** Mid-March - October.

Directions: Site is on side road leading east out of Kobarid, just beyond so-called Napoleon's Bridge, well signed on the left.

Camp Soca
Soca 8, 5232 Soca

From Kranjska Gora an amazing road runs southwest to the upper Soca valley. This road was built by Russian prisoners of war during WW1 in order to allow Austria to move troops and supplies towards the Italian frontier. Those with large units should note that it is tough going with over 50 hairpin bends! Those who successfully negotiate the 1,600 m. summit usually drop down to the busy small town of Bovec where there are several campsites. These have little to commend them except to canoeists for the turbulent waters of the Soca in this area are world famous among kayak enthusiasts. Fortunately for non-canoeists there is Camp Soca in the spec-tacular Lepena valley which is one end of a wonderful mountain trail, the other end of which is Bohinj (this trail was also opened by the Austrian army in WW1). Camp Soca is just off the main road on a shelving bluff formed by a wide curve of the Soca River. The site is literally theatrical as its two upper terraces and its large lower platform form a natural amphitheatre from which the mountains at the head of the Lepena valley can be admired. Those in need of a good restaurant or bar, a game of tennis or a ride on a Lipizaner can cross the Soca on a wobbly wire and plank bridge which leads through the woods on the opposite bank, to a small holiday resort.

Facilities: Small but well equipped toilet block. Small reception office/shop. Campsite owner Bostjan Komac and his father are usually on site and ready to give help and advice.

Charges guide

Per person	SIT 850 - 1000
child (7-14 yrs)	SIT 640 - 750
electricity	SIT 300

Tel: 065 89 318. **Reservations:** Contact site. **Open** May - September.

Directions: Site is on the main road between Kranjska Gora and Bovec, between the villages of Soca and Podklanec, just to west of the side road to Lepena.

Hotel-Camping Belvedere
Dobrava 1A, 6310 Izola

On paper, with the choice of no fewer than six sites, there should be no difficulty in selecting a recommended site for the Slovenian Riviera. In fact, it is very difficult, not because the sites are unsuitable, but because the sheer pressure of customers on restricted space is too heavy. Two factors exacerbate this situation. For the many Italians living in the Trieste area, and for Slovenes, the Slovenian Riviera is the nearest place for a cheap beach holiday. This is coupled with willingness by site operators to allow long seasonal letting of pitches. This not only means that touring visitors have difficulty in obtaining a satis-factory pitch, but also that it is very difficult for site operators to maintain standards. Of the six sites the only one which is not on the waterfront is our choice. During the Socialist period the site was developed into a massive leisure complex of which camping is a small part. Thanks to its loca-tion, it is the only coast site where the pressure on facilities is such that the management can maintain standards.

Facilities: Very comprehensive leisure facilities, including a huge swimming pool, restaurant, night club (can be very noisy late into the night) and hotel. Shop (25/6-1/9). **Off site:** Half mile's walk or drive from sea.

Charges guide

Per person	€ 3.58 - € 6.14
child (under 10 yrs)	€ 1.79 - € 3.07
electricity	€ 2.56
car	€ 1.53
local tax	€ 0.51

Tel: 05 6605 100. Fax: 05 6415 583. E-mail: belve@siol.net. **Reservations:** Contact site. **Open** May - October.

Directions: Follow the main A2 coast road west just beyond the Izola by-pass; the site is clearly signed but the exit is on a rather confusing summit road junction.

Camping Danica Bohinj

4265 Bohinjska Bistrica

Until recently the best site for those visiting the famous Bohinj valley, which stretches like a fjord right into the heart of the Julian Alps, was the Zlatorog campsite on the western tip of the lake. Zlatorog also happens to lie at the foot of a spectacular amphitheatre of Alpine peaks which rise seemingly sheer several thousand feet above the lake. However, the available waterfront is now so packed with Slovene campers that visitors from abroad are well advised to chose the more spacious Danica site which lies in the valley about 3 km. downstream of the lake. Danica was set up in 1989 to supplement the camping accommodation. Occupying a rural site that stretches from the main road leading into Bohinj to the bank of the Sava river, it is basically flat meadow, broken up by lines of natural woodland. There are 140 pitches, 125 for touring units.

Facilities: Small shop. Café. Fishing. Bicycle hire. **Off site:** Riding 1 km.

Charges 2002

Per person	SIT 1000 - 1400
child (7-14 yrs)	less 25-30%
electricity	SIT 400
local tax	SIT 100

Less 10% for stays over 7 days. **Tel:** 04 572 1055. Fax: 04 572 3330. E-mail: tdbohinj@bohinj.si. **Reservations:** Contact site. **Open** May - September.

Directions: Driving from Bled to Bohinj, the well signed site lies just behind the village of Bohinjska Bistrica on the right-hand (north) side of the road.

Camping Pivka Jama

Veliki Otok 50, 6230 Postojna

Postojna is renowned for its extraordinary limestone caves. Only 4 km. from the caves. Pivka Jama is a most convenient site, mid-way between Ljubljana and Piran and only about an hour's pleasant drive from either. The site is deep in what appears to be primeval forest, cleverly cleared to take advantage of the broken limestone bed-rock. The 300 pitches are not clustered together but nicely segregated under trees and in small clearings, all connected by a neat network of paths and slip-roads. The facilities are both excellent and extensive and run with obvious pride by enthusiastic staff. It even has its own local caves which can spare its visitors the commercialisation of Postojna.

Facilities: Extensive service and recreational facilities. Bicycle hire. **Off site:** Fishing 5 km. Riding 10 km. Skiing 10 km.

Charges 2002

Per person	€ 7.00 - € 8.00
child (7-14 yrs)	€ 5.00 - € 6.00
electricity	€ 3.00

Family packages available. **Tel:** 05 726 5382. Fax: 05 726 5348. E-mail: autokamp.pivka.jama@siol.net. **Reservations:** Contact site **Open** 1 March - 30 November.

Directions: Take the side road leading west from Postojna (just off the A10 trunk road) to neighbouring Pojnska Jama and on to Pivka Jama (all well signed).

Autocamp Jezica

Dunajska 270, 1000 Ljubljana

The Sava river slices across Slovenia from northwest to southeast, passing through the northern outskirts of Ljubljana. Jezica is actually on the south bank of the river but a thick hedge and a heavy wire fence means that many campers are unaware of the Sava's presence. The site is basically a large 3 ha. flat grass expanse, punctuated with birch trees. It is essentially a convenient base for visiting or passing through Ljubljana rather than a holiday centre.

Facilities: Large, modern and well designed, but poorly managed, toilet block. All facilities are basic **Off site:** Ample sporting facilities locally. Historic town centre only minutes by bus.

Charges guide

Per person	SIT 900
pitch	SIT 200 - 300
electricity	SIT 400

Tel: 061 371 382. Fax: 061 313 649. **Reservations:** Contact site. **Open** all year.

Directions: Follow the main road leading due north from the city, across the ring road, continuing straight ahead (not bearing right) towards Jezica suburb. Turn left immediately before the Sava bridge crossing; site is well signed.

Camping-Resnik

Maistrova 32, 1240 Kamnik

437

Nobody should visit central Slovenia without stopping off to wander around the unspoilt small country town of Kamnik which was once Ljubljana's main trade rival. The town is delightful and is only five minutes walk from the campsite, which is rather unprepossessing, comprising a small open field with two very basic prefabricated toilet units, However, there are compensations. Although the actual camping area is but 1 ha. it is only the edge of a much larger meadow, with sports centre adjoining. On the site is a friendly bar/café, patronised by both campers and players. Ljubljana is only an hour's drive to the south.

Facilities: Two very basic prefabricated toilet units, which are not as well serviced as they. Shop. Bar/restaurant. Site is part of Kamnik sports centre, which boasts large swimming pool and many tennis, badminton and squash courts. Outdoor pool. **Off site:** Pleasant family Inn opposite. The proprietor, Michael Resnik, also runs the campsite.

Charges guide

Per person	SIT 300
child (under 10 yrs)	SIT 150
pitch	SIT 200 - 400
electricity	SIT 300
local tax	SIT 100

No credit cards. **Tel:** 01 831 7314. Fax: 01 839 2243. **Reservations:** Contact site. **Open** 1 May - 30 September.

Directions: Site is 200 m. on the left along the main road leading north from Kamnik.

Camp Dolina Prebold

Vozlic Tomaz Dolenja vas 147, 3312 Prebold

440

Prebold is a quiet village about 15 km. west of the large historic town of Celje. It is only a few kilometres from the remarkable Roman necropolis at Sempeter. There are two small campsites in Prebold. Our choice, Dolina, is little more than the garden of the house (taking 50 units). It belongs to Tomaz and Manja Vozlic who look after the site and its guests with loving care. To the south of Prebold lies some of Slovenia's best walking country and to the north lies the upper Savinja valley. It is an easy drive up the Savinja to its spectacular source in the Logar Valley; beyond its semi-circle of 2,000 m. peaks lies Austria. There are other sites on the upper Savinja our preference is for Dolina.

Facilities: The small, heated toilet block would certainly qualify for Slovenia's 'best loo' award. Reception with bar. Small swimming pool (heated, 1/5-30/9). Sauna. Bicycle hire. **Off site:** Good supermarket and restaurant 200 m. Tennis and indoor pool within 1 km. Fishing 1.5 km.

Charges 2002

Per person	SIT 1000
electricity	SIT 500
local tax	SIT 150
dog	SIT 200

No credit cards. **Tel:** 035 724 378. Fax: 035 724 591. E-mail: dolina@email.si. **Reservations:** Contact site. **Open** all year.

Directions: Site is well signed in a small side street on the northern edge of Prebold. Best reached via a signed exit on the Ljubljana - Celje motorway.

Hotel Grad Otocec Camp

8222 Ototec

442

Unlike the turbulent Soca and Savinja upper rivers, the Krka flows slowly through the fertile farmland of southeast Slovenia. There are several well known campsites along its banks and, with one exception, these are part of large spa complexes which generally have little appeal to British travellers, however well equipped. The exception is a quiet wooded stretch of the Krka river, opposite the small island on which the 16th century fortress of Otocec is to be found. The fortress has recently been turned into a 5 star hotel. Campers have to drive or walk across the wooden bridge to register at the hotel's opulent reception. At weekends the campsite and neighbouring area liven up with Slovenes attracted for all the activities.

Facilities: Good toilet facilities are accessed by key supplied on registering at the hotel reception. **Off site:** Nearby canoeing, fishing, cycling and horse riding (equipment for all these can be readily hired)

Charges 2002

Per person (over 2 yrs)	SIT 600
caravan	SIT 400
tent	SIT 300
car	SIT 300
motorcaravan	SIT 600
electricity	SIT 440

Tel: 068 21 830. Fax: 068 23 413. **Reservations:** Contact hotel. **Open** May - September.

Directions: About 7 km. northeast of Novo Mesto on route 1 (E70), take the clearly signed Otocec exit on right. Cross the old road running along the north bank of the Krka river and on over the bridge to the island hotel (the campsite lies beyond on the south bank via a second bridge).

Spain

Spanish National Tourist Office, 22/23 Manchester Square, London W1M 5AP
Tel: 020 7486 8077   Fax: 020 7486 8034   Brochures: 09001 669920 (60p per minute)
E-mail: londres@tourspain.es   Internet: http://www.tourspain.es

Spain, which occupies the larger part of the Iberian peninsula, is the fourth largest country in Europe, with extremes of climate, widely contrasting geographical features and diversity of language, culture and artistic traditions. Spain's capital is, of course, Madrid, but the country is divided, like the USA or Germany, Austria or Switzerland, into 17 different federal states called 'autonomias', each with its own capital. For example the capital of Catalunya is Barcelona, that of Galicia is Santiago de Compostela; each federal state has its own government and parliament, and its own prime minister. The central government in Madrid retains power over the national economy and foreign affairs, for example, but other matters such as tourism are the exclusive preserve of the autonomias, which explains why there are different regulations for camping, caravanning and campsites in the various different autonomias. These differences extend to matters such as 'wild camping', 'overnighting' and even the classification (grading) of campsites.

So far as campsites are concerned, Spain has much to offer in terms of some of the best large sites in Europe, such as Playa Montroig, but it also has many attractive smaller sites which will appeal to many of our readers. There are quite a lot of sites which claim to be open all year, but services on most may well be limited to a minimum (eg. only one sanitary block operating and the shop open at weekends only). Even though all the sites featured in this guide have indicated positively that they will be open during the periods stated, we would still advise anyone contemplating a visit out of season to check first rather than rely entirely on information provided so far in advance! Readers should also bear in mind that a pitch of 80 sq.m. is considered to be large in Spain (worth remembering if you have a large outfit), although many sites, particularly in Catalunya, are now increasing pitch size to 100 sq.m. Finally we should mention that there has been a growing tendency in recent years for what we call 'Spanish weekenders' – domestic tourism, whereby the Spanish themselves take pitches for an extended period to use as a weekend holiday home – this tends to give some sites a rather strange appearance during the week when many pitches are occupied by caravans, tents, etc. but not a soul is to be seen.

Population

39,000,000, density 77 per sq. km.

Capital

Madrid

Climate

Spain has a very varied climate depending where you are and the time of year. Temperate in the north, which also has most of the rainfall, dry and very hot in the centre, subtropical along the Mediterranean coast. The average winter temperature in Malaga is 57°F.

Language

Castilian Spanish is spoken by most people with Catalan (northeast), Basque (north) and Galician (northwest) also used in their respective areas.

Currency

From January 2002, in common with 11 other European countries, the Spanish unit of currency has been the EURO (€).
€ 1 = Pesetas 166.39.

Time

GMT plus 1 (summer BST + 1).

Banks

Open Mon-Fri 09.00-14.00 Sat 09.00-13.00 (only certain towns). In tourist areas you will also find 'cases de cambio' with more convenient hours.

Post Offices

Offices (Correos) open Mon-Sat 08.00-12.00. Some open late afternoon, while some in the large cities open 08.00-15.00. Queues can be long and stamps can be bought at tobacconists (tabac).

Telephone

From the UK, the code is 00 34 followed by the internal area code, including the initial 9, and exchange number. To call the UK dial 07 44. Make international calls from 'telefone internacional' boxes or from 'Telefonica' offices.

Public Holidays

New Year; Epiphany; Saint's Day, 19 Mar; Maundy Thurs; Good Fri; Easter Mon; Labour Day; Saint's Day, 25 July;

Assumption, 15 Aug; National Day, 12 Oct; All Saints Day, 1 Nov; Constitution Day, 6 Dec; Immaculate Conception, 8 Dec; Christmas, 25 Dec.

Shops

Open Mon-Sat 09.00-13.00/14.00, afternoons 15.00/16.00-19.30/20.00. Many open longer.

Food: The Spanish in general eat much later than we do. Lunches start at 13.00 or 14.00 and evening meals 21.00-22.00, so the streets remain lively until late. You can go to a 'restaurante' for a full meal or to a 'bar' where you have a succession of 'tapas' (small snacks) or 'raciones' (larger ones). Fish stews (zarzuelas) and rice based 'paellas' are often memorable.

Motoring

The surface of the main roads is on the whole good, although secondary roads in some rural areas can be rough and winding and have slow, horse drawn traffic. In Catalan and Basque areas you will find alternative names on the signposts, for example, Gerona - Girona and San Sebastian - Donostia.

Last year (2002) saw the emergence of EU-funded roadworks in Spain on an unprecedented scale. In all 17 states there are huge programmes throwing the road system into confusion. The renumbering of major and minor roads has even foxed the locals! Great caution, therefore, should be taken with navigation and directions to sites, particularly when roadworks are evident. The information is currently changing with alarming speed.

Tolls: Payable on certain roads and for the Cadi Tunnel, Vallvidrera Tunnel (Barcelona) and the Tunnel de Garraf on the A16.

Fuel: Petrol stations on motorways often open 24 hrs. Credit cards are accepted at most stations.

Speed Limits: Built-up areas 31 mph (50 kph) or less for both car and car towing. Other roads 56/62 mph (90/100 kph). On motorways, 75 mph (120 kph). For cars towing: other roads 43/50 mph (70/80 kph), on motorways 50 mph (80 kph).

Parking: 'Blue' parking zones (zone azul) are indicated by signs and discs are available from hotels, the town hall and travel agencies. In the centre of some large towns there is a zone 'ora' where parking is allowed only against tickets bought in tobacconists.

Spain - Cataluña

Camping Cadaques

8005 Ctra. de Port Lligat 17, 17488 Cadaques (Girona)

Picturesque Cadaqués is only accessible by a long winding road over the hills behind Roses and has an air of isolation. The attractive promenade is lined with restaurants and you can sit and watch the fishermen land their catches. Camping Cadaqués overlooks Port Lligat where Salvador Dali constructed his famous home. This site is ideal as a stopover if you don't want the long drive in and out and wish to be able to walk to this magnificent house in its unusual setting or to enjoy the local cuisine and beaches. This is a basic site, mainly used by transit campers for short stays to visit the Dali attraction. Not recommended for holidays, it is included to give an easier overnight visit to this difficult location. There are 200 pitches of 60-70 sq.m, some with a slight slope, and a separate area for tents. The large pool is adjacent to the bar and restaurant with a terrace giving stunning views of the mountains, the Port of Lligat, Dali's house and the nature reserve. There are very few activities other than the pool and the site does look a little tired out of high season. The Port of Lligat is slowly being changed to accommodate the visitors to what is anticipated to become one of the most popular historic destinations in Spain.

Facilities: Restaurant/bar. Good, well stocked supermarket producing its own bread. Swimming pool (high season). Laundry service and ironing. Dogs are not accepted. **Off site:** Fishing 2 km. Golf 12 km. Riding 5 km. Bicycle hire 2 km.

Charges 2002

Per adult	€ 4.30
child	€ 3.20 - € 2.46
tent or caravan	€ 5.40
car	€ 4.30
motorcaravan	€ 8.00
electricity	€ 3.10

Plus 7% VAT. **Tel:** 972 258 126. Fax: 972 159 383. **Reservations:** Not generally necessary. **Open** Easter - 15 September.

Directions: Leave autopista A7 (Figueres - Girona) at exit 4 and take C260 to Roses and on to Cadaqués. It is a long, winding road and the return journey is along the same route.

Camping Castell Mar

8010 Playa de la Rubina, 17486 Castelló d'Empúries (Girona)

This busy, modern site is 350 metres from one of the very pleasant Gulf of Roses beaches, and within the large Aiguamolls of l'Empordà nature reserve. It is also convenient for (but quite separate from) the latest tourist development and facilities at Empuria Brava. With some 300 pitches, it is smaller than many sites in this part of Spain and is particularly suitable for families. There is a heated outdoor pool and an large open-air auditorium where a varied entertainment programme is provided. A roof-top, terraced area with a bar and restaurant enjoys pleasant views of the surrounding area. The pitches, most with electricity, are of a reasonable size for the Costa Brava and are on level ground with some artificial shade mainly for tents, and natural shade from the trees and hedges. There are opportunities for most watersports nearby and reception can arrange excursions by canoe through the nature reserve. Security is very good - if you want to leave before 8 am. you must make prior arrangements. There is a tour operator presence but it is not intrusive.

Facilities: The large, well maintained, modern toilet block is of a high standard. It provides some wash-basins in cabins, facilities for disabled visitors and dishwashing with hot water. Washing machines. Bar. Family restaurant/pizzeria. Supermarket. Large screen satellite TV/video. Children's play area. Table tennis. Swimming pools. Many organised activities and entertainment over a long season. Riding and children's donkey rides with cart. Exchange facilities. ATM. Torches required in some areas.

Charges 2002

Per person	€ 3.00
child (3-10 yrs)	€ 2.00
pitch incl. electricity	€ 6.00 - € 26.00

VAT included. No credit cards. **Tel:** 972 450 822. Fax: 972 452 330. E-mail: cmar@campingparks.com. **Reservations:** Necessary for July/Aug. and made with deposit (€ 12,02) for a min. of 8 days between 9/7-15/8. **Open** 11 May - 22 September.

Directions: From C260 Figueres - Roses road site is signed on the right (just after the turn off to the Empurio Brava complex); follow road for approx. 1.5 km.

Camping Internacional de Amberes

8020 Playa Salins, 17487 Empúria-brava (Girona)

Situated in the 'Venice of Spain', Empuria Brava is interlaced with inland waterways and canals, where many residents and holiday-makers moor their boats directly outside their homes on the canal banks. Internacional Amberes is large friendly site 50 m. from the wide, sandy beach, which is bordered on the east and west by the waterway canals (no access into them from the beach, only by car on the main road). The site can arrange temporary moorings for boats at Empuria Brava. The sea breeze here appears regularly during the afternoon so watersports are very good and hire facilities are available. Amberes is a surprisingly pretty and hospitable site where people seem to make friends easily and get to know other campers and the staff, led by the manager of over 20 years, Costa Verges. The site has 600 hedged pitches enjoying some shade from strategically placed trees, 550 with electricity and water connections, and there are pleasant views from some parts. Unusually the swimming pool is on an elevated terrace, raised out of view of most onlookers with sunbathing areas and a small children's pool adjoining. A shallow river runs through the site and children can amuse themselves catching the colourful crawfish that abound here.

Facilities: Toilet facilities are in four fully equipped and recently renovated blocks. Washing machines. Motorcaravan services. Supermarket. Restaurant/bar. Disco bar and restaurant. Takeaway. Pizzeria. Watersports - windsurfing school. Boat moorings. Organised sports activities, children's programmes and entertainment. Swimming pool. Children's playgrounds. Football. Table tennis. Tennis. Volleyball. Apartments. **Off site:** Bicycle hire, riding or fishing 500 m. Golf 12 km.

Charges 2002

Per person over 3 yrs	€ 2.80
pitch incl. electricity (55 sq.m.)	€ 7.00 - € 18.00
pitch 70 sq.m.	€ 9.00 - € 29.00
pitch 85 sq.m.	€ 10.80 - € 22.50
pitch 100 sq.m.	€ 12.00 - € 24.80

Less 20% for pensioners for stays of 15 days or over in low seasons. **Tel:** 972 450 507. Fax: 972 451 772. E-mail: info@inter-amberes.com. **Reservations:** Contact site for booking form. **Open** 1 April - 15 October.

Directions: Site is signed from main roundabout leading into Empuria Brava from Roses - Castello d'Empuries road (4 km. from Roses).

Camping Mas Nou

Ctra. Figueres-Roses, km 38, 17486 Castelló d'Empúries (Girona)

Some two kilometres from the sea on the Costa Brava, this is a surprisingly tranquil site. Split into two parts, one contains pitches and sanitary blocks and the other houses the impressive leisure complex. There are 450 neat, level and marked pitches on grass and sand, a minimum of 70 sq.m. but most 80-100 sq.m, and 300 with electrical connections (6/10A). The leisure complex is 80 metres from the main site across a very quiet road and features a huge L-shaped swimming pool with a paddling area. A more formal restaurant with ajoining bar, pleasant terrace crêperie and rotisseria under palms. Another barbeque/rotisseria in another part of the site offers takeaway meals (in season). The site owns the large souvenir shop on the entrance road. There are many traditional bargains here and it is worth having a good look around as the prices are extremely good. Lots of time and money goes into the cleanliess of this site and it is good very for families. Ask about the origin of the site coat of arms. The Bay of Roses and the Medes islands have a natural beauty and a visit to Dali`s house or the museum (the house is fascinating) will prove he was not just a surrealist painter.

Facilities: Three excellent, fully equipped sanitary blocks include baby baths, good facilities for disabled visitors. These are amongst the best we have seen. Dishwashing and laundry sinks. Washing machines. facilities. Supermarket and other shops close by. Bar/restaurant. Takeaway. Swimming pool with lifeguard (from 1/6). Tennis. Minigolf. Basketball. Volleyball. Football. Mini-club in dedicated building (July/Aug). Table tennis. Children`s playground. Electronic games. **Off site:** Riding 1.5 km. Fishing or bicycle hire 2 km. Beach 2.5 km. National Park. Aquatic Park. Romanica tour of famous local churches.

Charges 2002

Per person	€ 3.60 - € 5.10
child (4-11 yrs)	€ 3.00 - € 3.40
caravan or tent	€ 3.60 - € 5.10
car or motorcycle	€ 3.60 - € 5.10
motorcaravan	€ 7.20 - € 10.20
electricity	€ 2.60 - € 2.70

All plus 7% VAT. **Tel:** 972 454 175. Fax: 972 454 358. E-mail: masnou@intercom.es. **Reservations:** Write to site. **Open** 12 April - 28 September.

Directions: From A7 use exit 3. Mas Nou is 2 km. east of Castelló d'Empúries, on the Roses road, some 10 km. from Figueres.

Camping L'Amfora

Avenida Josep Tarradellas 2, 17470 San Pedro Pescador (Girona)

This is a friendly, colourful family site with a Greek theme, which is manifested mainly in the restaurant and pool areas. The site is clean and well kept and the owners are keen to operate in an environmentally friendly way. There are 850 pitches, all with electrical connections and most with a water tap, on level grass with small trees and shrubs. Of these, 64 pitches are large (180 sq.m.), made for two units per pitch and each with an individual sanitary facility. This feature consists of small blocks containing six units (toilet, shower and washbasin), each unit 'owned' by one pitch for their stay - virtually 'en-suite' camping. Further new, separated pitches of 90 sq.m. have been developed with limited shade as yet. An inviting terraced bar and self-service restaurant overlook two large swimming pools (and one for children) which are divided by an attractive arch and fountain. A third pool has been added recently with two water slides. Ambitious evening entertainment (pub, disco, shows) and children's animation are organised in season and a choice of water-sports activities is available on the beach.

Facilities: In addition to the individual units, the two main sanitary blocks (one heated) offer free hot water, washbasins in cabins, hairdryers and baby rooms. There is extra provision near the pool area. Access is good for disabled visitors. Laundry facilities. Terraced bar, self service and waiter service restaurants, takeaway and pizza service. Restaurant and bar on the beach with limited menu. Disco-bar for the young. Supermarket. Swimming pools, one new with slides. Table tennis. New tennis courts. Bicycle hire. Minigolf. Football. Volleyball. Playground. Entertainment and organised activities for children. Evening shows. Windsurfing school. Sailing. Riding (in season). Doctor daily in season. Exchange facilities. Internet point. Car wash. Torches required in beach areas.

Charges 2003

Per person	€ 2.90 - € 3.70
child (2-9 yrs)	free - € 3.00
pitch (100 sq.m.)	€ 11.50 - € 28.00
pitch with individual sanitary unit	€ 16.00 - € 38.00
large pitch (180 sq.m.) with sanitary unit	€ 18.50 - € 90.00
dog	€ 1.40 - € 3.40

Electricity (10A) included. Plus 7% VAT. Discounts for pensioners for longer stays. No credit cards. **Tel:** 972 520 540. Fax: 972 520 539. E-mail: info@campingamfora.com. **Reservations:** Made with deposit (€ 61) and fee (€ 15,03); write to site. **Open** 11 March - 28 September.

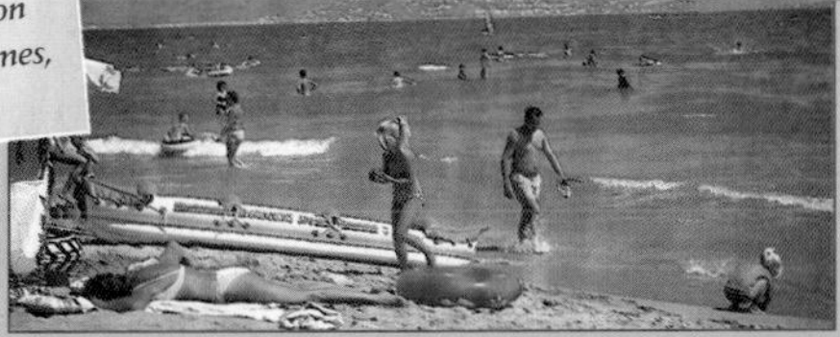

Directions: From A7 motorway take exit 3 (N-11) towards Girona/Barcelona. Exit for Figueres/Roses towards Roses on the C260 and, 9 km. before Roses turn right to Sant Pere Pescador. Site is signed through town.

Spain - Cataluña
Camping Nautic Almata

8030 Ctra. St Pere Pescador, km 11.6, 17486 Castelló d'Empúries (Girona)

Situated in the Bay of Roses, south of Empuria Brava and beside the Parc Natural dels Aiguamolls de l`Empordà, this is a site of particular interest for nature lovers (especially bird watchers). Beautifully laid out, it is arranged around the river and waterways, so will suit those who like to camp close to water or and those who enjoy watersports and boating. It is worth visiting because of its unusual aspects and the feeling of being on the canals, as well as being a high quality beach-side site. As you drive through the natural park to the site watch for the warning signs for frogs on the road and enjoy the wild flamingos alongside the road. It is a large site with 1,109 well kept, large, numbered pitches, all with electricity and on flat, sandy ground. There are some pitches right on the beach. The name no doubt derives from the fact that boats can be tied up at the small marina within the site and a slipway also gives access to a river and thence to the sea. Throughout the season there is a varied entertainment programme. The facilities on this site are impressive. Some tour operators use the site.

Facilities: Sanitary blocks all of a high standard, attractively decorated. include some en-suite showers with basins, taps to draw hot water for dishwashing, laundry sinks and baby baths. Good facilities for disabled visitors and ramps where necessary. Washing machines. Gas supplies. Excellent supermarket. Restaurant and bar (recently refurbished), rotisserie and pizzeria near pool. Two separate bars by beach where discos held in main season. Waterski and windsurfing schools. 300 sq. m. swimming pool. Tennis, squash, volleyball, fronton all free. Minigolf. Games room with pool and table tennis. Extensive riding tuition with own stables and stud. Children's play park (near river). Car, motorcycle and bicycle hire. Hairdresser. Torches are useful near beach. **Off site:** National Park and wetlands around site. Canal trips 18 km. Aquatic Park 20 km. Adventure sports 40 km. Excursions to Barcelona, Monserrat, Andorra and Dahli's museum.

Charges 2003

Per pitch	€ 16.50 - € 33.00
person (over 3 yrs)	€ 1.45 - € 2.90
dog	€ 3.60 - € 4.60
boat or jetski	€ 5.65 - € 7.90

All plus 7% VAT. No credit cards. **Tel:** 972 454 477. Fax: 972 454 686. E-mail: info@almata.com. **Reservations:** Write to site. **Open** 17 May - 21 September, including all facilities.

Directions: Site is signed at 26 km. marker on C252 between Castello d'Empuries and Vildemat, then 7 km. to site. Alternatively, on San Pescador - Castello d'Empuries road head north and site is signed on right.

Spain - Cataluña
Camping-Caravaning La Laguna

8015 Apdo. de Correos 55, 17486 Castelló d'Empúries (Girona)

La Laguna is a relaxed, spacious site on an isthmus within a Catalan national maritime park. It has direct access to the sandy beach and estuary of the river Muga. The new owners are spending much time and effort to improve the site. La Laguna as the name suggests has a large lagoon in two parts within the site. The approach is by a long (4 km), more or less, private road. This is quite an unusual site for this area, being laid out very informally among mature pine trees, in contrast to the other large, more formally designed sites nearby. The 793 pitches are clearly marked on grass and sand, all with 6A electricity (a long lead may be useful). The facilities, particularly the sanitary installations, are in quite elderly buildings but have been well renovated and are very clean. An attractive bar restaurant overlooks the lagoon and there is a pool (July/Aug) and a disco across the road from reception. The beach frontage is large and a sailing school operates from here. The river Muga running along one side of the site is hidden by a high bank with a path along the top and there are many pleasant walks in this area. With the planned improvements this will be a very pleasant, natural site but it is a pleasant site for family holidays now.

Facilities: Four toilets blocks, placed to avoid long walks, are simple in design. All recently renovated, they are adequate, with free hot water. Showers are unisex but we are assured that this will change. Plenty of dishwashing sinks. Well equipped laundry room. Bar. Restaurant. Supermarket. Swimming pool (15/5-30/9). Tennis (free in low seasons). ATM. Minigolf. Sailing school (July/Aug). Fishing. Mini-club. Bicycle hire. Riding. Dinner dance weekly. 24 hour photo service. Animation programme and competitions. **Off site:** Golf 15 km.

Charges 2002

Per person	€ 3.60 - € 6.25
child (3-10 yrs)	€ 2.95 - € 4.80
tent or caravan	€ 3.60 - € 6.25
car	€ 3.60 - € 6.25
motorcycle	€ 2.95 - € 4.80
motorcaravan	€ 6.85 - € 11.20
electricity	€ 2.95

Discounts for longer stays and pensioners. No credit cards. **Tel:** 972 45 05 53. Fax: 972 45 07 99. E-mail: info@campinglaguna.com. **Reservations:** Contact site. **Open** 1 March - 22 October.

Directions: Site is signed from Castello d'Empuries bypass (C260 Figures - Roses) and is on the junction with the road for Sant Pere Pescador (huge signs). Follow approach road for approx. 4 km.

Camping Aquarius

8050 Playa s/n, 17470 Sant Pere Pescador (Girona)

A smart and efficient family site, Aquarius has direct access to a quiet sandy beach that slopes gently and provides good bathing (the sea is shallow for quite a long way out). The site is ideal for those who really like sun and sea, with a quiet situation. One third of the site has good shade with a park-like atmosphere with the great variety of plants here being carefully labelled (Mr Rupp the owner is an enthusiast). An extension with less shade provided an opportunity to enlarge the pitches and they are now all at least 70-100 sq.m. which is good for Spain. A total of 447 are numbered with 400 electrical connections (6A). The owner has an architectural background and a wealth of knowledge on the whole Catalan area and culture. He has written a booklet of tours (from reception). The whole family are justifiably proud of their most attractive site and they continually make improvements. The fountain at the entrance, the fishponds and the water features in the restaurant are soothing and pleasing. A small stage close to the restaurant is used for live entertainment in season. The spotless beach bar complex with shaded terraces and minigolf has marvellous views over the Bay of Roses. The 'Surf Center' with rentals, school and shop is ideal for enthusiasts and beginners alike.

Facilities: Attractively tiled, fully equipped, large toilet blocks provide some cabins for each sex. Excellent facilities for disabled people, plus baths for children and hot water for sinks. A superb new block has under-floor heating and features family cabins with showers and basins. Laundry facilities. Gas supplies. Car wash. Motorcaravan services. Full size refrigerators. Supermarket with butcher. Pleasant restaurant and bar with terrace. Bar by beach serving snacks. Takeaway. Children's play centre (open all season and with qualified attendant), playground near the beach and games hall. TV room with giant screen and ample comfortable seating. 'Surf Center'. Table tennis. Volleyball. Minigolf. Bicycle hire. Football field. Boules. Barbecue and dance once weekly when numbers justify. Security boxes. Exchange facilities. ATM. Electronic games. Dogs are accepted in one section. **Off site:** Fishing 3 km. Riding 3 km. Golf 15 km.

Charges 2002

Per adult	€ 2.75 - € 3.20
child (2-12 yrs)	€ 2.00 - € 2.30
pitch acc. to season and facilities	€ 9.60 - € 27.75
Individual sanitary unit	€ 3.00 - € 9.50
electricity	€ 2.50
animal	€ 2.30 - € 2.50

All plus 7% VAT. Discounts for pensioners on longer stays. No credit cards. **Tel:** 972 520 003. Fax: 972 550 216. E-mail: camping@aquarius.es.
Reservations: made for any length with £50 deposit and £15 fee. (you are strongly advised to book early for any pitch near the beach). **Open** all year except 11 Jan. - 14 March.

Directions: Turn off main road by bridge south of Sant Pere Pescador and follow camp signs.

Camping Estartit

8075 Calle Villa Primavera 12, 17258 L'Estartit (Girona)

This friendly, Belgian run site has limited facilities, but is only 300 m. from Estartit town. A short walk down the hill brings you into the heart of the town which is extremely popular and very commercialised, although you can find authentic tapas bars and street entertainment. The site itself is surprisingly quiet, considering its proximity to the town. Set amongst tall pine trees (which provide complete shade), in a narrow valley, it has 160 terraced pitches, all with electrical connections (2/6A). These are best suited for campers with tents as there are some very steep drops between the terraces. However, there are two sand/gravel areas for a small number of motorcaravans and caravans (booking essential in high season), separated by a small drainage canal. The local beaches are extremely good but if the town is too frenetic the site has a very small pool plus a sunbathing area with loungers. An attractive shaded area has a terrace beside the bar. Access around the site could be difficult for disabled people.

Facilities: One modern, fully tiled sanitary block provides hot and cold showers (small fee for hot water), small laundry with washing machines and a separate baby area. Gas supplies. Bar/restaurant (1/6-15/9). Shop (1/6-15/9). Swimming pool (all season). Limited, small children's play area. Children's activities and adult social events (barbecue, bingo, etc). Excursions can be booked. Site is guarded day and night. Torches are necessary in the more remote parts of the site. Dogs are not accepted in high season (20/6-20/8). **Off site:** Fishing, bicycle hire and riding within 1 km. Golf 7 km.

Charges 2002

Per person	€ 2.34 - € 3.91
child (2-10 yrs)	€ 1.53 - € 2.52
caravan or family tent	€ 2.43 - € 4.21
car	€ 2.16 - € 3.16
motorcaravan	€ 4.33 - € 7.21
electricity (2/6A)	€ 2.10 - € 2.50
motorcycle	€ 1.53 - € 2.50

Plus 7% VAT. Less 10-30% outside high season (10/6-31/8). No credit cards. **Tel:** 972 751 909. Fax: 972 750 991. **Reservations:** Contact site. Winter address (15/10-15/3) Vrancken Joss, Plantenstraat 74, 3500 Hasselt, Belgium. **Open** Easter/1 April - 1 October.

Directions: Site is signed from Estartit town centre. Follow the one-way system.

Camping Las Dunas

Ctra S M d'Empuries - S Pere, 17470 Sant Pere Pescador (Girona)

8040

Las Dunas is an extremely large, impressive and well organised site with many on site activities and an ambitious programme of improvements. It has direct access to a superb sandy beach that stretches along the site for nearly 1 km. with a windsurfing school and beach bar. There is also a much used swimming pool with large double children's pools. Las Dunas is very large, with 1,500 individual hedged pitches of around 100 sq.m. laid out on flat ground in long, regular parallel rows. Electrical connections are provided on most pitches and shade is available in some parts of the site. Much effort has gone into planting palms and new trees here and the results are very attractive (find the 600 year old olive tree - it is easier than you think). Pitches are usually available, even in the main season. The large restaurant and bar have spacious terraces overlooking the swimming pools and you can enjoy a very pleasant more secluded cavern styled pub. A magnificent disco club is close by, in a soundproof building which has been cleverly painted to merge it with the blue skies of the Costa Brava backgound. It is reputedly the biggest on the Costa Brava and extremely popular. With free quality entertainment of all types in season and positive security arrangements, this is a great site for families with teenagers. Everything is provided on site and you do not have to leave during your stay. Used by British tour operators.

Facilities: Five excellent large toilet blocks (with resident cleaners 0700-2100 hrs) have British style toilets, controllable hot showers and washbasins in cabins. One block has underfloor heating and automatic doors for cooler weather. Excellent facilities for youngsters, babies and disabled people. Laundry facilities. Motorcaravan services. Extensive supermarket with superb butcher and other shops. Large bar with terrace. Large restaurant. Themed pub. Takeaway. Ice-cream parlour. Beach bar in main season. Disco club. Swimming pool (30 x 14 m) with children's pool. Playgrounds. Tennis. Minigolf. Football and rugby pitches. Basketball. Boule. Volleyball. Sailing/windsurfing school and other watersports. Organised programme of events - sports, children's games, evening shows, music and entertainment, partly in English (15/6-31/8). Exchange facilities. ATM. Safety deposit. Dogs taken in only one section mid June-mid Sept. Torches required in some areas.

Charges 2002

Per adult	€ 2.70
child (2-10 yrs)	€ 2.25
standard pitch incl. electricity	€ 11.72 - € 30.05
pitch with water and drainage	€ 12.92 - € 33.06
dog	€ 2.40 - € 5.50

All plus 7% VAT. **Tel:** 972 520 400. Fax: 972 550 046. E-mail: info@campinglasdunas.com. **Reservations:** made for numbered pitches with deposit and fee. Address for information: Apdo. de Correus 23, 17130 La Escala (Girona). **Open** 9 May - 25 September.

Directions: Use autostrada exit no. 5 towards Escala and turn north 2 km. before reaching La Escala at sign to St Martin de Ampurias. Site is well signed on this road.

Camping La Escala

Cami Ample, 17130 L'Escala (Girona)

8070

Under the same ownership as Las Dunas (no. 8040), but a complete contrast in terms of size, this is a neat, tidy and small site with limited facilities. It takes just five minutes to walk to either the very pleasant beach or to the centre of this modestly sized, lively, yet historic holiday resort. Here you will find most of the usual seaside attractions. The site has a canopy of fir trees giving excellent shade and the pitches are level and marked. They have managed to carve over 200 out of the area so they are small - just room for the car and caravan or tent - but all pitches have electricity, water and drainage. In season there is a bar and restaurant offering very good food with a pleasant enclosed terrace with a retractable candy-striped canopy. There is some road noise despite the very high wall between the site and the busy road alongside.

Facilities: The central toilet block is basic but clean, with British style toilets, washbasins (two in cabins for ladies), free hot water and 25 free showers. Dishwashing and laundry sinks with hot water. Shop, bar and restaurant (all high season). Basic children's play area.

Charges 2002

Per adult	€ 2.10
child (2-10 yrs)	€ 1.80
pitch incl. electricity	€ 10.60 - € 14.21
dog	€ 2.10 - € 2.70

All plus 7% VAT. **Tel:** 972 770 008. Fax: 972 550 046. **Reservations:** Not normally necessary. **Open** Easter - 25 September.

Directions: Site lies on the north side of the town and the beach. The access road feeds you to the beach road. Turn left into Cami Ample and site is on the right in 200 m. (watch for site name on wall and gate in high wall). Take care on the approach as there are few signs for this site in town.

Camping La Ballena Alegre 2

8060 San Pedro Pescador, 17470 San Pedro Pescador (Girona)

La Ballena Alegre 2, sister site to the Ballena Alegre south of Barcelona, is a big, relaxed site taking 1,675 units, partly in a lightly wooded setting, partly open, and with some 1,800 m. of frontage directly onto an excellent beach of soft golden sand (cleaned daily). The site has won Spanish tourist board awards and is keen on ecology. The grass pitches are individually numbered and of decent size (over 200 are 100 sq.m.). Electrical connections (5A) are available in all parts and there are 70 fully serviced pitches. There are restaurant and bar areas beside the pleasant pool complex. For those who wish to drink and snack late there is a pub open until 03.00 hrs. The soundproof disco has a covered approach and is firmly managed. A little train ferries people along the length of the site. Plenty of entertainment and activities are offered, including a well managed watersports centre, including windsurfing and sub-aqua, where equipment can be hired and lessons taken. You can also use a comprehensive open air fitness centre near the beach. A full animation programme is provided all season. A great site for families.

Facilities: All seven toilet blocks have been refurbished to a very high standard. These feature large pivoting doors for showers, wash cabins, etc, special low facilities for children, baby baths and facilities for disabled campers. Launderette. Motorcaravan services. Gas supplies. Supermarket. Chemist shop. Bar and self-service restaurant. Full restaurant (evenings all season). Takeaway. 'Croissanterie'. Pizzeria and beach bar in high season. Swimming pool complex (all season). Three tennis courts. Table tennis. Watersports centre. Fitness centre. Bicycle hire. Playgrounds. Sound proofed disco. Dancing twice weekly and organised activities, sports, entertainment, etc. all season but it is generally a quiet site. Safe deposit. Cash point. Resident doctor and site ambulance. Car wash. Dogs allowed in one zone. Internet point. Torches useful in beach areas. **Off site:** Go-karting nearby with bus service. Fishing 300 m. Riding 2 km.

Charges 2002

Per person	€ 3.30
child (3-9 yrs)	€ 2.40
pitch incl. electricity	€ 14.90 - € 30.50
serviced pitch plus	€ 6.00 - € 11.00

All plus 7% VAT. Discount of 10% on pitch charge for pensioners all season. No credit cards. **Tel:** 902 500 526. Fax: 902 500 527. E-mail: infb2@ballena-alegre.es. **Reservations:** made with deposit (€ 145), min. 10 days 10/7-10/8; contact site for details. Winter address: Ave. Roma 12, 08015 Barcelona. **Open** 15 May - 27 September.

Directions: From A7 Figueres - Girona autopista take exit 5 to L'Escala Cl623 for 18.5 km. At roundabout take sign to San Martin d'Empúries and follow camp signs.

Camping El Delfin Verde

8080 Ctra de Torroella de Montgri, 17257 Torroella de Montgrí (Girona)

A large, popular and high quality site in a quiet location, El Delfin Verde has its own long beach stretching along its frontage which campers have to themselves. A feature of the site is an attractive large pool in the shape of a dolphin with a total area of 1,800 sq.m. This has two island areas, one containing a huge fountain which can be lit at night. In the main season an elevated area with a large bar, full restaurant and a takeaway give wonderful views over the huge pool. There is a further restaurant with slightly cheaper, good value food in the main complex. This is a large site with nearly 6,000 visitors at peak times, well managed with friendly staff. Level grass pitches nearer the beach are marked and many are separated by small fences and newly planted hedging. All have electricity and access to water points and a stream runs through the centre of the site. There is shade in some of the older parts and a particularly pleasant area of pine trees in the centre provides marked but not separated pitches (sandy and not so level). El Delfin Verde is a large and cheerful holiday site with many good facilities and free family entertainment in season. Used by British tour operators.

Facilities: Six excellent large toilet blocks and a seventh smaller block, all with resident cleaners, have fully controllable showers using desalinated water and of good, comfortable size, and some washbasins in cabins. Laundry facilities. Motorcaravan services. Supermarket and other shops. Swimming pools (with lifeguard). Two restaurants, grills and pizzerias. Three bars - the main one closes 11 pm, pool bar open until 1 am; small bar by beach open in season. 'La Vela' barbecue and party area. Large sports area, football, volleyball, 8 tennis courts. 2 km. exercise track. Dancing and floor shows weekly in season. Disco. Excursions organised. General room with TV. Video room. Games room. Bicycle hire. Minigolf. Children's playground. Trampolines. Badminton. Fishing. Hairdresser. Car repairs, servicing and washing. Gas supplies. Dogs are not accepted in high season (15/7-18/8). **Off site:** Golf 4 km (20% discount). Riding 4 km.

Charges 2002

Per person	€ 3.00
child (2-9 yrs)	€ 2.25
pitch incl. electricity	€ 18.00 - € 33.00
dog (excl. 15/7-15/8)	€ 2.50

All plus 7% VAT. Special offers on long stays in low season. **Tel:** 972 758 454. Fax: 972 760 070. E-mail: eldelfinverde@drac.com. **Reservations:** Only a guarantee to admit - no specific pitch allocated. Write (all year) with deposit (€ 91). **Open** 23 March - 27 October, incl shops.

Directions: A very long approach road leads off the Torroella de Montgri - Palafrugell road (watch carefully for the sign); site is signed at the end of it.

Camping Castell Montgri

8007

Ctra Toroella - L'Estartit, km 4.7, 17258 Estartit (Girona)

This is a large bustling site with all the modern paraphernalia of holiday-making. With around 80% of the site dedicated to catering for tour operators, it may come as a surprise that we should choose to feature it in a guide for independent campers and caravanners. However, the site does include three designated areas for independent campers and these provide terraced and flat, pitches, some shaded but all with electricity. On arrival you are invited to find your own place. There is a busy bar/restaurant and terrace overlooking an attractive swimming pool with a pair of water slides (one large with attendant) close to these areas. The remainder of the site offers a very wide range of amenities and attractions, including one further, large pool with restaurant/bar and terrace areas higher on the site. There are also two independent mini-pools for toddlers around the site along with various play areas, disco, sports facilities and a live entertainment programme. This site could be of interest to families with teenagers, offering the possibility for parents to rest whilst the youngsters enjoy their own type of holiday within the confines of the site.

Facilities: Toilet facilities are quite adequate, if not that luxurious, each area of the site having its own block, with dishwashing (H&C) and laundry facilities. Cleaning is continual (06.00-22.00 hrs). Bars and restaurants. Pizzeria. Takeaway. Swimming pools. Supermarket and souvenirs. Football field. Tennis. Table tennis. Billiards. Volleyball. Minigolf. Children's playground. Large screen TV and videos. Disco. Entertainment programme and excursions. Exchange and safe deposit facilities. Car wash. Gas supplies. Free site bus to L'Estartit. Torches required in some areas. **Off site:** Fishing 300 m. Bicycle hire 1 km. Riding 500 m. Golf 10 km. Seaside entertainment in Estartit.

Charges 2002

Per person	€ 3.00
child (3-10 yrs)	€ 2.00
pitch incl. car and electricity	€ 7.00 - € 28.00

Prices include VAT. Minimum 7 day stay 6/7-18/8. Good discounts in low season. No credit cards. **Tel:** 972 751 630. Fax: 972 750 906. E-mail: cmontgri@ campingparks.com. **Reservations:** made with non-returnable deposit (€ 12,02), to guarantee admission only. **Open** 11 May - 6 October.

Directions: Site is on main Torroella de Montgri - L'Estartit road GE641 just north of the town, clearly signed alongside a huge complex called 'Jocs'.

Camping Les Medes

8072 Paratge Camp De L'Arbre, 17258 L'Estartit (Girona)

Les Medes is different from some of the 'all singing, all dancing' sites so popular along this coast and the friendly family of Pla-Coll are rightly proud of their award wining site. Set back from busy L'Estartit itself, it is only 800 m. to the nearest beach and a little train runs from near the site (June-Sept) to the town. With just 172 pitches, the site is small enough for the owners to know their visitors and, being campers themselves, they have been careful in planning their top class facilities. The level, grassy pitches range in size from 60-80 sq.m. All have electricity and the larger ones (around half) also have water and drainage. All are clearly marked in rows, but with no separation other than by the deciduous trees which provide summer shade. A cheery children's pool with fountains is behind the unusually shaped pool ringed by palms. This is part of an attractively landscaped feature producing a relaxing atmosphere in front of the old Catalan farmhouse buildings. A classy indoor pool (heated) with sauna and solarium and good access for disabled campers is a great option out of high season. The Medes islands are very pretty and worth exploring or a bad weather day could be used to visit Salvador Dali`s amazing house.

Facilities: Two modern, spacious sanitary blocks, can be heated and are extremely well maintained, providing washbasins in private cabins, top class facilities for disabled people and baby baths. Washing machines and dryer. Dishwashing and laundry sinks. Motorcaravan services. Bar with TV and snacks (all year). Restaurant (1/4-31/10). Shop (all year, but only basics in winter). Outdoor swimming pool and paddling pool (15/6-15/9) with drinks stall. Indoor pool with sauna, solarium (15/9-15/6). Masseur. Children`s play area with for games. Indoor children`s area. TV room. Internet terminals. Excursions organised in July/Aug. Diving activities arranged. Giant chess. Table tennis. Volleyball. Boules. Quality information folder on arrival. Bicycle hire. Diving organised from site. Tours arranged. Dogs are accepted in parts of two low season periods - check with the site. Environmentally friendly. Torches are useful. **Off site:** Fishing 800 m. Riding 400 m. Golf 8 km. Nearest beach 800 m. Estartit 2 km. Medes Natural Reserve 1.5 km.

Charges 2003

Per person	€ 3.00 - € 5.00
child (0-10 yrs)	€ 1.85 - € 3.60
pitch	€ 6.60 - € 11.20
electricity	€ 3.20
dog	€ 1.80

All plus 7% VAT. Discounts outside high season and special offers for low season longer stays. No credit cards. **Tel:** 972 751 805. **Fax:** 972 750 413. **E-mail:** campingslesmedes@cambrescat.es. **Reservations:** Advised for July/Aug. Write to site with € 31 deposit. **Open** all year except November.

Directions: Site is signed from the main Torroella de Montgri - L'Estartit road GE641. Turn right after Camping Castel Montgri, at Joc`s hamburger/pizzeria and follow signs.

A 2 km from l'Estartit, one of the most beautiful and ecological-minded villages of the Costa Brava, only 800m from the beach. On our family site you will enjoy a fabulous holiday in the midst of nature. We have high quality installations: modern sanitary instal. With baby-baths, install. for the handicapped and free hot water, swimming pool (also indoors heated) bar, restaurant and supermarket... Leisure activities for the whole family: children's playground, watersports, bicycles for rent and a large programme of activities for all ages. And to relax a dive in our swimming pool with solarium and sauna.

telf.+34 972 751 805 - fax.+34 972 750 413 - www.campingslesmedes.com - campingslesmedes@cambrescat.es
paratge Camp de l'Arbre, apartado de correos, 140 - 17258 l'ESTARTIT, Girona   COSTA BRAVA

Camping Paradis

8074 Avenida de Montgó 260, 17130 L'Escala (Girona)

If you prefer a quieter site out of the very busy resort of L'Escala then this site is an excellent option. This large, friendly, family run site has a dynamic owner Marti, who is a most pleasant man with excellent English and very keen to help. The site is divided by the beach access road and has its own private access to the very safe and unspoilt beach. The site has 646 pitches, all with electricity (10A), some on sloping ground although the pitches themselves tend to be flat. Established pine trees provide shade for most places with more coverage on the western side of the site. Non-stop maintenance ensures that all facilities at this site are of a high standard. There are three swimming pools, the largest with an idyllic and most unusual setting on the top of a cliff overlooking the Bay of Roses. The site operates its own well equipped sub-aqua diving school and campers can experience a free diving experience in the pool or more adventurous coastal diving where appropriate. A CCTV security system monitors the pools and general security from a purpose built centre.

Facilities: Modern, fully equipped sanitary blocks are kept very clean. Washing machines and dryers. Shop (1/4-30/9). Extensive modern complex of restaurants, bars and takeaways (1/4-30/9). Takeaway (1/4-15/9). Swimming pools (1/5-20/10). Pool bar. Play areas. Fishing. Basketball, volleyball and badminton. Kayak hire. Sub aqua school. Organised activities for children in high season. ATM machine. Private access to beach. **Off site:** Cala Montgo beach 100 m. with a charming bay of soft sand offering all manner of watersports, pretty restaurants and a disco in season. Road train service to town centre from outside site. Riding 2 km. Golf 10 km.

Charges 2002

Per adult	€ 2.45 - € 4.17
child (3-9 yrs)	€ 1.75 - € 2.95
pitch	€ 9.75 - € 19.75
electricity	€ 3.00

Plus 7% VAT. No credit cards **Tel:** 972 770 200. Fax: 972 772 031. E-mail: info@campingparadis.com. **Reservations:** advisable in high season. **Open** 17 March - 20 October.

Directions: Leave autopista A7 at exit 5 heading for Viladimat, then L'Escala. Site is well signed from the town centre.

Camping Cypsela

8090 Ctra de Pals - Platja de Pals, 17256 Platja de Pals (Girona)

This impressive, de-luxe site with lush vegetation and trees has many striking features, of which one is the sumptuous complex of sport facilities and amenities. This provides a fine large swimming pool, a good children's pool and playgrounds, two excellent squash courts, a tennis court, fitness room, and other entertainment rooms. These include a children's play-room with mini-club and organised enter-tainment (including video screen), an amusements room with pool tables, foot-ball tables, video games, and a luxurious air conditioned lounge for quality adult entertainment including piano concerts. This is not an exhaustive list. The 'Les Moreres' al fresco restaurant is very pleas-ant, with set meals at low cost, as well as a full menu, or there is another indoor restaurant offering a similar excellent serv-ice. You have the choice of a smart bar or the air conditioned cocktail bar. The main part of the camping area is pinewood, with 948 clearly marked pitches of varying cate-gories on sandy gravel, all with electricity and some with full facilities. The 202 'Elite' pitches of 120 sq.m. are impressive. Cypsela is a busy, well administered site, only 2 km. from the sea, which we can thoroughly recommend, especially for families. It is very efficiently run, with good quality fixtures and fittings, all kept clean. Several tour operators use the site.

Facilities: Four stylish sanitary 'houses' are of excel-lent quality with comprehensive cleaning schedules. Using solar heating, three have washbasins in cabins and three have amazing children's rooms with a battery of baby baths and larger ones for older chil-dren. Facilites for disabled people are superb. Serviced launderette. Ironing. Supermarket with great wines and other shops. Well appointed restaurant or cheaper meals served in cafeteria and a takeaway. Bar. Hairdresser. Swimming pools. Tennis. Squash. Table tennis. Football field. Minigolf. Fitness room. Air conditioned social/TV room. Barbecue and party area. Children's club. Comprehensive animation programme for children and adults in season. Organised sports and games activities. Games room with pool tables, electronic games etc. Free bus service to beach. Air conditioned telephone parlour. Business centre and internet centre. Doctor always on site; well equipped treatment room. Car wash. Gas supplies. ATM. Dogs are not accepted. **Off site:** Bicycle hire 150 m. Golf 6 km. Fishing 2 km.

Charges 2002

Per person	€ 5.10
child (2-10 yrs)	€ 4.10
pitch acc. to season and services	€ 24.75 - € 41.00
electricity	€ 2.70

Tel: 972 667 696. Fax: 972 667 300. E-mail: info@cypsela.com. **Reservations:** Contact site. **Open** 11 May - 22 September.

Directions: Cypsela is on the road from Torroella de Montgri to Bagur (Begur) to Platja de Pals.

Camping Playa Brava

8101 Avda. del Grau 1, 17256 Platja de Pals (Girona)

This is a pleasant site with an open feel which has access to a large sandy beach (200 m) and a freshwater lagoon. On both you can enjoy watersports and you may launch your own boat. The ground is level and very grassy with shade provided for the 500 pitches by a mixture of conifer and broad-leaf trees. Electricity is provided (10A) and about a third of the pitches (75-100 sq m) have water and drainage. The air of spaciousness continues around the large swimming pool and children's pool (lifeguard). There are no fences but huge grass sunbathing areas, the whole being overlooked by the restaurant and bar terrace. The restaurant is very pleasant and offers a most reasonable menu of the day including wine. An energetic entertainment programme runs during July and August. There are many interesting things to explore in the area including La Bisbal - famous for ceramics, Dali's Museum the Roman ruins at Empuries Girona and many more. A green and pleasant family site.

Facilities: Five modern, fully equipped toilet blocks include facilities for disabled visitors. Dishwashing facilities under cover. Washing machines and dryers. Bar/restaurant. Takeaway. Supermarket. Swimming pool (from 1/6). Tennis. Volleyball. Minigolf. Children's play area on grass. Fishing. Watersports on river and beach, including sheltered lagoon for windsurfing learners. Gas supplies. Torches required in some areas. Dogs are not accepted. **Off site:** Bicycle hire 3 km. Riding 5 km. 18 hole golf course 1 km.

Charges 2002

Per person	€ 1.40 - € 2.00
child	free - € 1.50
senior	free - € 2.00
75 sq.m. pitch incl. electricity	€ 19.20 - € 27.50
85 sq.m.	€ 22.40 - € 32.00

All plus 7% VAT. Discount for longer stays in low season. No credit cards. **Tel:** 972 636 894. Fax: 972 636 952. E-mail: info@playabrava.com. **Reservations:** Write to site. **Open** 19 May - 15 September.

Directions: Site is 3 km. north of village of Pals, in the direction of Platja de Pals. Follow road for 3 km. past golf course to beach; well signed.

Dreams can not be put into picture.

If you have ever dreamed about enjoying a deserved holiday, in a privileged surrounding, near the sea, in the middle of nature, with all the comfort,...
ask for our brochure and discover how your dreams can come true*

✉ CAMPING CYPSELA - 17256 PALS (Girona) SPAIN
☎ +34 972 667 696 - Fax +34 972 667 300
e-mail: info@cypsela.com http://www.cypsela.com

*Our special offers will make it even more easy for you.

Camping Mas Patoxas

Ctra Palafrugell-Pals, km 5, 17256 Pals (Girona)

8102

This is a mature and well laid out site for those who prefer to be apart from, but within easy travelling distance of the beaches (5 km) and town (1 km) in high season. It has a very easy access and is set on a slight slope with level terraces providing 450 grassy pitches of a minimum 72 sq.m. All have electricity (5A) and water, 150 have drainage as well. There are some very pleasant views and shade from a variety of mature trees. An air-conditioned restaurant/bar provides both waiter service meals and takeaway food to order (weekends only mid Sept - April) and entertainment takes place on a stage below the terraces during the high season. Both bar and restaurant terraces give views over the pools and distant hills. The restaurant menu is varied and very reasonable. We were impressed with the children's mini-club activity when we visited. There is a large irregular shaped swimming pool with triple flume, a separate children's pool (supervised) and a generous sunbathing area of the poolside and surrounding grass. Used by tour operators (40).

Facilities: Three modern sanitary blocks provide controllable hot showers, some washbasins with hot water, baby bath and three children's cabins with washbasin and shower. No specific facilities for disabled people, although access throughout the site looks to be relatively easy. Dishwashing facilities under cover (H&C). Laundry facilities. Restaurant/bar (1/4-30/9). Pizzeria. Takeaway. Well stocked shop (1/4-30/9). Swimming pool (15/6-30/9). Tennis. Table tennis. Volleyball. Football field. Entertainment in high season. Fridges for rent. Gas supplies. Torches useful in some areas. **Off site:** Bus service from site gate. Fishing, golf 4 km. Bicycle hire, riding 2 km

Charges 2002

Per person	€ 3.01 - € 4.81
child (1-10 yrs)	€ 2.40 - € 3.01
caravan pitch	€ 9.01 - € 15.03
tent pitch with car	€ 7.81 - € 12.02

Plus VAT @ 7%. Special low season offers. **Tel:** 972 636 928. Fax: 972 667 349. E-mail: info@ campingmaspatoxas.com. **Reservations:** Write to site. **Open** all year except 16 Dec - 18 Jan.

Directions: Site is east of Girona and about 1.5 km. south of Pals on the GE650 road to Palafugel.

Camping El Maset

Playa de Sa Riera, 17255 Begur (Girona)

8103

A delightful little gem of a site in lovely surroundings, El Maset has 109 pitches, of which just 14 are for caravans or motorcaravans, the remainder suitable only for tents. The owner of some 40 years, Sr Juan Perez is delightful, as is his secretary Josaphine. The site entrance is steep and access to the caravan pitches can be quite tricky. All these pitches have electricity, water and drainage with some shade. Access to the tent pitches, which are more shaded on attractive rock-walled terraces on the mountainside (more of a hill really!) seems quite straightforward, with parking for cars not too far away - of necessity the pitches are fairly small. All steep terraced pitches are safely fenced for children. A bar and homely restaurant offer excellent food. This small site provides the standard of service normally associated with the very best of the larger sites. It is in the tiny resort of Sa Riera with access to the beach (300 m), in a beautiful protected bay.

Facilities: Sanitary facilities are superb with marble tops, hair and hand dryers and soap. In three small blocks and very clean, they include new baby facilities. Top quality washing up area (H&C), industrial washing machines and dryers. Unit for disabled campers. Bar/restaurant, takeaway (all season). Shop (from May). Children's play area on astroturf. Area for football and basketball. Excellent new games room. Swimming pool (all season). Solarium. Dogs are not accepted. **Off site:** Fishing 300 m. Golf, bicycle hire 1 km. Riding 8 km.

Charges 2002

Per person	€ 3.90 - € 5.30
child (1-10 yrs)	€ 2.90 - € 3.90
caravan	€ 4.90 - € 6.60
tent	€ 3.20 - € 6.00
car	€ 3.90 - € 4.90
motorcaravan	€ 5.40 - € 7.20
electricity	€ 3.00 - € 4.00

Plus 7% VAT. Discount in low season for 7 day stay. **Tel:** 972 623 023. Fax: 972 623 901. E-mail: elmaset@jazzfree.com. **Reservations:** Write to site. **Open** 22 March - 24 September.

Directions: Site is 2 km. north of Begur (or Bagur). Follow signs for Playa de Sa Riera and site. Steep entrance.

CAMPING **EL MASET**

E-17255 BEGUR (Girona)
PLAYA DE SA RIERA COSTA BRAVA
Tel. (34) 972 62 30 23 Fax (34) 972 62 39 01
www.dlleure.com/Campings/elmaset.htm
elmaset@jazzfree.com

Only 300 yards from the beautiful Sa-Riera beach, with fabulous scenery and lovely surroundings, you will find Camping EL MASET, recommended for quiet, relaxing holidays with the whole family. Excellent, well-kept installations, free hot water, superm., bar-restaurant, games, sports, children`s playgr., comfortable studio-bungalows for 4-6 pers. (may be rented on a weekly basis). Totally independent terraced sites. English spoken. Free swimming pool . 10% discount in low season (after 1 week). In 1984 distinguished with the order for Touristic Merits by the Catalan Government. Facilities f. disabled. Caravans for hire.

Camping Relax-Nat

Montras, 17230 Palamos (Girona)

N8125

Enclosed by a perimeter wall, this extremely well maintained, small naturist site affords complete privacy. Set in pleasant countryside, eight hectares provide 300 pitches amongst a large variety of trees, spaced in such a manner as to provide sun and shade. There electricity hook-ups for all. Entering the site through the electronic gate, you will find English spoken at reception. From this point you overlook the terraces fronting the bar, shop and pools. Although the site does not have a restaurant, there are many in the area offering good Spanish cuisine. A small picturesque bay, typical of those to be found along the Costa Brava and only 6 km. from this base, is for use by naturists. Naturism is increasingly popular in Spain and reservation is advised.

Facilities: The main toilet block, completely refurbished to a high standard, provided partitioned hot showers (free), facilities for babies and a unit for disabled visitors. Shop. Bar. Snack bar. Swimming pools, one 30 x 12 m. from mid-May, a second smaller, heated one open all season with sun loungers, and a children's pool. Table tennis, boule, volleyball, basketball, football. Tennis (charged). Water activities. Minigolf. Two play areas and high season entertainment.

Charges guide

Per person	€ 3.91
child (under 10 yrs)	€ 2.94
pitch	€ 7.06 - € 11.72
electricity	€ 1.74

Plus VAT. **Tel:** 972 300818. Fax: 972 601100. E-mail: campingpal@grn.es. **Reservations:** Contact PB 19, 17230 Palamos (Girona) for details. **Open** 31 March - 30 September.

Directions: Travelling along road C31 Palafrugell - Palamos (formerly C255), site is on left just past km. stone 330 (opposite Mercamat store).

Kim's Camping

8120 Font d'en Xeco 1, 17211 Llafranc (Girona)

This attractive, terraced site is arranged on the wooded slopes of a narrow valley leading to the sea and there are many trees including huge eucalyptus. A steep lower area rises to a very pleasant plateau where all the amenities are located. With a total of 325 grassy and partly shaded pitches, many of the larger pitches are on the plateau enjoying great views. Pitches on the terraces are connected by winding drives, narrow in places. Most places have electrical connections (6A). The site has an excellent pool area with adult and small children's pools (lifeguard), a bar, charming restaurant with 'al fresco' eating. There are high standards of cleanliness and efficiency. The site is under 1 km. from the resort of Llafranc. This is a pleasant place for holidays where you can enjoy the bustling atmosphere of the town and beach, while staying in a quieter environment. The site provides an entertainment programme in high season and it is possible to organize a visit to the local sub-aqua schools for all levels of diving. There is an outstanding view along the coastline and of the Pyrenees from Cap Sebastian close by. English is spoken by the very friendly management and staff.

Facilities: Sanitary provision is adequate. Laundry facilities. Motorcaravan services. Well stocked shop. Bar. Croissanterie. Cafe/restaurant (15/6-20/9). TV room. Swimming pools (1/6-30/9). Tickets sold for the Girona bullfights. Excursions arrangesd - bus calls at site. Children's play areas. Torches required. Car wash. Gas supplies. **Off site:** Fishing, Glass bottomed boat in Lafranc. Bicycle hire 500 m. Riding 4 km. Golf 9 km.

Charges 2002

Per person	€ 2.52 - € 3.91
child (3-10 yrs)	€ 1.35 - € 2.10
pitch incl. electricity	€ 11.53 - € 18.03

Plus 7% VAT. Discounts for long stays and for senior citizens. **Tel:** 972 301 156. Fax: 972 610 894. E-mail: info@campingkims.com. **Reservations:** Made with deposit (€ 91). **Open** Easter - 30 September.

Directions: Turn off for Llafranc from Palafrugell - Tamariu road at turning signed 'Llafranc, Caella, Club Tenis'. Site is 1 km. further on, around a one-way circuit and is well signed.

1st. CATEGORY E-17211 LLAFRANCH

Tel: (34) 972 30 11 56 and 61   **Fax: (34) 972 61 08 94**
Internet: http://www.campingkims.com   E-mail: info@campingkims.com

CAMPING

KiM'S

LLAFRANC

COSTA BRAVA

1ᴬ CATEGORIA ★★★

One of the most beautifully situated camp sites on the Costa Brava in a landscaped green zone belt, at only 500m from the sea, with 2 swimming pools, children's playground, bar, restaurant, supermarket.

Only 325 sites (60-70-120 sqm) on a surface of 62,500 sq.m.

Bungalows and mobile homes for hire.

Open: Easter - 30.9

Camping Treumal

8140 Ctra 253, km 47.5, 17251 Calonge (Girona)

This very attractive terraced site has been developed on a hillside around the attractive gardens of a large, spectacular estate house which is close to the beach. The house is the focus of the site's excellent facilities, including a superb restaurant with terraces overlooking two tranquil beaches protected in pretty coves. The beaches are connected by a tunnel carved through solid rock through which you may safely walk. A multi-coloured, flower bedecked, and landscaped hillside leads down to the sea from the house with pretty paths and fishponds. There is a constant supply of fresh plants and flowers from the greenhouses which belonged to the house in yesteryear. In summer the house area is a blaze of colour and very appealing. The site which reaches back to the road has 572 pitches on well shaded terraces. Of these 444 are accessible to tourers and there are some 50 pitches on flat ground alongside the sea - the views are stunning and you wake to the sounds of the waves. There is a small (10 m) round swimming pool in the lower areas of the gardens, if you prefer fresh water. Cars may not park by tents or caravans in high season, but must be left on car parks or roads. Electrical connections are available in all parts.

Facilities: Three well maintained sanitary blocks have free hot water in the washbasins (with some private cabins) and the controllable showers, and a tap to draw from for the sinks. Washing machines. Motorcaravan services. Gas supplies. Supermarket. Bar. Takeaway. Good restaurant with attractive shaded terrace (15/5-15/9). Table tennis. Fishing. Children's play area and sports area. Games room. **Off site:** Bicycle hire 2 km. Riding, golf 5 km.

Charges 2002

Per person	€ 5.70
child (4-10 yrs)	€ 3.20
caravan, car and electricity	€ 20.80
motorcaravan and electricity	€ 19.20
tent, car and electricity	€ 19.90

Plus 7% VAT. Discounts in low seasons. No credit cards. **Tel:** 972 651 095. Fax: 972 651 671. E-mail: info@campingtreumal.com. **Reservations:** made to guarantee admission (needed more for caravans than for tents) with deposit. Contact site at Aptdo Correos 348, then address as above. **Open** 23 March - 30 September.

Directions: Access to site is signed from the C253 coast road 3 km. south of Palamos.

Camping Internacional de Palamos

8150 Apto. Correus 100, 17230 Palamos (Girona)

First impressions of this site are that it is unusual with a long perimeter wall covered with bright grafitti style murals. The site's strong point is the large swimming pool, plus children's pool, with attractive palms. It has a grass sunbathing area and its own modest white-washed bar/terrace in season. It might have space when others are full and has over 450 moderate sized, level, terraced pitches on a gentle slope. All pitches have a sink and variable shade, with electrical connections (6A) available in most parts. Access roads are gravel and may suffer in the case of heavy rain. Used by a tour operator (20). This is an improving site which is clean, welcoming and useful for exploring the local area from a peaceful base although it is pricey in high season.

Facilities: Three refurbished toilet blocks are fully equipped and include facilities for disabled people. Laundry room with washing machines, irons, etc. Small shop. Bar. Snack bar serving simple food and takeaway (from 1/6). Swimming pool (36 x 16 m.) with paddling pool. Torches necessary. **Off site:** Town 1 km. with hourly bus service. Nearest beach 400 m. Fishing 500 m. Bicycle hire or riding 1.5 km.

Charges 2002

Per person	€ 2.70 - € 2.98
child (under 10 yrs)	€ 1.98 - € 2.18
pitch for car and tent/caravan	€ 15.15 - € 31.37
tent pitch (motorcycle but no car)	€ 5.65 - € 12.51
electricity	€ 4.21

All plus 7% VAT. No credit cards. **Tel:** 972 314 736. Fax: 972 317 626. **Reservations:** Write to site with € 31 deposit. **Open** Easter - 29 September.

Directions: Cars can approach site from central Palamós, but town streets are too narrow for caravans which should turn off C255 road just outside Palamós to north by large garage, signed to Kings Camping and La Fosca, turn right just before Kings and from there follow Camping Internacional Palamos signs. Don't be confused by another site close by called Camping Palamos.

Camping Internacional de Calonge

8130 Ctra S Feliu/Guixols - Palamos km 7.4, 17251 Calonge (Girona)

This spacious, well laid out site has access to the fine beach by a footbridge over the coast road or you can take the little road train as the site is on very sloping ground. Calonge is a family site with two good sized pools on different levels, a paddling pool plus large sunbathing areas. These are overlooked by the restaurant terrace which has great views over the mountains. The site`s 800 pitches are on terraces and all have electricity (5A) with 167 available for winter use. A large proportion are suitable for touring units (the remainder for tents) being set on attractively landscaped terraces. Access to some pitches may be a little difficult. There is good shade from the tall pine trees and some views of the sea through the foliage, although the views from the upper levels are taken by the tour operator and mobile home pitches. A nature area within the site is used for walks or picnics. A separate area within the site is set aside for visitors with dogs.

Facilities: Generous sanitary provision in new or renovated blocks include some washbasins in cabins. One block is heated for winter use. Laundry facilities. Motorcaravan services. Gas supplies. Shop (Easter-30/10, supermarket 500 m). Bar/restaurant (Easter-30/10). Patio bar (pizza and takeaway). Swimming pools with lifeguard (1/4-30/10). Playground. Electronic games. Rather noisy disco two nights a week (but not late). Bicycle hire. Table tennis. Tennis. Volleyball. Hairdresser. ATM. Internet. Security boxes. Torches necessary in some areas. Good security. **Off site:** Fishing 300 m. Riding 10 km. Golf 3 km.

Charges 2003

Per adult	€ 3.30 - € 5.80
child (2-10 yrs)	€ 1.70 - € 3.30
caravan/tent incl. electricity	€ 11.75 - € 21.10
motorcaravan incl. electricity	€ 10.10 - € 16.80
dog	€ 3.00

All plus 7% VAT. Discounts for longer stays Oct - end May. No credit cards. **Tel:** 972 651 233. Fax: 972 652 507. E-mail: intercalonge@intercalonge.com. **Reservations:** Write with deposit (€ 37). UK contact: Mr J Worthington (0161) 799 9562. **Open** all year.

Directions: Site is on the inland side of the coast road between Palamos and Platja d'Aro take the C31 south to the 661 at Calonge. At Calonge follow signs to the C253 towards Platja d'Aro and on to site which is well signed.

Camping Cala Gogo

8160 Ctra St Feliu-Palamós, km 46.5, 17251 Calonge (Girona)

Cala Gogo is a large traditional campsite with a pleasant situation on a wooded hillside with mature trees giving shade to most pitches. A small cove of considerable natural beauty has a coarse sand beach and there is access to a further two small beaches along the sand. If you prefer fresh water there are two pools on the site. The campsite facilities are contained in a mature towering block which has a supermarket, shops, small restaurant and a bar all with an adjoining terrace enjoying views over the pools down to the sea. A second floodlit bar pleasant restaurant and a takeaway are on the beach and open in high season. The 665 shaded pitches vary in size in terraced rows, some with artificial shade, 300 have water and drainage (including chemicals). There may be road noise in eastern parts of the site. Some pitches are now right by the beach, the remainder are up to 800 m. uphill, but the two 'Gua gua' (South American Spanish for bus) tractor trains, operating all season, take people up and down and add to the sense of fun and energy that the site generates. It is an active, bustling place, with over 2,500 campers when full. A huge aqua-park close by offers amazing waterslides, wave simulation and all manner of water enjoyment and there is a bus from the site. Used by tour operators (52 pitches). This spacious, traditional site will appeal to some families.

Facilities: Seven toilet blocks are of a high standard and are continuously cleaned. Some washbasins are in private cabins. Laundry. Motorcaravan services. Gas supplies. Large supermarket. General shop. Restaurants and bars. Swimming pools (25 x 12 m.) and paddling pool with lifeguards. Playground. Crèche and babysitting service for smaller children (extra charge). Sports centre with tennis, volleyball, basketball, etc, plus a mini-club. Programme of animation including sports, TV and video programmes daily, tournaments, entertainment. Bicycle hire. Table tennis. Sailboards and pedaloes for hire. Fishing. TV/video room. Bureau de change. Medical service; nurse daily, doctor alternate days. Good 24 hr security service including video surveillance. Sponsored bus to local disco. Dogs are not accepted in July/Aug. **Off site:** Bicycle hire 4 km. Riding 10 km. Golf 4 km. Huge Aqua Park nearby with bus from site.

Charges 2002

Per person	€ 3.10 - € 5.95
child (2-9 yrs)	€ 1.50 - € 2.80
caravan or trailer tent	€ 5.00 - € 10.30
tent	€ 3.60 - € 8.50
car	€ 3.25 - € 5.95
motorcaravan	€ 5.50 - € 13.50
electricity (5A)	€ 3.20

Low season discounts. All plus 7% VAT. No credit cards. **Tel:** 972 651 564. Fax: 972 650 553. E-mail: calagogo@calagogo.es. **Reservations:** made for min. 1 week with deposit (€ 150). **Open** 27 April - 29 September, including amenities.

Directions: From A9 (Vidarus) take exit 9. Site is on inland side of coast road between Palamos and and Platja d'Aro on the C255 just south of Sa. Calogne and 4 km. South of Palamos and is well signed. If using the coast road, especially from the south, allow extra time as the road is very winding.

Spain - Cataluña
8232 Camping Bella Terra
17300 Blanes (Girona)

Our Spanish agent tells us that Camping Bella Terra is set in a shady pine grove facing a white sandy beach on the Mediterranean coast. It is a quiet and peaceful spot. The area is called 'Els Pins de Blanes' and is one of the prettiest places on the Costa Brava. It is easily accessible from the Spanish border and the city of Barcelona. A range of entertainment is provided under the supervision of experienced staff. There are 870 pitches with 590 for touring units, the rest taken by bungalows (some for rent). All pitches have 5/6A electricity and 24 are fully serviced.

Facilities: Fully equipped toilet facilities with provision for disabled visitors and laundry. Shop, restaurant, bar and takeaway (May - Sept). Outdoor swimming pool (May - Sept). Playground. Fishing. **Off site:** Golf 5 km.

Charges 2002

Per unit incl. 4 persons	€ 33.80 - € 87.40
incl. 6 persons	€ 42.20 - € 99.40

Tel: 972 348017. **Fax:** 972 348275. **E-mail:** cbellaterra@cbellaterra.com. **Reservations:** Contact site. **Open** 5 April - 30 September.

Directions: Site is south of Blanes. Follow signs from the town centre and site is just after Camping Blanes.

Camping Inter-Pals

Avda. Mediterrania, 17256 Platja de Pals (Girona)

8100

Sister site to no. 8170 and set on sloping ground, with tall pine trees providing shade and about 500 m. from the beach, this site has 625 terraced pitches (including 280 for touring units and 250 for tents), on terraces and levelled plots, mostly with shade. Some of the terraced pitches have views of the sea through the trees. The main entrance and its drive resembles a pretty village street as the bungalows are set on both sides of the street lined with traditional lamp-posts. Continuing the village theme is a row of shops where you will find most camper's needs. The site is close to Platja de Pals which is a long sandy unspoilt stretch of beach, a discreet area of which is now an official naturist beach. The formal restaurant with good value menu and choice of takeaway overlooks the pools. The pretty town of Pals is close by along with a good golf course. The site will assist with touring plans of the area.

Facilities: Three well maintained toilet blocks include individual washbasins, dishwashing and laundry sinks and facilities for disabled campers. Washing machines and dryers. Gas supplies. Fridge/TV rental. Medical centre. Excursions. ATM. Diving and watersport arranged. Shops. Restaurant/bar with Pizzeria/croissenterie with dancing and entertainment area. Cafe/bar by entrance. Swimming pool. Basketball, volleyball and badminton courts. Tennis. Children's playground and organised activities and entertainment in high season. Electronic games. Pool tables. Some breeds of dog are excluded - check with site. Torch useful. **Off site:** Fishing 200 m. Bicycle hire 500 m. Riding 10 km. Golf 1 km.

Charges 2002

Per person	€ 3.00 - € 4.20
child (3-10 yrs)	€ 2.00 - € 2.50
pitch	€ 14.00 - € 24.00
small tent and car	€ 12.00 - € 16.50
dog	€ 2.40

Plus 7% VAT. Discounts for long stays in low season. No credit cards. **Tel:** 972 636 179. Fax: 972 667 478. E-mail: interpals@interpals.com. **Reservations:** Made in the sense of guarantee to admit only, without deposit. Open 1 April - 30 September.

Directions: Site is on the road leading off the Torroella de Montgri-Bagur road north of Pals and going to Playa de Pals (Pals beach).

Camping Valldaro

8170 Apdo. Correus 57, Avda. Castell d'Aro, 63, 17250 Platja d'Aro (Girona)

Valldaro is 600 m. back from the sea at Platja de Aro, a small, bright resort with a long, wide beach and plenty of amusements. It is particularly pleasant out of peak weeks and is popular with the British. Like a number of other large Spanish sites, Valldaro has been extended and many pitches have been made larger, bringing them up to 80 or 100 sq.m. There are now 1,200 pitches with 800 available for tourers. The site is flat, with pitches in rows divided up by access roads. The newer section is accessed over a bridge and is brought into use at peak times. It has some shade and its own toilet block, as well as a medium-sized swimming pool of irregular shape with grassy sunbathing area and adjacent bar. You will probably find space here even at the height of the season. There are many permanent Spanish pitches but they are in a separate area and do not impinge on the touring pitches. The original pool (36 x 18 m.) is adjacent to the good Spanish-style restaurant which also offers takeaway fare.

Facilities: Sanitary facilities are of a reasonable standard, some with potted plants and patterned glass sink dividers. Children's size toilets. Individual washbasins with hot water and 136 free hot showers (temperature perhaps a bit variable). Two supermarkets and general shops. Restaurant. Large bar. Swimming pools. Tennis. Table tennis. Minigolf, with snack bar. Children's playgrounds. Sports ground with football and basketball. Organised entertainment in season. Hairdresser. Air conditioned telephone parlour. Gas supplies. Electrical connections throughout.

Charges 2002

Per person	€ 3.00 - € 4.50
child (2-10 yrs)	€ 2.00 - € 2.60
pitch incl. electricity	€ 14.00 - € 22.50
dog	€ 2.00

All plus 7 % VAT. Discounts in low seasons. **Tel:** 972 817 515. Fax: 972 816 662. E-mail: valldaro@ valldaro.com. **Reservations:** made only in the sense of guaranteeing admission without deposit. **Open** 15 March - 6 October.

Directions: Site entrance is off the road on which you approach Platja de Aro from Girona via Castillo de Aro. You can now also approach it from the Sant Feliu - Girona road.

Beach Camp El Pinar

8230 Avenida Villa de Madrid, 17300 Blanes (Girona)

Previously named Camping El Pinar, this is pleasant, family orientated site adjoining a good beach. The new name sums up the direction in which the owners are developing the site, with an emphasis on a more participatory approach to camping with an increase in the amount of activities and facilities offered - mostly directed towards sports. It is situated at the southern edge of Blanes beach, with direct access, and is about 2 km. from the town. The 690 pitches (250 on the new side), all with electricity and a minimum of 60 sq.m. are in two sections separated by the road with both sides having direct access to the beach. The older side is mostly shaded by pine or broad leaf trees, the newer part has young trees that do not offer a great deal of shade as yet. The newer side has its own modern sanitary block and a large swimming pool with a generous sunbathing area, plus a children's pool which are only used in July and August. This site will particularly appeal to families seeking easy access to a long beach (shelves quite steeply) and the attractions of a major resort.

Facilities: The sanitary blocks are tiled, have controllable hot showers, baby baths and open plan washbasins (all with hot water). The facilities on the original site are being refurbished for 2001. Dishwashing under cover. Laundry services. Motorcaravan services. Gas supplies. Bar/restaurant and takeaway. Small supermarket. Aerobic centre with professional instructor (but no gym equipment). Secure children's play area on grass. Swimming pool (small deposit for pass). Volleyball. Table tennis. Activities for adults and children organised in season (2/5-16/9) including dancing, bicycle excursions, aerobics, beach games. Excursions. Watersports near. No jetskis accepted. Regular bus service into the centre of Blanes.

Charges 2002

Per person	€ 3.61 - € 4.36
child	€ 2.85 - € 3.76
pitch incl. electricity	€ 10.52 - € 12.92

Plus 7% VAT. Discounts for pensioners and low season longer stays. **Tel:** 972 331 083. Fax: 972 331 100. E-mail: elpinar@mx3.redestb.es. **Reservations:** Write or phone site (no deposit). **Open** 31 March - 30 September.

Directions: Site is the last travelling south from Blanes town centre. Follow camping signs in Blanes until you see the El Pinar sign.

Camping Cala Llevadó

Ctra de Tossa a Lloret, km 3, 17320 Tossa de Mar (Girona)

8200

the travel service
TO BOOK

Ferry	✔
Pitch	✔
Accommodation	✗

01892 55 98 98

For splendour of position Cala Llevadó can compare with almost any in this book. A beautifully situated cliff-side site, it has fine views of the sea below. It is shaped something like half a bowl with steep slopes. There are terraced, flat areas for caravans and tents on the upper levels of the two slopes, with a great many individual pitches for tents scattered around. Some of these (no electricity) have fantastic settings and views. There is usually parking close to these pitches, although in some areas cars may be required to park separately. Electrical connections cover all caravan sectors and one tent area. High up in the site with a superb aspect, is the attractive restaurant/bar. One beach is for all manner of watersports and there is a sub-aqua diving school. Some other pleasant little coves can also be reached by climbing down on foot (with care!). Some fairly severe climbing and descending must clearly be expected on this site and this should be considered if older or disabled people are in your party. Cala Llevadó is luxurious and has much character and the atmosphere is informal and very friendly. Only 150 of the 650 pitches are accessible for caravans, so reservation in season is vital. It is peacefully situated but only five minutes away from the busy resort of Tossa. Some tour operator pitches (49).

Facilities: Four very well equipped toilet blocks are well spaced around the site, built in an attractive style, with some washbasins in cabins, well equipped showers, and baby baths. Washing machines and dryer. Laundry service. Motorcaravan services. Gas supplies. Fridge hire. Large supermarket. Restaurant/bar with terrace (5/5-28/9). Swimming pool (20 x 10 m.) and semi-circular children's pool. Three play areas. Entertainment for children (4-12 yrs). Sailing, water ski and windsurfing school. Fishing. Scuba diving. Excursions available. Torches are definitely needed in some areas. **Off site:** Bicycle hire 3 km. The site is alongside a larger complex where all manner of sophisticated sports and adventure activities are available. Campers can also use the other pools here.

Charges 2002

Per person	€ 4.40 - € 6.60
child (3-14 yrs)	€ 2.70 - € 3.65
caravan	€ 5.00 - € 7.05
tent	€ 4.40 - € 6.60
car	€ 4.40 - € 6.60
motorcycle	€ 4.40 - € 6.15
motorcaravan	€ 7.40 - € 10.50
electricity	€ 3.40 - € 3.50
dog	€ 3.15

Plus 7% VAT. **Tel:** 972 340 314. Fax: 972 341 187. E-mail: info@calallevado.com. **Reservations:** accepted with deposit and fee. **Open** 1 May - 30 September, including all amenities.

Directions: Cala Llevadó leads off the new Tossa-Lloret road about 3 km. from Tossa; the approach from either direction now presents no problems.

A first class site. **Fabulous situation** in the most beautiful part of the Costa Brava. Isolated and quiet. 4 beaches. Swimming pool, children's playground, bar, restaurant, supermarket, laundry, hairdressing, medical service. Exceptional sanitary facilities with free hot water.
Numbered pitches. Open from 1st. of Mai until 30th. of September.

Sports and animation:
Swimmingpool, tennis, basket ball, windsurfing and diving school, compressed air for divers, table tennis, minigolf, mountain bike.
Special activities for the children in July and August.

Reservation service.
Caravans and bungalows for hire.

Write to:
Camping **Cala Llevadó**
Postbus 34, E-17320 **Tossa de Mar**
COSTA BRAVA - Spain
Tel. 00 34 972 34 03 14
Fax 00 34 972 34 11 87
E-mail: info@calallevado.com
Web: www.calallevado.com

EMAS

ICICT CERT
Grupo TÜV Rheinland
UNE EN ISO 14001
Nº Reg.: 3.00.00018

Cala Llevadó
camping ★★★

Camping Sant Pol

8180

Doctor Fleming No.1, 17220 Sant Feliu de Guíxols (Girona)

Sant Pol is a small, family owned site and Anna Genover speaks excellent English, with a good understanding of campers needs. On the Costa Brava, this hillside site is on the edge of San Feliu, only 350 m. from the beach (may be some road noise on one side of the site). An attractive pool, bar and restaurant are the central focus of the site with shaded terraces and pitches of differing sizes curving down the slope. Higher terraces have the chalets and bungalows. There are only a few pitches for large units, but pleasant small terraces take tents and smaller units. The on site restaurant features regional dishes based on the best local produce available. San Feliu is an attractive seaside village with lots of cafés, restaurants and a crescent shaped white sandy beach. The local area has museums and archaeological sites. Dali's house is within driving distance (book ahead). A great site for exploring the area and short stays.

Facilities: One clean and modern sanitary block has British style WCs and hot water. WC for disabled campers, no shower (terrain would be difficult for wheelchairs). Washing machines and dryer. Motorcaravan services. Small supermarket for basics. Restaurant/bar. Swimming pools. Play area and animation for children in high season. Minigolf. Library. Internet point. Electronic games. Excursions. Torches needed in some area **Off site:** Large supermarket 300 m. Beach 350 m. Regular bus service into town.

Charges 2002

Per adult	€ 3.40 - € 7.10
child (5-10 yrs)	€ 2.15 - € 4.60
pitch	€ 6.75 - € 14.10
electricity	€ 2.75 - € 3.75
pitch incl. electricity and water	€ 10.75 - € 20.60

Discounts for stays over 21 days. **Tel:** 972 327 269. Fax: 972 327 211. E-mail: info@campingsantpol.com. **Reservations:** Contact site for details. **Open** 15 March - 30 November.

Directions: From the A7 take exit 7 to San Feliu de Guixols, turn at roundabout for S'Agaro, site is well signed.

Camping Botànic Bona Vista Kim

8240

Ctra NII, km 665, 08370 Calella (Barcelona)

While Calella itself may conjure up visions of mass tourism, this site is set on a steep hillside some 3 km. out of the town. Apart from perhaps some noise from the nearby coast road and railway, it is a quite delightful setting with an abundance of flowers, shrubs and roses (1,700 in total, all planted by the knowledgeable owner Kim, who has won several top Catalonian prizes for his roses). The site design successfully marries the beautiful botanic surrounds with the attractive views of the bay. The 160 pitches, all with electricity, are 60-80 sq.m. or more and are situated on flat terraces on the slopes, with some shade. On arrival, park at the restaurant and choose a pitch - Kim is most helpful with siting your van. The access road is steep, with many of the pitches enjoying lovely views. The bar/restaurant is close to reception at the bottom of the site and is unusual in the attractive choice of Spanish décor and in having a circular, central open-hearth fire/cooker. With two roof top terraces, the first level has a terrace with service from the restaurant and bar, above that (for over 16 year olds), is the sauna, jacuzzi with pool sized filter, a well equipped gym and a sun-bathing area, all enjoying views over the sea. There are quite good beaches just across the road and railway, accessible via a tunnel and crossing (including a naturist beach). The site has won environmental awards.

Facilities: The standard of design in the three sanitary blocks is quite outstanding for a small site (indeed for any site). Some washbasins in cabins in the newest block. Baby room. Dishwashing under cover. Washing machines. Motorcaravan services. Bar/restaurant, takeaway and shop (1/3-1/11). Sauna, solarium and jacuzzi. Large playground. Recreation park. Satellite TV. Games room. Barbecue and picnic area. No cycling allowed on site. **Off site:** Fishing 100 m. Bicycle hire 1 km. Riding, golf 3 km. Watersports near.

Charges 2002

Per person	€ 3.75
child (3-10 yrs)	€ 3.30
tent or caravan	€ 3.75
car	€ 3.75
motorcycle	€ 3.30
motorcaravan	€ 7.50
electricity	€ 3.00
dog	€ 2.25

All plus 7% VAT. No credit cards. **Tel:** 93 769 24 88. Fax: 93 769 58 04. E-mail: info@botanic-bonavista. net. **Reservations:** Write to site. **Open** 1 February - 31 October.

Directions: From N11 coast road site is signed travelling south of Calella (at km. 665), and is on right hand side of road - care is needed as road is busy and sign is almost on top of turning (next to Camping Roca Grossa). Entrance is very steep. From Barcelona, after passing through Sant Pol de Mar, go into outside lane shortly after 'Camping 800 m.' sign and keep signalling left. Site entrance is just before the two lanes merge.

Camping Montagut

9122 Ctra. Montagut-Sadernes, km 2, 17855 Montagut (Girona)

This is a most pleasant, small family site where everything is kept in pristine condition. Jordi and Nuria, a brother and sister team, work hard to make you welcome and maintain the superb appearance of the site. Flowers and shrubs abound, with 90 pitches on attractively landscaped and carefully constructed terraces or on flat areas overlooking the pool. A tranquil atmosphere pervades the site and drinks on the pleasant restaurant terrace are recommended, along with sampling the authentic menu as you enjoy the views over the Alta Garrotxa. There is much to see in the local area between the Pyrenees and the Mediterranean, for example a trip to the stunning village of Castellfollit de la Roca perched seemingly precariously on a precipice 60 m. above the Fluvia river. Or, on a different scale, the pretty Pont del Llierca which is a bridge in a most pleasant setting which the site has chosen to use on their logo. Walking and outdoor pusuits abound and the team will assist with bookings. This is a super site for relaxing and enjoying the peaceful situation and wonderful scenery.

Facilities: The modern sanitary block has free hot showers, washing and laundry facilities plus a modern section for babies and disabled campers; everything was spotless when seen. Motorcaravan services. Restaurant and bar (1/3-31/10). Supermarket. Medium sized swimming pool with large sunbathing area and children's pool (1/5-30/9). Playground. Soccer. Petanque. Volleyball. Barbecue area. Torches are useful in some areas and long electricity leads would be useful on the upper terraces.

Charges 2002

Per person	€ 3.60 - € 4.20
child (under 10 yrs)	€ 3.00 - € 3.60
caravan or tent	€ 3.90 - € 4.50
car	€ 3.30 - € 3.90
motorcaravan	€ 6.45 - € 6.75
small tent	€ 3.15 - € 3.60
electricity	€ 2.90

Plus 7% VAT. No credit cards. **Tel:** 972 287 202. Fax: 972 287 201. E-mail: camp.montagut@mx3.redestb. es. **Reservations:** Contact site. **Open** 1 March - 31 October.

Directions: Going west from Figueres on N260 Ripoll road, approx. 10 km. past Besalu, towards Olot, turn right towards Montagut. On reaching Montagut still follow the road to Sadernes and the site entrance is at the 2 km. marker.

Camping Stel

9144 Ctra N-152 Ramal-Llivia s/n, 17520 Puigcerdá (Girona)

Sister site to 8420 and 9143, this is an extremely efficient if pricey site. Part of a large, attractive building at the spacious entrance houses a modern reception (English is spoken). From here you will quickly be on your way to one of the flat, terraced pitches. Many of the pitches have shade and all are marked, clean and organized in rows with a water tap for each row. There is some road noise so, in order to avoid this and have views of the Cerdanya valley and the eastern Pyrenées, take one of the pitches on the upper terraces. We think it really is worth the trouble. The terrace closest to the facility block is occupied by new bungalows (2002). The rectangular pool with easy access is overlooked by the restaurant terrace, where you can enjoy a menu with local food, or the very reasonable menu of the day. You are very close to the French border here and thus you can enjoy sampling the two different cultures with ease. Visit Llivia, a Spanish village located on French soil where the oldest pharmacy in Europe is located and enjoy a trip to Andorra, famous for duty free shopping.

Facilities: Sanitary facilities in the main building are of very high standard with all the little luxuries and are kept very clean. A small, smart block serves the upper terraces. Both blocks can be heated. Separate modern unit with facilities for disabled campers. Washing machines and dryer in main block. Shop, Bar/restaurant (all season). Swimming pool (July-Sept). Boules. Table football. Snooker. Novel adventure style play frame for children (supervision needed). Adventure club organizes all manner of watersports, and outdoor activities such as biking, tours, climbing, hang gliding, indoor archery and many others. Animation in high season only. Drinks machines. Animals accepted in separate area. **Off site:** Fishing 7 km. Golf 7 km. Riding 5 km. Boat rental 2 km.

Charges 2002

Per pitch	€ 15.00
adult	€ 4.45
child (under 14 yrs)	€ 3.80
electricity	€ 3.00

All plus 7% VAT. No credit cards. **Tel:** 972 882 361. Fax: 972 140 419. E-mail: puigcerda@stel.es. **Reservations:** Advisable in July and August. **Open** all year.

Directions: From Perpignan take N116 to Prades and Andorra. At Puigcerdà take N152 to France (not the road with the security post) and the site is well signed.

Camping Pirineus

9143 Ctra. Guils de Cerdanya, km 2, 17528 Guils de Cerdanya (Girona)

This is a sister site to nos. 8420 and 9144, with a well organized entrance and one gets an immediate impression of space, green trees and grass - there is always someone watering and clearing up to maintain the high standards here. From the restaurant terrace you have fine views of the mountains in the background and the pool in the foreground. There is an open fire inside for cooler evenings and a huge mural of the mountains in case you cannot see the real thing out of the window. The pitches are neat, marked, of average size and organized in rows. Generally flat with some on a gentle incline, a proportion have water at their own sink on the pitch. There are many trees offering shade but watch overhanging branches if you have a high unit. There is much to see in the area but we do recommend a trip to the only cog railway in Spain which opened in 1931 (runs 15 July - 11 Sept). It leaves Ribes de Fresser and climbs 2,000 m. to the Sanctuary de Nuria where cars cannot go! It is a breathtaking trip. Try also the famous Catalonian gastronomy and experiment with the local wines and Cava.

Facilities: Two fully equipped, sanitary blocks of top quality and decorated with boxes of bright flowers, are kept spotlessly clean and can be heated when necessary. Smart washing machines and dryers. Motorcaravan service point. Shop (open all season). Bar/restaurant.(all season) TV room and well-equipped games room. Snooker. Heated swimming pool and circular paddling pool. Boules. Table football. Tennis. Table tennis. Basketball and five-a-side courts. Outdoor sports. Children's play area and clubhouse where youngsters can paint and play under supervision. Excursions. Entertainment (high season). Drinks machines. Dogs are not accepted. **Off site:** River fishing. Golf 6 km. Riding 4 km. Bicycle hire 2 km. French border and Andorra close by for duty free shopping.

Charges 2002

Per pitch	€ 15.00
pitch with water	€ 18.50
adult	€ 4.45
child (3-10 yrs)	€ 3.80
electricity (3A)	€ 3.00

All plus 7% VAT. No credit cards. **Tel:** 972 881 062. Fax: 972 882 471. E-mail: guils@stel.es. **Reservations:** Advisable in July and August. **Open** 22 June - 11 September.

Directions: From Perpignan take N116 to Prades and Andorra. Exit at Piugcerda and take the road to Guils de Cerdanya for 2 km. Site is well signed from the town.

Camping El Solsones

9123 Ctra. Sant Llorenc, km 2, 25280 Solsona (Lleida)

Situated on a hillside, 2 km. from Solsona, this all year site has pleasant views of the hills on three sides and lots of mature trees giving a pleasant green shady appearance. With a lovely Spanish feel, it would be a pleasant spot for a short stay during any season. There are many weekend units here, but still room for 100 pitches for caravans or motorcaravans and 100 for tents out of the total of 312 pitches. These are slightly sloping, with varying degrees of shade and 4, 6 or 10A electricity. The restaurant with its attractive stained glass screens and menu featuring Catalan style food is complemented by the large bar and casual eating area. A feature of the bar area is the central open fireplace. A large children's play area is provided, however parents are advised to supervise little ones as some of the equipment is of the older metal frame style which is not as child friendly as newer plastic play equipment. For winter visitors, the 'Ski Port del Conte' is 18 km. away. and there are facilities for riding, golf and walking in the vicinity. A friendly welcome is provided by the owner who has no English, but good French.

Facilities: Modern sanitary facilities are in two buildings, with free hot water to the showers, washbasins, laundry and dishwashing sinks. Motorcaravan services. Large supermarket with fresh food. Restaurant and bar - all open all year. Simple meals and snacks are served indoors and outside on the terrace overlooking the pool. Swimming pool (high season only). Excellent sports complex and minigolf. Bicycle hire. Children's play area (see above). Petanque. Fronton. Aviary. **Off site:** Golf, riding and skiing nearby.

Charges 2002

Per person	€ 4.21
child (2-10 yrs)	€ 3.91
caravan or tent	€ 4.21
car	€ 4.21
motorcycle	€ 3.50
motorcaravan	€ 7.82
electricity (4A)	€ 2.10

Plus 7% VAT. **Tel:** 973 482 861. Fax: 973 481 300. E-mail: campingsolsones@cbscat.com. **Reservations:** Contact site for high season (in French). **Open** all year.

Directions: Solsona is at the junction of the L301, C1410 and C149 in Lleida, 45 km. northwest of Manresa. The site is 2 km out of town on the LV4241 signed to Sant Llorenc de Morunys and Ski Port del Conte.

Spain - Cataluña
Camping de la Vall d'Ager
La Noguera, 25691 Ager (Lleida)

Ager is not on a through-route to anywhere so, if you are coming here, it is for a specific reason, hence the very peaceful situation. One of the main reasons for being here is that it is a hang-glider's paradise. The Montsec mountain range (1,677 m.) towers over the site in the Catalan pre-Pyrenees. Site activities revolve around flying - one of the launch points is just outside the perimeter and even the beer pump is in the form of a hang-glider! When you also consider that climbing, walking, mountain biking, canoeing and other water sports are all available in the vicinity, you may well wish to visit this pleasant site. There are 180 touring pitches on slightly sloping ground, marked out by trees and with some shade. Electricity (10A) is available to all. There is a pleasant large bar with snack area and a restaurant which offers local fare at good prices. The pool is very pleasant and most welcome as it is hot and a little dusty hereabouts in high summer.

Facilities: A central sanitary building provides good facilities, including large showers (with divider and lots of room to change). Separate rooms for disabled visitors, dishwashing (hot water) and laundry (cold) facilities, plus a washing machine and dryer downstairs. Bar, snack bar and restaurant (all year). Shop (main season only). Bicycle hire. Delta-wing store. Swimming pools (high season). Boule. Barbecue. Play area. Torches are required. **Off site:** Village 300-400 m. Summer parties in the village.

Charges 2002

Per person	€ 3.91
child (under 10 yrs)	€ 3.61
tent or caravan	€ 3.91
car	€ 3.91
motorcycle	€ 3.61
motorcaravan	€ 7.81
electricity (10A)	€ 4.21

Tel: 973 455 200. Fax: 973 455 202. **Reservations:** Unlikely to be needed. **Open** all year.

Directions: Site is on the northern edge of the village, which is on the L904, either direct from Balaguer (which is 28 km. NNE of Lleida) or from the C147 Balaguer/Tremp road. Either way, the L904 (which is being modernised) has old, narrow sections requiring caution.

Spain - Cataluña
Camping Repos del Pedraforca
Ctra. B400, km 13.5, 08699 Saldés (Barcelona)

Looking up through the trees in this steeply terraced campsite in the area of the Cadi-Moixero Natural Parc, you see the majestic Pedraforca mountain. A favourite for Catalan climbers and walkers, its amazing rugged peak in the shape of a massive stone fork gives it its name. The long scenic drive through the mountains to reach the site is breathtakingly beautiful. The natural beauty of the area, pretty villages, wild flowers, wonderful walks, and interesting local attractions including sea salt mountain and historic coal mines are what attract people to this area. The campsite owner, Alicio Fout, is a charming hostess who speaks English. She has created excellent summer and winter facilities including an indoor heated pool, sauna, jacuzzi and gym complex, a large outdoor pool, rooftop relaxation area, upstairs social room, excellent restaurant and popular bar. Access to the site is via a steep, curving road which could challenge some units. Pitches vary in size and accessibility, although there are excellent pitches for larger units.

Facilities: There are two clean, modern sanitary blocks. We found a low ratio of showers and toilet facilities, but all other sites in this area are the same. At peak periods there may be queues. British style WCs. Press button hot water and flowing cold water in the showers is a difficult system to manage, only one shower in each block has a privacy screen. Facilities for disabled campers. Washing machines and dryer. Restaurant/bar. Small supermarket for basic items. Heated indoor swimming pool, gym and spa. Outdoor pool. Children's play areas. Animation for children and adults in high season. Games and social rooms. Rooftop relaxation area. Table tennis. Electronic games. Itinerary suggestions for excursions in the area. Torches required. **Off site:** Motorcaravan service point close but not within site. Restaurants.

Charges 2003

Per adult	€ 4.45
child (1-10 yrs)	€ 3.65
pitch	€ 11.30
electricity (3-5A)	€ 3.20 - € 4.00
dog	€ 1.70

Discounts for stays of more than 3 nights and other offers for long stays (excluding high season). **Tel:** 938 258 044. Fax: 938 258 061. E-mail: pedra@ campingpedraforca.com. **Reservations:** Contact site for details. **Open** all year.

Directions: Site is approx 50 km. northwest of Girona. Access to the site is gained from the C-1411 Burga - La Seu / Puigcerda road. 2 km. south of Guardiola de Berga turn west to Saldes and site is well signed. It is 12 km. to site from the C-1411.

Camping La Ballena Alegre

8310 Autovia Castelldefels, km 12.5, 08840 Viladecans (Barcelona)

La Ballena Alegre is a large site with good facilites, popular with the Spanish and other Europeans. About 16 km. from the centre of Barcelona, it has all the facilities for an extended holiday plus a superb sandy beach more than a kilometre long and 100 metres wide. Some may prefer the extremely pleasant lagoon style swimming pool complex with slides and jacuzzi. It is a shaded, well laid out site, mostly covered by a pinewood and divided into 1,450 pitches of about 70 sq.m. with 1,250 for touring units. Space is not usually a problem, certainly outside July/August. There is an attractive bar and a white linen restaurant with a terrace overlooking the pool and entertainment is staged here in high season. A self service restaurant is close by serving great food, with some real Spanish dishes included at attractive prices if you have a large family. A further bar is open late near the entrance. The site has a lively atmosphere in high season, but with no noise after midnight. The airport is not far away and there is thus some aircraft noise and there is some road noise on one side of the site from the road. However, the site is full of fun and would be ideal for families seeking a holiday with a Spanish flavour. Used by tour operators (75 pitches).

Facilities: The toilet blocks are all good, varying in size and type. Two are new (these have some private cabins). Units for disabled visitors. Cleaning is good - a cleaner is on duty at each block during the day. Dog showers. Washing machines. Motorcaravan services. Large supermarket and other shops. Restaurant (24/6-30/8), and adjoining bar, snack bar and self service restaurant plus additional late bar near entrance. Swimming pool complex with slides and jacuzzi (25/5-25/9). Organised sports activities: aerobics, squash, roller skating, bicycle track, swimming, football etc. Open area where folk dances, shows etc. are staged twice weekly (24/6-30/8). Soundproofed disco. Sports area with football. Children's playground. Tennis. Fishing. Garage (petrol and servicing) by entrance. Hairdressers. Bureau de change. Good treatment room with nurse; doctor calls daily. Gas supplies. **Off site:** Bicycle hire 6 km. Riding 3 km. Golf 2 km. Regular bus service to Barcelona.

Charges 2002

Per person	€ 3.61
child (under 10 yrs)	€ 1.80
pitch incl. car and electricity	€ 9.02 - € 18.63
motorcycle with tent	€ 9.02 - € 12.02
dog	€ 1.80

All plus 7% VAT. **Tel:** 902 500 516. Fax: 902 500 527. E-mail: ballena1@ballena-alegre.es. **Reservations:** only made in the sense of guaranteeing admission. **Open** 1 April - 30 September.

Directions: From Barcelona on N11 either turn off on C245 road to Gava and Castelldefels or take motorway A2 spur towards Castelldefels - El Prat de Llobregat and continue to Castelldefels. Entrance leads directly off C246 dual-carriageway 'Autovia Castelldefels' on coast side of the road by a service station.

Costa Brava

The Costa Brava was the archetype Spanish destination in the early years of mass tourism and the tower blocks in some of the resorts are a dubious testimony to the days of the £50 package holiday. Fortunately package holiday trends changed before the developers could wreak total havoc and many villages and resorts remain very attractive and retain their charm, helped enormously by the towering cliffs and sheltered coves which give this coast its name – the 'Wild Coast'. There are of course some distinctly lively resorts, such as Lloret, Tossa and Calella in the province of Barcelona, but also several quieter ones. The coastal scenery is often spectacular and the climate pleasant – somewhat less hot than further south – making this one of the most attractive areas for the British, particularly for those who drive through France, since it is possible to reach the Costa Brava with only one night stop en-route.

CAMPING BEGUR

In the heart of the Costa Brava

Camping Begur, placed in a nice and shaded pine wood, only 10 minutes far from the beautiful beaches of Begur, is ideal to spend a quiet holidays in an area of great natural beauty, where silence and bird songs are the best sound. Enjoy of our environment, and visit some pintoresque villages like Begur, Pals, Peratallada with an excellent mediterranean cuisine.

CTRA. D'ESCLANYÀ KM.2 17.255 BEGUR - COSTA BRAVA - SPAIN

www.campingbegur.com - info@campingbegur.com ☎ / Fax: +34 972 623 201

Camping El Garrofer

8392 Ctra. C246 km 39, 08870 Sitges (Barcelona)

This a large, pine covered site, alongside fields of vines, is 800 m. from the beach, close to the pleasant town of Sitges. It has over 500 pitches of which 415 are for tourers and including 15 fully serviced pitches for large motorhomes. Everything is kept clean and the pitches are tidy and shaded, all with electricity (6A). Dino is the young, dynamic, English speaking manager who has a vast programme of improvements which will make this a most attractive site. The permanent pitches are grouped in a completely separate area and the amenity buildings are along the site perimeter next to the road which absorbs most of the road noise. A varied menu is offered in the cosy restaurant, complemented with the wines of the Penedes DO made hereabouts (the restaurant has a local reputation and is used by non-campers - the menu of the day is great value). A traditional bar is alongside and from here you can see the pretty mosaic clad play area. An ambitious animation programme is conducted for children in summer. A small pool with sunbathing areas is welcome on the hot summer days or you can walk to the very pleasant beach. Open most of the year the site offers all manner of adventure activities (extra charge) which may be organized through reception and there are many things to see here - we especially recommend a visit to Monserrat.

Facilities: Three sanitary blocks with ample facilities are mature but clean - one is of a good standard, and another was to be replaced in 2002. Good facilities for disabled campers. Laundry. Bar/restaurant. Shop (reception in low season). Swimming pool. Golf packages. Practice golf. Tennis. Older children's play area with dated equipment, modern plastic module for toddlers. Boules. Car wash. **Off site:** The town of Sitges is an attractive resort with seaside entertainments and is well worth exploring. Bus link from outside site to Barcelona airport and city.

Charges 2002

Per person	€ 2.31 - € 3.88
child (1-9 yrs)	€ 1.53 - € 3.10
pitch incl. electricity	€ 9.47 - € 13.00
motorcycle	€ 2.13 - € 3.56
dog	€ 1.79

Plus 7% VAT. **Tel:** 938 941 780. Fax: 938 110 623. E-mail: garrofer@interplanet.es. **Reservations:** Contact site. **Open** 17 January - 17 December.

Directions: Sitges is roughly 30 km. southwest of Barcelona and the site is accessed from the C-246 km. 39, 2 km. from town towards Vilanova i la Geltrú.

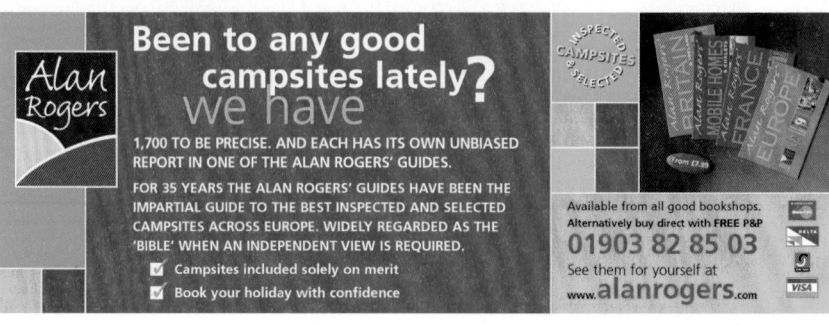

Camping Vilanova Park

Ctra. de l'Arboc, km 2.5, 08800 Vilanova i la Geltru (Barcelona)

This large, modern, hillside site has been equipped with costly installations of good quality. The most remarkable feature is the excellent pool complex with one very large pool where there are water jets and a coloured floodlit fountain. Together with a smaller children's pool, this covers an area of some 1,000 sq.m. and enjoys wonderful views over the sea. In the same area is the shopping centre and the large bar and restaurant, set around a thoughtfully executed extension and refurbishment of old Catalan farm buildings where dancing and entertainment take place. There is an ambitious animation programme throughout the high season, and at weekends for the remainder of the year. An unusual attraction is a Wildlife Park inhabited by deer and bird-life. Very pleasant, it has picnic areas and footpaths. At present there are 865 pitches with a very significant proportion occupied by a variety of well separated and screened static units. There are 150 pitches for touring units, located in separate areas with 120 having their own water supply. Marked and of 70-100 sq.m, all have 6A electricity and some larger pitches (100 sq.m.) also have water and drainage. The terrain, hard surfaced and mostly on very gently sloping ground, has many trees and considerable shade. Used by tour operators (57 pitches).

Facilities: All the sanitary blocks, including a new one, are of excellent quality, can be heated and have washbasins (over half in cabins) with free hot water, and others of standard type with cold water. Sinks for dishwashing and clothes. Serviced laundry. Motorcaravan services. Supermarket (Easter - 30 Sept). Souvenir shop. Full restaurant and larger bar where simpler meals served (both all year). Swimming pools (Easter - 15 Oct). Games room. Tennis. Bicycle hire. Tennis. ATM and exchange facilities. **Off site:** Golf 5 km. Fishing 4 km. Barcelona is easily accessible - buses every hour in the main season or electric train from Vilanova i la Geltru every 20 minutes. Vilanova town and beach are 4 km (local bus service).

Charges 2002

Per person	€ 3.64 - € 5.80
child (4-12 yrs)	€ 2.28 - 3.64
pitch incl. electricity	€ 10.91 - € 15.24
with water	€ 13.19 - € 17.52

All plus 7% VAT. Excellent deals for retired people on longer stays. **Tel:** 93 893 34 02. Fax: 93 893 55 28. E-mail: info@vilanovapark.es. **Reservations:** made in sense of guaranteeing to admit, with deposit. **Open** all year.

Directions: Site is 4 km. northwest of Vilanova i la Geltru towards L'Arboc. From Barcelona-Tarragona autopista take exit 29 and turn towards Vilanova. There is no exit at no. 29 from Tarragona direction; from here you must take exit 30, go into Vilafranca and turn right for Vilanova. The Vilanova bypass is now open so that one need not go into the town. Alternatively from the N340 from L'Arboc directly on attractive but very winding road for 11 km. signed Vilanova i la Geltru.

CAMPING VILANOVA PARK

Apartado (postbus 64)
Tel. (34) 93 893 34 02 • Fax (34) 93 893 55 28
E-08800 Vilanova i la Geltrú (Barcelona)

An elegant site with country club atmosphere!

50 km South of Barcelona, in the wine and champagne centre of Catalonia with more than 600 palm trees. Quiet situation. Very modern sanit. install. w. hot water everywhere. Swimming pool of 1.000 sqm and children's pool with big colour fountain (lighted in the evenings). Excellent restaurant "Chaine de Rôtisseurs" in old catalan mansion. Superm., shops, English press, children's progr., activities. Large pitches w. electr. conn. Private, large ecological park of 50.000 sqm. f. beautiful walks and picnics. Access: Motorway A-7, coming fr. Barcelona: exit 29; coming fr. Tarragona: exits 30 & 31; follow indic. Vilanova i la Geltrú/Sitges.

Open throughout the year. We speak English.

Camping Serra de Prades

8506 Sant Antoni, s/n, 43439 Vilanova de Prades (Tarragona)

On the edge of the village of Vilanova, nestling in granite foothills with superb views from its elevation of 950 m, this is a welcoming and peaceful site. The 215 pitches are on terraces formed with natural stone and with good access from resurfaced roads. The upper tent pitches have wonderful views although you have a trek to the sanitary facility on the lower level. Hedges and trees separate pitches providing a pleasant green environment and some shade, and 90% of the pitches have electricity. The site has won awards for its approach to ecology and solar power is used to supply hot water for the showers and to maintain the pool temperature. The elegant pool (supervised) has a terrace for sunbathing. The strength of this site is the range of adventure and outdoor activities on offer. These are professionally organized and climbing is a favourite followed by abseiling, paint ball, cycling, archery and a host of others. There is an impressive horse riding area within the site and guided treks are offered. The helpful staff will organize any activity and if it is not on offer here they have contracts with outside agencies for further extensive activities.

Facilities: The modern, well maintained sanitary block has British style WCs, hot water throughout and heating. Laundry facilities. Motorcaravan service point. Shop. Bar/restaurant. Swimming pool and children's pool (open and heated 1/4-15/10). Satellite TV. Archery. Basketball. Volleyball. Quad hire. Paint ball. 4 x 4 hire. Tennis. Riding with guided treks. Trekking and many more. Sports area. Entertainment organised in season. Safety deposit. Exchange facilities. Gas supplies. Torches required in some areas.

Charges 2002

Per person	€ 4.50
child (under 10 yrs)	€ 3.85
tent or caravan	€ 4.50
car	€ 4.50
motorcaravan	€ 9.50
electricity	€ 3.50

Plus 7% VAT. **Tel:** 977 869 050. Fax: 977 869 050. E-mail: info@serradeprades.com. **Reservations:** Write to site. **Open** all year.

Directions: From autopista A2 take exit 9 (Montblanc) and turn right on N240 towards Vimbodi. Turn left on T7004 to Vallclara, Vilanova and site. Alternatively from exit 8 (L'Albi) follow signs El Vilosell, Vallclara, then Vilanova de Prades.

Camping Stel

8420 Ctra. N340, km 1182, 43883 Roda de Bará (Tarragona)

Camping Stel is part of a group also consisting of sites 9143 and 9144. The group's high standards are maintained here in Playa Bara, between the pre-Littoral mountains and the sea. The rectangular site is between the N340 road and the excellent beach, with the railway running close to the bottom of the site. Beach access is gained through a gate and under the railway - there is rail noise on the lower pitches. The main facilities are grouped around the pools which are very pleasant with a large flume to an extension of the main pool (heated all season), an octagonal paddling pool and pleasant grass area carefully set out with palms. The central complex containing all the services is impressive with a large bar, terrace and snack area overlooking the pools. A small restaurant is behind the bar. The pitches are generally in rows with hedges around the rows but at the lower end of the site the layout is less formal. Many pitches have individual sinks. There is a separate area where no radio or TV is allowed ensuring peace and quiet. Just outside the gate is the famous Roman Arc de Bara which sits astride the original road.

Facilities: There are four clean, fully equipped, sanitary blocks. One has been totally refurbished (2002) and offers new crisp facilities for children, excellent facilities for disabled campers and four high standard private cabins. Baby baths in the ladies' sections of blocks. One block in the chalet area is available to campers. Laundry. Motorcaravan service area. Supermarket and tourist shop. Bar/restaurant and snack bar. Swimming pools (4/4-28/9) Outdoor sports area. Gym. Animation for children and some adult entertainment in high season. Electronic games. Internet bar. Hairdresser. ATM. Overnight area for late arrivals. Dogs are not accepted. Torch useful. **Off site:** Fishing from beach. Golf 4 km. Riding 4 km. Bicycle hire 4 km. Travel to the many attractions in the area is simple by the nearby autopista, rail or bus services.

Charges 2002

Per adult	€ 5.80
child (3-10 yrs)	€ 4.50
pitch incl. electricity	€ 16.40 - € 19.00
with water and drainage	€ 19.90 - € 22.20

All plus 7% VAT. **Tel:** 977 802 002. Fax: 977 800 525. E-mail: stel@stel.es. **Reservations:** Advisable in July/August. **Open** 4 April - 28 September.

Directions: Site is at 1182 km. marker on the N340 near Arc de Bara, between Tarragona and Vilanova.

Camping Playa Bara

8410 Ctra. N340, km 1183, 43883 Roda de Bará (Tarragona)

This is a most impressive site near the beach, which is family owned and has been carefully developed and designed over the years. On entry you find yourself in a tree-lined drive with an aroma of pine and woodlands and the sound of waterfalls close by. With over 850 pitches, it is still a very green and relaxing site with an immense range of activities. It is well situated with a 50 m. walk to a long sandy beach via a tunnel under the railway (some noise) to a new promenade with palms and a quality beach bar and restaurant. Much care with planning and in the use of natural stone, palms shrubs and flowering plants gives a most pleasing tropical appearance to all aspects of the site. The owners have excelled themselves in the design of the impressive terraced Roman-style pool complex, which is the central feature of the site. Sunbathe on the pretty terraces or sip a drink whilst seated at the bar stools submerged inside one of the pools or enjoy the panorama over the sea from the rooftop spa. Pitches vary in size, the older ones terraced and well shaded with pine trees, the newer ones more open, with a variety of trees and bushes forming separators between them. All have electricity (5A) and a sink with water. Arrive early to find space in peak weeks. Used by some British tour operators.

Facilities: Excellent, fully equipped toilet blocks are of different sizes and types. A number of private cabins for both sexes in some blocks, children's baths, basins and toilets and superb facilities for disabled visitors. A selection of good private sanitary facilities can be hired. Note: shower water is desalinated and thus rather salty but spring water is available from special taps. Washing machines and dryers. Motorcaravan services. Supermarket. Butcher. Bakery. Tabac. Souvenir shop. Full restaurant and larger bar where simpler meals and takeaway served, bars also in 3 other places, and bar/restaurant on beach. Swimming pools. Jacuzzi. Fronton and tennis courts (both floodlit). Roller skating. Football. Junior club. Sports area. Doctor on site. Windsurfing school. Volleyball. Basketball. Gym. Massage parlour. Petanque. Minigolf. Fishing. Entertainment centre: amphitheatre with stage and dance floor. Animation in several languages. Large busy games room; video room, films. satellite TV, cocktail bar/disco room open 11 to 4 am. (weekends only outside high season). ATM. Telephones. Deposit boxes. Hairdresser. Internet points. **Off site:** Bicycle hire 2 km. Riding 3 km. Golf 4 km.

Charges 2002

Per person	€ 3.87 - € 7.74
child (1-9 yrs)	€ 2.71 - € 5.42
tent or caravan	€ 7.74
car	€ 7.74
motorcaravan	€ 13.20
electricity	€ 3.00

All plus 7% VAT. Low season reductions for pensioners and sports charges reduced.**Tel:** 977 802 701. Fax: 977 800 456. E-mail: info@ barapark.es. **Reservations:** Contact site for details. **Open** 15 March - 29 September, with all amenities.

Directions: From A7 autoroute take exit 31. Site entrance is at the 1183 km. marker on the main N340 just opposite the Arco de Bara Roman monument from which it takes its name.

Camping Arc de Bara

8395 CN 340, km 1182, 43883 Roda de Bara (Tarragona)

In comparison to the gigantic sites along this coastline, this smaller site has only 300 pitches of which most are taken up with static holiday caravans. The site is 200 m. from the impressive Roman monument, Arc de Bara, and 60 m. from the superb beach. The beach is accessed by a rear gate in the site perimeter and is soft sand shelving gently. The 30 pitches for tourers are generally shaded, are of average size (60-70 sq.m.) and are somewhat set apart from the very extensive permanent pitches but there is a distinct feeling of compression. The unusual feature of this site, is the modernistic design theme used on many of the camp building exteriors and interiors. This theme is continued at the attractive large heated pool elevated above the site's ground level and forming a curved arrowhead shape. The shop, bar and restaurant close to the entrance are open daily between July and Sept. and at weekends only all other times of the year, as is the impressive bar/snack bar near the beach access (the site is open all year).

Facilities: Three very clean toilet blocks are of various designs (one a most unusual elevated circular building) and a fourth without showers. These offer free hot water to washbasins (some in cabins) and showers. Units for disabled visitors. Limited facilities for babies. Dishwashing and laundry (cold water only). A separate facility for disabled campers was under construction when we visited. Washing machines and dryers. Swimming pools. Bars. Restaurant. Snack bars. Supermarket. Small play area. Some animation in season. Torches required in some areas.

Charges 2002

Per person	€ 2.55 - € 4.09
child (3-9 yrs)	€ 1.56 - € 2.52
tent or caravan	€ 2.55 - € 4.09
car	€ 2.55 - € 4.09
motorcaravan	€ 4.09 - € 6.91
electricity	€ 2.52

Minimum charge € 20,44 per day for pitch and persons (1/7-31/8). All plus 7% VAT. **Tel:** 977 800 902. Fax: 977 801 552. E-mail: camping@ campingarcdebara.com. **Reservations:** Contact site. **Open** all year.

Directions: From A7 autopista take exit 31 towards Tarragona. Site is on CN340 Barcelona - Tarragona road at 1182 km. marker just 50 meters downhill from the Roman Arc which spans the road. Use the approach turn for Camping Stel.

Camping La Pineda de Salou

8482 Ctra. Costa Tarragona - Salou km 5, 43481 La Pineda (Tarragona)

La Pineda is just outside Salou towards Tarragona and this site is just 300 m. from the Aquapark and 2.5 km. from Port Aventura, to which there is an hourly bus service from outside the site entrance. There is some noise from this road. There is a medium sized swimming pool and children's pool, open from mid June, behind large hedges close to the entrance. A large terrace has sun loungers, and various entertainment aimed at young people is provided in season. The 366 flat pitches are mostly shaded and of about 70 sq.m. All have 5A electricity. The beach is about 400 m. The simple restaurant/bar is shaded and has a large cactus garden to the rear. This is a plain, friendly and convenient site, with reasonable rates, probably best used for visiting Tarragona and Port Aventura, or exploring the local area, rather than for extended stays. Note: the site is reasonably close to a large industrial centre.

Facilities: Sanitary facilities are mature but clean with baby bath, dishwashing and laundry sinks. Two washing machines in each block. The second building is opened in high season only. Gas supplies. Shop (1/7-31/8). Restaurant and snacks (1/7-31/8). Swimming pools (1/7-31/8). Bar (all season). Five-a-side soccer pitch. Small TV room. Bicycle hire. Games room with videos and drink and snack machines. Children's playground (3-12 yrs). Entertainment (1/7-30/8). Torches may be required. **Off site:** Fishing 500 m. Golf 12 km

Charges 2002

Per person	€ 3.20 - € 4.70
child (1-10 yrs)	€ 2.30 - € 3.50
tent or caravan	€ 4.50 - € 6.30
car	€ 3.00 - € 5.30
motorcaravan	€ 5.90 - € 9.30
electricity	€ 2.90
dog	€ 1.10 - € 2.20

All plus 7% VAT. **Tel:** 977 37 30 80. Fax: 977 37 30 81. E-mail: info@campinglapineda.com.
Reservations: Made for high season (min. 7 nights) contact site. **Open** all year except 1 Jan. - 22 March.

Directions: From A7 just southwest of Tarragona take exit 35 and follow signs to La Pineda and Port Aventura then campsite signs appear.

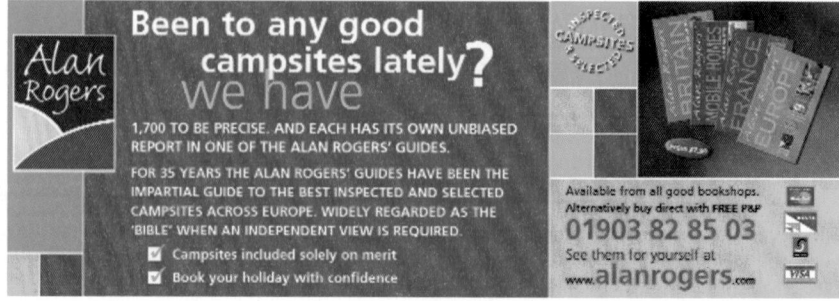

Camping La Siesta

Ctra. Norte 37, 43840 Salou (Tarragona)

8470

The palm bedecked site of La Siesta is only 250 m. from the pleasant sandy beach and close to the life of the resort of Salou. The town is popular with British and Spanish holidaymakers and has just about all that a highly developed Spanish resort can offer. For those who do not want to share the busy beach, there is a large, free swimming pool which is elevated above pitch level. La Siesta is divided into 470 individual pitches which are large enough and have electricity (10A), with smaller ones for tents. Many pitches are provided with artificial shade and within some pitches there is one box for the tent or caravan, and a shared one for the car. There is considerable shade from the trees and shrubs that are part of the site's environment. In high season, the siting of units is carried out by the management, who are friendly and helpful. Young campers are located separately to the rear of the site. The restaurant, which overlooks the pool, has a comprehensive menu and wine list, competing well with the town restaurants. A bar is alongside with TV and a large terrace part of which is given over to entertainment in high season. A suprisingly large supermarket caters for most needs in season.

Facilities: Three bright and clean sanitary blocks provide very reasonable facilities. Motorcaravan services. Supermarket. Various vending machines. Self-service restaurant and bar with cooked dishes to take away. Dancing some evenings till 11 pm. Swimming pool (300 sq.m; open all season). Playground. Medical service daily in season. ATM point. Torches may be required. **Off site:** Huge numbers of shops, restaurants and bars near. Port Adventura is close. Fishing 500 m. Bicycle hire 200 m. Riding or golf 6 km.

Charges 2002

Per person	€ 3.37 - € 4.72
child (4-9 yrs)	€ 2.64 - € 3.40
tent or caravan	€ 3.37 - € 4.72
car	€ 3.37 - € 4.72
motorcaravan	€ 6.31 - € 7.66
electricity	€ 2.34 - € 2.52

All plus 7% VAT. No credit cards. **Tel:** 977 380 852. Fax: 977 383 191. E-mail: siesta@tinet.fut.es.
Reservations: Advised 1 July - 20 Aug. and made in sense of guaranteeing a shady place, with electricity if required. Deposit required. **Open** 16 March - 3 November.

Directions: Leave A7 at exit 35 for Salou. Site is signed off the Tarragona/Salou road and from the one way system in the town of Salou. The site is in the town so keep a sharp eye for the small signs.

Camping & Bungalows Sanguli

Prolongacion Calle 'E' s/n, Apdo de Correos 123, 43840 Salou (Tarragona)

8480

Owned, developed and managed by a local Spanish family, Sanguli is a superb site boasting excellent pools and ambitious entertainment. It lies little more than 100 m. from the good sandy beach, across the coast road and a small railway level crossing (some train noise at times). Sister site to 8481, although large, Sanguli manages to maintain a quality family atmosphere due to the efforts of the very keen and efficient staff. There are four good sized, attractive pools (with children's pools), one near the entrance with a grassy sunbathing area partly shaded and a second deep one with water chutes that forms part of the excellent sports complex (with fitness centre, tennis and squash courts, a 'fronton', minigolf and football practice area). The third pool is the central part of the amphitheatre area at the top of the site which includes an impressive Roman style building with huge portals, containing a bar and restaurant with terraces. The amphitheatre seats 2,000 campers and treats them to very professional free nightly entertainment (1/5-30/9). All the pools have adjacent amenity areas and bars. The site is also fortunate to be placed near the centre of Salou and so can offer the attractions of a busy resort while still being private. It is only 3 km. from Port Aventura. The site is striving to achieve the 'Garden of Eden' that is the owners' dream. There are 1,472 pitches of varying size (75-90 sq.m) and all have electricity (7/10A). A wonderful selection of trees, palms and shrubs provides natural shade. A real effort is made to cater for the young including teenagers with a 'Hop Club' (entertainment tailored for 13-17 year olds), along with a Computer Club which includes use of the internet. This is a large, professional site providing something for all the family, but still capable of providing peace and quiet for those looking for it. Used by British tour operators (132 pitches).

Facilities: The quality sanitary facilities are constantly improved and are always exceptional, including many individual cabins with en-suite facilities. All are kept very clean. Launderette with service. Motorcaravan services. Bars and restaurant with takeaway. Swimming pools. Jacuzzi. Fitness centre. Sport complex with tennis, squash, football practice ground, Sports area and fitness room (charged). Children's playground. Mini club, teenagers club and computer club. New minigolf. First-aid room. Gas supplies. Dogs are not accepted. **Off site:** Fishing 100 m. Bicycle hire 100 m. Riding 3 km. Golf 6 km. Resort entertainment.

Charges 2002

Per adult	€ 4.50
child (4-12 yrs)	€ 3.00
pitch (70-75 sq.m.)	€ 13.00 - € 27.00
'special' pitch (90 sq.m.)	€ 13.00 - € 30.00
'master' pitch (incl. water)	€ 14.50 - € 32.00

Electricity included. All plus 7% VAT. Less 25-45% outside high season for longer stays. Special long stay offers for senior citizens. **Tel:** 977 381 641. Fax: 977 384 616. E-mail: mail@sanguli.es. **Reservations:** Advised for July/Aug. and made up to 1 March with sizeable booking fee; contact site. **Open** 15 March - 3 November.

Directions: On west side of Salou about 1 km. from centre, site is well signed from the coast road to Cambrils and from the other town approaches.

The Alan Rogers' Travel Service

We have recently extended The Alan Rogers Travel Service. This unique service enables our readers to reserve their holidays as well as ferry crossings and comprehensive insurance cover at extremely competitive rates. The majority of participating sites are in France and we are able to offer a selection of some of the very best sites in this country.

One simple telephone call to our Travel Service on 01892 55 98 98 is all that is needed to make all the arrangements. Why not take advantage of our years' of experience of camping and caravanning. We would be delighted to discuss your holiday plans with you, and offer advice and recommendations.

Share our experience and let us help to ensure that your holiday will be a complete success.

Alan Rogers Travel Service 01892 55 98 98 or www.alanrogers.com

Camping Cambrils Park

8481 Apartado de Correos 123, 43850 Salou (Tarragona)

A drive lined with palm trees and flowers leads from the large, very smart round reception building at this impressive modern site. Sister site to no. 8480, it is set 500 m. back from the excellent beach in a generally quiet setting with outstanding facilities. The 706 slightly sloping, grassy pitches of around 90 sq.m. are numbered and separated by trees. All have 10A electricity, 50 have water and waste water connections, some having more shade than others. The marvellous central lagoon pool complex is the main focus of the site with a raised wooden 'poop deck' sunbathing area that doubles as an entertainment stage at night. There is a huge bar/terrace area for watching the magnificent floodlit spectacles, along with an excellent restaurant and an adjacent takeaway. By day there is a small bar at a lower level in the pool where you can enjoy a cool drink from submerged stools, plus a dryer version on the far side of the bar or just relax on the spacious thick grassed sunbathing areas. There are a number of tour operator pitches and attractive thatched chalets. A fabulous jungle theme children's pool is nearer the entrance - they love it! This is a superb family site.

Facilities: Four excellent sanitary buildings provide some washbasins in cabins, superb units for disabled visitors, dishwashing, laundry and immaculate, decorated baby sections. Huge serviced laundry. Motorcaravan services. Car wash. Restaurant. Takeaway. Huge supermarket, souvenir shop and 'panaderia' (fresh-baked bread and croissants). Swimming pools. Minigolf. Tennis. Football. Multi-games court. Basketball. Volleyball. Petanque. Animation and entertainment all season. Mini-club. Doctor on site daily all season. ATM. Gas supplies. Dogs are not accepted. **Off site:** Fishing, bicycle hire 400 m. Riding 3 km. Golf 7 km. Port Aventura theme park 4 km.

Charges 2002

Per person	€ 4.50
child (4-12 yrs)	free - € 3.00
pitch incl. electricity	€ 13.00 - € 30.00
with water and waste water	€ 14.50 - € 32.00

All plus 7% VAT. Special offers, plus low season discounts for pensioners. **Tel:** 977 351 031. Fax: 977 352 210. E-mail: mail@cambrilspark.es. **Reservations:** Contact site. **Open** 22 March - 30 September, including all amenities.

Directions: Site is about 1.5 km west of Salou. The entrance is signed about 700 m. west of Camping Sanguli (8480), on the coast road from Salou to Cambrils. Watch for camping signs to Sanguli but note that they are not the normal tent type signs - just the name.

Camping Tamarit Park

8483 N340 km 1172, Tamarit, 43008 Tarragona (Tarragona)

This is an attractive, modern site, beautifully situated at the foot of Tamarit castle at one end of a 1 km. long beach of fine sand. The 710 pitches, 50 of which are virtually on the beach, are marked out on hard sand and grass and some are separated by a variety of shrubs, pines and palm trees. All have electricity (6A) and are 70, 90 or 100 sq.m. in area. Long electricity leads and metal awning pegs may be required in places but wide internal roads give good access for even the largest of units. A beach-side restaurant has superb views and the terrace has tables just a few metres from the sea. A vast lagoon-type pool with bar and sun terrace has been added. The site is approached by a long access road, rather narrow but with passing places, reached across a new bridge (6 m.) over the railway line (there is train noise on the site). This is a site with good facilities, albeit on the expensive side. Security is provided but the very low wall which is the site beach boundary must be viewed with caution. Tamarit would be a good choice for an active family holiday by the sea. The early morning sun shining on the blue sea and the golden stone of Tamarit castle high above is a memorable sight!

Facilities: Sanitary blocks (one heated) are modern and tiled, providing good facilities. An unfortunate recent economy feature in the showers is the introduction of push-button controlled hot water with tap controlled cold, leading to a confusing mixture of temperatures. Private bathrooms to rent. Dishwashing under cover with hot water. Laundry facilities including washing machines. Motorcaravan services. Gas supplies. Shop, bar/restaurant and takeaway service (all until 15/10). Swimming pool (15/5-15/10). Tennis. Volleyball. Petanque. Minigolf. Table tennis. Playground. Animation programme in season. Fishing. Exchange facilities and ATM. Barbecues not permtted on pitches. **Off site:** Bicycle hire 2 km. Riding 1 km. Golf 8 km.

Charges 2002

Per person	€ 4.00 - € 5.50
child (1-12 yrs)	€ 2.85 - € 4.25
pitch acc. to type and season	€ 15.00 - € 20.50
electricity	€ 3.60
dog	€ 1.00 - € 3.00

All plus 7% VAT. Discounts for students, pensioners, large families and longer stays in low season. **Tel:** 977 650 128. Fax: 977 650 451. E-mail: tamaritpark@tamarit.com. **Reservations:** Contact site. **Open** 1 March - 1 November.

Directions: From A7 take exit 32 towards Tarragona. At crossroads 'Urb. La Mora' go on towards Atafulla and after just 200 m. turn right to Tamarit. Site entrance is on left after 1 km.

Playa Montroig Camping & Bungalow Park

Aptdo 3, N-340 Km 1136, 43300 Montroig (Tarragona)

What a superb site! Playa Montroig is about 30 km. beyond Tarragona set in its own tropical gardens with direct access to a very long beach. Bathing, windsurfing, surfboarding two diving rafts, a diving school and many beach sports are available. The main part of the site lies between the sea, road and railway (as at other sites on this stretch of coast, there is some train noise) and there is a huge underpass. The site is divided into spacious, marked pitches with excellent shade provided by a variety of lush vegetation including very impressive palms set in wide avenues. There are 1,950 pitches, all with electricity and 330 with water and drainage connections. Some 48 pitches are directly alongside the beach - they are somewhat expensive and extremely popular. The site has many outstanding features. There is an excellent swimming pool complex near the entrance with two pools (one heated for children). A quality restaurant serves traditional Catalunian fare (seats 150) and overlooks an entertainment area where you may watch genuine Flamenco dancing and buffet food is served (catering for 1,000). A large terrace bar dispenses drinks or if you yearn for louder music there is a disco and smaller bar. If you prefer international food there is yet another eating option in a very smart restaurant (seats 500). Above this is the 'Pai-pai' Caribbean cocktail bar where softer music is provided in an intimate atmosphere. Children's activities are very ambitious - there is even a ceramics kiln (multi-lingual carers). 'La Carpa', a spectacular open air theatre, is an ideal setting for daily keep fit sessions and the professional entertainment provided. If you are 5-11 years old you can explore the 'Tam-Tam Eco Park', a 20,000 sq.m. forest zone where experts will teach the natural life of the area. You can even camp out for a night (supervised) to study wildlife (a once weekly activity). Adults are also allowed in to separate barbecues and other evening fun. This is an excellent site and there is insufficient space here to describe all the available activities. We recommend it for families with children of all ages and there is much emphasis on providing activities outside the high season.

Facilities: Fifteen sanitary buildings, some small, but of very good quality with toilets and washbasins, others really excellent, air conditioned larger buildings housing large showers, washbasins (many in private cabins) and separate WCs. Facilities for disabled campers and for babies. A 24 hour cleaning service operates. Water points around site (water said to be very pure from the site's own wells). Several launderettes. Motorcaravan services. Good shopping centre with supermarket, greengrocer, butcher, fishmonger, tobacconist and souvenir shops. Restaurants and bars. The 'Eurocentre', with 250 person capacity and equipped for entertainment and activities, large screen videos, films, shows and meetings (air conditioned). Fitness suite. Eco-park (see above). TV lounges (3) incl. satellite. Beach bar. Children's playground. Free kindergarten with multi-lingual staff. Skate-boarding. Jogging track. Sports area for volleyball, football and basketball. Tennis. Minigolf. Table tennis. Organised activities for children and adults including pottery and gardening classes. Windsurfing and water skiing courses. Surfboards and pedaloes for hire. Boat mooring. Ladies' and men's hairdressers. Bicycle hire. Bureau de change. Safety deposit boxes. Telephone service. Gas supplies. Dogs are not accepted. TVs are not allowed outside your vehicle. **Off site:** Riding or golf 3 km.

Charges 2003

Per person	€ 2.70 - € 5.00
child (under 10)	€ 2.10 - € 4.00
standard pitch with electricity	€ 16.23 - € 31.00
'premium' pitch	€ 18.63 - € 45.08

All plus 7% VAT. Discounts for longer stays and for pensioners. **Tel:** 977 810 637. Fax: 977 811 411. E-mail: info@playamontroig.com. **Reservations:** are possible and made with refundable booking fee (4,000 ptas). Contact Dept. de Reservas, Apdo 3. at site address. **Open** 1 March - 31 October.

Directions: Site entrance is off main N340 nearly 30 km. southwest from Tarragona. From motorway take Cambrils exit and turn west on N340 at 1136 km. marker.

Camping Club La Torre del Sol

8540 Ctra. N340, km 1136, 43300 Mont-Roig Del Camp (Tarragona)

the travel service
TO BOOK
Ferry ✓
Pitch ✓
Accommodation ✗
01892 55 98 98

A pleasant banana tree-lined approach road gives way to avenues of palms and you have arrived at Torre del Sol, a member of the French Airotel chain and the 'Yelloh' group of sites. Sister site to Templo del Sol (8537N), Torre del Sol is a very large site occupying a good position with direct access to the clean, soft sand beach, complete with a beach bar. Strong features here are 800m of clean beach-front and entertainment is provided all season. There is a separate area where the 'Happy Camp' team will take your young-sters to camp overnight in the Indian reser-vation plus they can amuse them two days a week in other activities. The cinema doubles as a theatre to stage shows all season. A complex of three pools, thoughtfully laid out with grass sunbathing areas and palms has a lifeguard. There is good shade on a high proportion of the 1,500 individual, numbered pitches. All have electricity and are mostly of about 70-80 sq.m. There is usually space for odd nights but for good places between 10/7-16/8 it is best to reserve (only taken for a stay of five nights or more). Part of the site is between the railway and the sea so there is train noise. We were impressed with the provision of season-long enter-tainment and to give parents a break whilst children were in the safe hands of the animation team.

Facilities: Four very well maintained, fully equipped, toilet blocks include units for disabled people and babies, and some tiled units at three blocks comprising private cabins with washbasins and hot showers. Washing machines. Gas supplies. Large supermar-ket, bakery, and souvenir shops at entrance, open to public. Full restaurant with soft-toy playpen area. Takeaway. Bar with large terrace where entertain-ment held daily all season. Beach bar. Coffee bar and ice cream bar. Pizzeria. Open roof cinema with permanent seating for 520; 3 TV lounges (satellite TV); separate room for films or videos shown on TV. Well-soundproofed disco. Swimming pools (two heated). Solarium. Sauna. Tennis. Table tennis. Squash. Volleyball. Language school (Spanish). Minigolf. Multi purpose hardcourt. Sub aqua diving from site (first dive in pool free!) Bicycle hire. Fishing. Windsurfing school; sailboards and pedaloes for hire. Children's playground and crèche. Fridge hire. Library. Ladies' and men's hairdresser. Car repair and car wash (pressure wash). Look for the traditional goods produced in the local villages displayed in reception. No animals are permitted. No jet skis accepted. **Off site:** Theme parks. Beach fishing. Riding 3 km. Golf 4 km.

Charges 2002

Per person	€ 3.00 - € 7.00
child (under 10 yrs)	€ 2.00 - € 5.00
pitch	€ 12.00 - € 20.00

All plus 7% VAT. Discounts in low season for longer stays. **Tel:** 977 810 486. Fax: 977 811 306. E-mail: info@latorredelsol.com. **Reservations:** Made only for Jul/Aug. before 15 June, in sense of guaranteeing admission, with booking fee (€ 18,03). **Open** 15 March - 22 October.

Directions: Entrance is off main N340 road by 1136 km. marker, about 30 km. from Tarragona towards Valencia. From motorway take Cambrils exit and turn west on N340.

Camping Marius

8520 Ctra. N340, km 1137, 43892 Miami-Playa (Tarragona)

Quiet, well tended and not too huge, this agreeable site has a family atmosphere and a personal touch. One perimeter is on a good sandy beach with direct access and no roads to cross - you can almost fall out of bed and onto the beach and a large beach bar will provide resuscitation when required! The site is divided into 345 indi-vidual pitches of adequate size so it does not become too overcrowded. They are quite shady with 300 electrical connections and 8 pitches with water and drainage. Dog owners go on one half of the site which is split down the centre by a wall and large storm drain gully (clean). The lively fishing port of Cambrils, where you can buy freshly caught fish, is about 7 km. It is an excellent watersports venue in high season. The use of TV sets outside your unit and the riding of bicycles on site is not permitted. Some train noise may be expected.

Facilities: Two of the sanitary blocks are dated but clean and a third is of an excellent standard. Free hot water in the showers and half the washbasins, plus 21 private cabins. Facilities for babies and disabled campers. Laundry room. Motorcaravan services. Bar and restaurant (1/6-30/9). Supermarket (15/4-30/9). Souvenir shop. Gas supplies. Children's club and playground. Hairdresser. Fishing. Table tennis. Torches required at night. **Off site:** Windsurfing, water ski and pedaloes nearby. Riding 4 km. Golf 10 km.

Charges 2002

Per person	€ 4.50 - € 6.00
child (1- 10 yrs)	€ 2.50 - € 3.50
pitch incl. electricity	€ 12.00 - € 16.00
dog	€ 2.50 - € 3.50

Plus 7% VAT. Less 10-20% for longer stays. **Tel:** 977 810 684. Fax: 977 179 658. E-mail: schmid@ teleline.es. **Reservations:** Contact site. **Open** 1 April - 15 October.

Directions: The site entrance is 28 km. from Tarragona on the Valencia road (N340).

CAMPING CARAVANING BUNGALOW RESORT

LA TORRE DEL SOL

Cat. 1 ★★★★

catalunya sud

E-43300 Montroig (Tarragona)
Tel. (34) 977 81 04 86
Fax (34) 977 81 13 06
E-mail: info@latorredelsol.com
www.latorredelsol.com

yelloh! VILLAGE
CAMPING VILLAGES

20 km south of Barcelona, on the Costa Daurada, directly by the sea.
pen: 15.3 - 22.10 with all install. and activities. Off-season discounts and spec. fees f. old-age pensioners.

Camping Naturista El Templo del Sol

43890 Hospitalet de L'Infant (Tarragona)

El Templo del Sol is a large, luxurious terraced naturist site with a distinctly Arabesque style and superb buildings in Moorish style. The owner has designed the magnificent main turreted building at the entrance with fountains and elaborate Moorish arches. The three large, tiered pools are wonderful with water cascading from one to the other and are part of a complex containing a huge luxurious jacuzzi with views over the sea, a large bar with snacks, plus a sunbathing area on the roof. The main building contains an impressive reception area and has an elegant restaurant with a terrace and a mosaic central, open area with a fountain and a luxury cinema. This grouping of services are said to be among the best in European naturist sites. The site has 435 pitches, mainly rather small (60/70 sq.m), but 85 fully serviced. Pitches are on terraces giving rewarding views over the sea and ready access to the sandy beach. There is some shade. Site lighting is provided from pleasing serpent shaped light assemblies. The site is under French management (the same as 8540 Torre del Sol) and English is spoken. There is some daytime rail noise especially in the lower areas where the larger pitches are located.

Facilities: The sanitary blocks are amongst the best you will find in Spain providing everything you could require and extensive services for disabled campers. Washing machines. Well stocked supermarket. Health shop. Souvenir shop. Bars. Restaurant and snack bar (1/4-10/10).Swimming pools (20/3-15/10). Jacuzzi. Cinema. Games area. Volley ball. Boule. Separate round children's pool and play area. Miniclub. Doctor available. Library. Safety deposit boxes. Professional entertainment includes genuine Flamenco dancing. Hairdresser. Bicycle hire. ATM. Animals are not accepted. No jet skis. **Off site:** Bicycle hire 3 km. Golf 2 km. Fishing 100 m. (night time only). Riding 7 km. Boat launching 3 km. Theme parks.

Charges 2002

Per person	€ 3.00 - € 6.50
child (under 10 yrs)	€ 1.80 - € 4.00
pitch incl. car and electricity	€ 11.00 - € 21.00
tent	€ 2.50 - € 4.50

Plus 7% VAT. Discounts for longer stays. **Tel:** 977 823 434. Fax: 977 811 306. E-mail: info@ eltemplodelsol.com. **Reservations:** Minimum stay in July/Aug. 5 nights, otherwise 3 nights. A naturist licence is required. Contact site for details. **Open** 28 March - 13 October.

Directions: From N340 south of Tarragona, exit at km. 1123 towards L'Hopitalet and follow signs.

Camping-Pension Cala d'Oques

43890 Hospitalet del Infante (Tarragona)

8535

Cala d'Oques - or Goose Bay - was where the migrant geese landed on return from wintering in South Africa, hence the geese featured on the camp logo and the three guard geese that watch the entrance to the site. This peaceful, and delightful site has been developed with care and dedication by Elisa Roller over 30 years or so. Part of its appeal lies in its situation beside the sea with a wide beach of sand and pebbles, its amazing mountain backdrop and the views across the bay to the town and part by the atmosphere created by Elisa, and staff - friendly, relaxed and comfortable. The restaurant with its homely touches has a super menu and a reputation extending well outside the site. The family type entertainment is in contrast to that provided at the larger, brasher sites of the Costa Daurada. There are 255 pitches, mostly level and laid out beside the beach, with more behind on wide, informal terracing. Odd pine and olive trees are an attractive feature and provide some shade. Electricity is available although long leads may needed in places. Gates provide access to the pleasant beach with useful cold showers to wash the sand away. For those interested, there is a naturist beach around the little headland just south of the site. This is a pretty place to stay and Elisa gives a personal service but do not expect 'Costa' type entertainment. Ask how the nearby village of Hospitalet del Infante got its name - it's a royal riddle! The village is well worth exploring and if you are here in June watch for the fireworks of the celebration of 'John and the Devil'.

Facilities: The main toilet facilities are on the front part of the building housing the restaurant, reception and the family home on the first level. Clean and neat, there is hot water to showers (hot water by token but free to campers - a device to guard against unauthorized visitors from the beach). An additional small block with clean toilets and wash-basins is at the far end of the site. Restaurant/bar and shop (1/4-30/9). Play area. Five-a-side soccer. Fishing. Internet point. Gas supplies. Torches required in some areas. **Off site:** Village facilities, incl. shop and restaurant 1.5 km. Bicycle hire or riding 2 km.

Charges 2002

Per person	€ 4.50 - € 6.25
tent or caravan	€ 4.50 - € 6.25
car or motorcycle	€ 4.50 - € 6.25
motorcaravan	€ 6.00 - € 12.20
electricity	€ 2.95
dog	€ 2.25 - € 2.40

Discounts for seniors and for longer stays. No credit cards. **Tel:** 977 823 254. Fax: 977 820 691. E-mail: eroller@nil.fut.es. **Reservations:** Contact site. **Open** all year.

Directions: Hospitalet del Infante is south of Tarragona, accessed from the A7 (exit 38) or from the N340. From the north take first exit to Hospitalet del Infante at the 1128 km. marker. Follow signs in the village, site is 2 km. south, by the sea.

CAMPING - PENSIÓN

Cala d'Oques

L'Hospitalet de L'Infant . E-43890 **TARRAGONA**
Tel. (34) 977 82 32 54 · Fax (34) 977 82 06 91
eroller@nil.fut.es · www.fut.es/~eroller/

You won't regret a visit to this very natural, and directly on the famous nudist beach 'Playa del Torn' located, quiet, clean, small and sympathetic family campsite, surrounded by mountains and considered by many clubs as one of the most beautifully situated site in Europe.
I also speak English. Welcome!

PATRONAT MUNICIPAL DE TURISME DE L'HOSPITALET DE L'INFANT

BANDERA AZUL DE EUROPA

Costa del Azahar

The 'Orange Blossom' Coast runs down the east coast from Vinaros to Almanzora, with the great port of Valencia in the middle. Orange groves grow right down to the coast, particularly in the northern section and the area is rich in fresh food from land and sea. Wine, fruit and flowers play large parts in the local economy and Paella and Zarzuela are said to have originated here. Most of the best beaches are found in the area of Peñiscola or to the south of Valencia and the area is very, very sunny.

Camping-Caravanning Ametlla Village Platja

8536 Apdo. Correus 240, Paraje Santes Creus, 43860 L'Ametlla de Mar (Tarrag (Tarragona)

This site within a protected area is new (2000), has been well thought out and is startling in the quality of service provided, the finish and the materials used in construction. The 373 pitches are on a terraced hillside above colourful coves with shingle beaches and two small associated lagoons (with a protected fish species). The site is environmentally correct, local planning regulations are extremely tight including the types of trees that may planted. The many bungalows here have been tastefully incorporated. There are great views, particularly from the friendly restaurant (which has a very good chef). Animation is organised for children in high season and there is a well equipped fitness room (free). There are quality pools (lifeguard) and a sub-aqua diving school operates on the site in high season and beginners may try a dive. This is a most attractive small site near the picturesque fishing village of L'Ametlla de Mar, famous for its fish restaurants, and within the Ebro Delta nature reserve. It is about 20 minutes from Europe's second largest theme park, Port Aventura, but as there is no regular bus service your own transport is required (the owners arrange free buses to the local disco each Wednesday). No transit traffic is allowed within the site in high season. Used by tour operators (30 pitches). This is a very good site for families or for just relaxing. There is some train noise.

Facilities: Three really good toilet blocks provide free hot water throughout, British style WCs, washbasins and some private cabins with WC and washbasin, plus others with WC, basin and shower. The showers in two blocks are adjustable, but those in the older block have a system of separate push-buttons for hot and cold water. Motorcaravan services. Gas supplies. Supermarket (1/4-30/9; small shop incl. bread at other times). Good restaurant with snack menu and bar with TV room (1/4-15/10). Swimming pool. Sub aqua diving. Kayaking. Fishing. Children's club and play area. Fitness room. Bicycle hire. Football. Basketball. Volleyball. Entertainment July/Aug. Barbecue area. Bicycle hire. Fishing. English is spoken. **Off site:** Golf 15 km. Riding 20 km. Boat launching 3 km. Theme parks.

Charges 2003

Per person	€ 2.06 - € 5.00
child (under 10 yrs)	€ 1.69 - € 4.10
tent or caravan	€ 2.18 - € 5.30
car	€ 2.18 - € 5.30
motorcaravan	€ 3.86 - € 9.40
electricity	€ 3.00 - € 3.50

All plus 7% VAT. Less for longer stays, especially in low season. **Tel:** 977 267 784. Fax: 977 267 868. E-mail: info@campingametlla.com. **Reservations:** Contact site. **Open** all year.

Directions: From A7 (Barcelona - Valencia) take exit 39 for L'Ametlla de Mar. Follow numerous large white signs on reaching village and site is 2.5 km. south of the village.

Camping Bonterra

8580 Avenida de Barcelona 47, 12560 Benicasim (Castelló)

If you are looking for a town site which is not too crowded and has good facilities this one may be for you as there are few quality sites in the local area and this is open all year. It is a 300 m. walk to a good, shady beach - and parking is not too difficult. Good beach for scuba diving or snorkelling - hire facilities are available at Benicasim. The site has 375 pitches (70-90 sq.m), all with electricity and a variety of bungalows on site. Bonterra has a clean and neat appearance with reddish soil, palms, grass and a number of trees which give good shade. There is a little road and rail noise. A well run, Mediterranean style site useful for visiting local attractions such as the Carmelite monastery at Desierto de las Palmas, 6 km. distant or the historic town of Castillion.

Facilities: Four attractive, well maintained sanitary blocks sensibly laid out, providing some private cabins, washbasins with hot water, others with cold. Showers have solar heating and include baby showers. Facilities for disabled campers. Laundry and motorcaravan services. Restaurant/bar. Shop (all year). Swimming pool, covered pool and children's pool. Playground (some concrete bases). Tennis. Multi-sport court. Table tennis. Disco. Bicycle hire. **Off site:** Town facilities. Fishing 500 m. Golf 10 km. Riding 3 km. Boat launching 5 km.

Charges 2003

Per adult	€ 2.03 - € 4.31
child (3-9 yrs)	€ 1.87 - € 3.95
pitch acc. to type and season	€ 7.50 - € 22.28
electricity	€ 3.13 - € 5.00

All plus 7% VAT. Less in low season and special long stay rates excl. July/Aug. **Tel:** 964 300 007. Fax: 964 300 008. E-mail: info@campingbonterra.com. **Reservations:** made if you write at least a month in advance. **Open** all year.

Directions: Site is east of Benicasim village, with entrance off the old main N340 road running a little back from the coast. Coming from the north, turn left at sign 'Benicasim por la costa'. On the A7 from the north use exit 45, from the south exit 46.

BONTERRA - PARK
CAMPING & BUNGALOWS

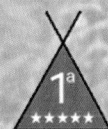

A campsite to spend wonderful holidays with your family, with high-quality installations, surrounded by a leafy Mediterranean wood.

Located in Benicàssim in front of the most acknowledged Almadraba beach, awarded with the blue flag, and close to the natural reserve Parque Natural del Desierto de las Palmas.

Bonterra has at its disposal several types of pitches, rental of bungalows, mobile-homes and wooden chalets.

On the campsite, you will find three swimming pools, bar, restaurant, cafeteria, shop, laundry and infirmary. It also has a large entertainment programme with an area for sport, a social club and a mini-club.

Our welcoming team is at your disposal so that you and your family can enjoy some unforgettable holidays in healthy, clean and safe surroundings.

Heated swimming pool, 28º C

Open all year

SPECIAL PRICES IN LOW SEASON

INFORMATION AND BOOKING
AVDA. BARCELONA Nº 47 • E- 12.560 • CASTELLON
TFNO: (34) 964-300 007 • FAX: (34) 964 300 008
info@campingbonterra.com • campingbonterra.com

Camping Vinaros

8558 Ctra. N340 km 1054, 12500 Vinaros (Castelló)

Taking its name from the seaside town nearby, this uncomplicated site now has 179 numbered pitches of average size on flat ground. Mature trees provide shade and neat hedges separate the pitches, all of which have an individual sink. The site entrance is directly off the N340, with a spacious drive and lots of outside parking, but there is traffic noise. A pleasant small swimming pool has a sunbathing area and a paddling pool (May-Sept). The restaurant is nicely decorated, has a reasonable menu and serves snacks all year. Large blocks of natural stone have been used for decoration in the site and the theme is continued in the spotless sanitary block. Petanque is played and indoor games are available in the bar. This site is ideal as an all year stopover site and normally has several long stay British customers enjoying the peace and good discounts in low season. Nathalie, the chirpy manager speaks good English and has a keen sense of humour. This area reputedly enjoys 300 days sunshine a year.

Facilities: Exceptionally clean, fully equipped, toilet block with clever use of marble and tiling creating a light crisp environment enhanced by potted shrubs. Some washbasins are in cabins. Washing machines and irons. Motorcaravan services. Camping essentials sold (tent pegs etc) and milk and bread can be ordered. Bar/restaurant (all year). Play area. Swimming pools (1/4-30/10). Petanque. Musical entertainment in season. Aviary. Fax machine. Ice for sale. **Off site:** Beach 800 m. Bus service outside gate. Rail station close by. Vinaros 500 m. with extensive choice of bars and restaurants. Golf 7 km.

Charges 2002

Per unit, all incl.	€ 12.40

All plus 7% VAT. Stay over 7 days in low season € 7.20 + 7% VAT. **Tel:** 964 402424. Fax: 964 402424. **Reservations:** Contact site. **Open** all year.

Directions: Take exit 43 (Ulldecona) from the A7. Switch to the N340 and head towards Barcelona. Site is at 1054 km. marker directly off N340.

Camping Playa Tropicana

8560 Playa Tropicana, 12579 Alcossebre (Castelló)

Playa Tropicana is the living dream of the owners Vera and Charlie. It has been given a tropical theme with scores of 'Romanesque' white statues around the site including in the sanitary blocks. It has a delightful position away from the main hub of tourism, alongside a good sandy beach which shelves gently into the clean waters. There is a shingle beach for fishing nearby and a pretty promenade in front of the site, with statues. It is a quiet position and it is a drive rather than a walk to the centre of the village resort. The site has 300 marked pitches separated by lines of flowering bushes under mature trees. The pitches vary in size (50-100 sq.m), most are shaded and there are electricity connections throughout (some need long leads). There are 50 places for motorcaravans with water and drainage and there is a scale of charges for the different pitches. The site has several large water features by the high quality restaurant (some are very cheeky!), aviaries and small monkeys. Visit the restaurant and enjoy the pictures of the owners with famous people.

Facilities: Two sanitary blocks delightfully decorated, fully equipped and of excellent standard, include 16 washbasins in private cabins. Baby baths, some units with WC, basin and shower, and facilities for disabled people. Washing machine. Motorcaravan services. Gas supplies. Large supermarket (all season). Superb restaurant, a little expensive (Easter - late Sept). Drinks served on terrace. Swimming pool (18 x 11 m.) and children's pool. Playground. Volleyball. Table tennis. Bicycle hire. Fishing. Torches necessary in some areas. No TVs allowed in July/Aug. Dogs are not accepted but cats are. **Off site:** Fishing and watersports on the beach. Golf 25 km. Riding 3 km. Boat launching 3 km.

Charges 2002

Per person	€ 6.35
child (1-10 yrs)	€ 5.00
pitch	€ 25.00 - € 35.40

Electricity and VAT included. Discounts up to 45% out of season. **Tel:** 964 412 463. Fax: 964 412 805. E-mail: info@playatropicana.com. **Reservations:** made for min. 10 days with deposit (25%). **Open** 15 March - 31 October.

Directions: Alcoceber (or Alcossebre) is between Peniscola and Oropesa. Turn off N340 at 1018 km. marker towards Alcossebre on CV142. Just before entering town take right turn signed 'platjes Capicorb'. Follow road for approx. 2.5 km. turning right at beach. Site is on the right.

Camping-Caravanning Moraira

8755 Camino Paellero 50, 03724 Moraira-Teulada (Alacant)

This small hillside site with some views over the town and marina is quietly situated in an urban area amongst old pine trees and just 400 m. from a sheltered bay. Terracing provides shaded pitches of varying size (access to some of the upper pitches may be difficult for larger units). A few pitches have water and waste water facilities and a few have sea and marina views. There are electricity connections (6/10A). A large, painted water tower stands at the top of the site. An attractive irregular shaped swimming pool with paved sunbathing terrace is below the small bar/restaurant with terrace. The pool has observation windows where you can watch the swimmers. The pool is used for sub-aqua instruction and the site runs a professional diving school for all levels (the diving here is good and the water warm even in winter). A sandy beach is 1.5 km.

Facilities: The high quality toilet block, with polished granite floors and marble fittings, is built to an ultra-modern design with extra large free hot showers. Washing machine and dryer. Motorcaravan services. Bar/restaurant and shop (main season). Small swimming pool. Tennis. Sub-aqua with site boat and instruction. Electronic games. Comprehensive security system. Torches may be required. **Off site:** Shops, bars and restaurants within walking distance.

Charges 2002

Per person	€ 3.60
child (4-9 yrs)	€ 2.70
pitch incl. car and unit	€ 9.91
electricity	€ 3.00

All plus 7% VAT. Less 15-60% in low seasons. **Tel:** 965 745 249. Fax: 965 745 315. **Reservations:** Write to site for details. **Open** all year.

Directions: Site is best approached from Teulada. From A7 take exit 63 onto N332. In 3.5 km. turn right signed Teulada and Moraira. In Teulada fork right to Moraira. At junction at town entrance turn right signed Calpe and in 1 km. turn right into road to site on bend immediately after Res. Don Julio. Do not take the first right as the signs seem to indicate otherwise you will go round a loop.

CAMPING - CARAVANING **MORAIRA**

E-03724 **MORAIRA-TEULADA (Alicante)** · Camino del Paellero, 50.
Tel. (34) 96 574 52 49 · Fax (34) 96 574 53 15
www.campingmoraira.com · e-mail: campingmoraira@campingmoraira.com
Motorway A-7, exit 63, direction Teulada.
Very nice, quietly situated camp site under pine trees with lots of shade and nearby the sea. Very original sanitary install. with hot water everywhere and beautiful swimming pool. Diving center at site. 15 to 60% discount in low season. Reservations possible.
Open throughout the year.

n o m i n a d o
PREMIO TURISMO
COSTA BLANCA '94
Campings

TROFEO DE LAS
NACIONES
Academie Europeenne de
Tourisme et Gastonomie
Bruselas 1995

Camping Cap Blanch

8687 Playa Cap Blanch, 03590 Altea (Alacant)

This well run site in a coastal location is open all year and very popular for winter stays. It is alongside the beach road and has direct access to the pebble beach and is within a few hundred yards of all Albir's shops and restaurants. Campers can join in a host of activities organised by the site, from physical ones such as tennis and walking to gentler ones such as painting or lessons in Spanish in the pleasant classroom. The site tends to be full in winter and is very popular with several nationalities, especially the Dutch. For winter stays, it would pay to get there before Christmas as January and February are the peak months. Although it is on the coast, the site is well sheltered and something of a sun-trap, the 250 pitches on flat, hard gravel are of a good size and well maintained with 5A electricity.

Facilities: The refurbished sanitary block can be heated and provides good facilities including some washbasins in private cabins, baby facilities and a room (locked) with facilities for disabled visitors. Motorcaravan services. Gas supplies. Laundry. Bar and restaurant. Children's playground. Tennis. Boules. Fitness centre. Organised entertainment and courses. ATM. **Off site:** Restaurants, shops and commercial centre close.

Charges 2002

Per person	€ 5.40
child (3-12 yrs)	€ 4.20
caravan/tent and car	€ 10.80 - € 12.00
motorcaravan	€ 8.40
electricity	€ 3.60

VAT included. Less 10-35% for low season stays 7-30 days, special rates for long stays. **Tel:** 965 845 946. Fax: 965 844 556. E-mail: capblanch@ctv.es. **Reservations:** Contact site. **Open** all year.

Directions: Site is on Albir - Altea coast road and can be reached from either end. From N332, north or south, watch for sign Playa del Albir and proceed through Albir until you reach the coast road. Site is on north side of Albir, well signed.

Kiko Park

8615 46780 Oliva (Valencia)

Kiko Park is a smart, modern site located alongside a magnificent beach (Blue Flag), nestled behind protective sand-dunes. Family owned and run, with well trained staff who form an enthusiastic team working hard to make your stay an enjoyable experience. Access to the beach is via several sets of tiled steps which take you over the bank between site and sea. The Kiko Port restaurant and beach bar are elevated in the northwest corner overlooking the beach. With architecture reminiscent of a ship, and the terrace covered with a huge canvas, the position, decor and menu make dining here a delightful experience. The site has direct access onto the spectacular, white, fine sandy beach that runs for miles - Kiko is towards the northwest end, which leads into a small marina and yacht club. Unfortunately the beach is not visible from the campsite itself, which is set at a lower level, behind a grassy bank. The 200 pitches all have electricity (16A, long leads may be needed), with shade provided by trees and tall hedges. Of variable size, access to them from the rather narrow roads could be difficult for larger units. This is an excellent site for watersports enthusiasts and medium sized boats can be launched. Windsurfing is reputed to be very good.

Facilities: Four modern sanitary blocks are very clean and fully tiled with free hot water, large showers, washbasins (a few in cabins), British style WCs and excellent facilities for disabled visitors (who will find a large part of this site flat and convenient). Laundry facilities. Motorcaravan services. Gas supplies. Restaurant. Bar with TV. Beach-side bar and restaurant (all year). Supermarket (all year, excl. Sundays). Children's playground. Watersports facilities Diving school in high season from mid-June. Mini club. Entertainment for children from mid-June. Petanque. Bicycle hire. Beach volleyball. Telephones. Exchange facilities. **Off site:** The yacht club offers its facilities of swimming pool, bar, restaurant and TV room to campers at Kiko. The footpath to the marina leads into the town - about a 10 minute walk. Golf 5 km. Riding 7 km. Indoor pool 1 km.

Charges 2002

Per person	€ 5.00
child (under 10 yrs)	€ 4.00
pitch acc. to services and season	€ 8.60 - € 24.00
electricity (16A)	€ 2.00
dog	€ 2.00

Tel: 962 850 905. Fax: 962 854 320. E-mail: kikopark@kikopark.com. **Reservations:** Write to site for details. **Open** all year.

Directions: From A7 north of Benidorm take exit 61 to the town and then the beach; site is at the northwest end.

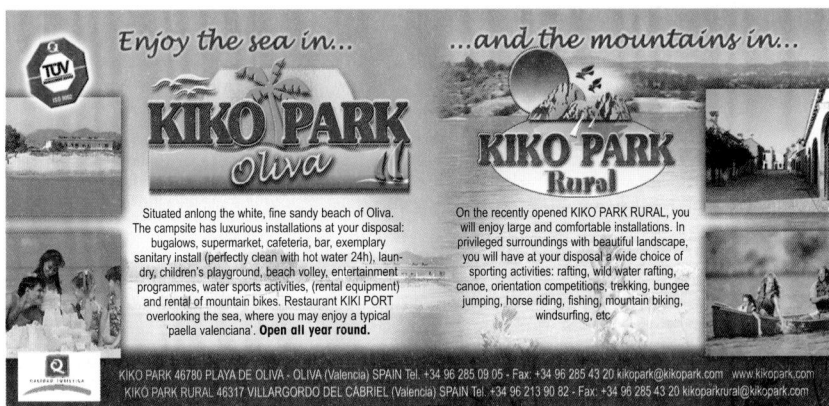
Spain - Communidad Valenciana

Camping Javea

8754 Ctra. Cabo de la Nao, km 1, 03730 Javea (Alacant)

The 200 m. access road to this site is a little unkempt as it passes some factories, but all changes on the final approach with palms, orange and pine trees, the latter playing host to a colony of parakeets. English is spoken at reception. The boxed hedges and palms surrounding this area with a backdrop of hills dotted with villas presents an attractive setting. Three hectares provides space for 246 numbered pitches with 146 for touring units. Flat, level and rectangular in shape, the pitches vary in size 60-80 sq.m. (not advised for caravans or motorhomes with an overall length exceeding 7 m). All have a granite chip surface and 8A electricity. Being a typical Spanish site, the pitches are not separated so units may be close to each other. Some pitches have artificial shade, although for most the pruned eucalyptus and pepper trees will suffice. The area has a large number of British residents so a degree of English is spoken at many shops and restaurants. Besides being popular for a summer holiday, Camping Javea is now open all year and could be of interest to those that wish to 'winter' in an excellent climate.

Facilities: Two very clean, fully equipped, sanitary blocks include two children's toilets plus a baby bath, dishwashing and laundry sinks. Two washing machines. Small bar and restaurant where in high season you purchase bread and milk. Large swimming pool and children's pool with lifeguard and sun bathing lawns. Children's play area. Table tennis. Boules. Five-aside football. Basketball. Electronic barriers (deposit for swipe card). **Off site:** Sandy beach 3 km. 'Old' and new Javea within easy walking distance with supermarkets and shops catering for all needs. Market Thursday.

Charges 2002

Per adult	€ 3.46 - € 3.85
child	€ 2.95 - € 3.95
pitch 60 sq.m.	€ 9.20 - € 10.22
pitch 70 sq.m.	€ 10.82 - € 12.02
pitch 80 sq.m.	€ 12.44 - € 13.82
electricity	€ 2.58

Good low season discounts for longer stays. **Tel:** 965 791 070. Fax: 966 460 507. E-mail: camjavea@ arrakis.es. **Reservations:** Necessary for high season. **Open** all year.

Directions: Exit N332 for Javea on A134, continue in direction of Port (road number changes to CV 734). On reaching roundabout and Lidl supermarket turn right signed Arenal Platges and Cabo de la Nao (also camping sign). Straight on at next roundabout to camping sign and slip road in 100 m. If you miss slip road go back from next roundabout.

Camping Villasol

8681 Avda. Bernat de Sarria, 03500 Benidorm (Alacant)

Benidorm is increasingly popular for winter stays and Villasol is a genuinely excellent, purpose built modern site. There is a small indoor pool, heated for winter use and a very attractive, large outdoor pool complex (summer only) featuring a lovely, sheltered free-form pool in a beautifully landscaped, grassy sunbathing area where palm trees and Mediterranean shrubs and flowers create a colourful and exotic atmosphere. The pool is overlooked by the bar/restaurant and restaurant terrace. Many of the 314 well separated pitches are arranged on wide terraces which afford views of the mountains surrounding Benidorm. All pitches (80-85 sq.m.) have electricity and satellite TV connections, with 160 with full services for seasonal use. Shade is mainly artificial as yet. The town and Levante beach are 1.3 km. within easy walking distance leaving your car on site. If you are looking for first class amenities in Benidorm, in pleasant and fairly quiet surroundings, this site would make an excellent choice. Reservation is advised even in winter. We hear that part of the site may be lost to a road widening scheme, but the owner is developing a new site elsewhere. We are following its progress.

Facilities: Modern, well fitted sanitary blocks provide free, controllable hot water to showers and washbasins and British WCs. Good facilities for disabled campers. Laundry facilities. Good value restaurant. Bar. Shop. Swimming pools, outdoor and indoor. Children's playground. Evening entertainment programme. Dogs are not accepted. **Off site:** Golf 8 km. Fishing, bicycle hire 1.3 km.

Charges 2002

Per person	€ 4.17 - € 5.64
child (1-9 yrs)	€ 3.24 - € 4.17
large tent or caravan	€ 4.35 - € 9.61
small tent	€ 4.35 - € 6.10
car	€ 4.17 - € 5.64
motorcaravan	€ 8.53 - € 15.26
electricity	€ 3.24

All plus 7% VAT. Good discounts for longer stays in winter. **Tel:** 965 850 422. Fax: 966 806 420.
Reservations: Only accepted for 3 month min. stay, starting 1 Oct. Write to site. **Open** all year.

Directions: From the autopista take Benidorm exit (no. 65) and turn left at the second set of traffic lights. After 1 km. at another set of lights turn right, then right again at next lights. Site is on right in 400 m. From northern end of N332 bypass follow signs for Benidorm Playa Levante. In 500 m. at traffic lights turn left, then right at next lights. Site is on right after 400 m.

Camping-Caravaning El Raco

8685 Avda. Doctor Severo Ochoa, s/n, 03500 Benidorm (Alacant)

This purpose built site (opened in '96) with excellent facilities and very competitive prices provides 685 pitches (100 for touring units). There is wide access from the Runcon de Loix road. The site is quietly situated 1.5 km. from the town, Levante beach and promenade. The road has both footpaths and a cycle track. There are wide tarmac roads and pitches of 80 sq.m. or more, separated by low, clipped cypress hedging, but there is not much shade as yet. Free satellite TV connections are provided to each pitch and there are 94 with all services with (5, 6, 10A) electricity available. The whole site is on a slight downward slope away from the entrance and affords excellent views of the rugged mountains in the hinterland, although this open aspect could be a disadvantage in windy weather. The restaurant, bar and elegant pools are all at the entrance, some distance from the touring pitches. There are large numbers of permanent pitches and many seasonal pitches are occupied by wintering campers (lots of British) and the site has a mature, cheerful atmosphere. This is a clean, tidy and good quality site.

Facilities: Three large toilet blocks are well equipped. Facilities for disabled people. Dishwashing sinks. Laundry facilities. Gas supplies. Motorcaravan services. Restaurant. Bar. Well stocked shop with reasonable prices. Busy bar with TV also open to public and good value restaurant. Outdoor swimming pool, no slides or diving board (1/4-31/10). Indoor heated pool (1/11-31/3). Playground. ATM. **Off site:** Beach 1 km. Bicycle hire 2 km. Golf 6 km. Theme parks.

Charges 2003

Per person	€ 4.30 - € 4.51
child (1-9 yrs)	€ 3.10 - € 3.31
tent	€ 4.66 - € 4.96
caravan	€ 5.41 - € 5.86
car	€ 4.06 - € 4.96
motorcaravan	€ 4.12 - € 9.02
motorcycle	€ 3.61 - € 3.91
electricity	€ 2.71 - € 2.86

Discounts for longer stays. VAT included. No credit cards. **Tel:** 96 586 8552. Fax: 96 586 8544. E-mail: campingraco@inicia.es. **Reservations:** Not accepted. **Open** all year.

Directions: From autopista take Benidorm exit (no. 65) and turn left at the second set of traffic lights. After 1 km. at another set of lights turn right, then straight on at next lights for 300 m. to site on right. From northern end of N332 bypass follow signs for Benidorm Playa Levante. In 500 m. at traffic lights turn left, then straight on at next lights for 300 m. to site on right.

Camping Armanello

8680 Av. de la Communidad Valenciana, 03500 Benidorm (Alacant)

This small, uncomplicated site is in a slightly scruffy area 1 km. back from the eastern Benidorm beach (the one on the other side of the town is less crowded), Armanello is quietly situated just far enough away from the main coast road to avoid excessive noise. It is a plain and mature site, with small pitches (60 sq.m.) marked out in bays of 10 or 12 in former citrus and olive groves. There is a small and much-used swimming pool. About 103 units are taken on flat ground with electricity available throughout (16A). The site is popular with long stay units in winter. The approach road from the main N332 is narrow and bumpy. The facilities here are rather basic and we see this as a site for transit stops and short stays, rather than as a holiday site, but the rates are good.

Facilities: Two heated toilet blocks (back to back) have some washbasins in cabins. Hot water for laundry and dishwashing. Facilities near reception include a washroom, shower and WC for disabled people. Washing machines and dryer. Gas supplies. Motorcaravan services. Shop (all year). Bar. Restaurant (high season). Swimming pool. **Off site:** Fishing, bicycle hire or riding 1.5 km. Golf 10 km.

Charges 2002

Per adult	€ 4.81
child	€ 4.21
pitch and car	€ 19.84
electricity	€ 2.70

Plus 7% VAT. Reductions in low season, plus special winter prices. **Tel:** 965 853 190. Fax: 965 853 100. E-mail: arenablanca@ctv.es. **Reservations:** Contact site for details (it also has much winter trade when reservation is advisable). **Open** all year.

Directions: From new bypass (N332) take Levante Beach road into Benidorm; watch for site signs after 1 km. directly off this road. From autopista junction 65 take Benidorm exit and at second traffic lights turn left. Site approach road is 1 km. on right. On leaving site turn right not left for the main road as the road becomes very rough and narrow.

Camping Benisol

8683 Avda. de la Comunidad Valenciana s/n, 03500 Benidorm (Alacant)

Camping Benisol is under new management and is being improved steadily. It is a mature and peaceful site with lush, green vegetation and a mountain background. Well developed hedging and trees give a good degree of privacy to each pitch and some artficial shade is provided. An excellent restaurant with a pretty, shaded terrace overlooks the pool. There are 298 pitches of which around 115 are for touring units (60-80 sq.m). All have electrical hook-ups (4/6A) and 75 have drainage also. All the connecting roads are now surfaced with tarmac. Amenities include a swimming pool with cascade and small water slides and the sports facilities listed below. The pool has a pleasant sunbathing area. Some day-time road noise should be expected.

Facilities: Modern sanitary facilities, heated in winter and kept very clean, have free, solar heated hot water to the washbasins, showers and sinks for laundry and dishwashing. Laundry facilities and clothes lines. Car wash. Gas supplies. Free satellite TV link. Restaurant with terrace and bar (all year, closed 1 day a week). Shop. Swimming pool (Easter - Nov). Sports ground. Small, old-style play area. Minigolf. Table tennis. Jogging track. Tennis. Golf driving range. Doctor's room. ATM. **Off site:** Bicycle hire 3 km. Fishing (sea) 3 km. Riding 1 km. Golf 14 km. Bus route.

Charges 2002

Per pitch	€ 11.45 - € 15.65
person	€ 4.20 - € 4.50
child (1-10 yrs)	€ 3.60 - € 3.90
electricity	€ 2.40

All plus 7% VAT. Less 15-60% in low seasons. No credit cards. **Tel:** 965 851 673. Fax: 965 860 895. **Reservations:** Contact site for details. **Open** all year.

Directions: Exit the N332 at 152 km. marker and take turn signed Playa Levant. Site is 100 m. on left.

Costa Blanca

The Costa Blanca (the White Coast) derives its name from its 170 miles or so of silvery-white beaches along the central section of the Spanish Mediterranean coastline. There are many sheltered bays and most beaches shelve quite gently. The countryside behind the coast remains largely untouched by mass tourism and is well worth exploring, as are places such as Alicante, Cartagena and Valencia. The most popular resort is Benidorm, which has very much shed its 'lager lout' image. Large sums of money have been spent building a beautifully paved promenade stretching the whole length of the beach, with palm trees at regular intervals. The beach itself is cleaned every night and the whole town presents a very well cared for image with plenty of police patrols in evidence. However, don't be too complacent as petty pilfering does occur. In the winter the town is filled with older people who never pose a problem, whilst in summer it is noisier and more boisterous with families and younger people on holiday.

Camping Playa del Torres

86889 Partida Torres Norte 11, Apdo. Correus 243, 03570 Villajoyosa (Alacant)

Jacinto and Mercedes have a pretty beachside site with the lower part set under eucalyptus trees. Reception is placed in one of the site's tasteful wooden buildings close to the beach (excellent English is spoken). The 85 lower pitches, some large, are on flat ground with shade. 10 good pitches are right alongside the beach fence (book early). All have electricity (16A), some are fully serviced and there are ample water fountains around the site along with efficient, modern lighting. The upper levels of the site have chalets and mobile homes. A modest sized pool is set in the centre of the site between the building housing the bar, cafeteria and shop and the separate clean sanitary block (a short walk from the beachside pitches). Boats can be launched from the sand and shingle beach, sub-aqua diving and other watersports can be organised. Benidorm with its beaches is close, along with many tourist activities including the Fuentes del Algar waterfall and the huge exiting new 'Terra Mitica' theme park. If you prefer a small sites away from the 'high rise' and bustle of Benidorm, this could be for you.

Facilities: The sanitary building is of a high specification, as are the fittings within, including excellent showers. Laundry. Bar. Cafeteria. Shop. Swimming pool. Children's play area. Petanque. Fishing. Barbecues. Freezer. Fridge hire. Reception will assist with all tourist activities. **Off site:** Riding 100 m. Golf 18 km. Serious or recreational walking and climbing is possible about 20 minutes away from the site. Benidorm is very close.

Charges 2003

Per person	€ 3.44 - € 3.82
child (4-13 yrs)	€ 2.57 - € 2.85
pitch	€ 3.22 - € 7.15
caravan	€ 3.57 - € 3.97
tent	€ 3.44 - € 3.82
car	€ 3.44 - € 3.83
motorcaravan	€ 6.44 - € 7.15
electricity (plus meter)	€ 3.31

Plus 7% VAT. Less 5-50% for low season stays of 7 days or more. **Tel:** 966 810 031. Fax: 966 810 173. E-mail: capto@ctv.es. **Reservations:** Contact site. **Open** all year.

Directions: From Villajoyosa on N332, 1 km. after town, 300 m. past traffic lights, sign on right, follow road 800 m. to site. From Benidorm after 3 km. site on left, but left turn prohibited. Proceed 400 m. to traffic lights, circle onto other carriageway, then as above. From autoroute leave at Benidorm or Villajoyosa onto N332, then as above. Do not confuse with two older sites (Hercules and Sartorium) which are adjacent beach sites.

Complejo Ecoturistico Marjal

8743 Ctra. N-332, km 73.4, 03140 Guardamar del Segura (Alacant)

MarJal is beside the estuary of the Segura river, alongside the pine and eucalyptus forests of the Dunas de Guardamar natural park. It is a new site with a huge lagoon-style pool and a superb sports complex. Reception is in a delicately coloured building topped by a weather-vane depicting the 'Garza Real' (heron) bird which frequents the local area and forms part of the site logo. There are 246 pitches on this award-winning site, all with water, electricity, drainage and satellite TV points, the ground covered with crushed marble making the pitches clean and pleasant. There is little shade as yet and the site has an open feel with lots of room. The large restaurant overlooks the pools and the river that leads to the sea in the near distance. This situation is shared with the taperia (high season) and bar with large terraces fringed by trees, palms and pomegranates. The impressive pool/lagoon complex (1,100 sq.m) has a water cascade, an island bar plus bridge, one part sectioned as a children's pool and a jacuzzi. The extensive sports area is also impressive with qualified instructors. No effort has been spared here, the facilities are of the highest quality. Entertainment is provided in season. The fine sandy beach can be reached through the forest (800 m).

Facilities: Three excellent heated sanitary blocks have free hot water, elegant separators between sinks, spacious showers and some cabins. Each block has high quality facilities for babies and disabled campers, modern laundry rooms with washing machines, dryers, ironing boards and dish-washing rooms (complete with drainers and paper drying rolls). Car wash. Well stocked supermarket. Restaurants. Bar. Large outdoor pool complex (1/6-31/10). Heated indoor pool (low season). Fitness suite and gymnasium. Sauna. Beauty salon. UV beds. Aerobics and aquarobics for the more mature camper. Play room for children. Minigolf. Floodlit tennis and soccer pitch. Volleyball. Bicycle hire. Games room. TV room. ATM. **Off site:** Riding or golf 4 km.

Charges 2002

Per person	€ 4.66 - € 6.91
child	€ 2.40 - € 4.21
caravan or tent	€ 5.11 - € 7.21
car	€ 3.61 - € 6.01
motorcaravan	€ 8.71 - € 13.22
motorcycle	€ 2.40 - € 4.81
electricity per kw.	€ 0.21
dog	€ 1.20 - € 2.10

All plus 7% VAT. **Tel:** 966 725 022. Fax: 966 726 695. E-mail: marjal@futurnet.es. **Reservations:** Contact site. **Open** all year.

Directions: On N332 40 km. south of Alicante, site is on the sea side between 73 and 74 km. markers.

Camping Internacional La Marina

8742 Ctra. N332 km 76, 03194 La Marina (Alacant)

Efficiently run by a friendly Belgian family, La Marina has 370 pitches of seven different types and size of pitch ranging from about 50 sq.m. for tents to 100 sq.m. with electricity (10A), TV, water and drainage. Artificial shade is provided and the pitches are extremely well maintained on level, well drained ground with a special area allocated for tents in a small orchard. The Lagoon swimming pool complex is absolutely fabulous and has something for everyone (with lifeguards). The quality restaurant and bustling terraces overlook the Lagoon making for a most relaxing meal. A fine fitness centre and covered, heated pool (14 x 7 m) is close by. A pedestrian gate is at the rear of the site to give access to the long sandy beach through the coastal pine forest that is a feature of the area. You can be assured of quality at La Marina and thus we recommend it very highly whatever type of holidaying camper you may be.

Facilities: The elegant sanitary blocks offer the very best of modern facilities. Heated in winter, they include private cabins and facilities for disabled visitors. These facilities are amongst the best we have seen on the Mediterranean coast. Laundry facilities incl. irons. Modern motorcaravan services. Gas supplies. Supermarket. Bar/restaurant serving traditional Spanish dishes (all year). Swimming pools (1/4-15/10). Indoor pool. Fitness centre with massage. Sauna. Extensive activity and entertainment programme. Tennis. Table tennis. Huge playground. Hairdresser. Good security. **Off site:** Fishing 800 m. Bicycle hire 8 km. Golf 7 km. Riding 15 km. Bicycle hire 8 km. Boat launching 5 km. Theme parks.

Charges 2002

Per person	€ 4.51 - € 5.41
child (under 10 yrs)	€ 3.31 - € 3.76
pitch acc. to type and season	€ 14.54 - € 27.05
electricity	€ 2.40 - € 4.00

Plus 7% VAT. Seven grades of pitch. Less in low season, plus good discounts for longer stays 16/9-14/6, excluding Easter. **Tel:** 965 419 051. Fax: 965 419 110. E-mail: info@camping-lamarina.com. **Reservations:** Made with deposit (€ 30,05), min. 5 days Easter and Aug. **Open** all year.

Directions: Site is 2 km. west of La Marina. Leave N332 Guardamara de Segura - Santa Pola road at the 75 km. marker if travelling north, or the 78 km. marker if travelling south. Site is well signed.

Camping Florantilles

8741 03193 San Miguel de Salinas (Alacant)

Florantilles is an unassuming site, some 4 km. behind the coast, with some views over the top of the neighbouring citrus groves to a distant salt lake. It is open all year and in winter and spring the delicious scent of orange blossom fills the air. Mimosa trees provide shade for the 271 good-sized pitches (around 90 sq.m.) which are laid out on wide terraces; some very large pitches are available at extra cost. Electricity connections (10A) are provided for each pitch, together with water and a raised drain. There are many long stay customers including lots of British. The entrance has a large parking area with car wash facilities, with the entrance to the camping area fitted with a barrier. Amenities include a good sized pool and a children's pool. There is a restaurant with a standard tourist menu. Some light entertainment may be organized in season. Many watersports are possible in the nearby noisy beach resort of Torrevieja and walking clubs are popular, also bird watching, cycling and golf (discounts available). There is noise from the new motorway on the north side of the site. We see this as a transit site or for short visits to explore the area, rather than for family holidays.

Facilities: Two main toilet blocks provide controllable hot showers. Several smaller blocks dotted around the site have toilets and showers but no hot water. Laundry facilities. Bar (all year). Restaurant (summer only). Shop (limited hours in low seasons). Swimming pool (supervised in peak season, closed in winter). Tennis. Boules. Children's playground. Only 20 dogs are accepted on the site so a call is advised to ascertain acceptability. Torches required in some areas. **Off site:** Golf 4 km. Fishing, bicycle hire 5 km. Major resort entertainment in Torrevieja.

Charges 2002

Per unit	€ 9.02
adult	€ 3.61
child (1-12 yrs)	€ 3.01
electricity	€ 2.70

All plus 7% VAT. Special low season discounts. **Tel:** 965 720 458. Fax: 966 723 250. **Reservations:** Contact site. **Open** all year.

Directions: Leave A7 Valencia - Alicante autopista at Crevillente exit 724 on to recently upgraded and renumbered A37 Alicante - Cartegena autopista. The exit for the camping is immediately after the first toll, exit 758 for Torrevieja (Sur). At the roundabout turn right (site is now signed), at 300 m. turn first right. Site is on left.

Caravaning La Manga

8753 autovia Cartagena-La Manga, 30370 La Manga del Mar Menor (Murcia)

The site is a very large well equipped, 'holiday style' site with its own beach and pool. With a good number of typical Spanish long stay units, the length of the site is impressive (1 km.) and a bicycle is very helpful for getting about. La Manga is a 22 km. long narrow strip of land, bordered by the Mediterranean on one side and by the Mar Menor on the other. There are sandy bathing beaches on both sides and considerable development in terms of hotels, apartments, restaurants, night clubs, etc. in between - a little reminiscent of Miami Beach! You cannot drive all round this narrow strip of land as there is a gap in the centre, however, the very end of the southern part is great for 'getting away from it all' (take a picnic for the beach and be sure to go over the little bridge for privacy). The campsite is situated on the approach to 'the strip' and enjoys the benefit of its own semi-private beach alongside the Mar Menor, with a sailing, canoeing and windsurfing school and the site's excellent restaurant (traditional Spanish Tapas and food) and bar right beside the beach. The beach is dotted with impressive tall palm trees and the sea is very shallow and warm, so it is ideal for families with small children or choose between the outdoor or indoor pools. There are some 1,000 touring pitches of two sizes (84 or 110 sq m), regularly laid out in rows on slightly sloping gravel. They are smart, separated and shaded by high hedges, all have electricity (10A) and water connections. This site's excellent facilities are ideally suited for holidays in the winter when the weather is very pleasantly warm. If you are suffering from aches and pains try the famous local mud treatment. November daytime temperatures are usually above 20°C.

Facilities: Seven clean toilet blocks of standard design well spaced around the site. They include washbasins (with hot water in five blocks), and covered cold water sinks (three with hot water) for washing up and laundry. Laundry. Gas supplies. Large well stocked supermarket. Restaurant. Bar. Snack bar. Swimming pool complex, supervised, (April - Sept). Indoor pool, gymnasium, sauna and jacuzzi. Open air cinema (April - Sept). Tennis. Petanque. Minigolf. Basketball. Volleyball. Football area. Play area. Watersports school. **Off site:** Golf, bicycle hire or riding 5 km.

Charges 2002

Per 84 sq.m. pitch incl.	
2 persons	€ 16.08 - € 21.34
3 persons	€ 17.88 - € 23.59
4 persons	€ 20.13 - € 26.59
Per 110 sq.m. pitch incl.	
2 persons	€ 19.08 - € 25.39
3 persons	€ 21.79 - € 27.95
4 persons	€ 23.59 - € 31.10

Electricity included. All plus 7% VAT. Prices for up to 8 persons available; child under 6 yrs free. Less 10, 20 or 25% for stays of more than 7, 14 or 21 days in low season. Special prices for long winter stays. **Tel:** 968 563 014. Fax: 968 563 426. E-mail: lamanga@caravaning.es. **Reservations:** Contact site. **Open** all year.

Directions: Use exit 15 from the MU312 dual-carriageway towards Cabo de Palos, signed Playa Honda (site signed also). Cross road bridge and double back on yourself. Site entrance is clearly visible beside dual-carriageway with many flags flying.

Camping Naturista El Portus

El Portus, 30393 Cartagena (Murcia)

N8752

Set in a secluded, mountain fringed, south facing bay, El Portus is a fairly large naturist site with direct access to a sand and shingle beach and enjoying magnificent views. With its own micro-climate, this part of Spain enjoys almost all year round sunshine. Mid-day temperatures which seldom drop below 20°C and water almost always warm enough for swimming makes this an ideal site for hibernating! There are some 400 pitches, half for tourers, ranging from 60-100 sq.m, all but a few having electricity (6A), mostly on fairly level, if somewhat stony ground. El Portus has a reasonable amount of shade from the trees and every pitch has views. Permanent units are situated on the hill-side above the site. A large, supervised swimming pool and paddling pool are sheltered and landscaped with grass areas for sunbathing. At other times there may be a smaller heated pool above the camping area. One of the bar/restaurants is open all year. This is relaxed site with welcoming, English speaking reception staff. There is much of historical interest in the area including the newly excavated Roman ruins, which include an amphitheatre close by in the ancient seaport of Cartegena.

Facilities: Five toilet blocks of varying styles are fully equipped. Opened as required, they are clean and bright, some unisex. Open plan dishwashing and laundry facilities showers all with hot water. Facilities may be a little busy in peak season. Unit for disabled visitors, key from reception. Washing machines. Motorcaravan services. Three drinking water points clearly marked near the steps to restaurant. Non-drinking water points well spaced around site. Well stocked shop. Bar with TV and libary. Restaurant with 'menu del dia' high season, snack bar by beach acts as restaurant low season. Swimming pools. Play area. Tennis. Volleyball. Table tennis. Petanque. Yoga. Scuba-diving club (high season). Windsurfing. Spanish lessons. Small boat moorings. Disco and entertainment (high season). **Off site:** Fishing from beach. Riding and golf 40 km.

Charges 2002

Per person	€ 5.23
child (3-9 yrs)	€ 3.85
pitch	€ 11.72
pitch with electricity	€ 16.38
dog	€ 3.55

Plus 7% VAT. Special discounts for longer stays and in low season. **Tel:** 968 553 052. Fax: 968 553 053. E-mail: elportus@elportus.com. **Reservations:** Made with € 181 deposit. **Open** all year.

Directions: Site is on the coast, 10 km. west of Cartagena. Follow signs to Mazarron then take E22 to Canteras. Site is well signed for 4 km. to El Portus.

Camping Sopalmo

Sopalmo, 04638 Mojacar (Almería)

8749

This is a tiny, homely, site run by a cheerful man called Simon and his charming mother Isabel. They are full of fun and determined that you will enjoy your stay. The site is on two levels, the upper site (be prepared for a fairly steep gravel track to the gates) for 20 tourers and the lower section for 12 tents. All pitches are marked, level and on gravel with electricity. It is unspoilt and has much rustic charm with the family house providing the focal point of the site. The attractive trees and shrubs around the site include olives, figs, mimosa and cacti. Reception is a pretty little room in the front section of the quaint house and a few steps take you into a small but typically Spanish bar. There is informal 'al fresco' gatherings and late barbecues on the lovely 'barbacoa' (terrace), especially at Christmas! We recommend the site for the more mature camper who wishes to get away from it all and be very much within a family atmosphere. Lots of British campers winter here! Ask to see the baby tortoises that Simon rescues and then releases back into the wild when mature.

Facilities: The small sanitary block is very clean and fully equipped. Facilities for disabled campers. Hot showers assisted by solar power. Basic laundry and dishwashing facilities in a pleasant roofed area near reception. Bar. Breakfast available in summer, and the baker calls at 10.30 daily. Torch useful. **Off site:** The beach is 2 km. (naturism permitted) and the nearest serious shops are 5 km. Riding and bicycle hire 10 km.

Charges 2002

Per adult	€ 3.70
child	€ 2.90
pitch	€ 7.40
electricity	€ 2.00

Plus 7% VAT. Reductions for low season and longer stays. No credit cards. **Tel:** 950 478413. Fax: 950 473002. **Reservations:** Contact site. **Open** all year.

Directions: Exit from main coast road (N340) at junction 520 (northeast of Almeria). Take the AL152 (formerly A150) to Mojacar Playa and continue south towards Carboneras. Site is 6 km south of Mojacar Playa, signed off the road.

Spain - Andalucia
Camping Cuevas Mar
8751 Cuevas del Almanzora, 04618 Palomares (Almería)

The site opened in 1995 is managed by Pedro, a friendly Frenchman and is gaining a reputation for its excellent service, comfortable facilities and immaculate appearance. Cuevas Mar is a welcome addition in a region very popular with British visitors who appreciate its year-round dry, sunny climate. Quietly situated just back from the coast road (a little road noise on the site) and 500 m. across the road from the beach, the site offers 200 large, smart pitches (80-100 sq.m), all with electricity connections (6A) and firm dry surfaces. The newer section for large motorhomes is closest to the road. The older pitches are screened by hedges and young trees which afford some shade and have easy access from wide roads (some artificial shade is provided). The most attractive sheltered, tiled, oval-shaped pool (14 x 9 m) is surrounded by a grassy sunbathing area and has a thoughtfully provided long ramp to help the elderly or infirm to enter the water. Although there are few additional facilities here it is a most pleasant site and there are good restaurants within easy walking distance.

Facilities: The well designed neat central sanitary block is generous in size, adequate and fully equipped. Good laundry and dishwashing facilities under cover. Washing machines and dryer (another block is planned for late 2002). Two drinking water points on site (note: in common with many other sites in this very dry area, drinking water is supplied from tanks refilled by tanker delivery and the remainder of the water on site is non-potable). Shop. Bar with terrace by pool. Snacks may be offered in high season. Swimming pool (May - Sept). Jacuzzi. **Off site:** Restaurants 200 m. Mojaca 7 km. for seafood and lively bars. Fishing from beach 200 m. Golf 4 km. Bicycle hire 3 km.

Charges 2002

Per person	€ 4.20
child	€ 3.20
caravan or tent	€ 4.20
car	€ 4.20
motorcaravan	€ 8.42
motorcycle	€ 3.01
dog	€ 1.80
electricity	€ 3.01

Generous discounts for longer winter stays. No credit cards. **Tel:** 950 467 382. Fax: 950 467 382. E-mail: cuevasmar@arrakis.es. **Reservations:** Contact site. **Open** all year.

Directions: From N340 (Murcia - Almeria) leave at 537 km. for Cuevas del Amanzora, then follow the road to Vera and Palomares. Site is signed from Vera.

Spain - Andalucia
Camping Mar Azul
8760 Playa de San Miguel s/n, 04711 Almerimar (Almería)

Right beside the sea, on flat ground and with direct access to a sandy beach, Mar Azul is in a dry and sunny area of Spain where there are few other camp sites. The landscape to the north is dominated by the Sierra Nevada (but is rendered unsightly on the approach and behind the site by local farmers use of acres of plastic cloches. This is the case for 120 km. along this part of the coast). The 890 individual, numbered pitches are quite attractively laid out with many palm trees and at 90 sq.m. are larger than most in Spain. Artificial shade is provided on most pitches. Some seviced pitches for large units have been added recently. A circular, unheated swimming pool with a terrace and sun-beds, is near the beach. There are two other pools - one is in the centre of the site, where there is a very large area set aside for many different sports, the other is near the entrance. The site lies out on its own, but the large development of Almerimar with golf course, large hotel, restaurant, some shops, etc. is little over 1 km. along the beach. The town of El Ejido is 8 km. with excellent shellfish restaurants and if you stroll through the sand dunes you will be treated to the spectacle of flamingos and other protected species in the adjacent lagoons.

Facilities: Four, fully equipped, toilet blocks of good quality are heated when required. Washing machines. Motorcaravan services. Gas supplies. Fridge hire. Comprehensive shopping facilities and supermarket. Bar. Restaurant. Swimming pools and children's pool. Tennis. Fronton. Squash. Table tennis. Fitness centre. Boules. Volleyball. Badminton. Basketball. Riding. Archery. Bicycle hire and circuit. Roller skating. Minigolf. Football practice area. Fishing. Windsurfing school and equipment for hire. Riding school. Children's club (Club Aire Libre) April - June. English is spoken. Torch useful. **Off site:** Golf 1.5 km.

Charges 2002

Per person	€ 3.13 - € 4.34
child (2-10 yrs)	€ 2.81 - € 3.91
tent or caravan	€ 3.13 - € 4.34
car	€ 3.13 - € 4.34
motorcaravan	€ 5.63 - € 6.88
dog	€ 0.78 - € 1.56
electricity	€ 2.66 - € 3.13

All plus 7% VAT. Reductions for longer stays (up to 60%). **Tel:** 950 497 585. Fax: 950 497 294. E-mail: info@campingmarazul.com. **Reservations:** Made for any length. **Open** all year.

Directions: Turn off main N340/E15 road at km. 409 for Almerimar. Follow signs to town - site is well signed as you approach town.

Camping Suspiro del Moro

9270

Ctra. Bailén - Motril, km. 145, Puerto Suspiro del Moro, 18630 Granada (Granada)

Suspiro Del Moro is 11 km. south of Granada just off the Motril road or, alternatively, can be approached on the scenic mountain road from Almunecar (lots of bends this way). Many places of interest are within reasonable distance of the site, including La Alhambra, Granada and the Parador of La San Francisco. Based high in the Sierra Nevada mountain range, the area offers spectacular views from just outside the site, with trees and fences inhibiting the views inside. The site is small and rectangular with a cool and peaceful atmosphere and noise from the road is reduced by the high perimeter wall. Family run, it is well kept with gravel paths leading to flat, grass pitches which all benefit from the shade of mature trees. The site is part of a business which includes a very attractive Olympic sized pool and there is a direct path from the site. Above this is a restaurant and bar both with terraces. The restaurant has an extensive menu and waiter service and it is a real treat to eat there whilst enjoying the views. This is an ideal site to investigate the local area and has the great advantage of impressive additional facilities.

Facilities: Three small toilet blocks are situated around the camping area with British WCs and free hot showers. Laundry and washing up facilities are of a good standard. Small shop. Small restaurant/bar (high season). Functions are sometimes held here which can be noisy until late at night. Bar. TV lounge. Swimming pool with children's end (high season only). Small play area on gravel. Table tennis. Table football. Pool table.

Charges 2002

Per person	€ 3.61
child	€ 2.40
pitch	€ 7.81
electricity	€ 2.40

Less 20% in low season. **Tel:** 958 555 411. **Fax:** 958 555 105. E-mail: suspirodelmoro@eresmas.com. **Reservations:** Contact site. **Open** all year.

Directions: Leave the new Granada to Motril road at junction 144 if from the south or 139 from the north and follow the un-named campsite signs. There is only one site here.

Camping Los Avellanos de Sierra Nevada

9275

Ctra. de la Fábrica s/n, 18152 Dilar (Granada)

This is a fascinating tiny business with a philosophy of peace and tranquillity, a world apart from other sites in southern Spain. This has been achieved by Pilar and her brother Idvier. The site is also called Camping Cortijo which loosely translates from the Spanish as a big house in grounds with animals, birds and produce where 'people work towards people'. There is a fabulous old house and 20 terraced pitches (mainly for tents) with amazing views enjoying the sound of water tinkling through the ancient irrigation channels on its way to the crops (cars are parked separately). You can pick fruit from the scores of fruit trees and collect the 'huevos corral' (free range eggs) or pick your own vegetables from the plot (small charge). The vine-covered patio overlooks the small raised pool and commands wonderful views of the mountains. The narrow approach roads are interesting for larger units and a few motorhomes may be accepted in an informal lower area where electricity can be supplied. A phone call is a good idea if you are driving a large unit- ask for Pilar as her English is very good. Expect a different experience here but we stress this is mainly for tents and better for summer.

Facilities: Toilet facilities are modern and clean. Pretty bar/restaurant serves typical local fare and sells basic supplies. (very limited in low season). Kitchen for hire. Restaurant/bar. Swimming pool (high season only). Table tennis. Darts. Bicycle hire. Riding. Fishing in river Dilar. Details of walks from reception. Torches essential. Excellent rooms to let. **Off site:** Tours of Granada (20 minutes away), especially the Alhambra, organised. Site also useful for ski-ing in Sierra Nevada in season.

Charges 2002

Per person	€ 3.16
child	€ 2.70
tent	€ 3.61
car	€ 3.01
motorcycle	€ 2.70

Electricity and larger units - price on application. All plus 7% VAT. No credit cards. **Tel:** 958 596016. **Fax:** 958 596016. E-mail: Avellano@Teleline.es. **Reservations:** Contact site. **Open** all year.

Directions: From Granada going south take the A323, then the GR05 road to Otura. Go through the town following signs for Dilar where you will find signs for the site. Note: do not stray from the route indicated by the signs through town, as the roads are extremely narrow.

Camping Las Lomas

9285 Ctra. de Sierra Nevada, 18160 Güejar-Sierra (Granada)

This site is high in the Güejar Sierra and looks down on the Patano de Canales reservoir. After a wonderful drive to Güéjar-Sierra, you are rewarded with a site having excellent facilities. It is set on a slope but the pitches have been levelled to a great degree and are quite private, with high separating hedges and with many mature trees giving good shade (some pitches have sinks and most have electricity). The large bar/restaurant complex has a patio with wonderful views over the lake and an impressive huge central fire that is lit in winter. The pools also share this view, and have a grassed area for sunbathing that runs down to the fence looking over the long drop to the lake below (safe fencing). A new feature is luxury rooms for hire, including one with a spa which is for hire by the hour. Iinfirm visitors will need a car to get around as the inclines are extreme.

Facilities: Pretty blue tiled sanitary blocks (heated in winter) provide clean facilities. First class facilities for disabled campers and well equipped baby room (key at reception). Spa for hire. Motorcaravan services. Supermarket. Restaurant/bar. Swimming pool. Play area. Table tennis. Minigolf. Basketball. Many other activities including parascending. Barbecue. Torches useful. **Off site:** Buses run from outside site to village and Granada (15 km).Tours of the Alhambra organised with guides if required. Winter ski-ing

Charges 2002

Per person	€ 3.01
child	€ 2.40
pitch	€ 7.81

VAT included. No credit cards. **Tel:** 958 484 742. Fax: 958 484 742. **Reservations:** Contact site. **Open** all year.

Directions: Using A323 (Jaén - Motril) take exit 135 at Granada to Sierra Nevada which brings you to the A395. At 4 km. marker take exit 5B for Sierra Nevada. Pass 7 km. marker and turn immediately right towards Cenes de la Vega and Güéjar-Sierra and right again after 200 m. onto GR420, then left to Güéjar-Sierra. Site is signed - drive uphill past the dam and enjoy the views to the site.

Güejar-Sierra, km 6,5
E-18160 GÜEJAR-SIERRA
Tel. 0034 958 48 47 42
Fax 0034 958 48 47 42

A first class site with all facilities. In quiet surroundings in midst of nature.

DISCOVER the SIERRA NEVADA and GRANADA Road...

Camping Sierra Nevada

9280 Avenida Madrid 107, 18014 Granada (Granada)

This is a good site either for a night stop or for a stay of a few days while visiting Granada and for a city site it is surprisingly pleasant. Quite large, it has an open feeling and, to encourage you to stay a little longer, an irregular shape pool with a smaller child's pool open in high season. There is some traffic noise around the pool as it is on the road boundary. Granada has much to offer for sightseeing, including the amazing La Alhambra. With 148 pitches for touring units, the site is in two connected parts with more mature trees and facilities to the northern end. Artificial shade is provided throughout the site if required. Electrical connections (10/20A) are available. There is a small tour operator presence but it is not intrusive.

Facilities: Two very modern sanitary blocks, with excellent facilities, including cabins, very good facilities for disabled people and babies. Additional high standard sanitary facilities by the pool made available at peak times. Washing machines. Motorcaravan services. Gas supplies. Shop (15/3-15/10). Swimming pools with lifeguards (15/6-15/9; charge € 1.50). Bar/restaurant by pool. Tennis. Table tennis. Petanque. Large playground. Doctor lives on site. **Off site:** Fishing 10 km. Golf 12 km. Bus station 50 m from site gate.

Charges 2003

Per person	€ 4.62
child (3-10 yrs)	€ 3.91
pitch	€ 10.50
electricity (10A)	€ 3.16

VAT included. **Tel:** 958 150 062. Fax: 958 150 954. E-mail: campingmotel@terra.es. **Reservations:** Made for camping or motel. **Open** all year.

Directions: Site is just outside the city to north, on road to Jaén and Madrid. From autopista, take Granada North - Almanjayar exit 123 (close to central bus station). Follow road back towards Granada and site is shortly on the right, well signed.

Nerja Camping

8711 Ctra. N340, km 297, 29787 Maro (Málaga)

This attractive site is set on the lower slopes of the Sierra Almijara, some 5 km. from Nerja and 2 km. from the excellent beaches. Nerja Camping is a delightful small site of 55 pitches (30 with 15A electricity and no statics) with impressive views of the surrounding mountains and the Mediterranean. Being situated slightly above but alongside the main coast road, it is easy to find - the price you pay is some traffic noise but this seems hardly to detract from the relaxing ambience. The pitches are on the small side and set on slopes with some terracing along with mainly artificial shade. The roads, although quite steep, are newly surfaced and should present little problem except perhaps for really huge motorhomes. Bar and cool restaurant where you can enjoy your meal on the terrace beside the magnificent Carob tree, cooked and served by the Irish owner Peter Kemp and his Spanish wife Make. They will help with all activities and also recommend restaurants in the area - try the inland meat speciality 'Cabrito Asado' which is roast kid. Many enthusiasts enjoy the walking hereabouts - join in or use the book available here written by a local English lady who loves walking.

Facilities: Single sanitary block of modern design and construction includes some free hot showers, washbasins (1 only with hot water), undercover dishwashing sinks (cold water) and laundry facilities. Small swimming pool and paddling pool (March - Sept). Bar/restaurant with simple fresh dishes and large breakfasts (March - Sept). Essentials from the bar. Pool table. **Off site:** Bus service nearby. Fishing 3 km. Bicycle hire or riding 5 km. Sub-aqua diving, parascending and watersports close by. Day trips to Granada or Gibraltar can be taken using tour operators. The newly opened Nerja limestone caves are just 1 km. away. Ski slopes of Sierra Nevada two hours.

Charges 2002

Per person	€ 4.00
child (2-10 yrs)	€ 3.25
caravan	€ 5.30
tent	€ 4.00 - € 5.30
car	€ 4.00
motorcycle	€ 3.25
motorcaravan	€ 6.00
electricity	€ 3.00

All plus 7% VAT. Less 20-40% outside 1/6-30/9. Special rates for long stays. No credit cards. **Tel:** 952 529 714. Fax: 952 529 696. **Reservations:** Write to site for details. **Open** all year except October.

Directions: Site is signed from main N340 coast road about 5 km. east of Nerja after the 296 km. marker. If coming from Nerja, go 500 m. past site entrance (opposite the red and white radio masts) to cross the extremely busy main road.

Camping-Caravaning Laguna Playa

8782 Prolongacion Paseo Maritimo, 29740 Torre del Mar (Málaga)

Laguna Playa is a pleasant and peaceful site run by a father and son team (the son speaks excellent English) who give a personal service, alongside one of the Costa del Sol beaches. Trips are organised to the famous Alhambra Mosque in Granada on a weekly basis and the site is well placed for visits to Malaga and Nerja. The pitches are flat, of average size and with good artificial shade supplementing that provided by the many established trees on site. All pitches have electrical connections (5/10A). The site runs a busy restaurant with a terrace offering value for money which many many locals use. The site organises various competitions including petanque in the summer. Good off peak discounts are available.

Facilities: Two well equipped, modern, sanitary blocks include baby baths and good facilities for disabled campers. Laundry facilities. Supermarket. Bar and busy restaurant also used by locals. All open all year. Adult and children's swimming pools (open high season). Children's play area. Drinks machine. **Off site:** Regular bus service 700 m. outside site.

Charges 2002

Per adult	€ 3.67
child	€ 2.91
caravan	€ 4.06
tent	€ 3.67
car	€ 3.67
motorcycle	€ 2.94
motorcaravan	€ 13.22
electricity (metered in winter)	€ 2.10

All plus 7% VAT. Less 10-30% in mid-season for extended stays, 20-50% in low season. No credit cards. **Tel:** 952 540 631. Fax: 952 540 484. **Reservations:** Write to site. **Open** all year.

Directions: Site is on the sea front, Paseo Maritimo, at Torre del Mar on the main N340 Malaga - Nerja road. Follow signs and take care not to enter the first camp site you meet on the beach as this is inferior and will be demolished in new development in the near future.

Camping Naturista Almanat

N8783 Carril de la Torre Alta s/n, 29749 Almayate (Málaga)

With direct access to a one kilometre grey sand and shingle naturist beach, this established, all year naturist site, set amongst agricultural land with mountain backdrop, is proving a firm favourite with many British seeking winter sun. The entire 2-hectare site is flat with a fine shingle surface on dirt. A large number of deciduous trees and thin conifers planted when the site opened in '98 have now matured. The conifers create pitch dividers whilst the larger trees provide shade in the summer months. Defrocked of their foliage in the winter allows the site to be bathed in sunshine. The 160 touring pitches with 16A electricity, vary in size and shape with the majority demanding some manoeuvring of caravans. Some pitches are long and narrow which could prevent awnings and you may feel quite close to your neighbour. The facilities on site are of a high standard. Delightful scenic routes inland take you to the Spain of yesteryear and a chance to explore Pueblo Blancos (white villages).

Facilities: The large, unisex toilet is fully equipped, regularly cleaned and all under cover. Good facilities for disabled campers near reception (approach surface may cause minor difficulty for wheel chair users). Bar/restaurant with terrace overlooking the sea. Small shop. Large unheated swimming pool. Play area. TV in bar. Sauna and fully equipped gym. Basketball, paddle tennis. Cinema (56 seats). Weather permitting, one is expected to be nude which is obligatory in the pool area and bar during the day. **Off site:** Torre del Mar is 2 km. Regular bus service from end of approach road (1 km).

Charges 2002

Per person	€ 3.75
child (2-10 yrs)	€ 3.00
pitch and car	€ 8.00
electricity	€ 2.25

All plus 7% VAT. No credit cards. **Tel:** 952 556 462. Fax: 952 556 271. E-mail: almanat@arrakis.es. **Reservations:** Contact site. **Open** all year.

Directions: Approaching this site from the east (Torre del Mar) requires a left turn to the single-track tarmac lane leading to the site. It is illegal to make that left turn - we recommend that whether travelling from the east or west exit the N340 autovia at exit 265 signed Cajiz Iznate and Costa 340a. Take the Costa direction and on reaching the coast turn left on 340a toward Torre del Mar. Site well signed in 4 km. on right after passing 'Bull' hoarding.

Camping La Buganvilla

8803 Ctra. N340, km 188.8, 29600 Marbella (Málaga)

A majority of the 300 pitches on this site are on large terraces, with mature trees affording shade to some of the pitches. In places the ground is slightly sloping, possibly uneven and appears a little unkempt. At the time of our visit the tarmac roads within the site were in a poor state of repair. However, the general facilities are sufficient to make this an acceptable base for exploring areas of the Costa del Sol and within an easy drive of the famous and picturesque Ronda Valley. Adjacent to the campsite a large area of common land provides pleasant walks amongst flora and fauna. A footbridge crosses the N340 allowing a gradual 400 m. downhill walk to the beach, dunes and a limited number of bars/restaurants.

Facilities: Three painted sanitary blocks are clean and adequate with laundry facilities. Large bar/restaurant with terrace overlooking the pool area. Mini supermarket. Play area. Basketball and tennis in high season. Dogs are not accepted in July/Aug. **Off site:** Bus service close to site entrance.

Charges 2002

Per adult	€ 2.50 - € 3.50
child (under 10 yrs)	€ 2.00 - € 3.00
pitch and car	€ 5.50 - € 9.00

All plus 7% VAT. Discounts in low season. **Tel:** 952 831 973. Fax: 952 831 974. E-mail: info@campingbuganvilla.com. **Reservations:** Contact site. **Open** all year.

Directions: Site is off the N340 between Marbella and Fuengirola. Access at 188.8 km marker on the N340 can only be achieved when travelling in a westerly direction (i.e. from Fuengirola). If travelling the opposite way continue past the site until reaching the 'cambio de sentido' signed Elviria. This enables a U-turn over the dual carriageway.

Camping Cabopino

Ctra. N340, km 194.7, 29600 Marbella (Málaga)

8802

This large mature site is alongside the main N340 coast road in the Costa del Sol, also known as the Costa del Golf, and fittingly there is a major golf course alongside the site. Just 600 m. from the beaches and dunes, a short walk over the road and down the hill brings you to a restaurant on the beach and an unofficial naturist area. You are 7 km. from Malaga which is extremely popular with the British and very commercialised, although you can find authentic tapas bars in the old town. The site is set amongst tall pine trees which provide shade, and the pitches are large and sandy (there are some huge areas for large units). The upper areas of the site are filled with permanent pitches and bungalows are scattered around the remainder. The 385 touring pitches all have electrical connections (10A) and there is a separate area on the west side for groups of younger guests. At the other side of the site you will find a fenced swimming pool with a grass sunbathing area. Close to the entrance, the terrace to the restaurant enjoys shade and is very pleasant. The white linen restaurant offers great food, good service and a reasonable wine cellar, competing well with the town restaurants. When we visited the site was undergoing a massive refurbishment programme and it would appear to be turning into a most comfortable, well equipped organisation.

Facilities: Four mature but clean sanitary blocks provide hot water throughout. washing machines. Bar/restaurant. Shop. Swimming pool (all season). Children's play area. Some children's activities and adult entertainment is planned for next year. Excursions can be booked. Torches necessary in the more remote parts of the site. **Off site:** Fishing, bicycle hire and riding within 1 km. Golf 7 km.

Charges 2002

Per person	€ 2.70 - € 3.90
child	€ 1.65 - € 3.30
caravan or family tent	€ 3.30 - € 5.10
car	€ 2.70 - € 3.90
motorcycle	€ 2.70 - € 3.90
motorcaravan	€ 3.45 - € 6.61
electricity (10A)	€ 2.94

Plus 7% VAT. Discounts outside high season. **Tel:** 952 834 373. Fax: 952 834 373. E-mail: info@ campingcabopino.com. **Reservations:** Contact site. **Open** all year.

Directions: Site is 7 km. from Malaga, take the Cabopino exit at the 194 km. marker. Site is off the roundabout at the top of the slip road.

Camping Marbella Playa

Ctra. N-340, km. 192,800, 29600 Marbella (Málaga)

8800

This large site is 12 km. east of the internationally famous resort of Marbella with public transport available to the town centre and local attractions. A sandy beach is about 150 m. away with direct access. There are 430 individual pitches of up to 70 sq.m. with natural shade (additional artificial shade is provided to some), and electricity (10/20 A) available throughout. A large swimming pool complex with a restaurant/bar with large patio, palm trees, banana plants and lush grass for sunbathing provides a very attractive feature. The site is busy throughout the high season but the high staff/customer ratio and the friendly staff approach ensures a comfortable stay. We recommend excursions to Gibraltar (via La Linea), and although an hour's winding drive is awaiting, a trip to Ronda is well worth the effort.

Facilities: Four sanitary blocks of mixed ages, are fully equipped and well maintained. Three modern units for disabled visitors. Laundry and dishwashing areas in good order. Large supermarket with butcher and fresh vegetable counter. Bar, restaurant and café. All open all year. Supervised swimming pool (free - April/Sept). Children's playground (on gritty sand). Torches necessary in beach areas.

Charges 2002

Per person	€ 3.55
child (1-10 yrs)	€ 3.01
caravan or tent	€ 6.01
car	€ 3.55
motorcaravan	€ 8.41
electricity	€ 2.46
minimum pitch fee	€ 9.02 - € 16.65

All plus 7% VAT. Reductions (up to 50%) for long stays and senior citizens outside 16/6-31/8. **Tel:** 952 833 998. Fax: 952 833 999. **Reservations:** Write to site. **Open** all year.

Directions: Site is 12 km. east of Marbella with access close to the 193 km. point on the main N340 road.

Camping El Sur

8809 Ctra. Ronda - Algeciras, km 1.5, Apartado de Correos 127, 29400 Ronda (Málaga)

The generous manoeuvring area and delightfully decorated entrance to this site are a promise of something different which is fulfilled in all respects. The very friendly family who run the site have worked hard for many years combining innovative thinking with excellent service. The 114 terraced pitches have electricity (5A) and water, and are partially shaded by olive and almond trees. Most have relaxing views of the surrounding mountains but at an elevation of 850 m. the upper pitches (the very top 45 pitches are for tents only) allow a clear view of the fascinating town of Ronda. The various leisure facilities are very clean, well maintained and the personal touches of the owners are obvious which make using them more enjoyable. This is one of the best small sites we have seen in Andalucia with prices that are extremely competitive. Enjoy the breathtaking 130 metre deep El Tajo gorge (where prisoners were thrown during the civil war) from the lovely 18th century bridge which joins the old and new parts of town. Look out also for the much-feared soldiers in tasselled red Fez headgear and green tunics. These are Franco's old crack unit; the infamous Spanish Africa Legion who are billeted here.

Facilities: The immaculate sanitary block is fully equipped (toilet paper purchased from reception). Laundry facilities in little separate blocks. Gas supplies. Bar and very large, high quality restaurant serving excellent food at reasonable prices (closed 7-15/1). Kidney shaped pool most welcome in summer as the temperatures soar (1/6-30/9). Children's playground and adventure play area. Separate camping area for groups. Minigolf. Dogs on leads with site permission. Barbecues on pitch with site permission. Off road bicycle hire. Internet terminal. **Off site:** The famous town of Ronda with all its attractions. The coast is approximately one hours drive. National parks to the north.

Charges 2003

Per person	€ 4.04
child (under 10 yrs)	€ 3.67
tent	€ 3.47 - € 4.50
car or motorcycle	€ 3.47
caravan	€ 4.74 - € 6.93
motorcaravan	€ 7.87 - € 11.02
electricity (5-10A)	€ 3.36 - € 4.81

Plus 7% VAT. Less 40% in low season. No credit cards. **Tel:** 952 875 939. Fax: 952 877 054. E-mail: info@campingelsur.es. **Reservations:** Advised for July/Aug. **Open** all year.

Directions: Site is well signed from the town centre (do not stray off the signed route as there are some very narrow roads) and it is off the Algeciras road, 1.5 km. south of Ronda.

Camping Chullera 2

8812 Ctra. N340, km 141.5, 29692 Sabinillas-Manilva (Málaga)

This is an uncomplicated site with a friendly owner on the Costa del Sol with an attractive 'al-fresco' type restaurant and bar close to the beach. The bar is a simple affair, the food is very good and cheap. The 8 km. of sandy beach is safe (shelving at low tide), clean, and a major attraction - there are a number of desirable pitches alongside the beach, with 6A electricity, where you wake to the sound of the waves. Most of the larger than average pitches have artificial or natural shade and are well cared for, some being on a gentle slope. There are a number of static pitches (30%) and weekends can be lively when the Spanish campers relax. If you wish to practice your Spanish it can be fun, but if you wish for something a little quieter then go to the sister site Chullera 3, just 1 km. east, where there are 250 touring pitches with similar facilities but no statics (Chullera I is under the building development to the west of Chullera 2!). We see this as a site for visiting the area rather than a family holiday site. There is some road noise in the northern part of the site.

Facilities: There are two mature sanitary blocks (cleaning may be variable). No facilities for disabled campers. Laundry facilities. Bar/café close to beach with TV. Well stocked supermarket by entrance. Basic children's play area. Torches advised in the beach areas. Bus service from outside site to Marbella/ La Linea (for Gibralta

Charges 2002

Per adult	€ 3.31
child (above 10 yrs)	€ 2.70 - € 3.31
caravan	€ 3.31
car	€ 3.31
motorcaravan	€ 6.61
electricity	€ 2.55

All plus 7% VAT. **Tel:** 952 890 196. Fax: 952 890 196. **Reservations:** Write to site. **Open** all year.

Directions: Site is well signed off the main N340 at the 141.5 km. marker, 16 km. west of Estepona.

Camping Los Alcornocales

11330 Jimena de la Frontera (Cádiz)

8889

Camping Los Alcornocales takes its name from the surrounding Los Alcornocales Natural Park which is one of Europe's largest Mediterranean forests. A small and charming new site, it is off the beaten track in unspoilt countryside. The site has been well planned and the owners have been environmentally strict in its construction and situation. The result is a most pleasant experience of nature if you tire of the beaches. There are magnificent views over the Natural Park and the river Hozgarganta, which is the last virgin Spanish river. It runs through the lower reaches of the site within easy reach, and presents a superb walking adventure. Within minutes you are in 170,000 hectares of park containing amazing landscapes, flora and fauna and you may spot otters, polecats, deer, wild boar, vultures and snake-eating eagles and others too numerous to mention. The 97 pitches 27 for tourers) have been thoughtfully hedged and grassed and all have electricity (16A). Trees such as catalpa, maple and hibiscus ensure a tranquil feeling. The administration building has a natural thatch roof (turf to us) and contains a superb restaurant with an open fire. The theme is continued throughout with a pretty bar using the natural wood and stone of the area and cleverly decorated with cork from the magnificent oaks, which abound. This is a superb site for those who love nature.

Facilities: The sanitary block is very much in keeping with the surroundings. It offers free hot water and the modern facilities include very large showers with excellent facilities for disabled campers. The mirrors used are genuine ships` portholes and are a pleasant touch. Small shop sells essentials but we recommend you stock-up. Bar/restaurant (all year). Children's playground. Football pitch. Swimming pool. English is spoken. No transit traffic is allowed within the site in high season. All forms of outdoor activity planned for 2003 but check before arrival. **Off site:** Walking in National park. Fishing 1 km. Golf 40 km. Riding 15 km. Bicycle hire 15 km.

Charges 2002

Per person	€ 3.60
child (2-12 yrs)	€ 2.40
car	€ 3.00
tent or caravan	€ 3.60 - € 4.00
motorcaravan	€ 6.00
electricity	€ 3.00

All plus 7% VAT. No credit cards. Discounts for longer stays over 1 month. **Tel:** 956 640060. Fax: 956 641290. E-mail: camping@arrakis.es. **Reservations:** Contact site. **Open** all year.

Directions: From N340 San Roque - Algeciras take exit 115. Follow C369 for approx. 30 km. then turn left on C3331 to Ubrique. Turn left after 80 km. marker signed Jimena de la Fronterra. Site is on the right. Don`t be put off if the gate is shut on arrival - someone will appear.

Camping Los Gazules

Ctra de Patrite km. 4, 11180 Alcala de los Gazules (Cádiz)

8890

On arrival at the mountain location of Los Gazules you gain the impression of space and clever planning with plenty of manoeuvring room. You park up leisurely to register in a dedicated reception block opposite a large grassed picnic/rest area. Just two years old in a peaceful setting this is a place where time can just slip by. The 180 large, mainly level pitches are level, well drained and planted out with young trees, although some existing mature trees do give some shade. All pitches have 16A electricity and there are plentiful water points. The circular restaurant is pleasant and has views of the surrounding hills and mountains. When we visited in low season it was very quiet and the company was attempting to begin a programme of mountain activities. Some of the buildings were in need of a spruce up but everything was clean inside, but do not expect too much support in low season.

Facilities: A circular sanitary block offers clean facilities. Facilities for disabled campers. Laundry equipment including washing machines dryers. Bar/restaurant. Supermarket.(high season) Swimming pool with life guards (May - Sep). Playground. Disco. Mountain bike hire. Riding. Canoeing organised. Tourist information. **Off site:** Site is well placed for exploring the local area and excursions to Cadiz.

Charges 2002

Per person	€ 2.85
child (0-10 yrs)	€ 2.25
caravan	€ 3.01
tent	€ 2.85
car	€ 2.85
motorcycle	€ 1.80
motorcaravan	€ 3.61
electricity (16A)	€ 2.10

Tel: 956 420 486. Fax: 956 420 388. E-mail: luisaf@ spa.es. **Reservations:** Not necessary. **Open** all year.

Directions: From A381 Algecieras - Jerez road take exit to Alcalá de los Gazules onto A375(C440). Continue around village on A375 to Ubrique and proceed to 42 km. marker. Then turn onto the road to Patrite; site is on the right at the 4 km. marker.

Camping Fuente del Gallo

8860

Apto. 48, 11140 Conil de la Frontera (Cádiz)

Fuente del Gallo extends a warm welcome to British visitors particularly as one half of the ownership is Irish. The site is well maintained with 235 pitches allocated to touring units. Although the actual pitch areas are generally a good size, the majority are long and narrow. This could, in some cases, prevent erection of an awning and your neighbour may feel close. In low season it is generally accepted to make additional use of an adjoining pitch. Each pitch has 10A electricity and trees create shade to some pitches. Good beaches are relatively near at 300 m. but elderly or disabled people may find access difficult due to the fairly steep, stony paths. A nearby development may lead to improved access. Helpful, friendly staff will assist in booking discounted trips to nearby attractions or even further afield to Africa. Cadiz, probably the oldest town in Spain, is worth a visit and in particular the old part with its narrow streets (many pedestrianised).

Facilities: Two modernised, clean sanitary blocks include excellent services for babies and disabled visitors. Two further (new in 2002) blocks provide additional areas for washing dishes and clothes (cold water only). Laundry room with two washing machines. Motorcaravan services. Gas supplies. Well-stocked shop. Attractive bar and restaurant (breakfasts served). TV and games rooms. Attractive swimming pool (lifeguard in high season when there is a small charge) with large grass area for sunbathing and children's pool. Play area. Excursions. **Off site:** Watersports on beach. Fishing 300 m. Bicycle and motor scooter hire 2 km. Riding 1 km. Golf 5 km.

Charges 2002

Per person	€ 3.70
child (3-10 yrs)	€ 3.20
caravan/tent and car	€ 6.20 - € 6.60
motorcaravan	€ 6.30
electricity	€ 3.00

All plus 7% VAT. Less 11-30% for longer stays (excl. July/Aug). **Tel:** 956 440 137. Fax: 956 442 036. **Reservations:** Write to site. **Open** week before Easter - 1 Oct, with all amenities.

Directions: From Cadiz-Algeciras road (N340) at km. 23.00, follow signs to Conil de la Frontera town centre, then shortly right to Fuente del Gallo and 'playas' following signs.

An ideal campsite in the ever sunny

Camping•Caravaning

FUENTE DEL GALLO

Urbanización Fuente del Gallo

E-11140 CONIL DE LA FRONTERA (Cádiz)

Tél. (34) 956 44 20 36 /956 44 01 37

Road CN-340, towards Conil at km 23 Situated at the marvellous 'Côte de la Lumière', at 300 m of naturel beaches. Watersports, windsurf, diving, etc. Modern installations, bar, restaurant, supermarket, children's playground, postal service, change and safe-deposit. Ideal situation for many interesting excursions.

www.campingfuentedelgallo.com   camping@campingfuentedelgallo.com

---

Camping Tarifa

8855

Ctra N340, km 78.87, 11380 Tarifa (Cádiz)

The long, golden sandy beach is a good feature of this site being ideal for windsurfing and, adjacent to the site with a private access, it is also clean and safe for swimming. The site has a pleasant, open feel and is reasonably sheltered from road noise. It has been landscaped and planted out with an amazing variety of shrubs and flowers and is remarkably clean. There is a smart, modern reception area with an attractive water feature close by. The 278 level pitches are of varying sizes and are surrounded by pine trees which provide ample shade. All have electricity. The pool complex has pleasant views of the distant mountain range. Tarifa is a little over 5 km. and is well worth a visit, also a drive inland to the traditional Pueblo Blancos (white villages) is rewarding.

Facilities: Two modern, fully equipped sanitary blocks include facilities for campers with disabilities and baby room. Motorcaravan services. Gas supplies. Supermarket and excellent bar/restaurant all open all year. Large patio and entertainment area. Swimming pool complex with bar. Large play area with modern activities. Good security. **Off site:** Fishing 100 m. Riding 300 m. Bicycle hire 5 km

Charges 2002

Per person	€ 4.81
child	€ 3.61
caravan/tent and car	€ 6.40 - € 6.71
motorcaravan	€ 4.81
electricity	€ 2.55

Plus 7% VAT. Discounts for long stays. **Tel:** 956 684 778. Fax: 956 684 778. **Reservations:** Advised for July/Aug. **Open** all year.

Directions: Site is on main N340 Cadiz road at the 78.87 km. marker, 7.5 km. northwest of Tarifa. There are large modern signs well ahead of the site with a deceleration lane if approaching from the Tarifa direction, large gaily coloured signs mark the approach to the site.

Camping Paloma

8850 Ctra Cadiz-Malaga, km 70, 11380 Tarifa (Cádiz)

A spacious, neat and tidy, family orientated site, Paloma is 700 m. from the nearest beach that has good facilities for swimming and windsurfing. The site has some 350 pitches on mostly flat ground, although the westerly pitches are sloping. The pitches are of average size with some extra large for big units, separated by hedges and some are shaded by mature trees; around 200 pitches have electrical connections (10A). A large restaurant and bar provide food and drinks at reasonable prices along with a huge TV. There is a small swimming pool with a paved sunbathing area and an attractive thatched, stone bar. There is a good restaurant at the road junction as you turn into the site. Ask for the 'menu-del-dia' - it is not advertised but it is extremely good value.

Facilities: There are two sanitary blocks, one of a good size, although it is a long walk from the southern end of the site. The other block is smaller and open plan, serving the sloping areas of the site. Amost all WCs are Turkish style, washbasins have cold water (cubicles and communal bidets for women). Facilities for disabled visitors are in the smaller block with access from sloping ground, also a baby room. Washing machine. Gas supplies. Shop. Busy bar and good restaurant. Swimming pool with adjacent bar (high season only). Playground. TV in bar. Excursions (June-Sept). **Off site:** Beach 700 m.

Charges 2002

Per person	€ 4.81
child	€ 3.91
caravan/tent and car	€ 6.32 - € 6.62
motorcaravan	5.11
electricity	2.70

Plus 7% VAT. Less 40% from 1/11-31/3 (no electricity). **Tel:** 956 684 203. Fax: 956 681 880. **Reservations:** made for one part of site, for any length and without deposit. **Open** all year (no electricity from Nov.- March).

Directions: Site is signed off N340 Cadiz road at Punta Paloma, about 10 km. northwest of Tarifa, just west of km. 74 marker. Watch carefully for the site sign - no advance notice. Follow signs down a sandy road for 300 m. and site is on the right.

Camping Playa Las Dunas de San Anton

8865 P Maritimo de la Puntilla, 11500 El Puerto de Santa Maria (Cádiz)

This site lies within the Parque Natural Bahia de Les Dunes and is adjacent to the long and gently sloping golden sands of Puntilla beach. A 10 minute walk takes you into the bustling heart of Puerto Santa Maria which claims to be the birthplace of the 'Flamenco', along with Cadiz. It is a traditional Spanish family resort with gastronomic delights in the local port area, supplemented by local wines and sherries produced in the immense white-washed warehouses (bodegas) which are open to visitors. This is a pleasant and peaceful site of some 400 separate marked pitches, with much natural shade and ample electrical connections (5/10A). Motorcaravans park in an area called the Oasis which is very pretty. The tent and caravan pitches, under mature trees, are terraced and separated by low walls. This is a spacious site with a tranquil setting and it is popular with people who wish to 'winter over' in peace. The proximity to the 'sherry triangle' is very useful if you are interested in this fascinating subject which has had considerable British influence in the past. Sir Francis Drake attacked Cadiz in 1587 and made off with 3,000 barrels of sherry along with firing most of the Spanish fleet! Indeed many of the wonderful bodegas were founded by British Catholic refugees in the sixteenth century - this explains the English churches hereabouts and the very British sounding companies producing sherry to this day.

Facilities: Immaculate modern sanitary facilities with separate facilities for disabled campers and a baby room. Laundry facilities are excellent. Gas supplies. Bar/restaurant (all year). Supermarket (high season). Swimming pool and toddlers' pool (high season). Play areas. Night security all year. **Off site:** Fishing 500 m. Riding or golf 2 km. Municipal sports centre close by offers all manner of sporting activities and the beach provides additional free sports facilities such as volleyball. Local buses for town and cities visits and a ferry to Cadiz.

Charges 2002

Per person	€ 3.37 - € 3.73
child	€ 2.88 - € 3.19
tentor caravan	€ 3.64 - € 4.06
car	€ 2.88 - € 3.19
motorcaravan	€ 4.81 - € 5.35
electricity (5A)	€ 2.43 - € 2.67

All plus 7% VAT. **Tel:** 956 872 210. Fax: 956 860 117. E-mail: campinglasdunas@terra.es. **Reservations:** Advised for August; contact site. **Open** all year.

Directions: Site is 5 km. north of Cadiz off N1V route. Take road to Puerto Santa Maria, site is signed throughout the town.

Camping Giralda

8871

Ctra. Provincial 4117, 21410 Isla Cristina (Huelva)

The fountains at the entrance and the circular 'thatched' reception building set the tone for this very large, well managed and pleasant site which is just a few years old. The 520 pitches are quite spacious on sand, most benefitting from the attractive mature trees which abound on the site. Most pitches have electricity (142 are for tents). Access to the excellent beach is gained by a short stroll, crossing the minor road alongside the site and passing through attractive pine trees. The many additional activities are listed below. There is a separate area within this huge site where organised groups come to enjoy the activities offered within a dedicated adventure area (low season only). A quiet site out of the main tourist area with good leisure and adventure facilities.

Facilities: Four large, modern, semi-circular 'thatched' sanitary blocks are very clean and fully equipped. Laundry. Shop, bar and snacks (all year). Restaurant (Apr-Sept). Swimming pools. Basketball. Archery. Volleyball. Petan. Soccer. Mountain biking. Beach games. Table tennis. Watersports school. Play area. Organised activity area for groups low season. Excursions booked. Site security all year. **Off site:** Beach 200 m. Fishing 200 m. Golf 4 km. Riding 7 km. Bicycle hire 1 km.

Charges 2003

Per person	€ 4.06
child (2-10 yrs)	€ 3.35
tent or caravan	€ 4.30 - € 5.00
car	€ 3.85
motorcaravan	€ 8.75
electricity	€ 3.00

Plus 7% VAT. Winter discounts. **Tel:** 959 343 318. Fax: 959 343 284. E-mail: campinggiralda@ infonegocio.com. **Reservations:** Advised for July/Aug. **Open** all year.

Directions: Site is off E1/A49 autoroute at junction 121 and N431 Portugal - Huelva road, 10 km. east of Ayamonte. Take the Isla Cristina road, (C4117) off to the left, pass through Isla Cristina then onto La Antilla and site is 600 m. on the left, well signed.

Camping Villsom

9081

Ctra. Sevilla - Cadiz, km. 554.8, 41700 Sevilla (Sevilla)

This is a fine city site that was one of the first to operate in Spain and it is still owned by the same pleasant family. The administrative building consists of an peaceful and attractive, bar with patio and satellite TV (where breakfast is served) and there is a pleasant, dedicated reception area. Minigolf and table tennis are available. There are no static caravans here, and the site has a nice homely feel. It is excellent for visiting Seville with a frequent bus service to the centre (20 minutes, bus stop close by) - this is especially useful if you wish to attend the superb April Feira which lasts for a week and takes place in the second half of the month. This is non-stop (24 hours) Spanish celebration including Flamenco, parades, social pavilions, singing, dancing and is amazingly intense. Some may also be interested in the bull-fighting in Seville in September which is supposedly the second best in Spain (Madrid being the first). Camping Villsom has around 180 pitches which are level and shaded. A huge variety of trees and palms are to be seen around the site and in summer the bright colours of the flowers are very pleasing. We are told that the oranges from the trees are sold to Britain for marmalade. The site has a most inviting, large, palm surrounded pool which is quite secluded. Temperatures can be hotter here than almost anywhere in Spain and the pool seems essential, as are the orange trees. It is essential to book if you intend to visit this site in peak weeks.

Facilities: An excellent new sanitary block supplements the recently modernised existing facilities. Laundry facilities. Small shop selling basic provisions. Bar with satellite TV (July/Aug). Swimming pool (June-Sept). Large minigolf course. Table tennis. Drinks machine. **Off site:** Restaurant and supermarket close.

Charges 2002

Per adult	€ 3.16
child	€ 2.76
caravan	€ 3.43
tent	€ 3.28
car	€ 3.28
motorcycle	€ 2.73
motorcaravan	€ 4.09
electricity	€ 2.04

All plus 7% VAT. **Tel:** 954 720 828. Fax: 954 720 828. **Reservations:** Write to site. **Open** all year.

Directions: This needs care as an error results in extensive driving along the main road to turn around. From Cadiz to Seville on NIV look for 'Carrefour' store and sign on left at the 554 km. marker and turn right signed Salida dos Hermanas, Isla Menor. Take the left to Isla Menor, and once you have passed under a concrete road bridge; the site is immediately on the right.

Camping Sevilla

Ctra N-IV, km 534, 41007 Sevilla (Sevilla)

9082

This site is ideal for visiting the fascinating city of Seville. It is just south of the perimeter of Seville airfield, by day with your ear defenders, you can practice your plane-spotting, but thankfully the usual mandatory respite exists at night, although you are fairly close to the main Seville - Madrid road. This is a flat, sandy site with 85 pitches of varying size for motorcaravans and caravans, plus 450 for tents. Electricity (6/10A) is available. Trees provide some pitches with shade, others havei artificial shade. There is the constant change-over bustle of all nationalities coming and going to visit Seville. The kidney shaped pool and paddling pool area are very welcome in the summer heat. The city of Seville is a must for anyone visiting southern Spain. From here came Carmen, Figaro and Don Juan and if you can we recommend the two great Feiras (fiestas) of Seville, one the week before Easter and the other in the last week of April. We see this site as ideal for a short stay to enjoy the fabulous city of Seville.

Facilities: Buildings housing the sanitary and supporting facilities are round in shape and a happy yellow colour. Half of the showers are cold water only. The remainder provide free hot (very) water, but only cold for all other washing. Blocks kept very clean. Supermarket, bar and restaurant (high season). Small bar/snack area (out of main season). Swimming pools (June - Sept; € 1,20 charge). Drinks machines. Electronic games. Two excellent motorhome service points. **Off site:** Bus service runs to city centre leaving from inside site (high season; in low season a short walk to municipal bus stop is necessary). 'Magic Island' theme park 3 km.

Charges 2002

Per person	€ 3.00
child (3-11 yrs)	€ 2.40
car	€ 3.00
caravan	€ 3.00
tent	€ 2.50 - € 3.00
motorcaravan	€ 4.50
motorcycle	€ 2.00
electricity	€ 2.00

Plus 7% VAT. No credit cards. **Tel:** 954 514 379. Fax: 954 514 379. E-mail: campingsevilla@wanadoo.es.
Reservations: Advised in July/Aug. **Open** all year.

Directions: From any route follow signs to the airport (very easy) and you will pick up signs for the campsite from any direction. Be sure to follow signs carefully If you miss the turn the quickest way to cross the autoroute is to go through the airport.

Camping Los Villares

Parque Periurbano, Avenida de l Fuen Santa 8, 14071 Cordoba (Córdoba)

9078

This is a site with a difference. Unusually it is part of one of Spain's natural parks and the environmental rules must be strictly followed when you stay here. If you wish for a peaceful, simple site with no frills then this may be your cup of tea. There are bountiful pine, olives, gums and other trees providing shade and, as the site is within the Parque, the setting is absolutely natural. Thoughtfully some natural stone tables and benches are scattered around the site. The natty little bar and restaurant provide a simple menu and drinks - practice your Spanish here! The 170 tent pitches are delightfully informal. Find your place with its considerable privacy or make your way to the fenced area for 30 caravans or motorcaravans - access is fine. The warden will assist as necessary. We played an interesting game of hunt the chemical disposal for a while (it is there and we did say it was different!). All touring pitches have electricity but you will certainly need torches as you find your way home through the strange noises emanating from the densely wooded area beyond the site. This is great site with reasonable prices for those who have there own transport for visiting the amazing city of Cordoba, or it will suit those who do not need the artificial entertainment of bigger sites and just wish to relax at one with nature.

Facilities: The single toilet facility is centrally located, provides free hot water and is of good quality. Washing machines. Restaurant/bar. Shop. Five-a-side soccer. **Off site:** Natural Parque (protected) - walks and wildlife.

Charges 2002

Per person	€ 2.55
child	€ 1.95
tent or caravan	€ 2.55 - € 3.91
car or motorcycle	€ 2.10
motorcaravan	€ 4.21
electricity	€ 2.40

No credit cards. **Tel:** 957 330145. Fax: 957 750463. E-mail: campingvillares@latinmail.com.
Reservations: Contact site. **Open** all year.

Directions: The site is about 7 km. north of Cordoba. It is on the north side of the river which bisects the city and it is simpler to go to the centre to find the small access road to Parque and site. Follow the Parador (state run hotel) signs if you cannot see the signs for the Parque Periurbano which have small camping sign inside the fairly large green edged signs. Also follow signs for municipal camping which help. All these will bring you past the municipal camping - then look for a major right turn and follow clear signs out of city. Site is a stiff climb of several thousand feet out of city - the views are great!

Camping Municipal El Brillante

9080 Avenida del Brillante 50, 14012 Córdoba (Córdoba)

For a municipal site this is impressive. Cordoba is one of the hottest places in Europe - the 'frying pan' of Spain - and the superb pool here is more than welcome. It is large and has pleasant terraced gardens where you can sunbathe as you admire the colourful flowers and shrubs. If you really want to stay in the city, then this site is a good choice. It has 120 neat pitches attractively spaced alongside the canal (securely fenced for safety) which runs through the centre of the site. The upper pitches are now covered by artificial and natural shade but the lower, newer area has little shade. Here the pitches are more spacious if you have a larger unit. The site becomes very crowded in high season. The entrance is narrow and may be congested so care must be exercised - there is a lay-by just outside and it is easier to walk in initially. The bar/restaurant is close to reception and there is a pleasant terrace bar/restaurant which overlooks the pool gardens in high season. Cordoba is a fascinating town and the Mosque/Cathedral is one of the great buildings of Europe and it is worth allowing two days here to investigate the area. Buses go from outside the site to town.

Facilities: The toilet blocks have been renovated and an impressive new block added with facilities for babies and disabled people. Motorcaravan services. Gas supplies. Bar and restaurant (1/4-30/9). Shop (all year). Swimming pool (15/6-15/9). Children's play area. **Off site:** Bus service to city centre from outside site. Large supermarket 300 m.

Charges 2002

Per unit incl. 2 adults	€ 15.93
extra adult	€ 3.45
child (1-10 yrs)	€ 2.58
tent and car incl. 2 adults	€ 14.72
tent without car	€ 10.97
electricity	€ 2.55

No credit cards. **Tel:** 957 403 836. Fax: 957 282 165. **Reservations:** are not made. It is essential to arrive early in high season. **Open** all year.

Directions: Site is on the north side of the river. Entering Cordoba by NIV/E25 road from Madrid, drive into city centre. After passing the Mosque/Cathedral, turn right onto the main avenue, continue and take right fork where the road splits, and follow signs for campsite and/or district of El Brillante. Keep a sharp eye out for camp signs as they are partially hidden behind foliage.

Camping Carlos III

9085 Ctra Madrid - Cadiz, km 430, 14100 La Carlota (Córdoba)

This is a good alternative site for Cordoba being 25 km. from the city. A very large, busy site especially at weekends, it has many supporting facilities including a good swimming pool for adults and separate children's pool. With the bar and catering services open all year, the site has a more open feel than the bustling municipal site in Cordoba. The touring areas are canopied by trees which offer considerable shade for the 300 separated pitches. On sandy, gently sloping ground, around two-thirds have electrical connections (5A). Permanent units, mobile homes and bungalows are in a separate area, where there are also sporting facilities. There may be some slight road noise.

Facilities: Sanitary facilities in two modern blocks have mixed British (40%) and Turkish WCs, with hot showers in the block near reception. Motorcaravan services. Bar/restaurant, shop (all year). Swimming pools (1/6-15/9). Aviary. Table tennis. Boules. Minigolf, Children's play area. Volleyball. Football. Hairdressers. **Off site:** Bus service outside site. Riding 500 m. Village 2 km.

Charges 2002

Per person	€ 3.60
child (under 12 yrs)	€ 2.70
caravan	€ 3.60
tent	€ 3.45
car	€ 3.30
motorcaravan	€ 4.95
electricity (5A)	€ 2.70

Plus 7% VAT. Discounts (10-20%) for longer stays in low season. **Tel:** 957 300 697. Fax: 957 300 697. E-mail: campingcarlos@navegalia.com. **Reservations:** Probably necessary in July/Aug. **Open** all year.

Directions: From N-IV Cordoba-Seville motorway take La Carlota exit at km. 429 point; site is well signed.

Camping Despenaperros

9089 Ctra Infanta Elena, 23213 Santa Elena (Jaén)

Despeñaperros is a very smart, new site in the heartland of La Mancha, run by a co-operative of five very friendly people who employ helpful staff. This site is an ideal break point for those travelling from Madrid towards the Costa del Sol, or those wishing to explore the local attractions. These include the narrow mountain Gorge of Despeñaperros (literally 'the throwing over of the dogs'); also Valdepeñas, acknowledged as the centre of the most prolific wine area of Spain. The site is located in a 30-year-old pine grove which is part of the Despeñaperros nature reserve. All 116 pitches are of a good size, have natural shade from the mature pine trees and unusually have their own electricity (10A), water, TV connections and waste water drainage.

Facilities: Two central sanitary blocks are of a high standard. Washing machines. Motorcaravan services. Gas supplies. Shop. Excellent bar (all year) and charming restaurant (12/3-20/10). Swimming pools (15/6-15/9). Tennis. First aid room. Caravan storage. Night security.

Charges 2002

Per adult	€ 2.85
child	€ 2.34
caravan	€ 3.01
tent	€ 3.01
car	€ 2.85
motorcaravan	€ 5.05
electricity	€ 2.70

All plus 7% VAT. **Tel:** 953 664 192. **Reservations:** Contact site. **Open** all year.

Directions: On N1V- E5 Autovia de Andalucia between Bailén and Madrid at km. 257, at the village of Santa Elena; site is well signed.

Camping Merida

9087 Ctra NV Madrid-Port, km 336.6, 06800 Mérida (Badajoz)

Mérida was the tenth city of the Roman Empire and it is purported that it contains the most Roman remains in all of Spain. The 60-arched Roman bridge, the amphitheatre and the National museum of Roman art are just some of the attractions that can be enjoyed here. In July and August the theatre festival stages classical Greek plays and Roman tragedies. Camping Mérida is situated alongside the main N-V to Madrid, the restaurant, café and pool complex separating the camping site area from the road where there is considerable noise. The site has 80 good sized pitches, most with some shade and on sloping ground, with ample electricity connections (long leads may be needed). No English is spoken, but try out your Spanish. Reception is open until midnight. Camping Mérida is ideally located to serve both as a base to tour the local area or as an overnight stop en route when travelling either north/south or east/west.

Facilities: Central sanitary facility include hot and cold showers, dishwashing sinks (H&C) and laundry sinks (cold only) under cover. Gas supplies. Small shop for essentials. Busy restaurant/cafeteria and bar. Medium sized swimming pool and children's pool with lifeguard (May-Sept). Bicycle hire. Children's playground. Caravan storage. Torches useful. **Off site:** Town 4 km.

Charges 2002

Per adult	€ 3.15
child	€ 2.70
tent or caravan	€ 3.15
car	€ 3.15
motorcaravan	€ 4.35
electricity	€ 2.70

All plus VAT. **Tel:** 924 303 453. Fax: 924 300 398. E-mail: proexcam@jet.es. **Reservations:** Write to site. **Open** all year.

Directions: Site is alongside road NV (Madrid - Lisbon), 5 km. east of Mérida, at km. 336.6 point.

Extremadura

Extremadura is a large and sparsely populated region in the west of Spain, bordering central Portugal and consisting of two provinces, both of which bear the name of their main town. Cáceres, to the north, has a fascinating old quarter, while Plasencia and the village of Arroyo de la Luz are also worth a visit. To the south is Badajoz, the second province and the largest in Spain, with its fortified main town (it lies on the border on the historic route from Lisbon to Madrid). Also of interest are Mérida, with Roman ruins and the ruined castle at Alburquerque. *See advertisement on page 445*

Camping Parque Natural de Monfrague

9027

Ctra Plasencia-Trujillo km 10, 10680 Malpartida de Plasencia (Cáceres)

Situated on the edge of the Monfrague National Park, this well managed site owned by the Barrado family, has fine views to the Sierra de Mirabel and delightful surrounding countryside. It would prove difficult to find a more suitable location for those that savour peace, quiet, study of yesteryear, flora and fauna. Created as a National Park in 1979, Monfrague is now recognised as one of the best locations for birdwatching. Many of the 128 good-sized pitches are grassed on slightly sloping terraced ground. Scattered trees offer a degree of shade, there are numerous water points and electricity is rated at 10A. Used by locals, the air-conditioned restaurant provides good quality food at acceptable prices. An evening meal on the veranda as the sunsets will install fond memories of a rewarding holiday. On rare occasions a train travels along the nearby railway line.

Facilities: Large modern toilet blocks, fully equipped, are very clean. Facilities for disabled campers and baby baths. Laundry. Shop. Restaurant, bar and coffee shop. TV room with recreational facilities and fire for cooler times. Swimming pools and children's pool (June - Sept). Play area. Tennis. Basketball. Bicycle hire. Riding. Animation for children in season. Barbecue areas. **Off site:** Large supermarket at Plasencia.

Charges 2002

Per adult	€ 3.20
child	€ 2.50
tent or caravan	€ 3.20
car	€ 2.50
motorcaravan	€ 4.50
electricity	€ 2.50

VAT included. **Tel:** 927 459 233. Fax: 927 459 233. **Reservations:** Write to site. **Open** all year.

Directions: Approaching on the N630 - From the north take the EX-208 (previously C524) Plasencia - Trujillo; site on left in approx. 6km. From the south turn right just south of Plasencia onto EX-108 (previously C511) towards Malpartida de Plasencia. Turn right at main junction onto EX-208 to site.

Camping Las Villueracas

9028

Ctra. Villanueva, 10140 Guadalupe (Cáceres)

This rural site nestles in an attractive valley northwest of Guadalupe. The pools and restaurant are of a very high standard (the locals eat there!) and the restaurant leads to a pretty patio with overhead vines and potted plants allowing elevated views of the pools. There is a separate patio across the village street which is pleasant for sitting out with drinks whilst the management provide a barbecue and more casual food. The 70 pitches are level and of a reasonable size; some are marked, although the logic of the numbering is difficult to follow in places and large units may have difficulty in getting into the more central pitches. There is limited shade from young trees and a more shaded area in a 'spinney'. A river runs alongside the site and we are told that the ground can be muddy in very wet periods. The site is co-located with hostel accommodation.

Facilities: The single toilet block is in the older style but very clean, one area for women and one for men, providing British type WCs, washbasins and free hot showers (although hot water is from a 40 litre immersion heater which could be overwhelmed in busy periods). No facilities for disabled campers as yet. Restaurant. Bar. Swimming pools. Shop. Tennis. Small playground. Barbecue area. Safe deposit. Medical post. Car wash. **Off site:** An ideal location for visiting the Monastery of Guadalupe, and the town of Guadalupe, an historic tourist town.

Charges 2002

Per adult		€ 2.40
child		€ 2.10
tent or caravan	€ 2.10 -	€ 2.40
car		€ 2.25
motorcycle		€ 2.10
motorcaravan		€ 3.61
electricity		€ 2.10

No credit cards. **Tel:** 927 367 139. **Reservations:** Write to site. **Open** all year.

Directions: From NV/E90 Madrid - Mérida exit at Navelmoral de la Mata. Follow south to Guadalupe on CC713 (approx. 83 km). Site is 2 km. from Guadalupe, near the Monastery.

There is so much

EXTREMADURA
Naturalmente

**JUNTA DE
EXTREMADURA**

Consejería de
Obras Públicas y Turismo
Dirección General de Turismo
C/ Santa Eulalia, 30 - 06800 MÉRIDA - España
Telf: 0034 924 38 13 68 - Fax: 0034 924 38 15 24
E-MAIL: turismo@mut.juntaex.es

EXTREMADURA

If you want to see it all, stop off in Extremadura. You will see things in Extremadura that cannot be found anywhere else: breath-taking scenery, gorges, lakes and Nature Parks, historical buildings, ancient towns and cities, action and relaxation, culture and cuisine... Everything in Extremadura will enchant you. You will experience everything with a new intensity allowing your imagination to roam free so that you never cease to marvel at all there is to see.
If you ask us for information, we will send you guides about everything you might be interested in (weeke-ends, spas, historic-artistic routes, museums, gastronomical routes,...).

to see Extremadura

THE PLAINS OF SANTIAGO: ALCORNOCAL — MONFRAGÜE: TAJO AND TIÉTAR RIVERS — PUERTO PEÑA: THE GUADIANA RESERVOIR

MONFRAGÜE: LEONADO VULTURE — LA ZARZA: GUADIANA RIVER — HERRERA DEL DUQUE: DEER

VALENCIA DE ALCÁNTARA: DOLMEN — MÉRIDA: ROMAN THEATRE — GUADALUPE: MUNDEJAR CLOISTER

CÁCERES: WOMAD FESTIVAL — MALPARTIDA DE CÁCERES: VOSTELL MUSEUM — BADAJOZ: MEIAC

IBERIAN "BELLOTA" HAM — CHEESE SALAD — WINE FROM EXTREMADURA

PIORNAL: THE JARRAMPLAS FIESTA — TRUJILLO: THE CHÍVIRI FIESTA — OLIVA DE LA FRONTERA: PASSION

Camping de Fuencaliente

9088 km.105, N420 Cordoba-Tarragona, 13130 Fuencaliente (Ciudad Real)

This quiet site nestles in an attractive valley between the Sierra Modrona and the Sierra Morena. It is ideal as a stopover if crossing Spain coast to coast, if you wish to visit the fascinating historic town of Toledo or finally if you are looking for a quiet 'away from it all' break. With very few other desirable sites in this region of Castilla - La Mancha, this one is open all year round and is very peaceful with good views through pined slopes. The site is spacious with some shade from young trees but most is provided by artificial means. The 91 well maintained pitches are generous at over 100 sq.m. and all have electricity (6A) and water. There are areas allocated for tents. The large swimming pool with a separate children's area is most welcome in summer, as this part of Spain gets very hot. The site has a good restaurant overlooking the pools, with very reasonable prices - the food was excellent when we visited. The local village of Fuencaliente is 5 km. south and provides the usual village facilities including some very good Spanish restaurants and bars.

Facilities: The large, modern toilet block has excellent facilities. Laundry sinks. Swimming pool (1/6-15/9; free). Restaurant/bar (all year). Supermarket. Children's playground. Barbecue facilities.

Charges 2002

Per person	€ 3.61
child	€ 3.31
caravan	€ 5.71
tent	€ 3.61
car	€ 2.10
motorcycle	€ 1.80
motorcaravan	€ 9.32

Electricity included. Plus 7% VAT. **Tel:** 926 698 170. **Reservations:** Advised for July/Aug. **Open** all year.

Directions: Site is on N420 road at 105 km. marker approx. 5 km. north of Fuencaliente.

Camping La Aguzadera

9094 Ctra. N-IV, km 197.5, 13300 Valdepeñas (Ciudad Real)

This is a small, unassuming site which will be useful to travellers, especially if you wish to enjoy some excellent Spanish fare in the restaurant. There are few other campsites open all year in this area. With pleasant views of the mountains, the site is part of a huge sports complex where there is lots of activity, although the site is quite separate with lots of room to manoeuvre. The 66 pitches are of average size and are on sloping sand with a few trees providing a little shade. There is some road noise as the site is just off the N4. The sophisticated restaurant overlooks a pool with terraces and sunbathing areas but food is also available in the bar. It is primarily a transit site but useful if you are following the Valdepenas wine route.

Facilities: The central sanitary block is average, unheated, but clean. Washbasins have cold water only. Restaurant plus bar and attached eating area. Essentials from bar. Swimming pool and paddling pools (high season only), Children's play area. Tennis. Large sports complex alongside (charges apply). Dogs are not accepted. Torches required.

Charges 2002

Per person	€ 3.55
child	€ 2.57
caravan	€ 3.95
tent	€ 3.01
car	€ 3.71
motorcaravan	€ 5.88
electricity	€ 3.01

Tel: 926 310 769. Fax: 926 311 402. E-mail: la-aguzadera@manchanet.es. **Reservations:** Contact site. **Open** all year.

Directions: Site is directly off N4 Madrid - Cadiz at 197 km. marker at Valdepenas exit. Look for the 'Angel of Peace' statue - the site is directly opposite and is well signed.

Camping El Greco

9090 Ctra CM-4000 km 0,7, Puebla de Montalban, 45004 Toledo (Toledo)

Toledo was the home of the Grecian painter and the site that bears his name boasts a beautiful view of the ancient city from the restaurant, bar and superb pool. The friendly, family owners make you welcome and are proud of their site which is the only one in Toledo. There is an attractive, tree-lined approach and ivy clad pergolas run down each side of the swimming pool. A large shaded terrace offers shelter from the sun which can be very hot here. The 150 pitches are of 80 sq.m. with electrical connections and shade from strategically planted trees. Most have hedges that separate and give privacy, with others in herring bone layouts that make for interesting parking in some areas. Access to some pitches may be tricky for caravans (narrow and at an angle). The river Tagus streches alongside the site but fishing in it is a better bet than swimming (it was being re-fenced when we visited). This site makes a relaxing base to return to after a hard day visiting the amazing sights of the old city of Toledo or for something different visit the Warners' Theme Park.

Facilities: Two sanitary blocks, both modernised include facilities for disabled campers and everything is modern and kept clean. Laundry. Motorcaravan services. Swimming pool (15/6-15/9; with charge). Restaurant/bar (1/4-30/9) with good menu and fair prices. Shop in reception. Volleyball. Playgrounds. Barbecues. Ice cube machine. **Off site:** Fishing in river. Golf 10 km. Riding 15 km. An hourly air-conditioned bus service runs from the gates to the city centre, touring the outside of the walls first. Warner Brothers movie theme park 40 mins. Madrid 1 hour drive.

Charges 2003

Per person	€ 4.40
child (3-10 yrs)	€ 3.70
caravan or tent	€ 4.24
car	€ 4.24
motorcycle	€ 3.50
motorcaravan	€ 8.49
electricity (6A)	€ 3.18

Plus 7% VAT. **Tel:** 925 220 090. Fax: 925 220 090. E-mail: elgreco@retemail.es. **Reservations:** Not necessary and not made. **Open** all year.

Directions: Site is on C4000 road on the edge of the town, signed towards Puebla de Montelban; site signs also in city centre. From Madrid on N401, turn off right towards Toledo city centre but turn right again at the gates to the old city. Site is signed from the next right turn.

Camping Lagos Coto Cisneros

9092 Ctra. Pte Arganda - Chinchon, 28500 Arganda del Rey (Madrid)

This is a large, lively site with a very simple Spanish flavour, 20 km. from Madrid, which could be used for exploring the capital or as a stopping point if travelling to the south as it is about half-way through Spain. The 340 marked pitches are of reasonable size, all have 5A electricity and most are shaded by mature trees. There is a large representation of permanent Spanish pitches but the touring pitches are generally separate and in pleasant surroundings. There are several lakes, two near the entrance and the other is surrounding more than half the site boundary. All are safely fenced but the friendly ducks have their own accesses and may well join you for a meal. The lakes are good for fishing and watersports are available (nothing involving engines). If you arrive late out of season persevere and the security guard will let you in. We see this mostly as a transit site but you can practice your language skills here and use it as a base to visit the new Warner Brothers Movie world theme park at San Martin de la Vega just 16 km. away.

Facilities: Unsophisticated, unheated sanitary blocks but clean and neat with facilities for disabled campers (note: one block has push button hot water with free flow cold water to the shower which is irritating). Staged area for animation in summer. Restaurant/bar (hours vary in winter and they may only open at weekends). Swimming pool and paddling pool (supervised in season). Play area. Watersports. Fishing. Football. Tennis. Bicycle hire. Petanque. Torch useful. **Off site:** Madrid 20 km. Theme park 16 km.

Charges 2002

Per person	€ 3.61
child	€ 3.01
caravan or tent	€ 3.61
car	€ 3.61
motorcaravan	€ 6.62
electricity (5A)	€ 3.31

No credit cards. **Tel:** 918 719 695. Fax: 918 719 695. **Reservations:** Contact site. **Open** all year.

Directions: From Madrid - Alabcete E901/NIII take the M832 Morata de T/Chinchon road at 20.5 km. from Madrid. Chincon. The site is 3 km. further on and well signed.

Caravanning El Escorial

9200

Apdo. Correos 8, Ctra. M600, km 3500, 28280 El Escorial (Madrid)

There is a shortage of good sites in the central regions of Spain, but this is one (if rather expensive). It is well situated for sightseeing visits especially to the magnificent El Escorial monastery which is a short drive. Also, the enormous civil war monument of the Valle de los Caidos is very close plus Madrid and Segovia both at c\50 km. El Escorial is very large, there are 1,358 individual pitches with artificial shade (ensure you get a pitch without a low tree canopy if you have a 3 m. high motorcaravan. Of these, 750 are occupied by permanent units but are totally separate from the touring and tent areas - weekends can be lively in the bar. There are another 250 pseudo 'wild' spaces for tourists on open fields, with good shade from mature trees (long cables may be necessary for electricity). The general amenities on site are good and include three swimming pools (unheated), plus a children`s pool in a central area with a bar/restaurant with terrace and plenty of grassy sitting out areas.

Facilities: Three large refurbished toilet blocks, plus two smart, small blocks for the 'wild' camping area, are all fully equipped with some washbasins in private cabins. Baby baths and facilities for disabled campers. The blocks can be heated in cool weather. Large supermarket (1/3-31/10) and souvenir shop. Restaurant/bar and snack bar (1/3-31/10). Disco-bar. Swimming pools. Three tennis courts. Two football pitches. Basketball. Fronton. Volleyball. Two well equipped children`s playgrounds on sand. ATM. **Off site:** Riding, golf 7 km. Town 3 km.

Charges 2002

Per person	€ 4.60
child (3-10 yrs)	€ 4.45
caravan or tent	€ 4.60
car	€ 4.60
motorcaravan	€ 7.90
electricity	€ 3.30

VAT included. **Tel:** 918 902 412. Fax: 918 961 062. E-mail: info@campingelescorial.com. **Reservations:** May be made in writing to guarantee admission. **Open** all year.

Directions: From the south go through the town of El Escorial, follow the M600 - Guadarrama road - the site is near the 8 km. marker, 3.5 km. north of town on the right. If approaching from the north use the A6 autopista take exit 47 and the M600 towards El Escorial town. Site is on the left.

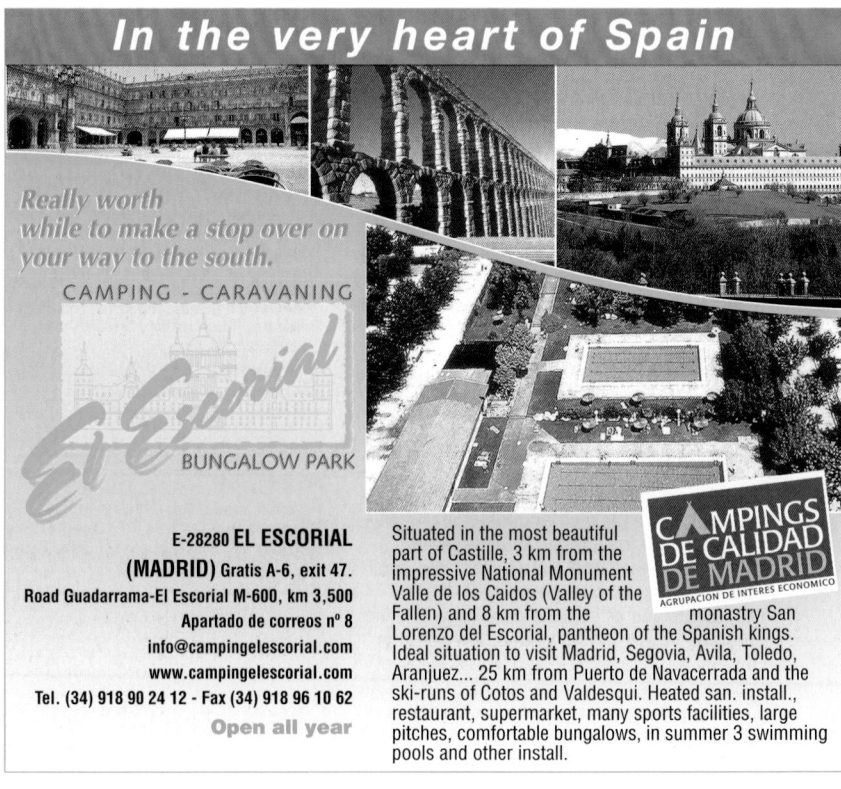

Camping Pico de la Miel

9210

Ctra. NI Madrid - France, km 58, 28751 La Cabrera (Madrid)

Pico de la Miel is a very large site 70 km. north of Madrid. It is well signed and easy to find, 2 or 3 km. southwest off the main N1 road, with an amazing mountain backdrop. Mainly a long-stay site for Madrid hence there are a huge number of very well established, fairly old statics. There is a small separate area with its own toilet block for touring units. The 60 pitches are on rather poor, sandy grass, some with artificial shade. Others, not so level, are under sparse pine trees and there are yet more pitches for tents (the ground could be hard). Electricity connections are available. Tall hedges and trees make it resemble a giant maze, no internal signs are provided and the long walk to the pool can be a challenge. The noise level from the many Spanish customers is high and you can practice your Spanish!

Facilities: Dated but clean tiled toilet block, with some washbasins in cabins and free hot water to laundry and washing up sinks. It can be heated and has an en-suite unit with ramp is provided for disabled visitors. Motorcaravan services. Gas supplies. Shop. Restaurant/bar (all year). Excellent swimming pool complex, supervised (15/6-15/9). Tennis. Playground. **Off site:** Bicycle hire 200 m. Riding 200 m. Fishing 8 km.

Charges 2002

Per person	€ 4.40
child (2-9 yrs)	€ 4.00
caravan or tent	€ 4.40
car	€ 4.40
motorcaravan	€ 7.00
electricity	€ 3.00

All plus 7% VAT. Less 10-25% for longer stays.
Tel: 918 688 082. **Fax:** 918 688 541. E-mail: pico-miel@sierranorte.com. **Reservations:** Contact site.
Open all year.

Directions: Site is well signed from the N1. Going south use exit 60, going north exit 59 or 60, and follow site signs.

PICO DE LA MIEL

E-28751 **LA CABRERA** (Madrid)
Tel. (34) 91 868 80 82
(34) 91 868 85 41

Access: N1/E5, excit 57 03 59

• 3 Swimming pools
• Restaurant - Cafeteria
• Supermarkt • First-aid room
• Washing machines
• Modern ablution blocks.

Ideal situation to visit Madrid, Segovia and El Escorial

First categorie site

Camping Municipal Soto del Castillo

9091

Soto del Rebollo s/n, 28300 Aranjuez (Madrid)

Aranjuez, supposedly Spain`s version of Versailles, is worthy of a visit with its beautiful palaces, leafy squares, avenues and gardens. It is 47 km. south of Madrid and 46 km. from Toledo, and this is therefore a useful and popular site, excellent for enjoying the unusual attractions or for an en-route stop. You can visit the huge, but slightly decaying Royal Palace or the Casa del Labrador which is a small neo-classical palace in unusual and differing styles. Two little tourist road trains run from the site to the palaces daily. This unusually well equipped municipal site is alongside the River Tajo in a park-like situation with mature trees. The 225 touring pitches, all with electricity (10A), are set on flat grass, unmarked. Siting is informal but pitches are of moderate size. There is a lockable moat gate to allow access to the river. There is good security backed up with CCTV around the river perimeter.

Facilities: The largest of three modern and good quality sanitary blocks is heated in winter and well equipped with some washbasins in cabins. Two smaller blocks of more open design have been refurbished. Washing up facilities have only cold water. Laundry facilities. Gas supplies. Small shop (15/6-15/9). Bar/restaurant (open to the public). Takeaway. TV room. Swimming pool (15/6-15/9). Play area. Bicycle hire. Canoe hire. Torch useful.

Charges 2002

Per person	€ 3.00 - € 3.91
child (3-10 yrs)	€ 2.55 - € 3.15
pitch	€ 5.25 - € 7.96
electricity	€ 3.30

Plus 7% VAT. Discounts for groups or long stays. **Tel:** 918 911 395. **Fax:** 918 911 395. **Reservations:** Write to site. **Open** all year.

Directions: Using the A305 Madrid - Aranjuez road, look for the 8 km. marker on the outskirts of town. Then follow campsite signs - these lead back onto the A305 (going north now) and the site is signed off right at 300 m. on the first left bend. Follow signs down narrow road for 400 m. From the south ensure that you have the A305 to Madrid - there are other roads signed to Madrid. If in doubt, ask as it is very confusing if the A305 road is missed.

Camping El Burro Blanco

9026 Camino de las Norias s/n, 37660 Miranda del Castañar (Salamanca)

Set on a hill top, within the Sierra Peña de Francia is the romantic walled village of Miranda del Castañar with its charming, crumbling castle. The winding, narrow streets are similar to the Arab medinas, with quaint mediaeval style houses which seem untouched by recent centuries where donkeys are still used as means of transport. The site has been developed by a Dutch team including husband and wife Jeff and Yvonne and their friend Paul. You are welcomed at the gate and are walked around the facilities. Then formal documentation is completed and 50% of the site fee is paid (cash only). A copy of the site regulations (three pages) is provided to all campers. The 48 shady pitches are 60 sq.m, with 2 at 130 sq m and are mostly level with some sloping and terracing but all with electricity. The pitches are set in 3.5 hectares of the most attractive woodland complete with rough tables and chairs made from local stone, unusual statues, a fountain fed by a well and a small stream which traces a route though the site. The owners keep an exhaustive list of all the birds and other wildlife spotted around the camp. By the lake there are luminous green tree frogs (you will hear their 'barking' at night in the mating season - May). As you leave your pitch will be inspected.

Facilities: One central modern sanitary facility, fully equipped includes a baby-bath. Two washbasins have hot water and one hot tap serves both the dishwashing and laundry sinks. Out of season part of the unit is closed and therefore facilities are unisex. Launderette. Gas supplies. Reading room with many books and a small bar. **Off site:** Restaurants, bars and shops in village 600 m. Municipal swimming pool nearby, river swimming and fishing 1.5 km. If you wish to explore some of the unique villages in the area avoid La Alberca which has been spoiled by over exploitation. Try instead Cepeda or Casas del Conde.

Charges 2002

Per person	€ 4.00
child (0-5 yrs)	€ 3.00
pitch	€ 9.00
electricity	€ 1.20

Plus 7% VAT. No credit cards. 50% of bill is requested on registration (cash only; ATM in village). **Tel:** 923 161 100. Fax: 923 161 100. E-mail: elbb@infonegocio.com. **Reservations:** Contact site. **Open** 1 April - 1 October.

Directions: Take C512 Salamanca - Coria road southwest for approx. 70 km. or C515 Bejar - Ciudad Rodrigo road turning south on C512. The road to Miranda del Castañar is approx. 7 km. northeast of the village of Cepeda.

Camping Regio

9025 Ctra. de Madrid, km 4, 37900 Santa Marta de Tormes (Salamanca)

Salamanca is one of Europe`s oldest university cities, and this beautiful old sandstone city has to be visited. Find the famous frog which is hidden in the fabulous University facade and discover what unusual Spanish fortune will be granted you! Or just enjoy the wonderfully accessible Salamantine architecture and the myriad of bars around the Plaza Mayor. This is also a useful staging post en-route to the south of Spain or central Portugal. The site is 7 km. outside the city on the old road to Madrid. It is behind the Hôtel Regio and campers can take advantage of the hotel facilities which include a quality restaurant, a somewhat cheaper cafeteria (discounts for campers), an excellent swimming pool and children`s pool (small charge). There is a pool bar and a shaded patio. The site itself has a small bar and restaurant. The pitches (with a large area for tents) are clearly marked on slightly sloping ground, with some shade in parts. There are plentiful electricity points (10A) in little red-roofed towers and many water points with unusual taps.

Facilities: Very large fully equipped sanitary block has very good facilities for disabled campers. Washing machines in a dedicated room - all very clean. Gas supplies. Excellent motorcaravan services. Restaurant, cafe and swimming pool at adjoining hotel. Bar. Supermarket (1/4-30/9). Play area. Tennis. Basketball. English is spoken. **Off site:** Bus to town terminates at hotel car-park. Town centre 7 km. Fishing 2 km. Golf 7 km. Bicycle hire 4 km.

Charges 2002

Per adult	€ 2.40 - € 2.90
child	€ 2.10 - € 2.55
tent or caravan	€ 2.40 - € 2.90
car	€ 2.40 - € 2.90
motorcycle	€ 2.10 - € 2.55
motorcaravan	€ 4.70 - € 7.20
electricity	€ 2.40 - € 2.90

Tel: 923 138 888. Fax: 923 138 044. E-mail: recepcion@campingregio.com. **Reservations:** Write to site. **Open** all year.

Directions: Take the main N501 route from Salamanca to Avila, then to St Marta de Tormes 7 km east of the city. Hôtel Regio is on the old road into St Marta on the left at the 90 km. marker. There are combined yellow camping signs through the city and on the roads to the east.

Camping La Pesquera

9019 Ctra. de Caceres - Arrabal, 37500 Ciudad Rodrigo (Salamanca)

This modest site has just over fifty pitches and is located near the Rio Agueda looking up to the magnificent fortress ramparts of Ciudad Rodrigo. A frontier city in its heyday, it has much of historic interest including the first Parador to be located in an historic building. The cathedral belfry still has shell marks caused by the Duke of Wellington's army during the 1812 war of independence. There are also wonderful treasures to be found in the golden stone buildings within the city walls. Entry to the site is through a municipal park with a large children's play area. Whilst the site is small it can take even the largest units, the centrally located facilities have all been refurbished to a high standard and include a unit for disabled visitors, the pitches are flat and grassy and the roads are well maintained gravel. The pitches are shaded by trees by day and there is site lighting at night however you may find torches useful due to the tree canopy. The reception and a small bar which serves snacks in the summer has a small shop which sells essentials is situated near the front of the site. There is a touch of old Spain directly alongside the site, an old farmhouse with its trailing grape vine and ancient well.

Facilities: Attractive new ochre/stone sanitary building with British WCs and free hot showers. Washing machine, dishwashing (H&C) and laundry (C) sinks. Facilities for disabled campers. Basics sold from bar in high season. Bar/snacks (Apr - Sep). Children's playground outside gates. Barbecue outside gate Torches useful. **Off site:** Fort in town to explore. Riding 5 km. River fishing 1 km. Superb walking area.

Charges 2002

Per adult	€ 2.80
child (up to 12 yrs)	€ 2.50
tent	€ 2.50 - € 2.80
caravan	€ 2.80
car	€ 2.80
motorcaravan	€ 5.00
electricity	€ 2.50
dog	€ 1.80

Tel: 923 481 348. Fax: 983 796 819. **Reservations:** Contact site. **Open** 25 April - 30 September.

Directions: Site is southwest of Salamancar close to Ciudad Rodrigo. From the E80 N260, any direction, take the 526 to Coria. Site is alongside river directly off the road and well signed.

Camping El Folgoso

9022 49361 Vigo de Sanabria (Zamora)

After a pleasant drive through the Sanabria National Park you reach this unspoilt site alongside a beautiful lake. It has green hills to the west and a lake of glacial origin to the east. It is a large site with the majority of the pitches given over to tents, as the terrain is rugged and strewn with enormous rocks, whilst being sheltered by fine dense oaks. The pitches are informal and tents are placed anywhere on terraces or the lower levels. Pitches for caravans and motorcaravans are in more formal lines at the far end of the site with (5A) electricity available. All buildings are primarily of wood and stone and designed to be in sympathy with the surroundings. The nearby lake shores are public areas but there are toilets along with picnic and barbecue facilities. There are magnificent walks all around the site and much to see in the area, from many spectacular canyons to Saint Martin's Monastery, the local castle or you can even venture into Portugal (25 km). The owners have another smaller site, also near the lake, if you prefer to really get away from it all.

Facilities: Three sanitary blocks, two refurbished and one new unit close to the restaurant, provide pre-set showers on payment (100 ptas coin slot), facilities for disabled campers and a variety of washing facilities but all with cold water. Bar with snacks (open all year). Self-service and full restaurants (April - Oct). Drinks machines. Torches essential. **Off site:** Supermarket (April - Oct.) just outside site. Children's playground very close. Gate at rear of site leads to lake 50 m. to fish, swim or enjoy the watersports.

Charges 2002

Per person	€ 3.46
child (under 10 yrs)	€ 2.55
caravan	€ 4.36
tent	€ 3.76
car	€ 3.31
motorcaravan	€ 5.26
electricity	€ 2.25

Tel: 980 626774. Fax: 980 626774. **Reservations:** not necessary. **Open** all year.

Directions: From the free N525 Orense/Ourense - Benavente autovia or the parallel A525, take any exit for Puebla de Sanabria and follow the signs for the Sanabria National Park. This will place you on the ZA 104 heading north. Pass through the villages of El Puente, Cubelo and Galende to 11 km. marker and site is signed to the right.

Camping El Astral

9029 Camino de Pollos 8, 47100 Tordesillas (Valladolid)

the travel
service
TO BOOK
Ferry ✓
Pitch ✓
Accommodation ✓
01892 55 98 98

The site is in a prime position alongside the wide River Duero (safely fenced). It is homely and run by a charming man, Eduardo Gutierrez, who has excellent English and is ably assisted by brother Gustavo and sister Lola. The site is generally flat with 154 pitches (on separated by hedges. They vary in size from 60 - 80 sq.m. with mature trees providing shade. We recommend a walk across the bridge to investigate the fascinating town of Tordesillas which is steeped in Spanish history. Also don't miss the Real Monasterio de Santa Clara known as the Alhambra of Castille - it is amazing. Visits to local Bodegas (wineries) can be organised. This is a friendly site ideal for exploring the area as you move through Spain. There is an electricity pylon tucked in the corner of the site but this does not detract from the pleasant ambience here and the quality stay offered.

Facilities: One attractive sanitary block including two cabins with WC, bidet and washbasin. Quality facilities provided for disabled campers, including ramps throughout site. Baby room in ladies' area. Washing machines. Motorcaravan services. Supermarket. Bar. Very good restaurant fequented by locals. Swimming and paddling pools (15/6-15/9; lifeguard at all times). New playground. Tennis. Minigolf. English speaking staff. Local bus service. Animation daily in high season. Torches are useful.

Charges 2003

Per person	€ 3.10 - € 3.95
child (0-12 yrs)	€ 2.45 - € 3.25
caravan or tent	€ 3.10 - € 3.95
car	€ 2.65 - € 3.40
motorcycle	€ 2.65 - € 4.40
motorcaravan	€ 5.25 - € 6.25
electricity (5A)	€ 2.80

Plus 7% VAT. Discounts in low season and for longer stays. **Tel:** 983 770 953. Fax: 983 770 953. E-mail: info@campingelastral.com. **Reservations:** Not necessary. **Open** 1 April - 30 September.

Directions: Tordesillas is 28 km. southwest of Valladolid. From all directions, leave the main road towards Tordesillas and follow signs to campsite or 'Parador' (a hotel near the campsite).

Camping Cañon del Rio Lobos

9251 Ctra. Burgos de Osma-S. Leonardo de Yagü, 42317 Ucero (Soria)

This is a smart and 'proper' site with vast amounts of flowers (a full time gardener keeps everything just so), set among attractive limestone cliffs of the Burgos canyons. The site is pricey but all facilities are immaculate and there are few others in the area. Reception is purpose built and control of the security barrier is from within - everything here is very organised. The camp logo depicts a bird of prey and you will see many of these wheeling above the site. You can practise your Spanish here as little English is spoken, but there is tourist information in English. The very attractive swimming pool is within a secure walled area, which again has many flowers and shrubs and is private from the road that runs alongside the site (some road noise). Children will need supervision in the pool as there is no barrier between the shallow and deep areas. If you wish to take advantage of the stunning scenery and explore the area the site staff will assist with routes and maps.

Facilities: Spotless fully equipped toilet blocks. Bar/restaurant (high season) or a set `menu del dia` in the bar. Basic shopping from bar. Swimming pool (extra charge). Two excellent tennis courts (extra charge). Play area. Bicycle hire. Fishing. Torch useful. **Off site:** Local bus service 1 km. on Wed./Sat.for town. Excellent walking routes.

Charges 2003

Per pitch	€ 11.60
adult	€ 4.20
child	€ 3.45
electricity	€ 4.30

All plus 7% VAT. **Tel:** 975 363565. Fax: 975 363565. **Reservations:** Contact site. **Open** March - November.

Directions: On N234 Burgos - Soria road take right fork in village of San Leornado de Yagüe. Turn right again after village signed El Burgos de Osma. Site is on this road and well signed south of Ucero.

Camping El Cantosal

9240 Ctra. de Santiuste, Km.2, 40480 Coca (Segovia)

On the 'Ruta de Mudejar' (route of Mudejar castles and buildings), near the nature reserve 'Hoces del Duraton' is this tiny campsite of fifty pitches. The setting has a fairy tale air about it - the magnificent fifteenth century Castillo de Coca can be seen from most of the site. The history of the village is fascinating and the climb to the tallest tower of the castle is rewarded with views of the village, its ancient bull ring and the surrounding countryside. Designed in sympathy with the surroundings the recently built stone buildings and all the facilities are of the highest quality. The grass and sand pitches are flat and shaded by tall trees in the daytime, and lit by pretty post lights at night. The bar serves snacks and excellent coffee and has a lovely open fire for cooler evenings. There is an arrangment for campers to use the local pool at a special rate, the campsite is set alongside a river where there are lots of wooden picnic tables under the trees and stone barbeques.

Facilities: Modern sanitary building with British style WCs and free showers is central. Washing machine, dishwashing (H&C) and laundry sinks under cover. Facilities for disabled campers. Shop (high season). Bar with snacks.(all season). Large playground just outside the site. **Off site:** Village with shops bars and restaurants. Fishing 2 km. Golf 20 km. Village of Coca with superb castle with attractive flowered gardens and bull ring 2 km.

Charges 2003

Per adult	€ 2.80
child (up to 12 yrs)	€ 2.50
tent	€ 2.60 - € 2.80
caravan	€ 2.80
car	€ 2.80
motorcaravan	€ 5.00
electricity	€ 2.55
dog	€ 1.80

Tel: 983 796819. Fax: 983 796819. **Reservations:** Write to site. **Open** Easter - September.

Directions: From Valladoid south on the N601 to Olmedo then east on the vp1105 road to Coca. At T junction marked Coca 2 km, Santiuste 7 km, turn into campsite road through stone pillars situated on the left and signed Zona De Picnic El Cantasol.

Camping Costajan

9250 Ctra. NI/E5, km 162, 09400 Aranda de Duero (Burgos)

This site is well placed as an en-route stop for the ferries, being 80 km. south of Burgos. It is the capital of the Ribera del Duero wine region that produces many fine wines of Spain competing with the great Riojas. The welcome is warm and friendly with 225 pitches provided all with electricity with around 100 available for all types of tourer. Large units may find access to the variably sized pitches a bit tricky among dense olive and pine trees and on the slightly undulating sandy ground but the trees provide good shade. In high season there is a good sized swimming pool to relax in. The river Duero runs close by and there is much of historical interest in the area. A café is here for snacks in season but there is a really good restaurant just 400 m. away any many more in the local area. There are many fascinating things to see in the area but we particularly recommend a visit to the suspended buildings at Gumiel de Izan for something different.

Facilities: Good, heated, modern sanitary facilities have hot and cold water, plus dishwashing and laundry sinks. Facilites for disabled people. Washing machine. Reception opens 08.00-14.00 and 18.00-22.00. Gas supplies. Shop with essentials (all year). Cafe with snacks and bar. Large swimming pool open to public (all 15/5-15/9). Tennis. Football. Minigolf. Torch useful. **Off site:** Fishing 3 km. Riding 2 km.

Charges 2002

Per person	€ 3.50 - € 3.65
child	€ 3.50
caravan	€ 3.50 - € 3.65
tent	€ 3.35 - € 3.65
car	€ 3.50 - € 3.65
motorcaravan	€ 5.50 - € 6.00
electricity	€ 3.50
dog	€ 1.60

Tel: 974 502 070. Fax: 974 511 354. E-mail: costajan@circulopyme.com. **Reservations:** Said to be unnecessary. **Open** all year.

Directions: From N1/E5 take exit to North signed Aranda de Duero at 164.5 km, follow N1 towards town and the campsite is at the 162 km. mark.

Covarrubias Camping

9252 09346 Covarrubias (Burgos)

This relatively new and peaceful site is surrounded by wooded hills of the Sierra de Covarrubias and is on a gentle slope (levelling chocks useful). Approaching from the south, the scenery through the lime-stone valleys is spectacular. The 136 numbered pitches are of a reasonable size, with electricity (5A) but generally without shade. The restaurant, off the bar, is pleasant with a reasonable menu and the bar has snacks and tapas with a large patio on the pool-side. There is much to see in the pretty town of Covarrubias and we suggest a visit to the Casa de Dona San and the ruins of San Pedro de Arlanza. The owner's son has published a delightful book of the 'rutas' (trails) in the area and horses can be hired to explore these delights.

Facilities: The fully equipped sanitary block is modern and clean. The pool side of the block has changing rooms. Washing machine. Shop - basics only (all year). Restaurant/café with full menu and snacks (all year). Bar (all year). Swimming pool with lifeguard (15/5-15/9). Tennis. Football. Minigolf. Bicycle hire. Riding. Torch useful. **Off site:** Fishing 3 km. Golf 28 km. Many superb walks. Restaurants, bars and shops in village 1 km.

Charges 2002

Per pitch	€ 6.50 - € 7.40
adult	€ 3.00
child	€ 2.10
electricity	€ 2.55

Tel: 947 406417. **Reservations:** Contact site. **Open** all year.

Directions: Nearest large city is Burgos. On N1/E05 Burgos - Madrid (N234) road take exit signed Soria at 230 km. On arriving at Hortigüela take exit to Covarrubias C110 and the site is on the left 1 km. out of village well signed.

Camping Municipal Fuentes Blancas

9021 Ctra. Cartuja - M'flore, km 3,5, 09000 Burgos (Burgos)

Burgos is an attractive city, ideally placed for overnight stop en route to the south of Spain. The old part of the city around the cathedral is quite beautiful and there are pleasant walks along the river banks. Fuentes Blancas is a comfortable municipal site within easy reach of the Santander ferries. There are around 350 marked pitches of 70 sq.m. on flat ground, 112 with electricity (6A) and there is good shade in parts. A small shop caters for most needs, the typically Spanish bar serves snacks and in the evening a restaurant is open. The site has a fair amount of transit trade and reservations are not possible for August, so arrive early.

Facilities: Clean, modern, fully equipped sanitary facilities in five blocks, but not all open outside July/Aug. Facilities for babies. Washing machine. Motorcaravan services. Small shop (all season). Bar/snack bar (all season). Swimming pool (15/5-15/9). Playground. **Off site:** Fishing 150 m. Bicycle hire 2 km. Bus service to city or a fairly shaded walk.

Charges 2002

Per pitch incl. caravan and electricity	€ 10.75
adult	€ 3.50
child (2-10 yrs)	€ 2.50

Plus 7% VAT. **Tel:** 947 486 016. Fax: 947 486 016. **Reservations:** Not made. **Open** 1 April - 30 September.

Directions: From north (Santander) follow signs for E5/N1 (E80/N620) Valladolid - Madrid on the main through road. Immediately after crossing river turn left at `Fuente Blancas Parc` signs leading to yellow camp signs and follow river east towards Cartuja de Miraflores for 3 km. Site is well signed on left.

Camping Camino de Santiago

9023 Casco Urbano, 09110 Castrojeriz (Burgos)

This tranquil and uncomplicated site lies to the west of Burgos on the outskirts of Castrojeriz, an unspoilt small Spanish rural town. In a superb location, almost in the shadow of the ruined castle high on the adjacent hillside, it will appeal to those who like peace and a true touring campsite and at a reasonable cost. Out of main season the bar/restaurant are closed but ask to be directed to the `Taberna` restaurant in town for a real treat of old Spanish cuisine. The 50 marked pitches are level, grassy and divided by hedges, with electricity (5A), water and drainage available to all. Mature trees provide shade and there is a pretty orchard in one corner of the site. English is spoken.

Facilities: Adequate sanitary facilities with showers (three hot per sex), British and Turkish style WCs, and washbasins with cold water only. Laundry and washing up sinks with hot tap. These facilities are in older style, but are well maintained and clean. Washing machine. Small shop (1/6-31/8). Bar. Cafeteria/coffee shop with two terraces (1/6-31/8). Games room. Tennis. Play area. Bicycle hire.

Charges 2002

Per person	€ 3.00
child	€ 2.00
pitch and car	€ 5.50 - € 6.00
electricity	3.00

All plus 7% VAT. **Tel:** 947 377 255. Fax: 983 359 549. E-mail: campingcastro@eresmas.com. **Reservations:** Contact site. **Open** 1 March - 30 Nov.

Directions: From N120 (Osorno-Burgos) road, turn onto BU404 for Villasandino and Castrojeriz. Turn left at crossroads on southwest side of town and then left at campsite sign.

Camping Picon del Conde

Ctra. NI, km 263, 09292 Monasterio de Rodilla (Burgos)

9253

This all year site is unusual, in that it has been amazingly decorated by the owner, Pedro Fasseler Sagredo who is extremely lively and friendly, as are his family. The experience begins as you drive under an art nouveau style entry arch and enter a pleasant site with a variety of unusual sculptures including Don Quixote and his companion Sancho Panza. The theme is continued in the friendly restaurant and bar with use of decorative local rock on most surfaces. The 60 level, grass pitches, all with electricity (5A), are of a reasonable size with separating hedges giving some privacy and trees offering some shade. There is some traffic noise from the busy N1 along-side the site and the picnic site and terrace directly outside the restaurant are always busy in season, the adjacent motel being responsible for some of this. Compared to other sites in the area this is a good option for a stopover if heading for the ferry or for exploring the area. If you visit at Christmas you will see the amazing nativity scene the father constructs - again all in the local stone which is full of holes like Emmental cheese, with a profusion of working models with lights and decorations.

Facilities: The first floor, unheated sanitary block is modern, very clean and fully equipped. A central elevated Venus de Milo statue is accentuated by mirrors and natural lighting. Good facilities for disabled campers are beneath the main sanitary facilities. Motorcaravan service point. Restaurant and friendly bar. Swimming pools. Play area. Tennis and fronton. **Off site:** Burgos 15 minutes away.

Charges 2002

Per adult	€ 2.90
child	€ 2.60
caravan	€ 3.20
tent	€ 2.90 - € 3.20
car	€ 3.20
motorcycle	€ 2.70
motorcaravan	€ 4.40
electricity	€ 3.10

Tel: 947 594 355. **Fax:** 947 594 355. **Reservations:** Contact site. **Open** all year.

Directions: Nearest town Monasterio de Rodilla (Burgos) From autopista A1 take exit 3 at Briviesca on the N1. Then exit 2 at Rubena heading north on N623 towards Irun. Site is on the N1 at the 263 km. marker, well signed midway between Burgos and Briviesca.

Camping Monumento al Pastor

Ctra. Madrid - Irun km 308, 09219 Ameyugo (Burgos)

9044

This is a very small simple site which makes a very good transit stop and is very special if you wish to sample traditional Spanish fare cooked to perfection whilst enjoying spectacular views. Look out for a 7 metre high white sculpture of the shep-herd boy towering 25 metres over the site and the road as you approach. The monu-ment is famous. The shepherd boy was killed by a thunderbolt in 1959 whilst tend-ing his sheep, accompanied by his dog who is also immortalised here, along with a lamb and a chapel dug into the rock. There are 15 pitches terraced on grass with one area allocated for tents. In high season there is a small hardstanding for two addi-tional vehicles. Electricity (5A) is available to all the grass pitches. There are also some 50 permanent pitches. In high season a small hut serves as reception, otherwise go to the bar. The site itself lays at the foot of Napoleon Hill. A large bar/restaurant provides magnificent views of the Obareues mountains and surround-ing hills which are designated to become a natural Park in the near future. The owner`s son speaks good English.

Facilities: Sanitary facilities are quaint, clean and adequate. Essentials sold in the bar. Fabulous stylish restaurant offering campers top Spanish cuisine or a special 'menu del dia', also very popular with locals. Playground. Basketball. 5-a-side soccer. **Off site:** Local bus/train service 3 km. Bilbao 70 km. Co-located superb restaurant with smart uniformed wait-ers, most impressive wine list and excellent food.

Charges 2002

Per adult	€ 2.84
child	€ 2.35
caravan	€ 3.05
tent	€ 2.40 - € 3.36
car	€ 2.84
motorcycle	€ 1.82
motorcaravan	€ 4.42
electricity	€ 2.25

Tel: 947 344355. **Fax:** 947 354290. **Reservations:** Contact site. **Open** all year.

Directions: Nearest large town is Miranda de Ebro. Site is very easy to find as it is on the N1 between Gastiez Vitoria and Burgos. Madrid - Irun (A68/E80 Bilbao - Burgos) road at 308 km. marker. The monument makes it impossible to miss the site, but take care as the access is can be dangerous if crossing the main road. A safer option is off the N625 250 m. from the main road access.

Camping Puerta de la Demanda

9254 Ctra. de Pineda, km. 2, 09199 Villasur de Herreros (Burgos)

This site is a new venture (2002) for the newly formed Unidos Group. This recently built site is being improved and shows great promise. On flat ground, it is over-looked on three side by the hills and mountains of the Sierra de la Demanda which give the site its name. There is little shade over 55 well marked large pitches all of which have electricity (5A) and drainage. The modern buildings are of local stone and wood in sympathy with the quiet surroundings, yet providing an excellent set of facilities. Just 300 m. away is a dam which may provide non-powered water sports and a river is very close for swim-ming and fishing. The whole site is securely fenced. When inspected the support facilities were being put into place but the owners assure us that everything will be in place for 2003. It is 11 km. from Atapuerca a most important historical find which will be opening shortly. Set in 50 unspoilt hectares it will show the origins of prehistoric man, his culture and his move from Africa to Europe. Burgos is close by with all its attractions.

Facilities: Attractive new ochre/stone sanitary build-ing with British style WCs and free hot showers. Washing machine, dishwashing (H&C) and laundry (C) sinks. Facilities for disabled campers. Basics sold from bar in high season. Bar/snacks (April - Sept). Children's playground outside gates. Barbecue outside gate. Torches useful. **Off site:** Fort in town to explore. Riding 5 km. River fishing 1 km. Superb walking area.

Charges 2003

Per person	€ 2.81
child (under 12 yrs)	€ 2.30
caravan	€ 2.91
tent	€ 2.62 - € 2.91
car	€ 2.91
motorcaravan	€ 4.90
m/cycle	€ 2.30
electricity	€ 2.30

Plus 7% VAT. **Tel:** 983 796819. Fax: 983 796819. **Reservations:** Contact site. **Open** Easter - September.

Directions: From the N120 Burgos - Lograno road, exit at Ibeas de Juarros (approx 7km east of Burgos) towards Villalbura, Arlanzon, Villasue de Herreros and site on road no. 8201.

Camping Los Manzanos

8942 Ctra. Sta Cruz - Meiras, km 0,7, 15179 Santa Cruz (A Coruña)

This large site is to the east of the historic port of La Coruña, not far from some ria (lagoon) beaches and with good communi-cations to both central and north Galicia - it is only an hour and a half drive from Santiago de la Compostela, for example. The site has a steep sloping access and is divided by a stream into two main sections, linked by a wooden bridge. Some huge interesting stone sculptures create focal points and conversation pieces. The lower section is on a gentle slope. Pitches for larger units are marked and numbered, all with electricity (10A) and, in one section, there is a fairly large, unmarked field for tents. The site impressed us as being very clean, even when full, which it tends to be in high season. Señor Sanjurjo speaks good English and visitors are assured of a friendly welcome. Some aircraft noise should be expected (but only six aircraft per day - none at night).

Facilities: Two good toilet blocks provide modern facilities including free hot showers. Swimming pool (clean, with lifeguard, free to campers, and open most of the day, evening and all season if you are tough enough!) Small shop with fresh produce daily. High quality restaurant/bar (Easter - Sept) serving good food and a range of wines at reasonable prices. Playground. Barbecue area. Telephone and post box. Medical post. Excellent bungalows for hire. **Off site:** Golf 8 km. Riding 8 km. Bicycle hire 2 km. Beach 800 m.

Charges 2002

Per adult	€ 4.40
child	€ 3.40
caravan or tent	€ 4.40 - € 4.80
car	€ 4.40
motorcycle	€ 3.60
motorcaravan	€ 8.80
electricity	€ 2.90

All plus 7% VAT. **Tel:** 981 614 825. E-mail: info@ camping-losmanzanos.com. **Reservations:** Write to site. **Open** Easter - 15 September.

Directions: Nearest large city is La Coruna. From A9/E1 going south, take exit 7 for Oburgo. The site is on the Santa Cruz - Meiras road, north of Oleiras and is well signed from there.

Camping As Cancelas

9024 Rue do 25 de Xulio 35, 15704 Santiago (A Coruña)

The beautiful city of Santiago has been the destination for Christian pilgrims for centuries and they now follow ancient routes to this unique city. The As Cancelas campsite is excellent for sharing the experiences of these pilgrims in the city and around the magnificent cathedral. It has 156 marked pitches (30-70 sq.m), arranged in terraces and divided by trees and shrubs. On a hillside overlooking the city, the views are very pleasant, but the site has a steep approach road and access to most of the pitches can be a challenge for large units. Electrical hook-ups (5A) are available. There are many legendary festivals here, the main one being on July 25, especially in holy years (when the Saint's birthday falls on a Sunday). Examine for yourself the credibility of the fascinating story of the arrival of the bones of Saint James at Compostela.

Facilities: Two very modern, luxurious toilet blocks are fully equipped, with ramped access for disabled campers. The quality and cleanliness of the fittings and tiling is outstanding. Dishwashing and laundry facilities. Mini market (July/Aug). Restaurant. Bar/TV (all year). Well kept, unsupervised swimming pool and children's pool. Small playground. **Off site:** Bus service runs into the city from the bottom of the hill outside site. Commercial centre (open late) five minutes level walk away.

Charges 2002

Per adult	€ 3.46 - € 4.00
child (up to 12 yrs)	€ 2.40 - € 3.07
pitch and car	€ 6.92 - € 8.48
electricity	€ 2.76

All plus VAT. **Tel:** 981 580 476. **Fax:** 981 575 553. E-mail: info@campingascancelas.com. **Reservations:** Write to site. **Open** all year.

Directions: From N550 La Coruna - Santiago road, at large roundabout (near petrol station),take exit to Lugo (C547)/La Coruña (A9), and take the left lane marked 'Santiago North historic'. Go straight on at first roundabout and take left lane. At the second, look for campsite sign pointing up a minor road. Turn right at sports stadium and site is 800 m.

Camping Los Cantiles

8940 Ctra. N-634, km. 5027, 33700 Luarca (Asturias)

Luarca is a picturesque little place with a pretty inner harbour and two sandy beaches. Los Cantiles is 2 km. to the east of town on a cliff top that juts out into the sea, giving excellent views from some pitches and the sound of the waves to soothe you to sleep. The owners speak excellent English and Hubert, who is Dutch, and Cornelia, who is German, are charming and eager that you enjoy your stay. The site is well maintained with no permanent units and is a pleasant place to stop along this under-developed coastline. The 230 pitches, 83 with electricity (3/6A) are most on level grass, divided by hedges of hydrangeas and bushes. There is a separate area for late arrivals in high season. You can take the car to the Laurca beaches and the small town is within walking distance downhill. This is a pleasant site as a base for exploring the area.

Facilities: Two modern, fully equipped sanitary blocks (one heated in winter) are kept very clean Mainly British style toilets. Large solar heating system ensures there is hot water throughout the facility including the units for disabled people and the baby bathroom. Water is recycled for flushing purposes and the owners have a 'green' attitude. Laundry. Freezer service. Gas supplies. Small shop (all year). Bar with hot snacks (15/6-1/10). Day room for backpackers with cooking facilities (less gas). Reading room. Bicycle hire. Torches are required. English is spoken. **Off site:** Indoor pool, sauna and fitness centre 300 m. Fishing 70 m. Riding 6 km.

Charges 2003

Per adult	€ 3.27 - € 3.50
child (4-10 yrs)	€ 2.85 - € 3.05
pitch and car	€ 6.31 - € 7.40
electricity	€ 1.82 - € 2.55

Plus 7% VAT. No credit cards. **Tel:** 985 640 938. Fax: 985 640 938. E-mail: cantiles@conectia.net. **Reservations:** Advised for mid July - end Aug and made by post with deposit. **Open** all year.

Directions: Turn off main N632 at 154 km. marker onto N634. At the km 502.7 point east of Laurca, site is well signed through an estate.

Camping Lagos de Somiedo

8945 Valle de Lago, 33840 Somiedo (Asturias)

This is a most unusual gem of a small site in the moutainous Parque Natural de Somieda. Winding narrow roads with challenging rock overhangs, hairpin bends and breathtaking views (for 8 km) finally bring you to the lake and campsite at an elevation of 1,200 m. This is a site for 4x4s, powerful small campervans, cars, backpackers of endurance - not advised for medium or large motorhomes - and caravans are not accepted. It is not a approach route for the faint hearted! The friendly Lana family make you welcome at their unique site, which is tailored for those who wish to explore the natural and cultural values of the Somiedo Natural Park without the support of 'normal' campsite amenities. There is no electricity, but in this extraordinary glacial valley you can leave reality behind in the exploration (on horseback if you wish) of the marvels of nature including bears, wolves, capercailles and a unique wild goat which frequents these mountains. A charming building, in keeping with the area, functions as reception, bar, restaurant, library and sanitary block and contains many items of natural interest. A small bar/restaurant set tight into the vertical rock face offers traditional Asturian food but be careful of the local's stilted wooden clogs scattered in the entrance. Here you will witness the cultural heritage of people living in harsh, though beautiful, surroundings. There is a cool wind here most of the time. A torch is essential.

Facilities: There are British style toilets and free hot water to clean hot showers, washbasins, laundry sinks and for dishwashing (outside, under cover). Facilities for babies and children. Washing machine. Combined reception, small restaurant, bar and reference section. Bread, milk and other essentials, plus local produce and crafts are sold in the site shop and bar. Horses for hire, trekking. Lectures on flora, fauna, history and culture. The river Valle runs through the site allowing trout fishing (licence required). Barbecue area. Small children's play area. Telephone. Gas supplies. **Off site:** The very small village is within 500 m. and it maintains the Spanish customs and traditions of this area.

Charges 2002

Per adult	€ 3.46
child	€ 2.85
tent with 3 or more persons	€ 4.06
tent incl. 2 persons	€ 3.46
motorcaravan	€ 6.01
car	€ 2.85
motorcycle	€ 2.40

All plus 7% VAT. **Tel:** 985 763 776. **Reservations:** not necessary. **Open** Easter - 15 October.

Directions: From N634 via Oviedo turn left at the 442 km. marker on AS-15 signed Parque Natural de Somiedo. At 9 km. marker past village of Longoria, turn left onto AS-227. At 38 km. marker, turn left into Pol de Somiedo, signed Centro Urbano. Follow signs for Valle de Lago and El Valle; 8 km. of hairpin bends from Pola, passing Urria on the left, brings you to the valley. Site is signed on the right.

Camping Costa Verde

8950 Playa de la Griega, 33320 Colunga (Asturias)

This busy site with a marked Spanish flavour is some 1.5 km. from the town of Colunga, has some very nice features and the owners aim to please. The most attractive feature, just outside the gate, is a spacious, supervised beach with a low tide lagoon which is ideal for younger children. The 160 regularly laid out pitches are very busy in high season. They are flat, but with little shade, and electricity (6A) is available throughout (long leads needed in places). A new sports and play area, with a dedicated barbecue and a picnic area is at the end of the site across a bridge. Whilst the river is mainly fenced off, children could possibly find their way to the river and thus should be supervised. This area is the real Jurassic Park with the footprints of dinosaurs having been discovered and preserved locally, along with some dinosaur fossil remains. Ask at reception for details and guides.

Facilities: The single toilet block is of a high standard with a mixture of British and Turkish style toilets (all British for ladies), large showers and free hot water throughout. Laundry. Well stocked shop. Bar/restaurant is traditional and friendly. Sports field. Barbeque. Playground. Torches needed. Little English spoken. **Off site:** Nearby towns of Ribadesella, Gijón and Oviedo. Excellent beaches. Fishing in river alongside site. Golf 18 km.

Charges 2002

Per adult		€ 3.70
child (over 5 yrs)		€ 3.15
tent	€ 3.25 -	€ 3.40
caravan		€ 4.20
car		€ 3.15
motorcycle		€ 2.85
motorcaravan		€ 6.00
electricity		€ 2.55

VAT included. **Tel:** 985 856 373. **Fax:** 985 856 373. **Reservations:** Essential for peak weeks and made for exact dates with deposit. Send for booking form. **Open** Easter - early October.

Directions: From Santander take the N634 road to Ribadesella, and continue for 21 km. along the N632 coast road towards Gijón. Take right turn towards Lastres from the centre of Colunga.

Camping-Caravaning Arenal de Moris

8955 Ctra. 632, 33344 Caravia Alta (Asturias)

This peaceful, rural site is close to three fine sandy beaches and is surrounded by mountains in the natural reservation area known as the Sueve. A hunting reserve, this is important for a breed of short Asturian horses. The famous mountains, Picos de Europa, are only 35 km. It is an ideal area for sea and mountain sports, riding, walking and cycling. Camping Arenal`s 350 grass pitches are of 40-70 sq.m. and electricity (5A) is available. With little shade, some pitches are terraced with others on an open, slightly sloping field with views of the sea. In the middle distance a new autoroute supported by concrete piers sculpts its way across the valley. There was little noise when we visited but this may be a possibility. The excellent beach is a short walk.

Facilities: Three sanitary blocks provide comfortable, controllable showers (no dividers) and vanity style washbasins, laundry facilities and external dishwashing (cold water). Supermarket. Restaurant. Swimming pool. Tennis. Children's play area in lemon orchard. English is spoken. **Off site:** Fishing 200 m. Golf 10 km. Riding 15 km. Shops, bar and restaurants in local village.

Charges 2003

Per person	€ 3.95
child	€ 3.70
caravan	€ 5.15
tent	€ 3.70 - € 3.95
car	€ 3.95
motorcycle	€ 2.90
motorcaravan	€ 6.50
electricity	€ 2.40

Tel: 985 853 097. Fax: 985 853 137. E-mail: camoris@teleline.es. **Reservations:** Contact site. **Open** 1 June - 31 August.

Directions: Site is signed from the N632 road (Ribadesella - Gijón) at km. 14 point.

Camping La Paz

8960 Ctra. N-634 Irun - Coruna, km. 292, 33597 Vidiago-Llanes (Asturias)

On arrival here you may well be reminded of the fortress towns of old Spain. The reception building is opposite a solid rock face, many hundred feet below the site, and the climb to the site is quite daunting. Staff will place your caravan for you, although motorcaravans will have an exciting drive to the top. Once there it is all worth it as the views are outstanding. The site is arranged on numerous terraces with lower areas in a valley floor. The way down to the beach is very steep but the views, both to the Picos de Europa and to seaward are most impressive. There are 434 pitches with electricity (6/7A) of between 30-70 sq.m, but many are only suitable for tents. An area back from the beach is more suitable for very large units. There is a cliff-top restaurant with commanding views over the ocean and beach. With the extreme slopes, we think it would appeal most to visitors who are not infirm. Children will require supervision.

Facilities: Four, first class sanitary blocks, with some interesting and unusual design features (such as being cut into solid rock), are modern, well equipped and spotlessly clean. They include hot showers with electronic controls and a baby bath. Full laundry and dishwashing facilities. Spring water is available from a number of taps throughout the site. Motorcaravan services. Mini-market. restaurant and bar. Lounge. Watersports. Table tennis. Games room. Fishing. Superb Beaches. Torches essential. English spoken.

Charges 2002

Per adult	€ 3.58
child	€ 3.34
tent	€ 3.40
caravan	€ 4.78
car	€ 3.58
motorcycle	€ 2.98
motorcaravan	€ 5.98
electricity	€ 2.52

All plus VAT @ 7%. **Tel:** 985 411 012. Fax: 985 411 235. E-mail: delfin@campinglapaz.com. **Reservations:** Advised for peak weeks. **Open** 1 June - 20 September.

Directions: From Santander take N634 towards Llanes. Site is signed from the main road at km. 292 point, before you arrive in Vidiago.

Camping Picos de Europa

8965 33556 Avin-Onis (Asturias)

It is said that, due to their proximity to the sea, the Picos (peaks) are called Europa as early navigators, on sighting them, knew they were again near the continent of Europe. Indeed, it is probably best to follow the coast to reach Cangas de Onis, the gate to the Picos, when first locating the site. Once settled you can explore these dramatic limestone mountains on foot, by bicycle, by horse, etc. The site itself is newly developed and the dynamic owner, Jose is very pleasant and nothing is too much trouble. There is direct access off the AS114 in a valley situation beside a pleasant, fast flowing river. Local stone has been used for the L-shaped building at the main entrance which houses receptionand a very good restaurant. The bar has an unusual circular window and small terrace overlooking the river. The 140 marked, smallish pitches have been developed in three corridor type avenues, on level grass backing on to hedging and with electricity to most. The tent area is over the bridge past the fairly small, round swimming and paddling pool. The site specialises in caving activities and is youthful.

Facilities: The main sanitary facilities are in the reception building. Additional toilet facilities, showers, baby bath, etc are in the tent area. Laundry and dishwashing facilities. Washing machine. Shop (July - Sept). Bar/restaurant serving a menu of the day at lunchtimes (all local fare, filling and very unusual). Swimming pool. Canoeing, riding and exceptional caving. Torches necessary. Excursions can be arranged in the mountains (on horseback if wished) and canoes can be hired. **Off site:** Site runs a most professional Speleology school with a hostel 3 km. away with 100 beds. Covadonga with its lakes and national park 13 km. Coast at Llanes 25 km. Golf 35 km. Riding 12 km.

Charges 2002

Per adult	€ 3.30
child (under 14 yrs)	€ 3.00
small tent	€ 3.30
large tent or caravan	€ 3.90
car	€ 3.00
motorcycle	€ 2.40
motorcaravan	€ 5.40
electricity	€ 2.40

All plus 7% VAT. **Tel:** 985 844 070. Fax: 985 844 267. E-mail: info@picos-europa.com. **Reservations:** Not needed outside July/Aug. **Open** all year.

Directions: Site is 15 km. east of Cangas on the AS114 road.

Camping La Isla

8962 Picos de Europa, 39570 Turieno-Potes (Cantabria)

La Isla is beside the road from Potes to Fuente Dé, with excellent mountain views and good shade, which makes it a popular site for families with young children. Established for over 25 years, a warm welcome awaits you from the owners (who speak good English) and a most relaxed and peaceful atmosphere exists in the site. The 160 unmarked pitches are arranged around an oval gravel track (one-way system), under a variety of fruit and ornamental trees. Electricity (3A) is available to all pitches, though some may require long leads. A small bar and restaurant is cleverly placed at a lower level, by the small river which runs through the site. Everything here is in the traditional style and very pleasing. There are opportunities for riding and 4x4 safaris (site provides details) in the region, together with all the other mountain sports and active outdoor pursuits.

Facilities: Single, clean and smart sanitary block retains the style of the site. It includes washbasins, laundry and dishwashing sinks all with cold water. Washing machine. Gas supplies. Freezer service. Small shop. Restaurant/bar with local dishes. Takeaway. Small swimming pool, bathing caps compulsory (15/5-15/10). Children's playground. Barbecue and picnic area. Fishing. Bicycle hire. Riding. Drinks machine. **Off site:** Interesting town of Potes, with Monday morning market 4 km. Monastery at Toribio nearby.

Charges 2002

Per adult	€ 2.91
child (0-10 yrs)	€ 2.37
caravan or trailer tent	€ 2.91
tent	€ 2.73
car	€ 2.73
motorcycle	€ 1.71
motorcaravan	€ 6.61
electricity	€ 1.98

All plus VAT. Low season reductions. **Tel:** 942 730 896. Fax: 942 730 896. E-mail: campicoseuropa@ terra.es. **Reservations:** Write to site. **Open** 1 April - 30 October.

Directions: Site is on right hand side, 4 km. outside Potes, on the N621 Potes to Espinama/Fuente Dé road.

Camping La Viorna

8963 Ctra. Santa Toribio, 39570 Potes (Cantabria)

The wonderful views down the valley from the open terraces of this site make it an attractive base from which to tour this region or to relax by the excellent swimming pool. It is popular with both familes and couples. There are beds of flowers and the trees are maturing, providing shade on many pitches. Access is good for all sizes of unit to the 110 pitches of around 70 sq.m, all of which have electricity (3 or 6 A). In high season, however, tents may be placed on less accessible, steeply sloping areas. The restaurant (fixed menu) has a terrace overlooking the pools. A pleasant feature is that all roofs are of the same design that is in sympathy with the town. This extends to a large picnic area behind the main block and even to small covered sitting out areas around the pool. All the buildings are in local stone with chunky wood fittings which look extremely attractive.

Facilities: Single, neat sanitary block of high standard, clean and modern. Washbasins with cold water. Facilities for disabled visitors double as unit for babies (key from reception). Laundry room has plenty of sinks, washing machine and ironing board. Dishwashing room with many sinks all cold water. Shop. Restaurant/bar with terrace. Heated swimming pool (23 x 13 m) and children's pool (bathing caps compulsory). Playground. Games room. Covered area with electronic games. Some English spoken. Many sporting activities can be arranged such as parascending, mountain biking, trekking, rafting, canoeing. **Off site:** Potes 2 km. (Monday market). Toribio Monastery close. Fuente Dé is a short, spectacular drive.

Charges 2002

Per person	€ 2.85
child	€ 2.40
caravan/tent	€ 2.85 - € 3.91
car	€ 2.85
electricity	€ 2.10

All plus VAT. **Tel:** 942 732 021. **Fax:** 942 732 019. **Reservations:** Write to site. **Open** Easter/1 April - 30 October.

Directions: Take road N621 from Unquera to Potes. After town take left fork signed Toribio de Liebana and site is on right after 800 m.

Camping Las Arenas-Pechon

8970 Ctra. Pechon - Unquera, km 2, 39594 Pechon (Cantabria)

This campsite is in a very quiet, but rather spectacular location bordering the sea and the Tina Mayor estuary, with views to the mountains and access to an excellent beach. Otherwise, enjoy the pleasant kidney shaped pool that also shares the views. Unusually there is yet another beach on the far side of the site, this for the more adventurous as the access path is a little steep. Las Arenas is a very green, 10 ha. site with lots of shade from acacias, oak and poplar trees, and is good value. Taking 337 units, half of the site is divided into marked, grassy pitches (60 sq.m) in various bays or on terraces with stunning sea and mountain views, with electricity available (5A) and connected by asphalted roads. There are some quite steep slopes to tackle - the restaurant along with reception is at the top. Children need to be supervised in some areas and infirm campers may find the slopes difficult.

Facilities: Clean, well tiled sanitary facilities are in the older style. Various blocks include showers (no divider), plus dishwashing, laundry sinks and washing machines. Well stocked supermarket Restaurant (open to public). Snack bar. (open when site open). Playground. Fishing. Opportunities for fishing, swimming, diving, windsurfing or cycling from site. Windsurfer and bicycle hire. Torches necessary. English is spoken. **Off site:** For older teenagers a disco/bar 1 km. Golf 28 km.

Charges 2002

Per adult	€ 3.60
child	€ 3.99
caravan	€ 4.80
tent	€ 3.00 - € 3.60
car	€ 3.60
motorcycle	€ 2.60
motorcaravan	€ 6.00
electricity	€ 2.15

All plus 7% VAT. **Tel:** 942 717 188. Fax: 942 717 188. E-mail: lasarenas@ctv.es. **Reservations:** Contact site. **Open** 1 June - 30 September.

Directions: Nearest large city is Santander. Turn off the N634, Santander - Coruna road, just east of Unquera onto the road to Pechon. Site is 4.5 km.

Northern Spain

This area includes the Costa Verde, the Basque Coast, the Pyrenees and inland Spain north of a line between Valladolid and just north of Burgos (lat. 42°). The Costa Verde is largely unspoiled, with clean water, sandy beaches and rocky coves against a backdrop of mountains including the magnificent Picos de Europa. The beaches and countryside on the Basque Coast are more developed in terms of tourism and industry and tend to be very popular, particularly in July and August. Both these areas are easily accessible from the ports of Santander or Bilbao. The Pyrenees stretch from the Bay of Biscay in the west (with the highest peaks) to the Mediterranean in the east, and include two spectacular natural parks, the Ordesa in Aragon and Aigues Tortes in Catalonia. The mountain gorges and valleys remain largely unspoiled.

Camping El Molino de Cabuerniga

8964 Sopeña de Cabuérniga, Ctra. C625, km 42, 39510 Cabuérniga (Cantabria)

Located in a peaceful valley with magnificent views of the mountains, beside the river Saja and only a short walk from the old and attractive village, this gem of a site is on an open, level, grassy meadow with trees. Wonderful stone buildings and artefacts are a feature of this unique site. There are 114 marked pitches, all with electricity (3/5A), although long leads may be needed and the site is lit at night. This comfortable site is very good value and ideal for a few nights (or you may wish to stay longer) whilst you explore the Cabuérniga Valley which forms part of the Reserva Nacional del Saja. The area is great for just resting or indulging in active pursuits with opportunities for mountain biking, climbing, walking, swimming or fishing in the river, riding, hunting, paragliding and 4x4 safaris.

Facilities: A single, modern sanitary block provides showers in curtained cubicles, washbasins with cold water only. Dishwashing (H&C) and laundry sinks outside. Washing machines and ironing. Facilities for disabled campers planned. Small shop for basics. Restaurant/bar (June - Sept). Wonderful children's playground in rustic setting - supervision recommended. Fishing. Bicycle hire. Barbecue. No English is spoken. **Off site:** Fishing 200 m. Riding 4 km.

Charges 2003

Per pitch	€ 6.61
adult	€ 3.31
child	€ 3.01
electricity	€ 2.10

All plus VAT. **Tel:** 942 706 259. Fax: 942 706 278. E-mail: c.m.cabuerniga@campingcabuerniga.com. **Reservations:** Contact site. **Open** all year.

Directions: From N634 at Cabezon de la Sal turn on C625, continue for approx. 10 km. to km. 42 where site is signed before Valle de Cabuérniga. Turn into village (watch out for low eaves/gutters on buildings), bearing right, watching carefully for small site signs through village (the locals always point for you!). automatic barrier at entrance arch.

Camping El Helguero

8961 Ctra. Santillana-Comillas, 39527 Ruiloba (Cantabria)

the travel service
TO BOOK

Ferry	✓
Pitch	✓
Accommodation	✓

01892 55 98 98

This site, surrounded by tall trees and impressive towering rock formations, caters for around 240 units on slightly sloping ground. There are many marked pitches on different levels, all with access to electricity (6A), but with only a little shade in parts. There are also attractive tent and small camper sections set close in to the rocks. The reasonably sized swimming pool and children's pool has an access lift for disabled campers. This is a good site for disabled visitors, in a peaceful location, and is excellent value out of main season. One can generally find space here even in high season, but arrive early. The site is used by tour operators and there are some site owned chalets. There is a large Spanish presence at weekends, especially in high season and if you do not wish to share the boisterous culture, choose one of the many pitches away from the restaurant area.

Facilities: Three well placed toilet blocks, although old, are clean and cared for, and include facilities for disabled visitors and children. Dishwashing, laundry sinks and washing machines. Motorcaravan services. Well-stocked supermarket (July/Aug. 9 am - 1 pm). bar snacks, separate more formal restaurant. Swimming pool with (limited opening with lifeguard on duty, caps compulsory - sold on site). Playground. Animation in high season. Games machines. Bicycle hire. ATM. Torches required. **Off site:** Restaurants in village. Fishing or riding 3 km. Santillana del Mar 12 km. Beaches near.

Charges 2002

Per adult	€ 3.00 - € 3.60
child (4-10 yrs)	€ 2.50 - € 3.10
caravan or tent	€ 3.00 - € 3.60
car	€ 3.00 - € 3.60
motorcaravan	€ 6.00 - € 7.20
electricity	€ 2.15

Tel: 942 722 124. Fax: 942 721 020. E-mail: elhelguero@ctv.es. **Reservations:** Write to site. **Open** 1 April - 30 September.

Directions: From the C6316 road from Santillana del Mar to Comillas, turn left at Sierra. Site signed as Camping Ruiloba (we don't know why) and is 200 m. on the left.

Camping-Caravaning Playa de Oyambre

8971 Finca Peña Guerra, 39547 San Vicente de la Barquera (Cantabria)

This exceptionally well managed site is ideally positioned to use as a base to visit the spectacular Picos de Europa or one of the many sandy beaches along this northern coast. The site is in lovely countryside (good walking and cycling country), with some views of the fabulous Picos mountains, and near the Cacarbeno National Park. The owner's son Pablo and his wife Maria are assisted by Francis in providing a personal service and both men speak excellent English. The 200 marked pitches are mostly of a good size (average 80 sq.m. with the largest ones often taken by tightly packed seasonal units). They are arranged on wide terraces with little shade and with electricity (10A) in most places. All pitches are flat and most have water and drainage. The site is well lit and a guard patrols at night (high season). The site gets busy with a fairly large Spanish community in season and there can be the usual happy noise of them enjoying themselves at weekends.

Facilities: Good sanitary facilities are in one, well kept block, with cleaners on duty all day and evening. Showers are spacious but have a frustrating mixture of push-button hot and ordinary cold controls. Facilities for babies and disabled visitors. Dishwashing (H&C) and laundry sinks (cold only). Washing machines (tokens from reception). Motorcaravan services. Well stocked supermarket open until 10 pm. with deliveries of fresh fish three days a week (15/6-15/9). Restaurant features fresh local dishes. Bar/TV lounge. Games area with machines. Swimming pools with lifeguard (1/6-15/9). Playground. Basketball. Football. **Off site:** Fishing 1 km. Riding 5 km. Superb beaches 1 km. San Vicente de la Barquera 5 km.

Charges 2002

Per pitch	€ 6.95
adult	€ 3.45
child	€ 2.95
electricity	€ 2.50

All plus VAT. **Tel:** 942 711 461. Fax: 942 711 530. E-mail: camping@oyambre.com. **Reservations:** Advised, particularly if you have a large unit. Write to site. **Open** Easter/1 April - 30 September.

Directions: Site is signed at junction to Comillas, at km. 265 on the E70, 5 km. east of San Vicente de la Barquera. The entrance is quite steep (take care with caravans). Exercise caution as there is another 'Camping Playa de Oyambre' within 500 m. (on the beach) which is not recommended.

Camping Santillana

8973 Ctra. de Comilias s/n, 39330 Santillana del Mar (Cantabria)

This is an attractive site on sloping ground 8 km. from the beaches of the north coast with full facilities. It has a fine swimming pool complex, a restaurant and self service café which operate all year. Pitches mostly for tents are informally arranged on a slope, with other pitches for caravans and motorcaravans on the lower part of the site. With numbered but unmarked pitches, some overcrowding may occur. Pitches alongside the road will experience some road noise as this is a busy arterial route. Many permanent types of accommodation on site and a large separate complex across a small street has many mobile homes. The site is directly off the main road and a fairly steep entry brings you to a reception where English is spoken. The site can be used en-route for the trip home or outbound or for exploring the northern areas of Spain. The centre of the charming medieval village of Santillana is near, and the Altamira caves are close.

Facilities: Well placed fully equipped sanitary facilities with facilities for disabled campers. Washing machines and irons. Supermarket. Souvenir shop. Bar/restaurant (popular with locals at weekends) and self service cafe (all year). Swimming pool complex with separate children's pool. Play area for toddlers and an inventive play complex for older children. Minigolf. Tennis. Bicycle hire. Satellite TV. Drinks machines. Electronic games. Film processing service. Entertainment in high season.

Charges 2002

Per person	€ 4.35 - € 4.80
child (6-10 yrs)	€ 3.45 - € 3.75
caravan	€ 4.65 - € 4.80
tent	€ 4.20 - € 4.65
motorcaravan	€ 5.40 - € 6.00
car	€ 4.20 - € 4.65
electricity	€ 2.85

Tel: 942 818 250. Fax: 942 840 183. E-mail: campingsantillan@ceoecant.es. **Reservations:** Advisable in July and August. **Open** all year.

Directions: Nearest large city is Santander. Site is directly off Santanilla - Comillas road (C6316) between the 5 km. and 6 km. markers. Exit the N634 west of Torrelavega.

Camping Los Molinos de Cantabria

8990 Ctra. Bareyo-Güemes, 39190 Bareyo (Cantabria)

Camping Los Molinos at Bareyo is an ideal site for families who wish to enjoy a tranquil setting with excellent views after or before the trials of a sea crossing, or for touring the local area. This is a sister site to Los Molinos Noja (8995) and a nice alternative to the fast moving seaside resorts. There is a large Spanish contingent on site and therefore, although the situation is peaceful, expect the normal Spanish exuberance at weekends and on their special days. This developing site is divided into two main areas, the lower established area with a large number of permanent units on a gentle slope and with southern mountain views. The newer, upper areas are terraced and planted with young trees which will eventually offer some shade. The higher the terrace the better the excellent inland views (long electricity leads may be required). The very top level is for tents at present (no electricity) and it offers wonderful views of the mountains inland and the sea to the north. There are 500 average sized touring pitches on the lower levels with some shade, and electrical connections.

Facilities: Modern sanitary buildings in pristine condition with British style WCs (no seats) and free showers are central. Cleaning can be variable. Washing machines, dishwashing (H&C) and laundry sinks are at the end of the blocks under cover. Facilities for disabled campers have access ramps. Shop (1/6-30/9). Restaurant/bar - great menu del dia and views (1/6-30/9). Swimming pools with lifeguard (25/6-7/9). Playground. Tennis courts. Volleyball. High season free bus twice daily to the beach and town. Safe deposit. Medical post with doctor daily in high season. Torches are required, especially on the steps between terraces. **Off site:** Golf 30 km. Riding 400 m. Bicycle hire 1 km. Beach 300 m.

Charges 2002

Per pitch	€ 6.50 - € 7.40
adult	€ 3.25 - € 4.00
child	€ 2.60 - € 3.00
tent	€ 3.90 - € 5.00
car	€ 1.70 - € 2.00
electricity	€ 2.45

No credit cards. **Tel:** 942 670 569. Fax: 942 630 275. E-mail: molinosdebareyo@ceoecant.es. **Reservations:** Write to site. **Open** Easter - September.

Directions: The site is 34 km. from Santander. Move south on Bilbao road to junction 11 then turn north on N141 via Somo to Bareyo. Look for good signs off to right by large church on hill - signed to 'Bareyo'.

Camping Los Molinos

8995 C/ La Ria S/N, 39180 Noja (Cantabria)

Camping Los Molinos is a sister site to Los Molinos at Bareyo (8990; which might be a quieter option). This site is ideally located for touring the local area and as an overnight stop en route when travelling by ferry via Bilbao or Santander. It is close to the village of Noja, a busy Spanish tourist resort in high season, on the coast of Cantabria and is near the Playa del Ris beach which has fine sand and clear water. The site is divided into two main areas, both with a large number of permanent units. There are 500 average sized touring pitches, on level ground, but with little shade; all have electricity. There is a large separate area for tents. Each half of the site has its own main building with catering facilities. The right side has the main restaurant/bar, disco, supermarket, while the left has the reception, café/bar, supermarket and the swimming pools. Unusually the site has its own karting complex.

Facilities: The fully equipped modern sanitary building is central and kept very clean. Washing machines, dishwashing (H&C) and laundry sinks under cover. Facilities for disabled campers have access ramps. Supermarket, butcher and fishmonger (1/6-30/9). Main restaurant/bar good decoration and tablecloths with cafe bar providing tapas, pizzas or takeaway food. (1/6-30/9). Swimming pool and children's pool with life guard (15/6-10/9). Playground. Basketball. Tennis. Team games. Medical room. Security at gate. ATM. Torch useful. **Off site:** Beach 300 m. Fishing 300 m. Golf 1 km. Riding 500 m. Bicycle hire 500 m. Boat launching 7 km. Indoor pool 100 m. Free bus hourly to the beach and town in high season.

Charges 2002

Per pitch	€ 6.50 - € 9.50
adult	€ 3.25 - € 4.40
child	€ 2.60 - € 3.40
tent	€ 4.50 - € 5.50
car	€ 2.00 - € 2.60
electricity	€ 2.45

No credit cards. **Tel:** 942 630 426. Fax: 942 630 725. E-mail: losmolinos@ceoecant.es. **Reservations:** Write to site. **Open** 12 February - 15 November.

Directions: From E70/A8 Bilbao -Santander, take exit 185, CA 147 to Noja take first right S403. It is 10 km. to Noja. In town look for multiple campsite signs going off to left. Follow signs to Playa del Ris. At beach roundabout turn left (the sign had gone when we visited) and look for a left turn at further large signs. Reception is in the building to the left.

Camping Playa Joyel

Playa de Ris, 39180 Noja (Cantabria)

9000

This very attractive, holiday and touring site is some 40 km. from Santander and 70 km. from Bilbao. It is a high quality, comprehensively equipped busy site, by a superb beach; providing 1,000 well shaded, marked and numbered pitches, including 80 large pitches of 100 sq.m. Electricity is available (3A with new blue Euro-sockets). The swimming pool complex with lifeguard is free to campers and the superb beaches are cleaned daily 15/6-20/9. One of the beach exits leads to the main beach, or if you turn left out of the other you will find a safe, placid estuary with water at rising tide. An unusual feature is the natural park within the site boundary which has a great selection of animals to see. It overlooks a protected area of marsh where European birds spend the winter. A 'no cycling on site' rule operates in July/Aug. There are security patrols at night. This good value, well managed site has a lot to offer for family holidays with much going on in high season when it gets very busy. Used by tour operators (150 pitches).

Facilities: Six excellent, spacious and fully equipped toilet blocks (voted amongst the cleanest in Europe) include baby baths and dishwashing facilities. Large laundry. Motorcaravan services. Gas supplies. Freezer service. Supermarket (all season). General shop. Kiosk. Restaurant (14/4-29/9). Bar, café take-away and snacks (14/4-28/9). Swimming pools, bathing caps compulsory (15/5-15/9). Entertainment organised with a soundproof pub/disco (July-Aug). Games hall. Gym park. Recreation area and sports field. Tennis. Playground. Riding.Fishing. Natural animal park. Barbecue area. Hairdresser (July/Aug). Pharmacy. ATM and money exchange. Torches necessary in some areas. Medical centre. Dogs are not accepted. **Off site:** Within 1 km. - large complex with multiple facilities including golf and indoor pool (fee). Bicycle hire 500 m. Golf 20 km.

Charges 2002

Per adult	€ 3.70 - € 5.50
child (under 10 yrs)	€ 2.50 - € 4.10
pitch	€ 9.90 - € 11.70
electricity	€ 2.45 - € 2.70

All plus 7% VAT. No credit cards. **Tel:** 942 630 081. Fax: 942 631 294. E-mail: campingplayajoyel@ yahoo.es. **Reservations:** made for 1 week or more. Early arrival or reservation is essential in high season. **Open** 23 March - 29 September.

Directions: From A8 (E70) toll-free motorway at Beranga (km.185) take the N634 then, almost immediately, take the S403 for Noja. Follow signs to site.

Only 40 km from Santander (ferry) and 70 km from Bilbao (ferry), easily and quickly reached along the magnificent, new, toll-free autovia and the coast roads.

A 25 ha. holiday site with a large (4 ha) recreation and sports area and a precious, 8 ha natural park with animals in semiliberty.

Modern, first category installations. Beautifull surroundings with direct access to wide, clean beaches. Surrounded by meadows and woods.

Service and comfort for the most exacting guests.Properly marked pitches.

English spoken. Open from Easter to 30th September.

Your beautiful holiday destination in SPAIN

CAMPING
PLAYA JOYEL

E-39180 NOJA (SANTANDER, CANTABRIA) SPAIN
Tel. (34) 942 63 00 81
Fax (34) 942 63 12 94

Camping Valderredible

8985 Ctra. Polientes - Ruerrero. S/n, Valderredible, 39220 Polientes (Cantabria)

This is a pleasant site owned by the Gutierrez brothers who designed and constructed this site using their past campsite experience. Jose and Jesus are very keen to welcome you to their establishment. If you approach the site from the east you will enjoy the vista of limestone valleys and pass a large ornate waterfall which is worth exploring. All facilities on site are modern and kept spotlessly clean. There are 100 flat pitches with 80 for tourers and 20 for tents. Most have electricity and trees have been planted, although there is little shade at the moment. The pools enjoy river and mountain views, as does the patio to the bar/restaurant. The bustling bar, with TV, is pleasantly decorated with local artefacts and offers a range of tapas in season. There are some lovely walks in this unspoilt area (ask for guidance). The site is about 80 km. south of Santander and is good as a stopover or for longer stays if you wish for a peaceful break. On the first Sat and Sun of August there is a Fiesta here with all night celebrations so the site is full and extremely noisy.

Facilities: The good central sanitary block is fully equipped and comfortable. Washing-up sinks outside but covered Two washing machines (free) and a dryer. No facilities for disabled campers. Small well stocked shop. Bar selling tapas and more formal restaurant, good service and reasonably priced. Swimming pool and children's pool (caps required; June - Sept). Play area (supervision required). Volleyball. Bar billiards. Table football. Torch useful. **Off site:** Canoeing and fishing in river Ebro 200 m. (March - June). Riding 15 km. Bicycle hire 15 km. Buses run to local village which has a few bars and some restaurants.

Charges 2002

Per adult	€ 3.15
child (3-10 yrs)	€ 2.79
tent	€ 3.25
caravan	€ 3.25
car	€ 3.25
motorcaravan	€ 5.26
electricity	€ 2.17

Plus 7% VAT. **Tel:** 942 776 138. Fax: 942 776 138. E-mail: valderrecamp@mundivia.es. **Reservations:** Necessary in August. **Open** 1 April - 4 November.

Directions: Exit from A623 Burgos - Santander road around the village of Quintanilla Escalada onto minor road to Polientes. The site is clearly signed along the 21 km. of road and is just past the village of Ruijas. It is a spectacular drive in from the main road.

Camping Angosto

9045 Ctra. Villanane - Angosto No. 2, 01425 Villanañe (Araba)

This is a smart eco-friendly site with excellent facilities surrounded by wooded hills near the Valderejo National Park. It is just four years old (2002) and the facilities are improving every year remaining smart and clean. A keen young team run things here, and there is an emphasis on adventure sports. The site is occasionally busy with parties of local youngsters enjoying the various activities organised by the management (it can be noisy when this happens). With ample manoeuvring space, the 71 pitches are flat and of average size, 25 having electricity. There is a large area for tents. Young trees have been planted around the site and are beginning to provide shade. An attractive new pool has been built (2002) with a sliding roof for inclement weather. Attractive walks start just outside the site perimeter and we spotted deer several times, and the area has one of the largest colonies of vultures in Northern Spain. As the site is one hour from Bilbao we see it as a most pleasant stopover or a chance to sample the rustic simplicity of the area and enjoy the facilities and a tranquil setting.

Facilities: Central, fully equipped sanitary block of attractive design with facilities for disabled campers. Dishwashing sinks outside, under cover. Washing machine. Good shop also used by the local villagers. Stylish bar. Attractive and terraced restaurant. Small fenced play area close to entrance and grass toddler play area. Mountain bike hire. Fishing. Adventure sports incl. para-ascending organised. Table football. Table tennis. TV. Fishing. Ice machine. Drinks machine. Torches necessary in some areas. **Off site:** Heated municipal pool 1.4 km. Bus service from pretty local village 1 km.

Charges 2002

Per adult	€ 3.16
child	€ 2.70
tent	€ 2.85
caravan	€ 3.16
car	€ 2.85
motorcaravan	€ 4.81
electricity	€ 2.70

All plus 7% VAT. **Tel:** 945 353 271. Fax: 945 353 271. E-mail: info@camping-angosto.com. **Reservations:** Contact site. **Open** April - September (plus weekends Sept - March).

Directions: Nearest town is Miranda de Ebro. From Bilbao and the Longrono autoroute, exit at village of Pobes and take road to Salinas and Espejo (N625). Site is clearly signed. If towing a caravan continue to Miranda de Ebro proceed towards Burgos for one exit (no 4) and take the N1 to the N625 then north to Villanane.

Camping Portuondo

9035 | Ctra. Gernika - Bermeo, 48360 Mundaka (Bizkaia)

From some of the 119 pitches on site there are stunning views over the ocean and estuary. Among the lovely gardens the pitches are mainly for medium size vans and tents but there are 6 large pitches at the lower levels for caravans and motorhomes. In high season (July/Aug) it is best to ring to book your space. Before entering the site walk 20 metres up the hill and enjoy views that are difficult to beat on this coast (it is also a good idea to have a look at the approach before driving in). This well cared for, impressive little site could either be a very pleasant site to stay or a good base from which to explore the local area and the old Spanish town and the friendly owner Inmanol is keen to help you. The site is mostly terraced, with pitches split, one section for your unit the other for your car and there is shade in parts. Most pitches are very slightly sloping and all have electricity (6A, some may need long leads). Above the larger sanitary block the building becomes a lofty picnic area with long benches, open on all sides, but perfect for occupants of tents in periods of rain. There is a stylish swimming pool in the lower area of the site but no facilities for disabled campers. We stress that this site is on a steep incline.

Facilities: Two very good quality, fully equipped, sanitary units can be heated and include mostly British WCs and a smart baby bathroom. Dishwashing and laundry sinks outside under cover. Automated shop (all season). Bar and two restaurants, one open to public offering full range of meals and snacks, plus barbecue food (16/1-15/12). Takeaway (15/6-15/9). Swimming pools (15/6-15/9). Table tennis. Sky TV. Barbecue area. Bicycle hire. Washing machines and dryers. Caravan storage. Torches necessary. English spoken. **Off site:** Fishing 100 m. Beaches 500 m. bracing walk. Surfing on Mundaka beach (500 m.) is so good they hold international championships there. Boat launching 1 km. Sailing 5 km. Bicycle hire 2 km. Bars and restaurants 2 km.

Charges 2002

Per adult	€ 4.10 - € 4.55
child (under 10 yrs)	€ 3.50 - € 4.00
pitch	€ 8.80 - € 9.20
pitch with electricity	€ 11.85 - € 12.15

All plus 7% VAT. Less 5-10% for longer stays. **Tel:** 946 877 701. Fax: 946 877 828. E-mail: recepcion@campingportuondo.com. **Reservations:** Write to site. **Open** all year.

Directions: From N634 or autopista (S. Sebastian-Bilbao), turn at Amorebieta onto the C6315 road to Gernika - Bermeo. Approach site from Bermeo direction due to oblique, steep (18%) access.

Gran Camping Zarautz

9039 | Monte Talai-Mendi, Ctra. N634 San Sebastian - Bilbao, km 17, 20800 Zarauz (Gipuzkoa)

This friendly site sits alongside vines high in the hills to the east of the Basque town of Zarautz and has commanding views of the excellent beaches and the island of Isarria. Twenty percent of the 500 pitches are permanent which brings Spanish life and colour to the site at weekends. The pitches are of average size, shaded by mature trees, are reasonably level and have 5A electricity. We recommend a call to reserve one of the perimeter pitches which enjoy magnificent views over the bay. Between the site and the sea is a protected public area where flora and fauna flourish. You can enjoy birds and wildlife whilst exploring the ruins of a once busy iron ore works on the shore and the adjacent small island of Mollarri (children should be supervised in this area). On approaching the site you will pass a Bodega producing the local white wine, Txakoli (pronounced Char-coal-lee). The locals drink it young with shellfish. The town of Zarautz offers a cultural programme in summer and the promenade with modern sculptures is a good vantage point to enjoy the beach and surfers.

Facilities: Two sanitary blocks - the more modern is circular and open plan with facilities for disabled campers. Two washing machines. Restaurant/bar with TV. Well stocked shop. Play area. Drinks machines. Recycling bins. English spoken. **Off site:** Bus/train service 1 km. Two good restaurants very close by. Below site at beach level is a 9 hole golf course. For a special treat visit the ancient 'siderías' (cider houses). These open in January and offer tastings with superb traditional food until the cider runs out. Ask for assistance at reception.

Charges 2003

Per adult	€ 3.80
child (0-10 yrs)	€ 3.25
caravan or tent	€ 4.50
car	€ 3.80
motorcaravan	€ 8.30
electricity	€ 3.10

VAT included. **Tel:** 943 831 238. Fax: 943 132 486. **Reservations:** Contact site. **Open** all year.

Directions: From N634 Donastia - San Sebastian road at 17 km. marker take sign to Zarautz and site is well marked on the roundabout at the eastern side of town.

Camping Igueldo

9030 Paseo Padre Orkolaga no. 69, Barrio de Igueldo, 20008 San Sebastian (Gipuzkoa)

Igueldo has a commanding view of the area from its hilltop location to the western edge of San Sebastian. It is also quite a pleasant site in a part of Spain where Britons may find it difficult to find a decent campsite. Although it is not luxurious, it is good value, friendly and ideal for a transit stop. Although there are steep slopes, there are upper pitches on flat ground that are fine for those who may be a little infirm. The site has 289 terraced pitches, although they are not very large (70 sq.m.). They are of two types, 191 have electricity (5A) and water, and the remainder are tiny tent pitches of 20 sq.m. San Sebastian is a large, pleasant and quite fashionable town which has all the shops, restaurants, entertainment and night life that one could want, as well as some sandy beaches, which are usually busy in the season.

Facilities: Fully equipped, adequate sanitary blocks very clean when visited. Facilities for disabled campers are good. Shop. Restaurant with terrace, TV and bar. Takeaway (all year). Drinks machines. Torch useful. **Off site:** Local bus service. Nearest beach about 5 km. Fishing 4 km. Golf 8 km. Riding 7 km. Boat launching 6 km.

Charges 2002

Per unit incl. 3 persons, car and services	€ 21.60
without services	€ 19.10
small tent pitch	€ 11.00
extra adult	€ 3.35
child (3-10 yrs)	€ 2.20
electricity	€ 2.53

All plus 7% VAT. Special winter prices available. **Tel:** 943 214 502. **Fax:** 943 280 411. E-mail: garoaigueldo@telefonica.net. **Reservations:** None made. **Open** all year.

Directions: The turning to Igueldo is at the western end of the town sea-front promenade and is well signed. It is a 7 km. long and steep climb to the site but there are no access problems.

Camping Orio

9038 20810 Orio (Gipuzkoa)

This site has 260 pitches, with many long stay units and privately owned static units, but there should always be adequate space in the 190 pitches allocated for tourers. It is only 100 m. from the beach and there is little shade. The pitches are in rows divided by tarmac roads and hedges, all with electricity (5A). Like most of the north coast sites, it is fairly expensive in high season, with the cheaper pitches furthest from the beach, but the bonus is that they are closer to the sanitary facilities. The beach is in a pretty bay contained by towering hills which overlook the site. The beach is of soft sand (real sand-castle stuff) and shelves gently. Fishing is popular off the extremely long jetty or in the local river. This is a decent site for transit stops, west of San Sebastian or a little longer if you wish to enjoy the beach.

Facilities: The modernised main sanitary block is fully equipped and includes baby baths. Two additional smaller, older sanitary blocks are opened in the main season. Large kitchen with additional dishwashing and laundry sinks (cold water) outside under cover. Good facilities for disabled campers. Minimarket and good restaurant/bar attached to the site (open July/Aug). Swimming pools. Playground. Squash and tennis courts. Fishing. Barbecue area. Dogs are not accepted. Torches are necessary. Some English is spoken. **Off site:** Fishing 100 m. Golf 6 km. Sailing. Indoor pool. Aviary 100 m.

Charges 2002

Per unit incl. 2 persons	€ 12.70 - € 22.55
extra adult	€ 2.30 - € 3.65
child (2-10 yrs)	€ 1.80 - € 3.10

VAT included. **Tel:** 943 834 801. Fax: 943 133 433. E-mail: kampina@terra.es. **Reservations:** Write to site. **Open** 1 March - 1 November.

Directions: Turn off N634 road at the Orio junction and follow signs to site. The approach is straightforward.

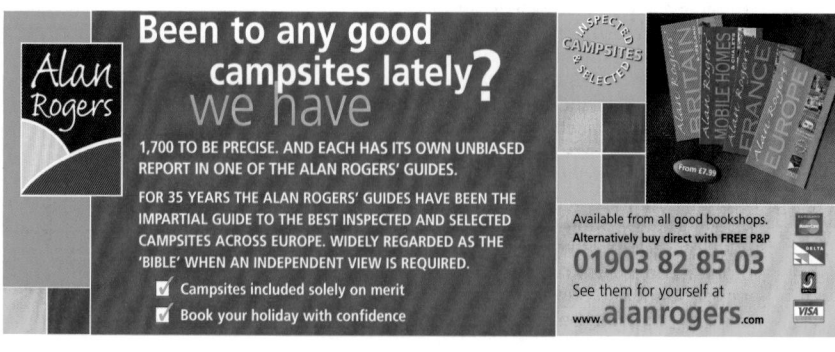

Camping de Haro

9040 Avenida Miranda 1, 26200 Haro (La Rioja)

This quiet riverside site is on the outskirts of the village of Haro, which is the commercial centre for the renowned Rioja wines. It is a family run site with excellent pools and good supporting facilities. There is considerable room to manoeuvre at the entrance with modern reception and a welcome from the cheery young owner, Carlos who speaks excellent English. The river Ebro running alongside the site can provide fishing, and there is secure fencing. Approximately 30% of the good sized pitches on level ground are occupied by permanent campers. The area is very popular with Spanish holidaymakers in summer. Electricity connections (3/5A) are provided, although long leads may be required on some pitches. The site gives information on the jewel of a town, and tastings at the Bodegas close by - there are some world famous names here and if you are keen on the superb Spanish wines they should not be missed. The famous Paternina within easy walking distance and Muga is 'on the doorstep'. There is insufficient space here to quote the rest but take advantage of the offer.

Facilities: Two modern sanitary blocks, one new in 2000 that incorporates excellent facilities for disabled campers. Laundry. All facilities were spotlessly clean and well maintained when visited. Mini market offers fresh bread in season. Restaurant, bar and supermarket (all in season only). Large smart adult pool Three toddler pools. Drinks and ice machine. New children's play area and animation in season. Fishing. Torch useful. **Off site:** Beautiful old town square with bustling bars, excellent restaurants and wine tastings. Order a 'Banda' in the bars, sold as a cheap house wine and be rewarded with a glass of 'Banda Azul' which is in fact a superb quality Rioja.

Charges 2002

Per adult	€ 2.93 - € 3.45
child	€ 2.31 - € 2.72
tent or caravan	€ 2.93 - € 3.45
car	€ 2.93 - € 3.45
motorcaravan	€ 5.06 - € 5.96
electricity (3A)	€ 2.05

Tel: 941 312 737. Fax: 941 312 068. E-mail: campingdeharo@fer.es. **Reservations:** Write to site. **Open** all year except 10 Dec. - 10 Jan.

Directions: Take E804 road from Bilbao south to Logroño; enter Haro at exit 9 and the site is well signed just west of the river on the western side of town.

Camping Etxarri

9042 Paraje Dambolintxulo s/n, 31820 Etxarri-Aranatz (Navarra)

Situated in the Valle de la Burunda the site is a peaceful oasis with superb views of the 1,300 m. high San-Donato Mountains. The approach to the constantly improving site is via a road lined by huge 300 year old beech trees, surrounding the tiny site, which nestles behind an enormous pool. Reception is a purpose built chalet with a touring reference library (mostly in Spanish). There are 100 average sized pitches on flat ground, 50 for tourers, with 6A electricity to all and water to 25. The site is well placed for fascinating walks in unspoilt countryside and is close to three recognised nature walks catering for all tastes and abilities. Animation is organised in August for children and there are many other activities available (see below). There is hostel accommodation for young Navarra students as part of their curriculum, and this is also used as standard accommodation especially at the time of the Fiestas de San Fermín (bull-running) in Pamplona. It is essential to make a reservation if you wish to stay for the thrilling week of 6-14 July. There is riotous non-stop celebration in Pamplona during this Fiesta, made world famous by Ernest Hemingway.

Facilities: Single, very modern sanitary block includes sinks and baby bath. Laundry. Gas supplies. Essential supplies available in high season. Bar. Restaurant with traditional fare at reasonable prices (1/6-30/9). Very large swimming pool plus children's pool (ex municipal and open to the public). Archery (small fee). Bicycle hire. Minigolf. Skateboarding. Table tennis. Small football pitch. Volleyball. Play area. Games room. **Off site:** Good bus services. Local village at 2 km. has bars, restaurants and shops. Pamplona is recommended - parking is difficult - try to the west of the bullring, then wander down to Plaza de Toros (renamed Plaza Hemingway), to savour the atmosphere. A useful tip: it is common to use dual-naming of places and roads - one in the Spanish language the other in Basque and it can be confusing - ask for advice if in doubt.

Charges 2002

Per adult	€ 2.75 - € 3.35
child	€ 2.50 - € 3.00
caravan	€ 3.40 - € 4.10
tent	€ 2.75 - € 3.25
car	€ 2.75 - € 3.35
electricity	€ 3.10

Tel: 948 460 537. Fax: 948 461 509. E-mail: info@ campingetxarri.com. **Reservations:** Contact site. **Open** 1 April - 1 October.

Directions: From A8 San Sebastian - Bilbao motorway take exit to Pamplona A15 at the junction at Irurzun (approx. 17.5 km. northwest of Pamplona) take N240 to Vitoria. At 40 km. marker take road to Etxarri-Aranatz where site is signed.

Camping-Caravanning Errota el Molino

31150 Mendigorria (Navarra)

9043

This is an extremely large, sprawling site set by an attractive weir near the town of Mendigorria, alongside the river Arga. Regardless of the mini-windmill (molino) at the entrance, it really takes its name from an old disused water-mill close by (try to find it when you have a moment spare). Reception is housed in the lower part of a large prefabricated building along with the bar/restaurant which has a cool shaded terrace, there is a large separate more formal dining room and a supermarket and other support facilities. The chirpy owner Anna Beriain will give you a warm welcome. The upper floor is dormitory accommodation for backpackers. The site is split into separate permanent and touring sections. The touring area is a new development which is divided into sections. There are good-sized flat pitches with electricity and water for tourers, however there is no electricity in the tent area. Many trees have been planted around the site but there is little shade as yet. There is a small tour operator presence and backpackers and campers abound during the festival of San Fermin (bull running) in July, made famous in Pamplona (28 km.) by Ernest Hemingway. Tours of the local bodegas (groups of 10) to sample the fantastic Navarra wines can be organised by reception.

Facilities: The single, fully equipped, toilet block is very clean and well maintained, with cold water to washbasins. Services could become busy during San Fermin but then access is allowed to the sanitary facilities on the permanent side. Dishwashing (cold only) and laundry sinks (H&C). Facilities for disabled campers. Washing machine. Large restaurant, pleasant bar. Supermarket (Easter - Sept). Superb new swimming pools for adults and children. Football. Table tennis. Volleyball. Golf. Bicycle hire. Riding. Weekly animation programme (July/Aug) and many sporting activities. Pleasant river walk. Sophisticated dock and boat launching facility, pedaloes and canoes for hire and an ambitious water sport competition programme in season with a safety boat present at all times. Torches useful. **Off site:** Bus for town 1 km. Tours to Pamplona.

Charges 2002

Per person	€ 3.40
child	€ 2.55
pitch incl. car and electricity	€ 9.32

Plus 7% VAT. Discounts outside high season.**Tel:** 948 340 604. Fax: 948 340 082. E-mail: info@ campingel-molino.com. **Reservations:** Made with 25% deposit. Advisable during San Fermin. **Open** all year.

Directions: From N111 Pamplona - Logroño road take exit to Puente la Reina. Take N6030 towards Mendigorria and after approx 6 km. take Larraga turn by the wide river Arga, where site is signed.

Camping Gavín

22639 Gavín (Huesca)

9064

Camping Gavín is set on a terraced, wooded hillside. At about 900 m, it is surrounded by towering peaks at the portal of the Tena Valley. One can enjoy the natural beauty of the Pyrenees and venture near or far along the great Pyrenean footpaths. The National Park of Ordesa, the valleys of Hecho, Broto and Tena and their associated ravines, lakes and rivers all offer a great variety of opportunities for physical activities. Visit the high mountain villages of Formigal, Panticosa and Balneario and watch the eagles soar overhead. The site offers 200 pitches of 80 sq m.in size and with electricity available to all. The main site buildings are built of natural stone. There are also 11 superb, balconied apartments for 4 to 6 persons. You will find a friendly welcome with English spoken.

Facilities: Shower and toilet facilities in three main buildings with subtle, tasteful décor include facilities for babies and disabled people. Dishwashing and laundry facilities. Bar and snacks. Well stocked supermarket. Swimming pool and children's pool. Tennis. Table tennis. Playground. **Off site:** Windsurfing, rafting, riding, fishing, walking and climbing in the vicinity. Day excursions to the Monastery of San Juan de la Pena or over the border into France possible.

Charges 2002

Per person	€ 3.25 - € 4.50
caravan or tent	€ 3.25 - € 4.50
car	€ 3.25 - € 4.50
motorcaravan	€ 5.50 - € 7.80
electricity	€ 4.50 - € 3.15
m/cycle	€ 3.00 - € 4.25

Tel: 902 485 090 or 974 485 090. Fax: 974 485 017. E-mail: info@campinggavin.com. **Reservations:** advisable for Holy week and July/Aug. **Open** all year.

Directions: Follow the N260 road and signs to site at Biescas. Site is off the N260, 2 km. after Biescas.

Camping Pirineos

9070 Ctra. N240, km 300, 22791 Santa Cilia de Jaca (Huesca)

This pretty, all year site is directly on the pilgrimage route to Santiago and pilgrims are a common sight. It has a mild climate, being near the River Aragon, not too high and convenient for touring the Pyrenees. The trees provide good shade. There is an attractive irregular shaped swimming pool and children's pool. The restaurant with a varied menu and a good value menu of the day has a large comfortable terrace and a patio for drinks and snacks. There is an open fronted room for barbecuing and all equipment is provided. A major feature here is the huge recreational area with all manner of sports and amusements. It is a friendly site which is useful for transit stops and off-season camping on the 250 large, level pitches all with electricity. There is some road noise along the north side of the site.

Facilities: One heated sanitary block is open all year, providing a quite satisfactory supply, including dish-washing and laundry sinks with hot water. A second, very modern block is open June - August only. Launderette. Restaurant (Easter - Oct). Bar (closed Nov). Supermarket (high season, otherwise essentials kept in bar). Swimming pools (July - Aug). Two tennis courts. Table tennis. Children's playground. Playroom with electronic games. Petanque. Bicycle hire. Gas supplies. 5-side-soccer. Torches required in some areas. Dogs are not accepted in high season. **Off site:** Fishing 200 m.

Charges 2002

Per adult	€ 4.50
child (2-9 yrs)	€ 4.15
caravan or tent	€ 4.50
car	€ 4.25
motorcaravan	€ 8.00
electricity	€ 3.50

All plus 7% VAT. **Tel:** 974 377 351. Fax: 974 377 351. E-mail: pirineos@pirinet.com. **Reservations:** Contact site. **Open** all year.

Directions: Site is 15 km. west of Jaca on N240 (65 km. northwest of Huesca).

Camping Lago Barasona

9125 Ctra. N-123a, km 25, 22435 La Puebla de Castro (Huesca)

This site, alongside its associated 10 room hotel, is beautifully positioned in terraces by the shores of the Lago de Barasona (a large reservoir), with views of hills and the distant Pyrenees. There are two excellent restaurants here one being in the hotel the other with a pretty terrace with wonderful views. The menu and cooking is outstand-ing, specialising in the regional cuisine. The very friendly, English speaking owner is keen to please and has applied very high standards throughout the site. The grassy, fairly level pitches are generally around 100 sq.m. with 35 high quality pitches of 110 sq m for larger units. All have electricity (6/10A), are well shaded and some have great views of the lake and/or hills. Waterskiing and other watersports are available in July and August. You may swim and fish in the lake which has a shal-low area extending for around 20 m. If you prefer, the site has a round outdoor pool plus the pleasant standard pool in the hotel (these open from as early as April when the weather is often quite warm). The disco is well away from the site by the lakeside. The local administration has put together some excellent tourist and walk-ing route information (in English) and the owner has matched this with his own qual-ity brochure. The recently discovered Roman town of Labitolosa currently under excavation is just 1.5 km. away. This is a most pleasant and peaceful site in a lovely area and will suit families who wish for quality and choice in their camping. The views really are beautiful.

Facilities: Two toilet blocks in modern buildings have high standards and hot water throughout including cabins (3 for ladies, 1 for men). Bar/snack bar and two excellent restaurants (all season). Shop (15/5-15/9). Swimming pools (15/5-15/9). Tennis. Table tennis. Mountain bike hire. Canoe, windsurfing motor boat and pedalo hire. Mini-club. Lake swimming, fishing, canoeing, etc. Facilities for volleyball, football and a new children's play area were under construc-tion. Walking (maps provided). Money exchange. Mini-disco. **Off site:** Riding 4 km.

Charges 2002

Per person	€ 3.50 - € 4.85
child (2-10 yrs)	€ 2.50 - € 3.95
caravan or tent	€ 3.50 - € 4.85
car	€ 3.50 - € 4.85
motorcaravan	€ 5.50 - € 7.85
electricity	€ 3.45

Plus VAT @ 7%. **Tel:** 974 545 148. Fax: 974 545 228. E-mail: info@lagobarasona.com. **Reservations:** Made with 25-50% deposit, but probably not needed outside mid-July - mid-August. Contact site for details. **Open** 1 April - 30 September.

Directions: Site is on the west bank of the lake, close to km. 25 on the N123A, 4.5 km. south of Graus (approx. 80 km. north of Lleida/Lerida).

Camping Peña Montañesa

Ctra. Ainsa -Francia, km 2, 22360 Labuerda (Huesca)

9060

A large, riverside site situated quite high up in the Pyrenees, near the Ordesa National Park, Pena Montanesa is easily accessible from Ainsa or from France via the Bielsa Tunnel, and is ideally situated for exploring the beautiful Pyrenées. The site is essentially divided into three sections opening progressively throughout the season and providing progressively less shade, although the trees in the newer section are growing. The 288 pitches on fairly level grass are of approximately 75 sq.m. and 10A electricity is available on virtually all. This is quite a large site which has grown very quickly and as such may at times be a little hard pressed. Grouped near the entrance are the facilities that make the site so attractive. Apart from a fair sized outdoor pool and children's pool, there is a heated, glass covered indoor pool with jacuzzi and sauna (open all year) and an attractive bar, restaurant (with open fire) and terrace with the supermarket and takeaway opposite. The complete town of Ainsa is listed as a national monument of Spain and should be explored while you are here, along with the national park.

Facilities: A newer toilet block, heated when necessary, has free hot showers but cold water to open plan washbasins, facilities for disabled visitors and a small baby bathroom. An older block in the original area has similar provision. Washing machine. Bar. Restaurant. Takeaway. Supermarket. Outdoor swimming pool and children's pool (March - Oct). Indoor pool with jacuzzi and sauna (all year). Children's playground. Boules. Minigolf. Table tennis. Bicycle hire. Riding. Rafting. Only gas barbecues are permitted. Torches required in some areas. **Off site:** Fishing 100m. Skiing in season. Canoeing near.

Charges 2002

Per person	€ 5.00
child (1-9 yrs)	€ 4.00
pitch	€ 14.00
electricity	€ 4.00
dog	€ 3.00

All plus 7% VAT. **Tel:** 974 500 032. Fax: 974 500 991. E-mail: info@penamontanesa.com. **Reservations:** are made for camping with € 60 deposit by visa or giro. **Open** all year.

Directions: Site is 2 km. from Ainsa, on the road from Ainsa to France.

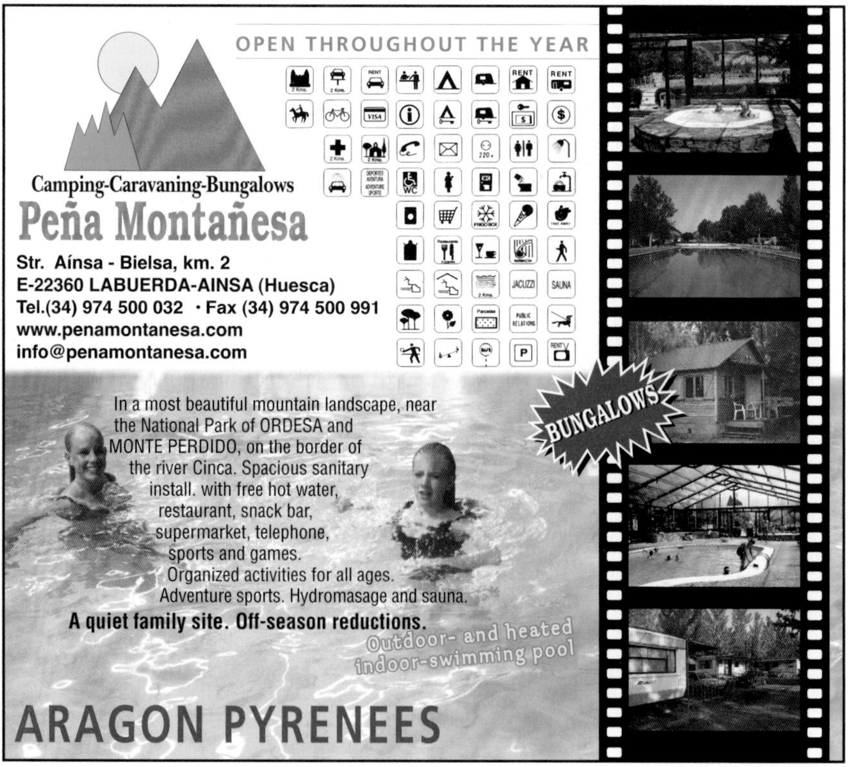

Camping Boltana

9062   Ctra. N-260, km 442, 22340 Boltaña (Huesca)

Nestled in the Rio Ara valley, surrounded by the Pyrennes mountains and below a tiny but enchanting, historic, hill top village, is the very pretty, thoughtfully planned Camping Boltana. Generously sized, grassy pitches have good shade from a variety of trees and a stream meanders through the campsite. The landscaping includes ten charming rocky water gardens (children loved the ducklings) and a covered pergola doubles as an eating and play area. A stone building houses the site's new reception, social room and supermarket. Opposite is a terrace for enjoying tapas, listening to music, casual eating, animation and games and above this is the charming stone and wood restaurant. Special meals, paellas and fideuadas can be ordered the day before for you to eat in the restaurant or take away. Angel Moreno, the owner of the site, is a charming host and has tried to think of everything to make his guests comfortable.

Facilities: Two modern sanitary blocks include facilities for disabled visitors and laundry facilities. Casual and formal restaurants. Supermarket. Swimming pools, children's pool and hydro pool. Children's playground. Covered summerhouse and barbecues. Full size soccer pitch. Animation for children, music at weekends in high season. Pentanque. Guided tours organized, plus hiking, canyoning, rafting, climbing, mountain biking and caving. Torches may be necessary in some parts. Local bus service.

Charges 2002

Per adult	€ 4.09
child (1-10 yrs)	€ 3.31
caravan or tent	€ 4.51
car	€ 4.51
motorcycle	€ 3.61
motorcaravan	€ 8.11
dog	€ 2.10

Tel: 974 502 347. Fax: 974 502 023. E-mail: boltana@svt.es. **Reservations:** Contact site for details. **Open** all year.

Directions: South of the Park Nacional de Ordesa, site is about 50 km. from Jaca near Ainsa. From Ainsa travel northwest on N260 toward Boltana (near 443 km marker). 1 km. from Boltana turn south toward Margudged. Camping Boltana is well signed and is approx. 1 km. along this road.

Camping Casablanca

9100   50012 Zaragoza (Zaragoza)

Although not a sophisticated site, Casablanca is considered acceptable for overnight or for a short stay to visit the fascinating city of Zaragoza - the bridge over the river Ebro is impressive, as is the Basilica of our Lady of the Pilar with its jewels, amazing altar and fine paintings including Goya's. Although a city site it is surprisingly quiet. On a flat meadow (with little grass), there are 192 pitches with 10A electricity. It can be very hot here in summer but there is some shade and the site has a pleasant medium sized swimming pool with a small area separated for children, although this is only open in July/August.

Facilities: The sanitary block is basic with hot water and could be hard-pressed at busiest times. British style WCs. Shop and restaurant/bar (July/Aug). Swimming pool (July/Aug). Children's play area. Torches required. **Off site:** Town shop 200 m.

Charges 2002

Per adult	€ 3.79 - € 4.12
child	€ 3.09 - € 3.41
tent or caravan	€ 3.79 - € 4.12
car	€ 3.79 - € 4.12
motorcycle	€ 3.34 - € 3.89
motorcaravan	€ 5.95 - € 6.62
electricity	€ 3.05

Tel: 976 753 870. **Reservations:** can be made to Campings Betsa, C/Nov. 139, 17600 Figueras (Gerona). **Open** 1 April - 15 October.

Directions: Site is just outside town to southwest in the Val de Fierro district; access roads lead off N11 Madrid road (km. 316a) or N330 Valencia road and are well signed. The site lays back from the road across apiece of open ground so keep a good lookout.

Camping Lago Park

9105 Ctra. Alhama de Aragon-Nuevalos, 50210 Nuevalos (Zaragoza)

Lago Park is situated in an attractive area which receives many visitors for the Monasterio de Piedra just 3 km. distant and it enjoys pleasant views of the surrounding mountains. The site has a rather steep access and slopes so is considered unsuitable for disabled campers. It is just outside the attractive ancient village, between lake and mountains, and suitable as a base for exploring this really attractive area. Set on a steep hillside, the 300 pitches (250 for tourers) are on terraces. Only the lower rows of terraces are suitable for large caravans. These pitches, are numbered and marked by trees, most having electrical connections (10A). Facilities on site include a large pool (unheated and chilly with its mountain water), a restaurant/bar and small shop. The restaurant is disappointing with restricted hours, mediocre cooking and is pricey, but there are many good restaurants in town. The site is suitable for transit stops or if you wish to visit the monasterio as it is the only one hereabouts and appears to make the most of that fact. It is not recommended for extended stays.

Facilities: The single sanitary block has Turkish and British style WCs. washbasins with hot water and controllable hot showers (no dividers). Restaurant/bar (June-Sept). Shop (all season). Swimming pool (late June-Sept). Play area. Gas supplies. Torches needed in some areas. **Off site:** Fishing 300 m. Riding 2 km.

Charges 2002

Per person	€ 4.21
child (up to 10 yrs)	€ 4.06
caravan	€ 4.66
tent	€ 4.51
car	€ 4.21
motorcycle	€ 3.16
motorcaravan	€ 8.11
electricity	€ 3.61

Tel: 976 849 038. Fax: 976 849 100. **Reservations:** Contact site. **Open** 1 April - 30 September.

Directions: From Zaragoza (120 km.) take fast A2/N11/E90 road and turn onto C202 road beyond Calatayud to Nuévalos (25 km). From Madrid exit A2 at Alhama de Aragón (13 km). Follow signs for Monasterio de Piedra from all directions.

Camping Ciudad de Albarracin

9095 Junto al Polideportibo, 44100 Albarracin (Teruel)

Albarracin, in southern Aragon is set in the 'Reserva Nacional de los Montes Universales' and is a much frequented, fascinating town with a Moorish castle. The old city walls towering above date from its days when it attempted to become a separate country within Spain. This neat and clean family site is set on three levels on a hillside behind the town, with a walk of 1 km. to the centre. It is very modern and has high quality facilities including a superb building for barbecuing (all materials provided). There are 130 pitches, all with electricity and separated by trees. Some require cars to be parked separately. The homely bar/restaurant, with terrace and TV, is open all season and has a limited but very pleasant menu. The site is good value, is well run and is a good bet for exploring the area or just enjoying the peace and quiet in this area of natural beauty.

Facilities: The two spotless, modern sanitary buildings provide British style WCs, quite large showers and hot water throughout. Baby bath in the ladies' and a smart area for dishwashing and laundry with washing machines. Bar/restaurant (all season). Essentials from bar. Special room for barbecues with fire and wood provided. Children's play area. Fronton. 5-a-side soccer. Torches required in some areas. **Off site:** Town shops, bars and restaurants 500 m. Municipal swimming pool 100 m. (high season).

Charges 2002

Per person	€ 2.40
child (under 14)	€ 1.80
caravan	€ 2.55
tent	€ 2.40
car	€ 2.30
motorcaravan	€ 4.35
electricity	€ 1.80

Plus 7% VAT. **Tel:** 978/710197 or 710107. **Reservations:** Contact site for details. **Open** 1 April - 31 October.

Directions: From Teruel north on the N330 for about 8 km. then west onto A1512 for 37 km. Site is well signed in town.

Why camp in Menorca?

Menorca, steeped in history and blanketed by mystery, is an enchanting island waiting to be explored. Roughly 270 square miles in area, you can easily trek, bike or drive round the island in no time. The building of leisure facilities is now heavily taxed by the regional government and the proceeds used to buy land for National Parks and Nature Reserves, thereby protecting the island for future generations.

The C721 highway provides the back-bone to the island, connecting modest market towns to Mahon (the main town) in the east and Ciutadella in the west. Mahon's classic Georgian style buildings, complete with sash windows, will endear them to the British traveller. Its impressive harbour was captured by the British in 1708 during the Spanish War of Succession. In complete contrast, Ciutadella has a more Gothic feel to it. A labyrinth of tiny streets entwine the 'little city', most of which can only be accessed on foot. Monte Toro stands proudly at the centre of the island surveying all. To the south a greener lush terrain exists with long, luxurious beaches, while to the north a giant rockery erupts riddled with caves and prehistoric finds.

So why camp in Menorca? Because you can and it's a super relaxed way of discovering and enjoying this marvellous, unspoilt Spanish island.

Spain - Menorca
Camping Son Bou
8000 Ctra. de San Jaime km. 3.5, Apdo. de Correus 85, Alayor, 07730 Menorca

When the owner of Camping Son Bou originally asked us to visit with a view to the site being included in the Europe Guide, we did not think it was worth following up being on a small island in the middle of the Mediterranean. However, we are glad that we did and the site is more than happy to arrange the overnight ferry crossing from Barcelona or Valencia with a 25% discount in low season and 15% in the high season. Yes, it is expensive and you would need to stay for a decent length of time to make it worth while but this beautiful island cries out to be explored. It is peaceful and tranquil, with its characteristic dry stone walls, its low white buildings with terracotta tiled roof, its beautiful coastline, ancient monuments and pretty villages with their cycle of fiestas of religious origin with the noble horse as the central element. The site was only opened in July 1996 and has been purpose built in local style providing a large irregularly shaped pool with marvellous views across to Monte Toro and overlooked by a pine shaded, terraced bar and restaurant. The 216 large pitches are arranged in circles radiating out from the main facilities and clearly edged with stones. Natural pine tree shade covers most but the outer ring. Drinking water and refuse points are well placed. Electricity (6A) is available on nearly all pitches. The ground is hard and devoid of grass except where special sprinklers operate. The site gets very busy with Spanish from the mainland in high season. Earlier in the year it is quieter and greener. If you do not fancy the ferry crossings the site has some neat wooden chalets and ready erected tents.

Facilities: Well designed toilet block of good quality, open plan in places. Some washbasins in cabins. Separate room with baby baths. En-suite facilities for disabled visitors and ramped access to other facilities on site. Washing up and laundry sinks all have cold water as do the washbasins. No washing machines but serviced wash available. Shop (from 1/5). Bar. Restaurant (open when site open). Outdoor pool (from 1/5). Tennis. Petanque. Football. Basketball. Volleyball. Children's play area. Bicycle hire. English spoken. Open air cinema most evenings. Occasional barbecue with guitarist. Comprehensive activity programme covering birdwatching, walking, mountain biking, canoeing, diving, windsurfing, water skiing and various excursions. **Off site:** Riding 3 km. The village of Son Bou itself is 0.75 km. away and very much a small tourist centre. The sandy beach is the longest in the island, well organised with lifeguards, snack bars, sun beds and umbrellas to hire with a naturist section at the far end.

Charges 2002

Per adult	€ 4.81 - € 5.82
child (3-13 yrs)	€ 3.46 - € 4.20
tent for 2 persons	€ 5.33 - € 6.44
tent for 1 person	€ 2.67 - € 3.22
car	€ 3.22 - € 3.86
motorcaravan	€ 8.55 - € 10.30
electricity	€ 3.22

All plus 7% VAT. **Tel:** 971 372 605. Fax: 971 372 605. E-mail: info@campingsonbou.com. **Reservations:** Contact site. The site can also arrange the ferries from Spain. **Open** 22 March - 31 October.

Directions: From Mahon (Mao) follow the main road to Ciutadella. Go past the town of Alaior (bypassed), for a further km. approx. Watch for restaurant on left and road sign for San Jaime/Son Bou. Turn left on this road (the surface is not as good as the main road). Continue for 3.5 km.and site on right.

Sweden

Swedish Travel and Tourism Council, 11 Montagu Place, London W1H 2AL
Tel: 020 7870 5600   Fax: 020 7724 5872 Brochures: 01476 578811
E-mail: info@swetourism.org.uk   Internet: www.visit-sweden.com

Sweden covers an area almost twice that of the UK but has a population only one seventh of ours, with over half the land surface covered by forests and lakes. Stretching from north of the Arctic circle for 1,000 miles to a southern limit about level with Glasgow, inevitably the roads are quiet and almost traffic free with a range of scenery varying from the vast, wild open spaces of Lapland to the rich forests of the south and a choice of climate to match. The very beautiful southwest region, the 'Swedish Lake and Glass country', makes a perfect introduction to this fascinating land. It is easily reached, either by a wide choice of ferries or overland from Norway. The area is dominated by the two great lakes, Vänern (2,000 sq. miles) and Vättern (750 sq. miles), Europe's second and third largest lakes. Stockholm, the capital, is a delightful place built on a series of fourteen small islands, housing monumental architecture and fine museums giving it an ageing, lived-in atmosphere and providing the country's most active culture and night life. Today Sweden enjoys one of the highest standards of living in the world and a quality of life to go with it.

Population

8,700,000, density 19.3 per sq. km.

Capital

Stockholm

Climate

Sweden enjoys a temperate climate thanks to the Gulf Stream. The weather is similar to Britain's, apart from the fact that there is generally less rain and more sunshine in the summer.

Language

English is fairly widely spoken but a phrase book is advised.

Currency

Swedish currency is the Krona (plural Kronor) made up of 100 öre. It comes in coins of 50 öre, 1 kr, 5 kr and 10 kr, and notes of 20, 50, 100, 500, 1,000 and 10,000 kr.

Banks

Open Mon-Fri 09.30-15.00. Some city banks stay open til 17.30/18.00. All are closed on Sats.

Time

GMT plus 1 (summer BST +1).

Post Offices

Open 09.00-18.00 on weekdays and 09.00/10.00 - 13.00 on Saturdays. You can also buy stamps at stationers and tobacconists.

Telephone

To dial Sweden from the UK, dial 00 46 followed by the area code (omitting the initial zero) followed by number. For Britain dial 009 44.

Public Holidays

New Year; Epiphany; Good Fri; Easter Mon; Labour Day; Ascension; Whit Sun/Mon; Mid- summer, Sat between 20-26 June; All Saints, Sat between 31 Oct-6 Nov; Christmas, 24-26 Dec.

Shops

Open Mon-Fri 09.00-18.00. Sat 09.00-13.00/ 16.00. In some large towns department stores remain open until 20.00/22.00.

Food: The Swedes generally eat fairly early. Lunch can start at 11.00, the evening meal at 18.00. A typical Swedish 'Smorgasbord' can be enjoyed all over the country.

Motoring

Roads are much quieter than in the UK. Secondary roads may be gravel surfaced but are still good. Dipped headlights are obligatory.

Speed Limits: Caravans and motorhomes (3.5 tons) 31 mph (50 kph) in built up areas; 50 mph (80 kph) on other roads for caravans. Motorhomes 44 - 56 mph (70 - 90 kph) on other roads and 56 - 69 mph (90 - 110 kph) on motorways.

Fuel: Away from large towns, petrol stations rarely open 24 hrs. Buy diesel during working hours, it is rarely available at self service pumps. Credit cards generally accepted except in some 24 hr stations where payment must be made in 20/100 kr notes.

Parking: Meters are in use in several larger towns.

Overnighting

Allowed in most areas, with the permission of the landowner.

Note: Mosquitos can be a problem in summer (from June) - go prepared.

Lisebergs Camping Karralund

Olbersgatan 1, S-416 55 Goteborg (Hallands Län)

Well positioned for visiting the city, this busy, well maintained site has 200 marked pitches, 150 with electricity (10A) and cable TV, 42 hardstandings, and several areas for tents. Pitches do vary in size, some are fairly compact and there are no dividing hedges, consequently units can be rather close together. Additionally there are cabins for rent, a budget hotel and a youth hostel. All this makes for a very busy site in the main season, which in this case means June, July and August. An advance telephone call to check for space is advisable. A breakfast buffet is served in low season and there is a restaurant 300 m. from the site entrance. Reception has a range of tourist information, can provide advice on travel in the city, the Liseberg Amusement Park, and sells the Göteborg Card. The nearby Delsjö Camping (also a Lisebergs campsite) is only open in July.

Facilities: Two heated sanitary buildings, the larger one fairly new, and a smaller, older one with limited facilities, are well maintained and cleaned. They provide all the usual facilities, with controllable hot showers, a good suite for small children, dishwashing sinks and a laundry, kitchens with cooking facilities, and a complete unit for disabled visitors. Motorcaravan services. Shop. Restaurant and takeaway. Playground. TV room.

Charges 2002

Per unit	Skr. 150 - 225
electricity	Skr. 40

Only pitches with electricity available in high season. **Tel:** 031 840 200. Fax: 031 840 500. E-mail: boende.lgab@liseberg.se. **Reservations:** Advised from mid-June to end of August. **Open** all year (full services 10/5-25/8).

Directions: Site is about 2.5 km. east of city centre. Follow signs to Kärralund and campsite symbol from E20, E6 or Rv 40.

Lisebergs Camping Askim Strand

Marholmsvagen, S-436 45 Askim (Hallands Län)

Within easy reach of city, this is a very pleasantly located site, close to a long gently sloping beach which is very popular for bathing. As a result the area behind the campsite is populated by many holiday homes and cabins. A very open site with very little shade, it has 276 mostly level, grassy pitches all with 10A electricity, plus two areas for tents. Many pitches are fairly compact, although there are some larger ones. The keycard entry system operates the entrance barrier and access to the buildings and there is a night security guard (June-Aug). Reception has a range of tourist information, and can provide details of reductions on bus and taxi fares to the city, also selling the Göteborg Card.

Facilities: Two heated sanitary buildings, the larger one fairly new, the smaller recently refitted. Both are maintained to a high standard and provide all the usual facilities, including a good suite for small children, dishwashing sinks, laundry, kitchens with cooking facilities, and a unit for disabled visitors. Hot water is free. Motorcaravan services. Small shop (24/6-8/8, 08.00-21.00). Snack bar (July). Children's playground. TV room.

Charges 2002

Per unit	Skr. 150 - 190
electricity	Skr. 40

Only pitches with electricity available for high season. **Tel:** 031 286 261. Fax: 031 681 335. E-mail: boende.lgab@liseberg.se. **Reservations:** Advised for June-Aug. **Open** 10 May - 25 August (full services 20/6-11/8).

Directions: About 10 km. south of Göteborg, take exit signed Mölndal S and ports (Hamnar). Take the Rv 159 towards Frolunda, and watch for a sliproad to the right, signed to Askim and follow signs to campsite.

We are always interested to hear about your experiences.

Why not write to us at: Alan Rogers' Good Camps Guides, Manor Garden, Burton Bradstock, Bridport, Dorset DT6 4QA

or e-mail us at editorial@alanrogers.com

Perhaps you have a site that you would like to recommend? Or your favourite site has made some changes? Please let us know.

Krono Camping Båstad-Torekov

S-260 93 Torekov (Skåne Län)

2640

Part of the Kronocamping chain, this campsite is 500 m. from the fishing village of Torekov, 14 km. west of the home of the Swedish tennis WCT Open at Båstad on the stretch of coastline between Malmö and Göteborg. Useful en route from the most southerly ports, it is a very good site and worthy of a longer stay for relaxation. It has 525 large pitches (325 for touring units), all numbered and marked, mainly in attractive natural woodland (mostly pine and birch), with some on more open ground close to the shore. Of these, 350 have electricity and cable TV, 77 also having water and drainage. The modern reception complex is professionally run and is also home for a good shop, two small boutiques, a snack bar, restaurant, pizzeria and a fishermen's style bar (Zorba's), open until 1 am. The spacious site covers quite a large area and there is a cycle track along the shore to the beach with bathing. Games for children are organised in high season and there is an outdoor stage for musical entertainment and dancing (also in high season). This well run site is a pleasant place to stay.

Facilities: Three very good sanitary blocks include a modern one of high quality and two refurbished older blocks. Hot water is free and there are facilities in each block for babies and disabled visitors. Laundry. Cooking facilities and dishwashing. Motorcaravan service point. Restaurant, pizzeria and snack bar with takeaway (7/6-15/8). Bar. Shop and kiosk. Minigolf. Sports fields. Children's play areas. Bicycle hire. TV room. Beach. Fishing. **Off site:** Tennis close. Golf 1 km. Riding 3 km. Games, music and entertainment in high season.

Charges 2002

Per unit	Skr. 135 - 210
electricity/TV connection	Skr. 35 - 60

Tel: 0431 364 525. Fax: 0431 364 625. E-mail: torekov@kronocamping.se. **Reservations:** Advised in high season, contact site for details. **Open** 16 April - 17 September.

Directions: From E6 Malmö - Göteborg road take Torekov/Båstad exit and follow signs for 20 km. towards Torekov. Site is signed 1 km. before village on right.

Skånes Djurparks Camping

Jularp, S-243 93 Höör (Skåne Län)

2650

This site is probably one of the most unusual we feature. It is adjacent to the Skånes Djurpark - a zoo park with Scandinavian species - and has on site a reconstructed Stone Age Village. The site is located in a sheltered valley and has some 90 large, level grassy pitches for caravans and motorhomes all with 10A electricity, a few with waste water drain, and a separate area for tents. The most unusual feature of the site is the sanitary block - it is underground! The fully air-conditioned building houses a superb and ample complement of facilities The site also has a number of underground, cave-man style, 8 bed (dormitory type) holiday units which can be rented by families or private groups (when not in use by schools on educational trips to the Stone Age Village). They open onto a circular court-yard with a barbecue and camp fire area and have access to the kitchens and dining room in the sanitary block. There are good walks through the nature park and around the lakes, where one can see deer, birds and other wildlife. Well placed for the new Copenhagen - Malmo bridge or the ferries, this is also a site for discerning campers who want something distinctly different.

Facilities: The underground block includes roomy showers, two fully equipped kitchens, laundry and separate drying room and an enormous dining/TV room. Facilities for disabled people and baby changing. Cooking facilities. Laundry. Mini-shop (April - Oct). Café (June - Aug). Small heated swimming pool (June - Aug). Children's playground. Stone Age Village. **Off site:** Fishing 1.8 km. Riding and golf 8 km. Bicycle hire 3 km. Restaurant just outside the camp entrance.

Charges 2002

Per unit	Skr. 130
electricity	Skr. 25 - 40

Tel: 0413 553270. Fax: 0413 200 61. E-mail: info@ grottbyn.com. **Reservations:** Advised for high season (July/Aug). **Open** all year (full services 15/6-15/8).

Directions: Turn off no. 23 road 2 km. north of Höör (at roundabout) and follow signs for Skånes Djurpark. Campsite entrance is off the Djurpark car park.

Tingsryds Municipal Camping

Mårdslyckesand, S-362 91 Tingsryd (Kronobergs Län)

2655

A pleasant, well managed municipal site by Lake Tiken, Tingsryds Camping is well placed for Sweden's Glass District. The 129 large pitches are arranged in rows divided by trees and shrubs, with some along the edge of a lakeside path (public have access). All have electricity (10A) and there is shade in parts. The facilities are housed in buildings near the site entrance, with the reception building having the restaurant, cafe, bar and a small shop. Adjacent to the site is a small beach, grassy lying out area, playground and lake swimming area and three tennis courts. Hire of canoes, fishing and minigolf are available on site (public access also). Two large supermarkets, a heated indoor 'Waterworld', bowling alley, and further shops and restaurants are in the town (1 km), which can be reached via a level footpath/cycle track directly from the site. The town hosts a Folk Festival and market in July each year. This site is an ideal place from which to explore the factories and shops of the 'Kingdom of Crystal'.

Facilities: Heated sanitary installations are in two well maintained buildings, one including showers, mostly with curtains (on payment, communal undressing), the other a campers' kitchen with hobs and dining area, plus dishwashing sinks with further sinks outside under cover (hot water from separate tap). Facilities for disabled people and family room. Laundry with free ironing. Motorcaravan services. Shop (1/5-15/9). Restaurant, cafe, bar (1/5-15/9). Tennis. Minigolf. Children's playground. Boules. Lake swimming. Beach volleyball. Canoe hire. Fishing. **Off site:** Bicycle hire 1 km. Golf 15 km.

Charges 2002

Per unit	Skr. 110 - 135
electricity	Skr. 25

Tel: 0477 10554. Fax: 0477 31825. E-mail: tingsryd. camping@swipnet.se. **Reservations:** Advised for high season. Write to site. **Open** 5 April - 20 October (full service 24/5-19/8).

Directions: Site is 1 km. from Tingsryd off road no. 120, well signed around the town.

Krono Camping Saxnäs

S-386 95 Färjestaden (Kalmar Län)

2680

Well placed for touring Sweden's Riviera and the fascinating and beautiful island of Öland, this family-run site, part of the Krono group, has 420 marked and numbered touring pitches. Arranged in rows on open, well kept grassland dotted with a few trees, all have electricity (10A), 320 have TV connections and 116 also have water. An unmarked area without electricity can accommodate around 60 tents. The site has about 130 long stay units and cabins for rent. Reception is efficient and friendly with good English spoken. In high season children's games are organised and dances are held twice weekly, with other activities on other evenings. The sandy beach slopes very gently and is safe for children. Nearby attractions include the 7 km. long Öland road bridge, Kalmar and its castle, museums and old town on the mainland, Eketorp prehistoric fortified village, Öland Djurpark and many old windmills.

Facilities: Three heated sanitary blocks provide a good supply of roomy private showers, washbasins, some washbasin/WC suites and WCs. Facilities for babies and disabled visitors. Well equipped laundry room. Good kitchen with cookers, microwaves and dishwasher (free), and dishwashing sinks. Hot water is free throughout. Gas supplies. Motorcaravan services. Shop (1/5-30/8). Pizzeria, licensed restaurant and café (all 1/5-30/8). Bar (1/7-31/7). Children's playgrounds and crêche. Bouncing castle. Boules. Beach with volleyball. Fishing. Bicycle hire. Minigolf. Family entertainment and activities. Football. **Off site:** Riding 2 km. Golf 10 km.

Charges 2002

Per pitch	Skr. 100 - 200
electricity/TV connection	Skr. 40

Weekend and weekly rates available. **Tel:** 0485 35700. Fax: 0485 35664. E-mail: saxnas@ kronocamping-oland.se. **Reservations:** Essential for high season (mid June - mid Aug). **Open** 7 April - 16 September.

Directions: Cross Öland road bridge from Kalmar on road no. 137. Take exit for Öland Djurpark/ Saxnäs, then follow campsite signs. Site is just north of the end of the bridge.

Lysingsbadet Camping

Lysingsvägen, S-593 53 Västervik (Kalmar Län)

One of the largest sites in Scandinavia, Lysingsbadet has unrivalled views of the 'Pearl of the East Coast' - Västervik and its fjords and islands. There are around 1,000 large, mostly marked and numbered pitches, spread over a vast area of rocky promontory and set on different plateau, terraces, in valleys and woodland, or beside the water. It is a very attractive site, and one which never really looks or feels crowded even when busy. There are 83 full service pitches with TV, water and electrical connections, 163 with TV and electricity and 540 with electricity only, the remainder for tents. Reception is smart, efficient and friendly with good English spoken. An hourly bus service to Västervik runs from the site entrance from May-September. On site facilities include a full golf course, minigolf, heated outdoor pool complex with water slide and poolside café, sauna and solarium, children's playgrounds, boat hire, tennis, basketball, volleyball and fishing. A licensed restaurant is supplemented by a café/takeaway and a range of on site shops. For children, Astrid Lindgren's World theme park at Vimmerby is an easy day trip away and for adults the delights of the old town of Västervik and its shopping.

Facilities: Ten modern sanitary blocks of various ages and designs house a comprehensive mix of showers, basins and WCs. All have good quality fittings and are kept very clean. Several campers' kitchens with dishwashing sinks, cookers and hoods, also 4 laundry rooms. Free hot water throughout and all facilities free of charge. Campers are issued with key cards which operate the entrance barriers and gain access to sanitary blocks, pool complex and other facilities. Motorcaravan services. Supermarket and shops (15/5-31/8). Restaurant and café/takeaway (1/6-15/8). Swimming pool complex (15/6-31/8). Golf. Minigolf. Tennis. Basketball. Volleyball. Bicycle and boat hire. Fishing. Entertainment and dances in high season. Children's playgrounds. Quick Stop service. Hairdresser. Bus service.

Charges 2002

Per unit	Skr. 120 - 190
electricity	Skr. 35

Tel: 0490 88920. Fax: 0490 88945. **Reservations:** Advisable for peak season (July/Aug). Write to site for details. **Open** all year.

Directions: Turn off E22 for Västervik and keep straight on at all junctions until first campsite sign. Follow signs to site.

Glyttinge Camping

Berggärdsvägen, S-582 49 Linköping (Östergötlands Län)

Only five minutes by car from the Ikea Shopping Mall and adjacent to a good swimming pool complex, Glyttinge is a most attractive site with a mix of terrain - some flat, some sloping and some woodland. A top quality site with enthusiastic and friendly management, it is maintained to a very high standard and flowers, trees and shrubs everywhere give it a cosy garden like atmosphere. There are 239 good size, mostly level pitches of which 125 have electricity (10A) and 28 are fully serviced. Children are well catered for - the manager has laid out a wonderful, fenced and very safe children's play area and, in addition, parents can rent (minimal charge) tricycles, pedal cars, scooters and carts. There is also a wet weather playroom. Adjacent to the site, the heated outdoor pool complex has three pools (charged). Attractions nearby include the old town of Gamla Linköping, Aviation Museum, Land Museum and the Ikea Shopping Mall. Also ask at reception about canal tours.

Facilities: The main, central toilet block (supplemented by additional smaller facilities at reception) is modern, well constructed and exceptionally well equipped and maintained. It has showers in cubicles, washbasin and WC suites, hand dryers, and soothing music! Separate facilities for disabled visitors. Baby rooms. Laundry. Solarium. Superb kitchen and dining/TV room, fully equipped. Motorcaravan services. Shop and takeaway (15/6-15/8). Minigolf. Football. Bicycle hire. Playground. Swimming pool complex adjacent (15/5-25/8). Fishing 5 km. Riding and golf 3 km.

Charges 2002

Per unit	Skr. 130 - 150
electricity	Skr. 30

Low season discounts for pensioners. **Tel:** 013 174 928. Fax: 013 175 923. E-mail: glyttinge@swipnet.se. **Reservations:** Advised for July/Aug. Write to site for details. **Open** 27 April - 1 October.

Directions: Exit E4 Helsingborg - Stockholm road north of Linköping at signs for Ikea and site. Turn right at traffic lights and camp sign and follow signs to site.

Grannastrandens Familjecamp

Box 14, S-563 21 Granna (Jönköpings Län)

2670

This large, lakeside site with modern facilities and busy continental feel, is set below the old city of Gränna. Flat fields separate Gränna from the shore, one of which is occupied by the 25 acres of Grännastrandens where there are 500 numbered pitches, including a tent area and some seasonal pitches. The site is flat, spacious and very regularly laid out on open ground with only a row of poplars by the lake to provide shelter, so a windbreak may prove useful against any onshore breeze. About 260 pitches have electricity (6/10A). Part of the lake is walled off to form an attractive swimming area with sandy beaches, slides and islands. Obviously the great attraction here is the lake. It offers beaches, bathing, fishing, sailing and superb coastal walks. Outstanding, however, is the 30 minute ferry crossing from the tiny harbour next to the site to Visingsö, the beautiful island reputedly inhabited for over 6,000 years. It is this excursion, complete with its gentle tour by horse drawn `remmalag' which alone warrants Grännastrandens as your base. Gränna is also the centre of hot air ballooning and on 11 July each year there are ascents from Sweden's only `balloon airport'.

Facilities: The large, sanitary block in the centre of the site has modern, well kept facilities including British style WCs, some with external access, wash-basins, and free hot showers, some in private cubicles. Dishwashing and laundry sinks. Laundry facilities. Provision for disabled people. A further small, older block is by reception. Cooking facilities. Motorcaravan services. Shop. TV room. Children's playground. Lake swimming area. Boating and fishing. **Off site:** Café outside site (1/5-31/8) or town restaurants close.

Charges 2002

Per unit	Skr. 150
electricity and satellite TV connection	Skr. 30

Tel: 0390 10706. Fax: 0390 41260. **Reservations:** Write to site for details. **Open** 1 May - 30 September.

Directions: Take Gränna exit from E4 road (no camping sign) 40 km. north of Jönköping. Site is signed in the centre of the town, towards the harbour and ferry.

Swecamp Rosenlund Camping

Villa Bjorkhagen, S-554 54 Jonkoping (Jönköpings Län)

2665

Overlooking Lake Vättern, Rosenlunds is a good site, useful as a break in the journey across Sweden or visiting the city during a tour of the Lakes. It is on raised ground overlooking the lake, with some shelter in parts. There are 300 pitches on well kept grass which, on one side, slopes away from reception. Some pitches on the other side of reception are flat and there are 200 electrical (10A), 100 cable TV and 40 water connections available. Jönköping is one of Sweden's oldest trading centres with a Charter dating back to 1284 and several outstanding attractions. These must include the museums of the 'safety match', ceramics and weaponry and, particularly, the superb troll artistry of John Bauer.

Facilities: Heated sanitary facilities include hot showers on payment (some in private cubicles) and a sauna, plus provision for disabled visitors and babies. Laundry. Dishwashing facilities. Motorcaravan services. Gas supplies. Well stocked mini-market. Restaurant (May - Sept). Playground. TV room. Bicycle hire. Minigolf. **Off site:** Swimming pool complex 500 m. Fishing 500 m. Riding 7 km.

Charges 2002

Per unit incl. all persons	Skr. 160
electricity/TV connection	Skr. 30

Prices may be increased if there is a local exhibition. **Tel:** 036 122863. Fax: 036 126687. E-mail: villabjorkhagen@swipnet.se. **Reservations:** Advised for July - write to site for details. **Open** all year (full services 1 May - 30 September).

Directions: Site is well signed from the E4 road on eastern side of Jönköping. Watch carefully for exit on this fast road.

Tidaholm-Hökensås Camping

2720 | Daretorp, S-522 91 Tidaholm (Västra Götalands Län)

Hökensås is located just west of Lake Vättern and south of Tidaholm, in a beautiful national park of wild, unspoiled scenery. The park is based on a 100 km. ridge, a glacier area with many impressive boulders and ice age debris but now thickly forested with majestic pines and silver birches, with a small, brilliant lake at every corner. This pleasant campsite is part of a holiday complex that includes wooden cabins for rent. It is relaxed and informal, with over 200 pitches either under trees or on a more open area at the far end, divided into rows by wooden rails. These are numbered and electricity (10A) is available on 130. Tents can go on the large grassy open areas by reception. The forests and lakes provide wonderful opportunities for walking, cycling (gravel tracks and marked walks) angling, swimming and when the snow falls, winter sports.

Facilities: The original sanitary block near reception is supplemented by one in the wooded area. Hot showers with communal changing area and some curtained cubicles are free. Separate saunas for each sex and facilities for the disabled and babies. Campers' kitchen at each block with cooking, dishwashing and laundry facilities (irons on loan from reception). Small, but well stocked shop with a comprehensive angling section. Café with takeaway. Children's playground. Tennis. Minigolf. Sauna. Lake swimming. Fishing.

Charges 2002

Per unit (more for Midsummer celebrations)	Skr. 110
electricity	Skr. 35 - 45

Tel: 0502 230 53. Fax: 0502 230 23. E-mail: info@hokensas-semesterby.com. **Reservations:** Write to site for details. **Open** all year (full services 20/6-11/8).

Directions: Approach site from no. 195 western lake coast road. at Brandstorp, about 40 km. north of Jönköping, turn west at petrol station and camp sign signed Hökensås. Site is about 9 km. up this road.

Borås Camping

2700 | PO Box 44022, S-500 04 Borås (Västra Götalands Län)

Borås Camping is in a park setting 2 km. north of the city centre. This pleasant municipal site is within easy walking distance of a swimming pool complex, Djurpark and shopping centre, and is convenient for ferries to and from Göthenberg. A tidy, well managed site, it provides 500 large, numbered, level pitches, carefully arranged in rows on well kept grass with good tarmac perimeter roads. Electricity (10A) provided to 300 pitches and there is some shade in parts. Many activities are available both on the site and nearby, many free to campers; the excellent outdoor heated pool complex, Alidebergsbadet, is only 400 m. Canoes and pedaloes are available on the small canal running through the site. The shopping precinct at Knalleland is only 500 m, the Zoo (Djurpark) is 400 m. The site can issue the 'Boråscard' which gives free and discounted access to city car parks, transport, museums and attractions during your stay.

Facilities: Six good, modern sanitary blocks are clean and heated. Facilities for babies and disabled people, in various combinations (the largest block new in '99). Good campers' kitchens have hobs, extractor hoods, and dishwashing sinks (free of charge). Laundry facilities. Motorcaravan service point. Shop. Cafeteria and takeaway (full services 6/6-9/8). Several children's playgrounds. Minigolf. Bicycle hire. **Off site:** Swimming, tennis, frisbee, badminton, football, croquet, table tennis, jogging tracks, basketball all nearby

Charges 2002

Per unit	Skr. 120 - 155
electricity	Skr. 30

Tel: 033 353 280. Fax: 033 140 582. E-mail: info@borascamping.com. **Reservations:** One should always find room here. **Open** all year.

Directions: Exit road no. 40 from Göthenberg for Borås Centrum and follow signs to Djurpark and road no. 42 to Trollhätten through the town. Turn left to site.

Krono Camping Lidköping

2710 Läckögatan, S-531 54 Lidköping (Västra Götalands Län)

This high quality, attractive site provides about 430 pitches on flat, well kept grass. It is surrounded by some mature trees, with the lake shore as one boundary and a number of tall pines have been left to provide shade and shelter. There are 274 pitches with electricity (10A) and TV connections and 91 with water and drainage also, together with 60 cabins for rent. A tour operator takes a few pitches and the site takes a fair number of seasonal units. Very good playgrounds are provided for children, together with a play field, TV room and an amusement and games room. The lake is available for watersports, boating and fishing with bathing from the sandy beach or there is a pool complex adjacent to the site.

Facilities: Excellent, modern sanitary facilities are in two identical blocks with under-floor heating, attractive decor and lighting (and music). Hot water is free. Make up and hairdressing areas baby room and facilities for disabled people. Dishwashing sinks outside each block. Good kitchens with cookers and microwaves. Motorcaravan services. Small shop. Coffee bar with snacks. Minigolf. Volleyball. Solarium. Children's playgrounds. TV room. Games and amusements room. Bicycle hire. Play field. Lake swimming, fishing and watersports. **Off site:** Swimming pool adjacent.

Charges 2002

Per unit	Skr. 140 - 170
electricity/TV connection	Skr. 40

Tel: 0510 26804. Fax: 0510 21135. E-mail: info@kronocamping.com. **Reservations:** Write to site for details. **Open** all year (full services 8/6-15/8).

Directions: From Lidköping town junctions follow signs towards Läckö then pick up camping signs turning right at second roundabout. Continue to site on left (0.5-1 km).

Laxsjons Camping och Friluftsgard

2740 S-660 10 Dals Långed (Västra Götalands Län)

In the beautiful Dalsland region, Laxsjöns is an all year round site, catering for winter sports enthusiasts as well as summer tourists and groups. On the shores of the lake, the site is in two main areas - one flat, near the entrance, with hardstandings and the other on attractive, sloping, grassy areas adjoining. In total there are 300 places for caravans or motorcaravans, all with electricity (10A), plus more for tents. The site has a good pool with minigolf, tennis, trampolines and a playground. A restaurant is at the top of the site with a good range of dishes in high season. In addition, there is a lake for swimming, fishing and canoeing. The site is located west of Lake Vänern, in an area of deep forests, endless lakes and river valleys.

Facilities: The main toilet block has hot showers on payment (communal changing), open washbasins, WCs and a hairdressing cubicle. With a further small block at the top of the site, the provision should be adequate. Facilities for disabled visitors. Laundry with drying rooms for bad weather. Cooking rooms for tenters. Restaurant (high season). Shop. Tennis. Minigolf. Sauna. Children's playground. Swimming pool. Lake for swimming, fishing and boating.

Charges 2002

Per unit	Skr. 115 - 135
electricity	Skr. 30

Tel: 0531 30010. Fax: 0531 30555. E-mail: info@laxsjonsfriluftsgard.com. **Reservations:** Advisable in peak season. Write to site for details. **Open** 1 April - 30 September (full services 22/6-15/8).

Directions: From Åmål take road no. 164 to Bengtfors, then the 172 towards Dals Långed. Site is signed about 5 km. south of the town 1 km. down a good road.

Ekuddens Camping

2730 Strandbadet, S-542 00 Mariestad (Västra Götalands Län)

Ekuddens occupies a long stretch of the eastern shore of Lake Vänern to the north-west of the town, in a mixed woodland setting, and next door to the municipal complex of heated outdoor pools and sauna. The lake, of course, is also available for swimming or boating and there are bicycles, tandems and canoes for hire. The spacious site can take 350 units and there are 230 electrical hook-ups (10A). Most pitches are under the trees but some at the far end of the site are on more open ground with good views over the lake. The site becomes very busy in high season.

Facilities: Sanitary facilities are in three low wooden cabins, all clean and well maintained. Free hot showers, some in private cubicles. Facilities for disabled visitors. Kitchens with cooking facilities. Shop. Licensed bar. Takeaway (high season). Canoes, bicycles and tandems for hire. Playground. Minigolf. TV room. Entertainment in high season.

Charges 2002

Per unit	Skr. 110 - 130
electricity	Skr. 30

Tel: 0501 10637. Fax: 0501 18601. E-mail: a.appelgren@mariestad.mail.telia.com. **Reservations:** Essential in high season. **Open** 1 May - 30 September (full services 15/6-15/8).

Directions: Site is 2.5 km. northwest of the town, well signed on the ring road. From E20 motorway Mariestad S. exit. Follow signs towards Marieholm.

Årjäng SweCamp Resort Sommarvik

Sommarvik, S-672 91 Årjäng (Värmlands Län)

A good quality site in beautiful surroundings beside lake Västra Silen, Sommarvik has some 250 large, separated and numbered pitches arranged in terraces on a pine wooded hillside, some overlooking the lake. There are 100 with electrical connections, 30 are all service pitches and there is an area for groups at one end. It offers much in the way of outdoor pursuits and peaceful countryside. A very large and smart restaurant offers a full range of meals, soft drinks, beers and wines, and takeaway meals. On site activities include swimming in the lake from a sandy beach (safe for children), canoe hire, windsurfing, rowing boats, fishing, sauna, tennis courts, football field, organised Elk safaris, minigolf, quizzes or guided walks. The site also organises local folk music during the main season. You can ride trolleys around the area on disused railway tracks or take a day trip to go gold panning. The site is within easy reach of the Norwegian border and Oslo. Skiing is also possible (when there is snow). This is a very scenic region and one which makes an ideal base for a family holiday with lots of activities and sightseeing trips available.

Facilities: Five sanitary units house a good mix of private shower cubicles (hot water on payment), washbasins (free hot water), WCs, family bathrooms, and facilities for disabled people and baby changing. All are kept clean. Good campers' kitchens with cookers and sinks. Laundry facilities. Motorcaravan services. Restaurant and takeaway (1/6-1/9). Shop (1/5-1/10). Minigolf. Lake swimming. Canoe, row boat and windsurfer hire. Bicycle hire. Fishing. Tennis. Sauna. Football field. Good children's playgrounds. Organised activities. 'Quick stop' pitches for overnight stays. A youth hostel and conference centre are also on site. **Off site:** Indoor pool complex 3 km. Riding 5 km. Golf 9 km.

Charges 2002

Per pitch with electricity and water	Skr. 110 - 120

Tel: 0573 12060. Fax: 0573 12048. E-mail: swecamp@sommarvik.se. **Reservations:** Advised for peak seasons (summer and winter). **Open** all year (full services 26/5-22/8).

Directions: Site is signed from roads nos. 172 and E18. It is 3 km. south of Årjäng Centrum.

Frykenbaden Camping

Frykenbaden PL 1405, S-655 00 Kil (Värmlands Län)

Frykenbaden Camping is in a quiet wooded area on the shores of Lake Fryken and takes 250 units on grassy meadows surrounded by trees. One area nearer the lake is gently sloping, the other is flat with numbered pitches arranged in rows, all with electricity (6/120A), and many with satellite TV and phone connections. Reception, a good shop and takeaway are located in a traditional Swedish house surrounded by lawns sloping down to the shore, with minigolf, a play barn and playground, with pet area, also close by. Tables and benches are near the lake, where swimming and canoeing are possible. A good value restaurant is at the adjacent golf club which can be reached by a pleasant walk. Fryken is a long, narrow lake, said to be one of the deepest in Sweden, and it is a centre for angling. Frykenbadens Camping is on the southern shore, and is a quiet, relaxing place to stay away from the busier, more famous lakes. There are plenty of other activities in the area (golf, riding, ski-ing in winter) and Kil is not too far from the Norwegian border.

Facilities: The main sanitary block is of good quality and heated in cool weather with showers on payment, open washbasins, a laundry room and room for families or disabled people. With a further small block with equally good facilities, the overall supply is better than average for Swedish sites. Well equipped camper's kitchen with ovens, hobs and sinks. Small shop. Snack bar and takeaway. Minigolf. Children's play barn and playground. Lake swimming. Canoes and bicycles for hire. **Off site:** Golf 500 m. Go-karts, riding, jogging track 3 km.

Charges 2002

Per unit	Skr. 100 - 120
electricity	Skr. 35
TV connection	Skr. 15

Tel: 0554 40940. Fax: 0554 40945. E-mail: frykenbaden@telia.com. **Reservations:** Write to site. **Open** all year (full services 17/6-13/8).

Directions: Site is signed from the no. 61 Karlstad - Arvika road, then 4 km. towards lake following signs.

Skantzö Bad u. Camping

Box 506, S-737 27 Hallstahammar (Västmanlands Län)

2820

A very comfortable and pleasant municipal site just off the main E18 motorway from Oslo to Stockholm, this has 180 large marked and numbered pitches, 165 of these with electricity (10A). The terrain is flat and grassy, there is good shade in parts and the site is well fenced and locked at night. There are 22 new alpine style cabins for rent with window boxes of colourful flowers. Reception is very friendly. Amenities include a very large, fenced, outdoor, heated swimming pool and waterslide (free), children's playground, tennis and minigolf (charged) and a games area complex. Direct access to the towpath of the Stromsholms Kanal and nearby is the Kanal Museum. The site provides hire and transportation of canoes for longer canal tours. There are good walks and cycle trails all around the area, and excellent tourist information is available.

Facilities: One sanitary block, located in the reception area, is maintained and equipped to a high standard, including free hot showers (in cubicles with washbasin), facilities for disabled people and baby changing. A new unit to the same high standards has been added at the far end of the site and both are heated. Good campers' kitchen with drying room and lines, washing machine and dryer. Motorcaravan services. Barbecue grill area. Cafeteria and shop (18/5-19/8). Swimming pool and waterslide (23/5-19/8). Minigolf. Tennis. Children's playground. Bicycle hire. Fishing. Canoe hire. **Off site:** Golf 9 km.

Charges 2002

Per unit	Skr. 115
electricity	Skr. 35

Tel: 0220 24305. Fax: 0220 24187. E-mail: turism@ hallstahammar.se. **Reservations:** Write to site for details. **Open** 1 May - 30 September.

Directions: Turn off E18 at Hallstahammar and follow road no. 252 to west of town centre and signs to campsite.

Stockholm Swecamp Flottsbro

PO Box 1216, S-141 25 Huddinge (Stockholms Län)

2840

Flottsbro is a neat, small site with good quality facilities and very good security, located some 18 km. south of Stockholm. There are 100 large numbered pitches for caravans and motorhomes and a separate unmarked area for tents. Pitches are arranged on level terraces, 65 with electricity (10A), but the site itself is sloping and the reception and restaurant are at the bottom with all the ski facilities and further good sanitary facilities with a sauna. The reception area is remote from the entrance but a very good security system is in place, campers have keys to the barrier and toilet blocks, there is a night guard and an entry phone/camera surveillance system on the entrance for good measure. Once you have negotiated the entry phone you will find a friendly and more personal service at reception. Do not be tempted to walk to reception from the gate, it is a long way down and a steep climb back. Other facilities on site include the ski slope and lift, restaurant which serves a selection of simple meals and snacks, beer, tea, coffee and soft drinks. The site has a small lakeside beach and grassy lying out area with a playground and plenty of room for ball games. The area is also good for walking, cycling and cross-country skiing.

Facilities: In addition to the facilities at reception, two other small sanitary units are on the camping area. Modern facilities include free showers, a suite for disabled people, baby facilities and a family bathroom. Excellent campers' kitchen with electric cookers and sinks with hot water, all free. Washing machine, dryer (charged for) and sink. Sauna. Restaurant. Minigolf. Volleyball. Frisbee. Jogging track. Canoe hire. Children's playground. **Off site:** Large supermarket and the local rail station are 10 minutes by car from the site.

Charges 2002

Per pitch	Skr. 110 - 175
electricity	Skr. 35

Tel: 08 449 9580. Fax: 08 449 9581. E-mail: info@ flottsbro.com. **Reservations:** Advisable for both summer and winter peak times. Write to site for details. **Open** all year (full services 1 June - 31 August).

Directions: Turn off the E4 at Vårby/Huddinge and turn left on road no.259. After 2 km. turn right and follow signs to Flottsbro.

Bredängs Camping

2842 Stora Sällskapets väg 51, S-127 31 Skärholmen (Stockholms Län)

Bredängs is a busy city site, with easy access to Stockhom city centre. Large and fairly level, with very little shade, there are 500 pitches, including 115 with hardstanding and 180 with electricity (10A), and a separate area for tents. Reception is open from 07.00-23.00 in the main season (17/5-29/8), reduced hours in low season, and English is spoken. They can provide the Stockholm card, or a three-day public transport card. Stockholm has many events and activities all year round, you can take a circular tour on a free sightseeing bus, various boat and bus tours, or view the city from the Kaknäs Tower (155 m). The nearest Metro station is five minute walk, trains run about every ten minutes between 05.00 and 02.00, and the journey takes about twenty minutes. The local shopping centre is five minutes away and a two minute walk through the woods brings you to a very attractive lake and beach.

Facilities: Four heated sanitary units of a high standard provide British style WCs, controllable hot showers, with some washbasins in cubicles. One has a baby room, a unit for disabled people and a first aid room. Cooking and dishwashing facilities are in three units around the site. Laundry with washing machines and dryers, and separate saunas (18.00-21.00). Motorcaravan services and car wash. Well stocked shop (1/5-30/9). Small café serving fast food (1/5-9/9). Sauna. Children's playground.

Charges 2002

Per person	Skr. 85 - 90
pitch	Skr. 160 - 190
electricity	Skr. 30

Discounts for pensioners in low season. **Tel:** 08 977 071. Fax: 08 798 7262. E-mail: bredangcamping@ swipnet.se. **Reservations:** Advised for main season. **Open** 15 April - 27 October.

Directions: Site is about 10 km. southwest of city centre. Turn off E3/4 at Bredängs signpost and follow clearly marked site signs.

Orsa SweCamp

2835 Box 23, S-794 21 Orsa (Dalarnas Län)

This quiet, budget priced site, adjacent to the Grönklitt Bear Park, is primarily designed for winter, with a ski slope adjacent. The site is a rather large and featureless, gravel hardstanding, providing room for more than 50 units with electricity (10A) available to all, but particularly good for larger motorcaravans. In summer, this quietly located site rarely has more than a dozen occupants, yet it is half the price of the crowded, often noisy sites in Orsa town 14 km. away. Reception is located in the holiday centre with its rental cabins, inn, tourist information and other services, about 1 km. below the camping area, and one should book in here and obtain a key for the sanitary unit before proceeding to the site. The Grönklitt Bear Park, with bears, wolves, and lynx is within a short scramble up the hillside from the site and there are magnificent views over this scenic lakeland area.

Facilities: The excellent, very modern, small sanitary unit is heated. It has one unisex WC with external access and, inside for each sex, there is one WC and washbasin cubicle, and two hot showers with curtains and communal changing area. Suite for disabled visitors. Drying room. Wel equipped kitchen with two hobs and two dishwashing sinks. All showers, hairdryers, hot water, drying and kitchen facilities are free of charge. Swimming pool (heated) and children's pool. Entertainment and activities for children. Jogging tracks. Minigolf. **Off** site: Nearest town 1 km.

Charges 2002

Per unit incl. all persons	Skr. 105 - 175
electricity/TV connection	Skr. 40

Families only for Midsummer. **Tel:** 0250 552 300. Fax: 0250 428 51. E-mail: fritid@orsa-gronklitt.se. **Reservations:** Not necessary. **Open** all year (full services 17/7-12/8).

Directions: From Orsa town centre follow the signs to Grönklitt and 'Björn Park'. Site is 14 km.

Mora Sweden Dalarna

2836 Mora Parkens Camping, Box 294, 79225 Mora (Dalamas Län)

Mora, at the northern end of Lake Silijan is surrounded by small localities all steeped in history and culture. On the island of Sollerön, south of Mora, is evidence of a large Viking burial ground. Traditional handicrafts are still alive in the region. Travel to Nusnäs and see the production of the brightly coloured wooden horse. Every household should have two for luck. Winding country roads lead you through rich farmland to the pretty half timbered houses in Bergkarlås/Vattnås. Mora is lively, friendly and attractive. The campsite is only 10 minutes walk from the town. The camping area is large, grassy, open and flat. It is bordered by trees and a stream. The pleasant staff speak English.

Facilities: Toilet facilities are fully equipped. Camper's kitchen. Laundry. Shop. Restaurant/bar. Sauna. Boat and bicycle hire. Fishing. Cabins to rent.

Charges 2002

Per unit	Skr. 120 - 140
electricity	Skr. 4

Tel: 460/250 27600. **Fax:** 460/250 12785. **E-mail:** moraparken@mora.se. **Reservations:** Contact site. **Open** all year (full services mid June - mid August).

Directions: Follow signs to centre of town. The campsite is clearly signed from the town centre and is next to Zorngården and Zorunuse Et (the Zorn museum).

Svegs Camping

2845 Kyrkogrand 1, S-842 32 Sveg (Jämtlands Län)

On the 'Inlandsvagen' route through Sweden, the town centre is only a short walk from this neat, friendly municipal site. Two supermarkets, a café and tourist information office are adjacent. The 160 pitches are in rows, on level grass, divided into bays by tall hedges, and with electricity (10/16A) available to 70. The site has boats, canoes, cycles and rickshaws for hire, and the river frontage has a barbecue area with covered seating and fishing platforms. Alongside the river with its fountain, and running through the site is a pleasant well lit riverside walk. Places to visit include the town with its lovely church and gardens and 16th Century Remsgården, 14 km. to the west.

Facilities: In the older style, sanitary facilities are functional rather than luxurious, providing stainless steel washing troughs, controllable hot showers with communal changing areas, and a unit for disabled visitors. Although a little short on numbers, facilities will probably suffice at most times as the site is rarely full. Kitchen and dining room with TV, four full cookers and sinks, plus more dishwashing sinks outside under cover. Washing machine and dryers, and an ironing board (iron on loan from reception). Children's play area. TV room. Minigolf. Canoe, boat, rickshaw and bicycle hire. Fishing.

Charges 2002

Per unit	Skr. 110 - 160
tent	Skr. 60 - 70
electricity	Skr. 30 - 40

Tel: 0680 10775. **Fax:** 0680 10337. **Reservations:** Contact site. **Open** all year.

Directions: Site is off road 45 behind the tourist information office in Sveg.

Ostersunds Camping

2850 Krondikesvagen 95, S-831 46 Ostersund (Jämtlands Län)

Östersund lies on Lake Storsjön, which is Sweden's Loch Ness, with 200 sightings of the monster dating back to 1635, and more recently captured on video in 1996. Also worthy of a visit is the island of Frösön where settlements can be traced back to pre-historic time. This large site has 300 pitches, electricity (10A) and TV sockets on 120, all served by tarmac roads. There are also 41 tarmac hardstandings available, and over 200 cottages, cabins and rooms for rent. Adjacent to the site are the municipal pool complex with cafeteria (indoor and outdoor pools), a Scandic hotel with restaurant and a filling station. A supermarket and bank are 500 m. and Ostersund town centre is 3 km.

Facilities: Toilet facilities are in three units, two including controllable hot showers (on payment) with communal changing areas, suites for disabled people and baby changing. The third has four family bathrooms each containing WC, basin and shower. Two kitchens, each with full cookers, hobs, fridge/freezers and double sinks (all free of charge), and excellent dining rooms. Washing machines, dryers and free drying cabinet. Very good motorhome service point suitable for all types of unit including American RVs. Playground.

Charges 2002

Per unit	Skr. 130 - 170
electricity	Skr. 30

Tel: 063 144 615. **Fax:** 063 144 323. **Reservations:** Contact site. **Open** all year.

Directions: Site is to the south of the town off road 605 towards Torvalla, turn by Statoil station and site entrance is immediately on right. (well signed from around the town).

Strömsund Swecamp

2857

S-83324 Strömsund (Jämtlands Län)

A quiet waterside town on the north - south route 45 known as the Inlandsväen, Stromsund is a good place to begin a journey on the Wilderness Way. This is route 342 which heads northwest towards the mountains at Gäddede and the Norwegian border. Being on the confluence of many waterways, there is a wonderful feeling of space and freedom in Stromsund. Beside the main bridge is an excellent open air museum with a collection of buildings dating back several centurys, in the forests there are well marked trails. Walk here alone at midnight on Midsummer's Eve in an intense blue light - nothing moves as the path ahead leads deeper into the dense forest - it is a memorable experience. The campsite is set on a gentle grassy slope backed by forest. Another part of the site, across the road, overlooks the lake. Cabins are set in circular groups of either six or seven. The staff are very friendly, happy and helpful.

Facilities: Excellent facilities include a shower block with underfloor heating (so floors of the showers are always dry) and are fully equipped. Laundry. Campers' kitchen. Bicycle and boat hire. Fishing. **Off site:** Municipal pool is next to the site.

Charges 2002

Per unit	Skr 90 -120
electricity	Skr 25 - 50

Tel: 460 670 164 10. Fax: 460 670 137 05. E-mail: stromsund.turism@stromsund.se. **Reservations:** Contact site. **Open** all year (full services mid June - mid August).

Directions: Site is 700 m. south of Stomsund on route 45.

Flogsta Camping

2855

S-872 80 Kramfors (Västernorrlands Län)

Kramfors lies just to the west of the E4, and travellers may well pass by over the new Höga Kusten bridge (one of the largest in Europe), and miss this friendly little site. The area of Ådalen and the High Coast, which reaches as far as Örnsköldsvik, is well worth a couple of days of your time, also Skuleskogen National Park, and Norfallsvikens, an old fishing village with many original buildings. The attractive garden-like campsite has around 50 pitches, 21 with electrical connections (10A), which are arranged on level grassy terraces, separated by shrubs and trees in bays of 2-4 units. All overlook the municipal swimming pool complex and attractive minigolf course. The non-electric pitches are on an open terrace nearer reception. The town centre is a 20 minute easy walk through a housing estate, and do use the excellent covered and elevated walkway to cross the main road and railway to the pedestrian shopping precinct with its floral arrangements and fountain.

Facilities: Excellent sanitary facilities comprise nine well equipped family bathrooms, each with British style WC, basin with hand dryer, shower (on payment). Laundry with washing machine and dryer. More WCs and showers are in the reception building with a free sauna. A separate building houses a kitchen, with hot-plates, fridge/freezer and TV/dining room (all free). The reception building has a small shop and snack-bar (staffed 07.00-23.00 hrs from 9/6-11/8 - outside these dates a warden calls daily). Children's playground. **Off site:** Swimming pools (one day free admission to campers).

Charges 2002

Per unit	Skr. 85 - 115
cyclist/hiker and tent	Skr. 55
electricity	Skr. 25

Tel: 0612 10005. Fax: 0612 150 35. **Reservations:** Contact site. **Open** May - end September.

Directions: Well signed from road 90 in the centre of Kramfors, the site lies to the west in a rural location beyond a housing estate and by the Flogsta Bad, municipal swimming pool complex.

Umeå Camping

2860

S-901 84 Umeå (Västerbotens Län)

An ideal stop-over for those travelling the E4 coastal route, or a good base from which to explore the area, this good quality municipal campsite is on the outskirts of this university city. It is 6 km. from the town centre, almost adjacent to the Nydalsjön lake, ideal for fishing, windsurfing and bathing. There are 320 grassy pitches arranged in bays of 10-20 units, divided by shrubs and small trees, all with electricity (10A), and some are fully serviced (electricity, water, waste water). Outside the site adjacent to the lake, but with direct access, are a small open-air pool with waterslide, minigolf, mini-car driving school, skateboard ramp, beach volleyball, a mini-farm and there are cycle and footpaths around the area. Umeå is also a port for ferries to Vasa in Finland.

Facilities: The large, heated, central sanitary unit is modern and well equipped including controllable hot showers with communal changing areas, and a sauna. Well equipped kitchen with large dining room adjacent. Laundry with washing machines, dryers and ironing boards. These facilities are supplemented in high season by a basic smaller unit, plus a 'portacabin' style unit both with WCs and hand-basins only. Shop and snackbar (summer only). Volleyball. Children's playgrounds. Bicycle hire. Boat hire. Fishing. **Off site:** Riding 15 km. Golf 18 km.

Charges 2002

Per unit	Skr. 150 - 160
unit with electricity	Skr. 180 - 190
serviced pitch	Skr. 200 - 210

Tel: 090 702 600. Fax: 090 702 610. E-mail: umea.camping@umea.se. **Reservations:** Contact site. **Open** all year (full services 11/6-12/8).

Directions: From the E4 on northern outskirts of the town, turn at traffic lights, where site is signed.

Camp Gielas

2865

Järnvägsgatan 111, S-933 22 Arvidsjaur (Norrbottens Län)

A modern site with excellent sporting facilities on the outskirts of the town, this site is well shielded on all sides by trees, providing a very peaceful atmosphere. The 150 pitches, 80 with electricity (16A) and satellite TV connections, are level on sparse grass and accessed by tarmac roadways. The sauna at the sports hall is free to campers, who may also use all the indoor sporting, gymnasium and solarium facilities at the usual rates. Also on site is a snack-bar. The lake on the site is suitable for boating, bathing and fishing and other amenities include tennis courts, minigolf, canoe and boat hire and playgrounds.

Facilities: Two modern, heated sanitary units provide controllable hot showers (on payment) and a unit for disabled visitors. Well equipped kitchens (free). Washing machine and dryer. The unit by the tent area also has facilities for disabled people and baby changing. Snack bar. Minigolf. Children's playgrounds. Sauna. Solarium. Sporting facilities. Boat and canoe hire. Lake swimming. Fishing. Winter golf course on snow on site. **Off site:** Bicycle hire 2 km. Riding 500 m. Golf 200 m.

Charges 2002

Per unit	Skr. 100
electricity/satellite TV connection)	Skr. 40
hikers tent	Skr. 70

Tel: 0960 55600. Fax: 0960 10615. E-mail: gielas@arvidsjaur.se. **Reservations:** Contact site. **Open** all year.

Directions: Site is well signed from road 95 in the town.

Jokkmokks Turistcenter

2870

Box 75, S-962 22 Jokkmokk (Norrbottens Län)

This attractive municipal site is just 8 km. from the Arctic Circle. Large and well organised, the site is bordered on one side by the river and with woodland on the other, just 3 km. from the town centre. It has 170 level, grassy pitches, with an area for tents, plus 59 cabins and 26 rooms for rent. Electricity (10A) is available to all touring pitches. The site has a heated open-air pool complex open in summer. There are opportunities for snow-mobiling, cross-country skiing in spring, or ice fishing in winter. Nearby attractions include the first hydro-electric power station with free tours between 15/6-15/8, Vuollerim (40 km.) reconstructed 6,000 year old settlement, with excavations of the ice-age village.

Facilities: Heated sanitary buildings provide mostly open washbasins and controllable showers - some are curtained with a communal changing area, a few are in cubicles with divider and seat. A unit by reception has a baby bathroom, a fully equipped suite for disabled visitors, games room, plus a well appointed kitchen and launderette. A further unit with WCs, basins, showers plus a sauna, is by the pool. Shop, restaurant and bar (in summer). Takeaway (high season). Swimming pools (25 x 10 m. main pool with water slide, two smaller pools and paddling pool). Sauna. Bicycle hire. Playground. Minigolf. Games machines. Fishing (licences sold).

Charges 2002

Per unit	Skr. 120 - 150
electricity	Skr. 30

Tel: 0971 12370. Fax: 0971 12476. **Reservations:** Contact site. **Open** all year.

Directions: Site is 3 km. from the centre of Jokkmokk on road 97.

Switzerland

Swiss National Tourist Office, 10 Wardour Street, London W1D 6QF
Tel: 020 7851 1700   Fax: 020 7851 1720
E-mail: stlondon@switzerlandtourism.com   Internet: http://www.MySwitzerland.com

This land locked country, with 22 independent Cantons sharing languages with its four neighbours, has some of the most outstanding scenery in Europe which, coupled with its cleanliness and commitment to the tourism industry, makes it a very attractive proposition. The Swiss are well known for their punctuality and hard work and have the highest standard of living of any country in Europe, which makes Switzerland one of the most expensive yet problem free countries to visit. The Berner Oberland is probably the most visited area with a concentration of picturesque peaks and mountain villages, though the highest Alps are those of Valais in the southwest with the small busy resort of Zermatt giving access to the Matterhorn. Zurich in the north is a German speaking city with a wealth of sightseeing. Geneva, Montreux and Lausanne on the northern shores of Lake Geneva make up the bulk of French Switzerland, whilst the southernmost canton, Ticino, is home to the Italian speaking Swiss, with the resorts of Lugano and Locarno.

Population

6,800,000, density 165.5 per sq.km.

Capital

Bern.

Climate

No country in Europe combines within so small an area such marked climatic contrasts. In the northern plateau surrounded by mountains the climate is mild and refreshing. South of the Alps it is warmer, coming under the influence of the Mediterranean. The Valais is noted for its dryness.

Language

The national languages of Switzerland are German 65% (central and east), French 18% (west), Italian 10% (south), Romansh - a derivative of Latin 1% (southeast), and others 6%. Many Swiss, especially those involved in tourism speak English.

Currency

The unit of currency is the Swiss franc, divided into 100 centimes, coming in coins of 5, 10, and 20 centimes and Sfr 0.5, 1, 2, 5. Notes are Sfr 10, 20, 50, 100, 500, 1000.

Time

GMT plus 1 (summer BST +1).

Banks

Open Mon-Fri 08.30-16.30. Closed for lunch in Lausanne and Lucerne 12.30-13.30/14.00

Post Offices

Open Mon-Fri 07.30-12.00 and 13.45-18.30. Sat 07.30-11.00 or later in some major city offices.

Telephone

From the UK, the code is 00 41 followed by the area code (omitting the initial zero) followed by number. Phone cards are sold.

Public Holidays

New Year; Good Fri; Easter Mon; Ascension; Whit Mon; Christmas, 25 Dec; Other holidays are observed in individual Cantons.

Shops

Generally open Mon-Fri 08.00- 12.00 and 14.00- 18.00. Sat 08.00-16.00. Often closed Monday mornings.

Food: The cost of food in shops and restaurants can be expensive; it may be worthwhile to consider 'stocking-up' on basic food necessities purchased in the UK, or elsewhere in Europe. Note that, officially, only 2.5 kgs per head of foodstuffs may be imported into the country. The local specialities to try if there is money in the budget are 'Fondue' or 'Raclette' in French speaking Switzerland and 'Rösti' in German speaking areas.

Motoring

The road network is comprehensive and well planned. If the roads are narrow and circuitous in parts, it is worth it for the views. An annual road tax is levied on all cars using Swiss motorways and the 'Vignette' windscreen sticker must be purchased at the border (credit cards not accepted), or in advance from the Swiss National Tourist Office, plus a separate one for a towed caravan or trailer.

Fuel: On motorways, service stations are usually open from 0600- 2200/2400. On other roads it varies 0600/0800-1800/2000. Outside these hours petrol is widely available from 24 hr automatic pumps - Sfr 10/20. Credit cards generally accepted.

Speed Limits: Cars in built-up areas 31 mph (50 kph), other roads 50 mph (80 kph), and motorways 75 mph (120 kph). For towing vehicles on motorways 50 mph (80 kph).

Camping TCS Pointe à la Bise

CH-1222 Vésenaz (Genève)

Ideal for visiting Geneva, Pointe à la Bise is directly on the lake and has superb views of it and the surrounding mountains which may well tempt you to stay longer. The 200 pitches for touring units, 70 with electricity (4/10A) are not marked so, although electricity boxes roughly determine where each unit goes, you do not have an exactly defined place which might make for crowding in high season. Tall trees provide some shade. There are a number of static caravans but these are grouped to one side of the tourist area. Being away from the main road, this is a quiet site with a relaxed atmosphere - no disco, but occasional light, live music entertainment during high season. Improvements in recent years have lifted this from a reasonable site to a good one where you should receive warm welcome.

Facilities: The single fully equipped sanitary block has been refurbished to a high standard. Baby room. Washing machines and dryers. Motorcaravan services. Gas supplies. Shop. Bar. Restaurant (open all day) with takeaway. Community room with TV. Children's pool (15/5-15/9). Playground. Lake swimming and watersports. Windsurfing and small boats under 10 h.p. may be used from site. Fishing. Bicycle hire. Programme of organised activities in July/Aug. **Off site:** Golf 3 km. Lido 5 km.

Charges 2003

Per person	Sfr. 5.20 - 6.20
child (6-15 yrs)	Sfr. 2.60 - 3.10
tent	Sfr. 7.50 - 9.50
caravan	Sfr. 16.00 - 19.00
motorcaravan	Sfr. 19.00 - 22.00
electricity	Sfr. 4.50
dog	Sfr. 2.00 - 3.00
local taxes	Sfr. 1.50

Tel: 022 752 12 96. Fax: 022 752 37 67. E-mail: camping.geneve@tcs.ch. **Reservations:** Contact site. **Open** Easter - 6 October.

Directions: Follow lakeside road from city centre towards Thonon (lake on left hand side) for about 6.5 km. and site is signed.

Camping Le Petit Bois

CH-1110 Morges (Vaud)

This excellent TCS campsite is on the edge of Morges, a wine-growing centre with a 13th century castle, on Lake Geneva about 8 km. west of Lausanne. Le Petit Bois is next to the municipal sports field complex with views across the lake to the mountains beyond. A good variety of flowers, shrubs and trees adorn the site and the neat, tidy lawns make a most pleasant place. The site has 175 grass pitches for tourists, all with 6A electricity and laid out in a regular pattern from wide hard access roads on which cars stand. There are 8 larger pitches for motorcaravans with electricity, water and drainage. Two tent like structures have electronic games in one with the other being used for entertainment. A fence separates the site from the lake with gates for access to the water. As well as being good for a long stay to explore this scenic and interesting region, it also makes a night stop when passing this way. The friendly managers speak good English, and will advise on local attractions.

Facilities: Two well built, fully equipped, modern sanitary blocks include hot water in half the washbasins and sinks and on payment in the showers. Separate block with excellent baby room and cosmetics room. Improved facilities for disabled visitors. Washing machines, dryers and irons. Motorcaravan services. First class restaurant (with service) and takeaway. Well stocked shop. Children's playground. Boules. Bicycle and scooter hire. Small general room. Internet point. Some entertainment in high season. Picnic area. **Off site:** Next to the site is the very good heated town swimming pool and open space for ball games. Small harbour adjoining site has some moorings for campers' boats. Town centre within walking distance.

Charges 2003

Per person	Sfr. 5.60 - 7.00
caravan	Sfr. 16.00 - 20.00
tent	Sfr. 7.80 - 8.80
motorcaravan	Sfr. 20.00 - 22.00
electricity	Sfr. 4.00
dog	Sfr. 2.00 - 3.00
local taxes	Sfr. 3.10

Tel: 021 801 12 70. Fax: 021 803 38 69. E-mail: camping.morges@tcs.ch. **Reservations:** Made for min. 1 week with deposit (Sfr. 80) and fee (20) **Open** 1 April - 19 October.

Directions: On Rue de Lac (B1); coming from Lausanne, leave Lausanne - Geneva motorway at exit 'Morges-ouest', from Geneva exit 'Morges'. Turn towards town and signs for site.

Camping De Vidy

927 chemin du Camping 3, CH-1007 Lausanne (Vaud)

The interesting and ancient city of Lausanne - its first cathedral was built in the 6th century - spills down the hillside towards Lake Geneva until it meets the peaceful park in which this site is situated. The present owners took the site over from the City council in 1987 and have enhanced its neat and tidy appearance by planting many flowers and shrubs. Although only minutes from the city centre, only a gentle hum of traffic can be heard and the site exudes peace and tranquillity. A public footpath separates the site from the lakeside, but there is good access. The World HQ of the Olympic movement is adjacent in the pleasant park, which is also available for games and walking. Hard access roads separate the site into sections for tents, caravans and motorcaravans, with 10A electrical connections in all parts, except the tent areas. Pitches are on flat grass, numbered but not marked out, with 245 (of 350) for tourists. The lakeside bar/restaurant (also open to the public) provides entertainment in season in the various rooms so that the young and not so young can enjoy themselves without impinging on each other. The keen young couple who manage the site speak good English, whom they welcome.

Facilities: Two excellent sanitary blocks, one near reception (heated) and one on the opposite side of the site, have mostly British, some Turkish style WCs, free hot water in washbasins, sinks and showers with warm, pre-mixed water. Facilities for disabled people. A third small block of the same standard has been added. Motorcaravan services (Euro-Relais; Sfr. 10 for overnight guests, 20 otherwise). Gas supplies. Well stocked shop and self-service bar/restaurant (1/5-30/9). Takeaway in high season. Children's playground. Evening entertainment in high season. Internet point. Lake swimming. Fishing. **Off site:** Frequent bus service into Lausanne. Boat excursions on the lake.

Charges 2003

Per person	Sfr. 6.50
student	Sfr. 6.00
child (6-15 yrs)	Sfr. 5.00
car	Sfr. 3.50
motorcycle	Sfr. 2.50
tent, caravan or motorcaravan	Sfr. 12.00 - 13.00
2 person tent	Sfr. 8.00
dog	Sfr. 2.00
local tax	Sfr. 1.30

No credit cards. **Tel:** 021 622 50 00. Fax: 021 622 50 01. E-mail: info@campinglausannevidy.ch. **Reservations:** Write to site. **Open** all year.

Directions: Site is left of the road to Geneva, 500 m. west of La Maladière. Take autobahn Lausanne-Süd, exit La Maladière, and follow signs to camp (very near). Care needed at motorway exit roundabout.

Camping Les Grangettes

922 CH-1845 Noville (Vaud)

At first sight, Les Grangettes appears to be filled with static caravans and, indeed, 245 of the 315 pitches have these. However, to one side there is a separate section of 70 places for touring units. These are good sized level pitches, separated by saplings, and back to back in regular rows on either side of rolled stone roads backed by trees leading down to the lake. All have electricity connections (10A). Musical entertainment is provided in the restaurant in high season but this is a quiet site in a scenic location with views across Lake Geneva. It could make a useful night stop when travelling from Montreux to Martigny, the Rhone Valley and Simplon Pass but is, perhaps, better for a longer stay when exploring this part of Lake Geneva.

Facilities: The well built, modern sanitary block is fully equipped with hot water (pre-mixed from a single tap) in washbasins and sinks and on payment in the showers. Facilities for disabled visitors. Washing machines and dryers. Motorcaravan services (Euro-Relais). Basic food supplies. Excellent bar/restaurant with terrace. Children's playground.

Charges 2003

Per person	Sfr. 6.00 - 8.00
child (2-16 yrs)	Sfr. 2.50 - 5.50
tent	Sfr. 5.00 - 8.50
caravan	Sfr. 7.00 - 10.00
car	Sfr. 2.00
motorcaravan	Sfr. 8.00 - 11.00
electricity (10A)	Sfr. 4.00
dog	Sfr. 3.00
local tax	Sfr. 1.00

Tel: 021 960 15 03. Fax: 021 960 20 30. **Reservations:** Contact site. **Open** all year.

Directions: From N9 Montreux-Martigny motorway, take Villeneuve exit, and follow signs to Noville and then site.

Camping Sémiramis

963 CH-1854 Leysin (Vaud)

Leysin came to fame at the end of the last century when it was found that the pure mountain air was conducive to the cure of turberculosis. The discovery of antibiotic drugs in 1955 made the lengthy natural treatment redundant and Leysin turned to tourism as a summer and winter resort. At 4,500 feet above sea level in the Vaudois Alps, there are spectacular views over the Rhône valley. Reputably enjoying more hours of sunshine than anywhere in Switzerland, Leysin has become a well equipped resort with ski-ing facilities including a cable way to a revolving restaurant. The village straggles up the mountain side and Sémiramis is at the start of this. With 120 pitches and on a slight slope with static caravans on the upper level, the meadow at the entrance provides 60 places for touring visitors. No places are marked out and long leads may be required for the electricity hook ups (6/15A). There is little shade but the views are breathtaking and mountains protect the campsite to the north. This neat, compact site has very friendly, English speaking management and provides an excellent base to enjoy the amenities of the region.

Facilities: The two sanitary blocks are heated in cool weather, one on the ground floor of the hotel and one next to the snack bar, shop and reception. Free hot water is dispensed through a single tap in wash-basins, showers and sinks. Washing machine and dryer. Gas supplies. Motorcaravan services. Shop (1/7-31/8). Bar and snack bar (closed May and Nov). Children's play area. TV room in bar. Boules. Sports centre. Table tennis. Badminton. **Off site:** Fishing 2 km. Bicycle hire or riding 1 km. Tennis courts and the town's large ice rink (open all year) are next to the site with restaurants and shops nearby.

Charges 2002

Per person	Sfr. 5.00 - 6.00
child (6-16 yrs)	Sfr. 2.50 - 4.00
caravan	Sfr. 6.00 - 7.00
tent	Sfr. 3.00 - 4.00
car	Sfr. 4.00 - 5.00
motorcycle	Sfr. 2.00 - 2.50
motorcaravan	Sfr. 10.00 - 13.00
electricity (max. 3 nights)	Sfr. 4.00
local tax	Sfr. 1.70 - 3.50

Tel: 024 494 3939. Fax: 024 494 2121. E-mail: info@hoteldusoleil.ch. **Reservations:** Write to site with deposit (Sfr. 50). **Open** all year.

Directions: Take Leysin road at Le Sepey on Aigle - Châteaux-d'Oex road and turn left immediately after the town sign (just past Subaru garage).

Camping Avenches Port-Plage

909 Camping-Port-Plage, CH-1580 Avenches (Vaud)

This is a large site by Swiss standards, located in a quiet, open situation directly on Lake Murten with its own marina and excellent access to the water. The site is well cared for, with 200 out of the 700 pitches available for tourists. These are of reasonable size (80 sq.m.) with shade in parts from tall trees and electrical connec-tions on most (6A). At the centre of the site is a large building which houses a general shop, butcher, baker and the main sanitary facilities. A separate restaurant is nearer the lake shore. With its location directly on the shores of the lake, there are many leisure opportunities including watersports, fishing and sandy beaches for swimming or relaxing.

Facilities: Three toilet blocks, one new, are of excel-lent quality with British style WCs. Motorcaravan services. Restaurant. Shop, butcher and baker. First aid room. Children's playground. Special events are organised for adults and children in July/Aug. Watersports, boating and lake swimming. Pedaloes.

Charges 2003

Per person	Sfr. 8.30
child (4-16 yrs)	Sfr. 5.20
caravan	Sfr. 11.40
tent acc. to size	Sfr. 7.25 - 11.40
motorcaravan	Sfr. 15.50 - 20.70
electricity	Sfr. 4.00
local tax	Sfr. 1.00

Tel: 026 675 17 50. Fax: 026 675 44 69. E-mail: camping@avenches.ch. **Reservations:** Write to site with Sfr. 20 fee. **Open** 1 April - 30 September.

Directions: Site is signed near Avenches on the Bern - Lausanne road no.1 (not the motorway).

Camping Paradis Plage

903 CH-2013 Colombier (Neuchâtel)

This area of Switzerland deserves to be better known as there is much of interest here near the French border. Paradis Plage is nicely situated on the shores of Lake Neuchatel, with access to the lake. The 160 pitches available to tourists are numbered and marked out on flat grass under a covering of tall, mature trees. All have electricity (10A) and some have gravel hardstanding for caravans and motorcaravans. There are separate areas of grass where pitches are not marked, including a small overflow section for individuals or groups. The 200 static pitches are occupied mainly at weekends and high season and are neatly set out together in rows. Although a motorway runs over the site near the entrance, we did not notice any undue noise as this seemed to be screened out by the trees. Access to the site is rather narrow but adequate. A very pleasant restaurant with a large terrace, well stocked shop and takeaway (all to end Sept) form the focal point in the centre with views through the trees to the lake. Friendly, English speaking management. The site is well placed for walking in the Jura or touring the Bernese Oberland.

Facilities: Three heated sanitary blocks, well sited around the site, have been refurbished and make a good provision. Baby room. Laundry rooms also have electric cooking rings for free use. Gas supplies. Motorcaravan services. Shop (1/3-25/9). Restaurant (all season). Small children's pool (20/6-20/8). New children's play area. Table tennis. Bicycle hire. Fishing. Boating. **Off site:** Sports complex nearby with indoor and outdoor tennis courts, squash, bowls and football. Riding 3 km.

Charges 2003

Per person	Sfr. 8.00 - 9.00
child (6-15 yrs)	Sfr. 3.00
pitch	Sfr. 8.00 - 15.00
car	Sfr. 2.00 - 3.00
motorcycle	Sfr. 1.00
electricity	Sfr. 3.50
local tax per pitch	Sfr. 2.00

Discounts for stays over 17 days (10%) up to 30 days (23%). **Tel:** 032 841 24 46. Fax: 032 841 43 05. E-mail: paradisplage@freesurf.ch. **Reservations:** Write to site. **Open** 1 March - 31 October.

Directions: Leave the short stretch of motorway at Colombier from where site is signed.

Camping Bois-du-Couvent

905 CH-2301 La Chaux-de-Fonds (Neuchâtel)

The road from Lake Neuchatel to Chaux-de-Fonds, which stands just inside the Swiss border with France in the northwest of Switzerland, has been greatly improved with parts to motorway standard. La Chaux-de-Fonds is the biggest watch and clock-making centre in Switzerland and one of the largest agricultural centres. Completely destroyed by fire in 1794, it was rebuilt to a geometric plan. Postage stamps for Switzerland and many foreign countries are printed here. Camping Bois du Couvent is situated at the southern end of the town on a hill-top with splendid views (1,060 m.). Most of the pitches are taken by static caravans but the 40 places for tourists, with 10A electrical connections, although not marked, are obvious, with an open lawn for tents. The site has a pleasant appearance and tarmac and gravel roads link the terraces, some of which have shade from tall trees. Very little English is spoken but the warden has good tourist information available. This is a good area for walking.

Facilities: Two fully equipped sanitary blocks provide free hot water in washbasins and on payment in sinks and showers. Washing machine and dryer. Restaurant (open all year except Tues, 08.00 - midnight). Children's playground. Some entertainment for children in summer. **Off site:** Bicycle hire and tennis 100 m. Minigolf 300 m. Heated pool 500 m. Supermarket 1 km. Clock museum 1 km.

Charges 2003

Per person	Sfr. 3.50 - 4.50
child (4-16 yrs)	Sfr. 1.50 - 2.00
pitch	Sfr. 6.00 - 15.00
electricity	Sfr. 3.00 - 8.00
dog	Sfr. 3.00
local tax	Sfr. 2.00

Tel: 079 240 50 39. Fax: 032 914 48 77. **Reservations:** Write to site. **Open** all year.

Directions: Site is signed and is at south end of La Chaux-de-Fonds. Coming from Neuchatel, turn left at second roundabout after tunnel.

Camping des Pêches

route du Port, CH-2525 Le Landeron (Neuchâtel)

904

This recently constructed, touring campsite is on the side of Lake Biel and river Thienne, and close to the old town of Le Landeron. The site is divided into two sections - on one side of the road is a well presented and neatly organised static caravan area, and on the other is the modern campsite for tourists. At the entrance an inviting reception building greets the visitor, also housing community room, small café and first-aid. The 200 pitches are all on level grass, numbered but not separated, a few with shade, all with electricity (10A) and many conveniently placed water points. All the facilities are exceptionally well maintained and in pristine condition during our visit throughout a busy holiday weekend.

Facilities: The spacious, modern sanitary block contains all the usual facilities including a food preparation area with six cooking rings, a large freezer and refrigerator. Payment for showers is by card. Baby room. Washing machines, dryers and irons. Motorcaravan service point. Swimming pool (16/5-1/9; charged). Children's playground. Bicycle hire. TV and general room. Treatment room. Card barrier. **Off site:** Golf and riding 7 km. Fishing 300 m.

Charges 2003

Per adult	Sfr. 7.00
child (6-16 yrs)	Sfr. 3.50
tent	Sfr. 7.50 - 9.50
caravan	Sfr. 10.50
motorcaravan	Sfr. 15.00
electricity	Sfr. 3.50
local tax per pitch	Sfr. 2.00

Tel: 032 751 29 00. Fax: 032 751 63 54. E-mail: info@camping-lelanderon.ch. **Reservations:** Contact site. **Open** 1 April - 15 October.

Directions: Le Landeron is signed from the Neuchâtel - Biel motorway and site is well signed from the town.

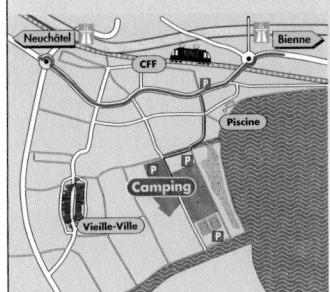

LE LANDERON «Camp des Pêches»****

Quiet and well equipped site for tourists (40'000m2) for a restoring holiday or a short stay in an attractive countryside:

- Idyllic mediaeval town with Gothic town hall, museum, castle, chapels and historic fountains – surrounded by gardens and well-known vineyards
- On the shores of the lake of Bienne with a picturesque harbour, heated olympique swimming pool and restaurant (300m)
- Nice promenades along the river Thielle and walking tours to the Chasseral (1609m)

Camp des Pêches, CH-2525 Le Landeron
Phone 0041-32-751 29 00, Fax 0041-32-75163 54
www.camping-lelanderon.ch

Camping Le Bivouac

Route des Paccots, CH-1618 Châtel-St-Denis (Fribourg)

930

the travel service TO BOOK

erry	✓
Pitch	✓
Accommodation	✗

01892 55 98 98

A nice little site in the mountains north of Montreux, Le Bivouac has its own small swimming pool and children's pool. Most of the best places here are taken by seasonal caravans (130) and there are now only about 30 pitches for tourists. Electrical connections (10A) are available and there are five water points. The site is also open for winter sports caravanning and all the sanitary facilities are heated. Entertainment is organised for adults and children in high season. This is a good centre for walking and excursions.

Facilities: The good toilet facilities include pre-set, free hot water in washbasins, showers and sinks for laundry and dishes. Baby room. New facilities in the main building have more showers, free hot water and laundry facilities. Gas supplies. Shop (1/7-31/8). Bar (1/7-31/8). Swimming pool (1/6-15/9). Room for general use adjoining. Table tennis. Fishing. **Off site:** Bicycle hire 2 km. Riding 4 km.

Charges 2003

Per person	Sfr. 6.00
child (6-16 yrs)	Sfr. 4.00
pitch	Sfr. 15.00
electricity	Sfr. 4.00
local tax (adults)	Sfr. 1.40

No credit cards. Possible discount on showing this guide. **Tel:** 021 948 78 49. Fax: 021 948 78 49. E-mail: bivouac@swissonline.ch. **Reservations:** Advised for July/Aug. and made for 1 week with deposit (Sfr. 50) and fee (10). **Open** all year.

Directions: From N12/A12 Bern-Vevey motorway take Châtel St Denis exit and turn towards Les Paccots (about 1 km).

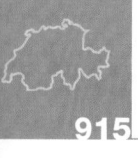

Camping Waldhort

900 Heideweg 16, CH-4153 Reinach bei Basel (Basel-Land)

This is a satisfactory site for night halts or for visits to Basel. Although there are almost twice as many static caravan pitches as spaces for tourists, this is a quiet site on the edge of a residential district, within easy reach of the city. The site is flat, with 220 level pitches on grass with access from the tarmac road which circles round inside the site. Trees are now maturing to give some shade. All pitches have electricity (6A). Owned and run by the Camping and Caravanning Club of Basel, it is neat, tidy and orderly and there is usually space available. An extra, separate camping area has been added behind the tennis club which has pleasant pitches and good sanitary facilities.

Facilities: The good quality, fully equipped, central sanitary block includes facilities for disabled people. Washing machine and dryer. Motorcaravan services. Small shop with terrace for drinks. Playground with two small pools. Table tennis. Swimming pool and tennis next to site. **Off site:** Reinach is within walking distance from where there is a tram service into Basel.

Charges 2003

Per person	Sfr. 7.00
child (6-16 yrs)	Sfr. 4.50
tent	Sfr. 11.00
caravan or motorcaravan	Sfr. 17.00

Electricity included. **Tel:** 061 711 64 29. Fax: 061 713 98 35. E-mail: camp.waldhort@gmx.ch.
Reservations: Made for main season; advance payment asked for single nights, otherwise no deposit. **Open** 1 March - 25 October.

Directions: Take Basel - Delémont motorway spur, exit at 'Reinach-Nord' and follow camp signs.

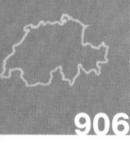

Camping Seebucht

915 Seestrasse 559, CH-8038 Zürich-Wollishofen (Zürich)

Being a smallish site only 4.5 km. from the centre of the important town of Zürich and in a pleasant situation with well kept lawns, Seebucht has more demands on space than it can meet. With 300 touring pitches (136 with 6/10A electricity), it may well pack units rather closely in season but there is much transit trade so there are usually plenty of vacancies each day if you are early (reservations not made). Caravans go on flat hardstandings (cars cannot always stand by them); tents, for which space may be easier to find, go on lawns. The grassy strip alongside the lake is kept free for recreational use

Facilities: The single sanitary block has been improved and has British style toilets, with some Turkish style for men, individual washbasins (cubicles for women) with cold water and hot water on payment for the showers. Motorcaravan services. Shop. Café for meals or drinks. Bar (1/6-31/8). Swimming is possible into fairly deep water. Fishing. Jetty where small boats can be launched. **Off site:** Golf 2 km. Bicycle 1 km.

Charges 2002

Per person	Sfr. 8.00
child (4-16 yrs)	Sfr. 5.00
pitch	Sfr. 16.00
car	Sfr. 5.00
electricity	Sfr. 4.00
local tax	Sfr. 1.20

Tel: 01 482 16 12. Fax: 01 482 16 60. **Reservations:** Not made. **Open** 1 May - 30 September.

Directions: Site is on southern side of town and western side of the lake, at Wollishofen; well signed from most parts of town and at motorway exit.

TCS-Camping Kappelenbrücke

906 CH-3032 Hinterkappelen (Bern)

This well established site, being just outside the Federal Capital, is conveniently placed either for an overnight stop or for exploring the city and surrounds. The 305 pitches (230 for touring) are numbered but not marked out and you choose your own place; cars are parked away from the pitches. All have electricity and there are special pitches for motorcaravans. There are some static units but there should always be room. The shop also serves drinks which can be taken to a pleasant rest room nearby or consumed on the terrace. It is a pleasant, well cared for site near a small lake which is unsuitable for swimming, however there is a pool on site. It is probably the best site for visiting Bern.

Facilities: Two new toilet blocks are of exceptional quality and fully equipped. One block is heated in cool weather. Sinks for laundry and dishwashing under cover. Baby room. Washing machines and dryers. Shop/bar. Swimming pool and children's pool (May - Oct). TV room. Day room. Playground. Table tennis. Fishing. **Off site:** Frequent bus service to city.

Charges 2002

Per person	Sfr. 5.80 - 7.20
child (6-16 yrs)	Sfr. 2.90 - 3.60
caravan	Sfr. 13.00 - 17.00
motorcaravan	Sfr. 13.00 - 20.00
electricity	Sfr. 4.00
local tax	Sfr. 1.90

Tel: 031 901 10 07. Fax: 031 901 25 91. E-mail: camping.bern@tcs.ch. **Reservations:** Write to site. **Open** all year.

Directions: Take Bethlehem exit from N1 motorway on western side of Bern, towards Aarberg, and site will be seen on right before river.

Camping Bettlereiche

CH-3770 Gwatt (Bern)

933

Bettlereiche is an ideal site for those who wish to explore this part of the Bernese Oberland and who would enjoy staying on a small site in a quiet area, away from the larger sites and town atmosphere of Interlaken. There are 90 numbered, but unmarked pitches for tourists, most with 4A electricity available, and about the same number of static units. There are hard access roads but cars must be parked away from the pitches. Although there are some trees, there is little shade in the main camping area. Direct access to the lake is available for swimming and boating. The site has a cared for air and the friendly management speak good English. Part of the restaurant is reserved for young people. Some animation in high season.

Facilities: Single, modern, well constructed sanitary block, fully equipped with hot water provided for washbasins in cabins (cold otherwise). Facilities should be adequate in high season. Room for disabled visitors. Washing machine and dryer. Motorcaravan services. Well stocked shop. Restaurant (no alcohol). Lake swimming and boating.

Charges 2002

Per person	Sfr. 5.40 - 7.40
child	Sfr. 2.70 - 3.70
caravan or motorcaravan	Sfr. 13.00 - 19.00
tent	Sfr. 6.00 - 7.00
dog	Sfr. 3.00
electricity	Sfr. 3.00
local tax	Sfr. 3.60

Tel: 033 336 40 67. Fax: 033 336 40 17. E-mail: camping.gwatt@bluewin.ch. **Reservations:** Contact site. **Open** Easter - 29 September.

Directions: From Berne-Thun-Interlaken autoroute, take exit Thun-Süd for Gwatt and follow signs for Gwatt and site.

Camping Grassi

CH-3714 Frutigen (Bern)

936

This is a small site with about half the pitches occupied by static caravans, used by their owners for weekends and holidays. The 70 or so places available for tourists are not marked out but it is said that the site is not allowed to become overcrowded. Most places are on level grass with two small terraces at the end of the site. There is little shade but the site is set in a river valley with trees on the hills which enclose the area. It would make a useful overnight stop en-route for Kandersteg and the railway station where cars can join the train for transportation through the Lotschberg Tunnel to the Rhône Valley and Simplon Pass, or for a longer stay to explore the Bernese Oberland. Electricity is available for all pitches but long leads may be required in parts. There is a kiosk for basic supplies, but shops and restaurants are only a 10 minute walk away in the village.

Facilities: The well constructed, heated sanitary block is of good quality. Washing machine and dryer. Gas supplies. Motorcaravan services. Rest room with TV. Kiosk (1/7-31/8). Children's play area and play house. Mountain bike hire and tours. Fishing. Bicycle hire. **Off site:** Riding 2 km. Outdoor and indoor pools, tennis and minigolf in Frutigen. Ski-ing and walking.

Charges 2003

Per person	Sfr. 6.40
child (1-16 yrs)	Sfr. 1.50 - 3.20
pitch	Sfr. 6.00 - 12.00
electricity (8/10A)	Sfr. 2.50
local tax	Sfr. 0.40 - 0.80

No credit cards. **Tel:** 033 671 11 49. Fax: 033 671 13 80. E-mail: campinggrassi@bluewin.ch. **Reservations:** Write to site. **Open** all year.

Directions: Take Kandersteg road from Spiez and leave at Frutigen Dorf exit from where site is signed.

Camping Manor Farm 1

Manor Farm AG, CH-3800 Interlaken-Thunersee (Bern)

942

Manor Farm has for many years had a large proportion of British guests, for whom this is one of the traditional touring areas. The site lies outside the town on the northern side of the Thuner See, with most of the site between road and lake but with one part on the far side of the road. Interlaken is rather a tourist town but the area is rich in scenery, with innumerable mountain excursions and walks available. The lakes and Jungfrau railway are near at hand. The flat terrain is divided entirely into 552 individual, numbered pitches which vary considerably both in size (60-100 sq.m.) and price with 10A electricity available and shade in some places; 144 are equipped with electricity, water, drainage and 55 also have cable TV connections. The ground becomes a little muddy when wet. Reservations are made, although you should find space except perhaps in late July/early August, but the best places may then be taken. Around 30% of the pitches are taken by permanent or letting units and there is a tour operator presence. Manor Farm is efficiently and quite formally run, with good English spoken.

Facilities: Six separate toilet blocks are practical, heated and soundly constructed. Fully equipped, they even include free hot water for baths. Baby rooms. Twenty private units for rent. Washing machine, dryer, ironing. Motorcaravan services. Gas supplies. Shop (1/4-15/10). Site-owned restaurant adjoining (1/3-30/11). Snack bar with takeaway on site (1/6-31/8). TV room. Football field. Children's playground and paddling pool. Minigolf. Bicycle hire. Table tennis. Sailing and windsurfing school. Bathing possible in the lake at two points and boats can be brought if a permit obtained. Boat hire. Fishing. Daily activity and entertainment programme in high season. Excursions. Tourist information. **Off site:** Golf 500 m. Indoor and outdoor pools 3 km. Riding 3 km. Area is good for cycling and walking.

Charges 2003

Per person	Sfr. 5.90 - 9.80
child under 6 yrs	free
child 6-15 yrs	Sfr. 2.75 - 4.60
pitch	Sfr. 7.80 - 38.00
dog (max 1)	Sfr. 2.40 - 4.00
boat	Sfr. 2.40 - 6.00
electricity (0.5, 4 or 6A)	Sfr. 0.80 - 4.50
local tax	Sfr. 1.60

Various discounts for longer stays. **Tel:** 033 822 22 64. Fax: 033 822 22 79. E-mail: manorfarm@swiss-camps.ch. **Reservations:** Taken for high season (min. 3 days) with booking fee (Sfr. 30). **Open** all year.

Directions: Site is about 3 km. west of Interlaken along the road running north of the Thuner See towards Thun. Follow signs for 'Camp 1'. From the motor road bypassing Interlaken (A8) take exit marked 'Gunten, Beatenberg', which is a spur road bringing you out close to site.

Camping Jungfraublick

Gsteigstrasse 80, Matten, CH-3800 Interlaken (Bern)

944

the travel service
TO BOOK
Ferry ✓
Pitch ✓
Accommodation ✗
01892 55 98 98

The Berner Oberland is one of the most scenic and well known areas of Switzerland with Interlaken probably the best known summer resort. This second site is offered here as a contrast from the larger one on the opposite side of town. Situated in the village of Matten and within walking distance of the town centre (about 1 km), Jungfraublick is a delightful, medium sized site with splendid views up the Lauterbrunnen valley to the Jungfrau mountain. The pink glow reflected from the sunset is a sight to behold when weather conditions allow. The motorway which bypasses the town runs in a deep cutting along one side of the site so traffic noise is screened out and an earth bank has been constructed alongside the access road reducing noise from here. The 100 touring pitches 60-75 sq.m. with electricity (2-6A) are in regular rows on level, well cut grass. A number of fruit trees adorn but do not offer much shade. The 35 static caravans are to one side of the tourist area and do not intrude. This is a very pleasant, quiet, tidy site with a friendly, English speaking owner who is pleased to advise on the attractions of the region.

Facilities: Fully equipped sanitary facilities are divided between two buildings near the entrance. Showers are on payment, as is hot water for dish-washing. Washing machines and dryers. Motorcaravan services. Shop for basic food requirements (from 25/5). Small swimming pool (12 x 8 m.) open mid-June - end-Aug. according to the weather. Heated rest room with TV and electronic games. Barbecues must be off the ground. **Off site:** Wilderswill train station is only 10 minutes walk. Restaurants and shops about 1 km. in the town. Bicycle hire 700 m. Golf, riding and fishing 4 km.

Charges 2003

Per person	Sfr. 5.80 - 6.80
child (under 16 yrs)	Sfr. 3.50 - 4.20
pitch acc. to size and season	Sfr. 10.00 - 28.00
electricity (2-6A)	Sfr. 1.10 - 3.20
dog	Sfr. 3.00
local tax	Sfr. 1.60

Tel: 033 822 44 14. Fax: 033 822 16 19. E-mail: info@jungfraublick.ch. **Reservations:** Write to site with deposit (Sfr. 30) and fee (10). **Open** 1 May - 25 September.

Directions: Take the Lauterbrunnen exit from the N8 motorway bypass, turn towards Interlaken and site is on the left hand side.

berner oberland
MANOR FARM 1

INTERLAKEN-THUNERSEE

A comfortable site for wonderful lake-and-mountain holidays and a perfect base for innumerable excursions on foot, by car or mountain railway.

The only camp site in Interlaken right on the shores of Lake Thun. First class facilities, restaurant, snacks, mini golf, boats hire, sailing and windsurfing school, camper stations.

MANOR FARM 1
CH-3800 INTERLAKEN-THUNERSEE

PHONE
0041 33 822 22 64
FAX 0041 33 822 22 79
www.manorfarm.ch
manorfarm@swisscamps.ch

Switzerland - Centre

Camping Aaregg

951 Seestrasse 26, CH-3855 Brienz (Bern)

Brienz is a delightful little town on the lake of the same name and the centre of the Swiss wood carving industry. Nearby at Ballenberg is the fascinating Freilicht-museum, a very large open-air park of old Swiss houses which have been brought from all over Switzerland and re-erected in groups. Traditional Swiss crafts are demonstrated in some of these. Camping Aaregg is a very good site situated on the southern shores of the lake with splendid views across the water to the mountains. There are 45 static caravans occupying their own area and 220 tourist pitches, all with electricity (10A). Of these, 15 are larger with hardstandings, water and drainage also. Pitches fronting the lake have a surcharge. The trees and flowers around the site make it an attractive environment. It could be useful as a night stop when passing from Interlaken to Luzern but would also make a good base from which to explore the many attractions of this scenic region.

Facilities: Well built, fully equipped, sanitary blocks refurbished to a high standard include some wash-basins in cabins and showers on payment. Laundry facilities. Motorcaravan services. Pleasant restaurant with terrace and takeaway in season. Enlarged play area. English is spoken.

Charges 2002

Per person	Sfr. 9.00
child (under 15 yrs)	Sfr. 4.50
pitch	Sfr. 10.00 - 18.00
dog	Sfr. 3.00
electricity	Sfr. 4.00
local tax	Sfr. 1.60

Low season less 20%. **Tel:** 033 951 18 43. Fax: 033 951 43 24. E-mail: mail@aaregg.ch. **Reservations:** Made with deposit (Sfr. 20); min. 14 days in July/Aug. **Open** 1 April - 31 October.

Directions: Site is on road B6 on the east of Brienz with entrance road between BP and Esso filling stations, well signed. From the Interlaken-Luzern motorway, take Brienz exit and turn towards Brienz, site then on the left.

Camping Jungfrau

CH-3822 Lauterbrunnen (Bern)

946

This friendly site has a very imposing situation in a steep valley with a fine view of the Jungfrau at the end. You can laze here amid real mountain scenery, though it does lose the sun a little early. There are naturally many more active things to do - mountain walks or climbing, trips up the Jungfrau railway or one of the mountain lifts or excursions by car. The site itself is quite extensive and is grassy with hard surfaced access roads. It is a popular site and, although you should usually find space, in season do not arrive too late. All 391 pitches (250 for touring) have shade in parts, electrical connections (10-15A) and 50 have water and drainage also. About 30% of the pitches are taken by seasonal caravans. The site is used by a tour operator and by groups of youngsters from many different countries - pitches at the top of the site may be quieter. The von Allmen family own and run the site and provide a warm welcome (English is spoken).

Facilities: Three fully equipped sanitary blocks can be heated in winter and include a good, new modern one at the far end of the site. The other two have been renewed and modernised. Facilities for disabled visitors, baby baths and footbaths. Cleaning and maintenance can be variable. Washing machine, spin dryer and ironing. Motorcaravan services. Supermarket (all year). Self-service restaurant with takeaway (May - end Oct). Good general room with wooden tables and chairs, TV, jukebox, drink vending machines, amusements, with second one elsewhere. Well equipped and maintained children's playgrounds and covered play area. Excursions and some entertainment in high season. Mountain bike hire. **Off site:** Free bus to ski station (in winter only).

Charges 2002

Per person	Sfr. 7.20 - 8.20
child (6-15 yrs)	Sfr. 3.60 - 4.10
pitch	Sfr. 12.00 - 18.00
car	Sfr. 3.50
dog	Sfr. 3.00
electricity (+ meter)	Sfr. 2.50
local tax	Sfr. 2.40

Discounts for camping carnet and for stays over 3 nights outside high season. **Tel:** 033 856 20 10. Fax: 033 856 20 20. E-mail: info@camping-jungfrau.ch. **Reservations:** Made for any period with deposit; write for details. **Open** all year.

Directions: Go through Lauterbrunnen and fork right at far end before road bends left, 100 m. before church. The final approach is not very wide.

Camping Gletscherdorf

CH-3818 Grindelwald (Bern)

948

Set in a flat river valley on the edge of Grindelwald, one of Switzerland's well known winter and summer resorts, Gletscherdorf enjoys wonderful mountain views, particularly of the nearby north face of the Eiger. The site has 120 pitches, 60 for touring units. Most are marked and have electricity connections (10A), with a few others in an overflow field. There is a good community room with tables and chairs. This is, above all, a very quiet, friendly site for those who wish to enjoy the peaceful mountain air, walking, climbing and exploring with a mountain climbing school in Grindelwald.

Facilities: Excellent small, heated, fully equipped, sanitary block. Washing machines and dryer. Motorcaravan services. Gas supplies. Small shop provides basic food items. Dogs are not accepted. A torch would be useful. **Off site:** Bicycle hire or golf 1 km. Indoor pool 1 km. Town shops and restaurants within walking distance.

Charges 2003

Per person	Sfr. 6.90
child (6-16 yrs)	Sfr. 3.50
pitch	Sfr. 6.00 - 17.00
electricity	Sfr. 3.50 - 4.00
local tax	Sfr. 2.30

Tel: 033 853 14 29. Fax: 033 853 31 29. E-mail: info@gletscherdorf.ch. **Reservations:** Essential for July/Aug. - contact site. **Open** 1 May - 20 October.

Directions: To reach site, go into town and turn right at camp signs after town centre; approach road is quite narrow and steep down hill but there is an easier departure road.

Grindelwald
Gletscherdorf 31 ✱✱✱

The especially quiet camping ground with lots of wonderful ramble possibilities. New sanitary block.
In winter only: seasonal caravan pitches.
Turn right after the village, follow the signs Gletscherdorf 31.

Fam. D. Harder-Bohren
Gletscherdorf
CH-3818 Grindelwald
Tel. 0041- 33 - 853 14 29
Fax 0041- 33 - 853 31 29
www.gletscherdorf.ch
E-mail: info@gletscherdorf.ch

Camping Eigernordwand

CH-3818 Grindelwald (Bern)

949

Grindelwald is a very popular summer and winter resort and Eigernordwand, at 950 m. above sea level, is dramatically situated very close to the north face of the famous mountain in a delightful situation. The slightly sloping pitches have gravel access roads but are not marked out. There are some trees around but little shade, although there are splendid views of surrounding mountain peaks. Being so high it can become cool when the sun goes down. Excursions to the Jungfrau and climbing or walking tours are organised. Some static caravans remain during the winter with about 140 places for tourists in summer. Electrical connections (6A) are available. There is a good quality restaurant and hotel at the entrance.

Facilities: A new sanitary block, heated in cool weather, is of excellent quality and includes a drying room and facilities for disabled people. Washing machines. Motorcaravan services. Restaurant. Hotel. Kiosk for basic supplies. Children's playground. Barbecue hut. **Off site:** Ski lifts, and cable cars near.

Charges 2003

Per person	Sfr. 8.00 - 10.00
child (3-12 yrs)	Sfr. 4.00 - 5.00
tent	Sfr. 7.00 - 9.00
caravan	Sfr. 11.00 - 12.00
car	Sfr. 3.00
motorcaravan	Sfr. 9.00 - 12.00
electricity	Sfr. 3.00
local tax	Sfr. 2.90

After 10 days, 1 day free. **Tel:** 033 853 42 27. E-mail: camp@eigernordwand.ch. **Reservations:** Write to site. **Open** all year.

Directions: 800 m. before entering Grindelwald bear right past Grund railway station. Turn right over bridge, follow railway line for 500 m. and cross stream to camp on right.

Camping Vermeille

CH-3770 Zweisimmen (Bern)

939

This small, well run campsite is about 1,000 m. above sea level, on a road followed by many tourists and can serve either as a night stop or as a holiday base for those who like a mountain site with many attractive excursion possibilities. In summer there are 40 pitches for tourists (limited shade), in winter 25 (the remainder of the 125 total being seasonal lets), with 130 electrical connections (from 6A) available. The site is equipped for winter sports camping and therefore a fair proportion of the available space consists of hardstandings for caravans on stony ground. However, there are also lawns for tents.

Facilities: Sanitary installations include a baby room and facilities for disabled people. In the main building, they are fully enclosed and heated in winter. A few washbasins are in private cabins, and hot water for washing up and showers is on payment. Washing machine. Motorcaravan services. Shop. New bistro. Small pool (mid-May - late Sept). Mountain bike hire.

Charges 2003

Per person	Sfr. 7.20
child (6-12 yrs)	Sfr. 3.80
pitch and car	Sfr. 14.00 - 17.50
electricity	Sfr. 2.00
local tax	Sfr. 1.00

Less 10% on person charge outside July/Aug. **Tel:** 033 722 19 40. Fax: 033 722 36 25. E-mail: info@ camping-vermeille.ch. **Reservations:** Made for min. 5 nights with deposit and fee. **Open** all year.

Directions: Site is north of town on no. 11 road. Turn off where signed and go past a different site on left of access road. From N6 motorway take exit for Wimmis/Spiez (from Spiez before town).

Camping International Lido

Lidostraße 8, CH-6006 Luzern (Luzern)

912

Luzern is a traditional holiday resort of the British and this site has many British visitors. It lies near the shore of Lake Luzern, just outside the town itself. Next to the site (you have to pay for entrance) is the Lido proper, which has a large sandy beach, bathing in the lake and sports fields. The site is divided into separate sections for caravans, motorcaravans and tents; the first two have hardstandings which, in effect, provide rather formal and small individual pitches with shade in parts. There are about 100 electrical connections (10A). Quiet in early season, from late June to late August it usually becomes full and, especially in the tent section, can at times seem rather crowded. Good English is spoken and the charges are reasonable.

Facilities: The sanitary installations are in three sections, two close to reception and all fully equipped with heating. Large, fully equipped modern block includes a rest room and cooking area with electric rings (pre-payment). Some washbasins in cabins for women, with hot water for showers and sinks on payment. Smallish shop. Takeaway. Community room. Organised excursions. **Off site:** Luzern 20 min. walk along the lake or nearby buses run into the town up to midnight.

Charges 2002

Per person	Sfr. 7.50
child (6-14yrs)	Sfr. 3.75
pitch and car	Sfr. 8.00 - 18.00
local tax	Sfr. 1.20

Tel: 041 370 21 46. Fax: 041 370 21 45. E-mail: luzern@camping-international.ch. **Reservations:** Advised 15/6-15/9. **Open** 15 March - 31 October.

Directions: Follow Lido signs out of Luzern and a large sign to Lido will be seen on right just outside of town.

Camping Vitznau

CH-6354 Vitznau (Luzern)

913

Camping Vitznau is in the small village of the same name, above and overlooking Lake Luzern, with splendid views across the water to the mountains on the other side. It is a small, neat and tidy site very close to the delightful village on the narrow, winding, lakeside road. The 120 pitches (max length 7 m.) have 15A electricity available to most. They are on level, grassy terraces with hard wheel tracks for motorcaravans and separated by tarmac roads, and although of sufficient rather than large size, with single rows on each terrace, all places have views. Larger units might have difficulty manoeuvring onto the pitches. Trees provide shade in parts and this site makes an excellent base.

Facilities: The single, well constructed sanitary block provides free hot showers (water heated by solar panels). Sinks for laundry and dishwashing are under cover with metered hot water. Washing machines and dryers. Gas supplies. Motorcaravan services. Well stocked shop. Games room and a well stocked shop. Small swimming pool (15/5-15/9). **Off site:** Village restaurants about five minutes walk. Fishing or bicycle hire within 1 km. Golf 15 km.

Charges 2003

Per person	Sfr. 8.00 - 9.50
child (4-14 yrs)	Sfr. 4.00
pitch acc. to size and season	Sfr. 14.00 - 22.00
electricity	Sfr. 4.00
local tax	Sfr. 1.90

Tel: 041 397 12 80. Fax: 041 397 24 57. E-mail: camping-vitznau@bluewin.ch. **Reservations:** Write with deposit (Sfr 20). **Open** all year.

Directions: Site signed from the centre of Vitznau.

TCS-Camping Seeland
CH-6204 Sempach-Stadt (Luzern)

911

Lucerne is a very popular city in the centre of Switzerland and Camping Seeland makes a peaceful base from which to visit the town and explore the surrounding countryside or, being a short way from the main N2 Basel - Chiasso motorway, is a convenient night stop if passing through. This neat, tidy site has 200 grass pitches for tourists, all with electricity (4A), a few with gravel hardstanding on either side of hard roads under trees with further places on the perimeter in the open. There are about 250 static caravans. A small river runs through the site with a connecting covered bridge. Activities are organised for adults and children during high season and the site can supply a map (freizeitkarte) which shows walking, jogging and cycle tracks around the district. Bern, Zurich and Interlaken are less than an hour's drive away. Excursion tickets for mountain trains are available. The friendly, English speaking wardens will be pleased to advise on local attractions.

Facilities: Two good quality sanitary blocks have the usual facilities including facilities for disabled visitors and a baby room. Washing machine and dryer. Motorcaravan service point. Excellent self-service bar/restaurant with pleasant terrace overlooking the children's play area, lake and surrounding tree covered hills. Shop. Children's paddling pool and playground, table tennis, fishing. Lakeside beach with lawn for sunbathing. **Off site:** Shops and restaurants a short distance away in the interesting and ancient village which has tennis courts, boats to rent and cycle hire, mini-golf and golf club. Hot air ballooning, river rafting and archery can be arranged and fishing (free) is allowed from the lake shore. Windsurfing school nearby.

Charges 2002

Per person	Sfr. 4.60 - 7.20
child	Sfr. 2.60 - 3.60
caravan	Sfr. 13.00 - 18.00
motorcaravan	Sfr. 13.00 - 20.00
tent	Sfr. 5.00 - 7.00
electricity	Sfr. 3.00
local tax	Sfr. 1.10

Tel: 041 460 14 66. Fax: 041 460 14 66. E-mail: camping.sempach@tcs.ch. **Reservations:** Write to site with Sfr. 100 (Sfr. 20 for admin, balance towards charges). **Open** 27 March - 6 October.

Directions: From the N2 take exit for Sempach and follow signs for Sempach and site.

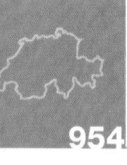

Camping Lido Sarnen
CH-6060 Sarnen (Obwalden)

954

Sarnen is about 20 km. south of Luzern on the main road to Interlaken and is, therefore, ideally placed for ski-ing in winter and sightseeing in summer. The summit of the well known Mt. Pilatus can be reached by mountain railway (the steepest of its type in the world) from Stansstad, about halfway between Luzern and Sarnen, and steamer trips on Lake Luzern can also be made from here. The site is on flat ground directly on the lake with lovely views of near and distant mountains. Suitable for long or short stays, it makes an ideal base for this part of Switzerland or for a night stop if passing through. The 220 pitches, 80 for tourists with electricity (10A), are of 80-90 sq.m. on grass with hard access roads (some narrow). There is shade in parts and the location is a quiet one on the edge of the small town. The site is part of the town Lido complex with a large, heated swimming pool and child's pool and facilities for non-powered boats. Narrow roads on site might make manoeuvring difficult for large units.

Facilities: Exceptionally good sanitary arrangements, heated in cool weather, include a special baby room are in main reception building. Hot water on payment in the showers and sinks. Facilities for disabled visitors. Washing machines and dryers. Shop. Restaurant with large terrace is self-service at lunch time and waiter service at night. Table tennis. Watersports. Swimming pools. Good playground. **Off site:** Tennis nearby. Pleasant walk along the lakeside.

Charges 2002

Per person	Sfr. 7.00 - 8.50
child under 6 yrs	free
child (6-11 yrs)	Sfr. 3.50 - 4.50
lakeside pitch	Sfr. 10.00 - 14.00
inland pitch	Sfr. 8.00 - 10.00
car beside pitch	Sfr. 3.00
electricity	Sfr. 3.00
local tax (over 12 yrs)	Sfr. 1.20

Tel: 041 660 18 66. Fax: 041 662 08 66. E-mail: camping.sarnen@bluewin.ch. **Reservations:** Advised for high season and made with Sfr. 30 deposit. **Open** all year.

Directions: Follow signs from southern junction where town road meets the main road from Interlaken.

Camping Eienwäldli

957 Wasserfallstraße 108, CH-6390 Engelberg (Obwalden)

This super site has facilities which must make it one of the best in Switzerland. It is situated in a beautiful location 3,500 feet above sea level and surrounded by mountains on the edge of the delightful village of Engelberg. Being about 35 km. from Luzern by road and with a rail link, it makes a quiet, peaceful base from which to explore the Vierwaldstattersee region, walk in the mountains or just enjoy the scenery. The area is famous as a winter sports region and summer tourist resort and Eienwäldli is open all year. The indoor pool has recently been most imaginatively rebuilt as a Felsenbad spa bath with adventure pool, steam and relaxing grottoes, Kneipp's cure, children's pool with water slides, solarium, Finnish sauna and eucalyptus steam bath. There is an extra charge to use this. Half of the site is taken up by static caravans but these are grouped together at one side. The camping area is in two parts - nearest the entrance there are 57 hardstandings for caravans and motorcaravans, all with electricity and beyond this is a flat meadow for about 70 tents. The reception building, as well as housing the pool complex, has a shop, a café/bar for simple meals, and rooms and apartments to rent. A Gasthof/restaurant is opposite the entrance.

Facilities: The excellent toilet block, heated in cool weather, has free hot water in washbasins (in cabins) and sinks and on payment in the showers. Washing machines and dryers. Shop. Restaurant. Café/bar. Small lounge. Indoor pool complex. Ski facilities. Children's playground. Torches useful. **Off site:** Golf driving range and 9-hole course near. Fishing and bicycle hire 1 km. Riding 2 km.

Charges 2002

Per person	Sfr. 8.00
child (6-15 yrs)	Sfr. 4.00
caravan or tent	Sfr. 8.50 - 12.00
car or motorcycle	Sfr. 2.00
motorcaravan	Sfr. 14.00
electricity (plus meter)	Sfr. 2.00
cable TV	Sfr. 2.50
dog	Sfr. 2.00
local tax	Sfr. 1.90

Credit cards accepted (surcharge). **Tel:** 041 6371949. Fax: 041 637 44 23. E-mail: info@eienwaeldli.ch. **Reservations:** Necessary for summer and winter high seasons. Made with Sfr 50 deposit. **Open** all year.

Directions: From N2 Gotthard motorway, leave at exit 'Stans-Sud' and follow signs to Engelberg. Turn right at T-junction on edge of town and follow signs to 'Wasserfall' and site.

Camping Buchhorn

CH-9320 Arbon (Thurgau)

This small but clean and pleasant site is directly beside Lake Bodensee in the town's parkland. There is access for boats from the campsite, but powered craft must be under a certain h.p. (take advice on this from the management). There are splendid views across this large inland sea and interesting boats ply up and down between Constance and Lindau and the Bregenz. The town swimming lido in the lake, with a restaurant, is quite close. The site is well shaded with pitches for tourists by the water's edge and an overflow field for tents next door. There are a number of static caravans but said to be room for 100 tourists. Pitches are on a mixture of gravel and grass, on flat areas on either side of access roads, most with 6A electricity. A railway line runs directly along one side but one gets used to the noise from passing trains - pitches near the lake should be requested. A single set of buildings provide all the site's amenities. This is a beautiful area and the site is well placed for touring around Lake Bodensee.

Facilities: Toilet facilities are clean and modern, and should just about suffice in high season. Washing machine, dryer and drying area. Fridge. Shop (basic supplies, drinks and snacks - all season). General room. Playground. Gates closed 12-14.00 hrs daily. Dogs are not accepted. **Off site:** Town swimming lido 400 m. Tennis 150 m. Watersports and steamer trips are available on the lake, walks and marked cycle tracks around it, Nature reserve is near.

Charges 2002

Per person	Sfr. 6.75
child (6-16 yrs)	Sfr. 3.10
large tent, caravan or motorcaravan	Sfr. 11.40
small tent	Sfr. 5.70
car	Sfr. 3.10
motorcycle	Sfr. 1.05
electricity	Sfr. 3.10

Tel: 071 446 65 45. Fax: 071 446 48 34.
Reservations: Write to site. **Open** 13 April - 5 October.

Directions: On Arbon-Konstanz road 13, signed 'Strandbad' and 'Strandbad Camping' on leaving Arbon.

Arbon

Camping Buchhorn

One of the finest camping sites on the shores of Lake Constance

- 100 yards of own sandy beach
- idyllic site under old, high trees
- perfect, new sanitary equipment
- shop with Camping-Gaz
- free entrance to the Lido, 200m.
- closed daily 12 to 2 pm

Edi+Lotty Hurter, CH-9320 Arbon   071 446 6545 Fax 071 446 4834

TCS-Camping Leebrücke

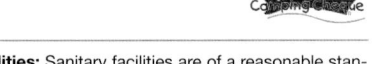

CH-9304 Bernhardzell (St Gallen)

Leebrücke is a long, narrow park in a small wooded valley beside the river Sitter. Permanent units are alongside most of the river, with tourers behind and tents in their own area at the far end. The 70 unmarked touring pitches are fairly flat, grassy or grass and gravel. In a country situation but only a few kilometres from Lake Constance, this could be considered as a quiet alternative to the very busy lakeside sites.

Facilities: Sanitary facilities are of a reasonable standard in the main building, with showers on payment (no cabins). Washing machine and dryer. Shop all season. Small snacks cooked daily. Covered terrace bar. Outdoor table tennis, pool table and table football. River swimming. **Off site:** Restaurant 2 km. Riding 5 km. Golf 10 km.

Charges 2002

Per person	Sfr. 4.80
child (6-15 yrs)	Sfr. 2.40
pitch	Sfr. 12.00 - 13.00
electricity	Sfr. 3.00

Tel: 071 298 49 69. **Reservations:** Contact site.
Open 20 April - 29 September.

Directions: Leave A1/(E60) at St Gallen, take turn towards Wittenbach and follow camp signs. In Wittenbach turn towards Bernhardzell and in 1 km. at bottom of hill, turn right just after passing over the river Sitter. There is a factory on one side of the river, the site is on the other bank.

TCS Camping Rheinwiesen

CH-8246 Langwiesen (Schaffhausen)

916

Rheinwiesen is a friendly site in a very pleasant setting on the banks of the Rhine, with some tall trees, amongst which are some attractive willows. It is level and grassy, the first half quite open and the rest of the touring area wooded, with numbered pitches (mostly small - up to 70 sq.m.), many under tall trees. There are many day visitors in summer as the site is ideally placed for swimming, canoeing and diving in the Rhine. Whilst here, you would not want to miss the impressive waterfalls at Schaffhausen, 150 m. wide and 25 m. high.

Facilities: For tourers, there is an old but clean building which might be under pressure at the busiest times. Washing machine and dryer. Two very deep, large waste collectors. Bar/snack bar with covered terrace open daily. Bread to order, some essentials kept. Pool room also used as wet weather rest room. Two shallow open air paddling pools, with play area close by. Table tennis, table football. Dogs are not accepted. **Off site:** Shop 500 m.

Charges 2002

Per person	Sfr. 4.40 - 6.40
child (6-16yrs)	Sfr. 2.20 - 3.20
caravan	Sfr. 12.00 - 15.00
motorcaravan	Sfr. 12.00 - 17.00
electricity	Sfr. 3.00

Tel: 052 659 3300. Fax: 052 659 3355. E-mail: camping.schaffhausen@tcs.ch. **Reservations:** Contact site **Open** 27 April - 29 September.

Directions: From Schaffhausen head east towards Stein am Rhein/Kreuzlingen for approx. 2.5 km. to Langwiesen where the site is signed. If coming from the east, it is a tight turn into the site.

TCS-Camping Neue Ganda

CH-7302 Landquart (Graubünden)

985

Situated close to the Klosters, Davos road and the nearby town of Landquart, this valley campsite provides a comfortable night-stop near the A13 motorway. The 80 tourist pitches are not marked or separated but are all on level grass off a central tarmac road through the long, narrow wooded site. All pitches have 6A electricity. The many statics are mostly hidden from view in small alcoves. The modern timber clad building at the entrance houses all the necessary facilities - reception, community room and sanitary facilities. The restaurant/shop adjacent is open all year.

Facilities: The toilet block is extremely well appointed and can be heated. Motorcaravan services. Washing machine and dryer. Drying room. Restaurant. Shop. **Off site:** Tennis, riding and canoeing nearby.

Charges 2002

Per adult	Sfr. 4.80 - 6.00
child	Sfr. 2.40 - 3.00
caravan	Sfr. 13.00 - 15.50
motorcaravan	Sfr. 13.00 - 18.00
tent	Sfr. 6.00 - 7.50
electricity	Sfr. 4.00

Tel: 081 322 39 55. E-mail: camping.landquart@tcs.ch. **Reservations:** Contact site. **Open** all year, except 23/3-8/4 and 10-15/12.

Directions: From A13 motorway take Landquart exit and follow road to Davos. After crossing large bridge, site is signed on right.

Camping St Cassian

CH-7083 Lenz/Lantsch (Graubünden)

984

Although St Cassian caters mainly for static holiday caravans, it has room for 40 touring units and is suitable for a night stop travelling to or from St Moritz, or for a longer stay. The site is on a gentle slope but the 40 touring pitches (out of 200) are terraced between the statics under a cover of tall pines. Being 1,415 m. above sea level in a north-south valley, this is a peaceful location surrounded by scenic views and abundant sunshine; 140 signed walking paths of various degrees of difficulty start from the site. Although there is no organised entertainment on the site, there are many opportunities at the holiday resort of Lenzerheide Valbella 3 km. Tennis, an 18-hole golf course, bars and discos, and a heated swimming pool.

Facilities: Small, heated, good quality sanitary facility with free hot water in washing troughs and sinks and on payment in showers. Washing machine and dryer. Dishwasher. Motorcaravan services. Gas supplies. Excellent restaurant. Shop for basics. Torches useful. **Off site:** Golf 500 m. Bicycle hire 1 km. Riding 2 km. Fishing 3 km. Good bus services (with a stop outside the entrance) serve the region.

Charges 2002

Per person	Sfr. 8.00
child (6-16 yrs)	Sfr. 4.50 - 6.00
caravan	Sfr. 9.50
tent	Sfr. 7.00 - 9.50
car	Sfr. 2.50
motorcaravan	Sfr. 12.00
electricity (10A)	Sfr. 3.00

Tel: 081 384 24 72. Fax: 081 384 24 89. E-mail: camping.st.cassian@bluewin.ch. **Reservations:** Made with Sfr. 20 deposit. **Open** all year.

Directions: Site is 20 km. from Chur on no. 3 Chur - St Moritz road, between Lenzerheide and Lantsch/Lenz.

Camping Pradafenz

Pradafenz 106, CH-7075 Churwalden (Graubünden)

982

In the heart of the village of Churwalden on the Chur - St Moritz road, Pradafenz makes a convenient night stop and being amidst the mountains, is also an excellent base for walking and exploring this scenic area. There are 38 ski lifts serving the district with one starting from the site entrance both for winter ski-ing and summer walking. The 'longest toboggan run in the world' is planned to be opened next year. Being at 1,200 m. above sea level and surrounded by pine-clad mountains, the views are breathtaking and the air fresh and clean. The absence of entertainment on site makes this a quiet, peaceful place although a variety of entertainment is offered in the region. At first sight, this appears to be a site for static holiday caravans but three large rectangular terraces at the rear take 50 touring units. This area has a hardstanding of concrete frets with grass growing through and 'super-pitch' facilities of electricity (10A), water, drainage, gas and TV sockets. A flat meadow is also available for tents or as an over-flow for caravans. Although the gravel road which leads to the tourers` terrace is not very steep, the very friendly German speaking owner will tow caravans there with his tractor if required.

Facilities: The main sanitary block is half underground, well appointed and heated. It includes some washbasins in cabins. Baby room and another with hair dryers. Another good, heated small block has been added in the tourist section. Washing machines, dryers and separate drying room. Boot drying room with freezer for ice packs. Motorcaravan services. Gas supplies. Small new restaurant serving good, simple meals and selling basic provisions. General room. Walking. Skiing. Bicycle hire. Torches useful. **Off site:** Restaurants and shops 300 m. in village. Municipal outdoor pool 500 m. Riding 3.5 km. Golf 5 km.

Charges 2003

Per person	Sfr. 6.50
child (up to 12 yrs)	Sfr. 4.40
local tax	Sfr. 0.80 - 1.80
caravan	Sfr. 10.00 - 13.00
tent	Sfr. 5.00 - 10.00
motorcaravan	Sfr. 12.00 - 15.00
car	Sfr. 3.00
dog	Sfr. 3.00
electricity	Sfr. 2.00

Tel: 081 382 19 39. Fax: 081 382 19 21. E-mail: camping@pradafenz.ch. **Reservations:** Advisable for winter; write to site. **Open** 28 May - 31 October and 15 Dec - 22 April.

Directions: Site is 300 m. from the main road, signed in the village centre.

Camping Sur En

CH-7554 Sur En / Sent (Graubünden)

983

Sur-En is at the eastern end of the Engadine valley, about 10 km. from the Italian and Austrian borders. The area is, perhaps, better known as a skiing region, but has summer attractions as well. At nearby Scuol there is an ice-rink and thermal baths, plus a wide range of activities including mountain biking, white water rafting and excursion possibilities. As you approach on road 27 and spot the site way below under the shadow of a steeply rising, wooded mountain, the drop down may appear daunting. However, as you drive it becomes reasonable, although the site owner will provide assistance for nervous towers. A level site, it is in an open valley with little shade. They say there is room for 120 touring units on the meadows where pitches are neither marked nor numbered; there are electricity connections for all (6A). The friendly, English speaking owner seems to have created a very pleasant atmosphere and although the site might be used for a night stay during transit, it could well attract for a longer period.

Facilities: The modern, heated sanitary block is of a high standard and there is a further small provision in the main building when required. Washing machine and dryer. Motorcaravan services. Shop and good restaurant (15/12-15/4 and 1/5-31/10) with covered terrace overlooking the children's play area so that adults can enjoy a drink and keep watch on their children whilst enjoying the mountain views. Takeaway (high season). Swimming pool (1/6-15/10). Bicycle hire. Fishing. Entertainment for adults and children is arranged in July/Aug. and a symposium for sculptors is held during the second week in July. Excursions are arranged in high season. Bus service to Scuol for train to St Moritz. **Off site:** Golf 8 km.

Charges 2002

Per person	Sfr. 5.80
child (6-16 yrs)	Sfr. 2.90
caravan	Sfr. 13.40 - 15.00
tent	Sfr. 9.90
motorcaravan	Sfr. 15.00
electricity	Sfr. 2.80
local tax	Sfr. 2.90

Tel: 081 866 35 44. Fax: 081 866 32 37. E-mail: w.bosshardt@bluewin.ch. **Reservations:** Not made. **Open** all year.

Directions: Site is clearly visible and also signed from main road 27 to the east of Scuol.

Camping Plauns

Morteratsch, CH-7504 Pontresina (Graubünden)

986

This is a mountain site in splendid scenery near St Moritz. Pontrasina is at the mouth of the Bernina Pass road (B29) which runs from Celerina in the Swiss Engadine to Titana in Italy. Camping Plauns, some 4 km. southeast of Pontresina, is situated in the floor of the valley between fir-clad mountains at 1,850 m. above sea level. A river runs through this long, narrow site with lovely views on each side with a small lake at one end. There are about 250 pitches for tourists in summer, all with electricity, some in small clearings amongst tall trees and some in a larger open space. During the winter the number is reduced to 40. They are neither numbered nor marked and size depends on the natural space between the trees. Being in a mountain valley, the grass is thin over a stony base with tarmac roads running through. This is a quiet site in a peaceful location and could make a useful night stop when travelling through or a base for exploring the region which is good walking country.

Facilities: Three fully equipped sanitary blocks, one old and two new, modern and excellent, and can be heated in cool weather. Some washbasins in private cabins and showers on payment. Facilities for disabled visitors. Washing machines and dryers. Small well stocked shop. Grill-snack bar for drinks or simple meals. Children's playground. Torch useful. **Off site:** Restaurant 1 km. Entertainment programme offered, winter and summer, at nearby Pontresina.

Charges 2002

Per person	Sfr. 8.50
child (6-11 yrs)	Sfr. 4.00
child (12-15 yrs)	Sfr. 5.50
caravan or motorcaravan	Sfr. 14.00 - 15.00
tent	Sfr. 9.00 - 11.00
electricity	Sfr. 3.50 - 4.50
local tax	Sfr. 1.00

Tel: 081 842 62 85. Fax: 081 834 51 36. E-mail: a.brueli@bluewin.ch. **Reservations:** Made with Sfr. 20 deposit. **Open** 1 June - 15 October and 15 December - 15 April.

Directions: Site is on B29 road about 5 km. southeast of Pontresina - well signed.

Camping Silvaplana

CH-7513 Silvaplana (Graubünden)

980

Silvaplana is situated at the junction of the road from Italy over the Malojapass, the road from northern Switzerland via the Julierpass, and the road which continues through St Moritz to Austria. Camping Silvaplana, therefore, might be useful for a night stop if travelling this way. Although the surrounding scenery across the lake is very pleasant, there is nothing remarkable about the site except that a wind blows along the lake most afternoons which is used by windsurfing enthusiasts. However, it is probably the best campsite in the area, with good walking and climbing possibilities. The site is mainly level and the 160 pitches for tourists are numbered and marked by posts or tapes, with 120 electrical connections (10A). A fenced river runs through but the lake shore is unprotected (with access for boats to the lake).

Facilities: The toilet block is old, but acceptable and heated, including hot water in washing troughs, sinks and showers. No washing machines but staff provide a laundry service. Motorcaravan services. Gas supplies. Shop for basics (15/5-15/9). Small play area. **Off site:** Restaurant outside site open all day (June-Oct). Facilities next to the site for volleyball or football and a windsurfing school. Tennis near. Lake swimming (pool 4 km. in St Moritz). Bicycle hire 200 m. Riding 5 km. Golf 10 km.

Charges 2002

Per person	Sfr. 9.70
child 5-12 yrs	Sfr. 4.50
child (12-16 yrs)	Sfr. 7.30
caravan	Sfr. 7.00
tent	Sfr. 5.00 - 7.00
car	Sfr. 8.00
motorcycle	Sfr. 3.00
motorcaravan	Sfr. 12.00
electricity	Sfr. 3.50

Tel: 081 828 84 92. **Reservations:** Write to site. **Open** 15 May - 15 October.

Directions: If coming from the Julier Pass continue through Silvaplana to junction with road to St Moritz, turn right and look for camp signs on your right. From St Moritz, continue along lakeside passing the village - camp signs are on your right.

Camping Rive-Bleue

960 Bouveret Plage, CH-1897 Bouveret (Valais)

At the eastern end of Lac Léman, the main feature of this site is the very pleasant lakeside lido only a short walk of 300 m. from the site and with free entry for campers. It has a new 'Aquaparc' pool with a water toboggan and plenty of grassy lying-out areas, a bathing area in lake, boating facilities with storage for sailboards, canoes, inflatables etc, sailing school, pedaloes for hire. Also here and, like the lido, under same ownership as the campsite, is a quality hotel which at the rear has a café for food and drinks with access from the lido. The site itself has 200 marked pitches on well kept flat grass, half in the centre with 6A electricity, the other half round the perimeter.

Facilities: Two decent toilet blocks have washbasins with cold water in the old block, hot in the new, and pre-set free hot showers. Shop, restaurant by beach (both all season). Bicycle hire. Fishing. Covered area for cooking with electric rings and barbecue. Drying room. Motorcaravan services (Euro-relais; Sfr. 12).

Charges 2003

Per person	Sfr. 7.40 - 9.10
child (6-16 yrs)	Sfr. 5.20 - 6.20
car	Sfr. 1.80
tent	Sfr. 6.40 - 10.10
caravan	Sfr. 8.10 - 11.20
motorcaravan	Sfr. 9.90 - 13.00
dog	Sfr. 2.00
electricity	Sfr. 3.20
local tax	Sfr. 0.80

Tel: 024 481 21 61. Fax: 024 481 21 08. E-mail: info@camping-rive-bleue.ch. **Reservations:** Are advised and made for any length with Sfr. 20 non-refundable reservation fee. **Open** 1 April - 30 September.

Directions: Approach site on Martigny-Evian road no. 21 and turn to Bouveret-Plage south of Le Bouveret.

RIVE-BLEUE, BOUVERET PLAGE   Lake Geneva

Tel: (information) 024/482 42 42
(reservation) 024/481 21 61
Fax: 024/482 42 40

1st category international tourist site Natural beach, heated swimming pool, tennis, sailboarding, shop and restaurant. Modern toilet blocks with free hot water.

AQUAPARK (100 m.)

TCS-Camping Les Iles

971 CH-1951 Sion (Valais)

Sion is an ancient and interesting town on the main route from Martigny to Brig and the Simplon Pass into Italy. Les Iles is an excellent, well organised and pretty site, useful for a night stop when passing through or for a longer stay to explore the region or relax in a pleasant area. Although it is near a small airport, it is understood that no planes fly at night. The rectangular site has 440 level pitches for tourists, 340 with 4A electricity and 22 serviced with water and waste water also. Well laid out, a profusion of flowers, shrubs and trees lead to a lake which supplements the pool for swimming and may be used by inflatable boats. A wealth of sporting activities nearby includes watersports, mountain biking, para-gliding, etc. Good English is spoken and the warden is pleased to give advice on places to visit.

Facilities: Six good sanitary blocks spaced around the site include baby rooms and provision for disabled people. Washing machines and dryers. Motorcaravan services. Well stocked shop. Popular restaurant (both open all year). Swimming pool (12 x 10 m. mid May - mid Sept). Two play areas. Football field. Table tennis. Good animation programme for both children and adults in July/Aug. and organised excursions (extra cost). Bicycle hire. **Off site:** Tennis 100 m. Golf and horse riding 6 km. Town 4 km.

Charges 2002

Per person	Sfr. 6.00 - 8.00
child	3.00 Sfr. 4.00
caravan	Sfr. 13.00 - 23.00
tent	Sfr. 6.00 - 9.00
motorcaravan	Sfr. 13.00 - 23.00
electricity	Sfr. 3.00
local tax	Sfr. 1.80

Tel: 027 346 43 47. Fax: 027 346 68 47. E-mail: camping.sion@tcs.ch. **Reservations:** Write to site. **Open** all year except 4 Nov - 15 Dec.

Directions: Site is about 4 km. west of Sion and is signed from road 9 and the motorway exit.

Camping Des Glaciers

966 CH-1944 La Fouly (Valais)

Situated at 1,600 m. above sea level, Des Glaciers is set amidst magnificent mountain scenery in a very quiet, peaceful location in the beautiful Ferret Valley. Being just off the main Martigny - Grand St Bernard route, it could make a night stop when travelling along this road but as this would entail a 13 km. detour along a minor road, it is more convenient for a longer stay. Those seeking peace, quiet and fresh mountain air or an opportunity for mountain walking would be well suited here. Marked tracks bring Grand St Bernard and the path around Mont Blanc within range, among many other possibilities with an abundance of flora and fauna for added interest. The site offers two types of pitches, about half in an open, undulating meadow with campers choosing where to go, the rest being level, individual plots of varying size in small clearings either between bushes and shrubs or under tall pines. A small stream runs through the site. Of the 170 places, 150 have 15A electricity so a small heater can be used if evenings become chilly. There are sports facilities and swimming pools at 18 and 25 km. but this is, above all, a campsite for those who wish to enjoy the mountain atmosphere, get close to nature or walk in the mountains where there are also refreshment stops at mountain huts. The charming lady owner, fluent in six languages, is always ready not only to welcome you to this peaceful haven but also to give information on the locality.

Facilities: Three sanitary units, all of exceptional quality and heated when necessary. The smallest is under reception, there is another in the centre of the open area and a block in the centre of the site. Hot water is free in all washbasins (some in cabins), showers and sinks. Washing machines and dryers in each block, one block has a drying room, another a baby room. Gas supplies. Motorcaravan services. Small shop. Recreation room with TV. Playground. Torches may be useful. **Off site:** Shop and restaurant 500 m. Bicycle hire 500 m. Riding 8 km.

Charges 2003

Per person	Sfr. 6.50
child (2-12 yrs)	Sfr. 3.50
baby	Sfr. 2.00
pitch	Sfr. 10.00 - 16.00
electricity	Sfr. 3.50
dog	Sfr. 1.50

Less 10% in June and Sept. **Tel:** 027 783 17 35. Fax: 027 783 36 05. E-mail: camping.glaciers@st-bernard.ch. **Reservations:** Made without deposit; write to site. **Open** 15 May - 30 September.

Directions: Leave Martigny-Gd St Bernard road (no. 21) at Orsieres and follow signs to La Fouly. Site is signed on right at end of La Fouly village.

Camping Gemmi

973 Briannenstrasse 4, CH-3952 Susten-Leuk (Valais)

The Rhône Valley is a popular through route to Italy via the Simplon Pass and a holiday region in its own right. Enjoying some of the best climatic conditions in Switzerland, this valley, between two mountain regions, has less rainfall and more hours of sunshine than most of the country. It is an area of vines and fruit trees with mountain walks and the majestic Matterhorn nearby. Gemmi is a delightful small, friendly site in a scenic location with 71 level pitches, all with 16A electricity, on well tended grass amidst a variety of trees, some of which offer shade. There are some pitches for motorcaravans with water and drainage. The pleasant, friendly owner speaks fluent English, maintains high standards and has bucked current trends by establishing a campsite for tourists with no resident static units.

Facilities: A modern, central sanitary block, part of which is heated, is of excellent quality and kept very clean. It includes some washbasins in cabins. Private bathrooms for hire on weekly basis. Washing machines and dryers. Motorcaravan services. Gas supplies. Well stocked shop. Small bar/restaurant where snacks and limited range of local specialities served. Terrace bar and snack restaurant. Playground. Tennis, swimming and walking near. **Off site:** Riding 2 km. Fishing 6 km. Golf 1 km.

Charges 2003

Per adult	Sfr. 6.50 - 7.50
child (1-16 yrs)	Sfr. 3.50 - 5.50
pitch	Sfr. 11.00 - 15.00
pitch with drainage	Sfr. 15.00 - 19.00
electricity	Sfr. 3.00
local tax (under 16 half price)	Sfr. 0.80

Tel: 027 473 11 54. Fax: 027 473 42 95. E-mail: info@campgemmi.ch. **Reservations:** Necessary for high season. **Open** 17 April - 11 October.

Directions: From east (Visp), turn left 1 km. after sign for Agarn Feithieren. From west (Sierre), turn right 2 km. after Susten by Hotel Relais Bayard, then after 300 m. right at sign for Camping Torrent.

Camping de Molignon

CH-1984 Les Haudères (Valais)

967

The uphill drive from Sion in the Rhône Valley is enhanced by the Pyramids of Euseigne, through which the road passes via a short tunnel. These unusual structures, cut out by erosion from masses of morainic debris, have been saved from destruction by their unstable rocky crowns. De Molignon, surrounded by mountains, is a quiet, peaceful place 1,450 m above sea level; although there may be some road noise, the rushing stream and the sound of cow bells are likely to be the only disturbing factor in summer. The 100 pitches for tourists are on well tended, level terraces leading down to the river. Some 72 have electricity (10A) and are marked by numbered posts. Although this is essentially a place for mountain walking (guided tours available), climbing and relaxing, there is a geological museum in Les Haudères, which has links with a British University, cheese making and interesting flora and fauna. Good English is spoken by the owner's son who is now running the site, who will be pleased to give information on all that is available from the site.

Facilities: Two fully equipped sanitary blocks, heated in cool weather, now include free hot showers. Baby room. Washing machines and dryer. Motorcaravan services. Gas supplies. Small shop for basic supplies (1/7-10/9). Restaurant good menu at reasonable prices (all year). Heated swimming pool (6 x 12 m). Playground. Guided walks, climbing, geological museum, winter skiing. Fishing. **Off site:** Tennis and hang-gliding near. Bicycle hire 3 km. Riding 15 km. Skiing and langlauf in winter.

Charges 2003

Per person	Sfr. 6.00
child (4-16 yrs)	Sfr. 3.20
pitch	Sfr. 8.00 - 15.00
dog	Sfr. 3.00
electricity	Sfr. 3.00
local tax	Sfr. 0.40 - 0.80

Less 10% in low season. **Tel:** 027 283 12 40. Fax: 027 283 13 31. E-mail: molignon@swisscamps.ch. **Reservations:** Contact site. **Open** all year.

Directions: Follow signs southwards from Sion for the Val d'Herens through Evolène to Les Haudères where site is signed on the right (3 km).

Camping Santa Monica

CH-3942 Raron (Valais)

977

We offer several different styles of campsite in the Rhône Valley and now add this pleasant, well tended site which stays open all year. The Simplon Pass is the only main route from Switzerland to Italy which avoids motorways and the need to buy the Swiss motorway vignette. It is also an easy pass for caravans which is only closed occasionally in winter and, even then, this way is possible by using the Brig-Iselle train ferry through the mountain. About half the site is occupied by static caravans and the site's own accommodation, but these are to one side leaving two flat, open meadows, bisected by the hard access road, so do not intrude on the tourist camping area. The 200 level pitches (100 for touring units) all have electricity (16A) and are roughly defined by saplings and the connection boxes. There is a small (12 x 4 m) pool and a shop/bar/snack bar (open in high season) in the reception building. Being right beside the main road 9 (some road noise), one does not have to deviate to find a night stop but it would also make a good base for exploring the area. With mountain views, close on south side, distant across the valley. it has an air of peace. Two cable ways start near the site entrance for winter skiers and summer mountain walkers.

Facilities: The single, heated sanitary block is towards the entrance, has free hot water in washbasins and sinks and on payment in the showers. Facilities for disabled visitors. Motorcaravan services (Euro-Relais). Gas supplies. Bar, restaurant and shop (1/6-15/10). Small pool and child's pool (15/6-31/8). Children's playground and play house. Table tennis. Bicycle hire. Ski room. Walking country, cable cars near. **Off site:** Shops and restaurants near. Tennis courts next door to site. Riding 10 km.

Charges 2003

Per person	Sfr. 5.00 - 6.00
child (6-16 yrs)	Sfr. 3.00 - 4.00
pitch	Sfr. 9.50 - 12.00
electricity	Sfr. 3.00 - 5.00
local tax	Sfr. 0.35 - 0.70
dog	Sfr. 3.00

Special offers in low season. **Tel:** 027 934 24 24. Fax: 027 934 24 50. E-mail: santamonica@rhone.ch. **Reservations:** Write to site. **Open** all year.

Directions: On the south side of road 9 between Visp and Susten, signed.

Camping Swiss-Plage

969 CH-3960 Sierre-Salgesch (Valais)

This is a good site and is well run by its English speaking owner and, although about half is occupied by static caravans, there are still 250 pitches for visiting tourists. The site is also slightly unusual in that much of the terrain has been deliberately left in its natural state. The wooded section gives good shade and tree formations and access roads determine where units go. There is a central open meadow and some quiet spots are a little further from the amenities. Most pitches, although unmarked, have 10A electric points available. One part of the site may be reserved but some space is usually available. The centre of the site has a natural lake which is kept dredged and clean and is suitable for small boats (not windsurfers) and for bathing - the site say the water is tested weekly. It is possible to stroll along the banks of the Rhône and good walks are nearby.

Facilities: In the centre of the site, the main sanitary block is of a high standard and heated in cool weather. Although the two other blocks are showing signs of age, the total provision should be sufficient. Free hot water in washbasins in the new block, cold in some of the others, and hot showers on payment. Washing machine and dryer. Motorcaravan services. Shop. Bar/restaurant and snack bar with grills and pizzas. Takeaway. Lake. Paddling pool. Playground. Table tennis. Fishing (on payment). Volleyball. Badminton. Some entertainment in high season.

Charges 2003

Per person	Sfr. 6.60
child (4-16 yrs)	Sfr. 3.30
pitch	Sfr. 15.00
electricity	Sfr. 2.50
local tax	Sfr. 0.30 - 0.60

Less 10% in low season. No credit cards. **Tel:** 027 455 66 08. Fax: 027 481 32 15. E-mail: info@swiss-plage.ch. **Reservations:** Necessary and made for any length with deposit. **Open** 7 April - 1 November.

Directions: From either direction on road no. 9 or more recent bypasses, follow signs for Salgesch which should bring you past site entrance 3 km. northeast of Sierre. Care is required to spot the first sign in Sierre at a multi-road junction; site is well signed from here.

Camping «SWISS PLAGE» **** SALGESCH

The only camp in the Valais region with its own bathing lake (entry free for campers), temperature around 18°C. Partly sunny, partly shaded pitches. Well maintained sanitary facilities. Restaurant, self-service shop. Starting point for innumerable excursions: Zermatt (Matterhorn), Saas-Fee, Aletsch glacier, Leukerbad. Attractive hiking possibilities in the nearby Pfynwald nature reserve, into Val d Anniviers and alongside the «Suolen» (water supply canals) etc.

Camping «Swiss Plage», Sierre-Salgesch
Tel. 0041-27-455 66 08, Fax 0041-27-481 32 15

Camping Bella-Tola

972 Waldstrasse 57, CH-3952 Susten (Valais)

An attractive site with good standards, Bella-Tola is on the hillside above Susten (east of Sierre) with good views over the Rhône valley. It boasts a good sized heated swimming pool and children's pool (both free to campers) which, like the restaurant and bar overlooking them, are also open to non-campers and so more crowded at weekends and holidays. In the low rain climate of the Valais the pool is naturally much used. Extensive terracing has been carried out and most of the pitches are now terraced and flat. Some 200 of the 260 individually numbered pitches have electricity connections. The fullest season is 10/7-10/8, but they say that there is usually room somewhere. Used by tour operators (20%). Guests are requested to comply with environmental rules by sorting rubbish as directed.

Facilities: Three good quality modern sanitary blocks should be quite sufficient, with some washbasins in cabins. Free hot water in showers and sinks for clothes and dishes, plus baby rooms. New facilities for disabled visitors. Washing machines, dryers and irons. Motorcaravan services. Shop. Restaurant/bar (1/5-30/9). Takeaway (1/7-31/8). Swimming pool (1/5-15/9). General room with TV. Films and guided walks in July/Aug. Torches advised. **Off site:** Riding and tennis near. Golf.

Charges 2003

Per person	Sfr. 9.80
child (2-6 yrs)	Sfr. 4.80
child (6-16 yrs)	Sfr. 6.80
pitch acc. to type and season	Sfr. 5.00 - 26.00
electricity	Sfr. 3.60
dog (max 1)	Sfr. 2.80
local tax	Sfr. 0.35 - 0.70

Less 25% on person/pitch fees outside July/Aug. **Tel:** 027 473 14 91. Fax: 027 473 36 41. E-mail: info@bella-tola.ch. **Reservations:** Will be made with deposit and fee. **Open** 10 May - 28 September.

Directions: Turn south from main road at Susten where site is well signed.

TCS-Camping Bois de Finges

968 CH-3960 Sierre (Valais)

The site is situated in the middle of the 'Bois des Finges' pine forest on a rocky wooded hillside. It is an attractive site, well maintained with much to offer for the naturalist. It lies in a protected area of changing forest and heathland with many walking and hiking possibilities. With 100 pitches cut out of the hillside, some are difficult to access but the manager will help. They can take units of up to 7 metres but mainly smaller units and tents in some parts. All pitches are well screened by trees and some 60 have 4A electricity connections (long leads are useful). Staff are welcoming and helpful but little English is spoken. Reception houses a café and a shop at the entrance but the toilet blocks are at the extreme ends of the site so a good walk for some.

Facilities: Two very clean and well maintained wooden toilet blocks are fully equipped. Freezer, washing machine and dryer. Motorcaravan service point. Well stocked but limited shop and snack bar. Outdoor heated pool (6 x12 m) and paddling pool. Well appointed play area. Tennis. Table tennis. Fishing (licence required). Barbecues are not permitted. Torches are useful. **Off site:** Town of Sierre 1 km. Walking and hiking area.

Charges guide

Per adult	Sfr. 4.80 - 5.80
child	Sfr. 2.40 - 2.90
pitch	Sfr. 10.00 - 16.00
electricity	Sfr. 3.00
dog	Sfr. 3.00 - 4.00
local tax	Sfr. 0.60

Tel: 027 455 02 84. Fax: 027 455 33 51.
Reservations: Contact site. Open 12 April - 30 September.

Directions: Leave motorway at Sierre East. Site is signed on the right within 200 m.

TCS Camping Parco al Sole

997 6866 Meride (Ticino)

Meride is a small village in the extreme south of Switzerland with the Italian border close on three sides. A little remote, Parco al Sole is on a slight slope 1 km. before the village, with a steep mountain face. Apart from a little traffic noise from the road running past, it is a peaceful place. Parco al Sole is better for a few days stay to explore the area rather than as a single night stop. There is space for 64 small units, with electricity. Pitches are not marked out and caravans are placed between tall trees or on an open space. Cars are parked near the entrance.

Facilities: A good quality sanitary block with the usual facilities, free hot water and a baby room is halfway up the site. Cafe with log fire during cool weather for drinks and simple meals. Limited basic food supplies. Heated swimming pool (12 x 6 m). Playground. TV (in cafe). Table tennis.

Charges 2002

Per person	Sfr. 5.60 - 7.40
pitch	Sfr. 6.50 - 16.00
electricity	Sfr. 3.00

Tel: 091 6464330. Fax: 091 6460992. E-mail: camping.meride@tcs.ch. **Reservations:** Write to site.
Open 12 April - 14 October.

Directions: From N2 motorway take exit for Mendrisio (near Chiasso). Head to Rancate then Basazio, Arzo and Meride. Site is 6 km. from the motorway exit. The bridge in the last few yards has an awkward angle.

Camping Al Censo

993 CH-3702 Claro (Ticino)

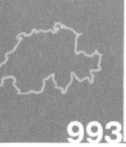

Now that most traffic uses the N2 motorway, the B2 Gotthard - Bellinzona one is used mainly by local vehicles and is, therefore, much quieter. Al Censo is a very pretty site with an abundance of flowers and shrubs and backed by a mountain face. Although the site is on a slope and levellers may be needed in places, the 90 tourist pitches, 52 of which have electricity (6A), are level and amongst mature trees with an overflow section just outside the entrance for tents. This is a useful site for a peaceful night away from the motorway - it may tempt for a longer stay from which to explore the Ticino. The friendly, live on site and will help with local attractions.

Facilities: Two small sanitary blocks, one enlarged to a good standard include warm pre-mixed water dispensed through a single tap and a baby room Washing machines and dryers. Self-service shop (limited), drinks served. Swimming pool (18 x 9 m), sauna and whirlpool (high season). Games room. Table tennis. No entry to site 12.00 - 14.00 hrs.

Charges 2003

Per person	Sfr. 7.00
child (1-12 yrs)	Sfr. 5.20
pitch	Sfr. 9.00 - 18.00
electricity	Sfr. 3.50
local tax	Sfr. 2.20

Tel: 091 863 17 53. Fax: 091 863 40 22.
Reservations: Made without charge. **Open** 1 April - mid-October.

Directions: Site well signed at northern end of Claro on old St Gotthard-Bellinzona road. From motorway going south, leave at Biasco exit, go into village and then south on B2. Heading north, take Bellinzona-Nord exit and go north on old pass road.

Camping Campofelice

CH-6598 Tenero (Ticino)

989

The largest site in Switzerland and, now that three of the toilet blocks have been rebuilt and the other three renewed, Campofelice must rank among the best. It is bordered on the front by Lake Maggiore and on one side by the Verzasca estuary, where the site has its own harbour. The beach by the lake is sandy, long and wider than the usual lakeside ones. It shelves gently so that bathing is safe for children. Campofelice is divided into rows, with 1,030 individual pitches of average size on flat grass on either side of hard access roads. Mostly well shaded, all pitches have electricity connections (10A) and some also have water, drainage and TV connections. Pitches near the lake cost more (these are not available for motorcaravans) and a special area is reserved for small tents. Sporting facilities are good and there are cycle paths in the area, including into Locarno. English is spoken at this good, if rather expensive site.

Facilities: The six heated toilet blocks are of excellent quality. Washing machines and dryers. Motorcaravan services. Gas supplies. Supermarket. Restaurant. Tennis. Minigolf. Bicycle hire. Playground. Doctor calls. Dogs are not accepted. **Off site:** Facilities nearby for waterskiing (6 km), windsurfing (1 km) and boat hire (5 km).

Charges 2003

Per unit incl. 2 persons	Sfr. 51.00 - 81.00
low season	Sfr. 36.00 - 57.00
extra person	Sfr. 7.00 - 11.00
child (under 2 yrs)	free

Electricity and taxes included. Some pitches have min. stay regulations. **Tel:** 091 745 1417. Fax: 091 745 1888. E-mail: camping@campofelice.ch. **Reservations:** Not made but there is usually space. **Open** 4 April - 25 October.

Directions: Site is very well signed on Bellinzona side of lakeside road no. 13 from Locarno.

Camping Lido Mappo

CH-6598 Tenero (Ticino)

988

Lido Mappo lies on the lakeside at the northeast tip of Lake Maggiore, about 5 km. from Locarno, and has views of the surrounding mountains and hills across the lake. A wide variety of trips can be made from here by car, lake steamer or mountain lift. The site has its own narrow beach with a frontage of some 400 m., mainly sandy, but the lake, shelving very gradually, has a stony floor. Boats can be brought and left on the shore or at moorings; a jetty has been constructed for these. The site is attractively laid out in rows of individual, numbered pitches, half for tents and half for caravans and mostly split up by access roads or hedges. The pitches (421 for touring) vary in size, those by the lake costing more and most are well shaded. Electricity (10A) is available on all pitches. Although reservations are only made for longer stays, there is always a fair chance of finding a vacant place. With helpful staff who speak good English, it is a quiet site.

Facilities: The five toilet blocks can be heated in cool weather and are always well kept, although some are newer than others. They have been improved with more individual washbasins, all in cabins for women and some for men. Facilities for disabled people. Baby room. Washing machines and dryers. Cooking facilities. Refrigerated compartments for hire. Motorcaravan services. Supermarket. Restaurant/bar. Takeaway (high season). Large playground. Bathing raft in lake. Fishing. First-aid post. Dogs are not accepted. **Off site:** Bicycle hire near. Riding 3 km. Golf 5 km.

Charges 2003

Per unit incl. 2 persons	Sfr. 33.00 - 51.00
extra person	Sfr. 6.00 - 7.00

Less 5% for stays over 10 days. **Tel:** 091 745 14 37. Fax: 091 745 48 08. E-mail: lidomappo@bluewin.ch. **Reservations:** Min. 1 week (2 weeks lakeside) July/August, or 2 weeks at other times. Large deposit and smaller fee. **Open** 4 April - 19 October, as are all amenities.

Directions: On Locarno side of Tenero, on Bellinzona - Locarno road, site signed to the south.

Camping Piccolo Paradiso

CH-6670 Avegno (Ticino)

987

Locarno, in the most southern of Swiss cantons, Ticino, is a popular holiday area with activities associated with lakes and mountains. Being on the south of Locarno, Avegno is also a good base from which to visit Lake Maggiore and this part of northern Italy. There are a number of very good sites to which we add this one. We were impressed with the friendly, happy atmosphere engendered by the owner who appears to know visitors who return year after year and greets them enthusiastically. The lively social life revolves around the central bar/restaurant and terrace (all noise has to cease at 11 pm). The 300 tourist pitches are on two level terraces in a river valley, marked by numbered stones set into the ground. Spaces are not over-large but seem to suffice.

Facilities: Three well placed sanitary blocks well spaced around the site should suffice. Hot showers on payment. Washing machines and dryers. Motorcaravan services. Self-service bar/restaurant (mainly Italian type fast food) with terrace. Shade in parts. Children's pool. Two children's play areas. River bathing (summer). Boating. Table tennis. Volleyball. Mountain bike hire. Entertainment in high season.

Charges 2002

Per person	Sfr. 7.00 - 8.00
child (4 -14 yrs)	Sfr. 5.00 - 6.00
caravan, motorcaravan or large tent	Sfr. 12.00 - 18.00
medium tent	Sfr. 11.00 - 15.00
electricity (10A)	Sfr. 4.00
dog	Sfr. 3.00

Tel: 091 796 15 81. Fax: 091 796 31 70.
Reservations: Write to site with Sfr. 50 deposit.
Open 1 March - 31 October.

Directions: From Locarno follow signs for Valle Maggia and then camp signs to site (6 km).

Camping Delta

Via G. Respini 7, CH-6600 Locarno (Ticino)

990

Camping Delta is actually within the Locarno town limits, only some 800 m. from the centre, and it has a prime position right by the lake, with bathing direct from the site, and adjacent to the municipal lido and sports field. Boats can be put on the lake and the site also has some moorings on an estuary at one side, with a jetty. It has 300 pitches on flat ground of 80-100 sq.m. of which 250 are available for touring units. They are marked out at the rear but have nothing between them. Delta is a well run and well situated site and Locarno is host to an International Film Festival, classical and jazz concerts and exhibitions.

Facilities: The single central toilet block is kept very clean and should be about large enough except perhaps at the busiest times. Hot water is free in the washbasins (some cabins for women), showers and sinks. Washing machine and dryer. Motorcaravan services. Small supermarket. Restaurant/bar with limited menu. Fitness room. Playgrounds. Table tennis and amusements. Entertainment and excursions. Fishing. Bicycle hire. Dogs are not accepted. **Off site:** Golf 200 m. Riding 4 km.

Charges 2003

Per person	Sfr. 11.00 - 18.00
child (3-15 yrs)	Sfr. 6.00
pitch acc. to type and season	Sfr. 21.00 - 57.00
electricity	Sfr. 5.00

Tel: 091 751 60 81. Fax: 091 751 22 43. E-mail: info@campingdelta.com. **Reservations:** Made for any length with deposit (Sfr. 50) and booking fee (50). **Open** 1 March - 31 October.

Directions: From central Locarno follow signs to Camping Delta, Lido or Stadio along the lake. Approaching from south there are also Delta signs which lead Albergo Delta in quite the wrong place.

Camping Riarena

CH-6516 Cugnasco (Ticino)

991

An agreeable site close to the route from the St Gotthard to the south, Riarena may appeal both to those who are looking for a convenient night stop and to those seeking a holiday site, as it has a medium sized swimming pool and children's pool. Most of the site is covered by tall trees and it is in a peaceful setting, far enough from the main road to be away from noise. The 210 pitches (150 for touring units) are now all individually marked with 10A electrical connections available. July is busiest; there is usually space at other times

Facilities: A fully equipped, good quality sanitary block includes a few washbasins in private cabins. Facilities for disabled visitors. Washing machines and dryers. Shop. Restaurant. Takeaway. Play area. Swimming pools (25/5-15/9). Mountain bike hire. **Off site:** Fishing 1 km. Riding 2 km.

Charges 2003

Per unit incl. 2 adults and tax	Sfr. 27.00 - 38.00
child (3-14 yrs)	Sfr. 3.00 - 5.00
electricity	Sfr. 3.50

Tel: 091 859 16 88. Fax: 091 859 28 85.
Reservations: Made without charge. **Open** 1 March - 25 October.

Directions: From motorway exit Bellinzona south in the direction of Locarno. After 10 km. at large roundabout turn to Gudo-Bellinzona for 2.5 km. and follow signs for Cugnasco from where site signed.

TCS-Camping Piodella

CH-6933 Muzzano (Ticino)

This modernised site, on the edge of Lake Lugano facing south down the lake must rank as one of the best in Switzerland. There are 265 numbered pitches (212 for touring units) of good size, with electricity connections in all areas (4/6A). There is shade in the older part nearest the lake and young trees in the new area. Cars must be parked in the car park, not by your pitch. Roads have been relaid and a marina has been built. A good, large swimming pool and a child's pool have been added and one can also bathe from the sandy beach. The site is a short way from the end of Lugano's airport but there appears to be no night flying or movements by large aircraft. Although the site is well placed for exploring Lugano, southern Switzerland and northern Italy, many will be content to stay put and enjoy the facilities of the site.

Facilities: In addition to the original refurbished sanitary block, a splendid new one has been added which includes a baby room, and bathroom for disabled visitors. Facilities are heated in cool weather. Washing machines and dryers. Motorcaravan services. Gas supplies. Shop. Bar/restaurant with pleasant terrace. Swimming pools (May - mid Oct). Day and TV rooms. Children's playground. Two tennis courts. Marina.

Charges 2002

Per person	Sfr. 6.40 - 8.40
child (6-16 yrs)	Sfr. 3.20 - 4.20
pitch	Sfr. 16.00 - 34.00
motorcaravan	Sfr. 21.00 - 29.00
electricity	Sfr. 3.00 - 4.00
local tax	Sfr. 1.25

Tel: 091 994 77 88. Fax: 091 994 67 08. E-mail: camping.muzzano@tcs.ch. **Reservations:** Write to site. **Open** all year except 31 Oct - 12 Dec.

Directions: Piodella is on Bellinzona-Ponte Tresa road; take motorway exit Lugano-Nord for Ponte Tresa and turn left at T-junction in Agno. Follow signs for Piodella or TCS. Site is at south end of the airport.

Liechtenstein

Liechtenstein is an independent principality, bounded on the north by Switzerland and Austria, and on the south and west by Switzerland. One of the smallest independent states in the world, it has a total area of 157 sq. km. (61 sq. miles). The climate is Alpine with mild winters; average temperatures range from -1.1° C (30° F) in January to 21.1° C (70° F) in July. Liechtenstein has a population of 29,868, of whom about one-third are resident aliens, with an overall density of about 190 people per sq.km. Native-born Liechtensteiners are descended from the Germanic Alamanni people and most still speak an Alamanni dialect of the official language, German. The country's close ties with Switzerland are also important; the Swiss franc is the official currency of Liechtenstein and the two states have operated a customs union since 1924. Liechtenstein is a constitutional monarchy governed by hereditary princes.

Camping Mittagsspitze

FL-9495 Triesen

Camping Mittagsspitze is attractively and quietly situated for visiting the Principality. Probably the best site in the region, it is on a hillside and has all the scenic views that one could wish. Extensive broad, level terraces on the steep slope provide unmarked pitches (a reader tells us that spacing causes problems in high season). There is little shade. Electrical connections (6A) are available. Of the 240 spaces, 120 are used by seasonal caravans. Liechtenstein's capital, Vaduz, is 7 km. Austria 20 km. and Switzerland 3 km.

Facilities: Two good quality sanitary blocks (the one near reception is new) provide all the usual facilities. Washing machine, dryer and ironing. Room where one can sit or eat with cooking facilities. Shop (1/6-31/8). Restaurant (all year). Small swimming pool (1/6-31/8), not heated but very popular in summer. Playground. Fishing. **Off site:** Tennis and indoor pool nearby.

Charges guide

Per person	Sfr. 8.50
child (under 14 yrs)	Sfr. 4.00
car	Sfr. 4.00
caravan or large tent	Sfr. 8.00 - 10.00
small tent	Sfr. 5.00
dog	Sfr. 4.00
electricity	Sfr. 5.00

Plus local tax 3.5%. Discounts: 8 days 5%, 15 days 10%, 21 days 15%. **Tel:** 392.36.77 or 392.26.86. Fax: 392.36.80. E-mail: engelbert.schurte@ bluewin.ch. **Reservations:** not made. **Open** all year.

Directions: Site is just off the main Vaduz - Chur road 2 km. south of Triesen.

Open All Year

The following sites are understood to accept caravanners and campers all year round. However, it is always wise to phone a campsite if you are visiting in the low seasons as, for example, the facilities available may be reduced.

Andorra
7143 Xixerella
7145 Valira

Austria
003 Holiday
004 Zugspitze
006 Natterer See
007 Hofer
009 Zillertal-Hell
010 Toni Brantlhof
011 Tirol Camp
014 Wilder Kaiser
016 Zell am See
017 Kranebitten
018 Woferlgut
019 Erlengrund
020 Sport Camp
022 Krismer
023 Waldcamping
036N Rutar Lido
044 Schluga
048 Burgstaller

Belgium
052 Blekker
052 Blekker
053 Waux-Hall
054 Orient
056 Lombarde
058 Memling
059 Gavers
062 Roosendael
066 Baalse Hei
067 La Clusure
070 Spa d'Or
078 Wilhelm Tell

Czech Republic
459 Lisci Farma
464 Areal Jadran
477 Dlouhá Louka
485 Sokol Troja
487 Morava
488 Roznov

Denmark
2020 Mogeltonder
2044 Hampen Sø
2140 Jesperhus
2150 Solyst
2215 DCU Odense

France
0608 Les Cigales
3605M Vieux Chênes
7303 Lanchettes
7610M Cany-Barville
8604 Futuriste
8804 Lac de Bouzey

Germany
3002 Karschau
3010 Röders Park
3015 Lüneburger
3020 Bremen
3025 Alfsee
3030 Trumapark
3035 Kur-Camping

3202 Grav-Insel
3210 Biggesee
3212 Wirfttal
3215 Goldene Meile
3222 Moselbogen
3235 Mühlenteich
3242 Schinderhannes
3254 Harfenmühle
3256 Hunsrück
3258 Sägmühle
3275 Seepark
3280 Teichmann
3402 Cannstatter
3405 Bad Liebenzell
3407 Schwäbische
3410 Aichelberg
3415 Adam
3420 Oberrhein
3430 Alisehof
3432 Bonath
3437 Hochsch'wald
3440 Kirchzarten
3445 Belchenblick
3450 Münstertal
3452 Sägmühle
3455 Gugel's
3470 Odenwald
3610 Nürnberg
3620 Romantische
3627 Ellwangen
3632 Altmühltal
3650 Gitzenweiler
3675 Richterbichl
3685 Allweglehen
3690 Wagnerhof
3720 Naabtal
3725 Bavaria
3820 Havelberge
3842 Schlosspark
3847 Auensee
3855 Oberhof

Hungary
515 Fortuna
517 Rosengarten
519 Farm Lator
521 Diófaház
526 Jonathermál

Ireland
874 Cong
916 Moat Farm

Italy
6053 Fusina
6060 Estense
6200 Olympia
6201 Antholz
6202 Toblacher
6220 Mombarone
6250 Lac de Como
6401 Dei Fiori
6403 Baciccia
6412 Valdeiva
6603 Ecochiocciola
6605 Mugello
6610 Panoramico
6623 San Marino
6665 Le Soline
6667 La Finoria

6810 Seven Hills
6815 Holiday Village
6830 Zeus
6832 I Pini
6850 Sea World
6858 Il Salice

Liechtenstein
758 Mittagspitze

Luxembourg
759 Belle-Vue
767 Ardennes
770 Gaalgebierg
785 Fuussekaul
788 Trois Frontières
786N Reenert

Netherlands
550 Pannenschuur
554 Katjeskelder
560 Delftse Hout
562 Duinrell
563 Koningshof
564 Kijkduinpark
573 Sikkeler
576 Kuilart
579 Kuierpadtien
584 Pampel
589 Klein Canada
591 Hertenwei
596 Wielerbaan
652 BreeBronne
656 Maasvallei

Norway
2315 Ringoy
2385 Sandvik
2400 Jolstraholmen
2455 Ballangen
2460 Prinsen
2475 Saltstraumen
2480 Bjorkedal
2490 Skjerneset
2505 Magalaupe
2510 Håneset
2515 Gjelten Bru
2545 Rustberg
2550 Strandefjord
2570 Fossheim
2590 Sandviken
2610 Neset
2615 Olberg

Portugal
803 Rio Alto
804 Vagueira
809 Figueira-Foz
810 Sao Pedro
813 Guincho
814 Monsanto
815 Caparica
816 Porto Covo
817 São Miguel
818 Milfontes
819 Sitava
820 Valverde
821 Albufeira
822 Quarteira
823 Olhao

833 Arganil
835 Markádia
836 Idhana
837 Cerdeira
838 Vilar-Mouros
841 Armacao
843 Sagres
844 Quintos
846 Vale Paraiso
848 Foz do Arelho

Slovakia
491 Turiec

Slovenia
410 Spik
415 Kamne
435 Jezica
440 Dolina Prebold

Spain
8390 Vilanova
8395 Arc de Bara
8506 Serra-Prades
8535 Cala d'Oques
8536 Ametlla Platja
8558 Vinaros
8580 Bonterra
8615 Kiko Park
8680 Armanello
8681 Villasol
8683 Benisol
8685 El Raco
8687 Cap Blanch
8689 Playa-Torres
8741 Florantilles
8742 La Marina
8743 Marjal
8749 Sopalmo
8751 Cuevas Mar
8752N El Portus
8753 La Manga
8754 Javea
8755 Moraira
8760 Mar Azul
8782 Laguna Playa
8783N Almanat
8800 Marbella Playa
8802 Cabopino
8803 La Buganvilla
8809 El Sur
8812 Chullera 2
8850 Paloma
8855 Tarifa
8865 Las Dunas
8871 Giralda
8889 Alcornocales
8890 Los Gazules
8940 Los Cantiles
8964 Molino
8965 Picos-Europa
8973 Santillana
9022 El Folgoso
9024 As Cancelas
9025 Regio
9027 Monfrague
9028 Villueracas
9030 Igueldo
9035 Portuondo
9039 Gran Zarautz

9043 Errota-Molino
9044 Monumento
9060 Peña M'ñesa
9062 Boltana
9064 Gavin
9070 Pirineos
9078 Los Villares
9080 El Brillante
9081 Villsom
9082 Sevilla
9085 Carlos III
9087 Merida
9088 Fuencaliente
9089 Despenaperros
9090 El Greco
9091 Soto-Castillo
9092 Cisneros
9094 Aguzadera
9121 Vall d'Ager
9123 El Solsones
9140 Pedraforca
9200 El Escorial
9210 Pico-Miel
9250 Costajan
9252 Covarrubias
9253 Picon-Conde
9270 Suspiro-Moro
9275 Los Avellanos
9280 Sierra Nevada
9285 Las Lomas

Sweden
2650 Skånes
2665 Rosenlund
2675 Lysingsbadet
2700 Boras
2705 Karralund
2710 Lidköping
2720 Hökensås
2750 Sommarvik
2760 Frykenbaden
2835 Orsa
2836 Mora Parkens
2840 Flottsbro
2845 Svegs
2850 Ostersunds
2857 Strömsund
2860 Umeå
2865 Gielas
2870 Jokkmokks

Switzerland
905 Bois-Couvent
906 Kappelenbr'ke
922 Grangettes
927 De Vidy
930 Bivouac
933 Bettlereiche
936 Grassi
939 Vermeille
942 Manor Farm
946 Jungfrau
949 Eigernordwand
954 Lido Sarnen
963 Sémiramis
967 Molignon
977 Santa Monica
983 Sur En
984 St Cassian

No Dogs

Since the introduction in 2000 of the Passports for Pets scheme many British campers and caravanners have been encouraged to take their pets with them on holiday, but not only are the Pet Travel conditions understandably strict, the procedure is quite lengthy and complicated, and may be modified again - you can check the current situation via the Passports for Pets web site: http://freespace.virgin.net/passports.forpets

There is also a help line: 0870 241 1710 or e-mail: passports.forpets@virgin.net.

For the benefit of those who want to take their dogs to Europe, we list here the sites which have indicated to us that they NEVER accept dogs.

Austria		6022	Portofelice	584	Pampel	**Slovenia**	
009	Zillertal-Hell	6025	Residence	586	Betuwestrand	423	Soca
042N	Müllerhof	6030	Dei Fiori	597	De Paal	442	Otocec
		6032	Cavallino	598	De Roos		
Czech Republic		6035	Mediterraneo	651	Schatberg	**Spain**	
469	Slunce	6040	G. Paradiso	679	Kienehoef	8005	Cadaques
475	Bila Hora	6055	Isamar	696	Klepperstee	8090	Cypsela
		6065	Tahiti			8101	Playa Brava
France		6256	Garda	**Norway**		8103	El Maset
0608	Les Cigales	6263	Bella Italia	2315	Ringoy	8420	Stel
1701	Bois Soleil	6265	Ideal Molino	2320	Odda	8481	Cambrils
8402N	Bélézy	6401	Dei Fiori	2325	Sundal	8530	Playa Montroig
8515	La Yole	6618	Stella Maris	2330	Eikhamrane	8537N	Templo del Sol
8521	Les Ecureuils	6624	Rubicone	2360	Ulvik Fjord	8540	Torre del Sol
Germany		6630	Montescudaio	2390	Kjornes	8560	Tropicana
3260	Bad Dürkheim	6636	Capanne	2435	Solvang	8681	Villasol
3405	Bad Liebenzell	6645	Delle Piscine	2445	Slettnes	8741	Florantilles
3440	Kirchzarten	6671	Argentario	2455	Ballangen	8751	Cuevas Mar
2685	Allweglehen	6800	Europe Garden	2465	Lyngvaer	9000	Playa Joyel
Hungary		6801	Holiday	2475	Saltstraumen	9038	Orio
509	Füred	6815	Holiday Village	2490	Skjerneset	9143	Pirineus
538	Venus	6820	Baia Domizia	2495	Vegset	9251	Rio Lobos
Ireland		6853	Athena	2550	Strandefjord	**Switzerland**	
951	Eagle Point	**Luxembourg**		2555	Lom	916	Rheinwiesen
Italy		782	Bon Repos	2600	Rysstad	918	Buchhorn
6000	Mare Pineta	**Netherlands**		2612	Holt	946	Jungfrau
6003	Pra' Delle Torri	568	Noordduinen	**Portugal**		948	Gletscherdorf
6010	Capalonga	574	S.Maartenszee	817	São Miguel	988	Lido Mappo
6015	Il Tridente	578	Zanding	819	Sitava	989	Campofelice
6020	Union Lido	582	Hertshoorn	838	Vilar Mouros	990	Delta
6021	Italy					993	Al Censo

SOMETIMES: The following sites do not accept dogs at certain times. We do advise phoning the site first to check – there may be limits on numbers, breeds, or times of the year when they are excluded.

Austria			**Italy**			
006	Natterer See	not July-Aug	6210	Steiner	not July/Aug	
040	Arneitz	not July-Aug	6660	Sans Souci	not 16/6-31/8	
			6813	Porticciolo	must reserve	
Belgium			6832	I Pini	not July-Aug	
055	Nieuwpoort	one per pitch	6842	Sant' Antonio	not Aug	
067	La Clusure	max 1 in July/Aug	6845	San Nicola	not high season	
France			**Netherlands**			
2301	Poinsouze	not 6/7-20/8	576	Kuilart	separate field	
2603	Grand Lierne	not 1/7-25/8				
4005	Col-Vert	small pets only	**Portugal**			
4012N	Arnaoutchot	small pets only	835	Markádia	not July-Aug	
8320	Les Pêcheurs	one only	837	Cerdeira	not July-Aug	
Germany			**Spain**			
3003	Wulfener Hals	Small dogs only	8072	Les Medes	not July-Aug	
3232	Family Club	not July/Aug	8075	Estartit	not 20/6-20/8	
3442	Herbolzheim	not 15/7-15/8	8080	Delfin Verde	not 15/7-18/8	
3465	Wirthshof	not July-Aug	8160	Cala Gogo	not 1/7-26/8	

We have had very favourable feedback from readers concerning our choice of naturist sites, which we first introduced in our 1992 editions. Over the last few years we have gradually added a few more.

Apart from the need to have a 'Naturist Licence' (see below), there is no need to be a practising naturist before visiting these sites. In fact, at least as far as British visitors are concerned, many are what might be described as 'holiday naturists' as distinct from the practice of naturism at other times. The emphasis in all the sites featured in this guide at least, is on naturism as 'life in harmony with nature', and respect for oneself and others and for the environment, rather than simply on nudity. In fact nudity is really only oblig-atory in the area of the swimming pools.

There are a number of rules, which amount to sensible and considerate guidelines designed to ensure that no-one invades someone else's privacy, creates any nuisance, or damages the environment. Whether as a result of these rules, the naturist philosophy generally, or the attitude of site owners and campers alike, we have been very impressed by all the naturist sites we have selected. Without exception they had a friendly and welcoming ambience, were all extremely clean and tidy and, in most cases, provided much larger than average pitches, with a wide range of activities both sporting and cultural.

The purpose of our including a number of naturist sites in our guide is to provide an introduction to naturist camping in Europe for British holidaymakers; we were actually surprised by the number of British campers we met on naturist sites, many of whom had 'stumbled across naturism almost by accident'. A Naturist Licence can be obtained in advance from either the British naturist association (see advert below), but are also available on arrival at any recognised naturist site (a passport type photograph is required).

The naturist sites featured in this guide (the site numbers are prefixed with 'N'):

www.insure④europe.com

Taking your own tent, caravan or motorhome abroad?

Looking for the best cover at the best rates?

Our prices considerably undercut most high street prices and the 'in-house insurance' of many tour operators whilst offering equivalent (or higher) levels of cover.

Our annual multi-trip policies offer superb value, covering you not only for your european camping holiday but also subsequent trips abroad for the next 12 months.

Total Peace of Mind

To give you total peace of mind during your holiday our insurance policies have been specifically tailored to cover most potential eventualities on a self-drive camping holiday. Each is organised through Voyager Insurance Services Ltd who specialize in travel insurance for Europe and for camping in particular. All policies are underwritten by UK Insurance, part of the Green Flag Group.

24 Hour Assistance

Our personal insurance provides access to the services of International Medical Rescue (IMR), one of the UK's largest assistance companies. Experienced multi-lingual personnel provide a caring and efficient service 24 hours a day.

European vehicle assistance cover is provided by Green Flag who provide assistance to over 3 million people each year. With a Europe-wide network of over 7,500 garages and agents you know you're in very safe hands.

Both IMR and green flag are very used to looking after the needs of campsite-based holidaymakers and are very familiar with the location of most European campsites, with contacts at garages, doctors and hospitals nearby.

Save with an Annual policy

If you are likely to make more than one trip to Europe over the next 12 months then our annual multi-trip policies could save you a fortune. Personal cover for a couple starts at just £90 and the whole family can be covered for just £110.
Cover for up to 17 days wintersports participation is included.

Low Cost Annual multi-trip insurance

Premier Annual Europe self-drive
including 17 days wintersports

£90 per couple

Premier Annual Europe self-drive
including 17 days wintersports

£110 per family

Low Cost Combined Personal and Vehicle Assistance Insurance

Premier Family Package
10 days cover for vehicle, 2 adults plus dependent children under 16.

£71-50*

Premier Couples Package
10 days cover for vehicle and 2 adults

£57-75*

* Motorhomes, cars towing trailers and caravans, all vehicles over 4 years old and holidays longer than 10 days attract supplements – ask us for details. See leaflet for full terms and conditions.

Belle FRANCE

Walking & Cycling Holidays

Discover rural France at its best

Belle France offers cycling and walking holidays through the most beautiful and interesting parts of France.

Your luggage is moved for you whilst you find your own way, at your own pace with our detailed maps and notes.

Relax in the evening in charming family run hotels, offering a good standard of accommodation and a warm and friendly welcome.

Call now for a free brochure
01892 55 95 95

www.bellefrance.co.uk

Paying too much

for your mobile home holiday?

Travel off peak and Pay Just £24.95 per night
with Holiday Cheque

Holiday Cheque gives you exclusive off peak access to quality mobile homes and chalets on nearly 85 of Europe's finest campsites. You'll find superb family facilities, including sensational pools, great value restaurants, friendly bars and real hospitality. And the kids can have the time of their lives! All for just £24.95 per night.

Fully equipped to the consistently high specification of our Quality Charter you'll find all the mod cons of a proper home from home, including bedlinen - while saving up to 50% of the normal rates

✓ 85 top campsites

✓ All just £24.95 per night

✓ High quality mobile homes

✓ Luxury high specification chalets

✓ Fully equipped - down to the corkscrew!

✓ Plus unbeatable ferry prices

Huge savings - but hurry

HOLIDAY CHEQUES COST JUST £24.95 PER NIGHT. THAT'S A SPECIAL PROMOTIONAL RATE, SAVING UP TO 50% OFF CAMPSITE'S STANDARD PRICES. BUT IT'S FIRST COME, FIRST SERVED, SO THERE'S NO TIME TO LOSE IF YOU WANT TO BOOK THE CAMPSITE OF YOUR CHOICE.

HOLIDAY CHEQUE

Call today for your FREE brochure
0870 7200 560

it will save you £££'s on your holiday

Alan Rogers

in association wit

www.holidaycheque.co.uk

ABTA
W161

go as you please

Grand Prix Racing

JUST TICKETS

As the largest suppliers of **Formula One** and **Le Mans 24 Hour** spectator tickets **we provide the best range of seats in this country**.

Our **TICKET ONLY** service covers general admission, grandstand seats and parking at F.1 circuits and Le Mans.

At **MONACO** we offer some of the **best viewing of all from private apartment terraces** located at the most advantageous points, and seats and hospitality at a trackside restaurant.

For **SILVERSTONE** we can book seats, hospitality marquees, adjoining private parking and helicopters.

JUST MOTORING

Offers inclusive self-drive arrangements with hotels at **European Formula One** events, plus for **Le Mans**, ferry bookings, parking, camping and hospitality marquees.

CAMPING

We hae made arrangements with camping areas at several circuits, also nearby sites at most of the others.

Just Tickets
1 Charter House
Camden Crescent
Dover, Kent
CT16 1LE
Tel: 01304 228866
Fax: 01304 242550
www.justtickets.co.uk

Mr/Mrs/Ms

Address

Postcode

Event

Ref GCG/03

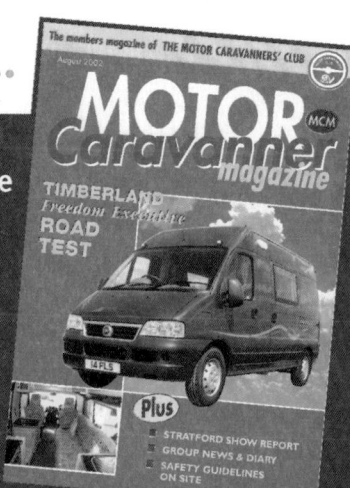

Reports by Readers

We always welcome reports from readers concerning sites which they have visited. Generally reports provide us with invaluable feedback on sites already featured in the Guide or, in the case of those not featured in our Guide, they provide information which we can follow up with a view to adding them in future editions. However, if you have a complaint about a site, this should be addressed to the campsite owner, preferably in person before you leave.

Please make your comments either on this form or on plain paper. It would be appreciated if you would indicate the approximate dates when you visited the park and, in the case of potential new parks, provide the correct name and address and, if possible, include a park brochure. Send your reports to:

Alan Rogers' Guides, Manor Garden, Burton Bradstock, Bridport DT6 4QA

Name of Site and Ref. No. (or address for new recommendations):

....

....

Dates of Visit: ....

Comments:

Reader's Name and Address: ....

....

....

....

Car Ferry Services

The number of different services from the UK to the Continent provides a wide choice of sailings to meet most needs. The actual choice is a matter of personal preference, influenced by factors such as where you live, your actual destination in Europe, cost and whether you see the channel crossing as a potentially enjoyable part of your holiday or, (if you are prone to sea-sickness) as something to be endured!

Below is a summary of the services likely to be operating in 2003, based on information available at the time of going to press (Dec 02), together with a number of reports on those services which we have used ourselves during the last two years. Detailed, up-to-date information and bookings for any of these services, and for campsite pitch reservations, travel insurance etc. can be made through the Alan Rogers Travel Service, telephone 01892 55 98 98.

Route	Frequency	Crossing Time
Brittany Ferries (Tel: 08705 360360)		
Portsmouth - Caen	Up to 3 daily	6 hours
Portsmouth - St. Malo	Daily	8.75 hours
Poole - Cherbourg (jointly with Condor)	Daily	2.25 hours
Poole - Cherbourg (conventional ferry)	Up to 2 daily	4.25 hours
Plymouth - Roscoff	Up to 3 daily	6 hours
Plymouth - Santander	Up to 2 weekly	24 hours
Condor Ferries (0845 345 2000)		
Poole - St. Malo	Daily	4.5 hours
Poole - Cherbourg (jointly with Brittany)	Daily	2.25 hours
DFDS Scandinavian Seaways (Tel 08705 333000)		
Harwich - Esbjerg	3-4 weekly	20 hours
Harwich - Hamburg	3-4 weekly	19 hours
Newcastle - Kristiansand	2 weekly	18 hours
Newcastle - Gothenburg	2 weekly	26 hours
Newcastle - Amsterdam	daily	14 hours
Eurotunnel (Tel 08705 353535)		
Folkestone - Calais	Up to 4 hourly	35 minutes
Fjord Line (Tel 0191 296 1313)		
Newcastle - Bergen	Up to 3 weekly	25.5 hours
Newcastle - Stavanger	Up to 3 weekly	18.5 hours
Newcastle - Haugestund	Up to 3 weekly	21 hours
Hoverspeed (Tel 08705 240241)		
Dover - Calais	Up to 12 daily	45 minutes
Dover - Ostend	Up to 7 daily	2 hours
Newhaven - Dieppe	Up to 3 daily	2 hours
Norfolk Line (Tel 0870 8701020)		
Dover - Dunkerque	up to 6 daily	2 hours
P&O North Sea Ferries (Tel 08701 296002)		
Hull - Rotterdam	daily	13.5 hours
Hull - Zeebrugge	daily	14 hours
P&O Portsmouth (Tel 0870 2424999)		
Portsmouth - Cherbourg (ferry)	Up to 4 daily	5 hours
Portsmouth - Cherbourg (Fast Craft)	Up to 3 daily	2.75 hours
Portsmouth - Le Havre	3 daily	5.5 hours
Portsmouth - Bilbao	2 weekly	27 hours
P&O Stena Line (Tel 0870 6000600)		
Dover - Calais	Up to 2 hourly	1.25 hours
Sea France (Tel 0870 5711711)		
Dover - Calais	15 daily	1.5 hours
Stena Line (Tel 0870 5707070)		
Harwich - Hook	2 daily	3.75 hours

Car Ferry Services

P&O Stena Line - Dover / Calais

With 20 sailings each way from October to March and 25 each way from April to September, fares at a reasonable level, the use of 'super ferries' which make the crossing in 75 minutes and a check-in time of 20 minutes, P&O are taking on the Channel Tunnel head on to ensure a competitive alternative to the latest method of reaching mainland Europe. Although prior booking is advisable, the space on each vessel means that, except perhaps at peak times, one can just turn up and cross on the next sailing. The A20 extension to the M20 Folkestone to the Eastern Dock entrance at Dover and the direct access to the French autoroute system at Calais with the pleasant 'cruise' across the channel in between, now make for a hassle free beginning to the holiday. This also helps the transition to driving on the right as, by the time one needs to use 'ordinary' roads, one has become used to overtaking on the left. Apart from these advantages, the ferries have been modernised to the highest standards with waiter and self-service restaurants, shops selling a wide range of duty-free and other goods, comfortable bars and lounges and Club Class at a small supplement for those who want peace and quiet away from the bustle on the decks below. Boarding and leaving the ships has been made simple by the use of double width ramps on two levels.

P&O North Sea Ferries Hull / Zeebrugge

Without claiming that these routes offer cruise-ship grandeur, this is something more than an exercise in merely travelling from A to B. There's a feeling of dignity here and a level of service that makes the overnight crossing a distinctly restful experience. For instance an opportunity to book free morning tea or coffee for delivery to your cabin door adds a nice touch to ease the burden of an early start to the day. Similarly the high quality restaurant service is worthy of mention with its large menu which should suit every taste. Little wonder then that many ferry users spend a few hours at the destination and then promptly return on the evening boat back to Britain - just for the pleasure of the cruise. For others with a long journey ahead, it's undoubtedly a good way to start a holiday.

Leaving the inner basin at Hull involves an intricate passage through a small lock; skilful seamanship means that many passengers are unaware of the manoeuvres as they 'settle in'. On the other hand, seeing how a large ship can be eased into such a small space is a spectacle worth watching. However, Hull's berthing facilities are currently being extended and this exercise will presumably become unnecessary. Similarly, Rotterdam's Europort is the current destination rather than the more familiar Hook of Holland port which lies slightly to the north. Certainly it's a straightforward drive after disembarkation at Europort and main routeways are easy to find.

Brittany Ferries - Plymouth/Santander

This service is operated by Brittany Ferries flagship, the 'Val de Loire'. Although this is a long crossing, which on the face of it appears relatively expensive, if you are travelling to Spain, Portugal or even the Basque area of France, the higher ferry cost may well be offset by the saving in fuel, autoroute tolls or overnight accommodation en route, so it's well worth making a comparative calculation of the total cost of your journey! Facilities on the Val de Loire are almost up to cruise liner standards, and the 24 hour voyage itself can be very enjoyable indeed, with plenty to keep you occupied or pleasantly relaxed – a good choice of restaurants, cinema, sun-decks, etc. all add to the 'cruising' atmosphere.

DFDS Seaways

Newcastle/Gothenburg and Harwich/Gothenburg

Travelling with DFDS Seaways from Newcastle to Gothenburg on board the 'Princess of Scandinavia' line added 22 hours cruising time to our journey. This leisurely crossing provided the perfect opportunity to relax. Once on board, we found all services to be efficiently run without fuss by a friendly crew. Our twin berth outside cabin with en-suite facilities was comfortable, airy and spacious. Catering facilities included an à la carte restaurant offering Scandinavian and German cuisine, the popular Smörgas-bord/carvery, a traditional Scandinavian feast, or the cafeteria and bistro is another option. The list of on board activities is equally extensive with live entertainment, disco, casino, cinema, sauna, solarium, pool, etc. There are shops and a bureau de change; vouchers, received with our travel documents, meant discount on certain duty free items. A most important factor on any journey is the cost, but with fare structuring and book in advance deals, we believe Scandinavian Seaways offers excellent value for money.

WE GO ──── THERE !

Offering more destination ports than any other UK ferry port, Portsmouth provides you with the best connections to France, Spain and the Channel Islands:

- ☑ **Direct access to the UK motorway network.**
- ☑ **Quicker access from the Midlands, North of England and Wales with the completion of the A34 Newbury bypass.**
- ☑ **Continental destination ports well placed for autoroutes and main links.**
- ☑ **A fast ferry service taking just 2 hours 40 minutes to Cherbourg, from April to September.**

So wherever you want to go for short breaks or longer holidays, go via Portsmouth. We put the continent within easy reach!

PORTSMOUTH

BRITAIN'S BEST CONNECTED FERRY PORT
www.portsmouth-port.co.uk

08705 360 360   **0870 2424 999**   **01305 761551**

CHERBOURG 〜 CAEN 〜 LE HAVRE 〜 ST. MALO 〜 GUERNSEY 〜 JERSEY 〜 BILBAO

Less driving,
more holiday

Why spend your holiday driving hundreds of unnecessary miles through France when we can take you and your car closer to your holiday destination? Not only do we offer the best choice of routes, you can also enjoy the finest on-board experience. And all for less than you'd expect.

Call 0870 366 9796 or visit *brittanyferries.com*

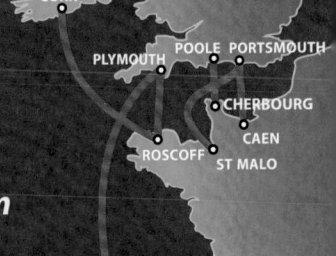

Plymouth - Santander | Plymouth - Roscoff | Poole - Cherbourg | Portsmouth - St Malo | Portsmouth - Caen | Cork - Roscoff

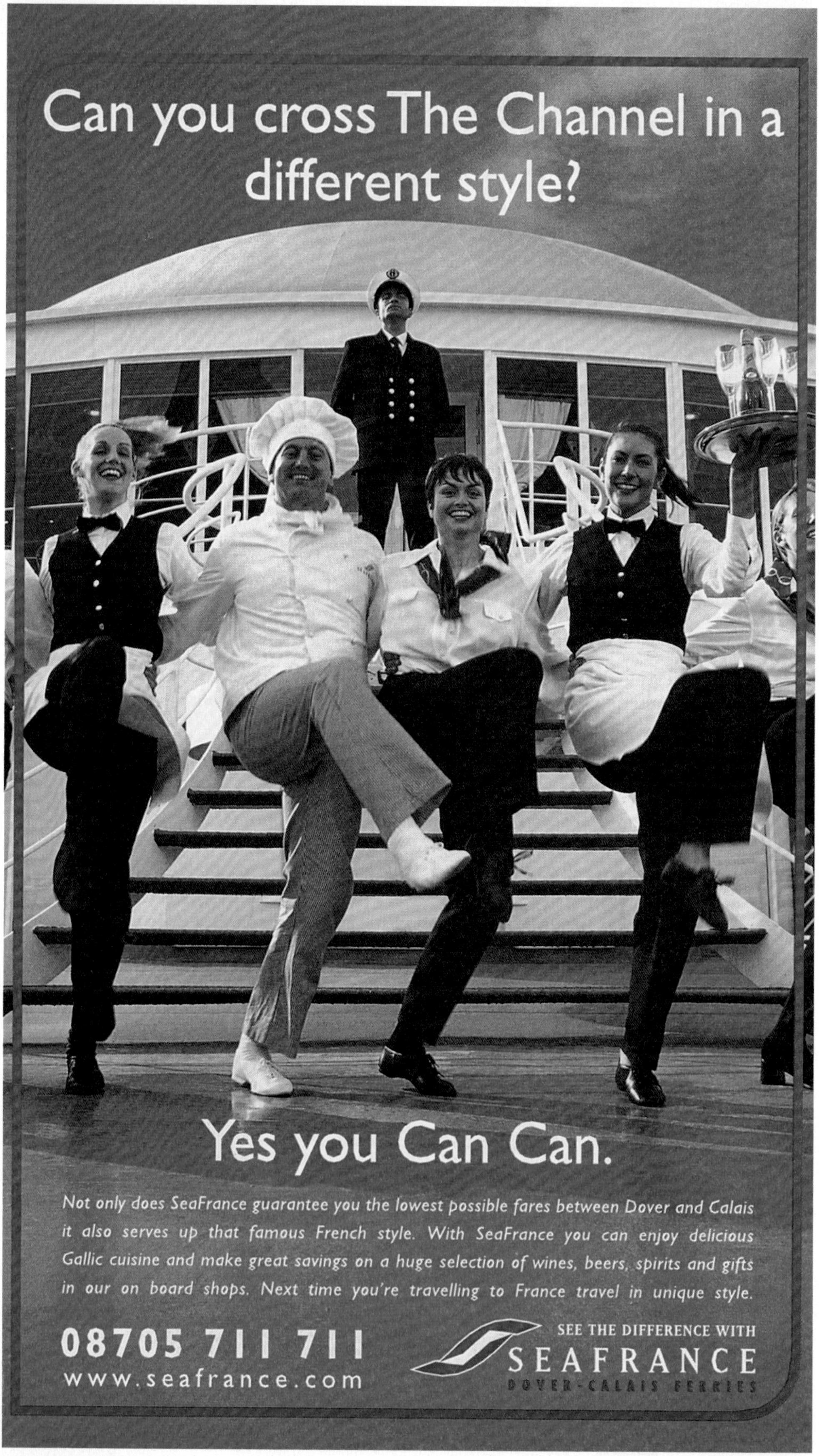
Can you cross The Channel in a different style?
Yes you Can Can.
Not only does SeaFrance guarantee you the lowest possible fares between Dover and Calais it also serves up that famous French style. With SeaFrance you can enjoy delicious Gallic cuisine and make great savings on a huge selection of wines, beers, spirits and gifts in our on board shops. Next time you're travelling to France travel in unique style.
08705 711 711
www.seafrance.com
SEE THE DIFFERENCE WITH
SEAFRANCE
DOVER-CALAIS FERRIES

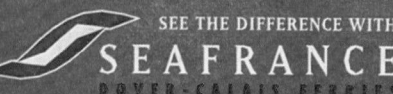

BILBAO, CHERBOURG, AND LE HAVRE: TWINNED WITH P&ORTSMOUTH

Sail with P&O Portsmouth and you'll enjoy easier access to your ferry. And disembark in the heart of France or northern Spain miles closer to your destination. On your crossing, you can relax as you enjoy not only our on board facilities but also the knowledge that you'll be pitching your tent or uncoupling your caravan far faster when you arrive. There can't be a better way to start your holiday. For a brochure call **0870 9000 212** (quoting AR). To book, call **0870 2424 999**, visit poportsmouth.com or see your local travel agent.

P&O
PORTSMOUTH

BILBAO   CHERBOURG   LE HAVRE

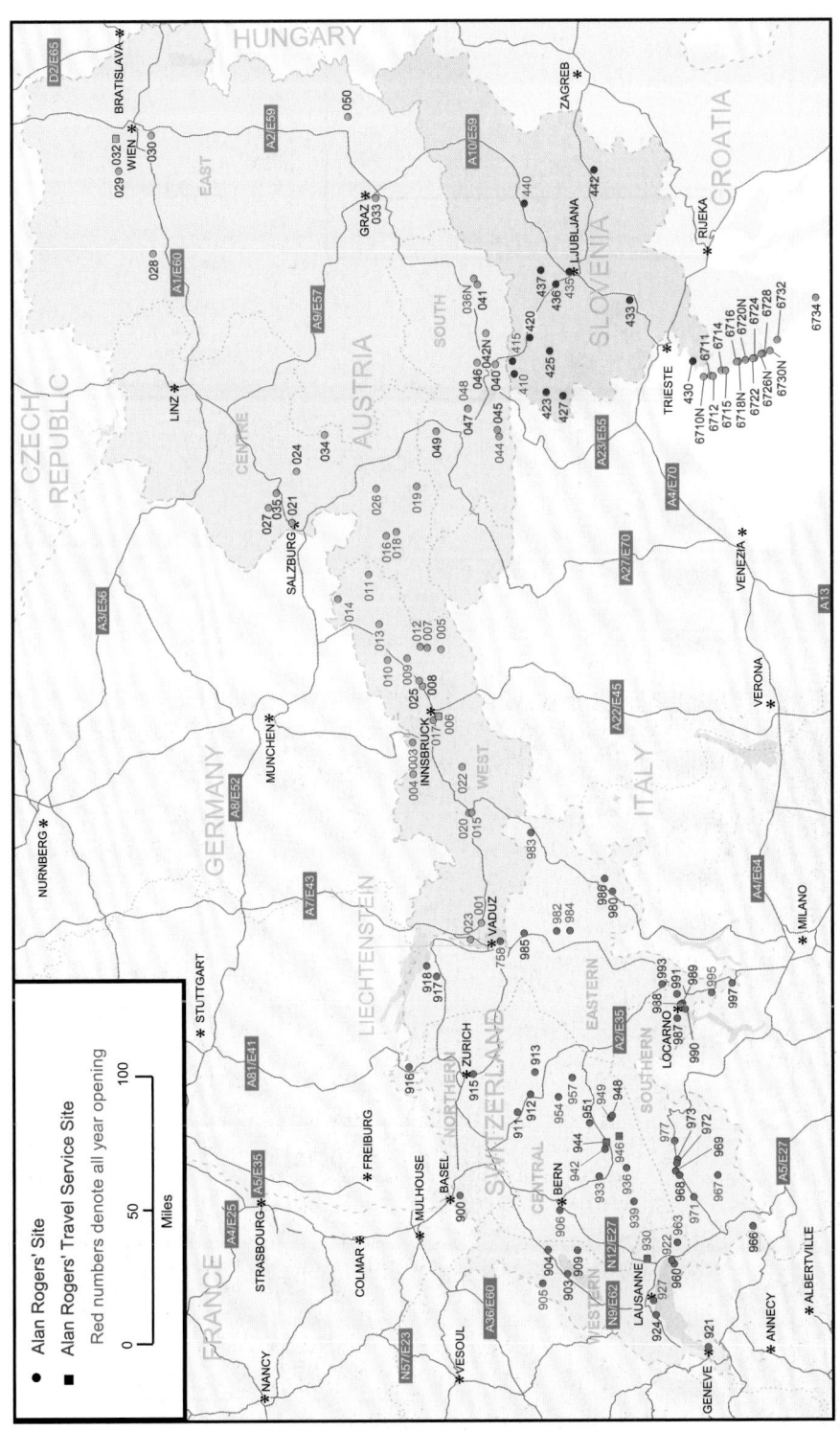

- ● Alan Rogers' Site
- ■ Alan Rogers' Travel Service Site

Red numbers denote all year opening

0   50   100

Miles

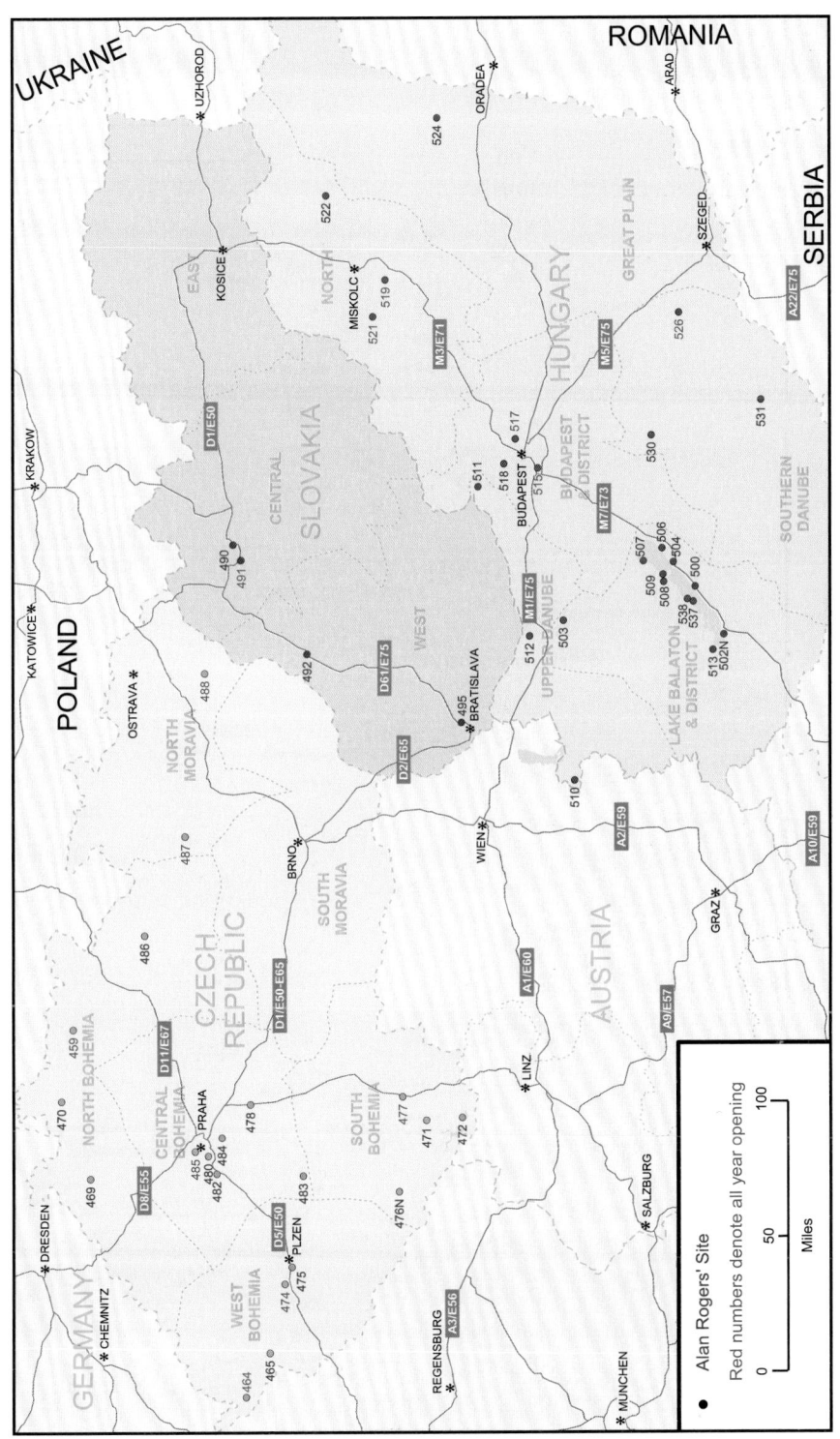

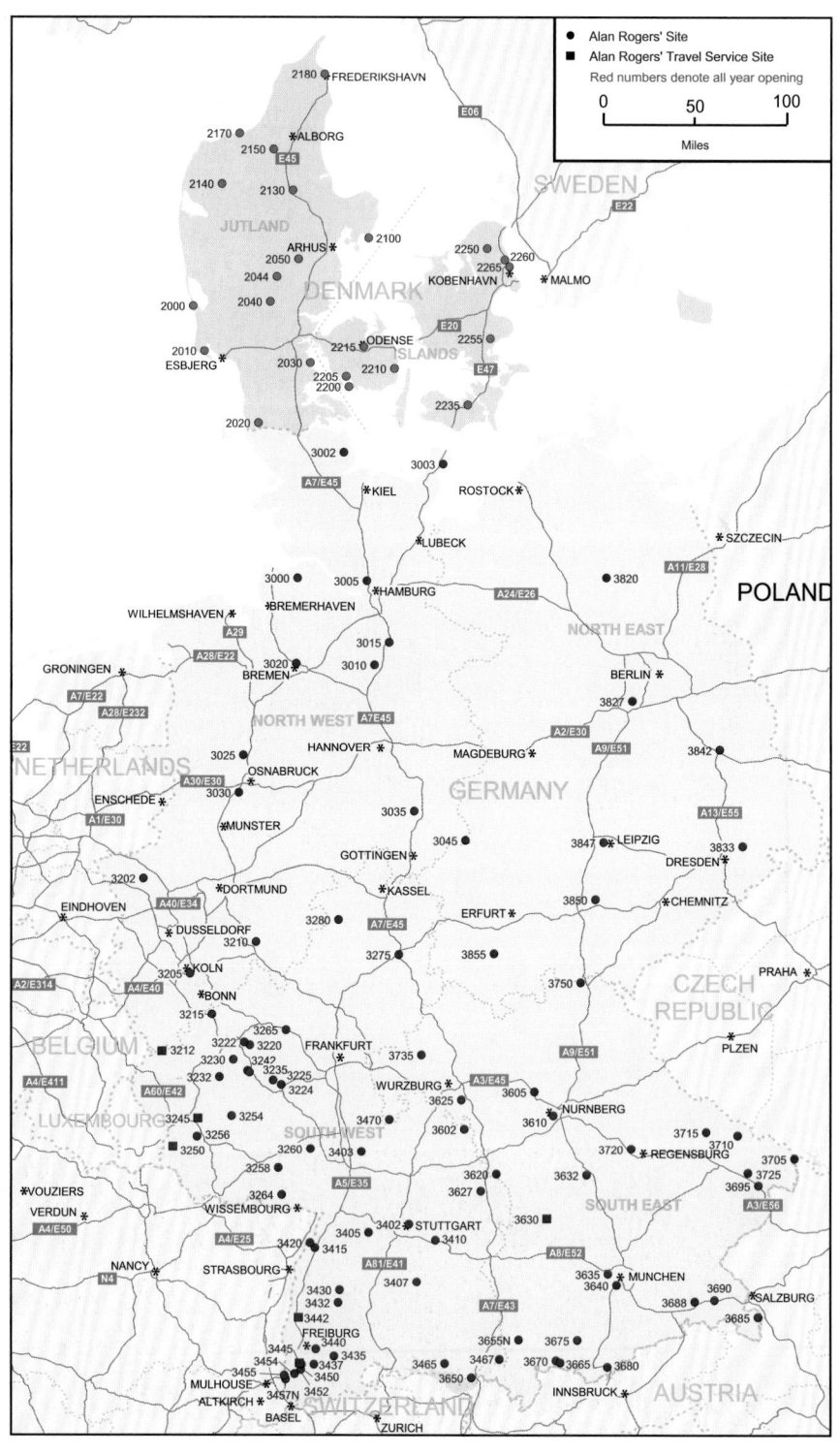

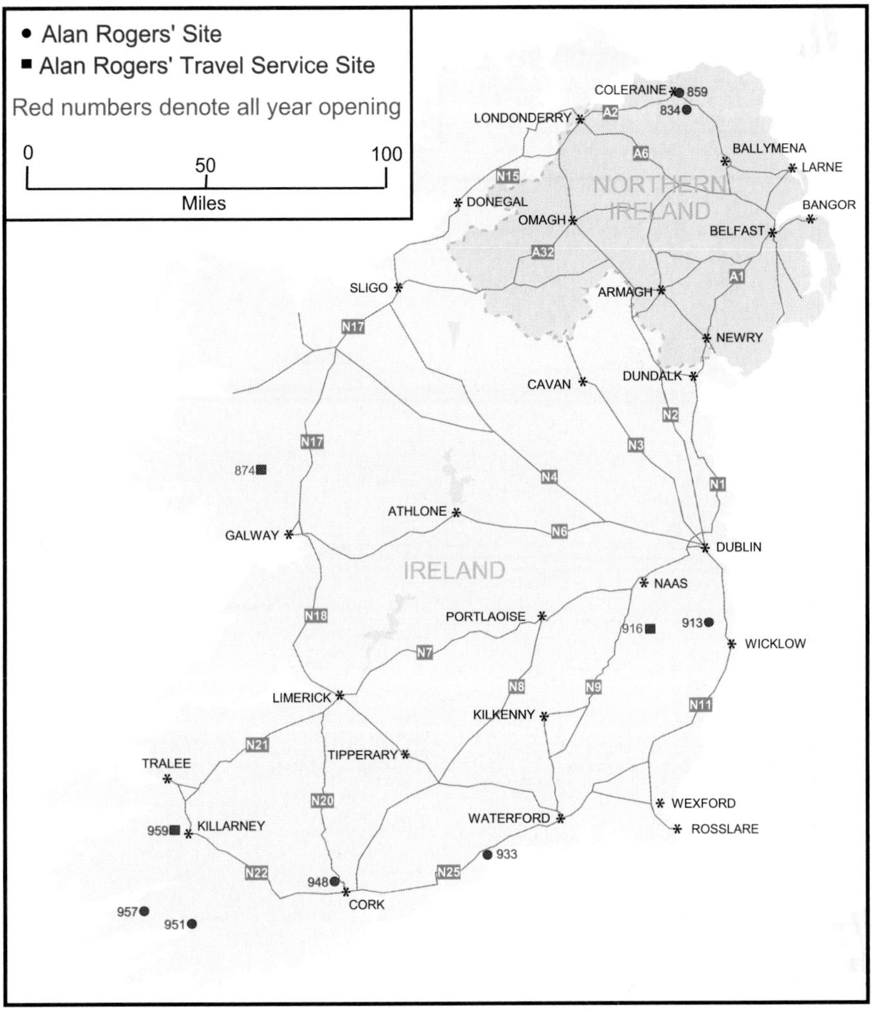

- Alan Rogers' Site
- Alan Rogers' Travel Service Site

Red numbers denote all year opening

0   50   100

Miles

COLERAINE 859
834
LONDONDERRY A2
A6 BALLYMENA
LARNE
N15
DONEGAL NORTHERN BANGOR
OMAGH IRELAND BELFAST
A32
A1
SLIGO ARMAGH
N17 NEWRY
DUNDALK
CAVAN
N2
N17 N3
874 N4
N1
ATHLONE
GALWAY N6
DUBLIN
IRELAND NAAS
N18 PORTLAOISE 913
916 WICKLOW
N7
LIMERICK N8 N9
KILKENNY N11
N21 TIPPERARY
TRALEE N20
959 KILLARNEY WEXFORD
WATERFORD ROSSLARE
N22 N25 933
957 948
951 CORK

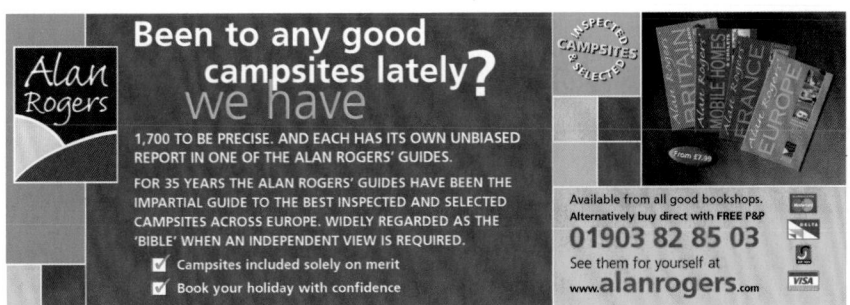

Been to any good campsites lately?
we have

1,700 TO BE PRECISE. AND EACH HAS ITS OWN UNBIASED
REPORT IN ONE OF THE ALAN ROGERS' GUIDES.

FOR 35 YEARS THE ALAN ROGERS' GUIDES HAVE BEEN THE
IMPARTIAL GUIDE TO THE BEST INSPECTED AND SELECTED
CAMPSITES ACROSS EUROPE. WIDELY REGARDED AS THE
'BIBLE' WHEN AN INDEPENDENT VIEW IS REQUIRED.

☑ Campsites included solely on merit
☑ Book your holiday with confidence

Available from all good bookshops.
Alternatively buy direct with FREE P&P

01903 82 85 03

See them for yourself at
www.alanrogers.com

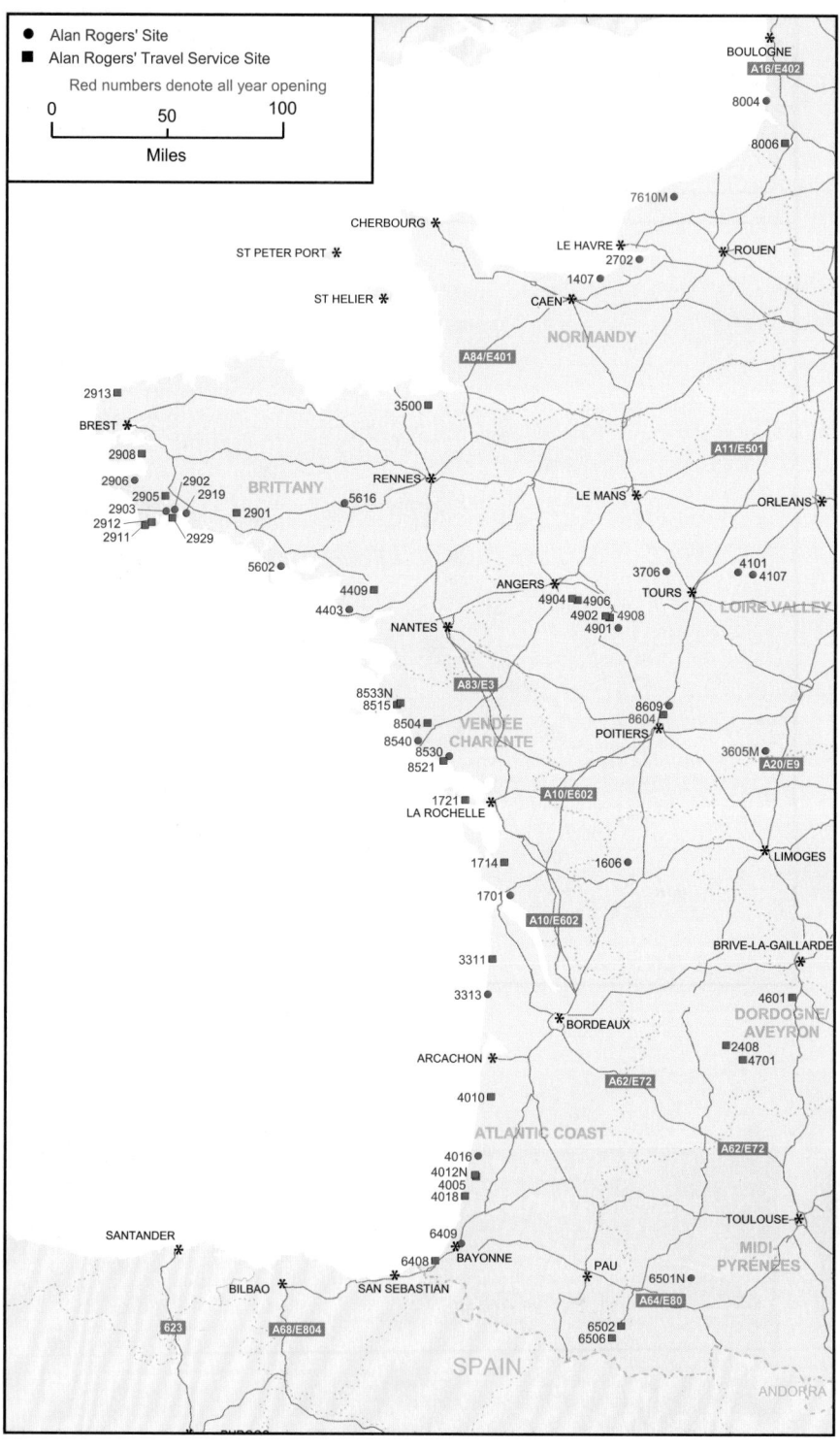

Alan Rogers' Site

■ Alan Rogers' Travel Service Site

Red numbers denote all year opening

0   50   100

Miles

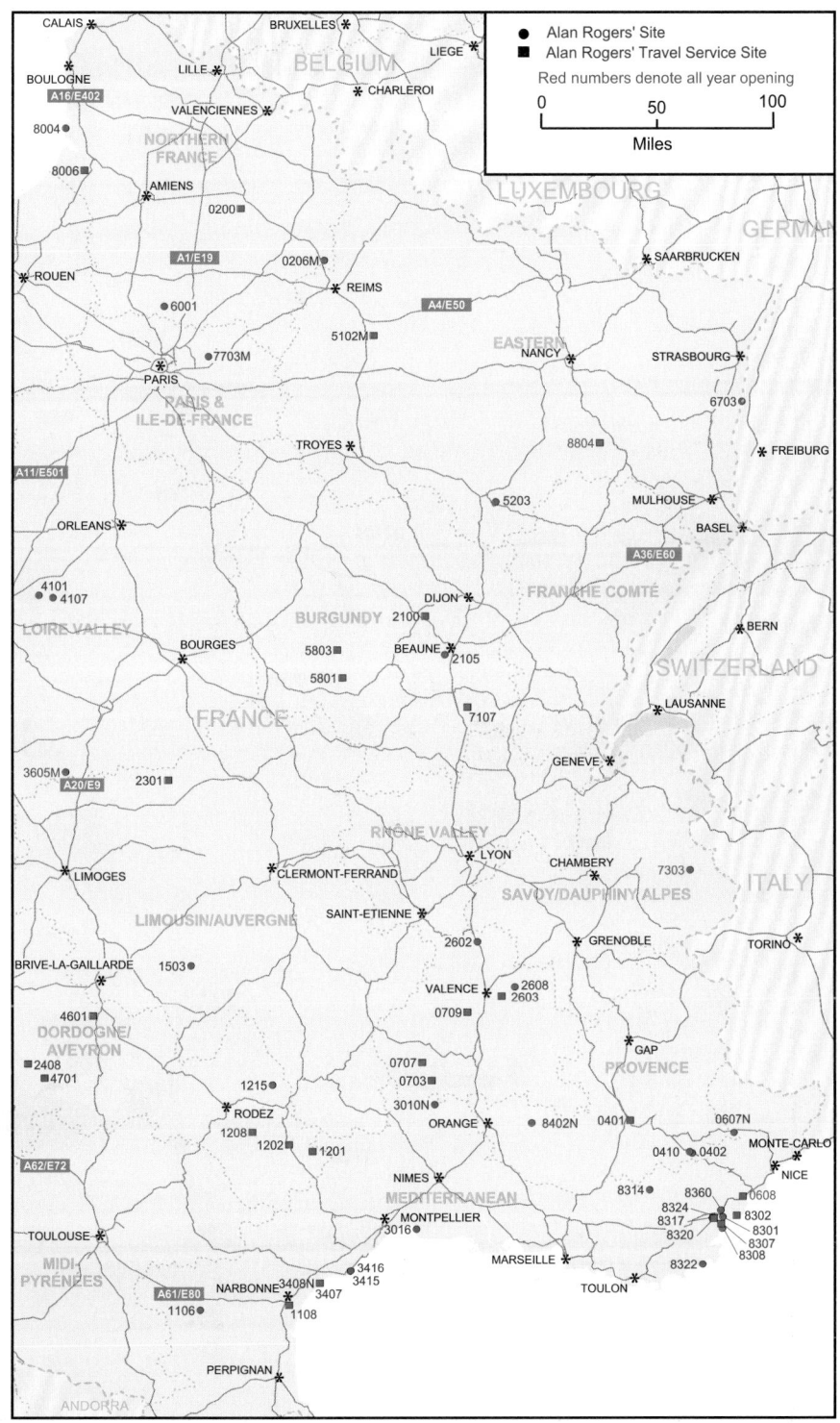

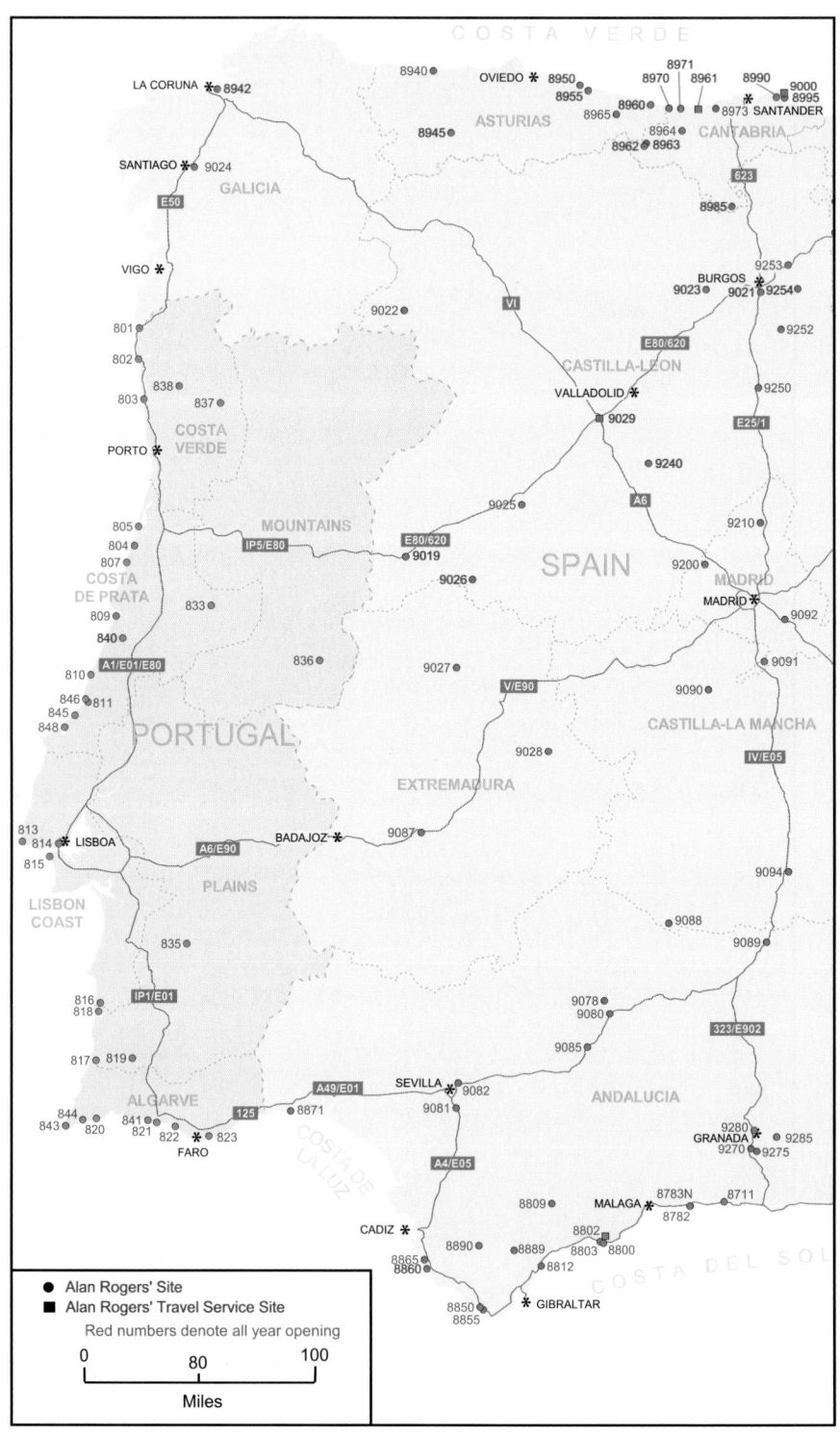

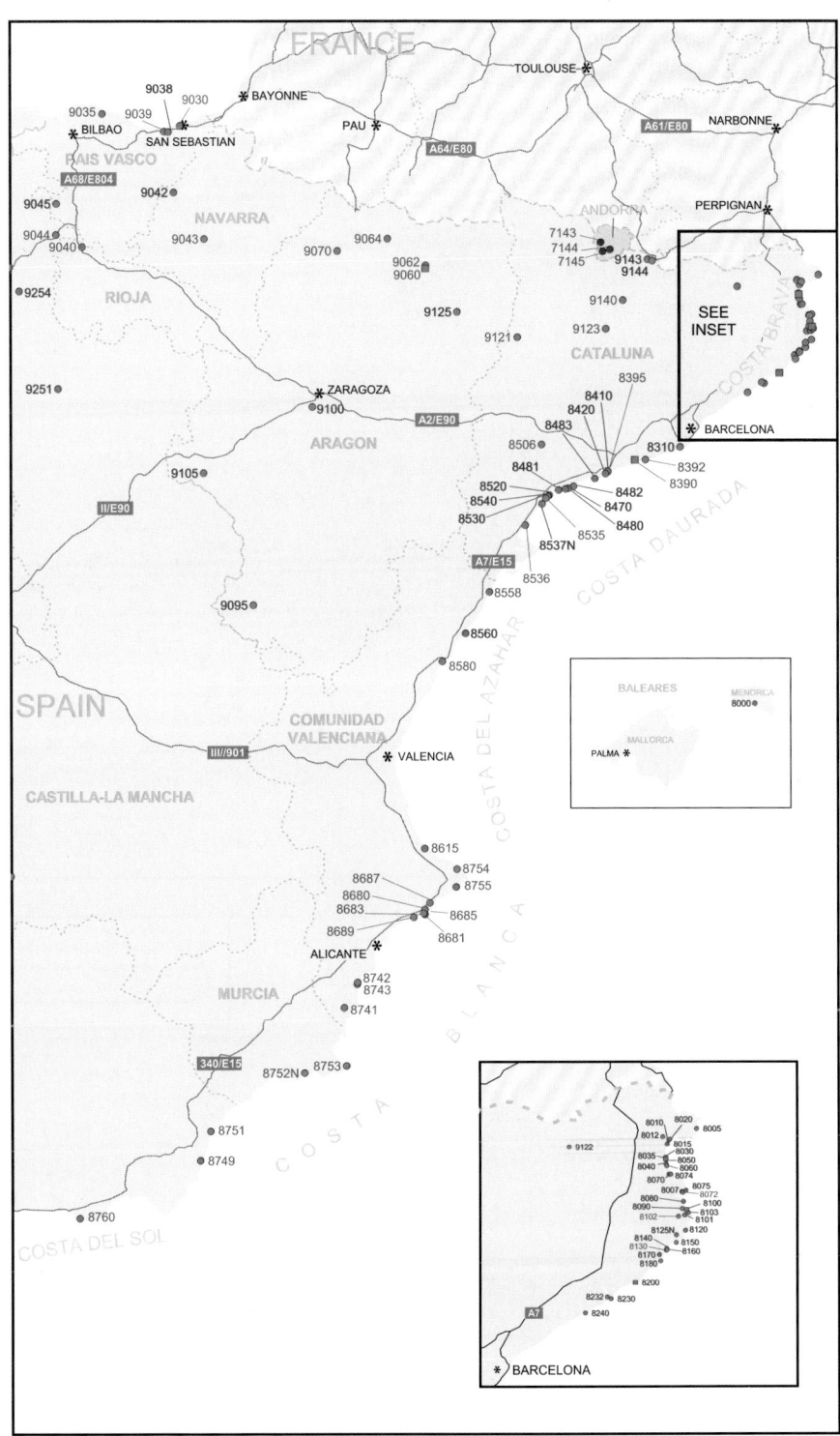

BASEL
ZURICH
INNSBRUCK
AUSTRIA
VADUZ
BERN
SWITZERLAND
A2/E35
A10/E59
6201
6200
6202
6205
6212
6210
NORTH EAST
A27/E70
A23/E55
A22/E45
LJUBLJANA
ZAGREB
SLOVENIA
6000
6007
6005
6010
6015
TRIESTE
6008
6003
6022
6021
6040
6028
6025
6020
6035
6030
6045
A4/E70
RIJEKA
CROATIA
6214
6230
6225
6227
6235
6232
6237
6250
LOCARNO
6240
6245
6247
6249
6246
6248
6258
6280
6275
6259
6270
6265
6284
6260
6277
6285
6283
6252
6263
6266
6254
6256
6255
6253
VERONA
A4/E64
A5/E27
6220
MILANO
NORTH WEST
6042
6032
6050
6053
VENEZIA
6055
A13
6060
6065
A22/E45
TORINO
A21/E70
PARMA
6602
BOLOGNA
6603
6063N
6622
6624
A14/E45
A7/E62
A6/E717
GENOVA
6410
6412
LA SPEZIA
CENTRAL
6623
SAN MARINO
6618
ANCONA
6605
6404
6403
6607
6600
6610
FIRENZE
6611
6612
6608
ITALY
6664
6663
6401
MONTE-CARLO
NICE
6630
6637
6632
6636
6635
6641
6640
6625
6665
6654
6653
6652
6655
6656
6645
6802
6801
6805
6800
PESCARA
6667
6660
6669
6662
6671
6860
6855
SASSARI
ISLANDS
SARDINIA
CAGLIARA
6811
6812
6813
6810
6809
6814
ROMA
SOUTH
6815
6820
NAPOLI
6830
6842
6835
6832

Alan Rogers' Site
Alan Rogers' Travel Service Site
Red numbers denote all year opening
0
50
100
Miles
6845
6848
6812
6813
6811
6809
6810
6814
ROMA
FOGGIA
6850
6856
BRINDISI
SOUTH
6815
6820
TARANTO
NAPOLI
6830
6842
6835
6832
6853
6865
6858
6852

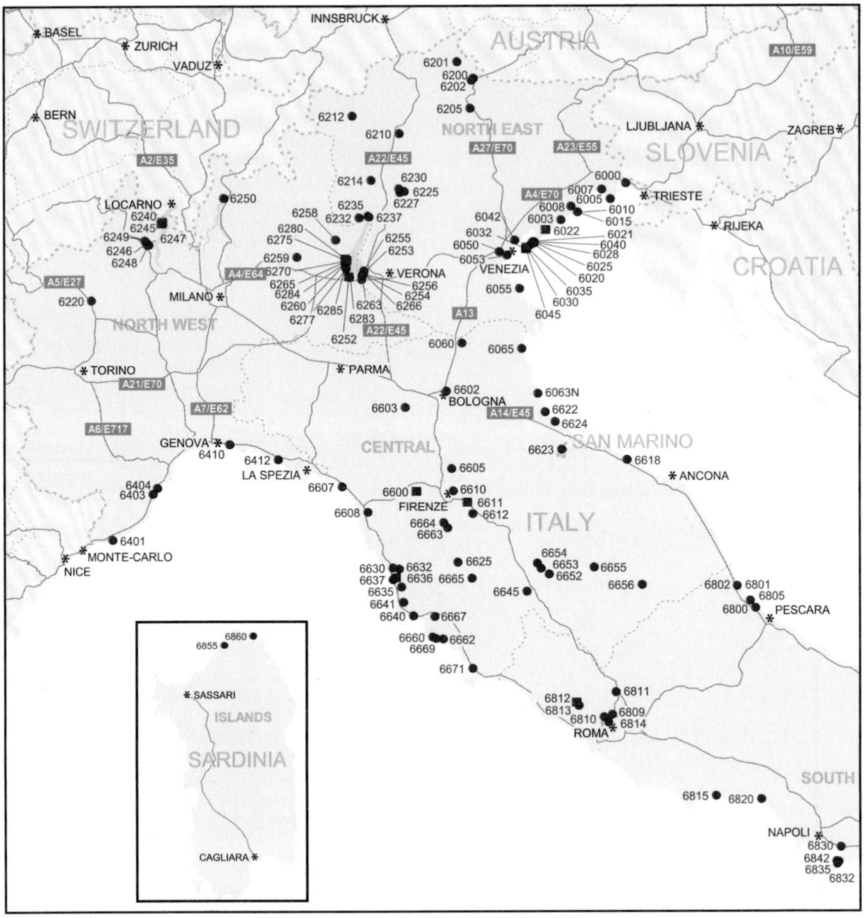

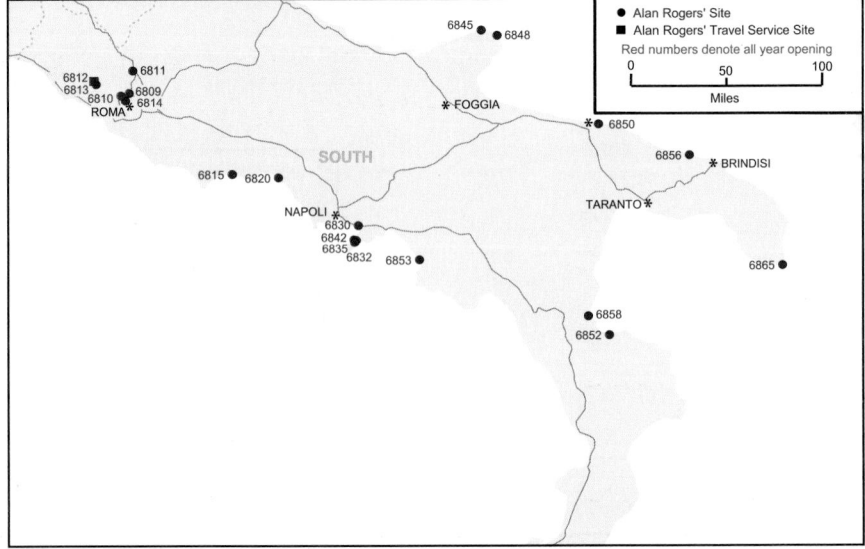

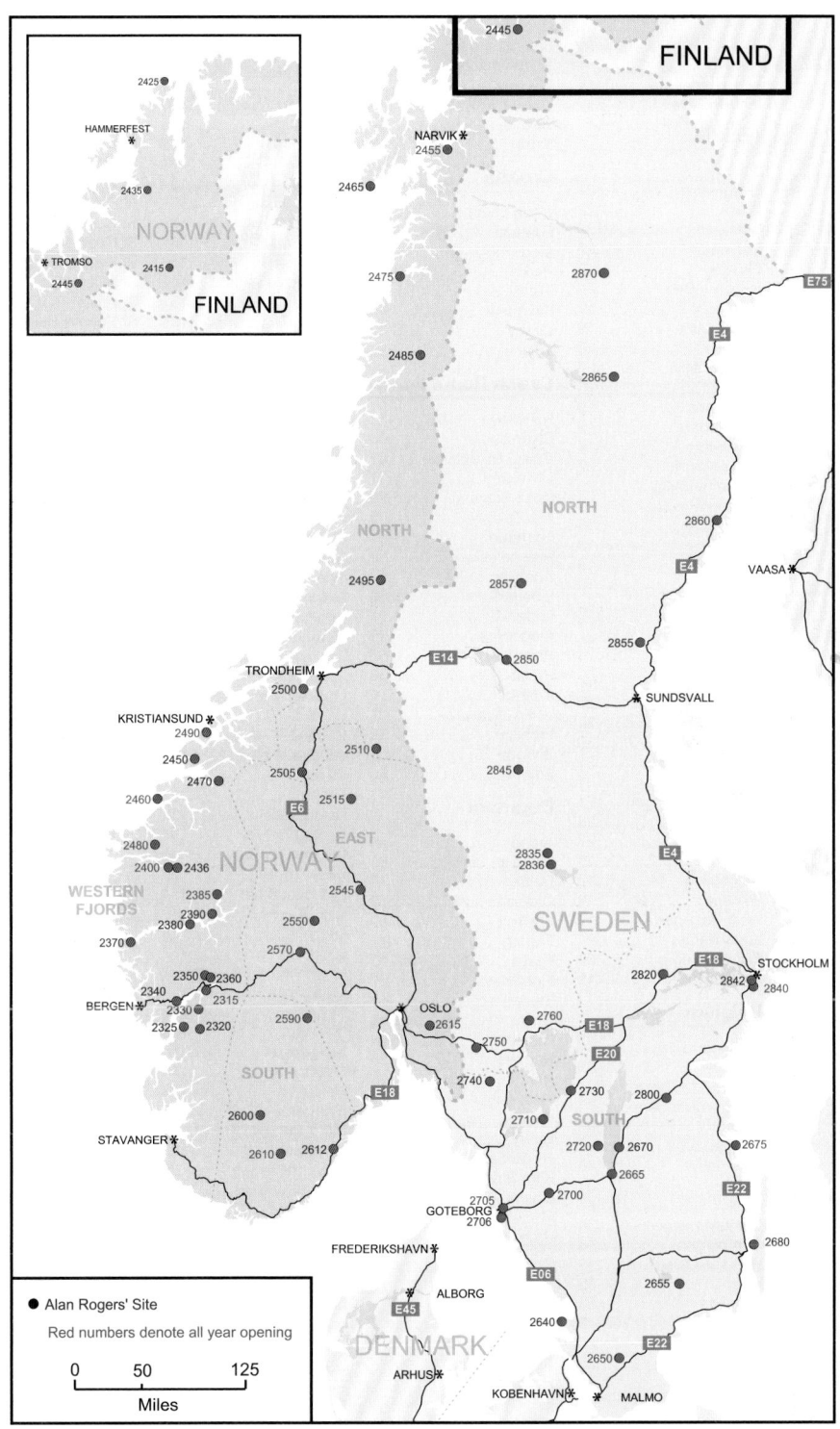

FINLAND

2445

2425

HAMMERFEST ✳

2435

NORWAY

✳ TROMSO
2445   2415

FINLAND

NARVIK ✳
2455

2465

2475

2485

2870

2865

NORTH

2860

E4

E4   VAASA ✳

2495

2857

2855

2850

SUNDSVALL ✳

E14

TRONDHEIM ✳
2500

KRISTIANSUND ✳
2490

2450

2470

2460

2480

2400 2436

WESTERN
FJORDS

2385

2390

2380

2370

2510

2505

2515

E6

EAST

NORWAY

2545

2550

2570

2845

2835
2836

SWEDEN

E4

2820

E18

STOCKHOLM

2842   2840

2350 2360

2340

2315

BERGEN ✳

2330

2325   2320

2590

OSLO
2615

2760

2750

E18

E20

STOCKHOLM

2842   2840

SOUTH

E18

2740

2730

2800

2600

STAVANGER ✳

2610   2612

2710

SOUTH

2720   2670

2665

2675

E22

2705
GOTEBORG
2706

2700

2680

FREDERIKSHAVN ✳

ALBORG

E06

2655

E45

DENMARK

2640

ARHUS ✳

2650

E22

KOBENHAVN ✳   ✳ MALMO

Legend
● Alan Rogers' Site

Red numbers denote all year opening

0   50   125

Miles

Town and Village Index

Town and Village Index

Campsite Index by site number

Campsite Index by Country and Region

There are three indexes in this guide:

On pages 548-551 campsites are indexed by Town. On pages 556-560 campsites are indexed by Country and Number. On pages 556-560 campsites are indexed by Country and Region.

Sites that are new to the guide this year are highlighted in bold text.

Municipal sites are marked 'M', Naturist sites are marked 'N'